New Systems and Architectures for Automatic Speech Recognition and Synthesis

NATO ASI Series

Advanced Science Institutes Series

A series presenting the results of activities sponsored by the NATO Science Committee, which aims at the dissemination of advanced scientific and technological knowledge, with a view to strengthening links between scientific communities.

The Series is published by an international board of publishers in conjunction with the NATO Scientific Affairs Division

A Life Sciences **B Physics**	Plenum Publishing Corporation London and New York
C Mathematical and Physical Sciences	D. Reidel Publishing Company Dordrecht, Boston and Lancaster
D Behavioural and Social Sciences **E Applied Sciences**	Martinus Nijhoff Publishers Boston, The Hague, Dordrecht and Lancaster
F Computer and Systems Sciences **G Ecological Sciences**	Springer-Verlag Berlin Heidelberg New York Tokyo

Series F: Computer and Systems Sciences Vol. 16

New Systems and Architectures for Automatic Speech Recognition and Synthesis

Edited by

Renato De Mori and Ching Y. Suen

Department of Computer Science, Concordia University
Montréal, Québec H3G 1M8, Canada

Springer-Verlag Berlin Heidelberg New York Tokyo
Published in cooperation with NATO Scientific Affairs Division

Proceedings of the NATO Advanced Study Institute on New Systems and Architectures for Automatic Speech Recognition and Synthesis held at Bonas, Gers, France, 2–14 July 1984

ISBN-13: 978-3-642-82449-4 e-ISBN-13: 978-3-642-82447-0
DOI: 10.1007/978-3-642-82447-0

Library of Congress Cataloging in Publication Data. NATO Advances Study Institute on New Systems and Architecture for Automatic Speech Recognition and Synthesis (1984 : bonas France) New systems and architecture for automatic speech recognition and synthesis. (NATO ASI series. Series F, Computer and system sciences ; vol. 16) "Proceedings of the NATO Advanced Study Institute on New Systems and Architecture for Automatic Speech Recognition and Synthesis held at Bonas, Gers, France, 2–14 July 1984" — T.p. verso. "Published in cooperation with NATO Scientific Affairs Division." Includes indes. 1. Automatic speech recognition — Congresses. 2. Speech synthesis — Congresses. I. De Mori, Renato. II. Suen, Ching Y. III. North Atlantic Treaty Organization. Scientific Affairs Division. IV. Title. V. Series: NATO ASI series. Series F, Computer and system sciences ; no. 16. TK7895.S65N375 1984 629.8'92 85-17228

Softcover reprint of the hardcover 1st edition 1985

Bookbinding: J. Schäffer OHG, Grünstadt
2145/3140-543210

TABLE OF CONTENTS

List of Participants

Mr. A. Aggoun
C.N.E.T.
B.P. 40
22301 Lannion
France

Dr. W. A. Ainsworth
Dept. of Communication and Neuroscience
University of Keele
Keele, Staffs. ST5 5BG
England

Mr. J. M. Benedi Ruiz
Departamento de Electronicae Informatica
Universidad de Valencia
Burjasot — Valencia
Spain

Prof. R. Bisiani
Carnegie-Mellon University
Dept. of Computer Science
Schenley Park
Pittsburgh, Pa 15213
U.S.A.

Dr. A. Cappelli
Istituto di Linguistica Computazionale
Via della Faggiola, 32
56100 Pisa
Italy

Dr. G. Chollet
E.N.S.T.
46, Rue Barrault
75634 Paris Cedex 13
France

Dr. A. Ciaramella
CSELT
Via G. Reiss Romoli 274
Torino 10148
Italy

Prof. G. Danserau
Université de Quebec à Hull
Dept. Informatique
CP 1250 succ. B
Hull, Quebec J8X 3X7
Canada

Prof. R. De Mori
Dept. of Computer Science
Concordia University
Montreal, Quebec H3G 1M8
Canada

Mr. Di Martino
C.R.I.N.
B.P. 239
54506 Vandoeuvre
France

Dr. D. Dours
U.E.R. de Mathématiques - Informatiques-Gestion
Université Paul Sabatier
118, Rue de Narbonne
31062 Toulouse Cedex
France

Mr. D. Fohr
C.R.I.N.
B.P. 239
54506 Vandoeuvre
France

Mr. N.J.A. Forse
British Telecom Research Laboratories
Martlesham Heath
Ipswich IP5 7RE
England

Dr. P. Frison
I.R.I.S.A.
Campus de Beaulieu
35042 Rennes Cedex
France

Prof. K. S. Fu
School of Electrical Engineering
Purdue University
West Lafayette, Ind. 47907
U.S.A.

Dr. R. Gubrynowicz
Université de Provence, Institut de Phonétique
29, Avenue Robert Schuman
13621 Aix en Provence Cedex
France

Prof. J. P. Haton
C.R.I.N.
Université de Nancy 1
B.P. 239
54506 Vandoeuvre
France

Dipl. Ing. H. Heckl
Siemens AG,
ZTI INF
Otto-Hahn-Ring 6
D 8000 München 83
West Germany

Dr. W. Hess
Lehrstuhl Für Datenverarbeitung
Technische Universität München
Arcisstr. 21
8000 München 2
West Germany

Prof. J. L. Houle
Ecole Polytechnique de Montréal
C.P. 6079 Succ "A"
Montreal, Que. H3C 3A7
Canada

Dr. A. Ingegnoli
C/O FACRC
Via Della Magione
00040 Pomezia (Rome)
Italy

Ing. B. Kammerer
Siemens AG, ZTI INF 111
Otto-Hahn-Ring 6
D 8000 München 83
West Germany

Dipl. Ing. W. Kulas
Lehrstuhl Fuer Allgemeine Elektronik
und Akustik
Ruhr-Universität Bochum
Universität Str. 150
D-4630 Bochum
West Germany

Prof. M. Kunt
Laboratoire de Traitement de Signaux
Ecole Polytechnique Fédérale de Lausanne
16, Chemin de Bellerive

Prof. P. Laface
Departimento di Automatica e Informatica
CORSO Duca Degli Abruzzi 24
10129 Torino
Italy

Mr. L. Leguennec
C.N.E.T.
B.P. 40
22301 Lannion Cedex
France

Prof. H. Leich
Faculté Polytechnique e Mons
31 Boulevard Dolez
7000 Mons
Belgium

Mr. P. Lockwood
Laboratoire de Marcoussis
91460 Marcoussis
France

Mr. U. Macdonald
Dept. of Computational
University of Saint Andrews
North Haugh, St. Andrews
Scotland

Dr. J. Manley
Centre for Research on Perception
and Cognition
University of Sussex
Brighton BN1 9QG
England

Dr. J. P. Martens
Laboratorium voor Electronica
St-Pietersnieuwstraat 41
9000 GENT
Belgium

Dr. G. Mercier
C.N.E.T.
B.P. 40
22301 Lannion Cedex
France

Dr. R. K. Moore
Royal Signals and Radar Establishment
St. Andrews Road
Great Malvern, Worcs. WRI4 3PS
England

Mr. J. Mudler
Institut für Nachrichtentechnik
TU Braunschweig
Postfach 3329
West Germany

Mr. R. L. Muhlfeld
IMMD 5
Universität Erlangen
Martensstr. 3
8520 Erlangen
West Germany

Dr. E. Mumolo
FACE RC
Via Della Magione 10
00040 Pomezia (Rome)
Italy

Dr. H. Ney
PHILIPS Gmbh
Forschungslaboratorium Hamburg
P.O. Box 540840
2000 Hamburg 54
West Germany

Prof. H. Niemann
Universität Erlangen-Nurnberg, IMMD
Martensstr. 3
8520 Erlangen
West Germany

Prof. J. Ohala
Phonology Laboratory
Department of Linguistics
University of California
Berkeley, CA 94720
U.S.A.

Dr. M. Ohala
Linguistics Program
California State
University at San Joseé
San Jose, CA 95192
U. S. A.

Mr. W. Ronnebrinck
Institut Für Nachrichtentechnik
Technische Universität Braunschweig
Schleinitzstr. 23
3300 Braunschweig
West Germany

Dipl. Ing. H. W. Rühl
Lehrsuhl für Allg. Elektrotechnik
und Akustik
Ruhr-Universität Bochum
Postfach 102148
4630 Bochum 1
West Germany

Dr. G. Ruske
Lehrstuhl für Datenverarbeitung
Technische Universität München
Franz-Joseph Str. 38
8000 München 40
West Germany

Prof. B. Sankur
Bogazici University
Dept. of Electrcal Engineering
Bebek, Istanbul
Turkey

Mr. E. G. Schukat
Universität Erlangen-Nurnberg
IMMD 5
Martensstr. 3
8520 Erlangen
West Germany

Dr. D. Sciarra
Electronica San Giorgio
Via Puccini 2
16154 Genova Sestri Ponente
Italy

Mr. N. Sedgwick
Acorn Computers Ltd.
Fulbourn Road
Cherry Hinton
Cambridge CB1 4JN
England

Dr. D. Sinclair
IBM Science Center
Athelstan House
St. Clement Street
Winchester, S023 9DR

Prof. W. Steenaart
Electr. Eng. Dept.
University of Ottawa
Ottawa, Ontario K1N 6N5
Canada

Prof. Ching Y. Suen
Dept. of Computer Science
Concordia University
1455 de Maisonneuve Blvd., West
Montreal, Quebec H3G 1M8
Canada

Mr. A. Tassy
E.N.S.T.
46, Rue Barrault
75013 Paris
France

Mr. E. Verdonck
Katholieke Universitat Leuven
CME — ESAT
De Croylaan 52
3030 Heverlee
Belgium

Mr. J. Verhoeven
University of Antwerp (UIA)
Dept. of Didactics & Criticism
Universiteitsplein 1
2610 Wilrijk
Belgium

Dr. E. Vidal Ruiz
Centro de Informatica
Universidad de Valencia
Burjasot — Valencia
Spain

Mlle. Nadine Vigouroux
Laboratoire CERFIA
(mr. Perennou)
118, Rte de Narbonne
31062 Toulouse, Cedex
France

Mr. D. Wood
GEC Research Laboratories
East Lane
Wembley, Middx
England

Prof. N. Yalabik
Computer Engineering Dept.
Middle East Technical University
Ankara
Turkey

FOREWORD

It is an established tradition that researchers from many countries get together on the average every three years for a two week Advanced Studies Institute on Automatic Speech Recognition and Synthesis. According to ASI policies the Institute is financed by NATO. This book contains the texts of lectures and papers contributed by the attendees of the ASI which was held July 2 — 14, 1984, at Bonas, Gers, France. Focussed on New Systems and Architectures for Automatic Speech Recognition and Synthesis, this book is divided into 4 parts:

(a) *Review of basic algorithms*

(b) *System architecture and VLSI for automatic Speech*

(c) *Software systems for automatic speech recognition,*

(d) *Speech synthesis and phonetics.*

Due to the international nature of the Institute, the readers will find in this book different styles, different points of view and applications to different languages. This reflects also some characteristics of the International Association for Pattern Recognition (IAPR) whose technical committee on Speech Recognition has organized this ASI.

Proposed contributions have been reviewed by an Editorial Committee composed of W. Ainsworth (Kent), R. Bisiani (Pittsburgh), J. P. Haton (Nancy), W. Hess (Munich), J. L. Houle (Montréal), P. Laface (Turin), R. Moore (Malvern), H. Niemann (Erlangen) and J. Ohala (Berkeley).

Typesetting of the book was performed using SYMSET facilities developed entirely by the Department of Computer Science at Concordia University. Special thanks are due to L. Lam, H. Monkiewicz and L. Thiel.

Montreal, Canada R. De Mori and C. Y. Suen

May 1985

AN OVERVIEW OF DIGITAL TECHNIQUES FOR PROCESSING SPEECH SIGNALS

Murat Kunt
Signal Procesing Laboratory
Swiss Federal Institute of Technology
16 Ch. de Bellerive
CH - 1007 Lausanne, Switzerland

and

Heinz Hugli
Mircrotechnique Institute
University of Neuchatel
Rue de la Maladière 71
CH - 2007 Neuchatel, Switzerland

ABSTRACT

This paper discusses major digital signal processing methods used in processing speech signals. Basic tools, such as the discrete Fourier transform, the z transform and linear filter theory are briefly introduced first. A general view of fast transformation algorithms and most widely used particular fast transformations are given. Linear prediction is then described with a particular emphasis on its lattice structure. A brief introduction to homomorphic processing for multiplied and convolved signals and to its applications in speech processing is given. Recalling some fundamentals of the speech signal, various speech analysis and synthesis models are described, showing which kind of processing methods are

NATO ASI Series, Vol. F16
New Systems and Architectures for Automatic Speech
Recognition and Synthesis. Edited by R. De Mori and C. Y. Suen

involved. Finally, two aspects of speech recognition are presented: feature traction and pattern matching using dynamic time warping.

1. INTRODUCTION

Because of its multidisciplinary character, digital signal processing became increasingly important in a number of scientific and technical areas. Continuous interaction between the methods and the particular applications have led to an avalanche on both sides. Increasingly sophisticated methods are developed to fulfil wider needs of a large number of applications. There is no doubt that one of the major application areas of digital signal processing is speech signals. Over the last two decades, considerable effort has been devoted to analyse, code, model, synthesize and recognize speech signals. A dozen of books are already available, presenting various aspects of digital speech processing.

This paper attempts to give a tutorial review of major digital signal processing methods used in processing speech signals. Because of space limitations and the wide range of the subject, in depth treatments are omitted. Essence of the methods and insight for the interpretation of the results are indicated whenever possible. In section two, basic methods are defined such as the discrete Fourier transform, correlation functions, the z transform, the convolution, and the linear system theory. A general view of fast transformation algorithms is given, showing structures for hardware and software. Commonly used fast transformations are also briefly indicated. The last part of this section presents the linear prediction models and tools for one dimensional signals and introduces its lattice structure, a structure that is modular and hence suitable for various implementations. In section three, homomorphic processing of multiplied and convolved signals is discussed with particular emphasis on its applications to speech signals, particularly for deconvolution. Section four gives an overview of the speech analysis and synthesis methods using previously defined tools. Speech recognition is summarized in section five with a particular emphasis on pattern matching. The objective, in these last two sections, is to point out particular digital signal processing methods used for reaching the goals.

2.0 BASIC METHODS

In this section basic signal processing methods are defined and their use in speech processing are discussed. Analysis and synthesis tools for digital signals, such as the discrete Fourier transform and the correlation function, and for systems, such as the z transform and the convolution are described first. A brief discussion on linear filters and fast transformations is presented next. The section ends with a rather detailed description of linear prediction. For more detail, the reader may consult [1] and [2].

THE DISCRETE FOURIER TRANSFORM

The discrete Fourier transform of a digital signal x(k) is a complex series defined by:

$$X(n) = \sum_{k=k_0}^{k_0+N-1} x(k)\exp(-j2\pi kn/N) \qquad (1)$$

with n = -N/2, ..., N/2-1

In this definition, only N consecutive samples of the signal are used starting at k = k0. The series X(n) is periodical in n with a period of N. The integer variable n represents discrete frequencies. For example n = 0 is the DC component and n = N/2 is the folding frequency, i.e. half of the sampling rate.

The inverse transform is given by:

$$x(k) = (1/N) \sum_{n=-N/2}^{N/2-1} X(n)\ \exp(j2\pi nk/N) \qquad (2)$$

with $k = k0, \ldots, k0 + N - 1$

Eq. (1) is referred to as the analysis of the signal, whereas eq. (2) is used to synthesize the signal from its Fourier Transform. From the complex numbers $X(n)$ two real sequences are obtained. The magnitude $X(n)$ plotted as a function of n is the magnitude spectrum. The argument $\arg[X(n)]$ is the phase spectrum. They inform on the frequency distributions of complex exponential signals composing the analysed signal $x(k)$. If the number of samples N is small compared to the total length of the signal, these spectra are called short term spectra. On a long signal, such as a speech signal, several short term spectra can be computed. Sections of the signal used in these computations may partially overlap or may be apart. If these spectra are plotted in three dimensions as a function of the frequency n and of the time (for example time instants corrresponding to the beginning of each signal section), the resulting surface is called spectrogram. It is usually represented as a black-and-white two level image on the (n,k) plane. Additional grey levels, if available, give more precise and detailed information on the frequency variations of various components of the signal. In section 1.6 fast algorithms for computing spectrograms will be discussed.

2.2 CORRELATION FUNCTIONS

The similarity of two signals $x(k)$ and $y(k)$ is measured by their cross correlation function defined by:

$$\varphi_{xy}(k) = \sum_{l=-\infty}^{+\infty} x(l)\, y(k+l) \tag{3}$$

For a given delay k of the second signal $y(k)$ with respect to the first signal $x(k)$, the cross correlation function is just the integral of the product of these two signals. It reaches its maximum value for the greatest similarity. If $x(k)$ is identical to $y(k)$, the cross correlation function is called autocorrelation function. It is given by:

$$\varphi_x(k) = \sum_{1=-\infty}^{+\infty} x(1)\ x(k+1) \tag{4}$$

Its maximum is at the origin k = 0. If this function is normalized by dividing it by the variance of the signal x(k), the result is called correlation coefficient. Its values lie between +1 and -1.

An equivalent way of computing correlation functions is obtained by taking the discrete Fourier transform of both side of eq. (3) or eq. (4). One obtains respectively;

$$\Phi_{xy}(n) = X^*(n)\ Y(n) \tag{5}$$

and

$$\Phi_x(n) = X^*(n)\ X(n) = |X(n)|^2 \tag{6}$$

These results can be proved easily. They are left as exercises to the reader.

2.3 THE z TRANSFORM

The discrete Fourier transform is a very powerful tool for analysing and synthesizing signals. It is not, however, suitable for studying signal processing systems. A more general transformation is needed. The z transform fulfils this need and becomes identical to Fourier transform in a particular case. The z transform of a signal is defined by:

$$X(z) = \sum_{k=-\infty}^{+\infty} x(k)\ z^{-k} \tag{7}$$

where z is a complex variable. A power series, such as this one, may not converge for all the possible values of z. The area of the complex plane z containing all the values for which eq. (7) converges is called convergence region.

The inverse transform is a complex integral given by:

$$x(k) = (1/2\pi j) \oint X(z)\, z^{k-1}\, dz \tag{8}$$

The integration contour must lie in the convergence region. Usually, the inverse z transform is computed by using partial fraction decomposition in which the inverse transform of each term is known. Since this transformation is linear, the sum of these partial signals gives the desired result.

It is interesting to note that if the z transform is computed on the unit circle of the z plane, i.e. for $|z|= 1$, the result is the continuous Fourier transform:

$$X(z)\Big|_{|z|=1} = X(f) = \sum_{k=-\infty}^{+\infty} x(k)\, \exp(-j2\pi kf) \tag{9}$$

If now, the continuous variable f is replaced by a discrete variable n with $f_n = n\Delta f = n/N$, or equivalently, if the z transform is computed on equally spaced points of the unit circle, the result is the discrete Fourier transform (1).

2.4 CONVOLUTION

Let us consider a signal processing system S which acts on the input signal x(k) to produce an output signal y(k):

$$y(k) = S[x(k)] \tag{10}$$

If it is required from the system to be linear, the superposition principle is satisfied, i.e.:

$$S[ax_1(k) + bx_2(k)] = aS[x_1(k)] + bS[x_2(k)] \tag{11}$$

An additional constraint may be required to be shift invariant. In this case, if the response to x(k) is y(k), the response to x(k-k0) is y(k-k0). Linear shift invariant systems are completely specified with their response to a unit sample, i.e. by their impulse response g(k). To see this, let us write the input signal in terms of unit samples:

$$x(k) = \sum_{1=-\infty}^{+\infty} x(1)\ d(k-1) \tag{12}$$

where d(k) is the unit sample having the value 1 at the origin k=0 and 0 elsewhere. Using eq. (12) as the input signal, we have:

$$\begin{aligned} y(k) = S[x(k)] \quad &= \sum_{1=-\infty}^{+\infty} x(1)\ S[d(k-1)] \\ &= \sum_{1=-\infty}^{+\infty} x(1)\ g(k-1] = x(k) * g(k) \end{aligned} \tag{13}$$

where g(k) is the response of the system to d(k). Eq. 13 is called convolution product or convolution. Notice the similarity between correlation and convolution.

By taking the Discrete Fourier transform of both sides of eq. (13) a simpler form is obtained:

$$Y(n) = X(n)\ G(n) \tag{14}$$

where G(n) is the frequency response of the system or the discrete Fourier transform of its impulse response.

A similar result is obtained by taking the z transform of both sides of eq. (13):

$$Y(z) = X(z)\ G(z) \tag{15}$$

where G(z) is the transfer function of the system.

2.5 LINEAR FILTERS

A linear shift invariant system with an impulse response g(k) is a filter. This terminology results directly from eq. (14). Since X(n) and the frequency response G(n) are simply multiplied, the selection of a particular function G(n) may attenuate or amplify some frequency components of the input signal to the detriment of others. For example, if G(n) is zero beyond a certain value of n, the output signal will not have any components at these frequencies. These components are filtered by the system.

Digital filters are divided into two broad classes depending on their impulse response. If the length of the impulse response is finite, i.e. if g(k) has only a finite number of non zero samples, the filter is called Finite Impulse Response (FIR) filter. In contrast, if the length of the impulse response is infinite, the filter is called Infinite Impulse Response (IIR) filter.

There are three equivalent ways of implementing a digital filter: 1) By convolution, using eq. (13) with finite number of samples. 2) By discrete Fourier transform, using eq. (14) and then taking the inverse transform of Y(n). 3) By using a difference equation of the following type

$$\sum_{n=0}^{N} a(n)\ y(k-n) = \sum_{m=0}^{M} b(m)\ x(k-m) \tag{16}$$

Eq. (16) seems to come out of the blue, but it is not. It is simply the inverse z transform of eq. (15) where the transfer function G(z) is a quotient of the polynomials in z, i.e..:

$$G(z) = \frac{\sum_{m=0}^{M} b(m)\ z^{-m}}{\sum_{n=0}^{N} a(n)\ z^{-n}} \tag{17}$$

Almost every transfer function can be written in this form. The rare cases where this is not possible, an approximation in the form of eq. (17) can be established by choosing N and M large enough. FIR filters are usually implemented using the convolution eq. (13). It is a simple form which can be analyzed easily. In contrast IIR filters are more suitable for a difference equation. In this case some cares must be taken. In particular, if the dynamic range of the input signal is bounded, it is desirable for the dynamic range of the output signal to be also bounded. Filters of this type are stable filters. Unstable filters do not produce any useful output, because the output signal diverges continuously.

So far, the filters that are described were shift invariant. Their characteristics (impulse response or frequency response or the coefficients of the difference equation) do not vary in time. These filters are convenient for processing stationary signals, i.e. signals whose statistical characteristics do not vary in time also. For nonstationary signals, however, such as the speech signal, it might be desirable to vary the characteristics of the filters. In this case, these filters are called time varying or adaptive. Rules must be established, of course, to find the new characteristics. Often, these rules are derived from the input signal itself, after detecting changes in its characteristics.

The main problem in filtering is to find samples of the desired impulse response or the coefficients of the differences equation in accordance with the filtering requirements. Methods for designing FIR and IIR filters are quite different. They have been investigated quite extensively over the last two decades. Because of their variety and the complexity of some of them, they will not be discussed in this text. The reader may consult [1] or [3] for detailed discussion of the subject. Presently, research efforts in digital filtering are rather oriented into implementation technologies such as VLSI and into multi-dimensional filtering. A brief discussion is included herein to emphasize basic problems related to the design and to the structures of digital filters.

When filtering is required, the frequency response of the desired filter is often a binary function: all the components within a frequency band should be completely attenuated and others in a different band should not be modified at all. Accordingly, the frequency response is a binary function switching between 0 and 1 on each cutoff frequency. These responses are impossible to match in practice. That is why they are called ideal frequency responses or ideal filters. Implementable filters can only approximate this behaviour according to an error criterion. Fig. 1 indicates major ideal frequency responses. In Fig. 2 tolerances

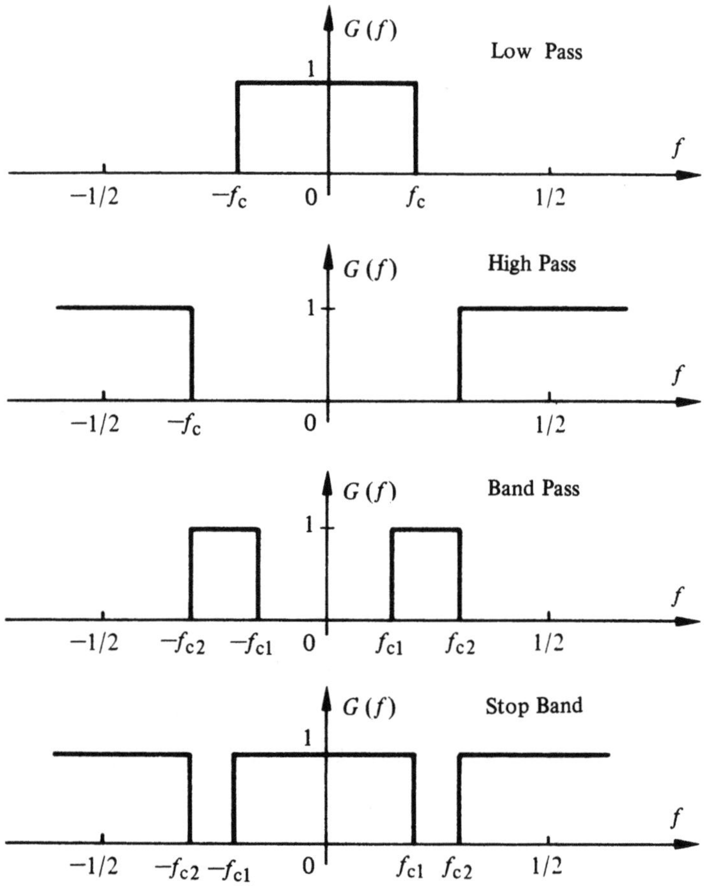

Fig. 1 Ideal frequency responses

are shown for a high pass filter. Instead of an ideal constant 1 in the passing band, oscillations within a band whose width is controlled by the parameter δ_2

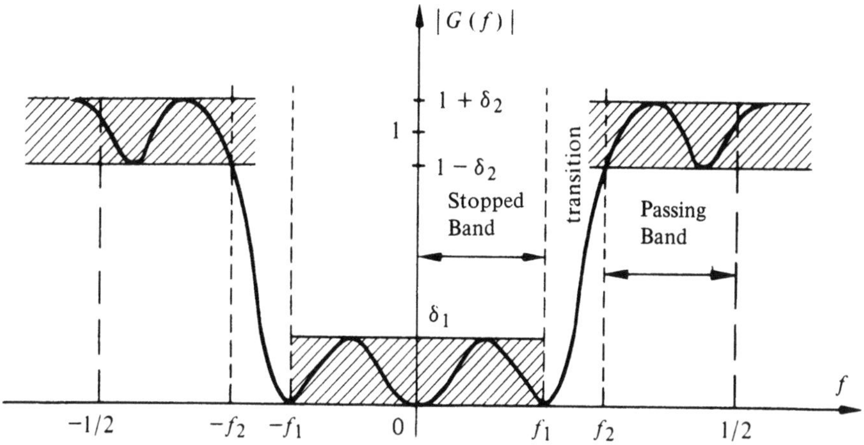

Fig. 2 Tolerance bands for a high pass filter

are tolerated. Similarly, in the stopped band, other oscillations are tolerated as regulated with the parameter δ_1. Finally, the transition between these two bands cannot occur at a unique frequency fc, but over a small frequency interval controlled with f1 and f2. Algorithms are then designed to find the impulse response or the transfer function of an implementable filter whose frequency response falls within this tolerance band.

Fig. 3 shows the block diagram of an FIR filter. This structure is quite simple and may conveniently be used with a variety of technologies (surface acoustic waves, switched capacitor circuits, charge coupled devices and VLSI). If a similar effort is produced to draw a block diagram for a difference equation, a structure is obtained as shown in Fig. 4a. This structure is not efficient because of the redundant number of delay elements. With a little algebra on the difference equation, it is possible to show that this structure is equivalent to that shown in Fig. 4b in which the number of delay elements is minimized. The big disadvantage of this last structure is its sensitivity to finite arithmetic. In fact, all the coefficients a(n) and b(m) and the signal samples must be quantized at a finite number of levels. Quantization error on one coefficient influence the entire frequency response and may unstabilize a stable filter. For this reason, especially when the number of quantization levels are not too large, this structure is divided

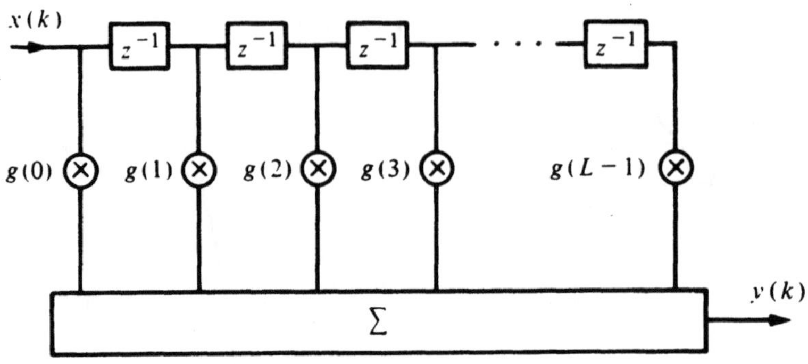

Fig. 3 Implementation structure for a transversal FIR filter

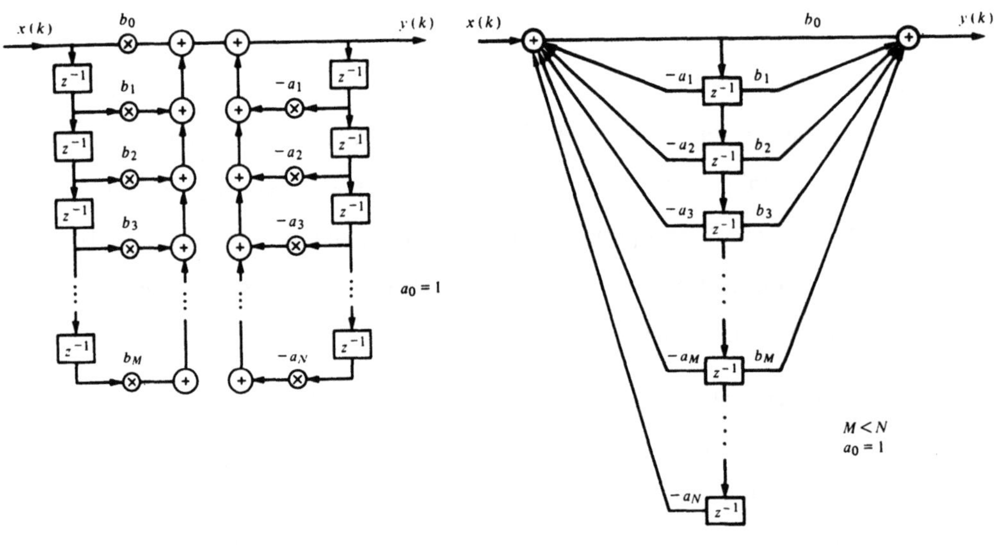

Fig. 4 Implementation structure for a recursive IIR filter. (a) structure as derived directly from a difference equation. (b) one equivalent canonical form.

into the cascade of first and second order sections.

2.6 FAST TRANSFORMATIONS

2.6.1 PRELIMINARY COMMENTS

Fast transformations play an increasingly important role in signal analysis, synthesis and coding. Since the reinvention of the fast Fourier transform in 1965, a number of complex methods that have not been used because of their computational cost, find increasingly wide applications and helped to solve various signal processing problems. With continuous progress in technology, a one-chip fast transform will soon find its socket in commonly used equipments.

What is meant by fast transformation is an algorithm which computes a linear transformation by using a minimum number of multiplications and additions. For example all the so-called fast Fourier transforms (FFT) compute the discrete Fourier transform given by eq. (1). Other linear transformations can also be computed with fast algorithms.

2.6.2 LINEAR TRANSFORMATIONS

A linear transformation of size N, transforms N samples of a signal into a set of N transform coefficients, each of them being a linear combination of the signal samples. From a mathematical point of view, a linear transformation can be expressed as:

$$X(n) = \sum_{k=0}^{N-1} a(n,k)\ x(k) \qquad (18)$$

with $n = 0, \ldots, N-1$

where x(k) are the signal samples, a(n,k) the kernel of the transformation and X(n) the transformed coefficients. By comparing this equation with eq. (1), it can be shown that the discrete Fourier transform is a particular case of eq. (18) with $a(n,k) = \exp(j2\pi nk/N)$.

In order to compute each transformed coefficient independently from the others, the kernel a(n,k) is required to have othogonal or orthonormal rows, i.e.:

$$\sum_{k=0}^{N-1} a(n,k)a^*(m,k) = \delta(n,m) = \begin{cases} 1 \text{ if } n = m \\ 0 \text{ otherwise} \end{cases} \tag{19}$$

where * represents the complex conjugate and $\delta(n,m)$ the Kronecker symbol. If X and x denote the coefficient and sample vectors respectively with:

$$X = (X(0),\ X(1),\ \ldots,\ X(N\text{-}1))^T \tag{20}$$

and

$$x = (x(0),\ x(1),\ \ldots,\ x(N\text{-}1))^T \tag{21}$$

Eq. (18) can be written as matrix vector product:

$$X = A\ x \tag{22}$$

where A is the matrix containing all the a(n,k). To recover the signal samples from the transform coefficients, A is required to be inversible. In this case, the following equation holds:

$$A\ A^{-1} = I \tag{23}$$

where I is the unit matrix. The matrix form of eq. (19) is:

$$A^H A = I \tag{24}$$

where H represents Hermitian transpose. Since A is unique, we have $A^H = A^{-1}$ and hence:

$$A\ A^H = I \tag{25}$$

If this last equation is written in series form, one obtains:

$$\sum_{n=0}^{N-1} a(n,k)\ a^*(n,l) = \delta(k,l) = \begin{cases} 1 \text{ if } n = m \\ 0 \text{ otherwise} \end{cases} \quad (26)$$

This equation implies that the columns of A are orthonormal too. A matrix A for which eqs. (19) and (26) hold, is called unitary. The transformation (18) is then a change in the N dimensional coordinate system in which x and X are expresed as vectors.

2.6.3 FAST ALGORITHMS

If the number of multiplications and additions required by a linear transformation such as (18) is counted, it is found to be $Nc = N.N = N^2$. Then, how this number can be reduced to a more or less theoretical minimum ? In general, this number is the minimum, unless there is some redundancy in the kernel so that some entries can be computed as functions of the others. Fast transform algorithms exist only for those transform matrices which have a structured redundancy. The discrete Fourier transform is one example.

Two classes of fast algorithms can be established based on the factorization of the number of samples N. In the first class, a repetitive basic structure in the algorithm, and hence in the corresponding hardware, can be found if N is an integer power of a small number such as $N = 2^m$, or $N = \alpha^m$. These algorithms are more suitable for VLSI implementations. In the second class, algorithms are designed for N factorized as a product of a series of various integer numbers such as N = N1.N2.N3....Nk. In this case the basic structure exists but changes its size according to the particular Nj in the factorization.

To see how a structured redundancy can be introduced in a transform matrix, let us consider the successive tensorial product of a set of ρ by ρ basic matrices Bi. We have:

$$A_n = \underset{i=0}{\overset{n-1}{\otimes}} Bi \otimes Bn\text{-}2 \otimes \ldots \otimes B0 \tag{27}$$

where x represents the tensorial product defined by $C = A \otimes B$:

$$A = \begin{pmatrix} a11 & a12 \\ a21 & a22 \end{pmatrix} \qquad B = \begin{pmatrix} b11 & b12 \\ b21 & b22 \end{pmatrix}$$

$$C = \begin{pmatrix} a11b11 & a11b12 & a12b11 & a12b12 \\ a11b21 & a11b22 & a12b21 & a12b22 \\ a21b11 & a21b12 & a22b11 & a22b12 \\ a21b21 & a21b22 & a22b21 & a22b22 \end{pmatrix} \tag{28}$$

The matrix A_n is of size ρ by ρ with only $n\rho$ non redundant entries. It can be shown [1] that A_n obtained with successive tensorial products can be factored into n matrices Cj, each of size ρ by ρ and having only ρ non zero entries per line. This result is known as Good's theorem and is expressed by:

$$A_n = \prod_{j=0}^{n-1} Cj = Cn\text{-}1.Cn\text{-}2 \ldots C0 \tag{29}$$

Eqs. (27) and (29) can be illustrated with the following example with $n = \rho = 2$.

$$A_2 = \begin{pmatrix} b_{1,0,0} & b_{1,0,1} \\ b_{1,1,0} & b_{1,1,1} \end{pmatrix} \otimes \begin{pmatrix} b_{0,0,0} & b_{0,0,1} \\ b_{0,1,1} & b_{0,1,1} \end{pmatrix}$$

$$= \begin{pmatrix} b_{1,0,0} & b_{1,0,1} & 0 & 0 \\ 0 & 0 & b_{1,0,0} & b_{1,0,1} \\ b_{1,1,0} & b_{1,1,1} & 0 & 0 \\ 0 & 0 & b_{1,1,0} & b_{1,1,1} \end{pmatrix} \cdot \begin{pmatrix} b_{0,0,0} & b_{0,0,1} & 0 & 0 \\ 0 & 0 & b_{0,0,0} & b_{0,0,1} \\ b_{0,1,0} & b_{0,1,1} & 0 & 0 \\ 0 & 0 & b_{0,1,0} & b_{0,1,1} \end{pmatrix} \tag{30}$$

A transformation using A_η as the transform matrix can be written as:

where the products should be carried out from right to left. A flow chart can be derived from eq. (31) which can be used to design various fast algorithms. Fig. 5 shows the chart of eq. (31). A basic structure is used twice. It is

$$\begin{pmatrix} X(0) \\ X(1) \\ X(2) \\ X(3) \end{pmatrix} = \begin{pmatrix} b_{1,0,0} & b_{1,0,1} & 0 & 0 \\ 0 & 0 & b_{1,0,0} & b_{1,0,1} \\ b_{1,1,0} & b_{1,1,1} & 0 & 0 \\ 0 & 0 & b_{1,1,0} & b_{1,1,1} \end{pmatrix} \cdot \begin{pmatrix} b_{0,0,0} & b_{0,0,1} & 0 & 0 \\ 0 & 0 & b_{0,0,0} & b_{0,0,1} \\ b_{0,1,0} & b_{0,1,1} & 0 & 0 \\ 0 & 0 & b_{0,1,0} & b_{0,1,1} \end{pmatrix} \begin{pmatrix} x(0) \\ x(1) \\ x(2) \\ x(3) \end{pmatrix} \tag{31}$$

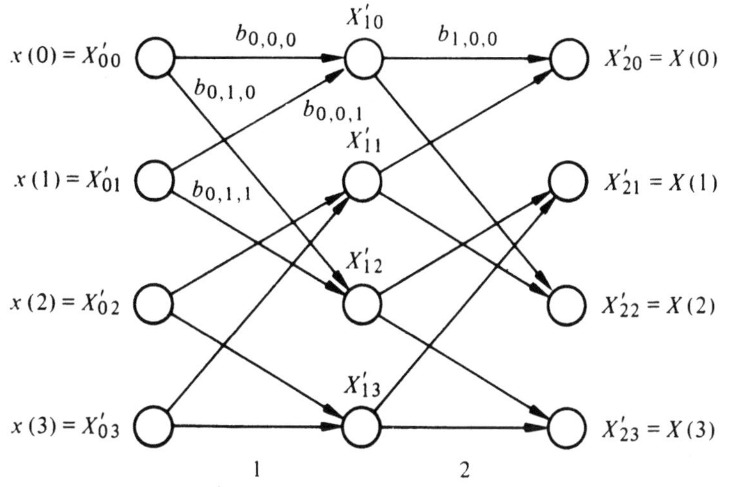

Fig. 5 Flow chart for a fast transform algorithm according to eq. (29).

possible to modify the flow charts provided that the information flow is not altered. For example, if the 2nd and 3rd lines of the rightmost matrix in (31) are swapped, the 2nd and the 3rd columns of the second matrix should also be permuted to keep the result unchanged. The corresponding flow chart is shown in Fig. 6. The basic structure of this flow chart is known as the butterfly operation which allows 'in-place' computation, i.e. the storage for input data is used for intermediary and final results.

In this scheme, the total number of multiplications and additions is reduced to Nf = ρNlog N if N is an integer power of ρ compared to Nc = N. For example, for N = 1024, which a very commonly used transform size, the saving is larger than a factor of 50 !

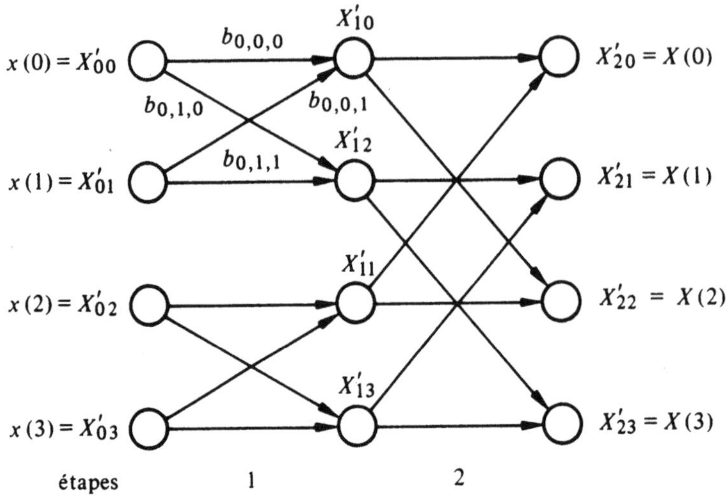

Fig. 6 Modified flow chart for 'in place computation'.

2.6.4 PARTICULAR FAST TRANSFORMS

Elaborating the general principles outlined in the previous paragraph, fast algorithms can be designed for the following particular transforms. Algorithms are not described due to the limited space of this text.

1) The discrete Fourier transform

Several fast algorithms exist for this transformation given by eq. (1). They are too specialized to be cited here. The reader may find details in [1] or [3].

2) The Hadamard transform

The Hadamard transform is perhaps the simplest transformation. Its transform matrix contains only +1's and -1's as entries. It is given by:

$$X(\beta) = (1/\sqrt{2^n}) \sum_{\alpha=0}^{N-1} (-1)^{\sum_{k=0}^{n-1} \alpha(k)\beta(k)} x(\alpha) \qquad (32)$$

with $\alpha \leftrightarrow \alpha(n\text{-}1) \ \ldots \ \alpha(1)\alpha(0)$

$\beta \leftrightarrow \beta(n\text{-}1) \ \ldots \ \beta(1)\beta(0)$

and $\alpha(k)$, $\beta(k) = 0$ or 1.

The coefficients $X(\beta)$ given by this equation are in the so-called natural order, as naturally given by the definition. They can be ordered in various ways such as bit-reversed order, sequency order or cal-sal order. Fast algorithms exist for each type ordering. A particular order is selected depending on the problem. For example, if even or odd symmetries are searched in the signal, cal-sal order is the appropriate ordering. If a parallel is made to the frequency as in Fourier transform, then sequency order should be used.

3) The R transform

This transformation is almost identical to Hadamard transform except that absolute values are taken after each substraction in the Hadamard transform flow chart. Because of this nonlinearity, this transform has no inverse. An interesting property of this transform is that the transform coefficients remain unchanged under cyclic translation of the input samples.

4) The Haar transform

A closed form analytical expression for this transform is cumbersome to write. The general form (18) remains valid here, where each a(k,n) are replaced by samples from the orthogonal set of Haar functions shown in Fig. 7.

5) The sine transform

The closed form analytical expression of the sine transform is the following:

$$S(n) = \sum_{k=0}^{N-1} x(k) \sin[\frac{(k+1)(n+1)}{N+1} \pi] \tag{33}$$

A similar form can be used depending on the even or odd numbers involved. This transform, along with the cosine transform as defined below, are used often for speech coding.

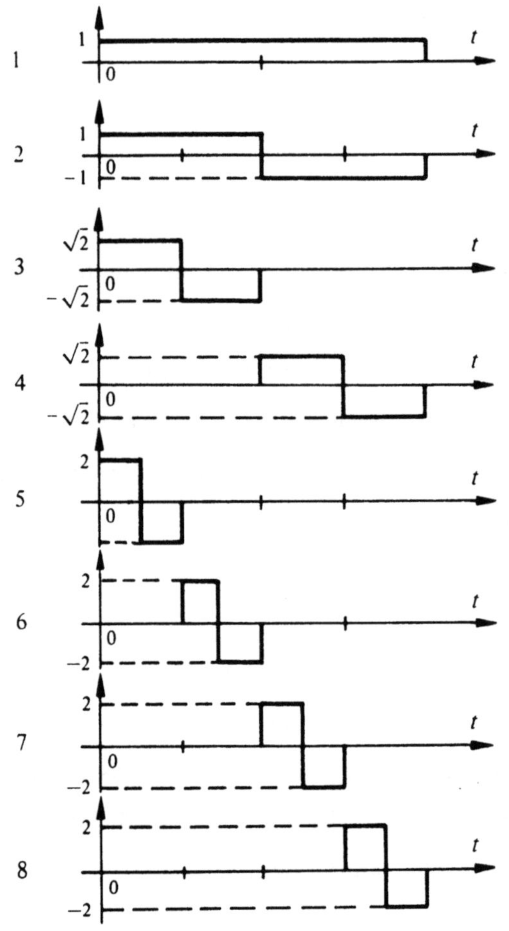

Fig. 7 Orthonormal set of Haar functions.

6) The cosine transform

The cosine transform is defined by:

$$C(n) = \sum_{k=0}^{N-1} x(k) \cos\left[\frac{\pi}{2N} (2k+1)n\right] \tag{34}$$

Note that sine and cosine transforms are byproducts of the discrete Fourier transform. Because they require real coefficients, instead of complex exponentials used in Fourier series, they are faster to compute and hence more suitable for real-time applications.

7) Slant transform.

As the Haar transform, the closed form analytical exprression for this transform is cumbersome to write. In this case a(n,k) are replaced by samples from the orthogonal set of slanted functions shown in Fig. 8.

2.6.5 THE KARHUNEN LOEVE TRANSFORM

Although there is no fast algorithm for this transformation, it is useful to describe it briefly because, in many cases, it is considered as the 'best' linear transform; best meaning whatever the reader thinks it means. The Karhunen Loeve transform, by definition, produces statistically uncorrelated coefficients, i.e. :

$$E[X(n)X*(m)] = \lambda_\eta \delta(n,m) \tag{35}$$

Substituting the general form (18) in (35), we have :

$$E[X(n)X*(m)] = E[\ \sum_k a(n,k)\ x(k)\ \sum_l a*(m,l)x*(l)\ ]$$

$$= \sum_k \sum_l E[x(k)x*(l)]\ a(n,k)\ a*(m,l) = \lambda[\eta]\delta(n,m) \tag{36}$$

The expectation $E[x(k)\ x^*(l)]$ is, by definition, the general entry of the correlation matrix $\varphi_x(k,l)$ of the signal. Eq. (36) is then :

$$\sum_k \sum_l \varphi_x\ (k,l)\ a(n,k)\ a^*(m,l) = \lambda_\eta \delta(n,m) \tag{37}$$

Comparing this result to eq. (19), we have :

$$\sum_k \varphi_x\ (k,l)\ a(n,k) = \lambda_\eta a(n,l) \tag{38}$$

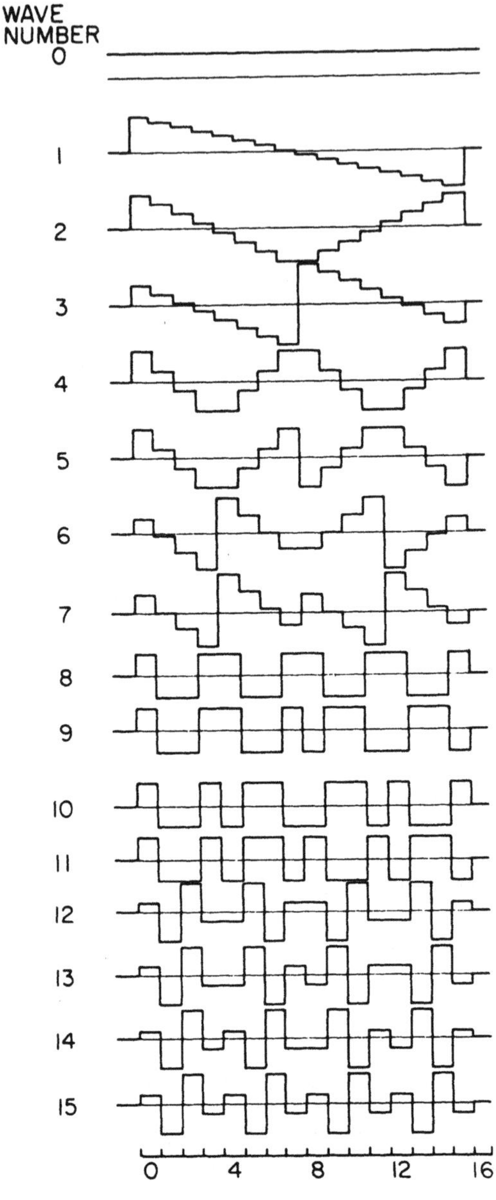

Fig. 8 Othonormal set of functions used in the slant transform.

In matrix notation, the equivalent form is :

$$\varphi_x A = \lambda_\eta A \tag{39}$$

which is the classical eigen-vector, eigen-value problem. The solution of eq. (39) gives the transform matrix which guarantees (35). To derive this transformation, the correlation matrix $\varphi_x(k,1)$ of the signal must be estimated first. Then a linear tranform requiring $Nc = N^2$ operations should be computed. Because of this computational load, the Karhunen Loeve transform is not very often used in practice. It gives an indication about the upper bound of what other transform cited earlier, computationally more efficient, should attempt to reach for decorrelating data samples.

2.7 LINEAR PREDICTION

2.7.1 PRELIMINARY REMARKS

There are several ways to introduce the linear prediction. The one which will be discussed here is based on the convolution, the z transform and linear systems described previously. Let us consider a linear system and its associated equations :

$$y(k) = x(k)*g(k) = \sum_{-\infty}^{+\infty} g(1)\ x(k-1) \tag{40}$$

and

$$Y(z) = X(z)\ G(z) \tag{41}$$

along with the convergence region.

The transfer function G(z) is then the ratio Y(z)/X(z). The roots of Y(z) is also the roots of G(z). In contrast, the roots of X(z) are the poles of G(z). The desired transfer function is often so idealized that various approximation forms are the followings :

1) Polynomial approximation.

In this case, the practical transfer function is given by :

$$G(z) = \sum_{i=0}^{M} b(i) \; z^{-i} \tag{42}$$

Substituting this particular form in (41) and taking the inverse z transform of both side of this equation, we have :

$$y(k) = \sum_{i=0}^{M} b(i) \; x(k-i) \tag{43}$$

which is nothing else than a particular form of the convolution (12) for FIR filters or systems. Note that in this case, each output sample is a weighted sum of a finite number of past and present input samples. The system is entirely described by m coefficients b(i). This type of system is also called all zero system since the transfer function has M zeros.

2) Inverse polynomial approximation

In this case, the practical transfer function is given by :

$$G(z) = \frac{1}{\sum_{j=0}^{N} a(j) \; z^{-j}} \tag{44}$$

It is possible to introduce a gain factor GO in (5) to replace the unity numerator. Substituting this particular form in (41) and taking the inverse z transform of both sides of this equation, we have :

$$y(k) = - \sum_{j=1}^{N} a(j)\ y(k-j) + x(k) \tag{45}$$

assuming $a(0) = 1$.

which is a particular form of the difference equation (16) for IIR filters or systems. Note that in this case, each output sample is a weighted sum of a finite number of past output samples and the present input sample. The system is entirely described by N coefficients a(j). These systems are also called all pole systems since the transfer function has N poles.

3) Ratio of polynomials

In the most general case, the practical transfer function is a ratio of two polynomials in z^{-1}. This is the case discussed in section 2.5 leading to the difference equation :

$$y(k) = - \sum_{j=1}^{N} a(j)\ y(k-j) + \sum_{i=0}^{M} b(i)\ x(k-i) \tag{46}$$

assuming again $a(0) = 1$

In this most general case, the output sample is a weighted sum of the past output samples plus a weighted sum of the present and past input samples. It is a mixed, pole-zero system.

In each of the preceeding approximations, the present output sample is expressed as a linear combination of past (and one present) samples. If the signal under investigation is associated to y(k), or equivalently if it can be viewed as the output of a known linear system (coefficients a(j)'s and b(i)'s known) whose input is a known signal x(k), eqs. (5), (6) or (7) can be used to predict the present sample of the output signal. Iterating these equations, the entire signal y(k) can be predicted. Since this prediction is done as a linear combination of other samples, it is called linear prediction.

There are several possible framework to study in detail linear prediction such as covariance method, autocorrelation method, lattice structures, inverse filtering, spectral estimation, maximum likelihood method, dot product method, etc.

Mathematical developpments for each of them are quite simple. But each step of the computation offer a pletore of possible interpretations. This results in a very rich, precise, reliable and robust technique.

2.7.2 LINEAR PREDICTION WITH ALL POLE SYSTEMS

Linear prediction with all pole systems has the most widespread use because of the following general properties.

Let y(k) denote the signal under investigation. If N past samples of this signal are used to predict its present value, we have :

$$\hat{y}(k) = \sum_{i=1}^{N} a(i)\ y(k-i) \tag{47}$$

It is hoped that $\hat{y}(k) \approx y(k)$. The predicted signal $\hat{y}(k)$ is thus produced with a linear system excited by y(k) and whose transfer function is P(z) given by :

$$P(z) = \sum_{i=1}^{N} a(i)\ z^{-i} \tag{48}$$

This result is obtained by just taking the z transform of both sides of eq. (47) and solving for the transfer function.

The prediction error e(k) is simply the difference between y(k) and $\hat{y}(k)$:

$$e(k) = y(k) - \hat{y}(k) = y(k) - \sum_{i=1}^{N} a(i)\ y(k-i) \tag{49}$$

Again, by taking the z transform of both sides of this equation, we obtain the transfer function Q(z) of the linear system that produces the prediction error signal when excited with the signal y(k). We have :

$$Q(z) = 1 - \sum_{i=1}^{N} a(i)\ z^{-i} = 1 - P(z) \tag{50}$$

Let us assume now the hypothesis that the signal y(k) is produced according to a linear prediction model given by :

$$y(k) = \sum_{i=1}^{N} \alpha(i)\ y(k-i) + GO\ x(k) \tag{51}$$

where the coefficients $\alpha(i)$'s are not known. The transfer function H(z) of this production model is obtained by taking the z transform of both sides of eq. (51) :

$$H(z) = \frac{GO}{1 - \sum_{i=1}^{N} \alpha(i)\ z^{-i}} \tag{52}$$

If the signal y(k) is produced with eq. (51) and if $a(i) = \alpha(i)$ with $i = 1,...,N$, then Q(z) is the inverse filter of H(z) :

$$H(z) = \frac{GO}{Q(z)} \tag{53}$$

In other words, systems characterized by the transfer functions H(z) and Q(z) have opposite effects. The first one produces the signal y(k) from a signal GO x(k), whereas the second produces the prediction error e(k) = GO x(k) from the signal y(k). This discussion is illustrated in Fig. 9. In this context, the prediction problem consists in finding the set coefficients a(i) from y(k) in order to represent this signal in the best possible way — according to a criterion — by eq. (52). Since in this equation Q(z) is a denominator polynomial, we have an all pole system for H(z).

2.7.3 COMPUTING THE PREDICTION COEFFICIENTS

The prediction coefficients are obtained by minimizing the energy of the prediction error e(k). This energy is given by :

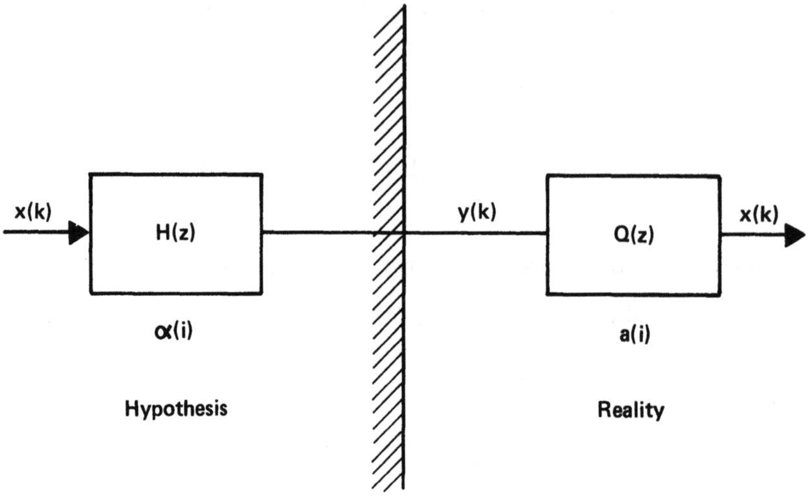

Fig. 9 Illustrating the prediction model.

$$W = \sum_{k=k_1}^{k_2} e^2(k) \tag{54}$$

Eq. (49) can be rewritten as :

$$e(k) = - \sum_{i=0}^{N} a(i)\ y(k-i) \tag{55}$$

with a(0) = -1.

Substituting (55) in (54), we have :

$$W = \sum_k \sum_i \sum_j a(i)\ y(k-i)\ y(k-j)\ a(j) \tag{57}$$

Defining the quadratic form

$$C(i,j) = \sum_{k=k_1}^{k_2} y(k-i)\ y(k-j) \tag{58}$$

we have

$$W = \sum_i \sum_j a(i)\ C(i,j)\ a(j) \tag{59}$$

Setting to zero all the derivaties of W with respect to a(i)'s :

$$C(0,j) = \sum_{i=1}^{N} a(j)\ C(i,j) \tag{60}$$

Particular cases are defined by constraining k_1, k_2 and y(k). For example, if C(i,j) is computed over an infinite interval ($k_1 = -\infty$ and $k_2 = +\infty$) and the signal y(k) is observed over a finite interal from k = 0 to k = N-1 (implicit rectangular window), the quadratic form C(i,j) becomes :

$$\begin{aligned} C(i,j) &= \sum_{-\infty}^{+\infty} y(k-i)\ y(k-j) = \sum_{-\infty}^{+\infty} y(k)\ y(k+|i-j|) \\ &= \sum_{-\infty}^{+\infty} y(k)\ y(k+|i-j|) = \varphi_y(|i-j|) \end{aligned} \tag{61}$$

In this case C(i,j) is the autocorrelation function and the method used to solve (60) for a(i)'s is called autocorrelation method.

If $k_1 = M$ where M is the order of the predictor to start the prediction with M initial conditions and $k_2 = N-1$, C(i,j) behaves like a covariance matrix. The method using this case to solve (60) is called covariance method.

Different polynomials Q(z) are obtained with different methods and analysis conditions. The autocorrelation method guarantees in theory the stability of H(z) given by (52) but requires a window on the signal which reduces the frequency resolution. On the other hand, the covariance method does not require any window, but does not guarantee the stability. The lattice method overcomes these problems, provides a quite general solution and guarantees the stability.

2.7.4 LATTICE METHOD [2]

The lattice method is obtained by computing two predictions on the signal, one for the future (which will be denoted by +) and one for the past (which will be denoted by -). Fig. 10 shows a signal x(k) and its samples to illustrate these predictions. Starting with the sample x(k-m) the future prediction is

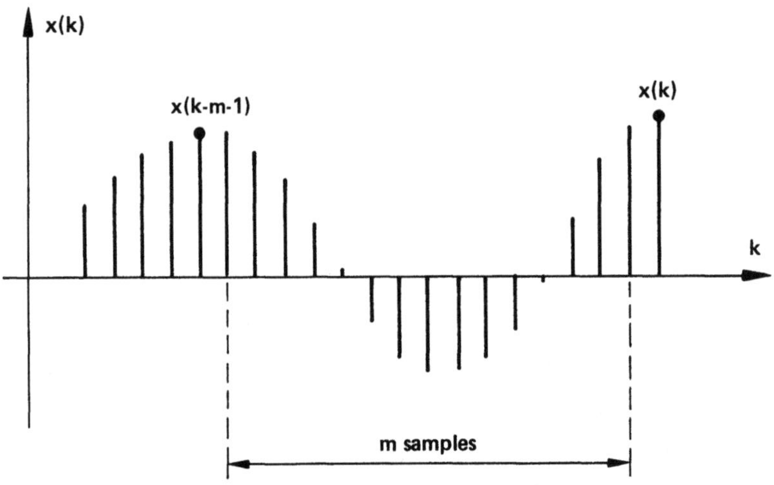

Fig. 10 Illustrating past and future predictions.

computed according to :

$$\hat{x}_{m+}(k) = - \sum_{i=1}^{m} a(m,i)\ x(k-i) \tag{62}$$

where m is a parameter taking the values 1, 2, ..., M. The prediction error is :

$$x_m^+(k) = x(k) - \hat{x}_{m+}(k) = \sum_{i=0}^{m} a(m,i)\ x(k-i) \tag{63}$$

with a(m,0) = 1. The past prediction is computed similarly :

$$\hat{x}_{m-}(k) = - \sum_{i=1}^{m} b(m,i)\ x(k-i) \tag{64}$$

leading to the past prediction error :

$$x_m^- = x(k\text{-}m\text{-}1) - \hat{x}_{m-}(k) = \sum_{i=0}^{m} b(m,i)\ x(k\text{-}i) \tag{65}$$

with $b(m,m+1) = 1$.

Note that in eq. (65) the error is computed at $x(k - m - 1)$ to have causal systems. The criterion used is the simultaneous minimization of the past and future prediction error energies, computed over the interval [k0,k1] :

$$W_+(m) = \sum_{k=k_0}^{k_1} |x_m^+(k)|^2 \quad \text{and} \quad W_-(m) = \sum_{k=k_0}^{k_1} |x_m^-(k)|^2 \tag{66}$$

with $m = 1, ..., M$

The transfer functions of the future and past predictors (62) and (64) are given respectively by :

$$A_m(z) = \sum_{i=0}^{m} a(m,i)\ z^{-i} \quad \text{and} \quad B_m(z) = \sum_{i=0}^{m} b(m,i)\ z^{-i} \tag{67}$$

It can be shown [2] that the simultaneous minimization of prediction error energies given by (66) leads the orthogonality of the polynomials $A_m(z)$ and $B_m(z)$ to z^{-j} :

$$\{A_m(z),\ z^{-j}\} = 0 \quad \text{and} \quad \{B_m(z),\ z^{-j}\} = 0 \tag{68}$$

where {.,.} represents the dot product.

The lattice structure is obtained by establishing iteratively the form of the polynomials $A_m(z)$ and $B_m(z)$ for $m = 1,...,M$ using two initial conditions $a(0,i) = b(0,i) = 1$. Iterations are governed by :

$$A_m(z) = A_{m-1}(z) + k_m B_{m-1}(z) \tag{69}$$

and by :

$$B_m(z) = z^{-1}[B_{m-1}(z) + k_m A_{m-1}(z)] \tag{70}$$

where k_m is given by :

$$k_m = (-1/W_{m-1}) \sum_{k=k_0}^{k_1} x^+_{m-1}(k)x^-_{m-1}(k) \tag{71}$$

and can be interpreted as partial correlation coefficient.

Taking the z transform of both sides of (63) and (65), substituting in this result (69) and (70) and taking the inverse z transform, we obtain the equations of the lattice structure :

$$x^+_m(k) = x^+_{m-1}(k) + k_m x^-_{m-1}(k) \text{ and } x^-_m(k) = x^-_{m-1}(k) + k_m x^+_{m-1}(k) \tag{72}$$

Fig. 11 shows the lattice structure of a filter equivalent to the filter characterized by the transfer function Q(z) given by (50) and producing the prediction error e(k). Because of the modularity contained in it, this structure is very suitable for hardware implementations.

2.8 HOMOMORPHIC PROCESSING OF SIGNALS

Homomorphic processing is a convenient tool to be used for processing signals combined by convolution or multiplication (modulation). Let us assume that the observed signal is given by $z(k) = x(k) \cdot y(k)$ or $z(k) = x(k) * y(k)$ where x(k) is the signal to be recovered. Clearly, in these cases linear filtering theory cannot be used, independently from its well known and powerful techniques. Two approaches can be envisioned. The first one consists in developing special methods to solve these problems, whereas the second attempts to transform these problems into other problems already solved, for example by using linear system theory. The second approach seems to be easier to develop and to apply, because it benefits from the large amount of available results in linear system

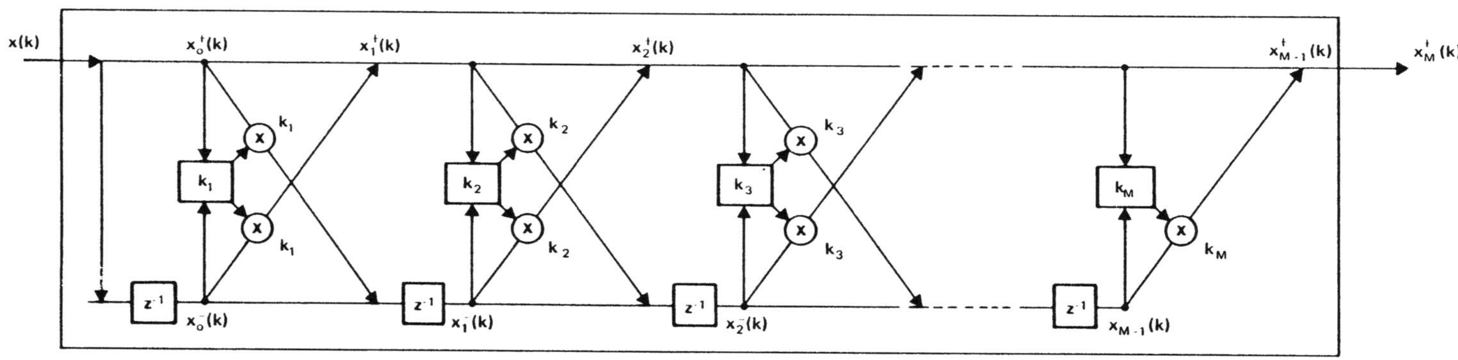

Fig. 11 Lattice structure for linear prediction

theory.

2.8.1 MULTIPLIED SIGNALS

If the observed signal is of the form :

$$x(k) = [x_1^{a_1}(k)]\ [x_{x[2]}^{a_2}(k)] \tag{73}$$

where a1 and a2 are two arbitrary constants, the well known way to transform this signal into a weighted sum is the use of logarithm. The real logarithm may be too restrictive because it can be used only for strictly positive signals or for signals which have been previously rescaled with the addition of a constant value to render them positive. The complex logarithm, however, can be used for bipolar or complex signals. In polar coordinates, a complex signal x(k) can be written as :

$$x(k) = |x(k)| \exp\ [j \arg(x(k)]$$

$$= \exp[\ln|x(k)| + j \arg x(k)] \tag{74}$$

The complex logarithm, denoted by ln[.], is then :

$$\ln[x(k)] = \ln|x(k)| + j \arg x(k) \tag{75}$$

As defined, the complex logarithm has an important disadvantage. It is not a one-to-one transformation. Its argument is defined modul 2π, i.e. adding multiples of 2π to the argument in (75) does not change the result. In other words, the phase is wrapped around the unit circle. To remove this ambiguity from the argument of the complex logarithm, all the arguments to be used need to be defined as continuous functions of x(k). With a continuous argument, the complex logarithm becomes a one-to-one transform. If ever, the former form of the argument is required, it is sufficient to compute it modulo 2π. Usually, what is given in the first place is the argument modulo 2π. There are several algorithms to transform such an argument into a continuous function. This operation is known as phase unwrapping. Fig. 12 shows wrapped and unwrapped versions of an argument.

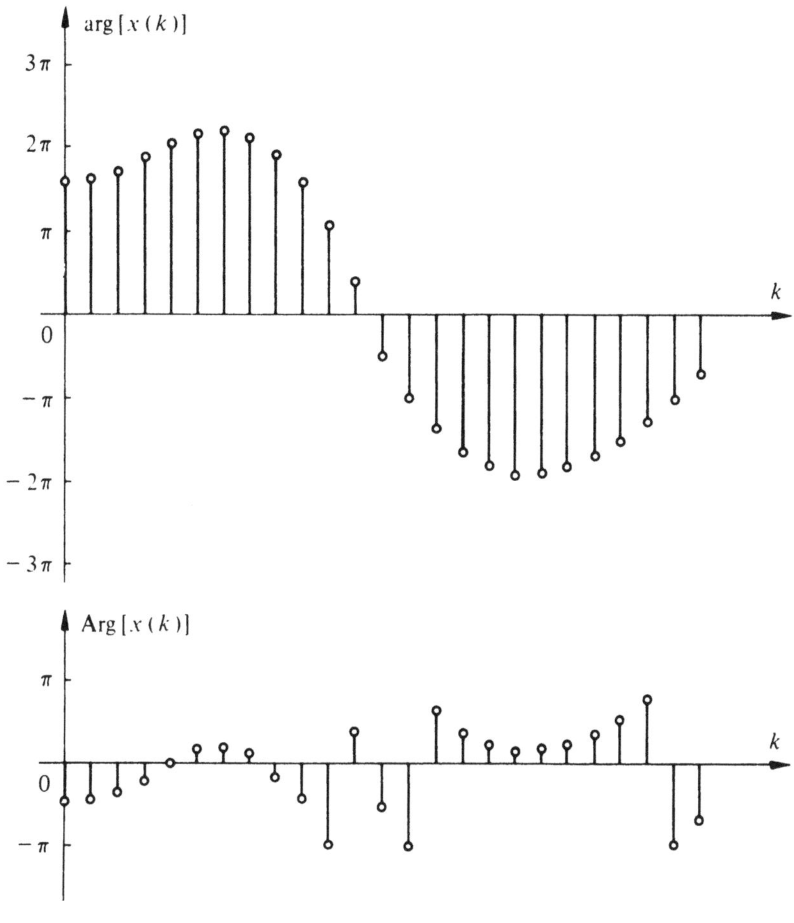

Fig. 12 Wrapped and unwrapped phase curve.

If the complex logarithm is now applied to the input signal x(k) given by eq. (73), the result is :

$$\hat{x}(k) = \ln[x(k)] = a1\ \ln[x_1(k)] + a2\ \ln[x_2(k)]$$

$$= a1\ \hat{x}_1(k) + a2\ \hat{x}_2(k) \qquad (76)$$

Notice that, now, the input signal x(k) is transformed into a signal $\hat{x}$ (k) which is a linear combination of other signals. Hence, according to the frequency content of $\hat{x}_1(k)$ and $\hat{x}_2(k)$, linear filtering may be used to recover for example $\hat{x}_1(k)$ or $\hat{x}_2(k)$ to the detriment of the other. Once the transformed version of the signal we are looking for is obtained, the signal itself is simply given by the inverse transform, i.e. :

$$x(k) = \exp[\hat{x}(k)] \tag{77}$$

The results of this section show that with a nonlinear one-to-one transformation, it is possible to transpose a multiplicative combination of signals into an additive combination, a familiar situation in which linear system theory can be used. Fig. 13 shows the block diagram of a homomorphic system for multiplied signals.

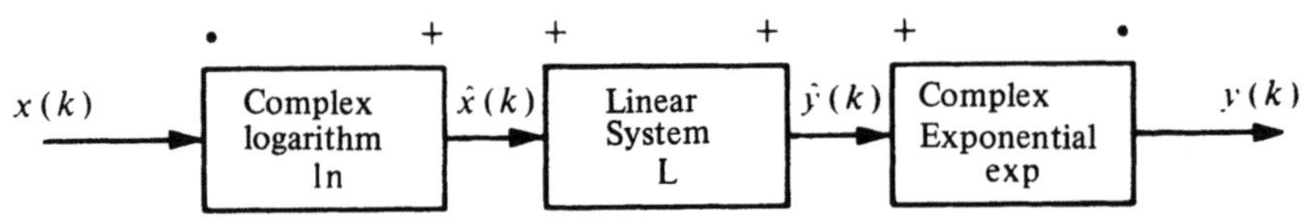

Fig. 13 Block diagram for homomorphic processing of multiplied signals.

As an example related to speech signals, let us consider the dynamic range handling. Whenever a speech signal changes its physical support, dynamic ranges on both supports should be measured and compared. Very often they are not compatible. It is therefore necessary to compress or expend the dynamic range before changing the recording media. The speech signal can be viewed as a low frequency envelope e(k) modulated with a high frequency carrier p(k). Hence, the input signal is :

$$x(k) = e(k) \cdot p(k) \tag{78}$$

Since e(k) is strictly positive, the complex logarithm leads to :

$$\hat{x}(k) = \ln e(k) + \ln|p(k)| + j \arg[p(k)] \qquad (79)$$

A linear filter can be used to compress or to expand the dynamic range of e(k) as given by :

$$\hat{y}(k) = a \ln e(k) + b \ln|p(k)| + jb \arg[p(k)] \qquad (80)$$

In practice, b = 1 because the carrier does not influence too much the dynamic range of e(k). If a is larger than 1, the dynamic range is expended. In contrast, if a is less than 1, the dynamic range is compressed.

2.8.2 CONVOLVED SIGNALS

In this case, the observed signal x(k) is the convolution of two signals x (k) and x (k), the former being the signal of interest.

$$x(k) = \sum_{l=-\infty}^{+\infty} x_1(l)\, x_2(k-l) = x_1(k) * x_2(k) \qquad (81)$$

The problem is now to recover $x_1(k)$ from x(k). Remembering eq. (14), if the discrete Fourier transform is applied to both sides of eq. (81), the result is a simple product :

$$X(n) = X_1(n) \cdot X_2(n) \qquad (82)$$

Notice that the use of the discrete Fourier transform for convolved signals, transform this problem into a problem that has just been solved, ie. the problem of multiplied signals. Since the discrete Fourier transform of a signal can be viewed as a complex signal, all that has to be done is to take the complex logarithm of both sides of eq. (82). We have :

$$\ln [X(n)] = \ln [X_1(n)] + \ln [X_2(n)] \qquad (83)$$

Now, the convolved input signal is transformed into a linearly combined signal for which the linear system theory may again be applied. Notice also that, in constrast with eq. (76), in this case signals are function of the frequency and not of the time. If a linear filter is to be used for eq. (83), it should be a filter whose impulse response is expressed in the frequency domain and its frequency response in the time domain. This is rather an uncomfortable situation in which it is not difficult to mix up time and frequency. To overcome this difficulty, the inverse Fourier transform of both sides of eq. (83) can be taken, leading to :

$$\hat{x}(k) = \mathcal{F}^{-1} \ln [X(n)]$$

$$= \hat{x}_1(k) + \hat{x}_2(k) \tag{84}$$

which is now a time domain equation for linearly combined signals. Linear filtering can be applied to this equation to recover $\hat{x}_1(k)$ or $\hat{x}_2(k)$. Then, to transform everything back to the original representation, a discrete Fourier transform should be computed first. Its result is then exponentiated and inverse Fourier transformed. Fig. 14 shows the block diagram of a homomorphic system for convolved signal. Notice that solving eq. (81) for $x_1(k)$ is the inverse of convolution. This operation is commonly referred to as deconvolution. Homomorphic processing is one of the possible ways to deconvolve a signal. The inverse Fourier transform of the complex logarithm of the Fourier transform of a signal is called cepstrum; a word obtained by scrambling the letters of the word spectrum. It finds a rather large number of applications in speech processing such as echo removal, pitch detection, speech parameters estimation and restoration.

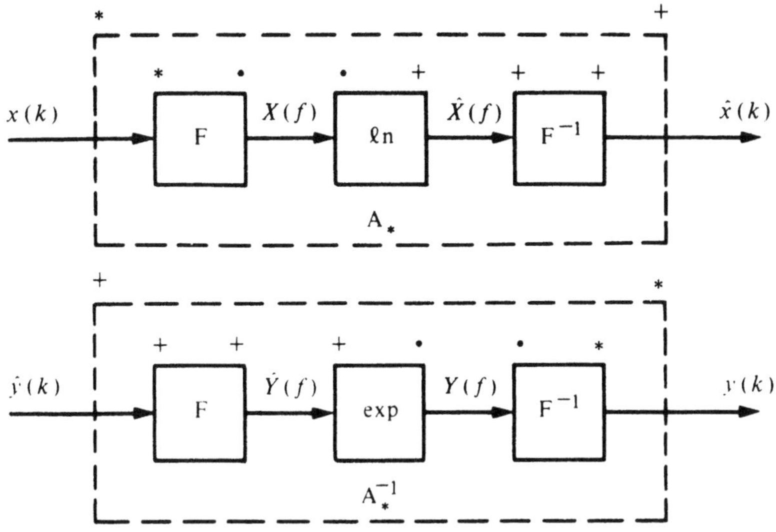

Fig. 14 Block diagram for homomorphic processing of convolved signals.

2.8.3 MAJOR APPLICATIONS OF THE CEPSTRUM

In this section three major applications of the cepstrum are given.

As a first case, let us consider a recorded signal x(k) resulting from several echos of the same initial signal $x_1(k)$:

$$x(k) = x_1(k) + \sum_{i=1}^{M} \alpha(i)\ x_1(k\text{-}ki) \tag{85}$$

where $\alpha(i)$'s are different attenuation factors and ki's the corresponding delays. Eq. (85) can be viewed as the convolution of the signal $x_1(k)$ given by :

$$x_2(k) = d(k) + \sum_{i=1}^{M} \alpha(i)\ d(k\text{-}ki) \tag{86}$$

where d(k) is the unit sample. For simplicity, let us consider one echo only, i.e. M = 1. The discrete Fourier transform of (86) is :

$$X_2(n) = 1 + \alpha(1)\exp[-j2\pi k_1 n/N] \tag{87}$$

Taking the complex logarithm, we have :

$$X_2(n) = \ln[1 + \alpha(1)\exp(-j2\pi k_1 n/N)] \tag{88}$$

This function is periodical of period $1/k_1$. Accordingly, the cepstrum $\hat{x}_2(k)$ will be nonzero only for integer multiples of k_1. In the cepstrum of the recorded signal, the non zero values of $\hat{x}_2(k)$ will appear as peaks. To surpress the echo, these peaks should be eliminated. This can be done with a comb filter applied to the cepstrum $\hat{x}(k)$ which recovers only the contribution of $\hat{x}_1(k)$. The inverse transform gives the original signal without any echo. Fig. 15 shows various functions involved in filtering the cepstrum for echo removal.

The second application of the cepstrum is its use in pitch detection and speech parametres estimation. A voiced portion of a speech signal can be modeled as shown in Fig. 16. The excitation signal e(k) containing a pulse train is filtered with a time-varying filter whose impulse response is h(k). A prefilter is also introduced to better represent vocal cords. Its impulse response is denoted by g(k). Accordingly, the produced speech s(k) is given by :

$$s(k) = e(k) * g(k) * h(k) \tag{89}$$

over a short period of time (10-30 ms). To avoid discontinuities at the ends of each speech segment, a window function w(k) is introduced, producing the windowed speech x(k) :

$$\begin{aligned} x(k) &= s(k) \cdot w(k) \\ &= [e(k)*g(k)*h(k)]w(k) \end{aligned} \tag{90}$$

Assuming that the window w(k) is smooth enough over the variation of g(k) * h(k), we have :

$$x(k) = e_w(k)*g(k)*h(k)$$

with

$$e_w(k) = e(k) \cdot w(k) \tag{91}$$

If the pitch period is k0, then :

$$e_w(k) = \sum_{m=0}^{M-1} w(mk0)\ d(k-mk0) \tag{92}$$

where M is the number of pulses seen through the window. The discrete Fourier transform of eq. (92) is given by :

$$E_w(n) = \sum_{m=0}^{M-1} w(mk0)\ \exp(-j2\pi nmk0/N) \tag{93}$$

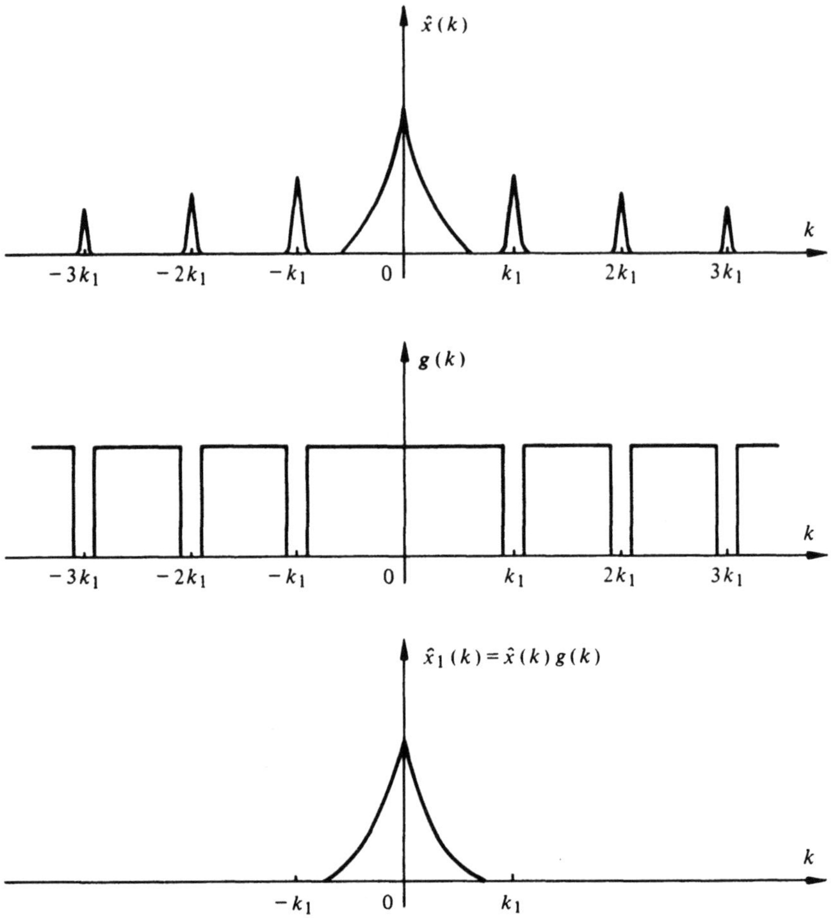

Fig. 15 Echo removal by deconvolution

This function is periodical with a period of 1/k0. The Fourier transform of the cepstrum ê(k) will also be periodical with the same period, since the logarithm is a memoryless monotonic function. Accordingly, the cepstrum ê(k) will be non zero only at integer multiples of k0. On the other hand, the duration of the composite impulse response $g(k) * h(k)$ does not exceed a few dozens of milli seconds. In the cepstral domain, the contribution of this composite impulse response is non negligible only over a short time interval around the origin. A high-pass time filter applied to the cepstrum will isolate e(k), whereas a low-pass time filter recovers the composite impulse response $g(k) * h(k)$. Fig. 17 illustrates, on a voiced speech section, various steps of this procedure.

The last application which will be described here concerns the restoration of old recordings. If s(k) denotes a speech signal or a song produced by an artist, its recorded version can be modeled as a convolution :

$$x(k) = s(k)*g(k) \tag{94}$$

where g(k) is the impulse response of the recording system. The only assumption of this method is that the length of the impulse response g(k) is much shorter than that of the signal s(k). If the recording is done with old equipment and if there is no way to repeat the recording with modern equipment, it is necessary to recover s(k) to avoid the effects of the recording system contained in g(k). In general s(k) is a nonstationary signal which excludes the use of classical filtering techniques. Homomorphic deconvolution can be applied in this case also. Taking the complex logarithm of the Fourier transform of both sides of (94) leads to :

$$\ln[X(n)] = \ln[S(n)] + \ln[G(n)] \tag{95}$$

The difficulty of this problem is that not only s(k) is not known but also g(k), and hence G(n). A possible way to estimate G(n) is the use of eq. (95) for several, uncorrelated recordings, so that after averaging the right side of eq. (95) will converge to G(n). The problem is that it is difficult, if not impossible, to find a large number of old recordings recorded with the same equipment under

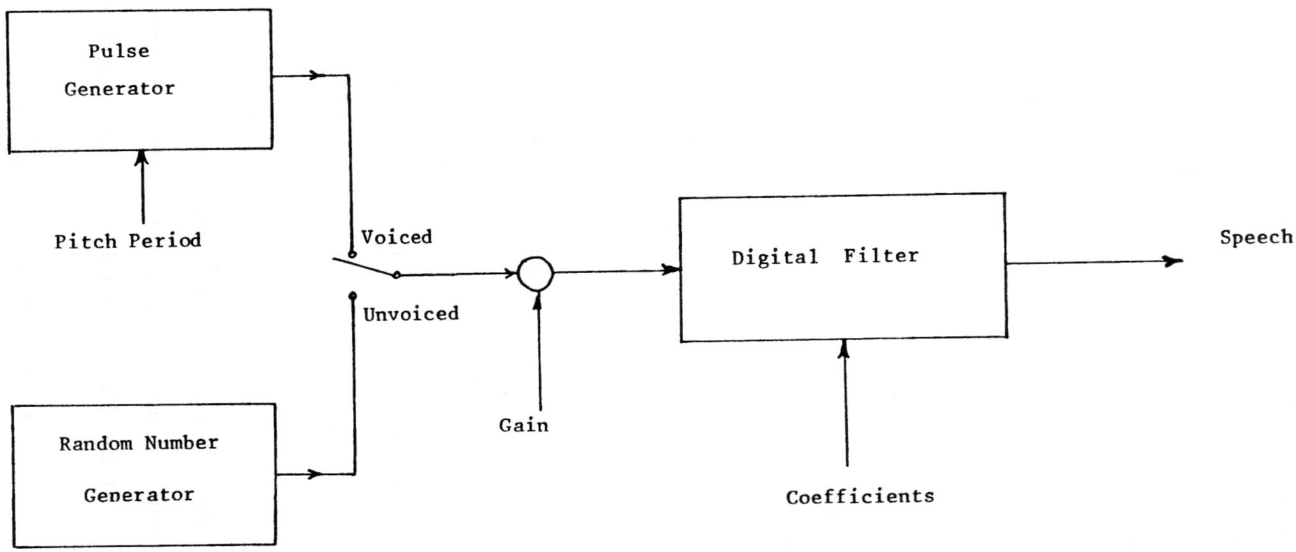

Fig. 16 Voiced speech production model

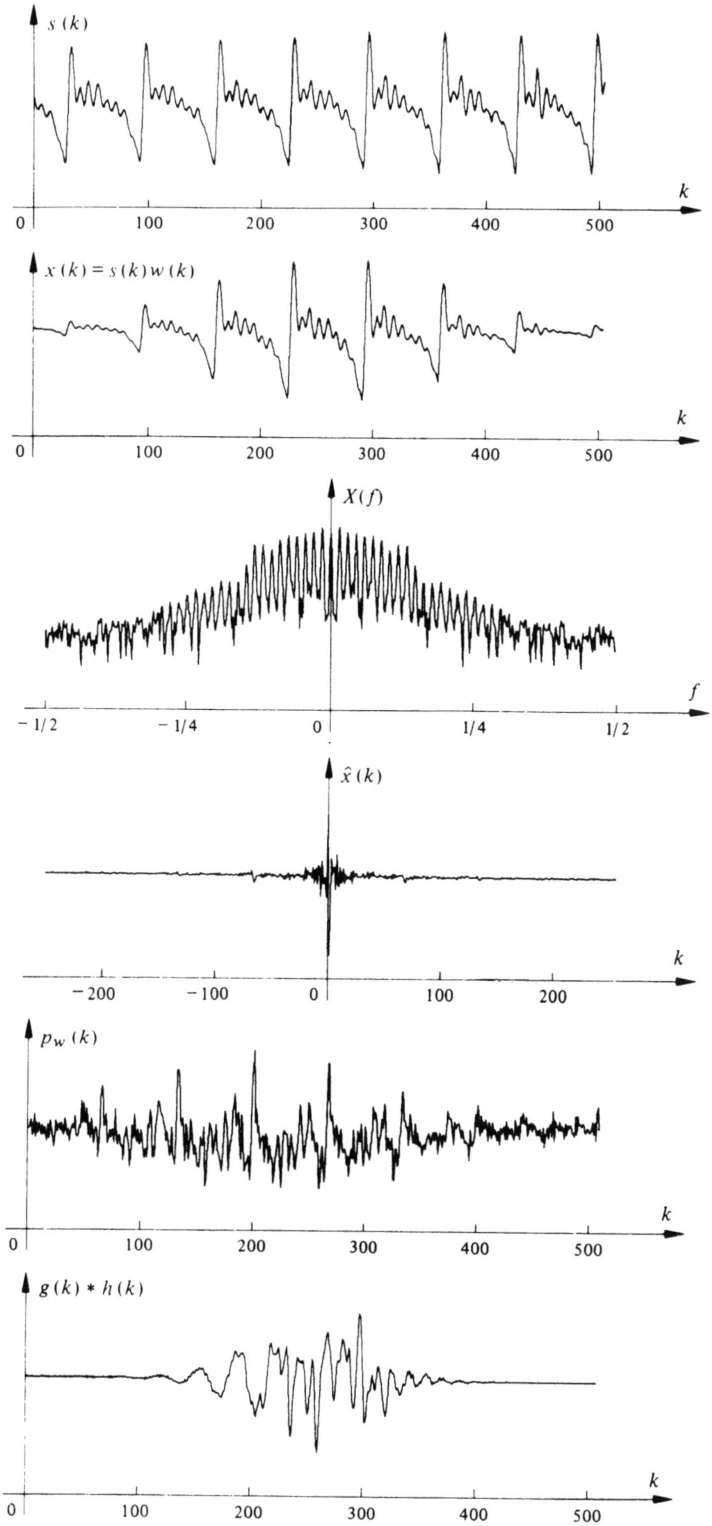

Fig. 17 Pitch period and parameter estimation

comparable conditions. This problem can be overcome if the recording x(k) is divided into several segments $x_i(k)$ of moderate length, a few seconds for example, longer than that of the impulse response g(k). Since each of these sections contains different s(k)'s, statistical filtering (averaging) may be applied. A given section $x_i(k)$ can be viewed as a windowed part of the signal x(k), i.e. :

$$x_i(k) = w_i(k)\ x(k) = w_i(k)[s(k)*g(k)] \tag{96}$$

Assuming that the window is smooth enough over g(k), we have :

$$\begin{aligned} x_i(k) &= [w_i(k)s(k)] * g(k) \\ &= s_i(k)*g(k) \end{aligned} \tag{97}$$

The complex logarithm of the Fourier transform of both sides of eq. (97) leads to :

$$\ln[X_i(n)] = \ln[S_i(n)] + \ln[G(n)] \tag{98}$$

If M denotes the number of section $x_i(k)$ in x(k), the average of both sides of eq. (98) gives :

$$(1/M) \sum_{i=1}^{M} \ln[X_i(n)] = (1/M) \sum_{i=1}^{M} [\ln[S_i(n)] + \ln[G(n)]] \tag{99}$$

The first term in the right hand side of eq. (99) is the estimate of the logarithmic power spectrum of s(k). It can be estimated by using a contemporary recording of the same song or speech recorded with modern equipment. For these systems G(n) is flat over a wide frequency range and equal to 1. So, if eq. (99) is used for a new recording, ln[G(n)] is zero and hence :

$$\frac{1}{M} \sum_{i=1}^{M} \ln[s_i(n)] = \ln[s(n)] \tag{100}$$

Substituting this in eq. (99) and solving with respect to G(n), we have :

$$\ln[G(n)] = (1/M) \sum_{i=1}^{M} \ln[X_i(n)] - \ln[S(n)] \tag{101}$$

Since the logarithm used is complex, eq. (101) should be written for the magnitude and for the phase. Neglecting the phase as a first approximation, we have :

$$\ln|G(n)| = (1/M) \sum_{i=1}^{M} \ln|X_i(n)| - \ln|S(n)| \tag{102}$$

The deconvolution is then obtained with a filter whose frequency response is the inverse of G(n), i.e. :

$$|G_r(n)| = 1/|G(n)| \tag{103}$$

The phase of $G_r(n)$ can either be obtained with the Hilbert transform or be neglected. Stokham used this method to restore old recodings from E. Caruso done in 1907 and obtained spectacularly good results [4].

To conclude this paragraph, notice that all the applications of the cepstrum are related to the deconvolution problem. The same ideas are also used for two dimensional signals, i.e. digital images.

3. SPEECH ANALYSIS-SYNTHESIS

In this section, we present principles and models of speech analysis and synthesis and show the use of signal processing methods in this context. After recalling the fundamentals of the speech signal, the principle of speech analysis-synthesis and speech short-time processing, we treat speech analysis and synthesis in two main sections. The first of them, spectral analysis, explores spectral envelope analysis and synthesis in the various speech synthesis models. The second is dedicated to pitch detection and pitch period measurement.

3.1 SPEECH SIGNAL

The speech signal is modeled after the speech production mechanism.

3.1.1 SPEECH PRODUCTION

Major elements of the vocal apparatus are: the lung, the larynx and the vocal tract:

a) The lung is the source of energy in form of air under pressure.

b) The larynx consists of three cartilages supporting the vocal cords which is an opening of variable size through which air from the lung flows. Voiced sounds are produced by adjusting the vocal cords in a way that they vibrate and modulate the air flow. Unvoiced sounds are produced by keeping the vocal cords open.

c) The vocal tract consists of: 1) the pharynx and oral tract which together from a tube, 17 to 20 cm in length, whose cross section varies with jaw, tongue and lips position; and 2) the nasal tract, 12 cm in length and of fixed cross section, which lies in parallel with the oral tract and is made active or inactive by displacing the velum.

Speech is the product of an original excitation, later modified by the vocal tract.

A first type of excitation, responsible for producing voiced sounds, is the airflow modulation produced by vibrating vocal cords. The excitation signal is periodic (pitch) and its spectrum displays harmonics whose power spectrum decreases with an average of 12 dB/octave.

A second type of excitation, responsible for producing unvoiced sounds, is the air turbulence provoked by a constriction somewhere in the vocal tract. The signal has noise characteristics.

The vocal tract acts as a resonator and modifies the excitation signal. For voiced sounds, the vocal tract usually shows 4 resonances which are called formants and which characterize the sound. Fig. 10 shows a typical spectrum of a voiced sound where both the periodic excitation spectrum and the formants are visible. When the nasal tract is also active then the overall transfer function also includes zeros call antiformants.

3.1.2 SPEECH MODEL

All speech production models have in common the separation of excitation features, which are accounted for by two pulse train generators and resonator features, which are accounted for by a time-varying linear system. Thus speech production is modeled after Fig. 18.

3.1.3 SPEECH ANALYSIS AND SYNTHESIS

The basic schema of a vocoder is given in Fig. 19. There are four main functions. The analysis functions are: detection and measurement of the pitch of fundamental frequency F_o, and analysis of the spectral envelope. The two synthesis functions are: generation of the excitation and restitution of the spectral envelope. Next sections will describe this function more in detail. However, compression of the data flow between analyser and synthesiser is not described further.

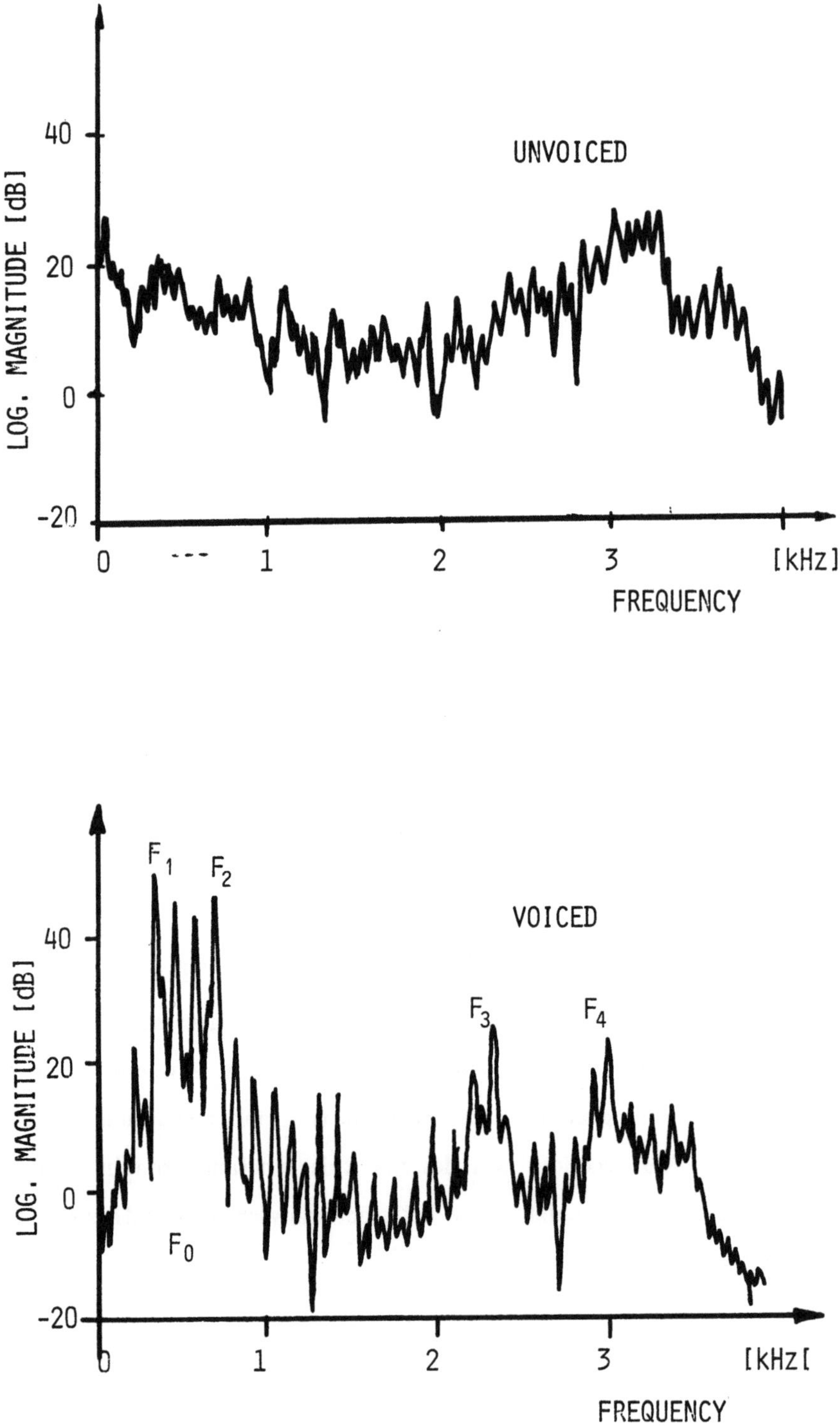

Fig. 18 Spectrum of a voiced sound

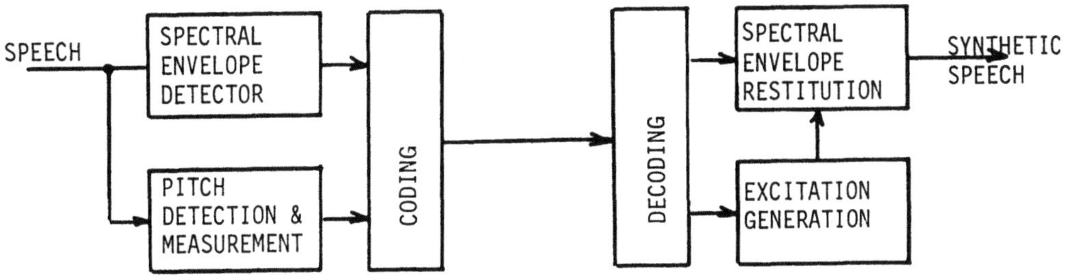

Fig. 19 Main functions of speech analysis and synthesis

3.1.4 SHORT-TIME SPEECH ANALYSIS

The properties of the speech signal change relatively slowly with time. This leads to short-time processing methods in which speech segments called frames are isolated and processed as if they had fixed properties. Such segments can be isolated by multiplication with a window sequence w(k) positioned at a location $k = \ell$. Windowing the speech signal x(k) using the time-domain window w(k) leads to the analysis sequence:

$$x_\ell(k) = x(k) \cdot w(\ell-k) \tag{104}$$

Two examples of short-time parameters are given. The short-time average magnitude is defiend by :

$$M(1) = \sum_{k=\ell}^{\ell+N-1} x(k) \cdot w(\ell-k) \tag{105}$$

The short-time average zero-crossing rate is defined by :

$$Z(k) = \sum_{k=\ell}^{\ell+N-1} c(k) \cdot w(\ell-k) \tag{106}$$

where : $c(k) = \begin{cases} 1 & \text{if } \operatorname{sign}(x(k)) \neq \operatorname{sign}(x(k-1)) \\ 0 & \text{else} \end{cases}$

3.2 SPECTRAL ANALYSIS-SYNTHESIS

We describe here the analysis and restitution of the spectral envelope. The various interpretations of short-time Fourier analysis are given and three vocoders are described.

3.2.1 SHORT-TIME FOURIER ANALYSIS

Three interpretations of the short-time Fourier transform are given. First it is defined as the normal Fourier transform of a sequence which is limited in time. Using the window sequence w(k) which is 0 outside the significant range $k = 1..N$, we find, using the definition of eq. (1), the short-time Fourier transform in its discrete form:

$$X_\ell(n) = \sum_{k=\ell}^{\ell+N-1} w(\ell-k) \cdot x(k) \cdot \exp(-j2\pi kn/N) \tag{107}$$

with : $n = -N/2, \ldots, N/2-1$

where N is the maximum width of the window sequence w(k). Note that it is a function of both the discrete frequency n and the position ℓ of the window. A first interpretation of X (n) is as follows. Eq. (107) can be seen as the DFT of a sequence $w(\ell-k) \cdot x(k)$ which itself, according to eq. (104) is the x(k) sequence observed through a window with impulse response w(k) displaced at position ℓ.

The second interpretation derives directly from eq. (107) by considering it as the convolution defined in eq. (3).

$$X_\ell(n) = [x(k) \cdot \exp(-j2\pi kn/N)] * w(k) \tag{108}$$

We thus obtain $X_\ell(n)$ by cascading a modulation of x(k) by exp(-j2πkn/N) and a filter with impulse response w(k).

To catch the third meaning of $X_\ell(n)$, we transform the equation above into the equivalent form:

$$X_\ell(n) = \exp(-j2\pi kn/N) \sum_{k=\ell}^{\ell+N-1} x(\ell-k) \cdot w(k) \cdot \exp(j2\pi kn/N) \tag{109}$$

which interprets as the result of modulating (exp(-j2πkn/N)) the output of a complex bandpass filter whose impulse response is w(k) exp(j2πkn/N). The practical consequence of this interpretation is that $X_\ell(n)$ can be obtained by filtering x(k) with a bandpass filter followed by a modulator. Moreover, in vocoders we are satisfied with the amplitude of the complex value $X_\ell(n)$. Using equation above, we find :

$$|X_\ell(n)| = \left| \sum_{k=\ell}^{\ell+N-1} x(1-k) \cdot w(k) \cdot \exp(j2\pi kn/N)\right| \tag{110}$$

which now has the following interpretation: $|X_\ell(n)|$ is obtained by cascading a bandpass filter with impulse response w(k)exp(j2πkn/N) and a RMS circuit. Also, it can be shown that an equivalent result is obtained if an envelope detector is used instead of the RMS circuit.

As a way to compare the interpretations given, we emphasize the respective role of the window in each form. It appears as a simple window function w(1-k) first, then as (low-pass) impulse response w(k) and finally as (bandpass) impulse response w(k)exp(j2πkn/N).

3.2.2 ANALYSIS AND SYNTHESIS METHODS

Spectral analysis is the transform of eq. (107). As shown right above, it can be realized either by linear filtering of x(k) according to eq. (110) or by FFT of w(l-k) · x(k).

Spectral synthesis is given by the inverse DFT of X (n) according to eq. 2. Three synthesis methods are now shown. To each corresponds a particular vocoder structure.

3.2.3 CHANNEL VOCODER

Principally, the speech spectrum is divided by a number of continguous bandpasses at the input and reconstructed by addition at the output. A channel is affected to each bandpass.

Practically, either a filter bank to implement digital filtering or FFT to implement DFT is being used both for analysis and synthesis. An other practical aspect is the division of the spectrum in several bands. Both uniform and non-uniform spectrum division is used. In the case of non-uniform spectrum division, the channel bandwidth increases with frequency (exponential law for instance) to account for the characteristics of the human ear.

Fig. 20 shows the principle of a channel vocoder using filter banks both for analysis and synthesis.

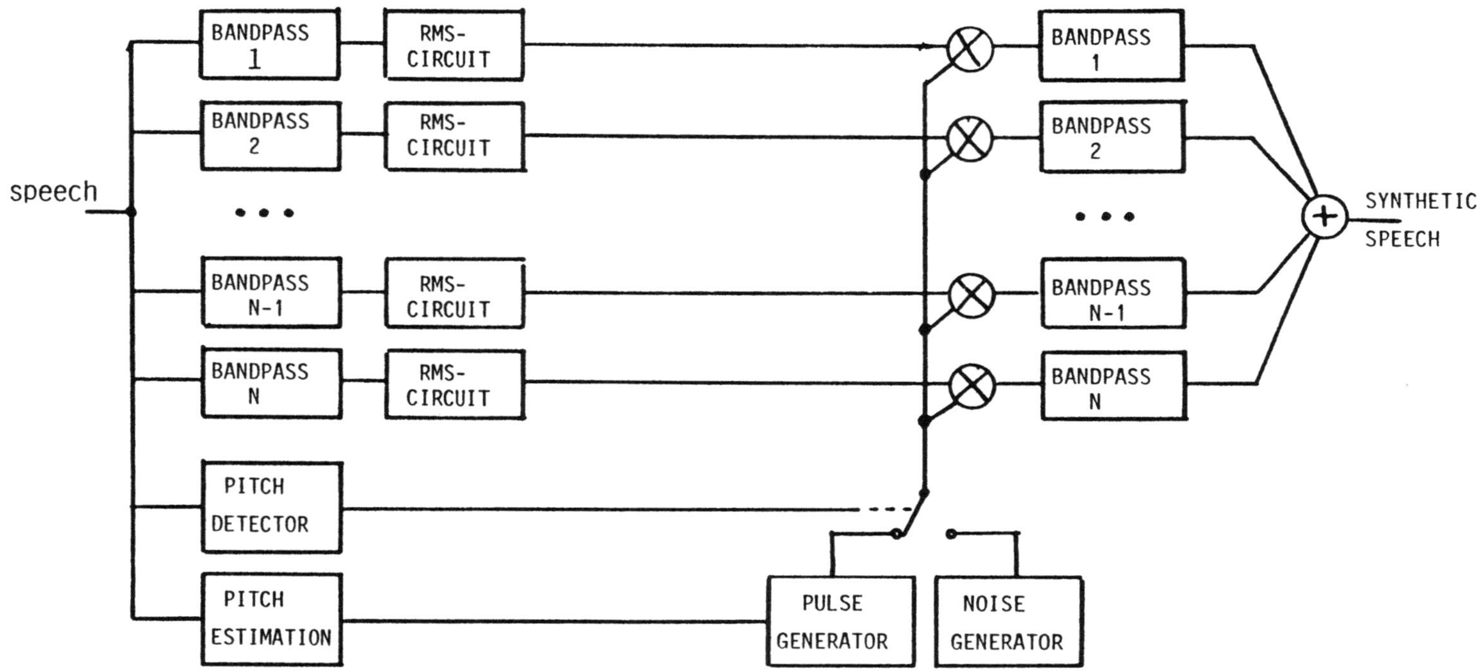

Fig. 20 Channel vocoder

3.2.4 FORMANT VOCODER

Rather than dividing the spectrum envelope in fixed contiguous bandpasses, this approach characterizes the spectral envelope by more specific information like the position, the amplitude and width of the formants. A better speech quality or better compresion factor is expected by this more specific approach.

Starting from a speech synthesis model which uses a cascade of digital resonators as a time-varying digital filter, the basic step is to find the model parameters fulfilling the following criteria: best match of the spectral envelope found by analysis, with the DFT of the system impulse response. For example, a system can use a 5 pole digital filter to account for voiced sounds and a 1 pole-1 zero digital filter for unvoiced sounds. The variable filter parameters are the pole positions F_1, F_2, F_3 for the voiced component and both the pole and zero position Fp and Fz for the unvoiced component.

A first analysis method directly finds the first three maxima of the short-time spectrum by simple peak detection. Practically, a rather large number of channels (30 to 50) is required in order to obtain a high enough spectral resolution to make those maxima detectable. Note that some kind of smoothing must be applied to the spectrum in order to remove the periodic pitch structure. By one method call cepstral smoothing, the pitch signal is filtered out from the cepstrum x (k).

A second, more simple analysis method divides the spectrum in three analysis channels by bandpass-filtering. The bandpasses are designed such as to capture each, one of the first formants F_1, F_2, F_3 and also, they are selected broad-banded enough to allow a sufficiently large variation of formant position. Then, the exact formant position and power is obtained by measurement of both the average zero-crossing rate eq. (106) as well as the average power in each channel.

A third method, called **analysis-by-synthesis**, proceeds by successive approximation. The model parameter are varied as long as to get, at the output, a good approximation of the input function.

Fig. 21 shows also an example of pole-zero locations for the two time-varying digital filters of the formant synthesizer.

3.2.5 LINEAR PREDICTION VOCODER

To remedy certain shortcomings encountered with the formant synthesizer, the filter model is now changed in that the cascade of second-order filters is replaced by a higher order linear system. The purpose of this system is to model together the excitation pulse shape, the vocal tract and other effects as well. The transfer function of the filter is of the form:

$$H(z) = \frac{1}{1 - \sum_{i=1}^{M} a_i \cdot z^{-i}} \tag{111}$$

where M is the filter order, typical values being 10 or 12; and $\{a_i, i = 1 \cdot M\}$ are the model parameter called the predictor coefficients. Their determination was shown in section 2.7.3.

Fig. 22 illustrates the corresponding linear predictive (LPC) synthesizer.

3.3 PITCH DETECTION AND PITCH PERIOD ESTIMATION

The purpose of pitch analysis is to provide the two pitch dependant parameters of the model: excitation mode (voiced/unvoiced) and pitch period value. The corresponding analysis procedures are pitch detection respectively pitch period estimation.

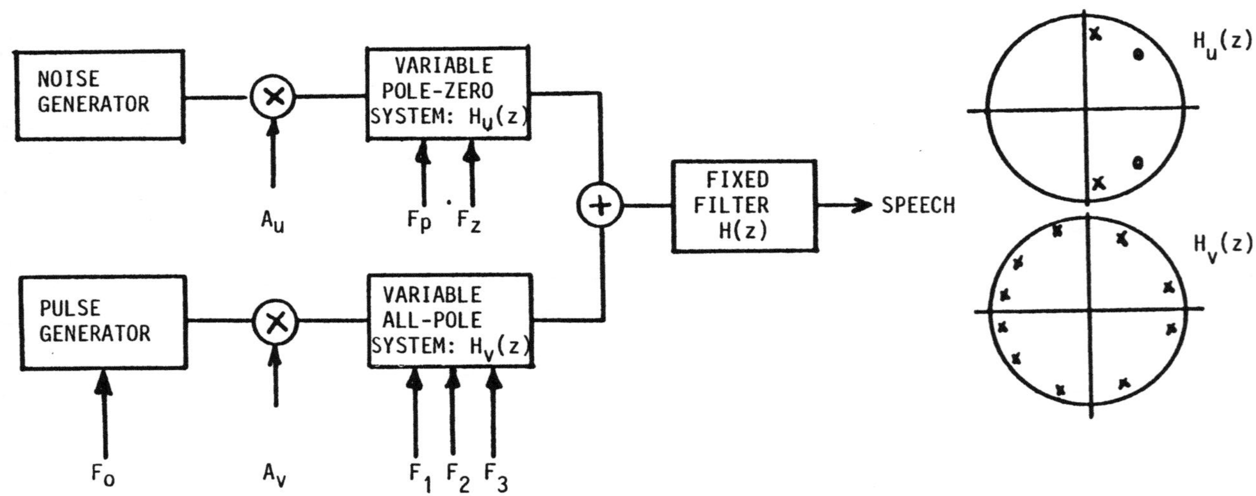

Fig. 21 Formant vocoder and typical pole-zero diagrams

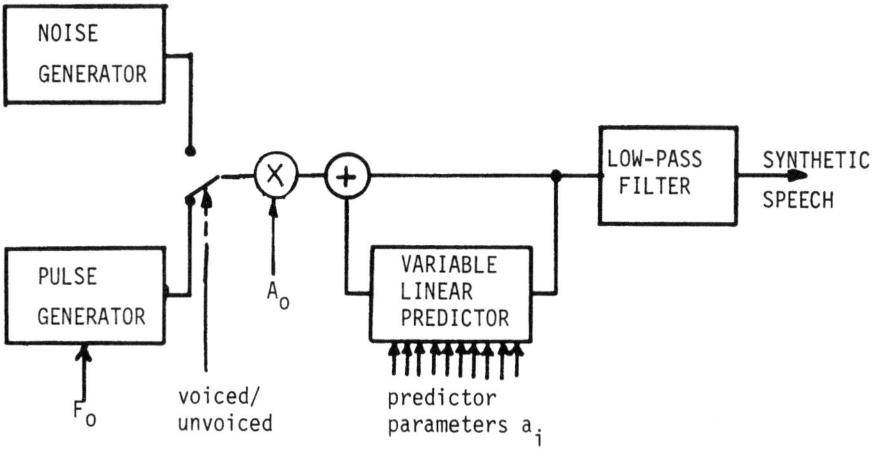

Fig. 22 Linear prediction synthesizer

Both because the human ear is very sensitive to the pitch and because the pitch contributes much to the naturalness of speech, correct pitch analysis and restitution is decisive for the quality of synthesized speech.

Pitch analysis methods are numerous and various and practical algorithms often combine seveal of them. For a comparison see for example [6] or [7]. We restrict this presentation to the basic methods. Also, note that for most practical methods, the effective processing is preceded by preprocesing like normalization, low-pass filtering or clipping and followed by postprocessing like smoothing, correction etc.

Pitch detection method can be divided in three categories: time-domain, frequency domain and hybrid methods.

3.3.1 TIME DOMAIN METHODS

The basic idea is to preprocess the quasiperiodic speech signal such as to reduce sufficiently the formant structure and then to use simple time domain methods to estimate the pitch.

3.3.1.1 ZERO CROSSING

The principle is: low-pass filtering followed by zero-crossing (eq. 106) measurements. A particularity however is that the useful pitch and the filter cut-off frequency are related, with the practical consequence of a limited pitch frquency range for a given filter configuration. To remedy that, adaptive filtering as a function of F can be performed.,

3.3.1.2 PEAK AND VALLEY MEASUREMENTS

The principel is: low-pass filtering followed by peak and valley detection and a final decision for the choice of the pitch. Practically, there are 6 parallel detectors: peak, valley, peak-to-valley, valley-to-peak, peak-to-previous-peak and valley-to-previous-valley detectors. The decision is made to guarantee correct pitch measurement in the case of a signal with both fundamental and second harmonic.

3.3.1.3 AUTOCORRELATION FUNCTION

This method uses the property of autocorrelation: the autocorrelation function of a periodic signal is periodic with the same period, i.e. it will show a peak at a lag value equal to the signal period. Further, the peak has same amplitude as the peak at the origin. For quasiperiodic signals, the peak is slightly reduced.

Practically, a window (eq. 104) is applied to the speech signal and the autocorrelation function from eq. 4 is computed:

$$\varphi_\ell(m) = \sum_{k=\ell}^{\ell+N-1} x(k) \cdot w(\ell-k) \cdot x(k+m) \cdot w(\ell-k-m) \qquad (112)$$

which can be computed directly or by FFT (see eq. 6). The lag value m corresponding to the first maximum of $\varphi_\ell(m)$ indicates the pitch period value.

The performance of this method is significantly improved by a non-linear preprocessing called central clipping which sets small relative values to 0.

Computation of the autocorrelation function can be simplified by quantizing the signal to the three levels +1, 0, -1. This eliminates all multiplications encountered with the normal computation of eq. 4 or 6.

3.3.1.4 AVERAGE MAGNITUDE DIFFERENCE FUNCTION

As the one just described, this method is a simple to implement approach to pitch detection. Compared to the autocorrelation function, it uses subtractions instead of multiplications. It takes advantage of the fact that for a periodic signal, $x(k)-x(k+p) = 0$ when p is a delay equal to one or several periods. The average magnitude difference function (AMDF) thus writes:

$$\mathrm{AVDF}(m) = \sum_{k=\ell}^{\ell+N-1} [x(k) \cdot w(\ell-k) - x(k+m) \cdot w(\ell-k-m)] \tag{113}$$

The detected pitch period is the lag value m for the first minimum of AVDF(m).

3.3.2 SPECTRAL METHODS

Frequency-domain pitch detectors use the property that, if the signal is periodic in time, then the frequency spectrum of the signal will consist of a series of impulses at the fundamental frequency and its harmonics. This harmonic structure, only present with voiced sounds, must be detected and the frequency interval between two lines must be measured.

3.3.2.1 CEPSTRUM METHOD

As we have seen, a basic step of the cepstrum computation is the logarithmic transform of the amplitudes in the spectral domain. The speech spectrum X(n) which is the product of the excitation spectrum E(n) and the vocal tract spectrum R(n) is thus transformed in the sum of two signals:

$$\ln|E(n) \cdot R(m)| = \ln|E(n)| + \ln|R(n)| \tag{114}$$

After inverse DFT we get the cepstrum $\hat{x}(k)$ which now, is the sum of the cepstra of e(k) resp. r(k): $\hat{x}(k) = \hat{e}(k) + \hat{r}(k)$. As the excitation e(k) is periodic, its cepstrum $\hat{e}(k)$ will display a strong peak, indicating the position of the pitch period, whereas the slow and aperiodic oscillation r(k) give raise to a much flatter curve.

Practical cepstral computation requires a good resolution in the spectral domain. Therefore difficulties arise for small values of F_o where the spectral lines are close to each other.

3.3.2.2 COMB FILTERING IN THE SPECTRAL DOMAIN

The principle is to filter the short-time speech spectrum $X_\ell(n)$ with a variable comb filter in the spectral domain. The comb filter is a function $C(n,n_o)$ where n_o is the interval between two teeth of the comb. The method looks for the maximum of the cross-correlation when the teeth interval n_o is varied. When this maximum is reached, the comb lies exactly on the harmonic lines of $X_\ell(n)$, and thus: $F_o = n_o$. This writes formally:

$$F_o = \underset{n_o}{\operatorname{argmax}} \left[\sum_{n=0}^{N/2-1} X_\ell(n) \cdot C(n,n_o) \right] \tag{115}$$

3.3.3 HYBRID METHOD

Hybrid methods use features of both the time- and the spectral domain.

3.3.3.1 SIMPLIFIED INVRESE FILTERING TECHNIQUE

The basic idea here is to first eliminate or reduce the effect on x(k) of the spectral envelope (which is a characteristic of the vocal tract, not the pitch) and then to detect the pitch by the autocorrelation method. Because the second of these two steps is described above, we concentrate on step one only.

Here then, the way adopted eliminates the effect of the spectral envelope by flattening it, which is also called signal whitening. Practically, this can be done in the time-domain by inverse filtering, i.e. by a filter which whitens the spectrum of x(k).

3.3.4 CONCLUSION

Basic pitch detection methods have been presented to give the reader an idea of principles and processing methods involved. To the subject, we keep in mind that pitch detection remains a difficult task.

4. SPEECH RECOGNITION

This section presents two aspects found in most speech recognition application: feature extraction and pattern matching.

4.1 FEATURE EXTRACTION

The most versatile methods can and have been used to extract features from the speech signal. Because most of them have already been encountered in this text, we give here just a list of feature extraction methods.

Time-domain methods:

— Average energy or amplitude
— Average zero-crossing rate
— Autocorrelation function

— Parcor or LPC coefficients
— Voiced/unvoiced, pitch value
— Amplitude distribution function

Transform methods:

— Fourier spectrum
— Hadamard transform
— Cepstrum coefficient
— Formants

4.2 PATTERN MATCHING

In either speech or speaker recognition, the basic principle of recognition used is pattern matching: the unknown speech pattern is compared to already available speech reference patterns, then, the best match is detected. If we denote D(T,Ri) the pattern distance measure for the unknown test pattern T and a reference pattern Ri, i = 1...I, then the recognition decision is:

$$i * = \underset{i}{\operatorname{argmin}} \ [D(T,Ri)] \tag{116}$$

Considering speech patterns as time sequence of feature vectors, i.e.:

$$T = \underline{t}(1),\ \underline{t}(2),\ ...,\ \underline{t}(m),\ ...,\ \underline{t}(M) \tag{117}$$

$$Ri = \underline{r}_i(1),\ \underline{r}_i(2),\ ...,\ \underline{r}_i(n),\ ...,\ \underline{r}_i(N)$$

and defining the distance measure of two feature vectors:

$$d_i(m,n) = \delta[\ \underline{t}(m),\underline{r}_i(n)\ ] \tag{118}$$

where δ is some adequate distance function, we will present the basic methods for matching the sequences.

The most obvious method establishes a one-to-one correspondence between both sequences (which thus must be of equal length M = N) so that the overall distance is :

$$D(T,Ri) = \sum_{i=1}^{M} d_i(m,m) \tag{119}$$

4.3 DYNAMIC TIME WARPING

The Dynamic time Warping (DTW) algorithm provides a procedure to align optimally in time the test and reference sequence and to find the optimal distance D (T,Ri) associated to the optimal warping path. The algorithm uses the principle of Dynamic Programming which is the theory telling how to find optimal paths in graphs. It operates in the two-dimensional field of $d_i(m,n)$ distances shown is Fig. 23, and finds under given constraints the optimal path leading from $d_i(1,1)$ to $d_i(M,N)$. If we define the cumulated distance at a given point of the path as :

$$C_i(m,n) = \sum_{j=1}^{J} d_i(m(j),\ n(j)) \cdot w(j) \tag{120}$$

where the pairs [k(j),1(j)], j = 1...J, describe a given path and w(j) is a given associated weighting function, then the optimal path is the one which minimizes $C_i(M,N)$, the cumulated distance at $d_i(M,N)$. Formally,

$$D_1(T,Ri) = \min_{\text{path}} C_i(M,N)] \tag{121}$$

The constraints used are various and fulfill two basic purposes: locally, limiting the range of the path slope; globally, limiting the path domain as shown for example in Fig. 23.

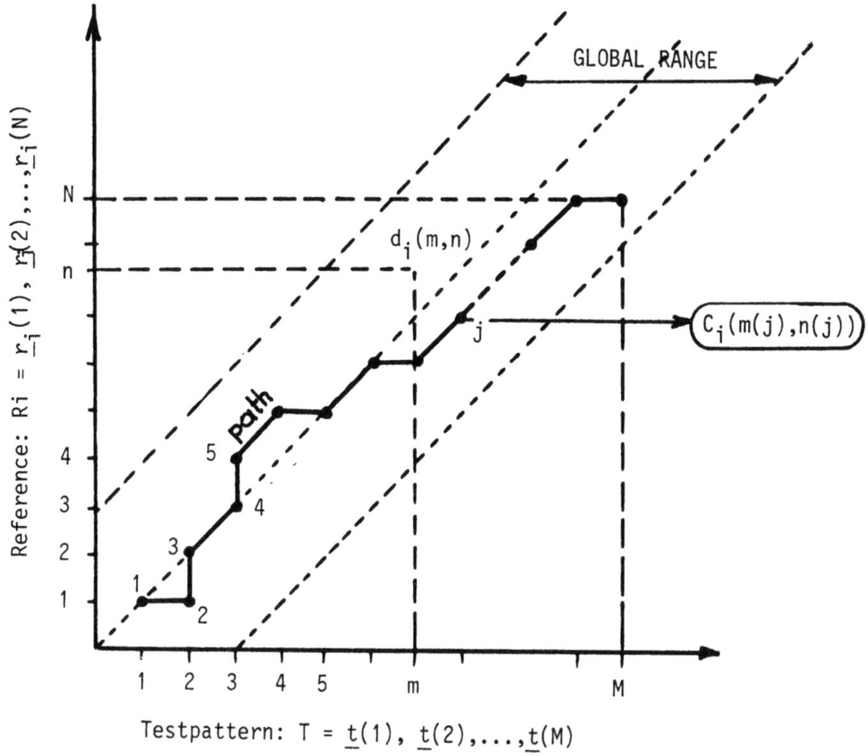

Fig. 23 Principle of DTW

4.4 CONNECTED PATTERN MATCHING

Connected pattern matching is useful to recognize connected speech patterns like connected phonemes or connected words. Again we consider the set of refrences 'Ri" and the unknown pattern T which, now, stands for a single pattern made of other patterns connected together. T must now be compared with all compound reference patterns made of connected references Ri. We call superrefernce R* such a compound reference. Using the notation and definition of :

$$R_i \otimes R_j = r_i(1),r_i(2),...,r_i(N_i),r_j(1),...,r_j(N_j) \quad (122)$$

for connected time sequences, we write the genral superreference as :

$$R*(\underline{q}) = R_{q(1)} \otimes R_{q(2)} \otimes ... \otimes R_{q(L)} \quad (123)$$

where $\underline{q}$ = [q(1),q(2),q(3),q(4),...q(L)] is the vector of reference indices.

With the brute force matching approach, the test pattern is compared by DTW with all possible superrefrences built from the reference set {Ri, i = 1...I}, resulting in $I + I^2 + I^L$ single matching operations.

4.5 TWO-LEVEL DTW

Starting from the DTW schema between T and Ri explained above, two levels are built by normalizing all references to a constant length $N_1 = N_2 = ... = N_0$ and thus considering fixed boundaries in the superreference. We give the indices 1 = 1,2,...,L to the boundaries. They appear as horizontal lines in Fig. 24. We call lower level processing, the one performed in-between the lines and upper level processing, the one which applies to operations performed on the boundary lines.

The principle of the algorithm is as in the case of simple DTW. The two-dimensional distance field can now be written as $d_i(m,n,1)$, m = 1,...,M; n = 1...N_0; 1 = 1...L. We search the optimal path leading from $d_i(1,1,1)$ to $d_i(M,N,1)$ where 1 = 1...L.

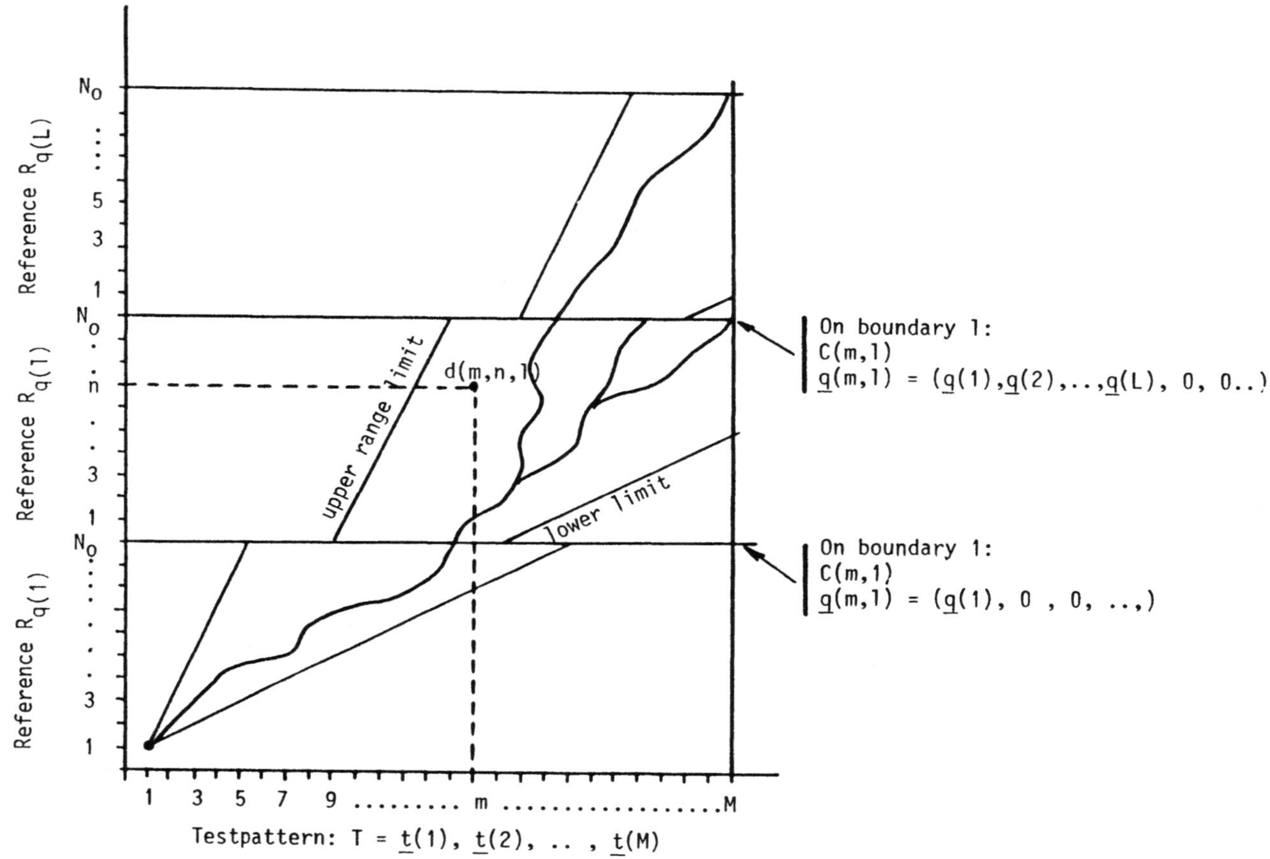

Fig. 24 Principle of two-level DTW

The upper level keeps track, at each boundary line 1 and for each position m of the test sequence, of the optimal path reaching that position in the form of the optimal cumulated distance C (m,1) as well as a path descriptor which can be the partial reference index vector $\underline{q}$ (m,1), by which we mean that, at the boundary 1, the vector components are defined up to component number 1.

The lower level performs normal DTW between T and {Ri} in the field bounded by two boundaries 1 and 1-1 with given boundary constraints. It finds, among all paths starting from the boundary 1-1 the best path reaching each position m of the boundary 1. Each lower level is repeated for each reference {Ri, i = 1...I} which ensures the optimality of the path found.

Upper and lower level processing once performed for each boundary 1 = 1...L, the final optimal path is the one given by :

$$D[T,R*(\underline{q})] = \min[C\ (M,1)] \qquad (124)$$

D [T,R*($\underline{q}$)] is the optimal distance for the two-level DTW and $\underline{q}$ is the index vector giving the optimal matching.

The advantage of Two-Level DTW compared to the brute force method is to drastically reducing the number of computations and to making thus connected pattern recognition possible. It requires computing I basic DTW whereas this number is $I+I^2+...+I^L$ in the case of brute force.

5. CONCLUSION

In this paper a short tutorial review of major digital signal processing methods used in processing speech signals is given. In depth treatments are omitted to the detriment of the essence and insight for interpretation. Following more than two decades of efforts in designing methods and algorithms, the present trend is in transposing these methods and algorithms into VLSI implementable architectures for better, faster and more reliable practical systems.

It seems reasonable to expect that now, algorithm designers and circuit designers will collaborate increasingly to design algorithms more suitable for VLSI and to develop technological tools and architectures more convenient for digital signal processing and hence speech processing.

REFERENCES

1. M. Kunt, "Traitement numérique des signaux" Presses Polytechniques Romandes, Lausanne, Switzerland, 1980.
2. J. D. Markel and A. H. Gray, "Linear prediction of speech" Springer-Verlag, New York, 1976.
3. L. R. Rabiner and B. Gold, "Theory and application of digital signal procesing", Prentice Hall, Englewood Cliffs, 1975.
4. T. G. Stockham, T. M. Cannon and R. B. Ingebretsen, "Blind deconvolution through digital signal processing" Proc. IEEE, VolL. 63, No. 4, April 1975, pp. 678-692.
5. L. R. Rabiner and R. W. Schafer, "Digital processing of speech signals", Prentice-Hall, N. J., 1978.
6. L. R. Rabiner et al., "A comparative study of several pitch detection algorithms", IEEE Trans. ASSP-24, pp. 399-413.
7. W. Hess, "Algorithmes et methodes pour la determination du fondamental", 12eme Journees d'Etude sur la Parole, Montreal, May 25-27, 1981.

SYSTEMS FOR ISOLATED AND CONNECTED WORD RECOGNITION

Roger K. Moore
Royal Signals and Radar Establishment
St. Andrews Rd., Malvern, U.K.

SUMMARY

This lecture is intended to provide an insight into some of the algorithms and techniques that lie behind contemporary automatic speech recognition systems. It is noted that, due to the lack of success of earlier phonetically motivated approaches, the majority of current speech recognizers employ whole-word pattern matching techniques. It is pointed out that these techniques, although rather shallow in concept, have enabled the development of commercial recognizers which exhibit useful and practical capabilities. A range of whole-word pattern matching algorithms are discussed, and in particular, key techniques such as dynamic-time-warping and hidden Markov modelling are explained in some detail. It is also shown how techniques for isolated word recognition may be extended to recognize connected speech. Each of the various methods is reviewed in the context of their computational implications as well as their recognition performance. It is also shown how suitable modifications to the basic algorithms can facilitate real-time operation. Where possible, specific techniqes are highlighted by reference to existing commercial recognition equipment. The lecture concludes by focusing on the key factors which limit the performance of current recognition tchniques, and by outlining some of the research work which may be relevant to future automatic speech recognition systems.

NATO ASI Series, Vol. F16
New Systems and Architectures for Automatic Speech
Recognition and Synthesis. Edited by R. De Mori and C. Y. Suen

1. INTRODUCTION

In 1952 Davis, Biddulph and Balashek published the first paper to describe a technique for recognizing spoken words automatically. Over thirty years later, related techniques still dominate the speech recognition field.

The purpose of this lecture is to review such techniques and to mark the progress of the latest developments. However, before doing so it is necessary (and illuminating) to note that many different approaches to automatic speech recognition have been attempted over the past thirty years, and of particular interest is the traditional pattern recognition approach, popular during the 1950's and 60's.

This early scheme was based on the apparently reasonable assumption that speech was a highly redundant signal consisting of a sequence of invariant information bearing elements called phonemes. As a consequence, the classical speech recognizer took the form of: a pre-processor to selectively reduce the quantity of data whilst retaining the relevant information, a feature extractor typically to identify formant frequencies, a segmentor to divide the signal into phonemic segments, and a classifier to recognize the individual phonemes from their features (see figure 1). Recognition of words was then simply a matter of looking up the sequence of recognized phonemes in a pronouncing dictionary.

Schemes of this type abounded, but all failed to a greater or lesser extent because of the basic inadequacy of the initial assumptions; a speech signal is not as easily characterized as one might wish. Indeed it exhibits properties which still make automatic speech recognition a major research topic.

The reasons why speech recognition is not such a straightforward endeavour may be summarized into four main problem areas:

First, speech signals are normally continuous. That is, there are no regular pauses between the words in a spoken sentence, nor are there any other acoustic markers to indicate where the word boundaries are. For example, figure 2 shows

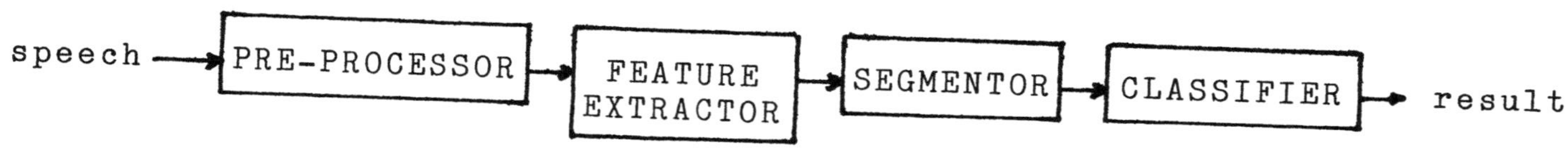

Figure 1 Typical structure of an early automatic speech recognizer.

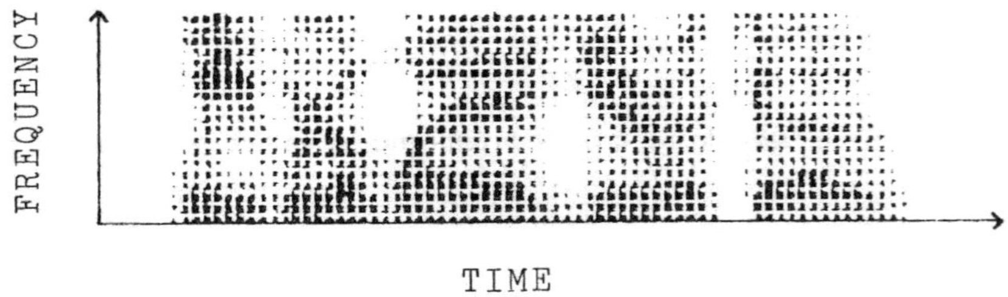

Figure 2 Speech spectrogram of the phrase "we were away a year ago".

a speech spectrogram for the phrase "we were away a year ago"; the only pause in this sentence is in the middle of the "g" in "ago", the rest is a continuously changing sound pattern. A recognition algorithm must therefore be able to recognize words even when embedded within a surrounding sentence.

Second, speech signals are highly variable in a number of ways. Obviously one person's voice can be very different to another's due to factors such as different sex, age or accent. But even a given speaker's voice will be different at different times since a speaker may speak softly or loudly or whisper, or might have a cold or be tense. In fact, it is virtually impossible for a speaker to say the same word in exactly the same way on two different occasions. For example, figure 3 shows the word "helicopter" spoken three times by the same person; note how the patterns are similar but not identical.

The continuity of speech is another source of variability. Since words flow smoothly one into another, the beginnings and ends of words can change significantly. For example, the phrase "bread and butter" may become "breb'm butter" if spoken quickly.

The inherent variability of speech is thus a very big problem for any technique which relies on invariance in the signal. A recognition algorithm must therefore be able to deal with pattern similarities rather than rely on the preservation of absolute identity.

The third problem area is ambiguity. For example, there is no acoustic difference between the words "to", "too" and "two". Similarly, "grey tape" sounds almost exactly the same as "great ape". A recognition algorithm must therefore be able to decide on the identity of a particular word whilst taking into account the identity of surrounding words.

The fourth problem area results from the fact that speech is just one component in the complex system of human language. Often it is the intention behind a message that is more important than the message itself. For example, the most useful answer to the question "Can you tell me the time?" is "10:15" not "Yes, I can".

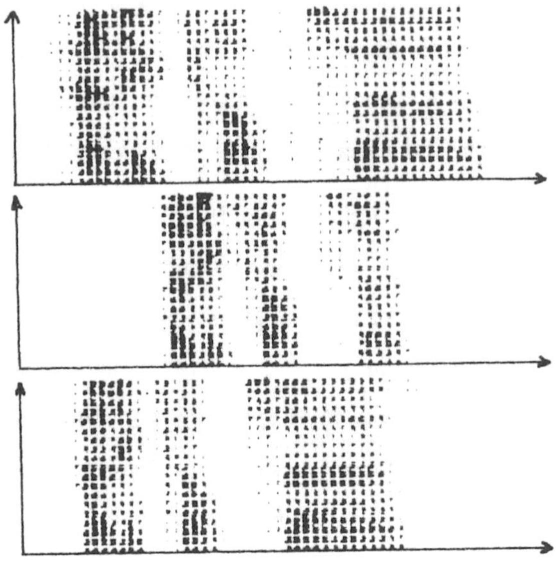

Figure 3 Three versions of the word "helicopter".

Faced with these problems, automatic speech recognition appears to be an almost unattainable goal. However, it turns out that by minimizing one's assumptions about the nature of speech signals, and by developing the rather simple principle exemplified by the 1952 recognizer, it has been possible to begin to derive some powerful (albeit only partial) solutions.

The basic principle underlying almost all current commercial speech recognition equipment is illustrated in figure 4. Speech which is to be recognized is compared with a set of pre-stored reference words (often referred to as 'templates'), and the identity of the stored patterns which most resemble the unknown pattern determines the result. In this scheme a pre-processor transforms the speech signal into some useful representation, a segmentor isolates the speech from the surrounding silence, and then a comparison module compares the unknown words with each of the templates, and outputs the result. Prior to recognition, such a recognizer is 'trained' by presenting it with examples of each of the words in its vocabulary at least once. The entire procedure is known as 'whole-word pattern matching'.

Notwithstanding the problems posed by variability and continuity, this approach relies on the patterns for different words being separable, and for words to be recognizable in context.

The rest of the lecture describes techniques for 'whole-word pattern matching' in detail.

2. PRE-PROCESSING

The range of signal processing techniques which may be applied to speech signals is very large [Schafer and Rabiner 1975, Flanagan 1972, Holmes 1982]. However, only a few have established themselves as standard techniques for automatic speech recognition. This section describes briefly the most popular techniques for producing a useful representation of a speech signal, and also the

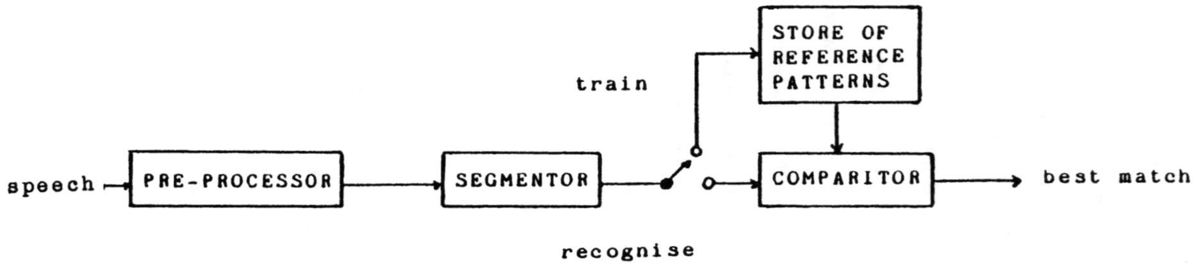

Figure 4 Structure of a contemporary automatic speech recognizer.

most common techniques for reducing the data rate of the pre-processor output.

2.1 Signal Representation

One of the most crucial factors which determines the success or failure of an automatic speech recognizer is the nature of the representation presented to the recognition algorithms.

Short-time Spectrum

The most common way to analyze a speech signal is to measure its short-time spectrum. This is possible because a speech signal can be considered to be stationary over a short time interval. Hence the spectrum can be estimated using the Fourier transform. One of the simplest methods for implementing short-time Fourier analysis is a bank of bandpass filters. Such an analysis is the basis of the UK channel vocoder analyzer [Holmes 1980] (see figure 5) which is used as a front-end to several automatic speech recognizers (and which was used to generate the spectrograms and other data presented in this paper).

In general, filter bank analyzers are easy to construct with analogue circuitry and the distribution of frequency bands can be readily modelled on the critical bands of the human ear. However, unless a very large number of channels is used, it is difficult to estimate the spectrum shape around spectral peaks.

Cepstral Analysis

The most useful spectral representation for speech recognition is the wide-band spectrum (which does not preserve pitch information). Such an analysis requires a short data window. However an alternative approach, which is able to use a wider time window is homomorphic or cepstral processing. This process is based on the assumption that speech is a convolution of an excitation function with a vocal tract impulse response. Figure 6 illustrates the scheme for separating these two components by liftering the cepstrum to obtain a smooth spectrum. In practice, the first few terms (excluding zero frequency) of a cosine

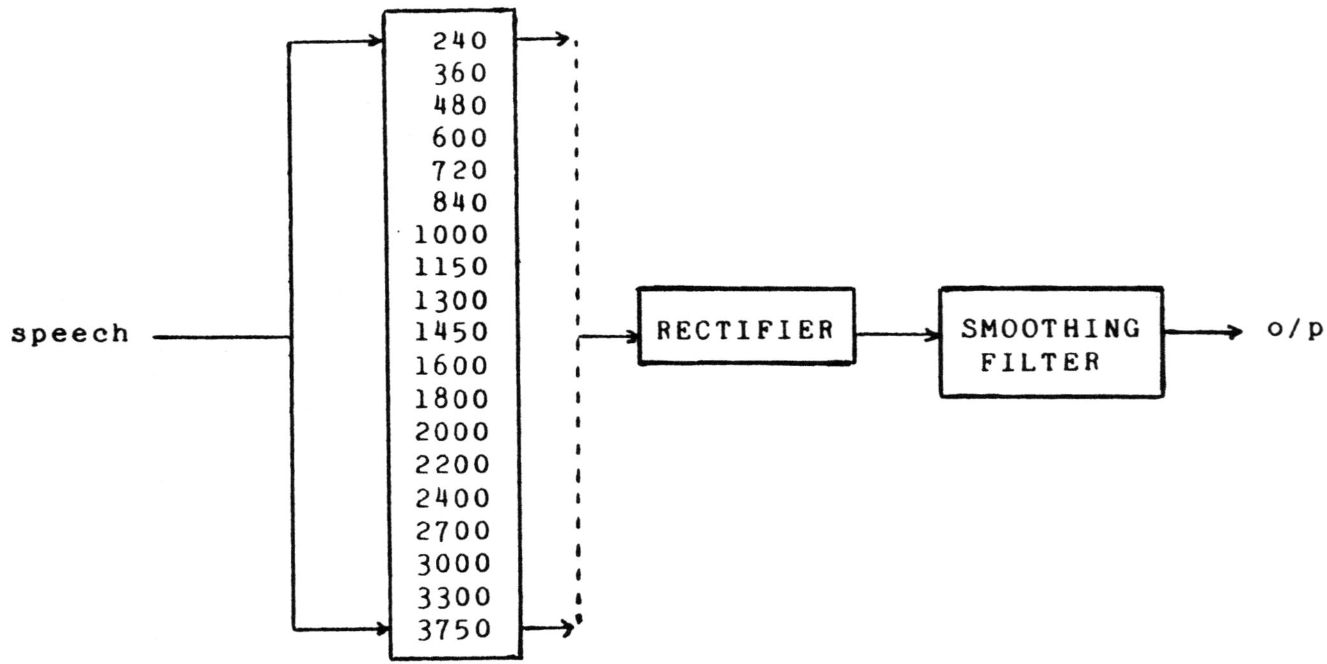

Figure 5 The JSRU channel vocoder analyser.

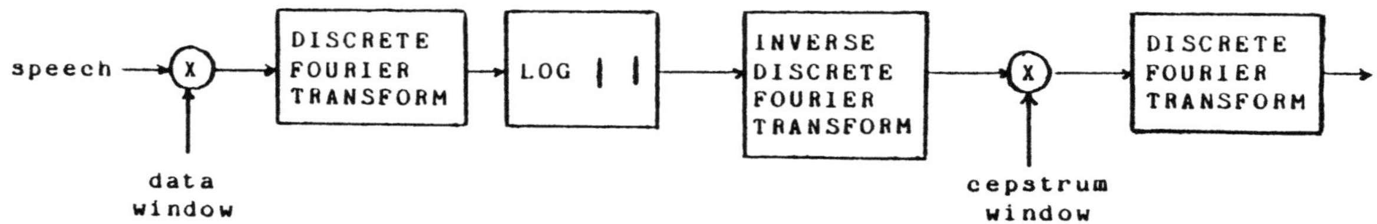

Figure 6 Cepstral analysis.

transform of the short-time log power spectrum may be used [Bridle and Brown 1974, Hunt et al 1980].

Linear Predictive Analysis

Linear predictive coding (LPC) is an analysis technique which is particularly attractive from the computational point of view. In this scheme the autocorrelation characteristics of the speech signal are exploited by estimating the value of the current sample using a linear combination of the past n samples. Figure 7 illustrates the principle. The all-pole properties of LPC analysis enable accurate estimations of spectral peaks to be made. However this is only true during speech sounds which conform to an all-pole model. During nasals and many consonant sounds LPC tends to overestimate the bandwidths of spectral peaks.

2.2 Data Reduction Techniques

The output of a typical front-end analyzer is thus framed data consisting of a sequence of vectors of a given size occurring a certain number of times each second. This data rate may be too high for subsequent processes to handle, hence techniques can be used for reducing the data rate by various forms of coding scheme.

Vector Quantization

Speech coding by vector quantization (or 'character string encoding' [White 1972]) is a technique whereby each frame of spectral data is coded in terms of the identity of a prestored reference vector called a 'codeword'. The collection of possible codewords is referred to as a 'codebook'. The spectral shape of an input vector is thus coded by identifying the particular codeword from the codebook that minimizes some predefined distortion measure. This means that a speech signal can be represented by a sequence of codewords with a bit-rate of b bits per vector if there are 2^b vectors in the codebook.

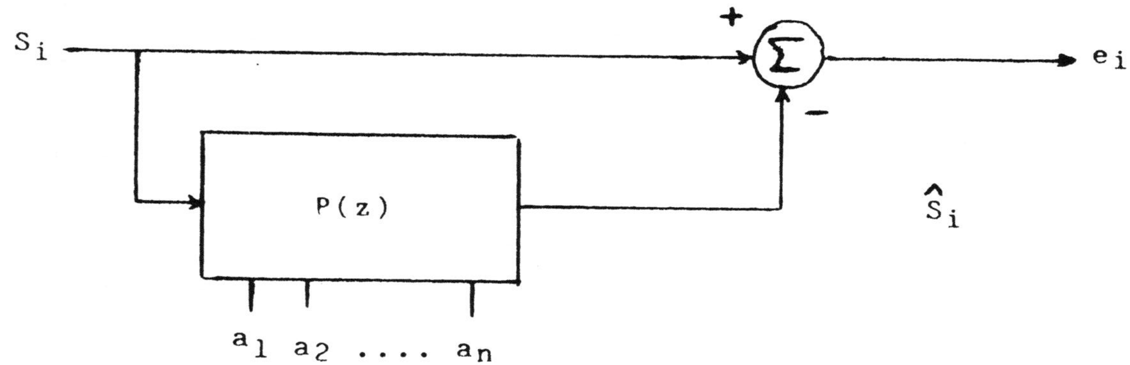

Figure 7 Liner predictive analysis.

A codebook is normally generated by a training procedure which minimizes the average distortion resulting from coding a suitably long sequence of vectors. This training procedure is essentially a cluster analysis; more codewords are allocated where the population of vectors is more dense.

Trace Segmentation

Trace segmentation is a 'data-adaptive frame rate' technique for reducing the number of vectors in a sequence. Each vector is viewed as a point in n-dimensional space (where n is the size of each vector) and the trace is the sequence of points drawn out by an utterance. The n-dimensional trace is subsequently resampled by calculating the total length of the trace, and then dividing the trace into a fixed number of uniformly spaced segments. By suitable choice of the new sampling rate, fewer vectors are required to represent a speech signal, and those vectors are better distributed (there will be more allocated when the spectrum is changing quickly than when it is changing slowly).

Variable Rate Coding

Variable frame rate coding is similar to trace segmentation in that the net result is a resampling of a speech signal according to the changing spectrum. However, trace segmentation relies on being able to determine the beginning and end of a trace. In circumstances where this might not be known (for example in the middle of a section of speech) variable rate coding techniques may be utilized.

The simplest scheme is to set a threshold such that a vector in a sequence is only retained if the distance between it and the last retained vector exceeds the threshold. Hence by adjusting the value of the threshold, the resampling rate can be varied to suit the circumstances; the higher the threshold, the fewer samples there will be in the more stationary regions of the signal.

More complex schemes have involved averaging vectors [Piereccini and Billi 1983] or multiple thresholds [Bridle and Brown 1982].

3. ISOLATED WORD RECOGNITION

Any approach to automatic speech recognition must overcome the continuity problem outlined in section 1. However, the simplest and most effective solution is obvious; ask the speaker to put artificial pauses between his words, thereby sacrificing naturalness in favour of greatly simplifying the recognition process. Each word is thus 'isolated' from its neighbours, and can be recognized individually.

Even for isolated words, the key to the success of the whole-word pattern matching approach lies in the comparison process (see figure 4). The rest of this section is concerned with techniques for implementing the comparison.

3.1 Absolute Pattern Match

The most basic comparison process is simply to correlate the time-frequency word patterns producd by the pre-processor in order to determine the 'distance' between an unknown word and each template. Unfortunately this is not possible because words are often different durations, hence their corresponding patterns are different sizes. However, by aligning the beginnings of all the patterns, and by correlating only over the areas of overlap, it is possible to generate a suitable measure of correlation (or distance: for example, the sum of the squares of the differences). The length difference can also be taken into account separately [White and Fong 1975].

Although rather simple minded, such a technique requires the minimum of computation: N vector comparisons per pattern match, where N is the number of vectors in the smallest pattern.

The performance of the technique can be gauged from White and Fong's experiments: the error rate for a test using a 54 word vocabulary, six band-pass filters (sampled every 10 ms) and vector quantization (32 codewords) was 7%. White identified misalignment of the beginnings of words as a source of some of the errors.

3.2 Best Absolute Time Alignment

An alternative to aligning the beginnings of words in order to perform an absolute comparison, is to adjust their relative timing to maximize the correlation of the overlap. This means starting with the beginnings aligned, then shifting the patterns with respect to each other until the ends align. The similarity of the pattern overlap is calculated at each shift, and the highest similarity is the output of the comparison.

Computationally this scheme is much more expensive: M*(N-M) vector comparisons, where N is the number of vectors in the longer pattern, and M is the number of vectors in the shorter pattern.

Recognition performance on the ten digit vocabulary, with a 16 channel filter bank (10 ms frame rate) was found to be only 82% using this technique [Moore 1980]. However, this level of performance is to be expected, since the behaviour of the algorithm for comparing different words is somewhat unpredictable.

3.3 Linear Time-Normalization

The problem with the two previous techniques is that they do not accommodate the fact that the same word is very rarely the same duration on different occasions. For example, in figure 3 it can be seen that the three versions of "helicopter" all have different lengths. A solution therefore, is to uniformly 'time-normalize' each pattern in order to make them the same size. Such a technique is referred to as 'linear time-normalization'.

Figure 8 illustrates the process on a pair of utterances of the word "helicopter". The two original patterns are shown at right angles to each other so that the two time scales can be compared. It is clear that the vertical utterance is much longer than the horizontal one. The rectangle on the right is prescribed by the lengths of the two words, and the diagonal line is the linear time-normalization relationship between the two. The third pattern is the result of stretching the horizontal one to the same length as the vertical one. The net result is that the two vertical patterns are more similar than the originals.

In practice, either the template patterns are time-normalized to the unknown word, or all patterns are time-normalized to a standard duration. In both cases the distance calculation involves a constant number of vector comparisons: N vector comparisons per pattern match, where N is the number of vectors in the input word (or in the standard length pattern).

The recognition performance of linear time-normalization can be quite useful if the vocabulary is kept reasonably small, 10 to 30 words for example. For the ten digits, one could expect recognition accuracies up to about 97% under ideal conditions. The actual performance obtained depends, amongst other things, on the inherent confusability of the words, the consistency of the speakers, the exact nature of the pre-processing and the number of training examples allowed per word.

In practice, the level of performance is such that several commercial speech recognizers employ the linear time-normalization principle.

EXAMPLE SYSTEM: Interstate Electronics VRM

Pre-processing:

— 16 channel analogue filter bank

— bandwith: 200 Hz to 7000 Hz

— 5 ms frame rate

— variable rate coding (user definable threshold)

— minimum number of frames per word: 16 (80 ms)

— maximum number of frames per word: 250 (1250 ms)

Segmentation:

— endpoint detection by spectral energy change

— user definable threshold

— minimum pause between words: 40 ms to 320 ms (user definable; default 160 ms)

Training:

— 40, 70 or 100 reference word patterns (depending on model)

— 32 bytes (256 bits) per reference pattern

Recognition:

— linear time-normalization (linear conversion from 250 frames to 256 bits)

— recognition based on number of bits in agreement between standard length patterns

— user definable reject threshold

Computation:

— CPU plus 4K ROM and up to 4K RAM (for references)

— processing time is 25+N ms, where N is the number of references

— response time is pause length plus processing time

Recognition accuracy:

— 2.9% error on Doddington-Schalk [1981] Texas Instruments (DSTI) data (20 word vocabulary; "zero" to "nine" plus ten command words, 8 men and 8 women, 5120 test tokens in total)

Cost:

— $2400

— latest product: VRT300 (512 bits/word, 200 words, $1295)

3.4 Non-Linear time-Normalization

For larger vocabularies, the recognition accuracy of linear time-normalization can drop significantly. The reason is that linear timescale distortion is not an adequate model of what actually happens when people make words longer or shorter. In reality some sounds are lengthened (or shortened) more than others. This effect is apparent from figure 8; although linear time-normalization has made the patterns the same lengh, it has still not made them particularly similar. In particular the technique is susceptible to 'endpoint detection' errors since correct normalization depends on the first and last frames being correctly aligned. In

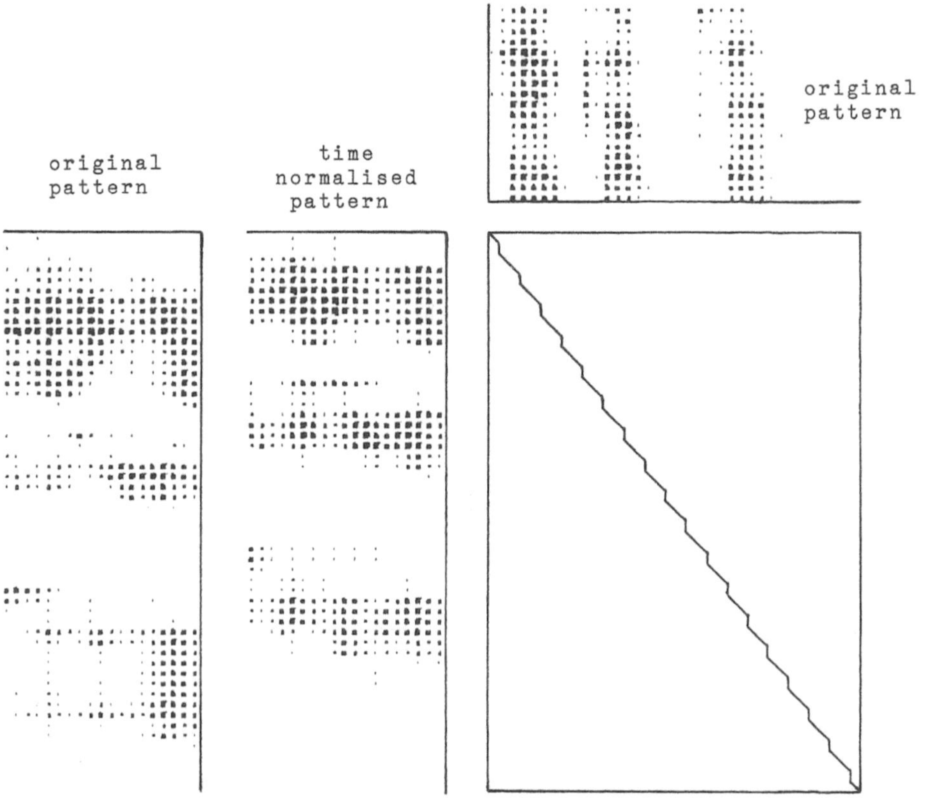

Figure 8 **Demonstration of linear time-normalisation between two versions of** the word "helicopter".

figure 8, the end of the horizontal pattern has been missed and extra silence has been included; it is clear that a better match would have resulted if the end of the horizontal pattern had been determined more accurately [Rabiner and Sambur 1975].

However, as suggested above, a better model of timescale distortion would be one which allows different sounds to be distorted differentially. By eye one can see from figure 8 that the patterns do have similar structures, and one can imagine that by distorting the horizontal pattern non-linearly, it could be made to look more like the original vertical pattern. Figure 9 shows such a non-linear time-normalization or 'time registration path'.

In fact, the time registration path in figure 9 was determined by eye, and it is obvious that it could be further modified to achieve a better match. Of course in practice it is necessary to find such a path automatically, but this involves a search space of many millions of possible paths! Luckily it is possible to use the mathematical technique of 'dynamic programming' (DP) to solve this optimization problem using only N*M operations (where N and M are the number of frames in the two patterns), and since DP is guaranteed to find the best solution, the result is optimal non-linar time-normalization or 'dynamic time warping' (DTW).

Figure 10 shows the result of using dynamic programming to find the best path; note how similar the vertical time-distorted version of the original horizontal utterance is to the original vertical utterance.

Dynamic time Warping

DTW is essentially a two-stage process; figure 11 illustrates the first stage. Two abstract speech-like patterns are shown, one vertically and one horizontally. Each pattern has time frames consisting of 3-element vectors; the vertical pattern has four frames, and the horizontal has five. The matrix in the centre is known as the 'distance matrix' and it contains numbers which correspond to the distance between each frame in one pattern and each frame in the other pattern. For example, the number "20" in the top right hand corner indicates that the first

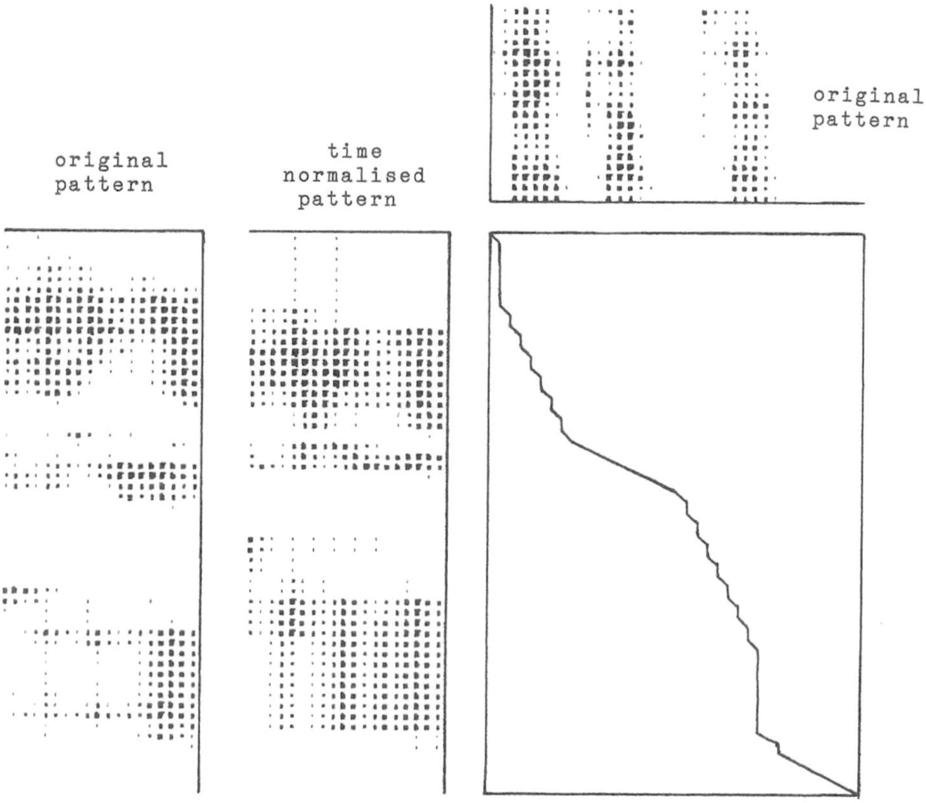

Figure 9 Non-linear time-normalisation (obtained by hand).

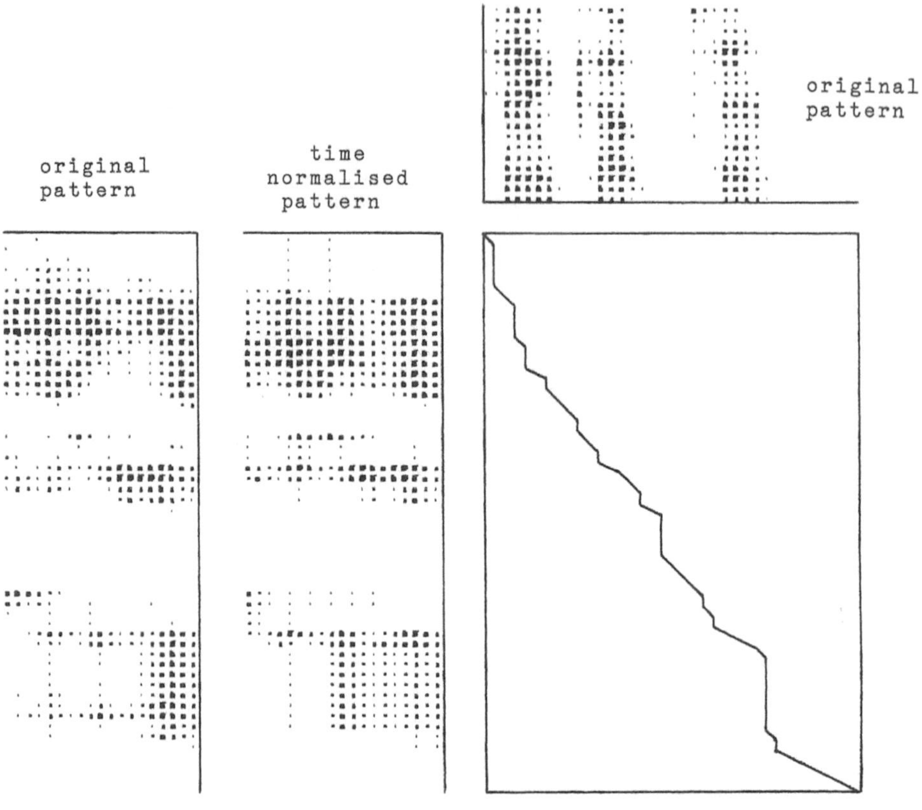

Figure 10 **Optimal non-linear time-normalisation obtained using dynamic programming.**

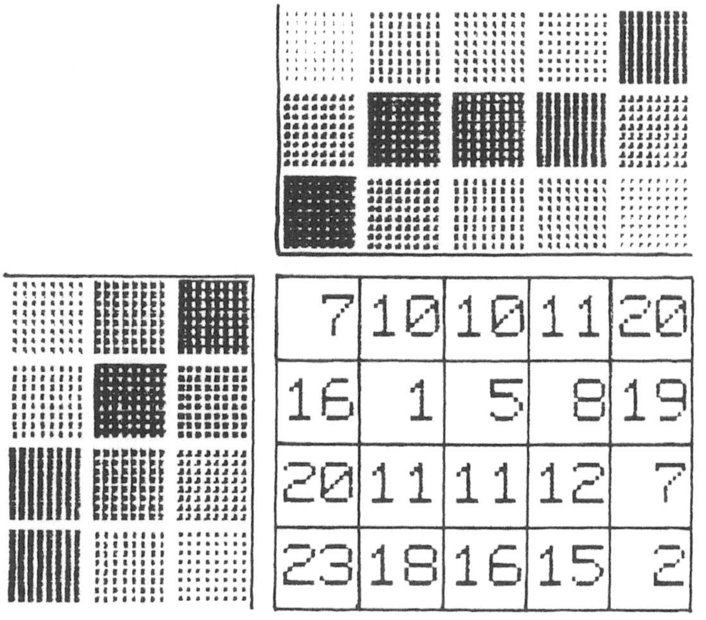

Figure 11 Distance matrix obtained by comparing two abstract speech patterns.

frame of the vertical pattern is quite different to the last frame of the horizontal pattern. Similarly, the "1" in row-2 column-2 indicates that the second frames of each pattern are very similar. The distances are actually calculated by taking the sum of the squares of the differences between each element of each pair of frames.

The second stage is to find the path through the distance matrix, from the top left hand corner to the bottom right hand corner, which has the minimum accumulated sum of distances along its length. This path is the required non-linear relationship between the timescales of these two patterns, and it is found by dynamic programming.

Dynamic programming involves the regular application of a local optimization procedure which ultimately leads to an overall global solution. In this case a 'local decision function' is used, together with the distance matrix, to construct a second matrix called the 'cumulative distance matrix'. Figure 12 illustrates the process. The local decision function is shown in figure 12a, and it defines that a path may arrive at any particular point either vertically, horizontally or diagonally. It is applied as follows:

For each point in the cumulative distance matrix, add the cheapest cost of getting to that point to the cost of being at that point, and enter it in the matrix. The cheapest cost of getting to a point is the smallest of the values in the previous entries (as defined by the local decision function) and the cost of being at a point is simply the value taken from the corresponding position in the distance matrix. Hence, if this process is applied iteratively, starting at the top left hand corner of the matrix, it is possible to complete all the entries in the cumulative distance matrix.

Figure 12b shows the cumulative distance matrix in the process of being filled in. The "?" indicates the point being considered, and the three previous points are highlighted. The cost of getting to the point is the minimum of 19, 13 or 21, and the cost of being at that point is 12 (from the distance matrix in figure 11). Hence the cumulative distance entered at that point is 25 (13+12).

Figure 12c shows the cumulative distance matrix completely filled in. The number in the bottom right hand corner is highlighted because this is the overall distance between the two patterns; it is the sum of distances along the least-cost path through the distance matrix. To find the path it is necessary to remember at each point in the calculation exactly which local decisions were made (horizontal, vertical or diagonal). Figure 12d shows all of these decisions and it can be seen that they form a tree radiating from the top left hand corner (where the calculation started). The actual minimum cost path is found by tracing back along the local decisions, starting at the bottom right hand corner (where the calculation ended).

Referring back to the distance matrix (figure 11), the calculation shows that the least-cost path takes the route 7+1+5+12+2; no other path has a cumulative sum less than 27.

The formulation for this dynamic programming calculation is the following recursive expression:

$$D(i,j) = d(i,j) + \min[D(i-1,j),D(i-1,j-1),D(i,j-1)]$$

where $1 \leq i \leq I$ and $1 \leq j \leq J$ (I and J are the numbers of frames in the two patterns being compared), d is a distance measure between two frames, and the initial condition is $D(0,0) = 0$. The overall distance between the two patterns is $D(I,J)$.

As an example of the same process applied to real speech patterns, figure 13 shows the comparison of two versions of the phrase "joe took father's shoe bench out". In this case the values in the distance matrix are shown as point densities; similar regions give rise to the highest density of points. From figure 13 the most likely route for the optimal time registration path can easily be seen by eye.

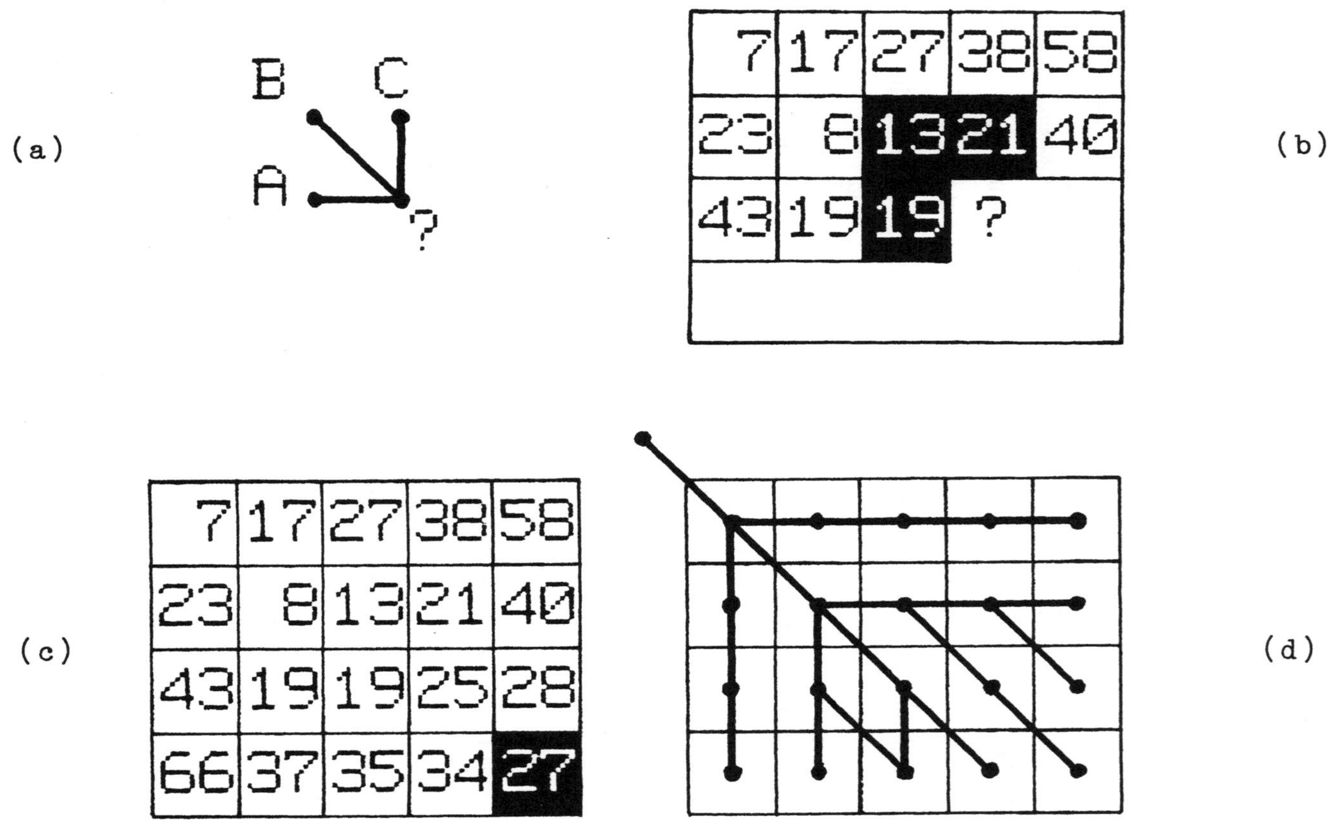

Figure 12 Demonstration of dynamic time warping; (a) local decision function, (b) partially completed cumulative distance matrix, (c) completed cumulative distance matrix and (d) record of local decisions.

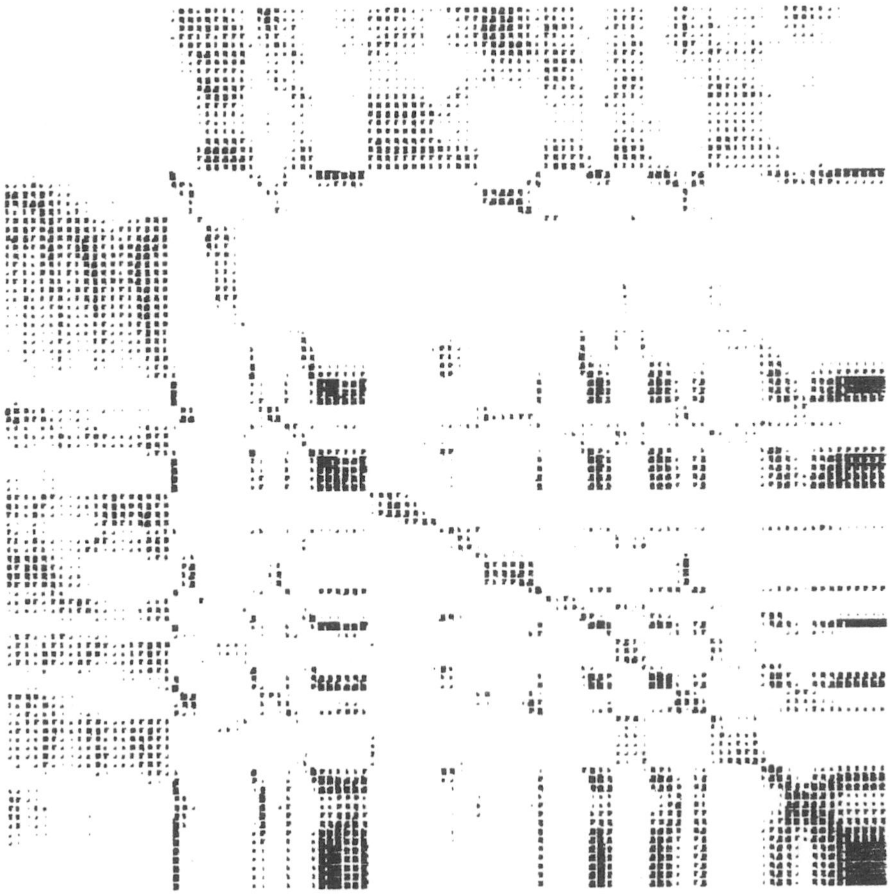

Figure 13 Distance matrix obtained by comparing two versions of the phrase "joe took father's shoe bench out".

Figure 14 shows the cumulative distance matrix corresponding to figure 13. The effect of the dynamic programming has been to form a rising valley of cumulative distances since high cumulative distances tend to lie well away from the likely route of the optimal path.

The matrix of local decisions is shown in figure 15. The complete tree is shown, and the best path, obtained by backtracking from the bottom right hand corner, is clearly visible. The result indicates that the "joe" in the vertical utterance was said much slower than in the horizontal, but the rest of the phrase has a more nearly linear temporal relationship.

Local Path Constraints

The technique described above is perhaps the simplest variant in the range of possible DTW algorithms, and it is termed the 'basic symmetric' algorithm. This refers to the shape of the local decision function which in this case is very simple, but in general may take many different shapes. For example, figure 16 shows several local decision functions which have been found to be useful. Essentially the local decision function determines the shape of possible time registration paths and hence the nature of the optimization that will be achieved. By varying the shape of the function, different properties can be introduced. For example, the basic symmetric function allows paths to have long horizontal or vertical stretches, and this might be considered to be undesirable. In this case it is possible to introduce extra limbs to the decision function such that a horizontal or vertical step can only be taken after a diagonal (see the 3rd function in figure 16).

In these circumstances the slope of the path is constrained by the shape of the local decision function, hence this property is referred to as the 'local path constraint' or 'slope constraint'. Similarly, the consequences for the total time registration path are that certain areas of the distance matrix are never visited. This effect is referred to as the 'global path constraint'.

Figure 14 Cumulative distance matrix for the example shown in figure 13.

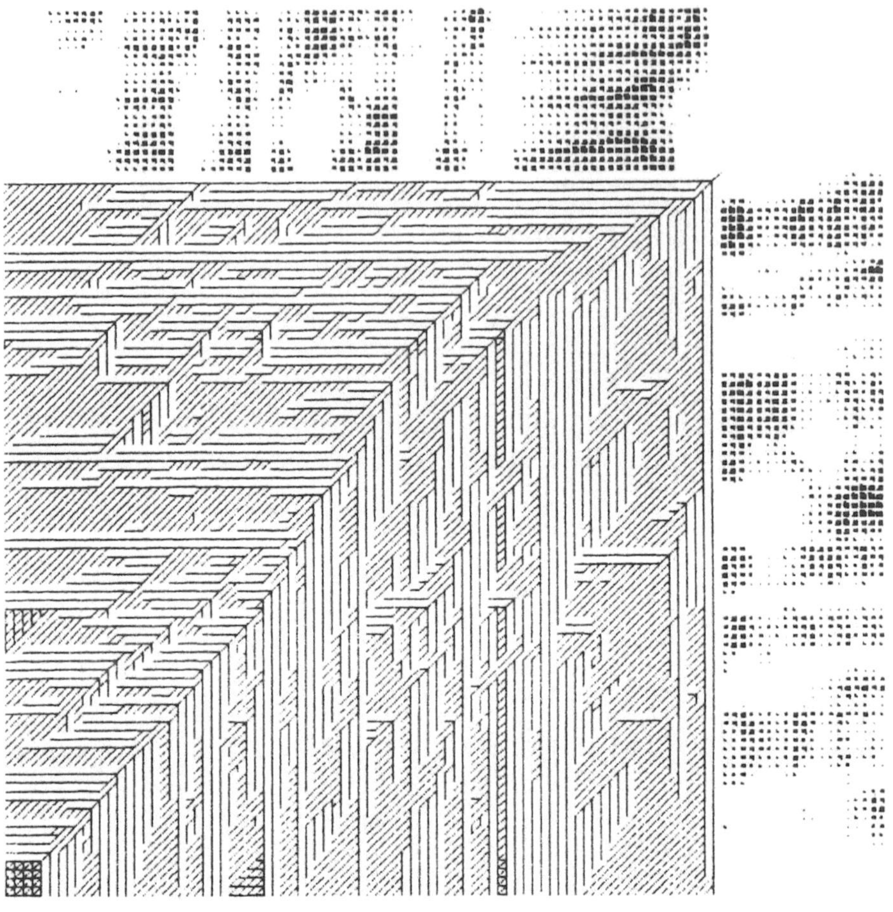

Figure 15 Local decision tree for the example shown in figure 13 and figure 14.

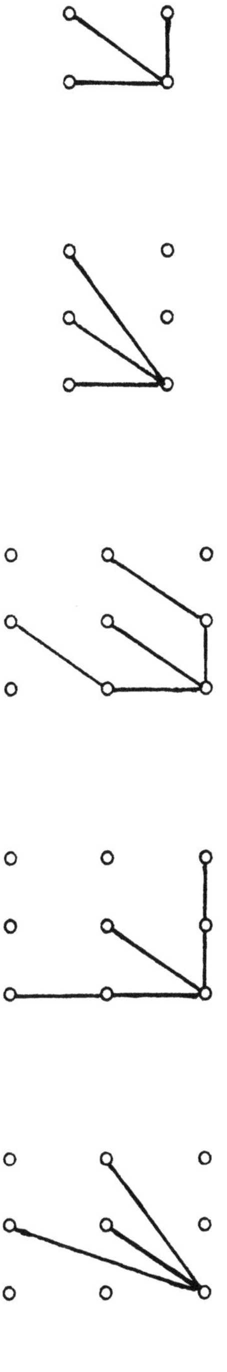

Figure 16 A selection of local decision functions.

In order to generalize these concepts, each limb of a local decision function is termed a 'production' [Myers et al 1980]. Hence a local decision function can be described as a list of productions, and a complete time registration path can be described by a sequence of productions.

Production Weighting

A softer form of path control is achieved by weighting the various productions in a local decision function. For example, in the case of the basic symmetric function, there is a natural bias towards paths which have more diagonal productions (since these paths will naturally have fewer distances) and this might be an undesirable property. Weighting the diagonal production by a factor of two cancels out this bias [White and Neely 1976, Sakoe and Chiba 1978].

In general each production may be weighted differently according to some predetermined path constraint requirement.

Path Length Normalization

The total cumulative distance along the optimal path will obviously depend on the total number of distances (and productions) which make up the path. Hence comparisons between long word patterns are bound to give rise to larger overall distances than comparisons between short patterns. To avoid this causing a problem, it is possible to normalize the final cumulative distance such that it represents the average distance per unit length of path.

Various normalizations are possible; Sakoe and Chiba suggest dividing the cumulative distances by I+J, where I is the length of one pattern, and J is the length of the other. It is also possible to divide by the actual length of the path, if such information is available.

Distance Measure

The entire DTW process ultimately depends on the choice of a suitable distance measure between two speech frames or vectors. Various alternatives may be used; for filter bank analyzer frames it is common to use either the 'city-block' metric, or the 'squared-Euclidean' metric. (The latter is squared so that the cumulative distance between two patterns can be interpreted as a global Euclidean distance between them.) In the case of an LPC analysis, it is common to use the log likelihood distance ratio proposed by Itakura [1975].

Isolated Word Recognition Using DTW

Figure 17 shows an example of isolated word recognition using optimal non-linear time-normalization. In the example there are three reference patterns, the digits "one", "two" and "three", shown vertically. The horizontal pattern is the word to be recognized (actually a "one"). The unknown word is compared with the three reference patterns using the techniques described above, and the three resulting non-linear time registration paths are shown. Also shown are the cumulative distances between the unknown pattern and each of the reference patterns. The best match is determined by the smallest distance, hence the unknown word is correctly recognized as "one".

The algorithm used in the example is the basic symmetric with no slope constraints and no path length normalization. To interpret the non-linear time registration paths, it should be noted that when matching two words which are the same, the distortions tend to be subtle variations on an essentially linear theme. On the other hand, when two different words are compared, the time registration paths tend to be extremely non-linear. This is because it takes a severe distortion of the timescales of two different words to make them even remotely similar. In fact, this is why slope constraints may sometimes increase recognition performance; in-class time registration paths will be unaffected, but out-class matches will be forced to be non-optimal (in comparison with the unconstrained condition) and thus further apart — hence less confusion.

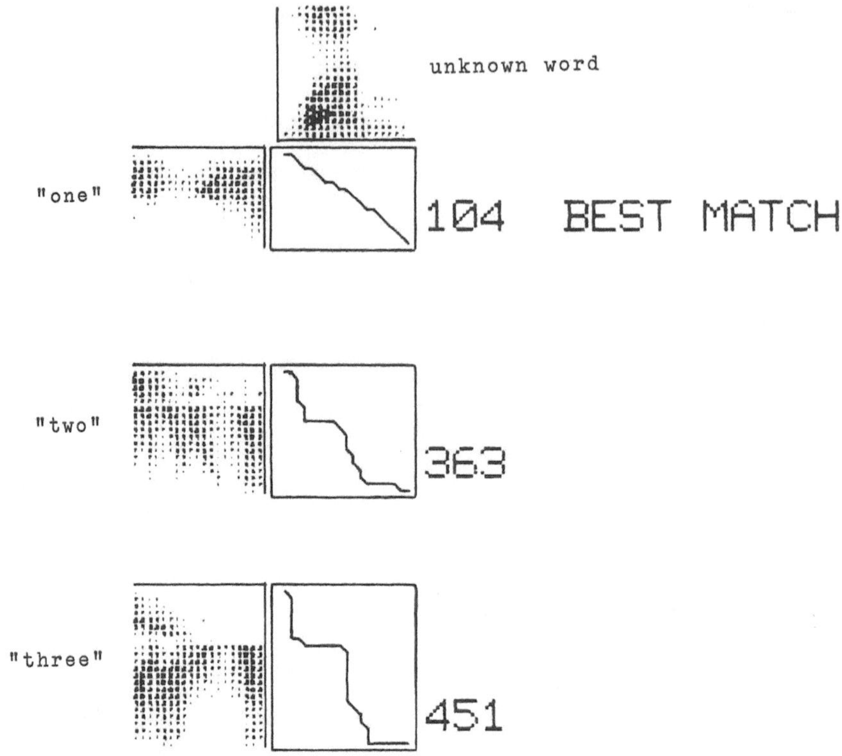

Figure 17 An example of isolated word recognition using dynamic time warping.

In practice it is possible to have more than one reference per word, and this enables more variability in pronunciation to be captured. Similarly, some training procedures involve averaging different examples to obtain a suitably representative reference pattern. The Bell laboratories 'robust' training procedure is a hybrid of the two, combining averaging with a statistical clustering technique [Rabiner and Wilpon 1980].

The computational requirement for DTW is composed of two parts: calculation of the distance matrix, and calculation of the dynamic programming optimization. It is not necessary for these two processes to be kept entirely separate (as in the example given above), but care must be taken to avoid calculating any of the distances more than once. A comparison of a word pattern of length M and a word pattern of length N therefore consists of M*N vector comparisons (the distance matrix) and M*N DP minimizations if there are no slope constraints. If there are slope constraints, then there will be fewer operations. The split between the distance matrix and DP calculation is approximately 80%:20% of the total time taken.

The recognition performance of isolated word recognizers based on DTW techniques is significantly better than that obtainable from linear time-normalization. This is because DTW provides a far more realistic timescale compensation process; greater variability can be accommodated, hence larger vocabularies may be used. Also by using relaxed endpoint constraints (the position where the timescale registration path is allowed to start and end), DTW does not suffer from the same dependency on endpoint detection as linear time-normalization. Hence the segmentor can be much simpler, and it is left to the DTW process to decide precisely where the words begin and end.

Typically, for the ten digits, one could expect recognition accuracies greater than 99% (the NEC DP-100 DTW based recognizer scored 98.8% on the DSTI test).

EXAMPLE SYSTEM: VOTAN V5000

Pre-processing:

— 16 channel filter bank

— bandwidth: 150 Hz to 4000 Hz

— 1000 bits for every 0.5 seconds of speech

— incorporates voice store and forward facility

Segmentation:

— pause between words: 500 ms

Training:

— 500 seconds of template storage

— maximum vocabulary: 256 words

Recognition:

— dynamic time warping

— second choice available

Recognition accuracy:

— 0.55% errors on DSTI data (test performed by VOTAN)

Cost:

— $5000 (V1000 board alone: $3200)

3.5 No Time-Normalization

The developing theme so far in section 3 has been the progressive relaxation of timescale registration constraints. Therefore, the next logical step from non-linear time normalization is to allow any assignment of time aligned points, without regard for temporal ordering at all — in other words, no time-normalization!

Although this idea sounds trivial, it is at least interesting to know how well it is possible to do by ignoring temporal information completely. In fact the very first recognizer (mentioned in the introduction) correlated word patterns without regard to the temporal sequence. More recently, Shore and Burton [1982] have pursued this concept in more detail.

The basic idea is that by using vector quantization, it is possible to set up a separate codebook for each word in the vocabulary. Recognition is then simply a question of which codebook best fits an unknown word (the fit being determined using the average distortion resulting from coding a word).

Computationally, each input vector has to be compared with all of the codewords in each codebook.

Surprisingly, the recognition performance obtained by Shore and Burton was excellent; 0.8% error on part of the DSTI database (which is comparable with the performance of DTW based techniques). The implications of this result are therefore important since it raises questions about whether DTW algorithms make the best use of the extra temporal information which they have at their disposal.

3.6 Stochastic Modelling

Perhaps one reason why Shore and Burton found such superior performance for recognition without time-normalization is that vector quantization is essentially a statistical data collection process. Hence by training their vector quantizer on all of the available training material, they were in a better position than DTW recognizers which could only use part of the training material. The implication is thus that automatic speech recognizers might achieve much better performance if they were statistically based; indeed one would be foolish to expect a recognizer to perform outstandingly well if its entire knowledge about speech is a single example of each word in its vocabulary. The recognizer ought at least to be given some information about the variability in the patterns.

One simple way of providing variability information is to use more than one example of each word. However, this leads to a large increase in the amount of computation required. An alternative is to use 'average' templates, but what this means for DTW based techniques is not absolutely clear. It is more constructive, however, to consider the statistical assumptions underlying the entire whole-word pattern matching process [Bridle 1979].

Statistical Pattern Recognition

In the completely general case, it would be possible to obtain the best classification of an observation vector 0 in terms of a set of classes C by finding for which j P(Cj|0) is a maximum:

$$0 \text{ is from } Ci \text{ if } P(Ci|0) = \max_{j} P(Cj|0)$$

Unfortunately it is difficult to measure P(C|0) directly, but using Bayes' theorem:

$$P(Cj|0) = P(0|Cj) * P(Cj) \;/\; P(0)$$

Thus by substituting, and by ignoring the a-priori frequencies of occurrence of the classes, a 'maximum likelihood classifier' is obtained: 0 is from Ci if

$$P(0|Ci) = \max_{j} P(0|Cj)$$

The advantage of this statement is that P(0|Cj) is easily measurable for each class. Hence, for an observation pattern which is a speech pattern 0(N,T) (where N is the size of the analysis frame and T is the number of time-frames in a word), if N and T are fixed (T being fixed by using time-normalization of some description), then it would be possible to construct the optimal statistical classifier. In practice, such a high dimensionality problem (N*T) would require an inordinate amount of training data and would therefore be unfeasable.

Therefore, to make the problem tractable it is necessary to introduce some assumptions·

a) assume multivariate normal distributions — this means that it is only necessary to measure class means and covariance matrices,

b) assume each frame and each element of the analysis vector are independent — this means that the covariance matrices are diagonal,

c) assume all variances are equal, and equal to 1.

These assumptions lead to the following consequences; 0 is from Ci if

$$P(0|Ci) = \max_{j} \prod_{n,t} P(0(n,t)|Cj)$$

where 0(n,t) is the scalar value of the speech pattern at element n of the vector at time t. Hence from the one-dimensional form of the normal distribution:

$$P(0(n,t)|Cj) = 1/\sqrt{2\pi} * \exp[-(0(n,t)-M(n,t|Cj))^2/2]$$

where M(n,t|Cj) is the mean value of the class j speech pattern at element n of the vector at time t. If, for convenience, logs are taken (and constant terms are ignored) then log P(0(n,t)|Cj) becomes log exp[$-(0(n,t)-M(n,t|Cj))^2$ which is:

$$-(0(n,t)-M(n,t|Cj))^2$$

and the product of terms becomes a sum. Hence 0 is from Ci if

$$\log P(0(n,t)|Ci) = \max_{j} - \sum_{n,t}(0(n,t)-M(n,t|Cj))^2$$

$$= - [\min_{j} \sum_{n,t}(0(n,t)-M(n,t|Cj))^2]$$

and this is the familiar nearest neighbour squared Euclidean distance. Hence such a classifier functions by finding the pattern match which results in the smallest sum of the squared differences over the entire patterns.

Thus whole word pattern matching is already operating in a statistical framework where a time-normalized example of an actual word is used to provide the values for M(n,t). So the question is not how to introduce statistics into whole word pattern matching, but how to relax some of the built-in assumptions.

However, more important is the reliance of the above statistical analysis on the use of time-normalized patterns. It explains how DTW is able to use minimum squared Euclidean distance as an optimization criterion, but it does not give an insight into capturing the average statistical behaviour of variable length patterns. A technique which does address this problem is 'hidden Markov modelling'.

Hidden Markov Models

Levinson et al [1983] describe a hidden Markov model (HMM) as follows: "A probabalistic function of a (hidden) Markov chain is a stochastic process generated by two interrelated mechanisms: an underlying Markov chain having a finite number of states, and a set of random functions one of which is associated with each state. At discrete instants of time, the process is assumed to be in a unique state and an observation is generated by the random function corresponding to the current state. The underlying Markov chain then changes states according to its transition probability matrix. The observer sees only the output of the random functions associated with each state and cannot directly observe the states of the underlying Markov chain, hence the term hidden Markov model."

Typically, hidden Markov models of speech employ vector quantization in order to reduce the random functions associated with each state to non-parametric distributions over a finite set of output symbols.

If H is a hidden Markov model with N states and M symbols, then H = (π,A,B) where π is an initial state probability vector (Nx1), A is a transition probability matrix (NxN), and B is a state output symbol probability matrix (NxM). These matrices completely specify the model. For example, $\pi(i)$ is the probability of starting at state i, a(i,j) is the probability of moving from state i to state j, and b(i,o) is the probability of observing output symbol o from state i.

To recognize a speech pattern, it is necessary to compare the sequence of observations 0 (0=o(1),...,o(T)) with each of the word models in order to find Hj which maximizes P(0|Hj). P(0|H) is found as follows:

A model can only generate an observation sequence of length T via a state sequence of length T. Hence if S is a state sequence (S=s(1),...,s(T)), then the joint probability of 0 and S given the model H is

$$P(0,S|H) = P(S|H) * P(0|S,H)$$

Now:

$$P(S|H) = \pi[s(1)]*a[s(1),s(2)]*a[s(2),s(3)]*...*a[s(T-1),s(T)]$$

and

$$P(0|S,H) = b[s(1),o(1)]*b[s(2),o(2)]*...*b[s(T),o(T)]$$

which by combining leads to:

$$P(0,S|H) = \pi[s(1)]*b[s(1),o(1)]* \prod_{t=2}^{T} a[s(t-1),s(t)]*b[s(t),o(t)]$$

To obtain the probability P = P(0|H) it is necessary to sum the probabilities P(0,S|H) over all state sequences of length T, and this may be achieved efficiently using dynamic programming. The required recursive expression is:

$$F(t,i) = [\sum_{j=1}^{N} F(t\text{-}1,j)*a[s(j),s(i)]] \; * \; b[s(i),o(t)]$$

where F(t,i) is the probability of o(1),...,o(t) finishing in state i at time t given the model H, and the initial condition G(1,i) is π(i)*b[s(i),o(1)]. Hence, since F(T,i) is the probability of 0 finishing in state i at time T:

$$P(0|H) = F(T,i)$$

Or, if H is a left-right model (one for which a(i,j) = 0 for j $\leq$ i: no backward transitions), then the final observation must come from state N and P(0|H) becomes F(T,N).

There are two distinct advantages of this type of statistical model for speech patterns. First, in addition to the variability within an analysis vector, it can model the temporal variability of speech data.
Second, there is an established technique for training the model: the 'Baum-Welch algorithm'.

The training procedure involves re-estimating the parameters of a model H in order to make P(0|H) larger, where 0 is now a training sequence. Intuitively, a good way to re-estimate the state transition probability from state i to state j, would be to measure the average number of transitions from i to j (given 0 and H) and to divide by the measured number of transitions out of i (given 0 and H). Similarly, the state output symbol probability of symbol s at state i can be re-estimated by counting the average number of observations of symbol s from state i, and dividing by the average number of observations of all symbols from state i.

Baums theorem [1972] gives a rigourous backing to these intuitive notions and proves that for the re-estimated model H':

$$P(0|H') \geq P(0|H)$$

In order to perform the re-estimation, it is necessary to introduce a second dynamic programming pass, but in the reverse direction. It is then possible, by a suitable combination of the forward probabilities F with the (new) backward probabilities to re-estimate the parameters of a model. This process is commonly referred to as the 'forward-backward' algorithm.

Isolated Word Recognition Using HMM

In the experiments described by Levinson et al [1983], a five state left-right model was used with limited, but regular, allowable state transitions. Figure 18 illustrates the model. The vector quantizer used a codebook containing 64 codewords.

The experiment itself consisted of a data base of two sets (training and test) of 1000 spoken words; one example of each of the ten digits, spoken by 50 men and 50 women. The training set was used to estimate the parameters of the vector quantizer and of the hidden Markov model, and the test set was then recognized. In addition, a comparison was made with a DTW based system using the same vector quantized data.

The results showed that there was almost no difference in recognition accuracy between the two approaches, both achieving slightly more than 96%. However, from a computational point of view the HMM requires an order of magnitude less storage and execution time.

The implications of hidden Markov modelling for automatic speech recognition are thus very important. Whereas DTW based techniques have a very simple training phase (just data collection) and a very complicated recognition phase, HMMs are just the reverse. It can be argued therefore that an HMM provides the correct balance for any practical system.

Figure 18 Typical structure of a 5-state hidden Markov model.

EXAMPLE SYSTEM: Dragon Systems

Pre-processing:

— 8-bit A/D conversion

— time domain featues

Training:

— 16/32 word vocabulary (Mark II: 96 words)

— any number of repetitions of each word (typically four)

Recognition:

— isolated words

— hidden Markov modelling

— result may be output before word is finished

Computation:

— software system

— runs on 6502 microprocessor (also 8086)

— response time may be negative

Recognition accuracy:

— 0.7% error on DSTI data (test performed by Dragon Systems)

Cost:

— $10 per unit to original equipment manufacturers

4. CONNECTED WORD RECOGNITION

The use of dynamic programming related techniques is obviously very important to achieving practical recognition performance from isolated word recognizers. However, this is not the only useful attribute; it turns out that it is possible to extend the techniques from isolated to connected words using relatively simple modifications to the algorithms.

To understand the principle behind these modifications, consider the isolated word recognition result illustrated in figure 17. Three time registration paths are shown, the best path (for the correct match) and two sub-optimal paths. If it were the case that only the best path were displayed, then it can be seen that the DTW process is one which finds the best explanation of the relationship between the unknown word and one of the reference patterns. Therefore, to recognize a sequence of connected words, it is necessary to find a time registration path which best explains the relationship between the unknown phrase and a sequence of reference patterns (a 'super' reference pattern).

This optimization can be achieved by a number of different techniques.

4.1 One-Pass Algorithm

Perhaps the simplest (yet very effective) connected word recognition algorithm has been described by Bridle and Brown [1979]. In this scheme the dynamic programming calculation is arranged such that the time registration path may leave the end of one reference pattern and enter the beginning of another. To do this it is necessary to use a slightly more complicated local decision function on the edges of the dynamic programming matrices than in the middles. Figure 19 illustrates the point. Essentially those productions on the top edge of a matrix, which would normally refer to non-existant data outside of the matrix, are duplicated and attached to the trailing edges of all the other matrices (including the same one). Paths are thus able to enter and leave reference patterns according to the local minimizations. As before, the best path is not known until all of the local decisions have been made; backtracking then reveals the result.

To avoid complicated recursions and also path length normalization problems, the local decision function is chosen to be asymmetric (in fact the second example in figure 16). The asymmetry is arranged such that each production takes a path from one input vector to the next. Hence all possible paths will have the

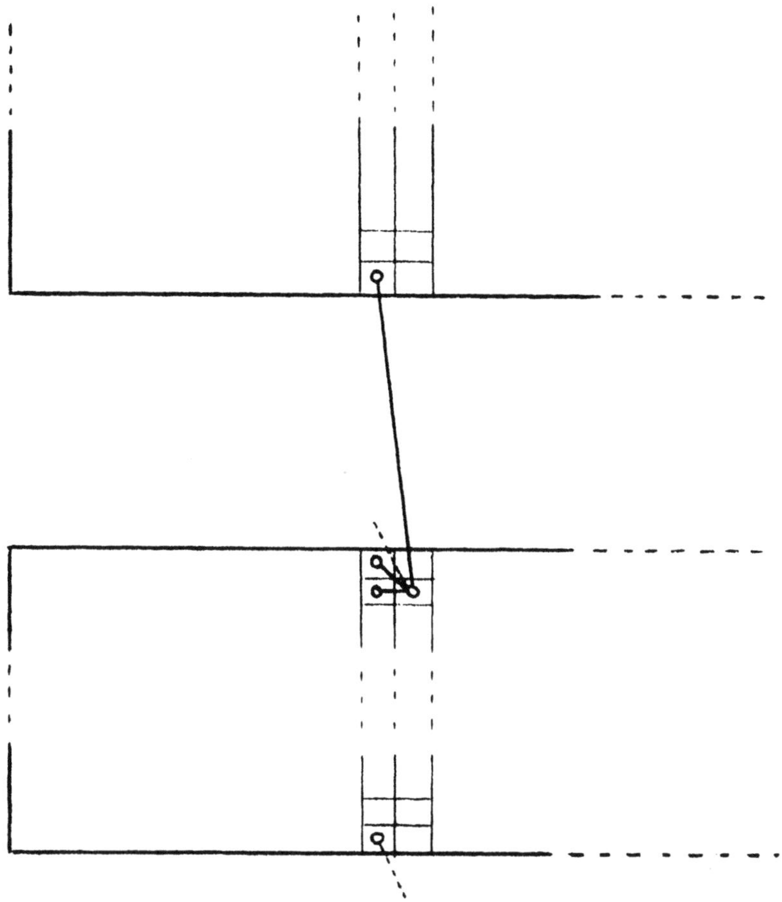

Figure 19 Arrangement of the local decision function at word boundaries in the one-pass connected word recognition algorithm.

same number of distances along their length, that number being equal to the number of frames in the unknown phrase. This also means that the computation may be performed on a column by column basis, hence processing one input vector with all of the reference data at each step.

Figure 20 shows an example of connected word recognition using the one-pass algorithm. The reference patterns are the same words as in figure 17, but the unknown pattern consists of a sequence of words (actually "11213"). The best path, determined by DTW, is shown, and it can be seen jumping around from template to template. The trajectory reveals that the phrase is correctly recognized as "11213".

(In comparing figure 20 with figure 17 it should be noted that there is only one path in figure 20: the optimal path, whereas in figure 17 three paths are shown: the optimal one and two sub-optimal ones.)

The computational requirement of the one-pass connected word recognition algorithm is exactly the same as for a DTW based isolated word recognition algorithm apart from the small amount of extra work needed to process the additional productions at template boundaries. Hence there are T*R*V vector comparisons, and the same number of DP minimizations, where T is the number of frames in the test pattern, R is the average number of frames per reference pattern and V is the number of reference patterns.

The recognition accuracy of the technique depends on a number of factors. First, the algorithm assumes that continuous speech is made up of isolated words spoken in sequence. Obviously this is not the case, hence the recognition accuracy will only be high if the user speaks carefully and avoids coarticulation effects at the word boundaries. Second, the asymmetric local decision function imposes a 2:1 slope constraint which can easily be broken when comparing connected speech with isolated training examples.

One way to overcome both of these problems is to use an 'embedded' training procedure whereby reference words are extracted from a carrier sentence [Rabiner et al 1982]. The beauty of this technique is that a connected word

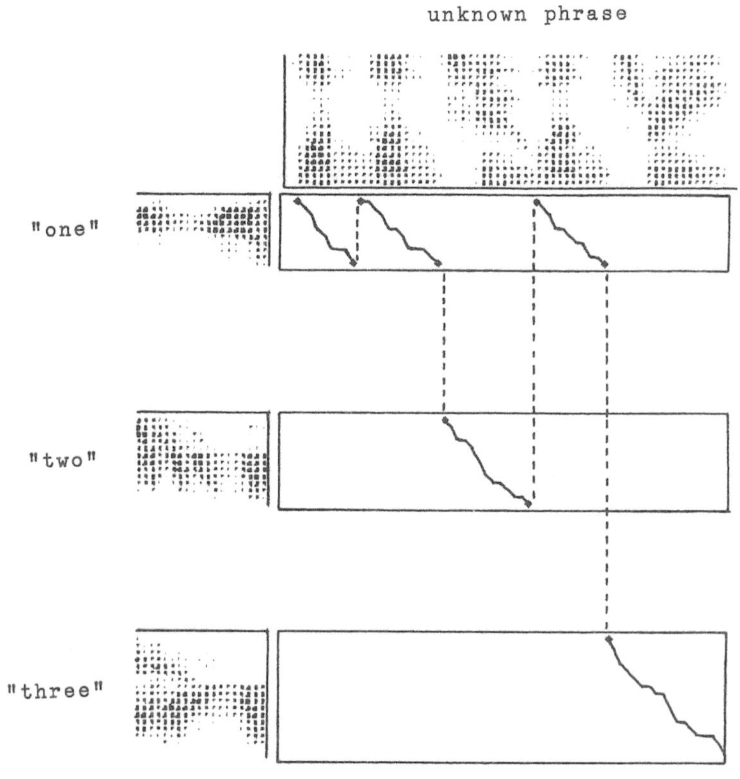

Figure 20 An example of connected word recognition using the one-pass algorithm.

recognition algorithm can be used to do the extraction. A simpler technique is to train such a connected word recognizer on isolated reference patterns which are spoken rather abruptly.

EXAMPLE SYSTEM: Marconi SR128

Pre-processing:

— 19 channel filter bank

Training:

— 128 seconds of template storage

— maximum number of templates: 240

— maximum length of a template: 2 secs.

— built-in digital mini-cassette recorder for long term storage

Recognition

— one-pass connected word recognition algorithm

— maximum length of a phrase: 8 secs.

Computation:

— recognition response time: 50 ms

Cost:

— £ 10000

4.2 Two-Level Algorithm

The two-level connected word recognition technique of Sakoe [1979] was the first practical attempt to extend DTW beyond isolated words. It operates by first finding the optimal reference pattern to match any part of the unknown phrase and then by finding the optimal way to connect together the partial matches. Consequently, two dynamic programming processes are required, one at the word level and one at the phrase level, hence the term 'two-level'.

At the first level a standard isolated word DTW algorithm is used to find the minimum cumulative distance between each reference pattern (r) and all possible start frames (s) and all possible end frames (e) in the test pattern: D(r,s,e).

At the second level a dynamic programming algorithm is used to find the path through D(r,s,e) which minimizes the total distance starting with s as the first frame of the test pattern, and ending with e as the last frame of the test pattern:

$$D'(n,e) = \min_{s} [\min_{r} [D(r,s,e)] + D'(n-1,s-1)]$$

where D'(n,e) is the cumulative distance obtained by matching the best concatenation of n reference patterns to the portion of the test pattern between frame 1 and frame e, and min[D(r,s,e)] over r is the distance resulting from the best reference pattern match between frames s and e of the test pattern.

The computation may be stopped once n is large enough to cover the maximum number of words expected in a phrase. The result can then be found by selecting the minimum value of D'(n,E) (where E is the last frame in the test pattern), and then backtracking through the local decisions (at the second level) to find the best sequence of n words.

Computationally the two-level algorithm is much more complicated than the one-pass algorithm (due to all the D(r,s,e) partial distance calculations); approximately $T*R^4*V$ DP minimizations, where T is the number of frames in the test pattern, R is the average number of frames per reference pattern and V is the number of reference patterns. However, the result of the different approaches should be identical. This is because ultimately they are both minimizing the same thing. However, the two-level algorithm does have the advantage that it is very easy to extract the recognition result for each value of n, that is, the scores for different length word hypothesese. Also, if required, it is easy to specify in advance how many words are in the unknown phrase.

Hence, errors of word deletion or insertion may be avoided. (It is possible to do the same for the one-pass algorithm, but it is much more complicated.)

EXAMPLE SYSTEM: Nippon Electric Company DP200

Pre-processing:

— 16 channel filter bank

— bandwidth: 120 Hz to 6000 Hz

Training:

— 4K bits per word

— vocabulary: 50 or 150 words

— built-in mini-floppy disk for template storage

Recognition:

— two-level connected word recognition algorithm

— up to five words per phrase

— 0.2 to 4.0 seconds per phrase

Computation:

— recognition result 300 ms from end of phrase

Recognition accuracy:

— 1.2% error rate on DSTI data (DP100 results)

Cost:

$15000

4.3 Level Building Algorithm

The level building connected word recognition algorithm, proposed by Myers and Rabiner [1981], is another technique for optimizing the match between a sequence of reference patterns and an unknown phrase. It is thus functionally identical to both the one-pass algorithm and the two-level algorithm.

In this scheme the term 'level' refers to the number of words in a hypothesized sequence. So to recognize a sequence of n words, at least n levels must be built. The first level corresponds to hypothesizing that the unknown phrase consists of a single word, the second level corresponds to two word hypothesese etc. Conceptually, at each level, DTW is performed between all of the reference patterns and all of the test patterns, and the results from each level are taken as inputs to the DTW calculations of the next level.

This means that at the end of the calculations for the first level, there will be associated with each frame of the test pattern a cumulative distance resulting from the best time registration path out of all of the references, and a pointer indicating which reference pattern it was. The time registration paths in this case will trace back to the first frame of the test pattern and the first frame of a reference pattern. This information then provides the starting point for the next level, and the new time registration paths will trace back to the first level, and so on.

The level building algorithm is computationally an order of magnitude more efficient than the two-level algorithm, but it has N times more dynamic programming minimizations than the one-pass algorithm (where N is the number of levels). However, like the two-level algorithm, the level building algorithm can easily find the best sequence of a given length.

4.4 Hidden Markov Models

The principle of hidden Markov modelling was in fact applied to connected word recognition before it was applied to isolated word recognition. Jelinek's team at IBM used HMMs to model phonetic speech segments, which could then be connected together to make words and then sentences [Jelinek et al 1982, Bahl et al 1983].

Exactly the same techniques may be applied to the connection of whole-word models, and the process is analogous to the one-pass algorithm described above. The advantage of this approach is that it becomes possible to train the word boundary information in context. However, the negative consequences of this feature are that the combinatorics require a large amount of training data.

EXAMPLE SYSTEM: Verbex 1800

Pre-processing:

— 32 channel filter bank

— bandwidth: 300 Hz to 3000 Hz

— autocorrelation coefficients

— eight input channels

Training:

— multiple training passes

— can train on word sequences

— vocabulary: 10 - 39 words

Recognition:

— connected word recognition

— hidden Markov models

Recognition Accuracy:

— 0.2% errors on DSTI isolated word data (best in the DSTI test)

Cost:

— $80000

5. REAL-TIME CONSIDERATIONS

Most of the algorithms discussed so far have been described without due regard to any short-cuts or other efficiency modifications. This section outlines some techniques which may be used to cut down the computational load and which may also affect the recognition performance (either for the better, or for the worse). For most of the algorithms, the introduction of efficiency usually means sacrificing optimality. Therefore, overall performance is often raised at the expense of making a few serious errors from time to time.

5.1 Syntax

As well as a definition of the words in the vocabulary, there will also be rules which govern the ordering of the words in most applications of automatic speech recognition. These rules define a grammar (or syntax) which may be used to reduce the computational requirement for an isolated or a connected word recognizer by limiting the number of alternative words at each point in a sentence.

The implementation of syntax for an isolated word recognizer is very easy; after each word is recognized, the active vocabulary is switched according to the rules of the grammar. For connected word recognition the process is more complicated, but it is possible to modify the algorithms such that time registration paths only connect words if such a connection is legal in the syntax. In this situation the syntax becomes an integral part of the overall optimization process, hence connected word recognizers with this facility are able to find the best syntactically valid interpretation of a connected utterance.

There are a number of ways of specifying a syntax, but the most common is in the form of a state transition diagram. Figure 21 shows a syntax for a voice controlled calculator. It can be seen that the diagram describes sentences such as "what is two plus four compute" and "put nine times alpha into beta compute". The overall vocabulary size is twenty-three, but the maximum number of words that need to be considered at any point is fourteen; in some places only one word is valid. The average number of legal words at any point is eight and this is known as the 'branching factor'. The ratio of branching factor to total vocabulary size gives an indication of the reduction in computation.

A low branching factor will also increase recognition accuracy because the number of potential word confusions is reduced. (In general, variability means that recognition performance goes down as the number of choices goes up.)

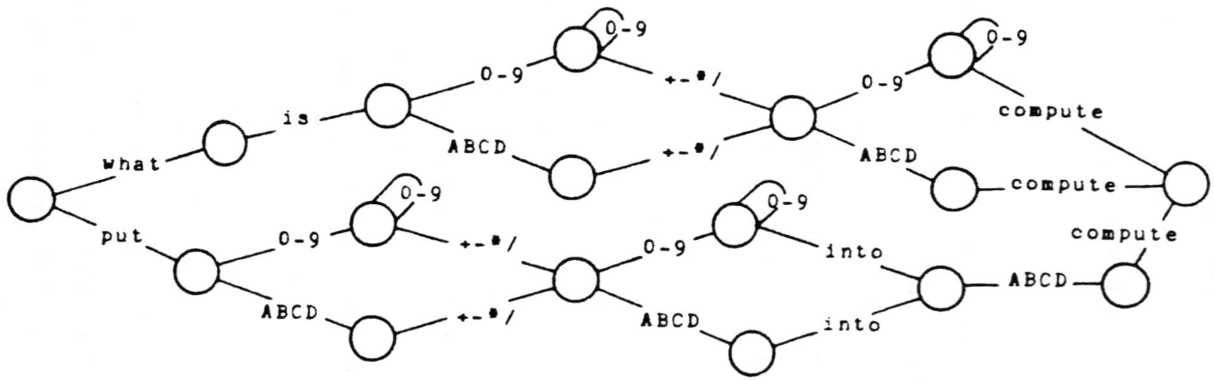

Figure 21 Syntax for a voice controlled calculator.

However, this gain in performance is balanced by the requirement that a user must be able to remember and use only allowable sequences of words. If a user says a word which is syntactically illegal, then a recognizer may be forced to misrecognize it, even if the word is in the overall vocabulary.

5.2 Fixed Search Window

In DTW based recognition algorithms the search for the optimal solution can often extend into regions which are extremely unlikely. Of course it is only by doing so, that the optimal solution can be guaranteed. Nevertheless, it is possible to achieve a reasonable reduction in computation, with only a small risk of reaching a non-optimal solution, by restricting the search in some way.

One way of achieving this restriction is to impose a fixed search window on the DTW process. Typically this might take the form of a range restriction on the total amount of time registration slippage that is allowed at any point. Hence in the calculation of the distance and cumulative distance matrices for isolated word recognition, the indices would be limited such that $|i-j| < W$, where i and j are the indices and W is the window width. Figure 22 illustrates the process (in this example the optimal path found in figure 15 has been lost).

For isolated word recognition it is possible to speed up the computation by a factor of 1.6 with no degradation in recognition accuracy [Moore 1980]. The same process may be applied to the two-level and the level building connected word recognition algorithms, and in these cases even larger savings in computation may be achieved.

5.3 Beam Search

A second technique for reducing the DTW search is not to have a fixed search window, but to have a dynamic window which is controlled by the search process itself. This technique is known as 'beam search' and it is based on the principle that at any point during the DTW process it is possible to measure the value of the best solution (minimum distance or maximum probability) so far. This means that on the next iteration of the processs, the search can be limited

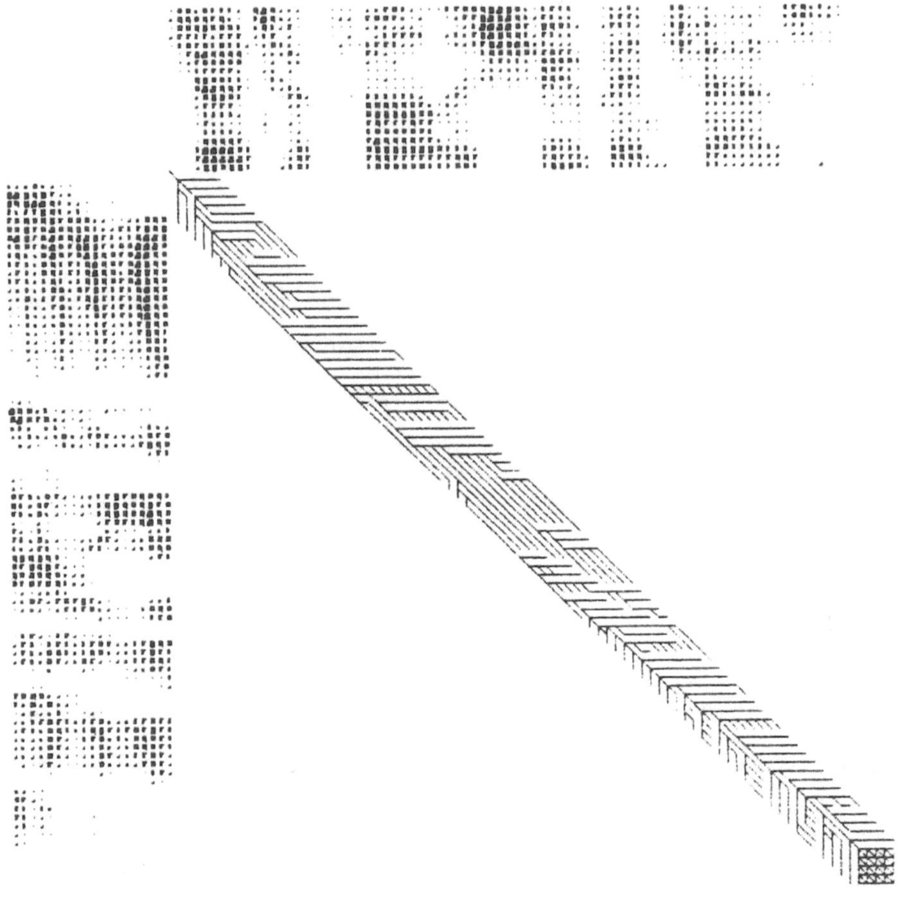

Figure 22 The effect of a fixed search window on dynamic time warping.

to solutions which lie within a given range of the current best solution.

The beauty of this technique is that when there is ambiguity there will be a range of solutions all fairly close to each other and the beam will be wide, but when there is little ambiguity there will be few competing solutions and the beam will be narrow. Hence the scheme ensures that most of the computation takes place where it is most needed. Figure 23 illustrates the effect on a single DTW word match.

The danger with the beam search technique is that if the beam is too narrow, then the optimal solution might be lost if there is a momentary bad fit in the data (after all, the main reason for using dynamic programming based algorithms is to exploit their property of overcoming local deficiencies). However, for isolated word recognition the technique is capable of speeding up computation by a factor of four without affecting recognition performance [Moore 1980].

5.4 Partial Traceback

Partial traceback is another technique for exploiting the intermediate properties of a dynamic programming type search [Spohrer et al 1980]. It is based on the idea that by continually tracing back during the DTW process (rather than waiting until the end) it is possible to discover a point in the past to which all backtraces lead. When such a point is found, no amount of further processing will change the trajectory of the path up to that point. Hence, the results of the DTW process up to that point may be output. Figure 24 illustrates the principle for an isolated word comparison.

The technique is particularly relevant to connected word recognition. If partial traceback is used in this situation, it becomes possible to output the initial words in a long sentence before the sentence has finished being spoken. More importantly, it is possible to run the entire DTW process continuously; the DTW optimization can continually take in new data, and the results are output (after a delay) by means of partial traceback [Bridle et al 1983]. (The amount of delay between input and output in such a system will depend on the ambiguity present in the signal.)

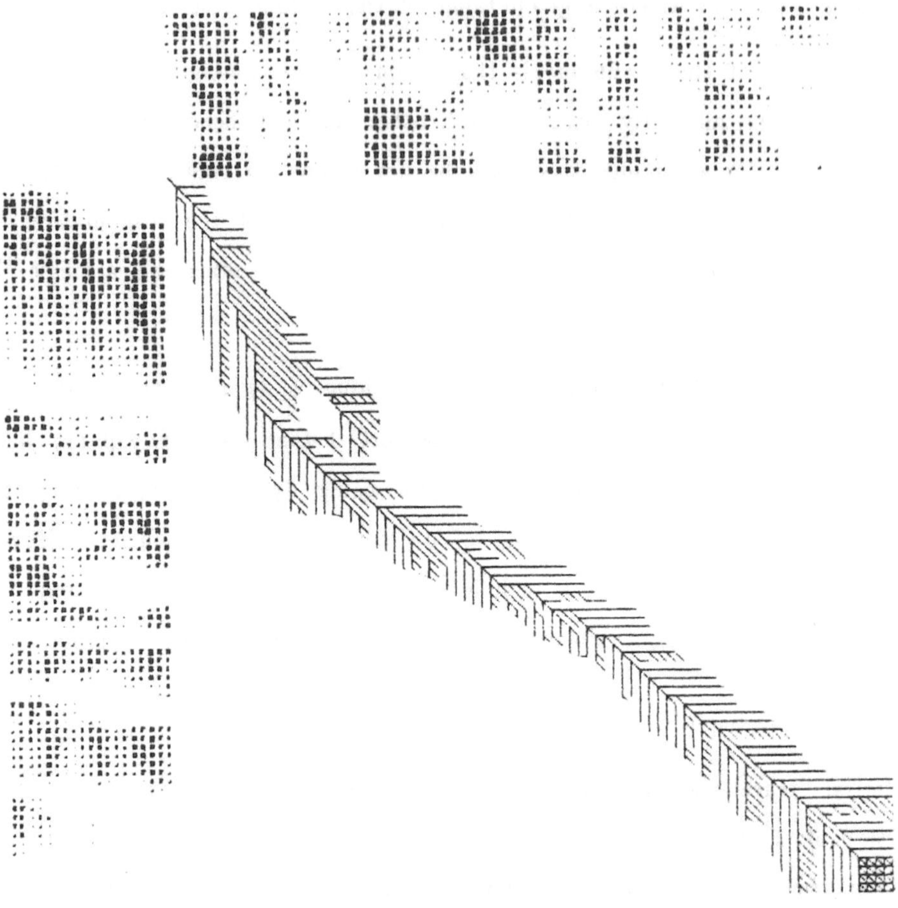

Figure 23 The effect of beam search on dynamic time warping.

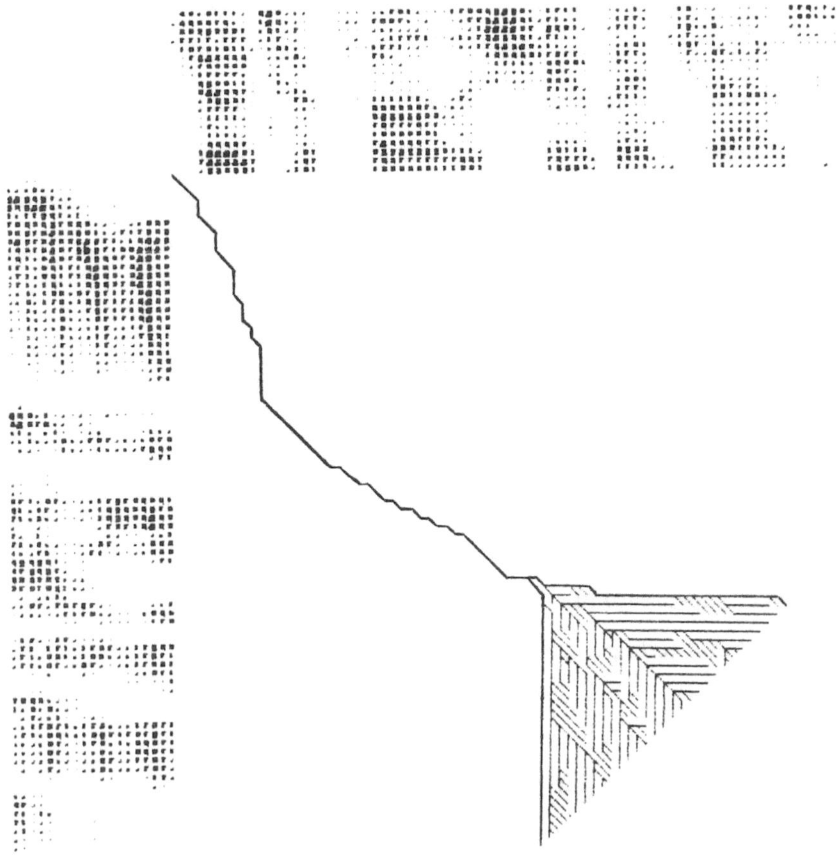

Figure 24 The effect of partial traceback on dynamic time warping.

If partial traceback is combined with beam search, then it is even possible to output the identity of a spoken word before it has been completely uttered. This will occur when competing words are sufficiently different that the beam falls totally within only one word. Partial traceback can detect this occurrence and output the word. However, if the beam is too narrow in this situation, it is possible to have a recognizer discriminating between two similar words before the deciding sounds have occurred.

EXAMPLE SYSTEM: Logica LOGOS

Pre-processing:

— 19 channel filter bank

— 200 frames per second

— variable rate coding

Training:

— embedded training (may be embedded in silence)

— uses concept of 'wildcard' frame

— storage for up to 2000 templates (minimum 64K bytes: 120 templates)

Recognition:

— continuous connected word recognizer

— one-pass connected DTW algorithm

— beam search

— partial traceback

— 5 second input buffer

— syntax (up to 256 nodes)

— number of active words: 20 (expandable up to 300 maximum)

— keyword spotting

Computation:

— separate DP processors for section of total vocabulary

— response: typically one or two words delay (depends on ambiguity)

Cost:

—£ 35000

6. FUTURE METHODS AND SYSTEMS

The foregoing sections have concentrated on established techniques for automatic speech recognition. This section is intended to focus on some of the key issues relating to future methods and systems.

From a user's point of view, perhaps the most immediate requirement is for systems with a high level of reliability for reasonable sized vocabularies regardless of whether they are isolated or connected word recognizers. Hence, work aimed at improving the discrimination power of recognizers is important. Second, users would ideally like not to have to spend too long training systems. Hence, work which is aimed at introducing more speech knowledge into systems is also important.

6.1 More Useful Representations

The beauty of the whole word pattern matching approach is that it provides a single (easy to characterize) interface between the speech patterns and the matching process. However, the performance of the approach ultimately depends on the exact nature of this interface and the quality of data that it uses. It can be seen from the preceding sections that nearly all of the recognizers employ a fairly coarse representation of the speech signal, usually equivalent to the analyzer section of a vocoder system.

Obviously such representations are in some sense appropriate for speech recognition (it is possible to understand the re-synthesized speech), but in no sense could they be described as high quality. It is therefore possible that one bottleneck in the performance of current systems is this reliance on low data rates at the front-end.

The question as to what constitutes a high enough quality representation is open to some debate, but it is reasonable to expect that work on auditory modelling has some relevance [Lyon 1982].

It might also be sensible to break away from the straightforward use of the 'raw' speech pattern, and instead to re-address the question of a suitable low-level featural description. Such an approach is currently being pursued by Cole et al [1983] using statistical pattern recognition techniques.

6.2 Better Models

In section 3.4 it can be seen how DTW is not a single well defined algorithm, but rather a principle which underlies a collection of alternative options and implementations. A lot of research effort has been directed towards manipulating the various parameters in a DTW algorithm, but it has resulted in very few insights into the meaning of DTW as a model of speech variability. On the other hand, hidden Markov modelling does provide a useful theoretical framework, but to what extent is it a 'good' model?

(It should be remembered that the purpose of a 'good' model is to take knowledge (perhaps in the form of training data) and 'generalize' that knowledge appropriately to assess previously unseen events. This can only be done by a proper understanding of the variabilities involved.)

Work at RSRE on 'timescale variability analysis' [Moore et al 1982 and Russell et al 1983] is an example of introducing into a DTW processs, knowledge about the expected local variation in the temporal structure of speech patterns. Essentially, the techniques replaces global path constraints with probabalistically conditioned local path constraints (it is analogous to training the state transition probabilities in an HMM). The result of providing DTW with a good model of temporal variability is that it is then better able to discriminate between different words, and is also able to discriminate between words where the difference is entirely temporal (something that normal DTW is unable to do). For example, using the 'locally constrained dynamic time warping' (LCDTW) algorithm, error rates for the two pronunciations of "close" (/kləʊs/ and /kləʊz/) were reduced from 40% (using DTW) to 1.5% (using LCDTW).

6.3 Improved Optimization

Assuming it is possible to arrive at a 'good' model, it is still necessary to train it (to optimize its behaviour). Hidden Markov models have an advantage here because they employ an algorithm (the Baum-Welch) which is guaranteed to improve the behaviour of the model. However, such an optimization is not guaranteed to find the 'best' solution, merely to find the best local optimum. As a consequence, the apparently straightforward handle-turning optimization process, is in fact rather more complicated.

In general, optimization techniques are becoming inherent to advanced automatic speech recognition algorithms. Hence, a better understanding of these processes is essential. An optimization technique which is able to avoid becoming trapped in local optima has been described by Kirkpatrick et al [1983]. In this scheme ideas based in statistical mechanics are used to implement an algorithm which simulates the cooling behaviour of a physical system: the annealing process. By introducing the notion of 'temperature' into an optimization problem, Kirkpatrick shows how the process can escape from local optima.

6.4 More Speech Knowledge

The performance of an automatic speech recognizer ultimately depends on the amount and quality of the training material. However, if the dimensionality of the representation is raised then recognizers are almost always going to be undertrained. It is therefore vital to know how the knowledge embedded in the training material can best be structured and hence utilized. One technique for obtaining this structured knowledge is to extract it from a human 'expert'. Unfortunately this raises questions about the usefulness of the knowledge thereby gained.

In theory, it ought to be possible to extract a great deal of structural information from the speech signal itself (humans seem to do it). So the question is how to use available speech data to the maximum advantage.

The work on 'discriminative networks' at RSRE [Moore et al 1983] shows how some of the problems associated with undertraining may be avoided. The technique is directed at the problems which arise from attempting to distinguish between two very similar words using whole-word pattern matching. Such similar sounding words are characterized by having extremely localized differences (for example, "stalagmite" and "stalactite") which are swamped by the irrelevant variability contained in the rest of the patterns.

If a recognizer was fully trained, then this variability would be characterized and it would be possible to optimally discriminate between the two words. However, since a recognizer is always undertrained (particularly if it has only one example of each word as a reference pattern), then it is possible to circumvent the undertraining by forcing the regions of the pattern which are irrelevant to the distinction to be identical. This is equivalent to deriving a network-type data structure for the two patterns (the discriminative network) which is able to focus the recognition process onto those regions of the patterns which are relevant to the distinction. The result is that the undertraining is supplemented with the a-priori knowledge that the two word patterns are supposed to be different.

The RSRE algorithm is able to derive the network structure for any pair of words automatically, and the networks assume the shapes one would expect given the phonetic structure of the component words. Figure 25a illustrates the expected discriminative network for "stalagmite"/"stalactite", and figure 25b shows the speech pattern network derived by the technique. For the same pair of words, a 40% error rate for normal DTW was reduced to no errors using the network shown.

6.5 Better Architectures

All of the techniques described in this lecture tend to be a mixture of sequential and parallel processes. Dynamic programming is essentially a sequential process since a set of partial results is needed before the next iteration can proceed. On the other hand, distance calculations may all be done in parallel since one distance does not depend on another. Suitable processing architectures

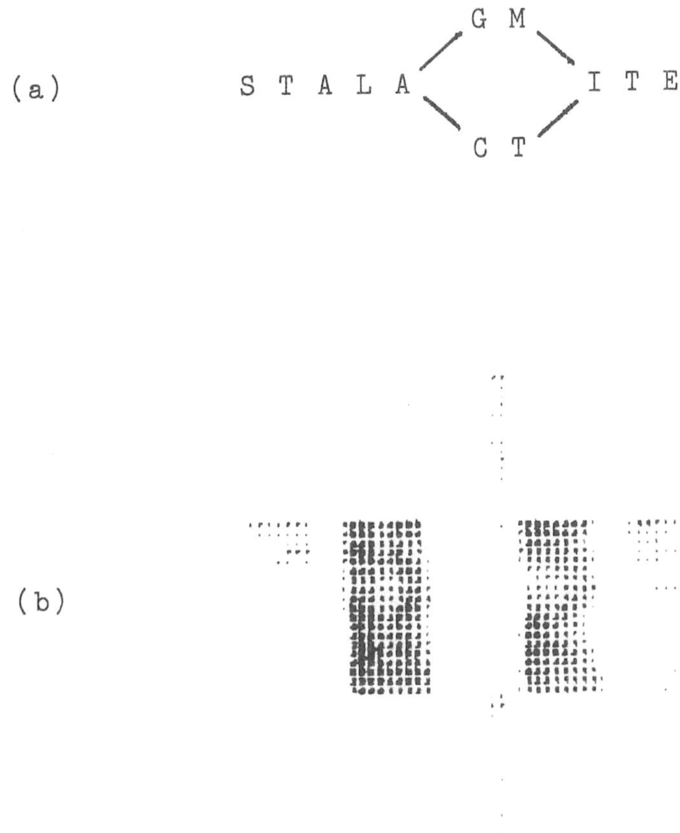

Figure 25 **Discriminative network for the words "stalagmite" and "stalactite";** (a) the expected network and (b) the experimentally derived speech spectrogram network.

are needed to exploit this mix, and in particular the parallelism that is possible.

A specific example of DTW being implemented on a parallel processing architecture is described by Simpson and Roberts [1983]. A highly parallel single-instruction multiple-data (SIMD) array signal processor with 32x32 processing elements and a 100 ns cycle time (the ICL distributed array processor: DAP) is shown to be capable of handling a 600 word vocabulary in real-time using the one-pass connected word recognition algorithm.

7. CONCLUSIONS

This lecture has attempted to describe in some detail many of the techniques which underlie contemporary isolated and connected word recognition systems. The main conclusion is that, far from being a 'dead-end', whole-word pattern matching techniques provide a baseline from which to develop new methods and systems.

The key to success in this area appears to be a proper separation between the knowledge which one might have about speech signals, the models in which one chooses to embody such knowledge, and the optimization techniques which are needed to load the knowledge into the models.

ACKNOWLEDGEMENT

I am particularly indebted to my colleague Dr. Martin Russell for his many helpful contributions to this lecture.

REFERENCES

1. L. R. Bahl, F. Jelinek and R. L. Mercer, "A maximum likelihood approach to continuous speech recognition", IEEE Trans. Pattern Analysis and Machine Intelligence, Vol. 5, 1983, pp. 179-190.
2. L. E. Baum, "An inequality and associated maximization technique in statistical estimation for probabalistic functions of a Markov process", Inequalities, Vol. 3, 1972, pp. 1-8.
3. J. S. Bridle and M. D. Brown, "An experimental automatic word-recognition system", JSRU Research Report No. 1003, 1974.
4. J. S. Bridle, "Pattern recognition techniques for speech recognition", Proc. NATO ASI on Spoken Language Generation and Understanding, 1979.
5. J. S. Bridle and M. D. Brown, "Connected word recognition using whole word templates", Proc. Inst. Acoustics Autumn Conf., 1979.
6. J. S. Bridle and M. D. Brown, "A data-adaptive frame rate technique and its use in automatic speech recognition", Proc. Inst. Acoustics Autumn Conf., 1982.
7. J. S. Bridle, M. D. Brown and R. M. Chamberlain, "Continuous connected word recoognition using whole word templates", The Radio and Electronic Engineer, Vol. 53, 1983, pp. 167-175.
8. R. A. Cole, R. M. Stern, M. S. Phillips, S. M. Brill, A. P. Pilant and P. Specker, "Feature-based speaker-independent recognition of isolated English letters", Proc. IEEE Conf. Acoustics, Speech and Signal Processing, 1983, pp. 731-733.
9. K. H. Davis, R. Biddulph and S. Balashek, "Automatic recognition of spoken digits", J. Acoust. Soc. Amer., Vol. 24, 1952, pp. 637-642.
10. G. R. Doddington and T. B. Schalk, "Speech recognition: turning theory to practice", IEEE Spectrum, Vol. 18, 1981, pp. 26-32.
11. J. L. Flanagan, *Speech Analysis, Synthesis and Perception*. New York: Springer-Verlang, 1972.
12. J. N. Holmes, "The JSRU channel vocoder", IEE Proc. Communications, Radar and Signal Processing, Vol. 127, Pt.F, 1980, pp. 53-60.
13. J. N. Holmes, "A survey of methods for digitally encoding speech signals", The Radio and Electronic Engineer, Vol. 52, 1982, pp. 267-276.
14. M. J. Hunt, M. Lennig and P. Mermelstein, "Experiments in syllable-based recognition of continuous speech", Proc. IEEE Conf. Acoustics, Speech and Signal Processing, 1980, pp. 880-883.
15. F. Itakura, "Minimum prediction residual principle applied to speech recognition", IEEE Trans. Acoustics, Speech and Signal Processing, Vol. 23, 1975, pp. 67-72.
16. F. Jelinek, R. L. Mercer and L. R. Bahl, "Continuous speech recognition: statistical methods", Handbook of Statistics, Vol. 2, Krishnaiah and Kanal, eds., North-Holland, 1982, pp. 549-573.
17. S. Kirpatrick, C. D. Gelatt, Jr. and M. P. Vecchi, "Optimization by simulated annealing", Science, Vol. 220, 1983, pp. 671-680.

18. S. E. Levinson, L. R. Rabiner and M. M. Sondhi, "Speaker independent isolated digit recognition using hidden Markov models", Proc. IEEE Int. Conf. Acoustics, Speech and Signal Processing, 1983, pp. 1049-1052.
19. R. F. Lyon, "A computational model of filtering, detection and compression in the cochlea", Proc. IEEE Conf. Acoustics, Speech and Signal Processing, 1982, pp. 1282-1285.
20. R. K. Moore, "An investigation into some fundamental problems in the automatic recognition of continuous speech", Unpublished Technical Report, 1980.
21. R. K. Moore, M. J. Russell and M. J. Tomlinson, "Locally constrained dynamic programming in automatic speech recognition", Proc. IEEE Conf. Acoustics, Speech and Signal Procesing, 1982, pp. 1270-1273.
22. R. K. Moore, M. J. Russell and M. J. Tomlinson, "The discriminative network: a mechanism for focusing recognition in whole word pattern matching", Proc. IEEE Conf. Acoustics, Speech and Signal Processing, 1983, pp. 1041-1044.
23. C. Myers, L. R. Rabiner and A. E. Rosenberg, "Performance tradeoffs in dynamic time warping algorithms for isolated word recognition", IEEE Trans. Acoustics, Speech and Signal Processing, Vol. 28, 1980, pp. 623-635.
24. C. S. Myers and L. R. Rabiner, "A level building dynamic time warping algorithm for connected word recognition", IEEE Trans. Acoustics, Speech and Signal Processing, Vol. 29, 1981, pp. 284-297.
25. R. Pieraccini and R. Billi, "Experimental comparison among data compression techniques in isolated word recognition", Proc. IEEE Int. Conf. Acoustics, Speech and Signal Processing, 1983, pp. 1025-1028.
26. L. R. Rabiner and M. R. Sambur, "An algorithm for determining the endpoints of isolated utterances", Bell Syst. Tech. J., Vol. 54, 1975, pp. 297-315.
27. L. R. Rabiner and J. G. Wilpon, "A simplified, robust training procedure for speaker trained isolated word recognition", J. Acoust. Soc. Amer., Vol. 68, pp. 1271-1276.
28. L. R. Rabiner, A. Bergh and J. G. Wilpon, "An improved training procedure for connected-digit recognition", Bell Syst. Tech. J., Vol. 61, 1982, pp. 981-1001.
29. M. J. Russell, R. K. Moore and M. J. Tomlinson, "Some techniques for incorporating local timescale variability information into a dynamic time-warping algorithm for automatic speech recognition", Proc. IEEE Conf. Acoustics, Speech and Signal Processing, 1983, pp. 1037-1040.
30. H. Sakoe and S. Chiba, "Dynamic programming algorithm optimization for spoken word recognition", IEEE Trans. Acoustics, Speech and Signal Processing, Vol. 26, 1978, pp. 43-49.
31. H. Sakoe, "Two-level DP-matching — a dynamic programming based pattern matching algorithm for connected word recognition", IEEE Trans. Acoustics, Speech and Signal Processing, Vol. 27, 1979, pp. 588-595.
32. R. W. Schafer and L. R. Rabiner, "Digital representations of speech signals", Proc. IEEE, Vol. 63, 1975, pp. 662-677.
33. J. E. Shore and D. Burton, "Discrete utterance speech recognition without

time normalization — recent results", Proc. 6th Int. Conf. Pattern Recognition, 1982, pp. 582-584.

34. P. Simpson and J. B. G. Roberts, "Speech recognition on a distributed array processor", Electronics Letters, Vol. 19, 1983, pp. 1018-1020.
35. J. C. Spohrer, P. F. Brown, P. H. Hochschild and J. K. Baker, "Partial traceback in continuous speech recognition", Proc. IEEE Int. Conf. Cybernetics and Society, 1980, pp. 36-42.
36. G. M. White, "Speech recognition with character string encoding", Proc. IEEE Conf. Decision and Control, 1972, pp. 111-113.
37. G. M. White and P. J. Fong, "k-nearest-neighbour decision rule performance in a speech recognition system", IEEE Trans. Systems, Man and Cybernetics, Vol. 5, 1975, pp. 389.
38. G. M. White and R. B. Neely, "Speech recognition experiments with linear prediction, bandpass filtering, and dynamic programming", IEEE Trans. Acoustics, Speech and Signal Processing, Vol. 24, 19776, pp. 183-188.

SYSTOLIC ARCHITECTURES FOR CONNECTED SPEECH RECOGNITION

Patrice FRISON
Patrice QUINTON

IRISA, Campus de Beaulieu,
35042 RENNES-CEDEX
FRANCE

July 1984

ABSTRACT

Systolic algorithm concept is introduced and three speech recognition algorithms are presented together with a systolic version. The first algorithm is based on the dynamic time warping algorithm which is applied directly on acoustic feature patterns. The second algorithm is the probabilistic matching algorithm which requires that the input sentence be preprocessed by a phonetic analyzer. The third algorithm is the connected word recognition algorithm that find the best matching word sequence. Finally, the architecture of a speech recognition machine using a VLSI chip, called API89, as the basic processor is presented.

NATO ASI Series, Vol. F16
New Systems and Architectures for Automatic Speech
Recognition and Synthesis. Edited by R. De Mori and C. Y. Suen

SYSTOLIC ARCHITECTURES FOR CONNECTED SPEECH RECOGNITION

Patrice FRISON
Patrice QUINTON

IRISA, Campus de Beaulieu,
35042 RENNES-CEDEX
FRANCE

1. INTRODUCTION

Speech recognition is a computationally intensive task which can be handled on conventional architectures only for small vocabularies. The use of pipeline and parallel architecture organizations increases the speed of the algorithms thus making realistic recognition of much larger vocabularies and broadening the range of application of vocal input.

Over the past few years, numerous attempts to map speech recognition algorithms on parallel architectures or to design dedicated parallel architectures supporting speech tasks have been reported [1]. Advances in VLSI have shown to be a determinant factor in this evolution as VLSI makes it feasible to implement complex parallel architectures on a few integrated circuits. Among the various parallel organizations that have been considered for that purpose, systolic array is a particularly appealing structure. A systolic array [2] is a special-purpose architecture made out of simple processing elements organized as a regular network. Processors are locally connected, operate synchronously, and data circulate throughout the network in a pipeline fashion.

Systolic arrays for speech recognition have been described recently. Weste, Burr and Ackland [3] present an orthogonal array of processors (40 × 40) that can support the dynamic time warping algorithm. The performances of this array permit real time isolated word recognition of a 20,000 word vocabulary. They also describe the VLSI implementation of the basic processor of this array. Yoder and Siegel [4] present various systolic schemes for dynamic time warping, including the use of a linear array. More recently, Feldman et al. [5] consider a wafer scale implementation of a two-dimensional systolic array for connected speech recognition.

This paper is based on an effort undertaken since the end of 1980 at IRISA to explore the potential of systolic architectures for connected speech recognition [6]-[9]. The algorithm that was originally considered in [6] is a probabilistic matching algorithm based on Bahl and Jelinek linguistic decoder [10]. The main difference with the dynamic time warping approach is that the speech signal must be preprocessed before applying the recognition, in order to recognize the phonemes in the speech. Our purpose in this paper is to present and discuss various systolic algorithms for connected speech recognition. In section 2 the systolic architecture concept is defined and an example presented. Moreover, a systematic design approach is shown. Section 3 presents three algorithms for which a systolic solution has been proposed: the dynamic time warping algorithm, the probabilistic matching and the connected speech recognition algorithm. In section 4, we describe a VLSI implementation of a continuous speech recognition systolic machine under developpement at IRISA.

2. SYSTOLIC ARCHITECTURE AND DESIGN METHODOLOGY

2.1. Definition and example

According to KUNG [2], a systolic architecture is defined in the following way:
- it is a special purpose parallel machine, made out of a small number of processor types (usually one);
- processors are regularly and locally connected;
- parallelism and pipeline processing are extensively used;
- computation is carried out in a synchronous way.

The convolution product is a good example to illustrate the systolic concept. Given a sequence $x(0), x(1), \cdots, x(i), \cdots$ and coefficients $w(0), w(1), \cdots, w(K)$, the convolution algorithm consists in computing the sequence $y(0), y(1), \cdots, y(i), \cdots$ where $y(i)$ is given by the following equation

$$y(i) = \sum_{k=0}^{K} w(k)\, x(i-k) \tag{1}$$

Fig. 1 shows a systolic architecture with three linearly connected processors ($K = 2$). For communication purpose, each cell is provided with four communication ports. The x values flow from left to right on the top communication lines and the partially computed y values flow on the bottom communication lines. Note that a delay is inserted on the x lines. Each processor contains a coefficient w. At each step of the computation, each cell receives two values, namely an x value and a y value. Internally, the following calculation is done:

$$y := y + w\, x$$

Then the two values x and y are sent out of the processor.

It is easy to show that the last processor gives the right sequence $y(i)$ assuming that K+1 cycles before, the values $x(i)$ and 0 were input on the first processor.

The above example is just an illustration of what a systolic machine is and how it works. It should be pointed out that the systolic concept is not a new architecture type since numerous parallel machines have been designed before the systolic term was proposed. The main idea is to combine efficiently parallel and pipeline processing and to use such machines as peripherals of a host computer in order to speed-up some very time-consuming tasks.

Moreover, the systolic idea is tightly related to the new types of applications highlighted by the VLSI technology. Indeed, a systolic machine has to be custom-designed for a given task. With new design methodologies [11], powerful and low design-cost integrated circuits can be fabricated. As explained in the following, the systolic concept is well-suited to VLSI:
- fast computation is obtained via parallelism instead of very fast technology;
- regular structure reduces the design task because only a few types of cells or processors need to be designed and tested;
- synchronisation problems are simplified due to local communications and

synchronous computation;
- by allowing multiple use of the same data, pipelining reduces communication bandwidth with the host computer, a major issue with most of the parallel computers.

2.2. Designing systolic algorithms

In this section, it is shown how systolic algorithms can be designed in a systematic way. The process of finding systolic arrays go through several steps that will be examplified on the convolution product. The first step, which unfortunately must be done by hand right now, consists in transforming the equations of the problem to be solved in such a way that they become a uniform recurrent system of equations. For some problems (like the convolution, or the matrix product), this is not very difficult. For other, in particular problems involving recursive computations, this may be very tricky. The second step consists in finding a timing-function for the uniform recurrent system. Finally, the last step consists in allocating the computations on a finite, regular array of processors. At IRISA, a system named DIASTOL based on these ideas is being implemented. In the next sections, starting from the example of the convolution product, we will examine these three steps in turn.

2.2.1. Transforming the equations

A first transformation of (1) consists in expanding the $\sum$ operator in such a way that only remain elementary calculations. These elementary calculations actually define the structure of the elementary cells of the systolic array. Equation (1) may be rewritten as:

$$\forall i,\ 0 \leq i\ ;\ \forall k,\ 0 \leq k \leq K:\ y(i,k) = y(i,k-1) + w(k)\, x(i-k) \qquad (2)$$

$$\forall i:\ 0 \leq i,\ y(i,-1) = 0$$

where $y(i,k)$ are partial accumulated values for $y(i)$. The basic idea is to consider these computations to be associated with points (i,k) of the plane, and more generally, to integer coordinate points of the Euclidean space. For any integer coordinate point (i,k) lying in the domain $D = \{\ 0 \leq i\ ;\ 0 \leq k \leq K\ \}$, we have to perform the elementary computation $y_{out} = y_{in} + w_{in} x_{in}$, the result of which will be $y(i,k)$ provided that y_{in}, w_{in}, and x_{in} are given correct values $y(i,k-1)$, $x(i-k)$ and $w(k)$.

As we want to express the computation as a flowgraph, it is necessary that each variable in (2) appear with all the indexes. We can see that w appears only with index k, and x only with index $i-k$. There are generally several ways to do that. Let us denote as $W(i,k)$ the new variable w, and $X(i,k)$ the new variable x. Equation (2) may be replaced by:

$$\forall i: 0 \le i \; ; \; \forall k: 0 \le k \le K$$

$$\begin{aligned} y(i,k) &= y(i,k-1) + W(i-1,k)\, X(i-1,k-1) \\ W(i,k) &= W(i-1,k) \\ X(i,k) &= X(i-1,k-1) \end{aligned} \tag{3}$$

with the following initial conditions:

$$\forall i,\ 0 \le i;\ \forall k,\ 0 \le k \le K:$$

$$y(i,-1) = 0; \quad W(-1,k) = w(k); \quad X(i-1,-1) = x(i); \quad X(-1,k-1) = 0$$

Such a system of recurrent equations is said to be uniform, since computation at point (i,k) depends only on values computed at points that are obtained by a translation which does not depend on i or k [12]. This system may be represented by a graph such as that of Fig. 2. The nodes of this graph represent the computations to be achieved and the edges represent values that are to be transmitted from one node to another.

2.2.2. Timing-functions

The next step consists in finding a schedule for the computations, called a **timing-function.** A timing-function is a integer mapping $t(i,k)$ which gives the time at which the computation associated with point (i,k) can occur. In DIASTOL, we only consider linear (or more exactly affine) functions for timing-functions.

In [12], it is explained formally how one can find a timing-function. Intuitively, there are two kinds of constraints to be considered. The first kind of constraints has to deal with the equations. If we want to be able to evaluate computation associated with point (i,k), it is necessary that all the computations involving input arguments of the equation be already done. Consider equation (3), computation at point (i,k) depends on results of computations at points $(i-1,k)$, $(i,k-1)$, and $(i-1,k-1)$. Therefore we must have:

$$t(i,k) > t(i-1,k)$$

$$t(i,k) > t(i,k-1)$$

$$t(i,k) > t(i-1,k-1)$$

The second type of constraints on the timing-function is related to the domain. If we want to be able to implement the problem on a real machine, it is necessary that the computation start once, i.e, that $t(i,k)$ have a minimum value over the domain of computation. Also there must be a bounded number of points to be computed simultaneously.

The timing-function is not unique but obviously some solutions are better than others (see [12] for details). For instance in the example we are dealing with, we obtain the timing-function:

$$t(i,k) = i + k$$

Fig. 3 shows the resulting schedule of the equations.

2.2.3. Allocation function

Once we have the schedule of the computations, it remains to map these computations on a finite machine, in a "systolic" way. A very convenient way to do so is to project the domain of computations along a direction defined by some conveniently chosen vector u. Each point of the resulting projected domain will represent a processor of the systolic architecture. Before giving more details about this step, consider again the convolution product example. A convenient way to project the domain (see Fig. 2), is to project it along the i-axis. In this way, all the points lying on lines parallel to the i-axis will be computed by the same processor. Since these points are computed at different times according to the timing-function we have chosen, a processor will never have more than a computation to do at a given time. The resulting architecture is the one already depicted on Fig. 1. To see how this architecture can be derived from the system, the timing-function, and the mapping, one can look at Fig. 3. Since the domain of computation has three lines parallel to the i-axis, there are only three processors. Let us call cell K the processor which takes care of the computations associated with points lying on line $k = K$. The data movement between the cells result from the data dependences shown on Fig. 2. Coefficients w stay on each processor. Values y and x go from processor 0 to processor 1 to processor 2. Note also that the x's move slower than the y's. This appears clearly by examining Fig. 2, since the x's move diagonally and therefore, reach a processor (i.e., a line $k=K$) every other time. This is the reason why the x's have to be delayed between two processors.

We denote as $a(i,k)$ the function that tells which processor execute the computation associated with point (i,k). This function is called the **allocation function.**

2.3. Another Example

To demonstrate the power of the previously explained method, and show that multiple solutions can be found for a specific problem, another systolic architecture for the convolution product is presented.

From the equation (1), there is another way to derive a system of recurrent equations. The idea is to expand the $\sum$ operator with the k indexes running from K to 0. Equation (1) may be rewritten as:

$$\forall i\colon 0 \le i\ ;\ \forall k\colon 0 \le k \le K$$

$$y(i,k) = y(i,k+1) + W(i-1,k)\, X(i-1,k-1)$$

$$W(i,k) = W(i-1,k)$$

$$X(i,k) = X(i-1,k-1)$$

with the following initial conditions:

$$\forall i,\ 0 \le i;\ \forall k,\ 0 \le k \le K:$$

$$y(i,K+1) = 0; \quad W(-1,k) = w(k); \quad X(i-1,-1) = x(i); \quad X(-1,k-1) = 0$$

Fig. 4 shows the dependence graph for that case with the corresponding timing function. The systolic array shown on Fig. 5 is obtained by projection along the i axis. Note that x and y values are input in the array every two cycles therefore indicating that each processor is idle every other cycle. Such an array would be convenient to compute two convolutions in interleaved way.

3. SYSTOLIC ALGORITHMS FOR SPEECH RECOGNITION

The systolic architecture concept presented above seems very attractive for applications such as signal processing as well as speech processing. In the following, we will see how this concept has already been used in the speech recognition area. We will also show that the systematic method for systolic architecture design can be applied very easily on realistic examples. In particular, we will see that the definition of the allocation function can depend on some constraints linked to the application.

Fig. 6 presents together the block-diagram of two connected speech recognition methods. The first one (Fig. 6A) is based on the DTW algorithm, and the second one (Fig. 6B) on a probabilistic matching algorithm. In both methods, the analog signal which results of an utterance is filtered, and acoustic features are extracted at constant intervals. Depending on the acoustic analysis method which is used, these features may be band energies, formant frequencies, cepstral coefficients, or linear prediction coefficients. Each vector of features, called a **frame**, encodes usually 20ms of speech signal and contains 8 to 15 values. Endpoints of the utterance are then determined by examining variations in the energy of the speech signal. At this point, the pronounced utterance is represented by a sequence of frames called the **acoustic test pattern.** Two different approaches are then possible. In the first one (Fig. 6A), reference words are memorized as acoustic patterns. Distance measures between reference words and every subsequence of the test pattern are calculated using the dynamic time warping algorithm. These distances are then combined in order to retrieve the original sentence. The other approach (Fig. 6B) consists in preprocessing the acoustic test pattern in order to encode it as a string of phonemes called the **phonetic test pattern.** The reference words, also represented as strings of phonemes, are then matched against the phonetic test pattern resulting in probabilities that are then used for the sentence recognition.

From the point of view of recognition accuracy, the DTW approach is superior to the probabilistic matching because the phonetic analysis that must be carried out before the probabilistic matching is a very inaccurate process. This explains why up to now only the DTW algorithm has been considered for practical application of speech recognition. However, in the long term, the second approach presents the two advantages of being less computation intensive and of needing less memory to store the reference words.

In the following, we describe in more detail the algorithms underlying each of these approaches. The DTW algorithm is first presented. Then we describe the connected word recognition algorithm based on DTW. Finally, the probabilistic matching algorithm is explained.

3.1. The dynamic time warping algorithm

The dynamic time warping algorithm is an application of the dynamic programming principle [10] to speech recognition. The following description is based essentially on the paper of Sakoe and Chiba [14].

3.1.1. Algorithm

Let $R = R(1) \cdots R(N)$ be a **reference word** and $T = T(1) \cdots T(M)$ be a **test utterance.** Given a pattern R, (word or connected word sequence), we shall denote as $R(i{:}j) = R(i) \cdots R(j)$ the subpattern of R from frame i to frame j and by $|R|$ the number of frames of R. Let $d(i,j) = \| R(i) - T(j) \|$ denote a distance between frame i of R and frame j of T. This distance may be the Chebischev distance, the Euclidean distance, or the log spectral distance depending on the type of acoustic feature considered.

Let C be a parametric curve of the plane defined by $C(k) = (i(k), j(k))$, $k = 1 \cdots K$, where $C(1) = (1,1)$ and $C(K) = (N,M)$ (Fig.7). The dynamic time warping distance between R and T is defined by:

$$D(R,T) = \min_{C} \left[\frac{\sum_{k=1}^{K} d(c(k)) \,.\, w(k)}{\sum_{k=1}^{K} w(k)} \right] \tag{4}$$

where $w(k)$ are weighting coefficients.

Various recurrent schemes have been proposed to compute $D(R,T)$ depending on restrictions made on the curve C. In the following, for sake of clarity, we will only consider a very simple recurrent scheme. Equation (4) may be solved by solving the following recurrence:

$$D(i,j) = \min \begin{cases} D(i-1,j) + d(i,j) \\ D(i-1,j-1) + d(i,j) \\ D(i,j-1) + d(i,j) \end{cases} \tag{5}$$

with the following initial conditions:

$D(0,0) = 0$; $D(i,j) = \infty$ if $i \leq 0$ and $j \geq 1$ *or* if $i \geq 1$ and $j \leq 0$

Assuming that $w(k) = 1$, It results immediately that:

$$D(R,T) = \frac{D(N,M)}{K}$$

Finally, a very common heuristics is that values $D(i,j)$ are computed only for the points (i,j) which lie in the band defined by:

$$| i - j | \leq r$$

where r is a given constant. This restriction avoids unreasonable stretching or compression of the reference pattern, and reduces the amount of computations to be carried out.

3.1.2. Systolic algorithm

The speech recognition algorithm that has been described has the property to be very regular in the sense that the basic computation to be executed at point (i,j) depends only on results provided by computations at neighboring points. This property makes it possible to implement the algorithms on systolic arrays. Fig. 8 shows the computation flow graph. The dependency graph for each point is depicted on Fig. 9. It shows that each point of the computation domain has to receive the previously computed D values as well as a reference frame R

and a test frame T. The distance value is then calculated and sent to the next points. The reference frame has to be sent to the next point to the right and the test frame is sent to the next point down. The timing function is:

$$t(i,j) = i + j$$

At this point, various systolic structure implementations are possible. The purpose of the next section is to explain how a two-dimensional array as well as a linear array can support this algorithm.

3.1.3. 2-D systolic implementation

The following presentation is based on [3]. The basic idea is to associate one processing element to the computation of each value $D(i,j)$. Consider an array of processors denoted $P_{i,j}$ connected as indicated by Fig. 10: $P_{i,j}$ has two input ports denoted I_v (vertical input) and I_h (horizontal input), and two output ports O_v and O_h (respectively vertical and horizontal output ports). I_v of $P_{i,j}$ is connected to O_v of $P_{i-1,j}$ and I_h is connected to O_h of $P_{i,j-1}$. Note that there is no diagonal connections since data flowing diagonallly have to be delayed during one systolic cycle before they are used (due to the timing function). Therefore, distance $D(i-1,j-1)$ may be routed through $P_{i,j-1}$, and then to $P_{i,j}$. In order to illustrate the explanation of the following, we assume that each processor has the architecture depicted by Fig. 11. A set of registers memorize the partial calculations performed by the arithmetic unit. We assume that the I/O operations are performed synchronously on the whole array. In the following, we successively describe the operation of the array on a single reference pattern and the pipeline mode.

3.1.3.1. Single reference operation

Consider the comparison between a reference pattern R and a test pattern T. The overall operation of the two-dimensional systolic array for the DTW algorithm is made on a diagonal basis. Assuming that the computation starts at time 0, then at time t, all the processors $P_{i,j}$ such that $i + j = t$ are active. In such a way, it can be easily checked that all the arguments needed for the computation of equation (5) have already been computed and have been routed correctly. The results $D(N,j)$ are obtained by the processors of the bottom row: $P_{N,j}$ delivers $D(N,j)$ at time $N + j - 1$.

In order to cope with variable length reference patterns, the array is dimensioned according to the longest reference word. Let $N_m = \max_{1 \le v \le V} N_v$ be the maximum number of frames of the reference words. The array has thus N_m rows and $N_m + r$ columns. The process remains essentially the same if the length N_v of the reference is smaller than N_m. In such a case, the final values $D(N_v,j)$ are computed by processors of row N_v, and must be transmitted to the bottom of the array. One way to solve this problem is to associate a flag with each reference frame $R(i)$. This flag is set to 1 for $i \ge N_v$ and set to 0 otherwise. A processor receiving this flag set to 1 from its left neighbor transmits the value $D(i,j)$ instead of $D(i-1,j)$ to its bottom neighbor, and $+\infty$ instead of $D(i,j)$ to $P(i+1,j+1)$. In such a way, the processors of the rows N_v, N_v+1, etc., propagate the final values $D(N_v,j)$ to the bottom boundary of the array.

3.1.3.2. Pipelining the reference words

Since only one diagonal of this network is active at a time for the computation of the DTW algorithm, several computations may be pipelined into the array as illustrated on Fig. 12. The pipeline operation of the array allows all the distances between any reference and any sub-pattern of T to be computed very efficiently. A sub-pattern $T(b : b+N_m+r-1)$ that enters the top of the array remains constant, and the successive reference patterns R_v, $1 \le v \le V$ enter the left part of the array. It can be seen that after a certain delay, each processor $P_{N_m,j}$ of the bottom row of this array will output values $D(R_v, T(b : b+j-1))$, for $1 \le v \le V$, one during each systolic cycle. For word spotting purpose, when all the vocabulary has been matched against the test pattern, it remains to shift the test pattern one position to the left before repeating the process. In the following, we will refer to the process of comparing the whole vocabulary with a sub-pattern of the test utterance as a **vocabulary cycle.**

3.1.4. 1-D implementation

Consider the comparison between a reference pattern R of N frames, and a test pattern T of M frames. We have to compute $D(i,j)$ for (i,j) such that $1 \le i \le N$, $1 \le j \le M$ and $|i-j| \le r$. For the sake of simplicity, we assume $r = 2q$ to be even. We have seen in section **3.1.2** that a simple way to order the calculations is to have $D(i,j)$ computed at time $t(i,j) = i+j$. A first linear systolic implementation is obtained by projecting the computation domain along the diagonal $j=i$. The architecture derived is made out of processing elements numbered P_i, that are two-way linearly connected as depicted on Fig. 13. Each processing element has two input ports denoted as I_l (input from the left) and I_r (input from the right) and similarly two output ports, O_l and O_r. The allocation scheme shows that processor P_k carries out all the computations $D(i,j)$ such that $i-j = k$. However, this implementation has the drawback that each processor is only working every other time. Another more interesting implementation consists in having P_k compute the values $D(i,j)$ such that $\left\lfloor \frac{i-j}{2} \right\rfloor$ (where $\lfloor x \rfloor$ denotes the greatest integer lower than or equal to x) as depicted on Fig. 14 (a). In such a way, the linear array has $r+1$ processors numbered P_{-q} through P_q.

3.1.4.1. Permanent regime

Let us first examine the operation of each processor when permanent regime is attained. P_k executes two different cycles depending on whether $i-j = 2k$ or $i-j = 2k+1$.

Case 1: $i-j = 2k$ **(Fig. 14 (b))**

In this situation, P_k has already the value $R(j)$ that was needed for the calculation of $D(i-1,j)$ during the previous cycle. It contains also the value $D(i-1,j-1)$ which was used two cycles before. Value $T(i)$ is provided by processor P_{k+1} and value $T(i-1)$ is sent to processor P_{k-1}. Well shall refer to this cycle as a T-cycle (for T transmit cycle) later on.

Case 2: $i-j = 2k+1$ **(Fig. 14 (c))**

Symmetrically, P_k contains already value $T(i)$ obtained during the previous cycle, and $D(i-1,j-1)$ obtained two cycles before. It remains to get $R(j)$ from processor P_{k-1}. This cycle is called a R-cycle (for R transmit cycle).

3.1.4.2. Initialization and termination

The initialization and termination process need to be examined carefully, since it is very important to keep the overall process regular: in particular, it is most important that data enter or leave the array only through the extremal processing elements, namely P_{-q} and P_q, in such a way that the number of connections with the other parts of the system are minimized.

During the initialization cycles, data enter the array in such a way that all the processing elements reach a consistent state and thus become able to perform their first computation. This is achieved by performing particular initialization cycles referred to as TI-cycle and RI-cycle. During a TI-cycle, processor P_k reads a test frame $T(j)$ from P_{k+1}, and initialization values for the registers D_v, d_v, D_d and D_p. During a RI-cycle the processor P_k reads a reference frame $R(i)$ and initialization values for the registers D_h and d_h. The initialization sequence consists of $q-1$ TI-cycles and q RI-cycles.

The termination process is carried out by making the final values $D(N,j)$ move to processor P_{-q} so that they may be output. After a processor has received the last reference frame $R(N)$, the processor does not compute value $D(i,j)$ which is not significant any more, but instead propagates during the T-cycles the value $D(i,j)$ it receives from its right neighbor. This termination scheme has the advantage that the data are output only by P_{-q} and also that no extra hardware is needed to send the results. However, since the last result $D(N_v,N_v+r)$ is produced by P_q, $2r$ cycles are necessary before this result reaches P_{-q}, introducing a significant overhead. Another way to proceed is to have each processor access a common output bus so that the results are sent directly to the outside. This is possible, since at a given time, at most one processor produces a final result.

The number of processors required to implement this scheme is $r+1$. The comparison between a reference R_V and a pattern T consists in $r-1$ initialization cycles and $2N_v+r-1$ calculation cycles, assuming that the results are output directly by each processor. Therefore, the total number of systolic cycles for one comparison is $2(N_v+r)$. This means that the array has $V\times 2(N_v+r)$ systolic cycles to perform for each test frame.

3.2. Probabilistic speech recognition

As mentioned earlier, another way to recognize speech is to preprocess the input data in order to identify the phonemes that have been pronounced. This process, called **phonetic analysis** is independent of the vocabulary chosen for the application, and reduces by approximately a factor of 5 the amount of information to be processed later on. Fig. 15 gives an example of the result of the phonetic analysis. The ideal transcription of the French sentence "liste des connecteurs" is presented together with the results of the phonetic analysis, as performed by the KEAL speech understanding system [15]. Each frame $T(i)$ contains a few phoneme candidates (three to five usually), with each of which is attached a probability (the probabilities are not represented on the figure for the sake of clarity). We denote as $x(i,k)$ the kth candidate phoneme of frame $T(i)$ and $p(i,k)$ the probability associated with this phoneme.

3.2.1. Algorithm

Let R_v be the words of the vocabulary, where the frames of R_v are now the phonemes of the ideal phonetic transcription of the word. The algorithm consists in retrieving the reference R that is most likely to have produced the test pattern T. Such a process may be carried out by the DTW algorithm provided that a distance is defined between frames of the reference words and of the test utterance. However, the information lost during the phonetic analysis makes it impossible to achieve a high recognition accuracy in this way.

Another way to proceed is to describe the behavior of the phonetic analyzer more accurately using the concept of Probabilistic Finite State Machine (PFSM) introduced by Bahl and Jelinek [10].

To each phoneme y is associated a PFSM (Fig. 16a) which describes how the phonetic analyzer is likely to deal with it. The PFSM has two states $S(0)$ and $S(1)$. Before reading y, it is in state $S(0)$, and may choose between three possibilities, namely **insertion, confusion** or **omission.** With each of these three possibilities is associated a probability denoted respectively $P_i(y)$, $P_c(y)$, and $P_o(y)$. If the insertion is chosen, the PFSM remains in state $S(0)$, and produces a phonetic label x, with a conditional probability $q_i(x \mid y)$. In the case of a confusion, the PFSM reads the phoneme y and outputs x with conditional probability $q_c(x \mid y)$. Finally, if the omission is chosen, the PFSM skips the phoneme y with probability $P_o(y)$. In order for the model to be consistent, we must have the following relationships for every phoneme y:

$$P_i(y) + P_c(y) + P_o(y) = 1$$

$$\sum_x q_i(x \mid y) = 1$$

$$\sum_x q_o(x \mid y) = 1$$

These probability distributions can be estimated from the actual results of the phonetic analyzer.

From the elementary PFSM's associated with each individual phonemes, it is possible to modelize the behavior of the phonetic analysis when dealing with a reference word $R_v = R_v(1) \cdots R_v(N_v)$ by concatenating the PFSM's associated to $R_v(1), \ldots, R_v(N_v)$ (Fig. 16b). It is convenient to assume that every reference word ends with a special marker denoted] whose PFSM is such that $P_i(]) = P_c(]) = 0$. This prevents the PFSM to produce any result when reading this special marker.

The recognition process may be carried out from this model as follows. Consider the likelihood that a test pattern T has been produced by analyzing a given reference $R = R(1) \cdots R(N)$. Let us denote by $L(i,j)$ the probability for the PFSM to enter state $S(i)$ after having produced $T(1{:}j)$. The PFSM may enter $S(i)$ after either inserting any candidate phoneme of $T(i)$ before reading $R(j)$, or after confusing $R(j)$ with one of the candidate phoneme of $T(i)$, or finally after skipping $R(j)$. As a consequence, $L(i,j)$ is given by the following recurrence equations:

$$L(i,j) = L_i(i,j) + L_c(i,j) + L_o(i,j) \tag{6}$$

$$L_i(i,j) = L(i,j-1) \times P_i(\, R(i+1)\,) \times \sum_k p(j,k)\, q_i(\, x(j,k) \mid R(i+1)) \tag{7}$$

$$L_c(i,j) = L(i-1,j-1) \times P_c(\, R(i)\,) \times \sum_k p(j,k)\, q_c(\, x(j,k) \mid R(i)) \tag{8}$$

$$L_o(i,j) = L(i-1,j) \times P_o(\ R(i)\ ) \tag{9}$$

where $L_i(i,j)$, $L_c(i,j)$ and $L_o(i,j)$ denote respectively the probability for the PFSM to enter state $S(i)$ after inserting $T(j)$, confusing $T(j)$ and $R(i)$, or missing $R(i)$. Equation (6) is valid when $1 \le i \le N$ and $1 \le j \le M$. If we add the following conditions:

$$L_c(i,0) = 0 \text{ if } i>0$$

$$L_c(0,j) = 0 \text{ if } j>0$$

$$L_c(0,0) = 1 \tag{10}$$

$$L_j(i,0) = 0 \ \forall i$$

$$L_o(0,j) = 0 \ \forall j$$

then (6) is still valid if $i = 0$ or $j = 0$.

As in the case of the DTW algorithm, one can restrict the computation of $L(i,j)$ to the points (i,j) which lie into a band of width r, i.e. such that $| i - j | \le r$.

3.2.2. Systolic implementation

In order to apply the design methodology described in section 2, the computation of the values $L(i,j)$ must be represented as a regular computation flow graph. In the case of the previous algorithm, finding the flow graph is not straightforward. Indeed, equations 6, 7, 8 and 9 altogether show that computation at point (i,j) $(L(i,j))$ depends on neighboring points $(i-1,j)$, $(i-1,j-1)$, $(i,j-1)$ (values $L(i-1,j)$, $L(i-1,j-1)$, $L(i,j-1)$ and $R(i)$, $T(j)$). However this computation needs also the value $R(i+1)$. Unfortunetly this does not agree with the flow graph approach since values $R(i)$ and $R(i+1)$ are needed for the point (i,j). To overcome this problem, computation at point (i,j) is done in a different way. Fig. 17 describes the dependency graph at point (i,j). Point (i,j) receives $T(j+1)$ and $L_o(i,j)$ from point $(i-1,j)$, $L_c(i,j)$ from $(i-1,j-1)$, and finally $R(i+1)$ and $L_i(i,j)$ from $(i,j-1)$. Using equation (6), point (i,j) computes $L(i,j)$. Then using equations (7), (8) and (9), it computes $L_o(i+1,j)$ which is sent together with $T(j+1)$ to $(i+1,j)$, then $L_c(i+1,j+1)$ which is sent to $(i+1,j+1)$, and finally $L_i(i,j+1)$ which is sent together with $R(i+1)$ to $(i,j+1)$. To summarize, R and L_i flow horizontally, T and L_o flow vertically and finally L_c flows diagonally.

3.2.3. 2-D implementation

The first systolic implementation of the algorithm is to assign a processor to each point (i,j). The overall operation of the array is similar to that of the DTW-algorithm. In particular, the pipelining scheme remains the same. Consider the comparison between a reference pattern R containing N phonemes (including the end of word marker]) and a test pattern T having M frames. We assume that the last test frame $T(M)$ is composed uniquely of the end-of-word marker], with probability 1. The array needed to implement such a computation has N rows and M columns. Processors are numbered $P_{i,j}$ where $0 \le i \le N-1$ and $0 \le j \le M-1$.

Note that this process still remains valid for processors at the boundaries of the array. As far as processors of the top row and the left column are concerned, equation (10) defines the initial values L_o, L_c and L_i that must enter these processors. Consider now processors $P_{N-1,j}$ for $j<M-1$. Since we assume that each reference word is terminated with a special marker], and since $P_c(]) = 0$, we can deduce from (9) that:

$$L(N,j) = L_o(N-1,j) \tag{11}$$

Therefore, the final value $L(N,j)$ is delivered by $P_{N,j}$ on its O_v port. Finally, consider the processors $P_{i,M-1}$ of the right column. Provided that we have $q_c(]|y) = q_i(]|y) = 0$ for all phoneme y, it can be seen that $P_{i,M-1}$ still delivers $L_o(i+1,M-1)$ on its vertical output port O_v. Therefore, from (11), $P_{N-1,M-1}$ provides $L(N,M-1)$ on its O_v port.

Note that this operation assumes that each processor knows the probabilities distributions P_o, P_c, P_i as well as q_o, q_c and q_i. However, the pipelining scheme described in the previous section helps to reduce significantly the amount of memory required, since the test pattern remains unchanged during a whole vocabulary cycle. As a consequence, processor $P_{i,j}$ receives the same frame $T(j+1)$ during V consecutive systolic cycles. This suggests loading the processors with the probabilities $q_c(x\,|y)$ and $q_i(x\,|y)$ only for the phonemes x which are in $T(j+1)$. Before every vocabulary cycle, these parameters are loaded into the first row of the array, then the second, etc., until the whole array is initialized.

3.2.4. 1-D implementation

Although it is possible to use the diagonal scheme to implement the probabilistic matching algorithm, this scheme has the main drawback that the probability values q_c and q_i have to be left-shifted every cycle, since the test frames flow from right to left.

A better scheme is to have processor P_j compute values $L(i,j)$, $(i = 1, \cdots, N)$, in such a way that frame $T(j)$ stays in P_j during a whole vocabulary cycle, thus minimizing data transfers between processors. In this implementation, called the **row scheme**, the linear array emulates successive rows of the two-dimensional array described in the previous section. Therefore, the linear array has M processors numbered P_0 through P_{M-1}. Fig. 18 shows the linear array for the probabilistic matching algorithm. Solid arrows indicate the communication lines during a vocabulary cycle. On these lines values R, L_i and L_c flow from left to right. Dashed arrows indicate the communication lines for the T values. Indeed, as explained before, the T values do not need to move during a vocabulary cycle. They have to be left shifted before a new vocabulary cycle.

To explain in more details the operation of the array, consider the comparison between a reference pattern of N frames and a test pattern T; assume that processor P_j is already loaded with $T(j+1)$ and the probabilities $q_c(x\,|y)$ and $q_i(x\,|y)$ for x in $T(j+1)$. During a basic cycle, P_j has to compute $L(i,j)$ according to equations (6), (7), (8) and (9) (see Fig. 18). $L_o(i,j)$, which has been computed by P_j during the previous cycle is already in P_j. Values $L_c(i,j)$, $R(i+1)$ and $L_i(i,j)$ are obtained from P_{j-1}. Processor P_j computes then $L(i,j)$, $L_i(i,j+1)$, $L_c(i+1,j+1)$ and $L_o(i+1,j)$. Values $L_i(i,j+1)$ and $R(i+1)$ are then sent to P_{j+1}. The probability $L_c(i+1,j+1)$ has to stay in processor P_j, since P_{j+1} will need it only two cycles later. Instead, $L_c(i,j+1)$ which was kept from the previous cycle is sent to P_{j+1}.

If we assume that the computation of $L(0,0)$ is done at time 0, then processor P_j computes $L(i,j)$ at time $i+j$. Final results $L(N,j)$ $(0 \leq j \leq M)$, are thus obtained respectively by $P_0, \cdots, P_j$ at time $N+j$.

In the context of connected speech recognition, as we will see in section 3.3, these results need not to be sent outside the array. During a vocabulary cycle, processor P_j computes successively the probabilities $L(N,j)$ for all the reference words of the vocabulary. P_j can therefore compute the maximum probability over the whole vocabulary.

The row scheme requires N_m+r+1 processors, assuming that N_m is the maximum number of phonemes of the reference words (final marker excluded). The number of systolic cycles for a single comparison is $2(N_v+1) + r$. Note however that the vocabulary cycles may be overlapped, since as soon as a processor P_j ends a vocabulary cycle, it can start the next one. In such a way, N_v+1 cycles are in fact needed for each comparison. Therefore, the array does $V\times(\overline{N}+1)$ cycles for each test frame, where $\overline{N}$ denotes the average number of phonemes of the reference words.

3.3. Connected speech recognition

The DTW algorithm may be used either for isolated word recognition, or as a basis for connected word recognition. We shall only consider the later case here. Algorithms for connected word recognition have been described by Banatre et al. [7], Bridle et al. [16], Myers and Rabiner [17], and Sakoe [18]. The algorithms described in [17] and [18] find the best matching connected word sequence considering successively sequences of one word, then two words, etc. The results are then compared and the best connected word sequence is determined. In [7] and [16], the best connected word sequence is found in a single pass of the algorithm. In [14], the DTW algorithm and the connected word algorithm are merged, which results in a very efficient but memory consuming algorithm. In [7], the DTW algorithm and the connected word algorithm are done separately. The following description is based on [7].

3.3.1. Algorithm

Let T be the pattern resulting from the acoustic analysis of a sequence of words taken from a given vocabulary. We denote as V the number of reference words of the vocabulary, and denote as R_v the vth reference word. The length of R_v is denoted as N_v. (The index v will be omitted when understood by the context). We call **super-reference** and denote as R^s the pattern obtained by the concatenation of a finite number of words R_v of the vocabulary. $||R^s||$ denotes the number of words of R^s (not to be confused with $|R^s|$, which is the number of frames of R^s).

With the above notations, the connected speech recognition algorithm consists, given a test sentence T, in finding the super-reference R^s which minimizes the distance $D(R^s,T)$. This process consists in two steps. First, one computes the quantity:

$$D^* = \min_{R^s} D(R^s,T)$$

Then one finds out the sequence of words whose concatenation achieves the distance D^*.

Let $D^{+}(b,e)$ be the minimal distance between any reference word and a sub-pattern $T(b:e)$ of T, i.e:

$$D^{+}(b,e) = \min_{1 \le v \le V} D(R_v, T(b:e)) \tag{12}$$

We denote as $v^{+}(b,e)$ the number of the reference pattern which minimizes (12). Let $D^{*}(e)$ be the minimum distance between any super-reference and $T(1:e)$, defined by:

$$D^{*}(e) = \min_{R^s} D(R^s, T(1:e))$$

Finally, let $D^{*L}(e)$ be the distance between a L-word length super-reference and $T(1:e)$. Since the recurrence scheme of equation (5) is considered, a L-word super-reference can match only a pattern having at least L frames. As a consequence, we have:

$$D^{*}(e) = \min_{1 \le L \le e} D^{*L}(e) \tag{13}$$

On the other hand, $D^{*L}(e)$ obey the following recurrence equation:

$$D^{*L}(e) = \min_{1 \le b \le e} \left[D^{*L-1}(b-1) + D^{+}(b,e) \right] \tag{14}$$

Substituting (14) into (13) gives:

$$D^{*}(e) = \min_{1 \le L \le e} \left[\min_{1 \le b \le e} \left[D^{*L-1}(b-1) + D^{+}(b,e) \right] \right]$$

By inverting the two minimum operations, we obtain:

$$D^{*}(e) = \min_{1 \le b \le e} \left[\min_{1 \le L \le e} \left[D^{*L-1}(b-1) + D^{+}(b,e) \right] \right]$$

or, equivalently:

$$D^{*}(e) = \min_{1 \le b \le e} \left[\left[\min_{1 \le L \le e} D^{*L-1}(b-1) \right] + D^{+}(b,e) \right]$$

which gives finally:

$$D^{*}(e) = \min_{1 \le b \le e} \left[D^{*}(b-1) + D^{+}(b,e) \right] \tag{15}$$

In this equation, the quantity $D^{+}(b,e)$ may be obtained by applying the DTW algorithm given by equation (5). For a given value b and a given word R_v, a single application of the algorithm allows all the quantities $D(R_v, T(b:e))$ to be computed for all values e lying in the interval $[e_1, e_2]$ where

$$e_1 = b - 1 + N_v - r$$

$$e_2 = b - 1 + N_v + r$$

According to equation (12) a first minimization over the index v gives then the distance $D^{+}(b,e)$. Finally, a second minimization over b by applying equation (15) gives the final result.

In order to retrieve the string of reference word numbers that minimizes $D^{*}(e)$, it is sufficient to keep track during the calculation of (15) of the index

$b^+(e)$ which achieve the minimum as well as the number $v^+(b,e)$ of the word which achieves the minimum distance $D^+(b,e)$. The string of word numbers $v^*(e)$ which minimizes $D^*(e)$ is then obtained by the following recurrence:

$$v^*(e) = v^*(\, b^+(e)\,)\,.\,v^+(\, b^+(e) + 1\,,\, e)$$

where $x.y$ denotes the concatenation of strings x and y.

The probabilistic model may be also adapted to connected speech recognition, in a very similar way as explained previously for the DTW algorithm. Suppose now that T has been produced by the phonetic analysis of a super-reference R^s. Denote as $L^*(e)$ the maximum probability of a super-reference R^s given a test $T(1{:}e)$, and as $L^+(b,e)$ the maximum probability of a single reference word given the test $T(b,e)$. By a similar reasoning, $L^*(e)$ can be estimated by:

$$L^*(e) = \max_{1 \le b \le e}\left[L^*(b-1) \times L^+(b,e)\right] \tag{16}$$

This equation is very similar to equation (15). The recurrent scheme for retrieving the pronounced utterance is the same as explained previously.

3.3.2. Systolic implementation

The computation of $D^*(e)$ given by (15) can be computed in exactly e steps with the following iterative scheme:

$$U_0(e) = +\infty$$

$$U_k(e) = \min\left[U_{k-1}(e), D^*(k-1) + D^+(k,e)\right] \tag{17}$$

with $D^*(0)$ initialized to 0. It is then clear that $D^*(e) = U_e(e)$. Replacing $D^*(k-1)$ by $U_{k-1}(k-1)$ in (17) gives:

$$U_k(e) = \min\left[U_{k-1}(e), U_{k-1}(k-1) + D^+(k,e)\right]$$

The dependency graph for the calculation of terms $U_k(e)$ is depicted on Fig. 19a. Fig. 19b is another representation of the same calculation but in this case data broadcasting has been removed. The timing function associated with this last flow graph is shown on Fig. 20. A systolic implementation is obtained by projecting the calculation domain along a diagonal.

The computation of $D^*(e)$ (defined by equation (15)) is carried out by a linear row of processors as depicted on Fig. 21. Every cell of the systolic array is structured as displayed on Fig. 22. It contains an adder and a comparator. The cell computes $U_k(e)$ using values $U_{k-1}(e)$, $U_{k-1}(k-1)$ and $D^+(k,e)$. Computation is achieved in the following way. In a first step, the cell inputs $D^+(k,e)$, $U_{k-1}(e)$ and $U_{k-1}(k-1)$. It computes $U_k(e)$. In a second step, the cell outputs values $U_k(e)$, $U_{k-1}(k-1)$.

3.3.3. Connected word recognition machine

Functionnally, the overall organization of a connected word recognition DTW machine is depicted on Fig. 23. The machine is built with three main array:
- the DTW array is used to compute distances between the reference patterns

and the test patterns sequences (values $D(R_v, T(b:b+j-1))$, see Fig. 12);
- the D^+ array computes during a vocabulary cycle, the best distances and memorize the words associated with them, that is:

$$D^+(b, b+j-1) = \min_{1 \le v \le V} D(R_v, T(b:b+j-1))$$

and $v^+(b:b+j-1)$;
- the D^* array is the CWR array described above.

In such a way, each step of the minimization is carried out in turn by the processors of the bottom row, from the left to the right. Note that the D^* array does not work according to the optimal timing function (Fig. 12). The reason is that the D^+ values that are necessary for the computation (Fig. 22) are provided by the D^+ array at the end of a vocabulary cycle. This shows that the computation is not done in parallel since the processors are activated in turn from the left to the right. A real implementation would be more efficient if both the D^+ and D^* were merged in a single array.

4. A VLSI IMPLEMENTATION CASE STUDY

4.1. The API89 chip

The following section is devoted to the structure of a special-purpose chip named API89 which implements one basic processor of the probabilistic matching systolic organization [9]. The design of this chip was made having in mind the following goals:
- try to have the maximum speed by using special-purpose elements required by the algorithms;
- reduce the layout space by implementing only the functions that are needed;
- keep the processor general enough to support the different variations that are commonly used in the class of speech recognition methods presented above.
- finally, choose a structure simple enough to avoid difficulties in designing and testing the chip.

4.1.1. Overall organization and Control

These ideas lead to the organization depicted by Fig. 24. The various elements of the circuit are organized around a single bus. These elements are:

a) Two input registers denoted as VR (vertical register) and HR (horizontal register);

b) One output register OR;

c) An Arithmetic Unit (AU) capable of performing addition, subtraction and incrementation on 16-bit values; the AU has an accumulator (ACC) and an input register (AR);

d) An array of 16 general purpose registers R[0] to R[15];

e) A 60 12-bit word memory with a Memory Address Register (MAR), a Memory Read Register (MR) and a Memory Write Register (MW);

f) A look-up table called the Z module, implemented using a PLA, for the summation of logarithms; this look-up table has an input register IZ and an output register OZ.

All the registers and the data paths are 16-bit wide in order to provide enough precision for the calculations as well as fast I/O. Operation of the processor is entirely synchronous and based on a two-phase nonoverlapping clock scheme. These two phases are denoted as φ_1 and φ_2 in the following.

The operation of the circuit is controlled by 10-bit micro-instructions which are generated outside the chip and expanded inside using a very simple control unit. Two types of micro-instructions have been defined as displayed on table 1. Microinstructions of the first type are executed during φ_1, and concern the transfers of data between the different modules through the bus. Microinstructions of the second type are synchronized on φ_2 and are used for I/O, memory and arithmetic operations. In order to increase speed, instructions are latched in a pipeline register thus allowing instruction decoding and execution to overlap. One instruction is thus executed every clock phase.

4.1.2. Description of the modules

Three modules of the chip need to be explained in more detail.

4.1.2.1. The memory

The memory is organized in such a way that the parameters necessary for the probabilistic matching algorithm can be memorized. We have seen that a processor need to keep track of the probabilities $q_c(x\,|\,y)$ and $q_i(x\,|\,y)$. However, since there are about thirty-five phonemes in a language as English or French, the amount of memory needed is too large to be reasonably implemented using the currently available technology. Hopefully, as explained in section 3.2.3., only a small amount of memory is used during a vocabulary cycle because only three phonemes x need to be considered at the same time. Moreover, two simplifications of the model are made according to an earlier software implementation of the algorithm [19]. First of all, it is assumed that the probability to insert a phoneme x is independent of the phonetic symbol y. Secondly, the probability to confuse a vowel and a consonant is assumed to be null. Therefore, for a given candidate phoneme x, it is only needed to memorize the quantities $q_i(x\,|\,y)$ and $q_c(x\,|\,y)$ for phonemes y which are of the same type (consonant or vowel) as x. Since we consider only three candidate phoneme for each test frame, the memory contains only 60 12-bits words, each candidate phoneme being represented on 20 words (this value has been chosen since there are 20 consonants in French). Each 12-bit word has two fields: a flag indicating the type of the phoneme, and a probability value coded on 11 bits.

The instructions for the memory are given by table 1. The RM instruction has a particular effect: if the type of the phoneme which has been loaded into the memory address register MAR and the type of the phoneme memorized in the memory word addressed are identical, then the value contained in that memory is loaded into the memory read register MR. Otherwise, the number representing probability 0 is loaded. In such a way, only one cycle is required to read a value $q_c(x\,|\,y)$ whatever the type of x and y are. Since the memory is implemented using dynamic memory cells, a particular instruction called RR is provided for memory refreshment.

4.1.2.2. Arithmetic Unit

The arithmetic Unit can perform addition, subtraction and incrementation as indicated on table 1. Two conditional instructions denoted as STR (star) and SBS (substar) are provided: STR complements the accumulator if the AU flag is set to 1; SBS subtract the AU input register to the ACC if the AU flag is set to 1. The AU flag is set to 1 when an arithmetic operation results in a negative number. As a consequence, the AU is capable to emulate comparison and absolute value instructions.

4.1.2.3. The Z module

Since the probabilistic matching algorithm has to perform multiplications, and manipulate very small values, the probabilities are coded using radix-2 logarithms. However, examining formulas (7), (8), and (9) reveals that we have to perform the calculation of $Log(a+b)$ given $Log\ a$ and $Log\ b$. This problem has been solved in the following way. Let Z be the real mapping defined by:

$$Z(t) = Log(1 + 2^t)$$

We have then:

$$Log\ (a+b) = Log(a) + Z(Log\ b\ - Log\ a) = Log(b) + Z(Log\ a\ - Log\ b)$$

Given the value of the function Z on the interval $[\ 0\ ,\ +\infty\ ]$, it is possible to compute $Log(a+b)$ from $Log(a)$ and $Log(b)$. Since the values are coded on 16 bits, it has been possible to implement the function Z using a PLA having only 128 product terms, with a good accuracy.

4.1.3. VLSI design of the chip

Two sets of chips have been fabricated. The first one using 4.5μ-NMOS technology was fabricated by the French MPC (Multi Project Chip) organization. The second set was fabricated by MOSIS using 4μ-NMOS technology. The chip contains approximately 12,000 transistors and measures 5mm by 6mm. The chip is housed in a 64-pin package since 16-bit wide parallel ports are used. The pin out is the following:

- 32 pins for the two input ports;
- 16 pins for the output port;
- 10 pins for the instructions;
- 4 pins for power and clocks.

Since the processor is microprogrammable, and since the inside decoding is reduced, access to the internal elements is relatively easy. A micro assembler has been written to compile tests programs and generate bit patterns for the circuit. Moreover, this micro-assembler is used for simulating the processor and thus generate a print out of the bit patterns expected on the output pads.

A first run has been returned from fabrication and tested. The test has been carried out easily as expected. Most of the modules of the chip work correctly except some minor details. The basic clock cycle has been measured to be about 700 ns for the 4.5μ version. This is slower than estimated (500ns) due to a bus design error. A new version has recently been sent for fabrication.

4.2. Example of systolic array implementation using API89

As an example, we show in this section how the chip can be used to implement the two-dimensional array for the probabilistic matching algorithm. Fig. 25 depicts the interconnection of the array, for $N = M = 3$. We assume, moreover, that the full array is implemented. The operation of the array is fully synchronous. A control unit (CU) broadcasts the microinstructions to all the processors of the array, and provides a separate flow of microinstructions for the connected word recognition array. Control lines are indicated by dashed arrows in the figure. Note that although each processor has only two input ports and one output port, all the logical connections needed can be emulated on this network, since the operation are synchronous. For example, vertical transmissions of data between processors are done by having all the processors load the output register with the value to be transmitted, and then read during the next cycle on the vertical input register. On the other hand, the left-to-right interconnection between the processors of the bottom row (see Fig. 21) is needed only for the broadcasting of the values $L^*(b)$ to compute equation (16). This can be emulated by having these values enter the last row of the array, move from left-to-right on this row, and be sent to the bottom processors.

A last remark that should be made concerns the synchronization of the connected word recognition row. Since the references are pipelined in the array, the operation of processor P^*_{j+1} is the same as the operation of P^*_j but occurs one cycle later. However, since each processor look for the maximum of the results $L(N,j)$ sent by the last row of the array, it is possible to align in time the connected word recognition array by having the network deliver values 0 when no significant comparison is done.

5. CONCLUSION

We have described several systolic arrays architectures which can implement two basic connected speech recognition methods.

The two-dimensional systolic array for the DTW algorithm leads to a 2,000 processor network when the full array is implemented, and to 925 processors when only the band of processors $P_{i,j}$ whith $|i - j| \leq r$ is implemented. This estimation is based on $N_m = 40$ and $r = 10$. Such a device would permit real-time recognition for a vocabulary of 5,000 words, based on a systolic cycle time of 4 microseconds, and a feature extraction interval of 20 milliseconds. This implementation is rather unrealistic for practical purpose due to the number of processors. It could only be considered if the number of processors were reduced by folding the computations. However, the control of this array would then be much more complicated.

The probabilistic matching algorithm may be run on a two-dimensional array having 180 processors if the full array is implemented, and 104 processors if the band is implemented. This estimation is based on $N_m = 10$ and $r = 4$. Executed on the API89 chip, the systolic cycle time is $s=50$ microseconds. Based on this parameter and assuming an average phoneme duration of 100 milliseconds, vocabularies of up to 2000 words could be handled in real time. The probabilistic matching implementation would be a good candidate for wafer-scale integration as presented in [5].

The linear systolic arrays are more realistic. The DTW algorithm implementation would permit a real time recognition of approximately 70 words, using 11 processors. On the other hand, 15 processors would allow the recognition of 250 words using the probabilistic matching algorithm. The difference of performances between these two systolic implementations comes from the fact that the initialization overhead is very significant in the case of the diagonal scheme. Although the row scheme could also be considered for the DTW algorithm, the number of processors would then be much higher, since N_m+r processors are needed. Both systolic arrays could be implemented on a single chip with the current available technology.

The API89 VLSI chip has been presented and it has been shown how such a chip can be used as the basic processor of these architectures. This study shows that there are many different ways to implement in parallel tasks such as connected speech recognition, even if one restricts oneself to a single type of architectures. Choosing between the different possibilities implies investigating in great details how the algorithm may be implemented, taking into consideration parameters such as the number of processors, the communications between the processors, and the complexity of the control. Our belief is that the new avenues opened by VLSI technology for special purpose hardware will become more and more practical, provided that more is known about the various ways to map an algorithm onto a parallel architecture.

REFERENCES

[1] L.J. Siegel, "Highly Parallel Architectures and Algorithms for Speech Analysis," *1984 Int. Conf. Acoustic., Speech, Signal Processing*, San Diego, March 1984, pp. 25A.1.1-25A.1.4 .

[2] H.T. Kung, "Why Systolic Architectures ?," *Computer*, Vol. 15, No 1, Jan 1982, pp. 37-46.

[3] N. Weste, D.J. Burr, and B.D. Ackland, "Dynamic Time Warp Pattern Matching Using an Integrated Multiprocessing Array," *IEEE Trans. Comp.*, Vol. C-32, Aug. 1983, pp. 731-744.

[4] M.A. Yoder and L.J. Siegel, "Dynamic Time Warping Algorithms for SIMD Machines and VLSI Processor Arrays," *1982 Int. Conf. Acoustic., Speech, Signal Processing*, Paris, May 1982, pp. 1274-1277.

[5] J.A. Feldman, S.L. Gaverick, F.M. Rhodes, and J.R. Mann, "A Wafer Scale Integration Systolic Processor for Connected Word Recognition," *1984 Int. Conf. Acoustic., Speech, Signal Processing*, San Diego, March 1984, pp. 25B.4.1-25B.4.4.

[6] J.P Banatre, P. Frison, and P. Quinton, "A Network for the Detection of Words in Continuous Speech," *Proceedings of the VLSI 81 Int. Conference*, Edimburg, Aug. 1981.

[7] J.P. Banatre, P. Frison, and P. Quinton, "A Systolic Algorithm for Speech Recognition," *1982 Int. Conf. Acoustic., Speech, Signal Processing*, Paris, May 1982, pp. 1243-1245.

[8] J.P. Banatre, P. Frison, and P. Quinton, "A Network for the Detection of Words in Continuous Speech," *Acta Informatica 18, pp. 431-448.*

[9] P. Frison, "Un Processeur Integre pour la Reconnaissance de la Parole," INRIA Research Report No. 215, July 1983.

[10] L. R. Bahl, and F. Jelinek, "Decoding for Channels with Insertions, Deletions, and Substitutions with Applications to Speech Recognition," *IEEE Trans. Informat. Theory*, Vol IT-21, No 4, pp 404-411, 1976

[11] C. Mead, L. Conway, *Introduction to VLSI Systems*, Addison Wesley Publishing Company Inc., 1980.

[12] P.Quinton, "The Systematic Design of Systolic Arrays," MCNC Technical Report, TR84-11, May 84.

[13] R. Bellman, S. Dreyfus, *Applied Dynamic Programming*, Princeton University Press, New-Jersey, 1962.

[14] H. Sakoe and S. Chiba, "Dynamic Programming Algorithm Optimization For Spoken Word Recognition," *IEEE Trans. Acoust., Speech, Signal Processing*, Vol. ASSP-26, No. 1, Feb. 1978, pp. 43-49.

[15] G. Mercier, A. Nouhen, P. Quinton, and J. Siroux, "The Keal Speech Understanding System," In: Spoken Language Generation and Understanding, J.C. Simon (Ed), Proc. NATO ASI, Bonas, 1980.

[16] J. Bridle, M. Brown, and R. Chamberlain, "An algorithm for Connected Word Recognition," *1982 Int. Conf. Acoustic., Speech, Signal Processing*, Paris, May 1982, pp. 899-902.

[17] C. Myers, and L.R. Rabiner, "A Level Building Dynamic Time Warping Algorithm for Connected Word Recognition," *IEEE Trans. on Acoust., Speech, Signal Processing*, Vol ASSP-29, No. 3, April 1083, pp. 351-363.

[18] H. Sakoe, "Two-Level DP-Matching - A Dynamic Programming-Based Pattern Matching Algorithm for Connected Word Recognition," *IEEE Trans. Acoust., Speech, Signal Processing*, Vol. ASSP-28, No. 4, Aug. 1980, pp. 588-595.

[19] L. Buisson, G. Mercier, J.Y. Gresser, M. Querre, and R. Vives, "Phonetic Decoding for Automatic Recognition of Words", *Speech Communication Seminar*, Stockholm, Aug. 1974

COMPUTER SYSTEMS FOR HIGH-PERFORMANCE SPEECH RECOGNITION

Roberto Bisiani*
Carnegie-Mellon University
Pittsburgh, PA 15232, USA

ABSTRACT

The object of this review and position paper is to draw a parallel between the field of high-performance speech recognition systems on one side and the field of computer systems (in particular computer systems for Artificial Intelligence applications) on the other. This paper gives a characterization of the computational requirements of speech recognition systems, and describes and exemplifies the classes of machines that could be useful in speeding up speech recognition systems.

---

*This research was sponsored by the Defense Advanced Research Projects Agency (DOD), ARPA Order No. 3597, monitored by the Air Force Avionics Laboratory Under Contract F33615-81-K-1539.
The views and conclusions contained in this document are those of the author and should not be interpreted as representing the official policies, either expressed or implied, of the Defense Advanced Research Projects Agency or the US Government.

NATO ASI Series, Vol. F16
New Systems and Architectures for Automatic Speech
Recognition and Synthesis. Edited by R. De Mori and C.Y. Suen

1. INTRODUCTION

The object of this paper is to present the inter-relationship between the state-of-the-art of system architecture research and speech recognition research. Our concern here is with the interplay of the recognition algorithms and the structure of the machines that execute them. We are therefore not concerned with the advancement of electronic technology per-se but with the possibilities of effectively exploiting the capabilities offered by such technology improvements.

Better computer systems can only improve the *cost* and the *speed* of a recognition system. We will immediately dismiss the cost issue, since it becomes relevant only in the context of a particular application and when a system with the correct accuracy has been demonstrated. Cost reduction is achieved by "simplifying" the algorithms while trying to keep accuracy constant; therefore, cost reduction is only meaningful when the required accuracy goal has already been achieved.

As far as speed is concerned, one should ask: *Why is speed relevant? Is it reasonable to consider optimizing the speed of recognition systems before having settled all the "speech science" issues?* The answer is a strong yes; it is indeed very important to be concerned with the speed of such systems in order to limit the turn-around time in the evaluation experiments since many are required simply to evaluate one version of a system. Moreover, the number of experiments required increases when the accuracy increases. For example, if one needs to measure the error rate with a confidence interval of 30% and a confidence level of 90%, 30 statistically independent errors are required. If a system has a .1% accuracy, it will need to process 30,000 sentences in order to get 30 errors. At 2 seconds per utterance, a real time system will take about 16 hours for each experiment. When we consider that most changes in a system influence the behavior of other parts of the system, we see that the number of experiments required grows combinatorially. Past experience has shown that if a system does not run close to real time, the feedback is not quick enough to allow researchers to efficiently evaluate their solutions. For example, if the Hearsay II system [11] had been two orders of magnitude faster, much more insights could have been gained from the effort by performing experiments that had been specified but were never carried out because of lack of time.

Section 2 describes the computational requirements of speech recognition systems. Two reasons prevent Section 2 from being as complete and conclusive as one might desire: first, the requirements of speech recognition systems change widely and in non-trivial ways when the task domain changes; second, there is no "correct" way to perform certain tasks and either worst-case analysis or highly speculative analysis are the only possible ways to proceed. Section 2 is structured according to one of the many possible system decompositions. It is virtually impossible at this point in time to prove or disprove that the speech recognition techniques suggested are the correct ones. However, unless some radically different approach is invented (a possibility that will appear unlikely to anybody that has worked with the speech problem for some time), the techniques evaluated are representative of future recognition systems.

Section 3 describes the classes of machines that might have an impact on speech recognition research. The classes considered are: *language-oriented machines*, *production system machines*, *general-purpose parallel machines*, *massively parallel machines* and *task-oriented machines*. For each class, the paper gives the underlying ideas, the expected performance of members of the class, and their typical applications.

2. CHARACTERIZATION OF THE SPEECH RECOGNITION TASK

The goal of this Section is to characterize the requirements of speech recognition systems from the point of view of the computer system that executes them. No matter what kind of system one considers, the computation required varies widely among the different components of the same system (e.g. signal processing vs. word hypothesization). The computation required is also influenced by the recognition task (number of words, grammar, etc.) that a system can deal with. For example, although numeric computation is usually a significant part of the computation, as the complexity of the task increases, memory access operations become prevalent. As of now, there is no agreement on which modules will constitute a satisfactory speech recognition system. For the sake of this paper, the computation performed by a speech recognition system will be divided into four components: Parameter Extraction, Acoustic/Phonetic Analysis, Word Recognition, Sentence Recognition. A realistic, high performance speech recognition system will have many more modules and much more refined intermediate representations of partial results; nevertheless, the four modules chosen are likely to be representative of most of the computation.

The computation characteristics are divided into three major categories:

- The *structure of the computation* includes all the features of the computation that interact with the architecture of a computer system. For example, the *kinds* of operations performed more often or the behavior of the control-flow.

- *The amount of computation and storage* are a (somewhat coarse) way of representing the raw requirements of a system. These characteristics depend at times on the *size* of the task a system can work with.

- *The available parallelism* is a fundamental characteristic since, in many cases, the amount of computation is beyond the capabilities of sequential systems.

The goal of creating a reasonable and meaningful picture is complicated by the fact that some of the requirements are influenced by the recognition task features and some of these features, like confusability of words, are hard to quantify. The parameters used in this paper are the number of vocabulary words and the word-grammar branching factor as defined by Goodman [14].

The characterization data presented in the paper is summarized in Tables 2-1 and 2-2. Each table is divided in four sections corresponding to the four major components that we are considering: *parameter extraction, acoustic/phonetic analysis, word recognition and sentence recognition.* The different categories in which each table is divided will become clear when the characteristics of the modules are explained.

2.1 PARAMETER EXTRACTION

Parameter extraction is the most tractable part of speech recognition because the computational problems it raises are shared by a large number of other, more mature applications and have therefore been studied in depth. With parameter extraction we indicate the initial transformations that are performed on the signal after it is sampled. This process is often identified with *signal processing* since most of the techniques employed are derived from classic signal processing algorithms (e.g. Fast Fourier Transform). Some form of parameter extraction is used in all systems and for many years most of the activity in speech processing was exclusively concerned with this kind of processing. The two mostly used parameter extraction procedures are (in chronological order) filter banks [19] and Linear Predictive Coding [22]. Initially, filter bank processing was mainly performed with analogic techniques (analogic filter bank processing has resurfaced for economic reasons with single-chip filter bank analyzers [7]). In both cases, a number of additional parameters like zero crossing and amplitude are often computed. The FFT is also often used in systems that need to extract very detailed information from the signal (e.g. FEATURE [8]).

Parameter extraction algorithms are highly regular and their control pattern is mostly data independent. This characteristic opens the possibility of using computer systems that are optimized for a given sequence of operations and data-flow. In the simplest case, the optimal computer structure for parameter extraction will have data paths optimized for vector and matrix operations and pipelined multiply-add. In the most complex and effective case, the architecture will have multiple functional units and data paths tailored for a given algorithm. For example, the systolic WARP processor [31] is one of such machines.

CHARACTERISTICS / COMPONENT	Control structure	Needs fast arithmetic: integer	Needs fast arithmetic: floating point	Needs efficient symbolic processing	Complexity of data structures	Data memory bandwidth
PARAMETER EXTRACTION	mostly regular and data independent	yes	no	no	low	medium
ACOUSTIC/ PHONETIC ANALYSIS	both regular and data dependent	yes	no	no	medium	low
WORD & SENTENCE RECOGNITION	mostly data dependent	no	no	yes	high	high

CHARACTERISTICS / COMPONENT	amount of computation in MIPSS				amount of storage	
	number of words				number of words	
	1,000		10,000		1,000	10,000
	branching factor					
	low	high	low	high		
PARAMETER EXTRACTION	30	30	30	30	less than 64K bytes	less than 64K bytes
ACOUSTIC/ PHONETIC ANALYSIS	.5	.5	.5	.5	less than 64K bytes	less than 64K bytes
WORD & SENTENCE RECOGNITION	3	30 to 300	15	100 to 1000	.5M bytes	.5M bytes

Figure 2-1 Tentative assessment of the requirements a speech recognition system poses on a computer system

CHARACTERISTICS / COMPONENT	parallelism			
	computation		communication	
	granularity size	number of parallel operations	structure	traffic
PARAMETER EXTRACTION	a few operators	up to 0(100) (in practice only a few)	regular	a few times signal bandwidth in samples/sec
ACOUSTIC/ PHONETIC ANALYSIS	large	a few	regular	low
	medium	0 (number of phonemes)		
WORD SENTENCE RECOGNITION	large	0(10)	random	high
	small	0(words)		

Figure 2-2 Tentative assessment of the requirements a speech recognition system poses on a computer system (cont.)

The most widely used primitives are integer arithmetic operators. Speech processing seldom requires more than 16 bits of precision (the input signal has a dynamic range of less than 11 bits). The reason why "floating point array processors" have been widely used for speech processing has to do with the ease of programmability that machines like the Floating Point Systems' AP-120B have when compared with most of the fixed point machines that have been built in the past. Therefore, recent technology improvements in integrated circuit design, that produced single chip processors like the Texas Instruments TMS32010, fulfill almost all the requirements of parameter extraction.

As one might expect, parameter extraction algorithms do not need very efficient symbolic (e.g. list) processing operators. The data structures used are very simple, mainly arrays, but the amount of load/store operations is very high. Since the access patterns are regular but at times complicated (e.g. the shuffling of FFT's) the performance of a system executing parameter extraction procedures depends on its ability to efficiently perform (or avoid) address calculations. For example, the author has observed an increase by a factor of 5 in the performance of an implementation of the FFT algorithm on a TMS32010 when the address computation and some of the data shuffling have been improved by additional hardware.

The amount of computation and storage is independent from the complexity of the task and ranges from about 1 to about 30 Millions of Instructions per Second of Speech (MIPSS). In some commercial systems, analog processing has been used in order to reduce cost but when detailed parametrization is required as in the Feature system [8], analog processing is not sufficient. The amount of memory that is necessary can be extremely small and is never much more than the number of samples that have to be kept around if non-local processing has to be performed (e.g. pitch tracking) or if the signal has to be re-examined in the context of some higher level constraint. The 64K byte figure in Table 2-1 is derived by assuming that a full 4-second-long utterance (16 bit values sampled at 16KHz) is kept in memory for delayed re-examination.

The parameter extraction computation can be easily parallelized because of its regular, predictable control and data-flow. When the control-flow is not data dependent, a very small granularity (e.g. "butterfly" operators) can be efficiently used. The degree of parallelism can also be very high, for instance in the order of hundreds of parallel operations. The communication structure can be quite complicated if the parallelism is pushed to its maximum, e.g. a fully parallel FFT. In practice, it is not necessary to exploit such parallelism because the necessary performance is already available from commercial high speed processors. In conclusion, speech recognition is not in the class of applications that one would define "signal processing intensive" by current standards.

2.2 PHONETIC ANALYZER

The phonetic analyzer comprises all the techniques that transform the parametric representation of the input speech into a phonetic description of the utterance. This component is not present in small systems that perform a template matching directly at the parameter level. Typically, this component contains a mixture of arithmetic computation (e.g. computation of distance) and data-dependent, branching programs (e.g. segmentation algorithms). The typical data structures that are used in this component are neither too complex (they would require special instructions to work fast) nor too simple (a signal processing architecture could be used). Therefore, this component is the one that matches best with "general-purpose" architectures.

The amount of computation and memory required are independent of the task characteristics and depend on the level of refinement necessary. For example, the Harpy segmenter and labeler used about .5 MIPSS and used less than 64K bytes of memory. Most current systems perform little or no phonetic analysis, relying on pattern matching of some kind of parameters, e.g. LPC coefficients. When feature extraction and classification techniques are used, as in the Feature system [8], there is the possibility that a lot of computation be required if complex combinations of features that vary over time have to be evaluated.

A limited amount of parallelism could be exploited in this module. For example, a number of "segment detectors" could work in parallel on the incoming data, each segment detector specialized in identifying a different set of acoustic characteristics. Each segment detector could be independent or cooperate very little with other segment detectors. A continuous speech acoustic front end that has these characteristics has never been built, and it is impossible to accurately evaluate the amount of computation involved since it will depend on how well one will be able to exploit the acoustic and phonetic knowledge.

2.3 WORD AND SENTENCE RECOGNITION

The word and sentence recognition component is the biggest unknown, both from the speech science point of view and from the computation point of view. The analysis is complicated by the fact that the computational requirements are influenced in a complex way by the characteristics of the task domain. We will examine increasingly complex techiniques that are used to perform this task. Although different techniques have different capabilities and performance from the point of view of recognition accuracy, this paper will not comment on this issue.

2.3.1 TEMPLATE MATCHING

In most of the current commercial systems and in some research systems, word and sentence recognition is performed by some kind of template matching. In the simplest (and cheapest) systems the pattern matching is performed at the parametric level, e.g. using LPC parameters [25]; in other cases the template matching is performed at a higher level [13]. In all these instances, highly regular architectures can be devised. For example see [30,6].

2.3.2 SEARCH-INTENSIVE SYSTEMS

For the purpose of this paper, search-intensive systems comprise all the systems that search a single large data structure in order to identify the "best matching" utterance. Usually these systems use an intermediate representation at the level of phonemes. Examples of this kind of systems are Harpy [21] and the IBM system [18].

One way to attack the analysis of the complexity of such systems is to extrapolate from the behavior of existing systems. For example, the Harpy system is a good example of a computationally very efficient, albeit limited system. The analysis of the Harpy system that was performed in order to build a tailored architecture [4] showed that:

- arithmetic operations were a small part of the total computation (< 5%);
- comparisons were also less than 10% of the total computation;
- more than 50% of the time was spent in accessing data structures;
- a static parallel decomposition was impossible because of the data dependent behavior of the algorithm.

Since the performance is a function of the task, one should be concerned with how the requirements will change when the task complexity increases. In the case of the Harpy system, the branching factor of the grammar and the number of words were the main factors controlling the number of instructions per second of speech required. Table 2-1 shows how the performance of the Harpy system (expressed in Millions of Instructions per Second of Speech, MIPSS) is influenced by changes in the number of vocabulary words or in the branching factor. The data shown are from [1] and were corrected to take into account the improvements to the Harpy system (about one order of magnitude) that we were able to obtain after the publication of [1].

The table shows a factor of three increases in the amount of computation when the number of words increases by a factor of four (from approximately 1 MIPSS and 250 words to 2.6 MIPSS and 1000 words). An increase of the static branching factor with the number of words (250) held constant caused an equal increase in the amount of computation required (.7 MIPSS to 6 MIPSS).

In order to extrapolate the results of these experiments to a 1000-word vocabulary where any word can follow any other word, we have to multiply the amount of computation (2.6 MIPSS) by the branching factor ratio of the two tasks (1000 versus 9.5 for the AIX05 grammar). This brings us to about 270 million instructions per second of speech. This should be considered an upper bound on the computational requirements of any system of this kind for such a

Grammar	MIPSS	Static branching factor	Vocabulary size
AIS10 (Harpy)	1	8.2	250
AIM12 (Harpy)	1.7	10.5	500
AIX05 (Harpy)	2.6	9.5	1000
AIX05 (Hearsay II))	60	9.5	1000
AIS06 (Harpy)	.73	4.6	250
AIS10 (Harpy)	1	8.2	250
AIS15 (Harpy)	1.4	11.9	250
AIS30 (Harpy)	4.5	33.3	250
AIS40 (Harpy)	6	39.5	250

Table 2-1: Effect of the vocabulary size and grammar branching factor on the performance of the Harpy and Hearsay II systems. The performance is measured in Millions of Instructions per Second of Speech (MIPSS)

task. In practice, the use of filtering based on coarse phonetic features and prosodic patterns can reduce the effective vocabulary size by one to two orders of magnitude with a corresponding decrease in the amount of computation required. Better parameter extraction and phonetic transcription modules will also help in limiting the amount of computation required. In general, a number of factors will contribute to reduce the amount of computation required, and will counterbalance the growth of computational requirements caused by the increase in the vocabulary size and in the branching factor.

2.3.3 HYPOTHESIZE-AND-TEST SYSTEMS

From table 2-1 we see that the Hearsay-II system needed much more computation than Harpy on the same task. Part of this increase in the computation was due to the less constrained recognition paradigm of Hearsay-II. For example, Hearsay-II could start searching an utterance at many different places while Harpy always performed a left-to-right search. The remaining difference in the amount of computation is due to inefficiencies encountered in executing a parallel system on a single processor. We can expect all the systems that use the same paradigm to incur a similar overhead. On the other hand, a system like Hearsay-II could benefit from executing on a really parallel system as suggested in Section 3.

Some more sophisticated algorithms that could exploit a large amount of parallelism have been proposed [10] but their effectiveness and their implementability still remain to be demonstrated.

3. COMPUTER SYSTEMS

In this Section, we will briefly describe a few classes of machines that might have an impact on the improvement the computational cost effectiveness of the previously described speech recognition system components. Machine classes will be presented in the order of their increasing departure from conventional "general-purpose" single-processor systems.

3.1 LANGUAGE-ORIENTED MACHINES

When executing a given algorithm, the easiest most cost-effective way to increase the performance of a machine is to tailor the instruction set to the task at hand. This generates a new "general-purpose" machine that behaves much better for some kinds of algorithms but can still be programmed to execute almost any kind of algorithm. This is at the basis of the current breed of LISP machines [15].

LISP machines make it reasonable to run large LISP based systems that require a lot of computation. For example, Boley [5] reports 3 to 12 fold improvement in speed by using a LISP machine instead of a "typical" LISP mainframe like the DECSystem-10. However, the success of LISP machines might in part be due to other features like their "window" system and their user interface.

LISP machines can be very good at executing some of the algorithms that might arise at the Word and Sentence Level (and sometimes at the Phonetic Analyzer Level), but their current value is more in the possibility to very quickly implement and test algorithms that is offered by a language like LISP when it is executed in a rich environment. This is currently one of the most important characteristics that a system for speech research should have.

The importance of the environment and the language are demonstrated by fine speech tools like SPIRE [26] and ISP [20]. LISP machines are necessary for tools like SPIRE because of their very good programming and user interface environment and not because of their processor. As a matter of fact SPIRE needs an attached array processor to perform some of its functions at an acceptable speed.

Prolog machines are also being proposed [32]. Since these efforts are trailing by a few years the similar LISP efforts, Prolog machines are not a possible research tool at this point. Some of the proposed parallel Prolog machines, if they will ever see the light, might be useful at the word and sentence level because of the processing power they will make available.

In conclusion, AI-oriented high-level language architectures are likely to have an impact on speech research not as an ultimate engine for speech recognition but rather as a very effective research tool, especially if integrated with other specialized computation engines and task-oriented architectures.

3.2 PRODUCTION SYSTEM MACHINES

Production Systems are widely used to build expert systems and to model intelligent behavior. In many respects, Production Systems could be a viable way of building speech recognition systems for which experts (e.g. spectrogram readers) channel their knowledge into rules that are executed by the system. It is hard to judge if this will ever be possible since the slow speed of execution of such systems has prohibited their use in domains requiring high performance and real-time response. This situation might change in the future if some ongoing research on machines for production systems [16, 23, 27] is successful.

A production system program contains rules (productions) that are activated depending on whether some conditions, that are specified with the rule, are satisfied. Production systems are constantly executing a three phase algorithm:

- *match*: the conditions are examined to identify the rules that can be executed;

- *conflict resolution*: one of the executable productions is selected;

- *act*: the production is executed, i.e. the memory is modified.

These three phases must be executed sequentially and cannot be "unfolded" as one might do with certain kinds of loops, since it is hard to predict whether any computation in a given iteration will depend on the result of previous iterations or not. The second and third phases require very little computation and are never a problem. The first phase seems to contain a large amount of parallelism since each condition could in principle be examined in parallel. Recent analysis of existing systems [16, 23] has shown that the amount of parallelism available is limited by the fact that a small set of productions (a few tens) is affected by the act phase. This result, if common to all kinds of production systems, would put the burden of speeding-up production systems on the improvement of the performance of the processors used in the match phase.

In conclusion, production systems are currently not a viable solution for speech processing but could become interesting in the future if suitable architectures are designed and built.

3.3 GENERAL-PURPOSE PARALLEL MACHINES

The next logical step away from language-oriented systems is to exploit parallelism as much as possible. We have already seen (in production systems) that this might not be easy and that the expected parallelism might not be there at the expected level. It is convenient to distinguish between algorithm level parallelism and machine level parallelism. Algorithm level parallelism is explicitly expressed *and managed* by the application algorithm, while machine level parallelism is visible only at a level different from the algorithm level and is *transparent* to the application algorithm. This distinction is important because the former kind of parallelism requires a known parallel algorithm, while the latter can improve any kind of algorithm.

If we exclude some massively parallel and hypothesize-and-test paradigms, most speech recognition paradigms are inherently non-parallel and even hypothesize-and-test can be truly parallel only if a satisfactory focus-of-attention policy is devised. It is therefore necessary to either restructure the algorithm in a parallel fashion *that fits the characteristics of a given multiprocessor* or to use a machine that can take advantage of the existing parallelism at a lower level.

In the past, the most taxing problem in adapting an algorithm to a general purpose multiprocessor has been the high overhead required for the synchronization of tasks. This required the algorithm to be partitioned in fairly large components which, in turn, caused poor load sharing and, ultimately, a speed-up curve that would sharply deviate from the linear speed-up after more than a few processors were used in the system [4]. For example, speech algorithms had the worst behavior over a number of other application-oriented algorithms when run on C.mmp and Cm* [24, 28].

One might ask if more modern multiprocessors would behave better. It is hard to tell at this point since no speech experiment has been performed on systems like the Denelcor's Heterogeneous Element Processor, the C-MU Parallel Processor Architecture (a shared memory multi-Vax system now being designed at C-MU in cooperation with an industrial partner) and the Ultracomputer [29]. Most likely these systems will require less synchronization overhead but, because of their "general-purpose" structure, their performance will be less than it could be obtained with a task-oriented system [4].

Modern general-purpose multiprocessors might, on the other hand, become the best vehicle for speech research if an hypothesize-and-test paradigm with independent knowledge source is used. The reason is that in this case the recognition process is implemented as a set of independent processes (the knowledge sources) whose interconnections can be implemented with protocols that do not guarantee complete correctness of the communication and, therefore, can be very efficient. For example, this paradigm is suitable for a distributed system of processors connected by a local area network.

Some machine level parallelism techniques like CPU pipelining and vector instructions do not make any use of the information contained in the representation of the algorithm and attain a limited parallelism regardless of the algorithm representation. If we describe an algorithm using a data-flow style language, the inherent parallelism is available all the way to the level of the atomic functions. Data-flow machines could efficiently exploit all this parallelism (if they have enough resources) and could therefore attain maximum effectiveness. Moreover, since computation resources in a data-flow machine are assigned while the machine is running, algorithms that have a control-flow that is highly data dependent can be dealt with as effectively as any other algorithm. For an in-depth treatment of data-flow machine issues see Arvind's article [2].

In conclusion, the highly data-dependent behavior of some speech algorithms seems to indicate that general-purpose data-flow machines might be more appropriate for speech recognition than vonNeumann style multiprocessors. Unfortunately, working data-flow machines are an almost empty class at this time. If one desires to use existing general-purpose multiprocessors, the use of an hypothesize-and-test paradigm can make it possible to build a recognition system on a loosely connected set of processors.

3.4 MASSIVELY PARALLEL MACHINES

Parallelism, rather than raw speed, seems the way the brain gets most jobs done and speech recognition is obviously one of these jobs. Massively parallel architectures are machines with a very large number of (perhaps small) processing elements connected by some ad-hoc network. Most of the computation consists in sending information to other elements and combining the incoming information. The connections between the elements are part of the "program" or the "knowledge" present in the machine.

These kinds of machines can be classified by the type of information that is passed among the elements: some simply exchange a marker [12], some exchange values [17], some exchange arbitrary messages [9]. Some components of a speech recognition system seem very suitable to massively parallel architectures. For example, word hypothesization could be performed by a system in which

- elements represent words or phonemes,
- phoneme-nodes are connected to word-nodes to represent the lexical knowledge, and
- "phoneme likelihoods" (values) *activate* words which, in turn, inhibit each other (e.g. sending negative values).

Massively parallel algorithms are not here yet and neither are massively parallel machines. In some way, even if the effectiveness of massively parallel algorithms could be demonstrated on a small task, massively parallel algorithms would become useful only if a machine could be built to execute them effectively.

3.5 TASK-ORIENTED MACHINES AND VLSI

*With the advent of Very Large Scale Integration (VLSI) comes the advent of the phrase: "With the advent of Very Large Scale Integration" (alas)**

The first part of this section dealt with the impact that various general-purpose architectures might have on the execution of speech algorithms. It is clear, though, that the current technology allows ultimate cost effectiveness to be obtained only if an architecture is specifically tailored to a given algorithm. Unfortunately, tailoring makes sense only when an algorithm has become well established. This does not mean that the algorithm cannot be further improved but simply that it has reached a satisfactory performance from the recognition accuracy standpoint. Among speech recognition components, parameter extraction techniques and template matching techniques are now sufficiently stable to be candidate for the design of dedicated architectures. Parameter extraction has been tackled by designing analog/digital components like filter banks [7] and specialized digital processors (e.g. LPC processors on a single chip). Template matching is dealt with in detail elsewhere in this book, suffice it to say that a regular and data-dependent control structure is the major characteristic of the Dynamic Programming algorithms that their systolic implementations exploit.

---

*From Mike Foster's plan file, Carnegie-Mellon University VLSI Vax

Some work has been done by the author at Carnegie-Mellon University in designing and building an architecture for the Harpy recognition system. This experiment showed that tailoring can dramatically improve the cost-effectiveness of a system. The system (Harpy Machine [4]), using five Digital LSI-11 multiprocessors executed in real time a task that a large mainframe like the Decsystem-10/KL-10 executed in double real time. The author is now working on a set of VLSI chips [3] that will improve the performance of the Harpy Machine by about two orders of magnitude. These chips will be used in the word hypothesizer of a connected, speaker independent system now being designed at C-MU. The reason why in this particular case it is reasonable to design VLSI chips for a partially unsettled algorithm is that a set of tools is being built at the same time allowing us to quickly design similar chips once the speech algorithms have stabilized.

VLSI, by itself, has little to do with improving the performance of speech recognition systems. The importance of VLSI stems from two facts: first, VLSI technology has made available fast signal processing devices that have satisfied all the requirements for signal processing including the case when an extremely high cost effectiveness is required (e.g. in a low performance, low cost application). Second, the possibility of designing and building a new architecture down to the logic circuit level (instead of the off-the-shelf microprocessor level) has given us the possibility to make real-time speech recognition in the context of complex tasks a reality.

4. SUMMARY

This paper has discussed the computational side of the speech recognition problem and described how some of the currently known computer architectures can influence the performance of speech recognition systems. Although speech recognition opinions take sometimes the flavor of articles of faith, too little is known about speech recognition to take any side and too little is known for the computer architect to design the ultimate speech recognition machine. Enough is known, though, to build increasingly interesting and fast systems.

REFERENCES

1. Speech Group, Summary of Results of the Five-year Research Effort at Carnegie-Mellon University, Computer Science Department, Carnegie-Mellon University, 1977.
2. R. A. Iannucci Arvind, "A critique of multiprocessing von Neumann style," 10th Annual International Symposium on Computer Architecture, 1983.
3. T. Anantharaman, M. Annaratone, R. Bisiani, "A family of custom VLSI circuits for speech recognition," IEEE International Conference on Acoustics, Speech and Signal Processing, March 1984.
4. R. Bisiani, H. Mauersberg and R. Reddy, "Task-oriented architectures," Proceedings of the IEEE, July 1983.
5. H. Boley, "A preliminary survey of artificial intelligence machines," SIGART, 72, July 1980.
6. R. A. Kavaler, T. G. Noll, M. Lowy, H. Murveit and R. W. Brodersen, "A dynamic time warp IC for a one thousand recognition system," ICASSP '84, IEEE, San Diego, March 1984.
7. R. D. Fellman and R. W. Brodersen, "A switched capacitor adaptive lattice filter," Journal of Solid State Circuits, February 1983.
8. R. A. Cole, R. M. Stern, M. S. Phillips, S. M. Brill, P. Specker, and A. P. Pilant, "Feature-based speaker-independent recognition of English letters," ICASSP '83 Proceedings, IEEE, 1983, pp. 731-734.
9. W. D. Hillis, *The Connection Machine*, MIT, 1981.
10. R. De Mori, R. Giordana, A. Laface, P. Saitta, "Parallel algorithms for syllable recognition in continuous speech," to be published.
11. L. D. Erman, F. Hayes-Roth, V. R. Lesser, D. R. Reddy, "The Hearsay-II speech-understanding system: integrating knowledge to resolve uncertainty," ACM Computing Surveys, 12, 2, June 1980.
12. S. E. Fahlman, NETL: A system for representing and using real world knowledge, Ph. D. Th., MIT, 1979.
13. P. Frison and P. Quinton, "A VLSI parallel machine for speech recognition," ICASP '84, IEEE, San Diego, March 1984.
14. R. G. Goodman, Language design for man-machine communication, Ph. D. Th., Carnegie-Mellon University, 1976.
15. R. Greenblatt, T. Knight and J. Holloway, *A LISP Machine, Fifth Workshop on Architectures for Non-numeric Processing*, Asilomar, March 1980.
16. A. Gupta and C. L. Forgy, *Measurements on Production Systems*, Carnegie-Mellon University, 1983.
17. S. E. Fahlman, G. E. Hinton and T. J. Sejnowski, "Massively parallel architectures for AI: NETL, THISTLE and Boltzmann machines," AAAI-83,

AAAI, Washington, DC, 1983.

18. L. R. Bahl, Das Das, P. V. De Souza, F. Jelinek, S. Katz, R. L. Mercer, M. A. Picheny, "Some experiments with large-vocabulary isolated word sentence recognition," ICASSP '84, IEEE, San Diego, March 1984.
19. J. N. Holmes, "The JSRU channel vocoder," IEEE Proceedings 127, February 1980.
20. G. E. Kopec, "The integrated signal processing system ISP," ICASSP '84, IEEE, San Diego, March 1984.
21. B. T. Lowerre, The Harpy Speech Recognition System, Ph. D. Th., Computer Science Department, Carnegie-Mellon University, 1976.
22. J. Makhoul, "Linear prediction: A tutorial review," Proc. IEEE 63, April 1975.
23. K. Oflazer, Partitioning in Parallel Processing of Production Systems, Computer Science Dept., Carnegie-Mellon University, Thesis Proposal 1984.
24. P. N. Oleinick, The Implementation and Evaluation of Parallel Algorithms on C.mmp. Ph. D. Th., Carnegie-Mellon University, Computer Science Department, 1978.
25. L. R. Rabiner, A. E. Rosenberg, S. E. Levinson, "Considerations in dynamic time-warping algorithms for discrete word recognition," IEEE Trans. ASSP ASSP-26, 6, December 1978.
26. D. W. Shipman, "SpireX: statistical analysis in the spire acoustic-phonetic workstation," ICASSP '83, IEEE, March 1983.
27. S. Stolfo, D. Miranker and D. F. Shaw, "Architecture and applications of DADO: A large scale parallel computer for artificial intelligence," International Joint Conference on Artificial Intelligence, 1983.
28. R. J. Swan, The Switching Structure and Addressing Architecture of an Extensible Multiprocessor: Cm*, Ph. D. Th., Carnegie-Mellon University, Computer Science Department, August 1978.
29. A. Gottlieb, C. P. Grishman, K. P. Kruskal, L. McAuliffe, L. Rudolph, "The NYU ultracomputer — designing an MIMD shared memory parallel computer," IEEE Trans. on Computers C-32, 2, February 1983.
30. J. A. Feldman, F. M. Gaverick, F. M. Rhodes and J. R. Mann, "A wafer scale integration systolic processor for connected word recognition," ICASSP '84, IEEE, San Diego, March 1984.
31. H. T. Kung, "Systolic algorithms for the CMU warp processor," Proceedings of the Seventh International Conference on Pattern Recognition, Quebec, Canada, July 1984.
32. D. H. D. Warren, "A view of the Fifth Generation and its impact," The AI Magazine, Fall 82.

VLSI ARCHITECTURES FOR RECOGNITION OF CONTEXT-FREE LANGUAGES

K. S. Fu
School of Electrical Engineering
Purdue University
W. Lafayette, Indiana 47907
U.S.A.

ABSTRACT

This paper presents two VLSI architectures for the recognition of context-free languages based on Cocke-Younger-Kasami's and Earley's algorithms. By restricting the context-free grammar to be free of null rule, it is possible to implement the two algorithms on triangular shape VLSI systems. For both parsing algorithms, the designed VLSI systems are capable of recognizing a string of length n in 2n time units. Extensions to the recognition of regular tree languages and finite-state languages are also discussed.

1. INTRODUCTION

The speed of formal languages recognition is frequently considered to be important in many applications such as syntactic pattern recognition [8], artificial intelligence [9], natural language processing [10], syntax analysis of programming languages [11], pattern matching [12], etc. With the continuing advances in Very Large Scale Integration (VLSI) technology making circuitry smaller and faster, many processors can now be put together on a single chip and communicate with

---

This work was supported by the NSF Grant ECS 80-16580.

NATO ASI Series, Vol. F16
New Systems and Architectures for Automatic Speech
Recognition and Synthesis. Edited by R. De Mori and C. Y. Suen

each other at on-chip speeds. This offers the opportunity in building low-cost, high-performance, special-purpose multiprocessor architectures to aid in the rapid solution of sophisticated language recognition of general context-free languages. These languages are most commonly used in the mentioned areas and their recognition methods have been well studied [1]. The recognition methods employed in this paper will be based on the Cocke-Younger-Kasami (CYK) algorithm and Earley's algorithm [1]. Multiprocessing and pipelining techniques are used in the architectures to execute the algorithm in parallel and they will be presented in the following sections.

The definition for context-free language is taken from [1]. N and Σ represent nonterminal and terminal sets, and $V = N \cup \Sigma$. Throughout this paper, Roman capitals A, B, ... denote elements of N while lower case a, b, ... are elements of Σ. Yet, n should always be the length of the string. Greek letters α, β, ... are elements of V^*, however, λ is specifically designated as the null or empty string.

Definition 1. A context-free grammar is a 4-tuple

$$G = (N, \Sigma, P, S)$$

where N is the set of nonterminal symbols denoted by upper case letters, Σ is the set of terminal symbols denoted by lower case letters, P is the set of productions of the form $A \rightarrow \alpha$, $A \in N$, $\alpha \in (N \cup \Sigma)^*$, and S is the start symbol. The grammar is said to be in Chomsky normal form if the productions are all of the form $A \rightarrow BC$ or $A \rightarrow a$. If α, β and γ are strings of terminals and nonterminals, then $\alpha A \beta \rightarrow \alpha\gamma\beta$ if and only if $A \rightarrow \gamma$ is a production. The language generated by the grammar is the set of strings of terminals w such that $S \xrightarrow{*} w$ where $\xrightarrow{*}$ is the transitive closure of $\rightarrow$.

2. VLSI ARCHITECTURE FOR CONTEXT-FREE LANGUAGES RECOGNITION BY CYK ALGORITHM

2.1 THE CYK ALGORITHM

Two major methods for context-free language recognition are known [1,2]. The first was proposed independently by Cocke, Younger and Kasami [1]. It requires a grammar in Chomsky normal form [1] with no null rule. The second major method was developed by Earley [3] which will work for context-free grammar of any form. Although the two algorithms appear to be quite different, both have the same time bound of $O(n^3)$ for general context-free languages. Valiant [14] had shown that the computation performed by CYK algorithm can be related to boolean matrix multiplication, and came up with a recognizer running in time $O(n^{2.81})$. This is the fastest known method on a sequential machine. About the same time, Kosaraju [15] showed that CYK algorithm can be used to recognize context-free languages in time O(n) on two-dimensional array automata, and in time $O(n^2)$ on one-dimensional array automata. In this section, the CYK algorithm for context-free language recognition will be discussed.

Algorithm 1 — CYK algorithm

Let $G = (N, \Sigma, P, S)$ be a context-free grammar in Chomsky normal form (with no null rule) and let $w = a_1 a_2 \ldots a_n$, $n \geq 1$, be a string where, for $1 \leq k \leq n$, $a_k \in \Sigma$. Form the strictly upper-triangular $(n + 1) \times (n + 1)$ recognition matrix T as follows, where each element $t_{i,j}$ is a subset of N and is initially empty. (note: 0-origin addressing convention is used for matrices).

```
Begin
     loop1:For i = 0 to n-1 do
          t_{i,i+1} = {A|A→a_{i+1} is in P};
     loop2:For d = 2 to n do
          For i = 0 to n-d do
               Begin
                    j = d = i;
                    t_{i,j} = {A|there exists k, i + 1 ≤ k ≤ j-1
                              such that A→BC is in P for some
                              B ∈ t_{i,k}, C ∈ t_{k,j}}
               End
End
```

If the element $t_{0,n}$ of the recognition matrix contains the start symbol S then the string is accepted, otherwise the string is rejected.

2.2 THE VLSI IMPLEMENTATION

The VLSI architecture for implementing the CYK algorithm in parallel can be divided into two parts: The preprocessing requirement and the hardware design. Preprocessing requirements are those tasks that are mostly input independent and therefore they are required to compute only once in the beginning. The hardware design is the part that uses the preprocesed results and performs the recognition in 2n time units.

(A) Preprocessing requirement

The preprocessing requirement has three parts. First, each distinct nonterminal of the grammar are numbered in ascending order. That is, if the nonterminal set is {S, A} then the corresponding numbered nonterminal set will be $\{A_1, A_2\}$ where $A_1 = S$ and $A_2 = A$. Similarly, we also number the terminals of the grammar in this way. That is, if the terminal set is {b, a} then the corresponding numbered terminal set will be $\{a_1, a_2\}$ where $a_1 = b$ and $a_2 = a$. With the production rules rewritten according to the numbered terminal and nonterminal sets, we can proceed to the next stage of the preprocessing requirement.

The next stage of preprocessing requirement is to construct a coded production table for the hardware. Assume we have s distinct nonterminals in the grammar labeled $A_1, A_2, \ldots, A_s$, then form the permutation of all possible nonterminal pairs in order (i.e. $A_1A_1, A_1A_2, \ldots, A_1A_s, A_2A_1, \ldots, A_2A_s, \ldots, A_sA_1, \ldots A_sA_s$). Following this order, for each of these pairs find the set of nonterminals that derives that pair. For example, if $A_1 \rightarrow A_2A_3$, and $A_4 \rightarrow A_2A_3$ then the set of nonterminals corresponding to the pair A_2A_3 is $\{A_1A_4\}$. Coded each of these sets with a corresponding binary word or bit vector of length s, if A_i is in the set then set bit i of the word to 1, otherwise set it to 0. For example, if the length of the binary word s is 4, the set $\{A_1,A_4\}$ will be coded as 1001. This bit vector representation will be used throughout the design. After completing the coding, we have a coded production table for the production matching operation. The table will then be loaded into the memory module of each cell in the architecture during the initialization phase. This will be further discussed when we come to the hardware design.

The last preprocessing requirement is to code every input string according to a special format. This task is corresponding to loop 1 of the CYK algorithm. First we build a code table similar to the one before except we use terminals this time. That is, assume we have n terminals labeled $a_1, a_2, \ldots, a_n$ then for each terminal find, in the order of labels, the corresponding set of non-terminals that derives it and code the set the same way as before. Now we can use this table to code the input strings by using table scanning. This table scanning job can be done either in the host computer or it can be done on-the-fly by a simple content addressable memory [4] which contains this code table.

Except the table scanning, all the other pre-processing tasks are input independent. Therefore, they are required to compute only once in the beginning and the rest of the recognition tasks will be carried out by the hardware.

(B) Hardware design

In order to implement the CYK algorithm efficiently in hardware, the VLSI structure is chosen to be the same as the strictly upper triangular recognition matrix T (See Figure 1). In this way, the data paths which are determined by the recognition matrix and the algorithm are explicitly incorporated in the processors' organization. On the other hand, data in each matrix element are represented by using a s-bit bit vector as described in the preprocessing tasks. In this way, the set membership representation of nonterminals can be done efficiently. The hardware design can be subdivided into two portions: The dataflow requirement and the functional units design. The dataflow requirement and the functional units design. The dataflow requirement takes care of the necessary data communications between cells whereas the functional units design handles the required operations on input data within a cell.

a) Dataflow requirements

The dataflow requirement is specified in loop2 of the CYK algorithm. It is easy to see that element (i,j) of the recognition matrix needs to receive data from elements (i,k) and (k,j), for $i < k < j$. Observe also that there is no data dependency among the elements on a particular diagonal of the recognition matrix, therefore we can compute the elements on a diagonal in parallel if the required data for each element is arranged to arrive at the right moment. It happens that this dataflow requirement is the same as the optimal parentization problems in [5]. Therefore, we have adopted their algorithm for such a dataflow requirement. An informal description of the algorithm is given as follows:

Let $t = j-i$ be the distance between cell (i,j) and the boundary (See Figure 1). The result of a cell at distance t will be ready at time 2t, the cell then transmits its result upwards and to the right. This result travels at a rate of one cell per time unit for t additional time units and then slows down to one cell in every two time units until the recognition is finished. Using this algorithm, a network with $n(n+1)/2$ cells will require 2n time units for the final result to be available.

To implement such a dataflow pattern, the method used in [5] is also adopted. Referring to Figure 1, each cell has three types of channel for data communications between its neighbors. The first one is called the fast belt, it can transmit one data value at a rate of one cell per time unit. The second one is known as the slow belt, it can transmit one data value at a rate of one cell

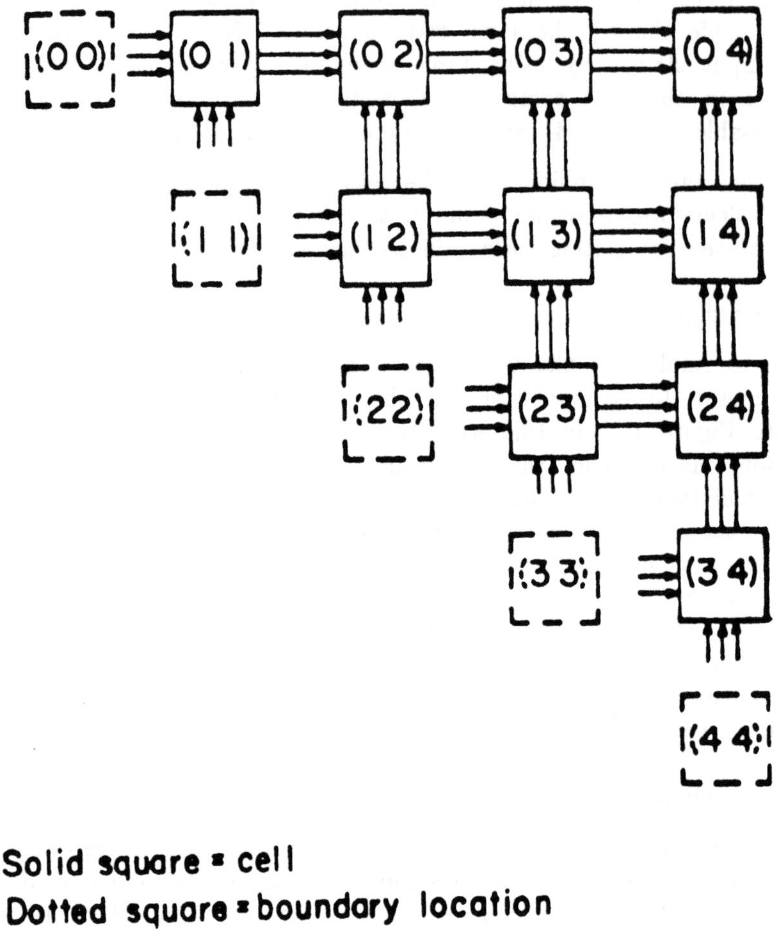

Figure 1. VLSI architecture for fast recognition of context-free languages (the case of n = 4 is shown).

in every two time units. The third one is a single bit control line, it is used for transmitting control signals between cells. There are five registers in each cell (See Figure 2): The accumulator (ACCUM.) where the current value of an entry of the recognition matrix is maintained, the horizontal fast (HORI.FAST) and vertical fast (VERT.FAST) registers for the implementation of the fast belts, and similarly the horizontal slow (HORI.SLOW) and vertical slow (VERT.SLOW) registers for slow belts implementation. Each of them is s-bits in length, where s is the number of distinct non-terminals in the grammar. In each time unit, the horizontal fast register receives data from its left neighbor while sending its old content to its right neighbor. On the other hand, the vertical fast register receives data from its neighbor below while sending its old content to its neighbor above. The horizontal slow and vertical slow registers behave exactly the same way except that the operation is done in two time units. That is, each of these registers has two stages. The incoming data enter the first stage, move the next stage at the next time unit and finally exit the cell at the following time unit. In each unit of time, a cell takes part in the belt motion as well as updating its accumulator. The new value of the accumulator is updated by the functional module FM (See figure 3) using the current contents of the five registers. This will be discussed later when we come to the functional units design. In addition, if the cell is at distance t away from the boundary, then at time 2t it will copy the contents of its accumulator into its fast horizontal and vertical registers. This is done by the data transfer module DT1. And finally, if it is at an even distance t = 2s from the boundary, then at time 3t/2 it will load the first stage of its horizontal (and vertical) slow register from the horizontal (resp. vertical) fast belt, ignoring its slow belts entirely. This is done by the data transfer module DT2. The timing of these transfers is controlled by the horizontal control line (HCTL) and vertical control line (VCTL) respectively. The accumulator to fast belt transfer (DT1) that occurs in cell (i,j) at time j-i is controlled by a rightward moving signal (HCTL) that moves at a rate of one cell every two time units. The fast to slow belt transfer (DT2) that occurs at time 3(j-i)/2 is controlled by an upward moving signal (VCTL) that moves at a rate of two cells every three time units. Using this implementation, the dataflow requirement is fulfilled.

b) Functional units design

In this part of the discussion, the emphasis will be on the design of the Functional Module (FM) such that the architecture can produce the required recognition matrix. Other functional units such as data transfer modules and various registers can be easily designed by using a few pass transistors and/or buffers [4], therefore they will not be further discussed.

The design of the Functional Module (FM) is shown in Figure 3. In order to simultaneously process data received from the register pair horizontal fast (HF) and Vertical Slow (VS) as well as the register pair horizontal slow (HS) and vertical fast (VS), the Functional Module has employed two Permutation Modules (PM1 and PM2). They are used to compute all possible right-hand side non-terminal pairs induced by data in each register pair (one PM for each pair).

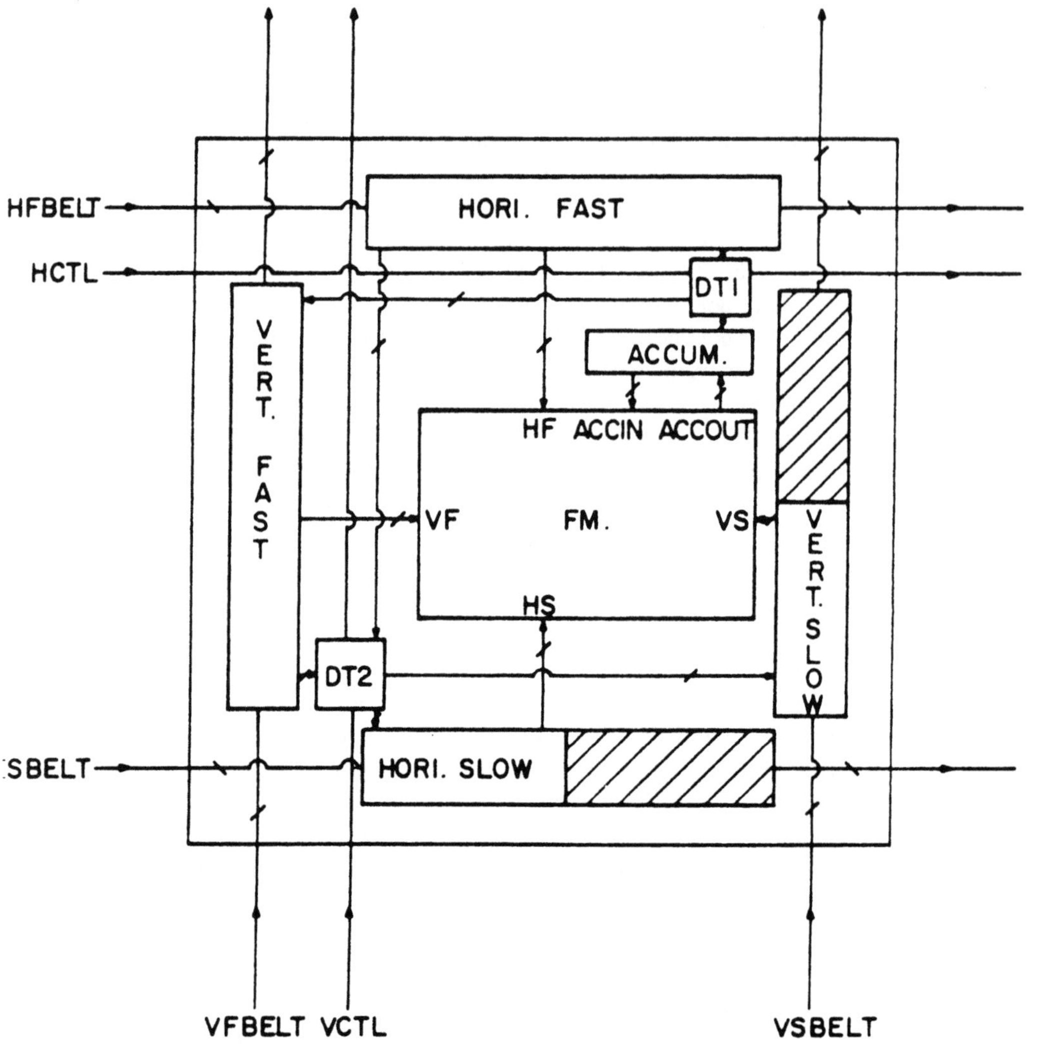

Figure 2. Cell design for CYK algorithm

Each Permutation Module simply performs the Boolean function $a_{ij} = b_i$ AND c_j for $1 \leq i, j \leq s$, where s is the number of distinct non-terminals in the grammar. Each b_i is from the input of its horizontal register whereas each c_i is from its vertical register and the output a_{ij} is arranged in the same order as the storage of the coded production table. Since we are interested in the right hand side non-terminal pairs induced by both of the register pairs together, the output of the two PM's are union together by the upper OR module in Figure 3 to form a single output of s^2 bit in length. That is, bit b_{ij} of PM1 is ORed with the corresponding bit c_{ij} of PM2 for $1 \leq i, j \leq s^2$. Now, in order to find the corresponding left-hand side non-terminal set simultaneously for each non-terminal pair, a Memory Module (MM) which stored the coded production table is used. The Memory Module has s^2 one-bit inputs and s^2 s-bit outputs, it will output the content of the memory cell (s bits in length) if the input is one and output zeroes otherwise. The outputs of the upper OR Module are directly connected to the inputs of the Memory Module so that the production table scanning process can be done simultaneously. The results of the table scanning (i.e. the outputs of MM) are then union together with the content of the accumulator (from ACCIN) to form the s-bit final result. This is done by the lower OR module (See Figure 3) which ORed bit i of every s-bit output of MM and ACCIN together, for $1 \leq i \leq s$. The output of the OR module (ACCOUT) will be sent to update the accumulator. In this way, the Functional Module in each cell will incorporate with the dataflow algorithm and produce the required recognition matrix in 2n time units.

To initialize the system so that it can behave properly, one requires to store the coded production table into the MM of every cell, reset every register in each cell to zero and have the coded input string loaded in the first diagonal. The loading can be done by sharing input data lines in each cell during the initialization phase. Now, start every control signal at the boundary (See Figure 1) and the architecture will run as desired. The next input string can be loaded overlappingly after the architecture has executed two time units and the next execution can start right after the completion of the present by properly resetting the registers and control signals. In this way, we can reduce the pin count by multiplexing input data lines and still can keep the system running continuously.

What is left now is to check the output of cell (0,n) and see if its non-terminal set contains the start symbol. This can be done by creating a mask with bit i equals to one if A_i is the start symbol and zero otherwise. We can then ANDed the output of cell (0,n) with this mask and test for zero. If the result indicates non-zero, we accept the string, otherwise we reject it. These operations can be done by using another simple module, we call this the Decision Module (DM). A simple design for such module is shown in Figure 4. Bit i of the input (IN) from the output of cell (0,n) is ANDed with bit i of the mask, for $1 \leq i \leq s$. The s bits result is then ORed together to form a single bit

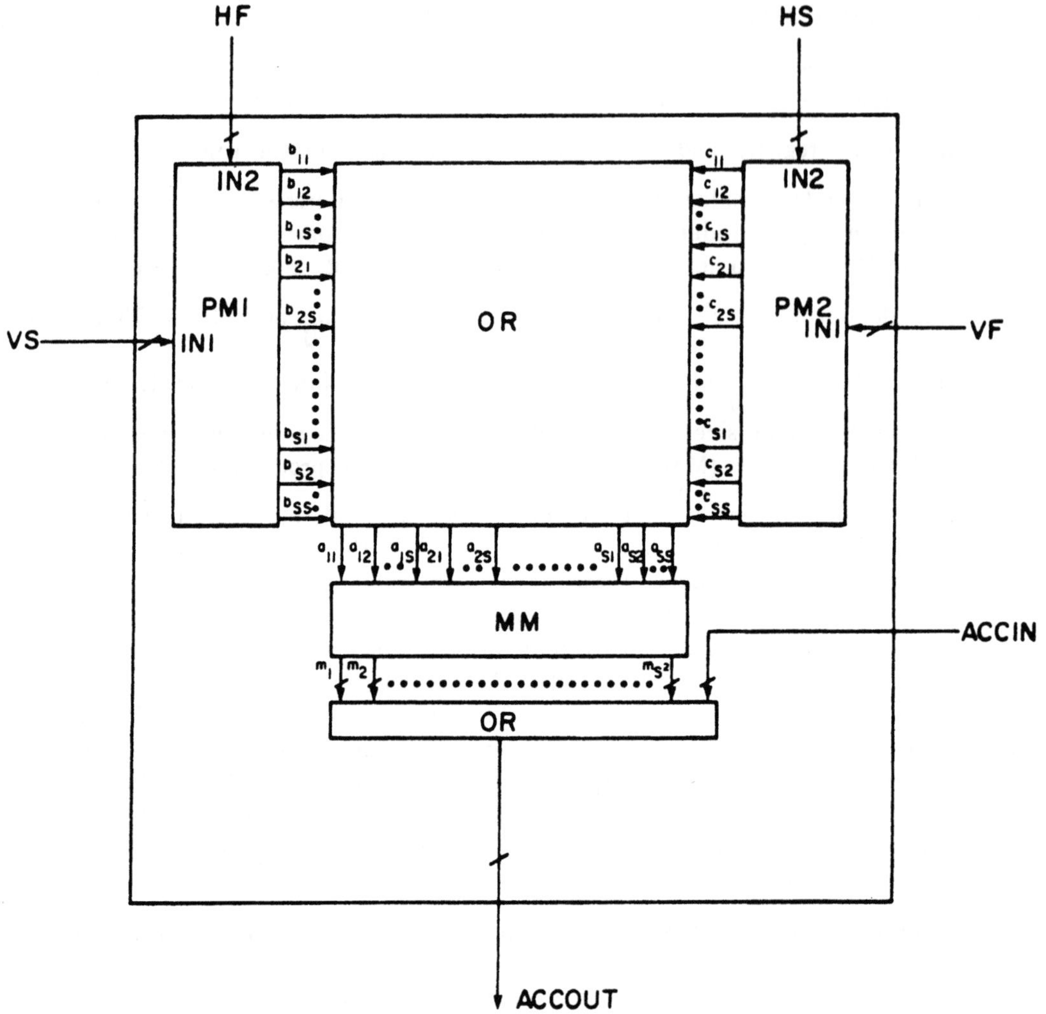

Figure 3. Functional Module (FM)

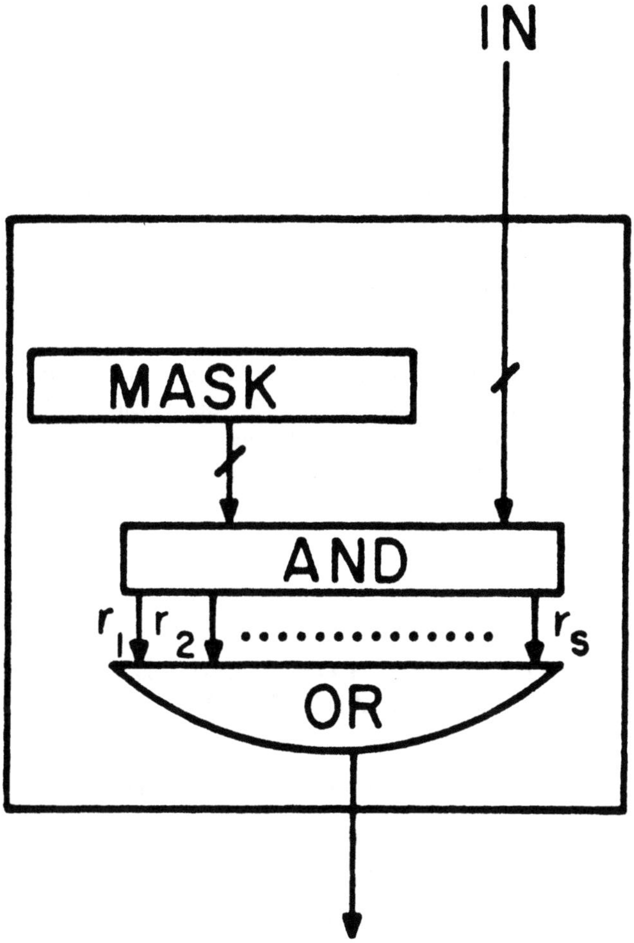

Figure 4. Decision Module (DM).

output. If the bit is one then the string is accepted, otherwise the string is rejected. With this module connected to the output of cell (0,n) of the architecture, the system can provide a 'yes' or 'no' answer in every 2n time units. In this case, the mask of DM is required to be computed and loaded by the host computer in the initialization phase.

A computer simulation has been carried out on the logic of the VLSI architecture. The purpose of this simulation is to make sure that the logic and the various timings of the architecture are designed correctly. The result of the simulation has demonstrated that the architecture is correctly designed to provide the recognition matrix in 2n time units [13].

A parse for a given input string is sometimes useful in syntactic pattern recognition because it provides the structural descriptions of the input string. Since the recognition matrix is generated during the recognition process, it is not hard to obtain a parse for an accepted input string by a simple parsing algorithm.

3. VLSI ARCHITECTURE FOR CONTEXT-FREE LANGUAGE RECOGNITION BY EARLEY'S ALGORITHM

It is known that Earley's algorithm recognizes general context-free languages in time $O(n^3)$. In 1976, Graham, et al [16] derived from Earley's algorithm a new on-line context-free language recognition algorithm. This algorithm allows an implementation with only $O(n^2/\log n)$ operations on bit vectors of length n, or $O(n^3/\log n)$ operations on a RAM. In the same year, Weicker came up with a similar result [17]. These two recognition algorithms are the fastest ever known.

Definition 2. For any rule $A \rightarrow \alpha\beta$ in P we will call $A \rightarrow \alpha \cdot \beta$ a *dotted rule*. The dot "." is a symbol not found in V and is used as a marker to indicate the position.

Definition 3. If $X \in V$, the predecessors of $X = \{A | A \overset{*}{\Rightarrow} X,\ A \in N\}$.

Definition 3. The $\times$ operator. Let Q be a set of dotted rules, then

$Q \times R = \{A \rightarrow \alpha U\beta \cdot \gamma |\ A \rightarrow \alpha \cdot U\beta\gamma \in Q,\ \beta \overset{*}{\Rightarrow} \lambda \text{ and } U \in R\}$, when $R \subseteq V$.

$Q \times R = \{A \rightarrow \alpha U\beta \cdot \gamma |\ A \rightarrow \alpha \cdot U\beta\gamma \in Q,\ \beta \overset{*}{\Rightarrow} \lambda \text{ and } U \rightarrow \delta. \in R\}$, when R is a set of dotted rules.

Definition 5. The $*$ operator. Let Q and R be sets of dotted rules, then

$$Q * R = \{A \rightarrow \alpha U\beta \cdot \gamma | A \rightarrow \alpha \cdot U\beta\gamma \in Q, \beta \overset{*}{\Rightarrow} \lambda$$

and there is some $U' \rightarrow \delta.$ in R such that $U \overset{*}{\Rightarrow} U'\}$.

Definition 6. Let $R \subseteq V$, define

$$\text{PREDICT}(R) = \{C \rightarrow \gamma \cdot \delta | C \rightarrow \gamma\delta \text{ is in } P, \gamma \overset{*}{\Rightarrow} \lambda,$$

$B \overset{*}{\Rightarrow} C\eta$ for some B in R and some $\eta\}$.

Graham, et al [16] rewrote Earley's algorithm in terms of dotted rule notation and the $\times$, $*$ operators. We called their algorithm the GHR algorithm as shown below:

Algorithm 2 — GHR Algorithm

$t_{0,0}$ = PREDICT({S})

for j = 1 *to* n *do*

begin [build col. j, given cols. 0,1,...,j-1]

[Scanner:]

for $0 \leq i \leq j\text{-}1$ *do*

$t_{i,j} = t_{i,j-1} \times \{a_j\}$

[Completer:]

for k = j-1 *downto* 0 *do*

begin $t_{k,j} = t_{k,k} * t_{k,j}$

for i = k-1 *downto* 0 *do*

$t_{i,j} = t_{i,j} \cup t_{i,k} \times t_{k,j}$

end

[Predictor:]

$t_{j,j}$ = PREDICT $(\cup_{0 \leq i \leq j-1}\, t_{i,j}$

end

Algorithm 2 constructs a recognition matrix $T = \{t_{i,j}\}$. All of its elements are sets of dotted rules. As Graham et al claimed, this algorithm has several advantages. The straightforward control and data structures used make it conceptually simpler than Earley's version. This algorithm also combined many steps in the Earley's version into one step. Therefore, Algorithm 2 can be implemented so as to take $O(n^2/\log n)$ bit vector steps on a bit vector machine or $O(n^3/\log n)$ steps on a RAM [16].

3.1 A PARALLEL EARLEY'S ALGORITHM

The computation in Algorithm 2 has one restriction, that is, no element of column $j + 1$ can be processed until $t_{j,j}$ is processed, and hence until all elements of column j are processed. This restriction is enforced by the Predictor, which ensures that $A \rightarrow \alpha \cdot \beta$ appears in the ith row only if $S \overset{*}{\Rightarrow} a_1 \ldots a_i A_\gamma$. Because of this restricted order in computation, Algorithm 2 can not be performed in parallel. However, it was mentioned by Graham [16] that with a weakened Predictor, Algorithm 2 will have the same form as CYK algorithm, except that the operation between elements is different. Based on this suggestion we developed a parallel version of Earley's algorithm and implemented it on a VLSI architecture.

(A) Removal of predictor

The function of the Predictor is to build up $t_{j,j}$ in the jth column after other elements in that column all have been processed. Suppose that we add some extra dotted rules which are not ordinarily there, the subsequent normal Scanner, Completer and Predictor operations may introduce extra dotted rules into columns to the right of j, but not above row j. In other words, this addition would have no effect on $t_{0,n}$, so we still have a correct recognizer. As a matter of fact, the Predictor can be replaced by the statement

$$t_{j,j} = \text{PREDICT}(N)$$

and the correctness is preserved. In doing so, the characterization theorem [1] would be changed to "$A \rightarrow \alpha \cdot \beta \in t_{i,j}$ if and only if $\alpha \overset{*}{\Rightarrow} a_{i+1} \ldots a_j$", which is analogous to the one for CYK algorithm. Since the diagonal elements would be all the same, independent of the input, they could be eliminated by a suitable combination of the operations $\times$ and $\cdot$. Earley's algorithm without the Predictor restriction is called *weakened Earley's algorithm.*

(B) Operator " $\times \cdot$ "

From Algorithm 2, we realized that eliminating the diagonal elements $t_{k,k}$ will also eliminate the * operation and leave the algorithm with only $\times$ operation. The $\times$ operation is the main computation for constructing the matrix elements and the * operation only applies to the element after it has completed its own computation and ready to assist the computations of other elements above it. Therefore, we can combine these two operations by attaching the * operator to a $\times$ operator. The formal definition is given below. Let Q and R be sets of dotted rules and Y = PREDICT(N), which replaces every central diagonal element.

$$Q \times \cdot R = \left\{A \to \alpha U\beta \cdot \gamma | A \to \alpha \cdot U\beta\gamma \in Q,\ B \overset{*}{\Rightarrow} \lambda \text{ and } U \to \delta . \in R\right\}$$

and

$$\{B \to \delta C\xi \cdot \eta | \gamma = \lambda,\ B \to \delta \cdot C\xi\eta \in Y, \text{ and } \xi \overset{*}{\Rightarrow} \lambda,\ C \overset{*}{\Rightarrow} A\}$$

if $R \subseteq V$, then

$$Q \times \cdot R = \{A \to \alpha U\beta \cdot \gamma | A \to \alpha \cdot U\beta\gamma \in Q,\ \beta \overset{*}{\Rightarrow} \lambda,\ U \in R\}$$

and

$$\{B \to \delta C\xi \cdot \eta | \gamma = \lambda,\ B \to \delta \cdot C\xi\eta \in Y, \text{ and xi } \overset{*}{\Rightarrow} \lambda,\ C \overset{*}{\Rightarrow} A\}$$

(C) The parallel weakened Earley's algorithm

After removing the Predictor restriction and substituting the central diagonal elements, we can write the weakened Earley's algorithm in terms of " $\times$ * " operator.

Algorithm 3 — Weakened Earley's Algorithm

for i = 1 *to* n *do*

$$t_{i-1,i} = Y \times \cdot \{a_j\}$$

for j = 2 *to* n *do*

begin

[Scanner:]

for $0 \le i \le j\text{-}2$ *do*

$$t_{i,j} = t_{i,j-1} \times \cdot \{a_j\}$$

[Completer:]

for k = j-1 *downto* 0 *do*

for i = k-1 *downto* 0 *do*

$$t_{i,j} = t_{i,j} \cup t_{i,k} \times \cdot t_{k,j}$$

end

This algorithm builds up a (n+1)X(n+1) upper triangular matrix. Figure 5 depicts the detailed computations of the algorithm. The Completer operation is to calculate $t_{i,j}$ based on the information from $t_{i,k}$ and $t_{k,j}$. Noted that for the maximum value $k = j-1 < j$ and $i = k-1 < k$, $t_{i,k}$ and $t_{k,j}$ are either to the left or below $t_{i,j}$. This characteristic suggests that we can construct the same matrix by calculating one diagonal from another and moving from the central diagonal towards the upper right corner as described in the following algorithm.

Algorithm 4

for i = 1 *to* n *do in parallel*

$$t_{i-1,i} = Y \times \cdot \{a_i\}$$

for j = 2 *to* n *do*

for i = 0 *to* n-j *do in parallel*

begin

[Scanner:]

$$t_{i,i+j} = t_{i,i+j-1} \times \cdot \{a_{i+j}\}$$

[Completer:]

for k = 1 *to* j-1 *do in parallel*

$$t_{i,i+j} = t_{i,i+j} \cup t_{i,i+k} \times \cdot t_{i+k,i+j}$$

end

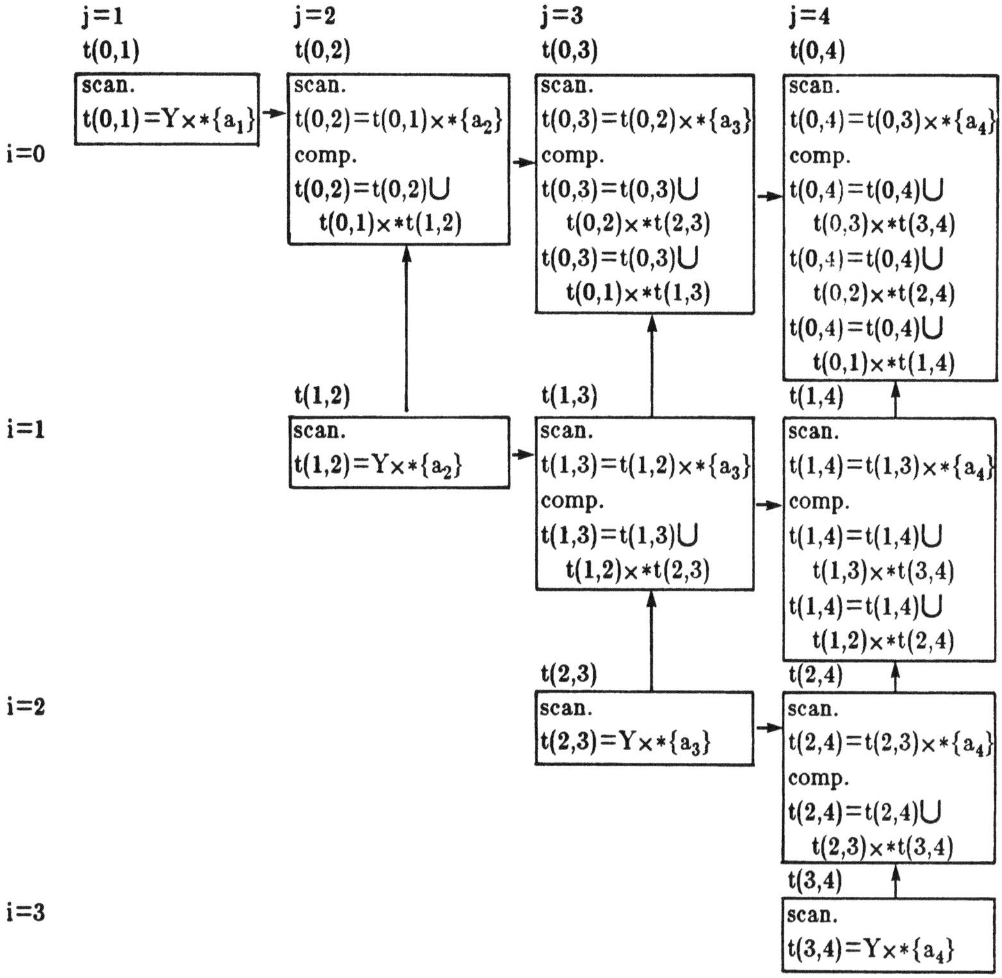

Figure 5. The computation of Weakened Earley's Algorithm (string length=4).

Algorithm 4 constructs the same matrix as Algorithm 3 does. From this parallel algorithm, we can see that j loop executes n times. Within j loop, all the i and k can be executed in parallel, provided we have enough processors to do so, hence this algorithm has time complexity O(n). Although we can break down the computation into (n-j+2) $\times$ (j-1) independent subjobs for each j loop and execute the algorithm on a MIMD system [18], yet it is not practical in real applications. For instance, if $n = 50$, when $j = 20$ the algorithm requries 608 processors to work simultaneously and when $j = 50$, only one processor is required while other processors have to be idled. This is a tremendous waste. Of course we can ease this situation by setting a loop for $k = 1$ to j-1 instead of executing in parallel. This arrangement reduces the number of required processors in the sacrifice of increasing the time complexity to $O(n^2)$. Besides, the rather complicate data exchange may also degrade the performance of this algorithm. A more efficient and promising architecture is still needed.

3.2 VLSI IMPLEMENTATION

For Algorithm 3, a direct implementation is to use the same VLSI system as the one for the CYK algorithm. Algorithm 3 has a regular communication geometry as shown in Figure 5, and the data movement can be kept simple and regular but, each processor does not perform constant-time operations.

(A) Constant-time operation

In Algorithm 3, only " $\times \cdot$ " operator was used. Recall the definition of " $\times \cdot$ " we notice that λ-production was considered in the operation, that is, we will add a dotted rule $A \rightarrow \alpha U\beta \cdot \gamma$ to the result instead of $A \rightarrow \alpha U \cdot \beta\gamma$, provided $\beta \overset{*}{\Rightarrow} \lambda$. Since the length of β is not known, we have to check the following symbols until the decision is made. This variable length of β makes the operation time different with different data and therefore hinders the implementation on a VLSI architecture. However, if we restrict our grammar to be λ-free, the " $\times \cdot$ " operation can easily be implemented on a dedicated hardware.

(B) Data representation

Bit vectors [20] are used to represent symbols in V and the matrix elements $t_{i,j}$. The former is easy to understand but the latter deserves further explanations. As we know, every matrix element $t_{i,j}$ is a set of dotted rules. Each dotted rule conveys the information about one production rule and its associated dot position. Since the production rules are given by the grammar, the matrix elements can only cover the dot position by bit vectors. For instance, one dotted rule with 5 symbols at its right hand side (RHS) and a dot between the second and the third symbol can be reprresented by a 6-bit bit vector with a 1 appears in the third bit and all the other bits are 0's. The extra one bit is reserved for the end marker of the RHS. Consequently, the matrix elements $t_{i,j}$ can be represented by an array of bit vectors. The dimension of the array equals the number of the production rules. We call this array of bit vectors the *cell data*, which represents the matrix elements and is transferred from cell to cell through data buses. This data structure contains all the information we need and has equal length for all elements hence indicates the uniform data transfer.

(C) Preprocessing

During the preprocessing stage, there are some information needed to be put into the VLSI system in certain forms. The grammar is coded into group of bit vector arrays and every array represents one grammar rule. If V has k symbols and each rule has at most m RHS symbols, then the array has m+1 bit vectors, each bit vector has k+1 bits. We also need to convert all the left hand side (LHS) symbols and its corresponding predecessors into array of bit vectors. Let Y = PREDICT(N) be a set of dotted rules. Since Y only depends on grammar, it can be calculated and converted into r(m+1)-bit bit vectors before hand, where r is the number of productions.

(D) The VLSI architecture

The VLSI system is similar to the one shown in Figure 1 except one extra vertical INP bus was used here to transfer input symbols. Every cell has identical structure. The system is controlled under a system clock (or unit time). It is assumed that during each system unit time, every cell can finish its computation and every bus can complete its data transfer operation. There are three vertical buses. VFB (vertical fast bus), VSB (vertical slow bus) and INP (input symbol bus), and two horizontal buses, HFB (horizontal fast bus) and HSB (horizontal slow bus). The fast buses and slow buses have the same transfer rate as discussed in the CYK algorithm, and INP bus has a transfer rate as that of a slow bus.

Each cell has three functions, namely, computing the " $\times \cdot$ " opeation, loading the data onto fast buses and shifting the data from the fast buses to the slow buses. The last two functions are essential for keeping the bus system work and are controlled by two control lines, VC (vertical control) and HC (horizontal control). The control lines only transfer one bit at a time. The transfer rate and functions of VC and HC are the same as the one mentioned in the previous section.

Initially, every cell has the information about grammar rules, LHS symbols and its predecessors and Y. Start from time 1, the input symbols are read into the system in parallel, as shown in Figure 1, and all the data buses are sending 0's except HFB is loaded with Y. The control lines start to send 1 from the central diagonal cells (which are not physically exist). The system is running in a pipelining and multiprocessing fashion. After 2n unit times the tester receives data from cell (0,n) through HFB and after one more time unit, the tester will tell whether or not the input string can be generated by the grammar. The tester stores a mask which contains the information $\{S \rightarrow \alpha. | S \rightarrow \alpha \in P\}$ in terms of array of bit vectors. After it receives data from cell (0,n), a simple AND operation can give us the result.

(E) Cell structure

In this section, we will discuss the implementation of the main cell function, the computation of " $\times \cdot$ ". Let us assume Q is a set of dotted rules. For convenience, when we say R1 of Q, we mean that R1 is an array of bit vectors and each vector represents the symbol appearing to the right of the dot, the dot position is specified by the cell data Q. Again, Y = PREDICT(N) and we can write $Q \times \cdot R$ into an eight-step procedure.

(1) Find the dotted rules which have the form $U_i \rightarrow \delta.$ from R and record the union of the LHS symbols U = union of U_i's.
(2) Compare U with R1 of Q and mark the dotted rule whenever a match occurs.
(3) Change Q by shifting those marked bit vectors one bit to the right and clear the other bit vectors.
(4) Find the dotted rules which have the form $U_i \rightarrow \delta.$ from Q and record the union of the LHS symbols U = union of U_i's.
(5) Find the predecessors for U.
(6) Compare predecessors with R1 of Y and mark the dotted rule whenever a match occurs.
(7) Change Y the same way as in step (3).
(8) $Q \times \cdot R$ = Y bit by bit ORing Q.

Recall from Figure 5, the Scanner operation only applies to the data from the left neighbor cell $t_{i,j-1} \times \cdot b$ and the same data is used in Completer operation as $t_{i,j-1} \times \cdot t_{j-1,j}$. It is very easy to combine the Scanner with the Completer, that is, after forming the U for $t_{i,j-1}$, we can OR U with the input symbol b and the remaining calculations are still the same. Therefore, instead of building up a Scanner, we can modify step (1) as follows:

(1) Find the dotted rules which have the form $U_i \rightarrow \delta.$ from R and record the union of the LHS symbols and the INP, U = union of U_i's and b.

The above procedure can be executed by the device shown in Figure 6. Figure 7 illustrates the architecture of the cell. In Figure 7, Operation 1 has the same structure as the one in Figure 6 while Operator 2 does not have the INP bus. The ACC will OR the results from both operators and itself. When the HC signal arrives, it will load the results to both HFB and VFB.

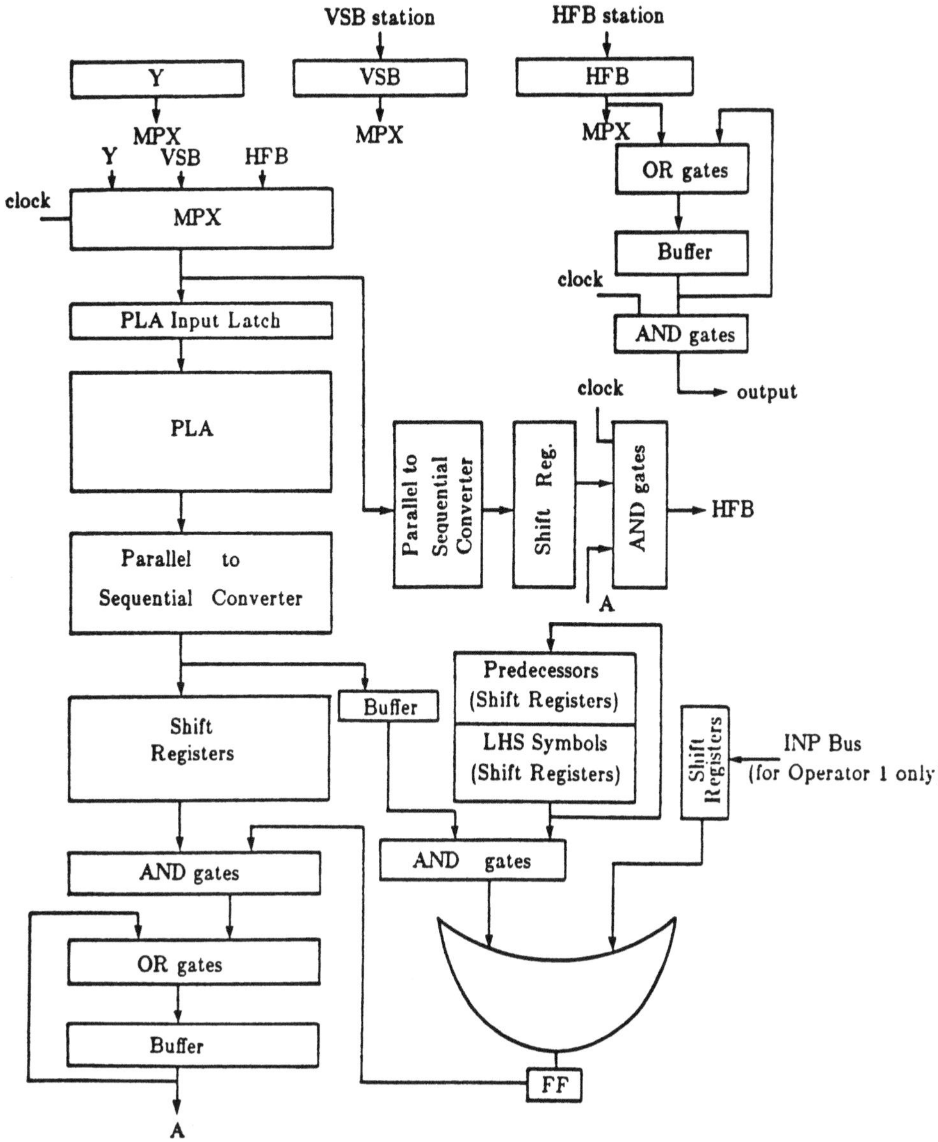

Figure 6. Structure of the operator for Earley's algorithm

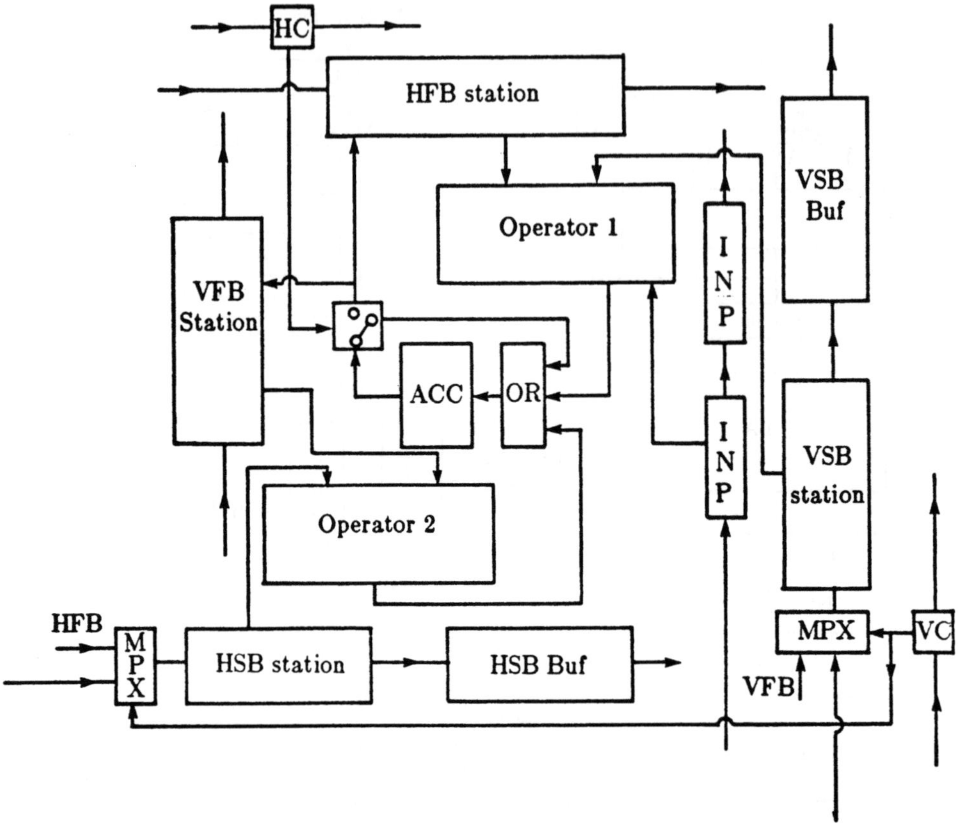

Figure 7. Structure of the cell (Earley's algorithm)

Following the parse extraction algorithm given in [1], it is possible to implement the algorithm on a processor array [21]. It is also possible to implement the minimum-distance error-correcting parse (a modified Earley's algorithm) on a VLSI system [21].

4. CONCLUDING REMARKS

It is interesting to see that although the VLSI systems for CYK algorithm and Earley's algorithm use the same triangular matrix structure, the cell designs in each system are different. Notice that the VLSI system for CYK algorithm has simpler cell design; however, the algorithm requires the grammar to be convered into Chomsky normal form. On the other hand, a more complex cell design is required in the VLSI implementation for Earley's algorithm that, however, has imposed no specific restrictions on the form of the grammar.

Since finite-state languages form a subset of context-free languages, the context-free parsing algorithms and hence the VLSI architectures described in Section 2 and Section 3 can also be used for the recognitin of finite-state languages. A more efficient method for finite-state language recognition, derived from the CYK algorithm, has recently been proposed. The VLSI architectur using this algorithm can be made to recognize a string of length n in constant time [13].

Tree languages are often used in sytactic pattern recognition for description of high dimensional patterns [8]. It has been shown that for a given regular tree grammar one can effectively construct an equivalent expansive tree grammar [8], and this equivalent grammar will have a form of context-free grammar in Griebach normal form [1]. Consequently, the VLSI architectures proposed in this paper can be employed for the recognition of regular tree languages.

Since Earley's parsing algorithm (or modified Earley's algorithm) has been commonly used in many fields, the proposed VLSI architecture for Earley's algorithm should find applications also in error-correcting parsing and high dimensional language recognition [8,22].

REFERENCES

1. A. V. Aho and J. D. Ullman, *The Theory of Parsing, Translation and Compiling*, Vol. I, Prentice-Hall, 1972.
2. M. A. Harrison, *Introduction to Formal Language Theory*, Addison-Wesley, 1978.
3. J. Earley, "An efficient context free parsing algorithm", Comm. ACM,

13(1970), pp. 94-102.

4. C. A. Mead and L. A. Conway, *Introduction to VLSI Systems*, Adison-Wesley, 1980.
5. L. J. Guibas, H. T. Kung and C. D. Thompson, "Direct VLSI implementation of combinatorial algorithms", Proc. Conf. on VLSI, Caltech, Jan. 1979, pp. 509-526.
6. H. T. Kung, "Let's design algorithms for VLSI systems", Proc. Conf. on VLSI, Caltech, Jan. 1979, pp. 65-90.
7. K. Q. Brown, "Dynamic programming in computer science", Carnegie-Mellon Univ., Tech. Report, CS-79-106, Feb. 1979.
8. K. S. Fu, *Syntactic Pattern Recognition and Applications*, Prentice-Hall, 1982.
9. N. J. Nilsson, *Principles of Artificial Intelligence*, Tioga publishing company, 1980.
10. D. L. Waltz and B. A. Goodman, "Writing a natural language database system", Coordinated Science Lab., Univ. of Illinois, Urbana, IL 61801.
11. A. V. Aho and J. D. Ullman, *Principles of Compiler Design*, Addison Wesley, 1978.
12. R. L. Hasin, "Hardware for searching very large text databases", Proc. 5th Workshop on Computer Architecures for Non-Numeric Processing, March 1980.
13. K. H. Chu and K. S. Fu, "VLSI architectures for high speed recognition of general context-free languages and finite-state languages", Proc. 9th Annual International Smposium on Computer Architecture, April 26-29, 1982, Austin, Texas.
14. L. Valiant, "General context free recognition in less than cubic time", J. Computer and System Science, Vol. 10, 1975.
15. S. R. Kosaraju, "Speed of recognition of context-free languages by array automata", SIAM J. Comput., Vol. 4, No. 3, Sept. 1975.
16. S. L. Graham, M. A. Harrison and W. L. Ruzzo, "On line context-free language recognition in les than cubic time", Proc. of the 8th Annual ACM Symposium on Theory of Computing, May 1976.
17. Reinhold Weicker, "General context free language recogntion by a RAM with uniform cost criterion in time $n^2 \log n$", Tech. Rpt. No. 182, Feb. 1976. Computer Science Dept., Pennsylvania State University.
18. Y. T. Chiang and K. S. Fu, "Parallel Processing for Distance Cmputation in Syntactic Pattern Recognition", Proc. IEEE Workshop on CAPAIDM, Nov. 1981.
19. M. J. Foster and H. T. Kung, "The design of special-purpose VLSI chips", Computer, Vol. 13, No. 1, Jan. 1980.
20. A. V. Aho, J. E. Hopcroft and J. D. Ullman, *The Design and Analysis of Computer Algorithms*, Addison Wesley Co., Reading, Mass., 1974.
21. Y. T. Chiang and K. S. Fu, "Parallel algorithms and VLSI implementation for syntactic pattern recogntion", IEEE Trans. Pattern Analysis and Machine Intelligence, Vol. PAMI-6, May 1984.
22. Q. Y. Shi and K. S. Fu, "Efficient error-correcting parsing for (attributed and stochastic) tree grammars", Information Sciences, Vol. 26, 159-188, 1982.

IMPLEMENTATION OF AN ACOUSTICAL FRONT-END FOR SPEECH RECOGNITION

Michele Cavazza, Alberto Ciaramella e Roberto Pacifici
CSELT - Centro Studi e Laboratori Telecomunicazioni
via Reiss Romoli, 274 - 10148 Torino, Italy

ABSTRACT

We describe the implementation of a programmable general-purpose acoustical front-end for speech recognition; its design keeps into account, as an example, the algorithm of centisecond cepstrum extraction for an acoustical signal sampled at a maximum rate of 12.8 kHz.

It consists of three boards, a master board controlled by a general purpose microprocessor, a slave board containing two digital signal processors working in parallel and an input/output analog board.

The overall system is connected to a general-purpose minicomputer, which constitutes the system host. The implementation details and its rationale (mainly reprogrammability and performance) are outlined. In cases of more demanding applications, the system could also be hardware reconfigured with cascade or parallel sections.

1. Introduction and requirements

In a speech recognition system, techniques for feature extraction have unusual interest. The algorithms used [1,2] are typical not only of most speech recognition systems [3] but also of systems used for speaker recognition [4] or certain kinds of speech coding systems [5], that is, in systems using a parametric representation of speech. Nevertheless, the algorithms for features extraction, though computationally rather demanding in a real time system, are highly regular and data dependent and use regularly structured data [6]. These algorithms are mainly spectral estimations [7] or LPC (linear prediction coded) parameter extractions [8] or cepstrum estimations [9].

Today DSP (Digital Signal Processor) technology is appropriate to the real time implementation of parameter extraction algorithms for speech and several types of these processors are presently available [10]. However, given the present memory and speed limits of these components, in several cases a number of DSP's is needed in order to perform a more complex algorithm [11] or to perform various kinds of parameter extraction in parallel. Moreover, in some cases of speech recognition the capability of changing the set of extracted parameters, depending on the context, would be welcome.

Taking these points into account, we implemented an acoustical front end for speeech recognition with the following requirements:

- high performance in a reduced space using current technology

NATO ASI Series, Vol. F16
New Systems and Architectures for Automatic Speech Recognition and Synthesis. Edited by R. De Mori and C. Y. Suen

- capability of being reprogrammed
- adequately modularized, so that every single block could also be used in different contexts, as described later.

Another requirement is a general-purpose interface to the host computer.

This acoustical front-end implements, as an example, the algorithm of cepstrum extraction via the FFT calculation followed by the DCT for an acoustical signal sampled at a maximum rate of 12.8 kHz. The computations are made over a window of 20 ms. with an overlap of 10 ms. This is useful from the recognition performance point of view [12], and exploits the computation and memory capability of the machine.

2. Architectural basic choices

The reprogrammability requirement (even in real time) leads to a software reconfigurable design and to a choice of a DSP based on an external program RAM. We chose the TMS320 [13] which, at the start of this project, was the only DSP with this characteristics. However, this DSP had other interesting characteristics,too, which have been exploited in many applications [14,15,16,17]. The basic configuration of the implementation is composed of three boards:

- a master board controlled by a general-purpose processor (Z80 in this case) and connected with the host through a high speed serial link,
- a slave board,containig two twins sections, each controlled by a TMS320,
- an input-output analog board.

This three board arrangement is the standard one, but, as we noted before, it can be not satisfactory for more demanding jobs. In these cases we can rearrange the same boards, basically in two ways:

- in "cascade" (or ripple) mode,
- in "parallel" mode.

The "cascade mode" has n blocks; the first is fed by the analog input and feeds the second; the second feeds the third and so on, this mode is useful when several stages are needed for a more complex computation (e.g. formant extraction for the sake of spectral evaluation). In "parallel mode", the analog input feeds in parallel all blocks performing different independent computations (e.g. spectral coefficients and pitch extraction).

3. Implementation details

The master is controlled by an 8-bit general purpose microprocessor, and can interface to external devices with two serial links controlled by a SIO (Serial Input Output): the first is used to communicate to the host (initially for program downloading and then for parameter passing), the second is used to communicate to a local terminal, mainly for debugging purposes. Data interchange with the slaves is controlled by two parallel input/output ports. Each also transforms the 8-bit data of the master into 16-bit data of the slave. A control register to the slaves issues suitable commands (e.g. for slave resetting). Direct data interchange is also possible from the A/D to the master and from the master to the D/A, although in the application implemented, this possibility is only used for initializing and debugging. A programmable counter (CTC) is used not only to control the speed of the serial line from/to host, but also to generate a programmable window for data acquisition. In fact, one input of the CTC is the sampling frequency, coming from the converter. The CTC and the surrounding logic divide this waveform by a programmable constant, generating two complementary square wave outputs, sent to slave 1 and slave 2, respectively, where the program synchronizes itself with the rising edge of this signal. In this way a programmable window rate (in every case the 50% overlap of windows is fixed) is obtained.

The slave board contains two twin TMS320. Since our goal was to build an efficient real time general purpose acoustical front end, we had to increase the basic input and memory capabilities of the signal processor. Regarding the first point, we note that the TMS320 has two basic input capabilities: an input line for interrupt and an input line (BIO) for sensing another status via a special conditional skip instruction, named BIOZ. Given that in our application there are many interrupting conditions, for example data ready from converter, data accepted by master, special signalling from master etc., all interrupts are suitably put in OR and then are polled by the BIO input via a multiplexer addressed by the program. This function is quite simple from the hardware point of view and introduces some overhead, though acceptable, as we will see later, in software implementation.

For the second pont, we augmented the basic program memory capabilities of the TMS320, since we relied fundamentally on software memory intensive techniques for giving general purpose real time efficiency to our system. In fact where needed we used "in line coding" [21] for increasing the efficiency of program control and "table look up" for increasing the efficiency of some address and data computations. These techniques are of course memory intensive.

In fact we chose not to add special purpose hardware to the system (e.g. for program control or address computation) for FFT only, since the front-end had to be general-purpose.

For our reference application, 4K words of program memory were not enough; hence the standard configuration was increased via bank switching. In fact, two output instructions select bank 1 and bank 2 of program memory respectively; however the first 1K of program memory is independently accessed by this selection and constitutes the bank 0 of program memory: in this way 1K of program memory is lost, but a flexible mailbox area is obtained for interchanging data between programs, independently of program page. This common area contains also, in a small ROM, the bootstrap. Bank 0 can allocate the bootstrap, interrupt programs and data to be exchanged between programs. In the first location of bank 1 and bank 2 we write the main program, which implements a loop. In this main program we can jump from page 1 to page 2 and vice versa, issuing suitable bank switching output instructions. Of course, we jump to the same address of the opposite page, for example from 4FF (hexadecimal) address in bank 2 to 4FF (hexadecimal) address in bank 1. At appropriate points of the main program, it jumps to a suitable subroutine, allocated of course in the same page (for example the routine for FFT computation). In practice the subroutines are allocated into pages 1 and 2, and then the main program is suitably written so as to allocate the calls to subroutines in the same page of the subroutine.

Details of the converter board are as follows. Strictly speaking, only the A/D section is needed for recognition purpose, although a D/A can be useful for prompting messages and diagnostic purposes. Furthermore it adds generality to the architecture for eventual uses in speech coding applications (analysis,synthesis). The board has multiple inputs and outputs for various purposes (microphone, loudspeaker, telephone) and is software reconfigurable via two command registers. By suitably loading these registers, various kind of transfers can be programmed, for example the digital loop, the A/D-D/A loop, the D/A-A/D loop. We can also program the sampling rate (8kHz. , 10kHz. ,12.8 kHz.), the input and output attenuation, and other options.

4. Programming and performance

After initial loading and testing, the master sends the calculated coefficients to the host; in our application we calculate 18 cepstral coefficients each centisecond frame. Given that each coefficient is represented with a word of 16 bits, we have to transmit to the host a net flux of 28.8 Kbit/s. over the serial link.

The computations performed by a slave can be distinguished into input/output programs, done in interrupt mode, and all the remaining computations, done in background mode. Two rotating buffers allocated in program memory are used for inputting samples: in fact, in interrupt mode one buffer is filled with samples which comprise frame n while at the same time the background program uses the contents of the other buffer which contains samples of frame n-2 in order to calculate cepstral coefficients. Of course, at the end of the frame, the contents of the buffer used for computation are not needed anymore, so this buffer becomes the input buffer for frame n+2 and the contents of the other buffer with frame n is used in background mode for computing cepstral coefficients.

Background programs perform:

- transfer of the buffer chosen for computing cepstral coefficients into a common buffer, with pre-emphasis,
- Hamming windowing of these data,
- 256 point complex FFT transform,
- modulus computation,
- band grouping,
- logarithm,
- direct cosine transform (DCT).

Given the data memory constraints of the TMS320, we performed the 256 point complex FFT transform by suitably combining 64 points complex FFT transforms (in fact this is the maximum block that can be contained in 144 words data memory); the elementary butterfly is a 4-points butterfly [18] (see also [19] for an example of efficient implementation on the TMS320).

We calculate logarithms via table look up, that is, the integer part of the logarithm is determined by searching for the most significant "1" in the binary word [20]; then the fractional part is calculated by using the remaining bits, suitably aligned, as addresses to a transform table, which in our case is composed of 128 entries.

Interrupt programs perform the input of the data and the output of calculated coefficients. There are also routines for handling special messages for master to host an vice-versa.

Fig.1 and Fig.2, respectively, summarizes program memory allocation and time performance of the application.

Memory has to be allocated to data and programs. Data in program memory are mainly the two rotating input buffers (maximum length for each: 256 words, for a 20 ms. window of signal sampled at 12.8 kHz.) and the intermediate buffer of 512 words (its double length is due to the fact that for increasing generality the input data for FFT are intended to be complex). All of these buffers together take 1K words of program memory. Tables for windowing data and for calculating logarithms via table look up plus other constants and data (e.g. output buffers) require a maximum of 0.5K words.

The program requiring the most memory is the FFT which is coded "in line" [21] for maximum speeed: this program therefore requires 2.5 K words of memory. All other programs taken together (that is, pre-emphasis, windowing, band grouping, modulus and logarithm computation, and DCT evaluation) occupy 1.9 K words, while the main and interrupting programs take a total of 0.4 k words.

Hence the total memory required is 6.3 K words. This a posteriori justifies the augmentation of the initial 4K words of available program memory to 7K words of bank switched program memory.

We also have to evaluate the computational load of the system in order to verify the fitness of the architecture for the real time implementation of the task. We can distinguish between the computational load due to background programs, independent of the sampling rate, and the computational load due to interrupting programs, proportional to the sampling rate. As we can see from Fig.2, the computational load due to background programs is 13 ms., and that due to interrupt programs is 3.2 ms. at the maximum sampling speed of 12.8 kHz. This comes from the fact that in this case every 78 μs. we use 14 μs. for the acquisition of the sample via interrupt (interrupt polling, loading of the data in the proper buffer location, controlling the advancement of buffer pointer). Hence, in total, we require 16.2 ms. every 20 ms. for the intended computation, which therefore can be done in real time.

We point out also that if data acquisition were done more automatically in hardware (with external FIFO for example) we would not still achieve a significant improvement in performance and in any case we would also need 2 DSP's.

5. Conclusions

The implementation detailed here stresses the limits of the state of the art in digital signal processing. Since we found that for the rather demanding but important task of cepstrum extraction, one DSP was not sufficient, we designed an efficient system based on two DSP, each of which controlling via bank switching an extended program memory, capable of performing the intended task, and of course less demanding tasks, as for example LPC coefficients extraction.

However in cases where the computational load overflows the basic system capability, the system is also expandable both in ripple, both in parallel way.

Acknowledgments

We acknowledge our colleagues M. Oreglia and F. Raineri, who have implemented the FORTRAN simulation of the logarithm via table look-up and who have succesfully compared its performance in a recognition task to the performance obtained via normal logarithm computation.

References

[1] Schafer R.W. and Markel J.D. (editors)
Speech Analysis
IEEE Press 1978

[2] Rabiner L. and Schafer R.
Digital Process of Speech Signals
Prentice Hall 1979

[3] Rabiner L. and Levinson S.E.
Isolated and Connected Word Recognition. Theory and Selected Applications
IEEE Trans. on Communication, vol. COM-29, N.5, May 1981, pp.621-659

[4] Foil J.T. and Johnson D.H.
Text Independent Speaker Recognition
IEEE Communication Magazine, Dec. 1983, pp.22-25

[5] Flanagan J.L., Schroeder M.R., Atal B.S., Crochiere R.E., Jayant N.S. and Tribolet J.M.
Speech Coding
IEEE trans. on Communications, Vol. COM-27, n.4, April 1979, pp.710-737

[6] Bisiani R.
Computer Systems for High Performance Speech Recognition
This issue of NATO Advanced Studies on New Systems and Architectures for Automatic Speeech Recognition and Synthesis, Bonas, July 1984

[7] Oppenheim A.V.
Speech Spectrograms Using the Fast Fourier Transform
IEEE Spectrum, August 1970, pp.57-62

[8] Makhoul J.
Linear Prediction: a Tutorial Review
IEEE Proceedings, vol 63, n.4, April 1975, pp.561-580

[9] Childers D.G. Skinner D.P. and Kemerait R.C.
The Cepstrum: a Guide to Processing
IEEE proceedings, vol. 65, n.10, October 1977, pp.1428-1443

[10] Burky D.
Digital Signal Processing Chips Move off the Designer's Wish
List and Enter into Everyday Use
Electronic Design, May 17,1984, pp.100-122

[11] Crochiere R.E. and Flanagan J.L.
Current Perspectives in Digital Speech
ICC 82- Philadelphia -June 1982

[12] Davis S.B. and Mermelstein P.
Comparison of Parametric Representations of Monosyllabic
Word Recognition in Continuously Spoken Sentences
IEEE trans. ASSP-28 (1980) pp.357-366

[13] Caudel E.R., Hester R.K. and Khen-Sang Tan
A Chip Set for Audio Frequency Digital Signal Processing
ICASSP-82 (Paris) , pp.1065-1068

[14] Daly D.F. and Bergeron L.E.
A Programmable Voice Digitizer Using the T.I. TMS320 Microcomputer
ICASSP-83 (Boston) 11.2 (pp. 475-478)

[15] Mehrgardt S.
Signal Processing with a Fast Microcomputer System
Signal Processing II: Theories and Applications- pp.351-354
EURASIP-1983

[16] Bryden B. and Hassanein H.
Implementation of a Full Duplex 2.4 kbps LPC Vocoder on a Single TMS320
Microprocessor Chip
ICASSP-84 (San Diego) 44.12

[17] Sweitzer S.
A Low Cost FFT Chip Set
ICASSP-84 (San Diego) 44.3

[18] Brigham E.O.
The Fast Fourier Transform
Prentice Hall 1974

[19] Morris L.R.
Digital Signal Processing Software
1983 DSPS

[20] Weste N. , Burr D.J. and Ackland B.D.
Dynamic Time Warp Pattern Matching Using an Integrated Multiprocessor
Array
IEEE trans. on Computers, vol. C-32, n.8 , August 1983, pp.731-744

[21] Morris L.R.
Automatic Generation of Time Efficient Digital Signal Processing Software
IEEE trans. ASSP, vol. ASSP-25, n.1, February 1977, pp.74-79

Data or programs	Kind of data or of program	words	V= variable, F = fixed }area
data	- buffer 1	256	V
"	- buffer 2	256	V
"	- internal buffer	512	V
"	- Hamming window coefficients	256	F
"	- Table for calculating logarithms	128	F
"	- other data and constants	≤128	V, F
data	partial total for data	≤1.5k	V, F
programs	- main and interrupts	0.4k	F
"	- FFT computations	2.5k	F
"	- other computations,	1.9k	F
	that is,		
	- pre-emphasis	≃ 40(*)	
	- windowing	≃ 30(*)	
	- modulus	≃ 132(*)	
	- band grouping	≃ 312(*)	
	- logarithm via table look up	≃ 260(*)	
	- DCT	≃1076(*)	
programs	partial total for programs	4.8k	
	total memory requirements	6.3k	

(*) data already taken into account in partial sum

Fig. 1 - Program memory requirements (in words)

Background or interrupt	Kind of function	Time
background " "	windowing FFT other background computations; that is - pre-emphasis - modulus - band grouping - logarithm - DCT	1 ms 7 ms 5.0 ms 1.4 ms (*) 2.3 ms (*) 0.3 ms (*) 0.6 ms (*) 0.4 ms (*)
background	partial for background	13 ms
interrupt	acquisition at sampling rate 12.8 kHz	3.2 ms
	total for background and interrupt	16.2 ms

(*) data already taken into account in partial sum

Fig. 2 - Time requirements (in ms) per frame

RECONFIGURABLE MODULAR ARCHITECTURE FOR A MAN-MACHINE VOCAL COMMUNICATION SYSTEM IN REAL TIME

D. DOURS - R. FACCA

CERFIA : Université Paul Sabatier
118, route de Narbonne
31062 TOULOUSE - FRANCE

ABSTRACT

The man-machine vocal communication requires autonomous, application-adaptable real time systems, whose cost is both reasonable and proportional to their efficiency.

The realisation of a vocal terminal having such characteristics, makes it necessary to choose a parallel architecture.

We present one architecture which is a combination of parallelism and pipelining. It makes it possible to get the best of the execution parallelism proper to the application class treating a continuous data flow.

It is a modular architecture, staticly reconfigurable, functionally distributed, monitored by the data and with a multi-levelled hierarchic control.

1. INTRODUCTION

We are on the eve on a new era where everyday-extending applications of man-machine vocal communication systems will change working conditions in the most diverse fields. But to avoid limiting their use, we shall have autonomous real time systems, adaptable to application so that their cost should be reasonable and proportional to their efficiency.

As far as we know there is no vocal terminal capable of such performances on the market today. However it would be interesting to have a flexible and modular machine structure, allowing on the one hand to implement in real time methods already existing in the field of man-machine spoken communication, and on the other hand to progressively take into account the

NATO ASI Series, Vol. F16
New Systems and Architectures for Automatic Speech Recognition and Synthesis. Edited by R. De Mori and C.Y. Suen

recent results of fundamental research.

But to have at one's disposal a vocal terminal functioning in real-time which would be at the same time evolutive and of a reasonable cost imposes constraints on the treatment methods as well as on the architecture that supports them.

Once discretised, the vocal signal can be considered as a continuous data flow and its treatment in real-time necessitates a dynamic treatment mode. The dynamic treatment is different from static methods in which the data dynamic is suppressed through their memorisation, which allows backtracking to reactivate treatments. In a dynamic method, the results must appear progressively as the data arrive which implies that only current data and data concerning a recent past can be treated, but that data concerning the future cannot be utilized at all. Speech recognition methods, analysing a vocal signal from left to right without backtraking, after the strategy of the "few best" in which only the most plausible solutions are kept and treated in parallel, are dynamic methods which can be implemented in real-time.

Thus the realization of a vocal terminal imposes constraints in the writing of algorithms and also in the choice of the architecture that executes them.

As soon as some vocal terminals, however elaborate they may be, are being studied, the treatments become so complex that it is no longer possible to execute them in real-time on a classical computer. One must then turn towards parallel structure systems on which several treatments can be run simultaneously.

This has been first attempted with the Cmmp multicomputers network [1] and the CM^* multiprocessors network [2] of Carnegie Melon University on which the Harpy system [3] has been implemented. It seems that the performances of these systems are insufficient for speech recognition in real time. The main reason for the relative failure appears to be the lack of adequation of the architectures used to the considered application. For, as Fennel and Lesser have underlined it, in their study on the measure of the parallelism that can be obtained by simulating the functioning in parallel of their Hearsay II system [4], the treatment speed may decrease when the number of processors increases, if the interconnections do not respect constraints related to the structure of treatments. Thus in order to satisfy these constraints, it seems preferable to define an architecture that takes into account the specificity of the data to be treated and of the derived treatments, rather than try to adapt the application to a predefined machine structure.

Overspecialized architectures, though they offer the advantage of being simple to implement, should be avoided, because their rigid structure does not allow future further system evolutions. One must then turn towards the definition of an evolutive modular structure.

This has been the aim of the "Architecture des Systèmes Parallèles" team, a section of the "Traitement Automatique de la Parole" group from the C.E.R.F.I.A. laboratory in Toulouse, whose studies have been first the definition and then the realization of a Reconfigurable Modular Architecture whose features meet the defined requirements.

2. RECONFIGURABLE MODULAR ARCHITECTURE

The discretized vocal signal can be considered as a continuous data flow which must be treated in transactional mode. The functional decomposition of this type of application brings to light treatments without any relation with each other, and treatments depending on the preceding ones only through the results obtained by them. Thus we have an application in which a continuous data flow may be treated by going through a series of stages each one being in charge of one part of the treatment. The successive pieces of information take each other's place according to the producer-consumer mode.

To define the architecture we took into account the specificity of the application. This architecture is indeed adaptable to the functional decomposition of the application to be implemented. The machine is built as a "Kit" starting from basic elements which are associated as required by the application.

We shall not give here any further detail about the architecture [5] and the physical realization [6] - [7], we shall only describe the general structure of a treatment processor as well as the way it works and the principle of an application implementation on this architecture.

2.1. STRUCTURE OF A TREATMENT PROCESSOR

The structure of a treatment processor is defined inductively from basic elements which are :

- a treatment processor (TP)
- an exchange processor (EP)
- a control processor (CP).

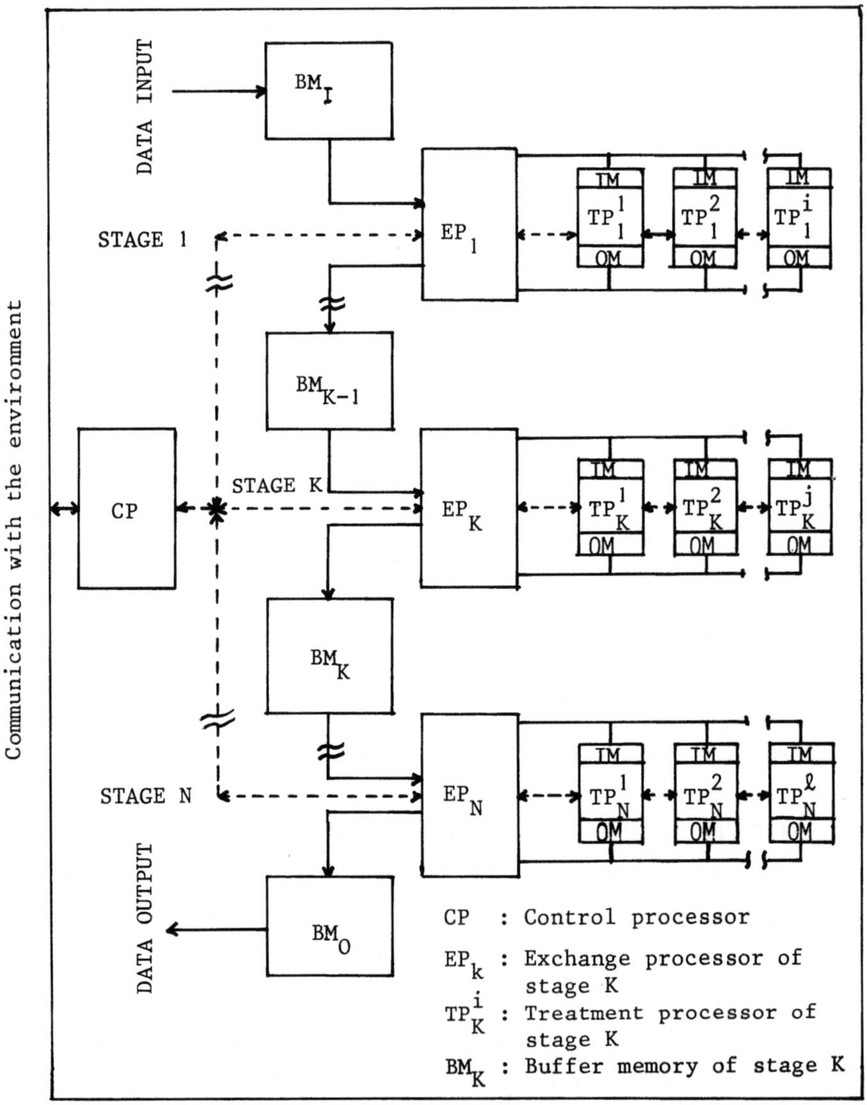

Fig. 1 - Functional structure

These elements are interconnected according to the topology defined in fig. 1. Treatment processors of the same level are linked to an exchange processor and constitute one treatment stage. Each processor ignores the other's presence and communicates only with the exchange processor. The communication is realized by a ring network for events and by two memories : the input memory (IM) in which the data to be treated are stored and the output memory (OM) in which the results to be transmitted are stored.

The distribution system in a stage is organized around two common buses, one for the input and one for the output, which allows a total parallelism for these two types of transfers.

A buffer memory (BM), with a double access port in mutual exclusion, makes it possible to store the data between two consecutive stages. The exchange processors are linked to the control processor by a ring network.

2.2. WORKING OF A TREATMENT PROCESSOR

When a treatment processor has finished carrying out the order for which it is specialized, it sends a data transfer request to the associated exchange processor and then waits. The latter transmits the request to the control processor which checks if the conditions for transfer are fulfilled.

For a stage K, these conditions are :

- input transfer possible if data have been stored in BM_{K-1} by EP_{K-1}
- output transfer possible if the data stored in BM_K have been taken by EP_{K+1}.

The control processor sends back an acknowledgement message to the exchange processor indicating the possible transfers. When receiving the message the exchange processor carries out the data transfers according to a description which specifies the links between two consecutive treatment. Afterwards, the exchange processor communicates with the treatment processor so that the task can be carried out again. Once all the data transfers in the stage have been carried out, the exchange processor informs the control processor so that the state progress, between the stages, can be updated.

When BM_I is empty or when BM_O has received some data, the control processor sends a message to the environment indicating either that some results are available or that some other data are required to carry out another treatment.

2.3. IMPLEMENTATION OF AN APPLICATION

The communication-execution-synchronisation separation simplifies the task of the user wanting to implement an application on this architecture. Indeed, he has to do only with the execution part and the descriptive processing relation between the different treatments. The synchronization and the communication are monitored by the system.

For a given application, the machine configuration principle is as follows :

Each functional task of the application is associated to a treatment processor. These processors are connected with exchange processor to make an upper level treatment processor.

The grouping of these processors must be made according to the topology defined by fig. 1 and adapted to the task to be executed. This approach is inductive. At the lowest level, to a so called elementary task (there is no subtler decomposition of the task) is associated an elementary treatment processor. At the highest level, a treatment processor is connected to I/O peripheral devices adapted to the application. For example, in the case of a vocal terminal monitoring an industrial process, a microphone and a loud-speaker, will be found for the vocal input and output, a specialized board for the system command and control, interface cards for the process control.

An elementary treatment processor is built with a MC 6809 microprocessor and its accessory circuits. Furthermore it has an input memory (I.M) and an output memory (O.M) a 128 K bytes (16 × 8k pages) memory where it is possible to plug either PROMs or RAMs (indifferently). A parallel I/O line makes it possible to connect specialized cards (FFT, LPC, filters,...) or cards to interface with peripheral devices or data processing systems. The treatment processor then behaves as a host computer.

When the machine is configured, a program is implanted on the PROMs, this program being associated to a treatment as well as the descriptive precising the connections between the different treatments. The control system then adapts itself automatically according to the number of implanted treatment processors and to the chosen configuration.

3. ADVANTAGES OF THIS ARCHITECTURE

The creation of a reconfigurable modular architecture which is adapted to the functional decomposition of the treatments allows the treatments to be carried out faster by increasing the degree of parallelism.

In effect, in this structure, a data flow undergoes a treatment by going through a series of stages, each of which being responsible for carrying out one part of the treatment, the information moving successively through the stages.

It should be noted that this type of parallelism can be particularly well adapted to the treatment of a continuous data flow.

The solution used here for processor interconnection reduces the complexity of the system from the point of view of topology, communication protocols, control and task sequencing.

The principles used here simply regulate the problems linked to parallelism :

- control of the flow of information,
- conflicts for access to the same unit,
- precedence and synchronization conflits.

The repetitive structure at all levels has the double advantage of modularity and flexibility. It is possible to increase the power of the system or to introduce new treatment algorithms without modifying the communication system. Furthermore, the repetitive structure has evident economic advantages since it minimizes the cost of the development and commercialization of a system designed with a small numbers of different cards.

4. CONCLUSION

The reconfigurable modular architecture which has just been described is that of a functionally distributed system, directed by the data and with hierarchy control over several levels.

The ease with which such a system can be realised allows us to think that there will be widespread developments of adapted systems making full use of the parallelism of one class of applications.

This is the reason why the CERFIA Laboratory thought of realising a parallel machine, based on this architecture, adapted to real time speech treatment. A prototype is now operational and the realization of a real time recognition system of isolated multi-speakers is in its final phase. The realisation of a real time analysis and recognition system for continuous speech (ARIAL project) is being studied. But this architecture can be used too for other applications, whether for image treatment, robot command or also in parallel compilation and more generally in any application treating a continuous data flow in real time.

REFERENCES

1 W.A. WULF, X.B. BELL : "C.mmp, a Multi-Mini-Processor" ; Proceeding AFIPS. FJCC. 1972

2 R.J. SWAN : "The Switching Structure and Adressing Architecture of an Extensible Multiprocessor" ; CM*, PH.D. Thesis, Carnegie Mellon University. 1978.

3 B.T. LOWERE : "The Harpy Speech Recognition System" ; PH.D, Thesis, Carnegie Mellon University, Pittsburg, USA. 1976.

4 R.D. FENNELL, V.R. LESSER : "Parallelism in Artificial Intelligence Problem Solving : A case Study of Hearsay II", IEEE Trans. Computer, Vol C26, n° 2, pp 98-111. 1977.

5 D. DOURS, R. FACCA, M. DALMAU : "ARMOR : Architecture Modulaire Reconfigurable pour le traitement d'un flot continu de données en temps réel ; "Rapport de contrat ATP-CNRS. 1983.

6 A. ALSUBAIDI, S. SOULAIMAN : "Système Multi-microprocesseur pour le traitement d'un Flot Continu de Données. Thèses de 3ème cycle, U.P.S. Toulouse. 1981.

7 M. DALMAU : "Système d'Exploitation pour la machine multiprocesseur ARMOR. Thèse de 3ème cycle, U.P.S. Toulouse, 1984.

A SURVEY OF ALGORITHMS & ARCHITECTURE FOR CONNECTED SPEECH RECOGNITION

D. Wood
GEC Research Laboratories
Hirst Research Centre
Wembley
U.K.
HA9 7PP

ABSTRACT

The paper surveys dynamic programming based connected speech recognition algorithms and architectures. A discussion of the computational complexities of the algorithms is given and suggests that the single pass algorithm of Bridle et al is the most suitable for real time operation. Currently available architectures for dynamic programming are discussed and it is shown that these are not suitable for the single pass algorithm in their present form. An alternative linear systolic architecture is described which is capable of matching vocabularies of up to 25000 words, in real time, using the single pass algorithm. The linear array has simpler data flows and uses fewer processing elements than most existing systolic structures.

NATO ASI Series, Vol. F16
New Systems and Architectures for Automatic Speech Recognition and Synthesis. Edited by R. De Mori and C.Y. Suen

INTRODUCTION

Dynamic time warping (DTW) has become a popular technique for pattern matching in some speech recognition systems. It has found application in both isolated and connected word recognition and good recognition accuracies have been reported. However, the DTW algorithm has a very high computational requirement and this can be a limiting factor when designing high vocabularies systems for real time operation. In such systems it becomes necessary to optimize computational throughput by exploring special purpose hardware structures and matching them to current algorithms. In this way, the most optimal combination can be identified.

DTW algorithms have a high degree of parallelism which can be exploited by using regular (or systolic) hardware structures. Over recent years, a variety of different options for systolic architectures have been proposed, such as Burr et al [1], Ciminiera et al [2] and Banatre et al [3]. These architectures have application in both isolated and connected speech recognition but vary with respect to the degree that parallelism and pipelining have been exploited. This leads to solutions with differing hardware requirements and complexities. It is apparent, when a global view is taken, that some architectures are only useful with certain algorithms and that some combinations may not be optimal in terms of number of processing elements, throughput and control complexity. It is important that the algorithm and architecture are considered together, the choice of algorithm can significantly affect the architecture (and vice versa!).

To give an architecture which is computationally efficient, simple to control and using the minimum of hardware requires that the right algorithm is chosen. This is reasonably straightforward with isolated word recognition but not so with connected word recognition because of its significantly higher complexity. A number of connected word matching strategies have been proposed, such as Banatre et al [3], Myers & Rabiner [4], Sakoe [5] and Bridle et al [6] which have differing architectural implications. A good algorithm is one which leads to a simple architecture that is as independent as possible of vocabulary and application. Computational flow should be simple and not too dependent on boundary functions (global path constraints) since this leads to simpler control.

The following sections summarize the considerations pertaining to the choice of algorithms and architecture comparing some of the available techniques. The first section discusses some of the alternative matching strategies with emphasis on their hardware implications. The second section discusses the available architectures with emphasis on their applicability to the algorithms and their practicality. The third section briefly describes an alternative, systolic architecture which implements Bridle's et al algorithm and shows that a very high throughput is possible. The final section concludes the paper with a summary of the most important points arising from this discussion.

ALGORITHMIC CONSIDERATIONS

The correct choice of algorithm is important since this can affect the complexity of the final implementation. This choice is not so straightforward in connected speech recognition because of the variety of matching strategies which can be employed. Matching strategy has a direct effect on computational complexity and the amenability of an algorithm for a hardware implementation. This section considers four algorithms covering a broad range of matching strategies and briefly assesses their suitability for an efficient hardware implementation.

Sakoe's [4] matching strategy, depicted in Figure 1, involves a two level process, the first level being word level matching, the second level being phrase level matching. Word level matching attempts to isolate the best word decision over each possible segment of the input speech. Segment boundaries are determined using an adjustment window. Phrase level matching uses the word level scores to determine the best concatenated sequence of word decisions over all possible concatenations and lengths.

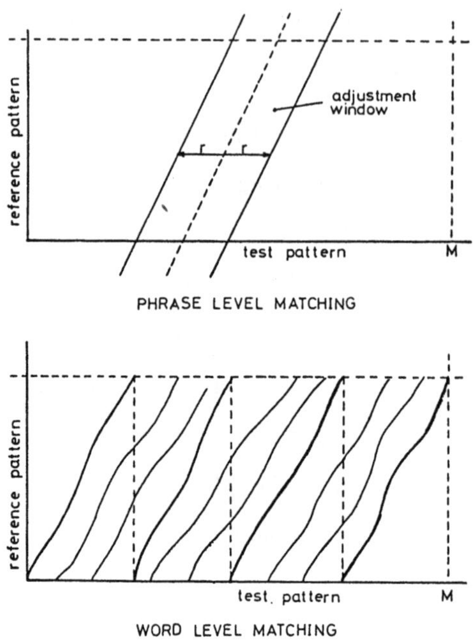

Figure 1: Sakoe's Matching Strategy

Myers' & Rabiner's [5] strategy, depicted in Figure 2, using a level building process. The number of levels is dependent on the maximum phrase length. Each level corresponds with an isolated word matching which is computed 'in strips'. The best scoring template ending at each strip is found and the scores used as initial conditions into the next level. Thus matching proceeds from level to level building up a series of word decisions at each level. Phrase level matching is implicit in the algorithm and the best phrase can be traced back from the end. A boundary function is used to restrict word level matching to a reasonable area of the warp grid.

Bridle's et al [6] algorithm, depicted in Figure 3, computes the best concatenated sequence of templates in a single pass through the input sequence. The strategy assumes templates can start and end at any input frame. Transitions between templates are from the end of the best scoring template ending at one frame to the start of all templates in the next frame (for a simple syntax). Phrase level matching is implicit in the process and the best sequence

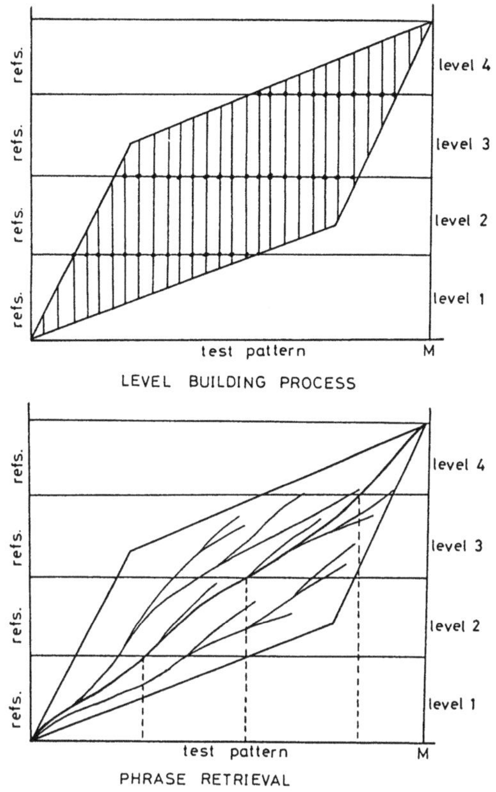

Figure 2: Myers' Matching Strategy

can be found by tracing back from the end.

Banatre's et al [3] algorithm, depicted in Figure 4, is similar to Sakoe's except that word level matching is not restricted by an adjustment window (although it can be). The vocabulary is matched to the input sequence and the best scoring template between a start point and a range of endpoints is found for all possible start and end points. The range of endpoints is determined by the dimensions of an isolated word warp grid. This grid slides through the input sequence in a similar fashion to the adjustment window of Sakoe's algorithm. Phrase level matching is done separately and concatenates the word decisions to form the best word sequence. Phrase length need not be specified.

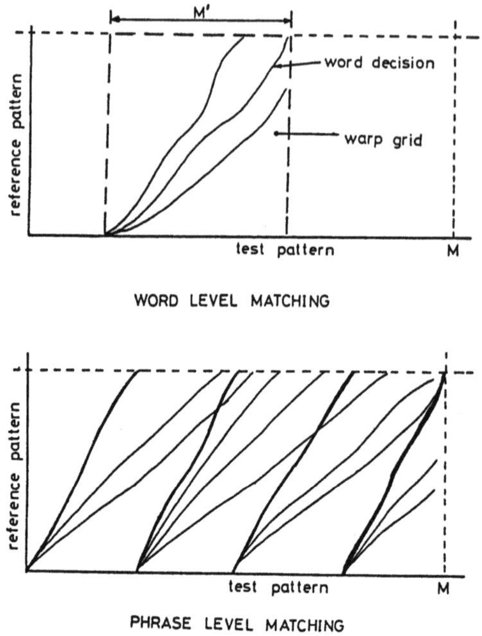

Figure 3: Bridle's Matching Strategy

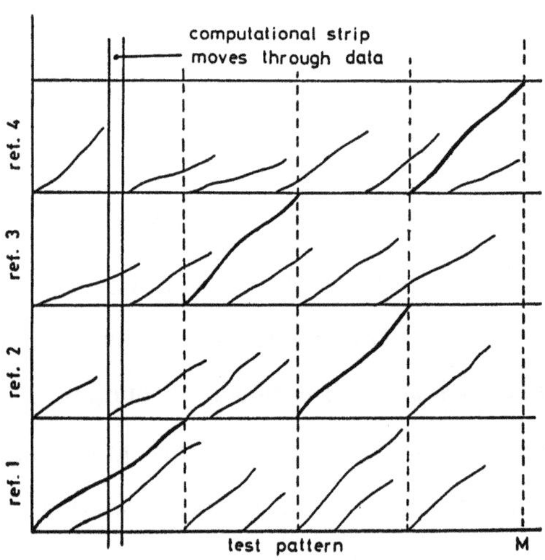

Figure 4: Banatre's Matching Strategy

The matching rate of a connected speech recognition system is dependent on how fast isolated word matching can be done. This depends on the matching strategy. Sakoe's algorithm (in 'real time mode') computes word decisions backwards from an end frame to a range of start frames given by the adjustment window. The width of the adjustment window depends on the template length. In hardware it is necessary to fix this width so that the largest template can be accommodated. A number of previous input frames must be saved and the same interframe distances re-calculated a number of times. This leads to computational inefficiency. A further restriction is that a maximum phrase length must be specified.

Myers' algorithm computes word level matches over varying lengths of the input sequence depending on the level. This is because isolated word matching is done in strips and the number of strips varies because of the boundary function. This leads to vocabulary dependent variability which is unsuitable in hardware for control complexity reasons. A further problem, especially for real time operation, is that a section of the input sequence must be entered before matching can start. Some interframe distance calculations are repeated since levels 'overlap', this leads to computational inefficiency. The removal of the boundary function may remove some of these problems. Finally, the specification of a phrase length introduces a further restriction.

Bridle's algorithm is perhaps the most efficient since interframe distances are only computed and used once. Input frames need not be saved since a single sweep is used and it is not necessary to return to an earlier section of input. Computational flow is sequential which can further simplify hardware.

Banatre's algorithm is as computationally expensive as Sakoe's algorithm since the same interframe distance must be calculated and used a number of times. The warp grid dimensions are determined by the length of the longest reference, this determines the number of PEs required. Input frames must also be saved.

ARCHITECTURAL CONSIDERATIONS

The choice of architecture has the most effect on the size of the final implementation, i.e. number of processing elements (PEs). However, the algorithm can also influence this by restricting the applicability of each structure. The final choice of algorithm and architecture should lead to a solution with a low number of PEs and simple control complexity but still offer high computational throughput. This section considers the mapping of the algorithm into an architecture using the architectures described by Burr et al [1], Ciminiera et al [2] and Banatre et al [3] as examples.

Banatre [3] described an architecture to implement the systolic algorithm, which is based on similar ideas to Burr et al [1]. This is shown in Figure 5 and

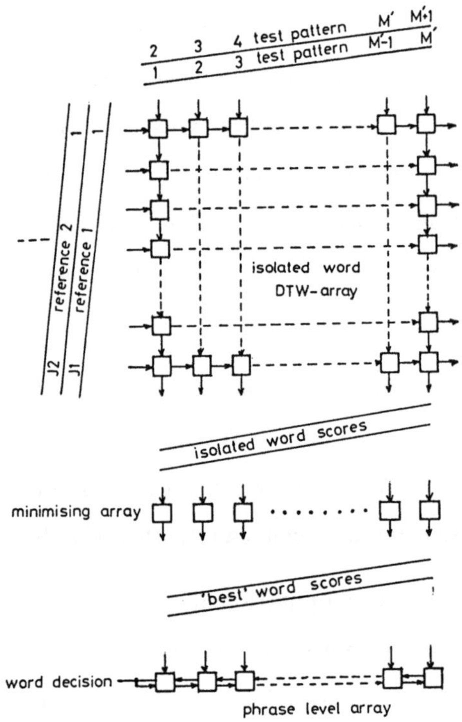

Figure 5: Banatre's Architecture

consists of the three arrays. The first is a two dimensional DTW array whose dimensions are determined by the height and width of the warp grid, these depend on the length of the longest template, Rmax. This DTW array calculates the isolated word matches. The second array takes the isolated word scores and finds the minimum over all templates. The third array computes the phrase level match. The disadvantage with this architecture is that it requires a huge number of PEs, approximately Rmax.M′, where M′ is the width of the grid, and also requires three types of processing element to be designed. If there are V vocabulary words then the time taken to complete the match is 0 (VM) 'operations', where M is the length of the input sequence and one operation is a distance calculation and a DP match. A reduced array (say a single strip) would require Rmax PEs but the time taken to complete the match would be $0(VM^2)$ operations. The number of PEs can also be reduced by removing those which lie outside of an adjustment window but this does not affect time complexity. However, the architecture integrates phrase level and word level matching quite well with a very regular data flow but is only suitable for Banatre's algorithm, and possibly Sakoe's.

Sakoe's [4] algorithm would probably be best computed using a single diagonal of processing elements as proposed by Ciminiera et al [2] since this is more appropriate to calculation of isolated word matches using an adjustment window. A further array must be added which minimizes the DP scores between start and endpoints and computes the phrase level match. The width of the window, and hence the diagonal, is (2r+1) where r is a fraction, x, of the length of the longest reference. The phrase level array would probably consist of the same number of PEs. A possible configuration is given in Figure 6. The time taken for the architecture to match V vocabulary words to an input sequence of M frames is 0((1+x)RmaxMV) operations, i.e. much slower than Banatre's architecture, but using fewer PEs. Data management and control could be a problem since the architecture must 'move through the data' hence the correct timing must be provided.

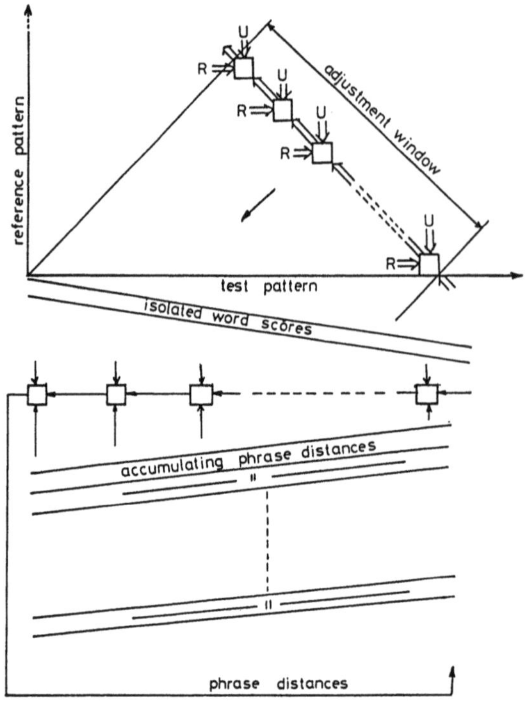

Figure 6: Possible Architecture for Sakoe's Algorithm

Myers' algorithm is practically unimplementable (in hardware) in its standard form. However, with the boundary function removed the ideas of Burr et al [1] may be appropriate here. A number of possible array configurations have been described by Burr, the most amenable to this algorithm seems to be a horizontally moving reduced array, see Figure 7. This sweeps out each level taking input conditions from the lower level and passing final scores to the higher level. Some means of minimissing the 'strip' scores over all templates must be incorporated. The number of sweeps is equal to the number of levels. The array height is governed by the length of the longest template and the width is two processing elements, giving a total of 2Rmax PEs. The time taken for a complete match is 0(1VM) operations where 1 is the number of levels. Control and data management could be expensive since the architecture requrires that

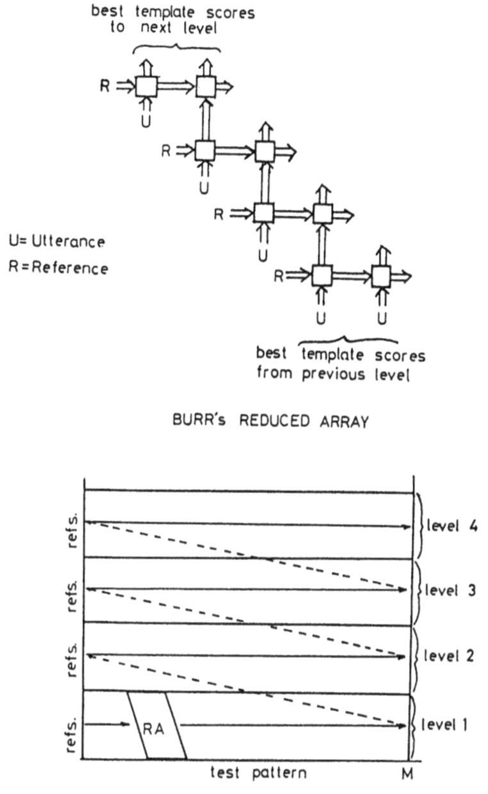

Figure 7: Possible Architecture for Myers' Algorithm

frame interactions are correctly synchronized. A further disadvantage is that the whole input sequence must be saved.

Bridle's algorithm is more sequential than the others because of its single pass nature. The pass is done one input frame at a time hence true real time operation is possible if all calculations can be done between successive input frames. None of the architectures proposed by Burr et al [1] or Ciminiera et al [2] appear suitable for this algorithm since they require the whole or part of the input sequence to be saved. The next section describes an alternative architecture and shows it to outperform those considered above.

SYSTOLIC ARCHITECTURE FOR THE SINGLE PASS ALGORITHM

The single pass algorithm of Bridle's et al [6] requires an architecture which can compute path scores using only the present input frame. Square array architectures or single diagonals are not suitable since these require a number of input frames in the calculation. This section describes such an architecture and compares its performance.

The architecture is a linear chain of PEs, shown in Figure 8, which has a

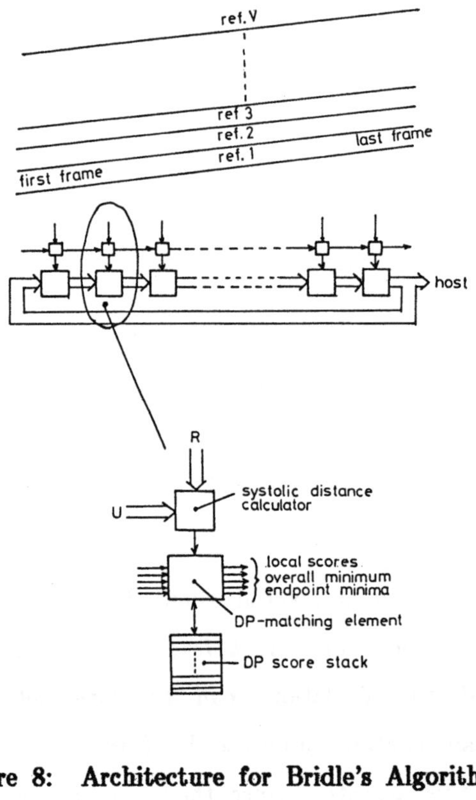

Figure 8: Architecture for Bridle's Algorithm

length determined by the longest template (Rmax). The input frame enters the left hand end of the array and meets with each frame of the reference templates as it is passed along the chain. Template frames enter in reference serial/frame parallel starting with the first frame of each template. At each PE, the interframe distance is calculated and added to the local minimum. The score is then stacked for use at the next input frame. The length of the stack is the same as the number of vocabulary words and all memory is sequentially accessed. The score is also used to find an overall minimum score and a minimum endpoint score (if the present template frame is an endpoint). Each PE performs the same operations simultaneously and passes local scores overall minimum and endpoint scores to the next PE on the right for updating the next frame. When all templates frames have passed through, the last PE contains the overall minimum and the endpoint minimum. These are passed to the left hand end of the chain as initial conditions to start templates at the next input frame. Tracepoint labels are also passed to host to aid phrase retrieval. Matching rate is independent of the number of frames in each reference. The architecture is described in more detail in [7].

The highest performance results when fixed hardware is used although this is very restrictive on the algorithm's 'internal' flexibility. The slowest computation is distance calculation which can be speeded up in the case of city block and squared Euclidean, using architectures similar to those described in [8]. The PE can thus be split up into a special purpose distance calculator plus a DP-matcher. The systolic array distance calculator can compute the distance in a time independent of the data dimensionality. However, time is dependent on data bit precision. The DP matcher must complete its calculations between successive distances. Any structure can be used assuming it is fast enough. A serial structure interfaces well with the distance calculator but requires a fixed algorithm. A parallel, ALU based architecture interfaces well with the stack memory and offers some algorithmic flexibility. In either case, latency is not important since the architecture operates sequentially. The architecture computes the complete match in a time of 0(VM) operations. Only V matches must be performed between successive input frames. If data widths are B bit then distances can be calculated in 2B cycles.

Assuming a 20 ms frame rate and B=8 bits then a vocabulary of approximately 12500 words can be matched at a 10 MHz clock frequency. With a serial structure it may be possible to push this to 20 MHz hence giving a maximum matching rate of 25000 words. Thus it can be seen that this architecture outperforms those described in the previous section on a throughput per processing element basis.

CONCLUSION

This paper has shown there is more to defining hardware for real time connected speech recognition systems than just specifying an architecture. It is not much use specifying an architecture with a high computational throughput which is then wasted on a computationally inefficient algorithm. This means that a large number of PEs must be used or low matching rates result. It is unfortunate, for instance, that Banatre et al, having developed a good regular architecture for the connected speech problem chose an inefficient algorithm to work from. For a solution which has a low number of procesing elements, low control and data management complexity, and high performance both the algorithm and the architecture must be carefully chosen.

A comparison of the algorithms shows that Bridle's, Sakoe's and Banatre's are suitable for true real time operation. Myers' algorithm requires the whole of the input sequence to be stored before matching commences. Bridle's algorithm, however, is much more efficient than Sakoe's and Banatre's since all the matching computations use only a single input frame, hence no computations are repeated. Sakoe's and Banatre's algorithm, requires that a number of previous input frames are stored since matching is 'guided' by an adjustment window or a warp grid. Banatre's, Sakoe's and Myers' algorithms also repeat inter-frame distance computations, the former two being the worse examples. Myers' algorithm also suffers because matching is guided by a boundary function which cannot be efficiently mapped into hardware. A final restriction imposed by Myers' and Sakoe's algorithms is that a maximum phrase length must be specified. Hence it can be concluded that Bridle's single pass algorithm is the most computationally efficient and the least dependent on vocabulary and application. The single pass nature allows simple and easily controllable sequential operation with low storage requirements (only one DP score and word link per frame must be stored).

A comparison of architectures shows that square arrays as proposed by Burr and also Banatre have the dual disadvantages of only implementing the less efficient algorithms and requiring inordinately large numbers of processing elements. Full size square arrays not only restrict template length (as do other hardware structures) but also restrict input sequence length. Reduced arrays and 'diagonals' of processing elements as proposed by Burr and also Ciminiera require fewer PEs and are less restrictive on input sequence length. However, the application of these types of array is still restricted to the less efficient algorithms and also require increased data management complexity to ensure that frames interact correctly. All the above structures require the input pattern to be stored over a number of input frames or the whole sequence.

Since none of the hardware structures proposed to date are suitable for implementing Bridle's algorithm an alternative structure based on a linear systolic array has been described. The architecture efficiently maps the sequential nature of the algorithm and is capable of very high throughput, i.e. 25000 words at input frame rates.

Such high throughputs suggest applications in systems with high computational requirements, such as:

(a) systems using multiple templates per word for (limited) speaker independence.
(b) systems for multi-channel operation using a single, multiplexed recognizer
(c) systems which require the tracking of sub-optimal paths for improved accuracy
(d) combinations of the above.

Incidentally, if very high throughput is not important, the length of the chain may be reduced with a proportional reduction in throughput. Other applications of this architecture are in isolated word recognition and string matching using the Levenshtein distance.

REFERENCES

1. D. J. Burr, B. D. Ackland, N. Weste, "Array configurations for dynamic time warping" IEEE Trans. ASSP, Vol. 32, No. 1, pp. 119-127, February 1984.
2. L. Ciminiera, C. Dematini, A. Serra, "A VLSI structure for pattern matching" Proc. 6th Int. Conf. on Pattern Recognition, 1982, pp. 380-383.
3. J. P. Banatre, P. Frison, P. Quinton, "A systolic algorithm for connected word recognition" Proc. ICASSP, pp. 1243-1246, 1982.
4. H. Sakoe, "Two-level DP-matching — a dynamic programming-based pattern matching algorithm for connected word recognition", IEEE Trans. ASSP, Vol. 27, No. 6, pp. 588-595, December 1979.
5. C. S. Myers, L. R. Rabiner, "A level building dynamic time warping algorithm for connected word recognition", IEEE Trans. ASSP, Vol. 29, No. 2, pp. 284-297, April 1981.
6. J. S. Bridle, M. D. Brown, R. M. Chamberlain, "An algorithm for connected word recognition", Proc. ICASSP, pp. 899-902, 1982.
7. D. Wood, R. B. Urquhart, "An architecture for a connected speech recognition algorithm" Proc. 7th Int. Conf. on Pattern Recognition, pp. 1197-1200, 1984.
8. R. B. Urquhart, D. Wood, "Efficient bit-level systolic arrays for inner product computation", GEC Journal of Research, Vol. 2, No. 1, 1984, pp. 52-55.

KNOWLEDGE-BASED AND EXPERT SYSTEMS IN AUTOMATIC SPEECH RECOGNITION

Jean-Paul Haton

CRIN - Université de Nancy 1

B. P. 239

54506 Vandoeuvre, France

I INTRODUCTION

Artificial Intelligence (AI) has recently advanced to the point that practical applications are now existing in several domains. Most of the results obtained are not due to general problem solving techniques but to the use of specific, domain-dependent knowledge. Formalizing and incorporating specific knowledge into a system makes it possible to reach the level of expertise comparable to that of a human expert in some specialized field. Such knowledge-based and expert systems have been extensively used in various domains like chemistry, medicine, geology, etc. The basic idea in these systems is to clearly distinguish between the knowledge base which usually incorporates rules and meta-rules about the domain of expertise and the control structures which manipulate this knowledge. That ensures great modularity and flexibility and makes it easy to modify and update a system [11].

This approach is very attractive in all cases where knowledge is incomplete or ill-formalized and where it does not exist algorithmic solutions. Automatic Speech Recognition and Understanding (ASR) obviously represents a typical example in which, moreover, it is necessary to combine many diverse knowledge sources.

NATO ASI Series, Vol. F16
New Systems and Architectures for Automatic Speech
Recognition and Synthesis. Edited by R. De Mori and C. Y. Suen

This chapter is devoted to the discussion of the impact of knowledge-based approaches in ASR. In section II the principles and interest of knowledge-based and expert systems are briefly exposed. The areas of ASR in which these approaches could be used are also presented.

Section III concerns the use of expert systems at the phonetic and phonological processing levels whereas section IV addressses the more general problem of designing and implementing an ASR system by using knowledge-based architectures.

II KNOWLEDGE-BASED SYSTMES

II.1. Basic principles

It is now widely admitted — although it has not been the case for years — that the automatic recognition and interpretation of a spoken sentence can only be achieved through the optimal use of a large number of very diverse knowledge sources, from acoustics to pragmatics. A similar situation can be found in others domains of AI such as computer vision or natural language understanding. The cooperation and synchronization of as many knowledge sources as available make it possible to emit and/or cancel hypotheses until reaching the final solution, according to the general paradigm of hypothesis-and-test.

It is not easy to give a definition of knowledge as useful in a knowledge-based system. A first characteristic is that knowledge is highly domain-dependent. Abstractly speaking knowledge is made up of descriptions, relationships and procedures corresponding to a given domain of activity. In practice knowledge can take many diverse forms. It roughly consists of the symbolic descriptions of "objects" and their relationships in a domain together with the procedures and heuristics for manipulating these descriptions. We will see later on that a very popular and efficient way of expressing and manipulating knowledge is under the form of simple production rules.

Three main problems are associated with the design of knowledge-based systems in any domain:

- *knowledge acquisition* — it is very difficult and time-consuming to extract knowledge from human experts. This remains an open problem in AI and the best that can be hoped is a computer-assisted system since a fully automatic acquisition of human knowledge by a system seems far ahead. Knowledge acquisition necessitates a long and careful interaction between the expert(s) and a knowledge engineer. Efficient schemes have been designed in specific domains, e.g. in speech spectrogram reading. The use of an expert system can be of valuable help since that makes it easier to test and update the knowledge, to detect contradictions, etc. In the case of speech recognition knowledge acquisition implies collecting and observing large data bases. This work is made easier by the use of dedicated computer facilities such as automatic segmentation or semi-automatic labelling of the speech wave, digital spectrograms display, etc.,

- *knowledge representation* — one is usually faced with the two complementary problems of what is to be represented and how. Classical AI representation techniques such as logic, semantic nets, production rules can be used, according to the peculiarities of the domain. An important aspect is the necessity of incorporating a certain amount of meta-knowledge, i.e. knowledge about knowledge. Meat-knowledge constitutes a fundamental aspects of human expertise and it is directly related to the reasoning strategies used by the expert,

- *control structures* — this point is related to the manipulation of knowledge and of its optimal use in order to solve a given problem. Once again techniques developed in other areas of AI can be used successfully.

II.2. An overview of expert systems

Instead of the usual two-tiered organization (data structures and program) knowledge-based and expert systems introduce a more flexible, three-level structure: data, knowledge and control structures. These systems therefore introduce a clear separation between knowledge and the programs which manipulate it.

Figure 1 illustrates the overall organization of such a system.

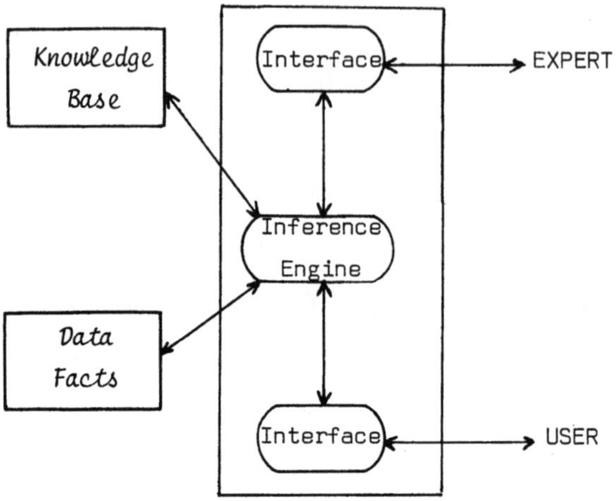

Figure 1 Architecture of a Knowledge-Based System

The data level stores a priori knowledge and facts about the domain and the particular problem to solve together with pieces of information which have been gained or deduced during the problem-solving process.

The control structures, or inference engine, constitute the heart of the system. They use the knowledge available in the knowledge base and carry out inferences from this knowledge.

The optimal use of an expert system necessitates friendly interfaces with the experts on one hand and the users on the other hand. Since these people are usually not specialists of computers these interfaces integrate a certain amount of natural language processing.

The ability of such systems to solve a problem is mainly related to the quality of the knowledge base. This knowledge is usually represented in a declarative form by using one of the classical representation schemes. It is often given under the form of "pattern-invoked" operators. At each time the applicable operators are applied and produce changes in the knowledge base. This process is repeated until the problem is solved. Such pattern-directed knowledge invocation has proven to be very efficient in a number of applications. The operators we have just introduced may be complex programs. However the most popular form for operators is the so-called production rule paradigm [6]. A production rule is of the form

IF Condition THEN Action

when "Condition" generally consists of a conjunction of predicates and "Action" means a change in the knowledge base, i.e. the current state of the problem. Production rules make it possible to split a complex expertise into a large number of small knowledge parcels. This formalism presents several advantages: modularity, readability, ease of modifying or updating, possibility for the system to explain its reasoning. Moreover, a human expert often seems to use a production rule scheme while reasoning. The method presents however some drawbacks: production rules are not very powerful in terms of speed and efficiency, at least with present, general-purpose computers and it is sometimes difficult, if not impossible, to split knowledge in a particular domain into very small pieces.

The control structures of knowledge-based systems use classical AI techniques that can be classified into three categories:

— state-space search including backtracking and the use of heuristics in order to speed up the search,

— problem reduction which consists of decomposing a problem into several subproblems that can be solved separately; this technique was used in the MYCIN expert system for medicine [23],

— constraints propagation, related to state-space search but without the necessity of backtracking since each partial solution must satisfy the various constraints which appear during the rule applications. EL, an expert system in electricity, uses this kind of control structures [25].

Another issue in expert system design concerns the chaining of rules. There are basically two different solutions:

— a forward reasoning scheme which consists of starting from the data and of making successive deductions with the knowledge base (in case of production rules that corresponds to a left-to-right application of these rules),

— a backward reasoning scheme which consists of starting from the goal to be reached and of defining subgoals in relation with the technique of problem reduction.

It is often interesting to combine these two basic schemes in order to improve the overall efficiency of the system.

The development of a knowledge-based or expert system is a long and difficult task. Besides the problem already mentioned of the automatization of knowledge acquisition this development itself necessitates the use of specific, sophisticated tools. Several tools already exists and are widely used, such as EMYCIN, OPS 5, AGE, HEARSAY III, etc. However a large amount of work is still needed in this area.

II.3. Applications to Automatic Speech Recognition

Automatic Speech Recognition, like other fields of AI such as computer vision, is characterized by a close interaction between a low-level processing, i.e. the acoustic-phonetic decoding, which represents the perceptive aspect of the problem, and a high-level (linguistic) interpretation which represents the cognitive aspect (figure 2). Knowledge engineering techniques can be helpful at both levels even though they must be considered carefully and constitute by no ways a miraculous solution for yet unsolved problems. In fact these techniques can be considered at two levels:

— they represent a flexible tool for solving specific problems especially when human experts possess an explicit knowledge about the domain (e.g. acoustic-phonetic decoding, phonology, prosody, etc.),

— they provide a general framework for designing the architecture of a speech recognition system, e.g. blackboard-like systems, production systems, expert societies, etc.

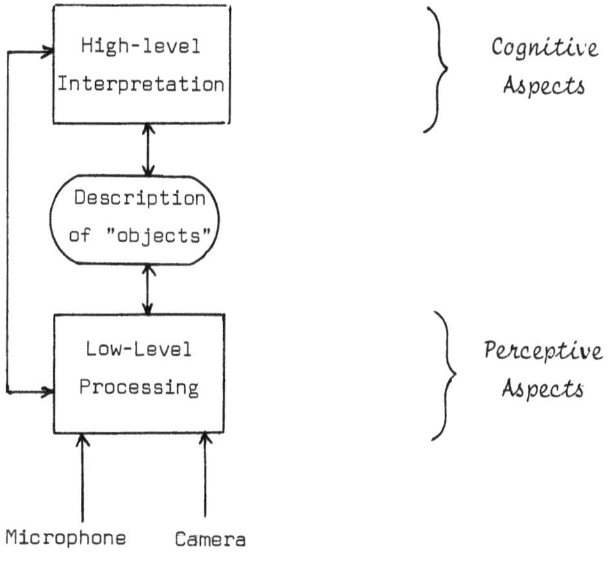

Figure 2 Principles of a Computer Understanding System (Speech or Vision).

We will now review with more details these different aspects.

III PHONETIC AND PHONOLOGICAL ASPECTS OF SPEECH RECOGNITION

III.1. Acoustic-Phonetic Decoding of Speech

The acoustic-phonetic decoding of speech, i.e. the mapping of the acoustic speech wave into discrete phonetic units, constitutes a major bottleneck in the design of large scale speech recognition systems, especially in multi-speaker environment. Prototype-based approaches using classical pattern-matching methods have proved to be unsufficient in order to obtain a high accuracy. On the other hand a rule-based recognition yields good results but cannot take into account large amounts of training data which are necessary for getting better performances. That can be done either by using a stochastic approach (for instance with a hidden Markov model) or by capturing the expertise accumulated over the years by phoneticians and speech scientists especially in reading speech spectrograms [27] or other kinds of parametric representations of speech such as LPC spectra, tables of numerical measurements [3] or temporal evolution of energy and formants [19].

There are several strong motivations for adopting a knowledge-based approach in phonetic decoding:

— first of all the existence of human expertise: a trained phonetician can transcribe a sentence by inspecting its spectrogram with a 85% accuracy which is far better than the present recognition rate of automatic systems and, moreover, this knowledge is to a large extent speaker-independent,

— this human expertise is conscious and can be formalized by a set of rules and meta-rules,

— the expertise will be useful not only for phonetic decoding but also for very important tasks such as segmentation or gross phonetic classes determination.

In the SYSTEXP project we are presently developing in our group [5] we aim at developing an expert system for automatic reading of speech spectrograms in order to improve our present speech recognition systems and eventually develop new sytems. A major point concerns the acquisition of human expertise in close interaction with the expert. We have particularly emphasized this aspect of the problem and we have developed special procedures for this purpose [4].

It is interesting to see how the expert proceeds. His process is usually made up of two successive steps:

— a global overlook on the spectrogram in order to determine the energy variations and a mean vowel duration (directly related to the speech rate of the speaker). These parameters are then integrated in the strategy of the expert,

— a local analysis which is carried out either by direct pattern matching or (most commonly) by visual analysis and reasoning on one phonemic segment and its two neighbours (whenever the segmentation seems reliable, otherwise an island-driven strategy is adopted).

According to the characteristics of the task the following guidelines have been used in the implementation of our expert system:

— most rules are contextual since the decision of the expert on a given segment relies on its neighbourhood,

— it is necessary to implement both a forward and a backward chaining of the rules,

— several kinds of rule are used concurrently [12]:

- gross phonetic class identification rules,
- exclusion rules,
- phoneme identification rules,
- meta-rules related to the knowledge of the expert about his own phonetic knowledge and enabling him to choose a strategy,

— at the strategy level any hypothesis never relies on just one, even very strong, cue. More generally it is necessary to postpone any decision until enough certainty exists. This "delayed decision" strategy is of general interest in speech recognition, not only at the acoustic-phonetic level.

It should also be noted that rule-based reasoning does not exclude in some cases the use of pattern-matching techniques with stored prototypes. The human expert sometimes uses this method and, therefore, both methods have to be mixed in the implementation of a system.

SYSTEXP is presently implemented in LISP on a Motorola 68000 machine and extensive tests are now being performed.

We have already mentioned several projects on related topics. [18] proposes a slighly different approach which consists of implementing an expert system using the expertise of a specialist of automatic speech recognition with a channel vocoder. [15] describes an interesting architecture for a speech spectrogram reading expert system. The model is based on the idea of experts cooperation and it is made up of three complementary modules:

— a visual reasoning expert which finds or verifies visual features on the spectrogram,

— an acoustic-phonetic expert which has to relate visual features to phonetic units,

— a phonetics expert which reasons about possible phoneme sequences and phoneme transformations.

Another actual application of expert systems in phonetic transcription is in the recognition of large vocabularies (several thousand of words). It is obvious that such systems have to be speaker-independent and cannot be handled by global pattern recognition techniques such as dynamic time warping. It is therefore necessary to take an analytical approach which consists of transcribing a word into a phonetic lattice and of matching this lattice against the phonetic transcriptions of the words in the lexicon. For sake of efficiency it is interesting to limit this comparison to a small subset of the lexicon. Experiments carried out for English [14] and for French [12] have shown that the selection of a sub-vocabulary for an unknown word can be done by describing the words in terms of gross phonetic classes (vowel, voiced plosive, sonorant, etc.). The results for a 1000 word vocabulary show that the mean size of the subvocabulary is around 10 for about 6 phonetic classes [17]. A rule-based decision is well suited for such a gross phonetic classification and it is then very attractive to use an expert system approach. In fact many rules used by expert phoneticians are expressed in terms of phonetic classes, e.g.

* IF Formant 1 ϵ [250 - 325 Hz]
  AND Formant 2 ϵ [1200 - 1500 Hz]
  THEN NOT Vowel

* IF Visible Energy = Voicing Bar
  AND Global Energy Decreases Rapidly
  THEN Voiced Plosive

Moreover these broad classes usually related to the manner rather than the place of articulation. They tend therefore to be more robust and speaker-invariant. Figure 3 shows the architecture of our large vocabulary isolated word recognition system with the role played by the knowledge-based system both for gross phonetic classification and phonetic transcription of a word.

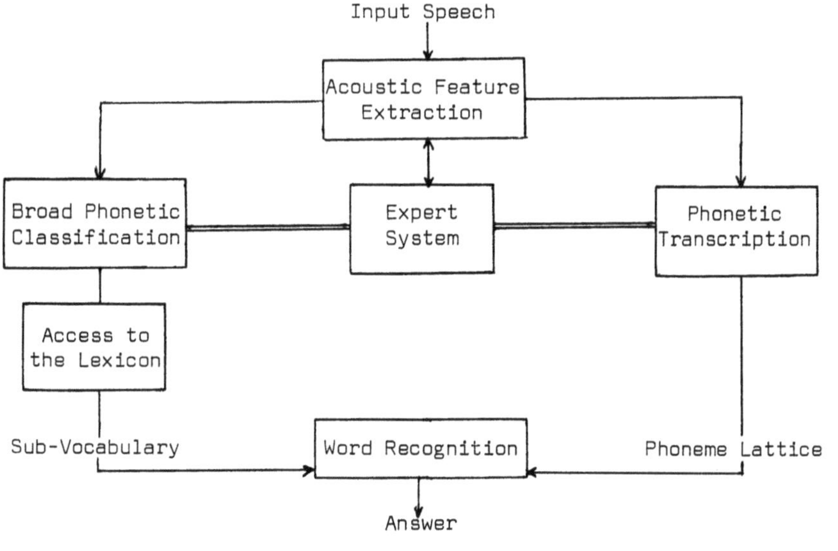

Architecture of a Large Vocabulary Isolated Word Recognition System

Figure 3

III.2. Use of frame grammars in control structures

We have just seen that the acoustic-phonetic knowledge base can be splitted into a large number of production rules. An alternative approach, though not exclusive, consists of defining the control structures of a knowledge-based system as a grammar of frames. In that case the selection of a rule or operator to be applied at any time is controlled by a planning system described by a frame grammar.

Frames were initially introduced for natural language understanding. A frame can be defined as a basic knowledge structure composed of a frame name and of a variable number of slots. The slots are the holder of particular pieces of information. The frame language is used for representing knowledge and how to use it.

There are several advantages to adapt this formalism to speech recognition. First that allows the activation of different acoustic analyses according to the context. Second these control structures are compatible with a rule-based description of knowledge. Third that makes it possible to introduce the important notion of planning in the speech recognition process.

De Mori [7] has proposed a frame language for extracting acoustic cues from the speech signal. Good results have been obtained for English, French and Italian. We are presently developing in Nancy a more general system using a frame language for the phonetic decoding of speech in relation with our phonetic expert system.

III.3. Phonology and Lexicon

A major activity in automatic speech recognition consists of emitting word hypotheses. The lexical level therefore plays a central role in a system. The great amount of variation in normal, continuous speech makes this process difficult since a word can be realized in a number of diverse ways according to the context, speaker characteristics, rate of speech, etc.

Fortunately, much of this variation appears systematically and can be formalized in contextual production rules called phonological rules [24]. In fact phonological knowledge links together the phonetic segments given by lower processsing levels and the morphological units used in the lexicon to describe the words.

A knowledge-based approach can be adopted in order to capture and use phonological rules [21]. An important contribution can be expected at the levels of knowledge acquisition in interaction with linguists and of sophisticated control structures for activating phonological rules.

There are roughly two extreme solutions for incorporating phonological knowledge in a speech rrecognition system:

— an analytical method which consists of applying the rules to the output of the acoustic-phonetic decoder at each access to the lexicon,

— a generative method which consists of expanding the lexicon by precompilation of the phonological rules. That yields a "phonological lexicon" including the various allophonic forms of words in context.

The latter is much more efficient in terms of processing time but it also presents some important drawbacks. First it is expensive in memory space (the expansion factor of the lexicon can be as large as 8). Second it is difficult to assign a likelihood measure to each production in the lexicon and a problem appears for inter-words rules. Finally the nature of phonetic variability is lost during the expansion process (for instance unstressed syllables are usually more sensitive to variations than stressed syllables).

It can be considered that a certain amount of rules should be used for generating the lexicon whereas other analytical rules should be applied during the recognition process.

IV KNOWLEDGE-BASED ARCHITECTURES FOR SPEECH UNDERSTANDING

IV.1. General Overview

We have already seen that the automatic recognition and interpretation of a sentence can only be achieved through the cooperation of all available knowledge sources, from acoustics to pragmatics. An important issue in the design of a system is therefore to define architectures which allow such an interaction between very diverse knowledge sources KSi each having its own monitor Mi, as illustrated in figure 4. Each knowledge source contains its own knowledge representation scheme and its own procedures for making hypotheses.

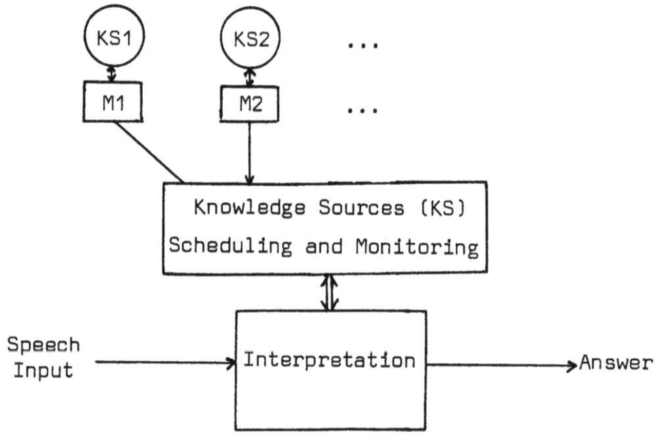

General Architecture of a Speech Understanding System

Figure 4

Various approaches have been proposed to solve this problem. Although it is an oversimplification we can distinguish between three classes of approaches:

— the first class consists of integrating all available knowledge sources into a simple structure. This is for instance the case of HARPY system which integrates a finite state network as will be seen later on,

— the second class uses some kind of stochastic modeling. We have already mentioned the use of Markov models at the phonetic level. This approach can be generalized to all knowledge sources, as for instance in the system developed by IBM [1] or in the DRAGON system [2],

— the third class is based on the classical AI paradigm of hypothesis-and-test which consists of emitting hypotheses on the basis of available knowledge and of verifying these hypotheses. This process is made necessary by the various errors and ambiguities which may be produced by a nonperfect pronunciation or during the word boundaries detection, etc. This "AI approach" is the one we are most concerned with in this paper. It clearly involves three kinds of problems which are not yet completely solved:

- knowledge representation,
- hypothesis evaluation,
- interpretation control and scheduling.

In fact the cooperation of various knowledge sources emitting hypotheses at various levels and at different instants during the interpretation of a sentence can be viewed as a parallel, synchronous or asynchronous access to a three-dimensional data base which contains the various concurrent hypotheses. The three dimensions are time, levels of interpretation and hypotheses.

IV.2. Distributed knowledge sources

There are basically two extreme models in order to implement the architecture suggested in figure 4, i.e. a heterarchical model in which each KS is connected to and interact with all other KSs and a hierarchical model in which a supervisor controls the operation and interaction of all KSs.

A straightforward implementation of a heterarchical model is not interesting for efficiency and cost reasons though attractive on a theoretical point of view. A good compromise is the blackboard model as used in HEARSAY II [16]. In this system the various knowledge sources are considered as independent processes which, theoretically, are not aware of each other and which asynchronously post hypotheses at their own level (acoustic feature, phoneme, syllable, word, phrase, sentence) to a global data base called the blackboard. This complex data structure thus contains a description at different levels of the sentence to be recognized. The blackboard constitutes the only link between the knowledge sources and its role is twofold:

— it transmits a message (i.e. an hypotheses) between two knowledge sources. An hypothesis emitted by KSi can trigger KSj. The activation of a KS is therefore data directed: a certain number of preconditions have to be fulfilled in the blackboard in order to enable a given knowledge source to access the blackboard for creating, modifying or cancelling one or several hypotheses. The action of a KS on the blackboard makes it possible to activate new KS_s, and so on,

— it contains the representation of the current interpretation of a sentence under the form of a set of hypotheses and of their relationships.

The global structure of a knowledge source in the blackboard model is thus of type "Condition-Action". It constitutes in that sense a generalization of the production rule models. However there exist considerable differences between HEARSAY II and production rule expert systems like for instance MYCIN, especially at the levels of reasoning schemes, control, etc.

In HEARSAY II the activities of the KSs are scheduled by using a strategy called "focus of attention". This strategy makes it possible to assign priorities to the different competing KS tasks according to the value of a weighting function based on several principles concerning the validity of data, the reliability of a KS, etc.

The general architecture of the HEARSAY II system is illustrated in figure 5.

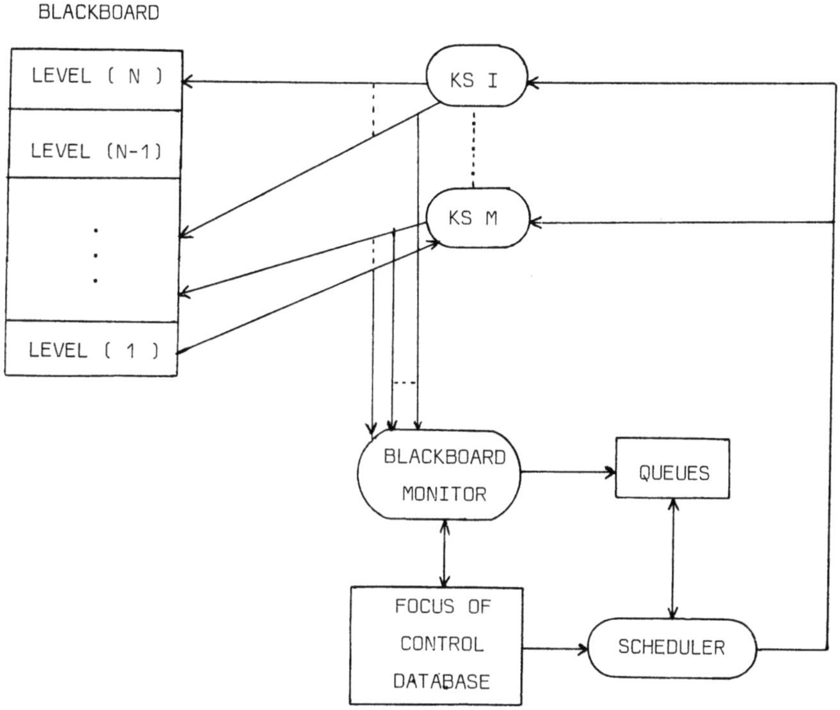

Figure 5 Architecture of HEARSAY II (after [Erman 80])

This architecture can be successfully used for implementing expert systems in complex domains with multiple, uncertain knowledge sources such as computer vision [22].

In a hierarchical model of speech understanding architecture the processing is controlled by some kind of supervisor. The supervisor activates the various available knowledge sources in contrast with the pattern-invocation of the blackboard model. This model is the most commonly encountered in practical systems.

A good example illustrating this model is the HWIM system [26]. This system uses a bottom-up, top-down strategy with island-driven focus of attention which appears to be one of the most powerful strategies available.

Another interesting way of implementing the distributed problem solving scheme necessary in automatic speech recognition is to define a society of experts. Each expert in the society is assigned a particular task which has been identified during a preliminary task decomposition [8]. That makes it possible to have a parallel execution of tasks suitable for real-time operation, with an efficient cooperation of the various experts different of the one which exists in the blackboard model. This model has been used for implementing a phonetic feature hypothesizer in the framework of a continuous speech recognition system [9]. It has now to be extended to the overall recognition process.

IV.3. Finite state networks and production rules

We have seen in par. IV.1. that a method for representing the various knowledge sources necessary in the speech recognition process was to integrate this knowledge into a single finite state network. To each state in this stochastic network is associated a phone template and a set of transitions to states representing phones that can follow it in time. The network therefore represents all allophonic variations of all possible sentences in the language. The interpretation of an input sentence consists of finding the path through the network with maximum likelihood according to the phone transcription of this sentence. In order to reduce the computational complexity of the recognition a beam search strategy has been adopted in order to keep active only a limited number of the possible states at each step of the search. Although non admissible this strategy is very efficient for speech recognition.

The stochastic network of HARPY contains all the available knowledge. It can be described by a set of stochastic rules

$$S(i) \xrightarrow{P(i,j)} h\ S(j)$$

where P(i,j) is the transition probability of going from state S(i) to state S(j) and h a current hypothesis. Such stochastic rules represent pieces of knowledge which can be transformed into production rules of the type [20]:

IF S(j) is an active state
AND h is a hypothesis
THEN Compute the likelihood of reaching S(j) from S(i).

HARPY can therefore the rewritten into a production system. Production rules can thus be applied not only for solving specific problems (phonetic decoding, phonological variations, etc.) but also for implementing speech recognition architectures. However the complexity of the task does not guarantee the efficiency of a pure production system for recognizing and interpreting a sentence.

V CONCLUSION

Knowledge-based and expert systems have been successfully used during the past few years in a number of domains. An important aspect of such systems is to provide a functional distinction between the knowledge base concerning the domain of expertise considered and the control structures which manipulate this knowledge.

Knowledge engineering techniques can be also very helpful in ASR. On one hand they help solving specific problems where there exists an important but ill-formalized human expertise. A typical example is the acoustic-phonetic decoding of speech, a major bottleneck in the design of ASR systems. Capturing the expertise of phoneticians reading speech spectrograms makes it possible to substantially improve the phonetic decoding of speech as well as speech segmentation or gross phonetic class identification. Similar techniques can be used for formalizing and using phonological knowledge in ASR.

On the other hand knowledge-based systems provide a good framework for implementing ASR system architectures. The blackboard model used in HEARSAY II is an efficient way for having multiple knowledge sources cooperation. Other schemes, like production systems or expert societies present also interesting features.

In conclusion knowledge engineering techniques do not solve all open problems in ASR but they definitely help getting substantial improvements in the domain.

REFERENCES

1. L. R. Bahl et al, "A maximum likelihood approach to continuous speech recognition", IEEE Trans. PAMI, Vol. 5, No. 2, pp. 179-190, 1983.
2. J. Baker, "The DRAGON system: An overview", IEEE Trans. ASSP, Vol. 23, pp. 24-29, 1975.
3. M. A. Bush, G. E. Kopec and V. W. Zue, "Selecting acoustic features for stop consonant identification", Proc. IEEE Int. Conf. ASSP, Boston, pp. 742-745, 1983.
4. N. Carbonell, M. O. Cordier, D. Fohr, J. P. Haton, F. Lonchamp, J. M. Pierrel, "Acquisition et formalisation du raisonnement dans un système expert de lecture de spectrogrammes vocaux", colloque A.R.C., 1984a.
5. N. Carbonell, D. Fohr, J. P. Haton, F. Lonchamp, J. M. Pierrel, "An expert system for the automatic reading of French spectrograms", Proc. IEEE-ICASSP, San Diego, 1984b.
6. R. Davis and J. King, "An overview of production systems", Machine Intelligence, Vol. 8, pp. 300-332, 1977.
7. R. De Mori, "Extraction of acoustic cues using a grammar of frames", Speech Comunication, Vol. 2, pp. 223-225, 1983a.
8. R. De Mori, *Computer Models of Speech Using Fuzzy Algorithms*, Plenum Press, 1983b.
9. R. De Mori et al, "Phonetic feature hypothesization in continuous speech", IEEE-ICASSP 83, Boston, pp. 316-319, 1983c.
10. L. D. Erman et al, "The HEARSAY II speech understanding system. Integrating knowledge to resolve uncertainty", Computing Surveys, Vol. 12, No. 2, pp. 213-253, 1980.
11. F. Hayes-Roth et al, editors *Building Expert Systems*, Addison-Wesley, 1983.
12. J. P. Haton, "Present issues in continuous speech recognition and understanding", in *Towards Robustness in Speech Recognition*, W. A. Lea, editor, in pres, 1984a.
13. J. P. Haton, "Accès lexical et reconnaissance de grands vocabulaires", 13èmes Journées d'Etude sur la Parole, GALF, Bruxelles, 1984b.
14. D. P. Huttenlocher and V. W. Zue, "Exploring phonotactilexical constraints in word recognition", J. Acoustic. Soc. Am. Suppl. 1:74, 1982.
15. J. Johannsen et al, "A speech spectrogram expert", IEEE ICASSP 83, Boston, pp. 746-749, 1983.

16. V. R. Lesser et al, "Organization of the HEARSAY II speech understanding system", IEEE Trans. ASSP, 23, pp. 11-23, 1975.
17. J. F. Mari and J. P. Haton, "Some experiments in automatic recognition of a thousand word vocabulary", Proc. IEEE ICASSP, San Diego, 1984.
18. G. Mercier et al, "From KEAL to SERAC: a new rule-based expert system for speech recognition", NATO ASI on New Architectures and Systems for Speech Recognition, Bonas, July 1984.
19. R. Mizoguchi and O. Kakusho, "Continuous speech recognition based on knowledge engineering techniques", Proc. 7th Int. Conf. Pattern Recognition, Montreal, pp. 638-640, 1984.
20. A. Newell, "HARPY, Production system and human cognition", in *Perception and Production of Fluent Speech*, R. A. Cole, ed., Erlbaum Associates, 1980.
21. B. Oshika, "Phonological rules for continuous speech recognition", in *Towards Robustness in Speech Recognition*, W. Lea, editor, Prentice-Hall, in press, 1984.
22. J. Prager et al, "Segmentation processes in the VISIONS system", Proc. 5th IJCAI, Cambridge, 1977.
23. E. H. Shortliffe, "Computer-based medical consultation: MYCIN", American Elsevier, 1976.
24. J. E. Shoup, "Phonological aspects of speech recognition", in *Trends in Speech Recognition*, W. Lea, editor, Prentice-Hall, 1980.
25. R. M. Stallman and G. J. Sussman, "Forward reasoning and dependency-directed backtracking in a system for computer-aided circuit analysis", Artificial Intelligence, Vol. 9, pp. 135-196, 1977.
26. W. A. Woods et al, "Speech understanding systems" Final Technical Progress Report, Report No. 3438, Vol. I.V., BBN, 1976.
27. V. Zue and R. Cole, "Experiments in spectrogram reading", Proc. IEEE Int. Conf. ASSP, Washington, pp. 116-119, 1979.

THE SPEECH UNDERSTANDING AND DIALOG SYSTEM EVAR

H. Niemann, A. Brietzmann, R. Mühlfeld, P. Regel, G. Schukat
Lehrstuhl für Informatik 5 (Mustererkennung)
Universität Erlangen-Nürnberg
Martensstr. 3
8520 Erlangen
West Germany

ABSTRACT

This paper gives an overview of a research effort whose goal is to develop a system which can carry out a dialog concerning a particular task domain using continuous German speech for input and output. The main processing phases are initial segmentation and labeling, finding words, understanding the meaning and giving an answer. Specialized processing modules for handling these four phases were developed or are being developed. The processing modules communicate via a common database.

1. INTRODUCTION

Speech is considered to be the most distinguishing human capability [1] — highly developed vision capability can be observed in many animals, but speech is mastered by human only; speech is also considered to be the most natural and efficient means of human communication [2]; and speech offers a communication channel which is fairly independent of hand and eye [3]. Therefore, it is no wonder that automatic speech recognition is an area of intensive research since

NATO ASI Series, Vol. F16
New Systems and Architectures for Automatic Speech
Recognition and Synthesis. Edited by R. De Mori and C. Y. Suen

several years, partly because of mere scientific interest, partly because of promising applications.

Basic tasks are recognition of isolated words or of a spoken text fairly independent of the speaker, and recognition of a speaker fairly independent of the spoken text. Recognition of a spoken text usually requires continuous speech recognition and the representation of the meaning of the speech. This field was initiated and treated with great engagement in the ARPA Speech Understanding Research Project. The role of high level syntactic, semantic, and pragmatic knowledge was stressed in this work, new system structures emerged in the HEARSAY II and HARPY architectures and several operational laboratory systems were completed. This work is reviewed in [4]. In addition, continuous speech recognition was investigated in many laboratories all over the world, and a review is given in [5]. Although this work brought significant contributions and improvements, additional work is needed in several respects, for example, more reliable phonetic segmentation, speaker independence, larger vocabularies, dialog strategies, syntactic, semantic and pragmatic reasoning and real time performance. A broad account of recent achievements is presented in [6]. It should be mentioned that also the isolated word recognition problem is treated furtheron, in particular the problems of speaker independence and large vocabularies [7].

At our institute research on understanding continuous German speech started around 1979. Our present research goals are as follows:

1. Develop a complete dialog system covering the tasks of recognition (of words), understanding (of the meaning), generation of further inquiries to the user, and generation of an answer, see Fig. 1.
2. Use a flexible system structure suited to carry out basic research.
3. Achieve speaker independence.
4. Limit the bandwidth to telephone quality.
5. Use a vocabulary of about 2000 words.
6. Apply high level syntactic, semantic and pragmatic knowledge.
7. Allow a large subset of German language.

8. Exclude dialects.

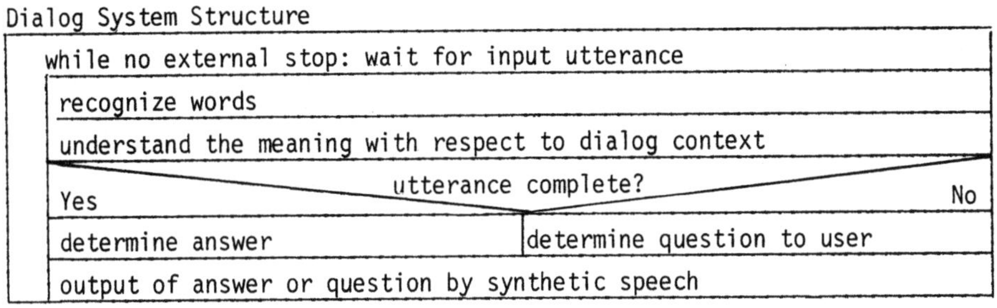

Fig. 1 The basic structure of a dialog system using continuous speech for input and output.

The system is called EVAR according to the German words for the four tasks mentioned in point 1 above. It should be noted that the 2000 words in point 5 are to be understood as cardinal forms. Since flexions of a word often sound very different from the cardinal form, all flexions of a word are also included in the lexicon and the total number of entries will be about 5 - 6000.

The system structure adopted for EVAR is according to a stratified linguistic model similar to the one given in [8], and the coordination of system modules is via a centralized data base and a control strategy as suggested first in HEARSAY II [4]. Fig. 2a,b show the present structure of the system, and this was also the structure used in former work about two years ago [9,10], but with some modifications. The two modules Word Hypothesization and Word Verification in Fig. 2a formerly were combined in only one module Lexicon. Furthermore, the module application meanwhile was split into the three modules Dialog, Retrieval, and Answer. The system as documented in [9,10] consisted of a relational data

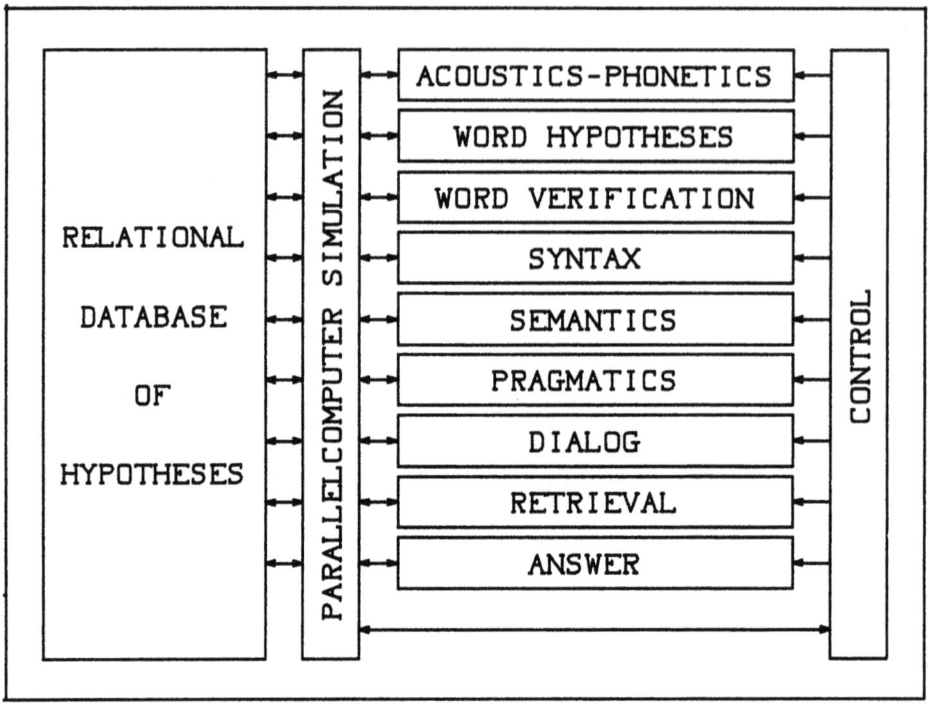

Fig. 2a The present structure of the speech understanding and dialog system EVAR

base, an Acoustics — Phonetics Module [11], a Lexicon Module, and a simple Control Module; a first version of a Syntax Module was available, but not yet integrated into the system. Inquiries about schedules of German intercity trains were chosen as an example of a task domain.

Incorporated in the system EVAR is the following knowledge:

1. A sample of hand-segmented and hand-labeled continuous German speech.
2. A lexicon with spelling, pronunciation, syntax and semantics.
3. Rules for generating inflexions.
4. Rules for generating pronunciation variants.
5. An ATN-grammar of German language.
6. Semantic classification and compatibilities of some word classes.
7. A semantic net representation of the task domain.

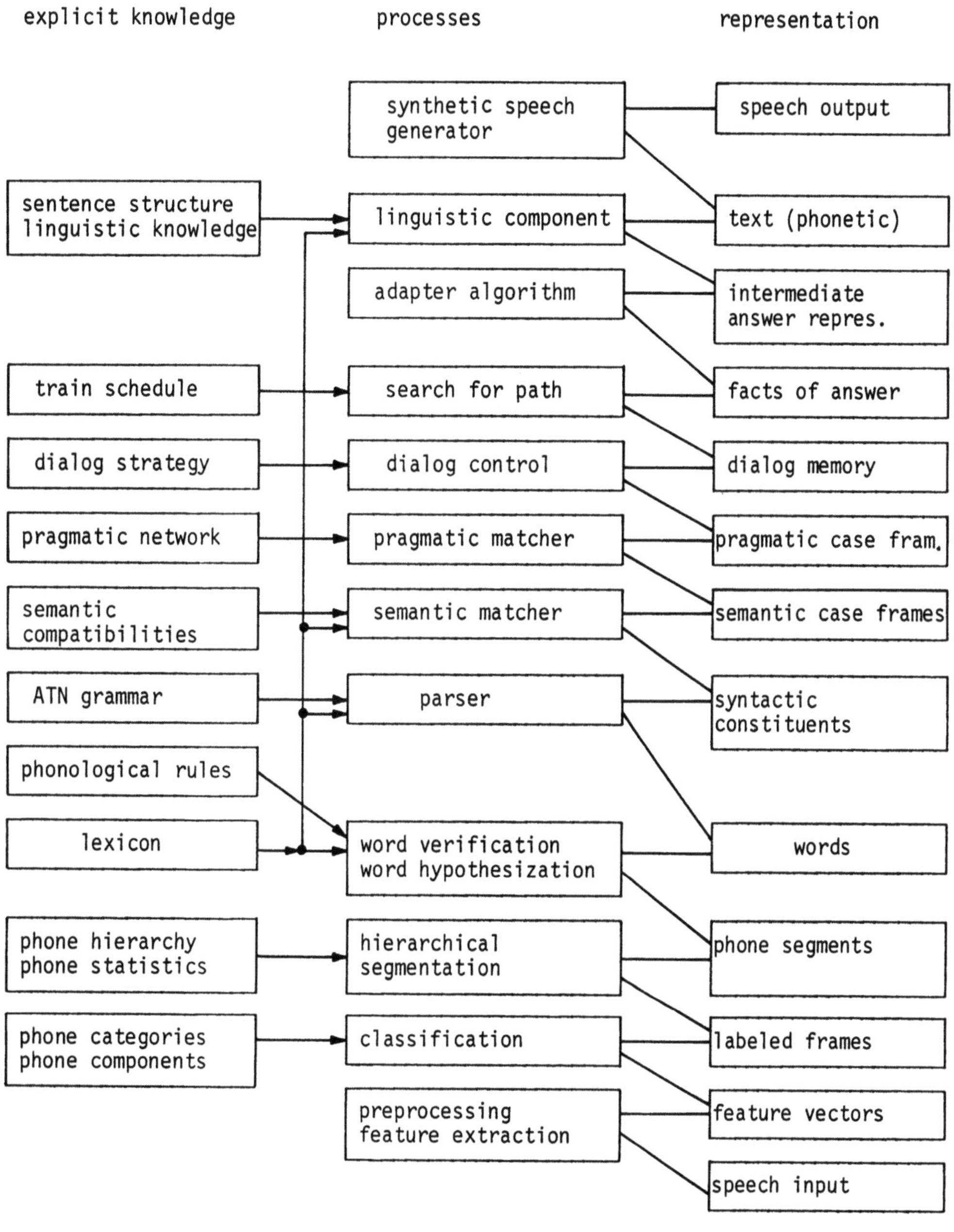

Fig. 2b The stratified linguistic model used in the system EVAR

8. An Inter City train schedule.
9. An ATN representation of the dialog strategy.
10. Linguistic knowledge for text generation.

This paper gives an account of the present status of EVAR. In Section 2 the initial segmentation and labeling of speech is treated which is performed by the Acoustics-Phonetics Module. The problem of finding words is handled by the Word Hypotheses and Word Verification Modules and discussed in Section 3. Section 4 gives an account of understanding the meaning of an utterance which is done in the Syntax, Semantic and Pragmatic Modules. First approaches to answer generation are treated in Section 5; this is done by the Dialog, Retrieval and Answer Modules. The concluding remarks in Section 6 give some directions of further work which we should like to explore. Because the intent of this paper is to give a survey of our recent and current work, mathematical details, which may be found in other and forthcoming papers, had to be omitted.

2. INITIAL SEGMENTATION AND LABELING OF SPEECH

In our system speech is bandlimited to 0.1 - 3.4 kHz, sampled at 10 kHz, and quantized with 12 bit per sample value. Segmentation of the speech into phones is done by the "classification, then segmentation" approach. This means that the whole utterance is subdivided into a number of frames, in our system frames are repeated every 12 ms and contain 20 ms of speech passed through a Hamming window. In a first classification step each frame is classified into the four categories silence, voiceless, voiced fricative and voiced nonfricative. In a second classification step the categories of a frame are classified into phone components. Examples of phone components are M, I, L, O in category voiced nonfricative, Z in category voiced fricative, and S, F, burst of t, aspiration of t in category voiceless. In most cases a phone component coincides with a phone, for example, the phone component I coincides with the phone I; but in some cases they do not, for example, the plosive [t] has the phone components silence, burst of t, and aspiration of t.

In both classification steps several alternative classifications are allowed. Since a Bayes classifier is used for classification, posterior probabilities are used to measure the reliability of alternatives. Each category of a frame which has a posterior probability greater than 2% is considered in further processing. Reliability of a phone component assigned to a frame is measured by the product of the posterior probabilities of the category and the phone component of this frame. The five most reliable phone components are used for further processing. Finally, several frames are combined to one segment which corresponds to a phone. This is done by several rules which merge adjacent similar frames to a segment part, determine essential segment parts, and extend essential segment parts as far as possible. Again, up to five alternative phone classes may be assigned to one segment. The final output is a string of segments, each labeled with up to five alternative phones and each phone rated by an assigned reliability. In addition, each segment also is assigned a measure of loudness and, if applicable, the pitch frequency. These two parameters are provided as prosodic features, but they are not used in the system presently. The structure of the Acoustics-Phonetics Module is given in Fig. 3, a labeled speech wave is shown in Fig. 4.

Acoustics-Phonetics Module

input: speech wave from microphone in unprepared room
0.1 - 3.4 kHz band pass filtering, 10 kHz sampling
mean energy normalization in time intervals
10 mel cepstrum features plus loudness
1. classification stage: 4 categories
2. classification stage: 40 phone components
obtain phone segments by hierarchical syntactic composition of phone components
output: string of segments, each with up to 5 phone labels and reliability, each with measure of loudness and pitch

Fig. 3 An overview of initial segmentation and labeling

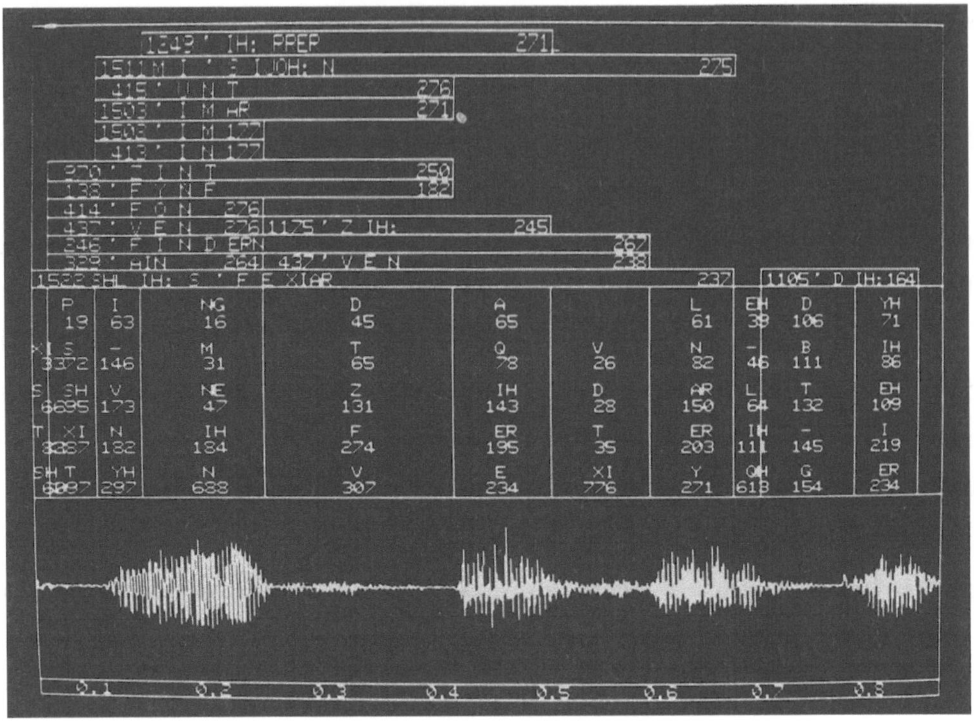

Fig. 4 An interval of continuous speech, showing the German word "Schließfächer (lockers)", its initial segmentation and labeling, and some of the word hypotheses generated.

An early version of the Acoustics-Phonetics Module is described in [11]. Meanwhile several additions, improvements and further investigations were carried out.

1. The sample of hand segmented and labeled speech was enlarged from 100 s spoken by 6 speakers to 600 s spoken by 12 speakers (6 male, 6 female).
2. Energy normalization was improved.
3. Several speaker normalization techniques reported in the literature were tested.
4. The number of phone classes was enlarged from about 30 to 40.
5. Experiments with several feature sets were made.

6. The suitability of nearest neighbour classification was tested.
7. Segments were built from frames by a hierarchical syntactic approach.

A detailed treatment of these points will be given in a forthcoming dissertation [12]. Only a short account of the major points can be given here.

Hand segmentation and labeling was done by one person who knew the spoken sentence, could listen to it and observe the speech spectrogram on a display. The sample of 600 s of speech spoken by 12 speakers is used to design the above mentioned classification stages for categories and phone components. Speaker independence is simulated by designing the system using data from 11 speakers and testing it with data from the one remaining speaker. This process is repeated 12 times in order to test all 12 speakers. Of course, 12 speakers probably are insufficient to judge system performance if many speakers are involved. But the present sample gives first estimates of system performance and may be the basis for obtaining larger samples by more automated approaches.

In the first experiments energy was normalized with respect to the whole utterance. This turned out to be less useful because usually energy tends to decrease at the end of an utterance. Therefore, energy now is normalized in time intervals whose length is small compared to the length of an utterance and large compared to the length of a phone segment. A time interval of 400 ms was found useful in several experiments.

Normalization of frequencies of the first two formants and of vocal tract length was employed in order to improve speaker independence. However, in our experiments the effect of these normalization procedures was negligible.

The initial set of phones consisted of 30 phones. This set was enlarged to 40 phones. A fairly complete list of phones used in German language contains about 60 phones. Nevertheless, a condensed set of only 18 phones is presently used in word hypothesization and is completely sufficient as mentioned in the next section. This condensed set is covered by the presently available 40 phones.

Initially, LPC based features were used for classification [11]. In addition mel-frequency and mel-cepstrum coefficients (mcc) were tested. The best results were obtained using mcc, and this result is in accordance with [13]. However, a slight modification was necessary in order to make mcc optimal also for classification of categories — loudness has to be used as an additional feature in this case. In our experiments the first 10 mcc turned out to be sufficient.

In [14] one finds the sentences "we should stop doing research on statistical decision theory ..." and the NN-rule is "simple to understand and to program, essentially distribution-free, and powerful in terms of performance". Since we have, in fact, evidence that there are deviations of feature distribution from the Gaussian distribution and since a more powerful classification procedure is always welcome, the NN-rule was tried as an alternative to simple Bayes classification using the normal distribution hypothesis. NN-rule prototypes were selected by editing a sample of speech spoken by 4 speakers, then condensing it and then reducing it. Tests were made with the sample from the remaining speakers, and this was compared to a Bayesian classifier designed and tested with the same samples [15]. Design time for NN-Prototypes far exceeds design time of the Bayes classifier, and recognition rate of the NN-rule was 45% with editing only and 41% with editing, condensing, and reducing compared to 51% of the Bayes classifier. A preliminary test gave no significant difference between NN-rule and edited NN-rule. Of course, there are some points which could be improved: we did not use Voronoi diagrams, and 4 speakers are not a representative sample.

A significant problem is the combination of phone components (that is classified speech frames) into larger phone segments. Initially a heuristic set of rules was used [11]. Meanwhile relaxation labeling and hierarchic syntactic combination was tested. Best results were achieved by the last approach. It starts on level 4 of the hierarchy with two broad classes of phone components which are voiced non-fricative and others. Frames are combined on this level by a formal grammar. Levels 3, 2, and 1 refine the classes to 7 vowels, 6 fricatives, 3 liquids, 3 nasals, 3 plosives, and silence and another formal grammar is used on every level. Finally on level 0 51 phone components are distinguished. A comparison using 23 phone components gave 47% correct segments with relaxation and 55% with syntactic segmentation; using 40 phone components we obtained 40% correct segments with heuristic segmentation and 46% with syntactic.

To summarize: The presently used version of the Acoustics-Phonetics Module distinguishes 40 phone classes, the first alternative is correct in 46%, errors consist of 12% insertions, 12% deletions, and 42% wrongly classified segments. The training set consisted of 520 seconds continuous speech spoken by 6 male and 3 female speakers, the test set consisted of 85 seconds spoken by 2 female speakers who were not in the training set.

Further work should explore the followig problems:

1. Steps towards automated sample set acquisition.
2. Speaker clusters to improve speaker independence.
3. Use of phonological rules and of larger time context.
4. Further improvement of classification and segmentation.
5. Some additional phone classes, in particular diphthongs and perhaps nasals.

3. FINDING WORDS

If an initial segmentation is available, the next step is to find words in the segmented speech. This requires that a lexicon of known words is prepared and made available to the system. The first approach to word recognition was a straight-forward dynamic programming algorithm which compared every word in the lexicon starting with every position in the utterance [9]. This allowed us to obtain first results, but, of course, is not sufficient for solving the word rcognition problem. Meanwhile the status reported in [9,10] was changed and improved as follows:

1. The lexicon was enlarged.
2. Word finding is done in the two phases of word hypothesization and word verification.

3. The algorithm and the data structure for word hypothesization was improved.
4. A first set of rules was developed to account for variations of pronunciation.

An initial version of the lexicon consisted of a basic vocabulary covering the most frequent German words, a task oriented vocabulary concerning the task domain of German Inter City trains, and an augmenting vocabulary containing numbers, cities, and week-days. This gave 306 cardinal forms. Adding all possible inflexions resulted in a lexicon with 1380 words. The lexicon is being augmented continuously and contains presently 3600 words. A word in the lexicon is represented by (spelling, number, pronunication, syntax, semantic). The number is a unique identification of every word, the spelling gives the usual text form, the pronunciation the standard phonetic representation. The entry syntax lists all possible syntactic classes and features of this word. The entry semantic lists, for every syntactic class, all relevant meanings together with case and valency information. Therefore, the information in the lexicon is a link between acoustics-phonetics, word finding, syntactic and semantic processing. Due to the large amount of syntactic and semantic information it is fairly time consuming to build up the lexicon. Up to now inflexions were added manually to the lexicon, but now it will be sufficient to enter the cardinal form and the inflexions will be generated by a program. Inflexions do not contain syntactic and semantic information, but have a pointer to the cardinal form where this information can be found. In addition a lexicon of about 8000 words without syntactic and semantic information is available [16] and is used up to the word recognition level.

The lexicon is to be considered as a raw information from which specialized knowledge used by various modules is derived. The type of specialization depends on the module and its processing algorithm and will be discussed as necessary.

As suggested, for example, in [3] the problem of finding words was split into the two problems of hypothesizing a small subset of words and verification of that subset. The subset should be hypothesized quickly, be as small as possible, and should contain the correct word with high probability. A word hypothesis consists of the three essential components (position, word, score),

and several auxiliary components like syntactic word class, status of the hypothesis, or a unique number. The three essential components have to be determined in the process of word hypothesization. After a subset of words is obtained all the words in it are carefully verified with respect to the utterance. Basically, the verification process should refine the essential components of the word hypothesis, in particular give high score to the correct word and low to the wrong ones.

Two approaches to word hypothesization are investigated which will be referred to as compressed lexicon tree (CLT) and feature addressed lexicon (FAL). A CLT is obtained by combining similar phone classes to superclasses. This reduces the number of confusions and also reduces the size of the lexicon since certain words become identical if they are represented by phone superclasses. Compression of the lexicon by means of broad phonetic classes was also suggested in [17] and the set of words becoming identical after compression was called a cohort. After some comparisons we obtained best results by using the transinformation as a criterion for deriving phone superclasses — in fact, this criterion is much better than error rate and also gave better results than a heuristic approach. The derivation of superclasses starts with a phone confusion matrix provided by the Acoustics-Phonetics Module. One may view the spoken phones as symbols entered into a channel and the recognized phones as symbols at the output of a channel. The transinformation gives the amount of information passed correctly from the input to the output, and it may be computed from the phone confusion matrix. Phone superclasses are obtained by merging two or more rows and columns of the phone confusion matrix in such a way that the transinformation is maximized. If the error rate is used as a criterion, rows and columns are merged to minimize error rate. Experiments showed that the error rate as a criterion tends to yield very few and very large superclasses whereas transinformation yields fairly many and small superclasses. This is a first hint that phone superclasses derived from maximization of the transinformation should be useful; this idea was confirmed by experiments with compression of the lexicon and by several cohort statistics. The size of a cohort, that is the number of words becoming identical when represented by phone superclasses, should be small. Table 1 gives some cohort statistics for superclasses obtained from maximization of transinformation, minimization or error rate, and a heuristic approach. This shows clearly the superiority of transinformation with

List of tables

	transinformation phone super classes		error rate phone super classes		heuristic
	5	18	5	18	5
Maximal cohort size	9	13	157	31	14
average cohort size	1.31	1.09	10.1	1.6	1.58
number of cohorts	928	1113	122	755	770

Table 1 Some cohort statistics obtained from a lexicon with 1222 words using 5 and 18 phone superclasses derived by three criteria

respect to cohort statistics. But also the five heuristically determined classes of vowels, fricatives, plosives, nasals, and remainder is quite satisfactory.

Presently, experiments are made using 18 phone superclasses which contain 87% of the initial transinformation in the full set of 40 phonemes (5 superclasses contain 58% of the initial transinformation). The lexicon is compressed to cohorts using these 18 classes and represented by a tree which is stored as a linear string of phonetic symbols together with some bookkeeping information; in particular, for each node of the compressed lexicon tree (CLT) representing a cohort this information contains a number identifying the cohort. From the cohort number the set of words in it can be determined. The CLT is matched with the phonetic string of the input utterance and for each word we compute the probability of observing the phonetic string when this word is pronounced [18]. This computation takes care of insertion and deletion errors in the phonetic string. The various transition probabilities are trained iteratively [19]. The result is a position of the word within the phonetic string and a probability of the word. The main steps of the algorithm are given in Fig. 5. However, the

Word Hypothesization Module
input: string of phone segments
transcription of phones to superclasses
match cpmpressed lexicon tree with input by stochastic automaton approach
select n best word positions
expand cohort hypotheses into word hypotheses
computation of word score
output: m best scoring word hypotheses

Fig. 5 The main steps of word hypothesization in the CLT

probability of a word is not used as a measure of priority for further processing because it depends highly on the length of a word. Instead, a score is computed by estimating mean and variance of word probabilities for each length and then normalizing probabilities with respect to mean and variance.

A first experiment with 20 sentences and a small lexicon of 100 words gave an average inverse rank [20] of word hypotheses equal to 0.46. Computation time on a PDP11/34 is about 2 minutes per sentence with a lexicon of about 1400 words. An example of some word hypotheses is shown in Fig. 4.

The CLT approach described above is basically a top-down approach because every cohort in the CLT is matched to the input utterance. A truly bottom-up approach is the feature addressed lexicon (FAL). The idea is to use phonetic features like phone tripels as entries in a FAL where each entry gives the set of words having this feature. By using several features, for example several phone tripels, the set of words having these features will become smaller. This approach is now being implemented and tested and results will be reported later.

The set of word hypotheses is then verified using the full set of phones and taking into account variations of pronunciation. Since word hypotheses contain the three components (position, word, score), the verificiation process can concentrate on a particular word and a particular interval of the utterance. Two versions of a Word Verification Module are under investigation; the first uses the string of phonetic segments provided by the Acoustics Phonetics Module, the second uses the string of labeled speech frames. The structure of the first version is given in Fig. 6. A set of about 140 phonological rules was developed

Word Verification Module (segment level)
input: string of phone segments, word hypotheses
select high scoring unverified word hypothesis
apply phonological rules to obtain pronunciation graph
match graph to interval of utterance
the word score is that of the best scoring pronunciation variant
output: (position, word, score, auxiliary information)

Fig. 6 The main steps of word verification on the segments level

to generate pronunciation variants of words from the standard phonetic representation contained in the lexicon. An average number of three variants per word is generated. The pronunciation variants and the standard pronunciation are represented by a pronunciation graph. Pronunciation variants occur often at word endings, voiced plosives and some frequently used words like articles, conjunctions and prepositions.

The pronunciation graph is used as input of a stack-decoding algorithm [18] which matches the graph to the relevant interval of the utterance by means of dynamic programming. This results in drastic improvements of scores of the correct word hypotheses in some cases, but also may result in improvements of the wrong word. This effect, which occurs if the correct word is pronounced clearly, needs further investigation and may require changes in some of the rules. The approach to word verification by matching a word hypothesis with labeled speech frames is presently being implemented and tested.

Further work should explore the following points:

1. Incorporation of pronunciation variants already on the hypothesis generation level.
2. Phonological rules to account for pronunciation variants between successive words.
3. Thorough experimental investigation of the performance of the various modules using lexicons of varying size.
4. Improved estimates of various parameters used in the matching algorithms, for example deletion, insertion, and confusion probabilities.
5. Take care of top-down word hypotheses generated from the Syntax Module, for example.

4. UNDERSTANDING THE MEANING OF AN UTTERANCE

The result of word matching is a set of word hypotheses which may have gaps, competing and erroneous hypotheses, and also may span the utterance by one or several sequences of (nearly) adjacent words. In the three main steps of syntactic, semantic and pragmatic analysis it is tried to find one unambiguous meaning for a spanning sequence of words or for some disjoint groups of words. This serves two goals. The first goal is to reduce the ambiguity of word hypotheses by using additional knowledge and thereby improving recognition of words. The second goal is to relate a sequence of words to the system's internal representation of linguistic knowledge, and by "understanding" we mean this process of relating an input to internal knowledge of the system.

In this paper the terms syntax, semantics, and pragmatics are used as defined in [21]. Syntax studies the formal relations of signs to one another. Consequently, the Syntax Module only treats properties of and relations between words and word classes. Semantics studies the relation of signs to the objects to which the signs are applicable. Therefore, the Semantics Module considers properties and relations of words and word classes resulting from their signifying certain objects, events, and concepts. Pragmatics deals with the relation of signs to interpreters. Therefore, the Pragmatics Module analyzes a word sequence with respect to the particular task domain. No task specific knowledge is available in the Semantics Module, and no knowledge about the general meaning of words is available in the Syntax Module. The advantage of this approach is a clear conceptual structure of the system and independence of modules — a change of the task domain would require a redesigned Pragmatics Module but no changes in syntax or semantics (probably the lexicon would have to be augmented by a task specific vocabulary, too). A disadvantage is a certain loss of processing efficiency. The three modules form a representational hierarchy in the sense that the Pragmatics Module requires a semantically interpreted word string, and the Semantics Module requires a syntactically analyzed string.

At present, the three modules are in different states of completion; the most advanced module is the Semantics Module, and this one will be described in some detail below. The early version of the Syntax Module is presented in [9,10]. It used a fairly elaborate ATN-grammar of German language and an island parser. The problem with this approach is the combinatoric explosion due to the fairly large number of word alternatives and the rigid constraints imposed by the ATN-rules, for example the case-number-gender agreement in noun groups. Therefore, we plan a redesign of the module according to Fig. 7. The two main points are that a fast prescanning of words will be done to detect a few sequences of words belonging to syntactically allowed word classes and that the rigidity of syntactic constraints will be dependent on the score of words. For example, the case-number-gender agreement may depend only on some endings of words which are hard to recognize and, therefore, this should be checked only for

Syntax Module
input: verified word hypotheses
determine triples of words with syntactically allowed sequences of word classes
determine larger sequences of words with syntactically allowed word class sequences
select some high scoring sequences of words
perform syntactic analysis with score - dependent rules
generate top-down word hypotheses in gaps of syntactic analysis
output: syntactic constituents of sentences represented in a syntax analysis tree

Fig. 7 The structure of the module for syntactic analysis

very high scoring words.

As shown in Fig. 8, the Semantics Module takes as input syntactic constituents and gives a semantic interpretation represented in a semantic net structure. Fig. 8 treats the case that a syntactic constituent spans the utterance,

Semantics Module
input: syntactic constituents spanning the utterance
select high scoring syntactic constituent
perform local interpretation of immediate constituents
instantiate case frames of the verb
match immediate syntactic constituents to case frames
interpretation of adjuncts
determine top-down word or constituent hypotheses from open case slots
select best scoring case frame
output: semantic net representation of interpreted constituent structure

Fig. 8 The structure of the module for semantic analysis of syntactic constituents spanning an utterance

but also constituents spanning only part of the utterance can be processed. The semantic nets are structured as suggested in [22]. Two basic components of a semantic net are the concept and the instance. Both consist of attributes which describe parts as well as properties (both may be concepts themselves). A concept is a definition of a word like 'tomorrow', or a class of objects like 'mammals', or an action like 'to eat', or a relation like 'left to'. An instance represents an individual member of a class defined by a concept. It is also possible to derive a concept as a specialization from a more general concept. The specialization inherits all attributes of all those concepts which are more general, except the attributes which are explicitly modified or differentiated. The semantic nets were implemented using GRASPE as an extension of SIMULA.

The 'raw knowledge' about semantic properties is manually prepared and stored in a dictionary, where each word has an entry as described in Section 3. By semantic analysis the dependencies and relations within a sentence are investigated and a formal representation of the meaning is obtained. The meaning concerns functional and logical or deep case relations within a sentence, the dependency structure or the valency of word groups, and aspects of text consistency and coherence. The main idea is that the structure of a sentence is determined by the leading verb, the so called nucleus. This is the topic of the valency and case theory. The nucleus has the ability to attach dependent constituents, and this ability is called its valency. The obligatory and optional dependent constituents of the nucleus largely determine the structure of a sentence. Often, different meanings of a verb give rise to different structures. In case theory the functional roles and logical relations of parts of a sentence are treated with respect to the nucleus. The structure implied by a certain meaning of the nucleus is represented in a case frame, and an example is given in Fig. 9. A case frame of a verb is a concept in a semantic net and obtained by a preprocessor from the lexicon containing the raw semantic knowledge.

The tasks of semantic analysis are to choose an appropriate meaning of a word out of the different meanings represented in the dictionary (different meanings of 'to get', for example, in 'get up', 'get started'), to recognize semantic ambiguities (in sentences like 'he wants a train to go to Munich'), to point out semantic anomalies (which may arise due to competing alternatives in word

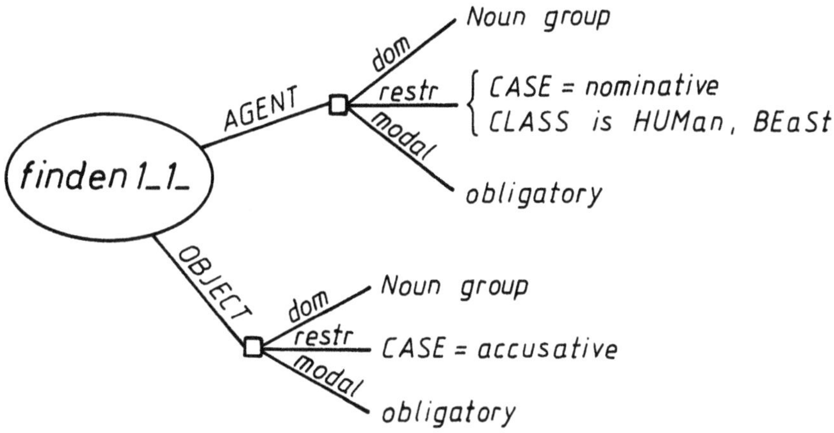
finden 1_1_
AGENT
dom
Noun group
restr
CASE = nominative
CLASS is HUMan, BEaSt
modal
obligatory
OBJECT
dom
Noun group
restr
CASE = accusative
modal
obligatory

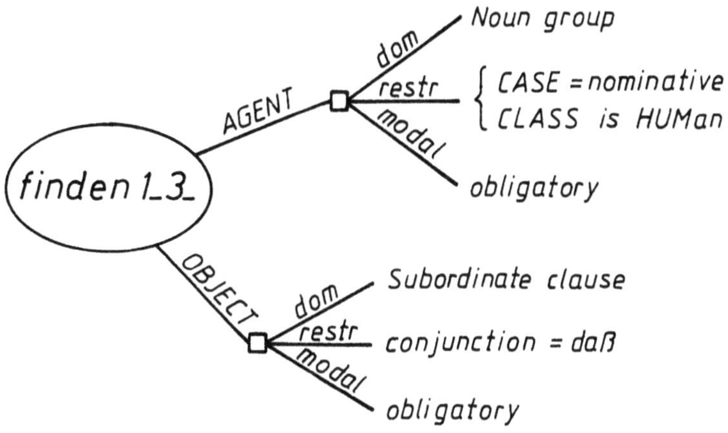
finden 1_3_
AGENT
dom
Noun group
restr
CASE = nominative
CLASS is HUMan
modal
obligatory
OBJECT
dom
Subordinate clause
restr
conjunction = daß
modal
obligatory

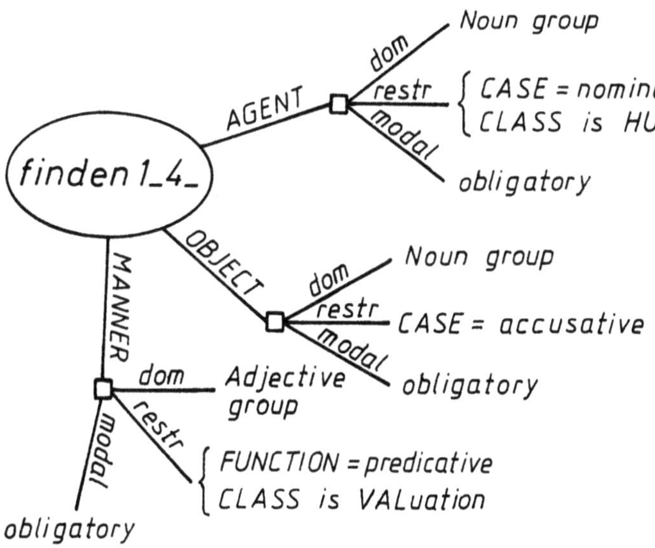
finden 1_4_
AGENT
dom
Noun group
restr
CASE = nominative
CLASS is HUMan
modal
obligatory
OBJECT
dom
Noun group
restr
CASE = accusative
modal
obligatory
MANNER
dom
Adjective group
restr
FUNCTION = predicative
CLASS is VALuation
modal
obligatory

recognition), to relate paraphrases (that is to map differently worded sentences with equivalent meaning to the same representation), and to support recognition by generation of top-down hypotheses. This is accomplished by three fundamental operations of the Semantics Module which are local interpretation, contextual interpretation, and top-down hypotheses. The realization and performance of these operations will be treated in the following. The reader should note that all examples which follow are taken from German language and are translated word by word. Therefore, the examples may sound awkward to the English speaking reader.

Local interpretation operates on syntactic constituents provided by the Syntax Module. Presently the five constituent types noun group NG, prepositional noun group PNG, adjective group ADJG, verbal group VG, and sentence S are available. The basic idea with local interpretation of the first three constituent types is that certain word classes (like prepositions) impose semantic constraints on other word classes (like nouns) with which they can be combined. These constraints are expressed in the dictionary by the feature SELECTION, which means that a preposition used with a certain meaning 'selects' a noun with a certain meaning.

For example, in the PNG 'mit der Bahn (with the train)' the word 'mit (with)' has four meanings in the dictionary, among them only one with class 'INSTRUMENT' and selection 'THING'. The word 'Bahn (train)' has five meanings, among them only one with class 'TRANSPORT'. Class TRANSPORT is a specialization of class THING, and therefore, the INSTRUMENT meaning of 'mit' is compatible with the TRANSPORT meaning of 'Bahn'. By checking all possible combinations of the different classes and selections, all consistent interpretations are obtained. In the above example it turns out that there is only one compatible combination. Even without a larger context the compatible alternative meanings of a constituent are much less than the combinatorial number. A compatible combination is given two features, the semantic class of the noun and that of the preposition.

Local interpretation of a constituent type VG only consists of generation of case frames of the form shown in Fig. 9. For each meaning of a verb in the dictionary a separate case frame is generated by a preprocessor. This is all that can be done by using the local information of VG only. If a constituent type S is locally interpreted, each individual constituent, that is NG, PNG, ADJG, and VG, is locally interpreted as described above.

The basic idea of contextual interpretation of a sentence or a major part of a sentence is to take the case frame obtained from local interpretation of a VG and to try to match the constituents PNG, NG, ADJG, also obtained from local interpretation, to attributes of the case frame. For a particular verb there usually will be several meanings associated with different case frames. The word 'finden (to find)' has five meanings listed in the dictionary, and the case frames of three of them are shown in Fig. 9. When matching constituents to case frames the number of successful matches will depend on whether a case frame fits to the intended meaning of the verb in the sentence or not. Therefore, a score is computed for each contextual interpretation, and the best scoring interpretation is selected.

The contextual interpretation is realized by three main functions: Frame Sentence Match (FSM), Frame Constituent Match (FCM), and Supplement Contextual Interpretation (SCI). We discuss these functions using the example sentence 'Er findet seine Fahrkarte nicht (word by word translation: He finds his ticket not)'. The Syntax Module yields a syntactic representation which is mapped to the network structure shown in Fig. 10. Since word recognition of the system is not perfect, there may be competing and erroneous word hypotheses which will give rise to several competing syntactic hypotheses. Every syntactic hypothesis has a score which is an estimate of its reliability and importance. The function FSM selects a good scoring syntax hypothesis of type S (sentence), which already was processed by the local interpretation operation. For every case frame of the verb in S an inexact matching operation of type 'concept-instance' is started. The type 'concept-instance' means that the concept of the case frame is matched with the instance S, and as many empty attributes of the case frame

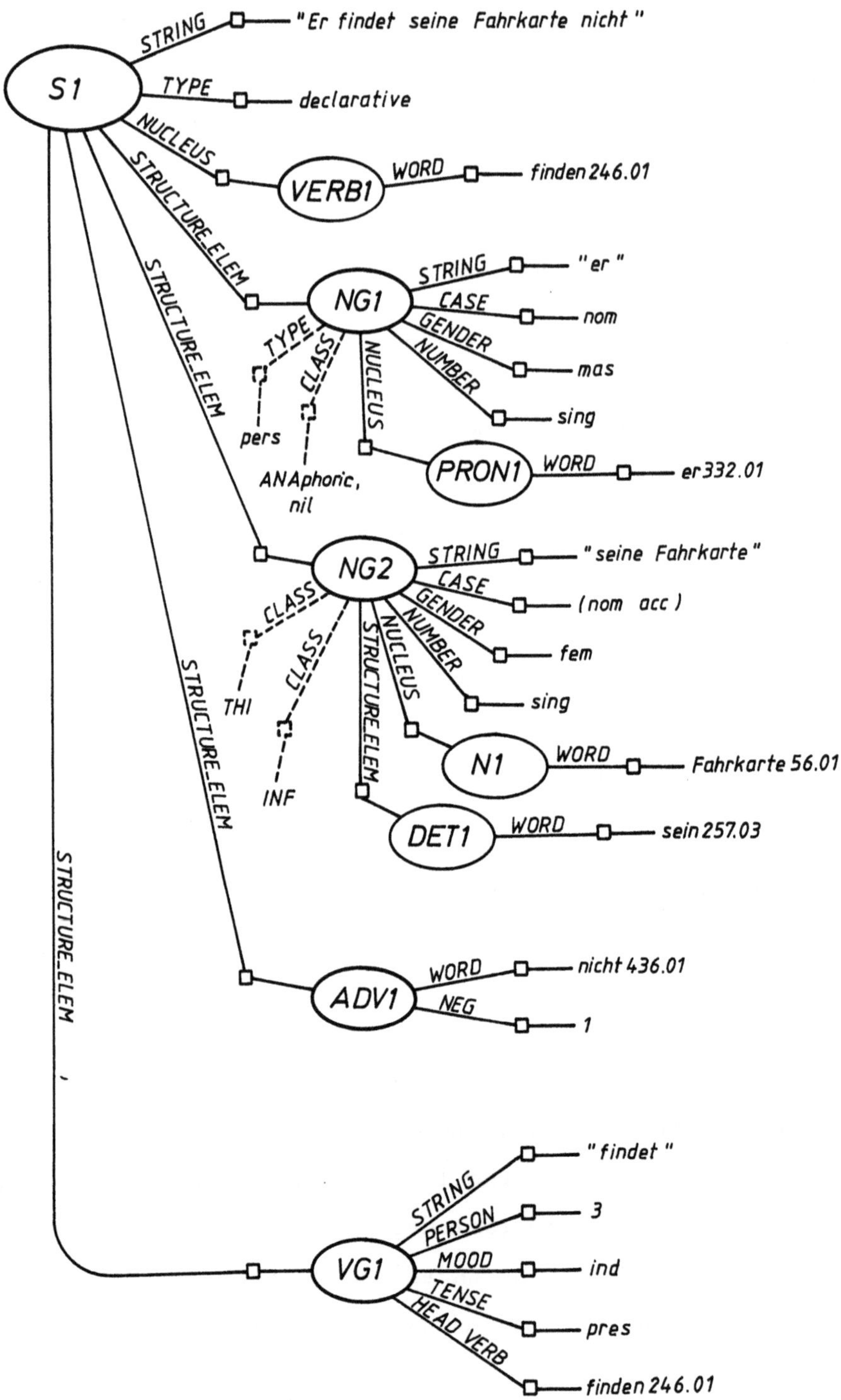

Fig. 10 Network representation of the syntax of an example sentence

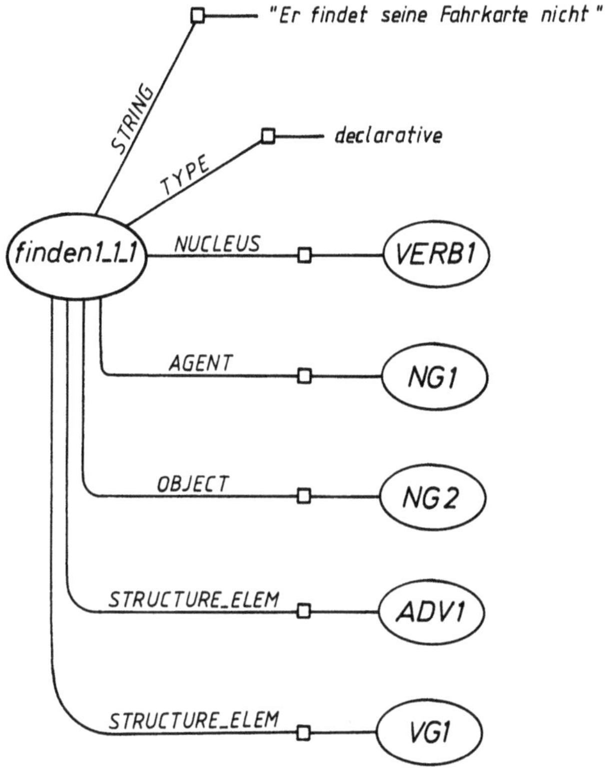

Fig. 11 Result of matching a sentence to a case frame of a verb

are filled by constituents in S as possible. The result is shown in Fig. 11. It is apparent that the agent and object attribute of the case frame 'finden 1_1' is matched by NG1 and NG2, respectively, of the sentence S. If 'finden 1_4' were used, the obligatory attribute 'manner' of the case frame could not be matched by S. Therefore, this match is scored less than that of 'finden 1_1' and the meaning of 'finden 1_1' is selected.

Whereas the function FSM requires a syntax hypothesis of type S, the function FCM also accepts syntactic constituents and does not require a complete sentence. FCM was implemented in order to process also intermediate results of the syntax module. The function SCI is used to attach constituents which are not part of the case frame but occur additionally in the sentence (see ADV1 in Fig. 11).

The semantic interpretation is done by local and contextual interpretation as described above. Generation of top-down semantic hypotheses is a feature which is supposed to be useful in speech undertanding but whose performance was not yet tested. The idea is to make predictions on the basis of so far unmatched obligatory attributes of a case frame.

The Pragmatics Module has not yet been implemented, but its operation is specified as shown in Fig. 12. Whereas the Semantics Module extracts general

Pragmatics Module
input: instantiated case frames
select high scoring case frame instance
perform matching of semantic categories to domain dependent concepts
perform matching of semantic deep cases to pragmatic concept roles
infer inquiry type from role structure and from situation dependent expectations
try to fill obligatory attributes of the inquiry concept by inferences and data base requests
output: semantic net representation of user inquiry

Fig. 12 The main steps of pragmatic analysis

linguistic information, the Pragmatics Module relates this to internal task specific knowledge. In our system we chose inquiries about train schedules as an example of a task domain. The relevant knowledge is represented in a semantic net containing five general concepts for five general types of inquiries, for example, inquiries about train connection or seat reservation. Each of the concepts has several obligatory and optional attributes. For example, the concept 'train connection' has obligatory attributes 'source' and 'goal'. Pragmatic analysis will try to match the obligatory attributes of a concept in the pragmatics net to attributes found by semantic analysis (see Fig. 11, where, for example, no source or goal attribute is present). If an obligatory attribute cannot be matched, this will be used to derive a question which the system asks the user.

Pragmatic analysis completes what is meant here by understanding the meaning of an utterance. If this analysis is successful, the acoustic signal is related to the system's internal knowledge.

Future work should explore the following points:

1. Efficient realization of syntactic and pragmatic analysis.
2. Refinement of the ATN grammar.
3. More general and powerful semantic analysis.
4. Thorough experimental investigation of the three modules.

5. GIVING AN ANSWER

Up to now the system always considered only one utterance and tried to recognize and understand it. Obviously this is not sufficient for a system which is supposed to carry out a dialog with a user. In the following short example S refers to utterances of the system, U to those of the user:

U1: When is there a train to Munich?
S1: At what time would you like to start?
U2: As soon as possible.
S2: You may take the train at 12:30 hours.
U3: When does it arrive there?
S3: At 13:45 hours.
U4: Does it have a dining car?
S4: Yes.

These few utterances demonstrate that a dialog is possible only if both partners can assume that some general and common knowledge is available and if they both relate and understand a sequence of utterances, not just one isolated utterance at a time. For example, in U1 the user assumes that the system has a reasonable default value for the starting point of the journey, and so does the system because it does not ask back. In U2 the user also assumes that the system has knowledge about time. Furthermore, U2 (or also S3, S4) are not understandable as isolated utterances, but only in the context of the dialog. The objects referred to by "it" and "there" in U3 have to be determined from S2. With S1 the system pursues a certain intention which is to give the user the train best fitting to the user's goals. There is a uniform topic through U1 to S3 which may be called "inquiries about train schedules", and there is a change of the topic in U4, S4 to "inquiries about an object", in this case about a particular train.

The above few examples demonstrate that finding an answer by the system raises a bulk of new problems. In EVAR these problems are treated by the following modules:

1. The Dialog Module. — It memorizes the context and meaning of a sequence of utterances and relates a new utterance to the former ones, and it determines the components of an adequate answer.
2. The Retrieval Module. — It retrieves the facts (in our case, for example, a departure time) meeting the requests determined by the Dialog Module.
3. The Answer Module. — It translates the internal representation of an answer to a German text. The text may then be printed or spoken by a speech synthesis device. The Dialog Module is specified and an interactive test facility was realized. The main structure of the module is shown in Fig. 13. Some of its functions still have to be realized. The Retrieval Module is presently under development. A version of the Answer Module using an intermediate representation of the answer was realized, but the translation of the output of the Dialog Module to this intermediate representation is not yet available. Fig. 14 gives the main steps of answer generation. Since finding an answer still needs a good deal of additional work, it seems premature to give further details in this paper.

Dialog Module

input: semantic net representation of user inquiry generated by the Pragmatics Module
resolve references and complete elliptic phrases
update memories of syntactic and semantic structures, of actual topic, and of mentioned objects
draw inferences from expectations on actual discourse move
match utterance to discourse scheme in order to determine actual dialog state
choose system reaction: determine content of answer if inquiry is complete, else ask back
update memories by system utterance
output: internal semantic network representation of system utterance

Fig. 13 An overview of the dialog facility in EVAR

Answer Generation Module

input: internal network representation of system utterance
translate network representation to caseframe-oriented intermediate structure
determine morphological surface structure from valency features and deep case rules: noun inflection; pro-form, question form, article selection
generate ellipsis and anaphora
inflect verb by tense and mood
determine phrase order
transform dependency tree to terminal string
output: textual form of answer

Fig. 14 An outline of answer generation

6. CONCLUDING REMARKS

We are convinced that speech understanding and dialog systems will become standard devices at some time, but we are careful not to predict at what time because this will depend to a good deal on the effort of research and development which can be afforded.

The modular structure of EVAR makes the system extremely suited to a multiprocessor realization, but we do not have the resources to achieve this. Presently, the processing up to the word level is done on a DEC PDP 11/34, the remaining processing is done on a CDC CYBER 845.

Concerning the whole system future work will have to consider the following points:

1. Enlargement, refinement, and correction of available linguistic data bases from which specialized knowledge of the modules is derived.
2. Incorporation of prosodic information.
3. Evaluation of user parameters (speak too loud, too fast and so on).
4. More efficient common data base.
5. Investigation and comparison of different control strategies.
6. Improvement of the available processing modules.

ACKNOWLEDGEMENT

The work reported here was partly sponsored by the German "Bundesministerium für Forschung und Technologie (BMFT)" under grant 08 IT 1019. Only the authors are responsible for the contents of this publication.

REFERENCES

1. K. R. Popper, J. C. Eccles, "Das Ich und sein Gehirn," R. Piper, München Zürich, P2.15 und E4.31, 1982.
2. A. Chapanis, "Interactive Human Communication," Scient. American, 232, No. 3, 36-42, 1975.
3. W. A. Lea (ed.), *Trends in Speech Recognition*, Prentice Hall, Englewood Cliffs, N. J., 1980.
4. D. H. Klatt, "Review of the ARPA Speech Understanding Project," J. Acoustical Soc. of America, 62, 1345-1366, 1977.
5. R. De Mori, "Recent Advances in Automatic Speech Recognition," Proc. 4, Int. Joint Conf. Pattern Recognition, Kyoto, Japan, 106-124, 1978.
6. R. De Mori (ed.), Special Issue on Speech Understanding, Information Sciences.
7. L. Bahl, "Recognition of Isolated Word Sentences from a 5000-Word Vocabulary Office Correspondence Task," Proc. ICASSP 83, Boston Mass., 1065, 1983.
8. T. Winograd, *Language as a Cognitive Process*, Vol. 1, Syntax, Addison Wesley, Rading Mass., 1983.
9. H.-W. Hein, Das Erlanger Spracherkennungssystem, Dissertation Universität Erlangen-Nürnberg, Arbeitsberichte des IMMD Band 15, Nr. 15, Erlangen 1982.
10. H. Niemann, "The Erlangen System for Recognition and Understanding of Continuous German Speech," in J. Nehmer (ed.), GI - 12. Jahrestagung, Informatik Fachberichte 57, Springer Berlin, Heidelberg, New York, 330-348, 1982.
11. P. Regel, "A Module for Acoustic-Phonetic Transcription of Fluently Spoken German Speech," IEEE Trans. ASSP-30, 440-450, 1982.
12. P. Regel, Akustisch phonetische Transkription für die automatische Spracherkennung, Dissertation, in preparation.
13. S. B. Davis, P. Mermelstein, "Comparison of Parametric Representations for Monosyllabic Word Recognition in Continuously Spoken Sentences," IEEE Trans. ASSP-28, 357-366, 1980.
14. J. Kittler, K. S. Fu, L. F. Pau, *Pattern Recognition Theory and Applications*, D. Reidel Publ. Comp., Dordrecht Boston London, 569, 1982.
15. J. John, R. Mühlfeld, P. Regel, G. Siller, "Vergleich von Klassifikatoren für die Lauterkennung," to appear in Proc. DAGM-84.
16. F. W. Kaeding (ed.), Häufigkeitswörterbuch der deutschen Sprache, Steglitz bei Berlin 1897-1898. We are grateful to Dr. Ruske who made available to us a tape with 8000 words.
17. D. W. Shipman, V. W. Zue, "Summary of Research in Speech Recognition," Res. Lab. of Electronics, M.I.T., Cambridge Mass., 1982.
18. L. R. Bahl, F. Jelinek, "Decoding for Channels with Insertions, Deletions, and Substitutions with Applications to Speech Recognition," IEEE Trans. IT-21, 404-411, 1975.
19. L. R. Bahl, F. Jelinek, R. L. Mercer, "A Maximum Likelihood Approach to Continuous Speech Recognition," IEEE Trans. PAMI-5, 179-190, 1983.

20. A. R. Smith, Word Hypothesization in a Large-Vocabulary Speech Understanding System, Ph.D. Dissertation Dept. Computer Science, Carnegie Mellon University, Pittsburgh, PA, 1977.
21. H. Niemann, *Pattern Analysis*, Springer Series in Information Sciences 4, Springer, Berlin Heidelberg New York, 1981.
22. R. J. Brachman, A Structural Paradigm for Representing Knowledge,

A NEW RULE-BASED EXPERT SYSTEM FOR SPEECH RECOGNITION

G. Mercier, M. Gilloux, C. Tarridec and J. Vaissiere
CNET
Route de Trégastel
22301 Lannion
FRANCE

I INTRODUCTION

SERAC (Expert System for Acoustic-phonetic Recognition) is an Expert System that applies Artificial Intelligence techniques to Automatic Speech Recognition.

Rule-based Speech Recognition Systems like the KEAL C.N.E.T. System MERCIER 82 have now become too much complicated to be implemented in the form of classical sequential programs. A new methodology is required to express the knowledge of human experts which is not always well formalized. Furthermore computer programs must be developed in an environment that makes it possible an incremental improvement of the knowledge.

The Experts Systems methodology has been successfully applied to such different problems as medical diagnosis MYCIN SHORTLIFE 76, mass spectrograms interpretation (DENDRAL BUCHANAN 71), geological classification (PROSPECTOR DUDA 82) and speech understanding (HEARSAY-II HAYES-ROTH 77, CARBONELL 84, DE MORI 82). These studies have shown that it is possible to build tools that can take into account great amounts of empirical knowledge to solve problems in very specific domains.

NATO ASI Series, Vol. F16
New Systems and Architectures for Automatic Speech
Recognition and Synthesis. Edited by R. De Mori and C.Y. Suen

The SERAC system was designed to structure the knowledge acquired with previous experience with the KEAL system and to provide a flexible tool for maintaining, improving and growing this knowledge. Since the whole knowledge required to build a Speech Understanding System is too wide to be taken into consideration all at once we decided to restrain our domain to the acoustic-phonetic analysis of the speech signal as a first step.

Our first task was to define a representation language for the KEAL acoustic phonetic knowledge. An object-oriented problem-driven rule-based language of the class of the OPS family (FORGY 81) appeared to be the most appropriate for this purpose. The production rule formalism was chosen for its ability to express domain expertise in a declarative way. A problem-driven forward chaining inference engine was introduced for encoding the problem resolution strategy into the language.

II REVIEW OF THE KEAL SYSTEM

II-1 SYSTEM ORGANIZATION

The KEAL Speech Understanding System has been developed to investigate the possibility of using voice as a communication support between a user and a computer for several tasks.

The present version of this system (Fig. 1) can be described as a set of components which successively perform the acoustic, phonetic, lexical and syntactic analysis in order to reconstitute the uttered sentence from the speech signal.

The comprehension part of the system involves a semantic interpreter and a dialogue manager able to perform automatic inquiry in a limited domain.

The speaker adaptation component of the system involves a matching program for extracting the new phonetic segment references and adjusting of the phonetic parameter representing the acoustic-phonetic knowledge. In the case of mapping errors (less than 10%) the limits of the segments have to be adjusted by

BLOCK DIAGRAM OF KEAL

Each step in the recognition process corresponds to a different type of analysis.

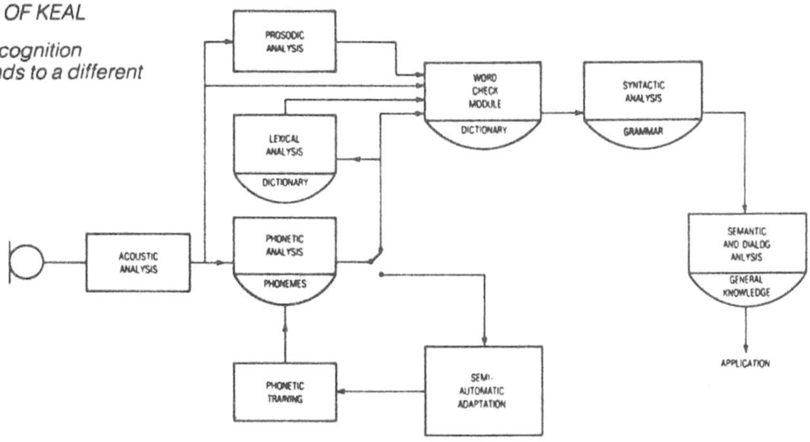

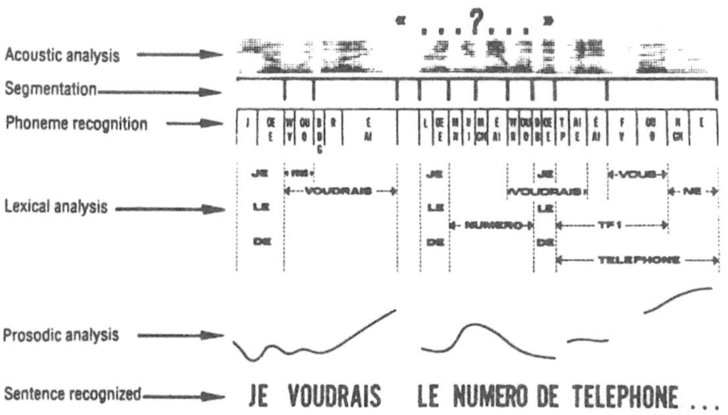

In this system, analytic speech recognition is a series of steps, as shown above.

KEAL means " IDEA " in the Breton language. It is also a set of initials for " Kenreizhadur Evit Anavezout Lavar " which, also in the Breton language, means automatic speech recognition system.

Fig. 1 THE KEAL SYSTEM

hand.

II-2 ACOUSTIC-PHONETIC DECODING

II-2-1 PREPROCESSING AND FEATURE EXTRACTION

Acoustic-phonetic decoding transforms the continuous speech signal into a series of discrete hypotheses. The units currently taken into account by the Keal phonetic analyzer are the syllable, the phoneme, the phone and the feature.

In a first step, a spectral analysis of the digitized signal is made every 13.3 ms using a simulated channel vocoder (14 or 16 filter banks). The energies within each frequency band are computed by a signal processing routine computing a 256-point D.F.T. and using a 20 ms window. This analysis results in a series of vectors with n components called samples or frames. In parallel, a few additional parameters are associated with each 13.3 ms frame, namely signal amplitude, pitch, energy and spectral center of gravity measurements within selected frequency bands.

The other parameters used are the spectral derivative with respect to time and the frequencies and amplitude of the first three maxima of the vocoder spectrum and the zero-crossings measurements.

Segmentation of continuous speech into phonetic units as well as labelling are progressively refined through the following steps (Fig. 2) by using this set of parameters.

II-2-2 CENTISECOND FRAME LABELLING

Based on a set of acoustic cues derived from these parameters, a set of phonetic features such as vowel, consonant, silence, fricative, open, closed, front, back, voiced, unvoiced, buzz-bar is assigned to each centisecond frame. The rules used for this primary labelling based on spectral information are speaker-independent and relatively simple.

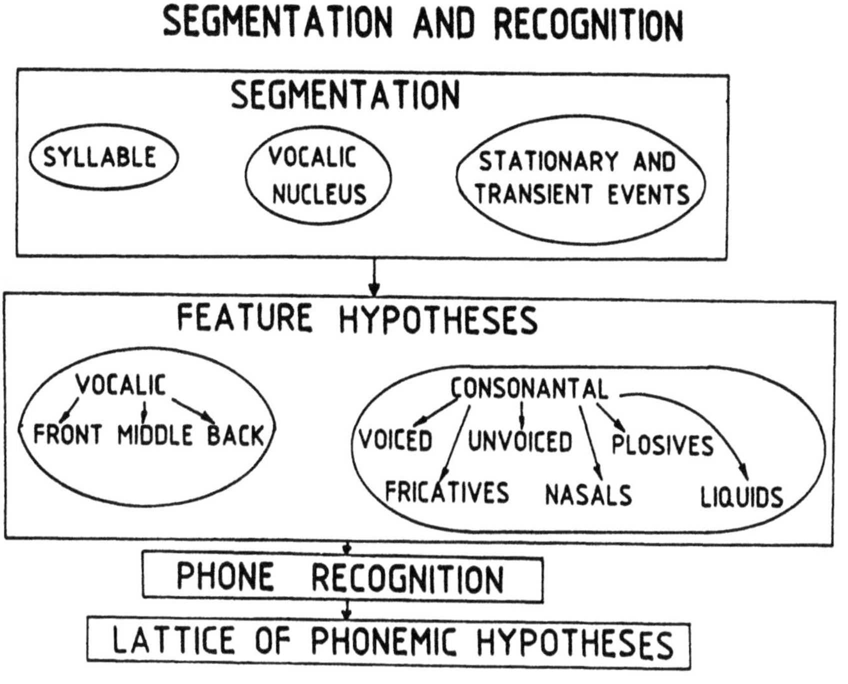
SEGMENTATION AND RECOGNITION
SEGMENTATION
SYLLABLE
VOCALIC NUCLEUS
STATIONARY AND TRANSIENT EVENTS
FEATURE HYPOTHESES
VOCALIC
FRONT
MIDDLE
BACK
CONSONANTAL
VOICED
UNVOICED
PLOSIVES
FRICATIVES
NASALS
LIQUIDS
PHONE RECOGNITION
LATTICE OF PHONEMIC HYPOTHESES

Figure 2

By computing linear decision functions between phone prototypes and a speech frame represented by the spectrum plus the additional parameters this classification is refined (Fig. 3).

II-2-3 SEGMENTATION INTO PSEUDO-SYLLABLES

The basic principle behind this segmentation is the search for the syllable's vowel nucleus; this is done in three steps:

1. First, the energy curve measuring the weighted energy in the frequency band 250-4200 Hz is split into consecutive segments computed each containing an energy maximum (Fig. 4). Consecutive segments, for which there is not a significant maximum of energy in low frequency (250-850 Hz) are concatenated.

2. These segments or pseudo-syllables, are then investigated in order to see whether or not they contain a vocalic nucleus. The following acoustic features are computed:

   — The low frequency energies measured at four instant of time corresponding respectively, to the peaks of the preceeding and current pseudo-syllables and to the minima of energy before and after the current peak of energy.

   — The amplitudes of the first formant computed at the same instants of time.

   — The number of "vowel" frames in the pseudo-syllables.

   — A measure of dissimilarity between the current potential vocalic nucleus and the preceeding one.

   — A feature indicating the presence of a significant proportion of "voiced" frames surrounded by "unvoiced" frames.

CENTISECOND PHONE LABELLING

SELECTION OF THE NUMBER OF PHONES: m
SPECTRAL FEATURE EXTRACTION AND SAMPLE VECTOR REPRESENTATION: $X(t)$
USE OF LINEAR DECISION FUNCTIONS: $Fi(t)=Ki(X(t))$
SELECTION OF THE THREE LARGEST VALUES $Fi(t)$, GIVING THE THREE MOST LIKELY PHONETIC LABELS.

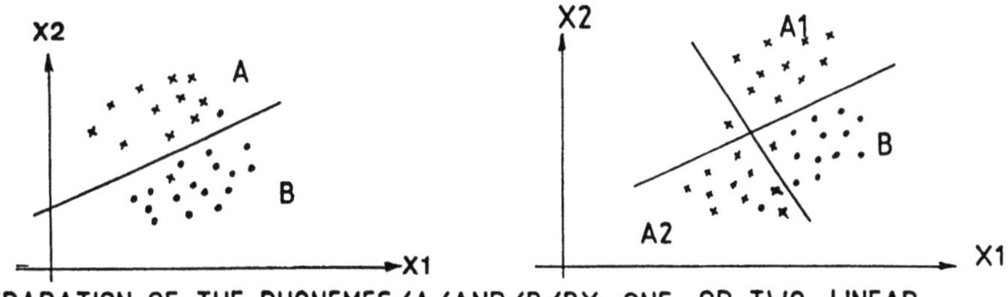

SEPARATION OF THE PHONEMES/A/AND/B/BY ONE OR TWO LINEAR FUNCTIONS

Figure 3

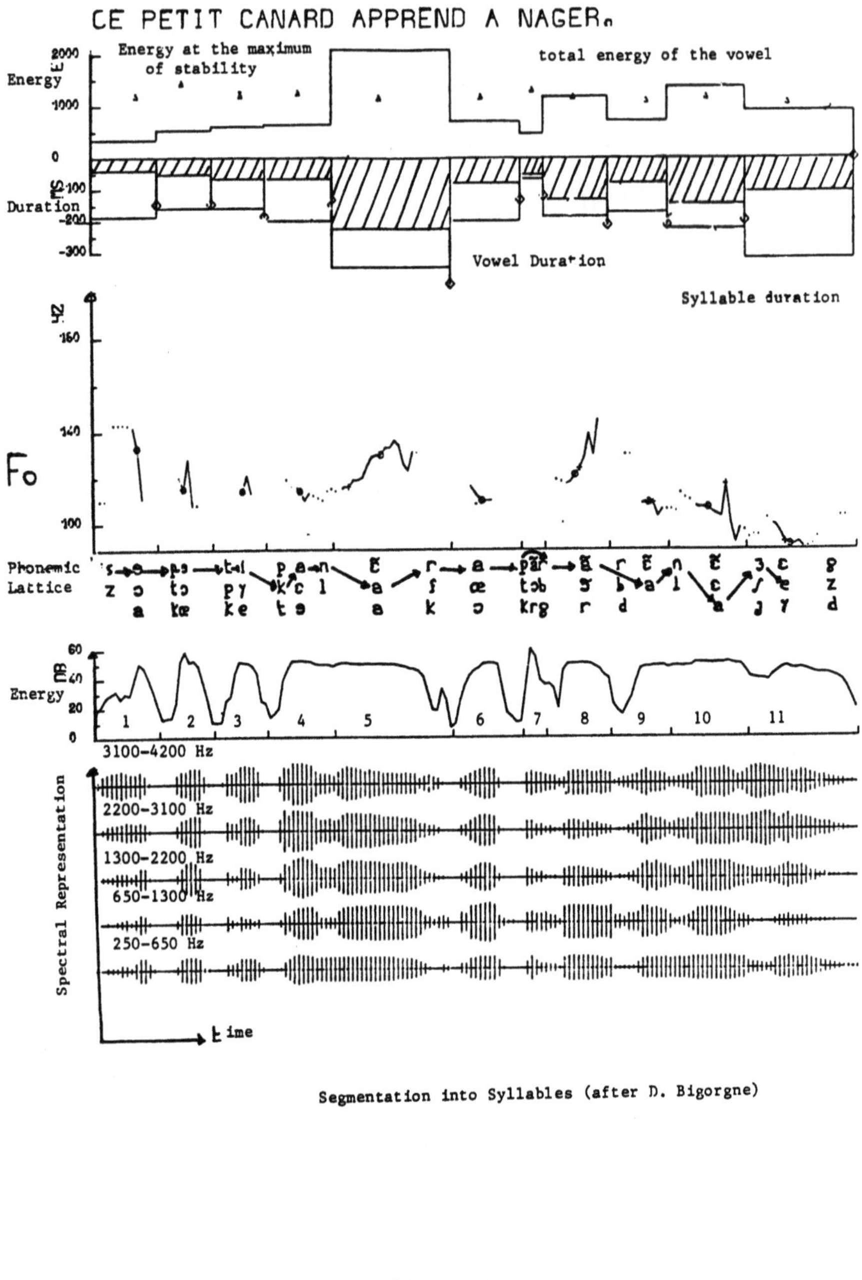

Segmentation into Syllables (after D. Bigorgne)

Figure 4

A value measuring the plausibility of there being a vocalic nucleus in the "potential" pseudo-syllable is computed by means of a linear combination of these features. When this plausibility value is equal to zero, the current segment is merged with the preceeding pseudo-syllable.

3. At the end of this process, the boundaries of the pseudo-syllable are determined. This is done by taking the stationary portion between two vocalic nuclei which contains the least energy and designating its first frame as the boundary.

Segmentation is about 95% correct when sentences are uttered normally. Results are little lower for rapid speech.

II-2-4 SEGMENTATION INTO PHONES

An obvious property of the speech signal is that it is composed of a sequence of stationary or transient events that can be displayed for instance, by the magnitude of the derivative with respect to time, P(t), of the spectral envelope (Fig. 5). Consecutive low values of P(t) delimit a stationary portion in the signal, which may contain the main features for certain phonemes, whereas high values of this curve indicate a transient event between phones which may include essential features of one or both of these phones.

In Keal, vowels are first located within the stationary zone around the maximum of energy of each syllable. In addition this zone must contain a sufficient proportion of vowel "frames". Then sequences of stationary and transient events are located between each vocalic nucleus. These segments form the new framework within which the main phonetic features will be identified.

II-2-5 VOWEL RECOGNITION

Based upon an idea proposed by STEVENS (1981) and adapted to our spectral data by R. Gubrynowicz (1983) acoustic cues measuring spectral areas between a line coresponding to the amplitude of the first formant (or the second formant) and the spectrum curve between some frequency band are used for

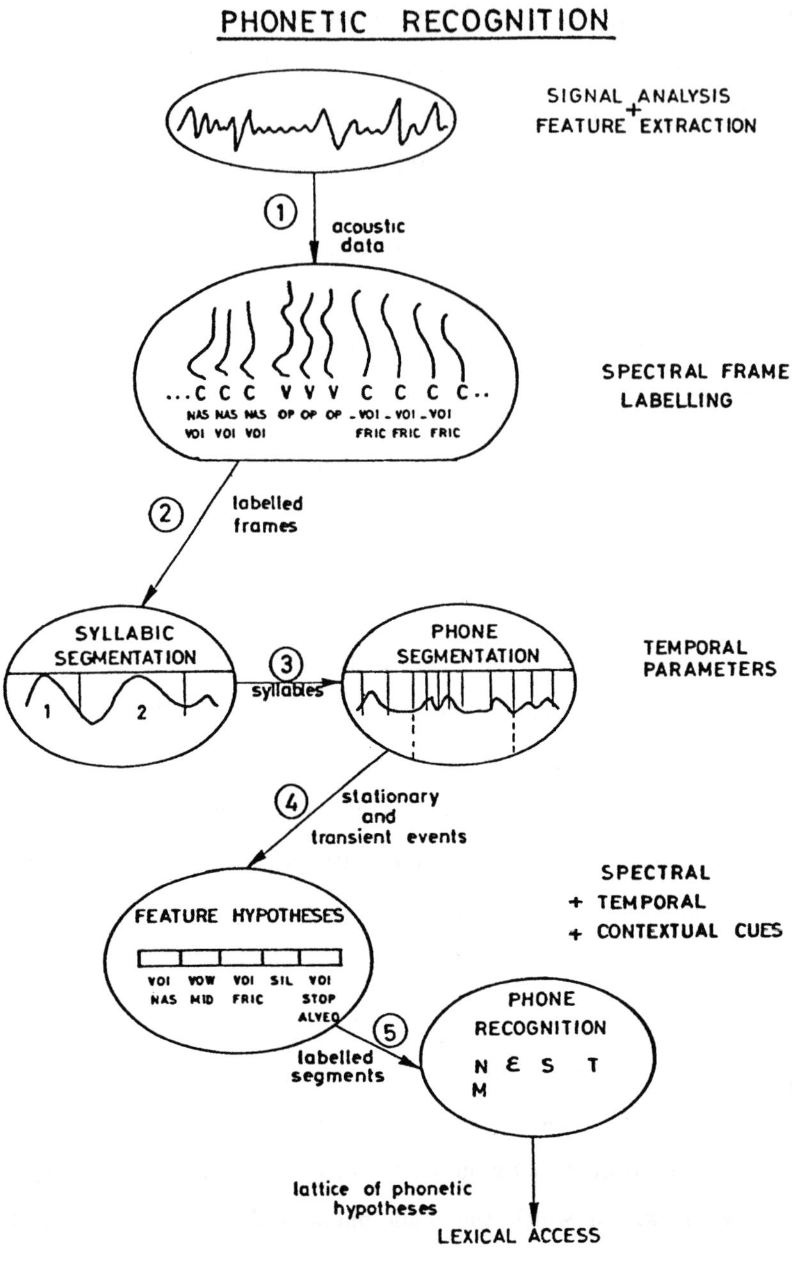
PHONETIC RECOGNITION
SIGNAL ANALYSIS + FEATURE EXTRACTION
1
acoustic data
...C C C V V V C C C C..
NAS VOI
NAS VOI
NAS VOI
OP OP OP
_VOI FRIC
_VOI FRIC
_VOI FRIC
SPECTRAL FRAME LABELLING
2
labelled frames
SYLLABIC SEGMENTATION
1
2
3
syllables
PHONE SEGMENTATION
TEMPORAL PARAMETERS
4
stationary and transient events
SPECTRAL
+ TEMPORAL
+ CONTEXTUAL CUES
FEATURE HYPOTHESES
VOI NAS
VOW MID
VOI FRIC
SIL
VOI STOP ALVEO
5
labelled segments
PHONE RECOGNITION
N Ɛ S T
M
lattice of phonetic hypotheses
LEXICAL ACCESS

Figure 5

separating the french vowels into the following categories: open, closed, mid and front, back, central. A second algorithm [ROSSI 81] based on the notion of distinctive vowel features, permits a hierarchical recognition of vowels. In a vowel recognition experiment using isolated words pronounced by three speakers, ROSSI found that the correct vowel was among the top two choices about 90% of the time.

This feature-based vowel recognition, which has to be improved for continuous speech, is not still completely integrated in the KEAL system. Speaker-dependent linear decision functions are used to assign one or more labels to each 13.3 ms frame. Labels that are assigned with a high frequency in the vocalic segments are stored in the final phonetic lattice. This procedure of frame labelling also makes it possible to detect diphthongs and sequences of two vowels that have been incorrrectly merged into a single segment (Fig. 6). We compute the temporal center of gravity along the time axis for each of the phone candidates. If the temporal center of gravity of any the phone candidates within a segment is sufficiently far away in time from those of other candidates, two segments may be detected. In order to confirm the existence of two segments in such a case, center of gravity, degree of opening or place of articulation parameters must have changed within the segment.

II-2-6 CONSONANT RECOGNITION

The following procedure is used for recognizing "consonant" segments.

— For each stationary segment placed between two vocalic nucleus, the proportion of "voiced" and "unvoiced" frames is measured. If this segment corresponds to a phone, then the degree of voicedness or voicelessness is given by this measure. Conversely, for stops, for instance, a second cue of voice onset time (V.O.T.) may be necessary when there is no buzz-bar. This cue is measured within the transient segment. In KEAL, V.O.T. is a function of the number of voiced or unvoiced frames at the beginning of the burst. The percentage of correct identification of the voiced-unvoiced feature is about 95%.

CENTISECOND LABELLING OF THE WORD
"MOINS": /m/o^w/ɛ̃/ /

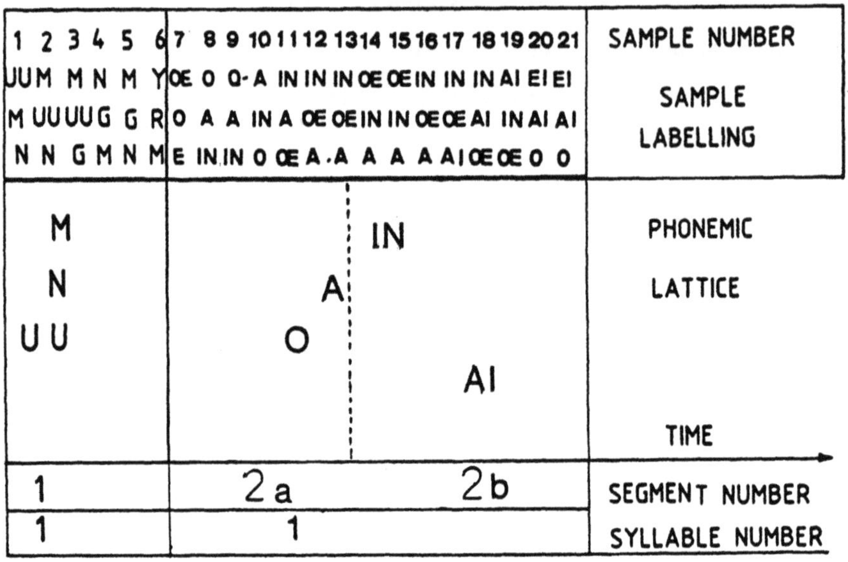

Figure 6

- The feature "stop is detected when a zone of silence or weak low frequency energy (buzz-bar) is included in the stationary segment and followed by a strong burst and a sudden variation of the spectral parameters (energies and centers of gravity of formants). The percentage of incorrect identification of this feature is about 5%.

- The feature "fricative" is assigned if the segment is composed of enough frames with the label "fricative"; and the rule condition for assigning the "fricative" label to a frame is: "The spectral center of gravity and zero-crossings must be higher than some fixed thresholds".

- A stationary segment will be labelled "nasal" if it is composed of enough "potentially nasal spectral frames" and if some contextual and temporal criteria hold for each frame (GUBRYNOWICZ, 1984).

- A liquid /l/ or /r/ will be detected after a plosive sound if there is at least one maximum in the energy curve together with enough energy at low frequencies. Fig. 7 gives performance of recognition of a few feature classes.

- Recognition of the place of articulation of plosives is under way. For the moment, three main cues are taken into consideration: change in the first spectral center of gravity, the frequency region in which the spectral maximum of energy of the burst is located and change in the amplitude of the signal during the burst. The current performance is about 70% correct identification for a few speakers continuous speech.

- A refinement of this ordered labelling and final generation of phonetic hypotheses is provided by a "pattern matching" approach where prototypes depend upon a speaker or upon a category of speakers if they are obtained by clustering methods.

PERFORMANCE OF A FEW FEATURE CLASSES

	TOTAL NUMBER OF SEGMENTS	NUMBER OF ERRORS	NO DECISION	NUMBER OF MISSED SEGM.	NUMBER OF SPEAKERS
VOICING	145	10	6		3: 1F, 2M
NASAL CONSONANT	116	16	0		8: 3F, 5M
VOICELESS FRICATIVE	77	0	1	1	5: 1F, 4M
VOICELESS STOP	78	1	1	1(Spreading)	3: 1F, 2M
VOICED STOP	39	2	15	0	3: 1F, 2M

DATA: Different Kinds of Continuous Speech Utterances (Mostly Phonetically Balanced French Sentences

Figure 7

Linear discriminant functions for the phone inventory are computed from twenty phonetically balanced sentences. These functions divide the R^n space where the phone references are represented and make it possible to assign a phone label to each phonetic segment found in the utterance. Within each segment, multiple phones candidates are ranked by their degree of confidence.

Following this procedure, a new set of rules combines the decisions of the feature-based hierarchical process and of the discriminant approach in order to get the final phonemic label.

II-2-7 BUILDING THE PHONEMIC LATTICES

The output of the phonetic analyzer is given in the form of segments, each with the following information: reliability value, beginning and ending time of the segment, candidate phonemes ranked by likelihood score, number of the syllable to which the segment belongs. This lattice is then given to a word spotter able to make hypotheses or verifications about the possible sequence of words in an utterance.

Fig. 8 gives an example of phonetic recognition obtained by the phonetic analyzer.

II-2-8 PHONETIC KNOWLEDGE ACQUISITION AND SPEAKER ADAPTATION

In order to evaluate the coefficients of the linear discriminant functions used to separate the phoneme classes, the following procedure has been designed.

— The phonetic segment references necessary for building the learning set are automatically extracted by using a matching program that maps the acoustic phonetic lattice given by the phonetic analyzer onto an ideal phonemic transcription of the words or sentences of the refrence data set and onto their corresponding acoustic representation (Fig. 9). In case of mapping errors (less than 10%) the limits of the segments have eventually to be adjusted (or deleted) by hand, then providing the correct acoustic samples (Fig. 10).

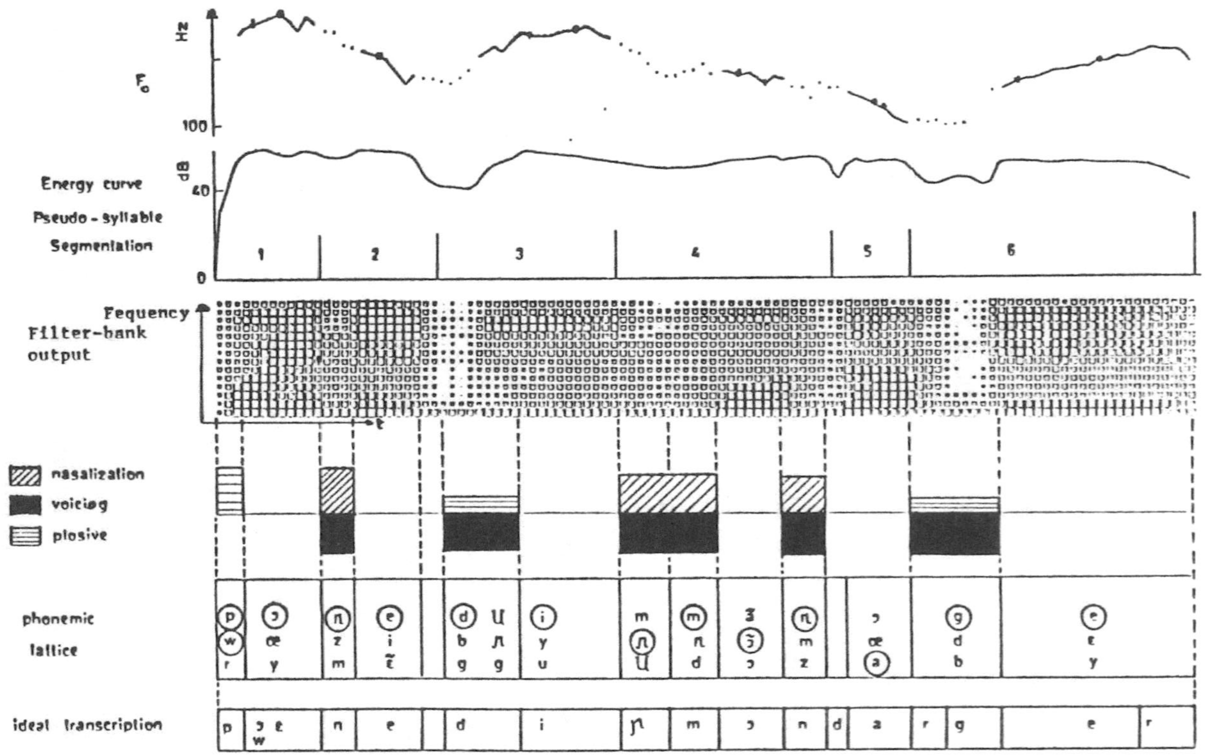

Results of applying KEAL to a Breton sentence : "poent eo diñ mont d'ar guer"...) "it is time to go home".

Figure 8

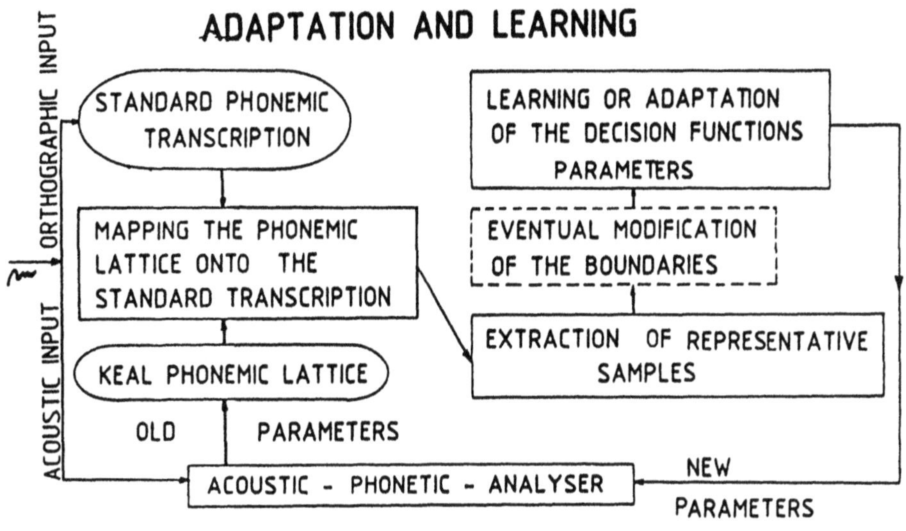
ADAPTATION AND LEARNING
ORTHOGRAPHIC INPUT
ACOUSTIC INPUT
STANDARD PHONEMIC TRANSCRIPTION
MAPPING THE PHONEMIC LATTICE ONTO THE STANDARD TRANSCRIPTION
KEAL PHONEMIC LATTICE
OLD PARAMETERS
ACOUSTIC - PHONETIC - ANALYSER
LEARNING OR ADAPTATION OF THE DECISION FUNCTIONS PARAMETERS
EVENTUAL MODIFICATION OF THE BOUNDARIES
EXTRACTION OF REPRESENTATIVE SAMPLES
NEW PARAMETERS

Figure 9

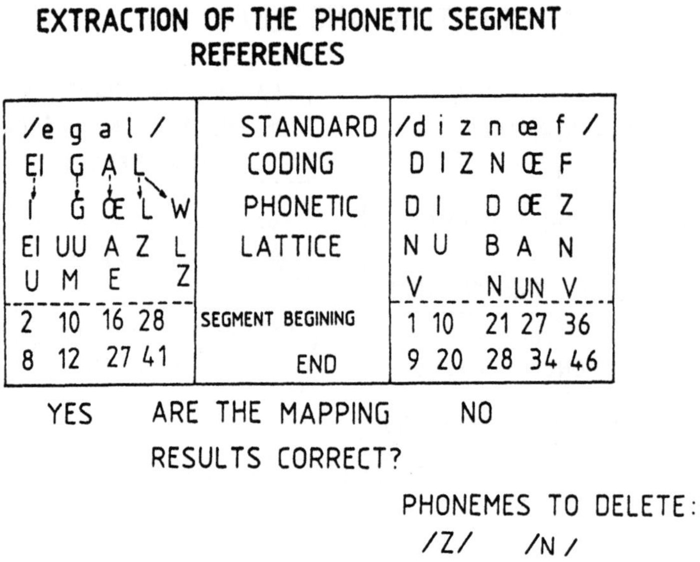

Automatic alignment of Speech with a Standard Phonetic Transcription

Figure 10

II-2-9 RESULTS

A recognition experiment was run on a few speakers' productions of continuously spoken, phonetically balanced sentences, without top-down information and using only the best choice for each segment in the phonemic lattice, a phonemic recognition rate of 55 to 60 percent was achieved. This rate is still too low, but what is interesting is that the recognition rate rises to 70% and 80% when the top two and three choices within the phoneme lattice are taken into consideration, respectively. Fig. 11 shows percentage of phonetic recognition and syllabic segmentation.

II-4 LEXICAL ANALYSIS

The role of the lexical analyzer is to match each word of the task vocabulary against the phonemic lattice, in order to detect the word in the sentence.

For achieving this goal, each word of the task vocabulary is given an ideal phonemic representation. If a word can have many pronunications, phonological rules are used to expand the lexicon in order to include all possible pronunciations.

During the matching process, a matrix is built, its rows corresponding to the phonemes of the word to be searched and its column to the consecutive segements of the phonetic lattice. An element (i, j) of the matrix is set to 1 if the phoneme lying in the ith row appears in the list corresponding to the jth column. Each 1 denotes a possible starting point for a detection of the word. Each 1 is a possible end point. The whole matrix is searched for paths which connect a starting point and an end point and pass through a set of (i, j) cells of the matrix. These cells must contain the number one and have increasing values of i and j. Each such path corresponds to a word detection. Each detection then receives a similarity score w (with $0 \leq w \leq 1$) which takes into account the degree of confidence for each segment and for each phoneme in the segment. Phoneme deletion, phoneme insertion, spreading or merging are also taken into account for computing this similarity score. The detection boundaries

PERCENTAGE OF PHONETIC RECOGNITION AND SYLLABIC SEGMENTATION

TOTAL NUMBER	220	385	695	635
RECOGNITION PERCENTAGE:1	60%	65%	55,1%	59 %
RECOGNITION PERCENTAGE:1+2	78,1	85,5%	74,6%	73.5 %
RECOGNITION PERCENTAGE:1+2+3	86,8	94,7%	85%	78.7
NUMBER OF SYLLABLES	85	232	275	
SYLLABIC SEGMENTATION	97,7%	96%	97,5%	
SPEAKER	1	1	2	3
TASK	RECOGNITION OF	NUMBERS		30 PHONETICALLY BALANCED SENTENCES

Figure 11

are then adjusted to the syllable boundaries in order to simplify the sentence recognition process. Only detections with scores higher than a fixed threshold are kept for the sentence recognition step, in a word-lattice.

II-5 PROSODIC ANALYSIS

Using both fundamental frequency values and the duration of the vocalic nuclei determined by the phonetic analyzer, the prosodic module is able to find the main boundary of a sentence in which no pause has been automatically detected. This algorithm works like this (Fig. 13).

— A window of the size of three syllables is used to determine whether the central syllable is carrying a basic prosodic primary (P.P.C.) in terms of the durational variations of the three successive nuclei within the window and in terms of a particular shape of Fo contour across the nuclei: the vocalic nuclei corresponding to a local peak of durational contrast, and/or to a local peak of Fo contrast, and the vocalic nuclei with using Fo modulation are selected.

— Then they are ranked by order of decreasing value at the level of the sentence.

— The vocalic nucleus of the sentence with the longest duration is selected and if this nucleus is located at the end of the sentence, then it is replaced by the second largest nucleus.

— If this vocalic nucleus contains the highest or the second highest Fo peak, or the largest or the second largest Fo rise on a vowel, then it is interpreted as the main boundary in the utterance.

On a total number of 253 sentences of various types spoken by 7 speakers this algorithm has correctly detected the main boundary for 80% of the sentences; 15% have not been segmented and there is 5% errors (VAISSIERE 83).

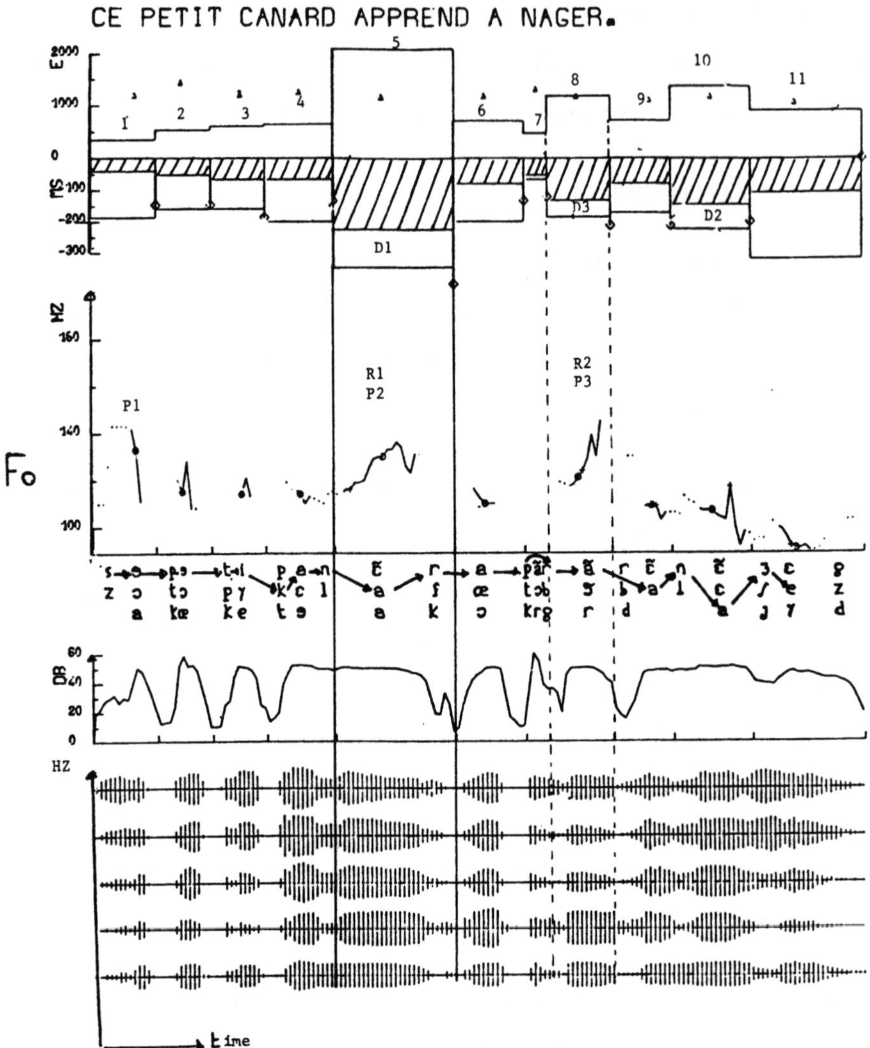

D1 + R1 + P2 = Main boundary

Dn	local peak of durational vocalic contrast
Pn	local peak of fo contrast
Rn	vocalic nucleus with rising fo modulation
n	rank of the nucleus

Figure 13

II-6 SYNTACTIC ANALYSIS

The role of the sentence recognizer is to search for the best sequence of word-detections of the word-lattice satisfying the grammatical constraints and to build the syntactic tree of the sentence. This algorithm has already been described in great detail (QUINTON, 1976). Briefly the language is described by a semantic context-free grammar and the parsing is based on EARLEY's algorithm. In addition, in order to avoid looking through the whole lexical lattice, only the best partial solutions are kept at each step, according to either a beam-search or a sequential decoding strategy. The result of the parsing, if any, is the recognized sentence associated with a score and a parse-tree.

Then the role of the semantic interpreter is to get from the parse-tree the information needed for the dialogue-controller. This is achieved by a set of transformation rules associated with the syntactic rules. The result of these transformations is a set of n-uplets containing only that in the sentence which is relevant to the dialogue. This comprehension part of KEAL has been described in detail in GILLET 1982.

II-7 RECOGNITION OF WORDS AND SENTENCES

Preliminary results, when using the lexical analyzer of KEAL, give a word recognition rate varying from 88% to 98% on a limited vocabulary (19 French digits and operands).

The programs corresponding to phonetic analysis, phonetic training, speaker adaptation and lexical word spotting are presently written in Fortran IV language and implemented on a SEMS M.225 mini computer. The speech data are digitalized through an A/D connected to a PDP 11/34 computer converter and the program simulating the channel vocoder and the pitch detection are implemented on an A.P. 120 B connected to the PDP 11/34. The spectral data are then transferred to the M-225 mini-computer.

Another version of KEAL including the syntactic analyzer is available on the U.T.S. systems of the new computer IBM 308 3/B of the computer center. It is written in C language. A Fortran version of this system has been tested on a set of randomly selected numbers composed of one to six digits spoken by three speakers. The results are shown in Fig. 14. Further testing will be necessary with this new version.

III SERAC SYSTEM ARCHITECTURE

III-1 GENERAL ORGANIZATION,

The SERAC system architecture uses the classical features of a rule production system. Rules that encode domain knowledge are stored in a data base, called Rule Memory, which is partitioned into sub-bases, each sub-base corresponding to a problem.

Objects that represent facts or event hypotheses are stored in an Object Memory which is divided into sub-memories corresponding to the different classes of objects.

Problem Memory contains interpretation problems whose solution will generate phonetic hypotheses such as segment boundaries detection, feature hypotheses, pseudo-syllable segmentation, vocalic nucleus detection and so on ...

Remaining entities like functions, parameters and acoustic data are encoded respectively under the form of Lisp functions, Lisp special variables (parameters) and files.

An inference Engine matches rules against problems and objects and decides which rules have to be triggered in a given circumstance.

The dialog between the user and the system is managed by an Interactive Editor. Edition of partial or complete results and triggering traces are handled by a special module.

SENTENCE RECOGNITION RESULTS

TASK	NUMBERS 0,...1000		
RECOGNITION PERCENTAGE	90%	75%	85%
NUMBER OF SENTENCES	50	40	40
SPEAKER	A	B	C

Figure 14

Fig. 15 shows the general organization of the SERAC system.

III-2 ACTIVATION

The "SERAC" phonetic recognition is decomposed into a sequence of step activations: initialization, labelling, segmentation and primary phonetic feature recognition.

The principal phases of these step activations are summarized in Fig. 16. Each module communicates with each other by means of acoustic objects like samples syllables, phonetic events and so on ... which are in the data base: these different steps are detailed in section VI.

IV THE LANGUAGE FOR EXPRESSING KNOWLEDGE

The expert's knowledge of acoustic-phonetic recognition consists of the following:

1. knowledge of domain objects (acoustic signal, samples, syllables, phonemes, etc...).

2. knowledge of the methods for phonetically transcribing the acoustic signal (algorithms, heuristics, etc...).

The objects represent the hypotheses elaborated or facts established during the recognition process and define, at a given instant the state of advancement of this process.

These objects are created or transformed through type 2 knowledge.

They are explicitly represented in a memory called the object memory.

Type 2 knowledge is coded in the form of:

— production rules

— Lisp functions evaluated in the rules

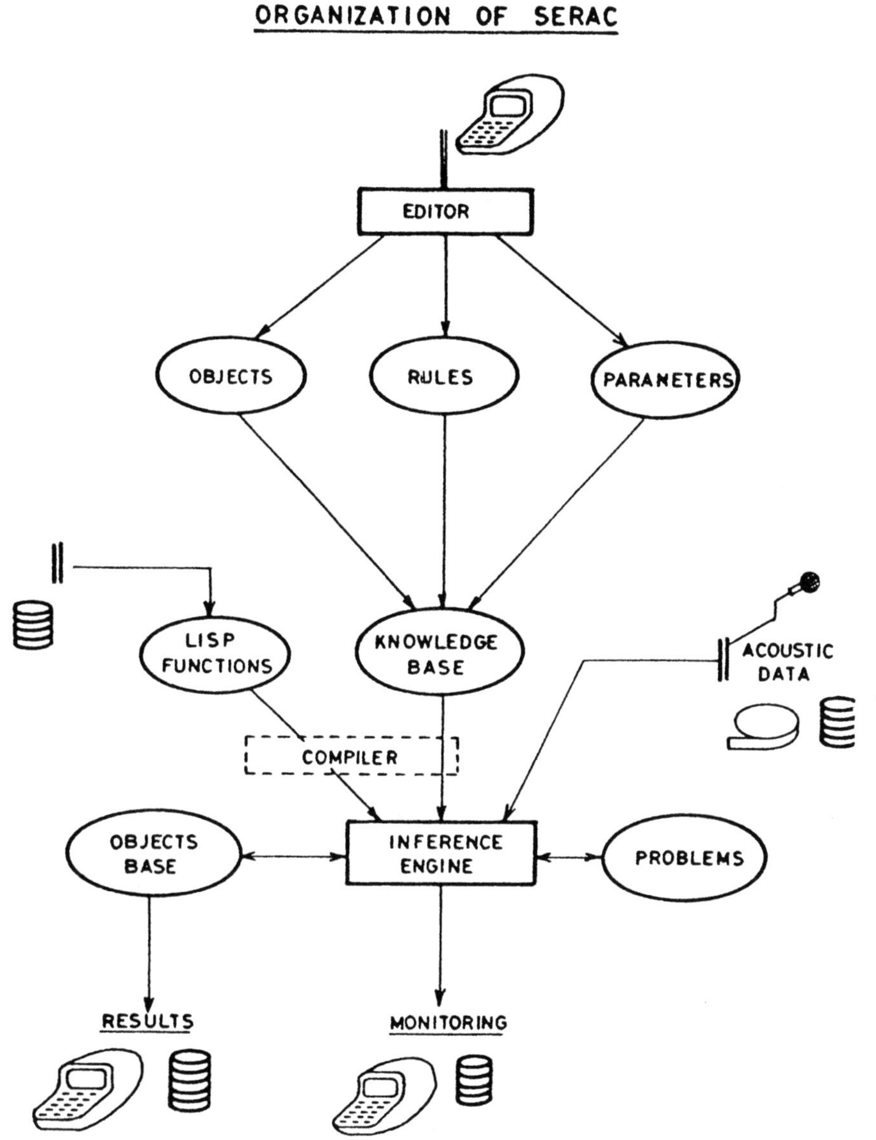
ORGANIZATION OF SERAC
EDITOR
OBJECTS
RULES
PARAMETERS
LISP
FUNCTIONS
KNOWLEDGE
BASE
ACOUSTIC
DATA
COMPILER
OBJECTS
BASE
INFERENCE
ENGINE
PROBLEMS
RESULTS
MONITORING

Figure 15

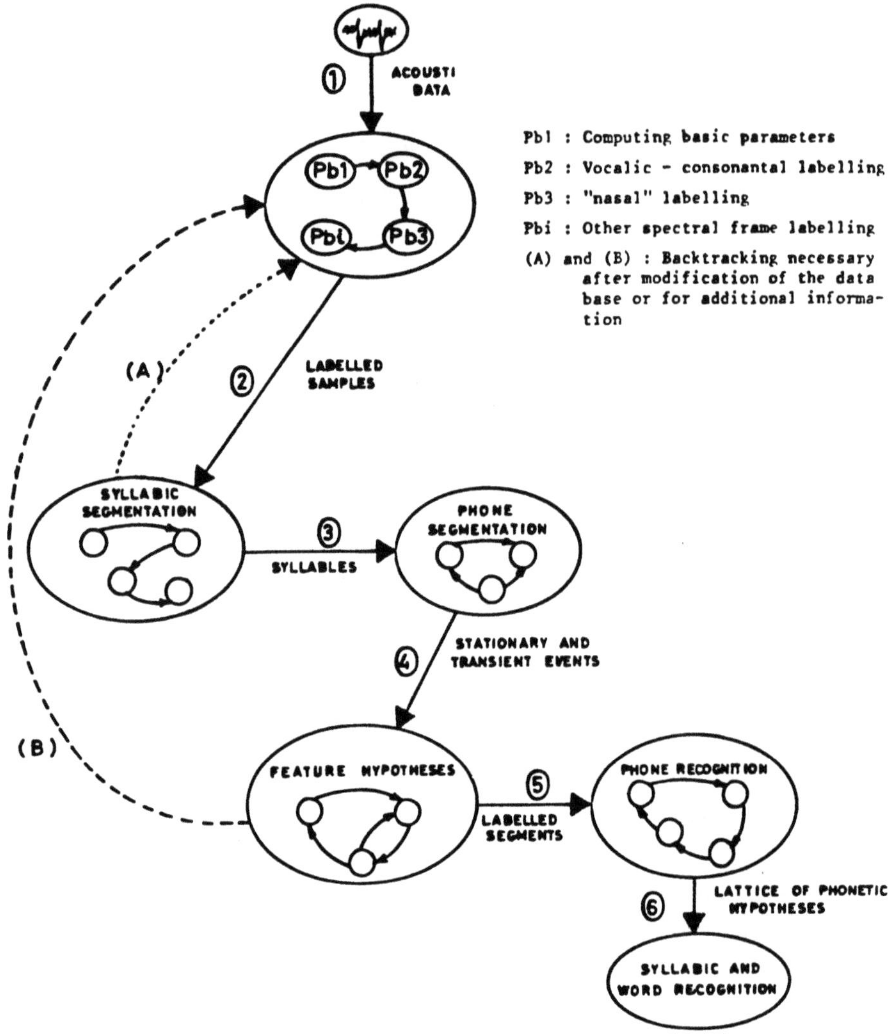

Main step activations of a rule-based phonetic recognizer

Figure 16

IV-1 THE OBJECTS

The objects are representatives or instances of structures in the form:

(< class > < atttribute 1 > ... < attribute n >)

as for a sample, for example:

(sample beginning end energy-vector ...)

A given sample will then be an object :

(sample 11 22 (1 2 0 3 4 0 2 3 2) ...)

Object structures are declared in a file (See functional architecture of the system) according to the syntax:

class = / attribute /+

IV-2 THE FUNCTIONS

IV-2-1 PRIMITIVE OPERATIONS OF THE LANGUAGE

Certain operations stem more from general knowledge than from expertise in the domain; these are, for example, arithmetic operations (+, – x, :), logical operations (and, or, negation), arithmetic predicatives (>, <, =, <>, ≥, ≤).

The operations are the primitives of the language expression knowledge, used as their Lisp equivalent.

IV-2-2 EXTENSIONS OF PRIMITIVES

Some expert knowledge corresponds to a purely algorithmic and procedural basic know-how of the domain which can easily be expressed in the form of Lisp functions, such as the computation of energy in a frequency band [f1, fh] from the vector v of energies in a sample,

This computation is made by the Lisp evaluation of:

(energy in the band fl fh v)

This use of functions permits access to value through computation rather than explicit storage, in the form of object attributes.

The expertise itself is expressed in the form of production rules:

condition ———— action

Modular knowledge can be easily expressed with this type of representation. Its accumulation can constitute a veritable expertise.

Moreover, the knowledge base, composed of the set of rules, evolves easily by removal or addition.

Lastly, each elementary part of the knowledge appears by itself within a rule and is therefore not lost, as an instruction would be in the heart of a fortran program, for example.

Rules are in the form:

NAME	sequence of characters used as mnemonic name for the rule in question
EXPERT	expert
PROBLEM	problem
IF	context
AND	condition
THEN	conclusion

Such a rule expresses that, for a data base situation (object memory, list of problems) which can be described by < expert >, < problem >, < context > and < condition >, this data bsse can be updated in compliance with < conclusion > directives.

IV-3-2-1 THE EXPERT

The knowledge base can be divided up into sub-bases made up of rules having the same expert name.

Each sub-base must both be able to be activated in parallel with the other sub-bases and to dialogue with them through the object memory.

Examples of sub-bases (or experts):

— beginning-and-end-of-speech-detector

— pseudo-syllable-detector.

IV-3-2-2 THE PROBLEM

Each expert possesses a list of current problems.

Each of these problems can be procesed by one of the expert's subsets of rules.

At a given instant only those rules for which the problem is one of the expert's current problems can be activated.

Example of problems for the "pseudosyllable-detector" expert:

— detection-of-the-beginning-of-a-pseudosyllable.

— detection-of-the-pseudosyllable-maximum.

— detection-of-the-end-of-the-pseudosyllable.

IV-3-2-3 THE CONTEXT

The context part tests the presence in the data base of objects described by patterns.

A data base situation can be described by the context part if:

— for each of the patterns, there exists an object in the data base which can be described by it.

— for each of the negative patterns, there is no object existing in the data base which can be described by it.

In these cases, the variables contained in the context part are related to the values of the objects or attributes which they describe.

IV-3-2-4 THE CONDITION PART

When the presence of certain objects in the data base has been tested by the context part, all of the pattern variables are bound.

The condition part, a logical conjunction of conditions, verifies then certain relationships between these variables.,

If, for example, the variables ?a and ?b are respectively bound to 10 and 20, the condition part:

(> ?b ?a)

is verified and the rule is applicable.

IV-3-2-5 THE CONCLUSION PART OR DIRECTIVES

When a rule is triggered, it carries out a certain number of actions (modifications in the object memory, list of problems, edition of results, etc...). These are expressed in the form of directives using the instanciations of variables realized in the context part : The main directives are : ADD, REMOVE, MODIFY objects; DO procedures; PRINT patterns; STOP; ADD, NEW or REMOVE Problems.

There is another very useful directive which allows to search for one or more objects within the data base by "pattern matching". This directive is the directive "FIND". It is possible for instance to find all the samples with the attribute "Fricative true" within the data base.

V THE RULE ACTIVATION

The rule interpreter is that part of the system which decides upon and carries out the activation of certain rules.

V-1 THE BASIC CYCLE

The basic cycle discussed in this paragraph is specific to a given expert and does not take into account the simultaneous activation of the different experts.

1. As long as there remains an applicable rule R

   1.1 search for the set of applicable rules

   1.2 choose one of these rules (conflict resolution)

   1.3 trigger the chosen rule (modifications in the object memory, in the list of problems).

2. Stop

V-2 APPLICABLE RULES

A rule is applicable if the problem that it deals with belongs to the current list of problems of the expert concerned and if the facts memory can be described by its context and conclusion parts.

V-3 CONFLICT RESOLUTION

When several rules are applicable during a given cycle of the rule interpreter, one of them must be selected for activation: this is the conflict resolution procedure.

This choice may be arbitrary or it may depend upon meta-knowledge.

The current version of SERAC (the first rule found) uses an arbitrary conflict resolution.

VI IMPLEMENTATION OF PHONETIC AND PROSODIC ANALYSIS IN SERAC

In the current version of SERAC two main experts corresponding to the first part of phonetic and prosodic knowledge have been implemented.

Current state of the phonetic analysis expert which includes more than three hundred rules is shown on Figure 17.

The phonetic recognition proceeds sequentially by step:

1. Reading each spectral sample and computing its attributes: spectral center of gravity, spectral standard deviation, low and high frequencies energies, derivatives, etc...
2. Detecting the sentence onset.
3. Setting the centisecond sample attributes: vowel, front, back, open, closed, consonant, nasal, fricative, silence.
4. Grouping of samples into pseudo-syllables.
5. Locating vocalic nuclei, detecting syllabic boundaries and computing their attributes.
6. Detecting the boundaries of stationary and transient events between the vocalic nuclei.
7. Computing the rudimentary phonetic attributes of these events: silence part, burst zone, fricative zone, nasal part, buzz-bar location, voicing segment...

These different steps are iterated each time it is possible until the sentence offset is detected and until the directive stop is given by one of the rules.

The implementation of the rules for discriminating between vowel attack and plosive burst, for recognizing the place of articulation of plosives and nasals and for refining the vowel identifiction is under way.

About fifty prosodic rules for detecting within a sentence the maxima and the minima of the vocalic durations, the peaks and the valleys of Fo, for ranking these attributes by decreasing order and for detecting the type of the sentence and its main boundary has been written in SERAC with the results given in Section II.5.

An example showing how the phonetic knowledge is represented in a rule is given in Figure 18.

VII FUNCTIONING OF SERAC

SERAC is written in NIL on a VAX 11-780 running VMS. An interactive editor allows us to add, create, modify rules, objects and parameters: During the running session it is also possible to have partial or complete traces of the instanciations of the rules and objects, to stop the execution, to save the data base memory, to modify rules or objects and to start again. Backtracking is also possible; i.e., it is possible to start one, two or n cycles before we stop. All these facilities are obtained through a "menu" organized like a tree.

The SERAC language is also compilable; each file can be compiled simultaneously or separately. This compilation makes an execution of the program much faster. For instance, the "SERAC" phonetic recognition as described in Fig. 17 takes about 1′ CPU time for analyzing a sentence composed of about 12 syllables. Digitalization and channel vocoder simulationa are done before and off-line on the PDP 11/34 and AP/120B processor. Current percentage of correct segmentation and primary phonetic feature recognition is similar to that obtained with the KEAL system.

CONCLUSION

Work is going on for including into SERAC the remaining rules which already exist in KEAL, for improving them and adding new ones possibly elaborated by other human experts. Then this new phonetic and prosodic knowledge base will be evaluated on a practical task.

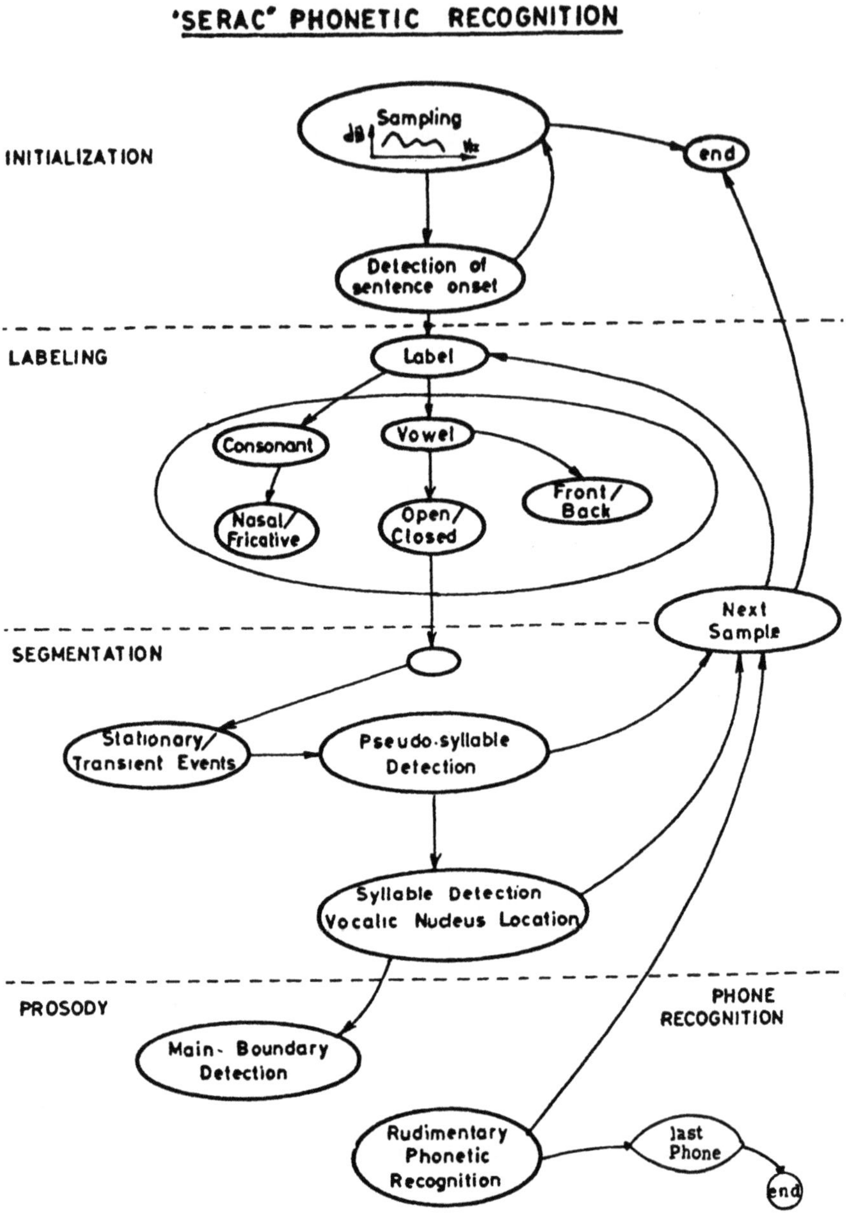
'SERAC' PHONETIC RECOGNITION
INITIALIZATION
Sampling
dB
Hz
end
Detection of sentence onset
LABELING
Label
Consonant
Vowel
Front/ Back
Nasal/ Fricative
Open/ Closed
SEGMENTATION
Next Sample
Stationary/ Transient Events
Pseudo-syllable Detection
Syllable Detection Vocalic Nucleus Location
PROSODY
PHONE RECOGNITION
Main- Boundary Detection
Rudimentary Phonetic Recognition
last Phone
end

Figure 17

(DEFRULE R1-NASALITY SAMPLE LABELLING	name of the rule name of the module current problem
IF (SAMPLE ?ECH (ENERGIES ?EN) (ENERGY-LOW-FREQUENCY ?PEB) (CENTER-OF-GRAVITY ?CDG)	CONTEXT PART OF THE RULE If there exists a sample represented by the variable ?ech, with spectral energies represented by the vector ?en, with the low frequency energy (250-450 Hz) represented by ?EB and with a spectral center of gravity represented by ?CDG
AND (> (– ?EB (MAX-ENERGY 450 1600 ?EN)) 1)	CONDITIONS: 1. The difference between the energy in the frequency range 250-450 Hz and the energy in the frequency range 450-1600 Hz must be higher than 1 (that is higher than 4 dB because the unit step of coding the energies is 4 dB)
(≥ (– ?EB (ENERGY 650 850 ? EN)) 3)	2. $E_{250\text{-}450HZ}-E_{650\text{-}850HZ} \geq$ 3x4db
(≥ (– ?EB (MAX-ENERGY 1600 4200 ?EN)) 2)	3. $E_{250\text{-}450HZ}-MAX(E_{1600\text{-}4200}) \geq$ 2x4db
(≥ (+ (– (ENERGY 450 650 ?EN) (ENERGY 650 850 ?EN)) 1) 0)	4. $E_{450\text{-}650HZ}-E_{650\text{-}850} \geq$ 4db
(OR (≥ (– ?EB (ENERGY 850 1050 ?EN)) 2) (≥ (– ?EB (ENERGY 1050 1300 ?EN)) 2)))	5. one of the 2 following conditions must be satisfied: $E_{250\text{-}450}-E_{850\text{-}1050} \geq$ 8db OR $E_{250\text{-}450HZ}-E_{1050\text{-}1300} \geq$ 8db
Then (MODIFY (SAMPLE ?ECH (NASAL1 TRUE))) (NEWPB (LABELLING-CONTINUE)))	Conclusion part The attribute NASAL 1 of the sample ?ECH becomes "TRUE" The new problem to be considered is LABELLING-CONTINUE

Fig. 18 An example of rule detection "nasality"

The SERAC system itself will be improved:

- A meta language will be included in order to make easier for an user to express the global strategy of phonetic recognition.
- The actual version does not take into account the parallel organization of speech recognition algorithms; this point will be integrated in the next version in order to speed up the recognition process and to distribute the knowledge over separated modules called experts. Cooperation between the different experts will be studied. A new implementation of SERAC into the special processor SM 90 is under way making possible to study this parallelism and cooperative aspects within an expert society.

ACKNOWLEDGEMENTS

We are very grateful to Jean Monne and Michel Querre for their assistance in implementing the KEAL programs on the PDP11/34, AP/120B and SEMS Mitra 225, allowing us to use this system on-line. We thank also M. Rossi, R. Vivès, D. Gillet, P. Quinton, J. Siroux, D. Bigorgne, M. Cloatre, L. Le Guennec for having written important modules in KEAL.

Many thanks also to M. Gerard and M. A. Simon for implementing a number of rules in SERAC.

We would like also to thank C. Cagnoulet, R. De Mori, R. Gubrynowicz, M. Vailly, M. Hautin, R. Descout, M. Cartier for helpful discussions and criticisms on this work.

Many thanks to M. N. Le Gall for printing this paper and to J. Le Denmat for her help along the year for making easier our work.

RFERENCES

1. B. Buchanan, R. O. Duda, "Principles of rule-based expert systems," Stanford University Comp-Science, STAN-CS-82-926, 1982.
2. P. Carbonell, D. Fohr, J. P. Haton, J. M. Pierrel, F. Lonchamp, "Systeme expert de decodage acoustico-phonetique et invariance," 13èmes J.E.P. Bruxelles, 1984.
3. R. De Mori, A. Giordana, P. Laface and L. Saitta, "An expert system for speech decoding," Proc. AAAI Conference, Pittsburg, P.A., pp. 107-110, 1982.
4. R. O. Duda, "The prospector consultation system," Final Report SRI 8172, 1982.
5. C. L. Forgy, "OPS5 user's manual," Department of Computer Science, C.M.U., Pittsburg, 1981.
6. D. Gillet, M. Gerard, "Integration of acoustic, phonetic, prosodic and lexical knowledge in an expert system for speech understanding," ICASSP 84, Vol. III, pages 42-9-1 to 42-9-4, San Diego, 1984.
7. D. Gillet, P. Quinton, J. Siroux, "From speech recognition to speech understanding: a case study of KEAL," IEEE ICASSP meeting, Paris, May 1982.
8. R. Gubrynowicz, "La détection des consonnes nasales dans le système de reconnaissance de la parole continue KEAL," R. A. CNET, Vol. II, pp. 91-107, 1983.
9. F. Hayes-Roth, V. R. Lesser, "Focus of attention in the HEARSAY II Speech Understanding System," 5th IICAI, pp. 27-35, 1977.
10. G. Mercier, A. Nouhen, P. Quinton, J. Siroux, "The KEAL speech understanding system," J. C. Simon, ed. *Spoken Language Generation and Understanding*, D. Reidel Publishing Company, Dordrecht, pp. 525-543, 1980.
11. P. Quinton, "Contribution à la reconnaissance de la parole, Utilisation d'heuristiques pour la reconnaissance de phrases," Thèse d'Etat, Université de Rennes, 1980.
12. M. Rossi, Y. Nishinuma, G. Mercier, "Indices acoustiques multilocuteurs et indépendants du contexte pour la reconnaissance automatique de la parole," Speech Com., Vol. 2, pp. 215-218, July 1983.
13. E. H. Shortliffe, *MYCIN: Computer Based Medical Consultations*, American Elsevier, New York, 1976.
14. R. N. Stevens, "Constraints imposed by the auditory system on the properties used to classify speech sounds: data from phonology acoustics and psycho acoustics," The Cognitive Representation of Speech, Myers, Laver, Anderson, North-Holland, pp. 61-74, 1981.
15. J. Vaissiere, "Suprasegmental effect on the velum movement in sentences," Abstract of the Tenth International Congress of phonetic sciences, Foris Publications, Dordrecht-Holland/Cinnamirson, U.S.A., 1983.
16. J. Vaissiere-Maeda, "A suprasegmental component in a speech recognition system," 104th ASA meeting, Florida, November 1982.
17. R. Vives, "Utilisation de l'information phonémique et syllabique pour la reconnaissance de mots prononcés isolément ou dans les phrases," Proc. 10 èmes J.E.P. Grenoble, pp. 375-384, 1978.

SAY - A PC based Speech Analysis system

P R Alderson, G Kaye, S G C Lawrence, D A Sinclair
B J Williams and G J Wolff

IBM UK Scientific Centre
Athelstan House
St Clement St
Winchester S023 9DR
ENGLAND

MOTIVATION FOR BUILDING A SPEECH ANALYSER

This paper is concerned with an experimental system of value to anyone interested in speech research in general, and in particular to those interested in speech input and output by computer. At the IBM UKSC we are building a system capable of converting text data to natural sounding speech. This embodies many of the features of an expert system since the system must understand and use the same rules of spelling, syntax, intonation, pronunciation and phonetics that a human speaker draws upon when talking. In building this system we must have a detailed understanding of normal human speech and a means of analysing synthetic speech to enable us to quantify the factors that determine intelligibility and acceptability. To achieve this we need a knowledge of both the physics and anatomy of speech production in the human articulatory system, and of the speech signal itself. We will need techniques for analysing synthetic speech and comparing it with its natural counterpart. An understanding of the process of speech perception, and of which parts of the speech signal carry the important perceptual information, is also relevant. A suitable system for the analysis of speech signals is thus an essential tool in this project and it is the development of such a speech analyser that is the subject of this paper.

NATO ASI Series, Vol. F16
New Systems and Architectures for Automatic Speech
Recognition and Synthesis. Edited by R. De Mori and C. Y. Suen

INTRODUCTION

SAY is an IBM Personal Computer (PC) based speech analysis tool intended for a diverse set of users engaged in the evaluation of natural and synthetic speech. The challenges involved in developing such a system include

- the recording, storage and manipulation of unlimited lengths of speech,
- provision of a flexible, easily understood interface for a very diverse set of users (eg linguists, phoneticians, speech therapists, engineers).
- provision of a high level of signal processing function (eg spectral and Linear Prediction Coefficient (LPC) analysis),
- provision of a simple method of extending the system function to fulfill a particular user's requirements.

The SAY system consists of a 640 Kbyte IBM PC-XT with 20 Mbyte hard disk, IBM 370 host connection together with special purpose digitisation and display hardware. Speech may be recorded and replayed from the hard disk at sampling rates up to 20 KHz. A vector display capable of showing two waveforms of up to 1024 points each is provided, together with waveform scrolling and editing facilities. There are two possible ways of editing the waveform:

1. The user may select, copy, delete or modify portions of the speech waveform - using a special control panel while viewing the results of this editing on the display and also listening to the results as required; or
2. System macros may be invoked to perform more complex operations on the selected portions of the waveform (eg cepstral analysis).

In the editing mode the user is provided with a special-purpose control panel containing keys allocated to the most common editing functions. These permit the user to display or replay portions of the edited or unedited wave and to scroll these waves across the display, selecting and manipulating portions by the use of a joystick and on-screen cursors. The system may either be menu or command driven according to the expertise of the user. The menu system provides a flexible interface for feedback of information to enhance ease of use.

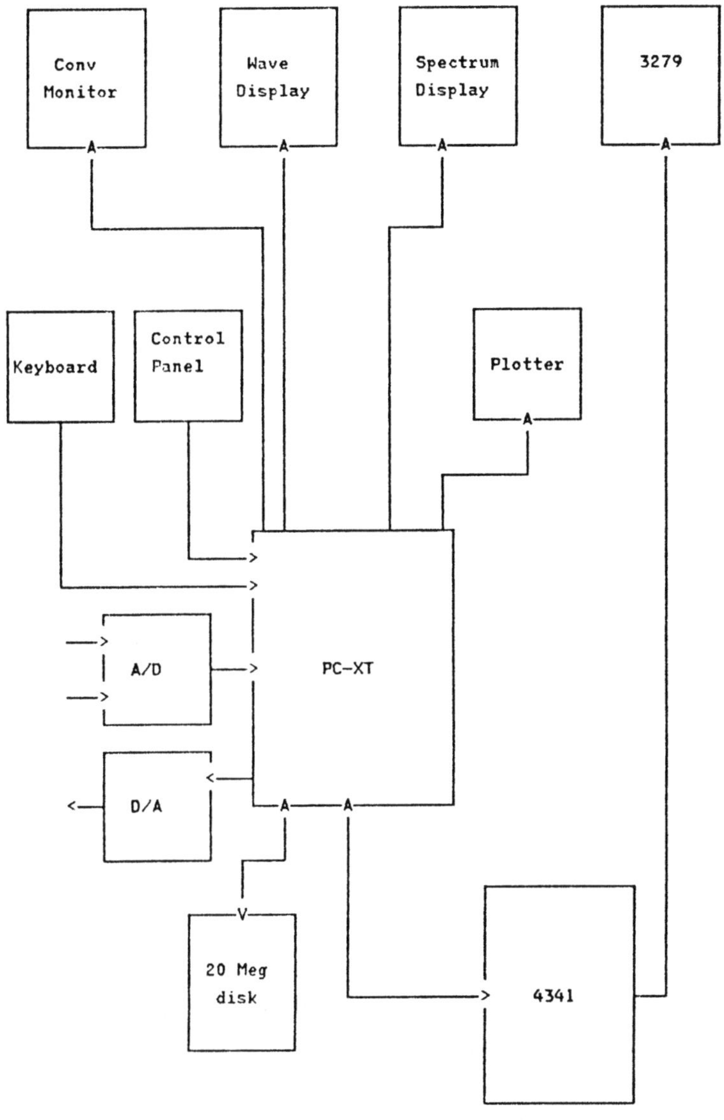

Figure 1. System Components

SAY provides a wide range of sophisticated signal processing facilites via a host link to the IBM UKSC IAX signal processing package (refs 2,3). These facilities include spectral and cepstral analysis, grey scale and colour spectrogram display, LPC analysis and pitch contour extraction. As the system is developed some of the signal processing facilites will move from the host into the PC. This will be achieved by the use of specialist signal processing hardware including a Discrete Fourier Transform (DFT) unit based on a prime radix transform and the attachment of a raster colour display.

SAY - SPEECH ANALYSER FUNCTIONAL DESCRIPTION

SAY provides the following facilities:

- Digitisation
- Editing
- Analysis
- Storage
- Replay

of speech signals. Since all its facilities, except for the actual speech acquisition and replay, can be applied to any one-dimensional digital signal, the system could usefully be applied to a range of non-speech applications eg seismic processing, time domain reflectometry, vibrational analysis.

It is intended that the system will have a wide range of users extending from computer specialists to linguists and phoneticians. Consequently it has a user interface that balances the flexibility needed by the computer professional with the ease of access appropriate to a linguist or other person with less computational experience.

This was achieved by adopting a largely menu driven system and by the provision of a special keypad containing dedicated controls for cursor functions, waveform scrolling and speech editing and playback. The more experienced user may overide the menu system and use a single or full screen command mode while still retaining the dedicated control panel key functions where required. Many of the more sophisticated facilities are built up from basic operations using this command interface (and interactions with the menu system where necessary). These facilities are provided by a library of system functions.

Examples are:

- Cepstrum processing to extract the vocal tract response
- Linear prediction to obtain vocal tract response
- Spectrum generation
- Pitch contour extraction

In implementing these functions extensive use has been made of the host resident signal processing functions provided by IAX. To this end a modified form of the PC Personal Editor has been produced. This can be invoked from SAY. It acts both as a command editor and an interface to the external command processors such as the PC DOS, the CMS environment in the host, and the interpretive IAX command processor within CMS in the host.

A block diagram of the system is shown in Figure 1and the main functional units are:

- Analog audio recording equipment
- Speech digitiser and playback
- Waveform display and editor
- Speech and waveform analysis system
- Spectrum display
- Speech synthesisers

The **PC-XT** controls all digitisation, editing, wave storage and playback functions. It is also used for the entry of all system commands and for the display of guidance information and alphanumeric feedback. It is connected to an IBM 370 host computer via a highspeed link. It is intended to enhance the function of the PC-XT with a specialist digital signal processing hardware to make a stand-alone system in the near future.

Conversational monitor

This is the PC monochrome display. It is used to display system menus and status information, such as the number of waves being edited, time of day. A typical menu is shown in Figure 2. Here the dual display mode is being used on the waveform to display two different sections of the same waveform. The top waveform shows an expanded region (along the time axis) of the waveform while the bottom regions shows a compressed region. The user is provided with information on the position of the cursors within the wave, the relative position of the cursor on the display and the position of the display window relative to the start of the wave. The overall duration of the wave in seconds, the original sampling rate and the total number of samples in the wave are also shown, together with an indication of the amount of horizontal and vertical scaling currently being applied to the display window. The user should be able to read all the facts he needs to know about the wave directly from the screen thus removing the need for tiresome mental arithmetic, say for instance in calculating the wave duration from the sample rate and total number of samples.

```
Speech Editing/Replay                                          26 Jun 1984 03-53pm
                         Number of waves being edited :  1
                                                         LEFT                RIGHT
                                                   edge     cursor     cursor     edge
Wave name . : POLITELY                  Display :        0       60        183      255
Sample rate : 10 Khz                    Wave. . :     9049     9109       9221     9304
Duration. . : 2.50 sec 25037 samples    Scaling : Horizontal :  4 Vertical :  1

Wave name . : POLITELY                  Display :        0                         2047
Sample rate : 10 Khz                    Wave. . :    15033                        17079
Duration. . : 2.50 sec 25037 samples    Scaling : Horizontal : -2 Vertical :  1

The information above shows:-

        1.  How many waves are being edited.
        2.  The name of the wave being edited.
        3.  The sample number of the right and left displayed samples.
        4.  The location of each cursor on the wave display and in the wave.
        5.  The scaling currently active.
                                                        More ...

F1 HELP  F3 EXIT  F4 WAVE  F6 DROP  F7 PLAY  F8 COMMAND  F9 STORE  F10 EXEC  SAY
```

Figure 2. Conversational monitor menu showing HELP facility.

At the bottom of all the system menus is a prompt line which indicates which of the PC keyboard programmable function keys are active at that time and what their effect is.

In the example menu it has been assumed that the user has pressed PF1 to obtain the HELP information for that menu. This displays information on the various options available within that menu. This is carefully positioned on the conversational monitor screen so that it does not obscure the primary menu fields.

Speech Digitisation

The speech sources are:

- Microphone
- Pre-recorded tape
- Output from a synthesiser

Digitisation sampling rate and filter can be selected under the control of commands issued from the PC keyboard. At present digitisation is performed by a Tecmar Labmaster attached to the PC. The input signal is low pass filtered by an analog antialiasing filter with an appropriate cut-off to allow 10kHz and 20kHz sampling. A new digitisation system that uses fast dual port memory to buffer the ADC into the PC memory space is currently being developed. This will allow digitisation concurrent with hard disk activity and will permit records of virtually unlimited lengths of speech at sampling rates of up to 40 kHz. Lower sampling rates are obtained by digital low pass filtering and downsampling to the required sample rate. In this way linear phase may be preserved in the overall system response.

The RECORD menu displayed on the conversational monitor is shown in Figure 3. All fields are initially filled in with defaults. The user may overtype these with new values if required. A simple recording level meter also appears

```
Speech Recording                                        26 Jun 1984 03-53pm

        Selected function:-
                             Recording
                             Editing and Replay
                             Command Processing
                             Synthesis

        External sample rate. : 10 kHz
        Antialiasing filter . :  5 kHz
        Internal sample rate. : 10 kHz      (10,20 kHz
        Recording source. . . : m           (m - microphone
                                            (t - reel-to-reel recorder
                                            (c - cassette recorder

        If incorrect change and press ENTER
        or press M4 to RECORD

        min                     ADC level                    max

F1 HELP  F3 EXIT
```

Figure 3. Record menu

on this menu so that the user may set the input level at an appropriate position to utilise the full ADC range.

Playback is through an appropriate reconstruction filter selected by the system according to the original sample rate. A dual port memory buffer (similar to that needed for digitisation) will be implemented to accomodate speech output direct from the hard disk.

The PLAYBACK menu displayed on the conversational monitor during replay of speech is shown in Figure 4.

Waveform Display

This is a high resolution X-Y directed-beam vector display capable of displaying one or two 1024 point windows on a speech waveform. The window may be scrolled along the waveform by the operation of a joystick on the control panel. The display has four levels of brightness (off, low, medium and high) and points may be made to blink as well. These brightness attributes are useful for delineating sections of the waveform that are being processed (eg deleted or copied).

Vertical zoom and horizontal zoom and compression are implemented using scaling factors of 2,4,8,16 and 32. It is very convenient being able to display two waveforms simultaneously at different resolutions, since this permits the user to have a global view of the speech waveform as well as a high resolution view of the particular area he is working with. A typical example of this is shown in Figure 5.

A pair of cursors are associated with each wave being edited. These may be manipulated from the control panel or by program control. They are used to mark sections of a wave for editing or replay purposes.

Help facilities

Help is provided for each function and facility in the system. It is displayed in either the lower or upper part of the conversation monitor screen as is most appropriate for the menu currently being displayed, and can be read whilst the user is completing the appropriate fields, or using the control panel. In general HELP is additive to what is currently displayed, and never overwrites a response field.

3279 Display

This is a colour output-only device and is used primarily as a 'soft' graph plotter. It is attached to IAX via the Grapical Data Display Manager (ref 4). Its primary purpose is to provide a rapid means of viewing, in graphical form, the results of various signal processing calculations eg to show a waveform and its corresponding pitch profile.

Graph Plotter

This is an A3 size eight-pen IBM Instruments XY-750 digital plotter. Its support software runs on the PC-XT. It provides a hard copy facilities as a counterpart to the 3279.

```
Speech Editing/Replay                                          26 Jun 1984 03-53pm
                         Number of waves being edited :  1
                                                    edge    cursor    cursor    edge
Wave name . : POLITELY                     Display :    0                        255
Sample rate : 10 Khz                       Wave. . :  9049                      9304
Duration. . : 2.50 sec 25037 samples       Scaling : Horizontal :  4 Vertical :  1

Wave name . : POLITELY                     Display :     0     546     1845     2047
Sample rate : 10 Khz                       Wave. . :  15033  15579    16877    17079
Duration. . : 2.50 sec 25037 samples       Scaling : Horizontal : -2 Vertical :  1

          Replay mode. . : s        (S,s Single / R,r Repeated
          Pause. . . . . : 0.5 secs
          Recorder . . . : 1        (t reel to reel recorder
                                    (c cassette recorder
                                    (l loudspeaker


F1 HELP  F3 EXIT  F4 WAVE  F6 DROP  F8 COMMAND  F9 STORE
```

Figure 4. Playback prompts on the conversational monitor: Replay of speech normally occurs when editing that speech.

Control Panel

The control panel provides a means of scrolling waveforms and of moving cursors. It also provides single key access to the commonest system functions. This means that the majority of editing activity can be performed under the control of one hand (usually the left) which leaves the other hand free for taking notes, adjusting tape recorder controls. It consists of 16 keys, a one dimensional joystick, two tracker wheels with rotary encoders and two sets of thumbwheel switches. The joystick is used for scrolling the active displayed waveform, the rate of scroll being proportional to the amount of joystick displacement. The tracker wheels are used to move the cursors on the waveform display. Two 3 digit thumbwheel switches are provided and these are used for specifying scaling factors for the region of the wave within and outside the area marked by the cursor. The function of each control panel switch is detailed below. The active action key mode is indicated on the control panel.

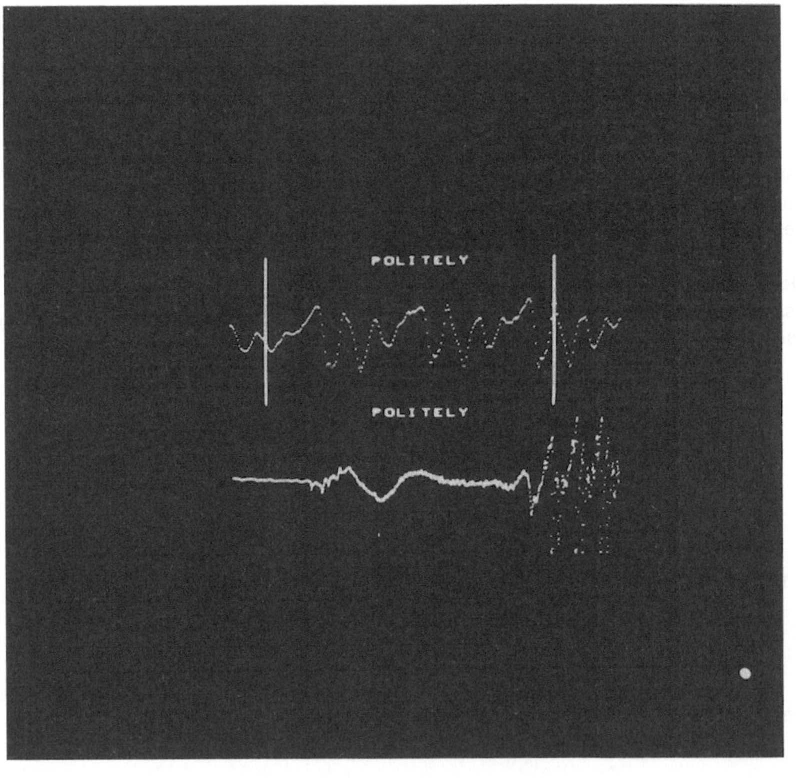

Figure 5. Waveform display: The top waveform shows the schwa at the end of 'better' in the digitised waveform of the utterance 'He had better speak politely'. The bottom waveform is an expanded view of the start of 'politely' showing the strong low frequency transient at the onset of the heavily aspirated 'p'.

M1	toggle to alternative function for A1-A8
M2	move to next wave in edit ring
M3	toggle between top and bottom displays
M4	select extended cursor mode
	record start/stop
P1	playback unedited active wave
P2	playback wave between cursors
P3	playback wave outside cursors
P4	playback displayed wave
A1	display edited wave
	select region between cursors
A2	display only selected regions within wave
	copy region between cursors
A3	display all but selected regions within wave
	mark point at left cursor
A4	toggle between dual and single wave display
	delete region between cursors
A5	increase wave vertical scaling
	reset cursor positions
A6	decrease wave vertical scaling
	reset selections
A7	increase wave horizontal scaling
	reset marked points
A8	decrease wave horizontal scaling
	select extended cursor mode

Figure 6. Control Panel Functions

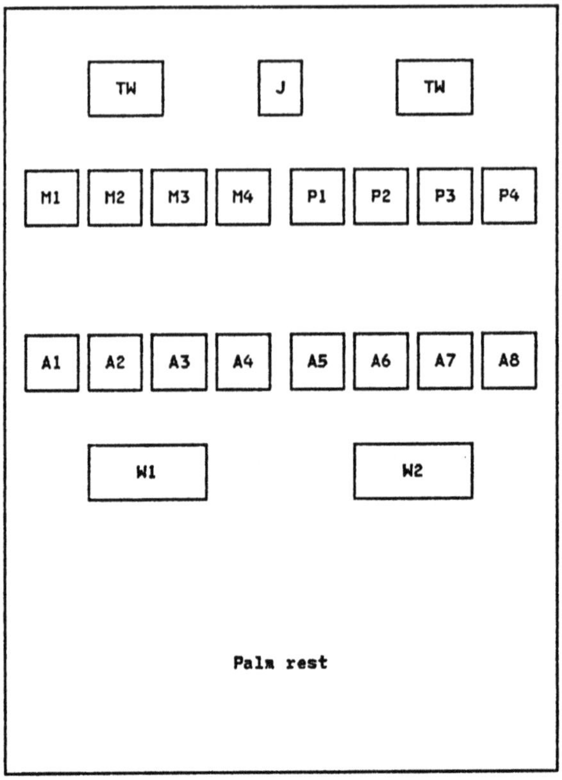

J Joystick
TW1 – TW2 Thumbwheels
M1 – M4 Mode setting keys
P1 – P4 Playback keys
A1 – A8 Action keys
W1 – W2 Tracker wheels

Figure 7. Control Panel

Speech Editing

A full range of waveform editing functions are provided. Up to six waves may be involved in the editing process at any one time. Sections may be copied and deleted from each of these waves freely.

The waveform editing facilities include:

- Delete a wave section
- Copy a section of a wave from one wave to another or within the wave
- Move sections of a wave within the wave
- Store wave on hard disk
- Select a segment of a wave for subsequent processing e.g.
  - Compute the Fourier transform of the segment
  - Play back only the selected segments
  - Play back ignoring the selected segments
  - Mark points in the wave for reference in subsequent processing

Spectrogram Computation and Display

Speech spectrograms can be computed using IAX and then displayed on a raster graphics display or on the 3279 colour terminal at present. It is intended to provide this facility eventually within the PC environment by the use of dedicated Fourier transform hardware.

Signal Processing

An extensive range of signal processing functions are available within IAX (refs 2,3) at the host. The user can invoke these functions directly from the speech analyser. In the first version the results may be displayed on the 3279, or on the wave and spectrogram displays. The command interface is via a modified form of the IBM PC Personal Editor. It provides both a command editor and a means of executing a single command or command list. Eventually it is intended to move the signal processing function provided by IAX into the PC environment by installing specialist digital signal processing hardware.

```
/* Routine to compute the spectrogram of a speech waveform */
/* Parameters :  1st  name of file containing speech waveform
                 2nd  width of FFT window
                 3rd  amount by which FFT window is stepped along waveform
                      for each spectrum time slot
                 4th  file name to receive calculated spectrum       */


/* first get parameters from command line */

"IAXLSTR"; IF RC¬=0 THEN EXIT RC; PULL name
"IAXLSTR"; IF RC¬=0 THEN EXIT RC; PULL width
"IAXLSTR"; IF RC¬=0 THEN EXIT RC; PULL ' step_size '_size
"IAXLSTR"; IF RC¬=0 THEN EXIT RC; PULL spectrum_file

/* compute Hamming window for selected FFT size */
'hamming=hamm('width')'
/* pad out the Hamming window with 0s to make overall window 512 points */
'pad= 0.('width' :511)'
/* reserve array space for resultant sonogram */
'r=0. (0:255 , 0:xs(' name ' )/'' step_size '_size'-1)'

/* main loop */
/* select the current portion of the speech waveform */
/* apply the Hamming window and take the FFT of the result */
/* take the log of the absolute magnitude and put in the result array */
/* repeat the loop, moving the FFT window slowly along the speech waveform */

'do i=0 by ' step_size ' to xs(' name ' )-' step_size '-1'
     'b=' name ' (i:i+' width ' -1)*hamming || pad'
     'c=ft(b)'
     'r(*,i/' step_size ')= log abs c(0:255)'
     'end'
/* orientate songoram + make max energy correspond to black rather than white */
'r=-r'
'r= cl range( r )'
'r=tr mir r'
/* put final sonogram in destination file */
'put r, ' spectrum_file ', IAX1,keep,repl'
```

Figure 9. Command list for the calculation of a spectrum

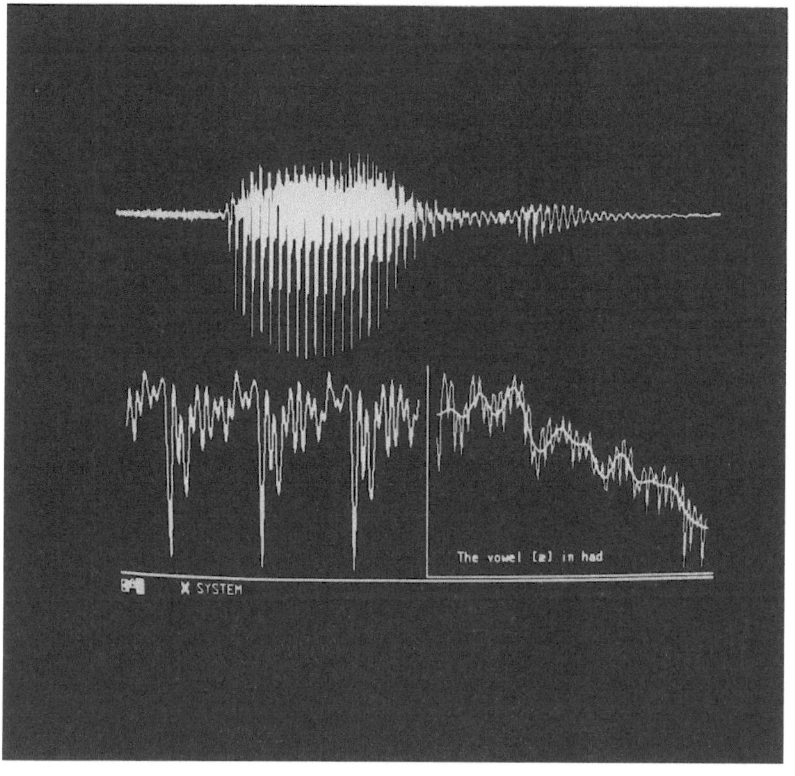

Figure 10. Cepstral calculation of the vowel a: in 'hard'

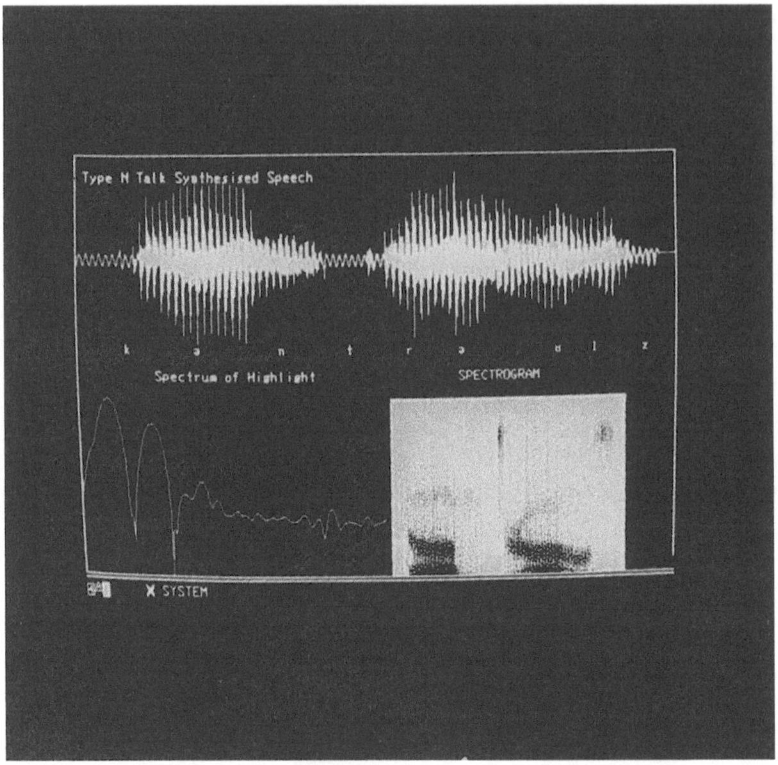

Figure 11. **Analysis of phoneme synthesiser spectrum:** The synthetic waveform is shown at the top. Bottom left is the spectrum of a portion of the dipthong in the second syllable of 'controls' while bottom left is a half tone spectrum of the entire word.

EXAMPLES FROM A SAY SESSION

SAY offers a wide range of signal processing functions. Here we will illustrate some of the simpler and more commonly used features. The spectrogram for the utterance 'Good morning how are you' is shown in Figure 8. This spectrogram was taken from the high resolution spectrogram display system within SAY and was computed using the hopping FFT technique shown in the SAY command list of Figure 9. The command list shows the simple, readable, high level form of the IAX language.

Figure 10 shows the type of graphical output that may be obtained from the 3279 soft graph plotter. Here the two formant peaks in the cepstrum of the vowel a: in hard can be clearly seen. (Note that this display would normally be in several contrasting colours but due to printing restraints a black and white image is shown here). By using a grey scale half-toning technique the 3279 can display spectrograms, albeit at rather lower resolution than the dedicated spectrogram display. This is useful when speech processing is being carried out under IAX but outside the normal SAY environment. An example is shown in Figure 11. This is a piece of synthetic speech - the word 'controls' generated by a simple phoneme synthesiser. It can be seen that the lower formants in the synthesiser output are approximately correct but the higher formant information is rather less well defined.

CONCLUSIONS

We have developed a multi-function speech analysis system, based on an IBM PC-XT, which is capable of a wide range of speech processing functions. The system function is being expanded to include local spectrographic calculation and processing of unlimited lengths of speech. The system is currently being used to evaluate human and synthetic speech in relation to our text to speech work.

Acknowledgements

We should like to thank all our colleagues at the UKSC for their help and

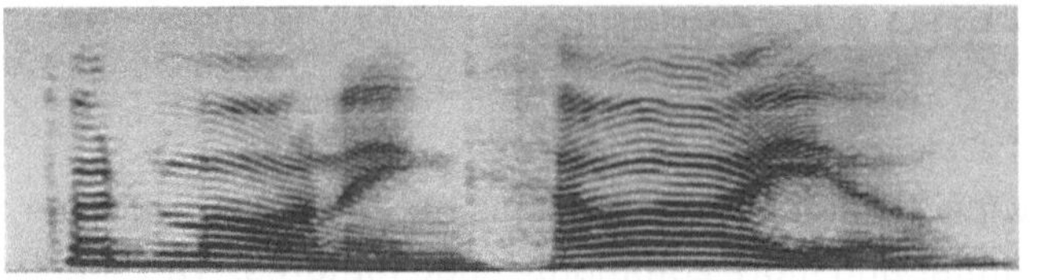

Figure 8. Narrowband spectrum of 'Good morning how are you'

criticism. We are especially grateful to Dr Paul Jackson for the help he has given us with the IAX package and to Nick Allen and Dilbagh Singh for the significant contribution they made in implementing the SAY code.

References

1. Tomorrow's Computers, IEEE Spectrum, vol 20 no 17, Nov 1983.

2. The IAX Image Processing Language. P H Jackson, UK Science Centre Report no 113, Feb 1983.

3. The IAX Image Processing Language - Functions and Commands. P H Jackson, UK Science Centre Report no 114, May 1983.

4. The GDDM General Information Manual. GC33-0100.

AUTOMATIC GENERATION OF LINGUISTIC, PHONETIC AND ACOUSTIC KNOWLEDGE FOR A DIPHONE-BASED CONTINUOUS SPEECH RECOGNITION SYSTEM

Anna Maria Colla
Donatella Sciarra
Central Research Department
Elettronica San Giorgio, ELSAG S.p.A.
Via G. Puccini, 2
16154 Genova Sestri
ITALY

ABSTRACT

An important issue in template-matching continuous-speech recognition systems is the right choice of the language model, together with an appropriate definition of the basic units to be recognized. The advantages of using a hierarchical transition network model with diphones and diphone-like elements as basic units are illustrated in the paper. However, a severe drawback in the use of sub-word units is an increased complexity in producing and managing the overall knowledge relating to language representation and template definition and extraction. An efficient solution to this problem is required especially when the recognition system is to be used by unskilled users in actual applications. For this purpose we have developed an automatic procedure for generating the linguistic, phonetic and acoustic data bases expressing the whole information required by the diphone-based system.

NATO ASI Series, Vol. F16
New Systems and Architectures for Automatic Speech
Recognition and Synthesis. Edited by R. De Mori and C. Y. Suen

1. INTRODUCTION

An important issue in template-matching continuous-speech recognition (CSR) systems is the choice of the basic units to be recognized. Economy and invariance with the surrounding units are the main requisites to be evaluated. We found that the diphones, as defined in the following, completely fulfil these requirements. In fact fewer than 400 diphones are sufficient to describe the whole Italian lexicon; moreover their fairly high insensibility to the context ensures that very few templates can adequately represent each unit. In this way the speaker-dependent template dictionaries are quite manageable even for complex applications. In fact such dictionaries need not comprise all the Italian diphones, but are tailored to a particular language: they only comprise the diphones appearing in the words of the lexicon, plus some elements that may be present at the junction between two fluently spoken words.

We have implemented two diphone-based CSR systems, obtaining satisfactory performances. One of them is described in [14]; the other one, which is referred to in this paper, has a real-time oriented, very simple architecture, consisting of two modules: an acoustic front-end and a linguistic decoder. The key point in this system is the choice of a good model of the spoken language: a *hierarchical transition network* (HTN), where the basic speech units are diphones [16]. The HTN language representation smoothly integrates the different knowledge sources involved: syntax and semantics describe the permitted sequences of words, while phonetic and phonological knowledge is used for generating the diphone subnetworks corresponding to words and for dealing with junctions. Acoustic knowledge is finally present in the sequences of spectra that make up the basic units and in the sound similarity measure.

With such a language representation, the recognition problem, formulated as that of finding the acceptable sequence of basic units that best fits the input signal [4], is turned into the search for the path through the network that obtains the maximum cumulative similarity score [16]. This task is accomplished by the *linguistic decoder*.

Such a diphone-based system led to high recognition performances [16] and proved to be more suitable for the treatment of complex languages than whole-word template matching systems; this is due particularly to the good discrimination between similar words, the small storage requirements and the fast training on new speakers. On the other hand, a drawback common to all systems that apply sub-word units is an increased complexity in producing the overall knowledge relating to language representation and template definition and extraction. With an HTN representation all the knowledge relating to an application must be conveyed into the linguistic, phonetic and acoustic data bases, corresponding to the high level networks, the diphone subnetworks and the template set, respectively (see Fig. 1). Both the building of the networks and the creating of the template set, which requires the identification, acquisition and extraction of the necessary units, are long and difficult tasks when complex languages are involved. It is hardly worth saying that manual network generation and template extraction are completely inadequate for practical applications. This spurred us to develop a completely automatic procedure (sketched in Fig. 1) that derives all the data bases relating to any language associated with a regular grammar, starting from the vocabulary and a Backus-Naur form (BNF) representation of the grammar. Besides building the high level and diphone networks, the procedure solves the problems of drawing up the inventory of the necessary diphones and correctly creating a set of templates, tasks which are not as straightforward as when dealing with whole words. The procedure derives a set of sentences containing occurrences of all the needed prototypes, which, uttered by any speaker, constitute the training material for that speaker from which the template extraction is finally accomplished by means of a *diphone bootstrapping* module.

The knowledge generation procedure, which produces all the pieces of information relating to an application and actually trains the system on new speakers, is the main subject of this paper. The diphones are defined, and their properties are illustrated in Section 2; the relevant phonological rules are described in Section 3. In Sections 4 and 5 the HTN language model and the linguistic

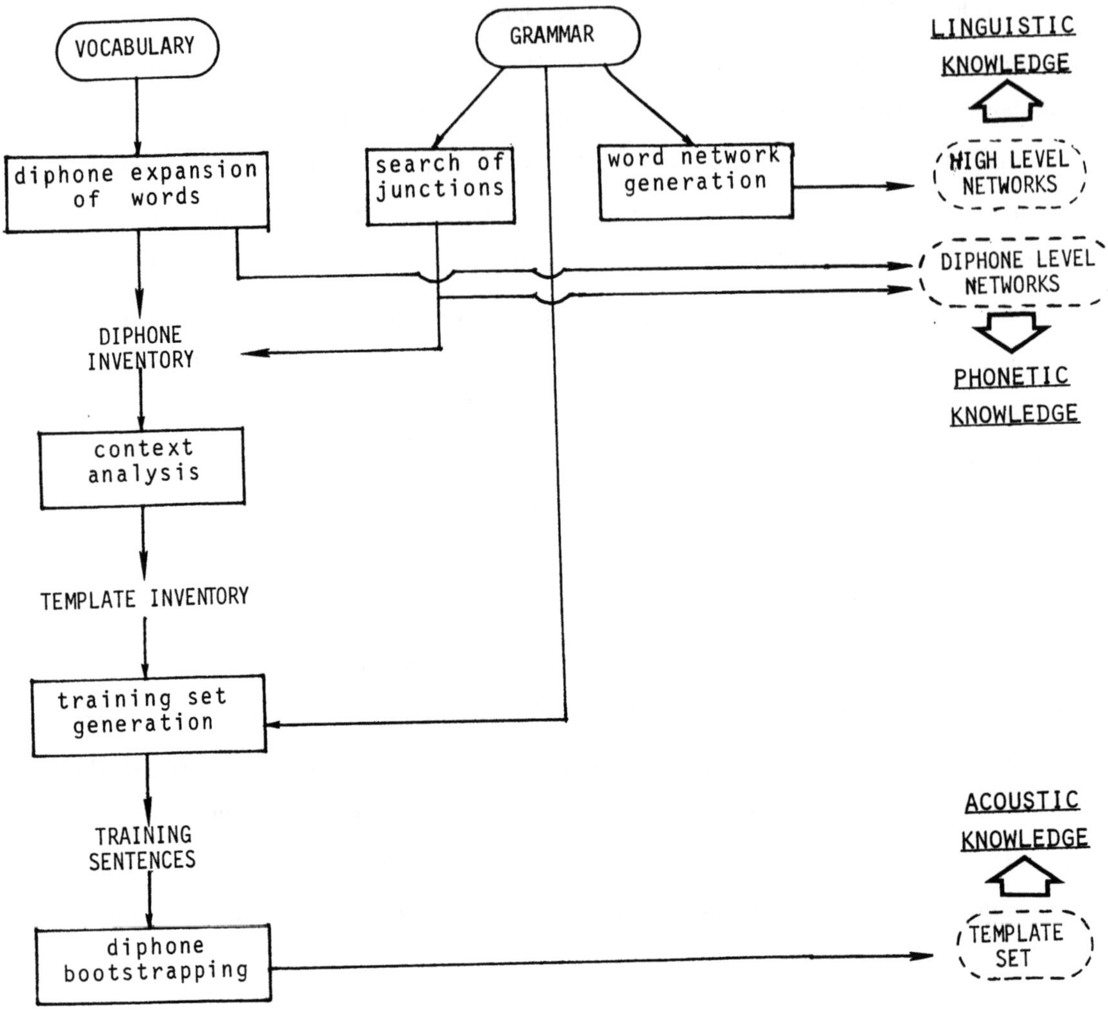

FIG. 1 : Generation of the linguistic, phonetic and acoustic knowledge for a given application from its vocabulary and grammar.

decoder are presented. The training phase of the system, consisting of the automatic generation of the training set and the extraction of the templates, is discussed in Section 6. Finally some experimental results obtained with data bases generated by means of our procedure are presented in Section 7.

2. THE DIPHONES: DEFINITION AND PROPERTIES

Diphone is a general name, used in order to avoid the proliferation of new terms, referring to three different types of units, whose common and major characteristic is the insensibility to coarticulation effects with the surrounding sounds. This means that a diphone keeps its identity regardless of the context in which it happens to be embedded; that is to say, a diphone is not influenced by adjacent diphones (although it may be influenced by prosodic factors such as the location within a word or the stress level). An important consequence of this feature is the economy of the diphone dictionaries, due to the very small number of templates required in order to represent each diphone adequately. In addition, the number of the diphones themselves is small (much smaller than that of syllables, for instance).

The different types of diphones are related to the main parts of fluent speech: steady-state sounds and transitions. With regard to the latter, we have chosen to take into account only the very transitions, that is, very short portions of the signal. Thus, as will be shown in the following, the matching with transition templates does not require any time warping [10] capability, necessary with longer units (words, demisyllables, and so on), which may sometimes cause misrecognition because of the allowance to skip spectral states. The resulting definition of "diphone" [15] is somewhat different from the classical one of "interval between the centres of adjacent phonemes" [8, 12, 17]. Our diphone dictionaries are made up of units representing:

1) stationary sounds corresponding to the steady-state part of some phonemes: vowels, silence and consonants other than plosives (we will

describe in Sect. 3 how plosives are dealt with);

2) true diphones, that is, transitions between two adjacent phonemes, the second one being sonorant: consonant → vowel, consonant → consonant, vowel → vowel; at present we do not make use of the vowel → consonant transitions;

3) triphones, that is, larger events embracing three phonemes, of which the central one is sonorant but not stationary (/r/ or semivowel).

The use of diphone-like units instead of the commonly used whole-word templates seems to be advisable in CSR systems. In fact the rather small size of the diphone template dictionaries ensures a smaller storage requirement and a lower computation time for the recognition system than those needed in whole-word template matching. Moreover, the time necessary to train the system on a new speaker is fairly low, since generally not all the words of the lexicon need to be comprised in the training set. Even for small vocabularies, such as the digits, the training set dimension for diphones is smaller than that required for whole words, if coarticulation effects are taken into account. When whole-word templates are used, different pronunciations or phonological variations of a word can only be taken into account by collecting many different templates. Here, one of the advantages in the use of diphones becomes clear: instead of adopting a unique description of each word, alternative and optional paths are allowed in the network, so that a highly accurate representation, endowed with greater flexibility and economy, is supplied. This kind of representation has a higher discriminative power on similar words as well, as no spurious differences in phonetically identical portions of such words may override true discriminative information. The diphones also provide a very natural way of dealing with junctions between adjacent fluently spoken words: these can be adequately represented by inserting optional transitional diphones such as diphthongs (see also [1]). As a final remark, we point out that the use of diphone-like units causes no penalty on recognition performance: actually, comparative tests have displayed better results with diphones than with whole words.

3. DIPHONE PHONOLOGY

The description of any word of a language in terms of a sequence of sub-word units is a rather easy problem to solve for the Italian language with the diphone-like units defined in Section 2.

The determination of the sequence(s) of diphones corresponding to any given word is accomplished in two steps: first a translation is performed from the orthographic form to a *phonetic transcription*; then the diphones relating to the sequence of phonemes are obtained. Table I shows the set of phonemes [11] pertaining to the Italian language.

The orthography of Italian words is closely related to their pronunciation, so that the phonetic transcription is quite an easy task. Generally there is a one-to-one correspondence between the phonemes making up an uttered word and the alphabetic symbols making up the same written word. The very few exceptions are easily dealt with in an automatic way.

The *determination of the diphone sequences* making up each word starts from the phonetic string corresponding to the word. It is based on rules likely to be applied not only to Italian, but also to any other syllable-timed language (such as Spanish or even German).

With regard to the three above mentioned diphone types, we point out that steady-state sounds are vowels, fricatives, nasals and liquid consonants, as well as the portions of affricates after the beginning of frication. Plosives generally have no "stationary" parts (/k/ may constitute an exception, as its burst may be long), whilst /r/ and semivowels may or may not have some. Plosives are simply rendered by means of a phonetic silence plus the transition to the following sonorant sound. Final plosives in names or foreign words (such as stop) are adequately represented by a transition to a "neutral" vowel /ə/. A phonetic silence may also appear before affricates. When a semivowel (/j/, /w/ following the notation of [11]) has a short steady-state portion, it is rendered by means of the corresponding vowel (/i/, /u/). In other cases a triphone is present. Only

NAME	SYMB.	TYPE	EXAMPLE
A	a	VOWEL	pane
E+	ɛ	"	sette
E-	e	"	cena
I	i	"	riso
O+	ɔ	"	storia
O-	o	"	pozzo
U	u	"	cura
L	l	LIQ.	lotta
L^	ʎ	"	glielo
R	r	"	ramo
M	m	NAS.	mano
N	n	"	notte
N^	ɲ		gnomo
F	f	FRIC.	folla
S	s	"	sano
S^	z	"	rosa
SH	ʃ	"	scia
V	v	"	vero
C	tʃ	AFFR.	ciao
J	dʒ	"	gioco
Z	ts	"	lenzuolo
Z^	dz	"	zero
B	b	PLOS.	bosco
D	d	"	donna
G	g	"	lega
K	k	"	cosa
P	p	"	parte
T	t	"	terra

TABLE I : The Italian phonemes.

very few triphones actually exist when the central phoneme is /j/, because of the intrinsic length of the overall transition "consonant → /j/ → vowel". Altogether, fewer than 400 different diphones are sufficient to cover all Italian words.

Each Italian syllable can be developed as a sequence of diphones by following the above mentioned rules. The development of each syllable contains:

1) the stationary consonant(s) (if any) and/or
2) the phonetic silence preceding plosives (if any);
3) the CC transition (if any) and/or
4) the CV transition;
5) the steady-state vowel(s);
6) the diphthong (if any).

For instance the syllables "sei", "ra", "ta", "spa", "fle" and "tro" can be decomposed as:

	sei	ra	ta	spa	fle	tro
1)	|S			|S	|F,L	
2)			|sil	|sil		|sil
3)					|FL	|TR
4)	|SE	|RA	|TA	|PA	|LE	|RO
5)	|E,I	|A	|A	|A	|E	|O
6)	|EI					

In the following we present the complete diphone sequences corresponding to the expansion of words containing the syllables of the above example. The diphones in parentheses (which correspond to diphthongs or "stationary" portions of /k/ or affricates) may be skipped. The couples of diphones in curly brackets can be replaced by the corrresponding triphones (i.e., "KUA", "TRO" and "ZIO").

<u>serata</u> → S - SE - E - RA - A - sil- TA - A

<u>sei</u> → S - SE - E -(EI)- I

<u>quattro</u> → sil- (K)-{KU -UA}- A -sil-{TR -RO}- O

i.e.:

quattro → sil- (K) < KU -UA / KUA > A -sil < TR -RO / TRO > O

<u>spazio</u> → S -sil- PA - A -sil -(Z)-{ZI -IO}- O

i.e.:

spazio → S -sil- PA - A -sil -(Z) < ZI -IO / ZIO > O

<u>flebile</u> → F -FL - L -LE - E -sil-BI - I - L -LE - E

We have also developed length rules for the diphones, to be applied in the generation of the network representation of the language.

4. LANGUAGE MODEL AND NETWORK REPRESENTATION

The adopted language model refers to a simple language type, the finite-state one, that can be associated with a non-recursive state transition network or finite-state automaton [6].

We make use of a hierarchical transition network representation [7], in which all the knowledge is partitioned into several levels. The specific knowledge pertaining to each level is contained in one or more networks whose nodes are related to an appropriate kind of unit (that is words, diphones or spectra). In all the levels except the lowest one each node points to a network belonging to the adjacent lower level, which may be considered as the expansion of the node in terms of simpler units. This provides a link between adjacent levels. Fig. 2 shows an example of a portion of a simplified HTN representation of a mini command language, with only one node in each level fully expanded through a lower level subnetwork. The language of the application is represented in terms of words in one or more high-level networks, where the syntactic and linguistic knowledge defines the correct sequences of words. The highest level may simply correspond to a network of words, or it may be convenient to introduce a number of upper levels (as in the example), whose nodes represent syntactic groups, each one associated with a different network. For complex and large

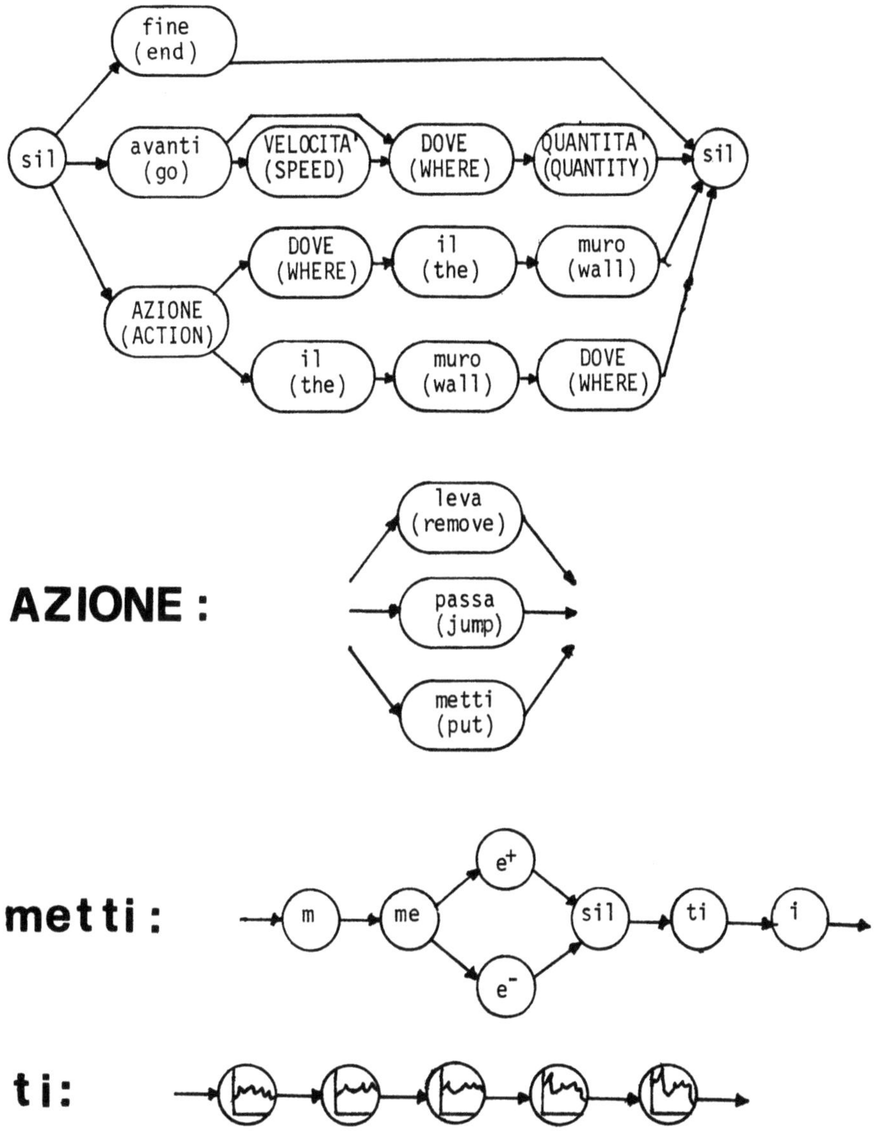

FIG. 2 : Hierarchical Transition Network representation of a mini command language. Only one node at each level is fully expanded through a subnetwork in the immediately lower level.

languages, in which the same groups appear in different positions, the latter representation is particularly useful because the repetition of their network representation is avoided. In this case the storage requirements generally decrease, while the computation effort required to manage this more complex structure grows. The initial and final states of the language correspond to the silence that precedes and follows any utterance; in adddition, an optional silence state may be included between any two consecutive words.

At a lower level, each word is described in terms of a network, whose nodes correspond to diphones, and which is built according to the phonetic knowledge. All the information about the possible alternative sequences of units in the word and their duration is contained in this diphone-level network. A node corresponding to a diphone can be described by means of a structure containing:

→ the diphone identifier

→ the position of the diphone in the word (initial, intermediate or final)

→ a steadiness flag

→ lower and upper duration bounds (only for stationary diphones).

Each transitional diphone can be simply represented by a sequence of spectral states, with no need to duplicate or skip any of them. In fact it is well known that the very transition between two sounds has a basically fixed duration, mainly determined by the articulatory time constants [3]. A duration variability is however allowed for steady-state sounds. The duration bounds depend on the particular sound, on the position in the word and on the stress level. Their accurate determination is very important in avoiding the erroneous recognition of abnormally short or long phonetic events. This model of temporal variability offers a better time warping capability than the common whole-word template matching methods with 2:1 maximum duration ratio between templates and test words [10]. Indeed the time alignment between input signal and templates thus achieved avoids possible misrecognitions due to the insertion or deletion of spectral states in the transitions, whilst the steady-state sounds can be shrinked or stretched to a greater extent within reasonable limits.

Phonological rules are also applied at the diphone level, to deal with junctions between words.

At the lowest level, in which the acoustic knowledge is present, a parametric representation of each diphone is given as the sequence of spectral states that make up its templates. Steady-state diphones are represented by one-spectral-state templates, while transitional diphones are represented each by one multi-frame template of appropriate length which exactly covers the transition.

The HTN representation can be automatically derived for any language generated by a regular grammar [6]. A procedure has been developed for the generation of the word network(s) (expressing the linguistic knowledge of the system, as shown in Fig. 1) from a BNF representation of the grammar where the type of recursion allowed in regular grammars may be present. Either one-level or multi-level organizations can be chosen for this representation. The insertion of optional silence states between consecutive words and the elimination of redundant states are automatically performed.

We have also developed a transcription procedure, which picks out the sequence(s) of diphones making up any Italian word simply from the orthographic form of the word itself. It is based on the rules presented in Section 3. Given a recognition task, with its lexicon and grammar, the procedure permits us to determine all the units needed for the representation of the vocabulary (including possible junctions between fluently spoken words). This in turns allows us both to derive the definition of the template dictionary (that is, how many and which units are needed, and how many and which templates for each unit) and to generate the diphone networks (expressing the phonetic knowledge of the system).

5. THE LINGUISTIC DECODER

In our diphone-based CSR system the HTN language model adopted yields a tight integration between signal and symbol processing, resulting in a simple organization. The entire system consists of only two processes: the acoustic front-end, providing a parametric representation of the speech signal, and the linguistic decoder, producing the interpretation of the utterance as a correct sentence of the language.

The speech signal, collected with a close-talking microphone, is low-pass filtered at 4.6 KHz and sampled at 10 KHz. Every 10 ms a 256-point Hamming window is applied to the signal and a parametric representation is derived. Different kinds of acoustic analysis are allowed; in the experiments being currently run we make use of 12 cepstrum coefficients derived by LPC analysis [13].

The HTN representation of the language is the database where all the knowledge relating to the recognition task is present at different levels. The recognizer basically performs a dynamic-programming search to find the path through the HTN which attains the highest cumulative similarity score with the input sentence. This path corresponds to a sequence of basic units, chosen from among all the acceptable ones that make up a sentence of the language. The multi-level organization requires the search to start from the highest level network, and to go downwards through the levels from a node to its expansion at the adjacent lower level, till the lowest level is reached. Here the similarity can be computed between input and template frames. Then the information is conveyed upwards through the levels to the highest one, and at each level a piece of knowledge is worked out, based on the information coming from the adjacent lower level. Any decision is deferred to the full-message level, where all the pieces of information, from acoustic-phonetic to lexical and syntactic, and possibly semantic, are available. Delaying decisions to the highest level reduces errors and, in addition, avoids the complications that arise in recovering from segmentation errors.

The recognizer makes use of a best-few search strategy without backtracking to update at each step the paths of the network being currently explored. The number of paths explored is kept small by a beam-search strategy similar to the one developed in the Harpy system [9]: those paths whose cumulative similarity score falls below the locally best one by more than a given threshold are pruned out. Preliminary tests were carried out to find the best pruning threshold, and the one which most restricted the number of paths retained without lowering the performance was chosen.

At each time interval an input frame is processed; a similarity measure is only computed between this frame and one template frame of the diphones associated with the current paths. The cumulative similarity for these paths is updated, and the best-few strategy is then applied to cut off low-similarity paths. The similarity score between an input frame and a template frame can be interpreted as an evaluation of the possibility that the input frame belongs to the relevant phonetic event. It can be obtained by calculating a distance between the two patterns, and transforming it into a number ranging between 0 and 1 as a linear function between two predefined distance thresholds, whose values depend on the analysis adopted. The distance chosen when using LPC coefficients is the Euclidean one.

The algorithm described is real-time oriented, as the decoding proceeds along with the similarity measurement. This means that a partial interpretation of early words in a sentence can be available when the input speech is still being processed, even before the speaker has finished talking. Indeed the decision on the recognized diphones does not have to be delayed until the end of the sentence; as soon as only one interpretation remains possible for a time interval, that is, only one path in the network is "alive" for it, the relative diphones and words are given, and a cleanup procedure eliminates dead paths, thus keeping the required memory storage to a minimum. Of course such a decoder cannot make use of pieces of information such as the length of the sentence; the decoder itself detects the end of the sentence when the last node in the best path corresponds to a final silence whose duration is longer than a predefined value. The segmentation process performed by the recognizer can be represented in graphic form, as a waveform where the boundaries of each recognized diphone are marked. An example is shown in Fig. 3.

The method appears to be robust, so that no particular care is required in the way the sentences are uttered. Moreover the simple algorithms and control strategy make a custom hardware implementation possible. An approximate evaluation of the computational power necessary for large vocabularies has revealed that it is well within the capability of present multiprocessor hardware. At present the linguistic decoder is implemented on a general-purpose mini-computer by means of Fortran routines.

6. AUTOMATIC TRAINING

When performing CSR with whole-word templates, the training set must comprise all the words of the lexicon in one or more occurrences; indeed, in order to correctly handle coarticulation effects between adjacent words, a different template is required for each context situation. When using diphones, the training sentences are only expected to include one occurrence of each diphone. As the lexicon size increases, the whole-word template set becomes larger and larger, whereas a diphone template dictionary remains fairly small in size. In the latter case both the amount of training material and the computational load are greatly reduced. On the other hand, the template extraction from the training sentences is undoubtedly more complex in the case of sub-word units, where a reliable segmentation is required to correctly isolate very small portions of the signal.

Since a different dictionary is necessary for each speaker and each language, however, the problem of determining the set of diphones for a given application and extracting the templates for a test speaker becomes crucial. Moreover, making the training phase completely automatic not only avoids a lot of manual work, but is also necessary for practical applications, if the recognition system is

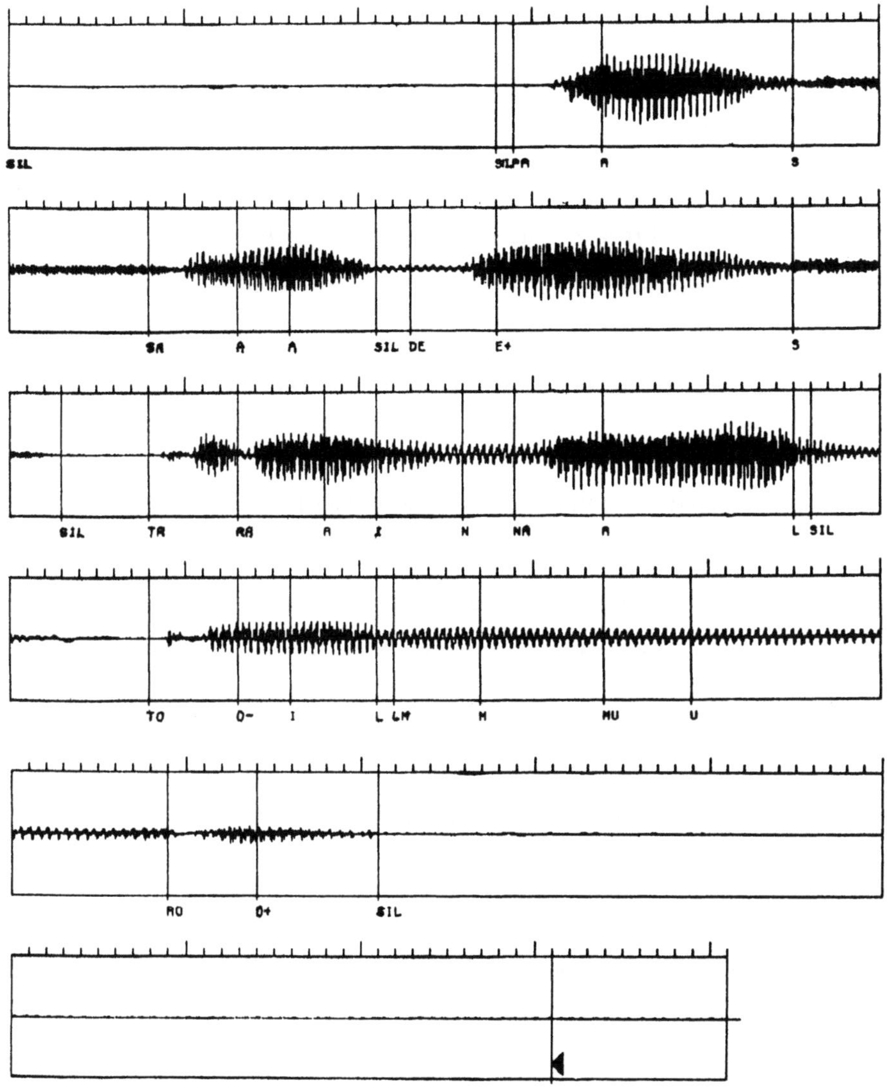

FIG. 3 : Output of the recognition of the utterance "Passa a destra in alto il muro" ("Jump the wall up right").

actually to be used by persons with no skills in phonetics or linguistics.

The training procedure necessarily consists of the following steps:

1) determination of the necessary units from the lexicon of the language and, for each unit, of the possible different context situations, i.e., determination of the number and types of the required prototypes;
2) generation of a suitable set of training sentences containing occurrences of all the prototypes needed;
3) extraction of the templates from the training sentences uttered by the test speaker.

We have developed a completely automatic method of performing these steps. It includes two modules:

→ generation of the training sentences (GTS). It performs steps 1 and 2;

→ diphone bootstrapping (DB). It performs step 3.

The GTS and DB modules can be used separately. For a given application, it is necessary to perform the GTS procedure only once and the DB procedure every time templates by a new speaker are needed.

GENERATION OF THE TRAINING SENTENCES

The input to the GTS module (see Fig. 1) consists of the vocabulary of the language and of a BNF representation of the grammar of the application, which must be a regular grammar. The main task performed by the procedure is the creation of the set of training sentences which, uttered by the test speaker, will constitute the training set and supply the templates. The procedure also produces the new diphone dictionary scheme, and a file which provides the DB module with the information necessary, i.e., the context of the diphones in each word and the transitional diphones that may be present at the junction between two consecutive words. It should be noted that it is possible to create a training set containing only some of the diphones of the application. This is useful if a dictionary of templates for the test speaker is available but a different application is required. This means that a number of templates already existing need not be extracted again; in this case it is convenient to enlarge the old dictionary by simply adding the missing units.

The GTS procedure was developed in a modular way, so that different routines perform a part of the whole task.

First a list of the necessary units is derived from the vocabulary by generating diphone expansions for each word using the rules described in Section 3. The procedure also finds out which stationary diphones appear in different prosodic situations and thus require multiple templates. At present multiple templates are only derived for sonorant sounds (vowels, liquids and nasals) if they appear in different positions in the words of the lexicon (initial / intermediate / final). For vowels the stress level is also considered. Altogether about 500 templates can represent the whole Italian lexicon for an individual speaker. A list of the junction diphones is derived by examining all the possible couples of consecutive words in the language to find out when an optional transitional diphone can be present at their junction. The junctions between words generally correspond to diphthongs (as usually Italian words end with a vowel), but they may also be consonant-vowel or consonant-consonant transitions, as shown for instance in Fig. 3 ("NA", "LM").

Another routine generates the set of training sentences that are expected to include one occurrence of each diphone. If a diphone can appear in different prosodic situations, at least one occurrence corresponding to each of them will be present, and it will be possible to extract each junction diphone between consecutive words. It is not necessary for the training set language to be the same as that of the application. A different grammar can be used that includes all the words of the lexicon; shorter or fewer training sentences can be obtained with a more flexible, less constrained training grammar, including a greater number of permissible sequences of word. This can be done for instance by allowing the elimination of some portions of sentences.

The input to the procedure for generating the training sentences consists of the training grammar and of a table containing, for each necessary template, a list of all the words that contain it. The procedure repeatedly creates groups of words, parts of correct sentences of the language, each group corresponding to the expansion of a non-terminal symbol in the grammar. This process stops as soon as all the templates are present in one or other of the groups. To go into detail, at each step the set of templates that have not yet been included in any group is examined. Only the templates that appear in a minimal number of words of the lexicon are considered: for each of these templates one of the words containing it is selected, namely the one comprising the greatest number of unselected templates. The groups of words are then arranged into a set, which must contain all the selected words; each group includes two or if possible more selected words, plus others chosen in such a way as to minimize the length of the group, while extracting as many templates as possible from it. When all the templates are present in one or other of the groups a set of complete sentences including all the groups is generated by adding as few words as possible.

DIPHONE BOOTSTRAPPING

Having generated a set of sentences containing occurrences of all the units needed for a given task by means of the above described GTS procedure, we have a complete training set. The actual template extraction is accomplished for each speaker through the DB procedure described in [2] (another example of a bootstrapping technique for deriving sub-word units, namely Japanese syllables, can be found in [5]).

The DB procedure, which is sketched in Fig. 4, consists of four steps, namely:

1) the acquisition and analysis of the training set;
2) a forced recognition of the training sentences, with hand-cut or automatically derived templates from a training speaker, by means of which the signal is

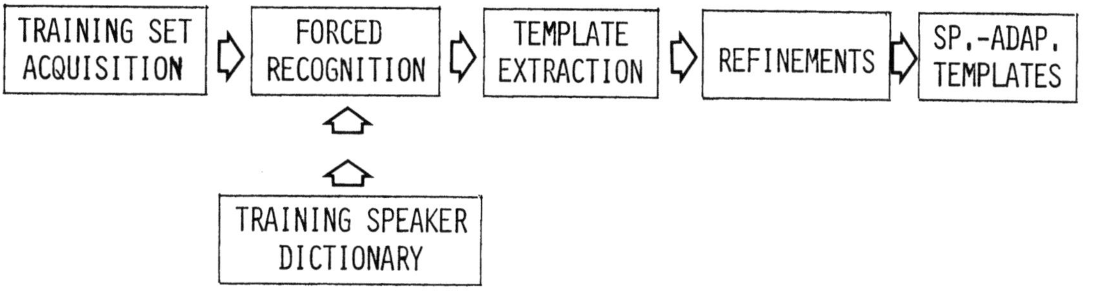

FIG. 4 : The Diphone Bootstrapping procedure.

segmented into diphones;

3) the template extraction;

4) a refinement session, for a check on the bootstrapped templates and, if necessary, the addition of any missing templates.

With regard to the *acquisition* (step 1), we must point out that the GTS procedure not only generates a complete training set (that is, all the templates needed can be extracted from it), but also makes the training session short and easy relative to the application. The training sentences are in fact fairly few; moreover, the fact that they are meaningful means that they can be uttered in a natural way. However, the speaker is allowed to utter every training sentence without any constraint on pronunciation. Each training utterance is sampled at 10 KHz and 12 Cepstrum coefficients are calculated every 10 ms.

The *forced recognition* of each training utterance (step 2) is accomplished by making use of one training speaker's prototypes as a reference set [2] and of a constrained network. The latter is obtained from the general network representation of the language by forcing the word sequence to be uniquely the correct one, while within each word all the valid sequences of diphones are permitted, and the general junction rules between adjacent words apply. Fig. 5-a

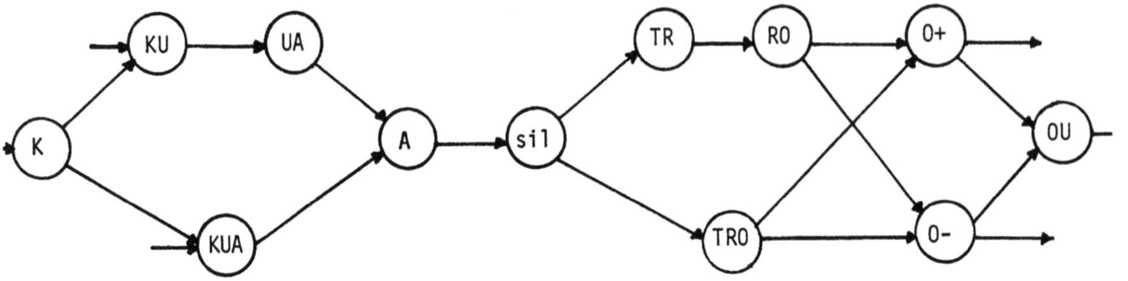

FIG. 5-a : Diphone network for the word "QUATTRO" ("four").

shows the network representation of the Italian digit "quattro" ("four"), with different paths corresponding to alternative allowed sequences of diphones. In particular, note at the end of the word the diphthong "OU" representing the possible junction with a word beginning with "U" (such as "uno"). The path in the network through "OU" is permitted but not forced, in order to take into account possible hesitations between words. Fig. 5-b shows a portion of a training utterance, containing the word "quattro", with the actual output of forced recognition. It corresponds to the sequence of diphones attaining the highest cumulative similarity score. Each diphone is delimited by its boundaries (marked with solid lines on the waveform). From each diphone occurrence a possible template for that diphone can be extracted.

The *template extraction* (step 3) is performed for a transitional diphone by taking the entire portion of signal corresponding to an occurrence, while for steady-state diphones only the central frame of an appropriate occurrence is

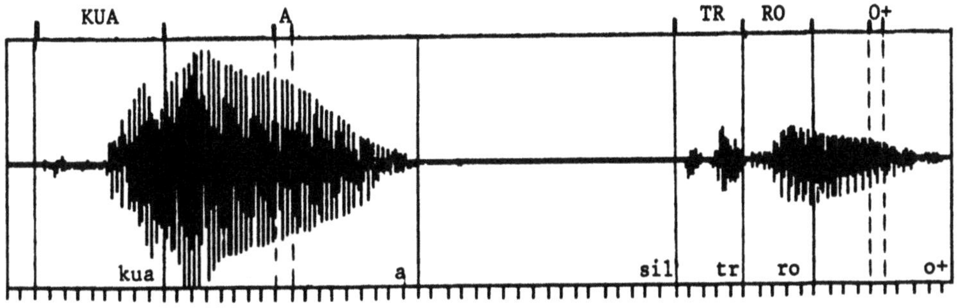

FIG. 5-b : Templates for some diphones in the word "QUATTRO" as detected by the forced recognition.

chosen (marked with dotted lines in Fig. 5-b). Only one template is derived for each different context of each diphone; the template is extracted from the first available occurrence of that diphone in the relevant context situation (for steady-state diphones occurrences shorter than a given duration are discarded). At present all diphones except steady-state ones corrresponding to sonorant sounds are considered mono-context; therefore multiple templates are derived only for vowels, nasals and liquids.

Finally (step 4) we apply two different kinds of *refinements*: template checking and dictionary filling. Although the segmentation produced by forced recognition is fairly accurate, we check the correctness of the location of the automatically derived templates. For steady-state diphones the steadiness of the intensity pattern and Cepstrum coefficients is checked against the surrounding environment of the template: the variation must not exceed a given threshold. For transitions the behaviour of spectral and energetic derivatives is examined. Any bad template for a diphone is dropped and, if possible, replaced with another convenient occurrence of the diphone. These checks, together with the reliability of forced segmentation, ensure that the templates for each diphone are derived from true occurrences of that diphone.

Finally, we provide a means for dictionary filling. In fact the procedure described does not guarantee the extraction of the whole set of templates from the training material. For instance a dropped template may not have been replaced, or none of the occurrences of a final vowel may be long enough, or a certain junction diphone may be missing due to non-fluent pronunciation. Missing templates (if any) are simply supplied by the training speaker's dictionary.

The output of the DB procedure is a manageable diphone template dictionary tailored for the speaker. This template dictionary provides a complete and correct representation of the lexicon relating to a given application and is part of the acoustic knowledge of the system.

7. EXPERIMENTAL RESULTS

Different applications are being tested in our Laboratory. Until now only one extensive experiment with automatically derived prototypes has been completed on the language of sequences of Italian digits. It was mainly performed in order to check the adequacy of the diphone bootstrapping procedure, but the whole described procedure of generation of the recognizer data bases was used. The recognition experiment with bootstrapped templates was done on 20 sequences of 5 connected digits, each uttered by 19 (9 male and 10 female) speakers. Each digit was present 10 times in different contexts in the test set. The training set was not acquired at the same time as the test set, thus proving that the efficacy of the template set was not influenced by environmental conditions. The three reference template dictionaries used for forced recognition contained hand-extracted prototypes from other speakers (two males and a female).

An average word recognition rate (WRR) of 99% corresponding to a rate greater than 98.5% with a confidence level of 99%, was obtained over the whole experiment, which included 1900 words. This corresponds to a 95.5% recognition rate on the 5-digit sequences. These results show the effectiveness of the training procedure, as they are only slightly below the average WRR of 99.5% obtained in a speaker-dependent recognition experiment with hand-extracted templates. Moreover they display a satisfactory improvement over the 88.9% average WRR obtained in a speaker-independent test with the training speakers' templates.

The above experimental results clearly show how our automatic training procedure produces reliable template sets (at least for small vocabularies). Moreover the procedure not only performed very well on the average, but also yielded homogeneous results on all the test speakers: even for the worst speaker 96 words out of 100 were correctly recognized.

8. CONCLUSIONS

We have presented a knowledge generation procedure for a diphone-based CSR system, which generates all the pieces of information relating to any given application in a completely automatic way. The procedure can also train the system on new speakers deriving a complete and correct template dictionary for each of them.

We make use of the procedure, which has proved to be both fast and reliable, as a tool for testing our system in new recognition tasks with a great number of different speakers. However, the main aim of the procedure is to enable the system to be used by unskilled users in practical applications. In fact none of the steps performed by the procedure require any intervention by the user, who only needs to supply the lexicon and a BNF representation of the grammar of the language.

The procedure has been developed in a modular way, so that it is possible to use the various modules separately, if only one specific task (such as the search for the diphone inventory, or the template bootstrapping) has to be performed.

REFERENCES

1. P. S. Cohen and R. L. Mercer, "The Phonological Component of an Automatic Speech Recognition System", in D. R. Reddy (Editor), *SPEECH RECOGNITION*, Academic Press, New York, p. 275, 1975.
2. A. M. Colla and D. Sciarra, "Automatic Diphone Bootstrapping for Speaker-Adaptive Continuous Speech Recognition", Proc. ICASSP 1984, (35.2), S. Diego, 1984.
3. J. L. Flanagan, C. H. Coker, L. R. Rabiner, R. W. Schafer and N. Umeda, "Synthetic Voices for Computers", IEEE Spectrum, 7, p. 22, 1970.
4. K. S. Fu, *SYNTACTIC METHODS IN PATTERN RECOGNITION*, Academic Press, New York, 1974.
5. H. Fujisaki, K. Hirose and T. Inoue, "Automatic Recognition of Connected Words from a Large Vocabulary Using Syllable Templates", Proc. ICASSP 1984, (26.9), S. Diego, 1984.
6. D. Hopkin and B. Moss, *AUTOMATA*, MacMillan, London, p. 5, 1976.
7. M. J. Hunt, M. Lennig and P. Mermelstein, "Experiments in Syllable Based Recognition of Continuous Speech", Proc. ICASSP 1980, Denver, p. 880, 1980.
8. D. H. Klatt, "SCRIBER and LAFS: Two New Approaches to Speech Analysis", in W. A. Lea (Editor), *TRENDS IN SPEECH RECOGNITION*, Prentice-Hall, Englewood Cliffs, p. 529, 1980.
9. B. T. Lowerre and D. R. Reddy, "The HARPY Speech Understanding System", in W. A. Lea (Editor), *TRENDS IN SPEECH RECOGNITION*, Prentice-Hall, Englewood Cliffs, p. 340, 1980.
10. C. S. Myers, L. R. Rabiner and A. E. Rosenberg, "On the Use of Dynamic Time Warping for Word Spotting and Connected Word Recognition", The Bell System Technical Journal, 60, 3, p. 303-325, 1981.
11. M. Onishi (Supervisor), *A GRAND DICTIONARY OF PHONETICS*, The Phonetic Society of Japan, p. 129, 1981.
12. J. E. Paul and A. S. Rabinowitz, "An Acoustically Based Continuous Speech Recognition System", IEEE Symposium on Speech Recognition, Carnegie-Mellon University, Pittsburgh, PA, p. 63, 1974.
13. L. R. Rabiner and R. W. Schafer, *DIGITAL PROCESSING OF SPEECH SIGNAL*, Prentice-Hall, Englewood Cliffs, p. 442, 1978.
14. C. Scagliola and L. Marmi, "Continuous Speech Recognition via Diphone Spotting: a Preliminary Implementation", Proc. ICASSP 1982, Paris, p. 2008, 1982.

15. C. Scagliola, "Continuous Speech Recognition Without Segmentation: Two Ways of Using Diphones as Basic Speech Units", Speech Communication, 2 (2-3), p. 199, 1983.
16. C. Scagliola, "Language Models and Search Algorithms for Real-Time Speech Recognition" (to appear on: International Journal of Man-Machine Studies).
17. J. E. Shoup, "Phonological Aspects of Speech Recognition", in W. A. Lea (Editor), *TRENDS IN SPEECH RECOGNITION*, Prentice-Hall, Englewood Cliffs, p. 125, 1980.

THE USE OF DYNAMIC FREQUENCY WARPING IN A SPEAKER-INDEPENDENT VOWEL CLASSIFIER

W. A. Ainsworth and H. M. Foster
Department of Communication & Neuroscience
University of Keele
Keele, Staffs., ST5 5BG
ENGLAND

ABSTRACT

A dynamic frequency warping algorithm has been used to match the spectra of the vowels of one speaker against the spectra of vowels of different speakers. Although the method resulted in a transformation which produced a good match, it was not accurate as a speaker-independent vowel classifier. With reference spectra from the vowels of male speakers and test spectra from the vowels of female speakers, and vice versa, the recogntion scores were only 33%, whilst with reference and test spectra from different utterances of the same speaker the mean score was 96%.

Various parameters of the spectra and the DFW algorithm have been studied. It was found that limiting the frequency range of the spectra to approximately telephone bandwidth (250-3200 Hz) increased the male-female scores by about 6%. Changing the frequency scale to barks or reducing the order of the linear prediction analysis reduced the recognition scores. Adjusting the warping window in the dynamic programming algorithm so that it was 160 Hz wide above the diagonal raised the male-female recognition score to 48.6%.

NATO ASI Series, Vol. F16
New Systems and Architectures for Automatic Speech Recognition and Synthesis. Edited by R. De Mori and C. Y. Suen

INTRODUCTION

The vowels of female speakers have higher formant frequencies than those of males because of their shorter vocal tracts. This causes no difficulty for a human listener, but the mechanism by which the compensation for different size vocal tracts occurs is not understood. It is possible that a value derived from the average fundamental frequency is used as a normalising factor, or that the average values of the formant frequencies are used. Perceptual experiments by Fujisaki and Kawashima (1968) and Ainsworth (1975) suggest that either or both of these factors are involved.

A more detailed examination of the formant frequencies of the vowels produced by male and female speakers, however, shows that a non-linear transformation is required to change the formant frequencies of a male vowel into those of a female vowel (Fant, 1975).

DYNAMIC TIME WARPING

In the time domain a superficially similar situation exists. Not only is the total duration of a fast utterance of a word shorter than that of a slow utterance of the same word, but the duration of certain sounds are relatively much shorter in the fast utterance. In automatic speech recognition systems it is possible to minimise the effects of these differences in duration by means of dynamic programming algorithms which compress and expand in the time scale of a test word in order to effect an optimal match with a reference word. This technique is known as dynamic time warping (Sakoe and Chiba, 1978; Myers, Rabiner and Rosenberg, 1980).

DYNAMIC FREQUENCY WARPING

In the present project a number of dynamic programming algorithms have been applied in the frequency domain to the problem of matching the vowels of one speaker against those of another speaker (Paliwal and Ainsworth, 1985).

Suppose that the log-power spectrum of a test vowel uniformly sampled at m frequency values, is:

$$\underline{a} = (a_1, a_2, \dots a_i, \dots a_m)$$

and the spectrum of a reference vowel (of another speaker) is:

$$\underline{b} = (b_1, b_2, \dots b_j, \dots b_m).$$

In order to obtain the optimum warping path between these spectra, the distance D ($\underline{a}$, $\underline{b}$) is computed along all possible warping paths between the points (1, 1) and (m, m) constrained by the warping window.

The distance D($\underline{a}$, $\underline{b}$) is computed as follows. The local distance between the ith component of the test spectrum and the jth component of the reference spectrum is given by:

$$d(i, j) = (a_i - b_j)^2.$$

The cumulative distance function at the point (i, j) is given by Sakoe and Chiba (1978):

$$g(i, j) = \min \begin{array}{l} g(i-1, j) + d(i, j) \\ g(i-1, j-1) + 2d(i,j) \\ g(i, j-1) + d(i,j) \end{array}$$

with the initial condition g(1, 1) = 2d(1, 1).

The distance D($\underline{a}$,$\underline{b}$) along the optimum warping path is computed from the final cumulative distance function by:

$$D(\underline{a}, \underline{b}) = g(m, m)/2m.$$

VOWEL ANALYSIS AND CLASSIFICATION

The eleven English vowels were spoken in /hVd/ context ten times by each of eight speakers (four male and four female). The waveforms were digitised at 10 kHz and displayed on a CRT. A 25.6 msec segment from the steady state part of each vowel was selected manually. The segment was weighted by a Hamming window function and a 10th order linear prediction analysis was performed using the autocorrelation method (Makhoul, 1975). The log-power spectrum was obtained from the resulting ten linear prediction coefficients by computing a 256-point discrete Fourier transform using the fast Fourier transform algorithm. Reference spectra were computed for each speaker by averaging the repetitions of the spectra of each vowel.

The above dynamic frequency warping (DFW) algorithm was applied to each pair of test and reference spectra. Vowel classification was achieved by choosing the reference class, p, for which:

$$D(\underline{a}, \underline{b}^p) < D(\underline{a}, \underline{b}^q)$$

for all q except $p = q$.

A number of parameters affecting the vowel spectra and the warping window were varied in order to study their effects on the performance of the vowel classification system.

SPEAKER-DEPENDENT AND SPEAKER-INDEPENDENT RECOGNITION

In order to provide base-line data, the vowel classifier was tested in both speaker-dependent and speaker-independent modes. The test patterns were the 128-point log-power spectra from each speaker. The reference patterns were the averaged spectra from each speaker. The system was trained with the vowels of each speaker one at a time.

The warping window was a region parallel to the diagonal bounded by $j = i - r$ and $j = i + r$, where r is the warping window length. It had been shown previously (Paliwal and Ainsworth, 1985) that recognition performance does not depend greatly on warping window length in the rang $r = 0$ to 8. (The units of r are the spectrum range (5 kHz)/no. of points (128) = 39 Hz.) It was found that when trained with one male speaker and tested with another, the recognition score deteriorated with increase in r, whereas when trained with a male speaker and tested with a female, the recognition score increased slightly with increase in warping window length. In the present experiment a value of $r = 4$ was employed.

The results are shown in Table 1. In speaker-dependent mode a mean recognition score of 96.1% was obtained for both the male and female groups of speakers. In speaker-independent mode, where the reference vowels have been excluded from the test set, the performance dropped dramatically. With male reference vowel spectra and female test spectra, or vice versa, the mean recognition score was about 33%.

TABLE 1

Recognition scores obtained with speaker-dependent and speaker-independent vowel classifiers using dynamic frequency warping.

Speaker	Reference vowels	Test vowels	Recognition score (%)
Dependent	Male	Same male	96.1
	Female	Same female	96.1
	Both	Same speaker	96.1
Independent	Male	Different male	53.4
	Female	Different female	44.0
	Male	Female	33.6
	Female	Male	32.2
	Both	Different speaker	39.7

NUMBER OF POINTS IN THE SPECTRUM

It has long been known that the most important factors for the discrimination of vowel sounds are frequencies of the first two formants (Pols, van der Kamp, and Plomp, 1969). These occupy the frequency range from about 200-3000 Hz. It is possible that only information in this range contributes to vowel recognition, and by ignoring information outside this range little deterioration in performance would result. The advantage of restricting the number of points is that the amount of computation is reduced.

The experiment described in the last section was repeated, but only using the first 80-points of each spectrum. This effectively reduces the frequency range to about 3200 Hz. The computation time was about halved.

The results are shown in Table 2. In speaker-dependent mode the recognition scores were reduced by about 3% to 93%. In speaker-independent mode, however, the mean recognition score increased by about 3% to 43%. The largest increase was found with male reference patterns and female test patterns, or vice versa, where the mean recognition scores increased by about 6% to 39%.

PSYCHOPHYSICAL SCALING

The points in the spectra are equally spaced in the physical frequency scale of Hertz. This was a consequence of employing the fast Fourier transform algorithm in the analysis. Perceptual studies, however, have shown that another frequency scale is more appropriate when listening to sounds. This is the Bark scale which effectively places the sampling points nearer together in the low frequencies and further apart in the high frequencies. An appropriate transformation is given by Schroeder, Atal and Hall (1979) as:

$$f = 650 \text{ sink } (x/7)$$

where f is the frequency in Hertz and x is the frequency in Barks.

TABLE 2

Recognition scores obtained for speaker-dependent and speaker-independent vowel classifiers using DFW with the frequency of the spectra limited to 0-3200 Hz.

Speaker	Reference	Test	Score
Dependent	Male	Same male	92.7
	Female	Same female	93.0
	both	Same	92.9
Independent	Male	Different male	48.7
	Female	Different female	46.4
	Male	Female	39.3
	Female	Male	39.2
	Both	Different speaker	42.8

Psychophysical spectra were constructed using this transformation, and the experiment with the vowel classifier was repeated with the vowels from all speakers forming the reference patterns and the vowels from the male speakers as the test pattern.

The results are given in Table 3. They show that the scores are about 5% less with the psychophysical spectra compared with the scores obtained with the physical spectra.

NUMBER OF LINEAR PREDICTION COEFFICIENTS

For the production of a neutral vowel the vocal tract can be modelled approximately by a uniform tube closed at one end (the glottis) and open at the other (the lips). The resonances of this tube are uniformly spaced. For a male speaker the formant frequencies are approximately at 500, 1500, 2500 Hz etc., making a total of five formants below 5000 Hz. For a typical female speaker the formant frequencies are about 20% higher, i.e. at 600, 1800, 3000 Hz etc. The female vowel has only four formants below 5000 Hz. One of the reasons why the male-female recognition scores are so low is that the DFW algorithm is attempting to match spectra having different numbers of formants, although they represent the same vowel class.

One way of reducing the number of apparent formants in a spectrum is to reduce the number of linear prediction coefficients in the analysis. This effectively models the vocal tract with a filter having less poles. In order to examine whether these simplified spectra are more useful for vowel recognition, the experiment was repeated with 6th order linear prediction analysis.

The results of this experiment are also shown in Table 3. It can be seen that 6th order linear prediction analysis is less useful than 10th order linear prdiction analysis for vowel spectra measured in either physical or psychophysical frequency units.

TABLE 3

Comparison of the recognition scores obtained with the spectra in Hz and in barks. The spectra obtained from the vowels of the male speakers were employed as the test patterns.

Reference patterns	10th order LPC		6th order LPC	
	Hz	Barks	Hz	Barks
Speaker-dependent males	92.7	86.1	88.0	78.4
Speaker-indpendent males	48.7	42.6	43.2	34.4
Females	39.2	33.2	36.4	33.5

LOW FREQUENCY LIMITATION

Although linear prediction analysis attempts to separate the source from the filter function of speech production, there are still major differences in the low frequency region of the spectra of vowels produced by different speakers. It is expected that the information in this region contributes little to the classification of the vowels of different speakers, so an experiment was performed in which the low frequency information was successively eliminated. The vowels from the male speakers were used to form the reference patterns and those from the female speakers were used as the test patterns.

The results are shown in Table 4. For the 3200 spectrum, there was a slight increase in the recognition score when the low frequency of the spectrum was limited to 250 Hz but this decreased at 500 and 1000 Hz. A similar pattern of results was obtained for the full spectrum (up to 5000 Hz) although there was little difference between 0 and 250 Hz.

SIZE OF THE WARPING WINDOW

All the experiments described so far have employed a warping window which is symmetrical about the diagonal. This is appropriate for a speaker-independent system. However, although the test speaker is unknown, the identity of the speaker who forms the reference patterns can be known. If he is a male speaker it might be expected that vowel spectra from another male speaker would need to be compressed or expanded with equal probability in order to obtain the test match. With vowel spectra from a female speaker, however, it would be expected that more compression than expansion would be required. To test this hypothesis an experiment was carried out with asymmetrric warping windows, with male reference patterns and female test patterns.

TABLE 4

The effect of low frequency limitation on recognition scores for the 3200 Hz and 5000 Hz spectra. Vowels from the male speakers were used as the refernce patterns and those from the female speakers as tet patterns.

Low frequency (Hz)	Recognition scores (%)	
	3200 Hz	5000 Hz
0	39.3	33.6
250	40.1	33.2
500	37.8	29.3
1000	29.4	24.8

With a symmetric warping window bounded by j = i - 4 and j = i + 4, a recognition score of 39.3% was obtained. With a warping window bounded by j = i and j = i + 8, the score increased to 47.0%. With a warping window bounded by j = i - 8 and j = 0, the score fell to 24.4%. Thus for male reference patterns and female test patterns an asymmetric warping window increases the recognition score.

A parametric study of the window size was performed next. The warping window was bounded by j = i + r and j = i, where r is the window size. The spectra were limited to a frequency rage of 250 to 3200 Hz. The results are shown in Table 5. A maximum recognition score of 48.6% occurred with a warping window size of r = 4, i.e. with a warping window 160 Hz wide.

CONCLUSIONS

A dynamic frequency warping algorithm has been studied as a method of recognizing the vowel sounds of different speakers. It was found to give good results (96.1% recognition scores) for a speaker-dependent system, but poor results (39.7%) in a speaker-independent system. In particular with reference patterns obtained from the vowels of male speakers and test patterns from the vowels of female speakers, and vice versa, the recognition scores were only 33%.

Limiting the high frequency of the spectra to 3200 Hz raised the male-female recognition scores to 39%, and this was increased to 40% by limiting the frequency range to 250-3200 Hz. It was found that changing to a psychophysical frequency scale (barks) or reducing the order of the linear prediction analysis both had a deleterious effect on the recognition scores.

The greatest increase in recognition score, to 48.6%, ws obtained for the male reference patterns and female test patterns by using an asymmetric warping window in the dynamic programming algorithm. It is suggested that further investigation into the optimum shape of the warping window is required.

TABLE 5

Recognition scores obtained with an asymmetric warping window bounded by $j = i + r$ and $j = i$. Vowels from the male speakers were used as the reference patterns and vowels from the female speakers as the test patterns.

Warping window size (Hz)	Recognition score (%)
0	38.4
80	44.4
160	48.6
320	47.0
480	43.8

ACKNOWLEDGEMENTS

We are indebted to Dr. K. K. Paliwal for writing the computer programs and collaborating during the early experiments. The work was supported by the UK Science and Engineering Research Council.

REFERENCES

1. W. A. Ainsworth (1975) "Intrinsic and extrinsic factors in vowel judgements", *Auditory Analysis and Perception of Speech*, (G. Fant and M. Tatham, eds.), Academic Press, London, 103-113.
2. G. Fant (1975), "Nonuniform vowel normalisation", *STL QPR*, No. 2-3, RIT, Stockholm, Sweden, 1-19.
3. H. Fujisaki and T. Kawashima (1968), "The roles of pitch and higher formants in the perception of vowels", *IEEE Trans. Audio. Electroacoust., AU-16*, 73-77.
4. J. Makhoul (1975), "Linear prediction, a tutorial review", *Proc. IEEE*, 63, No. 4, 561-580.
5. C. Myers, L. R. Rabier and A. E. Rosenberg (1980), "Performance tradeoffs in dynamic time warping algorithms for isolated word recognition", *IEEE Trans., ASSP-28*, No. 6, 623-635.
6. K. K. Paliwal and W. A. Ainsworth (1985), "Dynamic frequency warping for speaker adaptation in automatic speech recognition", J. Phonetics, Vol. 13, No. 1.
7. L. C. W. Pols, L. J. van der Kamp and R. Plomp (1969), "Perceptual and physical space for vowel sounds", *J. Acoust. Soc. Am.*, 46, 458-467.
8. H. Sakoe and S. Chiba (1978), "Dynamic programming algorithm for spoken word recognition", *IEEE Trans., ASSP-26*, No. 1, 43-49.
9. M. R. Schroeder, B. S. Atal and J. L. Hall (1979), "Objective measure of certain speech signal degradations based on masking properties of human auditory perception", *Frontiers of Speech Communication Research*, (B. Lindblom and S. Ohman, eds.), Academic Press, London, 212-229.

DYNAMIC TIME WARPING ALGORITHMS FOR
ISOLATED AND CONNECTED WORD RECOGNITION

J. di Martino
C.R.I.N. - Université de Nancy I
B.P. 239 - 54506 Vandoeuvre

ABSTRACT

In this paper we present a new formulation of the dynamic programming recursive relations both for word and connected word recognition that permits relaxation of boundary conditions imposed on the warping paths, while preserving the optimal character of the dynamic time warping algorithms.

I. INTRODUCTION

One of the most interesting approach for word recognition and connected word recognition is based on the dynamic programming approach. Several studies have shown that the technique of dynamic programming is very well suited for compensating for time distorsions due to the variability of elocution speed [1]-[8]. However, most of the algorithms that have been presented until now assume that the extraction of the vocal forms from the ambiant noise is error free and that the end-words are not too much corrupted by parasite noises. Unfortunately in practice such conditions are not always respected. For instance most of the speech detectors have great difficulties in capturing weak energy end-phonemes. Some attempts [1][3][4] have been made to take into account these problems, but all the strategies used failed in trying to maintain the optimality of the dynamic matching.

In this paper, after a brief summary of the dynamic programming technique, we introduce new dynamic recursive relations both for isolated word recognition and connected word recognition. These relations compensate for distorsions that may affect the end-words and at the same time preserves the optimality of the dynamic time warping algorithms. Preliminary experimental results in the case of isolated word recognition are given.

II. SOME NOTIONS ON TIME ALIGNMENT

Let $T = t(1), t(2), \ldots t(i), \ldots t(I)$
and
$R = r(1), r(2), \ldots r(j), \ldots r(J)$

be two speech patterns, where $t(i)$ and $r(j)$ are multidimentional feature vectors characterizing the speech signal at a given instant. The purpose of time alignment is to make a time registration between these vectors so as to synchronise the time scales of the two patterns. This registration can be formalized mathematically as the problem of finding among the functions :

$$W : \mathbb{N}_{I \times J} \rightarrow \mathbb{N}_I \times \mathbb{N}_J$$
$$k \longrightarrow W(k) = (i(k), j(k))$$

NATO ASI Series, Vol. F16
New Systems and Architectures for Automatic Speech
Recognition and Synthesis. Edited by R. De Mori and C. Y. Suen

- where $\mathbb{N}p = \{1, 2, \ldots p\}$ and $W(k)$ indicates that the kth coincidence associates the feature vector $i(k)$ of the pattern T with the feature vector $j(k)$ of the pattern R -

the optimal one that realizes the best mapping between the two patterns. The mappings W are called warping functions. In order for the warping paths to respect time fluctuations of the speech signal, the following monotonic conditions must be applied to the warping paths :

$$(1) \quad \begin{cases} i(k-1) \leqslant i(k) \\ j(k-1) \leqslant j(k) \,. \end{cases}$$

Furthermore, to eliminate possible unrealistic contractions or dilatations, local constraints, introducing continuity and slope conditions, must be applied. Relation (2) is an exemple of a local constraint due to Itakura [8] :

$$(2) \quad \begin{cases} j(k+1) - j(k) = 0, 1, 2 & \text{If} \quad j(k) \neq j(k-1) \\ j(k+1) - j(k) = 1, 2 & \text{If} \quad j(k) = j(k-1) \end{cases}$$

Finally, to avoid omission of word-end feature vectors through warping the end-frames of the two patterns are matched by the following boundary conditions :

$$(3-a) \quad \begin{cases} i(1) = 1 \\ j(1) = 1 \end{cases}$$

$$(3-b) \quad \begin{cases} i(K) = I \\ j(K) = J \end{cases}$$

- where K is the number of points of the warping path -

The optimal warping path is determined using the following metric on the set of warping functions :

$$(4) \quad D(W) = \frac{\sum_{k=1}^{K} d(i(k), j(k)) * P(k)}{N(P)}$$

- where : . K is the number of points of the warping path,
. $d(i(k), j(k))$ is a local distance between the $i(k)$'th vector of the pattern T and the $j(k)$'th vector of the pattern R ,
. $N(P)$ is a normalization factor that depends on the type of the weighting function used. The purpose of this factor is to compensate for the effect of K that is to say to make the metric independent of the length of the warping path.

The optimal path is then defined by :

$$(5) \quad \hat{W} = \underset{W}{\text{ARGMIN}} \; D(W) \,.$$

In combining relation (4) with relation (5) the problem of time normalization can be solved as :

$$(6) \quad D(\hat{W}) = \min_{K,\, i(k),\, j(k)} \frac{\sum_{k=1}^{K} d(i(k), j(k)) * P(k)}{N(P)} \,.$$

The typical weighting functions generally used are :

(7) $Pa(k) = i(k) - i(k-1)$

(8) $Ps(k) = i(k) - i(k-1) + j(k) - j(k-1)$.

The first is asymmetric since it is only function of the index of the projection of the pattern into the horizontal axis while the second one is symmetric being function of the indices of both the two patterns.

The motivation of this choice stems from the fact that if we define the normalization factor $N(P)$ by :

(9) $N(P) = \sum_{k=1}^{K} P(k)$,

then it is easy to show, by substituting relations (7) and (8) in (9) and in taking into account relations (3-a) and (3-b) that $N(Pa) = I$ and $N(Ps) = I + J$. Consequently, $N(P)$, for $P = Pa$ or $P = Ps$, is a constant, so can therefore be factorized in relation (6) :

(10) $D(\hat{W}) = \frac{1}{N(P)} * \min_{K,\, i(k),\, j(k)} \sum_{k=1}^{K} d(i(k), j(k)) * P(k)$.

Relation (10) can be solved by dynamic programming owing to the following local optimality principle introduced by Bellman [9]

- let $C[(1, 1), (i, j)]$ be the optimal path joining the point $(1, 1)$ and the point (i, j) , then for any point (i', j') belonging to $C[1, 1), (i, j)]$, the optimal path $C[(1, 1), (i', j')]$ is included in $C[(1, 1), (i, j)]$ as a portion of it.

Thus if we define $D(i, j)$ as the unnormalized distance associated with the optimal path $C[(1, 1), (i, j)]$, in applying the local optimality principle $D(i, j)$ can be expressed as :

(11) $D(i, j) = \min_{\substack{(i', j') \\ \in V(i, j)}} D(i', j') + dp((i', j'), (i, j))$

where (i', j') belongs to the neighbourhood $V(i, j)$ of the point (i, j) defined by the local constraint - for example in the case of the local constraint defined by relation (2) , $V(i, j)$ is the set $\{(i-1, j), (i-1, j-1), (i-1, j-2)\}$ - and $dp((i', j'), (i, j))$ is the weighted distance between the point (i', j') and the point (i, j) .

Consequently thanks to the recursive expression of $D(i, j)$ given by relation (11) the following simple algorithm evaluating $D(\hat{W})$ is easily obtained :

1) INITIALIZATION

$D(1, 1) = d(1, 1) * P(1)$
$D(1, j) = +\infty$ for $j = 2, \ldots, J$

2) DYNAMIC PROGRAMMING

FOR $2 \leqslant i \leqslant I$ Do
FOR $1 \leqslant j \leqslant J$ Do
COMPUTE RECURSIVELY $D(i, j)$
END FOR END FOR

3) EVALUATION OF THE DISSIMILARITY DISTANCE

$$D(\hat{W}) = \frac{1}{N(P)} * D(I, J) .$$

III. GENERALIZATION OF THE DYNAMIC PROGRAMMING RECURSIVE RELATIONS

We have seen previously that if the weighting functions are Pa or Ps and if the boundary conditions expressed by relations (3-a) and (3-b) are applied to the warping paths, then the normalization factor is a constant. From this result and from the local optimality principle we get the standard dynamic programming recursive relation given by (11) . If now we are interested in relaxing the boundary conditions so that the DP matching algorithm compensates for distorsions that may corrupt the end-words, then as in this case the length constancy property is not guaranted, it results that (11) does not hold. To make clear this point it is interesting to show that in general when the boundary conditions are relaxed the length constancy property is no more valid.

Let us make the assumption that the initial boundary conditions are relaxed - in this discussion we shall not consider the terminal boundary conditions because the results would be the same - and let us consider first the case of a symmetric local constraint. If the relaxation of the boundary conditions is authorized on the vertical axis, see figure 1-a , the lengths of the paths Cv1, Cv2, Cv3 starting respectively at the points (1, v1), (1, v2), (1, v3) with $vi \neq vj$ if $i \neq j$ and ending at the fixe point (I, J) are :

$$(12) \quad \ell(Cvi) = I + J - vi + 1 \quad \text{for} \quad i = 1, 2, 3$$

and as we have assumed that $vi \neq vj$ if $i \neq j$ we get $\ell(Cvi) \neq \ell(Cvj)$ if $i \neq j$.

In the same way, if the relaxation of the initial boundary conditions is authorized on the horizontal axis, see figure 1-b, the lengths of the paths Ch1, Ch2, Ch3 starting respectively at the points (h1, 1), (h2, 2), (h3, 3) with $hi \neq hj$ if $i \neq j$ and ending at the point (I, J) are :

$$(13) \quad \ell(Chi) = I + J - hi + 1$$

and as $hi \neq hj$ we get as previously $\ell(Chi) \neq \ell(Chj)$ if $i \neq j$. From these results we can already conclude that if the local constraint is symmetric then the length constancy property does not hold if the initial boundary conditions are relaxed.

Let us now consider the case of an asymmetric local constraint. If the initial boundary conditions are relaxed on the vertical axis the lengths of Cv1, Cv2, Cv3 are :

$$(14) \quad \ell(Cvi) = I \quad \text{for} \quad i = 1, 2, 3 .$$

On the other hand if the relaxation is realized on the horizontal axis, the lengths of Ch1, Ch2, Ch3 are :

$$(15) \quad \ell(Chi) = I - hi + 1$$

and here again we have $\ell(Chi) \neq \ell(Chj)$ if $i \neq j$.

In conclusion we have seen that whatever the type of the local constraint the length constancy property does not hold generally if the initial boundary conditions are relaxed. The only case where the property is still valid is when the relaxation is done in the vertical axis with an asymmetric constraint.

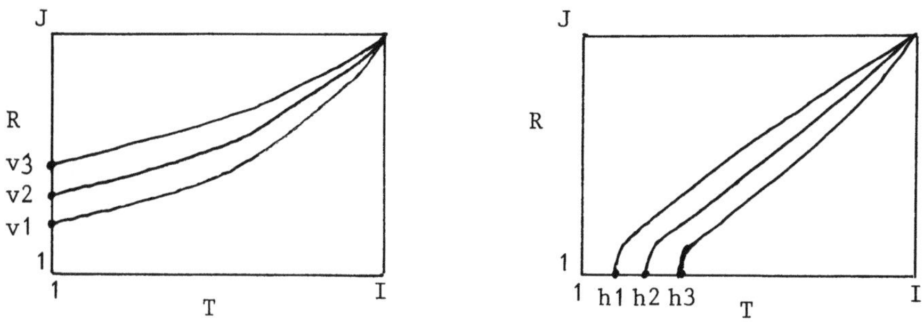

a- Vertical relaxation of the initial boundary conditions

b- Horizontal relaxation of the initial boundary conditions

Figure 1 : RELAXATION OF THE INITIAL BOUNDARY CONDITIONS.

In order to take into account variations of the path lengths when the boundary conditions are relaxed, a generalization of the optimality principle is needed :

- LET B be a sub-set of the matching plane PL , containing all the points that can be starting points of the warping paths,
- LET $p : PL \rightarrow B$ the function that gives at each point (i, j) the starting point of the optimal path ending at (i,j),
- LET C[p(i, j), (i, j)] be the optimal going from the point p(i, j) to the point (i, j) ,

THEN for each point (i', j') belonging to C[p(i, j), (i, j)] we have

1. p(i', j') = p(i, j)
2. C[p(i', j'), (i',j')] is included in C[p(i, j), (i, j)] , as a portion of it

With this new local optimality principle, to evaluate the accumulated distance D(i, j) recursively from the accumulated distances D(i', j') where the points (i', j') belong to the neighbourhood V(i, j) of the point (i, j) defined by the local constraint, it is necessary to use a two-phase dynamic programming strategy [10] [11] :

- in a first phase the point $(\hat{i}', \hat{j}') \in V(i, j)$ through which the optimal path goes must be determined in taking into account the length differences of the warping paths ending at (i, j). So a normalization of the accumulated distances by the length of the warping paths must be realized :

$$(16) \quad (\hat{i}', \hat{j}') = \underset{(i', j') \in V(i, j)}{\text{ARGMIN}} \frac{D(i', j') + dp\,((i', j'), (i, j))}{\ell(C[p(i', j'), (i', j')]) + \ell(C[(i', j'), (i, j)])}$$

$$(17)\quad D(i, j) = D(\hat{\imath}', \hat{\jmath}') + dp((\hat{\imath}', \hat{\jmath}'), (i, j))$$

$$(18)\quad p(i, j) = p(\hat{\imath}', \hat{\jmath}')$$

$$(19)\quad \ell(C[p(i, j), (i, j)]) = \ell(C[p(\hat{\imath}', \hat{\jmath}'), (\hat{\imath}', \hat{\jmath}')]) + \ell(C[(\hat{\imath}', \hat{\jmath}'), (i, j)]) .$$

Relations (16), (17), (18) and (19) can be considered as a generalization of relation (11) .

For example if the local constraint used is the symmetric Sakoe and Chiba local constraint [7] and if $\ell(i, j)$ denotes an abbreviation of $\ell(C[p(i, j), (i, j)])$ then relations (16), (17), (18) and (19) can be evaluated in the following manner :

1. FIRST PHASE

$$d = \text{MIN} \begin{cases} \dfrac{D(i-2, j-1) + 2 * d(i-1, j) + d(i, j)}{\ell(i-2, j-1) + 2 + 1} = d_1 \\[2ex] \dfrac{D(i-1, j-1) + 2 * d(i, j)}{\ell(i-1, j-1) + 2} = d_2 \\[2ex] \dfrac{D(i-1, j-2) + 2 * d(i, j-1) + d(i, j)}{\ell(i-2, j-1) + 2 + 1} = d_3 \end{cases}$$

2. SECOND PHASE

IF $(d = d_1)$ THEN
$$D(i, j) = D(i-2, j-1) + 2 * d(i-1, j) + d(i, j)$$
$$p(i, j) = p(i-2, j-1)$$
$$\ell(i, j) = \ell(i-2, j-1) + 3$$

IF $(d = d_2)$ THEN
$$D(i, j) = D(i-1, j-1) + 2 * d(i, j)$$
$$p(i, j) = p(i-1, j-1)$$
$$\ell(i, j) = \ell(i-1, j-1) + 2$$

IF $(d = d_3)$ THEN
$$D(i, j) = D(i-1, j-2) + 2 * d(i, j-1) + d(i, j)$$
$$p(i, j) = p(i-1, j-2)$$
$$\ell(i, j) = \ell(i-1, j-2) + 3$$

Owing to relations (16), (17), (18) and (19) it is possible to use a symmetric local constraint even when the boundary conditions are relaxed. That is the reason why we call the algorithm based on relations (16), (17), (18) and (19) using a symmetric local constraint UESLS "Unconstrained End-points Symmetric Local Strategy".

But in fact (16), (17), (18) and (19) are more general than that because they permit the implementation of local constraints weighted by any kind of weighting functions. For example if we consider the Sakoe and Chiba constraint weighted by arbitrary coefficients as indicated by figure 2 then relations (16), (17), (18) and (19) can be evaluated as follows :

1. FIRST PHASE

$$d = \text{MIN} \begin{cases} \dfrac{D(i-2, j-1) + a * d(i-1, j) + b * d(i, j)}{\ell(i-2, j-1) + a + b} = d_1 \\[2ex] \dfrac{D(i-1, j-1) + c * d(i, j)}{\ell(i-1, j-1) + c} = d_2 \\[2ex] \dfrac{D(i-1, j-2) + d * d(i, j-1) + c * d(i, j)}{\ell(i-1, j-2) + d + e} = d_3 \end{cases}$$

2. SECOND PHASE

IF $(d = d_1)$ THEN $D(i, j) = D(i-2, j-1) + a * d(i-1, j) + b * d(i, j)$

$p(i, j) = p(i-2, j-1)$

$\ell(i, j) = \ell(i-2, j-1) + a + b$

IF $(d = d_2)$ THEN $D(i, j) = D(i-1, j-1) + c * d(i, j)$

$p(i, j) = p(i-1, j-1)$

$\ell(i, j) = \ell(i-1, j-1) + c$

IF $(d = d_3)$ THEN $D(i, j) = D(i-1, j-2) + d * D(i, j-1) + e * d(i, j)$

$p(i, j) = p(i-1, j-2)$

$\ell(i, j) = \ell(i-1, j-2) + d + e$

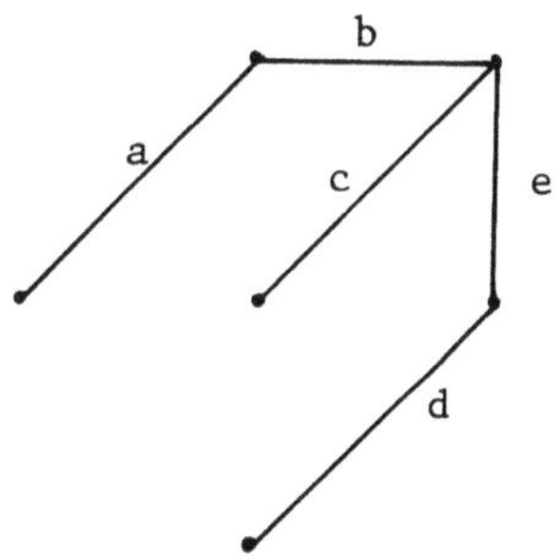

Figure 2 : THE SAKOE AND CHIBA LOCAL CONSTRAINT WEIGHTED BY ARBITRARY COEFFICIENTS.

IV. EXTENSION OF THE GENERALIZED DYNAMIC PROGRAMMING RECURSIVE RELATIONS IN THE CASE OF THE CONNECTED WORD RECOGNITION PROBLEM

IV.1. Introduction

One of the first attempt to solve the problem of the connected word recognition was undertaken by Sakoe [12]. He showed that the minimization process could be broken down into two dynamic programming levels, a word level where any portion of the input pattern is matched to all the reference patterns, and a phrase level where the best string of reference patterns is found owing to the best partial distances obtained in the word level. Myers and Rabiner [13], later showed that a computationnally more efficient method can be obtained in determining the optimal warping path in a "level building" fashion. The Myers-Rabiner algorithm, although an interesting improvment of the Sakoe algorithm is not very well suited for real time recognition. Recently Bridle et al. [14] and Nakagawa [15], independently proposed an algorithm that eliminates the weaknesses of the level building algorithm. This new algorithm is a one-stage algorithm, that is to say no backward jumps on the input pattern are necessary during the matching process, as is the case for the level building algorithm. Furthermore all the local distances are evaluated only once. However this algorithm is difficult to grasp because the formalism used clouded the useful analogy with the word recognition problem. In a recent paper, Ney [16] has presented a new formalism relying on the use of certain path constraints both in the word interior and at the end-words that links tightly the connected word recognition problem and provides a new and simpler formulation of the algorithm designed by Bridle et al and Nakagawa -hence forward refered as the Bridle-Nakagawa algorithm-.

IV.2. The pattern matching problem

Let T be the test pattern of length I in frames and V a set of N reference patterns R_K of length J_k that have been obtained by an isolated training procedure. The purpose of the connected word recognition is to find the best "super-reference" pattern :

$$SR(\ell, q) = R_{q(1)} \oplus R_{q(2)} \oplus \dots \oplus R_{q(\ell)}$$

defined as the concatenation of ℓ reference patterns that best matches the input pattern. In this problem, ℓ and the boundaries of the words are not known.

IV.3. The dynamic recursive relations of a one-pass algorithm for connected word recognition

The main idea of the one-pass algorithm relies in determining the optimal path in a three-dimensional space as illustrated by figure 3.

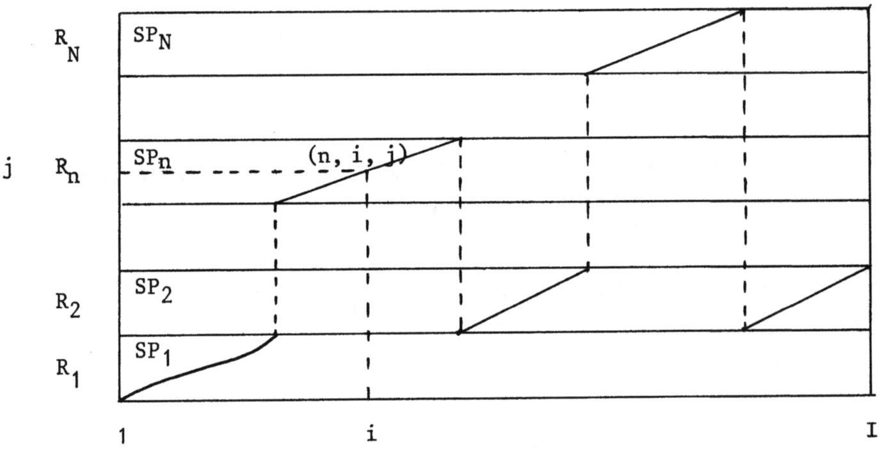

Figure 3 : ILLUSTRATION OF A WARPING PATH IN THE BRIDLE-NAKAGAWA MATCHING ALGORITHM.

Each point in this matching space can be represented by a triple (n, i, j) where n designates the sub-space SP_n relative to the reference pattern R_n ; i the current index of the input pattern, and j the j'th frame of R_n . With this formalism a warping path W is given as a sequence of points (n(k), i(k), j(k)) with k = 1, 2, ..., K , where K is the number of points of the warping path. The problem of the connected word recognition can now be stated in a similar manner as for the word recognition, that is to say, it can be solved by the following global metric minimization :

$$(17) \quad D(\hat{W}) = \underset{K,\, n(k),\, i(k),\, j(k)}{\text{MIN}} \frac{\sum_{k=1}^{K} d(n(k), i(k), j(k)).P(k)}{N(P)}$$

where d(n(k), i(k), j(k)) is the local distance between the i(k)'th frame of the input pattern and the j(k)'th frame of $R_{n(k)}$.

In the case of a symmetric local constraint, (17) depends on the length of the super-reference patterns that is obviously not constant, so that the normalization factor N(P) cannot be factorized. To get around the difficulty, only asymmetric local constraints with no relaxation of the boundary conditions has hitherto been considered. In that case N(P) is equal to the length of the input pattern and the minimization problem can be expressed as :

$$(18) \quad D^*(\hat{W}) = \underset{K,\, n(k),\, i(k),\, j(k)}{\text{MIN}} \sum_{k=1}^{K} d(n(k), i(k), j(k)) * P(k)$$

- the asterisk signifying that the global distance D is not normalized -

In order to solve (18) by a dynamic programming technique, by applying the optimality principle of Bellman, it is necessary to define for each point (n, i, j) of the matching space a minimum accumulated distance D(n, i, j) . And, as for the word recognition problem, the evaluation of this distance can be realized recursively as a function of the minimum distances associated to the points belonging to the neighbourhood V(n, i, j) of the point (n, i, j) defined by the local constraint used :

$$(19) \quad D(n, i, j) = \underset{\substack{(n', i', j') \\ \in V(n, i, j)}}{\text{MIN}} D(n', i', j') + d_p((n', i', j'),(n, i, j))$$

where $d_p((n', i', j'),(n, i, j))$ denotes the weighted distance of the local path going from the point (n', i', j') to the point (n, i, j). As was clearly shown in Ney's excellent tutorial paper [16] two types of neighbourhood must be defined : a whitin-template neighbourhood at the interior of a word and a between template neighbourhood at the boundaries of the words. Assuming the local constraint is the simple constraint with no slope conditions, shown in figure 4, then the within and between template neighbourhoods can be defined respectively by (20) and (21) :

$$(20) \quad V(n, i, j) = \{(n, i-1, j), (n, i-1, j-1), (n, i, j-1)\} \quad \text{with } j > 1$$

$$(21) \quad V(n, i, j) = \{(n, i-1, j), (n, i-1, Jn'), n' = 1, 2, \ldots N\} \quad \text{with } j = 1$$

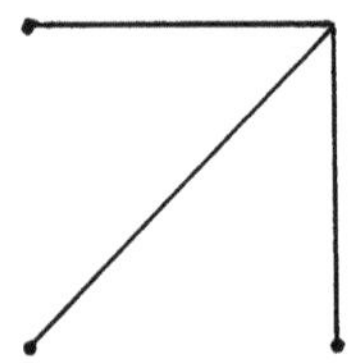

Figure 4 : A SIMPLE LOCAL CONSTRAINT WITH NO SLOPE CONDITIONS.

For further details, see [16]. Owing to relations (19), (20) and (21) the connected word recognition problem can be solved in a similar manner as the word recognition problem - the only differences lying in the introduction of another loop all over the reference patterns and of backtraking pointers -. It is in this last point that lies the original approach of Ney.

As now relation (19) can be regarded as just an extension of relation (11), the generalization of relation (19) in the case of a relaxation of the boundary conditions can be obtained by analogy with the relations we get for word recognition :

1. FIRST PHASE RELATION

$$(22)\quad (\hat{n}', \hat{\imath}', \hat{\jmath}') = \underset{\substack{(n',i',j') \\ \in V(n,i,j)}}{\text{ARGMIN}} \frac{D(n',i',j') + d_p((n',i',j'), (n, i, j))}{\ell(C[p(n',i',j'), (n',i',j')]) + \ell(C[(n',i',j'), (n, i, j)])}$$

2. SECOND PHASE RELATION

$$(23)\quad D(n, i, j) = D(\hat{n}', \hat{\imath}', \hat{\jmath}') + d_p(\hat{n}', \hat{\imath}', \hat{\jmath}'), (n, i, j))$$

$$(24)\quad p(n, i, j) = p(\hat{n}', \hat{\imath}', \hat{\jmath}')$$

$$(25)\quad \ell(C[p(n, i, j), (n, i, j)]) = \ell(C[p(\hat{n}', \hat{\imath}', \hat{\jmath}'), (\hat{n}', \hat{\imath}', \hat{\jmath}')]) + \ell(C[(\hat{n}', \hat{\imath}', \hat{\jmath}'), (n, i, j)])$$

where $p(n, i, j)$ denotes the starting point of the optimal path going through the point (n, i, j) .

In order to illustrate how relations (22), (23), (24) and (25) can be implemented in a practical case let us assume that the local constraint used is the simple local constraint with no slope conditions weighted by arbitrary coefficients - figure 5 - and distinguish the two types of neighbourhoods. The notation $\ell(n, i, j)$ is an abbreviation of $\ell(C[p(n, i, j), (n, i, j)])$.

Case of a within-template neighbourhood $(j > 1)$:

$$d = \text{MIN} \begin{cases} \dfrac{D(n, i-1, j) + a * d(n, i, j)}{\ell(n, i-1, j) + a} = d_1 \\[2ex] \dfrac{D(n, i-1, j-1) + b * d(n, i, j)}{\ell(n, i-1, j) + b} = d_2 \\[2ex] \dfrac{D(n, i, j-1) + c * d(n, i, j)}{\ell(n, i, j-1) + c} = d_3 \end{cases}$$

$$
\text{IF } (d = d_1) \text{ THEN } \begin{aligned} D(n, i, j) &= D(n, i-1, j) + a * d(n, i, j) \\ p(n, i, j) &= p(n, i-1, j) \\ \ell(n, i, j) &= \ell(n, i-1, j) + a \end{aligned}
$$

$$
\text{IF } (d = d_2) \text{ THEN } \begin{aligned} D(n, i, j) &= D(n, i-1, j-1) + b * d(n, i, j) \\ p(n, i, j) &= p(n, i-1, j-1) \\ \ell(n, i, j) &= \ell(n, i-1, j-1) + b \end{aligned}
$$

$$
\text{IF } (d = d_3) \text{ THEN } \begin{aligned} D(n, i, j) &= D(n, i, j-1) + c * d(n, i, j) \\ p(n, i, j) &= p(n, i, j-1) \\ \ell(n, i, j) &= \ell(n, i, j-1) + c \end{aligned}
$$

Case of a between-template neighbourhood (j = 1) :

$$
d = \text{MIN} \begin{cases} \dfrac{D(n, i-1, j) + a * d(n, i, j)}{\ell(n, i-1, j) + a} = d_1 \\ \underset{n'}{\text{MIN}} \dfrac{D(n, i-1, Jn') + b * d(n, i, j)}{\ell(n, i-1), Jn') + b} = d_2 \end{cases}
$$

$$
\text{IF } (d = d_1) \text{ THEN } \begin{aligned} D(n, i, j) &= D(n, i-1, j) + a * d(n, i, j) \\ p(n, i, j) &= p(n, i-1, j) \\ \ell(n, i, j) &= \ell(n, i-1, j) + a \end{aligned}
$$

$$
\text{IF } (d = d_2) \text{ THEN } \begin{aligned} \hat{n}' &= \underset{n'}{\text{ARGMIN}} \frac{D(n, i-1, Jn') + b * d(n, i, j)}{\ell(n, i-1, Jn') + b} \\ D(n, i, j) &= D(\hat{n}, i-1, J\hat{n}') + b * d(n, i, j) \\ p(n, i, j) &= p(\hat{n}', i-1, J\hat{n}') \\ \ell(n, i, j) &= \ell(\hat{n}', i-1, J\hat{n}') + b \end{aligned}
$$

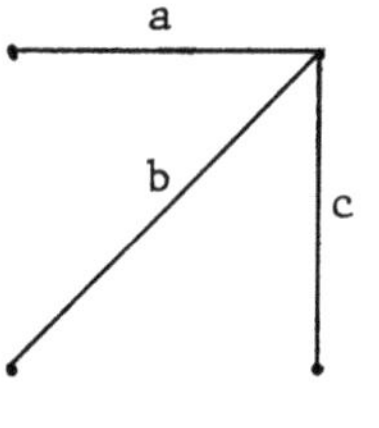

Figure 5 : THE LOCAL CONSTRAINT WITH NO SLOPE CONDITION WEIGHTED BY ARBITRARY COEFFICIENTS.

V. SOME CONSIDERATIONS ON TIME-SPACE COMPLEXITY

In order to compare our algorithms with the classical DTW algorithms from the point of view of time space complexity we will restrict the discussion to the problem of isolated word recognition - the discussion relative to the connected word recognition would be similar -.

Let N be the number of references, I the length of the test utterance, J the mean length of the references, β the number of bytes necessary to represent a word of data of integer type in the machine used, α the ratio of the time necessary to carry out a floating point division to the time needed to evaluate a local distance. For the standard DTW algorithm, in the case of a full search of the optimal path in the matching $N*I*J$ local distances must be evaluated and $N*J*\beta$ bytes of data are necessary to store the accumulated distances. In the case of our algorithm $N*I*J(1+3\alpha)$ "local distances" must be evaluated and $2*N*J*\beta$ bytes of data are necessary to store both the accumulated distances and the lengths of the partial optimal path ending at each point. From the expression of the number of local distances for our algorithm, we see that the computational effort necessary to implement our algorithm depends critically on the parameter α . If the time necessary for calculating a floating point division is greater or equal than the time necessary for evaluating a local distance - as it is the case in a general computer- the computational effort is multiplied by a factor of 4 or more. It is clear that our algorithm needs a special hardware configuration including an array processor or a digital signal processor. The comparison of the expressions giving the space of the data memory both for the two algorithms shows that our algorithm needs twice as much memory space as the standard algorithm. This is the minimum memory space requirement imposed by our method and there is no way of compression it further.

VI. SOME PRELIMINARY EXPERIMENTAL RESULTS ON WORD RECOGNITION

We have implemented on a mini-computer, MITRA 125, the algorithm we have called previously UESLS using the symmetric Sakoe and Chiba local constraint. The speech signal was analysed by a 16 chanel vocoder with a sampling frequency of 50 Hz. The vocabulary of words considered was the ten french digits. The mismatch in duration, tm , was a parameter of the algorithm. Only one reference was used for each word. Each word was pronounced 20 times. For tm = 0 ms we get 3 % of error rate and for tm = 60 ms we get 1 % of error rate. Consequently an increase in performance seems to appear when the boundary conditions are relaxed. But these experiments are not sufficient to give a final judgment on the performance of the method employed. For a more precise evaluation of the accuracy of the new class of DTW algorithms, both for isolated and connected word recognition, proposed in this paper, extensive experiments are under course in our research group. Detailed results will be given in a companion paper.

VII. CONCLUSION

In this paper we have presented a new formulation of the DTW recursive relations both for word recognition and connected word recognition. The new recursive relations presented are able to take into account possible warping path length variation which may result either from a relaxation of the boundary conditions or from the assignment of arbitrary weighting coefficients to the arcs of the local constraint employed. Preliminary experiments for word recognition indicate an improvment in performance in the case of the ten frech digit vocabulary when the boundary conditions are relaxed.

REFERENCES

[1] L.R. Rabiner, A.E. Rosenberg, S.E. Levinson, "Considerations in Dynamic Time Warping Algorithms for Discrete Word Recognition", IEEE Trans. Acoust., Speech, Signal Processing, vol. ASSP-26, N° 6, pp. 575-582, December 1978.

[2] J.P. Haton, "Contribution à l'Analyse et à la reconnaissance Automatique de la Parole", Thèse d'Etat, Université de Nancy I, January 1974.

[3] S.K. Das, "Some Experiments in Discrete Utterance Recognition", Proc. ICASSP, Denver, Co, 1980, pp. 178-181.

[4] A. Waibel, B. Yegnanarayana, "Comparative Study of Nonlinear Time Warping Techniques in Isolated Word Speech Recognition", Carnegie-Mellon University, Computer Science Department, 1982.

[5] C. Myers, L.R. Rabiner, A.E. Rosenberg, "Performance Tradeoffs in Dynamic Time Warping Algorithms for Isolated Word Recognition", IEEE Trans. Acoust. Speech, Signal Processing, vol. ASSP-6, N° 6, pp. 623-635, December 1980.

[6] H. Sakoe, S. Chiba, "A Dynamic Programming Approach to Continuous Speech Recognition", In Proc. Int. Congr. Acoust., Budapest, Hungary, 1971.

[7] H. Sakoe, S. Chiba, "Dynamic Programming Algorithm Optimization for Spoken Word Recognition", IEEE Trans. Acoust., Speech, Signal Processing, vol. ASSP-26, pp. 43-49, February 1978.

[8] F. Itakura, "Minimum Prediction Residual Principle Applied to Speech Recognition", IEEE Trans. Acoust., Speech, Signal Processing, vol. ASSP-23, pp. 67-72, February 1975.

[9] R. Bellman, "Dynamic Programming", Princeton, N.F. : Princeton, Univ. Press, 1957.

[10] J. di Martino, J.P. Haton, M.C. Haton, "Evaluation d'Algorithmes en Reconnaissance Automatique de la Parole", In Proc. Int. Congr. Acoust., Paris, France, 1983.

[11] J. di Martino, "Contribution à la Reconnaissance Globale de la Parole : Mots Isolés et Mots Enchaînés", Dr. Ing. thesis, Université de Nancy I, April 1984.

[12] H. Sakoe, "Two-Level DP-Matching-A Dynamic Programming Based Pattern Matching Algorithm for Connected Word Recognition", IEEE Trans. Acoust., Speech, Signal Processing, vol. ASSP-27, pp. 588-595, December 1979.

[13] C.S. Myers, L.R. Rabiner, "A Level Building Dynamic Time Warping Algorithm for Connected Word Recognition", IEEE Trans. Acoust., Speech, Signal Processing, vol. ASSP-29, pp. 284-297, April 1981.

[14] J.S. Bridle, M.D. Brown , R.M. Chamberlain, "An Algorithm for Connected Word Recognition", in Proc. 1982, IEEE International Conference on Acoustics, Speech and Signal Processing, Paris, pp. 899-902, May 1982.

[15] S. Nakagawa, "A Connected Spoken Word Recognition Method by O(n) Dynamic Programming Pattern Matching Algorithm", In Proc. 1983, IEEE International Conference on Acoustics, Speech and Signal Processing, Boston, pp. 226-299, April 1983.

[16] H. Ney, "The Use of a One-Stage Dynamic Programming Algorithm for Connected Word Recognition", IEEE Trans. Acoust., Speech, Signal Processing, vol. ASSP-32, pp. 263-271, April 1984.

AN EFFICIENT ALGORITHM FOR RECOGNIZING ISOLATED TURKISH WORDS

Neşe Yalabık and Fatih Ünal
Department of Computer Engineering
Middle East Technical University
Ankara, Turkey

ABSTRACT

In this study, a computationally efficient speaker independent isolated word recognition system for Turkish language is designed and implemented. The approach used is a combination of whole-word matching techniques with segmentation into phonetic units before classification. Linear Predictive Coding (LPC) coefficients for an eight-pole model of the short-time signal are used as feature vectors. Computational costs are reduced by a two-step classification strategy where unlikely words are eliminated in the first step by comparing only the first syllable. The Dynamic Time Warping (DTW) method is used in comparisons at both levels.

CPU time spent for word comparisons is reduced by about 40% compared to the time that has to be spent for a one-step whole-word classification without degrading the system performance.

I. INTRODUCTION

Many isolated word recognition systems for single speaker case process the incoming speech in real time. If speaker independence is also a desired feature, the extra processing that is needed may raise the computational costs significantly. This is caused by the fact that higher numbers of features and higher numbers of training samples need to be used in the classification to compensate for the variations among different

NATO ASI Series, Vol. F16
New Systems and Architectures for Automatic Speech
Recognition and Synthesis. Edited by R. De Mori and C. Y. Suen

speakers' speech.

In the whole-word template matching classification approach this means that usually more than one template per word is needed for comparisons.

This study makes use of a two-step classification strategy to reduce the number of whole-word comparisons, thus obtaining significant reduction in computational costs. The vocabulary is segmented into groups of dissimilar words. In the first step, a candidate from each group is selected by considering only the first syllable, thus avoiding the comparison cost for the rest of the word. In the second step, selected candidates which are few in number are compared with the unknown word as a whole to select the most likely one.

The block diagram for the system is shown in Figure 1. It has an 18-word vocabulary consisting of Turkish digits and arithmetic operators like plus, equal, etc. The speech signal is filtered by an analog low-pass filter to eliminate high-frequency noise and to prevent aliasing effects before it is digitized and stored in an LSI 11/2 microcomputer. The system software can mainly be divided into learning and recognition phases, as will be discussed in the following sections.

II. FEATURE EXTRACTION AND PATTERN SIMILARITY

Many different features are used for recognizing isolated words. Among them are short-time spectrum, cepstrum, LPC coefficients, etc. The LPC method, which was selected to be used in this work, is presently a widely used technique because it provides accurate estimates for spectral features of most sounds in a computationally feasible amount of processing time(1). LPC analysis relies on a model of the digitized speech signal s_n where it can be approximated by a linear combination of p past samples as follows:

$$s_n = \sum_{k=1}^{p} a_k \, s_{n-k} \qquad (1)$$

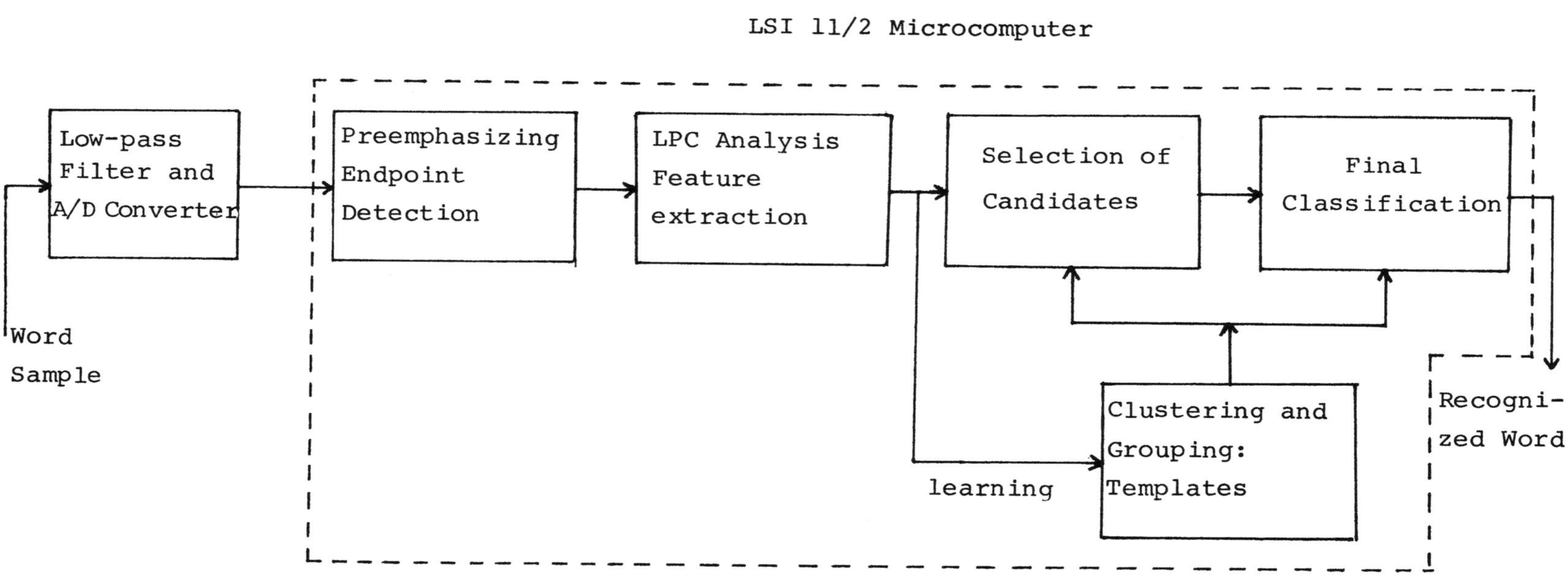

Figure 1. Sequential Speaker Independent Word Recognition System

This corresponds to a speech generation mechanism modeled as a p-pole digital filter whose input is a periodic train of impulses for voiced speech and a random sequence of noise for unvoiced speech. The filter is time invariant only for a short interval of time (about 30 msec) due to the vocal-tract properties. Hence the signal for a whole word is divided into a number of frames. Here, the frame width is selected to be 40 msecs, succesive frames overlapping by two thirds to compansate with the filtering problems at the sides. The p parameters $a_1, a_2, \ldots, a_p$ represent the properties of each frame. $p = 8$ is found to be good enough for this particular application.

Fig.1. shows that the digitized speech signal is first preprocessed for pre-emphasizing the high-frequency components and detecting the endpoints. The endpoint detection algorithm makes use of the zero crossing rate and energy measures, which is described in (2). After the preprocessing operations, the LPC parameters for each frame are estimated using the autocorrelation method of linear prediction(2,3).

Several distance measures between the two words which are represented by a sequence of LPC parameters have been proposed in the literature. Initially a distance measure between the two compared frames of two corresponding words has to be defined. Here the Itakura distance(4) is used, which is mainly the log ratio of the normalized autocorrelation functions of the LPC coefficients of test and learning samples.

Once the distance measure between the two corresponding frames has been determined, a time warping of two words to achieve an optimum match is employed. Main problems arise due to the fact that the number of frames in two compared words may not be the same, in addition to the problem that repetitions of the same word might have different durations for the same phonetic units. These problems were tackled by Dynamic Time Warping(DTW) alignment, which nonlinearly shifts the frames to get a best match between the two words or other compared units (5). An optimum solution is found by dynamic programming methods and allows different-length samples.

III. CLUSTERING

The last step in learning is setting a classification rule which makes use of reference patterns. The Nearest-Neighbor Rule classifies the unknown sample as belonging to the category closest reference pattern belongs to. However, computational costs involved in comparisons and storage make it impossible to use this classifier without any modification for most of the applications, as it is the case in word recognition problems. Only a few representative ones between the learning samples of each category is selected. These patterns are called templates. In the speaker independent recognition problem it is desired that the number of templates be more than one for each word to obtain acceptable results. To select the representative templates, possible clusters of feature vectors are selected. Here, a clustering algorithm which is proposed by(6) is used. The original algorithm creates a variable number of templates according to the structure inherent in the training set. The total number of clusters need not be known or specified a priori.

For determining the first template, a single pattern is selected from all the replications of that word in such a way that the maximum distance to any other sample is minimum. This point is called the minimax center. After the first template is selected, a cluster is formed around this point by including all the points that are closer to it than a predefined threshold. The samples which are not covered by the first cluster are considered for the determination of the second template and the second cluster, using the same procedure. The procedure can be repeated until all the words in the same class are covered.

IV. SEQUENTIAL CLASSIFICATION

One way to reduce the computational costs for the comparisons is to use a smaller number of frames. Obviously, this would cause some loss of information and an increase in the error rate. However, if the classification discriminates between distant (dissimilar) words, only a portion of the complete feature set might be used with acceptable results. The idea utilised here is as follows: Divide the words in the vocabulary into a number

GR-1	GR-2	GR-3	GR-4	GR-5
SIFIR/səfər/	ALTI /ä l tə/	İKİ /iki/	BİR /bir/	DÖRT /dœrt/
YEDİ /jedi/	SEKİZ/sekiz/	DOKUZ/dokuz/	ÜÇ /yt /	BEŞ /beʃ /
NOKTA/noktä/	TOPLA/toplä/	EŞİT /eʃit/	AÇ /ä tʃ/	ÇARP /tʃärp/
KAPA/käpä /	ÇIKAR/tʃəkar/		BÖL /bœl/	

Table 1: Grouping of the Turkish words in the vocabulary.

This approach differs from other sequential methods in the sense that dissimilar words, rather than similar are grouped together. Once advantage of this is that it might give better results when the vocabulary allows a uniform distribution of reference templates over the pattern space, rather than forming distinct clusters. The grouping of words in Table 1 is performed by making use of the confusion matrices obtained by the experiments performed on a one-step classification process in a previous study(2). For example YEDİ,SEKİZ and EŞİT are found to be confused mostly so they fall in different groups.

Here, one concern in determining the number of groups is to keep it small enough to allow a considerable reduction is computational cost but large enough so that the system performance is not degraded. This is performed heuristically here. Other factors that

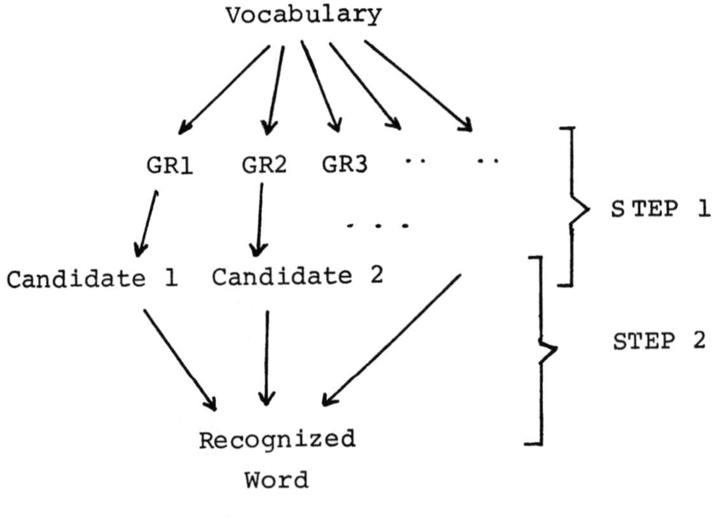

affect the groupings are the syllabic properties of the Turkish language. Words that are in the same group have the same number of syllables. Also, it was shown in previous(7,8) that segmentation of a word into its syllables is not as difficult as in many other languages. This fact is utilised in forming the following two-step classification rule (Fig. 2): A candidate is selected from each group. The frames that are taken into account in this selection approximately correspond to the first syllable of each word. The syllabic segmentation is performed by making use of energy values during the endpoint detection procedure. The reason for selecting the first syllable arises from the fact that the average duration of the first vowel, and hence the first syllable is shorter than the following ones in general for the Turkish language. Also, plosives such as /p/ and /t/, which appear at the end of the words in general generate bursts of energy, which result in peaks and causes a confusion of these sounds with vowels. Considering only the beginning of a word will avoid this problem.

The candidate selection from each group is performed by dynamically time-warping the selected frames of the words as discussed above. Once this has been done, the final classification is performed among the selected candidates, this time making full use of all the frames, using DTW matching.

V. RESULTS AND CONCLUSION

The word templates were generated by 16 different speakers (8 males and 8 females of different ages). About 300 words generated by other speakers were used for testing. In an earlier study (2) using the single-step dynamic time warping approach with two templates per word, a recognition rate of 80% was obtained. The approach discussed in the previous sections allowed for an improvement of 40% in recognition time while keeping the recognition rate at the same level. The earlier experiments showed that using three templates rather than two improves the recognition rate considerably (to approximately 87%), so that the savings

REFERENCES

(1) Makhoul,J., 'Linear Prediction: A Tutorial Review', Proc. IEEE, 63, 1975, pp.583-587

(2) Ünal,F., 'A Speaker Independent Isolated Turkish Word Recognition System', M.S. Thesis, METU, Ankara, Turkey, 1983.

(3) Rabiner,L.R., Schafer,R.W., 'Digital Processing of Speech Signals', Prentice-Hall, 1978.

(4) Itakura,F., 'Minimum Prediction Residual Principle Applied to Speech Recognition', IEEE Trans. Acoust. Speech and Signal Processing, Vol. ASSP-23, 1975, pp. 67-72

(5) Sakoe,H., Chiba,S., 'Dynamic Programming Algorithm Optimization for Spoken Word Recognition', IEEE Trans. on Acoust. Speech and Signal Processing, Vol.ASSP-26, 1978, pp. 43-49.

(6) Rabiner,L.R., Wilpon,J.G., 'Considerations in Applying Clustering Techniques to Speaker Independent Word Recognition', J. Acoust. Soc. Am. 1979, pp. 663-673

(7) Tőreci,E., 'Statistical Investigations on the Turkish Language Using Digital Computers', M.S. Thesis, METU, Ankara, Turkey, 1974

(8) Özmen,H., 'A Microcomputer Based System for the Recognition of Spoken Turkish Digits', M.S. Thesis, METU, Ankara, Turkey, 1981.

A GENERAL FUZZY-PARSING SCHEME FOR SPEECH RECOGNITION.

Enrique Vidal *
Francisco Casacuberta *
Emilio Sanchis *
Jose M. Benedi **

(*) CENTRO DE INFORMATICA
(**) DEP. ELECTRONICA E INFORMATICA FAC. FISICAS
UNIVERSIDAD DE VALENCIA
SPAIN

ABSTRACT.

In this paper a Speech Recognition Methodology is proposed which is based on the general assumption of "fuzzyness" of both speech-data and knowledge-sources. Besides this general principle, there are other fundamental assumptions which are also the bases of the proposed methodology: "Modularity" in the knowledge organization, "Homogeneity" in the representation of data and knowledge, "Passiveness" of the "understanding flow" (no backtraking or feedback), and "Parallelism" in the recognition activity.

The proposed methodology is formally presented, and algorithms to develop actual systems on general pourpose hardware are given. An implementation example as well as the results obtained with it are also presented.

1.- INTRODUCTION.

Automatic Speech Recognition (like other human-like perceptive and cognitive problems aimed at being solved by digital computers) has proved to be a dificult task. The main dimensions of the dificulty are variability and noise of data and ambiguity and uncertainty of knowledge; in fact, all these are of a nature which is very far from the exact-like principles under which all modern Von-Newman-machine based computers work. Most implementations of Speech Recognition Systems are, in reality, computer-simulated mathematical models which aim at accounting for the inexact nature of the problem. Among the theories which have been adopted as background for modeling inexactness is the Fuzzy-Sets Theory. It has been used in several Artificial Inteligence areas (12) and, in

NATO ASI Series, Vol. F16
New Systems and Architectures for Automatic Speech Recognition and Synthesis. Edited by R. De Mori and C. Y. Suen

particular, it has proved to be a consitent mathematical support for quite different problems in Speech Recognition (1)(2)(3)(13)(14).

The work presented in this paper is based on the above introduced general assumption of fuzzyness of both knowledge and data, and uses the Fuzzy-Sets Theory as the primary frame-work for developping a general model of perception and cognition with direct application to Speech Recognition.

Besides the fuzzyness principle there are four other fundamental assumptions under which the presented model is being developed: namely modularity, homogeneity, pasiveness and paralelism. "Modularity" stands for the organization of the knowledge, which is assumed to be structured into levels of understanding (acoustic, phonetic, lexical, etc.). The "Homogeneity" principle assumes knowledge and data to be uniformly represented at all the levels. "Passiveness" refers to the "understanding flow" which is thought to progress just as a parsimonious bottom-up systolic flow, without backtracking or feedback. The "Parallelism" principle, represents the way in which understanding activity is performed; both inter-level (all levels can work concurrently) and intra-level (several elements in each level can hold a parallel activity, cooperating to the in-level understanding process).

All these ideas agree closely with certain psycho-cognitive "connectionist" theories more or less based on speculative assumptions on the actual neuronal hardware (4) (5) (6). In these theories, it is considered that all encodings of importance are in terms of relative strengths of synaptic connections, and individual neurons do not transmit large ammounts of symbolic information; rather they communicate with each-other in a simple way. Complex concepts are thought to be held by an appropiate interconection scheme between several elemental units, and the apparent rule-based nature of cognition is considered as an illusion based on statistical properties of mass neuronal interactions.

The cognitive model presented in this paper, like all those related to "connectionist" theories (and many other models of speech understanding), are especially well suited for implementing with massively parallel machine architectures which are not technologically available at present, but which seem to be the target

model introduced, algorithms have been developped which can run satisfactorily on present general-pourpose (mini) computers, and there seem to be many potential (and actual) applications which can run on general pourpose hardware.

Under a more classical perspective the work presented in this paper can be viewed as a "pasive" system with the different knowledge sources structured into levels. In general, this kind of system produces important information reductions at each level, by "interpreting" the data coming from the lower level(s). This information reduction (which is very interesting from a computational point of view) is the main cause of a degradation in results produced by the presence of ambiguity and noise, which makes it impossible to get the "clean" interpretations usually aimed for at each level. The alternative proposed renounces explicitly to handle "clean" data, and aims to reduce the degradation by minimizing the loss of information associated with the interpretation process at each level. Fig 1.1. shows an intuitive illustration of the proposed methodology. Level-0 is a special level which obtains a fuzzy symbolic description of the parametric representation of speech. Level-1 fuzzy-interprets this fuzzy-symbolic description in terms of (broad) phonetic categories. This fuzzy-interpretation is processed in its turn by Level-2 which fuzzy-interprets it in terms of lexical categories. The process continues in a similar manner at all the levels, "focalizing" the incoming data into the most likely interpretations in terms of the categories associated with each level, but without significative dropping of information about low-scored interpretations which will therefore be available for the higher levels if there is low compatibility of the most likely data with the corresponding knowledge sources.

For most applications, the knowledge associated with each level can be homogeneously represented by fuzzy finite-state networks, and the same fuzzy-parsing scheme can be (concurrently) applied to all levels.

2.- THEORY AND ALGORITHMS.

In this section we will deal with a formal presentation of the

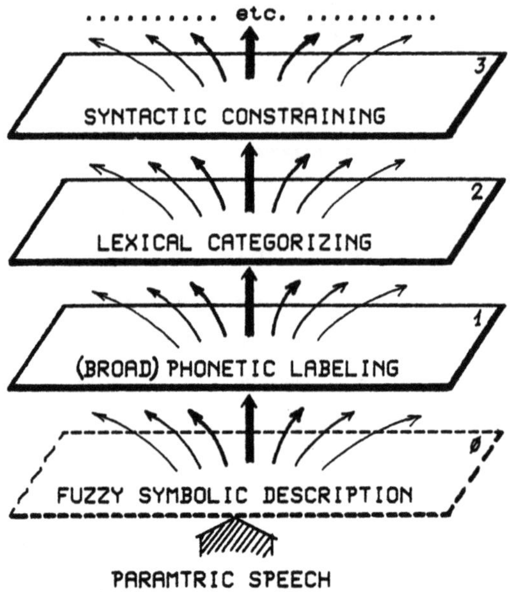

Fig 1.1. Multilevel fuzzy-interpretation process.

```
PARAMETERS: CONTIN_MODE, STARTING_SCORE, STATE_THD, RECOGN_THD,
            CONTINUITY_THD, NON_CONTINUITY_PENALTY.

INITIALIZATION:

  Make all current_state scores = 0;
  Make all next_state scores = 0;
  Make initial_state score = STARTING_SCORE;
  Make utterance_time = 0;

RECURSION:

  repeat
    input the current_fuzzy_label;
    for all current_states with score > STATE_THD:
        find all next_states;
        for each next_state:
            evaluate transition_evidence =
                  = I(current_state,current_fuzzy_label,next_state);
            if next_state score < current_state score □
                                                    transition_evidence
            then make next_state score = current state score □
                                                    transition_evidence;
        end for;
    end for;
    for all next_states:
        if next_state score - current_state score < CONTINUITY_THD
        then decrement next_state score by NON_CONTINUITY_PENALTY;
        if next_satate score < STATE_THD then make this score = 0;
    end for;
    make all current_state scores = next_state scores;
    {prunning may be necesary for large networks}
    for all final_states with score > RECOGN_THD:
        output these states and their scores as the fuzzy set
                                          of recognized categories;
    end for;
    {decimation can be applied for saving resources in next level}
    if CONTIN_MODE then make initial_state score = STARTING_SCORE;
    increment utterance_time by the time_unit;
  until utterance_time is exhausted.
```

Fig 2.2. The fuzzy-parsing algorithm.

As introduced in first section, each level accepts a sequence of a certain class of fuzzy-symbols produced by the lower level(s), and outputs another sequence of "fuzzy-symbols" corresponding to the associated symbol repertory. All these "fuzzy-symbols" are modeled as fuzzy subsets over the output alphabet corresponding to the categories associated with each level.

The output sequences of fuzzy-symbols are produced at all the levels, by a general "fuzzy-interpretetion process" and the knowledge needed for this interpretation is assumed to be represented by fuzzy finite-state networks. The exception is the lowest level, which must extract its corresponding sequence by means of a different "fuzzy-description process" (14) applied to a parametric representation of speech.

Let Ψ be a finite alphabet, and G the set of all fuzzy subsets over Ψ. We define a Ψ-fuzzy-finite state machine as a five-tuple $\underset{\sim}{A}$

$$\underset{\sim}{A} = (Q,\ q_I,\ F,\ \underset{\sim}{R},\ \underset{\sim}{T})$$

where:

1) Q is a finite set of states.
2) $q_I \in Q$ is the initial state.
3) $F \subseteq Q$ is the set of final states.
4) $\underset{\sim}{R}$: $Q \times Q \longrightarrow G$ are the arcs with their confidence values.
5) $\underset{\sim}{T}$: $Q \times G \times Q \longrightarrow [0,1]$ defined as:

$$\underset{\sim}{T}(q_i,\underset{\sim}{D},q_j) = \underset{\sim}{D}\,\Delta\,\underset{\sim}{R}(q_i,q_j)\ ;\ q_i,q_j \in Q;\ \underset{\sim}{D} \in G$$

The fuzzy relation $\underset{\sim}{T}$ aims at representing the "transition evidences" by considering the contribution of both the fuzziness of data $\underset{\sim}{D}$, and knowledge $\underset{\sim}{R}$. The simbol "Δ" is a generic composition operator which (depending on the requirements) can accept several different definitions:

- the max-min function:

$$\underset{\sim}{D}\,\Delta\,\underset{\sim}{R}(q_i,q_j) = \bigvee_{\forall e \in \Psi} \mu_{\underset{\sim}{D}}(e) \wedge \mu_{\underset{\sim}{R}(q_i,q_j)}(e)$$

- a normalized Hamming distance:

$$\underset{\sim}{D}\,\Delta\,\underset{\sim}{R}(q_i,q_j) = \frac{1}{\mathrm{card}(\Psi)} \sum_{\forall e \in \Psi} \left| \mu_{\underset{\sim}{D}}(e) - \mu_{\underset{\sim}{R}(q_i,q_j)}(e) \right|$$

$$\underset{\sim}{D}\Delta\underset{\sim}{R}(q_i,q_j) = \frac{1}{\sqrt{\mathrm{card}(\Psi)}}\left[\sum_{\forall e\in\Psi}\left(\mu_{\underset{\sim}{D}}(e) - \mu_{\underset{\sim}{R}(q_i,q_j)}(e)\right)^2\right]^{1/2}$$

Over $\underset{\sim}{A}$ we can define a "configuration" $\underset{\sim}{C}$ as a fuzzy subset of Q, and a state $q\epsilon Q$ is said to be "λ-active" in a configuration $\underset{\sim}{C}$ if $\mu_{\underset{\sim}{C}}(q)>\lambda>0$. A "move" between configurations can be defined as a function M: L x G $\longrightarrow$ L, where L is the set of configurations over $\underset{\sim}{A}$.

$$\underset{\sim}{C}_j = M(\underset{\sim}{C}_i,\underset{\sim}{D}) : \mu_{\underset{\sim}{C}_j}(q) = \bigvee_{\forall q'\in Q}\left(\mu_{\underset{\sim}{C}_i}(q')\,\square\,\underset{\sim}{T}(q,\underset{\sim}{D},q')\right) \ ; \forall\, q \in Q$$

where "$\square$" is another generic composition operator. A simple definition of this operator is the <u>min</u> function; however, this definition is not adequate to describe the evolution of configurations in all the cases, since it is too "local": that is, the configuration $\underset{\sim}{C}_j$ at a given time is made to be only dependent on the last configuration $\underset{\sim}{C}_i$ and the present transition evidence $\underset{\sim}{T}$. In order to enable more "global" operator definitions, a new concept must be introduced:

A trellis X_a over $\underset{\sim}{A}$ for an input string $a\in G^*$ $(a=\underset{\sim}{D}_1\underset{\sim}{D}_2\ldots\underset{\sim}{D}_{|a|})$ is defined recursively as the sequence of configurations of $\underset{\sim}{A}$:

$$\underset{\sim}{C}_0 = \left\{(q,\mu_{\underset{\sim}{C}_0}(q)) \ / \ \mu_{\underset{\sim}{C}_0}(q) = \begin{cases} 1 & \text{if } q = q_I \\ 0 & \text{if } q \neq q_I \end{cases}\right\}$$

$$\underset{\sim}{C}_{k+1} = M(\underset{\sim}{C}_k,\underset{\sim}{D}_{k+1}) \ , \ k=0,1,\ldots,|a|-1$$

In this case other alternative formulations for the operator can be given:

* The "global" running average:

$$\mu_{\underset{\sim}{C}_k}(q')\,\square\,\underset{\sim}{T}(q,\underset{\sim}{D}_{k+1},q') = \frac{k\,\mu_{\underset{\sim}{C}_k}(q') + \underset{\sim}{T}(q,\underset{\sim}{D}_{k+1},q')}{k+1}$$

* The "time decaying" windowed local average:

$$\mu_{\underset{\sim}{C}_k}(q')\,\square\,\underset{\sim}{T}(q,\underset{\sim}{D}_{k+1},q') = \alpha(\mu_{\underset{\sim}{C}_k}(q') + \gamma\,\underset{\sim}{T}(q,\underset{\sim}{D}_{k+1},q'));\ 0<\alpha<1;\ \gamma = 1/\sum_{n=1}^{\infty}\alpha^n$$

In most cases it is of great importance to constrain the set of λ-active states to those which receive <u>continuous</u> evidence

modification can be applied to the definition of M:

$$\underset{\sim}{C}_j = \hat{M}(\underset{\sim}{C}_i,\underset{\sim}{D}): \hat{\mu}_{\underset{\sim}{C}_j}(q) = \begin{cases} \mu_{\underset{\sim}{C}_j}(q) & \text{if } \mu_{\underset{\sim}{C}_j}(q)-\mu_{\underset{\sim}{C}_i}(q) > \varepsilon \\ \mu_{\underset{\sim}{C}_j}(q)-\eta & \text{if } \mu_{\underset{\sim}{C}_j}(q)-\mu_{\underset{\sim}{C}_i}(q) \leqslant \varepsilon \text{ and } \mu_{\underset{\sim}{C}_j}(q)-\eta \geqslant \lambda \\ 0 & \text{otherwise.} \end{cases}$$

where $\mu_{\underset{\sim}{C}_j}(q)$ is the above defined membership funcion, and ε and η are a "continuity-threshold" and a "non-continuity-penalty" respectively.

With this formulation, the trellis for a given input string can be interpreted as the time evolution of activity of states and the concept of λ-active states can be used as a pruning criterium for implementing the parsing algorithms. Depending on the definition of the "move" function M, the set of λ-active states can be reduced to a small subset of Q which changes dynamically with the evolution of configurations in the trellis. As will be shown later, this feature allows the implementation of efficient fuzzy-parsing algorithms over sequential general-pourpose hardware. It is worth-noting that the pruning methods introduced here have nothing to do with the well known beam-search technique used for parsing in large finite-state networks like Harpy (10); morever, this technique could be further applied over the methods presented in this paper.

In some cases it may be of interes to know how well a given input string is accepted by the Fuzzy-Automata $\underset{\sim}{A}$; in these cases we can say that a $\in G^*$ is λ-recognized by $\underset{\sim}{A}$, if the configuration $\underset{\sim}{C}_{|a|}$ of X_a contains at least one final state q $\in$ F such that $\mu_{\underset{\sim}{C}_{|a|}}(q) > \lambda$.

The fuzzy parsing scheme here presented can be easily extended for the aimed <u>fuzzy-interpretation process</u>. Let $\underset{\sim}{Z}$ be a fuzzy translation scheme defined as the triplet $\underset{\sim}{Z}=(\Phi,\underset{\sim}{A},H)$ where:

1) $\underset{\sim}{A}$ is a fuzzy finite state machine.
2) Φ is an output alphabet.
3) $H : Q \longrightarrow \Phi^*$.

H represents the asignement of at most one string over the output alphabet for each state of $\underset{\sim}{A}$.

Let $\mathcal{L}_Z$ be the finite language defined by H, that is $\mathcal{L}_Z = \{b/b \in \Phi^*, \exists q \in Q: H(q)=b\}$. If $a \in G$ $(a=D_1 D_2 \ldots D_{|a|})$, and the

$$\mu_{\underset{\sim}{E}_i}(H(q)) = \mu_{\underset{\sim}{C}_i}(q) \qquad \forall q \in Q \text{ , } 1<i<|a|$$

In most cases, this translation scheme can be simplified by modelling the network to have one final state per considered category at the corresponding level. In this case the output alphabet can be mapped with these categories, the langage is reduced to single-simbol strings, and (relaxing the notation) the definition of H can be simplified to: $H : F \longrightarrow \Phi$, where F is the set of final states of $\underset{\sim}{A}$.

Fig 2.1 summarizes the fuzzy interpretation process introduced above: for a sequence of fuzzy subsets over a finite input alphabet Ψ, the interpretetion process produces another sequence of fuzzy subsets over another finite output alphabet Φ. Although the length of both sequences is the same, in most cases the output categories can be described with a much coarser time resolution than the input ones (e.g. a 0.05 sec. resolution for phonemic-labeling versus 0.5 sec. for word-labeling). To take advantage of this feature, subsampling can be used for saving resources at the next level.

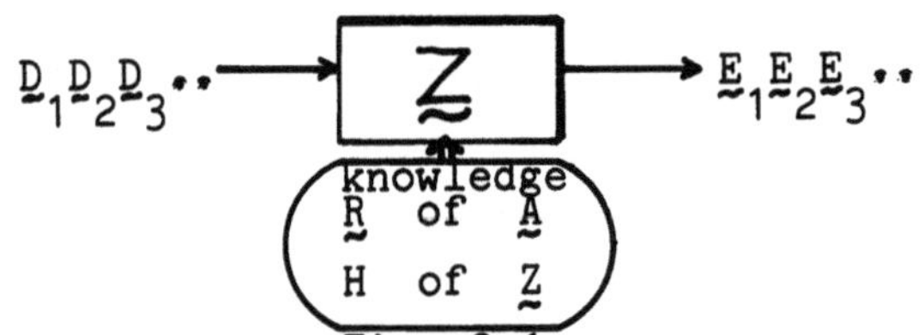

Fig. 2.1.

The Fuzzy-parsing and translation scheme introduced above, is implicitly associated with an abstract massively parallel machine. Though much recent research effort is being spent on such a kind of parallel hardware (8) (9), at present, only more or less sequential general-pourpose hardware is practically available. The algorithm developed for an efficient implementation of the methods presented in this section on general-pourpose computers (fig. 2.2) is based on the Viterbi algorithm (11), from which we have taken the structure of the trellis. The main differences in our algorithm are: 1) The weights of the arcs, which here represent the transition evidences $\underset{\sim}{T}$, and 2) The score accumulation method, which is based on the definitions of the "move" function M between configurations. The latter (which is the main contribution to the aimed fuzzy-parsing task) leads to a formalized pruning method which can be used both for memory and processor-time saving, and is the base of the real efficiency of the algorithm.

3.- THE LEVEL STRUCTURE: CURRENT DEVELOPEMENTS.

The fuzzy interpretation process introduced in last section can be applied to Automatic Speech Recognition in two basic ways: 1) Encoding all the knowledge into a single network which interprets the speech data directly in terms of syntactic-semantic categories, or 2) Structuring the knowledge into levels of understanding, and modeling each level as a local small network. The first alternative would lead to a large network system with all its well known advantages and drowbacks. The second alternative, which is the one adopted in this work, has the attractive features of modularity and (potential) inter-level parallelism, without dropping the general principles of passiveness and homogeneous representation of knowledge and data.

Structuring knowledge into levels of understanding is not a straight-forword task, and usually responds more to implementational reasons then to fundamental assumptions. Some of the levels which have been assumed in modern Speech Understanding Systems are the following: microphonetic, pseudophonetic, phonetic, diphonetic, pseudosyllabic, syllabic, lexical, syntactic, semantic and pragmatic. Not all the systems have used all the levels, rather, a subset of them has been implemented in each system. In the work presented in this paper some different structures will be suggested; however, in order to make a preliminary test of the theoretical assumptions above presented, only a very simple example has been implemented. In this implementation just three levels (microphonetic, lexical and syntactic-semantic) are assumed, and a very crude parametric representation of speech is used; this permits an easy test of different issues without spending too much effort in implementational aspects. In the rest of this section some details and results of this implementation will be given and different alternatives that arise will be discussed.

3.1.- Parameter extraction.

This is the first step in all Speech Recognition Systems. In that presented here, only three elemental short-time parameters have been used: signal average-magnitude (Amplitude) (A), Signal Zero-Crossing (Z), and signal-derivative zero-crossing (D). These parameters are extracted through a non-overlapping 15 ms. rectangular window, using a previously estimated threshold to avoid fluctuations in Z and D due to environnemental noise, and normalizing A to the most stressed vowel contained in the signal input buffer. This crude representation has been adopted for two main reasons: computation simplicity, which allows easy and efficient implementation on general pourpose hardware, and low spectral descriptive power, which is a challenge for the recognition methods, which must then work mainly on the basis of accurate temporal feature description of the acoustic patterns. As these temporal features of speech data respond basically to general phonological constraints, multispeaker operation is expected to be achieved easily. The drawbacks of this kind of representation are obvious, and for many real-applications the use of a more powerfull spectral representation would be necessary.

3.2.- Fuzzy-symbolic description.

The first task after a parametric representation of speech is obtained, is to derive an elemental Fuzzy-symbolic description of this representation. This description can be obtained by the methods introduced in (14). Each parameter must be divided into (several) overlapping intervals, and each interval must be assigned both a name and a membership function. The number of intervals, and the shapes of the membership functions, depends on the parameters to be described and also on the categories which must be derived from this description in next level. Fig 3.1 shows these functions and names for each of the three parameters used in the example presented. These functions have been obtained by hand-smoothing-and-merging the results of the statistical distributions over the three parameters of the different microphonetic categories to be used.

3.3.- Fuzzy microphonetic labeling.

Once a fuzzy-symbolic description is available, the general fuzzy-interpretation process presented in section 2 can be applied to interpret this description in terms of the categories wanted. In the example presented a set of broad-phonetic classes, which corresponds to the phonetic-labels to be assigned to each frame, is associated with the first level.

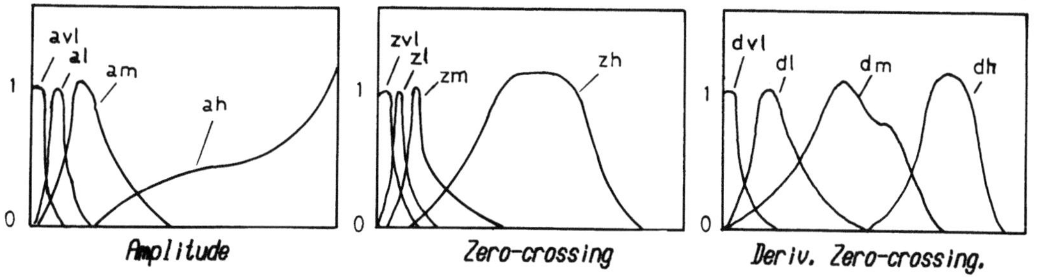

Fig 3.1. Membership functions for the fuzzy-description of parameters a,z,d.

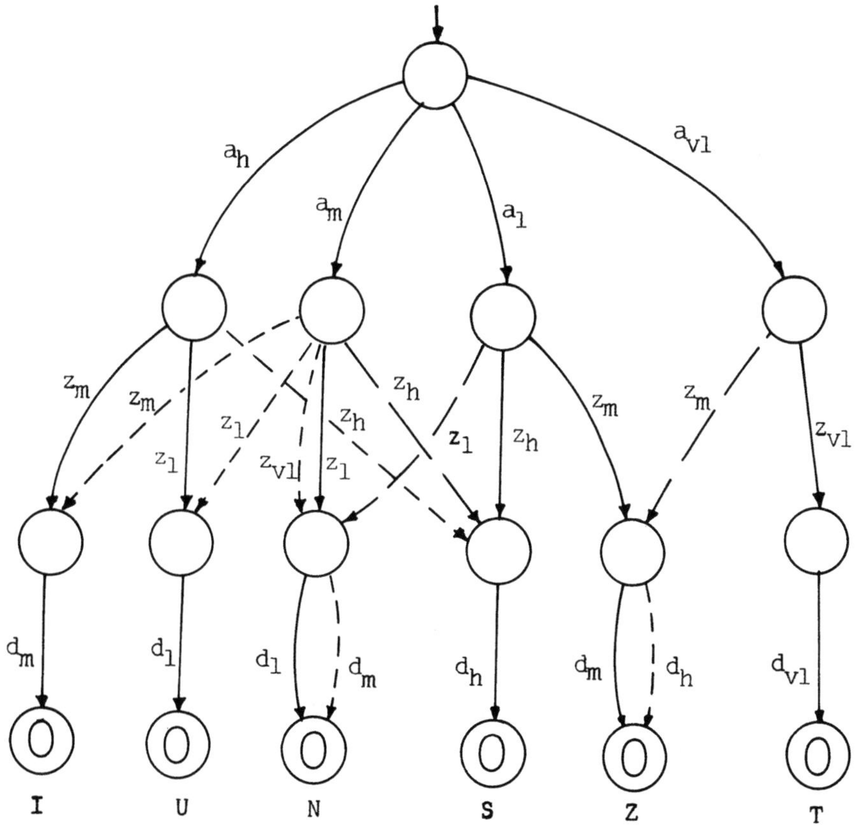

Fig 3.2. Broad-phonetic categories network.

(evidences of the arcs are represented by the diferent dashing of lines).

The broad-phonetic categories and symbols are the following:

"I": Front-vowel (/i/, /e/, /a/, some segments of /l/).
"U": Back-vowel (/u/, /o/).
"N": Weak-sonorant (/n/, /m/, /ɳ/, /ʎ/, some segments of /l/, most segments of voiced stops).
"S": Strong-fricative (/s/, hissing segments of /c/).
"Z": Weak-fricative (/θ/, /f/, /x/, some segments of /β/).
"T": Silence (/p/, /t/, /k/, some voiced stops, stop segments of /c/) .

Fig 3.2. shows the network used to obtain an interpretation of each frame in terms of the categories considered above. It must be pointed-out that the interpretation process at this level is "parameter-indexed" in opposition to the following levels in which the process is "time-indexed". The general operators used in this level are:

Δ= max-min function; $\square$= min function.

3.4 The lexical level: isolated and connected word recognition.

The output of the micro-phonetic-labeling level is a time series of fuzzy-broad-phonetic labels. From this series, several phonetic-like or syllabic-like intrerpretations are possible. However, for moderate lexical sizes (as considered in the example), it is also possible to achieve a direct lexical categorizing without intermediate levels. Fig. 3.3 shows the network used for the spanish digits lexicon.

The fuzzy lexical access obtained at this level, can be used as an input to higher levels. Nevertheless, there are also applications in which the results of this level can be used directly: namely, isolated and connected word recognition (IWR, CWR). For IWR, the silence anterior and posterior to the words can be modelled as part of the network (dashed-line final states and T-arc in initial state of fig. 3.3), and the "systolic-like" progression of the configurations is restricted to just one "systole" per expected word; that is, activity in the network is initiated just once, at the beginning of recognition by making λ-active the initial state at the initial time. The activity (score) of the final states at the

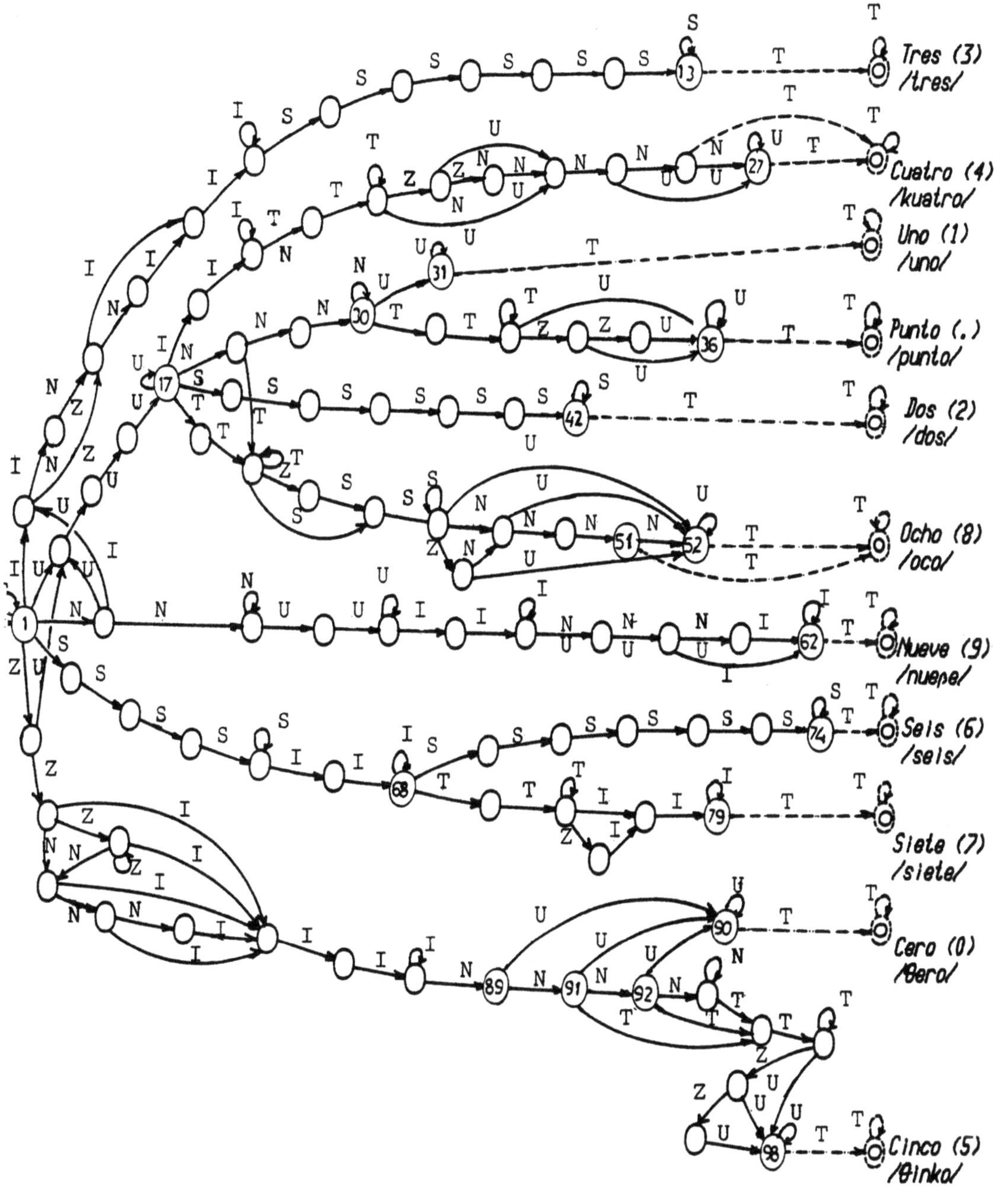

Fig 3.3. The spanish digits lexicon network.

be the word coresponding to the final state with greatest activity. For the IWR and CWR tasks the Δ operator is again the <u>max-min</u> function and the $\square$ operator can be implemented as either the "global running average" or as the "time-decaying" local average with delays (α) greater than the maximum expected word duration. Since neither normalization nor upper-limit bounding are necesary for IWR, it is also posible in this case to implement $\square$ as a global accumulation (algebraic summation).

The problem of connected word recognition can be aproached via the metodology introduced in two ways. The first and easier way is to extend the lexical network by introducing a "nil" labeled arc from each final state (like the ones drown with continous lines in Fig. 3.3) to the initial state. This allows the one "systole" activity flow, to feed-back the initial state every time some final-state has become λ-active, thus efectivelly initiating a new "systole" of recognition activity. The main and obvious drawback of this method is that recognition activity may be stopped if recognition fails for some word and no final-state becomes λ-active. The other way is to use the lexical network for continuously fuzzy-hypotesizing words in the continuous string of fuzzy microphonetic labels, producing an output string of fuzzy sets of recognized words ("multiword spotting"). This goal can be easily achieved by continuously making the initial state λ-active, thus allowing a continuous flow of systolic recognition activity, which starts a new "systole" whenever some compatibility of the data with the network is found. The errors of the output string can be minimized at the next level if syntax is associated with the language. For the CWR problem, no syntax is available, but a pragmatic-like level can be implemented to take into account the durational constraints of the string of connected words (e.g. the "presence" of the spanish word /kuatro/ is not possible before 0.6 sec. after the "presence" of any other word, etc.).

Fig. 3.4 shows the complete description and interpretation process for the spanish connected words /nueβepuntooco/ ("nine-point-eight"). The state-space evolution is also represented, showing the systolic-like progression of configurations and the time-decaying non-continuity-punished state deactivation feature.

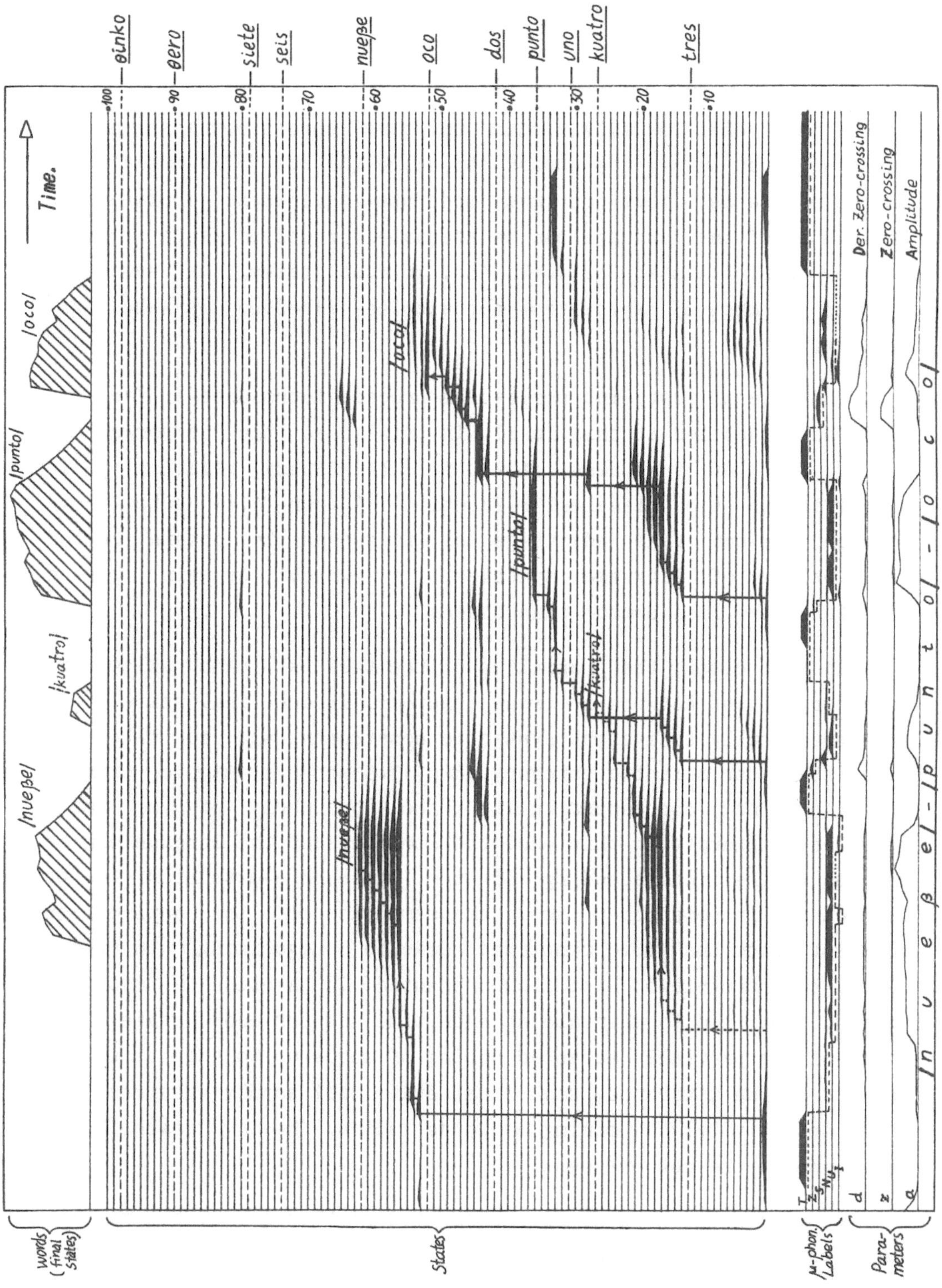

Fig 3.4. Activity at different levels while uttering the connected words

achieved by the recognition algorithm.

3.5.- Syntactic-Semantic level in task-oriented applications.

This level is usually assumed to have word-hipothesis as an input and must supply the phrase structure and the "corrected" words in the phrase as output. For many moderate-requirement applications the syntax of the language can be adequately modelled as a regular grammar or finite state network and, in most cases, the semantics (and/or pragmatics) of the task can also be embedded in the same network.

The general fuzzy-interpretation process introduced so far can be directly applied at this level. In this case the networks are usually free of fuzzyness; that is, the fuzzy relation $\underset{\sim}{R}$ is simplified to the classical δ-function of non-fuzzy automatas. However, one can take advantage of fuzzyness to obtain better descriptions of language syntaxes, in which certain phrase structures are less common than others.

In most cases, the pragmatics of the task at hand allow the modelling of the network to group together, in one final state, all the semantically equivalent syntactic constructs, and to have one final state per semantic category. Fig. 3.5 shows a simple example of this kind, corresponding to the protocol of a small telephone-exchange. In this case the semantics of the langage can be reduced to the understanding of the thelephone-extension to be connected. In some other cases, the semantics of the application does not allow the above mentioned semantic categorizing. In those cases, the recognition algorithm presented in section 2 must be somewhat modified to maintain at each time and for each state, the trace of the partially accepted string of words up to this time. At the end of the utterance, each final state will supply (besides its score or activity) the string of words which, having reached it, have matched the network best.

Concernig the general operators used at this level, the max-min function for Δ and the global average or the global accumulation for $\square$ seem appropiate. As different utterances can easilly be isolated from each-other at the acoustic level (inter-phrase silences), it is adequate to select the "one systole" type recognition flow, which is achieved, as in IWR, by making the initial state λ active just once

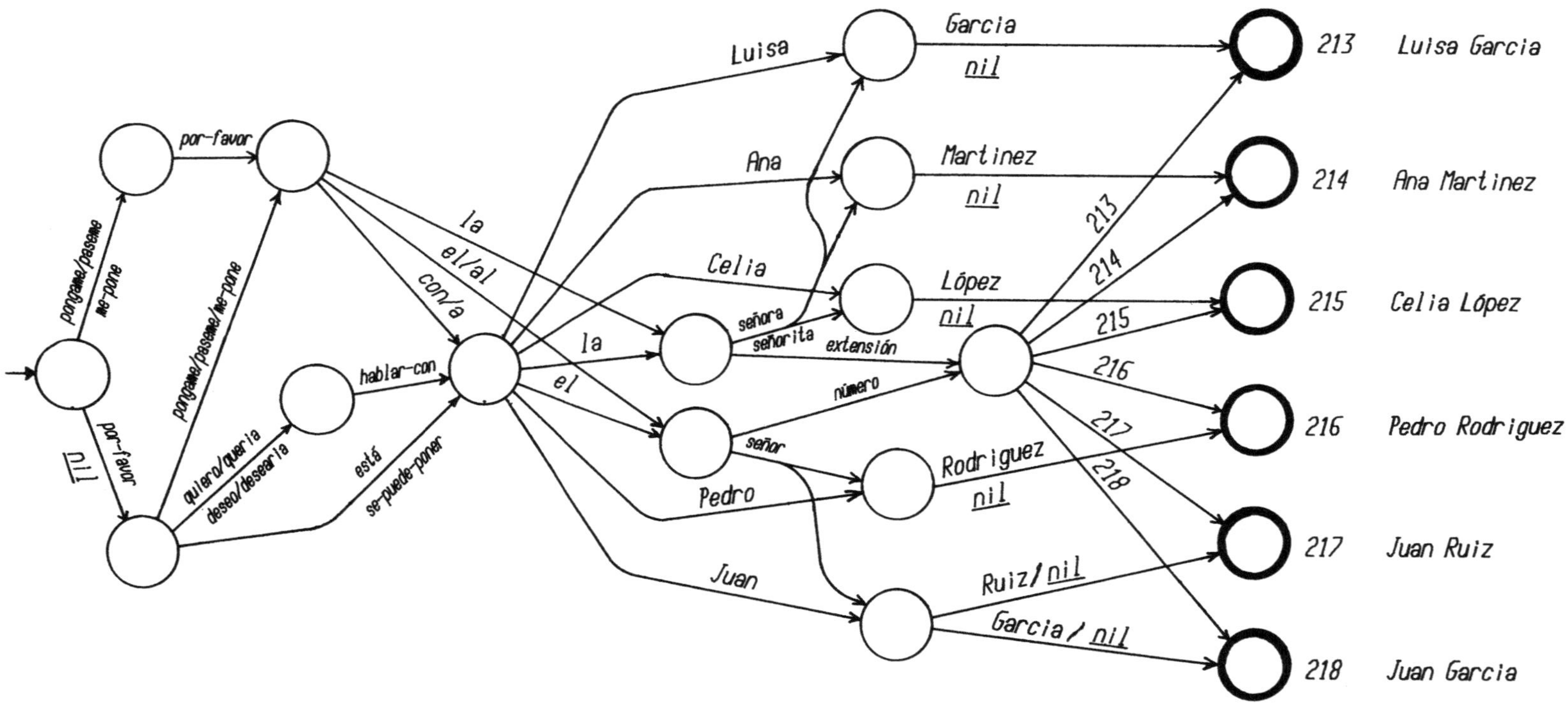

Fig 3.5. A simple example of syntactic-semantic level network: the 'telephonist language'.

at the initial time.

3.6.- The problem of building the networks.

The networks associated with the different levels must be built on the basis of phonological/grammatical rules, and/or inferred from actual speech data. At some levels (syntactic-semantic) the network can be obtained from the language grammar in a straight-forward enough way; at other levels (microphonetic-labeling, phonetic, syllabic, lexical) the network can also be obtained by the use of phonological rules. However, in these cases, several problems arise which make the task difficult. The first problem is that the fuzzyness of the network must be accurately generated, due to the dependance of the performance of these levels on it. The second problem is that the rules needed to obtain the networks, are usually not very well known, and depend on the type of parameters and categories associated with the different levels. The third problem arises from the fact that, even if the rules needed were well known, there are always non-standard phonological phenomena which are not accounted for by the rules.

One way of resolving the problem of network building is to proceed in two stages: 1) top-down rule-based arquetype network-building, and 2) bottom-up learning-based refinement of the built networks.

The first stage can be performed by means of an expert-systems methodology. For the example presented in this paper, a production system has ben implemented which supplies the regular expressions needed to build the lexical-level arquetypical networks. These expressions are automatically obtained from the ortographic word-spelling, by applying a set of $\sim$100 phonological rules. These rules (which summarize expert-like knowledge abaut the problem) can be easilly updated, and so the problem of partial knowledge of the rules is somewhat minimized.

The second learning-based refinement stage is much more difficult and, at present, is not performed automatically. Nevertheless, the importance of this stage is realized, and some research effort is being spent in order to develop good learning-based refinement methods.

4.- RESULTS AND DISCUSSION.

The simple examples which are being implemented on the basis of the methods presented so far, show very encouraging performance results. At lexical level, recognition results are in the range of 94-99% for the speakers involved in the process of inferring the different knowledge sources (membership functions, microphonetic network, lexical network), and are greater than 85% for the other speakers tried. These results are obtained in IWR experiments with three lexicons of similar complexity (spanish digits, catalan digits, telephone-exchange protocol), and with reconition times of the order of real time with a general pourpose 16 bits 0.7 mips minicomputer. For connected words, no reliable results are available at this moment, because the tests have been made with the same lexicon networks used for IWR, which should have been significantly modified for the CWR task. Nevertheless, the preliminary experiments show an adequate and efficient behaviour of the fuzzy-parsing algorithm, though the need of finer speech parameters and phonetic-labeling has been manifested for some of the lexicons tested. The need of an intermediate level between the micro-phonetic and lexical levels, which would alleviate the work of building the lexical networks, has also been detected.

This level is being introduced in the next system implementation, aimed to support realistic applications. This implementation also incorporates a finer spectral parameter set, as well as a more complete phonetic repertory at the microphonetic level. The intermediate level has diphones as output chategories and so, the lexical networks will be built (from the ortographic word-spelling) in terms of diphones. One of the conveniences of the introduction of this level is that the set of rules through which the lexical networks must be built, are much better known than the phonological rules at present required for the microphonetic-based lexical nets. All the problems of partial knowledge of rules and learning-based network-refinements are thus shifted one level down, but with the advantage that the diphonetic level network has to be correctly built just once, while the lexical nets are application-dependent and must then be able to be changed easily.

Other issues which have arisen through the development of the model introduced here, and which are currently under investigation are: 1) the need of a <u>learning</u> method, able to carry-out the network refinement procedure; and 2) the extension of the fuzzy-parsing scheme with an "inhibitory" mechanism, which has been found to be necessary for accurate modeling of durational constraints, and is thought to lead to improved results in all the levels.

REFERENCES.

(1) R. De Mori, P. Laface, "Use of fuzzy algorithms for phonetic and phonemic labeling of continuous speech", IEEE Trans. PAMI-2, 136-138, 1980.

(2) M.Allerhard, F. Fallside, P. Hinds, "Constrained recognizer using duration", 11-ICA, Toulouse Satellite Symposium, 1983.

(3) R.K. Moore, M.J. Russell, M.J. Tomlinson, "Locally constrained Dynamic Programming in Automatic Speech Recognition", ICASSP-82, pp 1270-1273.

(4) J.R. Anderson, "Cognitive psicology", Artificial Intelligence, 23(1984) 1-11.

(5) J.A. Feldman, D.H. Ballard, "Connectionist models and their properties", Cognitive Sciences 6(1982), 205-254.

(6) D.H. Ballard, "Parameter nets" Artificial Inteligence 22(1984) 235-267.

(7) J.A. Feldman, "A connectionist model of visual memory", in G.E. Hinton and J.A. Anderson (Eds.) Parallel models of associative memory, 1981.

(8) W.D. Hillis, "The connection machine (Computer architecture for the new wave)", AI memo 646, MIT, Cambridge, MA, 1981.

(9) G.E. Hinton, "Shape representation in parallel systems", Proc. 7th. IJCAI, Vancouver, B.C. (1981) 1088-1096.

(10) B. Lowerre, "The HARPY speech recognition system", Carnegie-Mellon Univ. memo, 1976.

(11) G.D. Forney, "The Viterbi Algorithm", IEEE proc. 3(1973), 268-278.

(12) L.A. Zadeh, "Fuzzy Sets and Their Applications to Cognitive and Decision Processes", Academic Press, 1975.

(13) E. Vidal, E.Sanchis, F.Casacuberta, "A speaker-independent Isolated Word Recognition System for specific dictionaries", SWSPA proc., 1,pp.B2/3(8p) Sitges, 1983.

(14) R. De Mori, L. Saitta, "Automatic Learning of fuzzy Naming Relations over finite languages". Information Sciences, Vol. 21, pp 83-139, 1980.

LINGUISTICS AND AUTOMATIC PROCESSING OF SPEECH

John J. Ohala
Phonology Laboratory
Department of Linguistics
University of California
Berkeley, CA 94720, U.S.A.

INTRODUCTION

To build a bridge it is helpful to know something about the physics of stress and vibration, about materials science, and so on. To cure sickness, it is helpful to know something about the nature and causes of disease, i.e., microbes, metabolism, etc. This is not to say that it is impossible to build bridges and cure sickness without such knowledge. Indeed, some bridges were built and some sicknesses cured centuries before anyone knew anything about the physical and physiological principles involved. However, it must be admitted that the bridges were modest, most sickness was not alleviated and successes in both areas owed more to trial and error or an intuitive understanding of the relevant principles than to any sort of systematic, scientific, knowledge. From the time that knowledge in these areas was put on a firm scientific basis, taking into account the factors underlying the behavior of materials and microbes, much more impressive bridges and cures were possible.

Similarly, to automate the production and the recognition of speech, it will be helpful to know something about the structure of speech and language and about the processes used by humans to produce and understand speech. Again, it may be possible to achieve limited success in these practical areas without knowing very much about the nature of speech but if the history of bridge

NATO ASI Series, Vol. F16
New Systems and Architectures for Automatic Speech
Recognition and Synthesis. Edited by R. De Mori and C. Y. Suen

building and medicine is any guide, progress should be greater once this knowledge is obtained and applied to the solutions of these problems.

Although some information about the nature and behavior of speech has been accumulating for some 2300 years since the time of the Hindu grammarian Panini and the early Greek philosophers, it was only in the beginning of the 19th century that linguists had their first success in providing answers to some of the questions that had occupied them — answers which, I think it is safe to say, may properly be characterized as being "scientific", i.e., obtained with care and provided with rigorous empirical support. The question they answered was "how do languages evolve?", i.e., they were able for the first time to reconstruct the history of languages, especially their phonological history. Since that time a considerable treasure of data about changes in pronunciation has accumulated.

Change in pronunciation over time, or *sound change*, as it is usually called, manifests itself in many ways. Discrepancies between the pronunciation implied by a conservative orthography and the actual pronunciation, e.g., English *laugh*, pronounced [læf],[1] is an indication of sound change. Differences in the pronunciation of cognate words in different dialects or languages is another, for example, in the history of French the original Latin word *cantus* changed to [tʃant] and then to [ʃã], the modern pronunciation. English borrowed this word from French when it had the intermediate form (at the time of the Norman invasion in 1066 A.D.), and has not changed it substantially since then; thus we have the current English pronunciation [tʃænt]. Variation in the phonetic form of

---

[1] The phonetic transcription used throughout this paper follow the principles of the International Phonetic Association as of 1979, except that retroflex consonants are indicated by a dot underneath the letter. The arrows '>' and '<' stand for 'changes to' and 'comes from', respectively. Citation of cognate forms from sister dialects lack arrows because, strictly speaking, one is not derived from the other but both are derived from a common parent, not cited. In this case, however, it is assumed that the form on the left reflects the phonetic form of the parent language. Other expository simplifications have also been made, e.g., the citation of Classical Latin, instead of the more appropriate Vulgar Latin, as the origin of words in French and other Romance languages.

the same morpheme in different grammatical contexts is yet another example, e.g., the English words *native*, *nature*, and *natural* have the same stem in the different phonetic shapes [neǐt], [neǐtʃ], and [nætʃ], respectively. (For further examples, see Ohala, 1980, 1983a.)

In this paper I suggest how this wealth of information might be harvested and put to use in automatic speech recognition (ASR) and in the synthesis of speech (SS). One motivation for doing this is that although there is relatively wide (but by no means universal) recognition of the applicability of many other areas of linguistics for tasks in automatic processing of speech and language, e.g., syntax, semantics, pragmatics, sociolinguistics, lexicography, morphology (see, e.g., Lea, 1980), there seems to be little awareness of the applicability of historical linguistics, especially historical phonology, to the same tasks.

It is understandable that historical phonology would be overlooked in this domain. First, the documentation of language change is expressed in a rather obscure jargon, using an inconsistent notation, and based on an intricate set of (usually) unstated assumptions. It is therefore very difficult for the newcomer to penetrate this literature. Second, many of the speculations on the causes of sound change were such as would suggest that the phenomenon held little interest for ASR and SS. For example, some suggested that sounds change because speakers' vocal anatomy changes over time, because the climate or terrain affects speech, because infants with their immature vocal organs are incapable of pronouncing words in the same way as adults and some infantile pronunciations persevere, because speakers tend to adopt "easier" articulations or articulations which are more distinct and thus easier to hear, because speakers try to simplify or optimize their grammars, or because pronunciation is subject to the whims of fashion in the same way that styles of clothing or furniture are.

Although there is little I can do about the first problem — the impenetrability of the historical phonological literature — the second problem I propose to deal with by offering a different account of the nature of sound change. Specifically, I propose that the majority[2] of sound changes result from errors of transmission of pronounciation from one speaker to another. Most of these errors are perceptual. If this is accepted, then the relevance of a study of sound change to the tasks of ASR and SS is obvious: in the same way that destructive tests are of value in materials science, sound change, being a breakdown of normal speech behavior, can give us valuable clues about the structure of speech production and perception. Of course, these clues must always be followed up by systematic laboratory investigations.

There are good reasons for rejecting the earlier theories of sound change which propose that it stems from factors specific to a given terrain, a given time, culture, etc. or that it is introduced willfully by speakers (i.e., that it is at heart a teleological phenomenon). These reasons are the following:

1. The majority of sound changes occur in virtually the same form in languages distant from each other in time, geography, family history, and structure (Ohala, 1974, 1983a; Hombert, Ohala, & Ewan, 1979). Examples will be provided below.

2. The "seeds" of many such sound changes can be found in presentday speech. That is, laboratory study of a modern speaker of virtually any language which possesses the relevant sounds reveals the *same* kind of variation (either randomly or conditioned by rate of speaking, the phonetic context, etc.) as is found in sound change.

3. These "seeds" can, in most cases, be attributed to universal physical and physiological causes (or, in some cases, to universal psychological causes).

---

[2] I say 'majority' because there are changes in pronunciation due to such factors as spelling (e.g., English *sound* with a final [d] even though its source, Norman French *soun*, had no [d]), and the regularization of grammatical paradigms (e.g., the past tense of English *dream* as *dreamed* [dr̩imd], replacing the earlier irregular form *dreamt* [drɛmpt].

The implication of this is that universal "extralinguistic" factors exist which are responsible for variation in speech; some of these variations eventually get "fixed" or "fossilized" (in ways to be described below) and thus lead to sound change.

The way this happens, I suggest, is similar to the way that noise invades electronically-transmitted signals, as schematized in Fig. 1. A message source sends a message, x, to an encoder which emits a signal x' which is an encoded

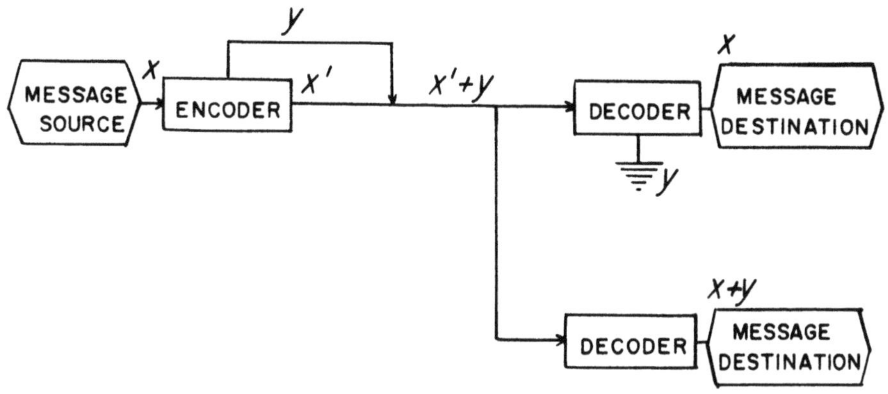

Figure 1. Schematic representation of a transmission line used as an anologue of speech production and perception; see text.

form of x. Added to the signal x', however, is noise, y. Usually communication engineers are concerned with noise added from the environment but to make the analogy applicable to the present case the noise arises from the workings of the encoder itself. The composite signal $x' + y$ is received by a decoder which ideally must factor out the noise y and then translate the encoded signal x' back into the intended message x and deliver it to the message destination. If the decoder is not able to factor out the noise y from the composite signal, then the message sent to the message destination will be contaminated with this noise component (see the lower branch of Figure 1).

By the analogical connections I wish to draw, the message source and message destination are the brains of the speaker and listener, respectively. The encoder is the anatomical elements used to produce speech, including not only the peripheral anatomical structures such as lips, tongue, soft palate, and larynx, but also the underlying muscular, neuromuscular, and neurological structures which control them. It is these structures which, due to their inherent physical and physiological constraints, impose certain distortions on the intended speech signal. The decoder is the listener's auditory system, including higher-level neurological structures. (These have their own physical constraints which may also distort the signal they receive but this is not represented in the figure.)

An example may clarify some of this. Consider a case where a speaker intends to produce the sequence /tju/. When encoded, i.e., articulated, the stop frequently becomes slightly affricated to [tʃju]. This occurs due to the physical constraint whereby the degree of turbulence and thus the amplitude of the noise spectrum increases as the channel through which airflow is forced becomes smaller. Glides and high, close, vowels provide the narrow channel which leads to increased turbulence. Normally the listeners are accustomed to such distortions (due to their long experience in listening to speech) and they factor out the inadvertent affrication, thus reconstructing the intended /tju/. However, if the listener fails to factor out this distortion, then the pronunciation is taken to be /tʃju/ and this is the pronunciation the listener aims at when he/she produces this word. Originally the amplitude and duration of turbulence would vary continuously as a function of the peculiar aerodynamic conditions created by the sequence of *stop* + *glide*; after this change the turbulence (affrication) would be an invariable part of the pronunciation of the word. In fact, this very sound change is quite common. It is responsible for the dialectal variants in American English of [tjuzdi] and [tʃuzdi] *Tuesday*, for the pronunciation [æktʃuəl] for *actual* (originally [æktjuəl]) as well as many changes from Latin to French, e.g., *fortia* > *force* (i.e., [fɔʁs]) and *palatium* > *palais* (where the final *s* was once pronounced). In the latter two cases we assume the sequence of sound changes [tj] > [ts] > [s].

It must not be supposed that because the term 'distortion' is used to describe these physically-caused excrescences on the speech signal, and because the experienced listener is said to factor them out, that these perturbations are therefore completely ignored by the listener. On the contrary, the more we investigate the acoustic cues utilized by listeners, the more we find that they are able to take advantage of any acoustic details which show some greater-than-chance probability of being associated with given contrasts. In a somewhat similar way, although the characteristic "hum" of an automobile engine is not what the engineer designing the engine was intending to produce, this sound is still used by the experienced motorist to diagnose its malfunctions. These features are 'distortions' in speech in the sense that they are variable in their appearance and therefore listeners must learn not to incorporate them purposely in their own mental lexicons where the instructions for pronunciation are stored.

The imporant aspect of this account of sound change is that the changes are non-purposeful (i.e., non-teleological). We may assume that speakers speak in a way which, as far as they know, conveys the pronunciation of words that is "standard" in the given speech community and conveys them in a way such that other listeners will be able to figure out the intended pronunciation.

What has been given above is an account of what might best be called "mini-sound changes" because as described they would only apply to changes that occurred due to the misapprehension of a single listener about the pronunciation of a single word. To link this with the "maxi-sound changes" that linguists study, i.e., sound changes characteristic of whole linguistic communities or even whole languges and affecting typically a vast number of words with similar phonetic shape, requires in addition the following assumptions:

1. That the listener's misapprehensions are not corrected. Although this type of misapprehension due to a failure in the error-correcting process is fairly common, most such errors eventually get corrected by virtue of the listener usually having access to other sources of information about how words are

pronounced, e.g., other speakers, the orthography. Nevertheless, it seems safe to assume that some small fraction of such errors escape eventual correction.

2. That the speech of the person who initiated the change serves as the model for other speakers' pronunciation. The extent to which a given speaker's speech is imitated by others depends on their social position, how much they meet other people, etc. Again, it seems safe to assume that situations will arise where a single speaker will influence the speech of a great many other speakers who will therefore copy and perpetuate any innovation this speaker may have initiated.

3. That, optionally, the change which manifested itself on one word then spreads to other similar words in the vocabulary. How this would occur is not precisely clear, although several hypothetical "scenarios" can be constructed (but will not be discussed here).

It might seem that if sound changes are similar across languages and are due to universal physical and physiological factors, then languages should converge towards the same phonological shape. It is fair to say that the macro-structure of all human language *is* quite similar (e.g., all languages use stops, all languages' vowels are roughly equally distributed in the vowel space) but differ largely in their micro-structure (e.g., whether they permit consonant clusters or not). The reason for the variation is that there are so many degrees of freedom in the "design" of a vocal communication system that languages' phonologies can be modified — and are modified by sound change — in numerous ways and still not converge. Likewise, although all living things are similar in being based on chemical processes involving carbon, oxygen, and hydrogen, nevertheless a great variety of different life forms, showing no tendency towards convergence, can be found in any given habitat even though the physical and environmental constraints are uniform. It sometimes happens that in the history of a given language, what one sound change creates, another destroys, and vice-versa. For example, in the evolution of Sanskrit into Prakrit, and its other descendants, almost all intervocalic consonant clusters were eliminated, see Table 1a (based on data from Misra 1967). However, in Hindi, one of the modern descendants of Sanskrit, medial consonant clusters have re-appeared due to the action of a sound change which deleted the vowel [ə] in certain environments, see Table 1b (from M. Ohala, 1983). Such cyclicity of phonological processes is not the rule in linguistic history but neither is it rare.

TABLE 1

A. The loss of Sanskrit medial consonant clusters in its linguistic descendants (data from Misra 1967; a macron above a vowel signifies it is long).

Sanskrit		Prakrit		Hindi	Translation
ʃuṣka	>	sukk^{h}a	>	sūk^{h}a	dry
karpūra	>	kappūra	>	kapūr	camphor
aṣṭa-	>	aṭṭ^{h}a	>	āṭ^{h}õ (oblique plural)	eight
karma-	>	karma-	>	kāmõ (oblique plural)	deed

B. Creation of medial consonant clusters in Modern Hindi (data from M. Ohala 1983).

Stem	Translation		Inflected/Derived Form	Translation
nəmək	salt	>	nəmkin	salty
purəb	east	>	purbi	Easterner
sɪsək	to sob	>	sɪski	a sob

To summarize: variations or distortions in the speech signal start out as phonetically dependent and potentially continuous. Then, due to the misapprehension of the listener these distortions become independent of the phonetic causation and they manifest themselves in an invariable way.

I will now list some of the clues a study of sound change provides us which may be of use in the tasks of ASR and SS.

CLUE 1: The sources of variation in speech.

The first clue provided us may seem obvious:

Variation in speech may be due to two different causes: (a) the physically-caused variation arising from the physical constraints (inertial, aerodynamic, etc.) of the speech mechanism and (b) sound change.

As mentioned, although basically similar (since the latter are drawn from the set comprised of the former), these will have different characters. The former will generally be a continuous function of phonetic context (rate of speaking, loudness, etc.). They will also be potentially universal in that, e.g., all sequences of /tj/ in any language will be subject to affrication if the /t/'s and /j/'s are articulated in similar ways. Therefore the rules for implementing this type of variation in synthesized speech (to achieve greater naturalness) will have the form of equations referring to parameters which may vary continuously e.g., that in (1), from Lindblom (1963) which predicts the F2 value of a vowel, given the target F2 of the vowel ($F2_{target}$), the F2 of the flanking consonants ($F2_{cons}$), the duration of the vowel (t), and two constants (k,b).

(1) $$F2 = k(F2_{cons} - F2_{target}) \cdot e^{-bt} + F2_{target}$$

The same rules — perhaps with different constants — could be used in different languages.

Variation due to sound change, however, will be discrete (the change is implemented or not — it would not have intermediate values) and might be a function of such non-phonetic factors as speaking style. The rule in (2) is an example; this involves the change in English of the vowel /ɚ/ to /ə/ when it

(2) ɚ → ə / --- Cr

appears before a cluster of *consonant* ('C' in (2)) + /r̩/, e.g., *surprise* as [sɚpr̩aɪz] or [səpr̩aɪz]. (The motivation for this rule will be discussed below.) Such rules, which reflect the action of sound changes, although found in numerous languages, will be language-, dialect-, and possibly speaker-specific. It might be imagined that it should be a simple matter to differentiate these two types of variation in speech but this is not the case. It may be easy to detect the action of sound change when variants occur in different languages, or different dialects but not necessarily when they occur within a given language in different grammatical or stylistic environments. Who can say whether the intrusive stops in words like *warmth* [wɔr̩mp̠θ] and *strength* [str̩ɛŋk̠θ] are physically caused or due to a sound change (see Ohala, 1981c)? Nevertheless, this is the kind of determination that must be made for optimal ASR and SS.

CLUE 2: Secondary Cues.

It is well known that many phonemic contrasts, although characterized by linguists as differing primarily by a single phonetic distinction, in actual fact show several phonetic differences. For example, in English the words *pat* and *bat* differ in the ways listed in Table 2. Presumably the more such features are included in synthetic speech, the more natural and the more intelligible it will be. Likewise, if these features can be detected it will enhance the success of a feature-based ASR effort. The problem is, how does one find out what these features are? A study of sound change can help. Many sound changes are of the type where a feature which was previously physically-caused and accessory to a sound is re-interpreted as a primary feature of the sound or sound sequence. A survey of the kind of re-interpretations which are possible for a given distinction will reveal what some of these accessory features are. For example, it is well documented that in the evolution from Middle Chinese to the pre-cursors of the modern Chinese languages, what was previously a contrast of voicing in initial stops changed into a tonal distinction on the following vowels. Table 3 gives comparable data from dialects of Kammu, spoken in Laos (data from Lindell, Svantesson & Tayanin, 1976).

TABLE 2

Some of the differences between the initial stops in *pat* and *bat*.

pat	*bat*
c. 60 msec VOT	c. 0 msec VOT
short transitions	long transitions
higher burst intensity	lower burst intensity
high falling FO on following vowel	level or low rising FO on following vowel
lower starting amplitude of of following vowel	higher starting amplitude of following vowel

TABLE 3

Data showing that tone in Northern Kammu corresponds to a voicing contrast in Southern Kammu (from Lindell et al. 1976).

Southern Kammu	Northern Kammu	Translation
kl*aaŋ*	kl*áaŋ*	eagle
gl*aaŋ*	kl*àaŋ*	stone

All languages which have segments contrasting in voicing and which have been subjected to instrumental study, show an FO difference of just this sort on the following vowels (Meyer, 1895; Hombert et al., 1979). Evidence exists that in the absence of other cues, English listeners can differentiate syllables such as /kɛ/ and /gɛ/ on the basis of the former having a falling FO on the vowel and the latter a rising FO (Fujimura, 1971). Apparently in the languages immediately descendant from Middle Chinese and the parent language of Northern Kammu, listeners took the FO contour as the intended difference between syllables with voiced and voiceless initial consonants. Perhaps this happened when the voicing contrast was made weakly or was not detected for some other reason.

The evidence which sound change provides us on the interaction of consonants and FO is quite specific, in fact. It also can tell us that sonorants like /m, n, l, j, w/ do not perturb FO, that implosives /ɓ ɗ/ in spite of their being heavily voiced, elevate the FO on following vowels, and that only glottal consonants such as /h ʔ/ affect the FO of both the preceding and following vowels (Hombert et al., 1979; Ohala, 1979).

Another similar case involves consonantal effects on vowels. There is much data of the sort in Table 4, which presents samples of sound changes in Tibetan

TABLE 4

Data from Tibetan showing the fronting influence of apical consonants on back vowels.

Written Tibetan (c. 8th century)		Lhasa Tibetan	Translation
drug	>	ṭhuu	six
thog	>	thɔɔ	roof
nub	>	nuu	west
but:			
bod	>	phøø	Tibet
ston	>	tø̃	autumn
lus	>	lyy	body
spos	>	pøø	incense

(from Michailovsky, 1975). The forms in the left column are those of written

Tibetan which reflect pronunciation in the 8th century; those in the right column, the pronunciation of present-day Lhasa Tibetan. The data show what happens to back rounded vowels when a final consonant is lost: when it was labial or velar there was no substantial change in the quality of the vowel, but when it was dental the preceding back vowel became fronted, retaining its rounding, i.e., /u/ to /y:/ and /o/ to /ø:/. The "seed" of this particular sound change has been phonetically documented in a variety of languages, e.g., English (Stevens, House & Paul, 1966), Swedish (Lindblom, 1963), French (Chollet, 1976), and Japanese (Umeda, 1960). The addition of the apical constriction to that proper to the back rounded vowel causes the F2 of the resulting sound to raise; the resulting vowel sound is not articulated as a front rounded vowel but it *sounds* like one. For the sound change to have taken place, some listeners must not have been able to factor out this fronting distortion (quite an understandable failure if this final consonant was weakly articulated and thus not readily detected — which must have been the case since the final consonant was lost) and so reinterpreted what they heard as a front rounded vowel (see also Ohala, 1981a).

Other sound changes reveal that labial consonants tend to make front vowels more back, especially labial velar consonants like /k͡p g͡b w ʍ/; /l/, especially the velarized or "dark" lateral, tends to shift vowels toward a mid or high back position; various types of /r/ tend to centralize vowels and/or make them lax.

CLUE 3. What are the units of speech perception?

It is a striking fact that most sound changs usually occur in very specific environments. Consider, for example, the fate of the Latin /l/ in French, as presented in a simplified way in Table 5. The /l/ changed to an [u]-like sound only in the environment *vowel_______consonant*: in intervocalic position and word-initial position it was preserved without change.

From this we can conclude that it is not phonemes which change (otherwise the phoneme /l/ would have suffered the same fate no matter what the environment). On the other hand, whole syllables or words are not the typical domain of change, either. The likely candidates which remain are something in

TABLE 5

Data showing the fate of /l/ in the evolution of Latin to French.

Latin		French
alter	>	autre
caldus	>	chaud
but:		
malus	>	mal
lactis	>	lait

between, i.e., drawn from a set intermediate in size between these two extremes; perhaps allophones or diphones (and related constructs). Without reviewing the literature which might bear on this question, I would venture the opinion that the primary units of speech perception are those regions where rapid acoustic modulations occur, i.e., what are commonly called the "transitions" between phonemes. (This does not mean that phonemes have no reality; they may be inferred from the evidence presented by these more basic perceptual units in the same way as objects like cups, faces, and tables may be inferred by cognitive processing of what are undoubtedly the primary elements of visual perception: edges, shadings of light and dark, etc. Phonemes are also very possibly the units used to represent words in the mental lexicon.)

Units of this sort, i.e., diphone, demi-syllables, etc., which consist of those stretches of speech *between* the periods of minimum rate of change and which therefore include the transition, have been quite successful as a basis for SS, even though they require an order of magnitude more stored units than would be the case with phonemes. It is often thought that their success is due to the fact that they sidestep the problems inherent in figuring out how phonemes are to be joined in the acoustic domain since they "pre-compile" these junctions. However, if my guess is right, their success may be due to the fact that, more than any other unit used in SS, they closely match the units human listeners' ears are tuned to.

CLUE 4: Sounds and Features have Varying Degrees of Salience and Confusability.

If communication engineers were set the task of designing a signalling system using the vocal-auditory channel, they would no doubt select units or ciphers for transmission which were as different from each other as possible in order to avoid confusions or other errors of reception. Human speech wasn't designed this way and it turns out that, based on the evidence of sound change, some sounds or features are more susceptible to reception errors than others. The cues for *manner of articulation* seem to be more robust than those for *place of articulation*. *Nasal consonants* in initial position survive unchanged more often than oral obstruents in the same position (Ohala, 1975). Weak fricatives, e.g., [f, v, θ, ð, x, ɣ], change more often than strong fricatives, e.g., [s, z, ʃ, ʒ, ʂ, ʐ]. These patterns may all reflect the high degree of salience of the amplitude parameter in comparison to other acoustic parameters and, obviously, the greater salience of any spectral parameter when it occurs on a part of the signal that has high intensity.

Also, although many sounds are salient by themselves, they are acoustically similar to other sounds and are thus susceptible of being confused. Table 6 provides one example, the shift of palatalized labials to apical or palatal sounds because the two have similar spectral patterns.[3]

CLUE 5: Perceptual Confusions tend to be Asymmetrical.

[3] When reading this and subsequent tables, it should be kept in mind that consonants can become phonetically palatalized or labialized by being adjacent to palatal and rounded vowels, respectively.

TABLE 6

Examples of the sound change whereby palatalized labials are confused with and become apical or palatal sounds (Ohala 1978).

Standard Czech	East Bohemian	Translation
m^{j}ɛstɔ	nɛstɔ	town
p^{j}ɛt	tɛt	five

Lungchow	T'ien-chow	
pjaa	tʃaa	fish

Latin		Intermediate Form		Spanish	
amplu	>	ampju	>	antʃo	large, spacious

Roman Italian	Genoese	
pjeno	tʃena	full
bjaŋko	dʒaŋku	white

Latin		French	
sapiens	>	saʒ	wise
rubeus	>	ʁuʒ	red

Proto-Bantu		Zulu	
pia	>	-tʃha	new

A puzzling meta-pattern found in sound change is the frequent asymmetry in the direction of change (see also Ohala, 1983b, c). Table 6, above, presents one such case; shifts in the reverse direction, of palatal or apical sounds to palatalized labials, are much less common. Other such asymmetrical sound changes are the shift of labialized velars to labials (e.g., Proto-Indo-European *ekwōs* became *hippos* in Classical Greek) and the shift of palatalized velars to apical affricates (e.g., Latin *radikina* "root" became /raditšinə/, and subsequently, French *racine* [ʁasin]). Such shifts are understandable given the great similarity in the spectral patterns of the sounds involved in each pair (Durand, 1955; Halle, Hughes & Radley, 1957).

These same asymmetries have been found in speech perception experiments (which reinforces the claim that these sound changes have a phonetic basis). Table 7 presents some results from a study by Winitz, Scheib and Reeds (1972) involving listeners' identification of CV sequences.

TABLE 7

Asymmetries of confusion in a speech perception study by Winitz et al. (1972), where ' > ' means 'was misidentified as'.

Error type			Incidence		Error type			Incidence
[pi]	>	[ti]	34%	but	[ti]	>	[pi]	6%
[ki]	>	[ti]	32%	but	[ti]	>	[ki]	6%
[ku]	>	[pu]	27%	but	[pu]	>	[ku]	16%

If one of these pairs of sounds changes into the other because they are acoustically similar and listeners mistake which one they are hearing, then it should be the case that the sound changes could go in either direction. The fact that they don't requires some explanation. A clue to the solution to this puzzle may be found in analyses of data from visual perception studies which also exhibit asymmetrical confusions. Gilmore, Hersh, Caramazza and Griffin (1979), for example, found the following kinds of asymmetries in subjects' misidentification of the capital Roman letters when presented under conditions which degrade perceptual performance, as shown in (3), (where '>' means the letter on the left was misidentified as that on the right more often than the reverse):

(3) Q > O E > F R > P

B > P P > F J > I

The letters in each pair are structurally similar to each other except for some extra distinguishing feature. In the case of E and F, for example, both are identical except for the "foot" of the E — missing in the case of F. If this distinguishing feature is missed when the letter on the left is viewed, then it will appear to be the letter on the right. When the righthand letter is viewed, however, it is less likely that this extra distinguishing feature will be mistakenly "filled in". Herein lies the basis for the asymmetry in confusion (Garner, 1978).

Pursuing the implications of this clue, it must therefore be the case that the pairs of speech sound sequences which exhibit asymmetries in sound change and in speech perception studies are acoustically similar except that the ones which are more susceptible to change have one or more extra distinguishing features which are lacking in the more stable sounds. Research is needed to identify these features but some candidates features immediately suggest themselves. For example, comparison of the smoothed spectra of the bursts of [gi] and [di] (see Fig. 2 from Stevens and Blumstein, 1978) reveals that each pair is quite similar except for a sharp peak at about 3 kHz in the case of [gi].

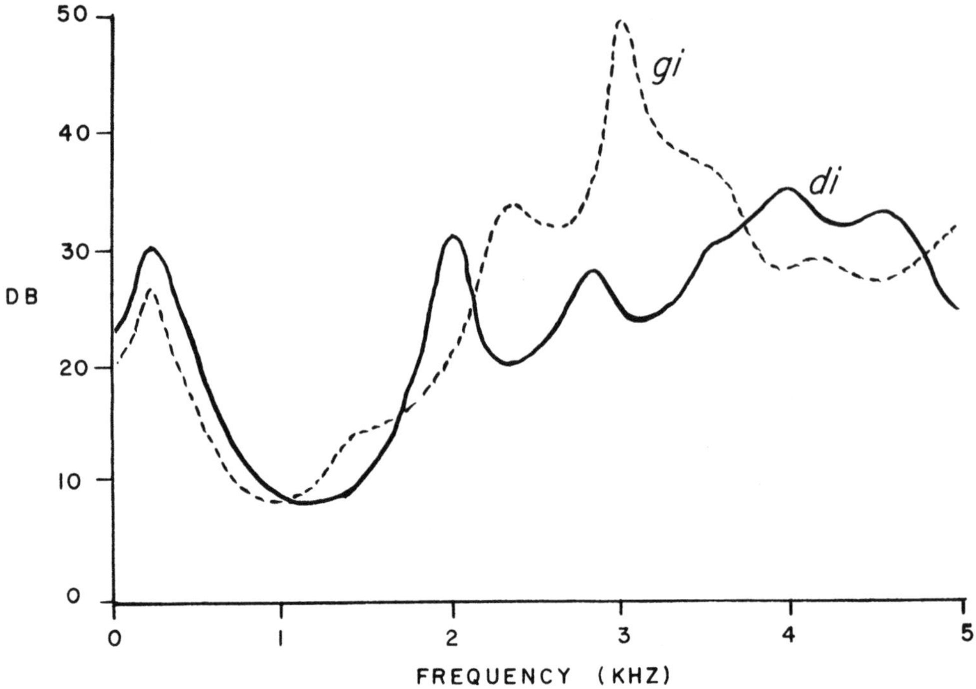

Figure 2. Spectra of the stop bursts of the syllables [di] (solid line) and [gi] (dashed line). (Redrawn from Stevens and Blumstein, 1978.)

It is obvious that these features which distinguish one sound from another must be discovered if SS is to be successful. But these perceptual asymmetries have more profound implications for ASR. The metric which compares the unknown input with a series of known templates should be capable of accommodating or reflecting this inherently asymmetrical nature of speech perception. That is, it should be the case that an input [di] would be shown to be more similar to a reference [gi] than would an input [gi] when referred to a [di]. This reflects the fact that it is easier to turn a [gi] into a [di] (by deleting the sharp peak in the burst) than it is to turn a [di] into a [gi] (which could only be done by *adding* that spectral peak). The assumption is made that accidental loss of certain features is more likely than their accidental introduction.

Current comparison metrics used in ASR, e.g., dynamic time warping, can be made inherently asymmetric by attaching different weights to paths which skip over or which repeat frames in the reference template (cf. R. Moore, this volume).

This is certainly a step in the right direction but the evidence I have reviewed here suggests that the asymmetrical comparison must also apply to the comparison of individual spectral frames or arrays of distinctive features (which cannot be done by just skipping or repeating spectral frames) and that the asymmetries — the differential weights attached to permitted operations which transform the input into the reference template — may be specific to certain sounds or sound sequences.

CLUE 6: Many Distinctive Features may be Non-Orthogonal.

In a maximally efficient signalling system the values assumed by any parameter should be completely independent of other parameters. Speech, by this criterion, is not maximally efficient. An examination of the record of sound changes in the history of many languages — including their segment inventories, which have been shaped by sound change — reveals a number of interdependencies among features.

Place of articulation and the feature of voicing interact as shown by, among other evidence, the stop inventories of over 570 languages (surveyed by Sherman, 1975; see also Gamkrelidze, 1975); Table 8 shows the incidence of stop gaps among languages which used a voicing contrast in at least one place of articulation for stops.

TABLE 8

Incidence of gaps in the indicated place of articulation in the stop inventories of over 570 languages (from Sherman 1975).

Place of articulation:	Labial	Apical	Velar
Voiceless	34	0	0
Voiced	2	21	40

(Many of these languages did not have a voicing contrast on stops; in the vast majority of these cases the stops were voiceless. This also demonstrates interdependence between the features 'stop' and 'voice'.) As can be seen, among voiceless stops, the labial stop /p/ is most often missing; among voiced stops, the velar, /g/ is the most common gap. Among languages lacking a /p/ (in native vocabulary) are Arabic, Yoruba and Vietnamese; Japanese uses a [p] only in very restricted phonological environments. Some languages lacking a /g/ are Dutch, Czech and Thai. Insofar as we know the history of these languages, the missing sounds were present at one time but subsequently changed either in the feature of voicing or stoppedness. What was once a [g] in Dutch, for example, is now an uvular fricative [χ].

The physical causes of these patterns are reasonably well understood: In the case of the voiceless consonants, the stop burst, which is one of the major cues to the presence of a stop, is of much lower intensity in the case of /p/ since, unlike the other stops, it has little or no resonating cavity in front of the point of release (where the burst is created) to reinforce it. In the case of the voiced consonants, the smaller air cavity behind back-articulated stops is less able to accommodate the glottal airflow with the result that the rapid accumulation of air behind the constriction diminishes the transglottal pressure drop and hence the rate of glottal airflow and thus voicing (Ohala, 1983a).

Voicing also doesn't sit comfortably on fricatives. Voiced fricatives require a delicate aerodynamic balancing act: for optimal frication the pressure drop across the consonantal constriction should be high; for the sake of optimal voicing, the pressure drop across the glottis should be high. These two requirements are represented in (4). Since atmospheric pressure cannot be manipulated and

(4) For optimal frication: P atmospheric < P oral

For optimal voicing: P oral < P subglottal

subglottal pressure cannot be easily altered in the short interval (c. 60 msec) required for the production of a single obstruent, the only one of these pressures that is amenable to modification is the oral pressure. But for one purpose it should be as high as possible while for the other as low as possible. Both cannot be done simultaneously. Therefore, to the extent that voiced fricatives have intense frication, e.g., [s,z,ʃ,ʒ] the so-called "strong fricatives", they have a tendency to become devoiced, while to the extent that they have robust voicing, e.g., [β, v, ð, ɣ, ʁ, ʕ], the "weak fricatives", they tend not to have very much frication.

Rules for SS need to take account of these non-orthogonalities by, e.g., modifying the degree of voicing or noise intensity depending on what other features they co-occur with. Natural sounding synthetic /g/'s in American English will not only be typically voiceless but will even have up to 20 msec of aspiration, even in pre-stress intervocalic position (Ohala, 1981b). Feature-extracting algorithms for ASR will not be able to use quite the same methods in the detection of, say, all voiced obstruents or all fricatives.

It should also be mentioned that non-orthogonality of features may appear not only due to articulatory, but also acoustic-auditory factors. It is not physiologically difficult to add pharyngealization (a secondary constriction in the pharyngeal region) to consonants having primary place of constriction in the labial and apical regions. However, Arabic, noted for its pharyngealized or "emphatic" sounds, uses this contrast primarily (some would say 'exclusively') on apical sounds. The reason is that the acoustic manifestation of pharyngealization is a lowering of some of the higher formants but labials already have lowered formants and so would not manifest this effect in an optimal way; apical sounds, on the other hand, have maximally high F2 and so would manifest pharyngealization's lowered formants quite clearly. (For further discussion, see Ohala, in press b; Ohala & Kawaskai, in press.)

CLUE 7: Listeners Perform Error-Correction in Speech Perception

In the introduction I suggested that the speech signal is a composite of the intended message (pronunciation) plus unintended distortions caused by the physical constraints of the speech production apparatus and that one of the tasks of the listener is to strip away the distortions in order to recover the canonical form of the message. If this is accepted, it has rather important implications for

ASR, namely, that successful speech recognition by machine will have to duplicate the listener's performance. Given that variability is at the heart of the problems facing ASR, developing this error-correcting capacity may be the key to successful ASR. That human listeners *do* have this capacity need not be simply assumed; there is evidence for it from sound change. I argue that some sound changes, those said to exhibit "dissimilation", are caused by the listeners inappropriately applying their error-correcting rules.

To begin discussion of this topic, we note first that assimilation can sometimes extend over relatively long stretches of speech. In a C_1 VC_2 sequence, for example, not only the intervening V but also C_1 can assimilate to some of the features of C_2. An example of this may be found in Kaiwa, an indigenous language of Brazil (Harrison & Taylor, 1971). The phrase /d^{y}uʔi ŋ^{w}e/ "frog" may appear in casual speech as [ɲũʔĩ ŋ^{w}e] where the nasalization of the [ŋ^w] has spread all the way to the beginning of the phrase to change /d^y/ to [ɲ] (the palatal nasal). We assume that this kind of distortion presents no difficulty for listeners because they can factor it out. Now, however, consider the evolution of the Latin word *quĩnque* [kwĩŋkwe] in its various daughter languages; see (5a). The stages in the evolution of this word from Latin to Italian, for example, is as given in (5b).

(5) (a) Latin *quĩnque* → French *cinc* | Spanish *cinco* | Italian *cinque*

(b) kwĩŋkwe

↓

kĩŋkwe

↓

tsiŋkwe

The initial labialized velar lost its labialization (and subsequently changed to an apical affricate — for the reasons discussed earlier). The second labialized velar survived a bit longer. Why should this dissimilation, a /kw/ changing to /k/ before another /kw/, occur? I claim it is due to the listeners erroneously attributing the labialization on the first syllable as due to the spreading labialization from the second syllable. In other words, they treated this labialization as a distortion and factored it out. In their own most careful pronunications, this word would not have any labialization in the first syllable. Presumably, similar reasons underlie the sound change mentioned above in (2) whereby a retroflex vowel [ə] becomes de-retroflexed before another retroflex sound.

In the terms of the schematization given above in Fig. 1, the process of dissimilation may be represented as in Fig. 3. Here the intended pronunciation includes $x + y$ but the decoder interprets y as noise and so strips it from the reconstructed signal x.

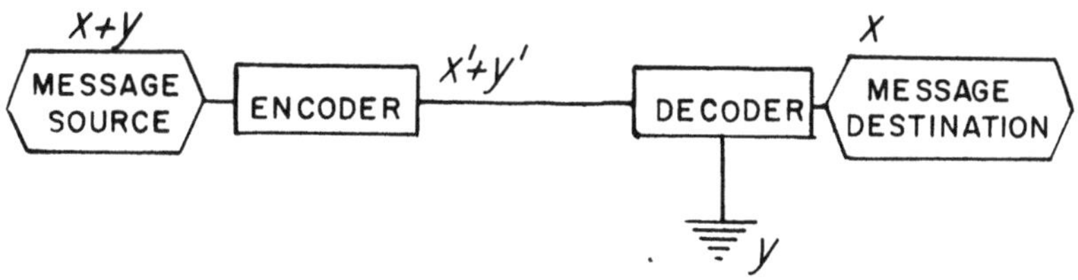

Figure 3. Schematic representation of a transmission line used as an analogue of speech production and perception to explain the process of dissimilation; see text.

There are a number of pieces of evidence supporting this account of dissimilation. First, it would predict that the only phonetic features which could be subject to dissimilation would be those features which are known to spread like a prosody over large stretches of speech, e.g., palatalization, retroflexion, aspiration, labialization, etc., but not features like stop or affricate which by their nature cannot spill over onto adjacent segments. By and large, this prediction is borne out (see Ohala, 1981a, 1983b, in press a). Second, there is supporting evidence from speech perception studies. Ohala, Kawasaki, Riordan, & Caisse (forthcoming) (as reported in Ohala, 1981a) had listeners identify as /i/ or /u/ stimuli of the sort /sVt/, /fVp/ where the vowel, V, was one of 9 steady-state vowels synthesized to range at regular increments between (and including) /i/ and /u/. Naturally listeners' judgements shifted from being predominantly /i/ to predominantly /u/ somewhere in the middle of this continuum. However, the location of this crossover point was further towards the front of the vowel space (i.e., towards /i/) when the vowels appeared in the /s__t/ context than the /f__p/ context. That is, a more front vowel was accepted as a good /u/ when it appeared in a phonetic environment known to cause fronting of back vowels (see above). Presumably, listeners attributed some of the frontness of the vowels to the surrounding apical consonants, /s/ and /t/, and thus factored it out in deducing its intended quality. Several other speech perception studies have also shown that listeners identify speech sounds after taking into account possible distorting effects of the phonetic environment they are found in (see Ohala, 1981a, 1983b, in press a, for references).

There is as yet no suggestion as to how human listeners perform this error-corrrection but a number of approaches are possible for algorithms that would do the same thing in an ASR task. One might be to take equations such as those of Lindblom's, presented above in (1), and turn them around so that target formant frequency of vowels could be computed given the rate of speaking, the formant frequencies of the adjacent consonants, and the measured formant frequencies of the spoken vowel. Another, more qualitative, approach — appropriate, perhaps, to an "expert system" for ASR — would be statements of the sort in (6).

(6) If: F2 of vowel > 1500 Hz and preceding or following consonants are alveolar or palatal,

Then: vowel has .60 probability of being a back vowel.

CONCLUSION

Some very challenging goals face those working in speech synthesis and automatic speech recognition: in speech synthesis, natural-sounding speech from unlimited text and in machine recognition of speech, the accurate recognition of large vocabulary continuously-spoken speech by any native speaker. I believe that the solution to these problems will entail learning as much as possible about how speech is structured and how human speakers and listeners accomplish their tasks in handling spoken language. One largely untapped but very rich source of clues about how speech works is the documentation linguists have accumulated over the past 2 centuries of *sound change*, i.e., the changes in pronunciation over time. I regard sound change as Mother Nature's speech perception experiment. All we have to do is to try to interpret the record of sound change for our purposes. In this paper I have given some examples of how one might do this.

ACKNOWLEDGEMENTS

I gratefully acknowledge the helpful comments, data, and bibliographical advice given by Mariscela Amador and those attending the NATO ASI at Bonas, July 1984, especially Renato De Mori and Manjari Ohala.

REFERENCES

1. G. Chollet, "Effects of coarticulation, syllable type and stress on acoustic French vowel targets", J. Acous. Soc. Am., Vol. 60, S44, 1976.
2. M. Durand, "Du rôle de l'auditeur dans la formation des sons du langage", J. de Psych., Vol. 52, pp. 347-355, 1955.
3. O. Fujimura, "Remarks on stop consonants: Synthesis experiments and acoustic cues", in L. L. Hammerich, R. Jakobson & E. Zwirner (eds.), *Form and substance. Phonetic and linguistic papers presented to Eli*

Fischer-Jørgensen. Copenhagen: Akademisk Forlag, pp. 221-232, 1971.

4. T. V. Gamkrelidze, "On the correlation of stops and fricatives in a phonological system", Lingua, Vol. 35, pp. 231-261, 1975.
5. W. R. Garner, "Aspects of a stimulus: features, dimensions and configurations", in E. Rosch & B. B. Lloyd (eds.), *Cognition and Categorization*, Hillsdale, N. J., Erlbaum, pp. 99-133, 1978.
6. G. C. Gilmore, H. Hersh, A. Caramazza and J. Griffin, "Multidimensional letter similarity derived from recognition errors", Perception & Psychophysics, Vol. 25, pp. 425-431, 1979.
7. M. Halle, G. W. Hughes and J.-P. A. Radley, "Acoustic properties of stop consonants", J. Acous. Soc. Am., Vol. 29, pp. 107-116, 1957.
8. C. H. Harrison and J. M. Taylor, "Nasalization in Kaiwa", in D. Bendor-Samuel (ed.), *Tupi studies I*, Norman, Oklahoma: Summer Institute of Linguistics, pp. 15-20, 1971.
9. J.-M. Hombert, J. J. Ohala and W. G. Ewan, "Phonetic explanations for the development of tones", Language, Vol. 55, pp. 37-58, 1979.
10. W. A. Lea (ed.), *Trends in Speech Recognition*, Englewood Cliffs: Prentice-Hall, 1980.
11. B. Lindblom, "Spectrographic study of vowel reduction", J. Acous. Soc. Am., Vol. 35, pp. 1773-1781, 1963.
12. K. Lindell, J-O. Svantesson and D. Tayanin, "Phonology of Kammu dialects", paper presented at the 9th International Conference on sino-Tibetan Languages and Linguistics, Copenhagen, 1976.
13. E. A. Meyer, "Zur Tonbewegung des Vokals", Phonetische Studien, Vol. 10, pp. 20ff, 1896.
14. B. Michailovsky, "On some Tibeto-Burman sound changes", Proceedings of the Annual Meeting, Berkeley Linguistics Society Vol. 1, pp. 322-332, 1975.
15. J. J. Ohala, "Experimental historical phonology" in J. M. Anderson & C. Jones (eds.), *Historical Linguistics II. Theory and Description in Phonology*. Amsterdam: North Holland, pp. 353-389, 1974.
16. J. J. Ohala, "Phonetic explanations for nasal sound patterns", in C. A. Ferguson, L. M. Hyman and J. J. Ohala (eds.), *Nasalfest: Papers from a symposium on nasals and nasalization*, Stanford: Language Universals Project, pp. 289-316, 1975.
17. J. J. Ohala, "The production of tone", in V. A. Fromkin (eds.), *Tone: A Linguistic Survey*, New York: Academic Press, pp. 5-39, 1978.
18. J. J. Ohala, "The application of phonological universals in speech pathology", in N. J. Lass (ed.), *Speech and Language. Advances in Basic Research and Practice*, Vol. 3, New York: Academic Press, pp. 75-97, 1980.
19. J. J. Ohala, "The listener as a source of sound change", in C. S. Masek, R. A. Hendrick and M. F. Miller (eds.), *Papers from the Parasession on Language and Behavior*. Chicago: Chicago Linguistic Society, pp. 178-203, 1981a.
20. J. J. Ohala, "Articulatory constraints on the cognitive representation of speech", in T. Myers, J. Laver and J. Anderson (eds.), *The Cognitive Representation of Speech*, Amsterdam: North Holland, pp. 111-122, 1981b.
21. J. J. Ohala, "Speech timing as a tool in phonology", Phonetica, Vol. 38, pp.

204-212, 1981c.

22. J. J. Ohala, "The origin of sound patterns in vocal tract constraints", in P. F. MacNeilage (ed.), *The Production of Speech*, New York: Springer-Verlag, pp. 189-216, 1983a.
23. J. J. Ohala, "The direction of sound change", in A. Cohen & M. P. R. v. d. Broeck (eds.), *Abstracts of the Tenth International Congress of Phonetic Sciences*, Dordrecht: Foris, pp. 253-258, 1983b.
24. J. J. Ohala, "The phonological end justifies any means", in S. Hattori & K. Inoue (eds.), *Proceedings of the XIIIth International Congress of Linguists, August 29 — September 4, 1982, Tokyo*. Distributed by Sanseido Shoten, pp. 232-243, 1983c.
25. J. J. Ohala, "Phonological evidence for top-down processing in speech perception", in J. Perkell et al. (eds.), *Invariance and Variability in Speech Processes*, Hillsdale, N. J.: Erlbaum, in press, a.
26. J. J. Ohala, "Around *flat*", in V. Fromkin (ed.), *Phonetic Linguistics*, New York: Academic Press, in press, b.
27. J. J. Ohala and H. Kawasaki, "Phonetics and prosodic phonology," *Phonology Yearbook*, in press.
28. J. J. Ohala, H. Kawasaki, C. Riordan & M. Caisse, Forthcoming. The influence of consonantal environment upon the perception of vowel quality.
29. M. Ohala, *Aspects of Hindi Phonology*, Delhi: Motilal Banarsidass, 1983.
30. D. Sherman, "Stop and fricative systems: A discussion of paradigmatic gaps and the question of language sampling", Stanford Working Papers in Language Universals, Vol. 17, pp. 1-31, 1975.
31. K. N. Stevens and S. E. Blumstein, "Invariant cues for place of articulation in stop consonants", J. Acous. Soc. Am., Vol. 64, pp. 1358-1368, 1978.
32. K. N. Stevens, A. S. House and A. P. Paul, "Acoustical description of syllabic nuclei: an interpretation in terms of a dynamic model of articulation", J. Acous. Soc. Am., Vol. 40, pp. 123-132, 1966.
33. N. Umeda, "Influence of consonants on vowels", J. Acous. Soc., Japan, Vol. 16, pp. 87-93, 1960.
34. H. Winitz, M. E. Scheib and J. A. Reeds, "Identification of stops and vowels for the burst portion of /p,t,k/ isolated from conversational speech", J. Acous. Soc. Am., Vol. 51, pp. 1309-1317, 1972.

SYNTHESIS OF SPEECH BY COMPUTERS AND CHIPS

Ching Y. Suen and Stephen B. Stein
Dept. of Computer Science
Concordia University
1455 de Maisonneuve Blvd., West
Montreal, Quebec H3G 1M8
Canada

ABSTRACT

Speech of unlimited vocabulary can be synthesized from systems which can produce the basic set of about 40 phonetic sounds of a language. However, the quality of the speech output is highly dependent on the method used in the system. Good synthesized speech requires good phonetic rules to give an accurate transcription of the input texts. A description of an accurate unrestricted text-to-speech algorithm will be described. An evaluation of speech synthesizers and the experimental results will be discussed. Further addition of prosody features will make the synthesized sound more and more natural. Some new systems developed in recent years and their characteristics will be presented.

INTRODUCTION

Speech is the primary mode of human communication. The great variety of applications of synthetic speech has already been described in the literature, see e.g. references [5-7, 10, 13-15, 19, 21, 22, 30, 33]. In this paper, we examine the role that synthetic speech can play in the man-machine interface.

NATO ASI Series, Vol. F16
New Systems and Architectures for Automatic Speech
Recognition and Synthesis. Edited by R. De Mori and C. Y. Suen

Methods of synthetic speech production may be grouped in the following manner:

1. Those which involve the storage, processing and coding of actual human speech such as those using linear predictive coding, see e.g. [3, 13, 17, 20, 23].
2. Those which involve the synthetic production of speech from formant type of synthesizer (usually equipped with flexible filters) and speech from a set of rules, see e.g. references [1, 2, 4-6, 8, 9, 12, 21, 25, 26, 28, 29, 31, 32, 34].

The former method may employ magnetic tape recordings or the digitization and machine processing of speech stored in solid state memory. In either case, with or without an encoding process, these methods which are commonly used in the manufacturing of talking toys, calculators, and watches are appropriate to only those applications where a small finite vocabulary is needed.

The latter method must be used where the ability to produce a large number of different vocabulary items is required. Such is the case in the development of reading machines for the blind or an auditory component to a computer assisted learning package.

The Concordia Speech Project (CSP) is involved in the development of a "speech by rule" system that produces speech with a high degree of intelligibility, yet is compact enough to be run on a microcomputer. The software was developed on a large mainframe, CDC's Cyber 172 computer, and drives a Votrax VS-6 synthesizer [26, 28, 29].

The Votrax synthesizer is an electronic analogue to the human vocal tract. It consists of two sound generator circuits. One produces voiced sounds and the other produces fricative sounds. These two outputs are joined and passed through a set of filters to simulate the vocal tract's resonance. The synthesizer has the ability to produce any of sixty-one phonemes, and is hardware controlled. All that is required to run it is a sequence of phonetic codes represented in six bit words. The VS-6 model which is used for this research has four set levels of intonation which control the phonemes, pitch and amplitude, requiring an additional two bits. Therefore, the entire command word has eight bits.

The Votrax synthesizer was chosen for this research because its operation requires a bit rate of only 70 bits per second and it provides a valuable research tool to develop phonetic rules to make it speak unlimited English. In microcomputer applications Votrax's single chip synthesizer (the SC-01) can be substituted for the VS-6 to which it is supposed to be identical. The major shortcoming of the synthesizer is that the lack of software control over pitch, speech rate and amplitude makes control of the suprasegmental aspects of speech rather limited.

This paper will present the speech rule system developed at Concordia University with experimental results and a comparison of performance with another synthesizer, the Type 'N Talk text-to-speech synthesizer. It also gives a description of new devices and speech synthesis chips available in the market. This paper is mainly addressed to the synthesis of spoken English, synthesis of other languages may be found in references [27, 16, 18].

PRINCIPLE OF TEXT TO SPEECH CONVERSION

The development of an algorithm to convert a string of orthographic symbols to a string of phonetic symbols needed by the Votrax synthesizer presents a problem with many facets. This is particularly true if the algorithm must be small enough to be run on a microcomputer.

Perhaps the simplest workable approach to the problem is that taken by Elovitz et al. [6]. In this system, a word is scanned from left to right and letters are assigned phonetic symbols solely on the basis of 329 letter-to-sound rules. The algorithm is very compact and can be easily implemented on practically any microcomputer. The absence of stress rules and problems of phonetic accuracy, however, impair the general intelligibility of the output.

At the other end of the simplicity continuum are systems such as those developed by Allen [2] and Hertz [8, 9]. Both these systems employ parametric synthesizers rather than the Votrax synthesizer used in the CSP. A parametric synthesizer is typically more expensive to run but allows much greater control over the realization of stress and intonation. In Allen's system words are broken up into their constituent morphemes. The pronunciation of these morphemes is checked against a dictionary of 12,000 entries. In the final output, adjustments are made in the cases where affixation affects the pronunciation of root morphemes. Those words for which no entries are found are sounded out as a human would upon encountering a new word.

While there can be little doubt that Allen's system is an excellent one, incorporating all known aspects of speech production, its size and complexity precludes its implementation on a small microcomputer.

THE CSP SYSTEM

The CSP system must be considered as one based on stress. It became apparent in the early stages of the project that much of the variation in a vowel's pronunciation depends more upon whether it is stressed than on its immediate segmental environment. The stress assignment algorithm used in CSP has three major functions:

1) It aids in the overall intelligibility of words,
2) It allows for the separate application of rules to stressed and unstressed vowels,
3) It enables the system to capture the most salient characteristic of English phonology: namely, that unstressed vowels generally reduce to "schwa".

In the CSP system, a word is first read in and checked against a prelexicon. The prelexicon contains the phonetic code for words which are exceptions to both the rules of English pronunciation and affixation. An example of this is the word "island", for which the correct pronunciation cannot be established by sounding out the word as a whole or by removing the suffix "land" and pronouncing "is" in isolation.

If the word is found in the prelexicon, the phonetic code is sent to the Votrax synthesizer. If it is not found, the word is syllabified by counting the number of vowel clusters. Of course, not all sequences of vowels are vowel clusters, and the system employs a set of rules to distinguish between words such as "noun" and "neon" assigning the former a syllable count of one, and the latter a syllable count of two. In addition, the detection of final silent "e" is necessary to avoid an inflation of the syllable count. It should be noted here that because the assignment of stress requires only that the number of syllables be known, the system does not establish syllable boundaries within a word.

Following syllabification, all external affixes are removed from the word. An external affix is defined as one which does not affect the placement of stress. Examples of these are the suffixes "ness" and "ment". This procedure has the advantages of simplifying stress assignment and aiding in the detection of silent medial "e". In the word "basement", for example, removal of "ment" places the silent "e" in final position where the final silent "e" rule can apply to the word "base". In addition, the removal of external affixes makes it possible to limit the size of the lexicon. The lexicon is consulted after affixes are removed, and therefore need only contain root words. The lexicon entries are words whose pronunciations are exceptions to general English rules, but allow for external affix removal. Therefore, although a word like "island" must be placed in the prelexicon, the correct pronunciation of "Thailand" requires only that "Thai" be a lexicon entry.

If a root word is not found in the lexicon, stress is assigned to it. The rules of stress assignment are based on principles of English stress described in Chomsky and Halle [4] as well as those in Wijk [32]. Although the Chomsky and Hall rules are rather elegant, they could not be taken over wholesale because of their reliance on the part-of-speech values of words. The CSP system, which does no grammatical parsing could not employ them.

Once stress has been established, two sets of text to speech rules translate letters to phonetic codes. One set of rules is reserved solely for stressed vowels, and the other provides phonetic code for unstressed vowels and consonants. Detailed descriptions of these rules can be found in Stein's thesis [26].

Before the final output, the phonetic code for any affixes that were removed is attached to the word. The code for affixes is derived using the same set of rules as the root word.

Finally, the entire word is sent to the Votrax buffer. The synthesized speech is produced using normal audio speakers.

Although the sets of stressed and unstressed rules specify different phonetic codes for the orthographic representation of vowels, they are identical in organization. The rules are organized by grapheme. Thus, there are blocks of 'A' rules, 'B' rules, etc.

For example, to determine the phonetic code for the word 'CAT', the system must first search linearly through the 'C' rules, then the stressed 'A' rules and finally the 'T' rules. The fact that a linear search is carried out through a rule block enables us to control the application of rules by ordering them within the block. In our example, the 'C' rule that applies is: [C] = /K/. This rule is simply read: "The letter 'C' is pronounced /K/". Because the rule specifies no special environment for its application, it must occupy the last position in the rule block. Otherwise, it would traverse through all other rules which come below it. All rules must be ordered, therefore, from the most specific to the most general.

In addition to specifying the pronunciation of a single letter, a rule may specify the pronunciation of a cluster of letters. The rule block into which such a rule is placed, however, must correspond to the first letter of the cluster. For example, the rule that states that [CHR] at the beginning of a word is pronounced /KR/ is found in the 'C' rules.

The fact that rules must be placed in letter blocks leads to some interesting consequences when one tries to capture some of the generalizations of English phonology. This can be seen in Figure 1 in which the system's output for the word 'COMPUTERS' is displayed. Here the palatalization of the letter 'P' is captured by the 'U' rule that is read: "If a stressed letter 'U' is preceded by one or more consonants but not (TH,ST,SH,CH,N,X,Y,S,Z,J,L or R) and if it is followed by one and only one consonant followed by at least one vowel, then it is pronounced /YU/.

FIGURE 1
EXAMPLE 1 (using the word 'computers')

```
WORD % 'COMPUTERS'
C  C
V  O
C  MP
V  U
C  T
V  E
C  RS

        THERE IS/ARE 3 SYLLABLE(S)

        PREFIX/SUFFIX RULE(S) NUMBER(S)-7
        3 SYLLABLE(S) IS/ARE CONSIDERED IN RULE
        AFTER STRESS RULE, WORD BECAME % COMPUTER
        STRESS 1 AFTER THE PREFIX % U
        RULE 19

MAIN WORD
[C]=/K/
[/0(S1);0/]=/UH3/
[M]=/M/
[P]=/P/
(C1)/TH;ST;SH;CH;N;X;Y;S;Z;J;L;R/^[U](C1,1)(V1)=/Y U/
[T]=/T/
[/E(V1);E/]=/EH3/
[R]=/R/
SUFFIX
%(C1)/T'/^[S]#=/Z/
```

Figure 1 exemplifies the operation of the algorithm described above. The word is first divided into consonant and vowel clusters. All affixes are identified and stress is assigned to the appropriate vowel. It is the knowledge that all vowels except the 'U' are unstressed that allows the lax pronunciation to be assigned to the 'O' and 'E'.

In this case the plural morpheme 'S' is seen as an external affix because it does not affect the placement of stress within the main word 'COMPUTER'.

PERFORMANCE

All of the first five thousand most frequently used words in the Brown corpus are pronounced correctly by the CSP system, within the hardware limitations of the Votrax synthesizer.

This was ascertained by listening to the synthesized version of each word and by looking at the phonetic transcription that was being produced to drive the synthesizer.

It was decided, however, that if the true performance of the CSP system were to be evaluated, a test situation more closely approximating the actual conditions under which the system would be used was needed. An experiment was therefore devised to test the performance of the CSP system against that of a human speaker and another, simpler, system — Votrax's Type 'N Talk. This synthesizer is based on the SC 01 chip, and its repertoire of phonemes is nearly identical to that of the VS 6. Both synthesizers are made by the same company. However, the Type 'N Talk contains its own built-in algorithm for text to speech conversion.

It was envisioned that the comparison of the CSP system to the Type 'N Talk would yield information on whether the greater complexity of our system actually produces significantly more intelligible output than a simpler, and therefore less expensive, algorithm.

they do not allow the listener to successfully employ any word expectancy strategy.

The nine lists of ten words were presented by means of a tape recording at approximately 60 dB to three randomly assigned groups of subjects. Three lists were read by a human, three by the Type 'N Talk, and three by the CSP. After each sentence was read, the subjects were required to write down exactly what they had heard. The test situation was therefore very similar to a standard dictation exercise.

The variables being manipulated were speaker (CSP, Type 'N Talk, human) and practice for each condition (first, second and third set of trials).

The design was a fully counter-balanced 3 x 3 factorial design with repeated measures on both factors.

After the subjects had completed the dictation task, each group was asked to subjectively rate the reading of an article from Time magazine by one of the three speakers in terms of overall intelligibility. The subjects were given a numerical rating range from zero to one hundred.

Results

A two way analysis of variance with factor trial (1st, 2nd, 3rd) and system (CSP, Type 'N Talk, human) with repeated measures on both factors was done. The main effect for system was $F(2,178) = 4231$, .001. The main effect for trial was $F(2,178) = 95$, .001, while the interaction between system and trial was $F(4,356) = 9.96$, .001.

These results are represented graphically in Figure 2.

The subjective ratings of the magazine article reading for each of the three speakers yielded the following results on a scale of 1 to 100: Human = 91; CPS = 64; Type 'N Talk = 32.

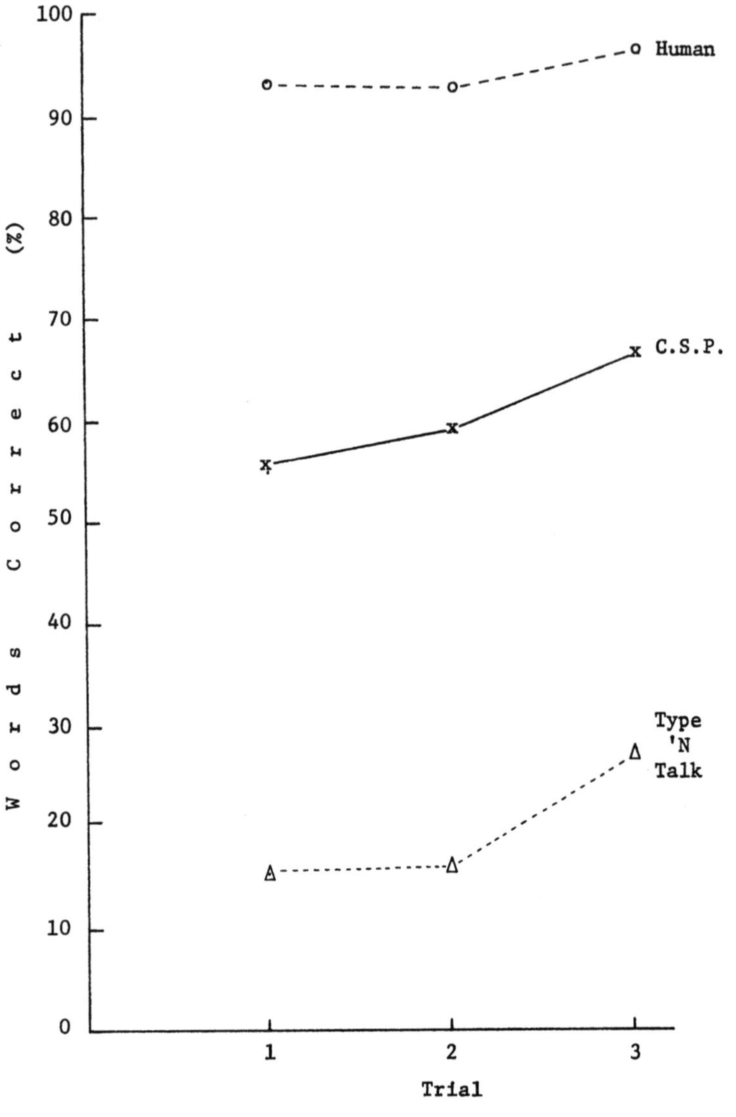

Percentage of correct words for each system.

Figure 2

DISCUSSION AND PRELIMINARY ERROR ANALYSIS

The large difference in words correct for CSP and "Type 'N Talk" was not expected. It would be convenient to attribute all the difference between the two systems to the fact that CSP uses a more sophisticated algorithm. Although this certainly is an important factor it does not account for all the results obtained in the experiment.

Spectrographs taken of the sentence "The tiny girl took off her hat.", spoken by all three systems show some important differences between systems. The spectrographs were made from the tapes actually used in the performance test.

The formant transitions produced by the Votrax VS-6 synthesizer, used in the CSP, tend to be smoother than those of the "Type 'N Talk". Much more information is available from the speech produced by the Votrax VS-6 at the higher frequencies than that of the "Type 'N Talk".

It is our aim at the CSP to use the results of this experiment to point to areas in which improvement to the CSP system is most needed. Preliminary analyses have revealed some interesting tendencies. It seems to us that the vast majority of errors are a result of 'semantic filling'. It is probable that in processing the sentences, the cadets did not recognize each word as they heard it, but rather, formed a general impression of the meaning of the sentence based on the key words that they did recognize. For each sentence then, the previously unrecognized words were filled in to construct a syntactically correct sentence that would be consistent with this meaning. The use of this strategy can be detected precisely because it did not work. The sentences used in the experiment were constructed so as not to allow the listener to build the entire sentence using only partial information. Had normal sentences been used, the semantic filling strategy would have undoubtedly been more successful.

Our observations have thus far been consistent with this explanation. Relatively few errors were made in the recognition of open-class words (nouns, verbs, adjectives and adverbs) whereas errors were frequently the result of the substitution of one preposition for another or the switching of article forms (a, the). Even where errors in open-class words were made, evidence points to semantic filling. In the sentence, "The Friendly gang left the drug store", 'gang' was changed to 'man' by a great many subjects listening to the CSP version. The most plausible explanation for this is that one generally does not expect a gang to be friendly.

Although we must emphasize that our error analysis results are preliminary, the concept of comprehension threshold promises to play an important role in the evaluation of synthetic speech systems. The Type 'N Talk system seems to be below the threshold for the recognition of open-class words. The CSP system seems to be at present below the threshold for the complete comprehension of closed-class words, in the absence of syntactic or semantic redundancy. We are currently investigating the role that increased phonetic redundancy could play in improving the intelligibility of the CSP output.

NEW SPEECH SYNTHESIS SYSTEMS AND CHIPS

As research and technologies advance in the field of speech synthesis and micro-electronics, new integrated circuit chips have been developed by a number of manufacturers [22]. Some of them perform the specific function of speech synthesis while others also include a text-to-speech algorithm. Obviously those presented in the following table do not necessarily exhaust all the speech synthesis systems and chips which exist in this rapidly growing market, anyhow, this list should provide the readers with sufficient leads to explore them further., As expected, most speech synthesizers accept ASCII texts and convert them to spoken English or other languages. they also provide controls (either discrete levels by software or external adjustment) on both pitch, speed and amplitude. These devices can be interfaced to most computers easily through the serial port. Several speech synthesis systems incorporating the synthesizer chips already exist in the market, e.g. the Type 'N Talk by Votrax, Intex-Talker by Intex Micro Systems Inc., and the Sweet Talker II by The Micromint Inc., all built around the Votrax SC-01A chip; while the SynPhonix speech articulator by Artic Technologies is built from a Silicon Systems Inc. SSI 263 phoneme synthesizer.

TABLE 1 New speech synthesis systems and chips from different manufacturers.

Manufacturer	Model	Synthesis Technique	Vocabulary	Feature
Covox, Inc.	Voice Master	Waveform processing and coding	Up to 64 numbered words or phrases, or other sounds	
Digital Equipment Corp.	DECtalk	Computer model of the vocal tract	Unlimited	Can produce voices from old male to a female, to a young child
General Instrument	VSM 2032	Linear prediction		
Hewlett-Packard Co.	82967A	Linear prediction	1500 words	
Infovox, Sweden	SA101	Formant synthesis	Unlimited	English, French Spanish, Italian German, Swedish
National Semiconductor	Digitalker	Waveform processing and synthesis	256 words or phrases	
	Microtalker	Concatenation of waveforms and processing	256 words	
NEC America, Inc.	AR-10	ADPCM coding		
Oki Semiconductor	MSM 6202 MSM 6212	ADPCM	Ability to select up to 125 phrases stored on chip ROM	Can store 12-40 sec. of speech

Silicon Systems Inc.	SSI 263	Formant synthesis	Unlimited	64 phonemes each with 4 different duration settings
Speech Plus Inc.	Prose 2000 Prose 2020		Unlimited	
	Text 5000		Unlimited	IBM PC compatible also through toned telephone
Street Electronics Corp.	ECHO GP		Unlimited	Stand-alone unit with own on-board microcomputer
Texas Instruments Inc.	TMS 5200	Linear prediction	Unlimited	
Vynet Corp.			Information "Spoken" by the computer as prede-termined voice messages from a program or database	For IBM PC as a voice response unit
Votrax Division, Federal Screw Works	SC-01A	Formant synthesis	Unlimited	64 phonemes plus 3 silences
	VS-B	Formant synthesis	Unlimited	64 phonemes plus 3 silences, French and German

CONCLUDING REMARKS

Speech synthesis by computer has been investigated by many researchers in the past two decades. This field has advanced from the simple method of split and concatenation to highly sophisticated methods of coding and employing powerful phonetic rules. As demonstrated in this paper, computer synthesis of spoken English, probably the most difficult one among European languages [25], due to immense variations and inconsistencies between English spelling and pronunciation, has been developed successfully. Additional research on prosodic and suprasegmental features will improve the naturalness of synthetic speech. Syntheses of other languages also exist in the market. The emergence of VLSI (Very Large Scale Integrated) circuits has added a new dimension to the field of speech synthesis. Indeed, as shown in this paper, several speech synthesizer chips have been manufactured. This new era has widely opened up the consumer market for speech synthesizers in toys, cars, teaching aids, computer terminals, automatic telephone answering, alarm systems, disabled aids and message systems [19]. The consumer market has attracted the attention of several leading computer manufacturers. It is anticipated that speech synthesizers will become popular built-in attachments to computers and peripherals, and daily utilities. It is not surprising that they will form standard peripherals to most personal computers in the near future.

ACKNOWLEDGEMENTS

This research was supported by the Department of Education of Quebec. The authors wish to thank Ms. T. Rossman, Mr. C. L. Yu, Mr. G. Liben, and Prof. N. Segalowitz for their help and comments in the experimental study of this project.

REFERENCES

1. W. A. Ainsworth, "A system for converting English text into speech", IEEE Trans. Audio Electroacoust., Vol. AU-21, 288-290, 1973.
2. J. Allen, "Synthesis of speeach from unrestricted text", Proc. IEEE, Vol. 64, 433-442, April 1976.
3. B. S. Atal and S. L. Hanauer, "Speech analysis and synthesis by linear prediction of the speech waveform", J. Acoust. Soc. Amer., Vol. 50, 637-655, August 1971.
4. N. Chomsky and M. Halle, *The Sound Pattern of English*, Harper and Row, New York, 1968.
5. S. Ciarcia, "Build a third-generation phonetic speech synthesizer", Byte, 28-46, March 1984.
6. H. S. Elovitz, R. W. Johnson, A. McHugh and J. E. Shore, "Letter-to-sound

rules for automatic translation of English text to phonetics", IEEE Trans. Acoust., Speech, Signal Processing, Vol. 24, 446-459, December 1976.
7. J. L. Flanagan, "Talking with computers: synthesis and recognition of speech by machines", IEEE Trans. Bio-Med. Engng., Vol. BME-29, 223-232, April 1982.
8. S. R. Hertz, "The 'morthology' of English spelling: a look at the SRS text-modification rules for English", Working Papers of the Cornell Phonetics Laboratory, No. 1, 17-28, December 1983.
9. S. R. Hertz, "From text to speech with SRS", J. Acoust. Soc. Am., Vol. 72, 1155-1170, 1982.
10. D. R. Hill, "Spoken language generation and understanding by machine: a problems and applications oriented overview", in J. C. Simon (ed.), *Spoken Language Generation and Understanding*, Proc. NATO Advanced Studies Institute, D. Reidel Publishing Co., Dordrecht, 3-38, 1980.
11. J. N. Holmes, "Formant synthesizers: cascade or parallel", Speech Communication, Vol. 2, 251-273, 1983.
12. S. Hunnicutt, "Phonological rules for a text-to-speech system", Technical Report, Research Lab of Electronics, MIT, 1979.
13. L. M. Koehler and T. C. Mackey, "Speech output for HP series 80 personal computers", Hewlett-Packard Journal, 29-36, January 1984.
14. J. A. Kuecken, *Talking Computers and Telecommunications*, Van Nostrand Reinhold, New York, 1983.
15. D. L. Lee and F. H. Lochovsky, "Voice response systems", Computing Surveys, Vol. 15, 351-374, December 1983.
16. S. C. Lee, S. Xu and B. Guo, "Microcomputer-generated Chinese speech", Computer Procesing of Chinese & Oriental Languages, Vol. 1, 87-103, December 1983.
17. K.-S. Lin, K. M. Goudie, G. A. Frantz and G. L. Brantingham, "Text-to-speech using LPC allophone stringing", IEEE Trans. Consumer Electronics, Vol. CE-27, 144-152, May 1981.
18. W. C. Lin and T.-T. Luo, "On synthesis of Mandarin by means of Chinese phonemes and phoneme-pairs (JIFH)", to appear in Computer Processing of Chinese and Oriental Languages, an international journal of the Chinese Language Computer Society.
19. G. C. Lyman, III, "Voice messaging comes of age", Speech Technology, Vol. 2, 45-49, August/September 1984.
20. J. D. Markel and A. H. Gray, *Linear Prediction of Speech*, Springer-Verlag, New York, 1976.
21. M. D. McIlroy, "Synthetic English by rule", Computer Science Tech. Report 14, Bell Laboratories, Murray Hill, Ner Jersey, March 1974.
22. N. Morgan, *Talking Chips*, McGraw-Hill Book Co., New York, 1984.
23. F. S. Mozer, "Method and apparatus for speech synthesizing", US Patent No. 4,214,125, July 1980.
24. *1965 Revised List of Phonetically Balanced Sentences (Harvard Sentences)*, IEEE Trans. Audio Electro-acoust., Vol. AU-17, 238-246, 1969.
25. B. A. Sherwood, "Fast text-to-speech, algorithms for Esperanto, Spanish, Italian, Russian and English", Int. J. Man-Machine Studies, Vol. 10, 669-692,

1978.

26. S. B. Stein, "A unrestricted text-to-speech algorithm for the Votrax synthesizer", M. Comp. Sc. Thesis, Concordia University, Montreal, March 1982.
27. C. Y. Suen, "Computer synthesis of Mandarin", Proc. IEEE Int. Conf. Acoustics, Speech and Signal Processing, 698-700, April 1976.
28. C. Y. Suen, T. Rossman, S. Stein, M. G. Strobel, C. Charbonneau and L. Santerre, "Computer speech synthesis at Concordia University", Proc. Int. Electrical, Electronics Conf. & Expo, 176-177, 1981.
29. C. Y. Suen, S. B. Stein, M. G. Strobel and L. Santerre, "An unrestricted text-to-speech algorithm for the Votrax synthesizer", Proc. 10th Int. Cong. Phonetic Sciences, 394, August 1983.
30. E. R. Teja, *Teaching Your Computer to Talk*, TAB Books Inc., Blue Ridge Summit, PA, 1981.
31. N. Umeda, "Linguistic rules for text-to-speech synthesis", Proc. IEEE, Vol. 64, 443-451, 1976.
32. A. Wijk, "Rules of pronunciation for the English language", London, 1966.
33. I. H. Witten, *Principles of Computer Speech*, Academic Press, New York, 1982.
34. I. Witten and J. Abbess, "A microcomputer-based speech synthesis-by-rule system", Int. J. Man-Machine Studies, Vol. 11, 585-620, 1979.

PROSODIC KNOWLEDGE IN THE RULE-BASED SYNTHEX EXPERT SYSTEM FOR SPEECH SYNTHESIS

A. Aggoun, C. Sorin, F. Emerard, M. Stella
C.N.E.T. — Lannion
Route de Trégastel
BP 40
22301 Lannion Cedex
France

1. INTRODUCTION

Speech synthesis is the transformation of a written text into an acoustic signal.

The speech synthesis system by diphones developed at C.N.E.T. (Centre National d'Etudes des Télécommunications de LANNION) is complete and is described in [14, 23]. The synthetic speech produced by the system is intelligible, but lacks more naturalness. The improvement of the intelligibility and naturalness depends in particular on progress carried out in segmental and prosodic rules. At the moment, experiments with new rules and in particular prosodic rules are not easy.

During the last few years, different speech synthesis systems from a written text have emerged. Some of these systems are written in classical programming languages (FORTRAN, etc...), which makes modification and improvement difficult.

More recently, the use of knowledge based systems as a framework has spread into new areas, such as speech recognition [15] and natural language understanding; the methodology of the expert systems facilitates an incremental

NATO ASI Series, Vol. F16
New Systems and Architectures for Automatic Speech
Recognition and Synthesis. Edited by R. De Mori and C. Y. Suen

transfer of knowledge from the human to the machine.

In this paper, we discuss the SYNTHEX (System SYNTHesis EXpert) system developed at C.N.E.T. The design of SYNTHEX is an example of the use of Artificial Intelligence techniques in order to study various problems related to speech synthesis from a written text [1, 2]. The main aim of this project is to develop a tool able to formalize knowledge related to the problem of speech synthesis from written text and to improve this knowledge.

II. TEXT-TO-SPEECH

Speech synthesis systems combine a given method with a given technique [9, 11, 23]. The technique permits the reconstruction of the acoustic signal containing the characteristics of the speech sound from certain parameters. The "text-to-speech" method consists of generating the above parameters from a given written text, such as synthesis by word, synthesis by rule [3, 7, 8, 16] or synthesis by concatenation of preanalysed units [14].

The speech synthesis system (fig. 2) is composed of:

— a grapheme-to-phoneme conversion module [12] which produces a string of phonetic symbols based on information in the written text;
— a prosodic module [14, 20, 24] which processes rules (expert rules) to produce prosodic parameters (pitch, duration and loudness);
— a conversion module which converts prosodic parameters into appropriate parameters in order to drive the synthesizer;
— a synthesizer to reconstruct the acoustic signal using various techniques [23].

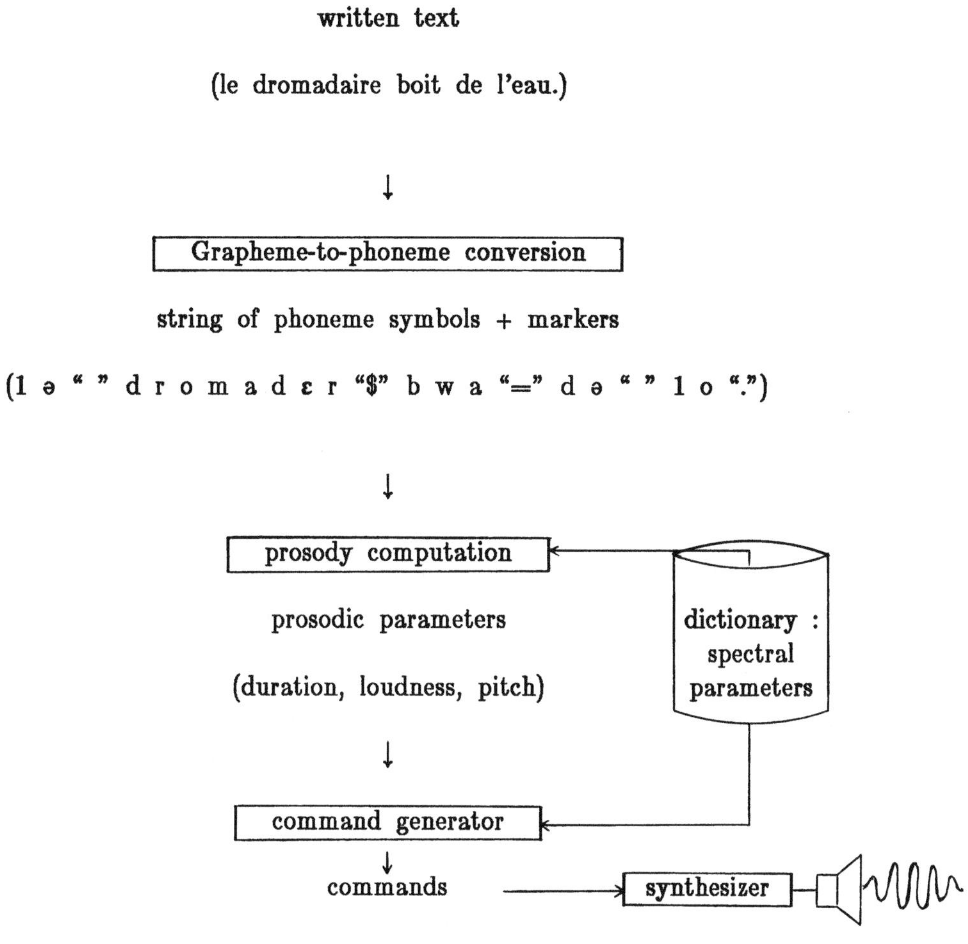

Fig. 1: Text-to-speech synthesis
The translation of the french sentence "le dromadaire boit de l'eau." is "the dromedary drinks water."

<u>N.B.</u>: Phoneme codification used in the example:
phonemes: l, d, r, m, b, w, ə, o, a, ɛ,
markers: " ", "$", "=", "."

III. PURPOSE OF THE SYNTHEX EXPERT SYSTEM

The SYNTHEX system has been developed originally to provide investigation in the speech synthesis domain. From the beginning, the goal of this system was to formalize the prosodic module (fig. 1) of the speech synthesis system.

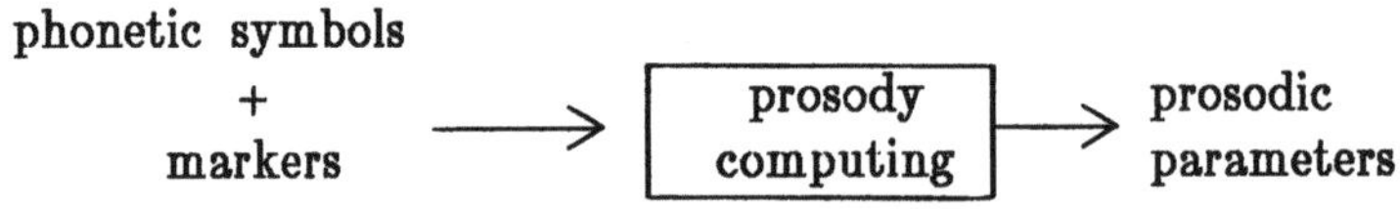

Fig. 2 Prosodic module

The system accepts as input a string of phonetic symbols (grapheme-to-phoneme conversion) and prosodic markers, and delivers as output prosodic parameters such as pitch, loudness and duration. Some markers are delivered implicitly in the text, such as punctuation markers and spaces between words. The remaining markers indicate syntactic points in the sentence such as the end of the preverbal group.

Some of the existent systems are written in an ad hoc manner, so their adaptation and maintenance are difficult. Other software packages are parameterized, but they can not solve problems caused by adding new knowledge, neither those caused by modifications of the existing rules.

In recent years, different languages adapted to phonetic and linguistic terminology have been proposed for synthesis by rules [3, 7, 8, 16, 22]. These languages are easy to use, but it is difficult to take into account the syntactic structure of the sentence.

The SYNTHEX expert system has been developed to fulfil the following goals:

— simplicity is essential, since speech synthesis experts are not necessarily programming specialists;
— independence from the language being synthesized (French, English, etc...) and

the synthesis technique;

- paraphrase and reformulation of the rules expressed by the speech experts to avoid any ambiguity;
- explanation of the reasoning adopted by the system during execution;
- formalization of the speech experts knowledge;
- introduction of methods for improving this knowledge.

IV GENERAL ARCHITECTURE OF THE SYSTEM

SYNTHEX is an expert system based on production rules [4, 17, 19, 21]. These rules defined by the user are stored in knowledge bases. Briefly an expert system is composed of:

- knowledge bases (methods, facts, assertions, relevant assertions, metaknowledges, etc...)
- inference engine (pattern matcher, knowledge modifiers, etc...)
- working memories (current goals, current hypotheses, etc....)

V KNOWLEDGE EXPRESSION LANGUAGE

To facilitate the transfer of the experts synthesis knowledge in the system, we have devloped a formalism adapted to the expert's needs. One of the basic criteria of this system is its simplicity. It should be easy to use by non programming specialists.

In this chapter we describe the external formalism.

The corresponding internal formalism will be illustrated in V. 2.

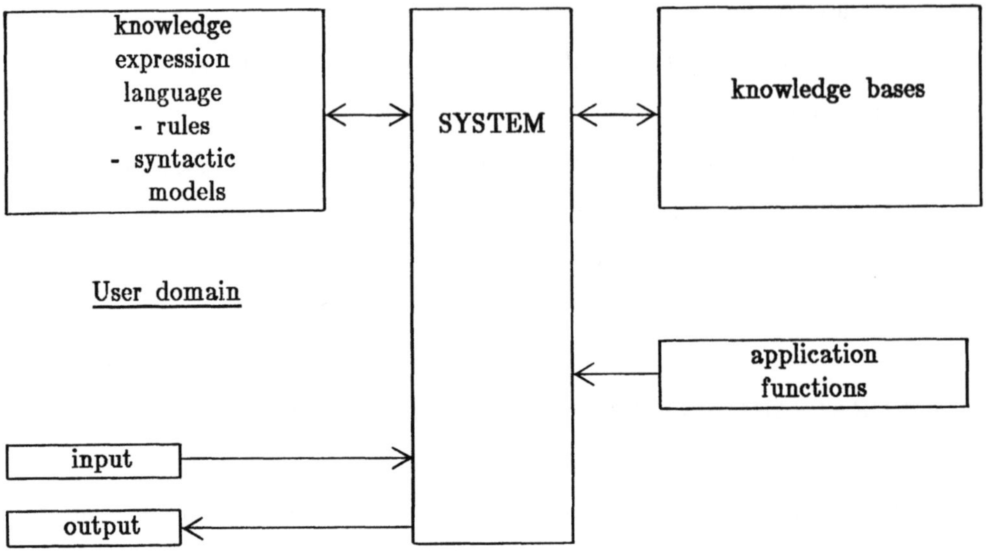

Fig. 3: General architecture of the SYNTHEX system

V.1 EXTERNAL FORMALISM

This formalism permits the expression of the two following entities:

— syntactic models which express the application concepts

— prosodic rules, as production rules.

V.1.1 SYNTACTIC MODELS

Those are essentially composed of syntactic structures, definitions, object descriptions and dictionaries containing the specific application data.

The "syntactic structure", "definition" and "object description" models should allow for the construction of a syntactic tree from a sentence composed of phonetic symbols and markers.

The various prosodic rules are applied to this tree. These concepts are derived from the study of speech synthesis. The syntax is carefully chosen to be as close as possible to the formalism used by synthesis experts.

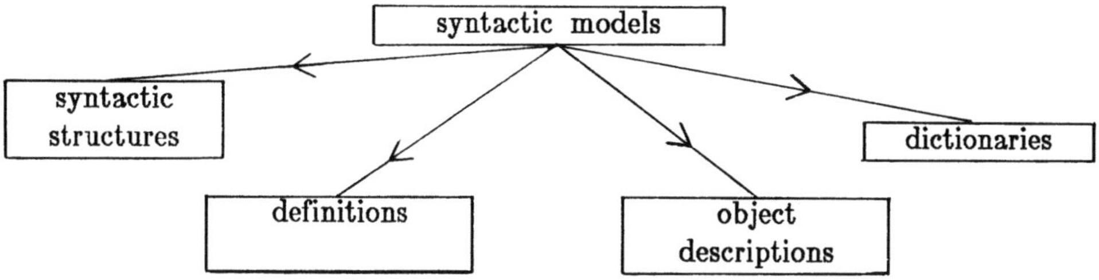

Fig. 4: Syntactic models

SYNTACTIC NOTATION

— the strings of underlined lower characters represent terminals,

— the strings of upper case characters represent non-terminals

— {A} n, * if n = 0 => the symbol A is optional

if n ≠ 0 => 1 or many times the symbol A

* => means many times

V.1.1.1 - SYNTACTIC STRUCTURE

syntax : (syntax: ({OBJECT} 1, *)

Where: OBJECT :: string-of-characters

EXAMPLE :

(syntax : (sentence word syllable phoneme frame))

(syntax : (sentence marker))

This example describes a syntactic tree where the root (ancestor) is sentence. The descendants of the root are either word nodes or marker nodes. Each word node can be broken down into smaller descendants, for example syllables, etc...

This syntax permits the user to define the different structures required for his application.

V.1.1.2 - DESCRIPTIONS

syntax : (description : OBJECT {ATTRIBUT} 0, *)

Where ATTRIBUT :: string-of-characters.

EXAMPLES:

(description : word (number-of-syllables type))

This model describes in terms of attributes each object declared in the syntactic structures. In the above example, the object "word" is characterized by the two attributes "number-of-syllables" and "type" (the type of a word may be lexical, grammatical, etc...). The system uses these models which define each node and its attributes to generate the syntactic tree from a written text. The attributes of the objects are instantiated in the second phase when rules are applied.

V.1.1.3 - DEFINITIONS

syntax : (definition : OBJECT
DOMAIN
REWRITING-RULES)

Where : DOMAIN : define the set of values of the object

REWRITING-RULES: these rules permit the input sentence to be structured in accordance with the syntactic pattern described by the user.

EXAMPLE:

In figure 7, the domain of the object marker is:

(belong to (" " "$" "=" "."))

The rewrite rules are expressed in an adequate formalism. The following rules are used to structure each word into syllables (Fig. 5).

EXAMPLE:

[consonant consonant vowel consonant vowel] →

[consonant consonant vowel) (consonant vowel]

[consonant vowel consonant vowel] →

[consonant vowel) (consonant vowel]

[consonant vowel consonant end} →

[consonant vowel consonant]

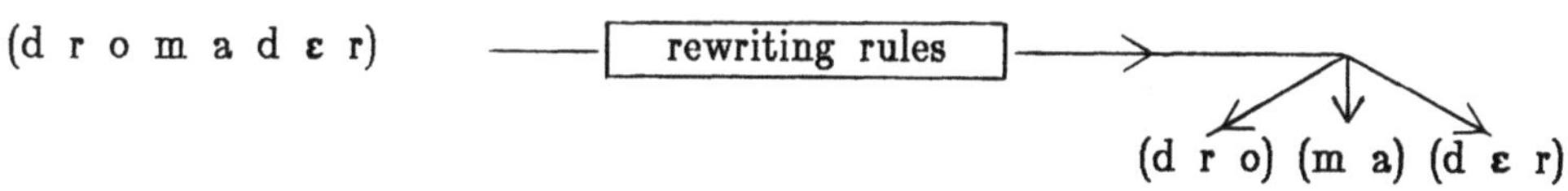

Fig. 5: Results once the rewrite-rules above are applied

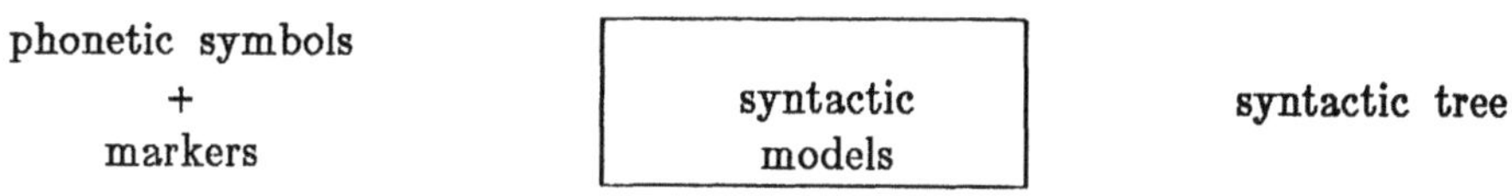

Fig. 6: Syntactic models interpretation

As shown in fig. 7, the string of symbols placed at the first level of the tree represents the instance of the object "sentence". The system produces the descendants of the root derived from the object "sentence" and information obtained from syntactic models. The second level is composed of:

— objects of type "word": (l ə), (d r o m a d ɛ r), (b w a), (d ə) and (l o)

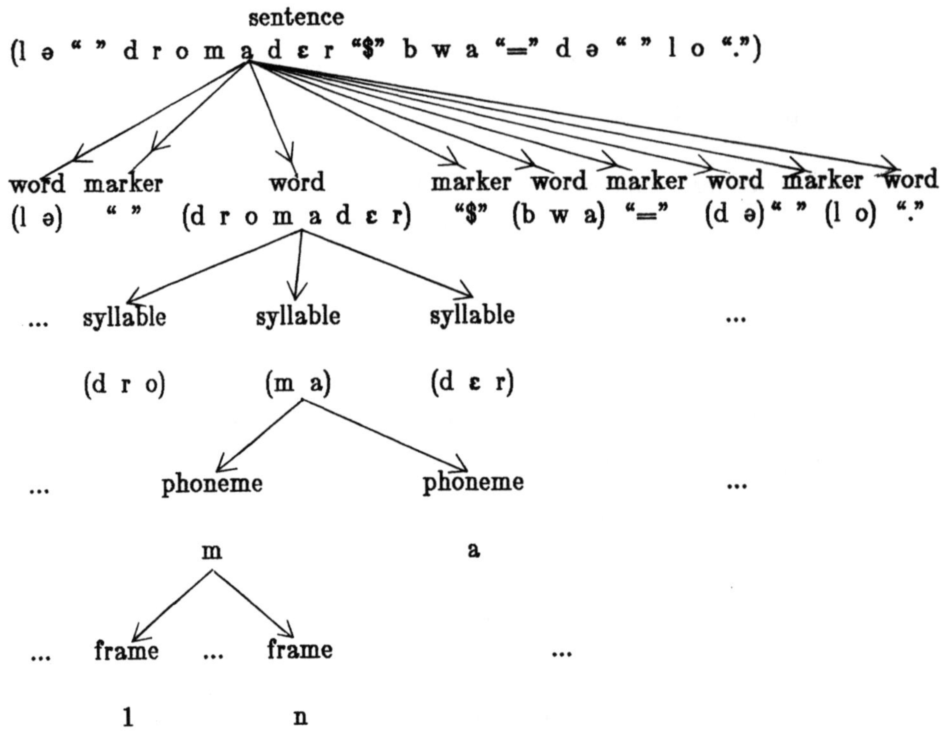

Fig. 7: The generated syntactic tree once syntactic models are performed the input of the interpreter system is:
(l ə " " d r o m a d ɛ r "$" b w a "=" d ə " " l o ".")

— objects of type "marker" : " ", "$", "=" and "."

Once objects of the second level are generated, the system performs rules to decompose each instance of word into syllables. In this example, "(d r o m a d ɛ r)" is composed of three syllables with their respective values "(d r o)", "(m a)" and (d ɛ r). The same process is repeated at each level until the syntactic tree is completed. The group of objects obtained constitute working data base to which prosodic rules can be applied.

V.1.1.4 - THE DICTIONARIES

The dictionary is a store of knowledge base which consists of the specific application data (the dictionary of diphones or phonemes, the phoneme features, etc...). The acquisition of this knowledge can be achieved by an adapted programming tool.

V.1.2 - PROSODIC RULES

As we have already indicated, all vocal synthesis systems include a prosodic module. In the SYNTHEX system this part is referred to as "prosodic rules". These rules take into account the statements of the syntactic models.

syntax:

```
    (problem : IDENTIFIER
        {if
            {- PREMISE }n, *
        then} *
            {- ACTION }n, *)
```

Where :

IDENTIFIER :: string of characters which identifies the problem.

PREMISE : a condition which has to be satisfied

ACTION : an action to be carried out.

semantic:

case 1: the premises are not omitted

```
    (problem : toto
        if
            - p1
            - p2
        then
```

- al

- a2)

the associated semantic is :

<u>if</u> (p1 <u>and</u> p2) <u>then</u> (a1 <u>and then</u> a2)

<u>case 2:</u> the premises are omitted

(<u>problem</u> : toto

- a1

- a2)

The associated semantic is :

<u>do</u> a1 <u>and then</u> a2.

SYNTHEX differs from other similar experiment systems in this domain in that it permits the speech synthesis expert to use his natural language when formalizing a problem. In fact, in the prosodic rules, the "PREMISES" and "ACTIONS" are expressed in a pseudo-natural language, i.e. in the form of sentences using a restricted french grammar (sub-grammar) augmented by variables. We know, based on the research done by several teams on the comprehension of natural languages [13, 10], that problems presented by "anaphoras" and pronominal reference are particularly difficult to carry out. The notion of variable allows such difficulties to be solved elegantly and simply without making speech synthesis expert's task more difficult. In a written text, a variable is a string of characters preceded by the special character "*". The "prosodic rules" component is organized as a set of knowledge bases, each one regrouping different problems. Each problem regroups a set of rules.

<u>EXAMPLE</u>:

exp-base is the name of the knowledge base in the figure below.

This knowledge base (fig. 8) includes four problems : number-of-syllables, first-consonant-duration, initial-duration and pause. Each of the first problems contains one related rule while the fourth one contains two rules.

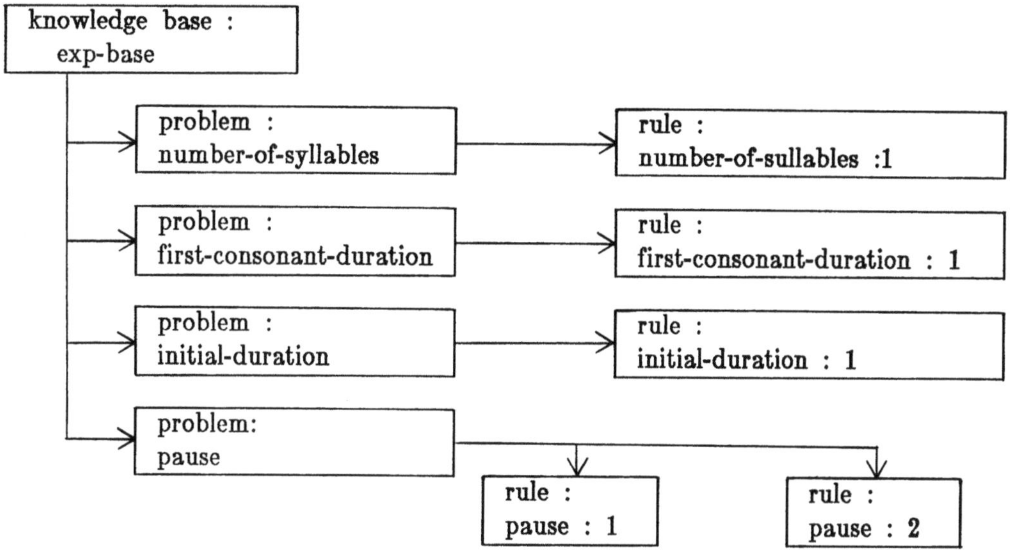

Fig. 8 Example of knowledge base

According to the external formalism, the first rule of the knowledge-base is described below:

(problem : number-of-syllables

if

- there exists a word *x

then

- count in *1 the number of phonemes whose instances are vowels
- attribute to the number-of-syllables of the word *x the value of the variable *1)

Remarks :

*x is a variable used to reference the object typed "word",

*1 is another variable which contains intermediate results,

premise :

if there exists a word in the syntactic tree

actions :

first action : count in the variable *1 the number of phonemes whose instances are vowels

section action : gives to the attribute "number-of-syllables" of the word above the value of the variable *1.

V.1.3 - EXAMPLES

For reasons of simplicity, it is assumed the statement below is true:

(description : phoneme (instance))

(description : frame (duration))

(description : marker (instance duration))

Example : 1

(problem : initial-duration

if

- there exists a word *m

then

- attributes to the duration of all frames of the word *m the value 26 multiplied by 0.85).

Remark

The rule gives to the attribute "duration" of all phoneme frames of each sentence's word the value 26 multiplied by 0.85.

Example : 2

(problem : first-consonant-duration

if

- the instance of the first phoneme *p1 of a word *w is consonant
- the instance of adjacent right phoneme *p2 of the phoneme *p1
  in the word *w is vowel.

Then

- print ("rule : frame's durations of the first phoneme")
- multiply the duration of all frames of the phoneme *pl by the value 1.15
- display the instance of the phoneme *pl
- display the duration of all frames of the phoneme *pl).

Remarks

If the first phoneme of a word possesses the characteristic "consonant" and if its immediate successor in the same word has the characteristics "vowel", then the following actions can be applied successively. First print the parameter text of the primitive "print", then multiply by 1.15 the value of the attribute "duration" of all phoneme frames.

Example : 3

(problem : pause

if

- the instance of a marker *x belongs to the list ("*" "+" "&")

then

- attribute to the pause of the marker *x the value 65).

(problem : pause
if
- the instance of a marker *x belongs to the list ("." "?" "!").

then
- attribute to the pause of the marker *x the value 400)

Remarks

The problem "pause" contains the two rules : pause : 1 and pause : 2 (see fig. 8). The system tries all the problem rules scucessively, except those frozen dynamically by commands.

first rule : if the value of a marker belongs to the list ("*" *+" "&"), then the associated pause is 65 ms.

second rule : if the value of a marker belongs to the list ("." "?" "!"), then the associated pause is 400 ms.

EXAMPLE 4 :

(problem : duration-and-pause
- execute initial-duration
- execute first-consonant-duration
- execute pause).

Remarks

This rule is not a prosodic rule, but is used to define the order in which the prosodic rules are applied, i.e. first the rules concerning initial-duration, next those concerning the first-consonant-duration and lastly those concerning pause. This approach allows several problems to be regrouped under the same name.

V.2 - INTERNAL FORMALISM

The internal formalism is the formalism of Horn clauses (PROLOG clause). The PROLOG language [18] is used as a knowledge representation language and also as a programming language to perform the translation of external formalism into the internal formalism.

In fact the language used is LISLOG [5, 6] which integrates the two programming languages LISP and PROLOG.

The internal formalism is directly executable. The LISLOG interpreter plays the role of the inference engine of the system.

VI SPEECH SYNTHESIS : USER DOMAINS

Fig. 9 The user domain

N.B. : A speech synthesis expert can be a user.

We have shown that experts in speech synthesis express their knowledge in a pseudo-natural language, and the system generates the corresponding internal forms (HORN clauses).

As soon as the SYNTHEX system has gathered enough expertise, one can use the system to synthesize sentences (i.e. check rules, evaluate results obtained, etc...).

Example : By applying the rule which counts the number of syllables in each word, the attribute "number-of-syllables" of each word is given an appropriate value.

word : 1	number-of-syllables : 1
word : 2	number-of-syllables : 3
word : 3	number-of-syllables : 1
word : 4	number-of-syllables : 1
word : 5	number-of-syllables : 1

SYNTHEX provides a number of facilities for the development of synthesis rules. SYNTHEX's editor is interactive. The form of all commands is simplified.

Syntactic patterns and prosodic rules are structured in knowledge bases. The user can define, store, edit, execute and then (possibly) improve the rule.

The user can also change by commands the ordering of the rules to be applied. The system possesses control commands which permits dynamically to freeze, activate and execute rules.

SYNTHEX's debugger facilitates the check of rules; it permits to display the text of the rule with the instances of the variables of applied rules.

Example : assume that we want to apply the "pause" rules to the sentence (fig. 7) and we specify by command to debug the pause : 2 rule, the debugger display the following text :

(problem : pause : 2

if

- the instance of a marker 5 belongs to the list ("." "?" "!")

then

attribute to the pause of the marker 5 the value 400).

VII CONCLUSION

The main aims of the development of the SYNTHEX system are : to give a method for formalizing the knowledge in the speech synthesis domain (prosody of vocal synthesis) and to study methods for improving this knowledge.

The system is written entirely in LISLOG which allows us to use logic programming in different forms.

The SYNTHEX system is being experimented on. Different extensions are being studied in order to explain the rules and the control mechanisms.

The translation of the written rule to the internal formalism takes about five seconds of run time (the run time for the rule in example V.1.3 is about 2 seconds on a DPS/8 machine) for each rule. The run time of each applied rule is about one second.

SYNTHEX was designed on the multics system.

ACKNOWLEDGEMENTS

The authors thank M. Dincbas, S. Bourgault, J. P. Le Pape and M. Guyomard for helpful discussions.

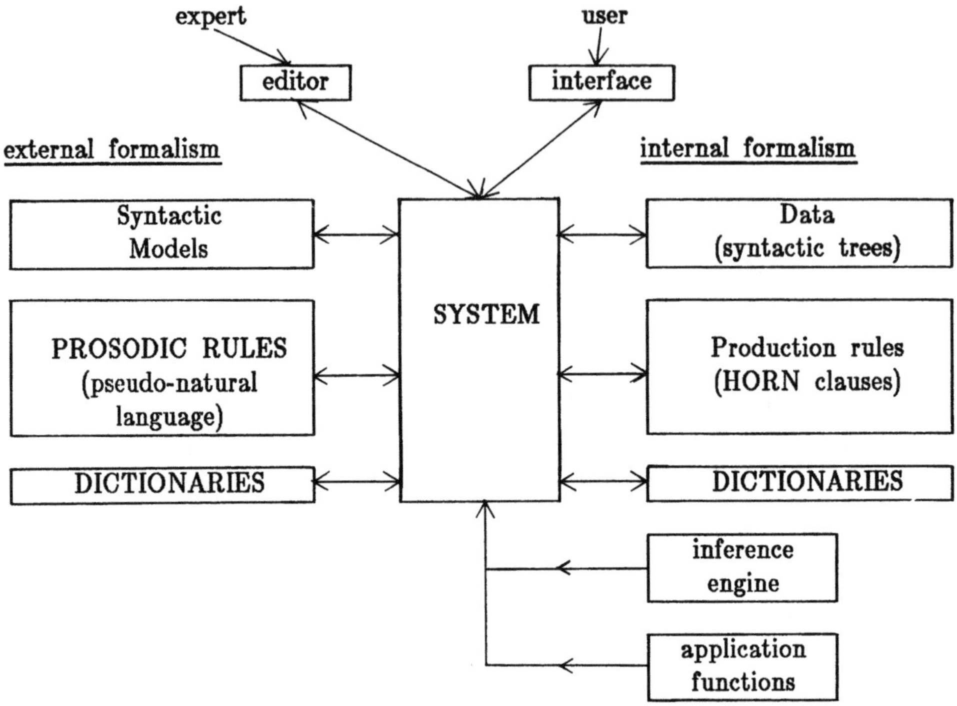

Figure 10: The complete architecture of the system SYNTHEX

REFERENCES

1. A. Aggoun, "A computer language adapted to the programming of prosodic rules". Arabic school on science and technology, Applied Arabic linguistics and signal and information processing. September 26 - October 1983, p. 208 à 210, RABAT (Maroc).
2. A. Aggoun, S. Bourgault, M. Guyomard, "SYNTHEX: un système expert pour la synthèse vocale à partir du texte". Séminaire sur la programmation en logique. Avril 1984, Plestin-les-Greves, France.
3. M. Barioglio, "Progetto di un compilatore per un linguaggio diserittiro di regole prosodicke struttura del sistema di sintesi". Thèse soutenue à l'Université de Turin, 1980.
4. A. Bonnet, "Applications de l'intelligence artificielle : les systèmes experts". Rairo Informatique/Computer Science, Vol. 15, no. 4, 1981, p. 325 à 341.
5. S. Bourgault, M. Dincbas, J. P. Le Pape, "Manuel Lislog". Note Technique NT/LAA/SLC/159, Janvier 1984, CNET LANNION, France.
6. S. Bourgault, M. Dincbas, D. Feuerstein, J. P. Le Pape, "LISLOG: l'an II", Séminaire sur la programmation en logique, PERROS-GUIREC, 22-23 mars 1983, France.
7. C. P. Browman, "Rules for demisyllabic synthesis using lingua, a language interpreter", Proc. 1980, conf. ASSP, p. 561-564.
8. R. Carlson, B. Granstrom, S. Hunnicutt, "A multi-language text-to-speech-module", Proc. 1980, conf. ASSP, p. 1604-1607.
9. R. Carre, J. P. Haton, J. S. Lienard, "Reconnaissance et synthèse de la parole, état de la recherche et du développement, IRIA - 1979.
10. A. Colmerauer, "Un sous-ensemble intéressant du Français", RAIRO Informatique, Theoretical Informatics, Vol. 13, No. 4, 1979, p. 309 à 336.
11. R. Descout, "Les techniques de synthèse de la parole, Note Technique NT/LAA/TSS/RCP, avril 1982, CNET LANNION - France.
12. M. Divay, M. Guyomard, "Conception et réalisation sur ordinateur d'un programme de transcription graphemo-phonétique du Français", Thèse troisième cycle, Université de Rennes, avril 1977.
13. P. Saint-Dizier, "Contribution à la transformation des langues naturelles en logique", Thèse troisième cycle 1983, Université de Rennes.
14. F. Emerard, "Synthèse par diphones et traitement de la prosodie", Thèse troisième cycle, Université de Grenoble, mars 1977.
15. M. Gilloux, F. Hautin, C. Tarridec, A. Vailly, D. Gillet, G. Mercier, "Note avant-projet d'un Système Expert en Reconnaissance Acoustico-phonétique : SERAC", Note Technique NT/LAA/SLC/119, NT/LAA/SLC/151, janvier 1983, CNET LANNION, France.
16. S. Hertz, "From text to speech with S.R.S.", J.A.S.A. 72(4), October 1982.
17. D. Kayser, "Examen de diverses méthodes utilisées en représentation des connaissances", Quatrième congrès de reconnaissance des formes et intelligence artificielle, 25-27 janvier 1984, Paris, p. 115 à 144.

18. R. Kowalski, "Predicate logic as programming language", Proceeding IFIP 74.
19. J. L. Lauriere, "Les systèmes experts, représentation et utilisation des connaissances, T.S.I. no. 1, 1982, p. 25-42, T.S.I. no. 2, 1982, p. 109-133.
20. P. Martin, "Phonetic realisations of prosodic contours in french", Speech Communication, Vol. 1, no. 34, December 1982.
21. S. Pinson, "Représentation des connaissances dans les systèmes experts", Rairo Informatique/Computer Science, Vol. 15, No. 4, 1981, p. 343-367.
22. S. Sandri, E. Vivalda, "A formal language for the generation of prosodic rules", The fourth F.A.S.E. symposium 81, Venezia, Italy.
23. M. Stella, "Synthèse de parole", l'Echo des Recherches No. 15, 1er trimestre, p. 21-32, 1984.
24. J. Vaissière, "The search for language-independent prosodic features", A paper presented at the first international congress on the perception of speech, No. 7-20, December 1980, Florence, Italy.

SYNTEX - UNRESTRICTED CONVERSION OF TEXT TO SPEECH FOR GERMAN

Wolfgang Kulas
Hans-Wilhelm Rühl
Ruhr-Universität Bochum
Lehrstuhl für Allgemeine Elektrotechnik und Akustik
Federal Republic of Germany

ABSTRACT

This paper is intended to give an overview over the SYNTEX system, a text-to-speech software for the German language designated to control phoneme synthesizers. Descriptions of the algorithms used for word structure analysis, letter-to-sound conversion, computing of word accent, sentence parsing, and generating an intonation contour are given. The software runs on a small microprocessor system much faster than real-time.

GENERAL DESCRIPTION

The general structure of SYNTEX is depicted in fig. 1. It is a construction of modules for text preprocessing, for processing at word level, for sentence level analysis and for control of prosodics and coarticulations. It is designed to drive phoneme or allophone based synthesizers.

The text preprocessing module converts unrestricted German text into a limited set of characters containing only upper case letters and some word boundary markers like blanks, commas, periods, etc. This means for example

NATO ASI Series, Vol. F16
New Systems and Architectures for Automatic Speech
Recognition and Synthesis. Edited by R. De Mori and C. Y. Suen

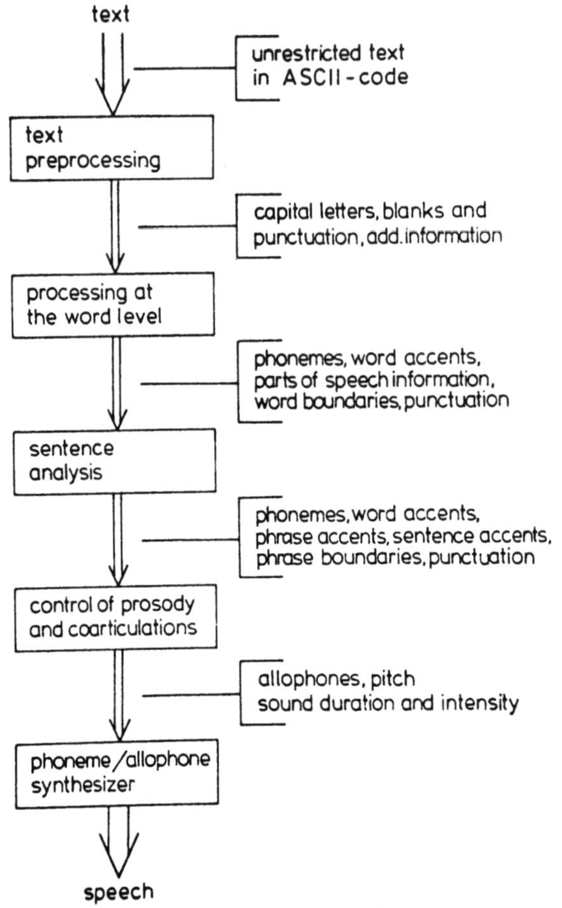

Fig. 1: The concept of the SYNTEX text-to-speech software

that strings of digits used to code integer, decimal or ordinal numbers, date, time, year or price are "spelled out" as strings of letter characters in the appropriate format. Input may be in upper case or lower case only, like a usual computer dialogue, or preferably in standard German orthography with initial capital letters for nouns and for the beginning of a sentence, lower case letters elsewhere. Standard orthography with nouns marked by capitals is useful for sentence analysis.

The input may be in standard ASCII code or in the German ASCII character set, which means that the German "Umlaute" 'Ä' , 'Ö', 'Ü' and the character 'ß' may be either represented as national ASCII characters or in standard ASCII as 'AE', 'OE', 'UE' and 'SS'. The set of characters may be selected statically by escape sequences as well as dynamically by software. In the dynamic mode rules based on adjacent characters are used to determine the meaning of characters having different meanings in both character sets.

Word level processing includes an analysis of word structure, a letter-to-sound algorithm and a generation of word accent patterns. As the German language tends to form compound words, the word structure analysis is based on an algorithm for finding morpheme boundaries by rules which employ a recognition of affixes. As the pronunciation of German words is based on a morpheme decomposition, 72 rather simple rules are sufficient to convert letters to phonemes. Word accent is computed by rules as well as by data included in the affix dictionaries.

At the sentence level we have been concentrating on the generation of an FØ-contour by rule. The calculated intonation is a function of utterance length, sentence type and number of phrases within a sentence. To detect phrases, we use an incomplete sentence parsing, as time is limited for real-time text-to-speech conversion. Parsing is done in three steps: first by assigning valences to function words, then by combining words to groups with paying attention to valences and third by verifying these phrases. The parser also determines the most significant word for each phrase and the most significant phrase of a sentence which is to carry the sentence accent. Having parsed a sentence in this way, each group is associated an FØ-contour which is similar to the hat-shaped patterns proposed by Cohen and t'Hart [7] to describe intonation.

ANALYSIS OF WORD STRUCTURE

German pronunciation rules are rather simple compared to English ones, provided that the rules can be expresssed at the morpheme level. Unfortunately, parsing words into morphemes is a rather difficult task, as German tends to form compounds more frequently than English. Expressions written in English as separate words (e.g. "word structure") are written as one word ("Wortstruktur") in German. Compounds acccount only for about 4% of the content words in running text, but most of the less frequent words are compounds, and they make up more than 50% of the words in a standard dictionary. Hence, for a low error rate, an analysis of the word structure is absolutely necessary.

Simple words containing one root can be decomposed by stripping off affixes only. But a compound processed by this affix detection remains as an unsolved cluster that starts and ends with roots, and perhaps contains affixes and further roots between the bracketing roots. Morpheme based pronunciation rules applied to such a cluster of morphemes will produce a lot of errors.

To perform a word structure analysis including a root recognition, algorithms based on a complete grammar and a large morpheme dictionary have been used, e.g. by Allen [1,2] for American English. This proceeding results in complex and slow programs with an extensive need for memory. For this reason we developed a decomposition algorithm which is not based on the recognition of all morphemes but on the recognition of affixes. It is used together with an algorithm called cluster analysis which is able to find boundaries between morphemes.

CLUSTER ANALYSIS

This algorithm called cluster analysis is based on the findings of W. Kästner [3], who decomposed all German morphemes into basic clusters. Basic clusters are strings of adjacent vowels or consonants. The morpheme "Flasche" for example decomposes into fl — initial basic consonant cluster

a — medial basic vowel cluster

sch — medial basic consonant cluster

e — final basic vowel cluster.

Kästner found that only 52 different basic initial consonant clusters and 120 basic final or medial consonant clusters are used to form German morphemes and that only few of the initial consonant clusters may be used in medial or final positions. He also found some twenty vowel clusters in different positions but these are not important for word analysis because most of the German roots have consonant clusters in initial and final position. Hence most of the morpheme boundaries fall between consonants.

In order to find morpheme boundaries within a word the cluster analysis tries to find medial clusters that are no basic ones. In the word "Weinflasche" for example, this test would find the cluster "nfl". Clusters like "nfl" are called boundary areas, because there has to be a morpheme boundary within the area of this cluster. In order to determine the exact position of the boundary, all possibilities are evaluated to split the cluster into basic initial and final clusters. "nfl" is neither an initial nor a final basic consonant cluster, hence boundaries before or after "nfl" are impossible. But "n-fl" and "nf-l" both split the medial cluster into basic clusters. In many cases, only one boundary leads to a valid basic cluster, which is a clear result and causes the cluster analysis to stop. But with several possible boundaries as in the example "Weinflasche", additional rules have to be employed for a decision.

In cases where there is more than one valid boundary, there can be no decision about the correct boundary without further knowledge and context-dependent rules. But even without knowledge of the context, a decision can be taken which boundary will produce least errors by examining the frequencies of the basic clusters. In our example, the basic clusters "n" and "l" have a very high frequency in German morphemes, "fl" is rather frequent and "nf" occurs seldom. Therefore a boundary between "n" and "fl" would be correct in more cases than a boundary between "nf" and "l". This relationship can be represented by attaching a number to each basic cluster representing a logarithmic frequency of occurrence. To get the most plausible boundary only the logarithmic frequencies of the resultant basic clusters have to be added for each possible boundary, and the boundary with the highest result will be selected. For our example, this decision algorithm marks a correct boundary between "Wein" and "Flasche".

The cluster analysis is able to find most boundaries between roots, due to the fact that most German roots begin and end with consonant clusters. For this reason, about 90% of the boundaries between roots are detected. Less than one third of the undectected boundaries cause pronunciation errors that reduce intellegibility. A main accent on a wrong syllable occurs very seldom, a mismatched boundary usually only causes a missing secondary accent. The typical pronunciation error that has to be expected when applying morpheme based letter-to-sound rules to words is a wrong vowel length for vowels preceding a final consonant cluster or a morpheme boundary. This error is very rare when cluster analysis is used.

THE ARCHITECTURE OF THE WORD STRUCTURE ANALYSIS BASED ON CLUSTER ANALYSIS

Cluster analysis is well suited to find morpheme boundaries between consonants. But a lot of German affixes either start or end with a vowel cluster, hence many boundaries adjacent to affixes are not detected. This would be a severe problem if there were no other ways of finding the missing boundaries. But not every boundary needs to be marked. The affix recognition starts at the beginning and at the end of a word recursively looking for the longest affix. It is also capable of starting at the boundaries detected by the cluster analysis looking to the left and the right for the longest affix. So all we need is one detected boundary within or adjacent to an affix cluster embedded between roots, and every affix within this cluster can be recognized. Examining every possible

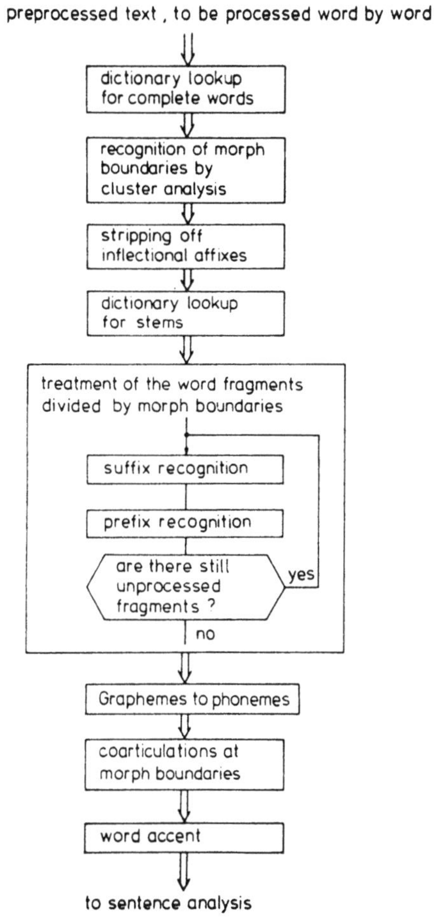

Fig. 2 Processing at the word level

combination of affixes between roots in the expressions

root1 — 1 or more suffixes — root2

root1 — 1 or more prefixes — root2

root1 — 1 or more suffixes — 1 or more prefixes — root2

we found that in the worst cases 'root1 — prefix — root2' the chance of detecting at least one boundary is 89%, in every other case the chance is more than 90%, which is sufficient for our purposes.

Hence, the general proceeding of word structure analysis is:

— Mark morpheme boundaries by cluster analysis
— Strip off inflectional affixes appearing only at the end of the word.
— Strip off prefixes at the beginning of the word and suffixes at the end of the word.
— Look for morpheme boundaries marked by the cluster analysis. If you find one, look for prefixes and suffixes to the right and to the left of the boundary.

This procedure is depicted in fig. 2. The chances of finding every affix within a word by using this procedure are very high. For this reason, every fragment not matched by affix recognition and not split by morpheme boundaries can be treated as a root.

AFFIX RECOGNITION

In a word decomposition algorithm based on a morpheme dictionary, the usual way of getting the correct decomposition of a word is to evaluate every possible combination of morphemes and then to score which combination fits best [2]. In most cases, there will be just one sequence of morphemes that matches the whole word and the algorithm to resolve ambiguities will be needed only in exceptional cases.

In our word structure analysis the problem of how to match morphemes within a word is different: we do not have all the "chips" to completely solve the "puzzle", nevertheless the few "chips" (= affixes) we have should be placed correctly. Attempts to match affixes are supported by word and morpheme boundaries and the beginnings and endings of recognized affixes that serve as points of departure for the matching process. But in each word there has to be at least one gap (= root) that cannot be verified by looking it up in a dictionary nor can it be decided without further rules whether the affixes to the right and to the left of a gap are correct. For this reason when recognizing affixes, the affix and the remaining word fragment have to fulfill some conditions for the recognition to be correct.

If the remaining word fragment is considered to be a root, it has to fulfill some general conditions: it should consist at least of one consonant cluster and one vowel cluster; it should at least consist of three letters (roots with only two letters are very rare), and it should start with a basic initial cluster and end with a basic final cluster. These general rules sometimes prevent incorrect matches, but in many special cases they still allow the recognition of parts of a root as an affix.

Hence special rules have been introduced for affixes to be recognized. These rules define an environment at the boundaries of the affixes, and by controlling the environment of the actual match it can be decided whether an affix is recognized or not. This leads to an organization of the affix recognition in the following way.

— Start at a marked boundary and look for the longest affix.
— When a character string is found that is a potential affix, apply the environmental rules in order to verify the affix.
— If the affix is verified, mark the resultant boundary and return to the first step.
— If the affix is not verified, look for shorter matches.
— If a shorter match is found, return to the second step, else finish the search.

The verificiation rules which examine the environment are different for every affix, and they are enclosed in the dictionary together with the affix they belong to and additional information. The rules have the general form:

(action) (environment data)

where (action) describes, what to do with the following environment data and how the results of the action have to be interpreted. A typical rule e.g. is

Comp-R-N, ber, kul, ren, rin

which is used for the prefix 'her' to reject the recognition of an affix in the words "Herberge", "Herkules", "Herren" and "Herrin". The first part of the action describes the class of instruction, which in our example is a 'compare'-instruction. The next letter 'R' tells the instruction to search at the 'R'ight boundary, and the last letter 'N' specifies that if a match is found the string to be verified is 'N'ot an affix. Other instructions examine the morpheme class of adjacent morphemes and test whether the following inflectional affixes contain a vowel or similar things.

The number of rules to verify an affix is somehow dependent on the string length of the affix. While long affixes are rather unambiguous and need only few rules, affixes consisting of two or three characters often correspond to parts of a root, and therefore they need more rules to be verified. Our current affix dictionaries are based on some two thousand frequent words including 32 prefixes and 57 suffixes. The dictionaries occupy about 2 kbyte. An improved version based on a German standard dictionary will have several hundred entries and is in progress.

As the analysis of word structure is partially based on statistical rules, it has to be equipped with dictionaries for exceptions that include words which would cause pronuncation errors if they were decomposed and pronounced according to the rules. Currently, we use two dictionaries for exceptions, one for entire words and the second one for stems, i.e. words with their inflectional suffixes stripped off. Both lists currently contain only function words used for sentence analysis and a few very frequent exceptions.

Word structure analysis based on cluster analysis is insufficient as a linguistic tool for word decomposition, but it is a fast and very effective tool for purposes of speech synthesis. No root lexicon is needed, only a list of the basic clusters and an affix dictionary. Decomposition is done in far less time than is used to pronounce the word, and the analysis written in assembler needs only 3 kbytes of memory. A version written in C is in progress.

LETTER-TO-SOUND RULES AND WORD ACCENTS

Due to the preceding word structure analysis, well known letter-to-sound rules may be used. We chose a conversion of letters to sounds in two steps. This means for vowels, that in the first step only a vowel quality is computed while in the second step the same rules are applied to all vowels to determine whether the vowel is long or short. 23 rules are needed for the first step and 4 rules for the second step. For consonants, most part of the conversion is done in the first step with 36 rules, while in the second step 9 rules govern the devoicing of voiced fricatives and plosives, the selection of two 'r'-variants and the change of 'n' to 'ng'. These 72 rules have proved to be sufficient for a conversion based on morphemes.

The generation of word accent patterns is a three stage process. At first, with the aid of information provided by affix dictionaries and word structure, it is decided which affixes can carry an accent. Then for each root and its adjoined affixes, accent patterns are generated. The last step is to combine these accent patterns in order to form a word accent pattern for compound words.

While there are few and simple rules to perform the second and the last step, a lot of computation is needed in the first stage to get the accent for affixes. The "accentability" of affixes depends on the order of affixes within a word as well as on context rules. Frequently, German affixes in some words may carry the main accent and in other words they may have no accent at all. To resolve such ambiguities, similar rules as for the affix verification are being used.

These rules have the same limitations as the rules for affix verification: currently they are based on several thousand words only, but they will be improved to match a complete standard dictionary.

SENTENCE ANALYSIS

In the SYNTEX system, the syntactical analysis of a sentence is the presupposition for generating its prosody. When the syntactical analysis has identified the parts of the sentence, its constituents can be determined. On the basis of these constituents or phrases, the prosodic features of the spoken utterance are calculated. We decided to use only syntax for prosody, because there are considerable difficulties in taking content and context into account. The two main reasons for this are, that it is not yet possible to describe and detect semantic relations under unrestricted text conditions, and that too much processing time would be required to allow real-time text-to-speech conversion.

Earlier research on German syntax analysis with unrestricted text [4] demonstrated processing intervals of several minutes on a mainframe for the complete parsing of a single main clause. Most of the time was spent determining the parts of speech of content words and detecting the correct syntactical relations between the constituents of a sentence. As processing time of that order of magnitude is not acceptable for real-time applications, we decided to do without a complete syntax analysis. We gained evident savings in processing time, because we need not detect the part of speech for every word of the sentence, and because detecting one possible syntactical structure for a sentence is sufficient.

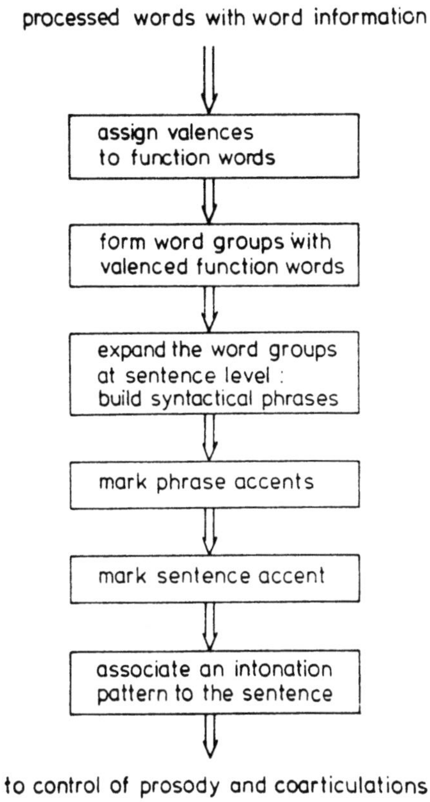

Fig. 3 Sentence analysis

INCOMPLETE SENTENCE PARSING

In written German only 512 words form about 60% of normal orthographic text [5]. Most of these words are function words to which we assign a valence. Valences mark the tendency of a word to be followed by certain parts of speech. With the help of function words and their valences sentences are decomposed into word groups (see fig. 3), by combining a function word and, dependent on the specified valence, some of the following unclassified words. There are 7 types of valences: no valence, and valences over 1, 2 or 3 words, which may be extended in a further step by adding trailing unclassified words to the valence group. These word groups correspond quite well to the beginning of German nominal phrases.

The problem arising with function words, which can carry either no valence or one or more valences, was solved by always assigning them no valence. Therefore, in order to determine the final length of a nominal phrase, an expansion of the word groups at sentence level is necessary. Looking at a whole sentence, sentence level rules are used to guess how far a word group can be expanded, provided that the group is marked with an extendable valence. The definition of the sentence level rules had to be done carefully, as they depend very much on the sort of text which is being processed. We determined our rules on the basis of German newspaper texts and found them to fit quite well for any kind of text.

Up to this point the sentence has been decomposed into a sequence of marked noun groups with unclassified words between them. In forming groups with these unknown words too, we define the groups marked so far to be the syntactically relevant phrases of the sentence.

MARKING ACCENTS ON PHRASE AND SENTENCE LEVEL

In German nominal phrases, there is a tendency to place the most important word of the phrase, which usually carries an accent, at the end. The nominal phrases of a sentence are detected by valence assignment to function words. So in every phrase detected with the help of valences the rightmost unclassified word, which is nearly always a contend word, is assigned a phrase accent.

The sentence accent can only be carried by a phrase which already has a phrase accent. If there is only one phrase accent, it automatically will be the sentence accent. If there are two phrase accents, the last phrase will get the sentence accent. If there are more than two phrase accents, the sentence accent is calculated on the basis of the rules given by J. Pheby [6], which rely on regularities in the sequence of German nominal phrases. For example, if there are two nominal phrases, one in the dative and the other in the accusative, the accusative phrase gets the sentence accent. The cases can be determined by analysing the function words and the word suffixes.

PROSODICS

At the prosodic level (see fig. 4) our main work concentrated on generating an FØ-contour by rule for a sentence. Therefore only simple timing rules like the shortening of the duration of function words are implemented at the moment. For the future, modules are planned, that control the speech rhythm depending on the speech rate and the number of phrases within a sentence. These modules will also consider coarticulations on the phrase and sentence level.

So at the moment, phoneme duration is determined by table only by considering the word structure, which means that sound lengthening occurs if there is a word accent. As function words carry no accent in the SYNTEX system, they are always shortened to a minimum length. This can be interpreted as a rhythmic component on phrase level which occurs in the system's output.

GENERATION OF AN FØ-CONTOUR

For the generation of an FØ-contour, we adapted a modified form of the hat-shaped pattern strategy proposed by Cohen and t'Hart [7]. For each utterance we calculate FØ by using a logarithmic scale which is measured in Cent (doubling FØ = 1200 Cent). The reference point for this scale is the lowest fundamental frequency normally produced in speech (55 Hz). This enables us to describe FØ-values that can be produced by the phoneme synthesizer.

SETTING THE BASELINE

In almost any language, there is a gradual fall of FØ in the course of an utterance. This is often explained by the decreasing air pressure in a speaker's lung which results in a diminishing of vocal cord tension [8]. We take account of this physiological effect by calculating an FØ-baseline which falls gradually with 200 cents per second in the first 1.5 seconds of an utterance and after that with 50 cents per second. A reduction of the FØ-fall in the second part of an utterance is necessary to prevent a too low FØ-value at the end of long utterances, that would affect the perception of the produced speech.

BUILDING FØ-PATTERNS

Like Cohen and t'Hart, we build the FØ-contour of an utterance by adding predefined FØ-movements to the baseline, in order to construct all perceptually relevant FØ-movements. We distinguish four FØ-movements:

— a steep fall with a fixed slope of 1200 cent per second and the FØ-change limited to 150 cent

— a steep rise with a fixed slope of 1200 cent per second and the FØ-change limited to 150 cent

— a gradual rise with variable slope and the FØ-change limited to 300 cent

— a gradual fall with variable slope and the FØ-change limited to 300 cent

Further on, there are two possible constant courses: one at baseline level ("low"), and the other 300 cent above the baseline ("high"). Frequently occuring sequences of FØ-movements may be combined to FØ-patterns. Among these FØ-patterns is the important "hat" shaped pattern" (low course - steep rise - high course - steep fall - low course).

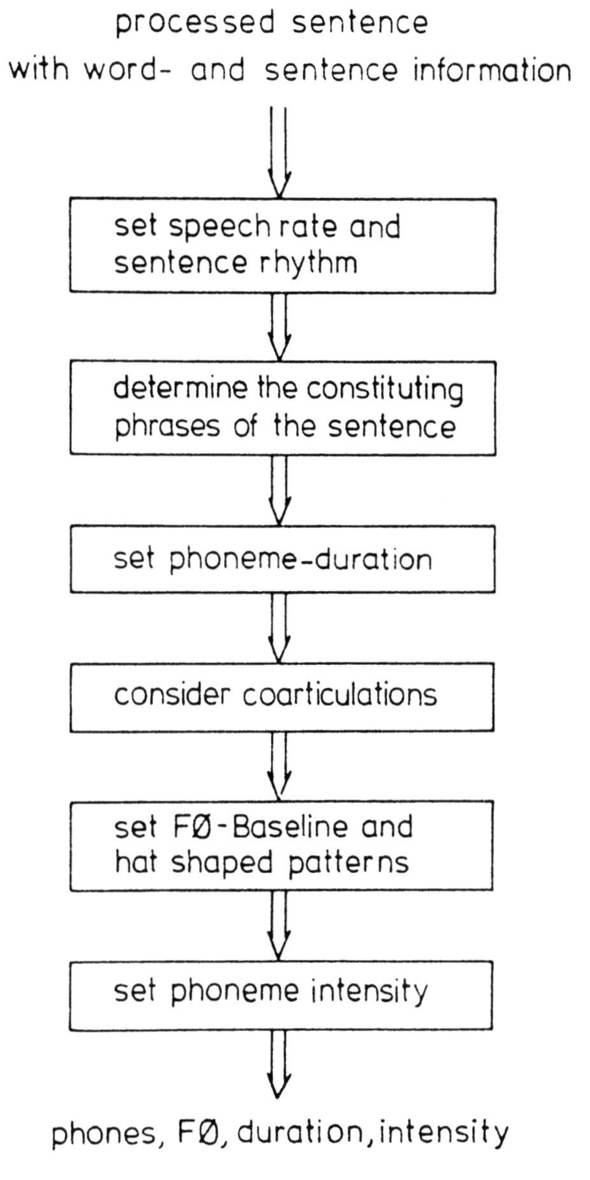

Fig. 4 Control of prosody and coarticulations

APPLICATION OF THE FØ-PATTERNS

Changing FØ at the end of a sentence is important for the perception of the characteristics of the sentence. The last phrase of an interrogative sentence is assigned the FØ-pattern "low course - steep rise - high course" and the preceding phrase has the pattern "high course - steep fall - low course". The two last phrases of a terminating sentence get the patterns "low course - steep rise - high course" and "high course - steep fall - low course". that means, that at the end of sentences there is always a hat shaped pattern either inverted or not. While developing the final patterns, we found that perception is increased by a slight modification of the patterns: a gradual fall or rise has to be added to the last syllable of a terminating or interrogative sentence respectively.

All preceding phrases of a sentence, if there are any, are handled by assigning the pattern "low course - steep rise - high course" without regard of the sentence characteristics. In the special case of a sentence consisting of only one phrase, this phrase is assigned the pattern "low course - steep rise -high course" for an interrogative sentence, or "high course - steep fall - low course' for a terminating sentence.

CURRENT STATUS

SYNTEX is a software system designed for microprocessors. Most routines have been written in assembler and are running on the Motorola 68XX microprocessors family. The software currently needs about 30 kbytes including 10 kbytes for dictionaries. Conversion of text to speech is done in less than 30% of the time used to pronounce the text. A 'C' version of the system is in progress.

While the development of algorithms at the word level is almost finished, the dictionaries are rather preliminary yet and have to be updated to match the whole German language. Analysis on sentence level and generation of intonation contours will be refined, too. Control of the prosodic features sound duration and intensity is planned.

Although up to date no high quality phoneme synthesizers for the German language are available, SYNTEX will not be expanded by the development of a phoneme synthesizer; only available phoneme synthesizers will be used to fill the gap between the phonemes and the spoken output. Up to now, driver programs for e.g. the Votrax VS6-G and the Votrax SC01 have been developed.

ACKNOWLEDGEMENTS

The authors wish to thank J. Blauert, who made this work possible at the Acoustics Laboratory of the Ruhr-University Bochum. We also thank M. Kugler, who helped us writing this paper, and the Deutsche Forschungsgemeinschaft (DFG), that supported essential parts of the research work.

REFERENCES

1. J. Allen, "Speech synthesis from unrestricted text" in J. L. Flanagan, L. R. Rabiner (eds.), *Speech Synthesis*, Dowden, Hutchinson and Ross Inc., Stroudsburg, pp. 416-428, 1973.
2. J. Allen, M. S. Hunnicutt and D. H. Klatt, MITalk-79, Notes for the M.I.T. summer course 6.69s, 1979.
3. W. Kästner, "Phonemisierung orthographischer Texte" im Deutschen, Helmut Buske Verlag, Hamburg, 1972.
4. Arbeitsgruppe MasA, "Zur maschinellen Syntaxanalyse", Forschungsberichte des Instituts für deutsche Sprache, Vol. 18.1, 18.2, 19, Mannheim, 1974.
5. H. Meier, *Sprachstatistik I/II*, Georg Olms Verlag, Hildesheim, 1964.
6. J. Pheby, "Phonologie: Intonation", in K. E. Heidolph et al, *Grundzüge einer Deutschen Grammatik* Akademie Verlag, Berlin, pp. 839-897.
7. A. Cohen and J. t'Hart, "Intonation by rule: a perceptual quest", J. of Phonetics, Vol. 1, pp. 309-327, 1973.
8. R. Collier, "Perceptual and linguistic tolerance in intonation", Int. Rev. Appl. Linguistics in Language Teaching, Vol. XIII/4, pp. 292-308, 1975.

CONCATENATION RULES FOR DEMISYLLABLE SPEECH SYNTHESIS

Helmut Dettweiler* and Wolfgang Hess
Lehrstuhl für Datenverarbeitung
Technische Universität München
Munich
Federal Republic of Germany

ABSTRACT

A system for speech synthesis by rule is described which uses demisyllables as phonetic units. The problem of concatenation is discussed in detail; the pertinent stage converts a string of phonetic symbols into a stream of speech parameter frames. For German about 1650 demisyllables are required to permit synthesizing a very large vocabulary. Synthesis is controlled by 18 rules which are used for splitting up the phonetic string into demisyllables, for selecting the demisyllables in such a way that the size of the inventory is minimized, and — last but not least — for concatenation. The quality and intelligibility of the synthetic signal is very good; in a subjective test the median word intelligibility dropped from 96.6% for a LPC vocoder to 92.1% for the demisyllable synthesis, and the difference in quality between the demisyllable synthesis and ordinary vocoded speech was judged very small.

---

* Dr. Dettweiler is now with BMW, Munich.

NATO ASI Series, Vol. F16
New Systems and Architectures for Automatic Speech
Recognition and Synthesis. Edited by R. De Mori and C.Y. Suen

1. PHONETIC UNITS AND THE PROBLEM OF CONCATENATION

Concatenation is a central problem in any system for speech synthesis by rule. It provides the link between the phonetic level, where the information to be synthesized is represented as a sequence of discrete phonetic and/or linguistic units, and the parametric level where the information is coded (Fig. 1).

In practice concatenation is controlled by a set of rules that act upon a data base of speech data. This data base may contain experimental data, such as a table of formant frequencies, but it may also consist of (parameterized) natural speech. The design of the concatenation component of a speech synthesis system is determined by a tradeoff between the number and complexity of the concatenation rules on the one hand and the size of the memory required for the data base on the other hand. The most important question in this respect is that of the phonetic units to be applied.

Viable phonetic units for speech synthesis are words, syllabic units, and phonemic units. Words as units for synthesis require a minimum of rules but a maximum of data memory; they are not realistic for synthesis of large or unlimited vocabularies. Phonemes, on the other hand, require a minimum of data memory since their number is limited to about 40, and their duration is rather short. It is well known, however, that phonemes cannot be simply concatenated; due to coarticulation effects, the information relevant for understanding speech is realized in the transitions between phonemes, and a great number of (language-dependent) concatenation rules are necessary to realize the transitions and to provide an acceptable quality and intelligibility. A lot of human work is thus required to establish and to test these rules (Allen, 1976; Klatt, 1980); nevertheless, the quality of the resulting speech is limited.

Considerable efforts have therefore been made towards designing speech synthesis systems that use larger phonetic units. In such systems many of the transitions and coarticulation effects are intrinsic to the stored data and need no longer be explicitly generated by rule. The number of concatenation rules necessary can thus be drastically reduced; this reduces the overall system

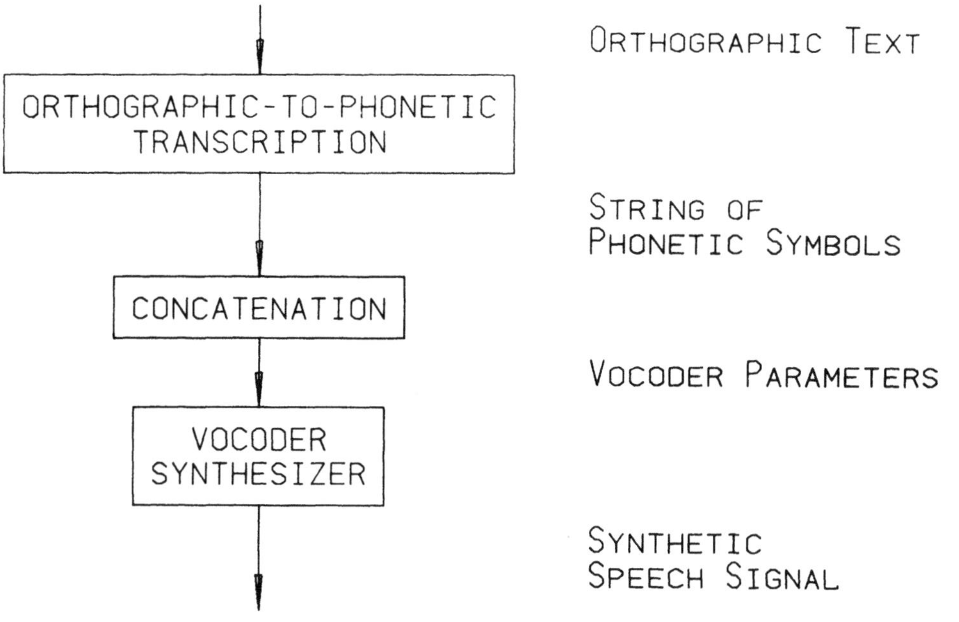

Fig. 1. **Block diagram of a speech synthesis system by rule. The components necessary for prosodic analysis and generation of prosodic control information have been omitted.**

complexity (in spite of the increase in data memory) and improves the quality of the synthetic speech at the same time, since any rule, even a very sophisticated one, can never completely replace natural speech. Diphones, i.e., units consisting of transitions between adjacent phonemes, have been applied in various systems, such as the one by Olive (1980) for American English, the one by Emerard (1977) for French, or the one by Endres and Wolf (1980) for German.

Besides diphones, syllabic units supply a viable data base for high-quality speech synthesis by rule. It has been shown that the influence of coarticulation strongly diminishes when a syllable boundary is crossed (Fujimura, 1981; Öhman, 1966). The number of complete syllables, however, is still too large (and, in addition, difficult to determine) to permit synthesizing an unlimited vocabulary with a reasonably small amount of memory. The number of elements, however, is drastically reduced when a syllable is split up into two *demisyllables* (DSs), as first proposed by Fujimura (1975, 1976a).

How can we suitably split up a syllable into two demisyllables? Usually a syllable is defined to consist of the *nucleus* (in German this is always a vowel or a diphthong) which is preceded and followed by a number of consonants, the so-called *consonant clusters* (CCs). The consonants preceding the syllabic nucleus form the *initial consonant cluster*, and the consonants following the nucleus represent the *final consonant cluster*. According to Fujimura's proposal a syllable is now split up into demisyllables in such a way that the initial CC and the beginning of the syllabic nucleus form the *initial demisyllable*, whereas the remainder (i.e., the second part of the nucleus and the final CC make up the *final demisyllable*.

As already mentioned, demisyllables as units of speech processing were first proposed by Fujimura both for speech recognition (Fujimura, 1975) and for speech synthesis purposes (Fujimura, 1976a), and an experimental system for demisyllable synthesis of American English was designed and implemented (Fujimura et al., 1977; Macchi, 1980; Browman, 1980). For German demisyllables were taken up by Ruske and Schotola (1978) in connection with a speech recognition system; for speech synthesis they were first used by Dettweiler (1980, 1981).

There are two advantages of the demisyllable approach. First, due to linguistic constraints, the number of demisyllables actually used in a language is only a small fraction of the number of demisyllables one could think of just by arbitrarily combining consonants and vowels. Second, since the experiments suggest (Fujimura et al., 1977; Dettweiler, 1980) that the boundaries of the demisyllables coincide with temporal minima of coarticulation effects, a small number of relatively simple rules will be sufficient to concatenate the individual elements. In this paper we will show that about 18 rules and about 1650 demisyllables requiring a data memory of less than 0.5 MByte is sufficient to synthesize (nearly) unrestricted German text.

The remainder of this paper is organized as follows. In Sect. 2 the complete demisyllable inventory will be established, and we will develop the concatenation rules for the syllabic nucleus which enable us to synthesize monosyllabic words. In Sect. 3 suitable reductions of the inventory will be discussed. Section 4 describes a major part of the concatenation rules for CCs in order to synthesize words with more than 1 syllable. Section 5 finally presents the results of intelligibility tests for a list of about 180 frequent meaningful German words.

2. THE DEMISYLLABLE INVENTORY. SYNTHESIZING MONOSYLLABIC WORDS

A representative list of demisyllables for the German language was compiled by Ruske and Schotola (Schotola, 1980, 1984; Ruske, 1984; Ruske and Schotola, 1978) based on a list of the 8000 most frequent German words (Meier, 1967) and other investigations (cf. Schotola, 1984). The initial consonant clusters contain from zero to three consonants, whereas up to 5 consonants may be encountered in a final CC. Nevertheless, the number of CCs is extremely limited due to linguistic constraints: there are only 47 initial and 159 final CCs, a list of which is given in this volume (Ruske, 1984). Concerning the syllabic nuclei, 23 vowels and 3 diphthongs must be dealt with; a list is given in Table 1.

LONG VOWELS								
Tense	Closed	e:	i:	o:	u:	ø:	y:	a:
Tense	Open	ɛ:						a:
SHORT VOWELS								
Tense	Closed	e	i	o	u	ø	y	a
Lax	Open	ɛ	ɪ	ɔ	ʊ	œ	ʏ	a
Lax	schwa	ə						
DIPHTHONGS		a^{e}	a^{o}	$ɔ^{ø}$				

Table 1. German vowels and diphthongs. After Martens and Martens (1965).

Contrary to speech recognition, where syllabic nuclei and CCs can be treated separately (Ruske and Schotola, 1978), the transitions between the syllabic nuclei and the CCs are essential for the quality of the synthesized speech; they cannot be generated by rule and must thus be available as stored data. That means that the number of elements required for the complete demisyllable inventory* amounts to

$$N_C = 26.51 \text{ initial DSs} + 26.159 \text{ final DSs} = 5460.$$

This number is considerable so that efforts are necessary in order to reduce the number of elements without degrading the resulting synthetic speech. This question will be further dealt with in Section 3.

Each DS now consists of a CC and part of a syllabic nucleus. Concatenation of DSs at boundaries within the syllabic nuclei and within CCs are principally different tasks and must be treated by separate rules. For synthesizing monosyllabic words, we only need to concatenate demisyllables within the syllabic nucleus. This problem shall thus be treated first.

Since coarticulation shows a strong tendency toward anticipating future articulatory gestures (Öhman, 1966; Fujimura, 1981), it is adequate to locate the demisyllable boundary within the first part of the vowel. As the experiment shows, Fujimura's proposal (1976a) to place the boundary 50 ms after the beginning of the vowel can be applied to German as well (Dettweiler, 1980). This means that all the problems of vowel duration as well as the question of the diphthongs are confined to the final demisyllables. This leads to concatenation rule #1 (Fig. 2):

---

* The number of initial CCs rises from 47 to 51 due to four CCs which do not occur in word-initial position, but must be added to the set of initial CCS due to rule SR2. for more details see Section 4.1.

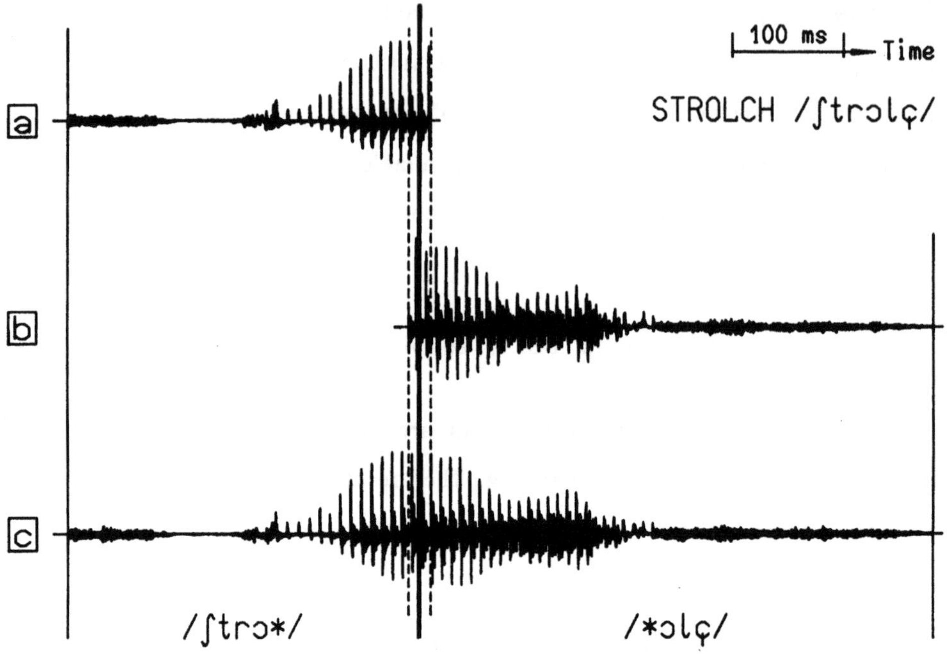

Fig. 2 a-c. Concatenation within the syllabic nucleus (rule CR1). (a) Initial DS, (b) final DS; (c) complete word after concatenation. The example shows the word "Strolch" ("lounger"); /ʃtrɔl$c/ -- > /ʃtrɔ*/ || /* lç/. In this and the following figures, the thick vertical line indicates the interconnection point; the smoothing interval is indicated by the dashed lines. The asterisk in the phonetic transcription refers to the position of the syllabic nucleus. All the signals were synthesized from the demisyllable data base (speaker HTD) using an LPC vocoder.

An initial demisyllable and a final demisyllable are concatenated after the first 50 ms of the vowel. Parameters are smoothed within ± 10 ms around the interconnection point. (CR1)

Like the system for American English (Fujimura et al., 1977), our system smoothes the transition by means of interpolation; i.e., frames within the smoothing area are obtained by interpolating between the parameter values of the adjacent frames on either side of the interpolation interval (which pertain to different demisyllables). A smoothing interval of ± 10 ms around the interconnection point has proved adequate.

3. INVENTORY REDUCTION

To reduce the number of demisyllables, two ways seem feasible: 1) vowel substitution, and 2) further splitting of consonant clusters. Both these possibilities have been implemented in our system. Three inventory reduction rules (RR1-3) and one splitting rule (SR1) have been developed for this purpose. Contrary to the concatenation rules that act on the parametric level, inventory reduction rules and splitting rules act on the phonetic level; they influence the selection of the demisyllables for a given input string of phonetic symbols.

3.1 VOWEL AND DIPHTHONG SUBSTITUTION

Inventory reduction rule #1, dealing with diphthongs, is a direct consequence of rule CR1:

Given a diphthong, CR1 states that most of it will be located in the final DS. The initial DS of the diphthong can thus be replaced with the initial DS containing the initial vowel of the diphthong. (RR1)

In standard German this is possible since the initial vowel of the diphthong is always well pronounced. If the substituted initial DS and the final DS which contains the diphthong do not match perfectly, this does not matter since the audible result of this mismatch will only be a further diphthongization.

The second rule refers to the short tense vowels which are always unstressed in German (and rather rare). Usually in German the long (stressed) vowels are tense, and the short vowels (whether stressed or unstressed) are lax and thus more open. These two categories of vowels must remain separated. The short tense vowels, however, can be derived from the corresponding long ones according to reduction rule #2:

A short tense vowel is obtained by concatenating the demisyllables with the corresponding long vowels and adequately decreasing the duration of the vowel.

(RR2)

The correspondence in German between the features "long" and "tense" on the one hand and "short" and "lax" on the other hand leads to a number of additional, well-known similarities between German vowels (Endres, 1971; Hess, 1972, 1976): /I/ and /e:/, /Y/ and /ø:/, /ʊ/ and /o:/ as well as /a/ and /a:/. In speech recognition, for instance, these vowel pairs become almost indistinguishable when duration is omitted as a cue (Hess, 1972). As the experiment shows, however, these vowel pairs are still somewhat different. Extending rule RR2 to them would thus lead to an undesirable diphthongization except for the case of /a/ and /a:/ where applying the rule does not degrade the synthetic speech. Hence, the two rules RR1 and RR2 reduce the number of vowels from 23 to 15 and eliminate the diphthongs from the initial demisyllables.

3.2 SPLITTING UP CONSONANT CLUSTERS. RUDIMENT AND SUFFIX

According to a later paper by Fujimura (1976b), certain consonants, when occurring in final position of a DS, may be split off from the DS and form separate units, the so-called *affixes*. According to Fujimura's proposal these are the consonants /θ/, /s/, /t/, /z/, and /d/ . Whereas for English this indicates a considerable inventory reduction, the effect is rather small for German since of these consonants only /s/ and /t/ occur in final position (the others do not exist in German, or they only occur in initial position). The fact that such a splitting is possible at all, however, indicates that fricatives and stops in final position, like vowels in the syllabic nuclei, represent a natural coarticulation barrier; i.e., sounds following this barrier do not (substantially) affect previous sounds. Looking for a different splitting scheme which is more efficient for German, Dettweiler (1980, 1981), arrived at the principle of rudiment and suffix (splitting rule #1; Fig. 3):

If a final demisyllable ends with /t/, /s/, /f/, /ʃ/ or a combination thereof, this part is split off and separately treated as a suffix. The remainder is defined to be the rudiment. (SR1)

It is obvious that /t/ and /s/ can be treated in a common way since their places of articulation - and with it the anticipatory coarticulation effects - are almost identical. In addition, the experiments have shown that there is no loss of intelligibility or quality when the rule is extended to /f/ and /ʃ/.

In practice the rudiment* is formed by uttering a demisyllable that contains

---

* According to the definition given in rule SR1, the term *rudiment* is used in connection with final demisyllables. For reasons of simplification, we also use this term in connection with final consonant clusters. To distinguish between a rudiment and an ordinary final DS or CC, any rudiment is marked by a '.' at the end.

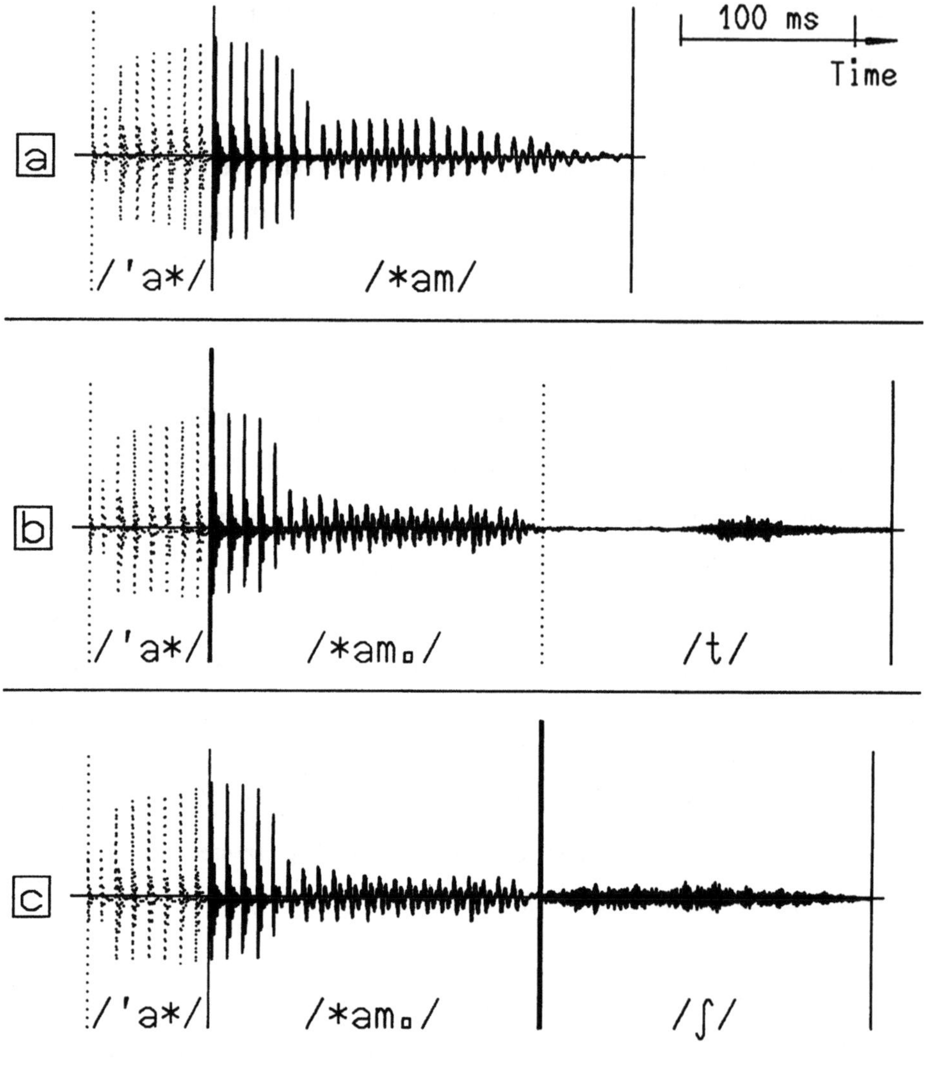

Fig. 3 a-c. The principle of rudiment and suffix. (a) Ordinary consonant cluster: example /*am/. (b) Rudiment and suffix: the demisyllable /*amt/ is split up into the rudiment /*am./ and the suffix /t/ (the dotted line represents the boundary). (c) Concatenation using rudiment and suffix (rule CR2): /*am./ || /ʃ/ -- /*amʃ/. The difference between the ordinary consonant cluster and the rudiment is clearly seen. The rudiment is shorter and ends more abruptly. In this and the following figures, signals drawn with dotted lines represent demisyllables that are needed to complete the word, but do not pertain to the demisyllables involved in the particular rule being explained.

the remainder of the consonantal cluster [without the suffix consonant(s)] plus a final /t/ and then removing the /t/ together with the pertinent silence before the burst (Fig. 3b). Since the rudiment contains all the coarticulatory influences by the following /t/, it is easy to see that the rudiment and the final DS containing an identical consonant cluster without the /t/ are different (cf. Fig. 3a,b). The concatenation rule for a rudiment and its suffix is simple:

A rudiment and a suffix are directly concatenated without any smoothing.

(CR2)

Applying the principle of rudiment and suffix thus leads to inventory reduction rule #3:

A final consonant cluster is split up into a rudiment and a suffix whenever possible, i.e., when it ends with /f/, /s/, /ʃ/, /t/ or a combination thereof.

(RR3)

This rule reduces the number of (ordinary) final consonant clusters from 159 to 23; in addition we obtain 23 rudiments and 26 suffixes (any combination of /f/, /s/, /t/, and /ʃ/ that occur in the final DSs of the full-size inventory). Table 2 contains a list of the reduced inventory of final CCs, rudiments, and suffixes. The total number of elements of the reduced inventory now amounts to

$$N_R = 51 \cdot 15 \text{ initial DSs} + 23 \cdot 19 \text{ final DSs} + 23 \cdot 19 \text{ rud.} + 26 \text{ suff.} = 1665 \ .$$

With an average duration of 0.3 s per element, the memory required for this inventory will be less than 0.5 MByte if a vocoder at or below 7.2 kbits/s is used.

FINAL CONSONANT CLUSTERS	-	r	l	m	n	ŋ	p	k	ç	x
RUDIMENTS	-▫	r▫	l▫	m▫	n▫	ŋ▫	p▫	k▫	ç▫	x▫
			rl	rm	rn		rp	rk	rç	
			rl▫	rm▫	rn▫		rp▫	rk▫	rç▫	
				lm	ln		lp	lk	lç	
				lm▫	ln▫		lp▫	lk▫	lç▫	
							mp	ŋk	nç	
							mp▫	ŋk▫	nç▫	
SUFFIXES	f	s	ʃ	t	fs	ft	st	ʃt	ts	tʃ
REDUCED SUFFIXES				t▫		ft▫	st▫	ʃt▫		
	fst	fts	sts	ʃst	tst	tʃt	tʃst			
	fst▫			ʃst▫	tst▫	tʃt▫	tʃst▫			

Table 2a,b. #(a) Final consonant clusters and rudiments, (b) suffixes for demisyllable synthesis of German text after inventory reduction (Dettweiler, 1980). The reduced suffixes represent some kind of "rudiment of a suffix"; they may be needed when a concatenation rule requires a rudiment in connection with a final demisyllable that ends with a suffix.

4. SYNTHESIZING POLYSYLLABLE WORDS

Polysyllabic words contain intervocalic consonant clusters between subsequent syllabic nuclei. This requires additional rules for the concatenation of consonant clusters (Dettweiler, 1980, 1984). The procedure is carried out in two steps. First (Sect. 4.1) an intervocalic CC is split up into a final CC followed by an initial CC, and the CCs are joined to the respective syllabic nuclei to form demisyllables. In the second step (Sect.4.2) the two DSs are concatenated. As in Sect. 3, the three splitting rules described in Sect. 4.1 act on the phonetic level where they define the syllable boundaries; the concatenation rules presented in Sect. 4.2, on the other hand, operate on the parametric level.

4.1 SPLITTING UP INTERVOCALIC CONSONANT CLUSTERS

The first rule (splitting rule #2) is necessary for the demisyllable principle to be applicable at all.

Given an intervocalic consonant cluster, this cluster must always be split up into a valid final consonant cluster and a valid initial consonant cluster. (SR2)

A CC is regarded as *valid* if it is contained in the demisyllable inventory.

If rule SR2 does not yield a solution, the inventory must be enlarged* so that a viable splitting can be provided. In German this applies to the four consonant "clusters" /s/, /x/, /ç/, and /ŋ/ which occur in final and intervocalic position, but not at the beginning of a word; these clusters must be added to the

---

* In order to enlarge the DS inventory, one must enter the new demisyllable(s) as specified in Section 5.1. This requires manual interaction and cannot be done at the same time as the (automatic) synthesis.

initial demisyllable inventory. If rule SR2, on the other hand, provides several solutions, the following experimental rule is applied:

If SR2 provides more than one valid solution, then the one is taken where as many consonants as possible are grouped within the initial consonant clu

This experimental boundary need not be identical to the syllable boundary requested by morphologic constraints (which, by the way, can be different for different words containing the same intervocalic CC). Inmost cases, however, the two boundaries are identical. The rule takes into account the anticipatory effect of coarticulation; a loss of quality was not registered when a demisyllable boundary, as established by Rule SR3, differed from a given morph boundary. The rule thus represents an adequate means to split up intervocalic CCs without requiring morphologic knowledge at this level.

A special case is given when the intervocalic CC only contains one consonant:

If the intervocalic CC contains one consonant only, and if this is neither a plosive nor /s/, /f/, or /ʃ/ (i.e., if it is a sustained consonant other than a suffix), then this consonant pertains to both the initial and the final demisyllables, and rule SR3 does not apply. (SR4)

This rule actually switches the system into a diphone mode.

The three splitting rules SR2-4 enable the system to split up any intervocalic CC into a final CC followed by an initial CC and to combine them with the preceding and subsequent syllabic nuclei to form a final DS followed by an initial one.

4.2 CONCATENATING CONSONANT CLUSTERS

The way in which an intervocalic CC is concatenated strongly depends on the consonants involved. Three principally different cases must be regarded: 1) the intervocalic CC contains at least one consonant, and there is no plosive at the interconnection point (Sect. 4.2.1); 2) the intervocalic CC is empty, i.e., two vowels that do not represent one of the diphthongs immediately follow each other (Sect. 4.2.2); and 3) the intervocalic CC contains one or several plosives at the interconnection point (Sect. 4.2.3).

4.2.1 THE INTERVOCALIC CC IS NOT EMPTY AND DOES NOT CONTAIN A PLOSIVE AT THE INTERCONNECTION POINT.

This case is handled by three concatenation rules which are rather self-explanatory. The most important point is that the anticipatory coarticulation effects within the initial DS are preserved; i.e., parts of the initial DS which are perceptually important must not be dropped nor smoothed out. The interval to be smoothed is thus situated asymmetrically around the interconnection point.

If the diphone mode applies, i.e., if the intervocalic CC contains one consonant other than /s/, /f/, /ʃ/, or a plosive, then the demisyllables are concatenated by cutting off the onset of the consonant in the initial DS and as much of the consonant in the final DS as necessary to obtain correct consonant duration. Smoothing is performed starting 30 ms before and ending at the first frame after the interconnection point. (CR3)

If the initial DS begins with /s/, /f/, /ʃ/, /z/, or /v/, and if the final DS does not end with one of these consonants, then the coarticulation effects between the demisyllables correspond to the case of Rule CR2. Therefore the final DS is replaced with the pertinent rudiment, and the initial DS is appended without smoothing. (CR4)

As this rule shows, the rudiment is not only suitable for inventory reduction; it can also be advantageously applied in such context where it represents a quasi natural way of coarticulation.

> *In all cases where rules CR3 and CR4 do not apply, the demisyllables are concatenated in such a way that the final part of the final DS (about 60 ms) and the onset of the initial consonant of the initial DS are dropped. Smoothing is performed in the same manner as in rule CR3, i.e., within -30 and +10 ms from the interconnection point.* (CR5)

Figures 4-6 show examples for these rules.

It is obvious that neither of these rules can be applied if there is a plosive at the interconnection point, i.e., if the initial DS starts or the final DS ends with a plosive. If a plosive, however, occurs only in internal position of a DS, then it is totally embedded in that demisyllable and does not pose any problems. For instance, the German word "Anspruch" ("claim"; see Fig. 5) is concatenated as

/'anʃprʊx/ < -- /'a*/ || /*an./ || /ʃprʊ*/ || /*ʊx/

according to the rules CR1 and CR3. The asterisk in the phonetic transcription of the demisyllables indicates the position of the syllabic nucleus, and the sign "||" stands for concatenation.

4.2.2 THE CONSONANT CLUSTER IS EMPTY

In this case two syllabic nuclei form a vowel cluster. A vowel cluster has to be distinguished from a true diphthong; the diphthong per definition represents a single syllabic nucleus (although in German a diphthong is orthographically represented by two letters), whereas a vowel cluster always represents a syllable with an empty final CC followed by a syllable with an empty initial CC. Acoustically such a cluster is realized by a rather long and slow transition; it can

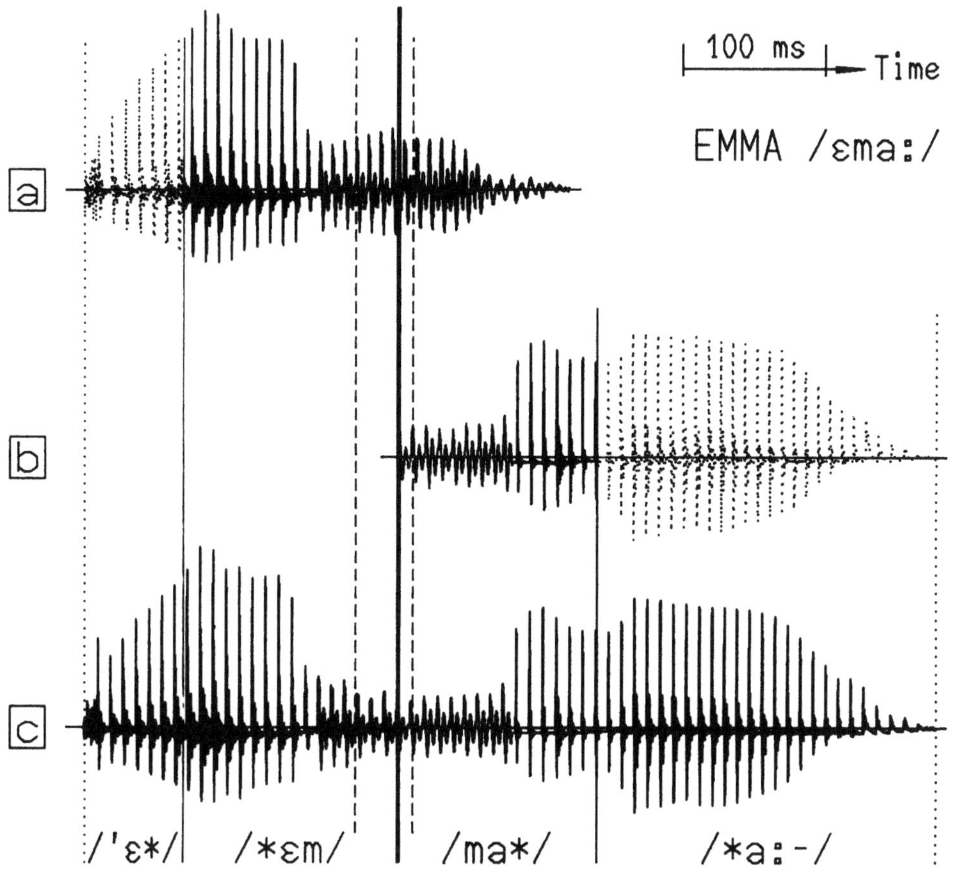

Fig. 4 a-c. **Concatenation of consonant clusters in diphone mode (rule CR3). (a) First syllable; (b) second syllable; (c) complete word after concatenation. The final consonant /m/ of the first syllable was shortened by 120 ms prior to concatenation. Example: /*ɛm/ || /ma*/ from the name "Emma" /'ɛma/.**

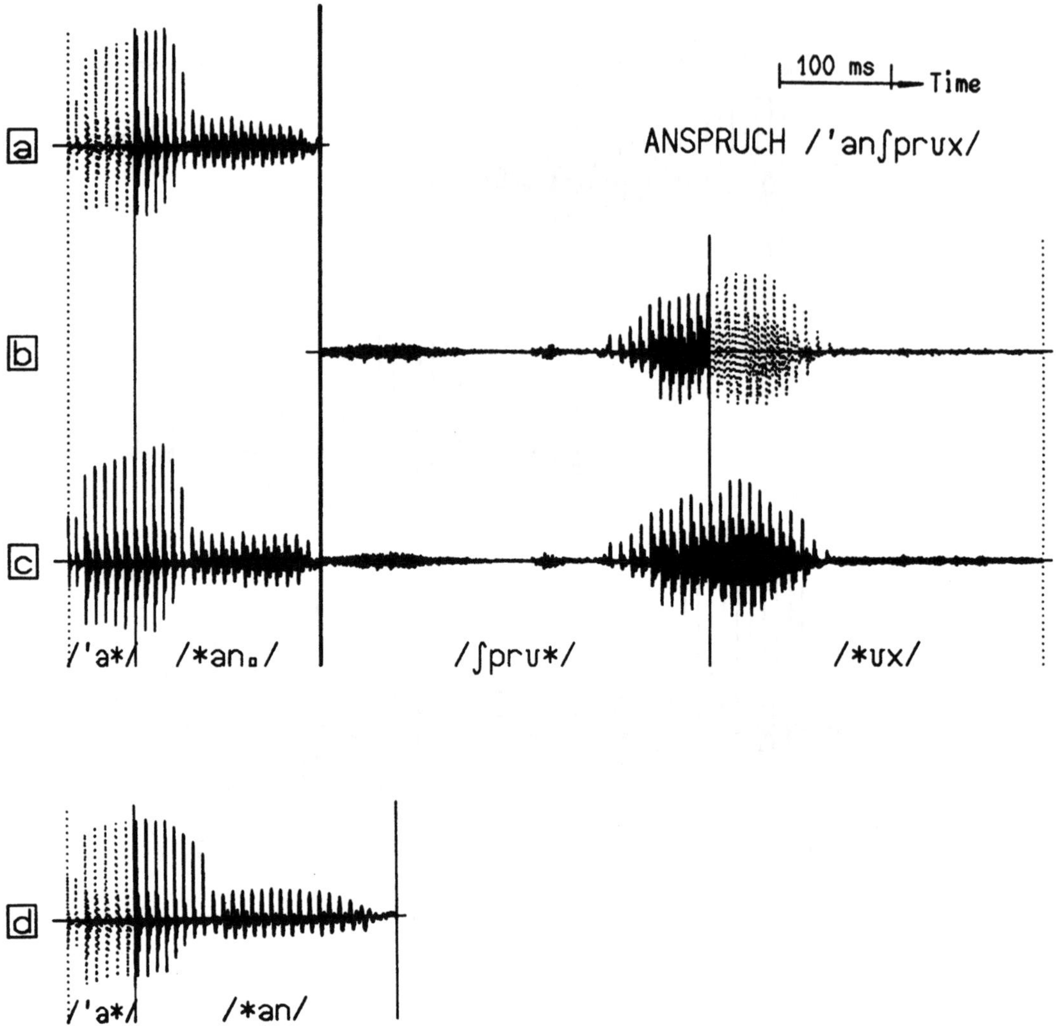

Fig. 5 a-d. (a-c) Concatenation of consonant clusters by rudiment (concatenation rule CR4). Example: /*an./ || /ʃprʊ*/ --> /*anʃprʊ*/ from "Anspruch" ("claim") /'anʃprʊx/; (d) DS with ordinary CC /*an/ for comparison. The thick vertical line indicates the interconnection point; there is no smoothing since a rudiment is involved.

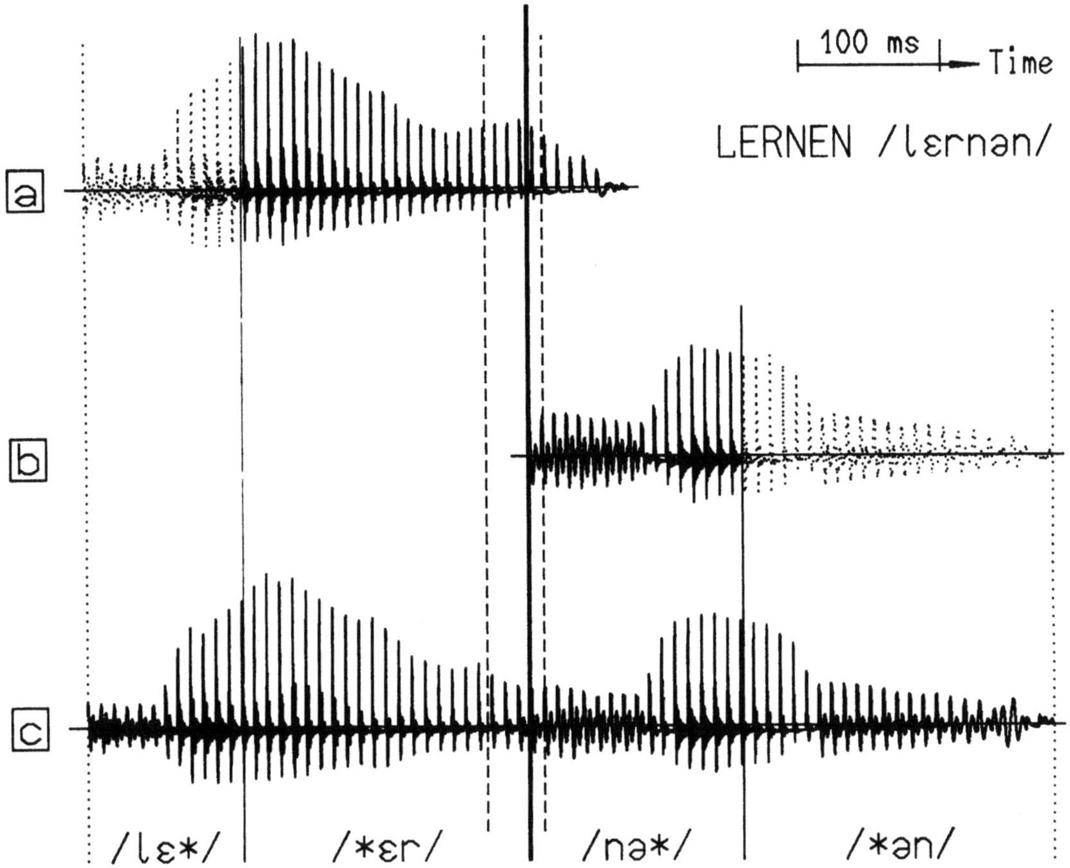

Fig. 6 a-c. Standard case of consonant cluster concatenation (rule CR5). Example: /*ɛr/ || /nɛ*/ -- /*ɛrnɛ*/ from "lernen" ("to learn") /lɛrnɛn/.

easily be synthesized by extended interpolation.

In the case of a vowel cluster the final DS consists of the first vowel followed by an empty final CC; the initial DS consists of the second vowel preceded by an empty initial CC. The two components are concatenated in such a way that the last 40 ms of the final DS are dropped. Smoothing by linear interpolation is performed within ± 30 ms of the interconnection point.

(CR6)

4.2.3 THE INTERVOCALIC CONSONANT CLUSTER CONTAINS ONE OR SEVERAL PLOSIVES AT THE DEMISYLLABLE BOUNDARY

German has 6 plosives: /b/, /d/, /g/, /p/, /t/, and /k/. All of them may occur in initial position whereas plosives in final position are always voiceless. In intervocalic as well as in final position two plosives may immediately follow each other.

Concatenating intervocalic CCs with plosives at the demisyllable boundary represents the most delicate case of demisyllable synthesis. The problems mainly result from the fact that plosives in initial and in final position are differently realized. A plosive in final or intervocalic position is characterized by 1) the sequence of the preceding transition, 2) the silent interval before the burst (which may be substituted by a voice bar in the case of a voiced plosive), 3) the burst, and - in nonfinal position - 4) the subsequent transition. In initial position, however, a (measurable) silent interval before the burst does not exist; it must therefore be substituted when an initial DS starting with a plosive is used for synthesizing an intervocalic CC. Five concatenation rules (CR7-11) are necessary to cover this task (Dettweiler, 1981, 1984). We first have to look at the position of the plosive (in the case of several subsequent plosives at the DS boundary we regard the last one). Three cases have to be distinguished.

1) The plosive pertains to the initial DS; appending it to the final DS, however, will result in a valid final CC as well. This case is also assumed to apply if the plosive is voiced (and therefore does not occur in final position) and the pertinent voiceless plosive (for instance, /p/ instead of /b/) can be appended to the final DS.
2) The plosive pertains to the initial DS and cannot be appended to the final DS.
3) The plosive pertains to the final DS and cannot be assigned to the initial DS.

Cases 1 and 2 must be further subdivided. In case 1 we must distinguish according to whether a) the plosive is voiceless, or b) the plosive is voiced; in case 2 we must look whether the final DS ends with another plosive or not.

The resulting five concatenation rules CR7-11 are not self-explanatory; discussing them in detail is not possible in this paper due to lack of space. Hence the discussion will be confined to case 1a (concatenation rule CR7) which is another good example how the rudiment can be advantageously applied.

> *If the initial DS starts with a voiceless plosive that can also be assigned to the final DS, the plosive is doubled, i.e., it is assigned to both the final and the initial DSs. The (extended) final DS is then replaced by the pertinent rudiment, and the initial DS is appended without smoothing.*(CR7)

The performance of this rule is illustrated using an example (Fig. 7) Rule SR2 splits the intervocalic CC /rk/ of the German word "Wirkung" ("effect") into the final CC /r/ and the initial CC /k/; this leads to the task of concatenating the DSs /*Ir/ and /kʊ*/. It is obvious that the silent interval before the /k/ is not contained in either of these DSs; it must thus be inserted. The concatenation

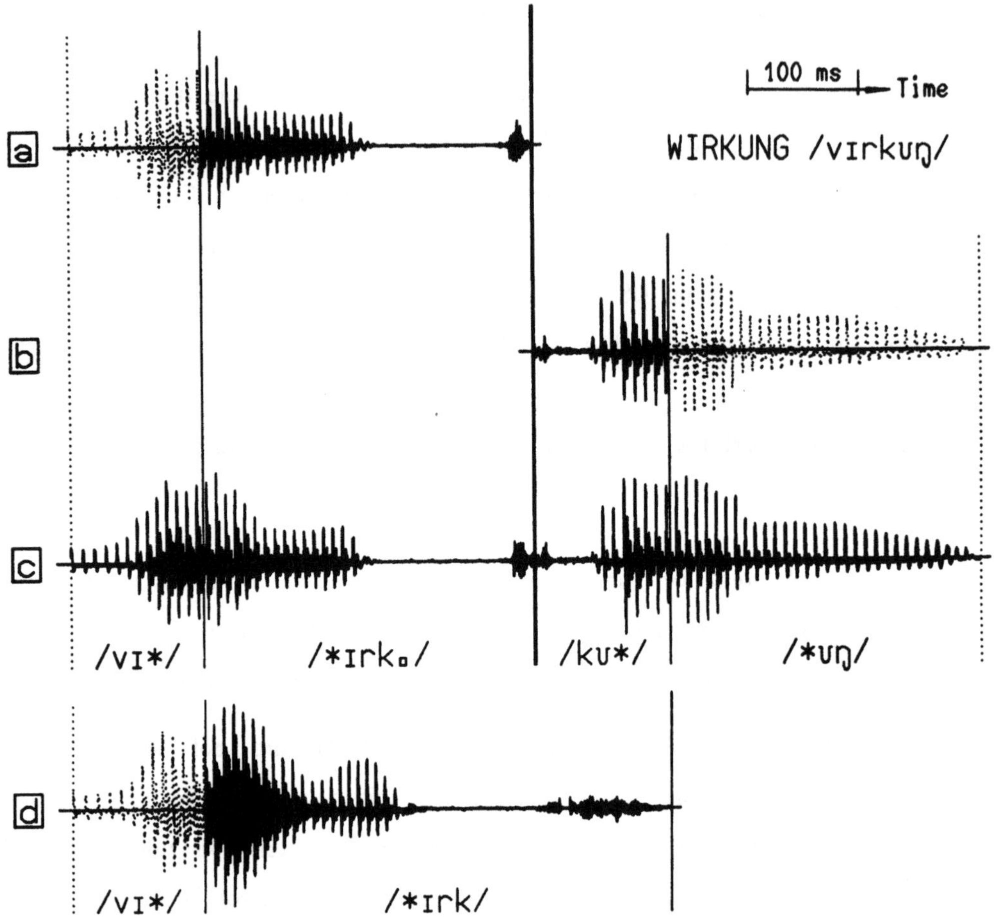

Fig. 7 a-d. Example of plosive processing (rule CR7). The rule applies when a voiceless plosive that can be assigned to both the initial and the final DSs occurs at the DS boundary. (a-c) Example: /*Irk./ || /kʊ*/ -- /*Irkʊ*/ from "Wirkung" ("effect") /vIrkʊŋ/; (d) DS with ordinary CC /*Iirk/ for comparison. Note that the /v/ in German represents a glide rather than a fricative.

/*Ir/ || "silence" || /kʊ*/ -- /*Irkʊ*/ ,

however, is not a good solution since the coarticulatory influence of the /k/ on the demisyllable /* r/ is disregarded. If we concatenate the final DS /*Irk/

/*Irk/ || /kʊ*/ -- /*Irkʊ*/,

contains both the silent interval and the coarticulatory influence of the /k/ on the /*Ir/ . However, the burst of the /k/ is now realized twice; it must thus be removed from one of the DSs, preferably from the final one. In this case, however, the beginning of the burst in the final DS must be exactly measured and marked. Of course this is undesirable.

A better solution is given when the rudiment /*Irk./ is taken instead of the true final DS /*Irk/. In the rudiment /*Irk./ the speaker is prepared to utter a /t/ subsequently to the /k/ so that the burst of the /k/ is very short (Fig. 7b). Removing the burst of the /k/ in the rudiment is thus unnecessary; if it is concatenated with the burst of the /k/ in the initial DS /kʊ*/, the two bursts are perceptually merged into one with slightly greater duration which only emphasizes the voiceless character of the plosive (Delattre, 1968). Therefore the concatenation

/*Irk./ || /kʊ*/ --> /*Irkʊ*/ ,

as specified by rule CR7, represents the optimal solution.

5. ACOUSTIC REALIZATIONS AND INTELLIGIBILITY TESTS

5.1 ACOUSTIC REALIZATION

An experimental system was realized using a 12th-order standard LPC vocoder with a constant frame interval of 10 ms and a signal sampling frequency of 10 kHz. Besides the 12 PARCOR coefficients which were available in unquantized form for the experiments, amplitude and normalized fundamental frequency were stored.

In principle it is not necessary to store fundamental frequency in a speech synthesis system since any prosodic effect of linguistic significance, regardless whether it influences amplitude, fundamental frequency, or duration, must be generated by a special rule system. Microprosodic effects, however, such as small F_0 inflections before and after plosives (which are rather difficult to be controlled by rule), as well as intrinsic pitch of vowels can be covered this way at the cost of a modest increase of the memory required (Dettweiler, 1980). As the experiments have shown, the use of microprosody as a stored parameter not only increases the naturalness of the synthesized speech, but also its intelligibility (Dettweiler, 1982).

For data acquisition the demisyllables were embedded in two-syllable meaningless words of the form /<initial DS>tYr/ and /gYt<final DS>/; the demisyllables were always in stressed position except for the demisyllables containing a schwa which were recorded in the form <initial CC> te:r/ and /ge:t <finalCC>/ in unstressed position. The data were LPC analyzed using a 20-ms Hamming window and the autocorrelation method of linear prediction (Markel and Gray, 1976). F_0 was determined by autocorrelation analysis of the LPC residual (Wagner, 1981); the influences of word prosody were removed from the F_0 contour, and the values of F_0 were normalized in order to yield equal values at the interconnection points within the syllabic nuclei. The DSs were then manually extracted using a display program and an interactive segmentation procedure.

5.2 INTELLIGIBILITY TESTS

A first test was carried out to investigate whether the use of rudiments and suffixes decreases intelligibility. For this test meaningless words of the form /gəa./||/<suffix>/ were offered to the listeners; the single consonants /t/, /f/, /s/, and /ʃ/ were used as suffixes. In a control experiment (which covered a part of the material) the same words were presented in a quasi-natural environment, i.e., LPC-analyzed and resynthesized by the same vocoder without further processing. The test showed systematic confusions between /f/ and /s/ which were mainly due to the high-frequency band limitation (5 kHz) of the vocoder. The two phonemes /ʃ/ and /t/ were clearly intelligible.

The main intelligibility test was carried out with a phonetically balanced list of 179 words (Dettweiler, 1984) pertaining to the 1000 most frequent German words (Meier, 1967; Ruske and Schotola, 1978); 9 meaningless words were added. The listeners were asked to exactly transcribe (phonetically or orthographically) what they heard; they were further told that there was a minority of meaningless words in the list (but not how many); so they could feel free to declare any word meaningless when they did not clearly understand it. In a control experiment the same words were offered as LPC-analyzed and resynthesized speech.

In the evaluation the meaningless words were excluded, and the transcription errors were counted with reference to the number of words, i.e., a word was regarded as wrong even when the transcription error was confined to a single phoneme. The result was very encouraging: for 18 listeners the median rate of correctly transcribed words was 92.5% for the demisyllable-synthesized speech and 96.6% for the vocoder alone. The median deviation from this value was 4.1%, and the median intelligibility loss per listener for the demisyllable-synthesized speech with reference to the vocoded speech was 3.4%. A number of errors were again due to the LPC vocoder, some more errors were due to incorrect demisyllable extraction and segmentation, particularly in connection with weak fricatives, and some additional errors might be due to the speaker who was not a professional speaker but one of the authors (HTD).

In summary, this test clearly shows that the degradation of intelligibility due to the concatenation by rule is almost negligible. This result is underligned by a subjective quality test where the subjective ranking of quality on a 10-rank scale (from "completely unnatural and unintelligible" to "fully natural") differed only by 0.3 points for synthetic and vocoded speech.

6. SUMMARY AND CONCLUSIONS

The concatenation component of an experimental speech synthesis system by rule was presented which uses demisyllables as phonetic units. The component consists of a rule framework and a data base with parameterized natural speech; it converts text given as a string of phonemes into a stream of parameter frames which control an LPC vocoder. The rule framework for demisyllable concatenation comprises 4 rules for splitting up the intervocalic consonant clusters into demisyllables, 3 substitution rules for demisyllable inventory reduction, and 11 concatenation rules. The data base comprises 1665 demisyllables which need less than 0.5 MByte of memory when used in conjunction with a 7.2-kbit/s vocoder. The quality of the synthetic speech was found nearly undistinguishable from vocoded speech using the same vocoder as the synthesis system; the degradation in word intelligibility (median value: 3.1%), compared to the vocoded speech, is rather small. Most of the errors found in understanding the synthetic speech were due to the LPC vocoder and to the stored demisyllable data, but not to the rules.

Future work thus will first aim at improving the quality of the vocoder in connection with the stored data. Since this kind of vocoder application needs a sensitive, high-quality vocoder rather than a robust or a fast one, complex speech analysis methods with high computing effort can be applied during the data acquisition phase. In particular, a signal bandwidth of 7 kHz requiring a sampling frequency of 16 kHz will eliminate the systematic confusions between the fricatives /f/ and /s/ present in the actual 5-kHz system, and a variable-frame-rate vocoder (Heiler, 1982) permitting a minimum frame rate of less than 5 ms without increasing the overall amount of memory will particularly improve the quality of synthetic stop consonants.

The question of prosody has been kept apart from the problem of concatenation as completely as possible. Microprosody, however, which influences the speech signal on a short-time basis very much alike to that of coarticulation, has been taken into account by adding normalized F_0 values to the stored data. On the syllabic level prosodic rules are necessary only to separate stressed and unstressed syllables. Since the whole material (except those DSs containing a schwa) was recorded using stressed syllables, one primitive rule (which has not been discussed in this paper) is necessary to reduce stressed demisyllables to unstressed ones whenever needed. All other questions of prosody must be dealt with at levels above that of concatenation.

The work described in this paper concentrates on the problem of concatenation, and in our opinion the experiments have shown that the use of demisyllables as phonetic units for speech synthesis solves the problem of concatenation to such an extent that the contribution of the concatenation component to the overall degradation of the quality and intelligibility of the synthetic signal becomes almost negligible.

ACKNOWLEDGEMENTS

The major part of this paper was extracted from the Dr.-Ing. dissertation of the first author (Dettweiler, 1984). The authors wish to thank Dr. G. Ruske for many fruitful discussions.

REFERENCES

1. J. Allen, "Synthesis of speech from unrestricted text", Proc. IEEE 64, 433-442, 1976.
2. C. P. Browman, "Rules for demisyllable synthesis using LINGUA, a language interpreter", Proc. IEEE Intern. Conf. on Acoustics, Speech, and Signal Processing (ICASSP-80), 561-564 (IEEE, New York), 1980.
3. P. Delattre, "From acoustic cues to distinctive features", Phonetica 18, 198-230, 1968.
4. H. Dettweiler, "Versuche zur Sprachsynthese deutscher Woerter mit Halbsilben", in *Fortschritte der Akustik*, Plenarvorträge und Kurzreferate der 7, Tagung der Deutschen Arbeitsgemeinschaft für Akustik (DAGA '80), München (VDE-Verlag, Berlin), 703-706, 1980.
5. H. Dettweiler, "An approach to demisyllable synthesis of German words", Proc. IEEE ICASSP-81, Atlanta, GA, 110-113 (IEEE, New York), 1981.
6. H. Dettweiler, "Sprachsynthese deutscher Woerter mit Halbsilben", in *Fortschritte der Akustik* (FASE/DAGA'82); 3. Kongress der FASE, 9. Tagung der DAGA, Goettingen 1982 (Goettingen), 1039-1042, 1982.
7. H. Dettweiler, Automatische Sprachsynthese deutscher Woerter mit Hilfe von silbenorientierten Segmenten (Diss., Technische Universität München), 1984.
8. F. Emerard, *Synth ese par diphones et traitement de la prosodie* (CNET, F-22301 Lannion), 1977.
9. W. K. Endres, "Die Uebergangslaute der deutschen Sprache als verbindende Elemente für eine Sprachsynthese", Proc. 7th Int. Congr. on Acoustics, Budapest 1971, Vol. 3, paper 25C14, 301-304, 1971.
10. W. K. Endres, "Speech synthesis for an unlimited vocabulary, a powerful tool for inquiry and information service", in *Spoken Language Generation and Understanding*, Proceedings of the NATO Advanced Study Institute held at Bonas, France, June 23 - July 5, 1979; ed. by J. C. Simon, (Reidel, Dordrecht), 1980.
11. O. Fujimura, "Syllable as a unit of speech recognition." IEEE Trans. ASSP-23, 82-87, 1975.
12. O. Fujimura, "Syllable as the unit of speech synthesis", unpublished Bell memorandum (Bell Labs, Murray Hill, NJ), 1976a.
13. O. Fujimura, "Syllables as concatenated demisyllables and affixes", J. Acoust. Soc. Am. 59 (Suppl.); paper XX3, 91st Meet. ASA, 1976b.
14. O. Fujimura, "Temporal organization of articulatory movements as a multidimensional phrasal structure", Phonetica 38, 66-83, 1981.
15. O. Fujimura, "Syllables as concatenative phonetic units", in *Syllables and Sequences*, ed. by A. Bell and J. B. Hooper (North-Holland, Amsterdam), 107-120, 1978.
16. O. Fujimura, M. J. Macchi, J. B. Lovins, "Demisyllables and affixes for speech synthesis", Proc. 9th Int. Congr. on Acoustics, Madrid 1977, paper I107, 1977.
17. J. Heiler, "Optimized frame selection for variable frame rate synthesis", Proc. IEEE ICASSP-82, Paris 1982, 586-589 (IEEE, New York), 1982.
18. W. J. Hess, Digitale grundfrequenzsynchrone Analyse von Sprachsignalen als

Teil eines automatischen Spracherkennungssystems (Diss., Technische Universität München), 1972.

19. W. J. Hess, "A pitch-synchronous digital feature extraction system for phonemic recognition of speech", IEEE Trans. ASSP-24, 14-25, 1976.
20. D. H. Klatt, "Software for a cascade/parallel formant synthesizer", J. Acoust. Soc. Am. 67, 971-980, 1980.
21. J. B. Lovins, M. Macchi, O. Fujimura, "A demisyllable inventory for speech synthesis", in Speech communication papers presented at the 97th Meeting of the Acoustical Society of America, Cambridge MA, June 12-16, 1979, ed. by. J. J. Wolf and D. H. Klatt, 519-522 (Acoustical Society of America New York, NY), 1979.
22. M. J. Macchi, "A phonetic dictionary for demisyllabic speech synthesis", Proc. IEEE ICASSP-80, Denver, CO., 565-567 (IEEE, New York), 1980.
23. M. J. Macchi, O. Fujimura, "The syllable and speech synthesis", J. Acoust. Soc. Am. 59 (Suppl.), 34; paper R3, 89th Meet. ASA, 1976.
24. J. D. Markel, A. H. Gray, "Linear prediction of speech", Communications and Cybernetics, Vol. 12 (Springer, Berlin), 1976.
25. C. Martens, P. Martens, *Phonetik der deutschen Sprache*, (Max Hueber, München), 1965.
26. I. G. Mattingly, "Syllable Synthesis", Speech Research 49, 111-119, (Haskins Labs., New Haven, CT), 1977.
27. H. Meier, *Deutsche Sprachstatistik*, (Olms, Hildesheim), 1967.
28. S. E. G. Öhman, "Coarticulation in VCV utterances: Spectrographic measurements", J. Acoust. Soc. Am. 39, 151-166, 1966.
29. J. P. Olive, "A scheme for concatenating units for speech synthesis", Proc. IEEE ICASSP-80, Denver, CO, 568-571 (IEEE, New York).
30. L. C. W. Pols, "Consonant intelligibility of speech produced by dyadic rule synthesis", unpublished Bell memorandum (Bell Laboratories, Murray Hill, NJ) 1979.
31. G. Ruske, "Demisyllables as processing units for automatic speech recognition and lexical access", this volume, 1984.
32. G. Ruske, Th. Schotola, "An approach to speech recognition using syllabic decision units", Proc. IEEE ICASSP-78, Tulsa, OK, 722-725 (IEEE, New York), 1978.
33. Th. Schotola, "Silbenanlautende und silbenauslautende Konsonantenfolgen als Entscheidungseinheiten für die automatische Spracherkennung (Diss., Technische Universität München), 1980.
34. Th. Schotola, "On the use of demisyllables in automatic speech recognition", Speech Commun. 3, 63-87, 1984.
35. M. Wagner, "Automatic labelling of continuous speech with a given phonetic transcription using dynamic programming algorithms", Proc. IEEE ICASSP-81, Atlanta, GA (IEEE New York), 1981.

ON THE USE OF PHONETIC KNOWLEDGE FOR AUTOMATIC SPEECH RECOGNITION

Renato De Mori
Concordia University
Department of Computer Science
1455 de Maisonneuve Blvd., West
Montreal, Quebec
H3G 1M8
Canada

Pietro Laface
Politecnico di Torino
Cens-Dipartimento di Automatica e Informatica
Corso Duca degli Abruzzi 24
10129 Torino
ITALY

ABSTRACT

A distributed rule-based system for automatic speech recognition is described.

Acoustic property extraction and feature hypothesization are performed by the application of sequences of operators. These sequences, called plans, are executed by cooperative expert programs.

Experimental results on the automatic segmentation and recognition of phrases, made of connected letters and digits are described and discussed.

NATO ASI Series, Vol. F16
New Systems and Architectures for Automatic Speech Recognition and Synthesis. Edited by R. De Mori and C. Y. Suen

INTRODUCTION

Machines for the automatic recognition of spoken words are now available. They perform well in a speaker-dependent mode on vocabularies of hundreds of words. Some of them may operate in a speaker-independent mode on more limited vocabularies. Some results have been obtained on the recognition of connected words for limited tasks, mostly in a speaker-dependent way [1,2].

Interesting results have also been achieved in researches on continuous speech in a speaker-dependent mode [3] or on highly constrained tasks in a speaker-independent mode [4].

Most of the systems proposed so far take advantage of the *redundancy* of the protocols they use. The most difficult and unsolved problems arise when tasks have little redundancy or when speaker-independence is required on complex tasks. Examples of such complex tasks are the recognition of letters and digits (isolated or connected) or of large vocabularies. In these cases, the use of a large variety of acoustic properties extracted with specific signal processing algorithms seem to be promising [5,6].

In many cases, acoustic property extraction is context-dependent. Context-dependencies impose precedence relations on the extraction processes. For example (see Demichelis et al. [7] for details), formant pseudo-loci are important cues for the recognition of plosive consonants in a Consonant Vowel (CV) or in a VC context, but their extraction can be performed only after having hypothesized the existence of a plosive sound before or after a vowel and having detected the voice onset interval and the formant loci of the vowel. Kopec [8] in a recent report on the speaker-independent recognition of unvoiced plosive consonants at the beginning of a syllable, has shown that the point of consonant release has to be detected before applying efficient recognition algorithms. Furthermore, acoustic properties of burst spectra, useful for the recognition of plosive consonants, can also be extracted with a specific algorithm in parallel with vowel formant loci.

Systems for extracting acoustic properties can be conceived in the framework of *distributed problem solving* in which acoustic properties are facts that drive computational processes to the achievement of goals consisting in hypothesis generation.

One motivation in favour of distributed systems is that they can be implemented with parallel computer architectures capable of reaching real-time performances that cannot be achieved by classical sequential computers.

Another important motivation is that if knowledge for problem solving is distributed into various sources, it is possible to update separately the knowledge of each source when new scientific results or new experience pertinent to it become available. Furthermore, different data structures and learning algorithms can be used for each source of knowledge. These algorithms can be, for example, syntactic or parametric.

A third motivation is that powerful control strategies can be used, for example, capable of scheduling the parallel execution of sensory procedures which extract new properties from the data when this is requested.

Based on these motivations, a system has been implemented for which the extraction of acoustic properties and generation of syllabic hypotheses is the result of a plurality of cooperating activities performed by many processes. This cooperation of computational activities has been conceived using the paradigm of an *Expert System Society* [9,10].

Each Expert is associated with a *Long Term Memory* (LTM) containing the specific Expert's knowledge and a *Short Term Memory* (STM) where data interpretations are written.

Experts are computing agents which execute reasoning programs using structural and procedural knowledge. The knowledge of each Expert is expressed by a set of *plans* some of which can be executed in parallel. Communication between cooperating tasks is performed by message passing. Some plans are executed as a result of a spontaneous data-driven activity. Other plans are executed on a request. In any case, each perceptual plan achieves a *goal* set by the system strategy. Plan definition will be given later on in this section.

The novelty of the knowledge based approach proposed here is that, descriptions of acoustic properties are extracted and related with phonetic feature interpretations using plans that are the result of a long learning effort in which a large number of patterns has been analyzed in order to extract invariant properties using knowledge about speech analysis, production and perception. For example, it is known that the burst spectrum of an alveolar plosive consonant should be compact but rules have to be inferred for detecting burst spectra and for characterizing compactness and statistics about their performances have to be collected.

Furthermore, rules may specify strategies for speech analysis that depend on incomplete feature hypotheses and model-driven predictions. These strategies involve variable-resolution spectral analysis (in the time and in the frequency domain), morphological analysis of the speech waveform, its loudness and pitch contour as well as the choice of a transfer function expression (selection of number of poles and zeros) for vocal tract modelling.

With this approach a phoneme PH_i is expressed by a set of phonetic features, i.e.

$$PH_i = (pf_{i1}, pf_{i2},\ldots,pf_{ij},\ldots,pf_{iJ}) \tag{1}$$

Each phonetic feature pf_x is represented by a relation R_x with a set of acoustic properties ap_x, i.e.

$$pf_x = R_x\,(ap_{x1}, ap_{x2},\ldots.ap_{xk},\ldots.ap_{xK}) \tag{2}$$

For example, the phoneme /p/ is represented as follows:

/p/ =

(nonsonorant-interrupted-consonant,tense,labial) =

(nit,labial).

The phonetic feature 'labial' in the context of 'nit' features is represented by the following relation R_k :

(relation R_k
(left-side
(feature (labial))
(feature context (nit))
(temporal context (followed-by front vowel)))
(right-side
(suprasegmental and time-domain properties)
(formant-transition properties)
(burst—spectra properties))) (3)

The rule for 'labial' takes into account different types of ***contextual dependencies.*** One contextual dependency is represented by the other features that appear with 'labial' in a plosive phoneme. The other contextual dependences are represented by the class of phonemes that can follow or precede the plosive phoneme under consideration. Relations are used by ***plans*** executed by the Expert System.

A ***plan*** is a sequence of items. Each item may contain a ***precondition expression*** for applying rules of the type R_k, ***operators*** containing sensory procedures, for extracting the properties used by R_k and an ***algorithm*** for evaluating the evidence of the hypothesis generated by R_k. In practice, a plan is a sequence of operators. Each operator is assoicated with a precondition and an action.

Sequences of phonetic feature hypotheses generated under the control of rules can be compared with prototypical sequences automatically generated from the orthographic form of a sentence using ***Dynamic Programming*** (DP). The result of the comparisons can be used for recognition or for segmenting continuous speech into words and for automatically learning different feature sequences corresponding to different pronounciation of a word. Sequences of phonetic feature hypotheses can also be used for computing the likelihood that a Markov source generates them when a sentence is pronounced. Bahl et al. [3] have proposed algorithms for this purpose.

STRUCTURE OF THE EXPERT SOCIETY

Interpretations of the speech waveform are generated by an Expert Society implemented on a VAX 11/780. Its structure is shown in Fig. 1.

EXP_1 is the Acoustic Expert (AE). It has the task of sampling and quantizing the signal, performing various types of signal transformations, extracting and describing acoustic cues. The term *acoustic cues* will be used for indicating spectral or signal properties describing aspects that are relevant for hypothesizing phonetic features. Examples of acoustic cues are formant loci, characteristics of burst spectra like "compactness", peaks and valleys of signal energy.

EXP_1 can perform, for example, an analysis based on Linear Prediction Coefficients (LPC) for segments labelled with vocalic hypotheses in order to find formant loci capable of describing the place and manner of articulation. EXP_1 can also perform a broad-band spectral analysis based on a Fast Fourier Transformation (FFT) when hypotheses of nonsonorant-continuant sounds have been made. EXP_1, as any Expert, may perform "spontaneous" *data-driven* activities and *expectation-driven* activities based on requests issued by other Experts.

Requests and control messages are exchanged among Experts through the "message exchange network" shown in Fig. 1. Data, cues, descriptions and hypotheses are written by an Expert into its own Short Term Memory (STM). Only the Expert that owns the STM can write into it, but any Expert can read any STM.

EXP_2 is the Phonetic and Syllabic Expert (PSE). It translates descriptions of acoustic cues into *phonetic feature hypotheses*. These features describe the *manner* and the *place* of articulation of each segment of the spoken language. This translation may involve the extraction of new acoustic cues by asking EXP_1

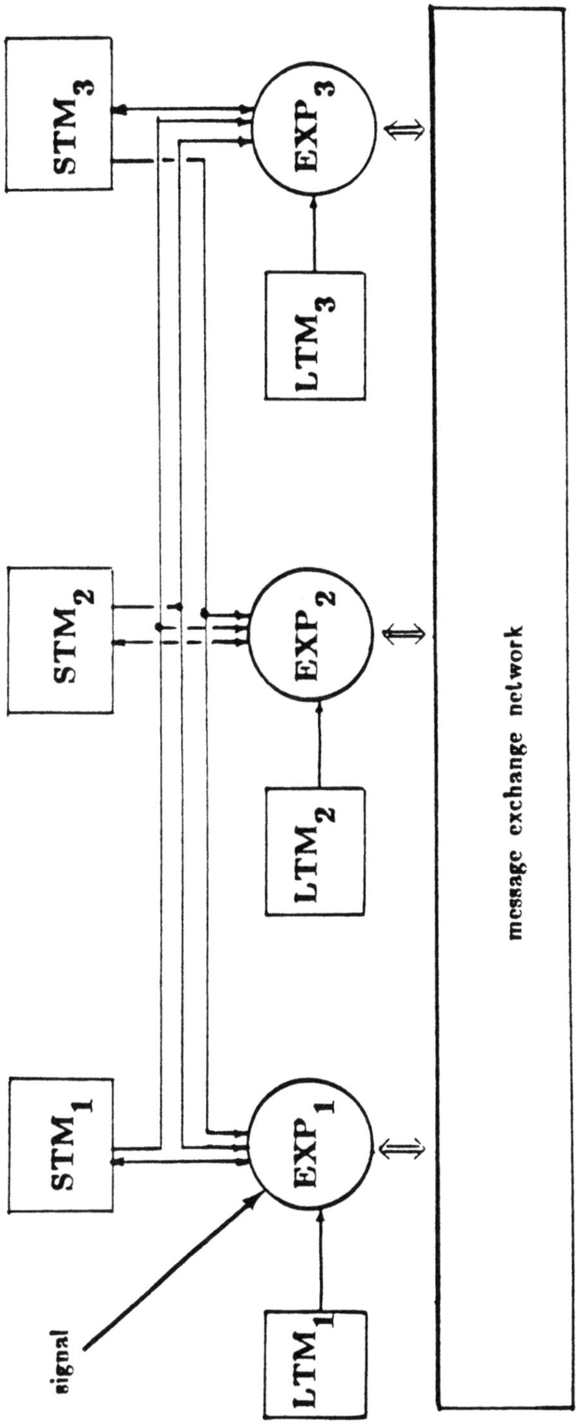

Fig. 1 - Structure of the Expert Society.

to execute sensory procedures.

Table I

Primary Acoustic Cues

Symbol	Attributes	Description
LPK	tb,te,m1,zx,	long peak of total energy (TE)
SPK	"	short peak of TE
MPK	"	peak of TE of medium duration
LOWP	"	low energy peak of TE
LNS	tb,te,zx	long nonsonorant tract
MNS	"	medium nonsonorant tract
LVI	tb,te,m1,zx	long vocalic tract adjacent to a LNS or a MNS in a TE peak
MVI	tb,te,m1,zx	medium vocalic tract adjacent to a LNS a MNS in a TE peak
LDD	emin,tb,te,zx	long deep dip of total energy
SDD	"	short deep dip of total energy
LMD	"	long dip of total energy with medium dep
SMD	"	short dip of total energy with medium de
LHD	"	long non-deep dip of total energy
SHD	"	short non-deep dip of total energy

Table II

Attribute description

Attribute	Description
tb	time of beginning
te	time of end
m1	maximum signal energy in the peak
emin	minimum total energy in a dip
zx	maximum zero-crossing density of the signal derivative in the tract

Table III

Primary Phonetic Features

Symbol	Primary Phonetic Feature
VF	Front vowel
VC	Central vowel
VB	Back vowel
VFC	Front or central vowel
VCB	Central or back vowel
VW	Uncertain vowel
NI	Nonsonorant interrupted consonant
NA	Nonsonorant affricate consonant
NC	Nonsonorant continuant consonant
SON	Sonorant consonant
SONV	A sonorant or the /v/ consonant
PP	Possible pause

There are some acoustic cues, like peaks and valleys of time evolutions of energies in fixed bands of the signal that can be extracted by context-independent algorithms. These acoustic cues will be called *Primary Acoustic Cues* (PAC) and the phonetic features related to them will be called *Primary Phonetic Features* (PPF). A definition of primary cues and features used in the system described in this paper is given in Tables I, II, III. These algorithms for extracting PACs generate descriptions of a time interval of the signal without being constrained by contextual information extracted from adjacent segments.

Examples of various types of PACs are shown in Fig. 2. The two curves in Fig. 2a represent the time evolution of the signal energy (—) and the zero-crossings counts (---) in successive intervals of 10 msec of the first derivative of the signal. The phrase is the sequence of letters and digits ECB3V. Fig. 2b shows the corresponding PAC description. Time unit is 0.01 sec. LONG and SHORT refer to the dip duration. DEEP, MEDIUM and HIGH refer to the height of the minimum energy in the dip with respect to background noise energy.

Other functions of EXP_2 are those of segmenting the speech signal into Pseudo Syllabic Segments (PSS) and of producing evidence measurements about phonetic hypotheses. The activity of generating PPFs is *data-driven*, the activities of extracting other phonetic features are *expectation-driven*. Expectations can be generated by a strategy inside EXP_2 or they can be requests transmitted by EXP_3.

EXP_3 is the Lexical Expert (LE) that generates lexical hypotheses based on prosodic features, phonetic hypotheses, syntactic and semantic constraints. As the design of the lexical component is still under development, it will be described in a future paper.

The behavior of the Expert Society can be summarized by the following algorithm written in Concurrent Pascal-like form.

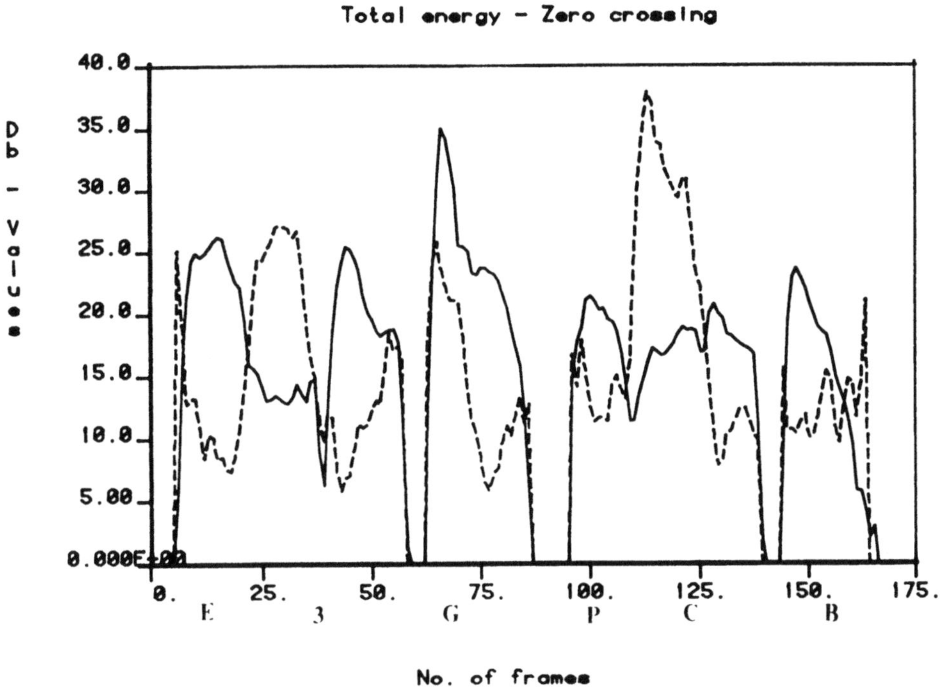

Fig. 2a Total energy (---) and zero-crossing counts (---) divided by 6 of the pronounciation of the sequence E3G PCB (time references are in tenth of milliseconds)

PAC	t_b	t_e
LDD	1	7
LPK	8	28
LNS	29	38
SPK	39	41
LPK	42	60
SDD	61	65
MNS	66	72
LPK	73	89
LDD	90	98
LPK	99	111
SMD	112	113
LNS	114	126
LVI	127	141
SDD	142	145
LPK	146	168

Fig. 2b Examples of PAC description for the sequence ECB3V

"Expert Society"

cobegin

acoustic-expert;

phonetic-and-syllabic-expert;

lexical-expert

coend

A more detailed task-decomposition can be performed for each Expert. This decomposition can either describe the parallel execution of operations on different segments of the speech signal or the parallel application of different pieces of knowledge stored into an Expert's LTM to the same segment. Details of EXP_1 and EXP_2 are given in [17]. An implementation of EXP_3 is described in the following section.

A PLANNING SYSTEM FOR CONNECTED WORD RECOGNITION

Canadian postal codes consisting of three sequences of one letter and one digit were considered. For this experiment, one speaker pronounced in English 500 postal codes randomly generated by a computer program. A finite state automaton for each symbol to be hypothesized was automatically generated. This knowledge source contains acceptable degradations of sequences of PPFs for each symbol. Segmentation was performed using dynamic programming for aligning sequences of corrupted strings of PPFs with sequences of prototypes. Coarticulation effects were taken into account in generating sequences of prototypes. The set of automata contains 250 states. The automata were merged into a network. Arcs of the network were labelled with PPF symbols. Some nodes of the network were associated actions for generating letter or digit hypotheses. At the beginning there is only one pointer that points to the root of the network.

As EXP_1 and EXP_2 generate PPF hypotheses, pointers move along the network. When a pointer cannot move from a node it is suppressed. When a pointer reaches a node with an output action associated to it, it generates an arc in a chart phase and a new pointer to the root of the network is created. Generation of hypotheses were performed on another 200 sequences using a parsing algorithm that generates a chart-parse for each analyzed sequence.

The following results were obtained:

Average number of partially overlapping hypotheses:
Percent of times the right hypothesis was missed:
Average number of branches in the chart-parse:

Results seem to be encouraging even if a more extensive training has to be done on coarticulation instances especially for very difficult cases like I1O and Y1I.

In order to reduce the number of branches of the chart-parse to 1 and to eliminate partially overlapping hypotheses, special disambiguation plans have to be developed.

PSS representations in terms of PPFs are used for preselecting a disambiguation plan. As the recognition of connected letters and digits is an extremely difficult problem, it was decided to investigate one disambiguation plan at a time. A plan PE1 was developed for recognizing the letters and digits described by sequences of PPFs corresponding to consonant-vowel syllables with consonants described by PPFs of the following set :

$$C1 = (PP, NI, NA, NC)$$

and vowels described as VF or VFC. The purpose of PE1 is thus that of discriminating among the elements of the following E1 set:

$$E1 = (P,T,K,B,D,G,C,V,E,3).$$

For the sake of generality plan PE1 was conceived in such a way that it is executed whenever PSS of the type C1 VF or C1 VFC are detected and it does not take into account any syntactic (top-down) constraint.

The idea behind the conception of plan PE1 is that a redundant set of acoustic properties for each phonetic feature is extracted by a chain of operators such that *redundancy* can compensate for lack of knowledge in using the properties or for errors in property extraction. With the actual system, it is easy to add or delete properties and a program is provided for collecting statistics about properties.

As the main purpose of this paper is that of describing the system, the choice of strategies for using detected properties will be discussed in a future work.

An overview of plan PE1 for the recognition of the E1 set is shown in Fig. 3. The plan is subdivided into sub-plans (Pe11, Pe12, ... , PE15).

PE11 produces an envelope description by analyzing the signal amplitude before and after preemphasis. Envelope samples are obtained every msec by and the absolute minimum of the signal in a 3 msec interval. The envelope description is made by the following alphabet . (˜ represents negation) :

EDA := SHORT—STEP(ST),
LONG—STEP(LST),
NO—STEP(NST),
STEP WITH HIGH LOW FREQUENCY ENERGY(BZ),
BURST—PEAK(BUR),
POSSIBLE—BURST(PBU),
NBZ=˜BZ,
NBU =˜BUR,
NPB=˜PBU.

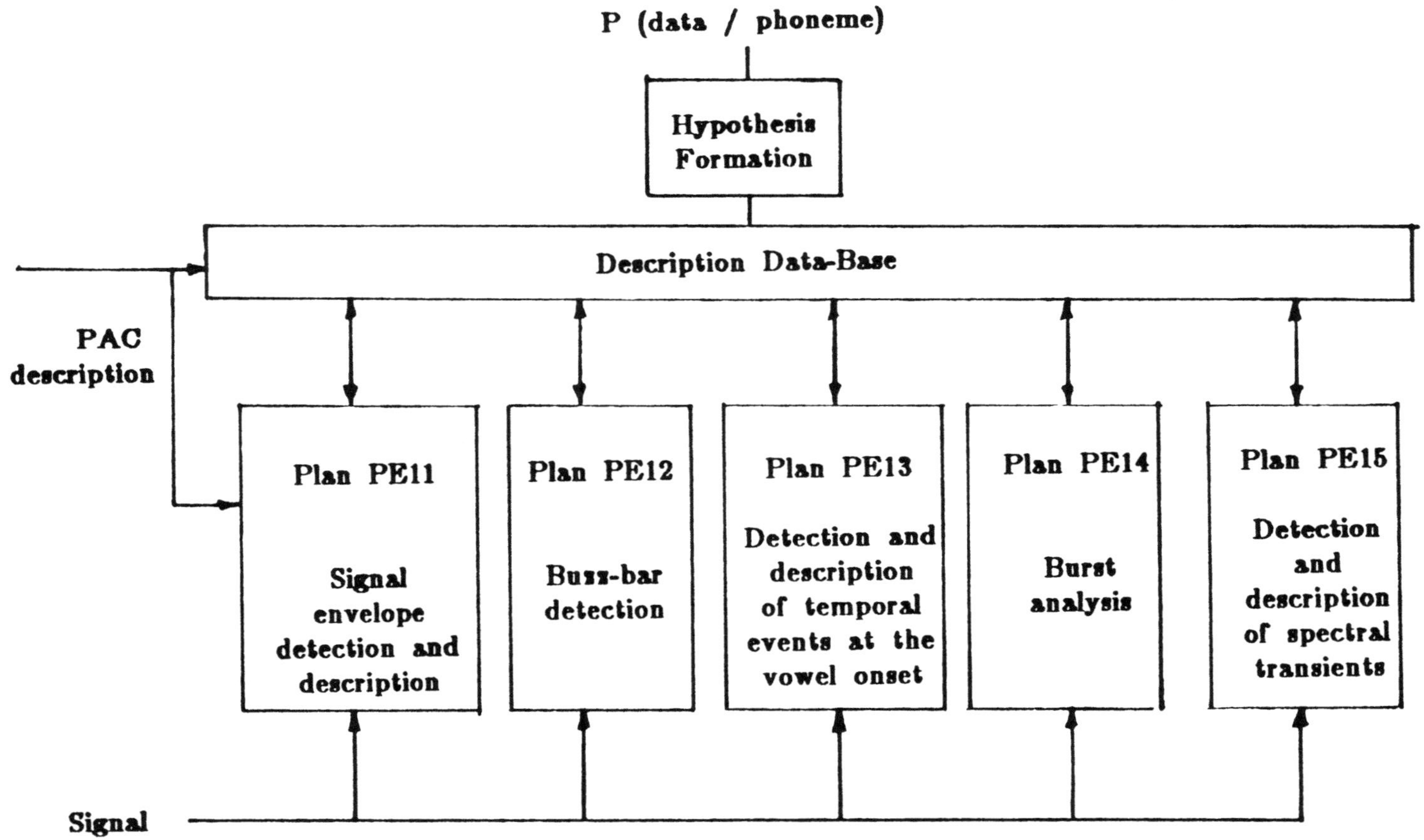

Fig. 3 Overview of plan PE1

PE12 detects a buzz-bar by analyzing the shape of FFT spectra before the voice onset. The alphabet of the descriptions it produces is :

BZA = {NOB,BU1,BU2,BU}

NOB means no buzz and the other three symbols describe degrees of buzz-bar evidence (BU1 : little evidence, BU : strong evidence)

PE13 analyzes temporal events at the voice onset. These events are related to voice onset time. They are :

D : the delay between the onset of low and high frequency energies,

ZQ : the duration of the largest zero-crossing interval of the signal at the onset,

ZR : the number of zero-crossing counts in the largest sequence of sucessive zero-crossing intervals with duration less than 0.5 msecs.

PE14 and PE15 perform respectively burst and formant transition analysis.

PE14 was not used in the experiment described in this sub-section.

PE15 was described in section V.

D is extracted and used according to a suggestion by Delgutte [15].

Preconditions for plan execution are learned with a general-purpose algorithm whose details are given in [13]. The following precondition expressions PRE_j $(1 \leq j \leq 5)$ have been inferred.

PRE1 = (LDD+SDD) * (LPK+SPK+MNS LPK)

PRE2 = LDD * (LPK+SPK)

PRE3 = (LDD+SDD) * (LPK+SPK)

PRE4 = SPK+BUR+PBU

PRE5 = LDD+LPK

Notice that '+' represents logical disjunction and A*B means that A preceeds B in time.

Expressions made of symbols extracted by subplans PE11 and PE12 and representing positive and negative information have been inferred for each PAC description and for each phoneme.

An example of such rules is given in the following :

E	:=	NBU	NBZ	NST	NBU	NPB
K	:=	NBU	NBZ	ST	BUR	PBU
B	:=	BU	BZ	ST	y	PBU

There are 96 of such rules in the plan corresponding to 24 sequences of PAC descriptions; y is a don't care condition.

A PAC description is used for indexing a set of rules that is matched against the input description produced by the plans. As rules and descriptions contain the same number of symbols, a similarity index S1 between a rule and a description is easily computed by the Algorithm Similarity that will be described in the following.

The parameters extracted by PE13 and PE15 are used in fuzzy relations. There is a fuzzy relation for each phoneme and the invocation of a fuzzy relation is conditioned by PAC, PE11 and PE12 descriptions. Fuzzy relations are conjunctions of disjunctions of fuzzy sets. A fuzzy relation computes another similarity index between phonemes and data extracted by subplans PE13 and PE15. A fuzzy relation can be seen as a conjunction of clauses. Each clause contains a disjunction of fuzzy sets defined over a parameter extracted by the planning system.

Fuzzy sets have been derived from a-priori probability distributions of parameters extracted by the plans. For each phoneme F, the membership function in the disjunction used in the relation of F is 1 in the interval in which 70% of the parameter values obtained by the pronounciation of F fall. The membership function then decreases toward zero and remains different from zero only in the interval in which fall 90% of the parameter values obtained by the

```
Algorithm Similarity (rule,description)
    begin
        c := 0;
        d := 0;
        for each i do
            begin
                if rule-symbol(i) matches
                    description-symbol(i)
                    then d := d + 1
                    else d := d - 1;
                c := c + 1
            end
        similarity := (d + c) / 2c
    end
```

pronounciation of F.

A similarity index S2 is computed by using the *max* operator for disjunctions and by summing the contributions of each clause and then dividing the sum by the number of clauses.

An example of clauses involved in fuzzy relations is the following :

E	:=	(short D)	(short ZQ)	(low ZR)
K	:=	(long D)	(short ZQ)	(high ZR)

where "short, long, high, low" are fuzzy sets. There are 43 such relations.

A-priori probabilities of the two similarity indices can be inferred from experiments for every phoneme. These probabilities can be supplied to the language model for further preprocessing or, they can be used in a Bayesian classifier. In the application described in this sub-section a simpler recognition strategy was used. It is described in the next sub-section.

Similarity measurements for the hypotheses generated by PE1 are averaged and the parameter $S12 = \frac{1}{2}(S1 + S2)$ is used for selecting the three candidates having the highest similarity with the data. Formant transitions are analyzed and a new similarity value S3 is computed for the three candidates. If the algorithm for analyzing formant transitions did not find plausible and unambiguous candidates, then S3 is not used, otherwise S3 is used for changing or confirming the ordering established based on S12.

S3 is used according to the rules of the following type. Horizontal formant patterns give a high S3 for E and bring E in the first position if E was second after B or P or third after both of them. There are five of such rules. Their details are omitted for the sake of brevity.

Bayesian classifiers or tree classifiers could be used for this approach. Nevertheless it was decided to experiment with a strategy in which expectation are built up using a-priori knowledge and parameter histograms. Candidates are then ranked according to how well they match expectations based on a voting criterion. Experimenting with other strategies is easy in this framework and will be done in the future. Various type of a-priori probabilities can be learned in this system and used in a recognition process based on an information theoretic approach as in [3].

Experiments on 1,000 samples of sequences of symbols in the E1 set pronounced by five male and five female speakers have given an error rate of 0.5% in *segmentation* without requiring any speaker adaptation.

Performances are shown in Fig. 4.

CONCLUSIONS

The following points summarize the most interesting aspects emerging from the experience described in this paper.

1) A distributed knowledge base system allows one to find a detailed

PRONOUNCED

RECOGNIZED

	P	T	K	B	D	G	C	V	E	3
P	93		1	2					2	
T		92	4		2	2			1	1
K		2	94						1	
B	5			93	4			3	1	
D		2		2	90			2		
G		3		1	2	97		1		1
C						1	100			
V				2	2			92		1
E	2		1					1	95	
3		1						1		97

INSERTION ERROR RATE: 0.5%
DELETION ERROR RATE : 0

Fig. 4 Performances on the recognition of the E1 set

explanation of the errors indicating along which directions the system should grow.

2) Speaker-dependent knowledge can be separated from the speaker-independent one.

3) Morphological features are useful ingredients for plan preconditions and for recognition.

4) Segmentation and recognition of place of articulation for vowels do not appear to be speaker dependent.

5) The good segmentation performances allows one to partition the difficulty of continuous speech recognition. Segmentation error are well explained.

6) Vectors of phonetic features can be mapped into symbols making this system similar to a vector quantizer where output can be used as an input to a recognizer based on DP-matching or on stochastic decoders.

7) Robust statistical algorithms can be used for clustering parameters used by plans. Clusters can be characterized by fuzzy sets.

8) Phonetic features are characterized by acoustic properties. Redundancies in this representation improve the recognition accuracy.

9) The research on connected letters and digits has potential applications in postal code recognition, in file directory access and in directory listing retrieval [16].

10) Planning can be systematically developed by listing the acoustic properties of phonetic features and the corresponding acoustic cues. Acoustic cues have to be described with a suitable formation (i.e. predicate calculus). Descriptions can be used for inductively learning rules [13].

ACKNOWLEDGEMENTS

This research was supported by the National Science and Engineering Research Council of Canada with grant no. A2439.

REFERENCES

1. G. R. Doddington and T. B. Schalk, "Speech Recognition, Turning Theory To Practice", IEEE Spectrum, Vol. 18, pp. 26-32, Sept. 1981.
2. L. R. Rabiner and S. L. Levinson, "Isolated and Connected Word Recognition. Theory and Selected Applications", IEEE Trans. on Communications, Vol. COM-29, No.5, pp. 621-659, 1981.
3. L. R. Bahl, F. Jelinek and R. L. Mercer, "A Maximum Likelihood Approach to Continuous Speech Recognition", IEEE Trans. on Pattern Analysis and Machine Intelligence, Vol. PAMI-5, No. 2, pp. 179-190, 1983.
4. L. R. Rabiner, J. G. Wilpon, A. M. Quinn and S. G. Terrace, "On the Application of Embedded Digit Training to Speaker Independent Connected Digit Recognition", IEEE Trans. on Acoustics, Speech and Signal Processing, Vol. ASSP-32, No. 2, pp. 272-279, 1984.
5. R. A. Cole, R. M. Stern, M. S. Phillips, S. M. Brill, A. P. Pilant and P. Specker, "Feature-Based Speaker-Independent Recognition of Isolated English Letters", IEEE Int. Conference on Acoustics, Speech and Signal Processing, Boston, Mass., pp. 731-734, 1983.
6. D. P. Huttenlocher and V. W. Zue, "A Model of Lexical Access Based on Partial Phonetic Information", IEEE Int. Conference on Acoustics, Speech and Signal Processing, San Diego, Cal., pp. 26.4.1-16.4.4, 1984.
7. P. Demichelis, R. De Mori, P. Laface and M. O'Kane, "Computer Recognition of Plosive Sounds Using Contextual Information", IEEE Trans. on Acoustics, Speech and Signal Processing, Vol. ASSP-31, pp. 359-377, 1983.
8. G. E. Kopec, "Voiceless Stop Consonant Identification Using LPC Spectra", IEEE Int. Conference on Acoustics, Speech and Signal Processing, San Diego, Cal., pp. 4211-4214, 1984.
9. M. Minsky, "A Framework for Representing Knowledge", In The Psychology of Computer Vision, Ed. by P. Winston, McGraw-Hill, 1975.
10. L. D. Erman, F. Hayes-Roth, V. R. Lesser and D. R. Reddy, "The HEARSAY-II Speech Understanding System. Integrating Knowledge to Resolve Uncertainty", Computing Surveys, Vol. 12, pp. 213-253, 1980.
11. R. De Mori, A. Giordana, P. Laface and L. Saitta, "An Expert System for Speech Decoding", Proc. AAAI Conference, Pittsburg, PA, pp. 107-110, 1982.
12. R. De Mori and P. Laface, "Use of Fuzzy Algorithms for Phonetic and Phonemic Labelling of Continuous Speech", IEEE Trans. on Pattern Analysis and Machine Intelligence, Vol. PAMI-2, pp. 136-148, 1980.
13. R. De Mori and M. Gilloux, "Inductive Learning of Phonetic Rules for Automatic Speech Recognition", Proc. CSCSI-84, London, Ont., pp. 103-105, 1984.
14. K. C. You and K. S. Fu, "A Syntactic Approach to Shape Recognition Using Attributed Grammars", IEEE Trans. on System, Man and Cybernetics SMC-9, pp. 334-345, 1979.
15. B. Delgutte, "Some Correlates of Phonetic Distinctions at the Level of the Auditory Nerve", in The Representation of Speech in the Peripheral Auditory System, Ed. by R. Carlson and B. Granstrom, Elsevier Biomedical, Amsterdam, pp. 131-149, 1982.

16. L. R. Rabiner, J. G. Wilpon and S. G. Terrace, "A Directory Listing Retrieval System Based on Connected Letter Recognition", IEEE Int. Conference on Acoustics, Speech and Signal Processing, San Diego, Cal., pp. 3541-3544, 1984.
17. R. De Mori, P. Laface, Y. F. Mong, "Parallel Algorithms for Syllable Recognition in continuous Speech IEEE Transctions on Pattern Analysis and Machine Intelligence. In press.

DEMISYLLABLES AS PROCESSING UNITS FOR AUTOMATIC SPEECH RECOGNITION AND LEXICAL ACCESS

G. Ruske
Division of Data Processing
Technical University of Munich
Federal Republic of Germany

1. INTRODUCTION

This paper describes a number of experimental investigations into syllable-based acoustic-phonetic analysis of German words; these methods can be used as a basic processing stage in a system for automatic speech recognition as well as for speech understanding. In this connection the importance of the syllable in speech processing by man and machine will first be discussed. Then several methods and experiments are presented involving segmentation into syllables and recognition of vowels and consonant clusters, as well as two methods for lexical access and lexical search using these units. The search in the lexicon is necessary in order to find the word in a word-list corresponding to the units recognized, or alternatively to determine the most similar word. The most salient feature of this system is that so-called demisyllables are used as the processing units.

A fundamental problem faced by every system is that of defining suitable segments in the speech signal which can be used for the analysis algorithms of the spoken utterance. Particularly when processing continuous speech and large vocabularies, some kind of segmentation is necessary, whether explicitly or implicitly. The introduction of smaller subword-units reduces the amount of training data and comes nearer to a phonetic description of the spoken utterance.

NATO ASI Series, Vol. F16
New Systems and Architectures for Automatic Speech
Recognition and Synthesis. Edited by R. De Mori and C.Y. Suen

It could be shown in previous experiments [1] that the use of smaller units in fact results in better performance than whole-word recognition when the vocabulary size increases.

If the segmentation is carried out explicitly in the signal domain or its parametric representation, the segmentation procedure is required to provide segments which on the one hand are readily found and isolated in the speech signal, and which on the other hand can be dealt with as independently of each other as possible. It is important to realize that the syntactic and semantic interpretation of a sentence can be carried out to best advantage at word level, since words fulfill grammatical functions as well as conveying the meaning. Seen in this light, it is thus advantageous at the first stage to aim to recognize words, or to form hypotheses about words. However, the explicit separation of words in continuous speech is an impossible task since words are linked and coarticulated with one another in much the same way as syllables. This leads immediately to the possibility of regarding syllables, and not words, as the elements with the greatest temporal extent from which every spoken utterance can be built up.

2. THE ROLE OF THE SYLLABLE IN SPEECH PROCESSING

In fact, there are a number of good reasons for regarding the syllable as the basic unit in speech processing. Evidence can be found from the areas of

- — speech production (articulation)
- — speech perception
- — technical realizability of the segmentation

In the following, each of these areas will be discussed briefly in turn. The basic gesture performed in speaking consists of a repeated opening and closing, or constriction, of the vocal tract. This is what lies behind the definition of the spoken syllable [2]. This basic speech gesture is responsible among other things for increased loudness within the syllable nucleus, a typical pitch contour, and a typical development in the quality of the speech sounds; this quality contour is most clear in the middle of the syllable. Finally, this production mechanism causes the strong coarticulatory effects, and thus the interdependency of the acoustic cues within the initial and final parts of the syllable.

Speech perception must also face the question of what units can be assumed. A variety of experiments indicate that consonants and vowels are not perceived independently of one another. For instance, experiments with consonant-vowel-consonant sequences (CVC) showed that both consonant and vowel information in a syllable is exploited to identify the vowel [3]. Such findings provide grounds for believing that consonants and vowels are not analyzed separately from each other, and that perception operates on units having at least the extent of a syllable. Of crucial importance is the practical realizability of the segmentation procedure in a speech recognition system if we intend to perform an explicit segmentation. Two facts facilitate the localization of syllable nuclei quite considerably: Firstly, a maximum in the sound pressure level, or to be more precise, in the psycho-acoustically defined 'loudness' can be expected [4,5,6]; secondly, the vocalic part of the syllable nucleus can be identified quite readily from the spectral distribution. These two procedures can be combined to produce a simple syllable detector; further details will be presented below. In contrast, the precise separation of consecutive syllables presents some problems. However, relative minima in the loudness contour can be regarded as suitable candidates for syllable boundaries [4,6].

3. DEMISYLLABLES AS PROCESSING UNITS

Since the inventory of syllables is very large, it seems sensible to divide every syllable into two *demisyllables*, namely into one extending from syllable boundary to syllable nucleus, and into one extending from syllable nucleus to the next syllable boundary, see fig. 1. The German language possesses more than 1000 initial and final demisyllables each. Demisyllable segments retain practically

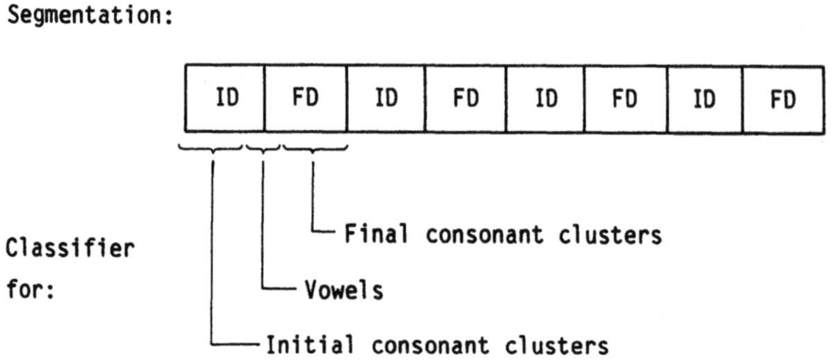

Fig. 1 Principle of demisyllable segmentation and recognition (ID = initial demisyllable; FD = final demisyllable).

all the advantages of complete syllables, are easy to locate, and include the strongest coarticulatory effects; in comparison, coarticulation between adjacent demisyllables is fairly weak.

A dramatic reduction in the number of classes can be achieved if the internal structure of a demisyllable is taken into account: Each demisyllable contains a part of the vowel forming the syllable nucleus as well as a *consonant cluster*, which can consist of any sequence of consonants permitted in syllable-initial or syllable-final position. It is thus appropriate to incorporate different classifiers, namely one each for the vocalic part forming the syllable nucleus, for the consonantal part at the beginning of the syllable, and for the consonantal part at the end of the syllable [4,6]. The decision units (classes) are thus defined to be vowels and consonant clusters. A precise separation of vocalic and consonantal parts is not absolutely essential for this purpose. It is sufficient for the part of interest to be emphasized and fed to the appropriate classifier.

In German, only about 47 initial consonant clusters occur [6,7], see fig. 2a. If extremely rare combinations (such as /dv/) and foreign words are included, the size of this inventory increases somewhat of course, but still remains within strict limits.

The number of final consonant clusters is significantly larger since a number of inflections can be appended. As depicted in fig. 2b, the inventory can amount to a maximum of 159 final consonant clusters, with many occurring very rarely indeed. If the vocabulary is limited to 8000 words then 103 final consonant clusters are enough, and with a vocabulary consisting of the 1001 most frequent German words this number drops to only 50 final consonant clusters [7]. With the consonant cluster inventory just described plus a maximum of 20 vowels (long vowels, short vowels, and diphthongs) it is possible to represent an almost unlimited German vocabulary, for both isolated words and continuous speech.

4. EXPERIMENTS WITH A SYLLABLE-BASED SPEECH RECOGNITION SYSTEM

A series of basic experiments with a syllable-based speech recognition system is described below; the system consists of the following stages: segmentation of individual words into demisyllables, classification of consonant clusters and vowels, and the subsequent correction of the recognition results with a phonetic lexicon.

Segmentation: Syllable-based segmentation is made easier if auditorily based pre-processing of the speech wave is carried out. Psycho-acoustic investigations have shown that the vowels in the syllable nucleus are normally experienced as being noticeably louder than their neighbouring consonants. In the following experiments a functional model of loudness sensation was thus implemented [8]. The analysis starts from a decomposition of the audible frequency range into 24 'critical bands' [9]. In each band (channel of a filter bank) the 'specific' loudness

(a)

'p t k b d g h f z ʃ m n l r v j

ʃpr pr ʃtr tr kr br dr gr pfr fr ʃr

ʃpl pl kl bl gl pfl fl ʃl ʃm ʃn kn gn

tsv ʃv kv ʃp ʃt pf ts

(b)

r l m n ŋ p t k f s ʃ ç x -

rl rm rn rp rf rt rʃ rk rç

lm ln lp lf lt lʃ lk lç

ŋk nf nʃ nç mp mpf mʃ

pf pʃ ft tʃ

} usually also with suffixes -s -t -st -ts

Fig. 2 Inventory of German initial consonant clusters (a), and final consonant clusters (b).

component $N_{\nu}(t)$ is calculated. We use 22 channels covering the range from 50 Hz to 8.5 kHz. The (total) loudness N(t) is formed from the sum of the specific loudness components over all 22 channels. In addition, a 'modified' loudness function $N_m(t)$ is derived as the difference between a lower (channels 3 to 15) and a higher (channels 20 to 22) frequency range. This modified loudness function is then smoothed by a low-pass filter with a cut-off frequency of about 10 Hz. Taken together with a rough vowel/non-vowel classification and a lower bound for the overall loudness it is then possible to infer the locations of the syllable nuclei directly from the maxima in the function $N_m(t)$. Fig. 3 shows as an example the German word 'Spracherkennung'; here the syllable nuclei (vowels) /a:/, /ɛ/, /ɛ/ and /u/ were picked out in this way. The maximum at /ʃ/ was

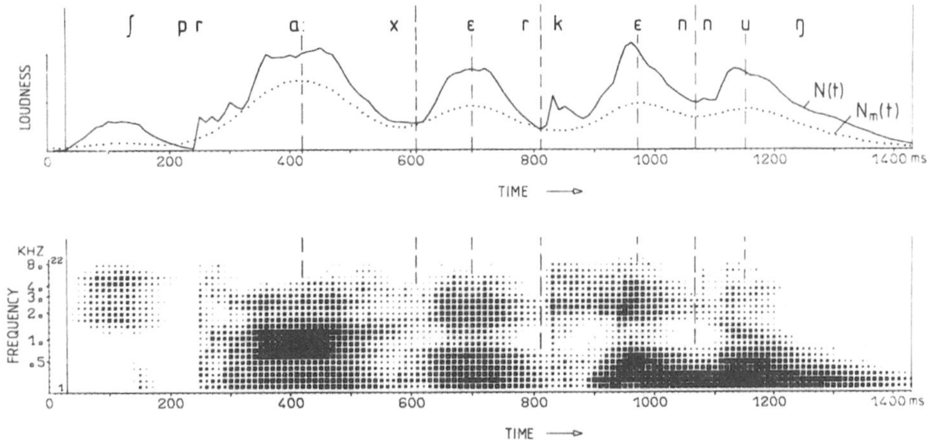

Fig. 3 Segmentation of the German word 'Spracherkennung' using the modified loudness function $N_m(t)$ and the (total) loudness N(t).

rejected since it did not fulfill the conditions for a vowel. The minima in the loudness contour N(t) show possible positions for the syllable boundaries. The experiments with a vocabulary of 1001 words spoken in isolation produced error rates of about 4% in the correct identification of the syllable nuclei.

Classification of consonant clusters and vowels: When classifying consonant clusters we are faced with the problem that the vocalic part must be suppressed or masked out as far as possible. The problem was solved in the following way. Each demisyllable segment covers a series of loudness spectra, which are measured at 10 ms intervals, the segments being of varying lengths. Using a so-called 'dynamic interpolation' procedure [4,6], this series is converted into a series with a fixed number of loudness spectra. Experiments show that conversion by interpolation into 12 spectra is sufficient. Suppression of the vocalic part is then achieved by dropping 3 interpolated spectra on the vocalic side; the 9 remaining spectra now represent the actual pattern for the consonant cluster. Classification of the interpolated patterns of the consonant clusters was carried out with the help of a geometrical distance measurement by using the 1-nearest-neighbour rule and a city-block metric. Previous experiments with German consonant clusters had resulted in recognition scores for initial consonant clusters in the order of 75% on average [6]; the average recognition scores for final consonant clusters amounted to 85%. Overall these results show that good recognition accuracy can be achieved using the concept of consonant cluster recognition and classification by template matching.

Classification of consonant clusters using feature vectors: Since knowledge about the phonetic structure could considerably reduce the dimensionality of the consonant cluster templates a second method was developed starting from a description of the relevant acoustic events within each demisyllable segment [10]. In a first step those spectral and temporal features or 'cues' are evaluated which can be objectively measured in the signal. The cues describe: the 'loci' of the first 3 formants of the syllable vowel, the formant transitions, formant-like 'links' for nasals and liquids, duration and spectral distribution of bursts and fricative noise ('turbulences'), pauses and the presence of voicing during pauses or turbulences.

A main problem is the dependency of most of the features on phonetic context; in this approach the context dependencies are taken into consideration by collecting the results of feature extraction within each demisyllable segment. This enables the contextual dependencies between the acoustic features to be determined statistically from representative speech material. The feature vector for an initial consonant cluster as well as for a final consonant cluster have a fixed number of components. In syllable-initial position 1 nasal, liquid or glide, and up to 2 fricatives or plosives are possible; in syllable-final position the maximum number of plosives or fricatives in the test speech material was 3.

Therefore, initial consonant clusters are completely described by 24 feature components and final consonant clusters by 31 components [10].

Feature extraction starts from a voiced/unvoiced/silence-decision for each spectral frame. Additionally, formant tracking is performed within voiced parts. Acoustic parameters are then derived from the energy in selected frequency bands, which allow a gross characterization of the spectral shape. Based on these parameters, a set of rules has been established in order to detect voiced and unvoiced turbulences and bursts, pauses, and liquid and nasal links. After detection the individual features are characterized by gross measurements of their spectral and temporal distribution (e.g. center of gravity as well as upper and lower cut-off frequency for turbulences, and the frequency values of spectral peaks for links) and used as components of the common demisyllable feature vector.

Classification of the feature vectors was based on Euclidean distance measurements within the feature space. For this purpose a special 'average normalized distance' was defined which allows the comparison of all feature vectors even if they differ quite considerably as to their current composition. For comparison, the same speech material was processed by a template matching method using a very fine temporal and spectral resolution; in this experiment 22 spectra with all 24 loudness components were used for each template giving 528 components altogether. The recognition results showed that the recognition scores for the feature representations were about 5-7% lower as compared to the template matching approach [10]. But when comparing both methods it has to be borne in mind that the feature vector for a consonant cluster has only 24 or 31 components whereas a corresponding template constructed from a series of consecutive spectra needs on average more than 500 components which have to be time normalized and compared by appropriate distance measurements. Therefore the two methods differ drastically in storage requirements and computation time. Thus feature components can in fact be seen as an efficient way of representing the units.

5. SYLLABLE-BASED SEARCH IN THE LEXICON

The quality of the search in the lexicon is decisively important for the performance of a recognition system. The effectiveness of the correction of wrongly recognized words is largely determined by the extent to which a-priori knowledge about the distribution of the classifier's wrong decisions can be utilized. The experiments to be described next will contrast two procedures, namely:

a) The words are stored in the lexicon in phonetic transcription in groups of consonant clusters and vowels (comparison based on phonetic symbols);

b) The individual demisyllables are given a spectral representation ('prototypes') both in the lexicon and at the output of the classifier.

In fig. 4a and 4b the two methods are contrasted. In the first procedure (fig. 4a), the similarity between recognition output and lexical entry is measured by using alternatives from a confusion matrix containing the a-posteriori probabilities; these typical confusions have been obtained in a training phase. The confusion matrices are set up separately for initial consonant clusters, final consonant clusters and vowels; the lexical entries are in phonetic transcription.

In the second procedure (fig. 4b), a geometric distance measurement using spectral representations ('prototypes') is carried out. The prototypes each consist of several consecutive loudness spectra from a complete demisyllable, and thus include the consonant cluster and the vowel up to the middle of the syllable [11]. The test material consisted of the 1001 most frequent German words and were spoken by one speaker three times.

The reference patterns for the classification of the consonant clusters and vowels were obtained from a training set. The classification was carried out using a distance measurement (1-NN rule with a city block metric). For each classified, unknown word the result is a sequence of labels (phonetic symbols) for initial consonant clusters, vowels and final consonant clusters. In this primary classification stage the average recognition rate for complete words amounted to

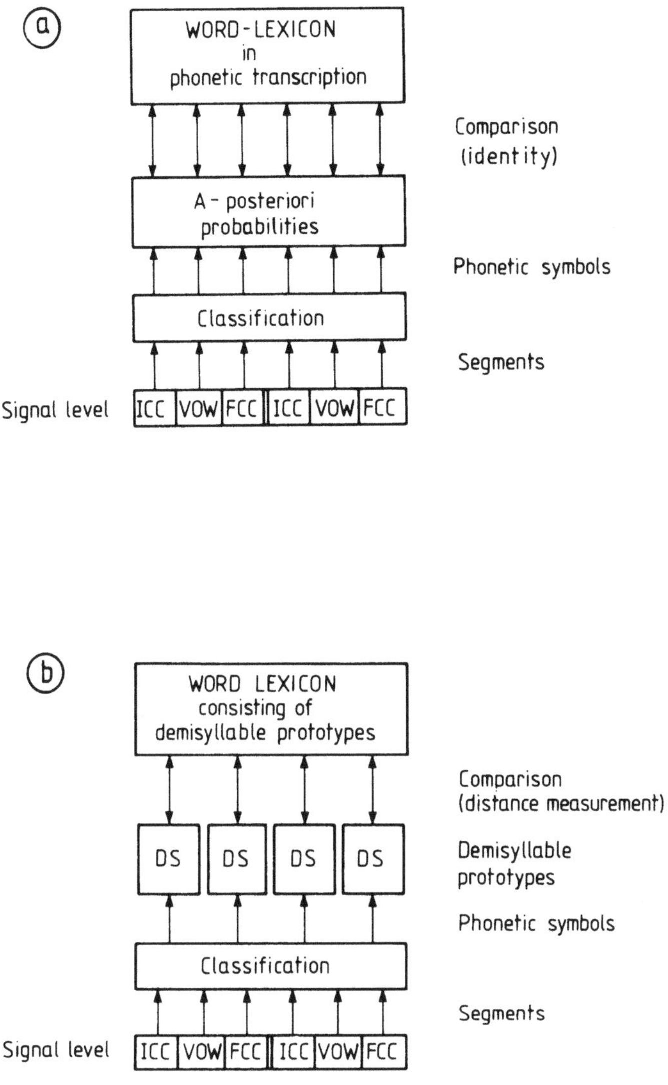

Fig. 4 **Principle of the lexical search, (a) using a-posteriori probabilities and (b) using spectral prototypes; (ICC=initial consonant cluster, FCC=final consonant cluster, VOW=Vowel, DS=demisyllable).**

50.1%; this means that for about half of the words every label in the complete word was correct.

Lexical search with a-posteriori probabilities: The confusion matrices were etablished by observing the confusions made by the classifier. If the given ('true') class membership of a unit is denoted by c, and the recognition result by k, the classification of a large sample of these units provides an estimate for the conditional probability $p(k|c)$. This result can be used to determine the a-posteriori probability of c for a given recognition result k:

$$p(c|k) = p(k|c) \cdot p(c)/p(k),$$

with

$p(c)$ and $p(k)$:	A-priori probabilities
$p(k|c)$:	Conditional probabilites (decisions of the classifier).

Let us consider now as an example the search for a monosyllabic word consisting of the 3 units: $C = \{c_1,c_2,c_3\}$. The classification output is given by: $K = \{k_1,k_2,k_3\}$. The lexical search has to find the word possessing the greatest overall a-posteriori probability for this particular recognition result. The a-posteriori probability for the word C of the lexicon when K was recognized, is expressed as:

$$p(C|K) = p(c_1,c_2,c_3|k_1,k_2,k_3) \ .$$

Assuming statistical independence of the three classification results we obtain the following expression:

$$p(K|C) = p(k_1,k_2,k_3|c_1,c_2,c_3) = p(k_1|c_1) \cdot p(k_2|c_2) \cdot p(k_3|c_3) \ .$$

Using Bayes' formula we get:

$$p(c_1,c_2,c_3|k_1,k_2,k_3) = \frac{p(k_1,k_2,k_3|c_1,c_2,c_3) \cdot p(c_1,c_2,c_3)}{p(k_1,k_2,k_3)}$$

$$= \frac{p(k_1|c_1) \cdot p(k_2|c_2) \cdot p(k_3|c_3) \cdot p(c_1,c_2,c_3)}{p(k_1,k_2,k_3)}$$

$$= \frac{p(c_1|k_1)p(c_2|k_2)p(c_3|k_3) \cdot p(k_1)p(k_2)p(k_3) \cdot p(c_1,c_2,c_3)}{p(c_1)p(c_2)p(c_3) \cdot p(k_1,k_2,k_3)}$$

The term $p(k_1,k_2,k_3)$ in the denominator and the product $p(k_1)p(k_2)p(k_3)$ in the numerator can be disregarded for the following considerations since they remain constant in the search. The expresion $p(c_1,c_2,c_3) = p(C)$ is the probability of occurrence of word C in the lexicon. Assuming the same probability of occurrence for all M words in the lexicon this term can also be left out for the search. In addition, it may be admissible to assume that the probabilities of occurrence of the classes $p(c_1)$, $p(c_2)$ and $p(c_3)$ in the lexicon are equally distributed, so that no class is preferred; in this case the lexical search becomes independent of the current distribution of the classes in the lexicon.

Let the j-th word in the lexicon be designated by $C_j = \{c_{1j},c_{2j},c_{3j}\}$. Based on the conditions outlined above, the lexical search chooses the word C_i for which the product of the a-posteriori probabilities is greatest:

$$\{k_1,k_2,k_3\} \in C_i, \text{ if } p(c_{1i}|k_1)p(c_{2i}|k_2)p(c_{3i}|k_3) > p(c_{1j}|k_1)p(c_{2j}|k_2)p(c_{3j}|k_3)$$

$$\text{for } j = 1...M,\ i \neq j\ ;\ M = \text{Number of words in the lexicon}$$

This expression means that the maximum of the products for all words in the lexicon must be determined. To this end, the individual classification results k_1, k_2 and k_3 are expanded to include all those 'alternatives' offered by the confusion matrices for these recognized units. The list of alternatives contains all those words to which an inference would be possible. Fig. 5 shows as an example the list of alternatives for the recognition result /' ai ls/. We see that several words in the lexicon will fit in here, e.g. 'als' (/'als/), 'teils' (/tails/),

RECOGNITION RESULT

'	aɪ	ls

↓ ↓ ↓

ALTERNATIVES FROM CONFUSION MATRICES

'	94.0	aɪ	73.0	ls	83.0
p	1.4	a	9.0	ts	6.0
t	1.2	ə	7.0	s	6.0
b	1.1	ɛ	6.5	nts	5.0
d	.9	a:	1.6		
g	.8	e:	1.2		
fr	.6	ɔʏ	.9		
		ɛ:	.7		
	[%]		[%]		[%]

Fig. 5 Expansion of the recognition result /' ai ls/ by using alternatives from confusion matrices together with their a-posteriori probabilities.

'Tanz' (/tants/) etc. Every word in the lexicon must now be compared with this list of alternatives to check for a match. The recognized word will be the one with the highest joint probability calculated from the product of the individual a-posteriori probabilities in the columns of this table.

In the present experiment with the 1001 word vocabulary a total recognition score of about 89.0% was achieved, see fig. 6a. The main problem resides in the determination of sufficiently precise confusion matrices and the corresponding a-posteriori probabilities.

Lexical search with spectral representations: When spectral prototypes are used it is also desirable for the confusions of the preceding classification to be represented as well as possible during the lexical search in order to make the best correction. This can be realized if the prototypes are represented in a feature space similar to the one underlying the classification. Representation in the form of demisyllable prototypes is particularly simple. A similar approach using

a)

EXPERIMENT 1 (Lexical search with phonetic symbols):

— Total recognition score (1001 words): 89.0%

b)

EXPERIMENT 2 (Lexical search with spectral prototypes):

— Total recognition score (1001 words): 90.3%

	Number of components:	22	12	6	3
Number of spectra	10	90.3	90.3	89.9	85.3
	5	90.2	90.3	89.9	85.1
	2	90.0	90.1	89.5	84.1

Fig. 6 (a) Recognition score of experiment 1 and (b) recognition scores of experiment 2 as a function of the temporal and spectral resolution of demisyllable prototypes for lexical search (in %).

diphone prototypes has already been proposed for English [12].

An example for the generation of demisyllable prototypes is depicted in fig. 7; the demisyllable segmentation procedure and dynamic interpolation is applied to each reference word. After that, the prototypes were constructed by averaging all demisyllables with the same label from the 2x1001 words of the training set. To handle the lexicon mentioned here about 200 prototypes each are required for the initial and final demisyllables. In the first trial each demisyllable prototype (in

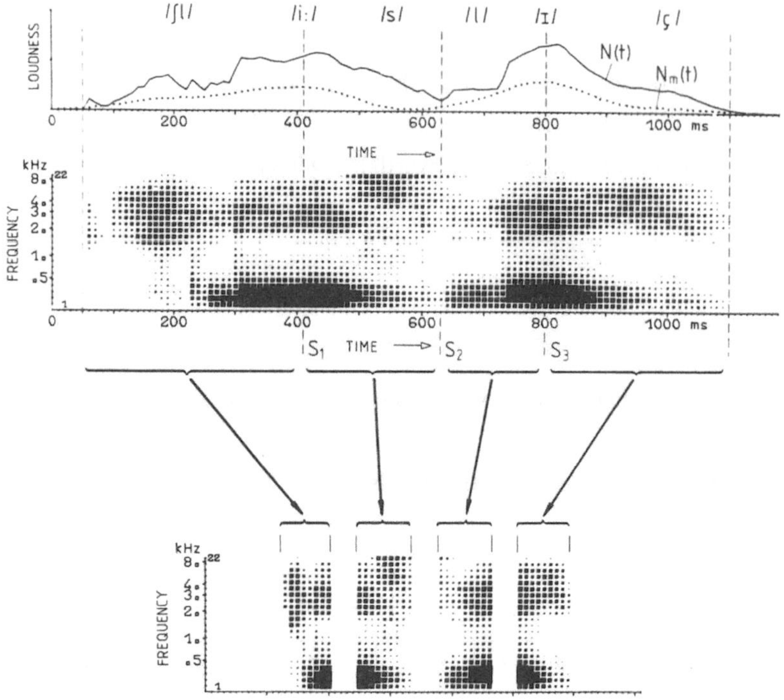

Fig. 7 Generation of demisyllable prototypes from the German word 'schließlich'.

the lexicon and the classification result) was represented by 10 spectra with 22 components. The total recognition rate was 90.3%, see fig. 6b.

It is not possible to improve the performance further by increasing the resolution of the prototypes, and this thus represents an upper bound. On the other hand, the table in fig. 6b shows that the spectral and temporal resolution of the prototypes can be reduced considerably without significant deterioration in correction performance. Even when the demisyllable prototypes were reduced to 2 spectra with six components, an overall recognition rate of 89.5% was still achieved [11]. In the present experiment lexical search with spectral representations thus attained practically the same recognition performance as a lexical search based on a-posteriori probabilities; the spectral representation method is even slightly superior as long as extremely low resolution in the prototypes is avoided. When judging the performance of the correction stage it must always be borne in mind that uncorrectable confusions and segmentation errors mean that the highest recognition result actually obtainable was 94.7%.

6. OUTLOOK

It is interesting to compare this 2-stage approach with whole-word recognition methods which can be considered as 1-stage methods. In other experiments we were able to show that the 2-stage method using a demisyllable segmentation and classification and a lexical correction stage, yielded better recognition scores when compared with whole-word recognition /1/. Further, it is an important advantage of the two-stage method that the recognition task is split up into two individual tasks, each of which can be realized with a substantially smaller number of components. The demisyllable segments thus consist of no more than 220 components (i.e. 10 spectra with 22 channels). The number of classes in the 1001-word list used here does not rise above an average of 41 consonant clusters and 19 vowels (with diphthongs); the representatives in the lexicon may consist of as few as 12 components (2 spectra with 6 channels). Within this feature space the classification can be realized easily using straightforward procedures. In contrast, for whole-word recognition a high-dimensional space is required in which the classification is to be performed.

The experiments discussed here were based on the speech material of one speaker, and were carried out with words spoken in isolation. The applicability of the demisyllable concept to the recognition of continuous speech has however already been demonstrated in some preliminary experiments [13]; under these conditions the number of syllable segmentation errors increases slightly.

Demisyllables have proven to be an appropriate choice of unit for the different processing stages. In sentence recognition syllable-based segmentation also has advantages for the subsequent processing stages. Pilot experiments have shown that it is advantageous to take well identified syllables as anchor points when generating hypotheses about words; on average, the first syllable only allows 40 words out of 1001 to be picked out as hypotheses. On this level it is possible to employ procedures which allow wrongly indicated syllables to be skipped or missing syllables to be inserted. For example, the comparison of the word hypotheses can be carried out back on the parametric level, this time without segmentation.

ACKNOWLEDGEMENTS

This research was supported by the 'Deutsche Forschungsgemeinschaft' (DFG).

REFERENCES

1. G. Ruske and T. Schotola, "The efficiency of demisyllable segmentation in the recognition of spoken words," IEEE Int. on Acoustics, Speech and Signal Processing, Atlanta, 971-974, 1981.
2. G. Hammarström, "Linguistische Einheiten im Rahmen der modernen Sprachwissenschaft," in *Kommunkation und Kybernetik in Einzeldarstellungen*, (H. Wolter and W. D. Keidel eds.), Volume 5, Springer-Verlag, 1966.
3. P. Mermelstein, "On the relationship between vowel and consonant identification when cued by the same acoustic information," Percept. Psychophys. 23, 331-336, 1978.
4. G. Ruske and T. Schotola, "An approach to speech recognition using syllabic decision units," IEEE Int. Conf. on Acoustics, Speech and Signal Procesing, Tulsa, 722-725, 1978.
5. M. J. Hunt, M. Lennig and P. Mermelstein, "Experiments in syllable-based recognition of continuous speech," IEEE Int. Conf. on Acoustics, Speech and Signal Processing, Denver, 880-883, 1980.
6. G. Ruske, "Auditory perception and its application to computer analysis of speech," in *Computer Analysis and Perception, Vol. II, Auditory Signals* (C. Y. Suen and R. De Mori, eds.), CRC-Press, Boca Raton, Florida, 1-42, 1982.
7. T. Schotola, "On the use of demisyllables in automatic word recognition," Speech Communication 3, North-Holland Publ., 63-87, 1984.
8. E. Zwicker, E. Terhardt and E. Paulus, "Automatic speech recognition using psychoacoustic models," JASA 65, 487-498, 1979.

9. E. Zwicker, "Subdivision of the audible frequency range into critical bands (Frequenzgruppen)", JASA 33, 248, 1961.
10. G. Ruske, "On the usage of demisyllables in automatic speech recognition," in *SIGNAL PROCESSING II: Theoreies and Applications*, H. W. Schüßler (Ed.), Elsvier Science Publishers B. V. (North-Holland), 419-422, 1983.
11. W. Schiele, "Korrektur falsch klassifizierter Halbsilben in einem Worterkennungssystem durch geometrische Abstandsmessungen", Report of the Division of Data Processing, Technical University of Munich, Germany, 1981.
12. D. H. Klatt, "Speech perception: A model of acoustic-phonetic analysis and lexical access," Journal of Phonetics 7, 279-312, 1979.
13. H.-J. Geywitz, "Automatische Erkennung fließender Sprache mit silbenorientierten Einheiten", Doctoral thesis, Division of Data Processing, Technical University of Munich, Germany, 1984.

DETECTION AND RECOGNITION OF NASAL CONSONANTS IN CONTINUOUS SPEECH - PRELIMINARY RESULTS

R. Gubrynowicz
L. Le Guennec
G. Mercier
Centre National d'Etudes des Telecommunications
22301 Lannion, France

1. INTRODUCTION

The problem of the detection, recognition or perception of nasal consonants in continuous speech signals is not frequently treated in the literature. Among the most significant works on this subject should be mentioned the classical ones such as [5,9,4] or more recently [11,3,2]. The principal reason that there are relatively few papers devoted to this subject is, perhaps, its complexity. In fact, from the acoustical point of view, the spectral structure of nasal consonants is rather complicated because their spectral envelope is formed not only by the resonants of the pharyngeal and nasal cavities but also by the anti-resonants of the oral cavity, which is closed during the articulation of nasals.

In general, the variations of resonants frequencies are not very great and are independent of the place of articulation. Only the variation of antiresonant frequencies are strictly connected with changes of articulatory parameters, which,

---

R. Gubrynowicz is also invited professor at Institut de Phonétique, Université de Provence, Aix-en-Provence, France.

NATO ASI Series, Vol. F16
New Systems and Architectures for Automatic Speech Recognition and Synthesis. Edited by R. De Mori and C. Y. Suen

in the first approximation, determine the length of the oral cavity branching the pharyngeal and nasal parts of the vocal tract. It is very often that the first anti-resonant (whose frequency is, for example for /m/, around 1,2 kHZ) involves the diminution or even total annihilation of the second formant which frequently is in the proximity of this anti-resonant. In addition, the individual voice characteristics of speaker can have a significant influence on the final form of the nasal consonant spectrum. In fact, the anatomical structure of nasal cavities varies from one speaker to the other, so it is difficult to identify the nasal consonant from their static acoustic properties determined mainly by the transfer function of pharyngo-nasal part of the vocal tract. The inadequacy of the approach based only on static parameters of speech is particularly evident in recognition systems, especially in those which are based only on general description of spectral properties as is the case with the vocoder, for example.

The purpose of our paper is to present a general scheme of the procedure for detecting and, in some particular conditions, for recognition of three French nasal consonants /m, n, gn/ spoken in continuous speech. This procedure is designed for the speech understanding system described in [8].

2. ARTICULATORY AND ACOUSTIC PROPERTIES OF NASAL CONSONANTS

In French, three nasal consonants are essentially distinguished, namely bilabial /m/, alveo-dental /n/ and palatal /gn/. The velar /gn/ is present only in words of English origin as it is in the case of the word "parking" (car-park). These consonants belong to the class of interrupted ones, for which the airflow in the oral cavity is stopped by closing lips or by forming lingual obstruction (with tongue blade or another part of the tongue body). This attribute is also characteristic of nasal consonants as a constant cue. In general, the articulatory properties of the same consonant spoken in a stream of sounds are modified by the context. In the case of nasals, the most important modifications are in the horizontal plane, especially concerning the place of articulation. But there are also some indications that alterations of the aperture in vertical plane are possible. The general rule, well established, says that the greater the important difference between the articulation forms of adjacent sounds, the more considerable is the influence of the following (or in specific cases, of the preceding) sound segment. In the case of nasals which are very sensitive to context. This influence is most visible for the nasal /n/, for example, pronounced in the vicinity of sounds with posterior place of articulation than of those with a more central configuration of the tongue body. Similarly, the palatal /gn/ as in the french word "agneau" (lamb) the place of articulation is more displaced to central region of the vocal tract in the vicinity of frontal sounds than for the others.

From an articulatory point of view, the basic attribute of nasals is the closing of the oral cavity and the opening of the velo-pharyngeal part which allows air to flow through nasal cavity. On the other hand, between pharyngo-nasal and oral cavities we observe a coupling which varies with the velum position and oral cavity configuration.

These articulatory properties result, in the acoustic domain, in the apparition of a very low first formant, typically between 200-300 Hz for adult's voices. Some acoustical attributes of nasals are independent of the adjacent vowel and are marked by a sharp change of total energy level at the release of the nasal segment, but this discontinuity is not very great (about 4 dB). The spectral changes are also rather sharp and generally, cover the total frequencies so that the presence of the nasal in sounds the stream is often easy to discriminate by eye on sonagrams, with one exception perhaps for the liquid /l/ which is frequently confused with this category of speech sounds. The spectral variations at the release of the nasal segment (in CV syllables) can be used for the distinction of its place of articulation, as suggested by [1] who demonstrated that the place of articulation can be characterized by the spectral energy distribution at the consonant release which in the case of alveolars is tilted towards high frequencies and for labials is either flat or else tilted towards lower frequencies. This tendency is visible on Figures 1 and 2 with sonagrams of bisyllabic

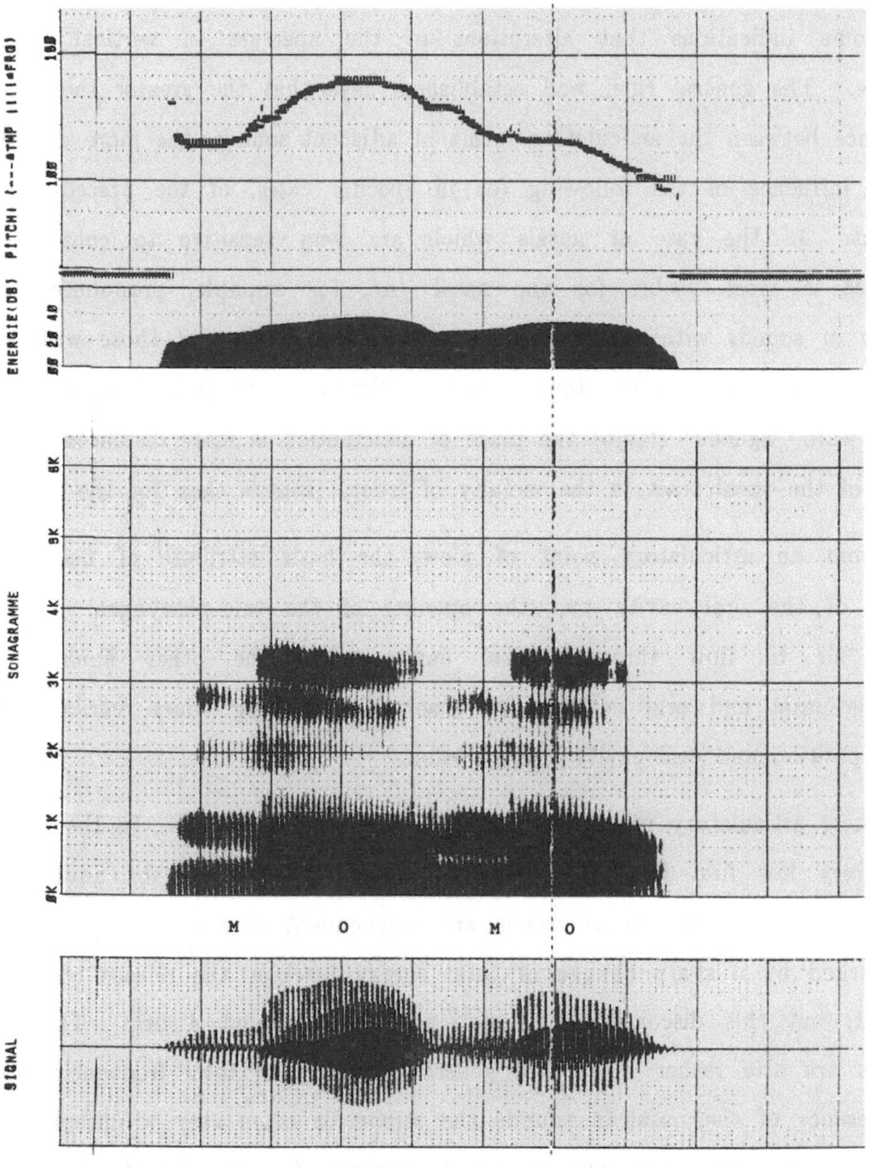

Fig. 1 Sonagram of the bisyllabic sequence /momo/ spoken in isolation by male speaker.

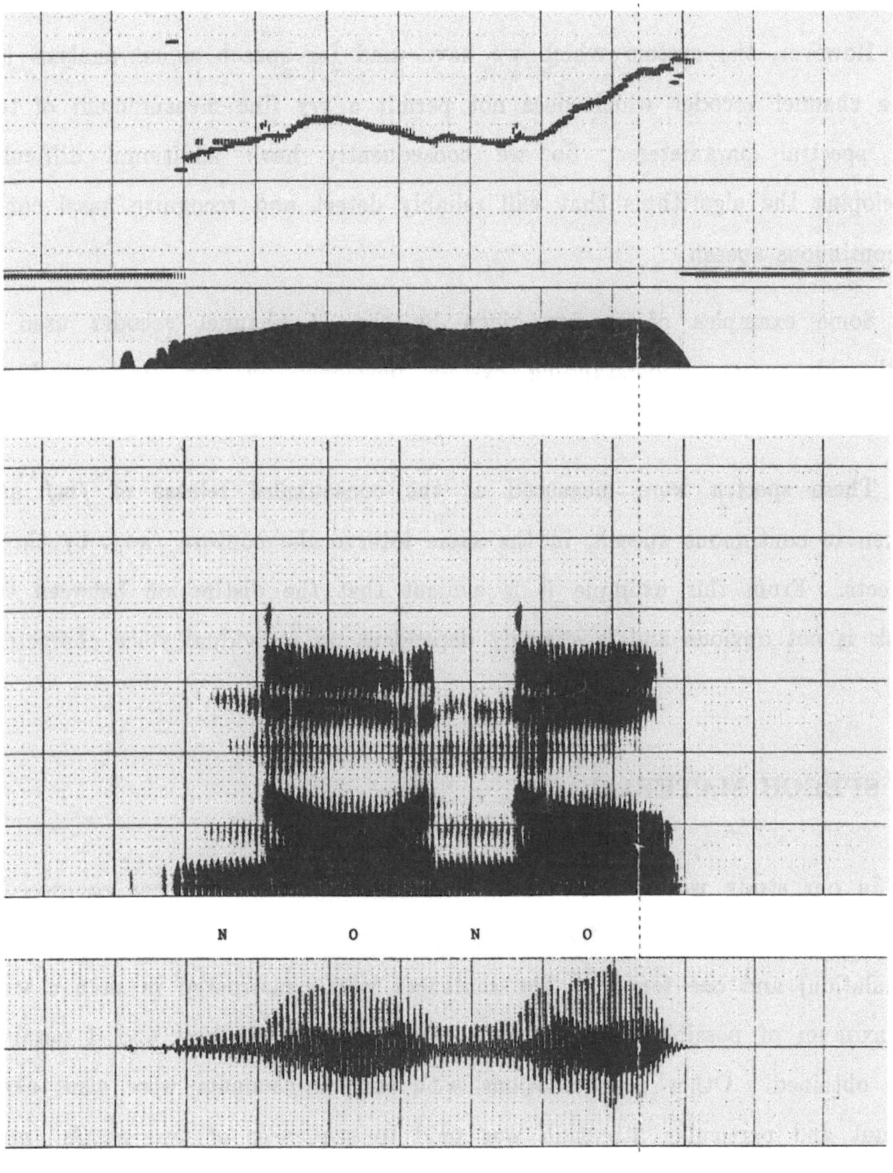

Fig. 2 Sonagram of the bisyllabic sequence /nono/ spoken in isolation by the same as in Fig. 1 speaker.

sequences /momo/ and /nono/ pronounced in isolation by a male speaker.

However, the system which we have used for speech signal analysis is based on a channel vocoder which does not permit a vry fine measurement of temporal and spectral parameters. So we consequently have additional difficulties in developing the algorithms that will reliably detect and recognize nasal consonants in continuous speech.

Some examples of spectra given by the 14 channel vocoder used in the continuous speech understanding system developed in the National Center of Telecommunication Studies (CNET) are presented in Figure 3.

These spectra were measured at the consonantal release of /m/ and /n/ spoken in continuous speech, in the same intervocalic context /a-i/, by three male subjects. From this example it is evident that the distinction between the two nasals is not obvious and is strongly dependent on individual voice characteristics.

3. SPEECH MATERIAL

In our study we used two sets of sentences. The first was composed of 44 sentences pronounced by five male speakers (two of them with a slurring articulation) and one female. The sentences were constructed in such a way that a maximum of possible coarticulations of nasals with 11 oral and 4 nasal vowels were obtained. Other coarticulations with some consonants were also taken into account and particular attention was paid to sequences of two nasals /mn/ and /nm/, nasals followed or preceded by a liquid /l/ or by a voiced fricative and stop consonants, because these cases turned out to be the most difficult for the nasal segment discrimination. The second set was composed of phonetically balanced sentences and of some other pronounced in Breton language for which the frequency of occurrence of nasals is relatively high. The overall number of subjects was equal to 8 male and 3 female speakers.

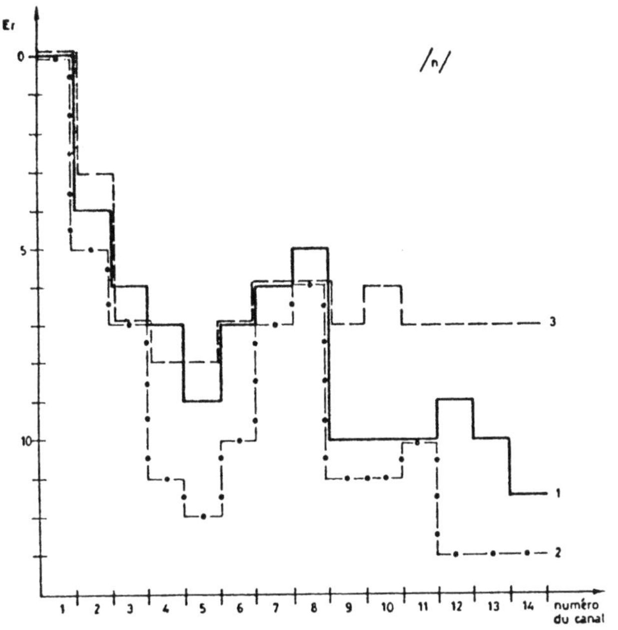

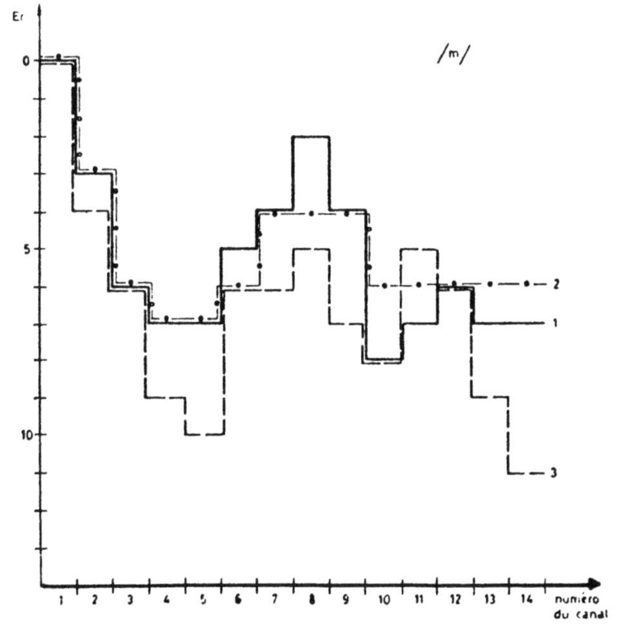

Fig. 3 Some examples of the nasal consonants' spectra evaluated at the release: a) of the /n/, of the /m/. The two nasals were spoken in the same intervocalic context /a-i/ by 3 male subjects.

In our study we distinguished three types of intervocalic contexts:

1) with no important change of the place of vocalic articulation,
2) with a relatively weak backward of forward movement,
3) with a strong change of the place.

In all we have analyzed 236 realizations of nasals: 108 of /m/, 109 of /n/ and 19 of /gn/.

4. SPEECH SIGNAL PROCESSING AND FEATURE PARAMETER EVALUATION

The speech signal was recorded in a sound treated studio, digitalized and coded by a 14 channel vocoder implemented on a VAX computer. After conversion each sentence is represented by a string of samples of 13.3 ms duration, each of them characterized by a set of 14 numbers which describes the spectral energy distribution. The data provided by vocoder were memorized and processed using a set of elaborate procedures.

Several features parameters were used for detecting nasals:

1) total energy of analyzed sample, obtained as a simple sum of channels' energy
2) a parameter called "pente" ('slope'-temporal derivative) which characterizes dynamic the spectral variations on two consecutive *samples* and was calculated by summing up the energy differences in corresponding channels,
3) the center of spectral gravity determined by formula:

$$CDGNO = \frac{\sum_{j=1}^{14} j\cdot(E_j - E_{min})}{\sum_{j=1}^{14} (E_j - E_{min})}$$

where $E_{min} = MIN(E_1,E_2,...,E_{14})$ for a given sample.

Our procedure is composed of two parts. The first, for segments previously classified as consonantal, determines the samples as potentially nasal. The detection of this class of samples is based on the gross spectral shape parameters, independently of the context. The principal condition which must be satisfied to consider the analyzed sample as potentially nasal, is the presence in the first channel (frequency band 250-450 Hz) of an energy peak dominating the others. Moreover, this peak in the case of nasals has a characteristic configuration which is described using some level differences (in the range of low frequencies, mainly below 1000 Hz, as it is presented on Figure 4. In Figure 5, the complete specification of parameters with the context-independent detection rule potentially nasal sample is given.

The following step of our analysis of the sequences of nasal samples is applied only for those segments whose duration is greater than 27 ms. Some realizations of the liquid /l/, a small perceptage of voiced stop /b, d, g/ and in individual cases voiced fricatives as /v/ and /z/ are classified as potentially nasal. In the last two last cases, the results of labelling are strongly speaker dependent. As mentioned, a stationary segment is labelled "nasal" if it is composed of enough "potentially nasal" spectral frames and if the following contextual and temporal criteria hold for each frame:

1. The energy within the 250-450 Hz bandwidth is less than or equal to that computed on the frame corresponding to the following vocalic energy peak.

2. The energy within the 450-650 Hz bandwidth is at least 65% of the energy in the same bandwidth computed on the vocalic energy peak.

3. At the point j corresponding to the maximum of instability between the nasal segment and the following (or preceding) vocalic segment the jump of energy is not too high: $E_{j+1} / E_j < 2.4$ where E_j is the energy of the jth frame.

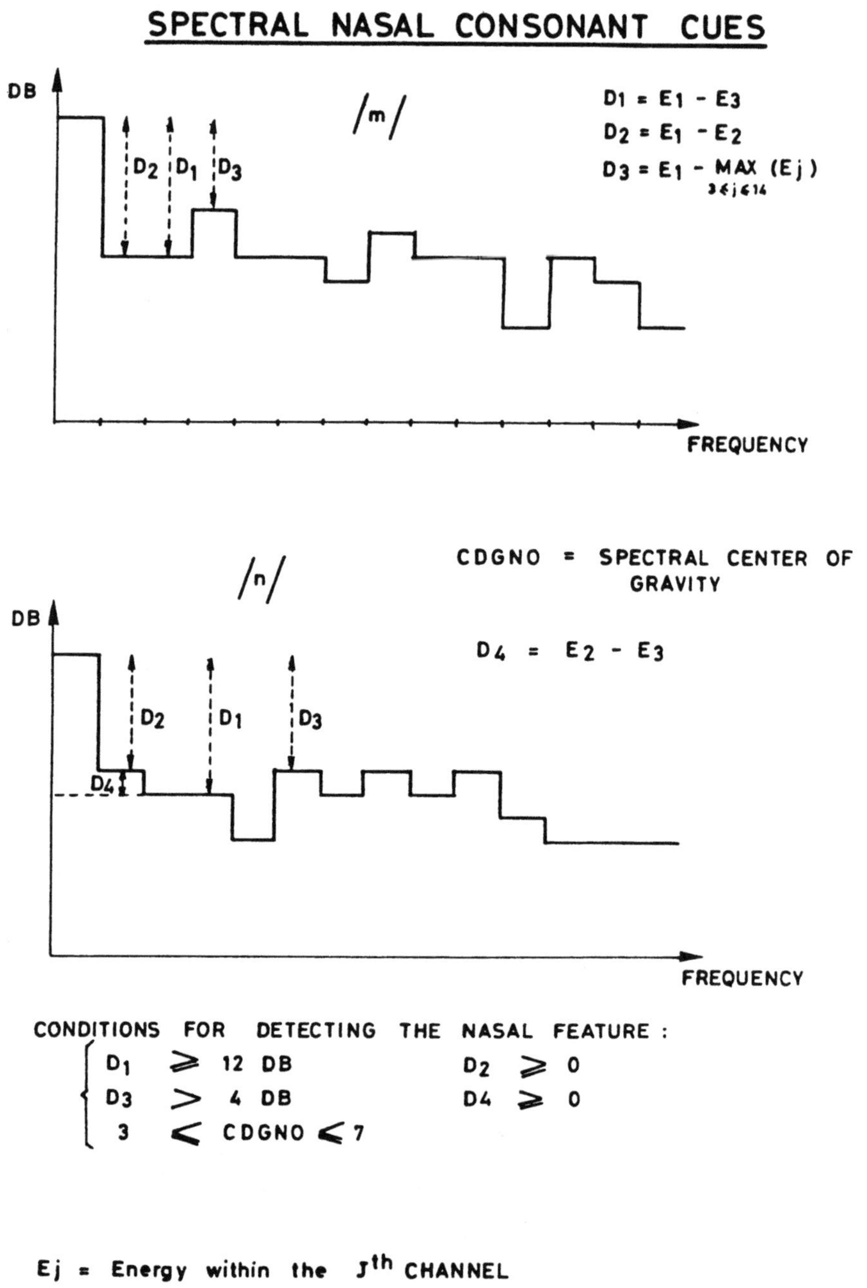

Fig. 4 Schematic representation of some spectral cues used for detection of 'potentially nasal' frames with examples of vocoder spectra obtained for /m/ and /n/.

NASAL 1: CALCULATED PARAMETERS

$D1 = E1 - E3$	$\Longleftrightarrow$	$E_{250\text{-}450} - E_{650\text{-}850}$
$D2 = E2 - \underset{2 \le j \le 6}{MAX(Ej)}$	$\Longleftrightarrow$	$E_1 - \underset{450\ -\ 1600}{MAX(Ej)}$
$D3 = E1 - \underset{7 \le j \le 14}{MAX(Ej)}$	$\Longleftrightarrow$	$E1 - \underset{1600\ -\ 4200}{MAX(Ej)}$
$D4 = E2 - E3$	$\Longleftrightarrow$	$E_{450\text{-}650} - E_{650\text{-}850}$
$D5 = E1 - E4$	$\Longleftrightarrow$	$E_{250\text{-}450} - E_{850\text{-}1050}$
$D6 = E1 - E5$	$\Longleftrightarrow$	$E_{250\text{-}450} - E_{1050\text{-}1300}$

RULE USED FOR NASAL SAMPLE DETECTION

$$(3 \le CDGNO \le 7) \wedge (D1 > 12DB) \wedge (D2 > 4DB) \wedge (D3 > 8DB) \wedge (D4 \ge 4DB) \wedge [(D5 \ge 8DB) \vee (D6 \ge 8DB)]$$

$\wedge$ — AND
$\vee$ — OR
E1: Energy in the channel 1 (250 to 450 HZ)

Fig. 5 Specification of static spectral cues used for detection of nasal frames.

4. The increase in energy within the 250-450 Hz bandwidth between the end of the "nasal" segment and the vocalic peak must not be too large (< 12 dB).

The conditions 1, 3, 4 are schematically presented in Figure 6.

This part of the algorithm eliminates most of voiced stops and fricatives classified previously as potentially nasal.

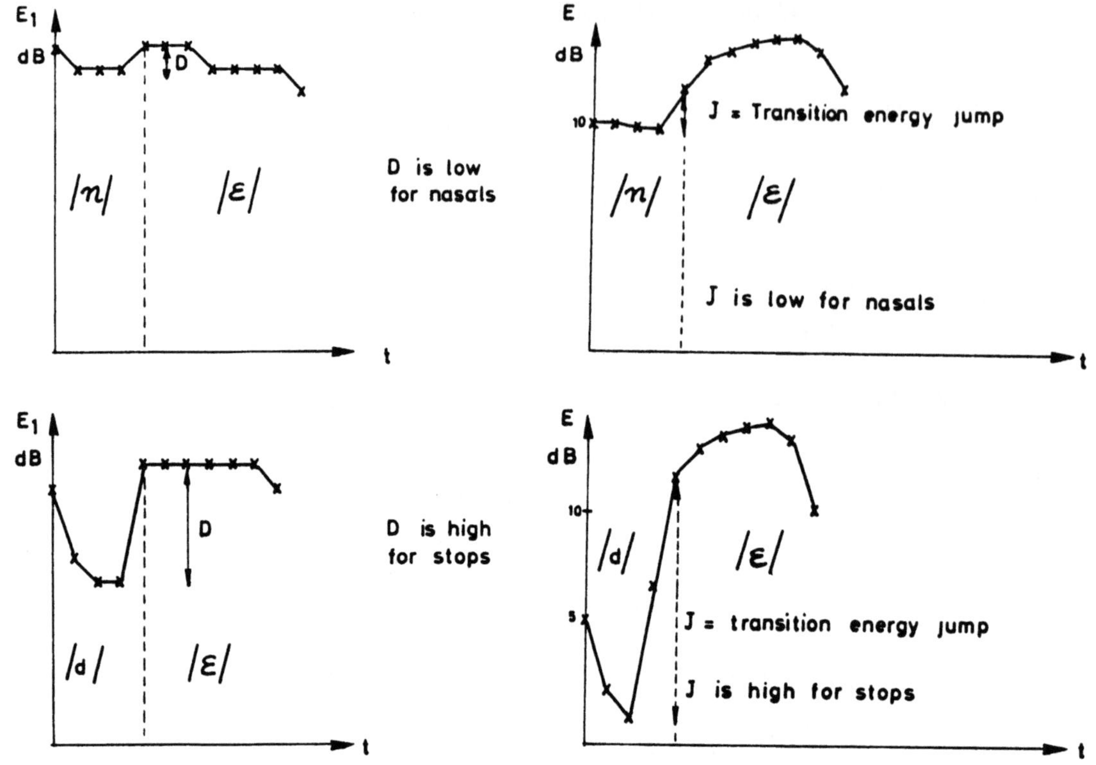

Fig. 6 Temporal cues used for detection of nasal consonants.

A preliminary study on the possibility of nasal consonants recognition has recently been begun. The first approach is based on a more detailed analysis of the spectral part in the frquencies band 820-1660 Hz. The algorithm is contextually dependent and begins with the analysis of time movements of the maximum in this frequency range, which in this case is divided in four bands (16 channel vocoder was used). The description of the peak movements is preceded by the evaluation of the place of articulation of the vowel which follows the nasal. Next, three types of time evolution, in the intervals starting 50 ms before and ending 50 ms after the limit separating the nasal and vocalic segments (determined by segmentation procedure of G. MERCIER with time sampling of 13,3 ms), in this range of frequencies are distinguished:

a) with rising frequency of the peak
b) with no changes
c) with frequency falling.

Another procedure was used to evaluate the mean level of energy in the 1180-1400 Hz band which in most cases is the region where the second formant and the first anti-resonant appear for the bilabial nasal /m/. The time variations of this parameter at the vicinity of the vocalic onset (30 ms before and after) were taken into account.

We have noted that for the nasal /n/ the rising of the peak frequency is more accentuated than for /m/, with exception however, for frontal vocalic context. In this case, no important variations were observed. It seems, that the mean relative level of nasal samples evaluated with regard to the energy spectral density can be used for final discrimination of nasals pronounced in prevocalic or intervocalic context. In the first approximation we have found that the samples of the nasal /n/, in most cases have an energy level in this frquency band higher than other nasals. A final version of the recognition procedure is under preparation.

5. RESULTS

The procedure of nasals detection based on the analysis of gross spectral shape parameters was tested on a relatively large sample of speech material in which about 240 nasal consonants realized in different contexts were present. Most cases of non-detection of nasals were due to the flatness of the low-frequency maximum, what is sometimes observed for opened and nasalized vowels context. In all the detection score of nasal consonants averaged of 80% ranging from one speaker to the other from 70% to 90%. Some difficulties in the discrimination of the liquid /l/ from the nasal, spoken in sequence have been noted, especially in the cases when these consonants were not separated by a schwa. Also for post-vocalic articulations, before a pause or at the end of the sentence similar problems were present. The mean error score for /l/ was about 20%. For other consonants such as voiced fricatives and stops the errors were less frequent, not exceeding 7%.

Some preliminary results of nasal consonants recognition obtained very recently for one male subject are presented on Figure 7.

Before the final recognition decision a weighting coefficient was calculated taking into account temporal variations of analyzed parameters evaluated in the vicinity of the following vowel onset. The results obtained for the nasal /gn/ are not satisfactory but we hope that some improvements of elaborated algorithms are possible, especially by introducing finer spectral description.

6. CONCLUSION

In our paper, we have presented some results of nasal consonants detection in continuous speech and of their recognition for the case when they were pronounced in bi-syllabic non-sense words. In the first case context-independent rules were used. It seems, that some improvements of nasal detection can be obtained by taking into account the properties of the adjacent vowel. In the

SPOKEN	RECOGNIZED M	N	GN
ma	6	0	4
na	4	10	9
mi	10	2	7
ni	2	5	4
mo	7	3	6
no	2	20	1
mu	7	2	7
nu	0	11	4
mon	6	0	2
non	2	19	2
man	6	0	4
nan	3	16	1
mou	9	3	11
nou	2	15	1
meu	7	0	8
neu	2	9	1
mei	9	0	5
nei	3	8	4
mai	6	0	0
nai	0	8	1
gna	8	5	18
gni	4	5	8
gno	4	5	6
gnon	3	6	7
gnan	5	5	7
gnou	6	3	6
gneu	7	2	7
gnei	7	8	9
gnai	5	8	9

SPOKEN	RECOGNIZED M	N	GN
ma	7	2	0
na	5	13	2
mi	20	9	1
ni	4	5	14
mo	7	2	12
no	4	8	0
mu	8	0	4
nu	5	6	4
mon	10	2	7
non	5	8	0
man	6	4	3
nan	4	18	3
mou	7	2	4
nou	8	7	8
meu	7	0	0
neu	2	6	1
mei	9	0	5
nei	1	8	2
mai	7	0	5
nai	0	8	1
gna	8	5	15
gni	3	8	15
gno	6	6	8
gnon	8	5	7
gnan	8	2	8
gnou	10	3	10
gneu	5	9	9
gnei	8	6	10
gnai	6	6	5

Fig. 7 Preliminary results of nasal consonants recognition in bisyllabic sequences /CVCV/.

case of nasal recognition the knowledge of context is strictly necessary, especially, for multi-speaker systems.

The algorithms for detection and recognition of nasals, are very simple and are based on the analysis of broad spectral cues, which generally make the elaborated rules more reliable than algorithms which make use of too precise and detailed acoustic properties which are often more context and speaker dependent.

REFERENCES

1. S. E. Blumstein and K. N. Stevens, "Acoustic invariance in speech production: Evidence from measurements of the spectral characteistics of stop consonants", JASA, Vol. 66, pp. 1001-1017, 1979.
2. P. Demichelis, "The automatic recognition of some sonorant consonants in continuous speech", Speech Communication, Vol. 1, No. 3-4, pp. 231-255, 1982.
3. R. De Mori, R. Gubrynowicz and P. Laface, "Influence of a knowledge source for the recognition of nasals in continuous speech", IEEE Trans. ASSP, Vol. ASSP-27, Vol. 5, pp. 538-549, 1979.
4. O. Fujimura, "Analysis of nasal consonants", JASA, Vol. 34, No. 12, pp. 1865-1875, 1962.
5. A. Malecot, "Acoustic cues for nasal consonants", Language, Vol. 32, No. 2, pp. 274-284, 1956.
6. G. Mercier, "Evaluation des acoustiques utilisés dans l'analyseur phonétique du système KEAL, ACTES 9èmes Journées d'Etudes sur la Parole, Lannion, pp. 231-242, 1978.
7. G. Mercier, "Acoustic-phonetic decoding and adaptation in continuous speech recognition, in: *Automatic Speech Analysis and Recognition*, Proc. NATO ASI Bonas, J.-P. Haton (ed.), Dordrecht, D. Reidel, pp. 69-99, 1981.
8. G. Mercier, "From KEAL to SERAC: a new based expert system for speech recognition", (see this book), 1984.
9. K. Nakata, "Synthesis and perception of nasal consonants, JASA, Vol. 31, No. 6, pp. 661-665, 1959.
10. K. N. Stevens, "Constraints imposed by auditory system on the properties used to classify speech sounds: .Data from phonology, acoustics and psychoacoustics, in : *The Cognitive Representation of Speech*, T. Myers, J. Laver and J. Anderson (eds), North-holland, New York, 1981.
11. S. Takeuchi, H. Kasuya and K. Kido, "A method for extraction of the spectral cues of nasal consonants", J. Acoust. Soc. Jap. Vol. 31, No. 12, pp. 739-740, 1975.

AUTHOR INDEX

NATO ASI Series F

Vol. 1: Issues in Acoustic Signal – Image Processing and Recognition. Edited by C. H. Chen. VIII, 333 pages. 1983.

Vol. 2: Image Sequence Processing and Dynamic Scene Analysis. Edited by T. S. Huang. IX, 749 pages. 1983.

Vol. 3: Electronic Systems Effectiveness and Life Cycle Costing. Edited by J. K. Skwirzynski. XVII, 732 pages. 1983.

Vol. 4: Pictorial Data Analysis. Edited by R. M. Haralick. VIII, 468 pages. 1983.

Vol. 5: International Calibration Study of Traffic Conflict Techniques. Edited by E. Asmussen VII, 229 pages. 1984.

Vol. 6: Information Technology and the Computer Network. Edited by K. G. Beauchamp. VIII, 271 pages. 1984.

Vol. 7: High-Speed Computation. Edited by J. S. Kowalik. IX, 441 pages. 1984.

Vol. 8: Program Transformation and Programming Environments. Report on an Workshop directed by F. L. Bauer and H. Remus. Edited by P. Pepper. XIV, 378 pages. 1984.

Vol. 9: Computer Aided Analysis and Optimization of Mechanical System Dynamics. Edited by E. J. Haug. XXII, 700 pages. 1984.

Vol. 10: Simulation and Model-Based Methodologies: An Integrative View. Edited by T. I. Ören, B. P. Zeigler, M. S. Elzas. XIII, 651 pages. 1984.

Vol. 11: Robotics and Artificial Intelligence. Edited by M. Brady, L. A. Gerhardt, H. F. Davidson. XVII, 693 pages. 1984.

Vol. 12: Combinatorial Algorithms on Words. Edited by A. Apostolico, Z. Galil. VIII, 361 pages. 1985.

Vol. 13: Logics and Models of Concurrent Systems. Edited by K. R. Apt. VIII, 498 pages. 1985.

Vol. 14: Control Flow and Data Flow: Concept of Distributed Programming. Edited by M. Broy. VIII, 525 pages. 1985.

Vol. 15: Computational Mathematical Programming. Edited by K. Schittkowski. VIII, 451 pages. 1985.

Vol. 16: New Systems and Architectures for Automatic Speech Recognition and Synthesis. Edited by R. De Mori, C.Y. Suen. XIII, 630 pages. 1985.

MIX
Papier aus verantwortungsvollen Quellen
Paper from responsible sources
FSC® C105338

If you have any concerns about our products, you can contact us on
ProductSafety@springernature.com

In case Publisher is established outside the EU, the EU authorized representative is:
Springer Nature Customer Service Center GmbH
Europaplatz 3, 69115 Heidelberg, Germany

Printed by Libri Plureos GmbH
in Hamburg, Germany

Dangerous Behavior in Clinical and Forensic Psychology

Series Editors

Greg Bohall, Innovative Psychological Solutions, Orange County, CA, USA

Mary-Jo Bautista, Innovative Psychological Solutions, Orange County, CA, USA

Sabrina Musson, State University of New York at Fredonia, Buffalo, NY, USA

This new series will close the gap between forensic rehabilitation and prediction/ intervention approaches. Taking a broad view of what is sometimes termed deviant behavior, the series will provide individual volumes on key problems such as domestic violence, bullying, homicide, and terrorism. Each topic will be handled in a systematic way that will cover major psychological concepts as well as policy issues, and clinical practice. Useful to a range of professionals who desire a brief evidence-based overview of problems critical to the health and well-being of individuals and society in general. It is particularly relevant to mental health professionals and forensic professionals as well as those in law enforcement.

Ruth J. Tully • Greg Bohall • David S. Prescott
Editors

Best Practices in Sexual Offender Assessment and Management

Springer

Editors
Ruth J. Tully
Tully Forensic Psychology Ltd.
University of Exeter
Nottingham and Exeter, UK

Greg Bohall
Innovative Psychological Solutions
Orange County, CA, USA

David S. Prescott
Continuing Education Center
Safer Society Foundation
Brandon, VT, USA

ISSN 2524-4051 ISSN 2524-406X (electronic)
Dangerous Behavior in Clinical and Forensic Psychology
ISBN 978-3-031-83137-9 ISBN 978-3-031-83135-5 (eBook)
https://doi.org/10.1007/978-3-031-83135-5

This Springer imprint is published by the registered company Springer Nature Switzerland AG
The registered company address is: Gewerbestrasse 11, 6330 Cham, Switzerland

Preface

When considering the rapid expansion of specialties within psychology coupled with disciplines outside of the behavioral sciences seeing the value of psychology in their day-to-day activities, researchers and clinicians alike are seeing "their place" in areas where they have traditionally not been before. For example, developmental psychologists whose expertise is in development across the lifespan may be involved in providing expert testimony on developmental factors as it relates to addressing various psycholegal questions. Sport psychology has typically centered on athlete performance; however, sport psychologists are implementing more clinical interventions as "grit", "determination", and "resilience" can only take an individual so far in their athletic performance. Clinical interventions to increase employee job satisfaction, improve employee motivation, and improve organizational communication have been sought from the clinical psychology specialty when it has not been as prominently involved historically (I/O psychology). Indeed, this expansion of ideas and researcher/clinician endorsement is exciting for the future of psychology.

Identifying and implementing various theories or clinical perspectives from these specialties to a central issue or population is an incredible benefit in psychology today. Moreover, many of these central issues or populations have not been explored from some of the various theories/perspectives or even within some specialties themselves; we believe the expansive nature of the volumes in this series provides an answer to that deficiency. As series editors, our goal was to identify these various clinical and forensic considerations in need of further exploration, identify the various components of each central issue or population, and help develop an expansive volume on the central issue or population where numerous perspectives are involved in order to improve understanding as well as how to effectively intervene.

The central issues and populations in this series were selected by the series editors; all have clinical and/or forensic aspects that make them important for publication at this time. Volume editors were selected for their specific expertise as it relates to the central issue or population. For this volume, Dr. Ruth J. Tully, Dr. Greg Bohall, and Mr. David S. Prescott have been appointed based on their expertise and willingness to direct this expansive project through its completion. Chapter authors were selected in the same manner to ensure that each volume will serve as a valuable reference for academics and clinicians alike. Through ongoing collaboration with the series editorial team, these volume editors have been able to strike a successful balance of authors that include those with a strong research background and/or a strong clinical background.

This volume synthesizes the important research and practice developments in the field of sexual offending. As the reader will review, sexual deviance and offending has undergone numerous conceptualizations over the past century and it continues to evolve in its understanding. The addition of various perspectives coupled with this unique approach to sexual deviance and offending makes this volume in the series titled *Dangerous Behavior in Clinical and Forensic Psychology* an essential resource for researchers and clinicians alike.

Orange County, CA, USA — Greg Bohall
Orange County, CA, USA — Mary-Jo Bautista-Bohall
Buffalo, NY, USA — Sabrina Musson

Contents

About the Editors and Contributors

About the Series Editors

Greg Bohall, Psy.D, CRC, MAC, ICADC, CADC-III Principal Series Editor Dr. Bohall is the co-owner of Innovative Psychological Solutions, A Professional Corporation, based in Orange County, California and is the current principal series editor of the series titled *Dangerous Behavior in Clinical and Forensic Psychology* through Springer. He earned a doctorate in psychology (Psy.D.) in clinical forensic psychology and provides consultation for numerous organizations throughout the United States. Dr. Bohall is currently internationally and nationally recognized as a Certified Rehabilitation Counselor (C.R.C.), as a Master Addiction Counselor (MAC), and as an International Certified Alcohol and Drug Counselor (ICADC). In the State of California, he is recognized as a Certified Alcohol and Drug Counselor-III (CADC-III). Dr. Bohall was the principal author in the co-authored textbook *The Psychologist's Guide to Professional Development* (2017). Furthermore, his work can be found in *The SAGE Encyclopedia of Psychology and Gender* (2017) and *The Complexity of Psychopathy* (2022) books. Additionally, Dr. Bohall has published journal articles in the *Journal of Family Violence, Aggression and Violent Behavior, BMJ Open,* and *Frontiers in Psychology.* Dr. Bohall also serves on the Editorial Board of the *Journal of Aggression, Maltreatment, & Trauma,* the *Journal of Family Trauma, Child Custody, & Child Development,* the *Journal of Child Sexual Abuse,* and the *Journal of Child & Adolescent Trauma.* Lastly, Dr. Bohall's academic and research interests include forensic assessment and intervention, crisis intervention and negotiation techniques, evaluation of interviewing, investigation, and interrogation procedures, psychopathy, and offender profiles and victimology of individuals involved in intimate partner violence cases.

Mary-Jo Bautista-Bohall, Psy.D. Associate Series Editor Dr. Bautista-Bohall is the co-owner of Innovative Psychological Solutions, A Professional Corporation, and is an associate series editor of the series titled *Dangerous Behavior in Clinical and Forensic Psychology.* Dr. Bautista-Bohall is an early career psychologist; she earned a doctorate in psychology (Psy.D.) in applied clinical psychology in 2013. She is a licensed clinical psychologist in the State of California and currently provides services for various state and government-funded agencies. Dr. Bautista-Bohall is an advocate for underprivileged populations and presents her work at national and international conferences promoting the need for mental health services for minorities. Her current projects include decreasing the stigma of mental health with Filipino Americans through the development of culturally specific interventions. Dr. Bautista-Bohall is also dedicated to educating practitioners on promising and effective interventions for individuals diagnosed with a neurodevelopmental disability. More specifically, she has extensive experience providing a variety of interventions for individuals with intellectual disabilities. In the forensic realm, Dr. Bautista-Bohall helps determine various capacities of individuals with a neurodevelopmental disability; this information is then used to determine ability to participate in the judicial process and to address other psycholegal questions. Dr. Bautista-Bohall's research interests include the identification of diversity factors that are associated with different deviant behaviors. Academically, she has been published three times in peer-reviewed works as well as her recent co-authored textbook, *The Psychologist's Guide to Professional Development (2017);* this text was designed to help students and fellow early career professionals reach their personal and academic goals.

Sabrina Musson, Ph.D., LMHC Associate Series Editor Dr. Musson is an associate editor of the series titled *Dangerous Behavior in Clinical and Forensic Psychology.* Dr. Musson has been an Assistant Professor in the Mental Health Counseling MS Program at the State University of New York at Fredonia since January 2024. Dr. Musson previously worked for the University of Buffalo's Research Institute on Addictions as a project director for various research studies funded by the National Institutes of Health from 2013–2018 and a Clinical Professor and Program Director at University at Buffalo's Mental Health Counseling MS program from 2018–2024. She presides on the Board of the non-for-profit Bridges from Borders since January 2021, assisting in mental health advocacy, training, supervision, and research within immigrant and refugee populations of Western New York. Dr. Musson served as the co-leader for the Western New York Chapter of the New York Mental Health Counseling Association from 2019–2021. She earned her master's degree in mental health counseling at Medaille College and her Ph.D. in counselor education at the State University of New York at Buffalo. She has over twenty years of experience working in the human services field. During this span, Dr. Musson has over ten years of clinical and research experience. Her fields of specialization include addictions, homelessness, intimate partner violence, crisis intervention, equity and inclusion, and clinical supervision. Dr. Musson also serves as a reviewer for the *Journal of Aggression, Maltreatment, & Trauma,* and the *Journal of Child and Adolescent Trauma.*

About the Volume Editors

Ruth J. Tully Volume Editor Dr. Ruth Tully [BSc(Hons), MSc, DForenPsy, CPsychol, EuroPsy, FBPsS, CSci, MAE] is a Consultant Forensic Psychologist in the UK. She is registered with the Health and Care Professions Council and Chartered by, as well as Fellow of, the British Psychological Society. Dr. Tully is Clinical Lead of Tully Forensic Psychology Ltd, where she and her team of Forensic and Clinical Psychologists work throughout the UK in the provision of psychological assessment, treatment/therapy, consultancy, expert witness services, and training. Dr. Tully's wider experience includes working with adults and young people in secure healthcare, social care, prison, and community settings. She has a particular interest in sexual, violent, and extremism offending as well as personality, intellectual disability, and clinical neuropsychology. Dr. Tully has an active research, publication, and public speaking profile. She is considered a leading authority on violence and sex offender risk assessment in relation to research, clinical practice, and training professionals.

Greg Bohall, Psy.D, CRC, MAC, ICADC, CADC-III Volume Editor Dr. Bohall is the co-owner of Innovative Psychological Solutions, A Professional Corporation, based in Orange County, California and is the current principal series editor of the series titled *Dangerous Behavior in Clinical and Forensic Psychology* through Springer. He earned a doctorate in psychology (Psy.D.) in clinical forensic psychology and provides consultation for numerous organizations throughout the United States. Dr. Bohall is currently internationally and nationally recognized as a Certified Rehabilitation Counselor (C.R.C.), as a Master Addiction Counselor (MAC), and as an International Certified Alcohol and Drug Counselor (ICADC). In the State of California, he is recognized as a Certified Alcohol and Drug Counselor-III (CADC-III). Dr. Bohall was the principal author in the co-authored textbook *The Psychologist's Guide to Professional Development* (2017). Furthermore, his work can be found in *The SAGE Encyclopedia of Psychology and Gender* (2017) and *The Complexity of Psychopathy* (2022) books. Additionally, Dr. Bohall has published journal articles in the *Journal of Family Violence, Aggression and Violent Behavior, BMJ Open,* and *Frontiers in Psychology.* Dr. Bohall also serves on the Editorial Board of the *Journal of Aggression, Maltreatment, & Trauma,* the *Journal of Family Trauma, Child Custody, & Child Development,* the *Journal of Child Sexual Abuse,* and the *Journal of Child & Adolescent Trauma.* Lastly, Dr. Bohall's academic and research interests include forensic assessment and intervention, crisis intervention and negotiation techniques, evaluation of interviewing, investigation, and interrogation procedures, psychopathy, and offender profiles and victimology of individuals involved in intimate partner violence cases.

David S. Prescott, LCSW, LICSW Volume Editor A mental health practitioner of 39 years, David Prescott is the Director of the Safer Society Continuing Education Center. He is the author and editor of 25 books in the areas of understanding and improving services to at-risk clients. He is best known for his work in the areas of understanding, assessing, and treating sexual violence and trauma. Mr. Prescott is the recipient of the 2014 Distinguished Contribution award from the Association for the Treatment and Prevention of Sexual Abuse (ATSA), the 2018 recipient of the National Adolescent Perpetration Network's C. Henry Kempe Lifetime Achievement award, and the 2022 recipient of the Fay Honey Knopp Award from the New York State Alliance for the Prevention of Sexual Abuse and New York State ATSA. He also served as ATSA President in 2008-09. Mr. Prescott currently trains and lectures around the world. His published work has been translated into Japanese, Korean, German, French, Polish, and Dutch. He has served on the editorial boards of four scholarly journals.

Contributors

Claire Barker Private Practice, Oxfordshire, UK

Greg Bohall Innovative Psychological Solutions, Orange County, CA, USA

Kelly Bonnar Department of Public Health & Human Performance, SUNY Potsdam, Potsdam, NY, USA

Sarah Brown Sexual Violence Research and Prevention Unit, University of the Sunshine Coast, Sunshine Coast, QLD, Australia

Chad Brownfield Private Practice, Rock Island, IL, USA

Elizabeth M. Bryant Psychology Department, Indiana University of Pennsylvania, Indiana, PA, USA

Mary C. Burke Department of Psychology, Counseling & Criminology, Carlow University, Pittsburgh, PA, USA

Adam J. Carter His Majesty's Prison and Probation Service, London, UK

Annalisa Castrechini Gestalt Therapy Kairòs Institute, Rome, Italy

Eunsuhk Choi Police Policy Research Division, Police Science Institute, Thornhill, ON, Canada

Korean National Police University, Asan-si, Chungcheongnam-do, Republic of Korea

Kevin Creeden The Whitney Academy, East Freetown, MA, USA

Rebecca Crookes Centre for Global Learning, Coventry University, Coventry, Warwickshire, UK

Rajan Darjee Centre for Forensic Behavioural Science, Swinburne University of Technology, Melbourne, VIC, Australia

Forensic Mental Health Service, Tasmanian Health Service, Hobart, TAS, Australia

Forensic Behavioural Assessment and Consultation Services (FBACS), Melbourne, VIC, Australia

Michael R. Davis Centre for Forensic Behavioural Science, Swinburne University of Technology, Melbourne, VIC, Australia

Department of Psychiatry, Monash University, Clayton, VIC, Australia

Department of Psychiatry, The University of Melbourne, Parkville, VIC, Australia

Samatha Etzi Graduate School of Social Work, University of Pittsburgh, Pittsburgh, PA, USA

Amanda Fenrich Graduate School of Arts and Sciences, Purdue University Global, West Lafayette, IN, USA

Ellen Gunst FIDES-R, Psychiatric Center Sint-Amandus, Beernem, Belgium

Zachary K. Hamilton Department of Criminology and Criminal Justice, University of Nebraska-Omaha, Omaha, NE, USA

Tamsin Higgs Department of Psychology, University of Montreal, Montreal, QC, Canada

Jonathan James Department of Psychology, University of Quebec in Trois Rivières, Trois Rivières, QC, Canada

Elizabeth L. Jeglic Department of Psychology, John Jay College of Criminal Justice, New York, NY, USA

Leah E. Kaylor PLLC, Uniontown, PA, USA

Raymond A. Knight Department of Psychology, Brandeis University, Waltham, MA, USA

Addison R. Kobie Department of Criminology and Criminal Justice, University of Nebraska-Omaha, Omaha, NE, USA

Tina Krolikowski Department of Psychology, Counseling & Criminology, Carlow University, Pittsburgh, PA, USA

Michael H. Miner Eli Coleman Institute for Sexual and Gender Health, Department of Family Medicine and Community Health, University of Minnesota, Minneapolis, MN, USA

Melanie Clark Mogavero Department of Crime and Justice Studies, Georgian Court University, Lakewood, NJ, USA

Elijah P. Morrow California Department of Corrections and Rehabilitation, Coalinga, CA, USA

Nicholas Newstrom Department of Marriage and Family Therapy, Syracuse University, Syracuse, NY, USA

Mark E. Olver Department of Psychology and Health Studies, University of Saskatchewan, Saskatoon, SK, Canada

Susan O'Rourke Center for Global Engagement, Carlow University, Pittsburgh, PA, USA

Sarah Paquette Department of Psychology, University of Portsmouth, Portsmouth, Hampshire, UK

Ragini Patel London, UK

Anthony D. Perillo Department of Psychiatry and Behavioral Sciences, University of New Mexico Health Sciences Center, Albuquerque, NM, USA

David S. Prescott Continuing Education Center, Safer Society Foundation, Brandon, VT, USA

Jean Proulx School of Criminology, University of Montreal, Montreal, QC, Canada

Kilby Raptopoulos School of Criminal Justice and Criminology, University of Arkansas-Little Rock, Little Rock, AR, USA

Emily K. Riemer Department of Psychology and Health Studies, University of Saskatchewan, Saskatoon, SK, Canada

Beatrice "Bean" E. Robinson Eli Coleman Institute for Sexual and Gender Health, Department of Family Medicine and Community Health, University of Minnesota, Minneapolis, MN, USA

Natalie A. Ross Psychology Department, Indiana University of Pennsylvania, Indiana, PA, USA

Lisa L. Sample Department of Criminology and Criminal Justice, University of Nebraska-Omaha, Omaha, NE, USA

Daniel Taggart Clinical Psychology Program, University of Essex, Wivenhoe, UK

Tusty ten Bensel School of Criminal Justice and Criminology, University of Arkansas-Little Rock, Little Rock, AR, USA

Gilian Tenbergen Department of Psychological Sciences, State University of New York at Oswego, Oswego, NY, USA

Carlo Tramontano Centre for Global Learning, Coventry University, Coventry, Warwickshire, UK

Ruth J. Tully Tully Forensic Psychology Ltd., Nottingham, UK

University of Exeter, Exeter, UK

Siebrecht Vanhooren Faculty of Psychology and Educational Sciences, KU Leuven, Leuven, Belgium

Kate Walker Northamptonshire NHS Foundation Trust (UK), Kettering, Northamptonshire, UK

Gerard P. Webster Institute of Contemporary Psychoanalysis, Los Angeles, CA, USA

Shannon White Department of Psychology, Counseling & Criminology, Carlow University, Pittsburgh, PA, USA

Hayley Wright Centre for Intelligent Healthcare, Coventry University, Coventry, Warwickshire, UK

Zachary Yeoman Somerset Psychological Group, P.A., Martinsville, NJ, USA

Chapter 1
Introduction to Sexual Offending

Ruth J. Tully, Greg Bohall, and David S. Prescott

Sexual offending and sexual harm are significant problems at societal level, with it generally being accepted that official crime statistics severely underestimate the scale of the problem. Sexual offending has the most important and clear impact on the people who are victimized, with significant psychological and physical harm being caused to them and often others associated with them (e.g. friends, family). There are additional costs to society, not limited to (but such as) the financial costs of criminal investigation, prosecution of cases through the court system, and costs associated with imprisonment and community long-term management of offenders (including risk reduction attempts and interventions).

This volume gives a wide-ranging view of topics that are essential to understand within sexual offending but due to the heterogeneity of both sexual offending (how it manifests) and the people who perpetrate sexual harm, it is important to note that there are areas of this topic, and subgroups of offenders, that are very much under-studied in the literature.

In relation to essential themes of understanding for sexual offending, Chap. 2 (Miner et al.) discusses human sexuality; an important aspect to aid our contextualization of sexual offending and sexual harm. Classification and typologies are discussed at length in Chap. 3 (Knight) including review of the methodological limitations affecting researchers' ability to categorize sexual offenders. Policymakers

R. J. Tully (✉)
Tully Forensic Psychology Ltd., Nottingham, UK

University of Exeter, Exeter, UK
e-mail: enquiries@tullyforensicpsychology.com

G. Bohall
Innovative Psychological Solutions, Orange County, CA, USA

D. S. Prescott
Continuing Education Center, Safer Society Foundation, Brandon, VT, USA

R. J. Tully et al. (eds.), *Best Practices in Sexual Offender Assessment and Management*, Dangerous Behavior in Clinical and Forensic Psychology,
https://doi.org/10.1007/978-3-031-83135-5_1

have differing views on where financial resources should be invested in this field; should society provide risk reduction treatment to those 'at risk' who have not offended (but may in the future), should finances be spent on risk reduction treatment for those who have offended, or should all resources go into treating victims? This is something that Morrow and Bonnar consider in detail in Chap. 24 from a public health perspective. Whilst the editors of this volume do not claim to have answers to these questions, in respect of sex offending and treatment, there are many psychological models that can be applied; Chap. 4 (Webster) examines the psychodynamic approach to understanding and treating sexual offending in detail, Chap. 5 (Gunst & Vanhooren) uses a meta-synthesis of 5 single case studies to explore experiential and existential dimensions of sex offender treatment, and Chap. 6 (Castrechini) addresses Gestalt analysis of sexual offending, including the use of a clinical case to illustrate this type of analysis. Whilst this series focusses largely on offenders and offending, the impact of sexual violence on victims is never forgotten. Importantly, Barker and Taggart (Chap. 23) discuss victimology and rehabilitation, considering some of the vulnerabilities around victims and the consequences of abuse.

As already mentioned, those who sexually offend are a varied group, and sexual offenders can be split into various subgroups. One such group is the juvenile group; Yeoman et al. in Chap. 7 discuss that even within the population of juveniles who engage in harmful sexual behavior, there is great heterogeneity, and their chapter takes a developmental approach in its discussion which concludes with consideration of the legal and policy implications of the literature. Kobie et al. in Chap. 18 further consider the juvenile population and discuss problem sexual behavior versus sexual offending behavior, as well as the assessment and treatment of juveniles. Juveniles are indeed a specific subgroup, but professionals also need to consider ageing and sexual offending to have the full picture; Crookes et al. in Chap. 20 provide a detailed review of the characteristics across the adult lifespan of those with sexual convictions. Chapter 8 (Tenbergen) provides insight into neuropsychological aspects of sexual offending and discusses issues around sexual preference for children in the context of impaired neuropsychological functioning while Chap. 16 (Mogavero et al.) discusses neurodevelopmental disorders and sexual offending, specifically autism spectrum disorder and intellectual disability.

A further very specific sub-group of those who sexually offend is the group of people who commit sexual homicide. Chapter 14 (Higgs et al.) gives careful consideration to best practices in the rehabilitation of those who fall within this group, considering the scientific knowledge as it currently stands, and its limitations. Olver and Riemer in Chap. 17 take on the topic of personality disorder and psychopathy and discuss the risk-relevance of these conditions to sexual offending. Females who sexually offend are an understudied group; most research is on males who sexually offend, although the literature has been growing regarding females in recent years. ten Bensel and Raptopoulos review the research in this area in Chap. 19 and focus on assessment and intervention considerations. Another very specific subgroup within sexual offending includes members of religious groups. Chapter 21 (Ross) gives special consideration to child sexual abuse by Catholic clergy, examining the available literature and identifying tends within such abuse.

Of critical importance in preventing future victims is risk assessment and therefore management of those who offend. Olver, in Chap. 9, discusses sex offender risk assessment including a comprehensive overview of the subject and best practice considerations. In respect of managing risk of offending, it is essential to understand sexual interests and paraphilias that may link to it. With this in mind, Chap. 11 (Kaylor & Jeglic) delves into voyeurism, exhibitionism, and frotteurism; consideration is given to diagnosis and issues such as comorbidity, assessment, and interventions are discussed. In Chap. 15, Burke et al. discuss human sex trafficking. Human trafficking is not a new crime; this has been happening globally for centuries. This chapter highlights the need to understand sex trafficking in detail to be able to provide accurate clinical assessment of both perpetrators and victims of this crime. Given the advances in technology over the years, the internet has added a new method of offending for those who are motivated to use it in this way. Chapter 22 (Paquette) discusses this field and issues such as the types of behaviors involved in this offending, with consideration for risk assessment and treatment being made. Added to 'how' people sexually offend, there is of course the issue of understanding what drives offending risk for them (i.e. the 'why'), which is central to risk assessment. In understanding this, is it of the utmost importance to be able to consider best practice in the assessment of offense-related sexual interests, or sexual deviance, along with the limitations of approaches to assessment, which is exactly what Yeoman et al. discuss in detail in Chap. 10. With that in mind, understanding presentations and risk associated with sexual sadism (Darjee & Davis, Chap. 12) and pedophilia (Davis & Darjee, Chap. 13) is essential; these two chapters take an extended deep dive into these topics with detailed analysis and discussion; these chapters are essential reading for those interested in this field.

Overall, the research into sexual offending continues to develop and aids our understanding, and therefore clinical practice, when working in this field. The body of work that has been brought together in this series is in-depth and comprehensive, but given the heterogeneity of the behavior involved in sexual offending and in the profiles of those who engage in it / subgroups, there is a critical need for more research. The chapters that editors have included here reflect developments and varied perspectives in this field, but it is also hoped that understanding of sexual offending, which is complex and harmful behavior, continues to develop further such that some of the most understudied groups may be better understood, to aid prevention of sexual offending and thus avoid future victimization.

Chapter 2
Sexology

Michael H. Miner, Nicholas Newstrom, and Beatrice "Bean" E. Robinson

2.1 Introduction

Sexology is defined as the scientific study of sexuality, particularly in human beings (American Psychological Association, 2022). In this chapter, the authors review insights gleaned from the scientific study of sexuality to address underlying concepts and current knowledge vis-a-vis sexual offending behaviors. The prevention and treatment of sexual offending is integral to societal sexual health.

The World Health Organization (WHO, 2006) defined sexual health as a state of physical, emotional, mental, and social well-being; not just the absence of disease. Furthermore, sexual health necessitates a positive and respectful approach to sexuality and sexual relationships where all individuals have a right to sexuality and sexual relationships that are free of coercion and violence. Additionally, the International Association for the Treatment of Sexual Offenders (IATSO) stated that "sex offender treatment is a basic human right" (n.d.). Taking WHO and IATSO definitions into account, sexual violence and abuse can be viewed within a public health framework and sex offender treatment is one important societal element needed to achieve community sexual health.

This chapter addresses current knowledge in sexuality and barriers to sexual health. Our perspective on sexual offender treatment is that sexual crimes are maladaptive sexual behaviors statutorily defined as crimes. Thus, it is important to understand what is known about sexuality and sexual behavior, sexual offending,

M. H. Miner (✉) · B. E. Robinson
Eli Coleman Institute for Sexual and Gender Health, Department of Family Medicine and Community Health, University of Minnesota, Minneapolis, MN, USA
e-mail: miner001@umn.edu

N. Newstrom
Department of Marriage and Family Therapy, Syracuse University, Syracuse, NY, USA

R. J. Tully et al. (eds.), *Best Practices in Sexual Offender Assessment and Management*, Dangerous Behavior in Clinical and Forensic Psychology,
https://doi.org/10.1007/978-3-031-83135-5_2

and other maladaptive behaviors that are not illegal, but lead to problems implicated in illegal sexual behavior. This chapter is not an inclusive review of sexuality, but addresses issues that the authors of this chapter believe have important implications for sexual offending behaviors and for the treatment of men and women who have engaged in violent and abusive sexual behavior. As such, sexual communication, culture, normative sexual behavior, gender identity, sexual dysfunction, and compulsive sexual behavior are discussed. For disorders and dysfunctions, what is known about presentation, etiology, and treatment is reviewed.

2.2 Sexual Communication

Paramount to sexual relationships, whether a casual encounter or an ongoing romantic relationship, is the ability for partners to communicate their intent and satisfaction during sexual interactions. Researchers have found that individuals who communicated their sexual likes and dislikes (i.e., sexual self-disclosure) reported increased sexual satisfaction with their partners (Jozkowski, 2013).

2.2.1 Sexual Script Theory

Sex researchers have used different theories to explain factors that influence sexual communication, including communication during sexual negotiation. Early sexologists, such as John Money (1986), pioneered the concept of "love maps" to describe ways people develop unhealthy sexual relationships or paraphilias, whereas Freund and Blanchard (1986) suggested paraphilias and sexual violence may arise from "courtship disorders," or disturbances that occur during the unfolding of dating relationships. Gagnon and Simon (1973) theorized that sexual behaviors are influenced by culture, interpersonal relationships, and intrapsychic scripts (i.e., sexual fantasy) which comprise one's sexual scripts; behaviors and expectations individuals have about their sexuality. Gagnon and Simon's Sexual Script Theory (1973) was pioneering in that their theory challenged the dominant psychodynamic theory, which tended to pathologize atypical sexual behaviors. In addition, their theory highlighted the importance of family, culture, and past sexual relationships as important factors that shape sexual communication.

2.2.2 Gender Roles, Sexual Scripts, and Consent

One application of sexual script theory was exploring the ways people give their consent to sexual behaviors. This research focused on gender differences, exploring how cisgender men and women consent to sexual behaviors, and found that women were more likely than men to rate verbal cues as more important during sexual consent negotiation (Humphreys & Herold, 2007). Men, on the other hand, were more likely to communicate consent through nonverbal behaviors, such as removing clothing (Jozkowski et al., 2013). Additionally, research indicated gender differences in how women and men interpret the behaviors of their partners in communicating consent for sexual activity. Men were more likely to interpret consent through their female partner's nonverbal cues, whereas women were more likely to interpret consent when their male partners asked them verbally to have sex and they were given the opportunity to respond (yes or no) to their partner's requests (Jozkowski et al., 2013).

In one of the most extensive studies of sexual consent, Hickman and Muehlenhard (1999) found that men were more likely to use nonverbal consent cues (e.g., touching, kissing, or caressing), whereas women were more likely to use indirect verbal cues to signal consent (e.g., asking if the other person has a condom) and indicate consent passively through "no response." Hickman and Muehlenhard (1999) also asked study participants to rate partner cues they would perceive as indicating consent for sexual behavior (consent perceptions). They found men rated direct verbal cues, direct nonverbal cues, indirect verbal statements, and statements about intoxication (e.g., "I'm really drunk") as more indicative of consent than female participants, although males also rated women's statements of intoxication as unlikely to be an indication of consent. These results suggest gender differences in giving and interpreting consent to sexual behavior. Thus, the chance for miscommunication between women and men can be high during sex negotiations, especially between individuals with no prior experience with each other.

Using Hickman and Muehlenhard's (1999) scales, Newstrom et al. (2021) found that women were more likely to rate their direct consent cues (e.g., "I want you") as indications of consent whereas men were more likely to rate their indirect verbal cues (e.g., "You ask if she has a condom") as indications of sexual consent. Additionally, relationship length and sexual self-disclosure did not affect how men and women communicated sexual consent in a hypothetical situation. Within-subjects gender differences were found between how the same behaviors were rated as an indication of consent if exhibited by the individual or perceived by the individual from their partners. Men indicated their use of indirect verbal behaviors (e.g., "Are you on birth control?") were not indications that they were consenting to sex, while they perceived such behavior by their partners as indicating consent. Women reported that they would be more likely to indicate consent through direct nonverbal behaviors (e.g., "You begin to take off your shirt"), but would not interpret such behavior as indicative of consent in their male partners. This finding suggests that men and women may be drawing conclusions about consent from behaviors they rate as less indicative of consent for having sexual intercourse, even though they would view the meaning of their use of such cues differently. In other words, women and men in this study may be perceiving certain cues as providing consent when their partners do not intend to signal affirmatively.

These studies of consent suggested gender differences in consent cues and consent perceptions that could influence how individuals might interpret a given sexual interaction. Within couples, one would expect that the more they know about each other's sexual likes and preferences (sexual self-disclosure) the less likely intentions would be misinterpreted. In one of the most thorough studies on sexual self-disclosure, MacNeil and Byers (2009) found that participants who reported higher rates of sexual self-disclosure were more likely to understand their partner's sexual scripts and report greater satisfaction with their sexual scripts. Additionally, when both partners engaged in mutual sexual self-disclosure there were higher reports of sexual satisfaction.

2.2.3 Future Research Directions and Clinical Interventions

The majority of the literature on sexual communication has focused on the sexual cues of cisgender men and women in opposite-sex relationships. Virtually all of the research on sexual communication between individuals in same-sex relationships has centered on how men communicate with their partners regarding safe sex practices (McDavitt & Mutchler, 2014; Prestage et al., 2006). More information is needed on sexual communication in diverse populations (e.g., those in same-sex relationships; transgender populations; older adults). Although Newstrom et al. (2021) investigated how relationship status influenced sexual communication, their study did not use couples, but simply asked individuals about their behavior in their coupled relationships. Research using couples as the unit of analysis needs to be conducted.

For individuals who have sexually offended, employment, housing status, and intimacy deficits (i.e., attachment style; poor relationships with others; negative peer influences) have been identified as dynamic risk factors for sexual perpetration and re-offending (Craissati & Beech, 2003). Treating unhealthy relationships and helping individuals who have committed sexual crimes to develop appropriate sexual communication skills could reduce the risk for sexual recidivism (Hanson & Harris, 2000). When appropriate, using exercises to improve sexual communication in couples may be useful when working with individuals who have committed sexual offenses and their partners (Gottman & Silver, 2015; Schnarch, 2009).

2.3 Sexuality, Culture, and Society

A person's cultural beliefs, the media messages they are exposed to, and their spiritual values are important factors that shape one's sexual behaviors. Early research on sexuality focused on the treatment of sexual dysfunctions/problems in mostly white samples (Parker, 2009). The 1970s and 1980s saw sex researchers adopt feminist theory into sexuality research and begin to study sexual minorities, such as gay, lesbian, bisexual, and transgender individuals (Parker, 2009). Contemporary sex research has focused on sexual health disparities faced by sexual, as well as racial and ethnic, minorities and is in line with the WHO and other international organizations affirming sexual health as a basic human right for all people (WHO, 2019).

2.3.1 Culture-Bound Conditions and Treatment Theory

The Dhat Syndrome, the belief that semen leaves the body when urinating, is one example of a culturally-specific syndrome listed in the ICD-11 (WHO, 2019), most commonly occurring in men from South Asian countries (Malhotra & Wig, 1975). Entrenched in Asian culture, seminal fluid is considered sacred and mystical and seen as a powerful "elixir of life" (Malhotra & Wig, 1975). Thus, the erroneous belief that one's semen is being eliminated through urine is anxiety producing and often made worse by untreated anxiety or depressive symptoms (Chadda & Ahuja, 1990). Since Western cultures do not understand the importance of seminal fluid in Asian culture, traditional Western-oriented sex therapy interventions, such as psychoeducation or cognitive behavior therapy may be ineffective and make men with Dhat Syndrome reluctant to return to therapy. Moreover, involving the client's partner may exacerbate the condition given the fact that sexual health topics are considered taboo in South Asian culture.

Contemporary interventions for addressing sexual dysfunctions usually include a sex-positive approach encouraging sexual pleasure, autonomy, and diversity (Williams et al., 2015). Practitioners who take a sex-positive attitude encourage self-exploration regarding sexual attitudes and beliefs, destigmatize sexual problems, and address relational problems (Williams et al., 2015). Given the *Black Lives Matter* movement and the attention that has been paid to anti-racism theory, psychotherapists have begun to think about new ways to address racial inequalities in the therapy room. Adopting intersectionality in clinical practice, research, and training is one such new idea. Intersectionality encourages scholars and practitioners to consider the impact of multiple disadvantaged statuses on a client's sexual and psychological problems by considering a client's social class, natal sex (sex assigned at birth), gender identity, and race when applying clinical interventions (Cole, 2009).

Applying a sex-positive therapy approach when treating a South Asian or other minority status client who has committed a sexual offense suggests the importance of exploring a client's cultural values around sexuality, spiritual practice, and past sexual experiences, all the while being sensitive to cultural differences in conceptualizing sexual dysfunction. Therapists incorporating an intersectionality perspective should explore a client's family and country of origin, standing within their community, immigration status, religious identification, and relationship status.

2.3.2 *Society, and Changes in Sexual and Dating Practices*

Societal values, attitudes, and behaviors around sexuality have shifted dramatically over time. Conservative Victorian era values, attitudes, and sexual practices restricted the discussion around sex to biological functioning (Zimmerman, 2016). Technological advances in effective contraception, legalized abortion, and the sexual revolution of the 1960s liberalized societal values, attitudes, and sexual practices. These changes shifted conversations about sexuality from a focus on the biological and medical aspects of sexuality to considerations around family planning and sexual pleasure. With the onset of HIV/AIDS, American society focused on sexually-transmitted infections (STIs) and safer sex practices (Zimmerman, 2016).

With the general availability of the personal computer and smart phone, the Internet has become a major source of information and entertainment for billions of people. Adults who experienced their childhood in the digital age have come to rely on the Internet for sex education and sexual entertainment (Scarcelli, 2018). This has allowed users to learn about sexuality, engage in virtual sexual behavior (e.g., using webcams to engage in sexual behaviors with others, watching pornography), and have casual, anonymous sex (Scarcelli, 2018). Dating practices have also changed. According to a 2016 Pew Research report, 15% of Americans found their partners through online dating websites (Smith, 2016), suggesting a growing shift to starting relationships virtually.

This easy access to sexuality over the Internet may pose problems for individuals convicted of sex offenses, specifically those convicted for child pornography offenses. Professional organizations, such as the Association for the Treatment of Sexual Abusers (ATSA), a network of researchers, sex offender therapists, advocates, and other similar organizations, can assist treatment providers in tailoring their treatment to the individual client who committed a sexual offense (ATSA, 2017). Treatment providers should help their clients adjust to changes in societal dating trends by teaching responsible Internet use. This includes following all supervision guidelines for Internet/computer use and encouraging honesty about apps and websites used. Therapists who treat individuals who have committed sex offenses should consider the changes in dating and socializing as digital technology advances in order to provide more effective treatment to their clients.

2.4 What Is Known About Sexual Behavior

Once an individual has committed a sexual crime, society is likely to view their sexual behavior and sexual development as deviant. For example, the first author reviewed the case of a 24-year old man committed to a sexual offender civil commitment program in the United States. This man engaged in sexual behavior with his younger, developmentally-delayed sister when he was 10 years old and was adjudicated delinquent at that time. He was placed in residential treatment and three years later, when he was 13 years old and living in a facility for children, he was playing co-ed touch football and touched one of the adolescent girls during the game on her breast. This was defined, in court documents supporting his civil commitment, as a sexual re-offense.

Before it can be determined what is problematic or deviant, what is usual in terms of sexual development and sexual behavior must be considered. This can be defined in terms of what is acceptable within a given population, what the majority of people are doing, or what a substantial number of people are doing. What is acceptable is defined by numerous cultural factors, so defining acceptable sexual behavior is highly population specific.

Over the years, there have been a number of surveys of sexual behaviors and attitudes in the United States. The first national sample, since the Kinsey studies (Kinsey et al., 1948, 1953), conducted in the United States was the 1991 National Health and Social Life Survey (NHSLS; Laumann et al., 1994) which provided important information on the prevalence of masturbation, vaginal intercourse, anal intercourse, oral sex, and the appeal of a range of sexual experiences among younger adults. Since NHSLS, there have been several surveys, but they have generally focused on sexual behaviors that confer risk of pregnancy and sexually transmitted diseases in younger populations (Eaton et al., 2008; Mosher et al., 2005) or the relational and sexual issues of older adults (Waite et al., 2008). The results of the most current survey of adolescents and adults in the United States, the 2015 Sexual Exploration in America Study (Herbenick et al., 2017), and similarly recent surveys from the United Kingdom (Mercer et al., 2013) and Australia (Richters et al., 2014) will be reviewed. While there have been similar studies conducted in other countries, our intent here is not to explore all the variations in sexual behavior around the world, but rather to highlight how recent changes, such as the rise in digital technology, may have influenced normative sexual behavior.

In a recent representative sample of 14 to 74 year olds in the United States, 1.9% of men and 3.6% of women self-identified as bisexual, while 5.8% of men and 1.5% of women self-identified as gay or lesbian (Herbenick et al., 2017). In a similar study in the United Kingdom, 1.1% of the sample (45% male) self-identified as gay or lesbian, while 0.9% of the sample self-identified as bisexual (Semlyen et al., 2016). Despite these low rates of self-identification as gay, lesbian, or bisexual, the UK survey indicates that 8% of men and 11.5% of women have had a same-sex experience at some time during their lifetime (Mercer et al., 2013). Thus, some level of experimentation with same sex behavior, is not as rare as self-identification as gay, lesbian, or bisexual.

Age of first sexual intercourse in the United States averages about 16 years, with boys and girls initiating sexual intercourse at about the same age (Zito & De Coster, 2016). The UK survey indicates sexual debut at 16 years as well, with similar ages for boys and girls (Mercer et al., 2013). Two trends are notable in the UK sample: (1) age of sexual debut has decreased steadily from those born between 1936–1945 to those born between 1986–1994 and (2) in the oldest age group (65–74 years old), men initiated sexual intercourse at a younger age than women, but this gender difference disappeared in more recent cohorts, those born in 1956 or later (Mercer et al., 2013).

Several sexual behaviors that may concern those working with individuals who have committed sexual crimes, are not uncommon in general adult populations. For example, 21% of adult men and women report having engaged in bondage, 29.5% of men and 34.1% of women report having spanked or been spanked by a sexual partner, and 16.2% of men and 13.8% of women reported having playfully whipped or been whipped by a partner (Herbenick et al., 2017). Additionally, 32.9% of men and 50.2% of women reported using a vibrator or dildo during their lifetime (Herbenick et al., 2017). About five percent of men have paid for sex in the last five years (Mercer et al., 2013). On average, men in the UK have had 6 lifetime sexual partners, while women in the UK have had 4 lifetime sexual partners (Mercer et al., 2013). In the United States, the number of sexual partners (males and females) reported by adults has increased from 7.2 in 1988 to 11.2 in 2012 (Twenge et al., 2015).

Digital technology has changed how individuals acquire sexual partners and how intimate partners communicate with one another after initiation of a relationship. In an Australian sample, the proportion of individuals who obtained a new sexual partner using Internet technology in the last year increased from 1.0% of men and 0.3% of women to 2.9% of men and 1.5% of women (Richters et al., 2014). In a recent study, Sawyer et al. (2018) reported that 39.5% of their sample reported using dating apps, with no difference between males and females. Those using dating apps reported higher rates of sexual behavior than those not reporting using such apps. Additionally, the number of adults using dating sites and apps has increased over the last few years. In 2017, 26.1 million adults in the United States reported using a dating site or app. This increased to 30.4 million by 2019 and is estimated to increase to 33.6 million by the end of 2021 (Statistica, 2020). Twenty-seven percent of adults in the United States reported having used, or continuing to use, dating sites or apps as of April 2020; this includes 36% of those 18 to 29 years old and 40% of those 30 to 44 years old (Statistica, 2020).

While it is relatively rare to engage in sexual behavior on platforms like Facetime or Skype (13.9% of men and 10.5% of women reported having sex using these platforms in their lifetime), sending nude or semi-nude pictures of oneself is far more common (24.0% of men and 26.9% of women), as is receiving nude or semi-nude pictures from someone else (41.0% of men and 27.0% of women). Additionally, more than one-third (39.9% of men and 36.1% of women) reported that they have flirted with others using SMS or chat functions (Herbenick et al., 2017).

2.5 Gender Identity

Transgender identities are gaining attention in clinical practice and research. Transgender individuals have long existed in different cultures throughout history (e.g., Hijra; "two spirit"). In the United States, laws that discriminated against individuals who identified as transgender were first passed in the 1850s (Stryker, 2008). In the 1920s, medical doctors began to research and provide clinical care for transgender individuals. Famed sexologist, Magnus Hirchfield, coined the term, "transsexual" to describe "sexual intermediaries," or, individuals whose gender does not align with their natal sex, and was one of the first doctors who performed sexual reassignment surgeries (Stryker, 2008).

An individual who identifies as male or female (in line with their natal sex) is referred to as *cisgender*, while someone who identifies as something other than their natal sex is referred to as *transgender* or *gender non-conforming*. Recently, there has been a move away from considering gender as a binary concept (male or female) toward viewing gender on a spectrum, leading to individuals who self-identify as *non-binary* (i.e., do not identify as male or female) or as *gender fluid* (i.e., not having a fixed gender). These new conceptualizations of gender have revolutionized transgender healthcare (Rider et al., 2019).

2.5.1 Diagnosis and Treatment Considerations

Psychiatrists and medical professionals first included a diagnosis of "transexualism" to describe gender identity disorder in the Diagnostic and Statistical Manual of Mental Disorders, 3rd Edition (APA, 1980). This was the first time that gender identity disorder was based on an empirical, medical model (Beek et al., 2016). Further editions of the DSM included language that gender identity disorder caused clinically significant mental health distress (dysphoria). Gender Identity Disorder was renamed Gender Dysphoria in 2013 to address the uncomfortable feelings that transgender individuals might have. This diagnosis also made clear that individuals who identify as non-binary can report dysphoria (Beek et al., 2016).

The first formalized standards of care to be adopted to treat individuals with gender dysphoria was published in 1980 by the *World Professional Association of Transgender Health (WPATH)*, a worldwide group of leading gender health researchers, physicians, clinicians, and advocates (Coleman et al., 2012; Stryker, 2008). These standards provide guidance regarding the administration of masculinizing and feminizing hormones and outline prerequisites for gender affirming surgeries for both adolescents and adults. Clinicians who work in sex offender treatment programs and who have clients that identify as transgender or non-binary should familiarize themselves with these guidelines, as they outline proper assessment of gender dysphoria and provide criteria that clients must meet in order to have letters of support written for gender affirming surgeries (Coleman et al., 2012).

2.5.2 *Gender Affirmative Lifespan Approach (GALA)*

Transgender individuals are at higher risk for adverse childhood experiences (ACEs) than cisgender gay men and women and have significantly higher rates of suicide (Clements-Nolle et al., 2006; Schnarrs et al., 2019). Although medical interventions are a critical part of transgender healthcare, individual and family therapy are also critically important to help transgender and non-binary individuals navigate social changes. Previous treatment theories of gender healthcare have been shaped by the binary nature of natal sex (e.g., female and male chromosomes) and were not informed by health disparities research. The Gender Affirmative Lifespan Approach (GALA) was developed by the National Center for Gender Spectrum Health at the University of Minnesota (Rider et al., 2019). The GALA model is comprised of five philosophical foundations and five components that guide treatment interventions based on the growing body of research on the nature of gender, transgender, and health disparities.

2.5.2.1 Philosophical Foundations

The five philosophical foundations include: (1) transgender-affirmative care (e.g., being transgender is an identity, not a disorder); (2) intersectionality (e.g., clinicians recognize that culture, race, sexual orientation, and other personality and developmental factors are intrinsically linked with a person's experiences); (3) transparency (e.g., in contrast to "doctor knows best", providers are encouraged to share health information); and (4) developmental differences in care across the lifespan (e.g., interventions are formulated with the developmental level of the client in mind; Rider et al., 2019).

2.5.2.2 Core Components

The five components of the model describe the overarching principles for clinical intervention:

(1) Developing gender literacy. Rider et al. (2019) describe this intervention component as helping clients identify and challenge "oppressive gender narratives" (e.g., gender identity only exists as male and female) that transgender and non-binary identifying individuals may encounter (Berg & Edwards-Leeper, 2018).
(2) Moving beyond the binary. Rider et al. (2019) describe how early transgender health interventions enforced binary genders within transgender health, neglecting the health needs of non-binary individuals. The interventions in this stage help clients explore their affirmed gender, positioning it on a spectrum of gender identity rather than encouraging a viewpoint that gender is comprised of only male and female identity.

(3) Helping transgender and non-binary clients foster resiliency. Interventions such as connecting transgender and non-binary patients to in-person and online transgender communities to support clients and share experiences with transition steps and stigmatization are common interventions.
(4) A unique component of the GALA model is pleasure-oriented positive sexuality/prioritizing pleasure and satisfaction. Traditional sex therapy interventions focus on the sexual pleasure of cisgender, heterosexual individuals (Spencer & Vencill, 2017). It is important to help transgender and non-binary clients prioritize pleasure and satisfaction regardless of the medical changes they choose to make.
(5) Making positive connections to medical interventions. Previous iterations of the *WPATH Standards of Care* have positioned therapists as gatekeepers of medical interventions (Stryker, 2008). Instead, the GALA model encourages providers to recommend competent transgender health providers and help clients obtain finances to pay for their transgender health treatments.

The GALA model is used as a guide to assist transgender and non-binary individuals in making social changes by legally changing their preferred gender pronouns and name and "coming out" as transgender to coworkers, family members, friends, and romantic partners. Working with a mental health therapist while pursuing these social changes may help ease dysphoria that could arise during this process. Sex offender therapists who are working in outpatient settings may find that applying all aspects of the GALA model may be difficult when working with those who identify as transgender or non-binary (e.g., supervision restrictions may prevent name change). For therapists working in secure treatment settings or providing sex offender treatment in prisons, helping individuals obtain hormone replacement therapy or a consult for gender affirming surgeries may be difficult. However, according to the *WPATH Standards of Care* (Coleman et al., 2012), individuals residing in secure institutions should be given the same treatment as non-institutionalized patients. At minimum, the *Standards of Care* make it clear that individuals who are in the process of transitioning to their affirmed gender should continue their transition while they are attending treatment and/or confined because of their sexual offenses (e.g., those participating in hormone replacement therapy should continue taking hormones while incarcerated). It is clear that these standards can be especially challenging to correctional and residential institutions. However, successful reintegration of individuals who are transgender or gender non-conforming requires compassionate attention to the unique needs of these individuals and inclusion of these issues into the individualized treatment plans of those in sex offender treatment.

2.6 Sexual Dysfunction

Sexual dysfunctions/disorders are prevalent in the general population in the U.S. and around the world, affecting about 43% of women and 31% of men (Rosen, 2000). Four major sexual dysfunctions in men have been identified in the DSM-5 (APA, 2013): delayed ejaculation (least common male sexual complaint); erectile disorder (one of the most common sexual complaints); male hypoactive sexual desire disorder (relatively rare in younger men); and premature (early) ejaculation (PE; large numbers of men report concern but a small number would be diagnosed with the disorder). All of these disorders increase in incidence with age except for PE. There is some recent research indicating that men may experience chronic urological pain but "research and clinical experience are not sufficiently developed to justify the application of this diagnosis to men" (APA, 2013, p. 439). Another common sexual problem that presents itself in couples is desire discrepancy (the disparity between an individual and their partner in the frequency of their desire for sexual activity), which our anecdotal experience indicates is often a complaint of men in sex offender treatment and a rationale they use for their offending behavior.

Historical research has suggested that sexual dysfunctions are present and prevalent in men who commit sex offenses, but it is not known whether this prevalence/incidence is greater or less than in the general population. The research examining this issue is 20+ years old and has not been updated since. For example, Raymond et al. (1999) found a lifetime prevalence of 24% and current incidence of 16% of sexual dysfunctions in a small sample of 45 men with pedophilia participating in residential and outpatient sex offender treatment. Types of dysfunctions present included PE, male erectile dysfunction (ED), inhibited male orgasm, sexual aversion, hypoactive sexual disorder, and sexual dysfunction not otherwise specified (Bownes & O'Gorman, 1991). Phillips et al. (2015) cite studies revealing a prevalence of sexual dysfunction among men who committed sexual offences ranging from 10 to 34% and note that erectile and ejaculatory dysfunction are the most reported sexual dysfunctions. Bownes and O'Gorman (1991) presented their data on the incidence and characteristics of sexual dysfunction in rapists as reported by 50 victims of rape: 16 (32%) of the victims reported that their rapist had experienced sexual dysfunction at some point during the attack. ED was most commonly reported (20% of all assaults) and delayed ejaculation or failure to ejaculate was reported in 12% of rapes. None of the victims reported that their rapist experienced PE. This research uses male dysfunction diagnoses based on previous editions of the DSM in effect at the time the research was conducted, in this case the Diagnostic and Statistical Manual of Mental Disorders, 3rd Edition—Revised (DSM-III-R; 1987) and the Diagnostic and Statistical Manual of Mental Disorders, 4th Edition (DSM-IV; 1994). These data are over 30 years old, thus it is argued that the incidence/prevalence of current sexual dysfunctions present in men who have committed various sex offenses is an important topic that warrants updated research.

Several authors raise concerns about the ethics of treating sexual dysfunctions in sex offenders, fearing that such treatment may increase the ability and tendency of sex offenders to commit sex crimes (Douglas, 2017; Federoff, 2015; Phillips et al., 2015). Others argue that such treatment will improve the sexual health of sexual offenders and deter or prevent sexual offending recidivism (Federoff, 2015; Plaut, 2015). Currently, there is no definitive or empirical answer to this debate. What is known is that men who have committed sexual offenses seek and receive treatment for their sexual dysfunctions (Phillips et al., 2015). Metz and Sawyer (2004) summarize their treatment philosophy for treating men who have committed sexual offenses and propose that:

> (a) sexual dysfunction is a prevalent co-occurring sexual disorder in sex offenders; (b) sexual dysfunction is, by definition, a lack of sexual health, which diminishes overall life satisfaction; and (c) sexual dysfunction can be a contributing factor for some in maintaining offense-related arousal patterns and therefore is a potential contributor to sex-offense risk. (p. 1)

In an outpatient program for the treatment of men who have committed non-violent sexual offenses, sex therapy was regularly provided to treat any sexual dysfunctions clients displayed, with good results (Dwyer, 1997; Dwyer & Amberson, 1985; Swinburne Romine et al., 2008).

In this chapter, treatment approaches of the most commonly reported sexual dysfunctions in men who have committed sexual offenses (i.e., ED, PE, and desire discrepancy) are provided with the goal of improving their relationships and quality of life. First, medical treatments for each disorder are provided and then general sexual therapy interventions are reviewed in order to assist in the treatment of all these disorders.

2.6.1 Erectile Dysfunction

ED is the "repeated failure to obtain or maintain erections during partnered sexual activities" for a significant amount of time (75–100% of the time) during the majority of sexual occasions and causes "clinically significant distress" (APA, 2013, p. 427). It can be caused by both physical and/or psychological problems, often interacting, and the list of causes is long. Physical causes include a myriad of diseases, many associated with aging (diabetes, arteriosclerosis, hypertension, heart disease, nerve diseases, kidney disease, stroke, prostate enlargement); injury or surgery to the pelvic area; common medications (e.g., high blood pressure, allergy, anti-depressants, antiarrhythmics, H2 blockers), as well as lifestyle choices such as alcohol and/or drug use (e.g., cocaine, heroin, methamphetamine, etc.); tobacco smoking; sedentary lifestyle; and lack of sleep (Porst et al., 2013; Shamloul & Ghanem, 2013; National Kidney and Urologic Diseases Information Clearinghouse, 2009; Shabsigh & Anastasiadis, 2003).

Common psychological factors include relationship difficulties, depression, individual reaction to erectile difficulties, performance anxiety, guilt, sexual myths, anxiety, inadequate sexual information and education, as well as lack of sexual attraction to adults. Most ED is caused by several factors interacting, such as when a man experiences increased difficulty getting or maintaining an erection due to some physical factor. This leads to increased worry and anxiety when approaching sexual activity, which exacerbates his problem with erectile functioning (Porst et al., 2013; Shamloul & Ghanem, 2013; National Kidney and Urologic Diseases Information Clearinghouse, 2009; Shabsigh & Anastasiadis, 2003).

Treatment for ED is most likely to include a combination of medical, lifestyle, and psychological strategies. Fortunately, there are numerous medical strategies for ED; the most of any sexual dysfunction for men or women. These include: using a PDE-5 Inhibitor; changing medications to those which have fewer sexual side effects; adding an antidote drug or oral PDE-5 inhibitors to counteract medication negative effects; vacuum constriction devices (penile pumps); surgical penile prostheses; penile vascular surgery; and medications applied to the penis (e.g., prostaglandin E1 (Alprostadil)). There are now 5 commercially available oral PDE-5Inhibitors (sildenafil—Viagra; Pfizer; tadalafil—Cialis; Lilly; vardenafil—Levitra, Staxyn; Bayer; avanafil—Stendra and Spedra; Vivus, Inc., Menarini, Metuchen Pharmaceuticals; udenafil—Zydena; Dong-A PharmTech; and mirodenafi—vix; SK Chemical (Porst et al., 2013; Shamloul & Ghanem, 2013; National Kidney and Urologic Diseases Information Clearinghouse, 2009; Shabsigh & Anastasiadis, 2003).

2.6.2 Premature Ejaculation

PE is a "persistent pattern of ejaculation occurring during partnered sexual activity within approximately 1 minute following vaginal penetration and before the individual wishes it" and causes "clinically significant distress" (APA, 2013, p. 443). This disorder is the most common sexual complaint in men. Causes are not well known but it seems to be more common in men with anxiety disorders, especially sexual anxiety. PE is also caused by genetic factors, ED, urinary tract symptoms, and emotional distress (APA, 2013; Rosen, 2000). Researchers have struggled to define what PE is, as it is related to partner satisfaction and preferences, and have questioned whether PE is a *true* dysfunction (Puppo & Puppo, 2016). The term "early ejaculation" was an attempt to pick a less judgmental term that demonstrates the more subjective nature of the problem. Recently many researchers have highlighted the distinction between lifelong and acquired PE (Serefoglu et al., 2014). Accepted medical treatments include daily treatment with serotonergic antidepressants, including paroxetine (e.g., Paxil, considered to be the most effective), clomipramine (e.g., Anafranil), sertraline (e.g., Zoloft), and fluoxetine (e.g., Prozac), and on-demand use of topical anesthetics and tramadol (Waldinger, 2007).

2.6.3 Desire Discrepancy

Sexual desire discrepancy is the disparity between an individual and their partner in the frequency of their desire for sexual activity. Although in long-term relationships it is common that one partner tends to experience lower desire than the other (Day et al., 2015), it is the inability to negotiate this discrepancy that contributes to this dysfunction. Similarly, while one partner may meet criteria for either female sexual interest/arousal disorder or male hypoactive sexual desire disorder, a sexual interest or desire diagnosis is not required for sexual desire discrepancy to cause problems in the sexual relationship. By definition, sexual desire discrepancy dysfunction is a couple dynamic that can lead to or cause lowered relationship and sexual satisfaction (Girard & Wooley, 2017). The discrepancy may occur as the result of one partner having low or high sexual desire or simply substantial incompatibility in levels of sexual desire. Relationship problems may lower sexual desire in one or both partners, leading to lowered sexual activity, which can then lead to further relationship dissatisfaction contributing to even less sexual intimacy, thus promoting an escalating cycle of sexual difficulty and relationship dysfunction (Brezsnyak & Whisman, 2004).

While there are some limited medical treatments for both women and men to increase low desire (Girard & Wooley, 2017) and there is no widely accepted treatment for sexual desire discrepancy dysfunction, psychotherapy is the usual treatment option. Several researchers suggest that since desire discrepancy is a couple issue, the couple should be treated systemically, not just the partner with (too) low/lower or (too) high/higher desire (Girard & Wooley, 2017). Several types of couple therapy and psychological strategies have been suggested to improve couple desire discrepancy dysfunction, including emotionally-focused therapy (EFT) and other forms of couple therapy, as well as sexual education. Suggested targets for therapy and education include strong communication between partners; having the expectation that sexual desire will ebb and flow over the course of a relationship; avoiding engaging in coercive "consensual" sex; making stress-free time for the relationship; being mindfully present, intentional, and invested in the relationship; developing care and motivation for one another's sexual needs (i.e., communal strength); rejecting sex kindly; developing/maintaining autonomy and an identity that is separate from the couple identity; avoiding stress and fatigue; avoiding monotony; creating novel and unexpected sexual encounters; and challenging restrictive sexual attitudes (Brezsnyak & Whisman, 2004; Day et al., 2015; Girard & Wooley, 2017; Kim et al., 2018).

2.6.4 *Sexual Therapy Approaches*

While *all* the sexual therapeutic approaches used to manage these common dysfunctions cannot be deliniated, some basic ideas and principles used by sex therapists the world over are listed here.

1. Broadening one's definition of sex/sexual intimacy to include and prioritize non-genitally focused activities; activities that do not center around vaginal/anal sexual intercourse nor rely on a hard or long lasting erection. These non-penetrative forms of pleasurable safer sex activities "came of age" in the HIV-prevention era and have been called "outercourse" (Bakaroudis, 2014). Such activities include, but are not limited to: hugging, kissing, giving or receiving massage, caressing breasts, undressing in front of a sexual partner, dry humping, mutual masturbation, using sex toys, rubbing the penis between the breasts/thighs/armpits/behind knee, showering/bathing together, watching pornography/erotica, sexy dancing, sucking/licking body parts other than vagina/penis/anus, wearing sexy clothes, making erotic eye contact, undressing in front of a sexual partner, rubbing bodies with clothes on, rubbing bodies with clothes off, manual stimulation, oral sex, writing love letters, sexual phone text messages, chat, or emails, thinking or fantasizing about sex, discussing sexual fantasies with someone in person or over phone/internet/SMS.
2. Challenging the fantasy model of sexual expectations for men that prescribe that "it's two feet long, hard as steel, and will knock your socks off" (Zilbergeld, 1999, p. 117), thus lowering anxiety, especially performance anxiety, and spectatoring, "the cognitive process of attending to negative self-perceptions rather than positive erotic cues during sex" (Wyatt & de Jong, 2020, p. 2983).
3. Improving relationship dynamics to enable the couple to set a relaxed and permissive mood when engaging in physical intimacy (Frederick et al., 2017; Mark & Lasslo, 2018).
4. Sex education, challenging myths about sexual activity (it comes naturally; women and men are the same sexually, understanding that sexual desire in women may be better conceptualized as "willingness" to start engaging in some sort of physical intimacy), and setting realistic expectations about sex (Metz & McCarthy, 2003).
5. Specific PE techniques focused on developing ejaculatory control, such as finding one's calm erection, practicing erection waxing and waning, learning pleasure toleration, stopping and starting, pacing individually and with one's partner, and initiating and acclimating to intercourse including progressive intercourse (Metz & McCarthy, 2003; Zilbergeld, 1999).

2.7 Compulsive Sexual Behavior

High frequency and out-of-control sexual behavior has been conceptualized in a number of ways, most frequently within the sex offender treatment community as sexual addiction (Grubbs et al., 2020). In the absence of strong empirical data supporting any specific conceptualization, Kafka (2010) proposed a general diagnosis of hypersexual disorder for the Diagnostic and Statistical Manual for Mental Disorders (DSM). Although the diagnosis was rejected, in part due to the relative lack of scientific support for the proposed criteria, the recently released edition of the International Classification of Diseases (ICD-11; WHO, 2019) recognized the diagnosis of compulsive sexual behavior disorder.

The challenge of arriving at some generally accepted nomenclature and set of diagnostic criteria for compulsive sexual behavior disorder is compounded by our limited understanding of its causes and determinants. Different terminologies are associated with different assumptions about underlying mechanisms (e.g., addiction, compulsivity, impulsivity; Bancroft & Vukadinovic, 2004; Coleman et al., 2018; Walton et al., 2017). In addition, the relative weight of the subjective experience of not feeling in control (and the distress associated with it) versus actual behaviors, and when to consider them to be excessive, further complicates matters.

The literature on the prevalence and possible causes of compulsive sexual behavior focused on different behaviors, depending on, among other factors, the sexual orientation of the participants. In heterosexual men and women, a substantial number of studies focused on pornography use, including its correlates and outcomes (e.g., on relationships, sexual function; Prause et al., 2015; Schmidt et al., 2017; Steele et al., 2013; Voon et al., 2014). Whereas almost no research exists on the experiences of bisexual and lesbian women, a large proportion of studies in men who have sex with men examine compulsive sexual behavior in the context of sex with others and its potential for associated risks (e.g., STDs/HIV; Coleman et al., 2010; Parsons et al., 2013; Yoon et al., 2016). Studies also exist that do not make such distinctions and include men and women of different sexual orientations and focus on high levels of pornography use and high numbers of sexual partners (e.g., Carvalho et al., 2015; Miner et al., 2016; Seok & Sohn, 2015; Stulhofer et al., 2016; Walton & Bhullar, 2018). This is consistent with the fact that most questionnaires that are used to assess out-of-control sexuality, more than 17 having been described in the literature (Hook et al., 2010), do not differentiate between different types of behaviors or problem areas. It remains to be established whether problems involving high levels of pornography use and those involving high levels of partnered sex are associated with similar etiologies, trajectories, and outcomes.

Individual differences in reward processing and sensitivity have been studied using, for example, Tellegen's (1985) personality theory, which distinguishes between three higher-order personality factors: *Positive Emotionality*, *Negative Emotionality*, and *Constraint*. Skegg et al. (2010) found that compulsive sexual behavior was related to higher scores on the *Stress Reaction* subscales and lower scores on the *Control* subscales of *Negative Emotionality* and *Constraint*, respectively. Miner et al. (2016) reported the results of personality testing from a larger study of 242 men with at least one male sexual partner in their lifetime. This study, which included cognitive tasks, psychophysiological assessment of sexual arousal under various emotional conditions, and self-report instruments assessing a variety of variables that have been hypothesized to be related to or cause compulsive sexual behavior, found that compulsive sexual behavior was related to higher *Negative Emotionality* and lower *Constraint*. Additionally, compulsive sexual behavior has been shown to be related to the "Big Five" (Digman, 1990) factor of *Neuroticism*, which is indicative of deficits in coping skills for stress and to vulnerability to depression and anxiety; and (negatively) to *Agreeableness*, which is indicative of individuals with a pattern of distrust, rudeness, manipulation, lack of cooperation, and lack of concern for others (Pinto et al., 2013). Further, *Neuroticism* was found to be highly correlated with scores on the *Sexual Compulsivity Scale* (Reid et al., 2008), and to mediate the relationship between shame and compulsive sexual behavior (Reid et al., 2011). Studies relating Tellegen's personality structure to the five factor model indicate that *Negative Emotionality* is a higher order factor that encompasses *Neuroticism* and the inverse of *Agreeableness* (Church, 1994). These findings consistently suggest that compulsive sexual behavior is positively associated with reactivity and difficulty coping with negative emotional states.

When it comes to mechanisms more directly relevant to sexuality, the *dual control model* (DCM) of sexual response provides a theoretical framework that has proven of value to our understanding of various aspects of sexual response and behavior, including sexual desire, sexual arousal, and sexual risk taking (Janssen & Bancroft, 2007). The model described sexual arousal and related processes as controlled by two underlying factors reflecting distinct neurophysiological systems, *sexual inhibition* and *sexual excitation* (Bancroft & Janssen, 2000). Individual differences in the propensity for *sexual excitation* reflect the tendency to experience motivation to engage in sexual behavior and heightened levels of sexual arousal when exposed to sexual cues. The *sexual inhibitory system* (SIS) is thought to suppress sexual response and behavior through two processes: inhibition due to threat of sexual performance failure and inhibition due to threat of likely outcomes of sexual behavior (Janssen et al., 2002). Consistent with the *dual control model*, some initial support has been found for the idea that compulsive sexual behavior is more likely in individuals with a high propensity for sexual excitation and a low propensity for sexual inhibition (Bancroft & Vukadinovic, 2004). Deficits in inhibition could indicate a more impulsive disorder, while high sexual arousability would be more consistent with the notion that compulsive sexual behavior may reflect the high end of a sexual motivation or responsivity dimension (Moser, 2011; Steele et al., 2013).

Sexual excitation, the ease with which an individual becomes sexually aroused, has consistently been found to be positively associated with compulsive sexual behavior, regardless of sexual orientation or gender (e.g., Bancroft & Vukadinovic, 2004; Miner et al., 2016; Muise et al., 2013; Parsons et al., 2016; Rettenberger et al., 2016; Walton et al., 2017; Winters et al., 2010). This well-replicated finding has played a role in discussions about whether compulsive sexual behavior should be considered part of a desire continuum, "a means of satisfying a strong sexual appetite" (Muise et al., 2013, p. 205), and has contributed to the observation that hypersexual individuals may be "neurologically and behaviorally predisposed to react sexually to specific cues/triggers which they feel unable to control" (Walton et al., 2017, p. 2242).

Consistent with work by Parsons et al. (2016), compulsive sexual behavior may be related to the affective response to and effects of such behaviors, not to the quantity or frequency of various sexual behaviors. Relevant to this observation, Bancroft et al. (2009) and Parsons et al. (2008) found a connection between negative affect (e.g., depression, stress) and compulsive sexual behavior. We, too, have found a connection between affect and compulsive sexual behavior, but it appears to be an interaction between negative affective arousal and positive affective arousal. In a study that combined a sexual daily diary procedure with an ecological momentary assessment of affect across the day, it was found that participants with compulsive sexual behavior were more likely to engage in sexual behavior when they experienced more than usual negative emotions, and the likelihood of this behavior increased with increased levels of positive affective activation (Miner et al., 2019). This interaction effect held for both partnered sexual behavior and for masturbation and pornography use.

There have also been a number of studies of neuroanatomical and neurological functioning differences between those with compulsive sexual behavior and those without. While a small study was conducted with men whose compulsive sexual behavior included partnered sex, the vast majority of this literature has focused on men who use visual sexual stimuli. While some studies have shown central nervous system circuits, most often related to the pleasure system (Gola et al., 2017; Voon et al., 2014), to be related to compulsive sexual behavior, other research indicated that physiological responses, including evoked potentials from electroencephalogram and penile tumescence, are more related to sexual excitation and sexual drive than to compulsive sexual behavior (Janssen et al., 2020; Prause et al., 2015; Steele et al., 2013).

The current literature supports the contention that there are men and women who present for treatment because they are concerned about the frequency or nature of their sexual behavior and perceive it as beyond their self-control. In many cases, these individuals experience interpersonal conflict, but they may also experience intrapersonal turmoil. Additionally, there appears to be consistent evidence that these individuals use sexual behavior, either with others or alone, to cope with negative affect. It is unclear if there is a unitary phenomenon that can be described as "addiction", although there is some evidence of central nervous system arousability in areas of the brain related to urges and wanting, but not necessarily liking, which is consistent with addiction. However, this arousability is also consistent with the argument that what is being described as sexual addiction or sexual compulsive behavior is more related to high sex drive and reactivity to sexual stimuli, rather than a lack of behavioral control.

Psychological treatment of individuals presenting with compulsive sexual behavior has been around for decades, but there is little empirical evidence for the effectiveness of most interventions. The most common treatments have been based on 12-step models used for substance abuse. There are numerous self-help groups, including Sexual Addicts Anonymous (SAA), which function similar to Alcoholics Anonymous, but they have not been rigorously studied for their effectiveness. A sex-positive and biopsychosocial intervention has been developed at the Center for Sexual Health (Coleman et al., 2018); this model, while based on frameworks with empirical support, has also not been rigorously evaluated for its effectiveness. In recent years, there have been random assignment studies addressing the outcome of treatments for compulsive sexual behavior. At least one has found positive effects for cognitive-behavioral interventions (Hallberg et al., 2019). There have also been some promising studies showing the effectiveness of the opiate antagonist, Naltrexone, for treatment of compulsive sexual behavior (Raymond et al., 2002, 2010; Savard et al., 2020).

2.8 Summary and Conclusions

Sexual offending, when viewed from a sexual health perspective, can be considered a maladaptive sexual behavior that happens to be illegal. It is our contention, therefore, that it is necessary to consider a range of individual, family, community, and societal factors when determining how various sexual behaviors fit into the development of sexual offending. In this chapter, our goal was to provide treatment providers with two general areas of information: (1) what is known know about sexual behavior, the factors that influence what most people do sexually, and what is considered appropriate, and (2) information and intervention options for gender and sexual health issues that those providing sexual offender treatment are likely to encounter.

Sexual communication is an important aspect of sexual health that can lead to abusive and illegal sexual behavior when done poorly. Consent for sexual behavior is communicated differently by men and women, and there is evidence that men imply sexual consent from behaviors that women report do not indicate consent. In general, consent is not often clearly stated, but is signaled through indirect verbal or non-verbal behavior. Thus, it is possible that men and women will miscommunicate and that men may assume that the sexual behavior was consensual, while women experienced it as coercive or abusive.

Over the last few decades, the age at which individuals, both men and women, initiate sexual intercourse has become younger. Currently, both men and women are likely to have their first sexual intercourse experience at 16 years old. This age of sexual debut is similar in the United States, the United Kingdom, and Australia. While in earlier generations, men experienced first sexual intercourse at earlier ages than women, this is no longer the case. However, sexual debuts prior to age 13 years are infrequent in both males and females. Many sexual behaviors, like bondage, discipline, and spanking, while relatively uncommon, appear to be more mainstream than sex offender treatment providers might assume. Thus, not all behaviors that have been considered deviant by the sex offender treatment community are, in fact, deviant.

The use of digital technology is more common in all populations and is changing the nature of sexual behavior and dating. It is becoming more likely that couples will meet through dating applications and communicate online for some period of time before meeting in person. Further, exchanging sexually explicit pictures between dating and romantic partners is becoming more frequent. It is likely that this manner of flirting and sexual communication will become more prevalent, and interventions attempting to discourage such exchange of images are likely to be ineffective. While these images are generally exchanged with the expectation of privacy, "revenge porn" and other non-consensual dissemination of images may violate those expectations. Interventions, rather than focusing on discouraging sexting, may be more effective if they focus, as with all sexual behavior, on the consent of the individual depicted in the images and their expectations for privacy.

Sexual issues treatment providers are likely to encounter when working with men who have committed sexual offenses who are being treated in either residential or outpatient programs has also been reviewed. Transgender and gender nonconforming individuals require some specialized knowledge and interventions; gender issues and gender dysphoria need to be addressed directly in the treatment program or with an appropriate referral. The World Professional Association of Transgender Health, *Standards of Care* is an importance resource for treatment providers and transgender clients.

Sexual dysfunctions, other than the specific offending behavior or paraphilia resulting in the sexual crime adjudication, are likely present in men being treated for sexual offenses at the same rate as in men in general. When looking at sexual offender treatment from a sexual health perspective, treating dysfunctions that are present should be part of sex offender treatment. Sexual dysfunctions may be a barrier to developing healthy romantic and sexual relationships, thus leading to increased risk for re-offending. Perhaps the only exception to this would be low sexual desire, which may make it easier for individuals with certain paraphilias to control their behavior. However, working with couples with desire discrepancies is likely to improve social support and relationship satisfaction.

There is controversy about the existence and nature of sexual addiction or compulsive sexual behavior. There is no doubt that there are individuals who perceive their behavior as out of control and either the nature or frequency of such behavior leads to emotional upset and/or social, relationship, and other interpersonal dysfunction. While such concerns are not present in all men or women who commit sexual crimes, there are some behaviors, like exposing, that have a component similar to what has been described as compulsive sexual behavior. There are also individuals in sex offender treatment who report they cannot control their sexual behavior. Being aware of the options for treatment, including opiate antagonists and psychotherapeutic interventions, provides the treatment provider with more tools in their toolbox.

In this chapter, information has been provided that allows us to put the etiological, developmental, and experiential components of our clients in perspective.

Further, some common issues and dysfunctions that treatment providers might confront when treating individuals who are undergoing treatment due to their criminal sexual behavior have been discussed. This chapter has attempted to put sexual behavior that is defined as a crime in the context of normative sexual behavior and within the cultural context that often determines what sexual behavior is illegal and what is socially acceptable.

References

American Psychiatric Association. (1980). *Diagnostic and statistical manual of mental disorders* (3rd ed.). American Psychiatric Association.

American Psychiatric Association. (1987). *Diagnostic and Statistical Manual of Mental Disorders, 3rd Edition*—Revised (DSM-III-R).

American Psychiatric Association. (1994). *Diagnostic and Statistical Manual of Mental Disorders*, 4th Edition (DSM-IV).

American Psychiatric Association. (2013). *Diagnostic and statistical manual of mental disorders* (5th ed.). https://doi.org/10.1176/appi.books.9780890425596

American Psychological Association. (2022). *APA dictionary of psychology*. https://www.dictionary.apa.org/sexology

Association for the Treatment of Sexual Abusers. (2017). *Association for the Treatment of Sexual Abusers*. https://www.atsa.com

Bakaroudis, M. (2014). Outercourse: Exploring nonpenetrative forms of pleasurable safer sex. *American Journal of Sexuality Education, 9*(3), 381–397. https://doi.org/10.1080/15546128.2014.944736

Bancroft, J., Graham, C. A., Janssen, E., & Sanders, S. A. (2009). The dual control model: Current status and future directions. *The Journal of Sex Research, 46*(2–3), 121–142. https://doi.org/10.1080/00224490902747222

Bancroft, J., & Janssen, E. (2000). The dual control model of male sexual response: A theoretical approach to centrally mediated erectile dysfunction. *Neuroscience & Biobehavioral Reviews, 24*(5), 571–579. https://doi.org/10.1016/S0149-7634(00)00024-5

Bancroft, J., & Vukadinovic, Z. (2004). Sexual addiction, sexual compulsivity, sexual impulsivity, or what? Toward a theoretical model. *The Journal of Sex Research, 41*(3), 225–234. https://doi.org/10.1080/00224490409552230

Beek, T. F., Cohen-Kettenis, P. T., & Kreukels, B. P. (2016). Gender incongruence/gender dysphoria and its classification history. *International Review of Psychiatry, 28*(1), 5–12. https://doi.org/10.3109/09540261.2015.1091293

Berg, D., & Edwards-Leeper, L. (2018). Child and family assessment. In C. Keo-Meier & D. Ehrensaft (Eds.), *Perspectives on sexual orientation and diversity. The Gender Affirmative Model: A new approach to supporting gender diverse and transgender children* (pp. 101–124). American Psychological Association. https://doi.org/10.1037/0000095-007

Bownes, I. T., & O'Gorman, E. C. (1991). Assailants' sexual dysfunction during rape reported by their victims. *Medicine, Science and the Law, 31*(4), 322–328. https://doi.org/10.1177/002580249103100408

Brezsnyak, M., & Whisman, M. A. (2004). Sexual desire and relationship functioning: The effects of marital satisfaction and power. *Journal of Sex & Marital Therapy, 30*(3), 199–217. https://doi.org/10.1080/00926230490262393

Carvalho, J., Stulhofer, A., Viera, A. L., & Jurin, T. (2015). Hypersexuality and high sexual desire: Exploring the structure of problematic sexuality. *Journal of Sexual Medicine, 12*(6), 1356–1367. https://doi.org/10.1111/jsm.12865

Chadda, R. K., & Ahuja, N. (1990). Dhat syndrome: A sex neurosis of the Indian subcontinent. *The British Journal of Psychiatry, 156*(4), 577–579. https://doi.org/10.1192/bjp.156.4.577
Church, A. (1994). Relating the Tellegen and five-factor models of personality structure. *Journal of Personality and Social Psychology, 67*(5), 898–909. https://doi.org/10.1037/0022-3514.67.5.898
Clements-Nolle, K., Marx, R., & Katz, M. (2006). Attempted suicide among transgender persons: The influence of gender-based discrimination and victimization. *Journal of Homosexuality, 51*(3), 53–69. https://doi.org/10.1300/J082v51n03_04
Cole, E. R. (2009). Intersectionality and research in psychology. *American Psychologist, 64*(3), 170–180. https://doi.org/10.1037/a0014564
Coleman, E., Bockting, W., Botzer, M., Cohen-Kettenis, P., DeCuypere, G., Feldman, J., Fraser, L., Green, J., Knudson, G., Meyer, W. J., Monstrey, S., Adler, R. K., Brown, G. R., Devor, A. H., Ehrbar, R., Ettner, R., Eyler, E., Garofalo, R., Karasic, D. H., et al. (2012). Standards of care for the health of transsexual, trans- gender, and gender-nonconforming people, version 7. *International Journal of Transgenderism, 13*(4), 165–232. https://doi.org/10.1080/15532739.2011.700873
Coleman, E., Dickenson, J. A., Girard, A., Rider, G. N., Candelario-Pérez, L. E., Becker-Warner, R., Kovic, A. G., & Munns, R. (2018). An integrative biopsychosocial and sex positive model of understanding and treatment of impulsive/compulsive sexual behavior. *Sexual Addiction & Compulsivity, 25*(2–3), 125–152. https://doi.org/10.1080/10720162.2018.1515050
Coleman, E., Horvath, K. J., Miner, M., Ross, M. W., Oakes, M., Rosser, B. R. S., & Men's INTernet Sex (MINTS-II) Team. (2010). Compulsive sexual behavior and risk for unsafe sex among internet using men who have sex with men. *Archives of Sexual Behavior, 39*(5), 1045–1053. https://doi.org/10.1007/s10508-009-9507-5
Craissati & Beech. (2003). A review of dynamic variables and their relationship to risk prediction in sex offenders. *Journal of Sexual Aggression, 9*(1), 41–55. https://doi.org/10.1080/355260031000137968
Day, L. C., Muise, A., Joel, S., & Impett, E. A. (2015). To do it or not to do it? How communally motivated people navigate sexual interdependence dilemmas. *Personality and Social Psychology Bulletin, 41*(6), 791–804. https://doi.org/10.1177/0146167215580129
Digman, J. (1990). Personality structure: Emergence of the five-factor model. *Annual Review of Psychology, 41*, 417–440.
Douglas, T. (2017). Refusing to treat sexual dysfunction in sex offenders. *Cambridge Quarterly of Healthcare Ethics, 26*(1), 143–158. https://doi.org/10.1017/S0963180116000712
Dwyer, M., & Amberson, J. I. (1985). Sex offender treatment program: A follow-up study. *American Journal of Social Psychiatry, 5*(4), 56–60.
Dwyer, S. M. (1997). Treatment outcome study: Seventeen years after sexual offender treatment. *Sexual Abuse: A Journal of Research and Treatment, 9*(2), 149–160. https://doi.org/10.1007/BF02674865
Eaton, D. K., Kann, L., Kinchen, S., Shanklin, S., Ross, J., Hawkins, J., Harris, W. A., Lowry, R., McManus, T., Chyen, D., Lim, C., Brener, N. D., & Wechsler, H. (2008). Youth risk behavior surveillance--United States, 2007. *Morbidity and Mortality Weekly Report. Surveillance Summaries (Washington, DC: 2002), 57*(4), 1–131.
Federoff, J. P. (2015). Editorial comment on "Sex offenders seeking treatment for sexual dysfunction—Ethics, medicine, and the law". *The Journal of Sexual Medicine, 12*(9), 1975–1976. https://doi.org/10.1111/jsm.12973
Frederick, D. A., Lever, J., Gillespie, B. J., & Garcia, J. R. (2017). What keeps passion alive? Sexual satisfaction is associated with sexual communication, mood setting, sexual variety, oral sex, orgasm, and sex frequency in a national U.S. study. *The Journal of Sex Research, 54*(2), 186–201. https://doi.org/10.1080/00224499.2015.1137854
Freund, K., & Blanchard, R. (1986). The concept of Courtship Disorder. *Journal of Sex and Marital Therapy, 12*(2), 79–92. https://doi.org/10.1080/00926238608415397
Gagnon, J., & Simon, W. (1973). *Sexual conduct: The social sources of human sexuality*. Aldine.

Girard, A., & Wooley, S. R. (2017). Using emotionally focused therapy to treat sexual desire discrepancy in couples. *Journal of Sex & Marital Therapy, 43*(8), 720–735. https://doi.org/10.1080/0092623X.2016.1263703

Gola, M., Wordecha, M., Sescousse, G., Sescousse, G., Lew-Starowiscz, M., Kossowski, B., Wypych, M., Makeig, S., Potenza, M. N., & Marchewka, A. (2017). Can pornography be addictive? An fMRI study of men seeking treatment for problematic pornography use. *Neurophychophamacology, 42*(10), 2021–2031. https://doi.org/10.1038/npp.2017.78

Gottman, J. M., & Silver, N. (2015). *The seven principles for making marriage work: A practical guide from the country's foremost relationship expert*. Harmony.

Grubbs, J. B., Grant, J. T., Lee, B. N., Hoagland, K. C., Davidson, P., Reid, R. C., & Kraus, S. W. (2020). Sexual addiction 25 years on: A systematic and methodological review of empirical literature and an agenda for future research. *Clinical Psychology Review, 82*, 101925. https://doi.org/10.1016/j.cpr.2020.101925

Hallberg, J., Kaldo, V., Arver, S., Dhejne, C., Jokinsen, J., & Görts-Öberg, K. (2019). A randomized controlled study of group-administered cognitive behavioral therapy for Hypersexual Disorder in men. *Journal of Sexual Medicine, 16*(5), 733–749. https://doi.org/10.1016/j.jsxm.2019.03.005

Hanson, R. K., & Harris, A. J. (2000). Where should we intervene? Dynamic predictors of sexual offense recidivism. *Criminal Justice and Behavior, 27*(1), 6–35. https://doi.org/10.1177/0093854800027001002

Herbenick, D., Bowling, J., Fu, T.-C., Dodge, B., Guerra-Reyes, L., & Sanders, S. (2017). Sexual diversity in the United States: Results from a nationally representative probability sample of adult women and men. *PLoS One, 12*(7), e0181198. https://doi.org/10.1371/journal.pone.0181198

Hickman, S. E., & Muehlenhard, C. L. (1999). "By the semi-mystical appearance of a condom": How young women and men communicate sexual consent in heterosexual situations. *The Journal of Sex Research, 36*(3), 258–272. https://doi.org/10.1080/00224499909551996

Hook, J. N., Hook, J. P., Davis, D. E., Worthington, E. L., Jr., & Penberthy, J. K. (2010). Measuring sexual addiction and compulsivity: A critical review of instruments. *Journal of Sex & Marital Therapy, 36*(3), 227–260. https://doi.org/10.1080/00926231003719673

Humphreys, T., & Herold, E. (2007). Sexual consent in heterosexual relationships: Development of a new measure. *Sex Roles, 57*(3–4), 305–315. https://doi.org/10.1007/s11199-007-9264-7

International Association for the Treatment of Sexual Offenders (IATSO). (n.d.). *Statutes and bylaws*. https://iatso.org/phocadownload/statutes%20and%20by%20laws_012017.pdf

Janssen, E., & Bancroft, J. (2007). The dual-control model: The role of sexual inhibition and excitation in sexual arousal and behavior. In E. Janssen (Ed.), *Psychophysiology of sex* (pp. 197–222). University of Indiana Press.

Janssen, E., Prause, N., Swinburne Romine, R., Raymond, N., MacDonald, A., III, Coleman, E., & Miner, M. H. (2020). Sexual responsivity and the effects of negative mood on sexual arousal in hypersexual Men who have Sex with Men (MSM). *Journal of Sexual Medicine, 17*(9), 1751–1760. https://doi.org/10.1016/j.jsxm.2020.05.005

Janssen, E., Vorst, H., Finn, P., & Bancroft, J. (2002). The Sexual Inhibition (SIS) and Sexual Excitation (SES) Scales: I. Measuring sexual inhibition and excitation proneness in men. *The Journal of Sex Research, 39*(2), 114–126. https://doi.org/10.1080/00224490209552130

Jozkowski, K. N. (2013). The influence of consent on college students' perceptions of the quality of sexual intercourse at last event. *International Journal of Sexual Health, 25*(4), 260–272. https://doi.org/10.1080/19317611.2013.799626

Jozkowski, K. N., Peterson, Z. D., Sanders, S. A., Dennis, B., & Reece, M. (2013). Gender differences in heterosexual college students' conceptualizations and indicators of sexual consent: Implications for contemporary sexual assault prevention education. *The Journal of Sex Research, 51*(8), 904–916. https://doi.org/10.1080/00224499.2013.792326

Kafka, M. P. (2010). Hypersexual disorder: A proposed diagnosis for DSM-V. *Archives of Sexual Behavior, 39*(2), 377–400. https://doi.org/10.1007/s10508-009-9574-7

Kim, J., Muise, A., & Impett, E. A. (2018). The relationship implications of rejecting a partner for sex kindly versus having sex reluctantly. *Journal of Social and Personal Relationships, 35*(4), 485–508. https://doi.org/10.1177/0265407517743084

Kinsey, A. C., Pomeroy, W. B., & Martin, C. E. (1948). *Sexual behavior in the human male.* W. B. Saunders Company.

Kinsey, A. C., Pomeroy, W. B., Martin, C. E., & Gebhard, P. M. (1953). *Sexual behavior in the human female.* W. B. Saunders Company.

Laumann, E. O., Gagnon, J. H., Michael, R. T., & Michaels, S. (1994). *The social organization of sexuality: Sexual practices in the United States.* University of Chicago Press.

MacNeil, S., & Byers, E. S. (2009). Role of sexual self-disclosure in the sexual satisfaction of long-term heterosexual couples. *The Journal of Sex Research, 46*(1), 3–14. https://doi.org/10.1080/00224490802398399

Malhotra, H. K., & Wig, N. N. (1975). Dhat syndrome: A culture-bound sex neurosis of the Orient. *Archives of Sexual Behavior, 4*(5), 519–528. https://doi.org/10.1007/BF01542130

Mark, K. P., & Lasslo, J. A. (2018). Maintaining sexual desire in long-term relationships: A systematic review and conceptual model. *The Journal of Sex Research, 55*(4–5), 563–581. https://doi.org/10.1080/00224499.2018.1437592

McDavitt, B., & Mutchler, M. G. (2014). "Dude, you're such a slut!" barriers and facilitators of sexual communication among young gay men and their best friends. *Journal of Adolescent Research, 29*(4), 464–498. https://doi.org/10.1177/0743558414528974

Mercer, C. H., Tanton, C., Prah, P., Erens, B., Sonnenberg, P., Clifton, S., Macdowall, W., Lweis, R., Field, N., Datta, J., Copas, A. J., Phelps, A., Wellings, K., & Johnson, A. M. (2013). Changes in sexual attitudes and lifestyles in Britain through the life course and over time: Findings from the National Surveys of Sexual Attitudes and Lifestyles (Natsal). *The Lancet, 382*(9907), 1781–1794. https://doi.org/10.1016/S0140-6736(13)62035-8

Metz, M. E., & McCarthy, B. W. (2003). *Coping with premature ejaculation. How to overcome PE, please your partner, and have great sex.* New Harbinger Publications, Inc.

Metz, M. E., & Sawyer, S. P. (2004). Treating sexual dysfunction in sex offenders: A case example. *Journal of Sex & Marital Therapy, 30*(3), 185–197. https://doi.org/10.1080/00926230490262384

Miner, M. H., Dickenson, J., & Coleman, E. (2019). Effects of emotions on sexual behavior in men with and without hypersexuality. *Sexual Addiction & Compulsivity, 26*(1–2), 24–41. https://doi.org/10.1080/10720162.2018.1564408

Miner, M. H., Swinburne Romine, R., Raymond, N., Janssen, E., MacDonald, A., III, & Coleman, E. (2016). Understanding the personality and behavioral mechanisms defining hypersexuality in men who have sex with men. *The Journal of Sexual Medicine, 13*(9), 1323–1331. https://doi.org/10.1016/j.jsxm.2016.06.015

Money, J. (1986). *Lovemaps: Clinical concepts of sexual/erotic health and pathology, paraphilia, and gender transposition in childhood, adolescence, and maturity.* Prometheus Books.

Moser, C. (2011). Hypersexual disorder: Just more muddled thinking. *Archives of Sexual Behavior, 40*(2), 227–229. https://doi.org/10.1007/s10508-010-9690-4

Mosher, W. D., Chandra, A., & Jones, J. (2005). *Sexual behavior and selected health measures: Men and women 15-44 years of age, United States, 2002* (No. 362). US Department of Health and Human Services, Centers for Disease Control and Prevention, National Center for Health Statistics.

Muise, A., Impett, E. A., Kogan, A., & Desmarais, S. (2013). Keeping the spark alive: Being motivated to meet a partner's sexual needs sustains sexual desire in long-term romantic relationships. *Social Psychological and Personality Science, 4*(3), 267–273. https://doi.org/10.1177/1948550612457185

National Kidney and Urologic Diseases Information Clearinghouse. (2009). *Erectile dysfunction.* U.S. Department of Health and Human Services. National Institutes of Health, NIH Publication No. 09-3923, June. National Institute of Diabetes and Digestive and Kidney Diseases.

Newstrom, N. P., Harris, S. M., & Miner, M. H. (2021). Sexual consent: How relationships, gender and sexual self-disclosure affect signaling and interpreting cues for sexual consent. *Sex Roles, 84*(7–8), 454–464. https://doi.org/10.1007/s11199-020-01178-2

Parker, R. (2009). Sexuality, culture and society: Shifting paradigms in sexuality research. *Culture, Health & Sexuality, 11*(3), 251–266. https://doi.org/10.1080/13691050701606941

Parsons, J. T., Kelly, B. C., Bimbi, D. S., DiMaria, L., Wainberg, M. L., & Morgenstern, J. (2008). Explanations for the origins of sexual compulsivity among gay and bisexual men. *Archives of Sexual Behavior, 37*(5), 817–826. https://doi.org/10.1007/s10508-007-9218-8

Parsons, J. T., Lelutiu-Weinberger, C., Botsko, M., & Golub, S. A. (2013). Predictors of day-level sexual risk for young gay and bisexual men. *AIDS and Behavior, 17*(4), 1465–1477. https://doi.org/10.1007/s10461-012-0206-1

Parsons, J. T., Rendina, H. J., Ventuneac, A., Moody, R. L., & Grov, C. (2016). Hypersexual, sexually compulsive, or just highly sexually active? Investigating three distinct groups of gay and bisexual men and their profiles of HIV-related sexual risk. *AIDS and Behavior, 20*(2), 262–272. https://doi.org/10.1007/s10461-015-1029-7

Phillips, E. A., Rajender, A., Douglas, T., Brandon, A. F., & Munarriz, R. (2015). Sex offenders seeking treatment for sexual dysfunction – Ethics, medicine, and the law. *The Journal of Sexual Medicine, 12*(7), 1591–1600. https://doi.org/10.1111/jsm.12920

Pinto, J., Carvalho, J., & Nobre, P. J. (2013). The relationship between the FFM personality traits, state psychopathology, and sexual compulsivity in a sample of male college students. *The Journal of Sexual Medicine, 10*(7), 1773–1782. https://doi.org/10.1111/jsm.12185

Plaut, S. M. (2015). Commentary on: Sex offenders seeking treatment for sexual dysfunction—Ethics, medicine, and the law. *The Journal of Sexual Medicine, 12*(7), 1601. https://doi.org/10.1111/jsm.12923

Porst, H., Burnett, A., Brock, G., Ghanem, H., Giuliano, F., Glina, S., Hellstrom, W., Martin-Morales, A., Salonia, A., Sharlip, I., & the ISSM Standards Committee for Sexual Medicine. (2013). SOP conservative (medical and mechanical) treatment of erectile dysfunction. *The Journal of Sexual Medicine, 10*(xx), 130–171. https://doi.org/10.1111/jsm

Prause, N., Steele, V. R., Staley, C., Sabatinelli, D., & Hajcak, G. (2015). Modulation of late positive potentials by sexual images in problem users and controls inconsistent with 'porn addiction'. *Biological Psychology, 109*, 192–199. https://doi.org/10.1016/j.biopsycho.2015.06.005

Prestage, G., Mao, L., McGuigan, D., Crawford, J., Kippax, S., Kaldor, J., & Grulich, A. E. (2006). HIV risk and communication between regular partners in a cohort of HIV-negative gay men. *AIDS Care, 18*(2), 166–172. https://doi.org/10.1080/09540120500358951

Puppo, V., & Puppo, G. (2016). Re: Simões Paço J, Jorge Pereira B.: New Therapeutic perspectives in premature ejaculation (Urology 2016; 88: 87–92). A rebuttal: Premature ejaculation is not a male sexual dysfunction. *Urology, 90*, 224. https://doi.org/10.1016/j.urology.2015.12.010

Raymond, N. C., Coleman, E., Ohlerking, F., Christenson, G. A., & Miner, M. (1999). Psychiatric comorbidity in pedophilic sex offenders. *American Journal of Psychiatry, 156*(5), 786–788.

Raymond, N. C., Grant, J. E., & Coleman, E. (2010). Augmentation with naltrexone to treat compulsive sexual behavior: A case series. *Annals of Clinical Psychiatry: Official Journal of the American Academy of Clinical Psychiatrists, 22*(1), 56–62.

Raymond, N. C., Grant, J. E., Kim, S. W., & Coleman, E. (2002). Treatment of compulsive sexual behaviour with naltrexone and serotonin reuptake inhibitors: Two case studies. *International Clinical Psychopharmacology, 17*(4), 201–205.

Reid, R. C., Carpenter, B. N., Spackman, M., & Willes, D. L. (2008). Alexithymia, emotional instability, and vulnerability to stress proneness in patients seeking help for hypersexual behavior. *Journal of Sex & Marital Therapy, 34*(2), 133–149. https://doi.org/10.1080/00926230701636197

Reid, R. C., Stein, J. A., & Carpenter, B. N. (2011). Understanding the roles of shame and neuroticism in a patient sample of hypersexual men. *The Journal of Nervous and Mental Disease, 199*(4), 263–267. https://doi.org/10.1097/NMD.0b013e3182125b96

Rettenberger, M., Klein, V., & Briken, P. (2016). The relationship between hypersexual behavior, sexual excitation, sexual inhibition, and personality traits. *Archives of Sexual Behavior, 45*(1), 219–233. https://doi.org/10.1007/s10508-014-0399-7

Richters, J., de Visser, R. O., Badcock, P. B., Smith, A. M., Rissel, C., Simpson, J. M., & Grulich, A. E. (2014). Masturbation, paying for sex, and other sexual activities: The Second Australian Study of Health and Relationships. *Sexual Health, 11*(5), 461–471. https://doi.org/10.1071/SH14116

Rider, G. N., Vencill, J. A., Berg, D. R., Becker-Warner, R., Candelario-Pérez, L., & Spencer, K. G. (2019). The Gender Affirmative Lifespan Approach (GALA): A framework for competent clinical care with nonbinary clients. *International Journal of Transgenderism, 20*(2–3), 275–288. https://doi.org/10.1080/15532739.2018.1485069

Rosen, R. C. (2000). Prevalence and risk factors of sexual dysfunction in men and women. *Current Psychiatry Reports, 2*, 189–195. https://doi.org/10.1007/s11920-996-0006-2

Savard, J., Görts Öberg, K., Chatzittofis, A., Dhejne, C., Arver, S., & Jokinen, J. (2020). Naltrexone in compulsive sexual behavior disorder: A feasibility study of twenty men. *The Journal of Sexual Medicine, 17*(8), 1544–1552. https://doi.org/10.1016/2020.04.318

Sawyer, A. N., Smith, E. R., & Benotsch, E. G. (2018). Dating application use and sexual risk behavior among young adults. *Sexuality Research & Social Policy: A Journal of the NSRC, 15*(2), 183–191. https://doi.org/10.1007/s13178-017-0297-6

Scarcelli, C. M. (2018). Young people and sexual media. In P. G. Nixon & I. K. Düsterhöft (Eds.), *Sex in the digital age* (pp. 35–45). Routledge.

Schmidt, C., Morris, L. S., Kvamme, T. L., Hall, P., Birchard, T., & Voon, V. (2017). Compulsive sexual behavior: Prefrontal and limbic volume and interactions. *Human Brain Mapping, 38*(3), 1182–1190. https://doi.org/10.1002/hbm.23447

Schnarch, D. M. (2009). *Passionate marriage: Keeping love and intimacy alive in committed relationships*. W. W. Norton & Company.

Schnarrs, P. W., Stone, A. L., Salcido, R., Jr., Baldwin, A., Georgiou, C., & Nemeroff, C. B. (2019). Differences in adverse childhood experiences (ACEs) and quality of physical and mental health between transgender and cisgender sexual minorities. *Journal of Psychiatric Research, 119*, 1–6. https://doi.org/10.1016/j.jpsychires.2019.09.001

Semlyen, J., King, M., Varney, J., & Hagger-Johnson, G. (2016). Sexual orientation and symptoms of common mental disorder or low wellbeing: Combined meta-analysis of 12 UK population health surveys. *BMC Psychiatry, 16*, 67. https://doi.org/10.1186/s12888-016-0767-z

Seok, J.-W., & Sohn, J.-H. (2015). Neural substrates of sexual desire in individuals with problematic hypersexual behavior. *Frontiers of Behavioral Neuroscience, 9*, 321. https://doi.org/10.3389/fnbeh.2015.00321

Serefoglu, E. C., McMahon, C. G., Waldinger, M. D., Althof, S. E., Shindel, A., Adaikan, G., Becher, E. F., Dean, J., Giuliano, F., Hellstrom, W. J. G., Giraldi, A., Glina, S., Incrocci, L., Jannini, E., McCabe, M., Parish, S., Rowland, D., Segraves, R. T., Sharlip, I., & Torres, L. O. (2014). An evidence-based unified definition of lifelong and acquired premature ejaculation: Report of the second International Society for Sexual Medicine Ad Hoc Committee for the Definition of Premature Ejaculation. *The Journal of Sexual Medicine, 11*(6), 1423–1441. https://doi.org/10.1111/jsm.12524

Shabsigh, R., & Anastasiadis, A. (2003). Erectile dysfunction. *Annual Review of Medicine, 54*, 153–168. https://doi.org/10.1146/annurev.med.54.101601.152212

Shamloul, R., & Ghanem, H. (2013). Erectile dysfunction. *Lancet, 381*, 153–165. Published Online, October 5, 2012. https://doi.org/10.1016/S0140-6736(12)60520-0

Skegg, K., Nada-Raja, S., Dickson, N., & Paul, C. (2010). Perceived "out of control" sexual behavior in a cohort of young adults from the Dunedin Multidisciplinary Health and Development Study. *Archives of Sexual Behavior, 39*(4), 968–978. https://doi.org/10.1007/s10508-009-9504-8

Smith, A. (2016, February 11). *15% of American adults have used online dating sites or mobile dating apps*. Pew Research Center. https://www.pewresearch.org/internet/2016/02/11/15-percent-of-american-adults-have-used-online-dating-sites-or-mobile-dating-apps/

Spencer, K. G., & Vencill, J. A. (2017). Body beyond: A pleasure-based, sex-positive group therapy curriculum for trans feminine adults. *Psychology of Sexual Orientation and Gender Diversity, 4*(4), 392–402. https://doi.org/10.1037/sgd0000248

Statistica. (2020). *Online dating in the United States*. Author.

Steele, V. R., Staley, C., Fong, T., & Prause, N. (2013). Sexual desire, not hypersexuality, is related to neurophysiological responses elicited by sexual images. *Socioaffective Neuroscience & Psychology, 3*(1), 20770. https://doi.org/10.3402/snp.v3i0.20770

Stryker, S. (2008). *Transgender history*. Seal Press.

Stulhofer, A., Jurin, T., & Briken, P. (2016). *Journal of Sex & Marital Therapy, 42*(8), 665–680. https://doi.org/10.1080/0092623X.2015.1113585

Swinburne Romine, R. E., Dwyer, S. M., Mathiowetz, C., & Thomas, M. (2008, October). *Thirty years of sex offender specific treatment: A follow-up study* [Poster presentation]. Poster presented at the 27th Annual Research and Treatment Conference of the Association for the Treatment of Sexual Abusers, Atlanta, GA.

Tellegen, A. (1985). Structure of mood and personality and their relevance to assessing anxiety, with an emphasis on self-report. In A. H. Tuma & J. D. Masters (Eds.), *Anxiety and the anxiety disorders* (pp. 681–706). Erlbaum.

Twenge, J. M., Sherman, R. A., & Wells, B. E. (2015). Changes in American adults' sexual behavior and attitudes, 1972–2012. *Archives of Sexual Behavior, 44*(8), 2273–2285. https://doi.org/10.1007/s10508-015-0540-2

Voon, V., Mole, T. B., Banca, P., Porter, L., Morris, L., Mitchell, S., Lapa, T. R., Karr, J., Harrison, N. A., Potenza, M. N., & Irvine, M. (2014). Neural correlates of sexual cue reactivity in individuals with and without compulsive sexual behaviours. *PLoS One, 9*(7), e102419. https://doi.org/10.1371/journal.pone.0102419

Waite, L. J., Laumann, E. O., & Das, A. (2008). Sexual activity, older age. In D. Carr, R. Crosnoe, M. E. Hughes, & A. Pienta (Eds.), *Encyclopedia of the life course and human development* (Vol. 3, pp. 362–366). Thomson/Gale.

Waldinger, M. D. (2007). Premature ejaculation. *Drugs, 67*(4), 547–568. https://doi.org/10.2165/00003495-200767040-00005

Walton, M. T., & Bhullar, N. (2018). Compulsive sexual behavior as an impulse control disorder: Awaiting field studies data [Letter to the Editor]. *Archives of Sexual Behavior, 47*(5), 1327–1331. https://doi.org/10.1007/s10508-018-1200-0

Walton, M. T., Cantor, J. M., Bhullar, N., & Lykins, A. D. (2017). Hypersexuality: A critical review and introduction of the "sexhavior cycle". *Archives of Sexual Behavior, 46*(8), 2231–2251. https://doi.org/10.1007/s10508-017-0991-8

Williams, D. J., Thomas, J. N., Prior, E. E., & Walter, W. (2015). Introducing a multidisciplinary framework of positive sexuality. *Journal of Positive Sexuality, 1*, 6–11. https://doi.org/10.51681/1.112

Winters, J., Christoff, K., & Gorzalka, B. B. (2010). Dysregulated sexuality and high sexual desire: Distinct constructs? *Archives of Sexual Behavior, 39*(5), 1029–1043. https://doi.org/10.1007/s10508-009-9591-6

World Health Organization. (2006). *Defining sexual health: Report of a technical consultation on sexual health, 28-31 January 2002, Geneva*. World Health Organization. https://www.who.int/reproductivehealth/publications/sexual_health/defining_sh/en/

World Health Organization. (2019). *International statistical classification of diseases and related health problems* (11th ed.). World Health Organization. https://icd.who.int/

Wyatt, R. B., & de Jong, D. C. (2020). Anxiousness and distractibility strengthen mediated associations between men's penis appearance concerns, spectatoring, and sexual difficulties: A preregistered study. *Archives of Sexual Behavior, 49*(8), 2981–2992. https://doi.org/10.1007/s10508-020-01753-4

Yoon, I. S., Houang, S. T., Hirshfield, S., & Downing, M. J., Jr. (2016). Compulsive sexual behavior and HIV/STI risk: A review of current literature. *Current Addiction Reports, 3*(4), 387–399. https://doi.org/10.1007/s40429-016-0121-z

Zilbergeld, B. (1999). *The new male sexuality: Revised edition*. Bantam Books.

Zimmerman, J. (2016). *Too hot to handle: A global history of sex education*. Princeton University Press.

Zito, R. C., & De Coster, S. (2016). Family structure, maternal dating, and sexual debut: Extending the conceptualization of instability. *Journal of Youth and Adolescence, 45*(5), 1003–1019. https://doi.org/10.1007/s10964-016-0457-7

Chapter 3
Classification Models for Individuals Who Have Sexually Aggressed

Raymond A. Knight

3.1 Introduction

Despite the wide prevalence of sexually aggressive behavior (Morgan & Oudekerk, 2019) and the serious consequences of sexual aggression for victims (e.g., Plichta & Falik, 2001; Paolucci et al., 2001; Weaver et al., 2007), the study of individuals who have sexually aggressed (ISAs) has remained meager relative to the study of other groups with deviant behavior. Theories about sexually aggressive behavior have often involved more speculation than empirical validation (Bryden & Grier, 2011). Driven by the critical need in the criminal justice system for guidance in making dispositional decisions about ISAs that enhance community protection, much of the research that has been conducted has focused on the creation of risk assessment tools, both empirical, mechanical actuarials and assessments of dynamic traits that should constitute the foci of intervention aimed at mitigating recidivism (Bonta, 1996; Cale, 2018). Much of this research to date has been inductive and atheoretical. Although reliable and pragmatic tools have emerged from this research, there is growing realization, even among those who have done the hard work of generating these measures, that the bottom-up, inductive approach to answering questions about sexual aggression has reached an asymptote, and further progress requires the generation and empirical validation of theoretical models of the core processes of such aggression and the mapping of the nomological network, etiology, and life course trajectories of these core factors (Cale, 2018; Thornton, 2016; Ward & Fortune, 2016).

In this chapter it is argued that research that has explored typological models of ISAs has laid the groundwork for the empirical investigation of theoretical models

R. A. Knight (✉)
Department of Psychology, Brandeis University, Waltham, MA, USA
e-mail: knight2@brandeis.edu

R. J. Tully et al. (eds.), *Best Practices in Sexual Offender Assessment and Management*, Dangerous Behavior in Clinical and Forensic Psychology,
https://doi.org/10.1007/978-3-031-83135-5_3

and has generated important data about sexually aggressive behavior that provide fundamental guidelines for generating and testing such theoretical models. The history of the attempts to create typological models of sexually aggressive individuals is briefly reviewed, the empirical and practical utility of the systems that have been proposed is critically evaluated, and the pros and cons of the major methodologies used to generate systems are discussed. Ultimately, it will be argued that although a number of speculative typological models have been proposed, most have not been rigorously tested and put at risk for disconfirmation (Meehl, 1978; Popper, 1972). Only one typological program (Knight, 2010a; Knight & King, 2012; Knight & Prentky, 1990) has provided sufficient operationalization and validation of its constructs to serve as a basis for moving forward in the search for optimal theoretical models. The important guiding principles that have emerged from this program, their potential contributions to treatment and disposition, and recommendations about where the field needs to go from here will be considered.

3.2 Brief Critical History of Typological Research for Sexually Aggressive Individuals

Classification is a fundamental cognitive process. Identifying the consistencies in the complexity of our perceptual and cognitive experiences is critical for negotiating our way through the world and surviving. Classification in scientific investigation mirrors its role in general cognition. The fundamental first step of any scientific investigation involves some kind of classification of the observed characteristics into homogeneous groups (Ghiselin, 1981). Such classification constitutes a precursor of scientific analysis and a necessary sustainer of the investigative progress (Hempel, 1965). The strategies for developing typologies include both empirical/inductive and rational/deductive methodological approaches (Blashfield, 1980; Meehl, 1979; Skinner, 1981, 1986), each with its advantages and disadvantages. Both strategies have been implemented independently, and they have also been programmatically combined to differentiate types of sexually aggressive individuals. Each strategy and their combined application are considered here in turn.

3.2.1 Rational Methods of Generating Typologies from Clinical Experience

Before we had empirical studies to guide our thinking and decision-making, clinicians working with ISAs were faced with a marked heterogeneity of symptoms and behaviors in the clients whom they evaluated and treated. One initial strategy available to them for making sense of this heterogeneity was to attempt to categorize clients into apparently homogeneous groups based on the behaviors and characteristics of the individuals they were assessing and treating. This classification strategy is a basic first step in any scientific endeavor (Ghiselin, 1981). It fits well with the daunting demands of clinical work, the necessity of making dispositional decisions when little scientific evidence is available, and the need to generate theoretical models that make sense of sexually aggressive behavior. The proposed rational typologies ranged from simple dichotomies that operationalized a distinction, applied it to a group, and examined the differences that emerged, to more complex multidimensional theoretical structures. Embedded in each proposed multidimensional system were implicit guesses about the variables that best discriminated among ISAs and about the covariation among the variables that were proposed to be critical for understanding ISAs and their sexually aggressive behaviors (Knight et al., 1985).

The history of these typologies (e.g., Cohen et al., 1971; Fitch, 1962; Gebhard et al., 1965; Groth et al., 1977; Guttmacher & Weihofen, 1952; Kopp, 1962; McCaghy, 1967; Prentky et al., 1985; Seghorn & Cohen, 1980; Swanson, 1971) has been described and evaluated previously (Blasko, 2016; Cale, 2018; Knight et al., 1985; Robertillo & Terry, 2007) with attempts to identify the consistencies and differences among proposed systems. The description and comparison of these typologies will not be reviewed in this chapter.

Although the simple generation of a system that has face validity and appears to reduce heterogeneity is certainly justified in the context of discovery (Reichenbach, 1958), such speculations are insufficient for the context of justification. Although the context of discovery is rich with possibilities, it lacks the guidance provided by a validation process that includes the operationalization of the categorization criteria for the proposed types, the classification of new individuals reliably into these types, and the testing of the validity of the types. Without such a validation process, the theoretical structure and the application of such typologies to clinical decisions are vulnerable to problematic cognitive distortions like confirmation bias, hindsight bias, availability bias, representational bias, and ascertainment bias that lead the unwary astray (Garb & Boyle, 2003; Grove & Meehl, 1996; Lilienfeld et al., 2003).

To date, except for simple dichotomous or trichotomous distinctions based on a single criterion like absolute and relative victim age (e.g., offenders with adult only, mixed, or child only victims), only the typology program begun at the Massachusetts Treatment Center (MTC) has generated and tested reliable operationalizations of rationally generated types. For the initial point of departure in this program all systems existing at that time were compared, the most representative types were selected, classification criteria were generated, and their reliability and validity were assessed (Knight et al., 1985). The initial types were found to have such poor reliability that they were considered disconfirmed, and discrepancy analyses led to revised typologies (Knight et al., 1985; Knight & Prentky, 1990).

It is important to point out that the Groth typologies (Groth & Birnbaum, 1979; Groth et al., 1977) were essentially identical to the types used as points of departure in the MTC program. Groth's typologies provided global, vague criteria for type assignment with no estimates of interrater reliability. These types and the parallel types developed in collaboration with Groth (Cohen et al., 1971; Seghorn & Cohen,

1980) were the only typologies other than those assessed in the MTC program that have generated any empirical scrutiny (Cohen et al., 1969; Hazelwood, 1987; Hazelwood & Burgess, 1987; Hazelwood et al., 1989). The first stage of the MTC program found that these systems had extremely low reliability, and preliminary empirical investigation of their validity revealed significant problems (Knight, 2010a; Knight & King, 2012; Knight & Prentky, 1990). Despite this disconfirmation, the Groth typologies continue to be cited as viable practical models. The MTC program will be reviewed later in this chapter.

3.2.2 Empirical/Inductive Clustering Methods of Typology Generation

Cluster analytic methods for exploring typological issues are inductive strategies that apply mathematical algorithms to a set of chosen variables and generate hypothetical groups in which the members in each group are more like each other on the input variables than they are like the members of other groups. The variables chosen can vary widely from measures that are theoretically chosen to define the expected groups (e.g., Rosenberg & Knight, 1988) to measures that are conveniently available, but only potentially relevant to sample differentiation (e.g., Bard & Knight, 1987). There was an explosion of cluster studies of psychopathological constructs in the 1970s, when computer programs became available to perform the complex calculations required. Since the 1980s, cluster analytic studies have become a popular strategy for generating speculations about ISA types, and they continue to be used today.

It is essential to recognize what exploratory cluster analytic algorithms can and cannot provide. As Meehl (1979, p. 567) astutely pointed out, "No accepted entity in psychopathology has owed its initial *discovery* to formal clustering methods, whether those invented by psychologists, biologists, or statisticians. In fact, I know of no agreed-upon instance where taxometrics has been mainly responsible for definitively *settling* a controversy about an already 'noticed' syndrome, e.g., as to its existence if disputed, its specific etiology, whether it should be sub-divided, or subsumed under another accepted category as a *forme fruste*, and so on." As we will see, today, more than four decades later, Meehl's observation remains true about the contribution of cluster analytic studies of ISAs. These analytic strategies can be useful in uncovering previously unrecognized distinctions, in challenging conceptions about hypothesized cohesions, and in suggesting avenues for further empirical scrutiny, as is evidenced in the MTC program. The results of the typical ISA clustering studies have, however, remained in the context of discovery, and like the original rational typologies, they have not progressed to reliable operationalization and cross validation of the resultant types. Consequently, they have yielded only hypothetical speculations about potential types without specific classification criteria, awaiting more rigorous validation in the context of justification.

Like the rational clinical typologies that have been proposed, an essential step in the validation of the "types" that cluster analyses generate is the independent operationalization of these "types" and the determination of whether individuals can be reliably sorted into these types. Once such reliable types have been established, rigorous construct validation should ensue on new samples. Simply comparing the groups that a cluster algorithm generated on a specific sample on variables external to the input variables used in the clustering solution is insufficient to corroborate either the structure or the validity of the types. Such results only tell us that external covariates operate in somewhat the same fashion as the input variables that were used in the cluster analysis. They do not provide classification criteria that can be applied reliably and independently of the particular cluster solution to allow us to identify other individuals who should purportedly be in the proposed groups. In short, they have little practical utility that can be applied to clinical decision-making, and they remain in the speculative context of discovery.

Another strategy for "validating" the types generated in cluster analyses of ISAs has been to compare the resultant types either to prior cluster solutions or to proposed rationally derived models. This strategy also remains in the context of discovery. It is often distorted by confirmation biases in which apparent salient consistencies are noticed, but disconfirmatory data fail to attract attention. The confirmation bias is also often exacerbated by jingle-jangle fallacies (Kelley, 1927) in which different constructs with the same name are erroneously assumed to represent the same underlying construct (jingle fallacy) or identical constructs with different names are labeled as distinct underlying constructs (jangle fallacy). Moreover, none of these theoretical comparisons of types has taken the follow-up step of operationalizing their hypothesized "types" and attempting to determine empirically that their type and the comparison type actually comprise the same offenders. Consequently, no attempt will be made in this chapter to speculate about the interrelation among the myriad types that these cluster studies have generated.

Examples of cluster analytic attempts to generate ISA types abound. The majority have been one-shot studies using a variety of algorithms to generate types using data of convenience available on large samples. They have neither created classification criteria nor cross-validated their resulting groups, so these remain sample-specific descriptions, very much the way exploratory factor analysis describes the linear composites that best account for a particular variance-covariance matrix. The greatest number of studies have applied agglomerative hierarchical cluster algorithms or k-means non-hierarchical algorithms, but more recently finite mixture modeling and latent class analysis (LCA) have been added. Multiple input sources have been used. These sources have included multiple personality/psychopathological tests such as the Minnesota Multiphasic Personality Inventory (MMPI; Flakenhain et al., 1999; Hall et al., 1991; Kalichman, 1990, 1991; Kalichman et al., 1989a; Kalichman et al., 1992; Kalichman & Henderson, 1991; Kalichman et al., 1989b; Schlank, 1995; Shealy et al., 1991; Smith et al., 1987), the Millon Clinical Multiaxial Inventory (MCMI; Bard & Knight, 1987), the Multiphasic Sex Inventory (MSI; Schlank, 1995), the Millon Adolescent Clinical Inventory (MACI; Higgins, 2008; Oxnam & Vess, 2006), and the California Psychological Inventory (CPI;

Worling, 2001), as well as crime-scene data (Brown, 2019; Hewitt et al., 2020; Ramírez et al., 2018) and dynamic risk factors (Mayburgh & Olver, 2021). Woessner (2010) entered a number of scales purportedly related to treatment readiness and targets. Several have used variables from multiple input sources. For example, Fargo (2008) examined offense characteristics, social-demographical variables, childhood experiences, substance abuse, and criminal behavior. Proulx and Beauregard (2014) used a two-staged hierarchical cluster analytic strategy. In their first stage they clustered offenders within five domains (modus operandi, precrime stressors, sexual behavior, general lifestyle symptoms, and MCMI personality traits), and in their second stage they used the output from Stage 1 to cluster the clusters of offenders. Most of these studies were atheoretical, using cluster algorithms to generate types from available psychometric instruments. Some have attempted to justify risk-related or treatment-oriented inputs, but only one program, which is discussed below, has used cluster analysis to explore the domains theoretically proposed as typology definers.

3.2.3 Dimension or Category?

A final problem of the exploratory cluster analytic solutions is that the resulting clusters have been treated as nonarbitrary categories or taxons that differ in kind from other "categorical types," rather than being considered groupings that differ quantitatively along one or more dimensions. The groups that emerge from traditional exploratory cluster analyses, even the more sophisticated LCAs that have recently become popular, cannot, however, be assumed to yield true, nonarbitrary taxons. LCA, like other clustering algorithms, does not differentiate between categorical and dimensional distributions (Meehl, 1995; Vermunt & Magidson, 2006; Walton et al., 2011).

The issue of determining whether a construct is better understood, analyzed, and used as a category or as a dimension has long plagued psychology, psychiatry, and criminality. Meehl and colleagues (Meehl & Yonce, 1994, 1996; Waller & Meehl, 1998) developed taxometrics' to address this important issue. Their solution to the taxonicity problem (Meehl & Yonce, 1994, 1996; Waller & Meehl, 1998) is consistent with Meehl's (1978, 1979, 1990, 1995) neo-Popperian epistemology and his realist, rather than fictionalist or instrumentalist, ontological perspective. The former demands that research should be embedded in theory and that all tests of theoretical hypotheses should put the theory at severe risk for disconfirmation. The latter affirms Meehl's goal of carving nature at its joints (Plato, 360 B.C.E./1952) rather than simply striving to create useful descriptions of convenience for communication and dispositional decisions. His solution of the taxon problem is also firmly anchored in his belief that construct validity is essential to the advancement of science and that consistent converging lines of evidence across multiple variables, multiple independent ways of measuring a construct, and multiple different samples or populations are the best ways to validate scientific constructs (Campbell & Fiske, 1959;

Cronbach & Meehl, 1955). The basic aim of taxometric analyses is to determine whether alternative methods that have semi-independent mathematical definitions of taxonicity and distinct theoretical bases yield consistent results about the latent structure of a construct (Ruscio et al., 2006). Coherence among nonredundant indicators provides strong corroboration of either taxonic or dimensional distribution, and consistency tests are essential. Thus, Meehl's taxometrics are most effective when theoretically driven and based on preexisting a priori hypotheses about latent and causal structure. Consequently, their application requires some theoretical and empirical justification before applying the methods (Lenzenweger, 2004). Simply throwing existing data at taxometric algorithms runs the risk of finding pseudo-taxa or of failing to identify a true taxon.

Meehl's taxometric algorithms have been widely used in psychiatry and psychology (Haslam et al., 2020), and the vast majority of scholars have accepted them as the optimal solution to the categorical/dimensional problem (Ruscio et al., 2006). The predominantly dimensional results of the application of these algorithms have corroborated the larger movement in psychopathology research aimed at replacing the DSM diagnostic categories with a dimensional, Hierarchical Taxonomy of Psychopathology (Krueger et al., 2018). Consistent with the findings about general psychopathology, the critical constructs underlying the varied manifestations of sexually aggressive behavior, with the possible sole exception of pedophilia, have been found to be distributed dimensionally. The critical studies about the taxonicity of four major domains related to sexual aggression—hypersexuality and the paraphilias, the facets of psychopathy, paraphilic coercion and sadism, and sexual age preference—are summarized next.

3.2.3.1 Hypersexuality and the Paraphilias

Walters et al. (2011a) were the first to use Meehl's taxometrics to examine the latent structure of hypersexuality. Assessing both a representative sample of the general population and a large group of ISAs, they found support for a dimensional interpretation of latent structure in both samples. In the ISA sample they had not only sexual drive measures but also items that assessed perceived loss of control over sexual fantasies or behavior. This problematic, compulsive aspect of hypersexuality was also found to be distributed as a dimension. These findings suggested that individual differences in both problematic sexuality and sexual drive (Knight & Du, 2021) are quantitative (matter of degree) rather than qualitative (difference in kind). Subsequent studies replicated these findings both on college students and community samples (Graham et al., 2015; Kingston et al., 2020) and corroborated these dimensional results not only on problematic and sexual drive measures, but also for both males and females. Thus, the data have consistently supported a dimensional interpretation of hypersexuality across disparate populations, using measures that assess both the sexual drive and the problematic aspects of hypersexuality.

As part of their analyses of sexual deviance in ISAs, Walters et al. (2011a) looked at several paraphilias and at a general paraphilia scale and found only evidence for dimensionality among men. In a large college sample and a male offender sample Thompson et al. (2025) replicated these dimensional results for men, but found indeterminant evidence about the distribution of paraphilias among women.

3.2.3.2 Facets of Psychopathy

Both psychopathy as a general construct and its specific facets have been found to be important constructs in understanding sexual aggression (Knight & Guay, 2006, 2018). In the more methodologically sound studies that have addressed the issue of psychopathy's latent distribution in adults (e.g., Edens et al., 2006; Guay & Knight, 2004; Guay et al., 2007; Marcus et al., 2004; Walters et al., 2007a, 2007b, 2008, 2011b, 2015) only dimensional results for the PCL-R total score, factors, and facets have emerged. Moreover, the majority of studies on youth have found that 'psychopathy variants' are also distributed dimensionally and vary only in severity (Edens et al., 2011; Murrie et al., 2007). The studies that have purported to have found a taxon (e.g., for adults: Harris et al., 1994, 2007; Skilling et al., 2001; and for youth: Vasey et al., 2005) have been criticized for both significant methodological and sampling issues (Guay et al., 2007; Marcus et al., 2011; Sellbom & Drislane, 2021; Walters et al., 2011b). Consequently, their results are questionable, and they do not provide any rigorous support for a taxonic distribution of any aspect of psychopathy.

3.2.3.3 Paraphilic Coercion and Sadism

Both paraphilic coercion and sadism have played a significant role in models of rape and child molestation (Knight, 2010a; Knight & King, 2012; Knight & Longpré, 2021). Knight et al. (2013) and Longpré et al. (2020) only found evidence of dimensionality for a self-report version of the Agonistic Continuum, which comprises paraphilic coercive (PC) fantasies at its lower end and sadism at its upper end, and for each of its PC and sadism subcomponents. Longpré et al. (2019a) replicated these Agonistic Continuum findings in non-sexual offenders, community controls, and college students. All these taxometric results are consistent with other data derived from archival sources that have found only dimensionality for measures of sadism (Longpré et al., 2018; Mokros et al., 2014).

3.2.3.4 Sexual Age Preference

Pedophilia is the only domain in sexual aggression in which more studies than not have found evidence for a taxonic distribution. The majority of taxometric studies that have directly tested pedophilia have found that it was distributed as a taxon (Brankley et al., 2022; three of four samples from McPhail et al., 2018; Schmidt et al., 2013). In their fourth sample McPhail et al. (2018) found overall "ambiguous" results, which nonetheless leaned in the taxonomic direction. Only two studies (Mackaronis et al., 2011; Stephens et al., 2017) have found evidence for dimensionality. The former used suboptimal measures of pedophilia (e.g., the Sexual Obsessions and Cognitive Distortions/Immaturity scales of the MSI [Nichols & Molinder, 1984]), and the latter was more likely testing for pedohebephilia than for pedophilia. Although the overall cumulative results across studies do not compel a firm conclusion, one could argue that they do provide overall support for the presence of a taxon, most likely capturing ISAs who are highly sexually fixated on prepubescent children, are possibly exclusive (low social competence), and manifest high emotional congruence for children (Brankley et al., 2022). It is noteworthy that even among offenders who have sexually abused children, psychopathy and its components have been found to be distributed dimensionally (Walters et al., 2016).

3.2.3.5 Taxometric Conclusions

The taxonomic studies have provided some clear guidelines about how to generate models for and study ISAs. For adult offenders against women category/typological models and exploratory clustering algorithms are suboptimal research strategies, and dimensional latent trait strategies should be preferred. For adult offenders against children focusing on the demarcation between pedophilia and other forms of child exploitation should be paramount. Determining the roles of other "facilitation" constructs like the various components of psychopathy (Daversa & Knight, 2007; Seto, 2018) should focus on dimensional latent trait research strategies. Exploratory cluster analyses are not likely to add to our knowledge base, but there might be some room for theoretically focused latent variable mixed modeling (Hillen, 2017).

3.2.4 The Integrated Approach to Generating and Testing Typological Models

3.2.4.1 Integration and Its Application

Each of the major strategies for generating typologies has its advantages and disadvantages (Blashfield, 1980; Meehl, 1978, 1979, 1990; Skinner, 1981, 1986). The inductive strategy generates a speculative typological structure empirically from the bottom up, but, as we have seen, before its structures can be considered to have validity and utility, additional steps of operationalizing the proposed types, creating reliable classification criteria, applying these criteria, and testing the validity of the types are required. The deductive strategy starts with a proposed structure generated either theoretically or empirically. Validation requires operationalization, creation of reliable classification criteria, assignment of appropriate participants to classes, and testing the construct validity of the resultant identified types. The deductive strategy is limited, however, in its ability to help the researcher break set and generate alternative structures, which, fortunately, the inductive, clustering approaches initially do well. Consequently, the two approaches are complementary, and an integrated approach that combines these two strategies in a programmatic, interactive, and iterative fashion uses the strengths of each to generate the best models. Following its neo-Popperian philosophical roots, such an integrated strategy iteratively generates theoretical models, operationalizes them, and puts them at severe risk for disconfirmation (Meehl, 1978; Popper, 1972).

As indicated earlier, the MTC typology program is the only one that has attempted to apply an integrated approach to the study of ISAs. It considers the results of both clustering strategies and the rational speculations about types to be in the context of discovery, still requiring operationalization, implementation of classification, validation, and integration across analytic strategies. This program and the methodological details of its execution have been extensively described elsewhere (Knight, 2010a; Knight & King, 2012; Knight & Prentky, 1990) and will not be repeated here. Rather, the core major findings that this program has generated and the lessons that it provides for moving forward in generating theoretical models for sexual aggression will be summarized. It is important to point out that although some speculation about juveniles who sexually offend emerged from this program (e.g., Knight & Sims-Knight, 2004; Knight & Prentky, 1993), it nonetheless focused predominantly on both criminal and noncriminal adult males.

3.2.4.2 Some Important Contributions of the Integrative Program

Over the more than four decades of its existence the MTC program has generated, applied, tested, and revised eight models, four each for sexual aggression against women and for the sexual abuse of children. In this process it has generated important results both about the theoretical structures of sexually aggressive behavior and about the ways in which, moving forward, sexual aggression should be studied. Five of the most important findings of this program and their implications for research and practice are discussed below.

3.2.4.2.1 Determining the Distribution of Core Variables Relevant to Sexual Aggression

The findings that have the greatest impact on how we should choose our future research strategies, how we should develop and calibrate our assessment tools, and how we should generate and investigate etiological hypotheses are those generated from the taxometric analyses of the domains most relevant to sexual aggression. Implementing these research guidelines has been an important part of the MTC program in the last decade and a half. Basically, as we have seen in the taxometric summary presented above, with the exception of pedophilia, all the major domains associated with sexual aggression have been found to be distributed dimensionally.

The consequences of these findings for how sexual aggression should be studied and assessed are explored next.

3.2.4.2.1.1 Generating Assessments for Decisions

The finding that most critical domains relevant to sexual aggression are distributed dimensionally and not categorically has important consequences for how we should develop scales for guiding clinical and dispositional decisions. When we create scales that measure a dimension, we must provide adequate discrimination along the entire continuum of the scale, rather than focusing on putative taxonic boundaries (Ruscio et al., 2006). Because we lack the nonarbitrary categorical cutoffs that taxonic distributions provide, when we use assessments of critical dimensional domains to make intervention and dispositional decisions about ISAs, we should be required to determine empirically the optimal cutoffs for particular decisions along the continuum and to address the difficult problem of the practical consequences of clinical and forensic decisions based on such cutoffs (Swets et al., 2000). The use of such cutoffs should be understood as arbitrary distinctions imposed for practical decision-making rather than as a "naturally" occurring differences in kind. The cutoff for determining who should be selected for an intensive sexual abuse prevention program in college should obviously not be the same as the cutoff for the civil commitment of a convicted ISA. Moreover, in general using the appropriate dimensional structure for our assessments should increase the reliability of the scales we use to make decisions. For instance, whereas many DSM-5 (American Psychiatric Association, 2013) diagnostic categories have not shown acceptable levels of interrater reliability (Regier et al., 2013), when measured dimensionally, which is how most DSM constructs have been found to be distributed (Haslam et al., 2020), these same "disorders" have often evidenced acceptable reliability (Markon et al., 2011).

These assessment guidelines are especially important for the Risk-Needs-Responsivity (RNR) model (Andrews & Bonta, 2010), whose principles have been found critical for the treatment of ISAs (Hanson et al., 2009). Not only are psychometrically sound measures that have been normed against both community and criminal samples necessary for the assessment-based component of RNR (Andrews et al., 2011), but also we need to provide clearly defined and empirically defended cutoffs for when the treatment of a particular criminogenic need is "essential" or "requires significant consideration." In addition, more differentiated scales with validation across the entire continuum assessed would be helpful for developing measures that are capable of mapping treatment improvement on criminogenic needs across their entire span.

In contrast, for the only sexual aggression domain that has been found to be distributed categorically, pedophilia, an intensive research effort is essential to nail down the maximal self-report, behavioral, and neurological indicators for its hypothetically nonarbitrary categorical boundary. Such an effort to identify its core components (e.g., fixation on prepubescent children, exclusivity, emotional congruence with children, neurological perturbations) should enhance the likelihood of determining the underlying psychological processes and physiological mechanisms that contribute to the etiology of this sexual preference and facilitate the search for its early indicators to maximize primary prevention efforts.

3.2.4.2.1.2 Research Strategies

Knowing the latent structure of a construct should guide our choice of the optimal strategies for researching that construct. Analyzing data by categorizing individuals into diagnostic groups focuses on categorical boundaries that are assumed to be the points at which groups are most reliably and optimally discriminated. In contrast, dimensional research strategies focus on the placement of individuals along the entire range of a continuum (Ruscio et al., 2006), and their sensitivity and power are optimized when one strives to create measures of constructs that have equivalent discrimination across an entire continuum. Preacher et al. (2005) demonstrated that a mismatch between the latent structure of a construct and the type of analytic strategy employed (e.g., using an extreme group analysis to study a dimensional construct) has a deleterious impact on measurement error and reduces discriminatory power.

Consequently, for the majority of domains relevant to sexually aggressive behavior, where only evidence for dimensional distributions have emerged, using latent trait dimensional research strategies for establishing the nomological network of behaviors should be preferred. Comparing typological groups is not an optimal research strategy for analyzing dimensional constructs. Moreover, the cluster analytic studies that have generated "types" that purportedly identify ISA categories that differ in kind, especially those focusing on sexual offending against adults, are not only problematic for the reasons described in the clustering section, but such studies now lack the theoretical justification that distinct types exist. Finally, the findings that most sexual aggression relevant domains are distributed dimensionally also provide support for the study of non-clinical/non-forensic samples with purportedly low base rates for sexually coercive behavior, such as community and college samples. This opens avenues for studying developmental trajectories, for exploring the influences of a range of etiological factors, and for exploring the nomological network among the domains relevant to sexually coercive behavior. This proposed movement away from a questionable categorical orientation to a more reliable and valid dimensional approach in studying sexual aggression is consistent with the larger movement in psychopathology to replace the DSM with a dimensional, Hierarchical Taxonomy of Psychopathology (Krueger et al., 2018).

3.2.4.2.1.3 Studying Etiology

Although taxometrics do not directly address questions about causality, they nonetheless aid in our search for causal processes. Whereas continuous phenotypic variation suggests that relevant etiology factors are likely numerous and additive in nature (Haslam, 1997; Meehl, 1992), taxonic outcomes suggest the possibility of a specific etiology. The findings that most domains related to sexual aggression were distributed dimensionally is consistent with Beauchaine and Constantino's (2017) recommendation that in psychopathology we embrace etiological complexity in our search for causal mechanisms. The findings that most sexual aggression domains are distributed dimensionally has transformed the MTC typology program from a focus on types to a completely dimensional model of rape (Knight, 2010a) and to a mixed model for child molestation (Knight & King, 2012). This dimensionalization of the models provided the foundation for the integration of our typological models with our structural equation etiological models (SEMs) of rape (Knight, 2010a; Knight & Sims-Knight, 2003, 2004, 2011, 2017) and child molestation (Daversa & Knight, 2007; Knight & King, 2012). It is noteworthy that the traits that emerged in our new dimensional models correspond to the major domains that are assessed in actuarials and dynamic risk assessment instruments (Brouillette-Alarie et al., 2018; Feigelson et al., 2018; Rohrer et al., 2018; Weydt, 2020). Prior to this integration, the MTC program had explored the SEM and typological strategies in parallel. A predominantly dimensional perspective now guides our current research program at the Brandeis Sexual Aggression Laboratory, which continues the work of the MTC program. Some of the major empirical and theoretical contributions of this recent research are described below.

3.2.4.2.2 The Role of Psychopathic Traits in Sexual Aggression

Psychopathic traits were introduced early in the MTC research program both to resolve typological inconsistencies (cf. Knight & Prentky, 1990) and to account for behavioral/attitudinal variance that was missed in extant etiological SEMs of sexually aggressive behavior against women (cf. Knight & Sims-Knight, 2003; Knight & Guay, 2006). Reviews of the literature on the role of psychopathy in sexual aggression (Knight & Guay, 2006, 2018) have since revealed that not only were the factors of psychopathy important in typological and etiological models of rape, but there was also substantial evidence (a) that sexual coercion was prevalent in rating scales for psychopathy and was found to be a covariate of psychopathy in the few studies that had examined this, (b) that high psychopathy was prevalent in ISAs, especially among those assaulting adult women, (c) that the factors of psychopathy were important in predicting recidivism among ISAs, and (d) scales measuring the components of psychopathy were important covariates of sexually coercive behavior in non-criminal populations. The psychopathic traits have not only been found to play consistently distinct roles in the SEM models we have generated, but, as is evident in the next section, they also interface differentially with other components in our models. The linkage of psychopathic traits to sexual aggression opens the study of sexual aggression to a substantial empirical and theoretical literature on psychopathy that not only facilitates the development of measures, but also enriches theoretical speculation and hypothesis generation.

3.2.4.2.3 Hypersexuality and Its Nomological Network

An unexpected covariation that we found between the subcomponents of psychopathy and hypersexuality highlighted inconsistencies in our third rapist typology, MTC:R3, whose structuring of types had assumed independence between these two constructs (Knight, 2010a). This substantial, originally unpredicted covariation between the Callous/Manipulative factor of psychopathy and the Hypersexuality latent trait consistently emerged in our SEM etiological models for rape across disparate samples (e.g., Knight & Sims-Knight, 2003, 2004, 2011; Schatzel-Murphy et al., 2009). Not only did it pose an explanatory challenge, but it ultimately contributed to the restructuring of MTC:R3 from a categorically oriented model to a dimensional model (see Knight, 2010a).

Our attempt to provide a theoretical explanation for the covariation between Callous/Manipulativeness and Hypersexuality followed a somewhat circuitous route that is a good example of how the iterative, disconfirmation-oriented strategy of the MTC program proposed models, challenged them, and learned from the data generated. Our first explanatory model for this covariation focused on the sexual drive aspects of the hypersexuality (Knight & Graham, 2017). Research generated to test the proposed criteria for the DSM-5 and studies subsequently inspired by the definitions of hypersexuality/sexual compulsivity included in the *International Statistical Classification of Diseases and Related Problems, 11th Edition* (ICD-11; WHO, 2019) found that their conceptualizations of hypersexuality covaried with the emotional dysregulated aspects of psychopathy and not with the callous/manipulative/risk taking aspects (see Knight & Du, 2021 for a review). To resolve this discrepancy, we hypothesized that, consistent with Carvalho et al.'s (2015) finding that hypersexuality had two subcomponents, Problematic Sexuality [PS] and Sexual Drive [SD], there were two correlated subdivisions of hypersexuality and each covaried differentially with the different aspects of impulsivity.

We created a hypersexuality/impulsivity survey and administered it to Mechanical Turk (MTurk) respondents and to college students to test this hypothetical resolution (Du & Knight, 2024). We corroborated Carvalho et al.'s (2015) two-dimensional model of hypersexuality, and we also generated factor-derived scales for the two dimensions of impulsivity that we had hypothesized (Du & Knight, 2024). Not surprisingly, the Problematic Sexuality factor comprised the three subcomponents—Sexual Compulsivity, Sexual Coping, and Sexual Consequences—that had consistently emerged in the factor analytic research that explored the subcomponents of the recently introduced Compulsive Sexual Behavior Disorder (CSBD) in ICD-11 (see Knight & Du, for a review). The second factor, Sexual Drive, included four scales (Hypersexuality [high sex drive], Sexual Preoccupation [high sexual fantasy involvement], Sociosexuality [predilection for impersonal sex], and Sexual Excitation [the propensity and ease of sexual arousal]).

The two subdimensions of hypersexuality differentially covaried with two types of impulsivity—a Risk-taking, Callous/Manipulative (RCM) factor and an Impulsive and Emotionally Dysregulated (IMED) factor. Consistent with our a priori hypotheses, SD covaried significantly more with RCM than it did with IMED, and PS covaried significantly more with IMED than did SD. Contrary to a priori hypotheses, however, PS had a high covariation with RCM that was equal to its correlation with IMED. This pattern of correlations, which was replicated in a second MTurk study, suggests that PS may be a final common outcome or equifinality (Cicchetti & Rogosch, 1996) of both RCM/sexual drive and IMED trajectories.

These findings have potential implications for the treatment of the hypersexuality. There is evidence that the two types of impulsivity may differentially respond to specific interventions (Baskin-Sommers et al., 2015), so the distinction could suggest specific avenues of treatment for the two subdimensions of hypersexuality. The distinction has also led to hypothesized and preliminarily tested modifications in the etiological SEM for rape (Knight & Longpré, 2019). Going forward, due to the new dimensional restructuring of MTC:R4 and its integration with our SEM model (Knight, 2010a; Knight & Sims-Knight, 2017), a latent trait analytic approach that explores covariation and interactions among the primary components of rape will be the strategy that guides our future research.

3.2.4.2.4 Sexual Sadism and the Agonistic Continuum

In the earliest SEM and typological models in the MTC program, aggressive sexual fantasies and sadism were critical constructs (Knight, 1997; Knight & Prentky, 1990; Knight & Sims-Knight, 1999). Sadism was a challenge to define and measure reliably from the beginning of the program (Knight & Prentky, 1990). The DSM definitions have consistently failed in their attempts to create criteria that reliably diagnose the construct (e.g., Graham, 2018; Levenson, 2004; Marshall & Kennedy, 2003; Perillo et al., 2014). In our initial attempts to achieve reliability, we generated a behavior-oriented crime-scene measure of the construct (Knight & Prentky, 1990) with somewhat better success. More recently, others have followed this strategy (Longpré et al., 2019b; Marshall & Hucker; 2006; Nitschke et al., 2009) with improved reliability and coverage. It is important to reiterate here the taxometric results of the studies of sadism that we reviewed earlier in which only evidence of dimensionality emerged; there is no evidence for any categorical distinctions. Although the various crime-scene scales have increased the objectivity and reliability of assessing sadism, they have tended to assess only the more salient extreme end of the sadism continuum because of their crime-scene focus, and they provide scant assessment of the power, control, or dominance that the perpetrator exerts over his victims, which has been theorized to be an important aspect of the construct (e.g., Fromm, 1977; Karpman, 1954; MacCulloch et al., 1983).

Recently, fueled substantially by prosecutors saddled with the requirement of identifying an "acceptable" mental disorder diagnosis for civil commitment hearings, the paraphilia sub-workgroup for the DSM-5 (American Psychiatric Association, 2013) proposed a distinct paraphilic mental disorder, Paraphilic Coercive (PC) Disorder, which hypothetically captured the sexual arousal to control/coercion in sexually aggressive behavior. In the debate that ensued, Knight (2010b) argued that the introduction of this distinct "disorder" was ill-advised, because PC was highly correlated with sadism and likely constituted the lower end of a sadistic continuum, but not a distinct "disorder." The proposed continuum not only had practical and assessment consequences, but it also challenged the two major theoretical models of the organization of the paraphilias (Freund & Blanchard, 1986; Money, 1986), both of which proposed that PC was not linked etiologically to sadism (see Knight & Longpré, 2021, for a review). We set about empirically exploring this continuum proposal about the relation of PC and sadism systematically. Using exploratory and confirmatory factor analysis, taxometrics, LCA, and Item Response Theory (IRT) on ISAs' responses to the Multidimensional Inventory of Development, Sex, and Aggression (MIDSA, 2011), we found consistently across two studies that the best model was a single Agonistic Continuum with items measuring PC dominating the lower end of the dimension and items measuring sexual arousal to victim harm, pain, and torture populating the upper end (Knight et al., 2013; Longpré et al., 2020). Longpré et al. (2020) found that those ISAs with scores at the high end of the Agonistic Continuum reported significantly more PC fantasies than those at the low end, disconfirming hypotheses that "sadists" were low in PC (Harris et al., 2012; Seto et al., 2012). Thornton (2019) has recently corroborated the dimensional nature of the Agonistic Continuum using plethysmographic assessment of both PC and brutality. The confluence of all these data argues that calling PC a distinct disorder from sadism is like calling Stage II cancer a different disorder from Stage IV cancer.

Building on this new structuring and expansion of sadism, our Brandeis lab has continued to work on validating the construct and searching for its underlying mechanisms. We are exploring the nomological network in which the Agonistic Continuum is theoretically embedded. The finding that the construct is distributed as a dimension and not as a taxon has allowed the exploration of "extreme" characteristics in wider, more representative samples, and the exploration of whether and how the characteristics of the "unrepresentative" group of incarcerated ISAs generalize to these other groups. We have corroborated covariations, previously identified in our SEM models, with hypersexuality (more highly correlated with the Problematic Sexuality than the Sexual Drive factor [Knight & Longpré, 2019]), with Callous/Manipulativeness (most strongly correlated with the Meanness and Machiavellian components of psychopathy [Knight & Longpré, 2019; Longpré et al., 2019a]), and with Emotional Dysregulation (Longpré et al., 2019a; Robertson, 2017; Robertson & Knight, 2014). In ISA samples the sadism, sexual violence, and other covariates of the Agonistic Continuum have also been found to covary substantially with one of the primary factors that has consistently emerged in factor analytic work of static actuarials, the Youthful Stranger Aggression factor, (Brouillette-Alarie et al., 2018; Knight et al., 2019; Rohrer et al., 2018), and sexual violence factors have emerged in the factor analyses of dynamic risk instruments (Feigelson et al., 2018; Weydt, 2020). Because of the importance of exploring the core mechanisms involved in this continuum, our lab has also been studying its covariation with cortisol indicators of emotional responsivity to interpersonal stress (Robertson, 2017) and its relation to low disgust sensitivity (Rohrer & Knight, 2025). In a large college student sample we have demonstrated with confirmatory factor analyses that sexual coercion and sexual harassment appear to be distributed on a single continuum (Knight & Sims-Knight, 2018). Although the Agonistic Continuum overlaps substantially with this Harassment/Coercion continuum, it nonetheless has unique independent variance that covaries with more extreme violence (Moloney et al., 2025).

3.2.4.2.5 The Integration of Developmental and Typological Models

The dimensionalization of our typologies has allowed the integration of this typological work with the SEM etiological models of sexual aggression that we began in the 1990s using self-report data from the MIDSA and its predecessors (Knight, 2010a; Knight & King, 2012; Knight & Sims-Knight, 2017; MIDSA, 2011). Our models exploring the key discriminators among ISAs and the investigation of their developmental antecedents have converged. Understanding the causal relations between early dispositional and experiential antecedents and the core traits essential to sexually aggressive behavior is a prerequisite for fashioning any effective preventative interventions (Moffitt, 2005). Therefore, the confluence of these separate typological and dimensional analytic strategies provides a solid empirical foundation for developing effective etiological theoretical models and helps to establish a firm empirical base from which to launch future prospective studies.

The MIDSA is a contingency base computerized inventory that captures extensive information about early developmental history. We have not only used the MIDSA responses of a variety of samples to help amend our original typological models, but we have also been using MIDSA responses to unpack the effects of early sexual, physical, and psychological abuse experiences as well as to explore the purported consequences of vicarious violence and caregiver instability on the major cross-temporally stable traits that covary with sexually aggressive behavior. Among our recent findings are the differential importance of both Emotional Abuse from significant male caregivers (Davis & Knight, 2019a, 2019b; Kingston et al., 2017) and Sexual Abuse experienced early (age range of 3 to 7 years) as opposed to later (Grabell & Knight, 2009) on the development of hypersexuality in males. Moreover, an interview format of the MIDSA Emotional Abuse scale has also been found to be a potent predictor of internalizing and externalizing behaviors in a sample of non-sex offending adolescents (Kosson et al., 2021). Also documented has been the role of the closeness in the relationship between sexually abusive perpetrators and their male victims in exacerbating negative outcomes for these victims in a number of adaptation domains (Berman & Knight, 2015).

These findings remain speculative. Because of the retrospective assessment that has generated them, they do not provide solid foundations for corroborating causality. As we describe below, large scale, prospective, genetically informed studies will be required to address the complex issues involved in corroborating the *causal* antecedents of sexually aggressive behavior. The research strategies that guided our search for typological solutions, but more recently morphed predominantly into latent trait modeling, can with the aid of our SEM MIDSA results provide a firm empirical base for initiating such an ambitious prospective program.

3.3 Conclusions

In addition to facilitating the operationalization of the complexity of domains relevant to sexually aggressive behavior and providing a platform to capture the similarities and differences that had emerged in clinical practice, the dual strategy in the MTC typology program also provided hypothetical structures that could be empirically investigated and corroborated or disconfirmed. When these structures were disconfirmed, the results furnished empirical cues about how to improve the models. This program led to many disconfirmations of clinical theorizing. For instance, it disconfirmed the existence and theoretical cohesion of the power reassurance type (Groth et al., 1977; see Knight & Prentky, 1990) and of proposed compensatory or displaced aggression types (Cohen et al., 1971; see Knight & Prentky, 1990). It also disconfirmed the proposed fixated versus regressed typological dichotomy in ISAs with child victims, demonstrating that among ISAs with child victims sexual fixation on children was independent of both low social competence and lack of relationships with age-appropriate partners, thereby failing to corroborate a major assumption of the proposed dichotomy (Groth et al., 1982; Lanning, 1986; see Knight, 1989, 1992). More importantly, however, it has also provided clear methodological and theoretical guidelines for the future study of sexual aggression.

Ultimately, this iterative process resulted in a radical shift away from taxonic, categorical models to a focus on multidimensional latent trait models. Although the current author agrees with Thornton (2021) that the MTC program "served an early function of mapping the field," even though it ultimately did not find the differences in *kind* for which it initially searched, he nonetheless disagrees, with the opinion that the program led to "a more realistic, but less theoretically interesting trait model" (Thornton, 2021, p. 6). As summarized earlier in describing the five most important methodological and theoretical contributions of this ongoing program, it has not only provided critical, foundational methodological guidance to direct future research, but it has also produced a promising theoretical structuring of the domains relevant to sexually aggressive behavior that can serve as a point of departure for the continuing exploration of empirically-based theoretical models. Moreover, it has provided preliminary evidence about potential developmental antecedents of these domains.

It is noteworthy that criterion validation (Nunnally, 1978) constituted the strategy for generating the current list of dynamic risk factors (e.g., Mann et al., 2010). Such an exclusively inductive strategy aims to maximize the prediction of a criterion, but it sacrifices theoretical cohesion of the predictors. Consequently, the identified risk factors lack both theoretical cohesion and specificity (Ward & Fortune, 2016). The models generated by our program stand in distinct contrast to this approach because of our emphasis on generating and testing theoretical models.

When the taxometric results changed our focus from types to dimensions, our neo-Popperian, model testing, construct validation orientation was still maintained. As we saw from the examples of our current work, we are both exploring the nomological network of traits in our models and working to identify the core mechanisms underlying these traits (Bechtel, 2008). Such a process-oriented approach (Knight, 1984) ultimately involves using multiple measures of the proposed traits from different levels of analysis (self-report, behavioral, biological/genetic, etc.: Cicchetti & Toth, 2009) to test constitutive mechanistic models (Kaiser & Krickel, 2017) that can provide the building blocks for improved theoretical models.

3.4 Future Directions

Not only does a process-oriented approach have the potential to increase our theoretical understanding of the varieties of sexually aggressive behavior, but it can also help to improve our measurement of relevant constructs for assessing both risk and treatment efficacy. More importantly, it can provide the critical foci for the investigation of the causes of sexual aggression. To turn well-defined constitutive mechanistic phenomena into etiological/causal distinctions (Kaiser & Krickel, 2017), we will have the daunting task of launching prospective, large sample, longitudinal research studies that are genetically informed (Moffitt, 2005; Viding, 2022) and that adequately assess multiple domains relevant to sexual aggression both within and outside of the developing persons across their lifetimes (Toth & Cicchetti, 2010). Such an ambitious strategy is essential to meet the call to explore antisocial trajectories over the life-course (Cale, 2018). It would allow us both to disentangle the potential multiple developmental trajectories leading to the equifinality of sexual aggression outcomes and to track the variety of outcomes (i.e., the multifinality) generated by particular genetic and developmental insults (Cicchetti & Rogosch, 1996; Cicchetti & Toth, 2009). The results of such an endeavor are critical to providing an empirical and theoretical foundation for intervention and for primary or secondary prevention initiatives (Ialongo et al., 2006). The results of programmatic, theory-focused research like that in our program can provide essential groundwork prerequisites for this ambitious research enterprise.

The results of our program are also a call to clinicians to move away from thinking about the individuals they assess and treat as exemplars of particular types and to focus on the core dimensions that should be the targets of assessment and treatment. This is the focus of the MIDSA, which assesses a number of dimensional criminogenic needs (e.g., hypersexuality, the emotional dysregulated, impulsive, and callous manipulative components of psychopathy, intimacy deficits). It locates individuals on these dimensions, which are standardized both relative to a relevant age ISA sample and to community controls, and it suggests preliminary cutoffs in comparison to both samples for treatment needs in each domain. Our future research on the MIDSA will be focused on improving existing self-report scales, on adding new scales that the empirical literature and our own research suggest, on developing better measures of change on the assessed domains, on providing risk metrics for these domains, and on continuing our search for the potential underlying mechanisms and developmental antecedents of each domain.

References

American Psychiatric Association. (2013). *Diagnostic and statistical manual of mental disorders* (5th ed.). https://doi.org/10.1176/appi.books.9780890425596

Andrews, D. A., & Bonta, J. (2010). *The psychology of criminal conduct*. Matthew Bender & Company, Inc.

Andrews, D. A., Bonta, J. L., & Wormith, J. S. (2011). Does adding the good lives model contribute to effective crime prevention? *Criminal Justice and Behavior, 38*(7), 735–755. https://doi.org/10.1177/0093854811406356

Bard, L. A., & Knight, R. A. (1987). Sex offender subtypes and the MCMI. In C. Green (Ed.), *Conference on the Millon inventories (MCMI, MBHI, MAPI)* (pp. 133–137). National Computer Systems.

Baskin-Sommers, A. R., Curtin, J. J., & Newman, J. P. (2015). Altering the cognitive-affective dysfunctions of psychopathic and externalizing offender subtypes with cognitive remediation. *Clinical Psychological Science, 3*(1), 45–57. https://doi.org/10.1177/2167702614560744

Beauchaine, T. P., & Constantino, J. N. (2017). Redefining the endophenotype concept to accommodate transdiagnostic vulnerabilities and etiological complexity. *Biomarkers in Medicine, 11*(9), 769–780. https://doi.org/10.2217/bmm-2017-0002

Bechtel, W. (2008). *Mental mechanisms: Philosophical perspectives on cognitive neuroscience*. Routledge.

Berman, A. K., & Knight, R. A. (2015). The relation of familiarity with sexual abusers to subsequent adaptation in youth who have sexually offended. *Sexual Abuse: A Journal of Research and Treatment, 27*(6), 587–608. https://doi.org/10.1177/1079063214544329

Blashfield, R. K. (1980). Propositions regarding the use of cluster analysis in clinical research. *Journal of Consulting and Clinical Psychology, 48*, 456–459. https://doi.org/10.1037/0022-006X.48.4.456

Blasko, B. L. (2016). Overview of sexual offender typologies, recidivism, and treatment. In E. L. Jeglic & C. Calkins (Eds.), *Sexual violence: Evidence based policy and prevention* (pp. 11–29). Spinger International Publishing. https://doi.org/10.1007/978-3-319-44504-5_2

Bonta, J. (1996). Risk-needs assessment and treatment. In A. T. Harland (Ed.), *Choosing correctional options that work: Defining the demand and evaluating the supply* (pp. 18–32). Sage.

Brankley, A. E., Knight, R. A., & Hanson, R. K. (2022). Pedophilia is a taxon among 706 adult males assessed at a civil commitment center. *Journal of Psychopathology and Clinical Science, 131*(2), 209–220. https://doi.org/10.1037/abn0000735.supp

Brouillette-Alarie, S., Proulx, J., & Hanson, R. K. (2018). Three central dimensions of sexual recidivism risk: Understanding the latent constructs of Static-99R and Static-2002R. *Sexual Abuse, 30*(6), 676–704. https://doi.org/10.1177/1079063217691965

Brown, A. (2019). Using latent class analysis to explore subtypes of youth who have committed sexual offenses. *Youth Violence and Juvenile Justice, 7*(4), 413–430. https://doi.org/10.1177/1541204018820578

Bryden, D. P., & Grier, M. M. (2011). The search for rapists' "real" motives. *Journal of Criminal Law and Criminology, 101*(5), 171–278. https://scholarlycommons.law.northwestern.edu/jclc/vol101/iss1/5

Cale, J. (2018). Classification of perpetrators of sexual offences: An overview of three generations of research and development. In P. Lussier & E. Beauregard (Eds.). *Sexual offending: A criminological perspective* (pp. 326–348). https://doi.org/10.4324/9781315522692-17

Campbell, D. T., & Fiske, D. W. (1959). Convergent and discriminant validation by the multitrait-multimethod matrix. *Psychological Bulletin, 56*, 81–105. https://doi.org/10.1037/h0046016

Carvalho, J., Štulhofer, A., Vieira, A. L., & Jurin, T. (2015). Hypersexuality and high sexual desire: Exploring the structure of problematic sexuality. *The Journal of Sexual Medicine, 12*(6), 1356–1367. https://doi.org/10.1111/jsm.12865

Cicchetti, D., & Rogosch, F. A. (1996). Equifinality and multifinality in developmental psychopathology. *Development and Psychopathology, 8*, 597–600. https://doi.org/10.1017/S0954579400007318

Cicchetti, D., & Toth, S. L. (2009). The past achievements and future promises of developmental psychopathology: The coming of age of a discipline. *Journal of Child Psychology and Psychiatry, 50*(1–2), 16–25. https://doi.org/10.1111/j.1469-7610.2008.01979.x

Cohen, M. L., Garafalo, R. F., Boucher, R., & Seghorn, T. (1971). The psychology of rapists. *Seminars in Psychiatry, 3*, 307–327.

Cohen, M. L., Seghorn, T. K., & Calmas, W. (1969). Sociometric study of the sex offender. *Journal of Abnormal Psychology, 74*(2), 249–255. https://doi.org/10.1037/h0027185

Cronbach, L. J., & Meehl, P. E. (1955). Construct validity in psychological tests. *Psychological Bulletin, 52*(4), 281–302. https://doi.org/10.1037/h0040957

Daversa, M. T., & Knight, R. A. (2007). A structural examination of the predictors of sexual coercion against children in adolescent sexual offenders. *Criminal Justice and Behavior, 34*, 1313–1333. https://doi.org/10.1177/0093854807302411

Davis, K. A., & Knight, R. A. (2019a). The relation of childhood abuse experiences to problematic sexual behaviors in male youths who have sexually offended. *Archives of Sexual Behavior, 48*(7), 2149–2169. https://doi.org/10.1007/s10508-018-1279-3

Davis, K. A., & Knight, R. A. (2019b). Childhood maltreatment experiences and problematic sexual outcomes in adult males who have sexually offended: Further evidence of the potency of male caregiver psychological abuse. *Child Abuse & Neglect, 96*, 104097–104097. https://doi.org/10.1016/j.chiabu.2019.104097

Du, R., & Knight, R. A. (2024). The structure of hypersexuality and its relation to impulsivity. *Archives of Sexual Behavior, 53*(6), 2277–2290. https://doi.org/10.1007/s10508-024-02828-2

Edens, J. F., Marcus, D. K., Lilienfeld, S. O., & Poythress, N. G., Jr. (2006). Psychopathic, not psychopath: Taxometric evidence for the dimensional structure of psychopathy. *Journal of Abnormal Psychology, 115*(1), 131–144. https://doi.org/10.1037/0021-843X.116.4.701

Edens, J. F., Marcus, D. K., & Vaughn, M. G. (2011). Exploring the taxometric status of psychopathy among youthful offenders: Is there a juvenile psychopath taxon? *Law and Human Behavior, 35*, 13–24. https://doi.org/10.1007/s10979-010-9230-8

Fargo, J. D. (2008). *An empirical taxonomy of incarcerated male sexual offenders using finite mixture modeling: Adult victims* [Paper presentation]. Proceedings of the North American Correctional & Criminal Justice Psychology Conference, Public Safety Canada.

Feigelson, D., Rohrer, D., & Knight, R. A. (2018, April). *A factor-analytic exploration of the Structured Risk Assessment Need Framework* [Poster presentation]. Joint Conference of the Massachusetts Adolescent Sex Offender Coalition and the Massachusetts Association for the Treatment of Sexual Abusers 20th Annual Meeting, Marlborough, MA.

Fitch, J. H. (1962). Men convicted of sexual offenses against children: A descriptive follow-up study. *British Journal of Criminology, 3*(1), 18–37. https://doi.org/10.1093/oxfordjournals.bjc.a048569

Flakenhain, M. A., Duckro, P., Hughes, H. M., Rossetti, S. J., & Gfeller, J. D. (1999). Cluster analysis of child sexual offenders: A validation with Roman Catholic priests and brothers. *Sexual Addiction & Compulsivity, 6*, 317–336. https://doi.org/10.1080/10720169908400201

Freund, K., & Blanchard, R. (1986). The concept of courtship disorder. *Journal of Sex & Marital Therapy, 12*(2), 79–92. https://doi.org/10.1080/00926238608415397

Fromm, E. (1977). *The anatomy of human destructiveness*. Penguin.

Garb, H. N., & Boyle, P. A. (2003). Understanding why some clinicians use pseudoscientific methods: Findings from research on clinical judgment. In S. O. Lilienfeld, S. J. Lynn, & J. M. Lohr (Eds.), *Science and pseudoscience in clinical psychology* (pp. 17–38). Guilford Press.

Gebhard, P. H., Gagnon, J. H., Pomeroy, W. B., & Christenson, C. V. (1965). *Sex offenders: An analysis of types*. Harper & Row.

Ghiselin, M. T. (1981). Categories, life, and thinking. *The Behavioral and Brain Sciences, 4*, 269–313. https://doi.org/10.1017/S0140525X00008852

Grabell, A., & Knight, R. A. (2009). Examining childhood abuse patterns and critical periods in juvenile sexual offenders. *Sexual Abuse: Journal of Research and Treatment, 21*, 208–222. https://doi.org/10.1177/1079063209333133

Graham, F. J., Walters, G. D., Harris, D. A., & Knight, R. A. (2015). Is hypersexuality dimensional or categorical? Evidence from male and female college samples. *Journal of Sex Research, 53*(2), 224–238. https://doi.org/10.1080/00224499.2014.1003524

Graham, N. (2018). *Examining the use of hebephilia and paraphilia non-consent in sexually violent predator evaluations* [Paper presentation]. Florida Sexually Violent Predator Program (SVPP) annual training. Tallahassee, FL.

Groth, A. N., & Birnbaum, H. J. (1979). *Men who rape: The psychology of the offender*. Plenum Press.

Groth, A. N., Burgess, A. W., & Holmstrom, L. L. (1977). Rape: Power, anger, and sexuality. *American Journal of Psychiatry, 134*, 1239–1243. https://doi.org/10.1176/ajp.134.11.1239

Groth, A. N., Hobson, W. F., & Gary, T. S. (1982). The child molester: Clinical observations. *Journal of Social Work and Human Sexuality, 1*(1-2), 129–144. https://doi.org/10.1300/J291v01n01_08

Grove, W. M., & Meehl, P. E. (1996). Comparative efficiency of informal (subjective, impressionistic) and formal (mechanical, algorithmic) prediction procedures: The clinical-statistical controversy. *Psychology, Public Policy, and Law, 2*(2), 293–323. https://doi.org/10.1037/1076-8971.2.2.293

Guay, J. P., & Knight, R. K. (2004, July). *A taxometric analysis of psychopathy using the MASA* [Poster presentation]. Developmental and Neuroscience Perspectives on Psychopathy Conference, Madison, Wisconsin.

Guay, J. P., Ruscio, J., Knight, R. A., & Hare, R. (2007). A taxometric analysis of the latent structure of psychopathy: Evidence for dimensionality. *Journal of Abnormal Psychology, 116*, 701–716. https://doi.org/10.1037/0021-843X.116.4.701

Guttmacher, M. S., & Weihofen, H. (1952). *Psychiatry and the law*. W. W. Norton & Company.

Hall, G. C. N., Graham, J. R., & Shepherd, J. B. (1991). Three methods of developing MMPI typologies. *Journal of Personality Assessment, 56*(1), 2–13. https://doi.org/10.1207/s15327752jpa5601_1

Hanson, R. K., Bourgon, G., Helmus, L., & Hodgson, S. (2009). The principles of effective correctional treatment also apply to sexual offenders: A meta-analysis. *Criminal Justice and Behavior, 36*, 865–891. https://doi.org/10.1177/0093854809338545

Harris, G. T., Lalumière, M. L., Seto, M. C., Rice, M. E., & Chaplin, T. C. (2012). Explaining the erectile responses of rapists to rape stories: The contributions of sexual activity, non-consent, and violence with injury. *Archives of Sexual Behavior, 41*(1), 221–229. https://doi.org/10.1007/s10508-012-9940-8

Harris, G. T., Rice, M. E., Hilton, N. Z., Lalumière, M. L., & Quinsey, V. L. (2007). Coercive and precocious sexuality as a fundamental aspect of psychopathy. *Journal of Personality Disorders, 21*(1), 1–27. https://doi.org/10.1521/pedi.2007.21.1.1

Harris, G. T., Rice, M. E., & Quinsey, V. L. (1994). Psychopathy as a taxon: Evidence that psychopaths are a discrete class. *Journal of Consulting and Clinical Psychology, 62*, 387–397. https://doi.org/10.1037/0022-006X.62.2.387

Haslam, N. (1997). Evidence that male sexual orientation is a matter of degree. *Journal of Personality and Social Psychology, 73*, 862–870. https://doi.org/10.1037/0022-3514.73.4.862

Haslam, N., McGrath, M. J., Viechtbauer, W., & Kuppens, P. (2020). Dimensions over categories: A meta-analysis of taxometric research. *Psychological Medicine, 50*(9), 1418–1432. https://doi.org/10.1017/S003329172000183X

Hazelwood, R. R. (1987). Analyzing the rape and profiling the offender. In R. R. Hazelwood & A. W. Burgess (Eds.), *Practical aspects of rape investigation: A multidisciplinary approach* (pp. 169–199). Elsevier.

Hazelwood, R. R., & Burgess, A. W. (1987). The behavioral-oriented interview of rape-victims: The key to profiling. In R. R. Hazelwood & A. W. Burgess (Eds.), *Practical aspects of rape investigation: A multidisciplinary approach* (pp. 151–168). Elsevier.

Hazelwood, R. R., Reboussin, R., & Warren, J. I. (1989). Serial rape: Correlates of increased aggression and the relationship of offender pleasure to victim resistance. *Journal of Interpersonal Violence, 4*, 65–78. https://doi.org/10.1177/088626089004001004

Hempel, C. G. (1965). *Aspects of scientific explanation*. Free Press.

Hewitt, A. N., Chopin, J., & Beauregard, E. (2020). Offender and victim 'journey-to-crime': Motivational differences among stranger rapists. *Journal of Criminal Justice, 69*, Article 101707. https://doi.org/10.1016/j.jcrimjus.2020.101707

Higgins, M. L. (2008). *A cluster-analytically derived typology of juvenile sex offenders* [Unpublished doctoral dissertation]. Auburn University.

Hillen, R. (2017). *Modeling psychological attributes: Merits and drawbacks of taxometrics and latent variable mixture models* [Unpublished doctoral dissertation]. Tilburg University, Netherlands.

Ialongo, N., Rogosch, F. A., Cicchetti, D., Toth, S. L., Buckley, J., Petras, H., et al. (2006). A developmental psychopathology approach to the prevention of mental health disorders. In D. Cicchetti & D. Cohen (Eds.), *Developmental psychopathology: Theory and method* (Vol. 1, 2nd ed., pp. 968–1018). Wiley.

Kaiser, I. M., & Krickel, B. (2017). The metaphysics of constitutive mechanistic phenomena. *The British Journal for the Philosophy of Science, 68*, 745–779. https://doi.org/10.1093/bjps/axv058

Kalichman, S. C. (1990). Affective and personality characteristics of MMPI profile subgroups of incarcerated rapists. *Archives of Sexual Behavior, 19*(5), 443–459. https://doi.org/10.1007/BF02442347

Kalichman, S. C. (1991). *A cluster analytically derived typology of incarcerated rapists based on the MMPI* [Unpublished doctoral dissertation]. University of South Carolina.

Kalichman, S. C., Craig, M. E., Shealy, L., Taylor, J., Szymanowski, D., & McKee, G. (1989a). An empirically derived typology of adult rapists based on the MMPI: A cross-validation study. *Journal of Psychology and Human Sexuality, 2*(2), 165–181. https://doi.org/10.1300/J056v02n02_11

Kalichman, S. C., Dwyer, M., Henderson, M. C., & Hoffman, L. (1992). Psychological and sexual functioning among outpatient sexual offenders against children: A Minnesota Multiphasic Personality Inventory (MMPI) cluster analytic study. *Journal of Psychopathology and Behavioral Assessment, 14*(3), 259–276. https://doi.org/10.1007/BF00962632

Kalichman, S. C., & Henderson, M. C. (1991). MMPI profile subtypes on nonincarcerated child molesters: A cross validation study. *Criminal Justice and Behavior, 18*, 379–396. https://doi.org/10.1891/0886-6708.6.3.201

Kalichman, S. C., Szymanowski, D., McKee, G., Taylor, J., & Craig, M. E. (1989b). Cluster analytically derived MMPI profile subgroups of incarcerated adult rapists. *Journal of Clinical Psychology, 45*, 149–155. https://doi.org/10.1002/1097-4679(198901)45:1<149::AID-JCLP2270450123>3.0.CO;2-1

Karpman, B. (1954). *The sexual offender and his offenses: Etiology, pathology, psychodynamics and treatment*. Julian Press.

Kelley, T. L. (1927). *Interpretation of educational measurements*. Yonkers-on-Hudson.

Kingston, D. A., Graham, F. J., & Knight, R. A. (2017). Relations between adverse childhood experiences and adult hypersexuality in adult sexual offenders. *Archives of Sexual Behavior, 46*(3), 707–720. https://doi.org/10.1007/s10508-016-0873-5

Kingston, D. A., Olver, M. E., Levaque, E., Sawatsky, M. L., Seto, M. C., & Lalumière, M. L. (2020). Establishing Canadian metrics for self-report measures used to assess hypersexuality. *The Canadian Journal of Human Sexuality, 29*(1), 65–78. https://doi.org/10.3138/cjhs.2019-0055

Knight, R. A. (1984). Converging models of cognitive deficit in schizophrenia. In W. D. Spaulding & J. K. Cole (Eds.), *Nebraska Symposium on Motivation, 1983: Theories of Schizophrenia and Psychosis* (pp. 93–156). University of Nebraska Press.

Knight, R. A. (1989). An assessment of concurrent validity of a child molester typology. *Journal of Interpersonal Violence, 4*, 131–150. https://doi.org/10.1177/088626089004002001

Knight, R. A. (1992). The generation and corroboration of a taxonomic model for child molesters. In W. O'Donohue & J. H. Geer (Eds.), *The sexual abuse of children: Theory, research, and therapy* (Vol. 2, pp. 24–70). Lawrence Erlbaum.

Knight, R. A. (1997, October). *A unified model of sexual aggression: Consistencies and differences across noncriminal and criminal samples* [Paper presentation]. Association for the Treatment of Sexual Abusers (ATSA) 16th Annual Meeting, Arlington, Virginia.

Knight, R. A. (2010a). Typologies for rapists: The generation of a new structural model. In A. Schlank (Ed.), *The sexual predator* (Vol. 4, pp. 17-1–17-28). Civic Research Institute.

Knight, R. A. (2010b). Is a diagnostic category for paraphilic coercive disorder defensible? *Archives of Sexual Behavior, 39*(2), 419–426. https://doi.org/10.1007/s10508-009-9571x

Knight, R. A., & Du, R. (2021). The structure, covariates, and etiology of hypersexuality: Implications for sexual offending. *Current Psychiatry Reports, 23*, 50. https://doi.org/10.1007/s11920-021-01260-w

Knight, R. A., & Graham, F. J. (2017). Hypersexuality: Equifinal, cohesive, clinical presentation or symptom cluster with multiple underlying mechanisms? *Archives of Sexual Behavior, 46*, 2261–2264. https://doi.org/10.1007/s10508-017-1089-z

Knight, R. A., & Guay, J. P. (2006). The role of psychopathy in sexual coercion against women. In C. J. Patrick (Ed.), *Handbook of psychopathy* (pp. 512–532). The Guilford Press.

Knight, R. A., & Guay, J.-P. (2018). The role of psychopathy in sexual coercion against women: An update and expansion. In C. J. Patrick (Ed.), *Handbook of psychopathy* (Vol. II, pp. 662–681). The Guilford Press.

Knight, R. A., & King, M. W. (2012). Typologies for child molesters: The generation of a new structural model. In B. K. Schwartz (Ed.), *The sex offender: Current trends in policy and treatment practice* (Vol. 7, pp. 5-1–5-33). Civic Research Institute, Inc..

Knight, R. A., & Longpré, N. (2019, November). *Exploring the structure and covariates of hypersexuality* [Paper presentation]. Association for the Treatment of Sexual Abusers (ATSA) 38th Annual Meeting, Atlanta, Georgia.

Knight, R. A., & Longpré, N. (2021). The structure and measurement of sadism: Implications for validation. In L. A. Craig & R. M. Bartels (Eds.), *Sexual deviance: Understanding and managing deviant sexual interests and paraphilic disorders* (pp. 207–221). John Wiley & Sons, Inc..

Knight, R. A., Longpré, N., & Rohrer, D. (2019, April). *The young sexual aggressor factor and the Agonistic Continuum* [Conference session]. Joint Conference of the Massachusetts Adolescent Sex Offender Coalition and the Massachusetts Association for the Treatment of Sexual Abusers 21st Annual Meeting, Marlborough, MA.

Knight, R. A., & Prentky, R. A. (1990). Classifying sexual offenders: The development and corroboration of taxonomic models. In W. L. Marshall, D. R. Laws, & H. E. Barbaree (Eds.), *The handbook of sexual assault: Issues, theories, and treatment of the offender* (pp. 23–52). Plenum Press.

Knight, R. A., & Prentky, R. A. (1993). Exploring the characteristics for classifying juvenile sexual offenders. In H. E. Barbaree, W. L. Marshall, & S. M. Hudson (Eds.), *The juvenile sex offender* (pp. 45–83). Guilford Press.

Knight, R. A., Rosenberg, R., & Schneider, B. (1985). Classification of sexual offenders: Perspectives, methods, and validation. In A. W. Burgess (Ed.), *Research handbook on rape and sexual assault* (pp. 222–293). Garland Publishing Inc.
Knight, R. A., & Sims-Knight, J. (2011). The developmental antecedents of sexual coercion against women: Testing alternative hypotheses with structural equation modeling. *Annals of the New York Academy of Sciences, 989*(1), 72–85. https://doi.org/10.1111/j.1749-6632.2003.tb07294.x
Knight, R. A., Sims-Knight, J., & Guay, J. P. (2013). Is a separate diagnostic category defensible for paraphilic coercion? *Journal of Criminal Justice, 41*, 90–99. https://doi.org/10.1016/j.jcrimjus.2012.11.002
Knight, R. A., & Sims-Knight, J. E. (1999, November). *Family and early behavioral antecedents of sexual coercion* [Paper presentation]. Society for Research in Psychopathology, Montreal 14th Annual Meeting, Quebec, Canada.
Knight, R. A., & Sims-Knight, J. E. (2003). Developmental antecedents of sexual coercion against women: Testing of alternative hypotheses with structural equation modelling. In R. A. Prentky, E. Janus, & M. Seto (Eds.), *Sexual coercion: Understanding and management* (pp. 72–85). New York Academy of Sciences.
Knight, R. A., & Sims-Knight, J. E. (2004). Testing an etiological model for male juvenile sexual offending against females. *Journal of Child Sexual Abuse, 13*(3–4), 33–55. https://doi.org/10.1300/j070v13n03_03
Knight, R. A., & Sims-Knight, J. E. (2017). A theoretical integration of aetiological and typological models of rape. In A. Beech & T. Ward (Eds.), *The Wiley handbook on the theories, assessment, & treatment of sexual offending* (pp. 73–102). Wiley.
Knight, R. A., & Sims-Knight, J. E. (2018, October). *The structure and covariates of sexual harassment and coercion* [Conference session]. Association for the Treatment of Sexual Abusers (ATSA) 37th Annual Meeting, Vancouver, British Columbia.
Kopp, S. B. (1962). The character structure of sex offenders. *American Journal of Psychotherapy, 16*, 64–70. https://doi.org/10.1176/appi.psychotherapy.1962.16.1.64
Kosson, D. S., Schraft, C. V., Brieman, C. L., McBride, C. K., & Knight, R. A. (2021). Parental Rejecting Behaviors: Validating a behaviorally based youth-report measure of parental emotional abuse. *Assessment, 28*(3), 899–917. https://doi.org/10.1177/1073191120918943
Krueger, R. F., Kotov, R., Watson, D., Forbes, M. K., Eaton, N. R., Ruggero, C. J., Simms, L. J., Widiger, T. A., Achenbach, T. M., Bach, B., Bagby, R. M., Bornovalova, M. A., Carpenter, W. T., Chmielewski, M., Cicero, D. C., Clark, L. A., Conway, C., DeClercq, B., DeYoung, C. G., Docherty, A. R., Drislane, L. E., First, M. B., et al. (2018). Progress in achieving quantitative classification of psychopathology. *World Psychiatry, 17*, 282–293. https://doi.org/10.1002/wps.20566
Lanning, K. V. (1986). *Child molesters: A behavioral analysis for law-enforcement officers investigating cases of child exploitation*. National Center for Missing and Exploited Children.
Lenzenweger, M. F. (2004). Consideration of the challenges, complications, and pitfalls of taxometric analysis. *Journal of Abnormal Psychology, 113*, 10–23. https://doi.org/10.1037/0021-843X.113.1.10
Levenson, J. S. (2004). Reliability of sexually violent predator civil commitment criteria in Florida. *Law and Human Behavior, 28*(4), 357–368. https://doi.org/10.1023/b:lahu.0000039330.22347.ad
Lilienfeld, S. O., Lynn, S. J., & Lohr, J. M. (2003). Science and pseudoscience in clinical psychology: Initial thoughts, reflections, and considerations. In S. O. Lilienfeld, S. J. Lynn, & J. M. Lohr (Eds.), *Science and pseudoscience in clinical psychology* (pp. 1–14). The Guilford Press.
Longpré, N., Guay, J.-P., & Knight, R. A. (2019a, July). *Latent structure and covariates of the Agonistic Continuum among a community sample and college students* [Paper presentation]. Australia and New Zealand Association for the Treatment of Sexual Abusers 9th Biennial Conference, Brisbane, Australia.

Longpré, N., Guay, J.-P., & Knight, R. A. (2019b). MTC Sadism Scale: Toward dimensional assessment of severe sexual sadism with behavioral markers. *Assessment, 26*(1), 70–84. https://doi.org/10.1177/1073191117737377

Longpré, N., Guay, J.-P., Knight, R. A., & Benbouriche, M. (2018). Sadistic offender or sexual sadism? Taxometric evidence for a dimensional structure of sexual sadism. *Archives of Sexual Behavior, 47*, 403–416. https://doi.org/10.1007/s10508-017-1068-4

Longpré, N., Sims-Knight, J. E., Neumann, C. S., Guay, J. P., & Knight, R. A. (2020). Is paraphilic coercion a different construct from sadism or simply the lower end of a continuum anchored at the high end by sadism? *Journal of Criminal Justice, 71*, Article 101743. https://doi.org/10.1016/j.jcrimjus.2020.101743

MacCulloch, M. J., Snowden, P. R., Wood, P. J. W., & Mills, E. W. (1983). Sadistic fantasy, sadistic behaviour and offending. *British Journal of Psychiatry, 143*(1), 20–29. https://doi.org/10.1192/bjp.143.1.20

Mackaronis, J. E., Strassberg, D. S., & Marcus, D. K. (2011). The latent structure of Multiphasic Sex Inventory-assessed pedophilic interest. *Psychological Assessment, 23*(4), 1017–1022. https://doi.org/10.1037/a0024625

Mann, R. E., Hanson, R. K., & Thornton, D. (2010). Assessing risk for sexual recidivism: Some proposals on the nature of psychologically meaningful risk factors. *Sexual Abuse: A Journal of Research and Treatment, 22*, 191–217. https://doi.org/10.1177/1079063210366039

Marcus, D. K., John, S. L., & Edens, J. F. (2004). A taxometric analysis of psychopathic personality. *Journal of Abnormal Psychology, 113*(4), 626–635. https://doi.org/10.1037/0021-843X.113.4.626

Marcus, D. K., Sanford, G. M., Edens, J. F., Knight, R. A., & Walters, G. D. (2011). Taxometrics and evolutionary theory: The case of the psychopathic sexuality taxon. *The Scientific Review of Mental Health Practice, 8*(1), 6–16. https://www.researchgate.net/publication/225285477

Markon, K. E., Chmielewski, M., & Miller, C. J. (2011). The reliability and validity of discrete and continuous measures of psychopathology: A quantitative review. *Psychological Bulletin, 137*, 856–879. https://doi.org/10.1037/a002367

Marshall, W. L., & Hucker, S. J. (2006). Issues in the diagnosis of sexual sadism. *Sexual Offender Treatment, 1*(2), 1–4. https://www.researchgate.net/publication/26585481

Marshall, W. L., & Kennedy, P. (2003). Sexual sadism in sexual offenders. An elusive diagnosis. *Aggression and Violent Behavior, 8*, 1–22. https://doi.org/10.1016/S1359-1789(01)00052-0

Mayburgh, J.-E., & Olver, M. E. (2021). A cluster analytic examination and validation of adult victim sexual offending subtypes in two Canadian samples. *Sexual Offending: Theory, Research, and Prevention, 16*, Article e3741. https://doi.org/10.5964/sotrap.3741

McCaghy, C. H. (1967). *Child molesters: A study of their careers as deviants*. Holt, Rinehart, & Winston.

McPhail, I. V., Olver, M. E., Brouillette-Alarie, S., & Looman, J. (2018). Taxometric analysis of the latent structure of pedophilic interest. *Archives of Sexual Behavior, 47*(8), 2223–2240. https://doi.org/10.1007/s10508-018-1225-4

Meehl, P. E. (1978). Theoretical risks and tabular asterisks: Sir Karl, Sir Ronald, and the slow progress of soft psychology. *Journal of Consulting and Clinical Psychology, 46*, 806–834. https://doi.org/10.1016/j.appsy.2004.02.001

Meehl, P. E. (1979). A funny thing happened on the way to the latent entities. *Journal of Personality Assessment, 43*, 564–581. https://doi.org/10.1207/s15327752jpa4306_2

Meehl, P. E. (1990). Appraising and amending theories: The strategy of Lakatosian defense and two principles that warrant it. *Psychological Inquiry, 1*, 108–141. https://doi.org/10.1207/s15327965pli0102_1

Meehl, P. E. (1992). Factors and taxa, traits and types, differences of degree and differences in kind. *Journal of Personality, 60*, 117–174. https://doi.org/10.1111/j.1467-6494.1992.tb00269.x

Meehl, P. E. (1995). Bootstraps taxometrics: Solving the classification problem in psychopathology. *American Psychologist, 50*(4), 266–275. https://doi.org/10.1037/0003-066X.50.4.266

Meehl, P. E., & Yonce, L. J. (1994). Taxometric analysis: I. Detecting taxonicity with two quantitative indicators using means above and below a sliding cut (MAMBAC procedure). *Psychological Reports, 74*, 1059–1274.
Meehl, P. E., & Yonce, L. J. (1996). Taxometric analysis: II. Detecting taxonicity using covariance of two quantitative indicators in successive intervals of a third indicator (MAXCOV procedure). *Psychological Reports, 78*, 1091–1227. https://doi.org/10.2466/pr0.1996.78.3c.1091
MIDSA clinical manual. (2011). Bend, OR: Augur Enterprises, Inc. Available at http://www.midsa.us/
Moffitt, T. E. (2005). The new look of behavioral genetics in developmental psychopathology: Gene–environment interplay in antisocial behaviors. *Psychological Bulletin, 131*(4), 533–554. https://doi.org/10.1037/0033-2909.131.4.533
Mokros, A., Schilling, F., Weiss, K., Nitschke, J., & Eher, R. (2014). Sadism in sexual offenders: Evidence for dimensionality. *Psychological Assessment, 26*(1), 138–147. https://doi.org/10.1037/a0034861
Moloney, E., Sims-Knight, J. E., & Knight, R. A. (2025). *Harassment, coercion, and the Agonistic Continuum: Exploring the structure of sexual aggression* [Manuscript in preparation]. Department of Psychology, Brandeis University.
Money, J. (1986). *Lovemaps: Clinical concepts of sexual/erotic health and pathology, paraphilia, and gender transposition in childhood, adolescence, and maturity*. Irving Publishers, Inc..
Morgan, R. E., & Oudekerk, B. A. (2019). *Criminal victimization, 2018* (NCJ 253043; p. 37). U.S. Department of Justice, Bureau of Justice Statistics. https://www.bjs.gov/content/pub/pdf/cv18.pdf
Murrie, D. C., Marcus, D. K., Douglas, K. S., Lee, Z., Salekin, T., & Vincent, G. (2007). Youth with psychopathy features are not a discrete class: A taxometric analysis. *Journal of Child Psychology and Psychiatry, 48*(7), 714–723. https://doi.org/10.1111/j.1469-7610.2007.01734.x
Nichols, H. R., & Molinder, I. (1984). *Multiphasic Sex Inventory manual*. Nichols & Molinder.
Nitschke, J., Osterheider, M., & Mokros, A. (2009). A cumulative scale of severe sexual sadism. *Sexual Abuse: A Journal of Research and Treatment, 21*(3), 262–278. https://doi.org/10.1177/1079063209342074
Nunnally, J. (1978). *Psychometric theory* (2nd ed.). McGraw-Hill.
Oxnam, P., & Vess, J. (2006). A personality-based typology of adolescent sexual offenders using the Millon Adolescent Clinical Inventory. *New Zealand Journal of Psychology, 35*, 36–44.
Paolucci, E. O., Genuis, M. L., & Violato, C. (2001). A meta-analysis of the published research on the effects of child sexual abuse. *The Journal of Psychology, 135*, 17–36. https://doi.org/10.1080/00223980109603677
Perillo, A. D., Spada, A. H., Calkins, C., & Jeglic, E. L. (2014). Examining the scope of questionable diagnostic reliability in Sexually Violent Predator (SVP) evaluations. *International Journal of Law and Psychiatry, 37*, 190–197. https://doi.org/10.1016/j.ijlp.2013.11.005
Plato. (1952). *Phaedrus* (B. J. Persons, Trans.) Britannica Great Books. William Benton (Original work published 360 B.C.E.).
Plichta, S. B., & Falik, M. (2001). Prevalence of violence and its implications for women's health. *Women's Health Issues, 11*(3), 244–258. https://doi.org/10.1016/S1049-3867(01)00085-8
Popper, K. R. (1972). *The logic of scientific discovery*. Hutchinson.
Preacher, K. J., Rucker, D. D., MacCallum, R. C., & Nicewander, W. A. (2005). Use of the extreme groups approach: A critical reexamination and new recommendations. *Psychological Methods, 10*(2), 178–192. https://doi.org/10.1037/1082-989X.10.2.178
Prentky, R. A., Cohen, M. L., & Seghorn, T. K. (1985). Development of a rational taxonomy for the classification of sexual offenders: Rapists. *Bulletin of the American Academy of Psychiatry and the Law, 13*, 39–70. http://jaapl.org/content/jaapl/13/1/39.full.pdf
Proulx, J., & Beauregard, E. (2014). Pathways in the offending process of extrafamilial sexual aggressors against women. In J. Proulx, E. Beauregard, P. Lussier, & B. Leclerc (Eds.), *Pathways to sexual aggression* (pp. 71–109). Routledge.

Ramírez, M. P., López, M. S., Giménez-Salinas, A., de Juan Espinosa, F., & de Juan Espinosa, M. (2018). Stranger rape: Classifying Spanish sexual offences using multiple correspondence and cluster analyses. *Journal of Sexual Aggression, 24*(2), 225–239. https://doi.org/10.1080/13552600.2018.1504554

Regier, D. A., Narrow, W. E., Clarke, D. E., Kraemer, H. C., Kuramoto, S. J., Kuhl, E. A., & Kupfer, D. J. (2013). DSM–5 field trials in the United States and Canada, Part II: Test–retest reliability of selected categorical diagnoses. *The American Journal of Psychiatry, 170*, 59–70. https://doi.org/10.1176/appi.ajp.2012.12070999

Reichenbach, H. (1958). *The philosophy of space and time* (M. Reichenbach & J. Freund, trans.). Dover Publications.

Robertillo, C., & Terry, K. J. (2007). Can we profile sex offenders? A review of sex offender typologies. *Aggression and Violent Behavior, 12*, 508–518. https://doi.org/10.1016/j.avb.2007.02.010

Robertson, C. A. (2017). *Psychopathic and sexually sadistic cognitions, traits, and behaviors: Relations with biomarkers and stress responses* [Unpublished doctoral dissertation]. Brandeis University, Waltham, MA.

Robertson, C. A., & Knight, R. A. (2014). Relating sexual sadism and psychopathy to one another, non-sexual violence, and sexual crime behaviors. *Aggressive Behavior, 40*(1), 12–23. https://doi.org/10.1002/ab.21505

Rohrer, D., Brouillette-Alarie, S., & Knight, R. A. (2018, April). *Replication of a three-factor solution: Exploring the underlying constructs of the Static 99-r and Static-2002* [Poster presentation]. Joint Conference of the Massachusetts Adolescent Sex Offender Coalition and the Massachusetts Association for the Treatment of Sexual Abusers 20th Annual Meeting, Marlborough, MA.

Rohrer, D., & Knight, R. A. (2025). *Exploring potential underlying emotional and behavioral mechanisms contributing to sexual sadism* [Manuscript in preparation]. Department of Psychology, Brandeis University.

Rosenberg, R., & Knight, R. A. (1988). Determining male sexual offender subtypes using cluster analysis. *Journal of Quantitative Criminology, 4*, 383–410. https://doi.org/10.1007/BF01065346

Ruscio, J., Haslam, N., & Ruscio, A. M. (2006). *Introduction to the taxometric method: A practical guide*. Lawrence Erlbaum.

Schatzel-Murphy, E., Harris, D., Knight, R. A., & Milburn, M. (2009). Sexual coercion in men and women: Similar behaviors, different predictors. *Archives of Sexual Behavior, 38*, 974–986. https://doi.org/10.1007/s10508-009-9481-y

Schlank, A. M. (1995). The utility of the MMPI and the MSI for identifying a sexual offender typology. *Sex Abuse: A Journal of Research and Treatment, 7*(3), 185–194. https://doi.org/10.1007/BF02258503

Schmidt, A. F., Mokros, A., & Banse, R. (2013). Is pedophilic sexual preference continuous? A taxometric analysis based on direct and indirect measures. *Psychological Assessment, 25*(4), 1146–1153. https://doi.org/10.1037/a0033326

Seghorn, T., & Cohen, M. (1980). The psychology of the rape assailant. In W. Cerran, A. L. McGarry, & C. Petty (Eds.), *Modern legal medicine, psychiatry, and forensic science*. Philadelphia, PA.

Sellbom, M., & Drislane, L. E. (2021). The classification of psychopathy. *Aggression and Violent Behavior, 59*, 101473. https://doi.org/10.1016/j.avb.2020.101473

Seto, M. C. (2018). *Pedophilia and sexual offending against children: Theory, assessment, and intervention* (2nd ed.). American Psychological Association. https://doi.org/10.1037/0000107-000

Seto, M. C., Lalumière, M. L., Harris, G. T., & Chivers, M. L. (2012). The sexual responses of sexual sadists. *Journal of Abnormal Psychology, 121*(3), 739–753. https://doi.org/10.1037/a0028714

Shealy, L., Kalichman, S. C., Henderson, M. C., Szymanowski, D., & McKee, G. (1991). MMPI profile subtypes of sex offenders against children. *Violence and Victims, 6*(3), 201–212. https://doi.org/10.1891/0886-6708.6.3.201

Skilling, T. A., Quinsey, V. L., & Craig, W. M. (2001). Evidence of a taxon underlying serious antisocial behavior in boys. *Criminal Justice and Behavior, 28*, 450–470. https://doi.org/10.1177/0093854801028004004

Skinner, H. A. (1981). Toward the integration of classification theory and methods. *Journal of Abnormal Psychology, 90*, 68–87. https://doi.org/10.1037/0021-843X.90.1.68

Skinner, H. A. (1986). Construct validation approach to psychiatric classification. In T. Millon & G. L. Klerman (Eds.), *Contemporary directions in psychopathology: Toward the DSM-IV* (pp. 307–330). The Guilford Press.

Smith, W. R., Monastersky, C., & Deisher, R. M. (1987). MMPI-based personality types among juvenile sexual offenders. *Journal of Clinical Psychology, 43*, 422–430. https://doi.org/10.1002/1097-4679(198707)43:4<422::AID-JCLP2270430414>3.0.CO;2-3

Stephens, S., Leroux, E., Skilling, T., Cantor, J. M., & Seto, M. C. (2017). Taxometric analyses of pedophilia utilizing self-report, behavioral, and sexual arousal indicators. *Journal of Abnormal Psychology, 126*(8), 1114–1119. https://doi.org/10.1037/abn0000291

Swanson, D. W. (1971). Who violates children sexually? *Medical Aspects of Human Sexuality, 5*, 184–197.

Swets, J. A., Dawes, R. M., & Monahan, J. (2000). Psychological science can improve diagnostic decisions. *Psychological Science in the Public Interest, 1*, 1–26. https://doi.org/10.1111/1529-1006.001

Thompson, L. M., Graham, F. J., & Knight, R. A. (2025). *Examining the latent structure of paraphilic behavior: Taxometric analyses of non-normophilic behavior in samples of convicted men and college students.* [Manuscript submitted for publication]. Department of Psychology, Brandeis University.

Thornton, D. (2016). Developing a theory of dynamic risk. *Psychology, Crime & Law, 22*(1–2), 138–150. https://doi.org/10.1080/1068316X.2015.1109092

Thornton, D. (2019, November). *Assessing sexual interest in rape* [Conference session]. Association for the Treatment of Sexual Abusers (ATSA) 38th Annual Meeting, Atlanta, Georgia.

Thornton, D. (2021). Sexual offending and classification. *Aggression and Violent behavior, 59*, 100436. https://doi.org/10.1016/j.avb.2020.101436

Toth, S. L., & Cicchetti, D. (2010). The historical origins and developmental pathways of the discipline of developmental psychopathology. *Israel Journal of Psychiatry and Related Sciences, 47*(2), 5–14. https://doctorsonly.co.il/wpcontent/uploads/2011/12/2010_2_2.pdf

Vasey, M. W., Kotov, R., Frick, P. J., & Loney, B. R. (2005). The latent structure of psychopathy in youth: A taxometric investigation. *Journal of Abnormal Child Psychology, 33*(4), 411–429. https://doi.org/10.1007/s10802-005-5723-1

Vermunt, J. K., & Magidson, J. (2006). Latent class cluster analysis. In J. A. Hagenaars & A. L. McCutcheon (Eds.), *Applied latent class analysis* (pp. 89–106). Cambridge University Press.

Viding, E. (2022, May). *Promises and limitations of genetics research for understanding the development and management of psychopathy* [Paper presentation]. Society for the Scientific Study of Psychopathy 9th *Biennial on-line meeting.*

Waller, N. G., & Meehl, P. E. (1998). *Multivariate taxometric procedures: Distinguishing types from continua*. Sage.

Walters, G. D., Brinkley, C. A., Magaletta, P. R., & Diamond, P. M. (2008). Taxometric analysis of the Levenson self-report psychopathy scale. *Journal of Personality Assessment, 90*(5), 491–498. https://doi.org/10.1080/00223890802248828

Walters, G. D., Duncan, S. A., & Mitchell-Perez, K. (2007a). The latent structure of psychopathy: A taxometric investigation of the Psychopathy Checklist–Revised in a heterogeneous sample of male prison inmates. Assessment, 14(3), 270-278. https://doi.org/10.1177/1073191107299594

Walters, G. D., Ermer, E., Knight, R. A., & Kiehl, K. A. (2015). Paralimbic biomarkers in a taxometric analysis of psychopathy: Does changing the indicators change the conclusion? *Personality Disorders: Theory, Research, and Treatment, 6*(1), 41–42. https://doi.org/10.1037/per0000097

Walters, G. D., Gray, N. S., Jackson, R. L., Sewell, K. W., Rogers, R., Taylor, J., & Snowden, R. J. (2007b). A taxometric analysis of the Psychopathy Checklist: Screening Version (PCL:SV): Further evidence of dimensionality. *Psychological Assessment, 19*(3), 330–339. https://doi.org/10.1037/1040-3590.19.3.330

Walters, G. D., Knight, R. A., & Långström, N. (2011a). Is hypersexuality dimensional? Evidence for the DSM-5 from general population and clinical samples. *Archives of Sexual Behavior, 40*(6), 1309–1321. https://doi.org/10.1007/s10508-010-9719-8

Walters, G. D., Knight, R. A., Looman, J., & Abracen, J. (2016). Child molestation and psychopathy: A taxometric analysis. *Journal of Sexual Aggression, 22*(3), 379–393. https://doi.org/10.1080/13552600.2016.1199742

Walters, G. D., Marcus, D. K., Edens, J. F., Knight, R. A., & Sanford, G. (2011b). In search of the psychopathic sexuality taxon: Indicator size does matter. *Behavioral Sciences & the Law, 29*(1), 1–17. https://doi.org/10.1002/bsl.964

Walton, K. E., Ormel, J., & Krueger, R. F. (2011). The dimensional nature of externalizing behaviors in adolescence: Evidence from a direct comparison of categorical, dimensional, and hybrid models. *Journal of Abnormal Child Psychology, 39*(4), 553–561. https://doi.org/10.1007/s10802-010-9478-y

Ward, T., & Fortune, C.-A. (2016). The role of dynamic risk factors in the explanation of offending. *Aggression and Violent Behavior, 29*, 79–88. https://doi.org/10.1016/j.avb.2016.06.007

Weaver, T. L., Allen, J. A., Hopper, E., Maglione, M. L., McLaughlin, D., McCullough, M. A., Jackson, M. K., & Brewer, T. (2007). Mediators of suicidal ideation within a sheltered sample of raped and battered women. *Health Care for Women International, 28*, 478–448. https://doi.org/10.1080/07399330701226453

Weydt, A. (2020). *Factor Analyses of the Juvenile Sex Offender Assessment Protocol-II (J-SOAP-II) and the Adult Sex Offender Assessment Protocol (A-SOAP): Comparing risk factors for juveniles and adult* [Unpublished honors dissertation]. Brandeis University, Waltham, MA.

Woessner, G. (2010). Classifying sexual offenders: An empirical model for generating type-specific approaches to intervention. *International Journal of Offender Therapy and Comparative Criminology, 54*(3), 327–345. https://doi.org/10.1177/0306624X08331213

World Health Organization. (2019). *International Statistical Classification of Diseases and Related Health Problems* (11th ed.). https://icd.who.int/

Worling, J. R. (2001). Personality-based typology of adolescent male sexual offenders: Differences in recidivism rates, victim-selection characteristics, and personal victimization histories. *Sexual Abuse: A Journal of Research and Treatment, 13*, 149–166. https://doi.org/10.1177/107906320101300301

Chapter 4
Psychodynamic Perspectives of Sexual Offending

Gerard P. Webster

4.1 Introduction

Father (Fr.) Paul was once a highly respected rising star for the Catholic Diocese in which he was a priest. He had a fine pedigree and was tipped to one day be ordained a bishop. His was the story of a quiet, well-behaved local altar boy who decided he had a calling from God to become a priest. His positive personal and academic qualities were soon recognized by Church authorities after he entered the seminary, resulting in his being chosen for advanced education at the Vatican. Fr. Paul first earned a degree in philosophy, then a theology degree, and then a doctorate in canon law while in Rome. He was ordained by Pope John Paul II and worked temporarily as a priest in Italy and England. Fr. Paul was swiftly appointed to the position of Bishop's Secretary when he returned to his rural diocese in the United States of America, a prestigious role for one so young. By all reports, he drew strong responses from his parishioners as he was given his own parishes to lead. As a parish priest, he was either admired by those who valued his sermons on love and forgiveness or hated by those who did not want to see his administrative plans implemented. But the Fr. Paul I met at the door for his first appointment did not embody the confidence, ease, and pride one might expect from such a person.[1]

[1] The author is grateful to the late Fr. Paul who consented to the use of material from his treatment both during his later years of life (Webster, 2017a, 2017b, 2017c, 2018) and after his death. He hoped that professionals might learn something from his story. While he was willing for this to occur without deidentification, the pseudonym, 'Fr. Paul,' has been retained to avoid confusion

G. P. Webster (✉)
Institute of Contemporary Psychoanalysis, Los Angeles, CA, USA
e-mail: gerard@gerardwebster.com

R. J. Tully et al. (eds.), *Best Practices in Sexual Offender Assessment and Management*, Dangerous Behavior in Clinical and Forensic Psychology,
https://doi.org/10.1007/978-3-031-83135-5_4

Although only in his 50s, Fr. Paul presented as a sickly and frightened man who nervously waited for my instructions about where he could sit. As with other recently released offenders, I wondered, “What am I to him, another guard that he must obey or at least appear to defer? What does he hope for and dread from me and from our time together?” Upon greeting each other I gestured toward his chair. Fr. Paul quickly impressed me as an unusually intelligent and articulate man despite his hesitancy. His nervousness was immediately apparent and not surprising given that this was his first session, but I also wondered if the more pressing concern was his desire to be seen as saying the right thing. I quickly came to the view that for us to progress he would need to feel safe in speaking openly about what he truly thought about his offending and felt about the things that mattered to him.

Fr. Paul completed a 12-month evidence-based custodial sex offender group program immediately before his release on parole—a program one might suspect Bonta and Andrews (2016) would highly approve. It was clear that Fr. Paul had benefited from the treatment he received. He was aware of his stable dynamic risk factors[2] and his relapse prevention plan. He was able to articulate the cognitive distortions that had enabled his crimes. He identified strategies that would interrupt his ‘offense chain’ (Pithers et al., 1989; Ward et al., 1995) and he was aware of effective and appropriate ways to meet his personal needs (Ward & Brown, 2004).

The end-of-treatment report described Fr. Paul’s participation in the group program in positive terms, noting that he actively worked towards and achieved the treatment goals. He was assessed as being at a moderate-high recidivism risk according to his static risk factors (Harris et al., 2003; Helmus et al., 2009) and dynamic risk factors (Hart et al., 2003) at the time of his discharge from the treatment program and subsequent release from prison. The post-release self-management plan developed between Fr. Paul and his psychologist comprised: (1) using positive coping strategies to deal with stress and problems; (2) developing and maintaining friendships with adults that are of equal power—considering their needs as well as his own; (3) maintaining healthy self-esteem; and (4) engaging in pro-social leisure activities. He was required to wear an electronic surveillance ankle bracelet, and to accept supervision from corrections caseworkers with weekly meetings. He was also required to attend a weekly post-release maintenance program for the entire eighteen months of his parole. Finally, he was mandated to maintain requirements

between early and later publications about his case. Further, demographic details have been modified to offer some protection to his known and unknown victims who may be distressed by some of the material discussed.

[2] Current literature on the assessment of the risk of reoffending endorses a multifaceted approach that includes an examination of static and dynamic risk factors. Static risk factors take into account the offender’s personal history and are therefore unchangeable, whereas dynamic risk factors consider the offender’s changeable but enduring personal characteristics. There are two types of dynamic risk factors: stable and acute. Stable risk factors are characteristics that are stable over time, such as the offender’s personality traits and disorders. Acute risk factors, on the other hand, are highly transient phenomena that can fluctuate more rapidly over a month or within days or hours, such as drug and alcohol abuse and being in an unstable intimate relationship (Chu & Ogloff, 2012).

to inform police of certain things given that he was a registered sex offender effectively for the remainder of his life.

Fr. Paul was transitioning from a halfway house to living alone in the community at the time we met. Having spent the last 14 years in prison and trained only to be a Catholic priest, he was ill-prepared for employment and almost completely devoid of community ties. His very public exposure as a high-profile child sex offender rendered him a *persona non grata* in the geographical region in which he had lived and offended. Further, his promise to his bishop that he would never return to the Diocese out of respect for his victims and their families meant that he could not effectively draw on past relationships with people who continued to care about his welfare. Fr. Paul moved to the capital city where I worked for his psychological and physical safety, where he was anonymous, had a couple of loyal friends, the promise of stable accommodation, and just enough money to get by if he was frugal.

Fr. Paul was under no obligation to see me. His participation in the maintenance program was considered sufficient to address his remaining treatment needs by the authorities. However, Fr. Paul reported aching for a deeper understanding of how he had come to be so deluded that he could harm so many people (children, their families, and the Church community) without being aware of the implicit and explicit destructiveness of his acts. The absence of understanding left him terrified that he might re-offend despite having all the correct answers he had learned in the previous 12 months. I was impressed by the fact that he had come to me for voluntary treatment, and openly admitted to countless (more likely thousands rather than hundreds) of sexual offenses against prepubertal boys and adolescents with whom he had fiduciary responsibilities. Fr. Paul was first interviewed by police about his crimes against a small number of these boys. He not only made admissions to these allegations immediately, but he later told police about as many of his undetected crimes as he could remember. He pleaded guilty to all charges in relation to dozens of boys and was sentenced accordingly.

Fr. Paul had only very rare contact with corrections psychologists for the first thirteen of his fourteen years in prison. He reported that he was enthusiastic about joining the group treatment program when it was offered towards the end of his sentence, but he never felt truly safe enough to express his private thoughts and feelings once the program began. Given his cautious approach to the group process and hearing him report verbatim the lessons he learned from the program, I grew concerned that Fr. Paul had only developed a superficial, intellectual understanding of his crimes and his gains in treatment. I was very concerned about his capacity for self-awareness of his emotions, fearing that he would be unable to recognize when his acute internal risk factors were on the rise.

Fr. Paul reported that he fully accepted the proposition that his sexual interactions with children were harmful, but he could not feel this to be true. He was acutely aware of the contradiction between his knowledge about the harm he had caused his victims and his subjective experience of his relationship with each child. Fr. Paul disclosed that he continued to feel his relationships with the children were based on "love" and his recollections of their "time together" as loving and mutually beneficial. Fr. Paul did not feel safe enough to share this with corrections psychologists or with fellow inmates in the group. While he was aware his open participation was encouraged in the program, he feared psychologists would shut down any attempts to explore this contradiction with an implicit or explicit axiomatic response that was familiar to him from his close involvement with the Church: "Thou shalt not speak about things that contradict the orthodoxy of the program. You will be punished if you do."

In addition to my concerns that Fr. Paul had not progressed as much as one might hope for such an investment in treatment, Fr. Paul reported that he was still suffering from the Depression and Generalized Anxiety Disorder he had experienced throughout his life. He was also experiencing Panic Attacks, secondary to his Post-traumatic Stress Disorder that resulted from multiple assaults and other inhumane behavior he sustained from both fellow inmates and corrections officers throughout the entire period of his incarceration. None of these issues had been addressed in his manualized custodial treatment program.

I formed the opinion that Fr. Paul would benefit from forensic psychodynamic treatment so that the gains he had made in his cognitive-behavioral treatment might be reinforced and augmented. In contrast to the exclusive targeting of criminogenic risk factors that Fr. Paul experienced in the custodial program that was based upon the Risk-Need-Responsivity model (Andrews et al., 2011; Craig et al., 2013; Grieger & Hosser, 2014; Ward et al., 2012), forensic psychotherapy would offer Fr. Paul a holistic treatment that was predicated upon the building of a safe and efficacious therapeutic relationship from which deep personal growth may occur. While the custodial treatment program was very likely to have been successful in addressing his recidivism risk, forensic psychotherapy would aim to build upon these advances by assisting Fr. Paul in reducing his psychological symptoms and adjusting to life in the community.

It was anticipated that by offering Fr. Paul a one-to-one therapeutic relationship he would become increasingly open to the emergence of a deeper therapeutic experience than he had in the past. By, together, spending a great deal of time thinking about and feeling into the conscious and unconscious issues that challenged and confronted him, Fr. Paul would for the first time in his life have an experience of someone being empathically attuned to his full range of thoughts and feelings without "collusion, disbelief (or) condemnation" (Symington, 1980, p. 295). By building an experience of being valued and understood by another as a unique and complex person, Fr. Paul might be better able to gain greater sensitivity to his internal experience (subjectivity) and the subjective experience of others. By building his self-awareness and greater victim empathy from a new foundation of another being aware of and empathic toward him, Fr. Paul might have greater freedom to respond quickly to impulses that could lead to re-offending. In addition, forensic psychotherapy would aim to deepen Fr. Paul's insight into his sexual feelings toward boys and his motives to sexually abuse them by enriching his attunement to his feelings and those of others, thereby enhancing his empathy for past and potential victims and raising the prospects of a meaningful and pro-social quality of life for his remaining years. It was clear that such an ambitious project would take time.

I provided forensic psychotherapy to Fr. Paul every week for 10 out of 12 years. His treatment was interrupted by two periods of imprisonment for sexual offenses against three other victims occurring in the same cluster of the crimes to which he had earlier been convicted. Fr. Paul entered pleas of guilt to each of these charges on the advice of his legal representatives, even though he denied committing them to me. This chapter will draw upon Fr. Paul's case to demonstrate the psychodynamic concepts that apply to the forensic population and, I believe, helped Fr. Paul to achieve significant gains in mental health that helped him lead a child-safe, meaningful and humble, rather than humiliating life in his final years.

4.2 The Psychodynamic Perspective

The term 'psychodynamic' as applied to psychological theory and practice is typically used interchangeably with the terms 'psychoanalysis' and 'psychotherapy' respectively. However, 'psychodynamic' can also be used in general terms to refer to any psychological system of thought that holds unconscious processes as the locus of inquiry and the focus of psychological intervention. This chapter will use the terms interchangeably.

The psychodynamic perspective is differentiated from other psychological perspectives by its focus on unconscious processes and the experience-near relationship of the patient and psychotherapist. Early iterations of psychodynamic theory conceptualized the unconscious mind purely as the internal world of an individual that is powered by instincts and dynamic drives. Considered in this way, instincts and drives determine the way a person experiences themselves and relates to the outside world. Contemporary psychoanalytic perspectives conceptualize unconscious processes in a more complex way where any division between the internal and external world is only partly representative of limitless influences in the psychic field that include the person's environmental and social (relational, cultural, and historical) matrices.

Dramatic changes have also taken place over the last 130 years in the way psychodynamic psychotherapists offer treatment. The early expert-practitioner rules of psychoanalytic practice considered it the patient's role to provide information for the psychoanalyst to interpret. The psychoanalyst's interpretation alone was considered curative. This approach has largely been replaced by a more 'relational,' mutual engagement between the psychoanalyst and their patient. Where once there was doctrine, now there are insights and guidelines for how to understand the patient and the psychotherapeutic process—a process that involves two subjects and two subjectivities. The exchange of words is no longer considered the single pathway to personality change. Instead, therapeutic action is considered to proceed due to the qualities of the therapeutic relationship which are always in a process of becoming through implicit and explicit mutual influence. Where once therapeutic technique was tightly prescribed, now psychoanalysts are free to make use of multiple theories and apply them in unique ways according to what is discerned to be most helpful to the patient at the time. The practice of psychodynamic psychotherapy is very personal, in the sense of being unique to each therapeutic dyad. A shift has therefore taken place from 'what works' to 'what works best for the patient at each particular moment.' The resulting diversity of psychoanalytic theories and the nuance of psychodynamic practice creates a challenge for researchers considering treatment efficacy.

Psychoanalysts, beginning with Freud, have studied the nonconscious processes that have led to the sexual abuse of children and other vulnerable people since the psychodynamic approach commenced almost a century and a half ago. Following Richard von Krafft-Ebing's research into sexuality and sexual aberrations (von Krafft-Ebing, 1886/2018), Freud was among the first theorists to conceptualize sexual offending not just as a serious crime and a departure from social rules and religious prohibitions, but as psychopathology. Freud's exploration of 'perversion' and sadomasochistic processes predates and informs psychology's current construct of the 'paraphilias.' As such, the psychodynamic approach has been an active contributor to the field of forensic psychology from the outset, predating the emergence of forensic psychology as a distinct subdiscipline of psychology.

It is necessary to examine historical developments in psychodynamic theory and practice to understand the range of psychodynamic perspectives about sexual offending and the treatment of sex offenders. The psychodynamic perspective emerged not long after the discipline of psychology embraced its cardinal value as a field of experimentation in the mid-nineteenth century. The earliest psychodynamic theorists enthusiastically shared psychology's aims and scientific method of inquiry: the aims being to understand human experience and alleviate mental suffering, and the method being to achieve these aims through careful observation and systematic analysis of data.

Psychodynamic theory and practice were given birth when Sigmund Freud (1856–1939) turned his attention from his successful research into neuroanatomy to the study of psychopathology. Freud was an established and published medical researcher at the Vienna General Hospital and a lecturer at the University of Vienna in the late nineteenth century before he turned his attention to psychopathology. His early research into the palliative effects of cocaine was provocative and his research about aphasia was highly regarded. The shift to studying nervous disorders such as hysteria required a change in research methodology from the examination of large samples of brain specimens to single case studies of deeply troubled people. The psychodynamic theories that Freud proposed were thereby steeped in the scientism of the late nineteenth century.

Freud was initially inspired to consider mental health from a psychological perspective after he began to consider the research of the French neurologist, Jean-Martin Charcot, in the late nineteenth century. Charcot was researching susceptibility to hypnosis and hysteria; the latter being considered a neurological condition affecting women. Freud quickly came to recognize the limits of Charcot's hypnotic method of treating hysteria and abandoned it after discovering that a more consistent and effective approach to symptom relief could be achieved by what he termed 'free association'—that is, allowing the patient to speak freely—and by interpreting reported dreams. By permitting patients to share their thoughts and experiences without deliberately controlling the conversation, Freud discovered a new source of data from which he could draw inferences and develop his theories.

Freud's theorizing was expansive and evolved throughout his life resulting in "a metapsychology of human development and behavior" (Abrahams & Rohleder, 2021, p. 16). His aim was "to discover what form the theory of psychical functioning will take if a quantitative line of approach, a kind of economics of nervous force, is introduced into it" (Freud, 1895, p. 296). He considered human psychology through the lens of energy proposing a "conception of neuronal excitation as quantity in a state of flow" (Freud, 1895, p. 296) which is governed by the biological principles of homeostasis. Freud drew from the then-popular economic model of the reflex that conceptualized incoming energy needing to be released to prevent a dangerous build-up in the system. Hence from the very beginning of his *Project for a Scientific Psychology* (1895), Freud considered his hypothesis of pain as being the result of built up energy in the psychic apparatus.

While the 'unconscious mind' was a topic of high interest to philosophers throughout the nineteenth century (von Hartmann, 1869/2014), Freud was the first to recognize its importance and centrality in human development and mental functioning. Freud proposed two models of the mind throughout his career that served as a launching pad for all psychoanalytic theories that came after his. Freud's *Topographical Model of the Mind* explicated three levels of consciousness: the System Conscious, the System Preconscious, and the System Unconscious (Freud, 1900/2001). This model has found considerable support and has been refined by infant and neuropsychological research over the last fifty years. While few contemporary psychodynamic theorists refer to the System Preconscious, the core principle remains that most of the workings of the human mind are unconscious. It is commonly held that any of a person's conscious thoughts, feelings, or behaviors are given rise by unconscious processes and that conscious phenomena, therefore, are only 'the tip of the iceberg.'

Freud discovered two species of mental functioning within his Topographical Model, comprising primary and secondary process thinking (Freud, 2011). *Primary process thinking*, he observed, takes place in the system unconscious and is irrational where there is no sense of time, and the events of the past and present are not distinguished. In contrast, *secondary process thinking* occurs in the system conscious and is rational, logical, and organized. Freud thereby anticipated neuropsychological evidence found in infant development and trauma research that recognizes the collapse of executive function operating in psychosis and that occurs in response to traumatogenic brain dysregulation and dissociation (van der Kolk, 2014).

Freud's second model was his *Structural Model* which provided a framework for considering the dynamic processes of the mind (Freud, 1920, 1923). Freud proposed that human beings are driven by two fundamental instincts, the sexual and the aggressive drives, both of which are at play in every aspect of our conscious thoughts, feelings, and behaviors. Freud considered sexual perversions and the criminal acts to which they give rise to be the result of an admixture of these two drives. In addition, Freud proposed three distinct, interacting agents in the psychic apparatus of the mind that manage these drives comprising *Das Es, Das Ich,* and *Das Über-Ich* (the Id, the Ego, and the Super-ego). Freud argued that these agents come into being during early childhood, with each remaining in continuous dialogue or conflict with the others throughout the lifespan—all in a struggle to achieve some satisfaction of the individual's desires for pleasure and the expression of aggression. The Id refers to instinctual sex and aggression drives that produce a hunger for the satisfaction of their related desires. The Super-ego represents the ever-watchful and critical aspect of personality that takes a moralizing stance concerning the Id, tending to be a strict or even punitive conscience. The Ego represents the organized, realistic aspect of the mind that mediates between the instinctual desires of the Id and the opposing morality of the Super-ego and operates at both conscious and unconscious levels. Freud proposed that the Super-ego and the Ego come into being during early childhood in response to developmental challenges.

Freud expanded his Structural Theory to include a theory of psychosexual development. This, his *Sexualtheorie*, is perhaps the most complex and challenging of his theories to consider. His five-stage theory of psychosexual development proposed that mental health is achieved only after individuals achieve developmental milestones in balancing their needs and desires with those of others, particularly those on whom they most rely. In childhood, the focus of conflict and achievement in relationships is found in the parent-child dyad, specifically with the mother. Freud proposed that pleasure-seeking libido becomes focused sequentially on different regions of the body throughout childhood until early adolescence. The five stages comprise the Oral, Anal, Phallic, Latency, and Genital stages.

Experiences of loss, fear, and helplessness are common during infancy and most often present in the form of relationship challenges. Freud's most famous representation of the mental and developmental challenges of early childhood was articulated in his conceptualization of the Oedipus Complex for boys and the Electra Complex for girls where the healthy child faces a conflict between his or her close bond with the mother and any other force that threatens that closeness (Freud, 1900/2001, 1910b). Freud conceptualized the resulting internal, unconscious conflict of love and hate in the context of a triangulation of relationships between the child, the mother, and the father (Freud, 1905/1949). However, subsequent theorists have expanded Freud's initial concept to focus on the conflict arising from other people or things having different kinds of relationships with the mother from which the child is excluded (Britton et al., 1989).[3] The resolution of these complexes became central to Freud's theory of psychological maturation and social responsibility.

Freud's publications in psychopathology and, to a lesser extent, treatment were controversial from the outset (Freud, 1896), drawing either interest or condemnation from both his colleagues and the general public (Breger, 2001). Douglas Kirsner asserts that "Freud's ideas became a pivotal part of the twentieth-century Zeitgeist.

---

[3]The author is deliberately softening the jargon and simplifying aspects of Freuds theories so it makes better sense to those who are not psychoanalytically educated. More conservative psychoanalysts might describe Freuds theories with different emphasis to those expressed here.

Even the strongest of the Freud-bashers has to reckon with, if not to adopt outright, many psychoanalytic concepts that have transformed our view of ourselves and our relationships" (2000, p. 250). Few can match Freud's influence on the field of psychology, nor his quantum of publications having authored more than 320 books, articles, and essays. While some of Freud's early theories have not stood up well against subsequent research findings and have thus been updated or replaced by contemporary psychoanalytic theories, many of his theories and innovative treatment techniques remain of interest and have been accepted across the discipline of psychology.

Jon Mills notes that "There is a cornucopia of empirical evidence in the cognitive neurosciences, the attachment field, infant-observation research, developmental psychology, and the therapeutic process that are corroborations, validations, extension, revisions, and emendations of Freud's contributions" (2012, p. 172). In terms of contributions to treatment technique, "Freud was the principal person to establish and articulate the basic technical principles of psychotherapy, including establishing rapport with patients; forming a therapeutic alliance; pointing out defenses and compromises in the service of resistance, self-protection, and repetition; forming an authentic manner of relatedness with patients; examining the transference; interpreting unconscious wishes and conflicts; and reaching the affect as part of the working-through process" (2012, p. 173). The astute reader will quickly recognize that most of these then innovative techniques have been adopted by most psychological treatment models including Cognitive Behavior Therapy, Mindfulness training, Eye Movement Desensitization & Reprocessing, to name but a few.

Freud attracted the interest of many mental health professionals as his reputation grew. These young colleagues were later to become the second generation of leaders in theory development and the establishment of an evolving code of practice referred to as the psychoanalytic technique. There were points of strong disagreement as up-and-coming psychoanalysts began to assert different views to those proposed by Freud. Famous examples of the schismatic consequences of these controversies are found in Alfred Adler's departure in 1911, Carl Gustav Jung's departure in 1912, and Otto Rank's departure in 1924. The point of contention in each case was these theorists' recognition that Freud's view did not adequately address the social constituents of the mind (Stern, 2017).[4] This issue and many similar controversies have continued over the last 130 years sometimes resulting in the creation of distinct schools of psychoanalysis. While bifurcation has resulted from the rigorous and sometimes bitter debate the results for psychoanalysis as a whole have mostly been positive. Freud held control over what was a single orthodoxy for the first three decades of 'his' psychoanalysis. However, subsequent years of theorizing, research, and internal scholarly debate have created a heterogeneity of contemporary

[4] Sándor Ferenczi was another of Freud's close protégées with whom the relationship ended in an irreconcilable breakdown and with Ferenczi's exclusion from the psychoanalytic community due to differences of opinion about theory and professional practice (Rudyntsky, 2022). Ferenczi held strongly to the view that his patients' accounts of sexual abuse during childhood were truthful well after Freud abandoned his Seduction Theory.

psychodynamic perspectives. A brief overview of the philosophical foundations of each school is necessary to understand the differences in theory and practice between them.

A scholar's theories about natural and human phenomena are predicated on her or his fundamental philosophical assumptions or worldview. The term 'paradigm' in the philosophical sense refers to "a pattern or model… a world view underlying the theories and methodology of a particular scientific subject" (*Oxford Dictionary of English*, 2010, p. 1287). A paradigm is an integrated set of worldviews that comprise beliefs about what is real, true, and important. Each philosophical framework and each theory about natural and human phenomena, including those developed in the study of psychology, have underlying assumptions that imply one paradigmatic pattern or another.

Modern developmental psychology for the most part holds that adult behavior and the personality characteristics of an individual are influenced or caused by the events of earlier life, particularly in the formative years. Early theorists attributed the cause of psychopathology to poor learning (Dollard & Miller, 1950; Skinner, 1938), irrational beliefs (Ellis, 1962), poor decision-making (Williamson & Darley, 1937), and unresolved intra-psychic conflict sometimes exacerbated by trauma as discussed above. Psychology's focus on the individual as the subject upon which life events impact, and upon which health professionals act, has earned this system of beliefs the label, Individualist. The Individualist Paradigm, also referred to as the Monologic Paradigm (Taylor, 1989), conceptualizes each person as a single entity in a world of other individuals. Since other individuals are identified as objects outside and separate, any contact an individual has with another is conceptualized as being through the mental representations he or she has within. The person's mind, or 'internal world,' is thereby made up of internal representations—that is, their thoughts, attitudes, beliefs, perceptions, motives, emotions, and, for the psychoanalyst, intra-psychic conflict.

As described above, Freud was a scientist, and his theories were steeped in the scientism of his day. Consistent with the rational experimentalism of the nineteenth century, Freud's ambition was to develop a system of knowledge about the human mind that presented a coherent and ordered arrangement of fundamental concepts that was capable of being accounted for by empirically observed phenomena using a methodology that sought to verify those concepts. Freud's philosophy of science was one of positivist materialism, a philosophical movement that emerged powerfully in the Age of Enlightenment.[5] His topographical and structural theories, described above, demarcate the individual's 'internal world' (comprised of their

[5]Like the discipline of psychology, the assertion that psychoanalysis is an established science has been rigorously debated since its inception. Challenging the view of psychoanalysis as a scientific endeavour, Kirsner states, "by almost any account, psychoanalysis is an experimental, subjective, personal and interpersonal exploration for which there are no validatng objective criteria. If anything, psychoanalysis is about unknowing, about the unconscious which is not known, about the uniqueness of individual discovery" (, p. 235). A thorough consideration of the complexities of this debate is beyond the scope of this chapter.

unconscious, partly conscious, and conscious Id, Ego, and Superego) as separate from the natural and social world in which they live. His is therefore an individualist, 'monadic theory of mind,' otherwise referred to as a 'one-person' psychology (Mitchell, 1988). As such, Freud's theorizing is predicated on the Individualist Paradigm that conceptualizes the person as primarily the subject of internal representations.

While the individualist model of the person has been dominant in psychology and throughout the history of Western philosophy, the 'social' interpretation of the human condition has been acquiring increased recognition within the discipline over the last century and has led to current developments such as race theory, queer theory, and intersectional theory. This alternate model has emphasized the socially and historically significant dimensions of personality and has been referred to in the philosophy literature as the social, dialogical, conversational, hermeneutic, or interpretive paradigm. Unlike individualist explanations, the Social Paradigm holds that personalities are never defined in terms of individual properties but are instead defined in terms of their social context. The social model of the person posits that the manner in which phenomena are experienced by a person is determined by the understanding she or he has of that experience; an understanding that has been socially constructed and embedded in social interaction. The Social Paradigm has disputed the assumptions of individualistic theories and claimed that human experience cannot be 'known' in the same way that science has claimed to know the characteristics of non-human phenomena. The social approach has argued that behavioral scientists (such as psychologists) cannot justifiably claim knowledge of human experience from a purely objective, third-person perspective. The sub-disciplines of critical psychology and critical psychiatry are predicated on the Social Paradigm.

Contemporary theories of psychoanalysis have, to varying degrees, adopted the Social Paradigm as the philosophical base for an interactional, relational theory of mind. At the very least, all schools of thought recognize the importance of relationships and environmental factors in psychological development, thereby breaking with the Individualist theories of the past, making contemporary psychoanalysis a two-person psychology. These two-person theories recognize "the bi-directionality of the analytic relationship and, alongside the patient's subjectivity, the centrality of the analyst's subjectivity" (Magid et al., 2021, p. 2). The "isolated mind" perspective of twentieth century psychoanalytic theories that reify the psychoanalyst as an autonomous, expert determiner of the goings on in another's 'internal world,' that implicitly or explicitly claims to be able to know what is occurring in the unconscious mind of the patient, has been challenged across all psychoanalytic schools. New iterations of these social theories are well underway and are referred to as Relational psychoanalytic approaches. With the distinction of individualist one-person and social two-person theories having been made, it is now possible to describe the schools that have stood on the shoulders of Sigmund Freud.[6]

---

[6] A more complex examination of the Individual and Social paradigms is not possible due to space limitations. Likewise, the following account of the distinguishing qualities of each psychoanalytic school is simplified for the purpose of clarity but risks misrepresenting a school of thought as

The contribution of Freud and his loyal contemporaries is now referred to as Classical Psychoanalysis. New schools of psychoanalysis have formed from earlier iterations over the last century. The first post-Classical school was Ego Psychology which focused upon and developed Freud's Structural Model of the Mind, remaining wedded to the Individualist Paradigm. Ego psychology was the predominant psychoanalytic approach in the United States during the middle decades of the twentieth century, but its dominance was soon challenged by other psychodynamic perspectives. Classical Psychoanalysis and Ego Psychology are the approaches often parodied and sometimes misrepresented as 'the psychodynamic perspective,' sadly even sometimes by our colleagues.

The Lacanian school of psychoanalysis was founded by the French psychoanalyst and psychiatrist, Jacques Lacan. From the 1950s to the 1980s, Lacan and his followers reconsidered Classical Psychoanalysis from a structuralist and post-structuralist philosophical perspective. Lacan expounded a theoretical system to explain the relationship between mind, behaviour, and culture, positing that the world of language, what Lacanians refer to as 'the Symbolic,' structures the human mind (Lacan, 1977/1998). Lacan focussed on three basic ontological structures of psychopathology previously identified by Freud—neurosis, perversion, and psychoses. Lacan argued that each structure originates as a fundamentally different way of solving the individual's problems of alienation, separation from their primary caregiver, castration, or having limits set by the law on the individual's '*jouissance*'[7] (Lacan, 2013).

The psychoanalytic school of British Object Relations evolved from Classical Psychoanalysis in three directions, thereby coming to hold three sub-systems of thought. The British school's 'trialectic' developed between the First and Second World Wars and was made up of (1) the Viennese tradition, initially led by Anna Freud; (2) the followers of Melanie Klein; and (3) the Independents, who recognized the strengths and shortcomings of both perspectives and did not want to side with either. Each of these systems of thought continues to hold to the classical fundamentals of psychoanalysis, including "the existence of the unconscious, the theory of instincts, childhood sexuality and development, defense, displacement, symbolization, symptom formation, repetition, transference, resistance, transference neurosis and working through" (Rayner, 1991, p. 9).

While Freud's theories were anchored in the Individualist Paradigm, he did begin to explore environmental instigators of neurosis later in his career (Freud, 1917,

homogenous when, in fact, all psychoanalytic schools of thought are heterogeneous and always in a process of becoming. The author agrees with Roy Schafer who once stated, "The problem of analyzing the structure of thought within any one school is so formidable that even analysts who belong to that school cannot agree altogether on which basic assumptions have to be made, on the mutual interrelations of the various key propositions of that school, on what constitutes evidence, and on what the relation of evidence is to the particular analytic methods that are practised" (Schafer, 1979, p. 667).

[7] '*Jouissance*' is a French word referring to physical or intellectual pleasure, delight, or ecstasy. In French psychoanalysis, the term refers to the dysregulation of an individual's desire for pleasure.

1926). Anna Freud's psychotherapeutic treatment of abandoned and neglected children led to advances in psychodynamic theory in the direction of the paradigm shift that was to become fundamental across psychoanalysis, but also to mainstream psychology half a century later. Anna Freud's study of traumatized children brought recognition to the deleterious impact of early disruptions to attachment in the development of psychological problems. Anna Freud's emphasis on environmental factors laid the foundation for later research into early childhood attachment.

In contrast, the theoretical developments of Melanie Klein took psychoanalysis more deeply into the Individualist 'Internal World' Paradigm. Drawing strongly on Sigmund Freud's instinct theory, Klein elaborated a theory of primitive instinctual impulses giving rise to unconscious 'phantasy' (Klein, 1975). Klein elucidated a stage theory of child development that was useful in understanding the unconscious dynamics of psychological disorders and she identified 'projective identification' as an unconscious defense that needed to be addressed in treatment (Klein, 1946/1975).

Other psychoanalysts, such as Donald Winnicott (1971), Harry Guntrip (1961), and others formed the third school of thought, referred to as the Middle School or the Independents. This group, along with Ronald Fairbairn (1943/1952) in Scotland, considered personality and psychopathology to arise from the individual's history of relationships with others, the mother-child relationship being the most important. The Independents argued that attachment is fundamental to the development of the self, be it healthy or pathological, thereby providing the basis for John Bowlby to develop his Attachment Theory (Bowlby, 1969/1999, 1973, 1980), which was subsequently and famously researched in children by Mary Ainsworth (Ainsworth, 1989; Ainsworth & Bowlby, 1991) and in adults by Mary Main and colleagues (Main, 1991; Main et al., 2005).

In one sense, British Independents increasingly transitioned psychoanalysis from a one-person to a two-person psychology. However, it is arguable that while recognizing environmental and relational influences, Object Relations theories, by and large, hold to the Individualist Paradigm as the child continues to be conceptualized as developing internal representations that take on a life of their own in their Internal World that go on for the rest of the individual's life. As important as the theoretical developments of the British trialectic have been to psychoanalysis, the question of whether the threshold from a one-person to a two-person psychology has been crossed remains debatable.

As will be discussed later in this chapter, the theories privileged by individual psychoanalysts have a profound influence on the way the analyst engages with their patient. While each psychoanalytic school promotesa particular model for understanding and responding to the patient—practice guidelines if you will—the practice of psychoanalysis in its contemporary forms is far from manualized. On the contrary, the uniqueness of what the patient and the psychoanalyst bring to the therapeutic relationship is not only recognized but deemed to be of great significance when exploring the patient's unconscious processes. While each member of the therapeutic dyad brings their subjectivity to the relationship, the psychotherapist brings their choice of theories and their unique way of transforming those theories into practice. While some psychoanalysts stay with the expert-practitioner model that amplifies the one-person quality of their theory, increasing numbers of psychoanalysts are joining with other contemporary psychoanalytic schools in taking a more collaborative and shared stance.

The outgrowths from Ego Psychology in America were arguably more radical than occurred in Britain. Interpersonal Psychoanalysis was founded by the American psychiatrist Harry Stack Sullivan in the 1950s in New York and was strongly influenced by the ideas of Sandor Ferenczi, another Classical psychoanalyst who found himself on the wrong side of Sigmund Freud due to his Social Paradigmatic leanings. Sullivan (1953) contended that each personality is ‘created and shaped’ by interpersonal interactions with others from infancy. Practitioners of Interpersonal Psychoanalysis seek to explore conscious and unconscious experience in great detail gleaned ‘mutually’ from the clinical experience rather than from a privileged position of the knowing analyst and the passive patient. The Interpersonal School can unambiguously claim the status of being a two-person psychology from its inception. The Interpersonal school introduced Field Theory to psychoanalysis and thereby became the catalyst of the ‘relational turn’ that has swept most, if not all psychoanalytic schools.

The school of Self Psychology developed in the 1960s, 70s, and 80s and was founded by Heinz Kohut in Chicago. Self Psychology seeks to understand individuals from within their subjective experience through a process he named ‘vicarious introspection.’ Kohut emphasized the concepts of empathy, self-object, mirroring, idealizing, alter ego/twinship, and the tripolar self (Kohut, 1971, 1977, 1984). Kohut’s spectacular departure from his much-loved Ego Psychology signaled for some, such as Teicholz (2021), an immediate breakthrough from a one-person to a two-person psychology. Others, such as Magid and colleagues (2021, 2022), have mapped a more gradual transition, but certainly, the relational turn did occur in Self Psychology by the last quarter of the twentieth century.

The Intersubjective Systems Theory perspective was founded by George Atwood and Robert Stolorow (1984) in New Jersey and Los Angeles who viewed one’s personal experience as always emergent, self-maintaining, and transforming in relational contexts. Intersubjective Systems Theory is predicated upon the philosophy of phenomenology that seeks to investigate and describe human phenomena as consciously experienced, without making claims of causal explanations and avoiding unexamined preconceptions and presuppositions. Practitioners of this school seek to identify the emotional convictions or organizing principles that systematize the self-experience of their patients, something akin to the construct of ‘implicit theories’ recently conceptualized in cognitive psychology.

While each of these schools argued its position of superiority over the other for several decades, a rapprochement began to emerge in the 1980s that saw the beginning of mutual valuing, rich discussion, and the sharing of ideas in what is referred to by psychoanalysts as the ‘relational turn.’ The relational turn represents the paradigm shift (Kuhn, 1962/2012) across almost all schools of psychoanalysis from being a one-person psychology. Where the analyst’s role was traditionally limited to interpreting the patient’s intrapsychic psychodynamics, the two-person psychology of relational psychoanalysis recognizes the analyst’s subjectivity not only influences what emerges in the patient-analyst dyad but the entire process of treatment is co-created by the subjectivity (intersubjectivity) of both.

Two distinct relational schools emerged from existing psychoanalytic theories over the following decades. The first school to form is known as Relational Psychoanalysis, which is typically predicated on the philosophy of social constructionism and draws together the social perspective of Interpersonal Psychoanalysis with object relations theory that emphasizes the internalized relationships with other people (Greenberg & Mitchell, 1983). Some relational psychoanalysts draw heavily from Lacan's theories and the structural and post-structural philosophies on which Lacanianism is based.

The most recent development of psychoanalytic perspectives is Relational Self Psychology, described well by Magid et al. (2021). Relational Self Psychology expanded the two-person psychology of Self Psychology, described above, with the more radical two-person psychology of Relational Psychoanalysis. Relational Self Psychology carries an interesting mix of influence of philosophical underpinnings given the strong influence of phenomenology coming from the incorporation of Intersubjective Systems Theory and the empiricism that underpins much of the infant and neuropsychological research upon which it relies for theory development and validation.

Both Relational schools draw from the system of ideas that preceded them—object relations theory and, for some, Lacanian theory for the school of Relational Psychoanalysis, and self psychology theory for the school of Relational Self Psychology. Orange (2014) captured what is perhaps the most significant change in the practice of psychoanalysis and psychotherapy resulting from the relational turn by quoting Peirce (1955/2014) in his admonition that we should hold our theories lightly. The Individualist top-down expert practitioner model that characterized early psychodynamic theories and practice has been largely replaced by a conceptualization of psychanalytic practice occurring in the context of a necessarily unequal but mutual, bi-directional therapeutic relationship. Theories about an individual's unconscious processes are co-created in the conversation between the psychoanalyst with the patient from the bottom up. Importantly, Aron (1990) notes: "The distinction between a monadic theory of mind (a one-person psychology) and a relational theory of mind (a two-person psychology) is crucial in understanding psychoanalytic concepts. However, some psychoanalytic theorists see these two models as essentially complementary whereas others see them as contradictory and irreconcilable… I propose that a two-person or relational field theory does not need to neglect or minimize the intrapsychic, the importance of fantasy, psychic reality, or the centrality of bodily and childhood experience" (p. 475). The current author would add that to manage the complexity of holding both paradigms lightly substantial psychoanalytic training is required.

4.3 Psychoanalytic Training

The psychodynamic perspective is not merely a set of ideas about how to understand and help human beings who are in a state of psychological distress or compromise. A more embodied definition describes the psychodynamic perspective as a set of ideas and practices that are held and continually rectified and refined by highly trained mental health practitioners committed to the well-being of their patients. The vast majority of formally trained psychotherapists and psychoanalysts have previously undertaken advanced training in psychology, psychiatry, or other relevant disciplines and are, thereby, bound by the ethics and codes of conduct of their profession. Forensic psychoanalysts and psychotherapists who work with sex offenders bear an additional commitment to community safety, specifically the protection of children and other vulnerable people. Forensic psychoanalysis is 'responsible' in that it calls upon the clinician to maintain a high degree of scholarship, with this scholarship informing his or her practice. Forensic psychoanalysts must be aware of current theoretical debates and best-practice guidelines, but also be the bearer of as many systems of thought as possible—systems of thought that come from the sciences, the humanities, and from the fine arts. The richer the psychoanalyst's array of conceptual subsystems, the richer can be the interaction between analyst and patient.

The international industry standard to qualify as a practicing psychanalyst or psychoanalytic psychotherapist requires trainees to undertake a substantial course in psychoanalytic theory and practice. Psychoanalytic institutes across the world are typically accredited by the International Psychoanalytical Association or the American Psychoanalytic Association. Both associations require trainees to undertake at least a four-year postgraduate level course of study to qualify as a psychoanalyst and at least a two-year postgraduate level course to qualify as a psychoanalytic psychotherapist. Training as a psychoanalyst typically involves acquiring extensive knowledge about established and emerging psychodynamic theories, attending weekly seminars and weekend conferences, giving and listening to clinical case presentations, engaging in group discussions, and writing a substantial dissertation. Some institutes require candidates to engage in infant observation where a newborn child is observed weekly over two years. In addition, candidates must undertake extensive supervised psychoanalytic practice (supervised weekly by a senior psychoanalyst) involving at least three cases where the patient is seen at least three, but more often four or five times a week. The candidate must engage in their own 'training analysis' for the duration of their training. This firsthand experience of being in an analysis with a senior psychoanalyst is often viewed as the most important aspect of training. The candidate not only learns from observing and experiencing their training analyst at work but also builds a greater psychological capacity to tolerate his or her own deeply held desires, anxieties, and defenses. As Teicholz (2021) explains, "before an analyst can be open to his patient's affective world, he needs free-flowing access to his own emotional life" (p. 320). The training analysis helps the analyst be more open to recognizing their influence on the patient and their responses to the patient (referred to as countertransference) so they have a greater capacity to lean into their patient's suffering to explore it, rather than defending against it and avoiding mutually confronting and aversive experiences.

Training in the psychodynamic perspective requires clinicians to build on their prior training and experience rather than reject it. There has always been dialogue between disciplines such as psychiatry and psychology with psychoanalysis as the vast majority of psychoanalysts are psychiatrists or psychologists. Hence, the psychodynamic perspective should not be considered to be in opposition to other psychological approaches but rather as adding complexity and different points of view about forensic psychological phenomena of shared interest. Heterogeneity of, and collaboration between perspectives create the preconditions for a fuller understanding of human experience. Likewise, advances in psychodynamic theory and practice do not require the practitioner to choose between one philosophical foundation or school of thought over other available options. It is the opinion of this author that a 'holding' of mixed models and even mixed philosophies are required for ongoing theory development. Perhaps the next generation of theorists and practitioners will discover new paradigms. Certainly, new schools of thought will emerge in both psychoanalysis and forensic psychology. New ways of thinking about and relating to patients will emerge as culture advances. Our understanding of sexual offending and our knowledge about what works best for individual offenders is and will continue to be enriched by openness to dialogue not only between multiple disciplines but between heterogeneous theoretical perspectives.

4.4 Review of Psychodynamic Theory Related to Sex Offending

> You are what your deep, driving desire is. As your desire is, so is your will.
> As your will is, so is your deed. As your deed is, so is your destiny.—Brihadaranyaka Upanishad (c. 700BCE/2016)

Psychanalysis is now best understood as a system of thought made up of multiple subsystems (schools of psychoanalytic thought or psychodynamic perspectives), each of which school is made up of hundreds or thousands of theorists challenging past ways of thinking and practicing and breaking ground on improved methods for intervening with patients suffering mental distress, disorders, or illness. With this now established, a brief review of how these perspectives have explored the phenomenon of sexual offending through the lens of perverse and sadomasochistic processes is discussed.

Freud was quick to observe that many of his patients engaging in free association reported childhood experiences of sexual abuse and he formulated his *Seduction Theory* accordingly. Freud initially believed these reports despite the public condemnation he faced when he began publishing his findings. He concluded that the psychoneuroses of hysteria and obsessional neurosis were the result of unconscious conflict arising from the internal struggle between one's innate sexual instinct, which is magnified by premature sexual experience, in opposition to one's conscience and internalized socio-cultural prohibitions (Breuer & Freud, 1895; Freud, 1896). Freud later came to believe that in some cases such memories were fantasies, the function of which was to fend off aversive unconscious thoughts of infantile sexual experience.

While abandoning the notion of equivalence between memory and reality, Freud maintained that infantile sexual scenarios whether real or imagined had a causative function for psychoneuroses, the pathogenic action being when such memories are repressed. The relevance of Freud's findings in these regards will not escape the attention of the forensic psychologist or legal professional. In the space of just a few years, Freud brought to professional and public attention (1) the prevalence of and harm caused by the sexual abuse of children, and (2) the possibility that reports of child sexual assault coming to conscious awareness in treatment environments may factually be false memories, but remain of great psychological, symbolic significance.

Freud turned his attention to the minds of those who abuse others immediately after he recognized the link between trauma and physical and psychological symptoms (Freud, 1905/1949). In so doing, Freud advanced the research by von Krafft-Ebing (1886/2018) on a wide range of aberrant sexual behaviors now referred to in the Diagnostic and Statistical Manual of Mental Disorders (2013a) as paraphilias. Freud and his contemporaries referred to sexual aberrations as 'perversions,' a term that is still used by some psychoanalytic theorists despite concerns about how it has come to carry pejorative overtones.

In the first of his *Three Essays on the Theory of Sexuality*, 'The Sexual Aberrations,' Freud (1905/1949) proposed that "every kind of perversion can be shown to exist as unconscious forces" (p. 231). Freud distinguished the *sexual object* that is desired by the person, such as a child or an animal, from the *sexual aim*—that is, the particular act a person might want to engage in with that object. In the case of pedophilia, for example, a child is the sexual object, and the aim can be any sexual act known to human imagination. As (Keogh, 2012) points out, "[w]ith offenses involving children, the non-normative nature of the child as the object required for sexual arousal, as well as the non-normative mode of sexual stimulation achieved through the offending, characterizes the perversion and the paraphilia that it represents. In the case of the adult rapist, the perversion and paraphilic nature of the behavior is characterized by the nature of the sexual object (e.g., a non-consenting and or an elderly or frail individual) and the sexually sadistic behavior" (p. 67).

In the second of his three essays, *Sexually Immature Persons and Animals as Sexual Objects*, Freud (1905/1949) challenges the views held by some of his contemporaries that the sexual abuse of children represents "severe aberrations of the sexual instinct to insanity" stating "[e]xperience shows that disturbances of the sexual instinct among the insane do not differ from those that occur among the healthy and in whole races or occupations. Thus, the sexual abuse of children is found with uncanny frequency among school teachers and child attendants, simply because they have the best opportunity for it" (pp. 148–149). Another of Freud's publications at the time included relatives and family friends as the perpetrators of sexual violence or misconduct (Freud, 1905). Freud's research and theorizing found that people who commit sexual offenses are not necessarily insane and, instead, the sex offender population is heterogeneous—observations that now have considerable empirical support.

Freud distinguished between types of sex offenders based on what motivates their sexual violence. He describes sexual acts that are "merely characterized by an active or violent attitude to the sexual object, and, on the other hand, cases in which satisfaction is entirely conditional on the humiliation and maltreatment of the object" (Freud, 1905/1949, p. 158). In other words, while all sex offenders' crimes are the expression of an admixture of sexual and aggressive impulses, some also give expression to sadistic motives that seek to humiliate the other, the latter meeting his definition of perversion. Yet, Freud also acknowledged that some offending occurs due to situational factors such as unavailable age-appropriate sexual partners and opportunities to offend due to unfettered access. An informed forensic clinician will be aware that many aspects of Freud's innovative theories, based on his observations from clinical practice, have now been tested as hypotheses finding strong empirical support. Freud thereby is rightly regarded as a founding father of forensic psychology and as one of the first major explorers in the process of evidence-based forensic practice.[8]

Freud's theory of psychosexual development was central to his examination of sexual offending but is now rarely considered by contemporary psychoanalysts. Freud proposed that sexual aberrations (deviations from normal sexuality and sexual behaviors) result from a disruption to the process of healthy maturation at one of the first four of his five stages of psychosexual development. Sexual 'perversions,' including those that lead to the sexual assault of children and vulnerable adults, develop when such disruptions result in fixation at one of those stages. In developing his Oedipal theory (where sexual and aggressive Id instincts dynamically drive for satisfaction in the unconscious mind, in opposition to the Superego unconscious conscience, being refereed by the hopefully strong enough Ego), Freud attempted to explain how healthy people come to not only *recognize* the importance of interpersonal and social boundaries, as might occur by observational learning, but *embrace* their importance in their unconscious mind, thereby experiencing them in a manner that carries a high emotional valance.

Freud held that an individual's resolution of the Oedipal Crisis produces a greater unconscious *desire* to comply with laws and social mores to build meaningful connections with others and not jeopardize such connections by destructive acts. The greater desire for closeness (over any competing hostile or selfish motives) provides the basis for a capacity that is fundamental to healthy sexual relating. Failure to accept the limits imposed on one's sexual and relational desires creates the

[8]The interested reader may want to compare Freud's *Three Essays on the Theory of Sexuality* (Freud, 1905/1949), bearing in mind the era and cultural context in which it was written, with the DSM chapter on *Paraphilic Disorders* (American Psychiatric Association, 2013b).

precondition for sexual offending. In other words, Freud considered the criminal sexual act to be predicated on a personality flaw originating in early childhood resulting from never fully accepting the 'no' for an answer articulated by others or by circumstances—others including individuals and society in the form of its lore and laws.

Had Fr. Paul been analyzed by Freud early in his career when he was formulating his Seduction Theory, great weight would have been placed on the fact that Fr. Paul had been sexually abused by an older boy beginning before his earliest memories and continuing well into his adolescence, by which time the perpetrator was an adult. Many of the details of the abuse were dissociated at the time of referral to me, but as we brought the memories more sharply into focus, the full meaning of the experiences was revealed. Initially, the sexual interactions were very aggressive with the force of the assaults causing young Paul considerable pain and emotional suffering. However, Paul came to experience the physical sensations as pleasurable and his relationship with the older boy ostensibly became one less characterized by domination and submission. Nevertheless, the unconscious psychodynamics of the relationship remained sadomasochistic.

Freud (1915) argued that criminality is one outcome of unconscious guilt. Freud might have interpreted Fr. Paul's sexual predation on children as being motivated by the unconscious guilt that resulted from the sinful pleasure he experienced during his period as a child victim of harmful sexual behavior. Fr. Paul was ordinarily a very methodical and orderly man who proved himself capable of achieving high academic performance and high status within the organization in which he worked, the Catholic Church. He was in no way insane, but he was prone to primary process thinking regarding his pattern of relating and conceptualizing his relationships with children. Fr. Paul considered children and young adolescent boys his equal and he considered their sexual activities as play or intimacy that was mutually initiated and enjoyed.

All victim statements would suggest the children's experience and recollections could not be more antithetical to Fr. Paul's conscious perception. By drawing attention to the many defense mechanisms Fr. Paul utilized throughout treatment, Freud would have most certainly identified the reversal of sadomasochism that Fr. Paul endured in childhood, to be the one who held power and control over the vulnerable boy he once was. Freud would have considered Fr. Paul to have an oral fixation based on the majority of evidence and the delight with which Fr. Paul occasionally re-experienced when talking about his offenses. Freud would have encouraged Fr. Paul to free associate while lying on the couch five times a week. In return, Freud would have listened closely and offered interpretations based on his theories with the expectation that his theories were correct, his interpretations were accurate and the insight that they imparted would have been sufficiently mutative to cause the amelioration of Fr. Paul's perversion.

The study of 'perverse' and 'sadomasochistic' unconscious processes that began with Freud continues to this day with each of the schools of thought identified above adding to the heterogeneity of insights and recommendations for treatment. For example, Lacan argued that the origin of perversion is not found in the fact of the individual engaging in habitually "abnormal" or transgressive sexual acts but, rather, of occupying a particular structural position in relation to the 'Other.' Correspondence with Lacanian theory and the case material provided by Fr. Paul in his psychotherapy sessions is found in his experience of alienation throughout his life, seeing himself as set apart from his peers and neighbours during childhood, and as inadequate throughout his adult life, and resulting in unconscious, disavowed psychic castration. Lacanians would conceptualise Fr. Paul's perversion as a result of excessive *jouissance* and a core belief that the law and social norms are weak, if not fraudulent. Fr. Paul's frank disclosures of his sexual experience with his victims strongly support the notion of him being in a state of dysregulated ecstatic pleasure when abusing them. No case material is found to support the notion that Fr. Paul consciously held essentially antisocial core beliefs. However, given that his criminal actions were unambiguously antisocial, for example, organising several pre-pubescent altar boys to engage in sexual activity in the sacristy as a group for his pleasure, it can be argued that he must have questioned the validity of law and lore about sexual violence toward children at least unconsciously.[9]

De Masi (2003) provides a useful grouping of three psychodynamic perspectives or viewpoints about sexual perversions, not including Lacan's contribution. He refers to theories that stayed close to Freud's drive theory and sexual stages of development as *First Paradigm Theories*.[10] Ego Psychologists W.H. Gillespie (1956), Mervin Glasser (1986), and Janine Chasseguet-Smirgel (1984) are fine examples of this perspective. *Second Paradigm Theories* comprise trauma and relational theories which conceptualize perversion as a way of repairing or defending against traumatic experiences held in the unconscious mind. Theorists who are listed in this grouping include the founder of Self Psychology, Heinz Kohut (1977), and Object Relations theorists, Donald Winnicott (1945) and Joyce McDougall (1995). *Third Paradigm Theories* conceptualize perversion as the sexualization of power and cruelty, resulting from a splitting of self whereby the perverse self dominates. Theorists in this grouping include Object Relations theorists, Melanie Klein (1932), Donald Meltzer (1973), and Herbert Rosenfeld (1987). De Masi places Object Relations theorist, Robert Stoller (1975) outside these categories and De Masi's theory as advancing beyond the three categories.

Perhaps with the exception of Heinz Kohut, each of these theories is predicated on the Individualist Paradigm in that they conceptualize the sex offender as the possessor of an isolated, damaged mind. Examples of these viewpoints are given below.

---

[9] A more comprehensive description of theory and application of Lacanian Psychoanalyis in relation to sex offending is beyond the scope of this chapter. Those interested in exploring the Lacanian approach to assessing and treating sex offenders are directed to Swales (2012) who explores the etiology, characteristics, symptoms, and fundamental fantasy of perversion. Presenting one case of a neurotic sex offender and another of a perverse sex offender, Swales proposes a guide to making differential diagnoses between psychotic, neurotic, and perverse patients, and offers a treatment model for working with either the structure of perversion or of neurosis.

[10] While De Masi uses the term 'paradigm,' perhaps 'viewpoints' or 'perspectives' would better describe his categorization, leaving the term 'paradigm' to remain faithful to its philosophical use as defined above.

As will be seen, these positions continue to hold value in understanding the internal world of the offender. The problem is not in the ideas themselves, as they have evolved over substantial periods of theory development. Each theory has found support from many clinicians who recognize the same or similar patterns played out in the offender's mental life and, at times, in the consulting room. The problem occurs when the ideas are absolutized and universalized and are thereby taken as axiomatic and complete.

No matter how helpful a theory may be, a doctrinaire omniscient approach to the application of that theory risks confirmation bias and closes down the psychoanalyst's thinking about other possible explanations. The top-down, theory-driven intervention style of the Individualist Paradigm has been challenged and replaced by a bottom-up approach of the Social Paradigm that, rather than rejecting the validity of theories, carries them lightly. Evidence can be found in the case of Fr. Paul that brings theories such as these to life, helping the analyst think about what unconscious processes *may* have led the individual offender to commit his or her crimes.

Ego Psychologist, Mervin Glasser (1986) developed Freud's (1905/1949) ideas of perversion as "the convergence of several motive forces" (p. 162), aggression being one, by proposing a 'Core Complex.' Noting Freud's recognition of the intimate relation between aggression and anxiety (Freud, 1926), Glasser (1979) considered aggression as essentially one of the ego's responses to threats to physiological or psychological homeostasis. Glasser (1986) elaborated that aggression always has a self-preservative function as "the aim of aggression is to eliminate, obliterate—essentially, to negate—the threat" (p. 9).

Taking Freud and Glasser's point of view, one that is held by Ego Psychologists and many contemporary psychoanalysts, sexual violence toward children or other vulnerable people arises as a defense against being overwhelmed by the threat of psychic annihilation. The powerful maneuver functions to alleviate unconscious anxieties that have arisen early in life from failure to adapt to developmental challenges, such as facing the limits of one's potency and having to tolerate going without when others get what they want—the Oedipus Complex. Instead of adapting normally to the developmental challenges of infancy, childhood, and adolescence (Erikson, 1963) the libidinal energy that powers the sex and aggression instincts become recruited to protect the self from the unconsciously perceived threat of annihilation. The merger of sexual and aggressive forces produces a defense where the other is psychically annihilated in the mind of the offender. With the treat defeated, unconscious anxieties remain unconscious and not faced.

From this perspective, Fr. Paul's sexual abuse of boys served to protect him from facing the repressed and denied aspects of his life that were overwhelming. Fr. Paul had an intense love for his mother whom he idealized. Ego psychologists would argue that every infant child seeks a complete merger with his mother as she is perceived as the one who can gratify all security needs. As the Oedipal Complex plays out, the child is forced to accept the mother's inevitable failures to meet these needs and individuate from her. Resentment toward the father for retaining the intimate relationship with the mother is also relaxed at this time when all goes well. But for the child who has a mother who also seeks merger and does not want the infant to individuate, the Oedipal challenge is all the greater.

The process of individuation is even more difficult for the child if the relationship between the parents is problematic. Such was the case in Fr. Paul's extremely violent home. Fr. Paul's father was alcohol dependent and might easily have met the criteria for Borderline Personality Disorder or Bipolar Disorder. During the first sessions with me, Fr. Paul was able to report incidents that occurred in his childhood such as witnessing his father forcing his mother to the floor choking her or seeing her bruises or the blood on the floor, or witnessing panicked neighbors run into the house to protect his mother. His emotional response was of great distress as one might expect. But these memories could not be thought about nor the meaning for him or the impact of these experiences considered. An ego psychologist might argue that Fr. Paul was never able to individuate from his mother due to the desperate circumstances in which she lived. Likewise, he was never able to face the truth of his much-loved father also being a violent wife-beater.

Reflections about these traumatic experiences throughout the psychotherapeutic treatment strengthened Fr. Paul's capacity to feel feelings that were prohibited—feelings of terror, powerlessness, love, and hate. By being more in touch with his feelings about these early traumatic issues, as was the case in exploring his experience as a sexually abused boy, Fr. Paul became increasingly able to recognize the feelings of terror, powerlessness, love, and hate that his victims had for him. This realization was antithetical to his previously held belief that the children involved were as powerful as he perceived himself to be, and they enjoyed their sexual encounters equally to him. Joyce McDougall's theory of perverse behavior is included as one of Di Masi's second paradigm theories that conceptualize perversion as a way of repairing or defending against traumatic experiences held in the internal world of the unconscious mind. McDougall (1995) argues that individuals who sexually abuse suffer from an unindividuated and poorly integrated self and are dependent upon others for a sense of integrity. Offenders are soothed by using others to gain a sense of self. Their dependence on the other to serve this function gives rise to the compulsive quality of sexual perversion.

Object Relations theorist, Timothy Keogh makes an important distinction between types of sex offenders and the usefulness of the theories of Joyce McDougall (1995) and Franco De Masi (2003). Keogh (2012) argues that McDougall's theory applies best to "sexual perversion which involves sensation-dominated (non-lexical) self, as seen in the attachment hungry pedophile, who engages in compulsive, sexualized behavior with an object that is used to maintain his sense of self" (p. 71), whereas De Masi's theory of perversion is best applied to understanding the more sadistic, psychopathic sex offender. De Masi contends that all psychoanalytic accounts of perversion, regardless of the viewpoint of the theorist have until now been inadequate in accounting for the sadomasochistic quality of some offending. De Masi proposed that perversion originates during infancy when the child learns to take flight from unwanted experiences by engaging in a psychic withdrawal and taking delight in the experience of sadomasochistic excitation resulting from being destructive. According to De Masi, the excitation in sadomasochistic perversion is directly related to the sexualization of primary, instinctual destructiveness.

Fr. Paul did not meet the criteria of a psychopath (Hare, 2003) although there was a schizoid quality to his presentation (self-state) under some circumstances (Fairbairn, 1940, 1944/52; Guntrip, 1952/1969, 1969). That said, it is not hard to imagine De Masi interpreting Paul's perverse excitation as being directly related to a sexualization of his instinctual destructiveness. Paul was exposed to a great deal of destructiveness in the home and, if there is such a thing as primary destructiveness as some psychoanalytic schools continue to contend, then Paul's instinctual destructiveness would certainly have been inflamed by his traumatic experiences during infancy. Evidence may be found in Paul being harmed by his own destructiveness which resulted in his inability to form a truly loving relationship that was not based on a less obvious sadomasochistic dynamic. However, while Paul's personality was clearly narcissistic he was not psychopathic. He could well be described as an attachment-hungry pedophile with a poorly integrated self who became dependent upon children and young adolescent boys for a sense of psychological integrity. He felt strong sexual arousal to them, to be sure, but he also spent many hours idealizing them as the kind of boy he never was—confident, cheeky, and full of vitality. The sheer number of his victims and the thousands of sexual offenses he admitted give strong evidence to the compulsive quality of his sexual perversion.

The theory of perversion offered by Robert Stoller is outside De Masi's three categories but is well worthy of mention. As the title of one of his many impressive books on psychoanalytic theory indicates, Stoller (1975) conceptualized perversion as the erotic form of hatred. As with Second Paradigm theorists, Stoller considered perversion as an adult triumph over the unconscious hatred arising from childhood trauma by sexualizing it. Again, Fr. Paul's life before entering the seminary was filled with trauma.

The five viewpoints described above (including De Masi's three paradigms, Stollar's theory, and De Masi's theory) are predicated on general theories of psychoanalysis postulated by the psychoanalytic schools wedded to the Individual Paradigm. These include Freud's (1900/2001, 1910b) Oedipus complex, Mahler's (1971) theory of separation-individuation, Klein's (1975) paranoid-schizoid and depressive positions, Kohut's (1977) idealizing, mirroring, and twinship longings, etc. In contrast, Social psychoanalytic theories do not postulate particular psychological contents of the individual's internal world, contents that are presumed to be universally salient in personality development and pathogenesis. From a social perspective, Individualist theorists too often make the mistake of absolutizing and universalizing one, two, or three important patterns they have identified that might explain human phenomena, declaring them to be causal of healthy or pathological development for every person. Social psychoanalytic theorists may value such "content" theories but mostly seek to build "process" theories that focus on the multiple bio-psycho-social and environmental systems that give rise to human behavior. By doing so, relational iterations of forensic psychoanalysis aim to provide a fuller understanding of sexual abuse phenomena including sex offending.

Contemporary psychanalytic field theorist, Andrea Celenza (2014), defines the term 'perversion' as "problematic and psychically harmful or deadened modes of relating" (p. 82). By conceptualizing perversion as intersubjective phenomenon—"a mode of relating"—Celenza corrects traditional psychoanalytic definitions that designate a specific behavior, comprising the sexual object and aim, as perverse. Celenza's definition of perversion not only supports the recognition of sexual violence as an interpersonal phenomenon but calls for a deeper analysis of sexual violence that explores the offender's experience, the victim's experience, and the co-created, emergent experience within the victim-perpetrator dyad.[11]

Celenza's definition of perversion as psychic harm includes occasions where perverse processes take place both interpersonally and intra-psychically. The psychoanalytic perspective of sexual violence as a 'perversion' not only includes interpersonal acts but goes further and deeper to include mental acts of violence upon the self (that may or may not lead to violence towards others at a later time) as well as leave open the possibility that even apparently accidental or reflexive acts may be the sequela of unconscious processes that cause harm. The harm of perversion can be that which is done to one's own body or the body of another, and one's own mind or the mind of another. This violence to self or other may be conscious or unconscious. Arguably, offenders are simultaneously harming themselves and the child—both mentally and socially—and, by extension, the community as a whole.

Whereas much has been written about the harmful effects of sexual assault there has been little exploration about the quality of victim-perpetrator relating. Even less has been written about the relationship of victim-perpetrator dyads to the communities from within which both people have emerged. That which has been written typically fails to consider the dynamics of sexual violence as bio-psycho-social phenomena in all their complexity. Psychoanalytic Complexity Theory addresses this deficiency by conceptualizing the child sex offender as a complex, dynamic, nonlinear, adaptive system that is only one part of a larger system of systems.

Psychoanalytic Complexity Theory is a metatheoretical framework that has emerged from the dialogue between contemporary, relational, two-person psychoanalytic schools and developments in complexity science. The current author has argued elsewhere that Psychoanalytic Complexity Theory compliments mainstream forensic approaches for treating sex offenders, adding depth to the therapeutic inquiry and broadening the treatment goals (Webster, 2015, 2017a, 2017c, 2018). Psychoanalytic Complexity Theory is predicated on and defines sex offending within the terms of the Social Paradigm.

> Sexual offending is conceptualized as an emergent property of a limitless multitude of systems and subsystems. The actual behavior perpetrated by an individual is understood as a patterned emotional experience that emerges and self-organizes in specific contexts, and

[11] Exploration of these kinds of questions should be conducted with due care by a well-trained forensic psychoanalyst or psychotherapist who recognises and reinforces the fact that sexual assault is solely the perpetrator's responsibility and that gaining a deeper understanding of the psychodynamics that have given rise to sexual offending is essential to expanding the offender's freedom to make child-safe decisions in the future particularly when vulnerable to recidivate.

> with the cooperation of many parts. Sexual offending emerges from not only the cognitive-affective-physiological subsystems that may be thought of as self-states in the individual… but also as systems made up of the embodied relational matrix – which may involve the subjectivity of the child [victim], his or her parents… other members of [the] community… [and] the wider social, historical and cultural systems are also recognized to be at play (Webster, 2018, p. 86).

Psychoanalytic literature is filled with the stories of people who have experienced intransigent symptoms, whether they be hysterical paralyzes, disturbing hallucinations, or commonplace depressions or anxieties. Taking into account the findings of complexity science, all living organisms make choices at every moment and every bifurcation point in the process of adaptation. Even a single-celled organism continually responds to the question: 'Do I repeat, or do I change?' (Capra & Luisi, 2014). As agentic beings, forensic psychotherapy from a psychoanalytic complexity perspective contends that sex offenders have the capacity to make choices that will affect the course of their lives—and, of course, the lives of others. Sex offenders, like the rest of us, make choices all the time with varying degrees of awareness even though they may not experience themselves as being agentic.

Forensic psychoanalysis from the perspective of Psychoanalytic Complexity Theory builds a sense of agency by facilitating a patient's awareness of their patterned behavior, its consequences, and its meanings. Such an evolution in the patient's conceptual subsystem not only changes his embodied system as a whole, but it builds, or rebuilds, awareness of his agentic capacity. Such an emphasis on change and relationship leads to a process of 're-humanization,' rather than to the 'dehumanization' that is often experienced by offenders as a result of the reactions of an angry and traumatized community.

In addition to the most obvious measure of effective treatment for the sex offender being the permanent cessation of such sexually abusive behavior, the 'effectiveness' of forensic psychoanalysis includes the analytic couple's confidence that a wider range of treatment goals have been achieved. Rather than these goals being limited to those defined and predetermined by reductive models such as the Risk-Need-Responsivity model (Andrews & Bonta, 2010; Bonta & Andrews, 2016), the desired outcomes of forensic psychoanalytic treatment are co-constructed in the emergent relational process established between the psychoanalyst and the patient (which is also informed by relevant research given the psychoanalysts forensic training). By forming a closely attuned, empathic, and challenging therapeutic relationship, forensic psychoanalysis promotes the sex offender's sense of dignity and worth by recognizing his uniqueness, and, therefore, meeting his unique treatment needs.

Fr. Paul had learned his lessons from the custodial treatment program well and he was quite rightly assessed as sufficiently rehabilitated to return to the community albeit on strict parole conditions. He wanted a deeper understanding of himself and felt this would help him achieve his goal of never reoffending. I assessed Fr. Paul as having a genuine motivation for treatment and the psychological capacity to make use of treatment guided by Psychoanalytic Complexity Theory. The goal of the joint endeavor was for Fr. Paul to gain greater leverage over his behavior and improve his mental life by helping him discover aspects of himself that he until then did not want to face or could not face alone. The method of achieving such leverage was by offering him a therapeutic relationship where his attachment needs for a safe, trustworthy, stable, and thoughtful other are met and form the basis for allowing prohibited material to come to consciousness awareness for analysis.

Fr. Paul was painfully aware of his conscious feelings at the time we began working together. It was the experience of being cared for and listened to that felt so alien. Over the first five years of treatment, I empathically tracked and inquired about Fr. Paul's affect. Gradually, a story unfolded that made sense of his many strengths, his emergent ‘perversion,’ and the choices that he had made. We discovered that beneath all of his sadness and shame, lay enormous unexpressed anger. He was not only angry about the things he was responsible for—what he had done to others and himself—but also angry about aspects of his upbringing over which he had had no control. These included his exposure to extreme domestic violence, his extensive experience of child sexual abuse perpetrated by an older boy throughout his childhood and adolescence, and his inculcation into the sexually oppressive and dogmatic culture of the Catholic Church.

Fr. Paul was free of his post-traumatic stress and anxiety symptoms within the first two years of treatment. He built healthy relationships with others and engaged in meaningful, age-appropriate, child-safe activities. With previously unavailable and unspeakable material out in the open, Fr. Paul began to build greater self-awareness and sensitivity about his impact on others. His awareness of his wrongdoing expanded with his growing capacity for empathy. His remorse became more other-centered, deeper, and excruciatingly painful. He never forgave himself for what he did to all those boys and regretted every perverse thought and act of abuse he perpetrated on them. He anguished over the harm he had caused each victim and prayed for their healing every day. The knowledge gained from his manualized cognitive treatment was integrated more deeply into his personality, thereby strengthening his protective factors against reoffending. No post-release allegations were made against Fr. Paul and only historical matters we alleged later in his life. His rehabilitation was holistic and, in the opinion of the author, successful.

4.5 Clinical Concepts Related to Sex Offending

Freud conceptualized the interpretation of unconscious material and processes as the single cause of therapeutic action. He considered that his patients' psychopathology would be cured by providing an insightful interpretation of their inner world that they, until then, could not have been aware of. Freud quickly recognized that patients can not only respond favorably to the ‘correct interpretation’ but resist it. In response, Freud famously developed the previously unheard-of, and now the commonly accepted and applied concept of ‘defense mechanisms.’ Defense mechanisms are unconscious psychological processes that function to protect the self/person from anxiety-producing thoughts and feelings arising from either internal conflicts or environmental stressors. A more contemporary view is that defense mechanisms function to fend off internal emotional dysregulation and preserve relational ties with others in the external world.

Freud identified ten defense mechanisms, as cataloged by his psychoanalyst-daughter, Anna. These comprised repressions, regression, reaction formation, isolation, undoing, projection, introjection, turning against one's own person, reversal into the opposite, and sublimation or displacement (Freud, 1937/2018). The conceptualization of these and more defense mechanisms have been elaborated by many theorists and researchers over the following decades, including that elicited from longitudinal research examined by George Vaillant and colleagues. Vaillant proposed a four-level, hierarchical classification of defense mechanisms. At the most severe level, Level I, are what he termed Pathological Defenses which include psychotic denial and delusional projection. At Level II are Immature Defenses which include fantasy, projection, passive aggression, and acting out. At Level III are Neurotic Defenses, comprising intellectualization, reaction formation, dissociation, displacement, and repression. And finally, at Level IV are the healthiest of defenses, the Mature Defenses of humor, sublimation, suppression, altruism, and anticipation (Vaillant, 1977/1998, 1994; Vaillant et al., 1986). Recognition of and discussion about unconscious defenses is now a staple of the psychotherapeutic process.

Traditional psychoanalysis was defined by patients laying on the couch, attending four or five sessions each week for many years, engaging in free association, and listening to the psychoanalyst's interpretations. However, the relational turn has radically changed how psychoanalysts engage with their patients. The traditional method of the patient laying on the couch with the analyst sitting behind is a very effective structure that supports the technique of free association. However, greater recognition of the benefits of face-to-face engagement between patient and psychoanalyst, and greater weight given to the patient's preferences have resulted in the couch being an option that now tends to be used judiciously and with flexibility. Most treatments occur with both the analyst and patient being seated.

Some patients need, want, and can afford up to five sessions a week, but the majority of therapies occur at lesser frequencies. Some treatments can last for years and still be productive while other treatments are more time limited. Some patients simply want their symptoms or troubles to be addressed and then terminate treatment, while others want more time in the therapeutic relationship to discover more about themselves or because their needs are ongoing and they value the unique support offered by a psychoanalytic experience.

Blagys and Hilsenroth (2006) delineated seven interventions that distinguish psychodynamic therapy from other forms of treatment in terms of techniques and processes. According to their research, psychodynamic therapy is distinguished by: "(1) a focus on affect and the expression of patients' emotions; (2) an exploration of patients' attempts to avoid topics or engage in activities that hinder the progress of therapy; (3) the identification of patterns in patients' actions, thoughts, feelings, experiences, and relationships; (4) an emphasis on past experiences; (5) a focus on a patients' interpersonal experiences; (6) an emphasis on the therapeutic relationship; and (7) an exploration of patients' wishes, dreams, or fantasies" (p. 167).

Otto Kernberg lists the four essential aspects of traditional psychoanalytic technique comprising interpretation, transference analysis, countertransference analysis, and technical neutrality. Interpretation refers to the verbal communication from the analyst to the patient of their hypothesis about the unconscious conflict that in their view is dominant, based on the contents of what the patient said during the session. Interpretations are typically about the patient's inner world defenses, followed by an interpretation of the context in which that defensive maneuver occurs, or the unconscious internal 'impulsive' relationship against which the defense is erected, and the analysis of what motivated the defensive process. Internal world psychoanalysts are trained in formulating interpretations according to a simple formula but one that is challenging to 'get right.' A good interpretation requires "a) clarification, by which the analyst attempts to clarify what is consciously going on in the patient's mind; b) confrontation, that is, tactful bringing into awareness nonverbal aspects of the patient's behavior; and c) interpretation proper, the analyst's proposed hypothesis of the unconscious meaning that relates all these aspects of the patient's communication to each other" (Kernberg, 2016, p. 287).

The importance of strict rules about interpretation as a technique has been challenged by relational psychoanalysts due to the restricted, top-down, knowing approach that is now considered counter-therapeutic, and mystifying to the patient. As indicated above, some contemporary psychoanalysts reject the internal world concept outright, so they would never 'presume' to make any claims about knowing what is going on in the mind of another. Their communication 'with' the patient is more mutual and therefore conversational. Relational psychoanalysts, such as those who have adopted Specificity Theory (Bacal, 2011), are open to engaging in both forms of communication with their patients, judging at the moment what is most likely to be the 'optimal response' (Bacal, 1985) at the time.

'Transference,' according to Kernberg (2016), refers to the patient's unconscious repetition of pathogenic conflicts from the past played out in the here and now within the therapeutic relationship. Where once the psychoanalyst relied exclusively on the verbal data provided by the patient, contemporary approaches reflect on the patient's total verbal and nonverbal, explicit and implicit communication designed to influence or affect the analyst in a certain direction. 'Transference' has traditionally been considered the main source of unconscious material requiring consistent exploration to illuminate aspects of the patient's internal world as it engages in the here-and-now relationship with the psychoanalyst. Analysis of the transference remains the defining quality and practice of psychoanalysis regardless of the paradigm or school of thought. However, the relational turn has brought a greater emphasis on making use of countertransference. Further, relational approaches recognize that both transference and countertransference are co-creating phenomena, shifting the focus from what occurs in the internal world of the patient to what unconscious processes take place between the patient and the psychoanalyst.

Freud was the first to formulate the concept of countertransference, seeing it as a problem, stating, "We have become aware of the 'countertransference,' which arises in him [the analyst] as a result of the patient's influence on his unconscious feelings, and we are almost inclined to insist that he shall recognize this counter-transference in himself and overcome it" (Freud, 1910a, pp. 144–145). Freud went on to advocate for emotional coldness in the response to the patient's transference, for both the analyst's protection and for the benefit of the patient. Freud insisted, "I cannot advise my colleagues too urgently to model themselves during psycho-analytic treatment on the surgeon, who puts aside all his feelings, even his human sympathy, and concentrates his mental forces on the single aim of performing the operation as skillfully as possible" (Freud, 1912/1958, p. 115). Whether Freud faithfully followed his directions for clinical distance is now considered doubtful (Lynn & Vaillant, 1998).

Countertransference refers to the psychoanalysts' moment-to-moment response in their engagement with the patient. From an internal world perspective, the psychoanalyst is represented as having an emotional reaction to the unconscious mind of the patient. In a sense, the psychoanalyst's experience is of being 'done to' by the patient, so their reactions to the patient are felt as a reaction rather than an emergent property of the analytic dyad. Even in the most contemporary view of internal world theories, "countertransference is that of a complex formation co-determined by the analyst's reaction to the patient's transference, to the reality of the patient's life, to the reality of the analyst's life, and to specific transference dispositions activated in the analyst as a reaction to the patient and his/her material" (Kernberg, 2016, p. 287). In contrast, a two-person description might go as follows: Countertransference is a psychological construct that represents the psychoanalyst's experience of the complex co-created, bi-directional, whole-person-to-whole-person exchange of implicit and explicit communication of conscious and unconscious processes, within the context of a dyadic system of mutual influence. Where the Individualist psychoanalyst will make transference interpretations about the goings on in the patient's internal world while being mindful of their personal reactions to the patient, the relational psychoanalyst will try to open a conversation about what might be happening for the patient and psychoanalyst with the benefit of clues that have been noticed by either one of them.

The golden rules of earlier iterations of psychoanalysis were anonymity, neutrality, and abstinence. These have been rejected in their extreme forms by contemporary psychoanalysts who embrace the Social Paradigm as being unrealistic at best, and abusive when applied without due regard to the patient's sensibilities. Before the relational turn, psychoanalysts were trained to strictly observe these rules of non-gratification that required them to avoid influencing the patient, giving no information about themselves to the patient (including about their emotional reactions), not agreeing or disagreeing with the patient, nor taking sides with the patient's internal conflicts, and offering nothing more than interpretations based on established theory. In the extreme, patients were not given a greeting at the door, offered a tissue when they cried, or a kind word when feeling terrible.

The intention of the 'blank screen' approach was a good one. It was thought that the patient's anxiety would be raised by not gratifying their wishes and that their reaction to this deprivation would expose their unconscious processes to the observing analyst. The psychoanalyst would interpret the material observed and the patient would be cured by this insight. Of course, any scientist will think of the observer effect identified in physics where it is recognized that the system being observed is disturbed by the act of observation. The traditional therapeutic relationship was far from a process of naturalistic observation. A key realization of relationalists has been the fact that patients know a lot more about us than we think even if we are cautious about what we disclose, so the idea of the analyst being a 'blank screen' is now recognized as a myth.

Otto Kernberg makes a strong case that perhaps most psychoanalysts would endorse when he says, "Technical neutrality implies a natural and sincere approach to the patient within general socially appropriate behavior, as part of which the analyst avoids all references or focus upon his/her own life interests or problems. The analyst cannot avoid that personal features emerge in the treatment situation, and do become the source of transference reactions. The patient's realistic reaction to realistic aspects of the analyst's behavior should not be considered a transference reaction: not everything is transference! Maintaining the definition of transference as an inappropriate reaction to the reality presented by the analyst, that reflects the activation of the patient's unconscious conflicts, should differentiate transference from other patient's realistic reactions to natural, as well as idiosyncratic, aspects of the treatment situation" (Kernberg, 2016, p. 287).

Regardless of how one conceptualizes transference and countertransference phenomena, psychoanalysts prioritize their attunement to the transference of the patient to gain a deeper understanding of what they are experiencing, how they think, and how they relate to others. This is no less the case for those who treat sex offenders. Sex offenders like any other cohort are bound to perceive the therapist and the therapeutic relationship in a wide range of ways, including positive, negative, and sexual transferences. Psychoanalysts engage with transference phenomena, albeit in different ways, as a crucial part of the 'working through' of as yet unresolved psychological issues. Patients whose sexual offending is given rise by perverse or sadomasochistic unconscious processes are likely to put pressure on the analyst to engage in perverse or sadomasochistic countertransference enactments. The interaction between patient and psychoanalyst may present at first glance anywhere from benign to malevolent but closer inspection may well reveal all is not what it seems. Failure to address transference and countertransference phenomena is destructive to the patient-psychoanalyst dyad, thereby hampering treatment progress or resulting in treatment failure. However, therapeutic action at least begins to take place when the analytic couple finds a way to make the pathological unconscious dynamics conscious.

Ogden (1996) suggested that the analysis of perversion may be seen as having evolved through three phases. First, it was fundamentally considered a process of decoding and interpreting the unconscious fantasies, anxieties, and defenses enacted in the perverse patient's sexual activity. Second, the analysis was viewed as centrally involving the understanding and interpretation of transference phenomena that were structured by the patient's perverse internal object world (Malcolm, 1970; Meltzer, 1973). Ogden provided the third phase, arguing that "the analysis of perversion necessarily involves the analysis of the perverse transference-countertransference as it unfolds in the analytic relationship… In analyzing perversion, one cannot hope to understand what the patient is attempting to communicate without to some extent entering into the perverse scene that is being created in the transference-countertransference" (Ogden, 1996, p. 1122). In Ogden's opinion, the therapeutic action of psychoanalysis would only truly take effect if both the analyst and patient recognize their contribution to and participation in the perverse intersubjective construction that is "powerfully shaped by the perverse structure of the patient's unconscious internal object world" (Ogden, 1996, p. 1121).

Forensic psychoanalysis, as conceptualized by this author, explores the conscious and unconscious processes of people who break the laws of society and thereby cause harm to others. Forensic psychoanalysis is, therefore, a study of the processes of relationships between victim and perpetrator within the socio-cultural context—the latter being embodied by the community within which both victim and perpetrator have emerged as "members of the human family" (United Nations General Assembly, 1948). Forensic psychoanalysis provides the basis for respectful, responsible, and effective rehabilitation initiatives that prioritize the human rights of all. This approach recognizes the offender's right to exist as a unique person, and his right to be treated justly and with dignity. These values augment, rather than contradict, the overriding value that every child has the right to protection from sexual abuse, and, as well, enhance society's goal to provide a safe environment in which all children can thrive (United Nations General Assembly, 1989).

Forensic psychoanalysis from a relational perspective draws from any or all of the psychoanalytic schools of thought and technique and is informed by current research and treatment models as they emerge in the disciplines of forensic psychology and criminology. More precisely, it is made up of a system of ideas and is, *coëxsistentia*, a conceptual sub-system of the whole system of scholarship that includes but is not limited to, psychology, sociology, anthropology, criminology, physiology, and philosophy. As a member of this scholarly network, forensic psychoanalysis is both informed by and informs other disciplines.

The application of forensic psychoanalytic theory in the clinical setting also occurs in a dialogic relationship with other treatment approaches, especially those supported by strong empirical evidence that has found broad acceptance across the field of forensic psychology. Fr. Paul had the benefit of successfully undertaking a manualized, evidence-based custodial treatment program by the time we met. This put me as his treating clinician in a position of advancing and deepening the gains he made in prison. There were many times that Fr. Paul raised for discussion the 'rules' he had learned in the cognitive behavioral therapy program, while never questioning their validity. We were able to personalize his experience of these truths by discovering how these same rules were obliterated by others during his childhood and corrupted his perception of reality when it comes to intimate human relationships.

Had Fr. Paul not had the benefit of the earlier treatment, the treatment goals as recommended by models such as the Risk-Need-Responsivity Model (Andrews & Bonta, 2010; Bonta & Andrews, 2016) *and* the Good Lives Model (Ward & Beech, 2006; Ward et al., 1995, 2012) would have been addressed both implicitly and explicitly. The goals would not have been pursued in a manualized manner but instead integrated as part of the holistic goals of treatment that emerged in the psychoanalytic process in the context of a therapeutic relationship. In this way, forensic psychotherapy must retain a 'both-and' inclusive but informed attitude toward theory and practice rather than limit itself to an 'either-or' binary attitude that limits understanding and promotes dogmatism that diminishes and disrespects ideas outside the orthodoxy. In this way, forensic psychoanalysis also retains its traditions of valuing uniqueness and wholeness of the person and challenges the culture of absolutism and universalization that has pervaded theories predicated on the Individualist Paradigm—be they from psychodynamic or other perspectives such as mainstream forensic psychology.

Contemporary forensic psychoanalysis, predicated on the Social Paradigm, recognizes that individuals are contextualized by their personal histories and culture, are embedded in relational matrices, and are subjects in a non-linear, dynamic process of becoming (Webster, 2018). Forensic psychoanalytic treatment creates a field within which a mutative relationship is co-created between two agents: (1) the professionally trained psychoanalytic psychotherapist who has developed scholarship in forensic issues; and (2) the person who has been or is currently accused of committing a criminal offense. The analytic couple enters a process that aims to build (a) a shared understanding of the particular conscious and unconscious bio-psycho-social processes from which the forensic patient's criminal behavior has emerged; (b) an appreciation of the impact of such behavior on the patient's relationships with significant others and with society as a whole; and (c) personal agency that drives and empowers pro-social behavior. The therapeutic relationship remains the defining medium of psychoanalytic interventions where the implicit and explicit processes of subject-to-subject relating are the locus of therapeutic action—the canvas, if you will, upon which the co-creative dyad lives out a process of 'becoming.' Part of that 'becoming' is a greater awareness of the patterns of feelings, organizing principles, and responses to the behaviors of others, as well as the impact of those responses on others.

Contemporary psychoanalysts recognize that any process that emerges within the analytic relationship can neither be predicted nor determined. Psychoanalysis has always been distinguished from other therapeutic approaches by creating and keeping open a non-directive space within which the patient can both discover and follow his or her path of personal growth. While the typical aim of a psychoanalytic journey is to become increasingly free to make better decisions (agency) that lead to an improved quality of mental life and enjoyment of the interconnectedness of human relationships, the more urgent aim of Forensic Psychoanalysis is for the patient to do no harm to themselves or others.

It is to be expected that perverse processes will be discovered within the therapeutic dyad, and here the author is in total agreement with Ogden in that these processes must be actively engaged. Forensic Psychoanalysis, therefore, has a mandate not only to offer support for and containment of charged affective processes associated with the patient's 'vulnerability' to perpetrate criminal acts against others, but also to directly engage, wrestle with, and confront perverse processes. Describing her work with one of her patients, Minne (2020), stated: "During sessions when he reported these ongoing activities and states of mind, it was crucial for me to sit with the gross disgust, terror, and anxiety, and occasionally let him know that he needed me to feel in our sessions just how he felt now but also, how he may have felt in earlier times—but without the excitement" (p. 18). Here, Minne is being truly present to her patient in body and mind, allowing herself to be open to true feelings without taking cover in the guise of 'professional distance.' By remaining 'experience near' to her patient and her own affective response and to what is occurring in the interpersonal field, at the same time maintaining her capacity for secondary process thinking, Minne can recognize the deeper, unconscious function and meaning of her intersubjective experience and communicate her insight to her patient.

While the sex offender's conscious thoughts, feelings, and behaviors are taken into account by the forensic psychoanalyst or psychotherapist, their greater value is found not in the explicit content of utterances or actions, but in the way these phenomena give clues to reveal the deeper workings of the offender's unconscious, dynamic processes—that is, their 'mind.' Engaging with the offender at this deeper level at which sexual violence toward children and other vulnerable people is given rise offers an opportunity not only to correct conscious attitudes and beliefs that promote sexual violence but access to the root causes of criminogenic unconscious processes, such as insecure attachment. While at times collaborators, and at other times challengers, the effective analytic couple must accept the relational challenge that inevitably means plunging into the abyss of perversion. This can present a psychic life-and-death struggle for the forensic patient and psychoanalyst—a struggle that is impossible to predict or to manualize. Insight and change can only come to light in a relationship that holds and welcomes all aspects of the person.

4.6 The Efficacy of Psychodynamic Treatment

Psychodynamic psychotherapy has received a lot of unfair criticism over the years with claims of inferiority to other treatments such as cognitive behavioral therapy. Eccleston and Ward (2006), for example, assert that "most therapists today acknowledge that psychodynamic approaches, which focus on helping child molesters gain insight into the causal mechanisms of their antisocial behaviors, are ineffective" (p. 224). Statements such as this, while not uncommon, are baseless except for the likely truth that "most therapists" believe such ill-informed claims to be true. The misrepresentation of psychodynamic theory and practice is reinforced when highly regarded researchers such as Eccleston and Ward whose reputation has been built on their outstanding research practices and theory development make such strong and sweeping claims without any reference to empirical evidence.

Descriptions of psychoanalytic theory and practice in forensic literature, when mentioned at all, are dated and fail to refer to the radical and diverse developments that have occurred in the field since the relational turn outlined in this chapter. Eccleston and Ward represent psychoanalytic practice as seeking only to assist sex offenders to gain insight into the causal mechanisms of their antisocial behaviors, a conceptualization of therapeutic action that has been obsolete for half a century, as described above. The notion of "causal mechanisms" is central to the Individualist Paradigm. Eccleston and Ward seem oblivious to the relational, postmodern turn described above. Similarly, Schwartz (2011) criticizes psychoanalysis for failing to incorporate social factors, thereby ignoring the paradigm shift that began at least three decades earlier, and the key concepts of contemporary psychoanalysis that have now long been embraced by almost all psychoanalytic schools. Perhaps "most therapists" would not be so confused about the shortcomings of psychoanalysis if highly esteemed leaders in the field did not perpetuate the logical fallacy of a straw-man argument where a position different to that which they are proposing is distorted into an extreme version of what is actually the case and then that extreme version is argued against.

The claim that psychodynamic approaches are "ineffective" is simply wrong. Not only has high-quality research produced favourable results in terms of treatment efficacy,[12] but reviews of studies that have found psychodynamic psychotherapy's treatment to be ineffective have exposed major shortcomings in research design and methodology (Wampold et al., 2017). In his review of the literature, Shedler (2018) identified problems in the research practices of studies that produced poor results for psychodynamic psychotherapy including sham control groups, cherry-picked patient samples, and suppression of findings that are contrary to the researchers' bias. Much of the efficacy research that has found the psychoanalytic perspective wanting does not distinguish what school of psychoanalysis or which psychoanalytic method is being tested, nor are trained psychoanalysts typically recruited to administer the procedure under examination.

Against a background of 'fake news,' considerable research has been undertaken to reestablish the standing of psychodynamic psychotherapy as an effective intervention. Perhaps the most robust and, therefore, convincing piece of research is the meta-analysis conducted by Steinert et al. (2017). This research aimed to systematically investigate the equivalence of psychodynamic psychotherapy to other established treatments by formally applying the logic of equivalence testing. Steinert et al. (2017) Steinert used "high methodological standards (e.g., controlling for researcher allegiance, applying the logic of equivalence testing, using one of the smallest margins ever suggested as compatible with equivalence, and using treatments established in efficacy as comparators)" (p. 7). The study included twenty-three randomized controlled trials involving 2751 patients and found psychodynamic therapy to be equivalent to treatments such as cognitive behavioral therapy that have established efficacy.

In a review of treatment efficacy literature, Solms (2018) concluded that psychoanalytic psychotherapy achieves at least as good as, and in some respects better outcomes than other evidence-based treatments currently used in psychiatry, including cognitive behavior therapy and psychopharmacological treatments. He argues

[12] The interested reader will find an extensive bibliography produced by the American Psychoanalytic Association addressing the compelling supportive evidence for psychodynamic perspectives on their website at https://apsa.org/research-bibliography.

that psychodynamic psychotherapy is a highly effective form of treatment in general with meta-analyses typically revealing effect sizes of between 0.73 and 0.85.[13] Agreeing with the findings of Steinert et al. (2017), Solms argues that psychoanalytic psychotherapy is equally effective as other forms of evidence-based psychotherapy. Further, Solms highlights evidence to suggest that the effects of psychoanalytic therapy last longer and may even increase after the end of the treatment. Solms cites a remarkable study from the prestigious Cochrane Database of Systematic Reviews undertaken by Abbass et al. (2006) into the efficacy of short-term psychoanalytic treatment yielded an overall effect of 0.97 in terms of general symptom improvement. Most remarkable is the finding that the effect size at follow-up increased to 1.51. A review of these findings was conducted eight years later by Abbass et al. (2014) who yielded an increase in overall effect size of 0.71. Again, the finding of maintained and increased effects at follow-up was reconfirmed.

Few examples of psychoanalytic treatment programs for sex offenders have been published. For example, Atascadero State Hospital in California was the first custodial treatment program for sex offenders in the United States. While it is reputed to have been successful in treating adult male sex offenders, publications to this effect are not readily available. An Australian residential treatment program for male clerical sex offenders, Encompass Australasia, was funded by the Australian Catholic Bishops Conference and the Australian Conference of Leaders of Religious Institutes between 1997 and 2008. Research into treatment outcomes was very positive (Cappo et al., 1998). The most famous of all sex offender treatment programs is that of the Portman Clinic which is an outpatient psychotherapy clinic of the United Kingdom's National Health Scheme, and part of the Tavistock and Portman NHS Foundation Trust in London. The Portman Clinic offers assessment and long-term psychotherapeutic treatment to children, adolescents (and their parents/carers), and adults who are diagnosed with paraphilia and engage in harmful sexual behaviors, criminality, or violence (Ruszczynski, 2016). However, outcome research for this program is difficult to locate.

While the research in favor of the efficacy of psychodynamic psychotherapy is strong for a range of mental problems, little research has been published by forensic psychoanalysts to contest negative assertions about the benefits of psychodynamic approaches when treating sex offenders. Unless one proffers an absurd argument that sex offenders are qualitatively different from other human beings, it is reasonable to assume that the evidence base that favors the benefits of psychodynamic treatment is just as applicable to offenders. Clearly, more research into the application of psychodynamic approaches to the treatment of sex offenders is warranted. Arguably, future efficacy studies will produce more accurate and nuanced findings as research methods improve. Much of the complexity of psychoanalytic treatment is beyond the ability of contemporary research methodologies to measure, such as changes in the therapeutic relationship and unconscious processes that are the loci

[13] An effect size of 0.8 is typically considered large, 0.5 is considered moderate, and 0.2 is considered small.

of therapeutic action. Perhaps forensic psychoanalysis (or any other form of treatment, for that matter) will be better able to give more definitive evidence of efficacy when greater gains have been made in complexity science to model complex systems, such as via system dynamics, non-linear models, and network theory (Colchester, 2015).

Riordan (2017) identifies three key areas in which psychodynamic psychotherapy currently plays an important role in forensic settings that are not specifically psychodynamic programs: assessment, treatment, and supervision. Riordan describes forensic psychotherapy assessment as attempting to "make sense of how a patient's early background and experiences (there and then) account for the patient's current predicament (here and now). The therapist is curious to know what state of mind the offender was trying to manage via their criminal act, including both conscious and unconscious aspects of the patient concerning "the index offense and other offending behavior; the 'meaning', symbolic and otherwise of the index offense; and an assessment of what psychological structures and defenses are in place" (Riordan, 2017, p. 227). Forensic psychotherapy assessments also include an assessment of the patient's treatability. Riordan notes the realistic position that "very few patients would be able to make use of traditional psychoanalysis," but considers psychodynamically informed therapy such as Mentalisation-Based Treatment (Allen & Fonagy, 2006; Fonagy, 2006) to be effective both in group and individual treatment. Finally, Riordan reports the benefit of forensic psychotherapists offering supervision to individual therapists or trainees who are directly treating patients. Forensic psychotherapists offering group supervision assist teams in the form of reflective practice groups or by working directly with teams at clinical meetings. Such consultations aim to "help teams better understand their patient, avoid perverse acting out, and to help manage strong countertransference reactions and the toll of working with these highly disturbed and disturbing patients" (Riordan, 2017, p. 228).

4.7 Conclusion

This chapter has described the heterogeneity found in psychodynamic perspectives particularly as applied to understanding and treating sex offenders. Classical and contemporary psychodynamic perspectives have been described in terms of their philosophical differences as is the impact of specific psychodynamic perspectives on the therapeutic relationship. The author has argued that psychodynamic perspectives contribute to a holistic approach to the rehabilitation of sex offenders that can assist in and augment the benefits achieved by time-limited, reductionistic, manualized treatment programs. A 'both-and' rather than 'either-or' attitude to the treatment of sex offenders is proposed that seeks to maintain a balance in recognizing the priority of recidivism risk reduction according to empirical research findings while appreciating the complexity of the sex offender's psychopathology which gives rise to criminal behavior. The practice of forensic psychoanalysis requires advanced training and extensive supervised practice to prepare the clinician for working from a mixed-model approach in an informed and ethically sound manner.

The key message of psychoanalysis to the field of sex offender treatment is that we, as clinicians, have to have the mental capacity, courage, and skill to lean into the unconscious experience of sex offenders to be able to understand why and how it is that they have developed behavioral patterns that are so destructive to the wellbeing of others and themselves. Our first goal is to form a working alliance with our patients rather than demand compliance. Once the collaborative therapeutic dyad has been formed, our goal is to meet our patients in the secret spaces of their minds where we can join them in the process of embracing a non-offending, child-safe future. We do this by recognizing the uniqueness and dignity of our patients, allowing them to speak freely, and inviting them into a genuine conversation about their lives and psychopathology, especially as it relates to sexual offending. We will meet the patient's resistance along the way and perversion is likely to be manifested in the therapeutic dyad as part of the process of change. However, through such intimate engagement, forensic psychoanalysis offers sex offenders a way forward that augments mainstream treatment approaches. Changes in the offender's unconscious processes, that result from coming to know and confront him or herself at the deepest level in the context of a long-term therapeutic relationship, make way for a more integrated personality, prosociality, and healthier relationships between the rehabilitated offender with other members of our shared human family.

References

Abbass, A. A., Hancock, J. T., Henderson, J., & Kisely, S. R. (2006). Short-term psychodynamic psychotherapies for common mental disorders. *Cochrane Database of Systematic Reviews, Issue 4*(Art. No. CD004687).

Abbass, A. A., Kisely, S. R., Town, J. M., Leichsenring, F., Driessen, E., De Maat, S., Gerber, A., Dekker, J., Rabung, S., Rusalovska, S., & Crowe, E. (2014). Short-term psychodynamic psychotherapies for common mental disorders (Review). *Cochrane Database of Systematic Reviews, Issue 7*(Art. No. CD004687). https://doi.org/10.1002/14651858.CD004687.pub4.

Abrahams, D., & Rohleder, P. (2021). *A clinical guide to psychodynamic psychotherapy*. Routledge.

Ainsworth, M. D. S. (1989). Attachments beyond intimacy. *American Psychologist, 44*, 709–716.

Ainsworth, M. D. S., & Bowlby, J. (1991). An ethological approach to personality development. *American Psychologist*(April 1991), 333–341.

Allen, J. G., & Fonagy, P. (2006). *Handbook of mentalization-based treatment*. John Wiley.

American Psychiatric Association. (2013a). *Diagnostic and statistical manual of mental disorders (DSM-5)* (5th ed.). American Psychiatric Association.

American Psychiatric Association. (2013b). Paraphilic disorders. In *Diagnostic and Statistical Manual of Mental Disorders (DSM-5)* (5th ed., pp. 685–705). American Psychiatric Association.

Andrews, D. A., & Bonta, J. (2010). *The psychology of criminal conduct* (5th ed.). Anderson Publishing Co..

Andrews, D. A., Bonta, J., & Wormith, J. S. (2011). The risk-need-responsivity (RNR) model: Does adding the good lives model contribute to effective crime prevention? *Criminal Justice and Behavior, 38*(7), 735–755.

Aron, L. (1990). One person and two person psychologies and the method of psychoanalysis. *Psychoanalytic Psychology, 7*(4), 475–485.
Atwood, G. E., & Stolorow, R. D. (1984). *Structures of subjectivity: Explorations in psychoanalytic phenomenology*. Analytic Press.
Bacal, H. A. (1985). Optimal responsiveness and the therapeutic process. *Progress in Self Psychology, 1*, 202–227.
Bacal, H. A. (2011). *The power of specificity in psychotherapy*. Jason Aronson.
Blagys, M. D., & Hilsenroth, M. J. (2006). Distinctive features of short-term psychodynamic-interpersonal psychotherapy: A review of the comparative psychotherapy process literature. *Clinical Psychology: Science and Practice, 7*(2), 167–188. https://doi.org/10.1093/clipsy.7.2.167
Bonta, J., & Andrews, D. A. (2016). *The psychology of criminal conduct*. Taylor & Francis Ltd.
Bowlby, J. (1969/1999). *Attachment* (Vol. 1, 2nd ed.). Basic Books.
Bowlby, J. (1973). *Separation: Anxiety & Anger* (Vol. 2). Hogarth Press.
Bowlby, J. (1980). *Loss: Sadness & Depression* (Vol. 3). Hogarth Press.
Breger, L. (2001). *Freud: Darkness in the midst of vision*. Wiley.
Breuer, J., & Freud, S. (1895). *Studies on hysteria*. Basic Books.
Brihadaranyaka Upanishad. (c. 700BCE/2016). *Brihadaranyaka Upanishad* (C. Johnston, Trans.). CreateSpace Independent Publishing Platform.
Britton, R., Feldman, M., & O'Shaughnessy, E. (1989). *The Oedipus Complex Today: Clinical implications*. Karnac Books.
Cappo, D., Taylor, G., Watson, D., Robinson, T., & Perritt, S. (1998, 4th October). *Towards Healing: An Australian approach to the problem of professional boundary violations by clergy and religious that encompasses both victim and offender*. Paper presented at the 4th International Conference on Sexual Misconduct by Psychotherapists, Other Health Care Professionals, and Clergy, Boston College, Boston MA.
Capra, F., & Luisi, P. L. (2014). *The systems view of life: A unifying vision*. Cambridge University Press.
Celenza, A. (2014). *Erotic revelations: Clinical applications and perverse scenarios*. Routledge.
Chasseguet-Smirgel, J. (1984). *Creativity and perversion*. Norton.
Chu, C. M., & Ogloff, J. R. P. (2012). Assessing alleged child sexual abusers in noncriminal contexts: Proposed guidelines for practice. *Psychiatry, Psychology and Law, 19*(4), 464–481.
Colchester, J. (2015). *Nonlinear systems: An overview*. Complexity Labs.
Craig, L. A., Dixon, L., & Gannon, T. A. (2013). *What works in offender rehabilitation: An evidence-based approach to assessment and treatment*. John Wiley & Sons.
De Masi, F. (2003). *The sadomasochistic perversion: The entity and the theories*. Routledge.
Dollard, J., & Miller, N. (1950). *Personality and psychotherapy*. McGraw-Hill.
Eccleston, L., & Ward, T. (2006). *Is risk management enough? Approach and avoidance goals in the treatment of sex offenders* (Vol. 19). Criminal Justice Press.
Ellis, A. (1962). *Reason and emotion in psychotherapy*. Lyle Stuart.
Erikson, E. H. (1963). *Childhood and society* (2nd ed.). Norton.
Fairbairn, W. R. D. (1940). Schoid factors in the personality. In *An object-relations theory of persoanlity*. Basic Books.
Fairbairn, W. R. D. (1943/1952). *An object relations theory of the personality*. Basic Books.
Fairbairn, W. R. D. (1944/52). Endopsychic structure considered in terms of object-relationships. In *An object-relations theory of the personality*. Basic Books.
Fonagy, P. (2006). A mentalisation-focused approach to social development. In J. Allen & P. Fonagy (Eds.), *Handbook of mentalization-based treatment* (pp. 53–100). John Wiley and Sons, Ltd.
Freud, A. (1937/2018). *The ego and the mechanisms of defence*. Routledge.
Freud, S. (1895). Project for a scientific psychology. In J. Strachey (Ed.), *Standard edition of the complete psychological works of Sigmund Freud* (Vol. 1, pp. 281–391). Hogarth Press.
Freud, S. (1896). The aetiology of hysteria. In J. Strachey (Ed.), *The standard edition of the complete psychological works of Sigmund Freud* (Vol. 3, pp. 191–221). Hogarth Press.

Freud, S. (1900/2001). The interpretation of dreams (J. Strachey, Trans.). In J. Strachey (Ed.), *Standard edition of the complete psychological works of Sigmund Freud* (Vol. 5, pp. 339–627). Vintage.
Freud, S. (1905). *Dora: An analysis of a case of hysteria*. Simon and Schuster.
Freud, S. (1905/1949). *Three essays on the theory of sexuality* (J. Strachey, Trans. Vol. VII). Imago Publishing Company.
Freud, S. (1910a). The future prospects of psycho-analytic therapy. In J. Strachey (Ed.), *The standard edition of the complete psychological works of Sigmund Freud* (Vol. 11, pp. 139–152). Hogarth Press.
Freud, S. (1910b). A special type of choice of object made by men (Contributions to the psychology of love I). In J. Strachey (Ed.), *The standard edition of the complete psychological works of Sigmund Freud* (Vol. 11, pp. 163–176). Hogarth Press.
Freud, S. (1912/1958). Recommendations to physicians practising psycho-analysis. In J. Strachey (Ed.), *The standard edition of the complete psychological works of Sigmund Freud* (Vol. 12, pp. 111–120). Hogarth Press.
Freud, S. (1915). *Some character-types met with in psycho-analytic work* (Vol. 14). Hogarth Press.
Freud, S. (1917). Mourning and Melancholia. In J. Strachey (Ed.), *Standard edition of the complete psychological works of Sigmund Freud* (pp. 243–258). Hogarth Press.
Freud, S. (1920). *Beyond the pleasure principle*. W.W. Norton.
Freud, S. (1923). *The Ego and the Id*. W.W. Norton.
Freud, S. (1926). *Inhibitions, symptoms and anxiety*. W.W. Norton.
Freud, S. (2011). *Formulation of the two principles of mental functioning* (Vol. 12). Hogarth Press.
Gillespie, W. H. (1956). The general theory of sexual perversion. *International Journal of Psychoanalysis, 37*, 396–403.
Glasser, M. (1979). Some aspects of the role of aggression in the perversions. In I. Rosen (Ed.), *Sexual deviation* (pp. 278–305). Oxford University Press.
Glasser, M. (1986). Identification and its vicissitudes as observed in the perversions. *International Journal of Psycho-Analysis, 67*, 9–16.
Greenberg, J., & Mitchell, S. (1983). *Object relations in psychoanalytic theory*. Harvard University Press.
Grieger, L., & Hosser, D. (2014). Which risk factors are really predictive? An analysis of Andrews and Bonta's "Central Eight" risk factors for recidivism in German youth correctional facility inmates. *Criminal Justice and Behavior, 41*(5), 613–634.
Guntrip, H. (1952/1969). The Schizoid personality and the external world. In *Schizoid phenomena, object relations and the self* (pp. 17–48). International University Press, Inc.
Guntrip, H. (1961). *Personality structure and human interaction: The developing synthesis of psychodynamic theory*. International Universities Press.
Guntrip, H. (1969). *Schizoid phenomena, object relations and the self*. International University Press, Inc.
Hare, R. D. (2003). *Hare Psychopathy Checklist - Revised (PCL-R)* (2nd ed.). Multi-Health Systems, Inc.
Harris, A. J. R., Phenix, R., Hanson, R. K., & Thornton, D. M. (2003). STATIC-99 Coding Rules Revised - 2003. In.
Hart, S. D., Kropp, P. R., Laws, D. R., Klaver, J., Logan, C., & Watt, K. A. (2003). *The risk for sexual violence protocol (RSVP): Structured professional guidelines for assessing risk of sexual violence*. Mental Health, Law, & Policy Institute, (Simon Fraser University); Pacific Psychological Assessment Corporation; and The British Columbia Institute Against Family Violence.
Helmus, L. M., Babchishin, K. M., Hanson, R. K., & Thornton, D. M. (2009). *Stalic-99 R: Revised Age Weights*. Retrieved from http://www.amyphcnix.com/docs/Static-99R-Revised-Age-Weights.pdf
Keogh, T. (2012). *The internal world of the juvenile sex offender: Through a glass darkly then face to face*. Routledge.

Kernberg, O. F. (2016). The four basic components of psychoanalytic technique and derived psychoanalytic psychotherapies. *World Psychiatry, 15*(3), 287–288. https://doi.org/10.1002/wps.20368
Kirsner, D. (2000). *Unfree associations: Inside psychoanalytic institutes*. Process Press.
Klein, M. R. (1932). *The psycho-analysis of children*. Hogarth Press.
Klein, M. R. (1946/1975). Notes of some schizoid mechanisms. In *Envy and gratitude and other works* (pp. 1–24). Delacorte Press/Semour Lawrence.
Klein, M. R. (1975). *Love, guilt and reparation and other works (1921-1945)* (Vol. 1). Karnac Books.
Kohut, H. (1971). *The analysis of the self: A systematic approach to the psychoanalytic treatment of narcissistic personality disorders* (Vol. null).
Kohut, H. (1977). *The restoration of the self*. New York.
Kohut, H. (1984). *How does analysis cure?* University of Chicago Press.
Kuhn, T. S. (1962/2012). *The structure of scientific revolutions* (4th ed.). The University of Chicago Press.
Lacan, J. (1977/1998). *The four fundamental concepts of psycho-analysis: Book XI of the Seminar of Jacques Lacan* (A. Sheridan, Trans. J. A. Miller Ed.). W. W. Norton & Company.
Lacan, J. (2013). *The ethics of psychoanalysis 1959-1960: The seminar of Jacques Lacan* (D. Porter, Trans. J. A. Miller Ed.). Routledge.
Lynn, D. J., & Vaillant, G. E. (1998). Anonymity, neutrality, and confidentiality in the actual methods of Sigmund Freud: A review of 43 Cases, 1907-1939. *American Journal of Psychiatry, 155*(2), 163–171.
Magid, B., Fosshage, J., & Shane, E. (2021). The emerging paradigm of relational self psychology: An historical perspective. *Psychoanalysis, Self and Context, 16*(1), 1–23. https://doi.org/10.1080/24720038.2020.1856111
Magid, B., Fosshage, J., & Shane, E. (2022). Response to Commentaries by Coburn, Gardner and Teicholz on "The Emerging Paradigm of Relational Self Psychology: An Historical Perspective". *Psychoanalysis, Self and Context, 17*(1), 1–7.
Mahler, M. S. (1971). A study of the separation-individuation process and its possible application to beorderline phenomena in the psychoanalytic situation. *Psychoanalytic Study of the Child, 26*, 403–424.
Main, M. (1991). Metacognitive knowledge, metacognitive monitoring, and singular (coherent) vs. multiple (incoherent) models of attachment: Some findings and some directions for future research. In P. Marris, J. Stevenson-Hinde, & C. Parkes (Eds.), *Attachment across the life cycle* (pp. 127–159). Routledge.
Main, M., Hesse, E., & Kaplan, N. (2005). Predictability of attachment behavior and representational processes at 1, 6, and 19 years of age: The Berkeley Longitudinal Study. In *Attachment from infancy to adulthood: The major longitudinal studies* (pp. 245–304). Guilford Publications.
Malcolm, R. (1970). The mirror: A perverse sexual phantasy in a woman seen as a defence against a psychotic breakdown. In E. Spillius (Ed.), *Melanie Klein Today* (Vol. 2, pp. 115–137). Routledge.
McDougall, J. (1995). *The many faces of eros: A psychoanalytical exploration of human sexuality*. Free Association Books.
Meltzer, D. (1973). *Sexual states of mind*. Clunie Press.
Mills, J. (2012). *Conundrums: A critique of contemporary psychoanalytic theory*. Routledge.
Minne, C. (2020). Sadomasochistic dynamics inside and outside the consulting room. *International Journal of Forensic Psychotherapy, 2*(1), 13–25.
Mitchell, S. A. (1988). *Relational concepts in psychoanalysis: An integration*. Harvard University Press.
Ogden, T. H. (1996). The perverse subject of analysis. *Journal of the American Psychoanalytic Association, 44*, 1121–1146.
Orange, D. M. (2014). And we shall be changed: To hold theory lightly is to surrender assumptions: Discussion of clinical narrative by Steven Stern. *International Journal of Psychoanalytic Self Psychology, 9*, 193–199.

Oxford Dictionary of English. (2010). (A. Stevenson Ed. 3rd ed.). Oxford University Press.

Peirce, C. S. (1955/2014). In J. Buchler (Ed.), *Philosophical writings of Peirce*. Dover Publications.

Pithers, W. D., Beal, L. S., Armstrong, J., & Petty, J. (1989). Identification of risk factors through clinical invterviews and analysis of records. In D. R. Laws (Ed.), *Relapse prevention with sex offenders* (pp. 77–87). Guilford Press.

Rayner, E. (1991). *The independent mind in British psychoanalysis*. Jason Aronson.

Riordan, D. (2017). Forensic psychotherapy. *Australasian Psychiatry, 25*(3), 227–229. https://doi.org/10.1177/1039856216689532

Rosenfeld, H. A. (1987). *Impasse and interpretation: Therapeutic and anti-therapeutic factors in the psychoanalytic treatment of psychotic, borderline, and neurotic patients*. Routledge.

Rudyntsky, P. L. (2022). *Mutual analaysis: Ferenczi, Severn, and the origins of Truama Theory*. Routledge.

Ruszczynski, S. (2016). A brief introduction to the history of the Portman Clinic. *Journal of Child Psychotherapy, 42*(3), 262–265. https://doi.org/10.1080/0075417X.2016.1238137

Schafer, R., (1979). On becoming a psychoanalyst of one persuasion or another. *Contemporary Psychoanalysis, 15*, 345-360.

Schwartz, B. K. (2011). *Handbood of Sex Offender Treatment*. Civic Research Institute.

Shedler, J. (2018). Where is the evidence for “evidence-based” therapy? *Psychiatric Clinics of North America*. https://doi.org/10.1016/J.PSC.2018.02.001

Skinner, B. F. (1938). *The behaviour of organisms*. Appleton-Century-Crofts.

Solms, M. (2018). The scientific standing of psychoanalysis. *BJPsych International, 15*(1), 5–8. https://doi.org/10.1192/bji.2017.4

Steinert, C., Munder, T., Rabung, S., Hoyer, J., & Leichsenring, F. (2017). Psychodynamic therapy: As efficacious as other empirically supported treatments? A meta-analysis testing equivalence of outcomes. *American Journal of Psychiatry, 174*(10), 943–953. https://doi.org/10.1176/appi.ajp.2017.17010057

Stern, D. B. (2017). Interpersonal psychoanalysis: History and current status. *Contemporary Psychoanalysis, 53*(1), 69–94.

Stoller, R. J. (1975). *Perversion: The erotic form of hatred*. Pantheon Books.

Sullivan, H. S. (1953). *The interpersonal theory of psychiatry*. Norton.

Swales, S. S. (2012). *Perversion: A Lacanian psychoanalytic approach to the subject*. Routledge/Taylor & Francis Group.

Symington, N. (1980). The response aroused by the psychopath. *International Review of Psycho-Analysis, 7*, 291–298.

Taylor, C. (1989). *Sources of the self: The making of modern identity*. Harvard University Press.

Teicholz, J. G. (2021). Relational self psychology: Could there be any other kind? A discussion of Magid, Fosshage & Shane’s Paper, the emerging paradigm of relational self psychology: A historical perspective. *Psychoanalysis, Self and Context, 16*(4), 319–326. https://doi.org/10.1080/24720038.2021.1945066

United Nations General Assembly. (1948). *Universal declaration of human rights*. United Nations General Assembly.

United Nations General Assembly. (1989). *Convention on the rights of the child*. United Nations General Assembly. Retrieved from http://www.refworld.org/docid/3ae6b38f0.html

Vaillant, G. E. (1977/1998). *Adaptation to life*. Harvard University Press.

Vaillant, G. E. (1994). Ego mechanisms of defense and personality psychopathology. *Journal of Abnormal Psychology, 103*(1), 44–50. https://doi.org/10.1037/0021-843X.103.1.44

Vaillant, G. E., Bond, M., & Vaillant, C. O. (1986). An empirically validated hierarchy of defence mechanisms. *Archives of General Psychiatry, 73*, 786–794.

van der Kolk, B. A. (2014). *The body keeps the score: Brain, mind, and body in the healing of trauma*. Viking.

von Hartmann, E. (1869/2014). *Philosophy of the unconscious* (W. Chatterton Coupland, Trans.). Routledge.

von Krafft-Ebing, R. (1886/2018). *Psychopathia Sexualis: A clinical-forensic study*. Franklin Classic.

Wampold, B. E., Flückiger, C., Del Re, A. C., Youlish, N. E., Frost, N. D., Pace, B. T., Goldberg, S. B., Miller, S. D., Baardseth, T. P., Laska, K. M., & Hilsenroth, M. J. (2017). In pursuit of truth: A critical examination of meta-analyses of cognitive behavior therapy. *Psychotherapy Research, 27*(1), 14–32. https://doi.org/10.1080/10503307.2016.1249433

Ward, T., & Beech, A. R. (2006). An integrated theory of sexual offending. *Aggression & Violent Behaviour, 11*, 44–63.

Ward, T., & Brown, M. (2004). The good lives model and conceptual issues in offender rehabilitation. *Psychology, Crime & Law, 10*(3), 243–257.

Ward, T., Louden, K., Hudson, S. M., & Marshall, W. L. (1995). A descriptive model of the offense chain for child molesters. *Journal of Interpersonal Violence, 10*(4), 452–472.

Ward, T., Yates, P. M., & Willis, G. M. (2012). The good lives model and the risk need responsivity model. A critical response to Andrews, Bonta, and Wormith (2011). *Criminal Justice and Behavior, 39*, 94–110.

Webster, G. P. (2015). *Psychoanalytic complexity and the perpetration of sexual abuse: Psychoanalysis, forensic psychology, and social change*. Paper presented at the Self Psychology in a Multidisciplinary World: Expansiveness and Constraints, Los Angeles, USA.

Webster, G. P. (2017a). *Forensic psychoanalysis: A process-relational approach to the treatment of child sex offenders*. (Ph.D. Theoretical). Institute of Contemporary Psychoanalysis, Los Angeles.

Webster, G. P. (2017b). *The Particularity of Paul: Paedophile, priest, and person*. Paper presented at the 14th Annual IARPP Conference - From the Margins to the Centre: Contemporary Relational Perspectives, Sydney.

Webster, G. P. (2017c). Who will sing with the perpetrator? *Psychoanalytic Dialogues, 27*(2), 164–171.

Webster, G. P. (2018). Psychoanalytic Complexity Theory: An application to the treatment of child sexual offenders. *Psychoanalytic Psychology, 35*(1), 83–92.

Williamson, E., & Darley, J. (1937). *Student personnel work: An outline of clinical procedures*. McGraw-Hill.

Winnicott, D. W. (1945). Primative emotional development. *International Journal of Psychoanalysis, 26*, 137–143.

Winnicott, D. W. (1971). *Playing and reality* (Vol. null). Routledge.

Chapter 5
Experiential and Existential Dimensions in Sex Offender Treatment

Ellen Gunst and Siebrecht Vanhooren

5.1 Introduction

Viktor Frankl (1967), the existential psychiatrist who survived the harsh conditions of Holocaust concentration camps, stated that there are three inescapable aspects of human life that cannot be denied without getting entangled in additional suffering: the experience of pain, the awareness of being mortal, and guilt. Although people are—existentially spoken—always free to a certain degree and responsible (Yalom, 1980), people who are guilty of offences are no longer free, but yet still responsible, explains Frankl (1967, p. 90): "What man has done cannot be undone… A man who failed by a deed cannot change what happened, but by repentance he can change himself. Through the right attitude he can transform [this] unchangeable suffering…"

Many offender therapists would probably agree with this quote of Frankl. Sexual offences leave a trace of harm in their victims, which often influences them for the rest of their lives. In the case of victims, recovering from traumatic sexual offences entails not only symptom reduction, but also an existential quest: they don't only have to make sense of what happened, but they also have to search for a new identity, which often entails resetting one's priorities and purpose in life (Calhoun & Tedeschi, 2013). For offenders, what has been done cannot be undone; the offence has taken place and nothing can be changed about that. However, Frankl suggests that this does not have to be the end on the part of the offender either. As victims have been unwillingly charged with a search for meaning, so are offenders, at least if they don't want to freeze their development as a human being by concealing their guilt and responsibility.

E. Gunst (✉)
FIDES-R, Psychiatric Center Sint-Amandus, Beernem, Belgium

S. Vanhooren
Faculty of Psychology and Educational Sciences, KU Leuven, Leuven, Belgium

R. J. Tully et al. (eds.), *Best Practices in Sexual Offender Assessment and Management*, Dangerous Behavior in Clinical and Forensic Psychology,
https://doi.org/10.1007/978-3-031-83135-5_5

An existential understanding of sex offending and sex offenders demands an approach that goes beyond the *Risk-Need-Responsivity model* (RNR; Andrews & Bonta, 2010), where the avoidance of situations, a change of distorted beliefs, improvement of self-control and social skills, or management of other risk factors are emphasized. As sex offenders are human beings in the first place, they have the same needs and are wrestling with the same existential challenges as others do. As Ward and Brown (2004) suggest in their *Good Lives Model* (GLM), offenders long to love and to be loved, to experience mastery and to have purpose and meaning in life. However, the way they try to fulfil these basic needs runs through antisocial behaviour, or by deviant or conflicting means. The GLM proposes the optimization of skills and capabilities and the removal of obstacles or conflicts in order to fulfil these needs differently. Clients are usually encouraged to follow training modules and take concrete steps in society in line with their strengths and interests, in order to realize valued outcomes in a personally fulfilling and socially acceptable way.

Notwithstanding these valuable approaches, existential, humanistic, and experiential approaches suggest a different, but complementary roadmap to explore and engage with offenders' needs (e.g. Gunst et al., 2019a; Pascual-Leone et al., 2011; Pascual-Leone et al., 2016; Polizzi & Draper, 2013; Vanhooren et al., 2017b, 2018). As Frankl (1967) already suggested, in order to live with a crime that cannot be undone, an offender not only needs to change behaviour to reduce harm and risk in the future, but also take the responsibility to engage in a profound self-search in order to make sense of what happened, of who one is, and who one wants to be.

Since numerous factors play a role in the development of sexually inappropriate behaviours, a combination of approaches is required to address the multiple problems inherent in this population. In this chapter, the existential approach will be used to widen the lens in order to acquire a deeper understanding of the dynamics of sex offending. More concretely, existential concerns and themes that are intertwined with sex offending, as well as how existential and experiential approaches can help to change one's course of direction, not only to reduce risk behaviour, but also to lead a more existentially fulfilling life will be explored.

5.2 Multiple Case Studies

In order to consider the role of existential concerns in sex offending and their potential role in offender therapies, the findings from multiple in-depth qualitative case studies were synthesized. Case studies that contain clients' lived experiences, have been found to be important sources of information concerning existential themes and dynamics (van Deurzen et al., 2019). Recent case studies have shown how existential concerns are intertwined with clients' problems as well as with the process of therapy itself (De Decker, 2020; Helsen, 2020; Vanhooren, 2019). Qualitative studies also have the potential to broaden our understanding of how existential aspects are imbedded in the lived experience of imprisonment (Vanhooren et al., 2017a, 2017b, 2018) and in offenders as such (Farrall, 2005; Gunst & Vanhooren,

2018). In order to learn how existential concerns could play a role in sex offending and how an existential and experiential view could show us paths of change in therapy, different single-cases of men who committed sexual offences were studied; each of them followed forensic treatment. Authors used meta-synthesis as a strategy to aggregate and synthesize the findings of the single-case studies through identification of shared concepts and themes across similar cases. Meta-synthesis aims at theory building and development (Iwakabe & Gazzola, 2009).

Authors selected five in depth case studies of sex offenders that have previously been published by the authors of this chapter (Gunst, 2015; Gunst et al., 2019b, 2020, 2022; Gunst & Vanhooren, 2018): Dave, Kevin, Nico, Patrick, and Bruno. The first four are men of average intelligence who had been convicted for sexual abuse of several minors. They followed an intensive long-term standard in-patient treatment based on RNR and GLM principles to which experiential psychotherapy has been added. The fifth case is a highly talented man who was guilty of downloading child abuse images. He followed a long-term weekly out-patient integrative treatment. They were all victimized in childhood (sexual, physical and/or neglect). For all of them, the sexual deviant interest and behavior had begun during adolescence.

Dave was referred for intensive in-patient treatment when he was in his forties because of severe and long-lasting abuse of his stepdaughter. His initial explanation was that suddenly becoming a father was very stressful and so, although he declared he had a satisfying sexual relationship with his wife, he needed more sex to channel this stress. He worked day and night which gave him the satisfaction to be a good financial provider. The relationship with his stepchildren was good but detached and he did not want them to call him father. The word father impacted his speaking and feeling, which was not yet clear, but his life story told an early loss of his father and extreme aggressive sexual behavior of an uncle who was his assigned guardian. The loss of his father was long since reprocessed, according to him, but the sexual abuse was unspeakable. He stated that it never bothered him before and seemed unhelpful for him to pay attention to. He did not want to link his own misbehavior to that situation. If he wanted to say something about being abused, he was overwhelmed and tended to relive the traumatic experience.

Kevin was 30 years old when he was admitted to the residential treatment unit. His background was characterized by a considerable amount of victimization and offending, which went all the way back to his childhood. He was scarred from physical and emotional abuse by his parents and was sexually abused by an adult male friend of the family at the age of 12. One year later, he had started to sexually abuse children and another year later, he attempted to commit suicide for the first time. Between the ages of 13 and 22, he molested nine children between 4 and 10 years old. As a result, he spent many years of his adolescence in youth institutions and 7 years in prison as an adult. A pattern of self-destructive behavior such as drug abuse, cutting, attempted suicide, and binge eating ran through his life.

As a child, Nico had been through several adverse experiences. Early on, he was sexually abused by his grandfather who taught him to soothe himself by stimulating his genitals, even long before he experienced sexual arousal. He was bullied in primary school and sexually abused by a neighbor over a two-year period at the age of 12. When aged 17, he started molesting young boys in his neighborhood. Later, he recruited boys via computer chats which led to obligatory out-patient treatment in his late 20s. Recidivism led to a referral to the in-patient treatment when he was 35 years old.

Patrick was 50 years old when he was admitted to the treatment unit because of sexual abuse of more than 10 children under the age of three for almost 10 years. His life narrative initially contrasted sharply with his offending history. Different than other clients, Patrick did not refer to adverse childhood experiences during the intake interviews. He grew up in a family with military discipline and harsh punishments, what he described as strict but fair. He believed his parents loved him and gave him everything he needed. He did not report traumatic losses or experiences at the beginning of treatment. He also did not mention any relational or professional problems.

Bruno, a 45-year-old man, was referred to an out-patient program for sex offenders by a child protection service. His wife alerted them after she discovered indecent child images on his computer. Since childhood, the client had an unhealthy interest in sexuality. Bruno had a history of severe sexual abuse by his mother and extreme harassment by his peers. Although he had a hard time coping with his traumatic history, he did not want therapy for his traumatic experiences. He kept his emotions under extreme control. Although he did not mention a problem of aggression at first, he often got absorbed by rage towards self and others.

5.3 Existential Givens

The mission of existential and humanistic psychologies and psychotherapies can be understood as the quest to develop a deeper understanding of what it means to be human, and how to help people lead more authentic, meaningful, and fulfilling lives (Angus et al., 2015; van Deurzen et al., 2019). Existential and experiential therapies posit that psychological suffering is often derived from not facing and not working through one's personal pains, which are caused by unmet existential needs and the person's own emotional reaction towards the situation in which these needs were and are unmet (Pascual-Leone et al., 2016). Frankl (1959) was among the first to acknowledge people's existential need for meaning in life, and to be of significance for others. However, there is more than humans' need for meaning. Based on Tillich (1952), Yalom (1980) speaks of four existential givens or ultimate concerns that people meet throughout their lifetimes. The challenge, says Greening (1992) is to acknowledge these existential concerns when they appear, and to make sense of one's own life while being confronted with these givens. Inspired by Greenings' reading of Yalom's existential givens, these givens are: (1) the fact that we are mortal but yet have to live with the awareness of being mortal, (2) that we are existentially isolated, and while we want to be outstanding, we also yearn for connection, (3) that we encounter meaninglessness, but that we have a desire for leading meaningful lives, and (4) that we are free, but are also determined and restricted, and responsible for our deeds.

There is a growing evidence that lopsided or unbalanced ways to cope with these existential challenges serve as trans-diagnostic factors. Greening (1992) gives examples how overly positive (e.g. life is always meaningful) or negative answers (e.g. there is no meaning in life) to these existential givens might lead to a more vulnerable position in life. It would create suffering in the long run. Current research demonstrates that skewed negative positions are robustly associated with psychopathology. For example, Iverach et al. (2014) show how death anxiety serves as a trans-diagnostic factor in different anxiety disorders, posttraumatic stress disorder, obsessive-compulsive disorder, and depression. Lower levels of meaning in life have been robustly associated with less mental well-being and psychopathology, especially with depression (e.g. Delle Fave, 2020; Glaw et al., 2017; Li et al., 2021). Existential isolation and loneliness have also been identified as experiences that are associated with psychopathology and have a strong impact on mental and physical health (e.g. Constantino et al., 2019; Maitland, 2020). When it comes to freedom and responsibility, research is largely non-existent. However, studies on the experience of not having agency over one's life, or experiencing an external locus of control, remind us of this existential challenge to experience freedom and responsibility while also feeling restricted or determined. Having an external locus of control has been associated with psychopathology and psychological symptoms, although differences are suggested between cultures (e.g. Cheng et al., 2013). When it comes to guilt, studies have been making a difference between adaptive and maladaptive feelings of guilt in its relationship to psychopathology (Taihara & Malik, 2016), but when it comes to offenders—and as already suggested by Frankl—experiences of guilt might play a different role.

5.4 The Existential Concerns of Sex Offenders

For this chapter, the five case studies described above were re-examined on the presence of existential concerns as defined by Yalom (1980) and Greening (1992) because little is known about existential aspects in forensic treatment. One qualitative study of experiential group therapy with sex offenders revealed that acceptance of responsibility of one's own change process and experiencing quality of life seems to be of higher importance (Willemsen et al., 2016), in contrast to Yalom and Leszcz' (2005) assertion that, in general, acceptance of mortality and going through life alone are most crucial. Moreover, a sense of existential well-being might be a protective factor for recidivism.

General case study research shows that Yalom's (1980) existential givens are highly present. In a total of 85 recent case studies of clients who were engaged for at least 15 sessions in person-centered therapies in Belgium (De Decker, 2020; Helsen, 2020), existential themes were most often presented in a very concrete *ontic* manner (e.g. 'what is the purpose of me doing this job', 'why did this happen to me') in the commentaries of clients on each session. Clients' descriptions of existential themes are usually interwoven with their lived experience of their existence, rather than appearing as *ontological* themes as such (e.g. 'what is the meaning of life'). In our current analysis, based on qualitative case studies, the subsequent ontic lived experienced expressions of the existential givens could be identified and illustrate how an existential and experiential approach could address these existential issues in sex offender therapies.

5.4.1 Life and Death

Greening (1992, p. 111) described the first existential challenge as coming to terms with life and death: "We are alive but we will die, and we live in a world that both supports and negates life." Similarly, Otto Rank, who heavily influenced existential-humanistic approaches, remarks that people are not only afraid of death, but are also afraid of living (Kramer, 2019). This life anxiety is expressed in the fear of being an identifiable individual, the anxiety of sticking out, being noticed and following one's own course in life. However, to live one's life and to take the risk of failure, a certain sense of *basic trust in life* is necessary. Frankl (1967) emphasizes the importance of this basic trust in life in order to actualize oneself.

The five clients under study struggle with life. Based on their early life experiences, they lack a basic trust that they are worth living. The qualitative comparison revealed maladaptive shame as a shared core maladaptive emotion scheme; a sense of worthlessness or a feeling of being disrespected. Besides that, the fact that they committed crimes put an extra burden on their—already—fragile experience of having the right to exist. Recurrent thoughts like 'I'd better be dead' express their experience of being a total failure and not being worthy of living. This might signal that they haven't been able to process their pain yet. However, this can also be understood as a form of evading responsibility, not being able to acknowledge and bear their guilt. In the face of death, a shift can arise in responsibility taking. When they have nothing left to lose, remorse can induce real acknowledgment of the wrongdoing towards the victims. It could be questioned whether more active confrontation of offenders in treatment with the reality of their mortality could promote responsibility. What would they want to do with their life if only one year would be left, like the main character of Yalom (2005)'s book 'The Schopenhauer Cure'?

For these five clients, the decision to follow treatment was actually a choice to make something out of life. However, this choice is more complicated, as the question of whether one feels worthy enough to be alive also entails the question of whether one deserves help in the first place. Feelings of worthlessness were processed on a deeper level in order to build an accepting and nurturing attitude towards one's own painful experiences and needs. Consequently, this helped in taking their existential needs seriously and helped them understand the difference between their needs—which are not 'wrong'—and the way they tried to satisfy these needs—which was maladaptive. As a result, this changed attitude increased the courage to also take responsibility for one's own mistakes. A warm and empathic strong therapeutic relationship served as a corrective and growth-promoting experience here.

Rogers (1980) explains how empathy can help clients to feel being part of humanity. He refers to the existential psychiatrist Robert Laing (1965) who studied experiences of the absence of this basic trust, or *ontological insecurity*. For Laing, rebuilding a sense of basic trust required being known by another person. The existential philosopher Martin Buber (1958) also states that our existence needs to be confirmed by another person. For Rogers (1980, p. 155), an empathic therapeutic relationship can indeed give the client "that needed confirmation that one exists as a separate, valued person with an identity." Laing (1965) also remarks on the importance of feeling not only confirmed in a relationship, but also to experience oneself as being embodied. As van Deurzen (1997) states, human beings are not just social, or psychological, or spiritual beings, but are also fundamentally grounded in the physical realm of existence. Therefore, having a basic trust in one's being also means building basic trust in one's bodily felt senses. For Gendlin (1973), contacting one's bodily felt senses opens the gate to one's actual lived experiences of one's existence. It helps to grasp the felt meaning of what it means to be one's self in the here-and-now, and also helps to acknowledge one's existential needs and which direction a person needs to follow in order to find what one needs. Gendlin (1978) called this embodied meaning-making or meaning-discovering process *focusing*.

The confirming therapeutic relationship can help form a new inner relationship on the side of the client and develop a capacity to listen to their bodily felt senses. Creating a safe climate (in the group) is essential (Willemsen et al., 2016) as well as constantly refocusing the attention of the client to his bodily awareness (Gunst et al., 2019a). Only then the therapist and client can dive into the focusing space (Depestele, 2004) characterized by a listening-accepting attitude to whatever comes.

> When the therapy started to concentrate on processing traumatic experiences, the therapist tried to help Bruno to make a distinction between his anger part, his inner child, and his observing self (that often disappeared). His rage was not only directed to his abusers and by extension the whole outer world, but also to his inner child. He wished he could beat this part to death in order to be released from his suffering. The therapist tried to contain his unbearable feelings and actively brought him back in the here-and-now. She needed to be directive in separating Bruno from his traumatic experience.

> It took two years of individual therapy for Bruno before there were little moments of focusing possible. In one of those early moments, words like 'remorse' and an image of a piece of burned wood came up when he listened to his vague bodily sensations. His first reaction towards these words and images was quite negative: 'Drop it, this is worthless.' When the therapist asked him to listen with openness and curiosity to this image, he was surprised to hear something inside like: 'Restore me.' (Gunst & Vanhooren, 2018).

Besides the lack of basic trust in life, the other side of the coin is *death anxiety*, which can be triggered by experiences of extreme threat and vulnerability in trauma (Arredondo & Caparrós, 2019; Iverach et al., 2014). For some clients, the sexual act is fused with aggression, arising from an experienced threat on a preconscious level. This was typically the case for one of the cases under study (Dave) but the aggressive urge was also prominently present in one other case (Bruno). According to

Crittenden (2008), the rationale for the behaviour cannot be easily detected because the threat is not consciously identified. It is a self-protecting response starting from the lower brain, which Siegel (2020) calls the low-road immersion. It is based on faulty information linked to exposure to life-threatening danger in the past, these people are confused about the present moment and the source of danger. Information processing did not reach the higher brain levels before action, leading to a lack of reflection and verbalisation. These people are often confused about affection and aggression, vulnerability, and power, and bring this in the present moment (Crittenden, 2008).

Early in treatment, Dave did not want to recount the past or make a link between the experience of abuse and his own wrongdoing. The few moments he did refer to it, he got immediately overwhelmed and tended to relive this traumatic experience with accompanied bodily sensations and gestures. He became anxious to feel the intense pain and anger. Only after one and a half years of intense group treatment and some individual sessions to install a workable distance towards his painful experience, he could explore the tension evoked by the word father. He always stated that his stepchildren could not call him father, but he could not explain the felt meaning of that blockage. He had to explore in treatment what led to the perception of threat in contact with his stepdaughter that suddenly turned into an unconscious self-protective reflex resulting in a violent sexual attack of the daughter he cared for.

For clients who react aggressively in response to an unconsciously experienced threat, Crittenden (2008) states that it is necessary to point our therapeutic interventions to the sequence leading to the perception of danger, because once in that perception, it is almost impossible to stop the self-protective reflex. It is experienced as terror.

In that exploration with Dave, he remembered how his stepdaughter was searching proximity and support because she was going through a rough time. The moment she came physically closer, something completely crashed. When he spoke out loud firmly that the first time something happened, he felt he had the power, he suddenly collapsed and seemed anxious. Quietly he said: "*I kept my soft side, but it was totally gone, hidden behind the attack. The defence comes from far away, the attack came from the defence against my uncle, a defence I lost. There could not be a soft side anymore, because it got stuck into defence, the defence was the attack, I could not show my soft side anymore, that was the problem. They always saw the beast in me who did not know that there was something soft in him. It is there, and now, after more than thirty years, I have connection again with what is behind the defensive attack, with my soft side, but in the meanwhile so much is destroyed* (Gunst, 2015)".

For the five offenders under study, who are also trauma survivors, maladaptive shame and anxiety seemed to be the main driving force behind the abuse. Although forensic therapists often claim or worry that clients may use their own trauma as an excuse, this did not seem to be the case for these five clients. On the contrary, when the trauma was acknowledged by the therapist, they had to overcome resistance and fear to integrate trauma work in forensic treatment. For these clients, intimacy was connected to anxiety, a basic sense of insecurity, although often not conscious. Processing of these maladaptive emotions (shame and anxiety) opened a window to primary adaptive emotions: mainly pain, sadness and loneliness linked to negative childhood experiences; and guilt related to own misbehavior (Gunst, 2019).

5.4.2 Connectedness and Existential Isolation

Another existential concern described by Yalom (1980) and Greening (1992) is the paradoxical tension between our need for connection and the fact that we are existentially isolated. Our human experiences can never fully be shared, which can lead to a deep feeling of utter loneliness, especially if we don't seem to be able to bridge our isolated position by connecting authentically to others. The ability and capacity to connect to others might be disturbed by our attachment history to our significant others. Interestingly, as attachment theories tell us, it is this attachment that helps us also to connect to ourselves. When we don't have the capacity to connect to ourselves, our experience of existential loneliness might be exacerbated (Yalom, 1980).

Children need to be convinced of the protective presence of the primary caregivers who provide attuned responses to the child's experience in order to feel safe in connection to others and to internalize an ability to contain their experiences and to modulate the intensity. Children normally seek proximity for protection from physical and psychological threats as well as to alleviate distress (Bowlby, 1998; Farnfield & Holmes, 2014; Mikulincer et al., 2003). In contrast, when attuned responses from attachment figures are lacking, children will develop secondary attachment strategies, other than proximity seeking, to ensure their needs for protection, comfort, safety, closeness, and predictability are met (Baim & Morrison, 2023; Crittenden, 2008). In these circumstances, children may learn to either suppress and ignore emotions and inner experiences (also known as deactivating or A-strategies), or to exaggerate their own emotions of fear, anger, sadness, or hopelessness (called hyperactivating or C-strategies; Crittenden, 2008). Crittenden's (2006) *dynamic maturational model* can be particularly relevant in professional work with forensic or other troubled clients (Baim & Morrison, 2023; Farnfield & Holmes, 2014), specifically in the work with sex offenders (Gunst et al., 2017). Crittenden (2006) and Crittenden et al., (2024) emphasizes the huge similarity between attachment and sexual behaviour. She perceives the boundaries between affection, aggression, and fear on the one hand, and sexual arousal on the other, as highly permeable. This suggests that high arousal in a state of anger or intense desire for comfort can be transformed into or experienced as sexual arousal. The onset of sexuality in puberty creates a challenge to integrate sexual desire with attachment needs and corresponding affects. A failure due to attachment difficulties can lead to isolation, promiscuity, or dangerous sexual incidents (Crittenden, 2006). Isolation, loneliness, and lack of intimacy have been described as important factors in people who commit sexual offenses (Seidman et al., 1994). Feelings of inadequacy and inferiority to others and a lack of the self-confidence and social skills, based on negative childhood experiences, might impede the building and maintaining of consensual intimate relationships with appropriate others. Low levels of intimacy and high emotional loneliness, withdrawal, and negative attitudes (such as anger and hostility) toward potential partners can lead to a progressive retirement from the real world and refuge in an internal world of deviant sexual fantasies in order to satisfy attachment-related needs for intimacy, emotional closeness, or power. This might be a predisposition to sexual offending (Maniglio, 2012).

For the five cases under study, it was clear that their sexual development was disturbed. While sexuality emerges in puberty in normal circumstances, four of them where sexually abused before puberty, which awoke early interest but also confusion. The latter was also true for the fifth client, although he did not experience sexual abuse. The only thing he remembered was the extreme taboo about sexuality or even physicality. For him, sexual interest and later desire had to be exiled to a secret world and could not be experienced in relation to someone else. All five clients did not succeed in integrating sexual desire with attachment needs and corresponding affects, the challenge in puberty described by the dynamic maturational model (Crittenden et al., 2024).

Furthermore, the dynamic maturational model using an attachment theory perspective provides a framework to understand why people under or over-regulate their emotions. Emotional self-regulation strategies that are endangering or damaging for self or others were once self-protective to meet basic attachment needs in childhood. While these strategies may be efficient or even essential to survive in times of distress and danger, they often lead to problematic bio-psycho-social functioning later in life when they are no longer necessary and become exaggerated or frozen (Baim & Morrison, 2023; Watson & Greenberg, 2017).

In forensic literature and treatment programs, regarding emotion regulation, the emphasis is on improving emotion regulation strategies in dealing with intense negative emotions. It has too long been ignored that many clients who committed sexual offences use distracting A-strategies that need a focus on improving awareness and acceptance of emotion rather than downregulating arousal (Gunst et al., 2017). Three of the five clients under study clearly showed A-strategies (Dave, Patrick and Nico), while the other two used a mix of A and C strategies (Bruno and Kevin).

Clients using A-strategies suppress their emotions with a risk of a sudden breakthrough. They often use drugs, alcohol, pornography, or sex to control and suppress their emotions. The core dilemma that characterizes the A-strategy is fear for intimacy versus fear for isolation. Some offenders seek sex without intimacy. Physical closeness is tolerated by keeping an emotional distance (Baim & Morrison, 2023). In this way, they cannot get hurt and they adhere to the idea that they don't need other people (self-reliance). The other is not seen as a person but is used to fulfil a sexual need. The consequence, however, is that emptiness and isolation continue to haunt the client internally.

> During his very early years (3–6), Nico was sexually abused by his grandfather, although he did not store this experience as negative. Traumatic for him was that the contact with his grandparents was suddenly broken without explanation, after his mother discovered this behaviour. The experience of being bullied exacerbated his shyness and insecurity. At the age of 12, he felt seen and safe in contact with his neighbour, who then sexually abused him

over a two-year period. At age 17, he started molesting young boys in his neighbourhood. Later, he recruited several boys via computer chats and paid them for sexual contact.

Nico's delict analysis early in treatment revealed that his fantasies of sex with minors were clearly linked to his own abuse, albeit he was now the abuser, not the abused. Also contacts with adults, both women and men, were based on sexual gratification and not on intimacy or connection. A half year later, he reported that his use of sex services and abuse of boys was not merely about sexual needs but also served as a relief from a lack of intimacy. The scarcity of bodily contact with his parents in contrast to the sexual abuse during childhood, as well as a sudden loss of a first partner in a car accident made him afraid of "truer" intimacy and engagement in relationships.

After one year treatment, he described in a client change interview: '*Before, I knew only one way to get rid of that bad feeling, and then it would have led to abuse or using sex services. [...] Now I felt the urge, but I also knew that this was not a good way to cope with bad feelings. [...] That I could express my feelings to someone was never taught to me. [...] Being abused, I blocked my thoughts, I was actually absent-minded, shutting everything down, but to feel disconnected felt good, and I linked that to sexuality. Since my childhood I have always fled from bad feelings into sexuality to shut down my thoughts and feelings. [...] This became a reflex.*" (to Gunst et al., 2020)

These offenders engage in what Buber (1958) calls *I–It relationships* which are exploitive and exist to serve the purpose of the "I" and at the expense of the objectified person (the "It"). Many of them have, during their youth, themselves been the objectified It and exploited for immediate gratification of someone else's need. According to Ronel and Segev (2014), one of the consequences of this objectification of the other is a growing lack of empathy. This leaves these clients in a vacuum of existential isolation and alienation. As a result, their basic existential needs such as love and meaning are often unmet (Vanhooren et al., 2017a, 2017b). The client is basically interpersonally disconnected. As the other is experienced as object-like, the way is open to engage in destructive behaviour in order to satisfy these unmet basic existential needs (Ronel & Segev, 2014; Vanhooren et al., 2017a). A central task of existential and experiential therapies is the development of a therapeutic relationship, which is characterized by what Buber (1958) calls *I–Thou relationship*-qualities. In this kind of relationship, both participants are genuine and equal, in which they are neither the objects nor perpetrators of "I–It" relationships. The I-Thou relationship is based on principles of presence, empathy, acceptance, and congruence (Geller & Greenberg, 2012; Greenberg & Watson, 2006; Rogers, 1959). This fully accepting relationship facilitates a focus on adaptive needs and validates the client's growth toward optimal complexity and adaptive flexibility (Greenberg, 2015).

Other clients with A-strategies only feel safe enough in relation to a child to experience closeness and intimacy. In fact, the need for comfort and intimacy is denied and projected to the child. The repressed need of the adult gets a sexual implementation and because of an experience merger, the need of the child is interpreted in that way too. Subsequently, the sexual behaviour is rationalized as affection and justified with so-called decent motives which are cognitive distortions. The perspective of the child is not seen as it is in reality. Crittenden (2008) describes these clients as people of which suppressed needs distort their perceptions.

It took one and a half years of intensive treatment before Kevin could recognize that all victims were children in need. By helping them, he felt recognized by someone. There was confusion between his needs and their needs. The close contact triggered his need for intimacy, protection, and to be meaningful to someone. In contrast to his lack of confidence in contact with adults, he felt safe and powerful in contact with children.

Through exploration of his life experiences, processing his own trauma and a self-reflective process of meaning making he was able to connect to the primary emotion of pain and loss leading to the need of being unconditionally regarded.

In the following session, Kevin mentioned anxiety and tension in his body. The therapist used focusing instructions to explore this bodily tension. This allowed him to start to formulate a deeper feeling of having missed out on so many good things in his life, such as good parents, a feeling of belonging.

T: You feel some relief, but also tension. Can you tell where in your body you feel the tension?

C: In my shoulders, my upper back, just to the middle.

Other client: As if you have to carry a heavy burden.

T: Does it feel like a heavy load that weighs?

C: It weighs and rests on my neck, it really feels like that. [Slowing down]

T: Do you have an idea what it is that weighs so heavily?

C: Most of all anxiety, I think, the memories, the lack, there is so much I have missed out on.

T: So, on the one hand there is anxiety, and on the other hand there is a wanting of everything you missed in your life. Maybe we can try to give these both parts some more words. Can you try that? And if you express the words, try to feel if they fit with your body.

C: Literally the fear that something bad could happen, that I cannot control, that fear is still there. [Client responds quickly and unconnected to his body.]

T: Try to feel how your back responds when you say that.

C: I feel that it is mentally correct, but I don't feel a shift physically, it is the fear that something could happen, I assume that it will happen, I am cursed. Although I know it has nothing to do with me, it does feel like that.

The therapist tried to help Kevin create more distance from his experience and asked him to try to listen to his feeling as if it were a friend who was telling something to him. When he asked his feeling on what it would need, the word "reassurance" came up. Kevin protested, because that was impossible given the fact that he had no control over external factors and what he really needed could not be fulfilled.

C: I cannot ask for another family … I cannot get other parents that care about me.

T: Here is the other part in you, the part that feels the missing.

C: That is the difficulty, how can you miss something that destroyed your life?

T: You say this sharply, "How can you miss something that destroyed your life?" If you say that to your [internal] *feeling of lack, how does it respond?*

C: [Speaking from the lack] *That, I see it different, that, I saw it many times in other people and every time I say "This is what I needed* [emotionally], *this could have made—how strange it might sound—my life normal."*

T: Of course, the feeling of lack is very natural [warmly].

C: It is so difficult, I miss parents, but I don't miss my parents, it is so confusing.

T: If you hear your feeling of lack say "it is strange, I don't miss my parents, but parents" what would you say then?

C: That I understand, it is a lack of a mother and a father that are really a mother and father, I never had that feeling and that is what I miss.

T: What message would you want to give to your feeling?

C: I would wish to meet a woman and have children, to feel part of a good, normal family.

T: To have the feeling to mean something, and feel loved, and give love [Client nodded]

This session was the onset to him expressing feelings of grief and hurt about everything he had missed out on in life, and he expressed a desire to start his own family. He felt a fear to stay alone and isolated, but also a desire to be of significance for others, for belonging and connection. Six months after discharge, Kevin reflected on the 25 months of treatment:

It gave me more stability. I came from prison with the idea that I was a stable person with solid footing. I was self-assured, too sure, not realistic. Now I can see what is unstable, what I have to take into account … I am changed as a person, but the risks stay the same. Now I realize, I am more than an offender … It is not me or the offender, it is together, it is a whole … What is very fragile and involves great risk is my self-esteem that I often lack, uh, the feeling that I am worth nothing … I have to take care of that. When that happens, then I become lonely and neglect myself. I think that is my biggest risk.

Kevin's emotion scheme of being worthless and shameful has shifted in small but important respects. Of major importance seemed that his capacity to give attention to his own needs had improved. During treatment, he had discovered that this altruistic tendency was actually part of his deficient emotion scheme and his so-called care for boys in need was actually a merger of his own need. *"I helped others not to be confronted with myself, to give myself a good feeling, to have meaning for someone."* It is of course a normal human desire to mean something to someone, but for Kevin it stays a risk factor to find that meaning in relation to a minor and it was a big challenge to experience that in relation to an adult, but at the end of treatment he met a girlfriend and was making plans for a future together (to Gunst et al., 2019a, 2019b).

5.4.3 Meaning and Meaninglessness

The struggle with meaninglessness for people who committed sexual offenses can be at least twofold. In the first place, meaninglessness and existential alienation is seen as a breeding ground for criminal behaviour and recidivism (Ronel & Segev, 2014). According to Frankl (1978), meaninglessness can manifest itself in a state of boredom. This is often mentioned as an emotional precursor to sexual offending and impulsive sexual behaviour (Stinson & Becker, 2018). In two recent studies by Moynihan et al. (2021), meaninglessness, boredom susceptibility, and sexual sensation-seeking with socio-sexual orientation was investigated in respectively 300 and 588 heterosexual and bisexual men. The second study also assessed if using sex as a coping mechanism plays a part in the proposed relationship while controlling for the Big-5 personality traits. Evidence was found for the *existential escape hypothesis* (Wisman, 2006) that meaninglessness is associated with men's increased endorsement of sensational and uncommitted sex via boredom susceptibility. Sex as a coping mechanism to deal with unpleasant affective states explained that relationship.

In the second place, creating a meaningful life can be a real challenge after a conviction for a sexual crime. Since the turn of the century, the focus in offender therapy has slowly been shifting from solely risk management to also supporting offenders to lead more fulfilling and meaningful lives (Wormith et al., 2007). The implementation of the GLM (Ward & Brown, 2004; Ward et al., 2007b) was the strongest catalyst for that change, besides positive criminology and humanistic approaches toward crime (Gunst et al., 2017; Polizzi et al. 2014; Ronel & Elisha, 2011). The GLM is based on the assumption that offenders have the same basic existential needs as any other individual, but because of a lack of capacities they achieve these needs through antisocial behaviour or by deviant or conflicting means (Ward & Brown, 2004). From this point of view, finding prosocial ways to meet these basic needs and living a meaningful life would help to decrease one's risk of reoffending (Ronel & Segev, 2014; Fortune et al., 2014). Putting more attention on existential issues and meaning in life in working with prisoners and offenders, is all the more important given the finding that half of the prisoners didn't experience meaning in life (Vanhooren et al., 2016) and that existential issues are often bypassed by therapists who work in correctional settings (Morgan & Winterowd, 2002). An experiential and existential therapeutic approach can encourage forensic clients to shift their 'empty' life goals into more self-transcendent and fulfilling purposes in life (Vanhooren et al., 2018).

For the cases under study, meaningfulness was highly related to having meaning for others. For two clients, the only reason to live was to be there for their children (Dave and Bruno). For another one, it was really important that he still was of significance to his wife, although he sometimes got overwhelmed by almost unbearable guilt feelings. The two clients who did not have a partner or children clearly struggled with finding meaning in life (Kevin and Nico).

A hindering factor to find meaning in life for all of the five clients was the interference of a self-critical voice that states that one does not have the right anymore to live a meaningful live, that one does not deserve to be happy anymore or does not deserve care for one's own traumatic injuries. The different case studies illustrate the integration of different parts in the self: victim or vulnerable parts as well as offender or destructive parts (Gunst et al., 2019a, 2019b; Gunst & Vanhooren, 2018). This is an important aspiration in offender treatment in order to let the client feel whole and be able to meet underlying needs in a way that is good for the self and others. This is in line with Bugental's (1978) central aim of existential therapy to strive for presence, which implicates the need for internal wholeness, or to repair the split and alienated self (Krug, 2009). Bugental (1976) emphasizes the importance of concentrating on inner awareness to recover one's lost sense of being and to discover one's "I-ness" (Krug, 2009). The presence and attuned responses of others, and so in treatment of the therapist, is a pre-condition in creating that sense of self. And in turn, that connection to internal wholeness can be seen as a prerequisite for empathy to others. The internalization of empathic attunement builds empathic capacity for the self and others. If clients becoming more empathic and responsive to themselves and others is desired, it is important that they internalize their therapists' empathy (Watson et al., 2014). Empathy training should therefore rely heavily on empathic attunement of the therapist to the affective experience of the client, rather than on psycho-education (Gunst et al., 2019a, 2019b).

Kevin expressed his wish and at the same time inability to be considered as a person, rather than merely be a victim or an offender, but he contrasted this need with a negative, shame-based evaluation of himself. The following fragment demonstrates that Kevin experienced this internal state of contradiction as both distressing and disorienting.

I want to be recognized for the person I am, but I cannot talk about other things because I only had misery. I want to be seen as a happy person but then I cannot allow it because I think I don't deserve it and at the same time I want it. It is so tiring to have that constant internal conflict.

In terms of Pascual-Leone and Greenberg's (2007) model for emotional processing, Kevin was stuck in the dialectic process of balancing out an existential need ("*I want to be recognized for the person I am*") and a core negative evaluation about the self ("*I don't deserve it*"), without being able to come to a synthesis of both. His *inner critic* interrupted contact with and exploration of his inner experience and needs. Eight months after he was checked into the hospital, Kevin started the emotion-focused group therapy. After a few sessions, the therapist invited Kevin to stay with his feeling of being not worthy to exist. As existential and experiential therapies suggest, it is by experiencing and exploring one's pain in the here-and-now situation that helps clients to process their wounded-ness and express their existential needs (Pascual-Leone et al., 2016):

T: *Can you try to stay with that, that there is a feeling in you that feels so undesirable, unwanted, that wants to hear "I am worthy." Can you say to that feeling that you noticed it and heard it?* [Client stays quiet.] *Where is that feeling in your body?*

C: *My throat.*

T: *Can you tell that feeling that you noticed it. That feeling of you needs to be taken care of.*

C: *It is very difficult to accept that because I also infected somebody else with it. I cannot tolerate it, because I don't deserve it.*

Kevin also had another argument why it was not possible to accept his need to be seen as a person rather than a monster. If he would be considered a genuine person, then the people who abused him as a teenager would also need to be considered genuine people, what is unacceptable for him. The anger towards his offenders also evoked anger towards his mother who blamed him for the abuse. When he was able to express disappointment and sadness for being blamed, it was the first time that he could tolerate his emotions and express his underlying need. What he missed was to find shelter in one's arms. He could stay with that desire for a little moment. Up until that moment, close connection to adults always had felt very unsafe and evoked a reaction of paralysis or freeze. Contact with children felt much safer.

Furthermore, forensic clients who are also victims of physical or sexual abuse were found to be more prone to experience low levels of meaning and low search for meaning (Vanhooren et al., 2016). A strong and warm working alliance is vital for the change process. Being fully seen and having the experience that there is still someone who believes in change and growth often marks the start of a deep search for meaning in forensic clients (Elisha et al., 2013; Maruna, 2001). Even if the client is in a state of 'pure' meaninglessness, Yalom (1980) believes that there is always a desire to be engaged in life somewhere within the client and that the best tool to remove obstacles that prevent the client from wholehearted engagement is the therapist's own engagement with the patient. The therapist can stay with and explore the deeper meaning of existential questions, integrate, and explore life experiences. In experiential and experiential-existential therapies, meaning-making will also typically run through methods such as *focusing*, where meaning is derived by attending the implicit bodily felt sense of the client. To create an offense-free life, it is crucial to find meaning in life, feel safe enough to build close and genuine connections, and feel valued as a person. This reminds us of Frankl's (1967) conviction that a meaningful life is only reached as people actually commit themselves to their purpose.

The case of Bruno revealed how the objectification of his external and internal relationships made him feel existentially isolated. Being cut-off from the experience of his basic existential needs such as love and intimacy, his life and other persons had no meaning, except his children. He wanted to be of significance for them. It was only with the emergence of his *self-in-presence* (Cornell & McGavin, 2008) and the possibility to focus on his anger that he became fully aware of his existential isolation and unfulfilled needs.

Later on, in a session near the end of treatment, Bruno interacted with the felt sense of his anger. Focusing again led to an unexpected result. At the heart of this anger, Bruno discovered something like his 'right to exist' and his 'urge to mean something and to matter to another person.' Focusing helped him to get in touch with his deep existential needs, which contradicted his previous coping style of isolating himself from others and from himself. For Bruno, his need for meaning and for being existentially significant to others became an important source of motivation for further change (Gunst & Vanhooren, 2018).

5.4.4 Freedom, Responsibility, and Guilt

The paradoxical given of freedom is primordial to clients in the forensic system. They live, compared to other people in the 'free world', more in a world that curtails their freedom while they still have a free will and choices to make in life. In some cases, violations are made of liberty rights, privacy rights, and health and well-being rights. However, "human rights provide an ethical scaffold or overlay to treatment that fuses the skills offenders learn and the values they acquire into a simple idea: pursue your own core and legitimate interests in a way that respects the human rights of others" (Ward et al., 2007a, p. 206). Being held accountable for the creation of a meaningful life or exploring the clients' existential guilt can be transformative for individuals through reconstruction of meaning (Clarke, 1989; Fischer, 1989; Elliott et al., 2021). Moreover, as Frankl (1967) states, the responsibility of offenders to change overrules their freedom because of their guilt. In order to live one's life authentically, facing one's guilt and taking responsibility over one's crime is a necessary condition.

A qualitative explorative study (Willemsen et al., 2016) with sex offenders revealed that it is crucial that individuals take responsibility for their life choices. In this study, 13 sexual offenders were interviewed who followed a residential treatment program which included experiential group psychotherapy. The semi-structured interviews included questions about what they considered as most important part of the experiential group psychotherapy, which difficulties they experienced, how it was to share personal things with the other participants, etc. The passages in which clients talked about helpful experiences were selected in the transcripts and categorized according to Yalom's description of the 11 therapeutic factors (Yalom & Leszcz, 2005). In the interviews, the factor of responsibility was mostly coded for instances in which clients described gaining insight into the fact that they themselves were the only ones capable of making change happen in their own lives. Clients often described initially feeling like it was the therapists' job to change their lives for them (as well as provide a name for their inner discomfort during sessions). Taking responsibility for their therapeutic process was noted as a key change. In this target population, acceptance of responsibility of one's own process and quality of life seems to be of higher importance.

> And now I've started to see – all because of experiential therapy – that it all has to come from you, that you're the one who has to find the answers. And that [therapist's name] doesn't have to do that for you. (Willemsen et al., 2016, p. 164)

Although one could expect that the lack of control and autonomy that comes with being on parole would play a part, this was not the case in this qualitative study. Other themes, such as dealing with the past, accepting or healing family bonds, and dealing with guilt and shame emerged frequently and spontaneously (Willemsen et al., 2016). Although this also holds true for the five cases under study, the meta-synthesis revealed a noteworthy obstacle in therapy. The entanglement of maladaptive shame (and trauma-related guilt) with the feeling of guilt for their own wrongdoing was found to be a hindering factor in treatment of sex offenders (Gunst, 2019). The four clients, described in this chapter, who were sexually abused in childhood, felt worthless and somehow ashamed and responsible for the sexual abuse they experienced as a child, which is often the case for trauma survivors (Paivio & Pascual-Leone, 2010). Guilt is usually understood as an adaptive experience as it leads to taking responsibility and reparative action, like confessing or apologizing. When guilt is fused with feelings of shame, the person is not only faced with tension and remorse over a specific behavior, but also saddled with feelings of contempt and disgust for a bad, defective self. Shame typically involves a negative evaluation of the global self (Tangney & Fisher, 1995). People with a core shame-based sense of self might block their therapeutic process by self-blame (they hold themselves accountable for their own maltreatment or feel they are not allowed anymore to receive care for being a victim), or might split off feelings of guilt, because it is too unbearable to face.

> Kevin expressed early on in treatment his struggle that he did *'not succeed in putting a barrier between being a victim and an offender. This is a daily conflict… having a desire for something you detest is inconceivable'*. The same confusion appeared towards what was done to him. He always had tried to suppress and ignore the negative impact. He blamed himself that he could have run away or defended himself (*'Did I want it? While there was also a feeling of disgust.'*). In treatment the struggle continued.
>
> *C: I never gave attention to it, although I could not go to the toilet or bath with a light on, I never made the association with the abuse. My struggle just began when I got a sense*

of guilt towards my victims. When I recognized what I did to that boy, I realized what happened to me. It became worse and worse. You don't want to block it because you don't want to stop the guilt feelings to your victim, you don't want to minimalize what you did, but at the same time feeling victimized becomes worse [client switched to the second person to control his intense experience and his voice is querulous and bated]. *Before, I almost never had problems with it and now when I am confronted with images or sensations, I become stuck in my feeling of being abused.*

For Nico, although there was a growing acknowledgment of his emotions and their value, after one year of treatment, he still expressed a continuing ambivalence to really engage in emotional work. In a working alliance dialog, treatment goals were discussed and there was agreement that working with his painful experiences to meet his underlying needs was most important.

Important for Nico in the experiential group therapy was a moment when he got a little emotional remembering how lonely he had been when he had shut down his emotions after being abused as a child, but it rapidly turned into anger towards his feelings. The moment he blamed himself for "having caved in for money" and "screwing everything up for myself", the therapist invited the client to engage in a two-chair dialog to build more self-compassion (Elliott et al., 2004). When the client was in the other chair, the therapist repeated the critic's voice explicitly and asked how it felt.

C: [in the other chair as "the experiencing self"] *I feel terribly lonely.*

T: Hm, you feel terribly lonely, what would you like to say to him? [to the "critic" in the other chair. The client cries, other client brings a tissue.] *It is so painful to feel that, right. Can you see if there is something you want to say or ask him from that pain or lonely feeling, what would you want from him?*

C: Do I have to stay my whole life in that tomb [cries deeply].

T: Will you leave me in that tomb my whole life? .... It sounds a bit like, it becomes time to get me out of here.

C: Yes! [sigh, cries deeply, overwhelmed].

The therapist invited the client to switch chairs again. The critic softened and affirmed that it was time to let "him" out. Nico was surprised that connecting to that part of himself felt helpful rather than threatening. This was an important shift. Nico continued to struggle to achieve balance between being completely distracted from his emotions or being too emotional, showing that this traumatic experience needed to be processed further. Another session, we worked further with on the one hand his destructive part, that searched for sex in order not to feel, and on the other hand, with his wounded, speechless part who just wanted to be hugged. From then, Nico was able to comfort and nurture that part.

An important step was for him to acknowledge his reactive secondary emotion of fear and shame that blocked his access to his underlying experience of pain, loneliness, and longing. A workable distance towards his experience was created (Pos & Paolone, 2019) using empathic affirmation responses, and helping him to make space by imagining putting his overwhelming or threatening experience at a distance. In addition to the improved adaptive self-soothing, at the end of treatment, he expressed gratitude towards the group members to whom he felt connected in a way that he had never felt before (Gunst et al., 2020).

Although the fifth client did not experience sexual abuse, threatening reactions of his father to everything related to the body or sexuality abandoned sexual desires to a secret world. As long as it was disconnected from self and others, the client did not experience shame nor guilt. However, these feelings came massively to the fore in therapy. For this client, the disconnection seemed to have paved the way for abusing minors without any discomfort:

> Patrick, being a perfect, law-abiding citizen in everyday life, abused several very young children 'in his secret world'. He found it real bad that he never had thought that he was doing wrong or felt bad when he was abusing children, not once. Breaking the secrecy and recognizing the harm he caused, led to an unbearable feeling of shame and guilt. These could overwhelm him suddenly when hearing a story of a victim in empathy training or when another client shared his story in experiential group therapy.
>
> He could "*not find a balance between* [on the one hand] *following and empathizing and otherwise keeping enough distance. It hurts too much*". It seemed as if he felt responsible for all the harm offenders caused to victims, raising the question of having the right to lead a happy life. However, after a while, the intense feelings could disappear just as quick.
>
> Patrick needed individual therapy to learn to find a workable distance towards his experience (not too far – not too close and overwhelming), to attend to his bodily awareness and differentiate his experience. In group sessions, he often said that he felt no connection to the stories of other clients (because he did not experience sexual abuse and did not recognize the impact of the frightening reactions of his father) or he became suddenly too overwhelmed.
>
> Later, he shared with the other group members "*The fact that I was completely stuck, that had a reason, it had nothing to do with your story, but much more, it had to do with your story and with mine, things are mixed up, and with the shame and the guilt about that, one big cocktail, if it overwhelms me, I get stuck, can't say a word. What I have done now is considering the pieces one by one; the shame and what's beneath it, the guilt, all the parts separately, and that makes it easier to talk about it and to hear stories of others without merging them with mine.*" He also described that he is able to be empathic, but something has turned that capacity off. "*I was convinced that I did not hurt these kids. If one did not want to be touched, it is hard to say, but I took another one. [...] I never used force or violence.*" Becoming more aware of his own lived experience, getting contact with his bodily experience was very important to him. "*If I did not have that change, I could speak about my offences like reciting an essay without being in touch with it.*" (to Gunst et al., 2022)

For offenders, it is important to take responsibility for their wrongdoing. To be able to do that, it is often important to free themselves from guilt feeling for what was done to them and overcome the suppression of their painful feelings. Shame and associated (trauma-related) guilt or self-blame can be described as recurrent factors in the five cases. Expression of the stifled emotional responses clarified the dysfunctional beliefs and mobilized unexpressed needs. All five cases illustrated that the sequence of approaching, allowing, and accepting pain and needs and combating dysfunctional beliefs results in change marked by a more self-nurturing and self-affirming stance. Therefore, they needed to take responsibility to fully (emotionally) engage in a therapeutic process. For the five cases under study, discovering underlying needs (e.g. the need for being valued and for intimate connection) was important in order to learn to respond in a way that takes the self and the other into account. A more positive relation to self and others made the guilt more shame-free, which improved taking genuine responsibility for their wrongdoing and for fulfillment of their needs in a pro-social way. As such, it is essential clients get connected with their underlying needs. The fundamental task of experiential and existential therapy for forensic clients is as such not different to other client populations—the symbolization of subjective emotional experience, to understand it and unfold its implicit action tendencies (Greenberg et al., 1993).

Concerning sexual traumatic experiences, processing trauma-related maladaptive emotions could be very worthwhile to interrupt the cycle of abuse. Experiential therapies help clients to face anxiety and pain, instead of abusing substances or others in order not to feel the unbearable inside. *Free will* is fostered by the improvement of affect regulation, self-awareness, and self-reflection based on the theory that adaptive emotions act as a guide in life (Elliott et al., 2004). The goal is to make more willful decisions about how to live in response to authentic inner needs.

5.5 Discussion

As evidence suggests that difficulties coping with existential challenges serve as trans-diagnostic factors, it is not surprising but appropriate that general case study research discovered that existential themes were highly present (De Decker, 2020; Helsen, 2020). However, research concerning existential issues in forensic clients, before and after they committed (sexual) offences, are rare. This meta-synthesis of different single-case studies (Iwakabe & Gazzola, 2009) revealed how Yalom's existential givens immerse in sex offender treatment and how existential and experiential psychotherapy can be of value as addition to risk management or a rehabilitation approach. Shared themes are systematically identified across similar cases. This way of comparing cases can aggregate and synthesize findings in order to build and develop theory and suggest implications for practice.

The first existential given about coming to terms with life and death was especially reflected in a lack of basic trust in life and the experience of death anxiety, both rooted in adverse childhood experiences. The five cases under study revealed maladaptive shame as a shared core maladaptive emotion scheme: a sense of worthlessness or a feeling of being disrespected. Besides that, the fact that they committed crimes put an extra burden on their already fragile experience of having the right to exist. For offenders who are also trauma survivors, maladaptive shame and anxiety might be seen as the main driving force behind the abuse. At its core, traumatic experiences are linked to death anxiety; the experience of being under extreme threat and vulnerability in trauma (Iverach et al., 2014). According to Crittenden (2006), experienced threat or a high desire for comfort is often mixed up with sexual arousal. Different case studies illustrated the confusion about affection and aggression, vulnerability and power, intimacy and sexuality.

The identified existential issues of basic trust and death anxiety in sex offenders remind us to pay attention to these dynamics in therapy. Building trust in oneself, others, and life is often a long-term effort including approaching and exploring the traumatic experiences. A safe therapeutic relationship is a prerequisite for achieving this goal, which brings us to the next existential given about connection and loneliness.

The importance of corrective experience through the empathic therapeutic relationship in existential and experiential psychotherapies is inspired by existential thinkers as Laing (1965) and Buber (1958) who emphasized the importance of being known by another person. The confirming therapeutic relationship can help forming a new inner relationship on the side of the client by developing the capacity to listen to their bodily felt senses, which was illustrated in the different case studies. Learning to attend to the (implicit) affective experience was of great importance in all the cases to grasp a sense of what is personally significant and to overcome the vacuum of existential isolation and alienation. After all, the capacity to connect to ourselves is related to our connection to others, both as source and result. Acknowledging one's existential needs helps to fulfil these needs with respect for oneself and others. The genuine, emphatic and respectful therapeutic relationship also served as an antidote for objectification. In this kind of I-Thou relationship, clients are neither the objects nor perpetrators of "I–It" relationships (Buber, 1958). The five clients under study confirmed the idea of existential thinkers and attachment theorists that a corrective therapeutic experience is of major importance in order to rebuild trust in their own inner compass and in connection to others.

Besides that, the presence and attuned responses of others is also a pre-condition in creating that sense of internal wholeness, which is seen as a central aim of existential therapy according to Bugental (1978). All the five cases illustrated the challenge of integrating different parts of self. Only when one is able to stand up and acknowledge that one is more than their traumatic experiences and more than their offences, can one bear their guilt (freed from maladaptive shame and trauma-related guilt). Building an accepting and nurturing attitude towards one's own painful experiences and needs was shown to be a precondition (to find the courage) to take full responsibility. Being freer to find their own inner truth improved their capacity to handle with respect to others and take responsibility for their deeds as well as for finding meaning in life.

This last existential concern about meaningfulness and meaninglessness was highly interwoven in the other existential dimensions. The experience of meaninglessness was rooted in the lack of trust in life, in others, and as a consequence in the own inner experience. For all the cases under study, meaningfulness was highly related to the experience of mattering to others. Family bonds, or more specifically the presence of children, are often the only reason to be still alive in the first place. Building trustful relationships within a safe therapeutic environment seemed to be a necessary stepping stone in order to create a connection to one's own needs as a guide to a more meaningful life.

5.6 Limitations

This exploration of existential dimensions emerging in people who committed sexual offences, before the onset of the abuse and during treatment, is only based on five qualitative case studies. More case studies are needed to deepen the understanding of existential factors in offending behavior and forensic treatment. A systematic study of more cases by more researchers can surely enrich the findings. Although it was an advantage that the cases were well-known by the performers of the meta-synthesis, it could also be an asset when researchers were involved without any connection to the original case study.

5.7 Conclusions

According to findings in general case study research, this meta-synthesis of different case studies of people who committed sexual offences also showed that existential themes were highly present before and after the offending behavior. For these five cases, a lack of basic trust in life was linked to poor connection to oneself and others. Experiencing genuine, respectful relationships and being of significance to others seemed to be of most importance to find meaning in life. Being able to integrate different parts of self and experiencing a sense of wholeness was in all the cases seen as precondition to taking full responsibility for their wrongdoing as well as to creating a meaningful life. This meta-synthesis is clearly a confirmation of the essential factor of a strong, empathic therapeutic relationship and an appeal to put more emphasis on therapeutic attunement to improve connection with the bodily felt experience and meaning.

References

Andrews, D. A., & Bonta, J. (2010). *The psychology of criminal conduct* (5th ed.). LexisNexis Matthew Bender.

Angus, L., Watson, J. C., Elliott, R., Schneider, K., & Timulak, L. (2015). Humanistic psychotherapy research 1990–2015: From methodological innovation to evidence-supported treatment outcomes and beyond. *Psychotherapy Research, 25*(3), 330–347.

Arredondo, A. Y., & Caparrós, B. (2019). Associations between existential concerns and adverse experiences: A systematic review. *Journal of Humanistic Psychology*. Advance online publication.

Baim, C., & Morrison, T. (2023). *Attachment-based practice with adults: Understanding strategies and promoting positive change*. Second edition. Pavilion Publishers.

Bowlby, J. (1998). *Attachment and loss*. Pimlico.

Buber, M. (1958). *I and Thou* (2nd ed.; R. G. Smith, Trans.). Scribner.

Bugental, J. F. T. (1976). *The search for existential identity*. Jossey-Bass.

Bugental, J. F. T. (1978). *Psychotherapy and process*. McGraw-Hill.

Calhoun, L. G., & Tedeschi, R. G. (2013). *Posttraumatic growth in clinical practice*. Routledge.

Cheng, C., Chueng, S., Chio, J. H., & Chan, M. S. (2013). Cultural meaning of perceived control: A meta-analysis of locus of control and psychological symptoms across 18 cultural regions. *Psychological Bulletin, 139*(1), 152–188.

Clarke, K. M. (1989). Creation of meaning: An emotional processing task in psychotherapy. *Psychotherapy: Theory, Research, Practice, Training, 26*(2), 139–148.

Constantino, M. J., Sommer, R. K., Goodwin, B. J., Coyne, A. E., & Pinel, E. C. (2019). Existential isolation as a correlate of clinical distress, beliefs about psychotherapy, and experiences with mental health treatment. *Journal of Psychotherapy Integration, 29*(4), 389–399.
Cornell, A. W., & McGavin, B. (2008). Inner relationship focusing. *The Folio. A Journal for Focusing and Experiential Therapy, 21*(1), 21–33.
Crittenden, P. (2008). *Raising parents: Attachment, parenting and child safety*. Willan.
Crittenden, P. M. (2006). A dynamic-maturational model of attachment. *Australian and New Zealand Journal of Family Therapy, 27*(2), 105–115.
Crittenden, P. M., & Landini, A. (2024). Sexual signals and behavior in children: Building hypotheses about the function of sexuality in childhood. *Human Systems, 4*(1), 21–49.
De Decker, N. (2020). Actuele existentiële thema's in cliëntgerichte psychotherapie Een kwalitatieve verkenning [Contemporary existential themes in person-centered psychotherapies: A qualitative exploration]. *Unpublished master thesis*. Leuven: KU Leuven.
Delle Fave, A. (2020). Meaning in life: Structure, sources, and relations with mental and physical health. *Acta Philosophica, 29*(1), 19–32.
Depestele, F. (2004). Space differentiation in experiential psychotherapy. *Person-Centered & Experiential Psychotherapies, 3*(2), 129–139.
Elisha, E., Idisis, Y., & Ronel, N. (2013). Positive criminology and imprisoned sex offenders: Demonstration of a way out from a criminal spin through acceptance relationships. *Journal of Sexual Aggression, 19*(1), 66–80.
Elliott, E., Watson, J., Timulak, L., & Sharbanee, J. (2021). Research on humanistic-experiential psychotherapies: Updated review. In M. Barkham, W. Lutz, & L. Castonguay (Eds.), *Garfield & Bergin's handbook of psychotherapy & behavior change* (7th ed.). Wiley.
Elliott, R., Watson, J. C., Goldman, R. N., & Greenberg, L. S. (2004). *Learning emotion-focused therapy: The process-experiential approach to change*. American Psychological Association.
Farnfield, S., & Holmes, P. (Eds.). (2014). *The Routledge handbook of attachment: Theory*. Routledge.
Farrall, S. (2005). On existential aspects of desistance from crime. *Symbolic Interaction, 28*(3), 367–386.
Fischer, W. F. (1989). An empirical-phenomenological investigation of being anxious. In *Existential-phenomenological perspectives in psychology* (pp. 127–136). Springer.
Fortune, C. A., Ward, T., & Polaschek, D. L. (2014). The Good Lives Model and therapeutic environments in forensic settings. *Therapeutic Communities: The International Journal of Therapeutic Communities*.
Frankl, V. E. (1959). The spiritual dimension in existential analysis and logotherapy. *Journal of Individual Psychology, 15*(2), 157–165.
Frankl, V. E. (1967). *Psychotherapy and existentialism: Selected papers on logotherapy*. Simon & Schuster.
Frankl, V. E. (1978). *The unheard cry for meaning*. Simon & Schuster.
Geller, S. M., & Greenberg, L. S. (2012). *Therapeutic presence: A mindful approach to effective therapy*. American Psychological Association.
Gendlin, E. T. (1973). Experiential psychotherapy. In R. Corsini (Ed.), *Current psychotherapies* (pp. 317–352). Peacock Publ.
Gendlin, E. T. (1978). *Focusing*. Everest House.
Glaw, X., Kable, A., Hazelton, M., & Inder, K. (2017). Meaning in life and meaning of life in mental health care: An integrative literature review. *Issues in Mental Health Nursing, 38*(3), 243–252.
Greenberg, L. S. (2015). *Emotion-focused therapy: Coaching clients to work through their feelings*. American Psychological Association.
Greenberg, L. S., Rice, L. N., & Elliott, R. (1993). *Facilitating emotional change: The momentby-moment process*. Guilford Press.
Greenberg, L. S., & Watson, J. C. (2006). *Emotion-focused therapy for depression*. American Psychological Association.

Greening, T. (1992). Existential challenges and responses. *The Humanistic Psychologist, 20*(1), 111–115.

Gunst, E. (2015). From self-in-prison to self-in-presence. In F. A. M. M. Koenraadt, K. 't Lam, L. Eurelings-Bontekoe, & M. Lance (Eds.), *Hechting of hechtenis?* Wolf Legal Publishers.

Gunst, E. (2019). *Facilitating emotional change in sex offenders: Lost cause or necessity?* Doctoral dissertation, Ghent University.

Gunst, E., Desmet, M., Watson, J., Willemsen, J., Loeys, T., & Vanhooren, S. (2022). Sexual pleasure as forbidden secret: A single-case study into emotion-focused therapy with an emotionally avoidant client who committed sexual offences. *Journal of Sexual Aggression*, 1–17.

Gunst, E., & Vanhooren, S. (2018). The destructive pattern: An experiential and existential theory-building case study. *Person-Centered & Experiential Psychotherapies, 17*(1), 1–18.

Gunst, E., Watson, J., Willemsen, J., Desmet, M., Loeys, T., & Vanhooren, S. (2020). A quest for self-soothing: A systematic case study into emotion-focused therapy with an emotionally avoidant client who committed sexual offenses. *Journal of Clinical Psychology, 76*(4), 676–687.

Gunst, E., Watson, J. C., Desmet, M., & Willemsen, J. (2017). Affect regulation as a factor in sex offenders. *Aggression and Violent Behavior, 37*, 210–219.

Gunst, E., Watson, J. C., Willemsen, J., & Desmet, M. (2019a). The role of affect regulation in the treatment of people who have committed sexual offenses. *Aggression and violent behavior, 44*, 99–110.

Gunst, E., Willemsen, J., Desmet, M., Watson, J. C., Loeys, T., & Vanhooren, S. (2019b). Into the wild, out of the woods: A systematic case study on facilitating emotional change. *International Journal of Offender Therapy and Comparative Criminology, 63*(15–16), 2586–2610.

Helsen, M. (2020). Actuele existentiële thema's in de cliëntgerichte psychotherapie: Een kwalitative verkenning [contemporary existential themes in person-centered psychotherapy: A qualitative exploration]. *Unpublished master thesis*. Leuven: KU Leuven.

Iverach, L., Menzies, R. G., & Menzies, R. E. (2014). Death anxiety and its role in psychopathology: Reviewing the status of a trans-diagnostic construct. *Clinical Psychology Review, 34*(7), 580–593.

Iwakabe, S., & Gazzola, N. (2009). From single-case studies to practice-based knowledge: Aggregating and synthesizing case studies. *Psychotherapy Research, 19*(4–5), 601–611.

Kramer, R. (2019). *The birth of relationship therapy: Carl Rogers meets Otto Rank*. Psychosozial-Verlag.

Krug, O. T. (2009). James Bugental and Irvin Yalom: Two masters of existential therapy cultivate presence in the therapeutic encounter. *Journal of Humanistic Psychology, 49*(3), 329–354.

Laing, R. D. (1965). *The divided self: An existential study in sanity and madness*. Penguin Books.

Li, J. B., Dou, K., & Liang, Y. (2021). The relationship between presence of meaning, search for meaning, and subjective well-being: A three-level meta-analysis based on the meaning in life questionnaire. *Journal of Happiness Studies, 22*(1), 467–489.

Maitland, D. M. W. (2020). Experiential avoidance and fear of intimacy: A contextual behavioral account of loneliness and resulting psychopathology symptoms. *Journal of Contextual Behavioral Science, 18*, 193–200.

Maniglio, R. (2012). The role of parent–child bonding, attachment, and interpersonal problems in the development of deviant sexual fantasies in sexual offenders. *Trauma, Violence, & Abuse, 13*(2), 83–96.

Maruna, S. (2001). *Making good*. American Psychological Association.

Mikulincer, M., Shaver, P. R., & Pereg, D. (2003). Attachment theory and affect regulation: The dynamics, development, and cognitive consequences of attachment-related strategies. *Motivation and Emotion, 27*(2), 77–102.

Morgan, R. D., & Winterowd, C. L. (2002). Interpersonal process-oriented group psychotherapy with offender populations. *International Journal of Offender Therapy and Comparative Criminology, 46*(4), 466–482.

Moynihan, A. B., Igou, E. R., & van Tilburg, W. A. (2021). Bored stiff: The relationship between meaninglessness, sexual sensation seeking, and promiscuous attitudes via boredom susceptibility. *Personality and Individual Differences, 168*, 110295.

Paivio, S. C., & Pascual-Leone, A. (2010). *Emotion-focused therapy for complex trauma: An integrative approach*. American Psychological Association.
Pascual-Leone, A., Bierman, R., Arnold, R., & Stasiak, E. (2011). Emotion-focused therapy for incarcerated offenders of intimate partner violence: A 3-year outcome using a new whole-sample matching method. *Psychotherapy Research, 21*(3), 331–347.
Pascual-Leone, A., Paivio, S., & Harrington, S. (2016). Emotion in psychotherapy: An experiential-humanistic perspective. In D. J. Cain, K. Keenan, & S. Rubin (Eds.), *Humanistic psychotherapies: Handbook of research and practice* (2nd ed., pp. 147–181). American Psychological Association.
Polizzi, D., Braswell, M., & Draper, M. (2014). *Transforming corrections: Humanistic approaches to corrections and offender treatment*. Carolina Academic Press.
Polizzi, D., & Draper, M. (2013). The therapeutic encounter within the event of forensic psychotherapy: A phenomenological hermeneutic of the givenness of the other within the therapeutic relationship. *International Journal of Offender Therapy and Comparative Criminology, 57*(6), 720–735.
Pos, A. E., & Paolone, D. A. (2019). Emotion-focused therapy for personality disorders. In L. S. Greenberg, & R. N. Goldman (Eds.), Clinical Handbook of Emotion-focused Therapy (pp. 381–402). Washington, D. C.: American Psychological Association.
Rogers, C. R. (1959). The essence of psychotherapy: A client-centered view. *Annals of Psychotherapy*.
Rogers, C. R. (1980). *A way of being*. Houghton Mifflin.
Ronel, N., & Elisha, E. (2011). A different perspective: Introducing positive criminology. *International Journal of Offender Therapy and Comparative Criminology, 55*, 305–325.
Ronel, N., & Segev, D. (2014). Positive criminology in practice. *International Journal of Offender Therapy and Comparative Criminology, 58*(11), 1389–1407.
Seidman, B. T., Marshall, W. L., Hudson, S. M., & Robertson, P. J. (1994). An examination of intimacy and loneliness in sex offenders. *Journal of Interpersonal Violence, 9*(4), 518–534.
Siegel, D. J. (2020). *The developing mind: How relationships and the brain interact to shape who we are*. Guilford Publications.
Stinson, J. D., & Becker, J. V. (2018). *Treating sex offenders: An evidence-based manual*. Guilford Publications.
Taihara, Q., & Malik, J. A. (2016). Is it adaptive or maladaptive? Elaborating conditional role of shame and guilt in the development of psychopathologies. *Psychological Studies, 61*(4), 331–339.
Tangney, J. P., & Fisher, K. W. (1995). *Self-conscious emotions: The psychology of shame, guilt and pride*. Guilford Press.
Tillich, P. (1952). *The courage to be*. Yale University Press.
van Deurzen, E. (1997). *Everyday mysteries: Existential dimensions of psychotherapy*. Brunner-Routledge.
van Deurzen, E., Craig, E., Längle, A., Schenider, K. J., Tentam, D., & du Plock, S. (2019). *The Wiley world handbook of existential therapy*. Wiley Blackwell.
Vanhooren, S. (2019). Struggling with meaninglessness: A case study from an experiential-existential perspective. *Person-centered & Experiential Psychotherapies, 18*(1), 1–21.
Vanhooren, S., Leijssen, M., & Dezutter, J. (2016). Profiles of meaning and search for meaning among prisoners. *The Journal of Positive Psychology, 11*(6), 622–633.
Vanhooren, S., Leijssen, M., & Dezutter, J. (2017a). Posttraumatic growth in sex offenders: A pilot study with a mixed-method design. *International Journal of Offender Therapy and Comparative Criminology, 61*(2), 171–190.
Vanhooren, S., Leijssen, M., & Dezutter, J. (2017b). Ten prisoners on a search for meaning: A qualitative study of loss and growth during incarceration. *The Humanistic Psychologist, 45*, 162–178.
Vanhooren, S., Leijssen, M., & Dezutter, J. (2018). Posttraumatic growth during incarceration: A case study from an experiential-existential perspective. *Journal of Humanistic Psychology, 58*, 144–167.

Ward, T., & Brown, M. (2004). The good lives model and conceptual issues in offender rehabilitation. *Psychology, Crime & Law, 10*(3), 243–257.
Ward, T., Gannon, T. A., & Birgden, A. (2007a). Human rights and the treatment of sex offenders. *Sexual Abuse: A Journal of Research and Treatment, 19*(3), 195–216.
Ward, T., Mann, R. E., & Gannon, T. A. (2007b). The good lives model of offender rehabilitation: Clinical implications. *Aggression and Violent Behavior, 12*(1), 87–107.
Watson, J. C., & Greenberg, L. S. (2017). *Emotion-focused therapy for generalized anxiety*. American Psychological Association.
Watson, J. C., Steckley, P. L., & McMullen, E. J. (2014). The role of empathy in promoting change. *Psychotherapy Research, 24*(3), 286–298.
Willemsen, J., Seys, V., Gunst, E., & Desmet, M. (2016). "Simply speaking your mind, from the depths of your soul": Therapeutic factors in experiential group psychotherapy for sex offenders. *Journal of Forensic Psychology Practice, 16*(3), 151–168.
Wisman, A. (2006). Digging in terror management theory: To "use" or "lose" the symbolic self? *Psychological Inquiry, 17*, 319–327.
Wormith, J. S., Althouse, R., Simpson, M., Reitzel, L. R., Fagan, T. J., & Morgan, R. D. (2007). The rehabilitation and reintegration of offenders: The current landscape and some future directions for correctional psychology. *Criminal Justice and Behavior, 34*(7), 879–892.
Yalom, I. (1980). *Existential psychotherapy*. Basic Books.
Yalom, I. (2005). *The Schopenhauer Cure*. Harper Collins.
Yalom, I., & Leszcz, M. (2005). *The theory and practice of group psychotherapy* (5th ed.). Basic.

Chapter 6
Gestalt Analysis of Sexual Offending

Annalisa Castrechini

6.1 Sexuality in the Gestalt Perspective

In all living species, except for humans, sexual activity and feeding oneself are unavoidable, spontaneous, and necessary needs for the survival of the species itself. They are biological and social "functions" that are "decisive for the organism" (Perls et al., 1997, p. 341) not only linked to instincts but both moved by internal regulatory instances (Salonia, 2015, 2019; Brotto, 2019). This means that humans eat and mate not only because they are pressed by their own needs, but because they decide it. This is what indissolubly binds the two functions of nature to logos, that is to a principle of self-determination in which the word—in the ability to say, to tell—that creates and defines our representation of the world coexists with the action of choosing that "*gives shape to something indefinite (…) and implies the passage from whatever is indistinct to something we can give a name to*" (Carofiglio, 2011, p. 111).

> It matters not how strait the gate, how charged with punishments the scroll. I am the master of my fate: I am the captain of my soul (Invictus, W.E. Henley, 2012).

Man asks himself questions about his existance ("what should I do?", "Why should I do it?"). Every time he is called to decide, and his capacity for judgment and autonomous action, germinated and supported only by an adequate path of emotional-relational growth and a healthy and ethical education, is linked to the

A. Castrechini (✉)
Gestalt Therapy Kairòs Institute, Rome, Italy

R. J. Tully et al. (eds.), *Best Practices in Sexual Offender Assessment and Management*, Dangerous Behavior in Clinical and Forensic Psychology,
https://doi.org/10.1007/978-3-031-83135-5_6

sense and causal power of responsibility.[1] It is up to his reflective self-awareness to direct him into moral actions and it is up to his freedom and to the nature of his human condition, the *ontological guilt* of being able to violate the order of the human world, as Buber would say, or to compromise the relationship with the others taking responsibility for it (Buber, 2008).

Endowed with self-awareness, he, in fact, has the privilege of accessing his internal experience and knows how to explain, evaluate, change his actions, unlike animals who "*cannot be aware of themselves as themselves and, therefore, do not have the ability to consider themselves responsible for what they do*" (Pacitto, 2012, p. 140).

In the human condition, according to the epistemological perspective of Gestalt Therapy, eros unfolds from the intertwining of two registers, the energetic one of action and the hermeneutic one of its meaning; only from their plot, our intentionality of contact will take shape and proceed clearly, fully realizing itself in an embodied action (Salonia, 2008. It will thus happen that an interest (Es function) will be evaluated and compared with our identity experiences (personality function) and from this polemòs we will arrive (Ego function) to a creative and new solution including the first two functions of the Self.

6.2 Maturity as an Evolutionary Task and Competence to Contact

Eros reveals us our incompleteness, as it compares us with the essential need of the other but also with his radical diversity which represents the constitutional limit of every human relationship (Salonia, 2004). The other is in fact 'other than me', as the bearer of connatural differences inscribed in the body and soul, but it is also 'other than me' that allows me to discover and play new parts (Cavaleri, 2007). Sexuality, in its intrinsic logic of donation and acceptance, thus becomes a place of true encounter and dialogue between Sein (Being) and Dasein (Being there) in a path of mutual integration (Salonia, 2011a).

The sexual experience, therefore, is "*the celebration and growth of the ability to be fully oneself and to be able to share one's own corporality and surrender to the inter-corporal traity*" (Salonia, 2015, p. 180). This is the ability that reveals sexual maturity which is the aim of an epigenetic path (Erikson, 1982); it proceeds through a fluid succession of evolutionary phases of development whose assimilation allows one to proceed towards the following ones, however preserving the immediately preceding state in a different form.

[1] According to the Theory of Self in Gestalt Therapy, the Personality Function—structure of the Self, together with the Es and the Ego—is the bodily and intimate instance, the result of all assimilated experiences and to it belongs the task of assuming responsibilities or to fulfill a contract. "Personality is the responsible structure of the Self": cifr. Salonia (2012a), p. 41.

According to the Gestalt perspective, every change in the evolutionary process concerns the body, a place of memory (Salonia, 2000) that preserves traces of our history, of our growth, of the transformations that have taken place, and it is always starting from the body that can start the acquisition of new ways of relating oneself. Within the coordinates of corporality and temporality we inscribe our existences because in the body "*the traditional dimension of time coexists: the present, the past (memories) and the future (hopes)*" (Romano, 2008, p. 26).

The itinerary of growth, along which we build our personality and our way of being in the world, begins with an experience of primary confluence with the mother's figure who, with her solid and loving body-relational presence, responds to the basic needs of the child and to the containment of his primitive anxieties. The basic securities that will be built will make the background for the subsequent developmental tasks of the child aiming towards the acquisition of the ability to come into contact in a healthy and nutritious way with the environment (Salonia, 2013a; Merenda, 2017).

> A child's life begins with expectation. Since the newborn does not have the ability to satisfy his own needs, he depends on his mother's milk and on the sensations that those who take care of him and help him grow can give him. In addition to milk, the baby also sucks the mother's deep emotions, the sense of well-being and her being there entirely in care of the body (Iacono & Maltese, 2012, pp. 15–16).

Retracing the evolutionary cycle (Salonia, 1989), from a fusional We, the child begins to learn the sense of the boundary between himself, the other (you) and the external reality, arriving to the development of an intimate ego (the sense of self, of one's uniqueness, the sense of the other). This corresponds to the beginning of the sense of the narrative-Self according to Stern, or the ability to narrate one's experiences (Stern, 1996), and which for Gestalt Therapy coincides with the phase of assimilation and the 'verbal' birth of the Personality-Function of the Self.

From a Gestalt perspective, the transition from one progressive moment to another will take place in a fluid and functional way if the child receives specific support from the parental figure: this figure, therefore, must be able to contain his natural anxieties and allow him to carry on his bodily tension towards contact. If, otherwise, this figure *inexplicably* disappears (Francesetti & Gecele, 2011), or loads anxieties on the child, or even adopts a confluent and confusing modality so as to "*not allow the existential distance for mutual recognition*" (Salonia, 2013b, 2014), depending on the time phase in which this will happen, the interrupted growth paths will compromise proper development of the sense of wholeness or the attainment of the experience of wholeness. The quality of the primary relationship is the foundation of a sure sense of self through the integration of the two existential polarities: being oneself and belonging. It is the unconditional acceptance of the parent and the emotional anchoring that will allow the child to experience himself in his strength and weakness, in dependence and separation, in the energy and need of the other (Mahler, 1996).

6.3 Sexual Violence and Its Forms

Sexual intercourse, which winds through the rhythmic waves of the intimate relationship between bodies (Salonia, 2015), is the conquest of the ability to meet the other in the vibrant fullness of an inclusive experience in which one's own boundaries, already built and then rediscovered, are lost.

The dimension of pleasure does not only have the function of releasing internal tensions: it is configured as a triadic experience (Ibidem) because through the sharing of pleasure, the person discovers his own subjectivity, discovers the presence of the other and the temporality. Pleasure, in fact, has and must always have an end so that we can return to ourselves, with a growth of autobiographical self, allowing us new assimilations. The intermission between one pleasure and another teaches us the 'place' to wait (Sichera, 2001), an indispensable territory for recognizing the other, where any forcing (prolongation or hasty closure) compromises the rhythmic flowing of the experience.

A disfunctional sexuality expresses an intentionality of contact blocked in the attempt to reach the other fully and tells of bodies in which an intimate knowledge has not developed, and, therefore, a sense of appropriation and fullness that would have made them vibrant and 'lived bodies' (Salonia, 1988, 2008; Sichera & Salonia, 2020). There was no conjunction between the 'what I feel' of the Es-Function and the 'who am I feeling' of the Personality- Function; only with this conjunction, the emotion is transfigured into a feeling that the body assimilates (background feeling) and the body identity of the partners is rewritten. In the context of severe dysfunctional contact processes, sexual violence is the most heartbreaking and painful form of border violation.

Under the heading 'sexual violence' there are various experiences in which the person is forced, by acts, prevarication or threat (explicit or implicit), to perform or suffer sexual acts against their will (Il Vocabolario Treccani, 1997). Among the most abject and aberrant forms of violence that will be addressed in this work, there is the abuse and sexual violence of minors and rape of adults. In the broad panorama of violent sexual behaviors, the theme of child sexual abuse will therefore be examined, through an analysis on the personality of the violent pedophile, and his dynamics of conduct, and that of sexual violence manifested through rape of adult subjects, examining the origin and dynamics of the violent relational modality according to the theoretical-clinical epistemology of Gestalt Therapy.

The choice to analyze child abuse and violence in the clinical picture of pedophilia arises from a precise consideration. Pedophilic perversion,[2] although distinct from violent sexual behavior, abuse and mistreatment of minors, has assumed coercive characteristics over time. Turning a careful look to the current historical-social

[2]According to the DSM-V (DSM-V, 2014), the Pedophile falls under paraphilic disorders. It is characterized by recurrent, intense sexually arousing fantasies, urges, or behaviors involving prepubertal or young adolescents (usually ≤ 13 years); it is only diagnosed in people ≥ 16 years of age and at least 5 years older than the child targeted by fantasies or behaviors.

background and its changes, we realize that, compared to the years in which the first studies on the subject were carried out, there are constantly ways characterized by forms of violence that in extreme cases lead to physical destruction of the child (Di Gregorio, 2016; Pacciolla et al., 2016; Frawley-O'Dea & Goldner, 2009). Pedophilia is a border area (Di Gregorio, 2016) where abusive behavior is mixed and masked by loving educational interests and practices. Therefore, in the following paragraphs, pedophilic sexual perversion will be explored in the cases in which the erotic sexualization of the relationship, as well as an expression of a deviated sexual orientation, contemplates aspects of cruelty to the point of assuming sadomasochistic connotations (Gulotta & Cutica, 2009; Mazzoni & Rotriquenz, 2012).

6.4 Origin of the Violent Pedophilic Relational Modality

> But the giant is standing now with his sword of love, and weeping he cuts the flower before it is trampled (Lucio Dalla, 1971).

For Gestalt Therapy, in the period of time between the confluence phase (birth—5/6 months) and introjection phase (from 5/6 months to the 9th month; Salonia, 1989), the child is fully cared in his vital needs by the significant figures that are near to him. In the phase of confluence there is a relational modality of 'We', characterized by undifferentiation and the absence of borders with the other, although already starting from the third month, as Stern states, an 'emerging sense of the Self' starts developing, as the child is in relation with his environment since the birth (Stern, 1987). In this phase, which Spitz called "pre-objectual" (Spitz, 1953) and Mahler "symbiotic" (Mahler, 1996), the mother's holding represents an organizer of the child's psychological birth (Ibidem). In the introjection phase, the infant introjects, or 'puts inside' the mother's food and experiences indiscriminately, and assimilates the first basic perceptual skills, necessary to define the boundaries between oneself and the other. In this period, in which the first experiences of differentiation[3] between one's own body and the mother's one begin to take shape, germinal attempts at separation-individuation are experimented. With dental development, emerges the first form of aggression (Perls, 1995) given by the evolution of the motor skills of the child (who now bites and chews food) and the refinement of taste (discriminates what he likes and what does not belong to him), resulting in the acquisition of a new competence in contact (From & Miller, 1997). If at this stage, the baby receives a negative bodily feedback from the mother, in terms of disqualification, punishment, abandonment, the new strength he is discovering becomes depressed, and the block of growth in positive experiences, produces "*ghosts of terror, destructiveness or of wickedness*" (Salonia, 2013d, p. 198).

---

[3]As Edith Jacobson argues, the ability to distinguish the external world (objects) develops before the ability to distinguish the self from the external world.

The genesis of pedophile behavior,[4] according to Gestalt Therapy, is specifically placed in the phase of addiction[5] (between the end of the confluence phase and the beginning of the introjection phase) in which the subject remains in a crystallized, frozen, passive and helpless mode of receiving; it does not pass, due to the absence of adequate parental support, in the natural and healthy assertive capacity of action/manipulation. The pedophile does not have adequate power of self-determination nor sufficient strength to live his internal experiences and peer relationships with complete affective-bodily-relational integrity. It is a force that, having no structure (because it has not been measured or defined), expresses itself in the subtle, manipulative seduction. This often starts with a delicate initial approach[6] with children or adolescents whose emotional difficulties are perceived and intercepted, or that the abuser himself knows, in which he identifies himself, and from which he sullenly takes advantage.

6.4.1 *The Impotence of the Body*

For Gestalt Therapy, the background from which the pedophile relational modality originates is characterized by an arrest in the condition of passive introjection, since the subject has not made the evolutionary leap given by the acquisition of the ability to deconstruct and assimilate.

> Biting, chewing and the very important functions of locomotion and the ability to contact are the main types of aggression that the child possesses (…). But if these biological activities are not employed in the service of the functions of growth (…), then the surplus of energy is discharged into types of displaced aggression (Perls et al., 1997, p. 463).

He has not been supported in the confidence in his own teeth and his energy, increased to carry on new intentionality of contact, and new paradigms of experience, is interrupted in the most archaic interactive mode: this mode belongs to a protected, sheltered, receptive dimension inside the confluent shelter of the dual

[4] In the broad panorama of chronophilia, we can distinguish between ephebophilia (primary sexual interest of an adult with regard to mid-late adolescence), from hebephilia (sexual preference towards individuals who have just entered the puberty stage, 12–14 years) and from pedophilia (primary or exclusive sexual interest in a prepubertal child, up to and not beyond 11–12 years). Although the numerous classifications on pedophilia will not be reviewed in this study, and the interesting difference between male and female pedophilia, the interpretative hypothesis of a latent form is supported (pedophiles animated by desire that remains in their mind or, at most , confined to acts of autoeroticism) and active in pedophilia ("child molester", molesters who actually pass to abuse after a phase of sexual fantasies or masturbatory acts that have children as protagonists). From many researches, we can affirm that the occasional pedophile is the most widespread type, and that not all those who experience pedophile fantasies carry them out, just as the obsessive pervert is relatively rarer.

[5] Salonia G., oral communication.

[6] We talk about Pedosadism when, on the other hand, mistreatment and torture are used to reach the peak of pleasure; practices that can culminate in the killing of the child.

mother-child unit. What is compromised, therefore, is the good formation of the ego function, the organismic function of the self appointed to "*identify and alienate what is me from what is not me*" (Salonia, 1989, p. 124). "*To accept an impulse as one's own means, in the sequence, to have it as part of the background in which the next figure will develop*" (Perls et al., 1997, p. 217).

Starting from the Gestalt assumption that the figure and the background are in a dynamic and changing relationship, in the pedophile we find a disturbed, chaotic background from which a clear figure or a clear and healthy intentionality directed towards a precise and adequate goal, cannot emerge.

Goodman writes: "*conflictual excitations lead to the dominance of alternative figures*" (Perls et al., 1997, p. 218). In fact, in the confused and ambiguous magma of the sensations felt, an erotic deviation can be configured towards an otherness that has the power to recall ancient, regressive aspects of the same subject. This can activate and satisfy needs that have remained unfulfilled and open: an experience that allows to free oneself from a seriously frustrating experience through the choice of 'another', whose peculiarities—being small—arouse attractive interest precisely because they facilitate the use of one's aggressive-manipulative energy. This is not the original goal (where intentionality should have unfolded), it is the object on which there is a shift of attention—on the erotic-sexual level—that takes on the contours of perversion (Freud, 2012). This orientation allows the avoidance of anxiety that would require an emotional-sexual relationship of an equal nature.

The split in his personal functioning is a specific *safety mechanism* (Perls et al., 1997) of the pedophile, which feeds himself, capable of separating the social dimension from the internal, consciously shameful one.

6.4.2 The Exercise of Power

> Please do what you have to do quickly, please do it quickly without hurting me. I swear to you I will have nothing to tell, But hurry up so I can breathe again (Pierdavide Carone, Dear Jack, 2018).

According to the Gestalt perspective, in pedophilia there is an exercise of power; that aggressive power that could not be tested in the inter-corporeal relationship with the mother and which was not assumed on an identity level, is rediscovered, actualizing itself in the relationship with the infant. It is within this relational unity that pedophiles feel and perceive their own body as larger than the evident body immaturity of a subject in the age of development, and can play a safer, actively enterprising sexuality, lived only on the register of the pleasure of the genital organ, compared to the unripe, unexplored and foreign sexuality of the other. In the contact process, the pedophile expresses the need of domination and control over the prey, as to compensate for their feelings of helplessness, left in the background.

On the psychogenesis of pedophilia, Gestalt Therapy presents similarities with the psychoanalytic conception. Starting from Freud (Freud, 2012, 2017) up to the most recent authors, pedophilia expresses the failure to achieve adequate adult sexuality, and is conceived as a form of perversion due to the insufficient empathic responses of the affective figure that impede a correct path of separation-identification and compromise the integrity of the Self (Salonia, 2001). At the extreme of this vision, there is the thought of Stoller (Stoller, 1978) who, in this regard, speaks of a conversion of 'childhood trauma into an adult triumph', for which the pedophile, urges to take revenge for the humiliating wounds inflicted by his parents during childhood, in turn dehumanizes and humiliates the partner in fantasy or perverse act.

6.4.3 The Plastic Form of Sexuality

An important aspect to consider is that sexuality, as well as food intake, are behavioral reactions with a *plastic form*[7] capable, therefore, of adapting to the background feeling of various emerging experiences; they are the extrinsic manifestation not only of needs or desires but also of tensions, internal agitations, negative emotions, and anxieties. We could say that the peculiarity of knowing how to model oneself on the internal and external inputs of the environment is the basis of the deviant and pathological behavior of the occasional pedophile, for example, or of those who do not have an exclusive preference towards children.

Moreover, the spread of a global network and technological advancement, while not directly responsible for the increase in pedophilia, contributes to and facilitates the expression of the sexual drive within a large virtual community that weakens the sense of shame, in a kind of widespread responsibility (Milgram, 2003; Darley & Latane, 1968).

6.4.4 Clinical Research on the Subject

In the study of the cases and, in particular of the personalities of the perpetrators of these crimes, research generally focused on the study of sex offenders rather than on the analysis of subjects diagnosed with pedophilic disorder. This for three reasons. The first is related to the tendency to deny. Those who have abused minors are able to recognize the indecent immorality of their acts and generally feel social shame, therefore, they do not reveal them. The second reason is the non-objectivability of the criteria (the criteria contemplate non-measurable experiences, as they are part of the internal reality of the subject; for this reason, they are affected by both the subject's capacity for self-observation and its ability to report them); thirdly, we find egosynthony (there is no perception of suffering from a discomfort and a pathological condition but of being invested by a benign, legitimate need).

[7] Salonia G., oral comunication.

Only witness evidence (which, however, will not be able to investigate fantasies, impulses, thoughts) and personal admission will allow the creation of a representative sample; in the absence of this, the studies are based, most of the time, on cases of recidivous offenders for sexual abuse of minors, found in prisons or rarely in private psychotherapy. The sample, therefore, will not be 'pure' but will be contaminated both by subjects with possible pedophilic disorders and by those with discontrol of sexual impulses.

6.5 Origin of the Violent Relational Modality: The Rapist

> Fleeting and empty is the pleasure stolen with force from a body and a soul (Giovanni Salonia, 2008, p. 56).

On the evolutionary level, according to Gestalt Therapy, the phase of introjection (discussed above) is followed by the phase of projection in which attention to what happens 'outside oneself' is a priority; vital space, experienced first as a container of one's emotions, then as a reality to be explored (Salonia, 1989). In this period, the skills are accompanied by additional skills such as exploration, manipulation, experimentation, and deambulation that allow better integration between the motor and sensory systems (Mahler, 1996) and allow the child to control his or her autonomous abilities. He is "*intoxicated by his own abilities, continually satisfied with the discoveries he makes in his expanding world, and is almost in love with the world and his own greatness and omnipotence*" (Salonia, 1989, p. 105). The emerging process of 'withholding and expelling' regarding food, background feelings and the products of his decision (feces), corroborates these sensations; the child discovers that he can hold and let go of the feces from his body, starting to experience a new relational paradigm qualified by the power over himself and others. It will therefore happen that if the parental body does not support the activation of the child's body and the emerging of feelings of excitement and ready to establish contact with the Environment, there will be an interruption of the increased and unprecedented aggressive energy.

In Gestalt Therapy, it is hypothesized that the origin of a violent dysfunctional contact modality—if not in relation to anthropological contexts and cultural mentality—is to be searched in the absence, (during the evolutionary phase) of a warm, solid, and congenial parental body with clear and defined boundaries that could accompany the growth of a preordained energy to carry out a congruent action in the Environment. According to the phenomenological-relational reading of Gestalt Therapy, we define it as a blocking in the phase of projection. Goodman writes about it: "*The individual who performs neurotic projections (...) cannot identify that free emotion as his own*" (Perls et al., 1997, p. 259).

If the child is not adequately supported in this new possibility (because the parent is absent, distressing or frightened himself) he will not learn the transition from feeling to acting in a fluid and appropriate way or to trust in the affective presence of the other, to which he can anchor; therefore, there can be the 'blocking of the gesture' (Salonia, 2008) that will remain crystallized in the body or the execution of a dissonant and disharmonic movement in relation to a feeling.[8]

As an adult, when the subject will be in contact with his own perceptual field, and will feel the intensification of his impulses and energy ("*the excitement is accepted and the environment is faced, one has the emotion*"; Perls et al., 1997, p. 259) he will not recognize these as his own (he will not appropriate them); it will be like feeling them in the air, he will feel prey of them, and so involved, so to let them overcome himself. Here, in the movement towards the environment, he will not experience himself as himself-in-action but will decline any form of responsibility (forgetting, hiding, even thinking of himself as someone who has suffered). In Gestalt Therapy, we say that there is a perfect coincidence and conjunction between need and action when there is an emotional and behavioral adjustment of *perception, sensation and movement* to a "possibility" that is looming in the Environment. For this reason, if there is a clear intentionality, the action will identify itself with the goal it wishes to achieve and in the orientation phase the body will respond "*very appropriately to contact with the environment compared to the simple awareness of the need*" (Cavaleri, 2010, p. 61).

In the projective relational modality "*the self that concentrates feels a gap in the experience*" (Perls et al., 1997, p. 346) as the intimate sense of self is lacking and, therefore, the "*proprioception, the feeling of one's movements*" (Ibidem). We pass, therefore, from the perception of the impulse—the most primitive emotional charge—directly to strong action; there is no orientation and manipulative capacity towards the environment because there is no awareness that takes place at the surface boundary in the relational field.

As Salonia writes: "*when the organism does not work, the self does not reach the contact boundary in a way that is appropriate to the context, that is, with the necessary awareness and energy*" (Salonia, 1989, p. 56).

In the case of sexual violence, the contact will be distorted and perverse, since it does not dwell on the border, in the place that contains and protects the organism and where the concrete experience of *inter-action* with the environment occurs. Therefore, there will be no relational self-regulation or assimilation of the novelty.

6.5.1 Sexual Violence According to Gestalt Therapy

The rapist is the one who lacks the warmth and sense of boundaries; a warmth that is neither felt nor able to be shared in the relationship with the other because unknown, given that, in the primary relationship, it was not possible to nourish oneself with the emotional, containing, and participating availability of the parent and

[8] For Salonia, the *missed gesture* not only expresses a bodily-emotional block (linked to a restrained emotion) but is equivalent to the interruption of a single, precise movement within a relationship.

trust in his firm and clear affective presence. Not having received the necessary support in the growing rising of excitement, the expressive and pertinent movement that would have allowed the achievement of the integrity and fullness of one's development remained frozen in the body (visible through muscle tension and contractions).

In primary experience, the coveted, rarely touched, and never fully experienced parental body becomes the missing experience, and constitutes the absence of a sensory ground from which needs should have clearly taken shape and so their fulfillment through action in the Environment. Not knowing how to act in the contact register, through sexual violence the subject carries out an assault in which he invades the boundaries of the other, remaining within them, with the aim of satisfying his needs (Pizzimenti, 2015). In the sacrilegious act of rape, one appropriates the body of the other by stealing his will and making him helpless and a slave to one's pleasure, in an exclusively individual perspective where the reality of the field made up of mutual self-regulation is absent.

According to the epistemological horizon of Gestalt Therapy, in sexual violence there is the coercive search/or the expulsion of sensations and emotions through the designated *object* of perversion (the victim of violence); it is believed that these sensations and emotions refer to the following specific situations:

1. It is hypothesized that the parts of himself that the child could not express because they appeared to the parent as *dirty, ugly and bad parts*, will end up to be denied (compromising a healthy and integrated growth) and being lived in a split way. In this divided background, the parts disregarded and despised by the same subject will be projected, and powerfully and brutally discharged through violence (Conte, 2013a).
2. The second condition, more specific than a narcissistic relational modality, is related to a subject unable to sustain an intimate relationship (Gecele, 2020; Conte, 2013a; Salonia, 2013e) and to be in the affective warmth. He frees, through sexual violence, unexpressed needs, longly silenced and retroflexed that, in life, have ended up taking on opposite connotations compared to the original experience. More clearly, the primary unfulfilled need to touch/receive/give heat takes the configuration of a fixation[9] and, consequently, of a perverse act of contact. Brutalizing the other becomes, therefore, the way to touch him, to get to him. In the background there is an experience of hostility, where the excitement lies in the sadistic and aggressive power exerted on the person. The rapist denies the humanity of the victim and feels his own sexual feelings experienced as an unbearable "*situation of need and vulnerability*" (Lowen, 1983, p. 53) (as intolerable; this condition, projected and captured in the victim, arouses an "*overexcitation of the genitals and leads to the act of rape*" (Ibidem).
3. In the third condition, however, the person feels in his body ambiguous and contrasting sensations and emotions as a result of original traumatic confusions

[9] By the word 'fixation', according to the Gestalt paradigm, we mean a rigid, unchanged, firm figure that does not recede into the background.

(Conte & Romano, 2010; Salonia, 2014), experienced in a painful way, and which will be expelled from his body with the aim of calming the anguish and internal tension.

6.5.2 Anthropological Traces

Clinical observations show that, in the context of violent action, the victim's fear feeds the aggressor's excitatory energy. Looking at the male/female relationship, and how history, characterized by continuous periods of emergency (hunger, wars, famines), has dichotomously defined the division of tasks, roles, and attitudes,[10] we can trace an anthropological origin of this phenomenon. In the time of danger, a division of functions and spaces between man/woman gradually was defined, which also led to a different register of existence (Salonia, 2004). Thus it happened that the woman, who lived in the shelter of the oikòs dedicating herself to the care of the family and the house, developed experiences of dependence and fear ("*she does not know what happens at the front, she is powerless on the progress of the situation, and therefore she feels the dependence growing within her, towards the one to whom salvation is entrusted*"; Salonia, 2004, p. 60), while the man, in the polis, forced to face danger, has developed more experiences of strength and courage: "*fighting against danger in a direct way gives a sense of control of the situation*" (Salonia, 2004, p. 60). It is hypothesized that, in the emotional-bodily-relational field between male and female, the perception of experiences of fear and anguish, by the woman, implicitly recalls the emergence of a bodily perception of protection, greatness and power, in man, which—in cases of violence—takes a different path bordering aggressive and sexual abuse.

6.5.3 The 'Rape Drug': Clinical Case

The clinical case that follows concerns the story of a prisoner, convicted of the crime of sexual violence, followed in a prison.

C. is a man of medium height and a small physique; he is quite pleasant in appearance and has thin, almost always dirty hands. Kind in his manner, he is formally polite, sometimes cloying, and poses as a little professor.

He was adopted in the first months of his life, a fact of which he becomes aware at school age from his adoptive parents and, in front of whom, he will always show a certain carelessness. He describes good relationships with his family but from his short narrations doesn't emerge a deep-rooted, deep emotional bond of reference,

---

[10] With postmodernity, the relationship orders have changed and decisive changes have taken place in the masculine-feminine grammar.

so that he always speaks about it with a certain detachment; he defines his father as rather anaffective and his mother obstinate and rigid in the rules which C. regularly disregarded, since he was a little boy. In his personal anamnesis, it is noted that he was approached to sexuality very early, in childhood, by some girls older than him, through erotic games and the viewing of pornographic films, and that these experiences lasted many years until C. undertakes the first romantic relationship. Trained in the best institutions, he boasts of possessing high cultural standards and a richness of language that celebrates more than it really is. Unable to study at university and poor in ambition, he ends up doing an office job because he wants to become independent. In young adulthood, he establishes few, but long-lasting, sentimental relations being, as he says, a lover of 'stability'.

The criminis event

Besides his work, with some friends, C. starts a collateral activity which consists in offering hospitality to tourists in their own home. C. and his friends often guide the guests visiting the main attractions of the city or to the clubs. At the end of the evenings, it often happens to entertain himself talking or drinking and, in some of these, C. decides to perform an act that gives him a perverse pleasure and which he will repeat again: he makes a 'drink spiking': he decides to administer anxiolytics, with sedative properties, in alcoholic beverages to induce a state of sedation along with disinhibition, and sexually abuses the girl with whom he is in company. C. has been convicted for abusing several girls in the same ways described.

Case analysis

C., in his family and relational life, was linked to dominant figures that he tried to please without enslaving his needs to theirs; rather, he manifested opposing behaviors tending to transgression with which in a clumsy and childish way he affirmed an immature identity on an affective-relational level, unable to experience reciprocity, to make amends for his mistakes or to anticipate the consequences of his actions. From the clinical investigation carried out in the penitentiary where he served his sentence, emerges the tendency to establish a confluence with the leaders;[11] *here he called his educator by name, and declared, as well, that he had been designated by the psychologist to follow a line of intervention with a co-inmate with significant clinical disorders, furthermore, considering their relationship to be equal and friendly. During the long months of treatment, the personality of C. was not completely clear: he showed good introspective skills, solidarity with others, active in re-education and adhering to disciplinary rules. The relationship he established with a co-inmate with a dependent relational style became significant; C. found in the difficult prison environment a friendly figure with whom he spent time, helping him in the many moments of crisis, finally becoming, for him, an undisputed reference. C. rose to a dominant role in which he wanted to be recognized; he imposed ways of doing things, choices, even what the other should have said or not said in the interviews. He was harsh, harsh and humiliating. C. exercised*

[11] He wanted to feel special and be looked at in a special way; he wanted to establish an equal relationship with the authorities.

a cold aggression, an autocratic power, and a sadistic pleasure of dominion over the other that so much recalled the dominion used in the abuses committed. C. spoke covertly with the therapist during the sessions (disconfirmations, disqualifications) and more openly in the relationship with others (harsh and severe judgments) when he did not feel seen, recognized, approved. What was striking was the apparent good functioning, the words and behaviors of righteousness and the active involvement but, on closer inspection, in everything, there was an excessive, obstinate need for zealous protagonism.

He was transferred before concluding the clinical and re-educational path started, and long before being able to take new paths together in the process of knowledge and care. It was important to be involved in various activities in which he was learning the co-centrality in the relationship (all unique, none unique) (Aparo, 2018*), so necessary for him, bearer of an abandoned experience never elaborated and of a loneliness linked to his own story.*

In therapy, even through dreams, windows of awareness have widened on the negative emotions that harbored within him, on the deep meaning and intimate direction of his aggressive energy (Perls, 1982*). Only the contact with his own experiences—through a slow and patient process of intrapersonal dialogue (Kimura, 2013)—has allowed a careful reading of his intentionality and the possibility of building and sharing new ways of encountering each other, guided by the inherent and vital self-regulating instance of the relationship.*

6.6 Peculiarities

In clinical work with subjects with severely disfunctional modalities such as those addressed, some specificities emerge.

In those who commit sexual abuse and violence there is an absence of an intimate verbal result.

The word is in deep connection with the body background, and from this it originates. On the evolutionary level, the absence of integrity and fullness, will ensure that words will be silenced and extinguished. From what emerges in the patients' narratives, it will therefore happen that, during the acts, generally no words will be spoken, but above all, no corporeal words will be uttered; those words that arise from a 'lived body' (Merleau-Ponty, 1979), able to feel "*sensations, emotions, experiences and meanings*" (Salonia, 2017a, 2008, p. 6) and to translate them into a congruent verbal expression.

The experience of pleasure does not pertain to the body in its entirety but is confined to only one part of it.

According to the hermeneutic perspective of Gestalt Therapy, sexuality, far from a reductive identification with genitality, represents a "*need for contact and exchange between differences, within a dimension of excitement and pleasure, connected to the genitals but not necessarily identified with them*" (Pizzimenti, 2015). Sexual behavior will therefore mean being in contact with one's sexual desire that takes into account the will and mutual intentionality of the other. The body experience of patients with violent sexual-relational modalities is that of a body not felt entirely, present and active in the genital area but alienated in its other parts. That is, it is a body that is not fully inhabited, and where the sexual experience will not be completely satisfying. It will therefore happen that when the impulse arrives, it will not flow smoothly into all the body structure; it will not be experienced as part of a whole but as an absolute need (Crolle Santi & Pintus, 2014).

'Going beyond' as an act of immediate pleasure and self-affirmation
In transgressing—from Latin transgrĕdi "to go beyond" (Il Vocabolorio Treccani, 1997)—is the immediate sense of gratification, "*because just when one rebels against a taboo and runs into a fatal danger it is possible to have a flash of spontaneous joy*" (Perls et al., 1997, p. 147). At the basis of research of a perverse transgression is the possibility of fielding an action that violates the rules of human and relational nature, and in the violation to carry out a consciously rough and dangerous act in which to be able to assert oneself against the 'other'. "*Deprivation and the forbidden seem to lead to more intense excitement (…) because they keep the connections open to resentment and anger and unconscious aggression against authority and, on a deeper level, with the desperate ability to risk something of oneself*" (Perls et al., 1997, p. 147).

The absence of Ordo Amoris (Salonia, 2013c)
If the contact leads to getting out from oneself to meet and accept the other in his diversity, the violent act does not arise from a genuine intertwining of reciprocal intentionality but from an assumed and self-justified power of the one who violates "*the sacred place of subjectivity in relation*" (Salonia, 2012b, p. 6) within a dynamic that takes place outside the contact process and in which the victim is reduced to a pure space of domination. The "relationship is reciprocity" (Buber, 1993), as the Jewish philosopher Martin Buber writes incisively, because it is the absence of any form of reduction of the self to you and vice versa. On the contrary, violence is the most sinister and deplorable dimension of subjugation, of "*predatory aggression*" (Hirigoyen, 2000, p. 127), deprivation of mutuality; it is a behavior in which the 'order' of the bond is missing (Hellinger, 2013; Salonia, 2013c; Buber, 2008), having destroyed a relational grammar that should take place within the vital interchange space built between the *self* and the *you.*

6.7 Therapeutic Paths

In the Gestalt theory of the Self, human growth is linked to the need to know how to combine two decisive and inseparable dynamics realities of existence: excitement and structure (Salonia, 2017b, p. 47). To enable the body to carry out its evolutionary project, the energy must flow smoothly, finding containment and direction within a flexible structure; otherwise, it would become chaotic agitation as well as a tight spot situation of the energy would cause the organism to block and devitalize (Salonia, 2017b). This means, for the human being, knowing how to listen to the background of sensations which will take the configuration of the emotion (Es-function), and knowing how to simultaneously operate a comparison with one's own body biography (Personality- Function); only in this way, the Self—the Organism in contact—will be able to orient itself towards the aim and make creative, healthy and coherent choices. Starting from these premises, the phenomenological-relational methodology of Gestalt Therapy (Francesetti et al., 2017), in the treatment of the two types of sexual aggressors that have been explained, does not have as its therapeutic aim the mere modification of deviant behavior, that is the extrinsic and ultimate manifestation of the path. In the same way, it is not based only on the search for causal origin since the sole attention to this would cause a block in the past and interfere with the assumption of responsibility of respect to the deviant experience. In the Gestalt perspective we pass from the *why* to the *how* which means bringing back to the understanding of meaning, therefore to organismic awareness. It works on bodily-emotional-relational experiences and aims primarily to restructure the bodily and cognitive evaluation of sensations and emotions, so that one learns how to symbolize and signify the emotional charge of the rising impulse, to discern the different levels of experience and to carry out a congruent action with one's own feeling and the intention of others.

6.7.1 Restore the Personality-Function of the Self

Performing acts moved by the charge of an impulse aiming to satisfy immediate and relationally blind bodily-emotional needs, reveals, both in the abusive pedophile and in the sex offender, a small and precarious identity, unable to establish an underground dialogue with itself (Salonia, 2012a), which becomes an inability to stop and observe one's own experiences, to assimilate them and to grow by virtue of them. This is a liquid identity (Bauman, 2006), blocked on an evolutionary level and not updated to one's own experiences, especially those concerning the violence carried out, as if the abuser had not been the subject himself, or as if the subject—and this happens in particular in sex offenders—has been pervaded and gripped by a force overwhelming his ability to hold it back. These patients suffer a clear disorder of Self Personality Function.

In the rapist[12]—if the victim is a woman, as in most cases—cognitive distortions are frequently recognizable, belonging to a male and male cultural background (Bozzoli et al., 2013), within which the behavior of others is read. These processes, accompanied by clear mechanisms of moral release (Merzagora Betsos, 2009), with

[12] Violence investigations portray women as the default victims of harassment, physical and sexual violence. The research highlights, however, the phenomenon of female violence, which is still rarely debated and which results above all in harassment, gaslighting, stalking, physical and emotional abuse, denial of paternity, limitations in the care of offspring.

which one is self-absolving ("it happened only once", "I didn't kill her", "she provoked me"), involves the rapist's perception of the female world. For example, bare breasts and legs are understood as sexual invitations. The difficulty and often the failure in the treatment of these patients—when the therapeutic treatment has not been autonomously decided by the subject but is institutionally foreseen by a rehabilitation plan, as in penitentiary contexts, in therapeutic communities, in anti-violence centers—lies precisely in the stubbornness and obstinate tendency to deny the event (the fact-crime); in fact, methods of neutralization are used to describe the incident such as the minimization of violence or the attribution of blame to the victim. This reluctance to open oneself, which does not only translate into the denial of what happened, determines a closure of protection that can prevent the construction of an authentic relationship—as there is an 'unsaid', supposed or certain (the violent sexual act), that burdens on the spontaneity and conditions the relationship itself—and the beginning of an adequate therapeutic path.

The therapeutic cure, oriented to the Personality-Function, aims to promote the construction of a healthy and solid body identity—capable of answering the question: "*who have I become?*"—and relational—capable of answering the question: "*who am I in front of you? And who are you in front of me?*"—through the development of an embodied awareness that takes into account the individual and intercorporeal feeling (Salonia, 1986); an awareness arising from the competence to narrate the experience, knowing how to attribute a specific name and a meaning to the experience that emerged, to perceive the emotion by grasping its quality (pleasant or unpleasant, interesting or not), to evaluate, through various criteria and levels, the experience.

In the work on the personality function of the self, the sensorial-perceptive dimension joins the symbolic-cognitive dimension of language and narration, in which the word is not empty and inconsistent as in the verbal exposures, often generic and vague, of these patients. Rather, it is the word that comes from the body and promotes contact and a modifying experience.

Starting from the experience "*I am aware of/that ...*"[13] means encouraging self-expression (of needs, emotions, etc.) and taking responsibility for this, drawing a form of self-support from it (Pacitto, 2007). Perls stated: "*Responsibility means the ability to respond: the ability to be alive, to feel, to exercise one's sensitivity*"(Perls, 1982 p. 110). Of course, awareness is inextricably linked to movement and action; therefore the question "what do you feel?" will be joined to the plan of intentionality "what do you want?" and to the pragmatic "what can you do?"

Only this path will allow the patient to connect the experiences to the here and now of the real situation and to fully appropriate the lived reality, feeling the responsibility—also in terms of consequences on the victims' lives—and to proceed, updating the autobiographical self.

---

[13] It is, as the founding fathers of Gestalt Therapy teach us, an experience that aims to 'direct awareness' to stimulate proprioceptive contact and orientation with respect to the Environment (Perls et al., 1997, cit.).

6.7.2 *Access the Sensory-Motor Register. The Es-Function of the Self*

The body is the constitutive dimension of our identity because our affective history is inscribed in it—in the posture, in the expression of movements, in the sound of the voice, in the tensions and desensitizations. It is the attention to bodily experiences and their meanings that inform and guide us on the present moment and the next, that is the step to take to achieve a healthy and nutritious encounter with the environment (Salonia, 2008).

The central task, in the treatment of abusive pedophiles and rapists, is to restore the healthy Es-Function of the Self[14] by supporting the awareness of intimate bodily experiences, so that we can properly read what happens inside the skin, and the flow of sensations, that exist between one's own body and the body of the other (intercorporeity; Salonia, 2011b).

Through the technique of concentration and body work with breathing, sentinel that guides us in the epiphanic discovery of our internal world, the subject establishes an intrapersonal contact with himself and learns how to answer to the underground question: "*what do I feel?*", "*what am I in contact with ?*", "*what feelings and emotions are going through me right now?*". Breathing and its blockages (Downing, 1995) (in the respiratory phases, in the breadth, in the depth) point out the presence of body defenses designed to suppress the emergence of sensations, emotions, memories, and threatening contacts. In therapy, the patient will therefore be advised to pay attention to the rhythm of his breathing movements because these will communicate his experience of withdrawal or opening to the world.[15] On this basis, the specific body work, for the abusive pedophile, will proceed with an introjective relational modality, aiming to supporting the fear linked to the identification of sensations and emotions and the maturation of his implicit reduced body scheme, incapable of trust in his own spontaneity and aggressive energy.

For the sex offender, a subject with a projective type of relational modality tending to cross over into abusive and violent behaviors with adult individuals, the body work will aim to accepting, signifying and containing the crescendo of excitement that emerges in the body background. Unable to fully recognize his own experiences, he in fact fails to assume paternity; he is unable to 'stay' with them, to contain them, regulate them and address them appropriately in the Environment. An Environment that he does not see but he wants to possess, destroying it and which, in the therapeutic process, he will learn to encounter, supporting the anguish that this entails.

[14] For Goodman, the Es-Function is the body background from which the orgasmic intentionality emerges (Perls et al., 1997, cit.).

[15] Breathing work becomes essential for the patient to expand—in perceptual terms—his body boundaries and feel that he can hold and contain the flow of the energy of excitement within a firmer structure. In therapy, the therapist's solid and containing presence will allow the patient not to feel overwhelmed by his own energy but to be able to feel it circulating throughout his body.

6.7.3 The Organism-Environment Contact: The Ego-Function of the Self

The impulse replaces the generation and the clear and correct movement of the Ego-function which cannot be anchored to the awareness of the background of sensations and emotions, because it is absent or scarce, nor to a solid and structured identity organization. When this happens, the precise and appropriate gesture that the Body would have liked to make or receive on its journey of encounter with otherness, stops, causing the onset of pathological discomfort. This is how the work on the Id function and the Personality function, and on their integration, constitutes the anchoring base for the I function to complete its trajectory, continuing the genuine contact with the Environment and making the creative adaptation for which it is designed.

If we start from the Gestalt principle that everything that is not completed is perpetuated, then the specific support for patients with violent relational-sexual modalities will concern:

- the development of a healthy Personality-Function—as an intimate regulatory instance and body memory of all assimilated contact experiences (Salonia, 2012a)—able to embody itself in every present situation and to be able to establish contacts that are affected by the nature of the relationship (symmetrical/asymmetrical) and of a faithful thought connected to one's own identity.
- completing an action that conforms to one's own feelings, capable of meeting the other in integrity and fullness. This means knowing how to answer the intimate question: "what do I really want? Where do I want to go? What do I need/desire?" but also to know how to question oneself on the intention of others. This attention, which constitutes a fundamental rule of relational grammar, enables us to carry out congruent actions and relationships of reciprocity.

The precious work on the Ego-Function, necessary to promote an adequate identification process, will allow the patient to be able to discriminate, in reality, what he can identify with (nutritious food) from what he must alienate and distance from himself because it does not belong to him. It will allow him to orient himself in relationships by making choices in line with what he needs and desires, in terms functional to his growth.

Supporting the emergence of a clear and vital Ego-Function means focusing on a concrete and specific use of language, characterized in particular by the more careful use of personal pronouns (Salonia, 2017b). The personal pronoun I, not adopted in a self-referential way but as a revealer of one's inner self, will thus facilitate the manifestation of oneself and overturn the "dominion over the self" (Perls et al., 1997, p. 487) so that the patient no longer feels possessed by an impulse that he cannot control but perceives himself architect of his own reality. As Perls would say: "*The ego is used as an antidote to it and develops the patient's sense of responsibility towards his feelings, thoughts and symptoms, the 'I am' is his existential symbol*" (Perls, 1977, p. 66).

6.7.4 Aggression and Sexuality

The patient with violent sexual modalities must be able to read his own aggressive energy that comes to life in a relational field, on the border between organism/environment. It is not, therefore, an individual phenomenon but a co-created experience in which the individual, in his going-towards movement, is influenced by the movement and presence of the other (Robine, 2006).

The difficulty in placing and regulating experiences on the border of contact with the other does not only concern the type of subjects analyzed, but is a sign of a discomfort linked to our time, and a growth challenge to which we are called. The current postmodern context, heir of a narcissistic society characterized by the weakness of belonging and by the exasperated search for self-affirmation, is characterized by increasingly uncertain, indefinite borders, presaging internal and relational confusions, and fragile and precarious identities. Thus subjectivity, increasingly dominated by chaos and emotional illiteracy, is accompanied by the inability to handle healthy and adequate instruments for comparison and dialogue, and failure in relationships (Conte, 1998, 2008).

Today relationships oscillate between dependence (I cannot live with you or without you) (Salonia, 2013e)—in which the other is seen only in the aspects that meet one's own need—and exasperated self-referentiality—in which the other is experienced as a limit to one's own affirmation or as a foreign presence, with which it is difficult to communicate. In both cases, the perception of the other in its entirety is missing. This process that also occurs in the rapist's violent sexual approach in which the other loses his characteristics of humanity and is objectified (Rollero & De Piccoli, 2013), dissected into his sexual functions which are, therefore, split off from the other identity components. The person, therefore, becomes pieces of himself perceived in isolation at the expense of the whole person.

In the reduction of man *to thing* is the tragic and ruthless aspect, and the metaphysical guilt, Jaspers would say, for which the sentimental matrix of the impulse to solidarity is lost. So, man loses the opportunity to recognize himself in his fellow man (Jaspers, 1996).

6.7.5 The Power of Hospitality

In the therapeutic relationship, the experience of acceptance has the value of transforming the patient's loneliness and silence, stained by his gross and ignoble actions, into the possibility of finding hospitality—perhaps for the first time—in a relationship where he can experience a new way of meeting the other. The solid, cordial and confined presence of the therapist, together with a climate of safety and trust, will be the safe haven in which he can feel recognized and fully express himself, to appropriate and integrate those parts of himself that are inaccessible and unexplored.

He discovers trust in his own corporeality, a place of experiences that find legitimacy, support and new forms of expression within a relationship of belonging.

However, in working with sexual aggressors, careful and delicate care is also required in the internal dynamics of the therapist himself, often accompanied by negative feelings, sometimes of disgust towards the patient. Loyal acceptance and awareness of one's emotional and affective energies constitutes a pre-understanding (Gadamer, 2000) of the relational experience that one is about to undertake. It is therefore essential that the therapist allow himself to be supported by a third, vicarious presence, such as that of the supervisor, who can help him maintaining a clear and healthy boundary in the relationship with the patient.

An elective context of growth for patients with violent sexual modalities is, in addition to individual psychotherapy, the group one. The group situation, a safe place of emergency (Perls et al., 1997) in which the individual learns how to recognize his most authentic needs, becoming aware of his own dysfunctional ways of contact and experiencing new ways of being in the world, relieves the individual from a situation of isolation and connects him with others with whom he can share his suffering. In the treatment process, Gestalt epistemology strongly supports the creative expression of oneself—a paradigm of a healthy creative adaptation (Sichera, 2011)—and the opening to new paths of growth. The psychotherapeutic path for patients with violent sexual modalities, carried out within a group treatment based on a multi-professional approach, may include various activities (Conte, 2013b). Therefore, active and dramatization techniques can be used to encourage reflection on oneself and mirroring; it will be possible to project themed films, and listen to readings of testimonies and lectures as a stimulus for discussion and sharing. They will constitute precious spaces for meeting and dialogue, and for relational maturation.

Finally, the pet therapy is an elective activity in treating patients with the methods described: a therapeutic and psychoeducational approach in which the animal—or rather, the relationship between man and animal—acquires curative value.

It is configured as an experience of intercorporeity (of bodies between bodies in interaction; Merenda, 2014) in which one learns to get in touch with another through body language, and to take care of them. Affective and relational skills that are at the basis of the dialogic and ethical dimension of responsibility.

References

Aparo, P. (Ed.). (2018). *Un fratello per Narciso*. Cittadella Editrice, Assisi.

Bauman, Z. (2006). *Amore liquido. Sulla fragilità dei legami affettivi*. Laterza, Roma-Bari.

Bozzoli, A., Merelli, M., & Ruggerini, M. G. (2013). *Il lato oscuro degli uomini. La violenza maschile contro le donne: modelli culturali a confronto*. Ediesse, Roma.

Brotto, F. (2019). *I ritmi dell'eros. Gestalt Therapy e sessuologia*. Il pozzo di Giacobbe, Trapani.

Buber, M. (1993) (ed. or 1954). *Il principio dialogico e altri saggi*. San Paolo Edizioni, Cinisello Balsamo.

Buber, M. (2008). *Colpa e sensi di colpa*. Apogeo Editore, Milano.

Carofiglio, G. (2011). *La manomissione delle parole*. BUR Extra, Milano.
Cavaleri, P. A. (2007). *Vivere con l'altro. Per una cultura della relazione*. Città Nuova Editrice, Roma.
Cavaleri, P. A. (2010). *La profondità della superficie. Percorsi introduttivi alla psicoterapia della Gestalt*. Franco Angeli, Milano.
Conte, V. (1998). Dall'appartenenza all'individuazione: come restare coppia. *Quaderni di Gestalt – Rivista semestrale di psicoterapia della Gestalt*, 26/29
Conte, V. (2008). Essere coppia nella postmodernità. In A. Ferrara & M. Spagnuolo Lobb (Eds.), *Le voci della Gestalt*. Franco Angeli, Milano.
Conte, V. (2013a). La modalità relazionale narcisistica nella postmodernità e il lavoro terapeutico. In *Rivista Internazionale di Psicoterapia GTK* n. 4.
Conte, V. (2013b). La Gestalt Therapy e i pazienti gravi. In G. Salonia, V. Conte, P. Argentino (Eds.), *Devo sapere subito se sono vivo. Saggi di psicopatologia gestaltica*. Il Pozzo di Giacobbe, Trapani.
Conte, V., Romano, R. G. (2010). Il paziente borderline: un'ostinata e sofferta richiesta di chiarezza. In *Rivista Internazionale di Psicoterapia GTK* n.1.
Crolle Santi, M. V., Pintus, G. (Eds.). (2014). *La relazione assoluta, Psicoterapia della Gestalt e dipendenze patologiche*. Collana L'Immaginale – Aracne Editrice, Roma.
Dalla, L. (1971). *Il gigante e la bambina in Storie di casa mia*. Sony Music.
Darley, J. M., Latane, B. (1968). Bystander intervention in emergencies: Diffusion of responsibility. *Journal of Personality and Social Psychology, 8*(4, Pt.1), 377–383.
Di Gregorio, L. (2016). *La voglia oscura. Pedofilia e abuso sessuale*. Giunti, Firenze.
Downing, G. (1995). *Il corpo e la parola*. Astrolabio, Roma.
DSM-V. Manuale diagnostico e statistico dei disturbi mentali (2014). Cortina Raffaello, Milano.
Erikson, E. (1982). *I cicli della vita. Continuità e mutamenti*. Armando, Roma.
Francesetti, G., Gecele, M. (2011). *L'altro irraggiungibile. La psicoterapia della Gestalt con le esperienze depressive*. Franco Angeli, Milano.
Francesetti, G., Gecele, M., Roubal, J. (2017). *La Psicoterapia della Gestalt nella pratica clinica. Dalla psicopatologia all'estetica del contatto*. Franco Angeli, Milano.
Frawley-O'Dea, M. G., Goldner, V. (2009). *Atti impuri. La piaga dell'abuso sessuale nella chiesa cattolica*. Raffaello Cortina, Milano.
Freud, S. (2012) (ed. or 1905). *Tre saggi sulla teoria sessuale*. Bollati Boringhieri, Torino.
Freud, S. (2017) (ed. or 1915). *Metapsicologia*. Bollati Boringhieri, Torino.
From, I., Miller, V. (1997). Introduzione. In F. Perls, R. Hefferline, & P. Goodman (ed. or 1994). *Teoria e pratica della terapia della Gestalt*. Astrolabio, Roma.
Gadamer, H. J. (2000). *Verità e metodo*. Bompiani, Milano.
Gecele, M. (2020). *Siamo tutti narcisi? Alla ricerca della relazione perduta*. Tangram Edizioni Scientifiche, Trento.
Gulotta, G., Cutica, I. (2009). *Guida alla perizia in tema di abuso sessuale e alla sua critica*. Giuffrè Editore, Milano.
Hellinger, B. (2013). *Ordini dell'amore. Un manuale per la riuscita delle relazioni*. Feltrinelli, Milano.
Henley, E. W. (2012). *Invictus in a book of verses*. Filiquarian Legacy Publishing.
Hirigoyen, M. F. (2000). *Molestie morali. La violenza perversa nella famiglia e nel lavoro*. Einaudi, Milano.
Iacono, D., Maltese, G. (2012). *Come l'acqua... Per un'esperienza gestaltica con i bambini tra rabbia e paura*. Il Pozzo di Giacobbe, Trapani.
Il Vocabolario Treccani. (1997). Istituto dell'Enciclopedia Italiana, Roma.
Jaspers, K. (1996) (ed. or 1946). *La questione della colpa. Sulla responsabilità politica della Germania*. Raffaello Cortina, Milano.
Lowen, A. (1983). *Il narcisismo, l'identità rinnegata*. Feltrinelli, Milano.
Mahler, M. (1996) (ed. or 1978). *La nascita psicologica del bambino*. Bollati Boringhieri, Torino.

Mazzoni, G., Rotriquenz, E. (2012). *La testimonianza nei casi di abuso sessuale sui minori.* Giuffrè Editore, Milano.
Merenda, A. (2014). *Incontri terapeutici a quattro zampe.* Il Pozzo di Giacobbe, Trapani.
Merenda, A. (2017). *Genitori con. Modelli di coparenting attuali e corpi familiari in Gestalt Therapy.* Cittadella Editrice, Assisi.
Merleau-Ponty, M. (1979). *Il corpo vissuto.* Il Saggiatore, Milano.
Merzagora Betsos, I. (2009). *Uomini Violenti.* Raffaello Cortina, Milano.
Milgram, S. (2003). *Obbedienza all'autorità. Uno sguardo sperimentale.* Einaudi, Milano.
Pacciolla, A., Romiti, M., Pacciolla, M. (2016). *Personalità, pedofilia e DSM-V. Come i sex offenders raccontano le loro storie.* Aracne Ed., Roma.
Pacitto, M. F. (2007). *Dal sentire all'essere.* Magi, Roma.
Pacitto, M. F. (2012). *Buoni si nasce, soggetti etici si diventa. La costruzione della mente etica tra neuroscienze, filosofia e psicologia.* Pendragon, Bologna.
Perls, F. (1977). *L'Approccio della Gestalt. Testimone oculare della terapia.* Astrolabio, Roma
Perls, F. (1982). *La terapia gestaltica parola per parola.* Astrolabio, Roma.
Perls, F. (1995). *L'Io, la fame, l'aggressività.* Franco Angeli, Milano.
Perls, F., Hefferline, R., Goodman, P. (1997) (ed. or 1994). *Teoria e pratica della terapia della Gestalt.* Astrolabio, Roma.
Carone Pierdavide, Dear Jack. (2018). *Caramelle, Artist First.*
Pizzimenti, M. (2015). *Aggressività e Sessualità. Il rapporto figura/sfondo tra dolore e piacere.* Franco Angeli, Milano.
Robine, J. M. (2006). *Il rivelarsi del Sé nel contatto.* Franco Angeli, Milano.
Rollero, C., De Piccoli, N. (2013). Modelli mediatici e oggettivazione maschile e femminile, La camera blu. *Rivista di studi di genere.*
Romano, R. G. (2008). *Ciclo di vita e dinamiche educative nella società postmoderna.* Franco Angeli, Milano.
Salonia, G. (1986). La consapevolezza nella teoria e pratica della Psicoterapia della Gestalt. In "*Quaderni di Gestalt*", n. 3.
Salonia, G. (1988). Itinerario bibliografico sul tema: il corpo in psicoterapia. In "*Quaderni di Gestalt*", n. 6/7.
Salonia, G. (1989). Dal noi all'io-tu: contributo per una teoria evolutiva del contatto. In "*Quaderni di Gestalt*", n. 8-9.
Salonia, G. (2000). *Respiro il corpo che parla di me in Messaggero Cappuccino – Periodico di cultura e formazione.*
Salonia, G. (2001). Tempo e relazione. L'intenzionalità relazionale come orizzonte ermeneutico della Psicoterapia della Gestalt. In M. Spagnuolo Lobb (Ed.), *Psicoterapia della Gestalt. Ermeneutica e clinica.* Franco Angeli, Milano.
Salonia, G. (2004). Femminile e maschile: vicende e significati di un irriducibile diversità. In R. G. Romano (Ed.), *Ciclo di vita e dinamiche educative nella società postmoderna.* Franco Angeli, Milano.
Salonia, G. (2008). La Psicoterapia della Gestalt e il lavoro sul corpo. Per una rilettura del fitness. In S. Vero (Ed.), *Il corpo disabitato. Semiologia, fenomenologia e psicopatologia del fitness.* Franco Angeli, Milano.
Salonia, G. (2011a). *Sulla felicità e dintorni. Tra corpo, parola e tempo.* Il Pozzo di Giacobbe, Trapani.
Salonia, G. (2011b). L'errore di Perls. Intuizioni e fraintendimenti del postfreudismo gestaltico. In *Rivista Internazionale di Psicoterapia GTK n.* 2.
Salonia, G. (2012a). Teoria del sé e società liquida. Riscrivere la funzione-Personalità in Gestalt Therapy. In *Rivista Internazionale di Psicoterapia GTK* n. 3.
Salonia, G. (2012b). *La grazia dell'audacia. Per una lettura gestaltica dell'Antigone.* Il Pozzo di Giacobbe, Trapani.
Salonia, G. (2013a). *Edipo dopo Freud. Dalla legge del padre alla legge della relazione. GTK Books, n. 1*

Salonia, G. (2013b). Disagio psichico e risorse relazionali. In G. Salonia, V. Conte, P. Argentino (Eds.), *Devo sapere subito se sono vivo: saggi di psicopatologia gestaltica.* Il Pozzo di Giacobbe, Trapani.

Salonia, G. (2013c). Ordo Amoris e famiglia di origine. In AA.VV., *Amare sempre o amare per sempre? Profezia della fedeltà creativa nel tempo delle relazioni liquide.* Il Calamo, Roma.

Salonia, G. (2013d). L'angoscia dell'agire tra eccitazione e trasgressione : la gestalt therapy con gli stili relazionali fobico-ossessivo-compulsivi. In G. Salonia, V. Conte, P. Argentino (Eds.), *Devo sapere subito se sono vivo: saggi di psicopatologia gestaltica.* Il Pozzo di Giacobbe, Trapani.

Salonia, G. (2013e). Pensieri su Gestalt therapy e vissuti narcisistici. In G. Salonia, V. Conte, P. Argentino (Eds.), *Devo sapere subito se sono vivo, saggi di psicopatologia gestaltica.* Il Pozzo di Giacobbe, Trapani.

Salonia, G. (2014). *La luna è fatta di formaggio. Terapeuti gestaltisti traducono il linguaggio borderline.* Il Pozzo di Giacobbe, Trapani.

Salonia, G. (2015). Eros e logos: La prospettiva gestaltica. In M. Pizzimenti (Ed.), *Aggressività e Sessualità. Il rapporto figura/sfondo tra dolore e piacere.* Franco Angeli, Milano.

Salonia, G. (2017a). Fragilità e disagi nella vita affettiva e sessuale. In P. Gambini, M. O. Llanos, & G. M. Roggia (Eds.), *Formazione affettivo-sessuale, itinerario per seminaristi e giovani consacrati e consacrate.* Edizioni Dehoniane, Bologna.

Salonia, G. (2017b). *Danza delle sedie e danza dei pronomi. Terapia gestaltica familiare.* Il Pozzo di Giacobbe, Trapani.

Salonia, G. (2019). Prefazione. In F. Brotto (Ed.), *I ritmi dell'eros. Gestalt Therapy e sessuologia.* Il Pozzo di Giacobbe, Trapani.

Sichera, A. (2001). Un confronto con Gadamer: per una epistemologia ermeneutica della Gestalt. In M. Spagnuolo Lobb (Ed.), *Psicoterapia della Gestalt Ermeneutica e clinica.* Franco Angeli, Milano.

Sichera, A., Salonia, G. (2020). Corpo, parola, corpo. Itinerario terapeutico della Gestalt Therapy, In *Rivista Internazionale di Psicoterapia GTK n.* 8.

Spitz, R. A. (1953) (ed. or 1962). *Il primo anno del bambino. Genesi delle prime relazioni oggettuali.* Giunti Barbera, Firenze.

Stern, D. (1987) (ed. or 1985). *Il mondo interpesonale del bambino.* Bollati-Boringhieri, Torino.

Stern, D. (1996). La nascita del sé. In M. Ammaniti (Ed.), *La nascita del sé.* Editori Laterza, Roma-Bari

Stoller, R. J. (1978) (ed. or 1975). *Perversione. La forma erotica dell'odio.* Feltrinelli, Milano.

Chapter 7
Developmental Considerations for Sexual Offending

Zachary Yeoman, Kevin Creeden, and Chad Brownfield

7.1 Introduction

As researchers and clinicians continue to grapple with our understanding of the heterogeneous group of adolescents who engage in sexually problematic behavior (SPB), there has been an increasing focus on taking a developmental perspective to examine the etiology of this behavior as well as determining what factors may differentiate the youth who persist in these behaviors from those who desist (Lussier et al., 2018; Lussier, 2017; Elkovitch et al., 2009; Chaffin et al., 2002). This developmental view can be seen in contrast to other research approaches that have sought to identify the specific traits associated with sexually abusive youth as a group and to differentiate this group from their delinquent peers who have not engaged in sexual offending behaviors or nonsexually abusive youthful offenders (Fox, 2017; McCuish et al., 2015; Seto & Lalumière, 2010; Knight & Sims-Knight, 2004). Arguably, a developmental approach encourages us to focus more on our clients as individuals, identifying those life experiences combined with genetic and social factors that have influenced their specific developmental trajectory and left them at greater (or lesser) risk for engaging in SPB. However, much of the theoretical underpinning for creating a developmental framework to examine SPB stems from an extensive body of work on developmental criminology (Farrington, 1995;

Z. Yeoman (✉)
Somerset Psychological Group, P.A., Martinsville, NJ, USA
e-mail: zyeoman@somersetpsych.com

K. Creeden
The Whitney Academy, East Freetown, MA, USA
e-mail: kcreeden@whitneyacademy.org

C. Brownfield
Private Practice, Rock Island, IL, USA

R. J. Tully et al. (eds.), *Best Practices in Sexual Offender Assessment and Management*, Dangerous Behavior in Clinical and Forensic Psychology,
https://doi.org/10.1007/978-3-031-83135-5_7

Loeber, 1990; Lussier, 2017; Moffitt, 1993) and similarly tends to focus heavily on risk factors (e.g., harsh parenting, impulsivity, poor school performance, antisocial peers, lack of parental supervision, etc.) and less on those protective factors that may foster resilience, promote positive outcomes, and in those who have already engaged in problematic sexual behavior, facilitate a pathway to desistance.

While figuring out "how we got here" (risk factors) is essential, it does not necessarily lead us to the answer for the question "how do we move forward" (intervention). Focusing on risk factors frequently obscures those individual traits, personal relationships, and social influences available to steer a particular youth back to a positive developmental trajectory (strengths and protective factors). The goal of this chapter is to take a developmental perspective on SPB that recognizes that for most children and adolescents, the arc of their developmental trajectory will move in a positive direction. The idea is not to ignore those personal traits, individual experiences, and social circumstances that create the risk for emotional and behavioral difficulties but to understand those risks in the context of the broader research around child development that identifies the core elements that lead to positive outcomes for children and adolescents (e.g., engaged parents, stable living environments, positive connections to school, good peer relationships, etc.). This shift allows us to view "risk factors" as obstacles to positive developmental outcomes that require creative and effective intervention rather than an ever-widening pathway to pathology. It also highlights the importance of considering the developmental timing of adverse experiences when considering their impact rather than just adding up the numbers (Cohodes et al., 2020; Smith & Pollack, 2020). It forces us to recognize how environment, experience, and timing affect neurodevelopment and consider the continued impact this will have on a child's capacity to regulate behavior, focus attention, and engage in adaptive problem solving to incorporate this awareness into our assessment formulations and treatment recommendations. A developmental perspective should steer us away from adopting "one size fits all" treatment programs and guide us towards individualized treatment that regularly incorporates parents and caregivers and is responsive to different learning styles and cultural differences (Creeden, 2020a, 2020b; Perry et al., 2018). Finally, assuming a developmental perspective on etiology and a developmental approach to treatment should move us away from viewing the goal of treatment as the "absence of bad" (recidivism) and move us towards a stance where treatment progress is equated with enhanced coping skills, greater personal and social competency, improved decision making, and increased prosocial interest and activity (Creeden, 2018; Masten & Coatsworth, 1998). In other words, treatment progress is developmental progress.

7.2 Adverse Childhood Experiences

A myriad of changing factors influences juvenile SPB. When trying to understand the etiology of this behavior, it is important to consider the developmental experiences common for this population, particularly adverse childhood experiences

(ACEs). ACEs are traumatic events during childhood or aspects of the child's environment that increase the risk of danger, instability, and disrupted attachment (The Center for Disease Control and Prevention, 2020). Sexually abusive youth and nonsexually abusive youthful offenders experience a high number and wide range of ACEs (Barra et al., 2018) and far more than youth in the general population (Baglivio et al., 2015). Because both groups share similar developmental experiences, there is no definitive set of factors that allows for a reliable determination of who will engage in SPB (Levenson et al., 2017). Nevertheless, examining those ACEs found most commonly in the lives of sexually abusive youth helps to advance our understanding of this population. Their histories most frequently demonstrate sexual victimization, physical abuse and maltreatment, early exposure to family abuse and violence, and general maltreatment (Rich, 2011).

7.2.1 Prior Sexual Victimization

Sexual victimization history is the most frequently discussed factor in explaining adolescent and adult sexual offending (Seto & Lalumière, 2010). As demonstrated in Table 7.1, many studies have found that a high percentage of sexually abusive youth were sexually victimized. Although there is a wide range in reported sexual victimization histories (13% to 79.4%), these rates are higher than the rate of sexual victimization in the general population of children and adolescents (Levenson et al., 2016). However, when the histories of nonsexually abusive youthful offenders are considered, the distinction between this group and sexually abusive youth is less clear. As demonstrated in Table 7.2, sexual victimization rates for nonsexually abusive youthful offenders range from between 0.1% and 46.7%. Overall, it appears that sexual victimization may be a significant predictor of juvenile delinquency in general and not specific to SPB.

7.2.2 Physical Abuse and Maltreatment, Early Exposure to Family Abuse and Violence, and General Maltreatment

Physical abuse and maltreatment, early exposures to family abuse and violence, and general maltreatment are also common in the histories of sexually abusive youth. These experiences are discussed here as a group because of the similarity in their relationships to conduct problems in youth. As shown in Tables 7.3 and 7.4, many studies of sexually abusive youth found a high percentage had these experiences, between 12.9% and 82%. Although this is a wide range, the median percentage is higher than the rate at which these experiences are reported in the general population of youth, approximately 25% to 34% (Costello et al., 2003; Dierkhising et al., 2013; Evans-Chase, 2014). However, like sexual victimization, rates of these

Table 7.1 Descriptive information for studies of sexually abusive youth regarding sexual victimization history

Study	Number of participants (N)	Type of sample	*% sexual victimization history*
Bagley and Shewchuk-Dann (1991)	382	Inpatient adolescent	28% of sexually abusive youth
Truscott (1993)	153	Inpatient adolescent	43.5% of sexually abusive youth
Milloy (1994)	256	Adolescent correctional	54% of sexually abusive youth
Moody et al. (1994)	38	Adolescent inpatient	77% of sexually abusive youth
Worling (1995)	90	Adolescent outpatient	75% with male victim, 25% with female victim
Borowsky (1997)	1674	Middle and High school students	46.7% of sexually abusive youth
Righthand et al. (2001)	96	Adolescent outpatient	58% of sexually abusive youth
Silovsky and Niec (2002)	37	Preschool outpatient	38% of sexually abusive youth
Burton et al. (2002)	471	Adolescent inpatient	79.4% of sexually abusive youth
Burton (2008)	127	Inpatient adolescent	69.6% of sexually abusive youth
Seto and Lalumière (2010)	17,248	Child and adolescent, inpatient and outpatient	46% of sexually abusive youth
Burton et al. (2011)	325	Inpatient adolescent	55% of sexually abusive youth
Carpentier and Proulx (2011)	351	Outpatient adolescent	50% of recidivists vs. 31.1% of non-recidivists
Wanklyn (2012)	224	Inpatient adolescent	20.8% of violent sexually abusive youth vs. 11.5% of sexually abusive youthful offenders
Aebi et al. (2015)	245	Community adolescents	42.4% of sexually abusive youth
Yoder et al. (2017)	860	Inpatient adolescent	55.1% of sexually abusive youth
Levenson et al. (2017)	69,135	Male juveniles arrested for sexual offenses	13% of sexually abusive youth
Barra et al. (2018)	332	Child and Adolescent	15.8% of sexually abusive youth

experiences for nonsexually abusive youthful offenders are also quite high, between 13% and 61.9%. While these ACEs may contribute substantially to the development of criminal behavior in youth, this behavior is as likely to be sexual as nonsexual. In the end, it appears that the most common ACEs experienced by sexually abusive youth are also commonly experienced by nonsexually abusive youthful offenders. As such, it cannot be assumed, for example, that sexually victimized children are

Table 7.2 Descriptive information for studies of nonsexually abusive youthful offenders regarding sexual victimization histories

Study	Number of participants (N)	Type of sample	*% sexual victimization history*
Truscott (1993)	153	Inpatient adolescent	13.7% of violent youthful offenders vs. 19.0% of youthful property offenders
Milloy (1994)	256	Adolescent correctional	5% of nonsexually abusive youthful offenders
Burton et al. (2002)	471	Adolescent inpatient	46.7% of nonsexually abusive youthful offenders
Burton (2008)	127	Inpatient adolescent	39.6% of nonsexually abusive youthful offenders
Seto and Lalumière (2010)	17,248	Child and adolescent, inpatient and outpatient	16% of nonsexually abusive youthful offenders
Wanklyn (2012)	224	Inpatient adolescent	5.5% of nonsexually abusive youthful offenders
Yoder et al. (2017)	1010	Inpatient adolescent	0.1% of nonsexually abusive youthful offenders
Levenson et al. (2017)	69,135	Male juveniles arrested for sexual offenses	5% of nonsexually abusive youthful offenders

any more likely to engage in SPB than non-sexually abusive criminal behavior. Given the current limitations of empirical research on this topic, theoretical perspectives may help advance our understanding of how maltreatment can result in SPB.

7.3 Theoretical Explanations

The outgrowth of SPB from sexual victimization is consistent with several well-established developmental theories. Bandura's (1977) social learning theory posits that we learn behavior by observing others' behavior, particularly within the family of origin. In the context of juvenile SPB, social learning theory supports the "victim to victimizer" explanation of this behavior. The sexually abused child or adolescent may learn through observation that adults can and do engage children sexually, that the interaction provides the victimizer with rewarding consequences, and that they are unlikely to be held accountable for wrongdoing. It is also likely that the victimized child is misled about the appropriateness of such behavior. As a result, the victim may come to believe that such behavior is acceptable (Seto, 2008; Garland & Dougher, 1990).

Social learning theory may also explain why youth who experience nonsexual ACEs may engage in SPB. Regularly witnessing and experiencing nonsexual violence and neglect can profoundly impact developing self-regulatory systems and cognitive schemas regarding themselves, others, and the world: domestic violence

Table 7.3 Descriptive information for studies of sexually abusive youth concerning histories of physical abuse and maltreatment, early exposure to family abuse and violence, and general maltreatment

Study	Number of participants (N)	Type of sample	% physically abused, exposed to family abuse and violence, and/or general maltreated
Smith and Monastersky (1986)	112	Outpatient treatment	26% of sexually abusive youth
Bagley and Shewchuk-Dann (1991)	382	Inpatient adolescent	28% of sexually abusive youth
Truscott (1993)	153	Inpatient adolescent	82.6% of sexually abusive youth
Ryan et al. (1996)	1600+	Juveniles referred for specialized evaluation and/or treatment following a sexual offense	63% of sexually abusive youth
Spaccarelli et al. (1997)	210	Chronic delinquents	43.6% of sexually abusive youth
Borowsky (1997)	1674	Middle and High school students	12.9% to 14.4% of sexually abusive youth
Welch et al. (2001)	78	Male and female youth who committed sex offenses with open cases with the Main Department of Human Services	64% to 72% (neglect and exposure)
Righthand et al. (2001)	96	Adolescent outpatient	44% of sexually abusive youth
Zakireh et al. (2008)	100	Residential and outpatient sexual and nonsexually abusive youthful offenders	80% of sexually abusive youth in residential placement
Wanklyn (2012)	224	Inpatient adolescent	66.7% of violent sexually abusive youth and 46.2% of sexually abusive youthful offenders

models aggression, poor-self regulation, and distorted-perceptions of intimate relationships. Dysfunctional households provide little opportunity to understand healthy relationships and emotional attachments, further limiting the ability to express sexual and romantic desires appropriately. Growing up around criminal behavior may also instill problematic beliefs about following the rule of law and respecting others' rights. Both experiences can manifest in feelings of disempowerment, enhancing the need for a sense of power and control (Ford et al., 2012). Youth who have these experiences may engage in SPB due to emotional regulation deficits, pro-offending cognitions, and the absence of an internal template for how to be sexual in a healthy way.

Table 7.4 Descriptive information for studies of nonsexually abusive juvenile offenders concerning histories of physical abuse and maltreatment, early exposure to family abuse and violence, and general maltreatment

Study	Number of participants (N)	Type of sample	% physically abused, exposed to family abuse and violence, and/or general maltreated
Bagley and Shewchuk-Dann (1991)	382	Inpatient adolescent	13% of nonsexually abusive youthful offenders
Truscott (1993)	153	Inpatient adolescent	74% of violent youthful offenders and 72.2% youthful property offenders
Spaccarelli et al. (1997)	210	Chronic delinquents	9.3% to 20.8% of low-violence delinquents
Zakireh et al. (2008)	100	Residential and outpatient sexual and nonsexually abusive youthful offenders	36% of nonsexually abusive youthful offenders
Wanklyn (2012)	224	Inpatient adolescent	33.3% of nonsexually abusive youthful offenders

Conditioning theories (Thorndike, 1901; Coon & Mitterer, 2008) can also explain why a sexually abused youth would sexually abuse others. If sexual stimulation occurs during the sexually abusive act, it may pair sexual arousal with sexual victimization (Burton et al., 2002). Masturbation to fantasies of these sexual experiences with adults can make them increasingly more arousing and, possibly, contribute to acting on these fantasies (McGuire et al., 1965). Then, these victims turned victimizers' actions may be conditioned by the reward of sexual gratification and the impact of sexual arousal and orgasm on negative mood (Marshall & Barbaree, 1990). Given the negative impact sexual victimization has on victims' psychological functioning, youth may develop a reliance on sexualized coping as a way of managing heightened levels of distress. It can also become a maladaptive strategy used to satisfy emotional needs such as intimacy, affection, attention, and control, which are unlikely to be met in families where sexual victimization occurs (Bushman et al., 2001; Levenson et al., 2016).

Although direct empirical support for existing attachment-related theories of SPB has been both mixed and inconsistent (Smallbone, 2006a, 2006b), attachment theory could advance our understanding of the development of juvenile SPB. Bowlby (1969/1982), the progenitor of attachment theory, posited that attachment or the affectional bond between a child and his or her attachment figure is essential to the healthy development of crucial psychological systems (e.g., self-regulation, interpersonal relations). Bowlby (1979, as cited in Cassidy & Shaver, 2008) highlighted romantic relationships as being strongly influenced by early attachments. Essentially, he believed that we develop a relational prototype that becomes the foundation for the course and quality of future love relationships. Although sexual behavior among children and adolescents is not necessarily romantic, it is evident at face value that similar mechanisms are at play when children and adolescents seek out sexual contact with each other.

Suboptimal attachment experiences often occur in unstable households with caregivers who have problems regulating emotions and behavior (i.e., sexual abuse, domestic violence, child abuse, criminality). When this happens, children may not form strong affectional bonds and become insecurely attached. When secure attachment is absent, a myriad of difficulties can develop. These children may develop maladaptive "internal working models" (Bowlby, 1973) or cognitive templates of what to expect from other people and the world, as well as how he or she can expect to be treated by others (Bowlby, 1969/1982). This can impede developing the interpersonal skills and empathy necessary for forming appropriate interpersonal relationships (Marshall & Barbaree, 1990). Youth may see the world as unresponsive to their needs and themselves as ineffective at meeting their own needs in a normal fashion, unable to compete with their peers for intimate relationships, and expecting rejection by others. When coupled with the underdeveloped self-regulatory systems of insecurely attached youth, they may engage in SPB with children or peers because they see no other pathway to meeting their intimacy needs, have trouble taking the perspective of others (particularly their victims), and they may be less averse to violating the rights of others (Seto, 2008; Miner, et al., 2010). Illustrating this point, Miner et al. (2010) concluded that youth who sexually abuse children disproportionately experience attachment anxieties, have difficulties forming relationships, have fewer friends, associate with younger children, feel isolated from peers, and feel socially inadequate, including a sense of masculine inadequacy.

While foundational developmental theories from established theorists such as Bowlby and Bandura have been crucial to our understanding of child development, they did not have access to the burgeoning neurodevelopmental research that has emerged over the last 25–30 years. Most theories examining the etiology of sexually problematic and abusive behavior have either not fully integrated neurological research into their models or have not focused on neurodevelopment at all, with the exception of Ward and Beech (2016) and less explicitly Grady et al. (2016). The impact of ACE's extends beyond "social learning" and insecure attachment. These harmful developmental experiences have a neurological impact that can change how a child or adolescent perceives, organizes, processes, and responds to the world around them.

ACEs have a notable and often pervasive impact on cognitive, behavioral, and psychological functioning that can be present throughout the developmental process (Chen & Baram, 2016; Teicher et al., 2016; de Bellis et al., 2013; Pechtel & Pizzagalli, 2011). A significant portion of the research examining the impact of childhood adversity and stress highlights functional changes in the hypothalamic-pituitary-adrenal axis (H-P-A) and the autonomic nervous system, as well as both structural and functional changes in the frontal lobe-limbic circuitry (Cohodes et al., 2020; Koss & Gunnar, 2018; Tottenham & Sheridan, 2010). These neural circuitry changes led to difficulties in self-regulation, expressions of anger, and the misreading of emotional cues from others, including an increased perception of threat in non-threatening situations (McEwen, 2017; Shackman & Pollak, 2014; Perlman et al., 2008). Further deficits in behavioral regulation stem from alterations in rewards processing, difficulty with flexible and adaptive problem solving, and attention bias (Harms et al., 2018; Novick et al., 2018; Romens & Pollak, 2012; Hart & Rubia, 2012).

Amidst these neurological considerations, the ingredients that place these children at greater risk for poor self-regulation, increased aggression, attention problems, poor behavior management, limited response to behavioral interventions, and impaired social relationships can easily be identified. This constellation of issues is frequently seen in children and adolescents with learning difficulties in school, higher levels of internal disorders like anxiety and depression, and those identified with conduct disorder and sexual behavior problems (McLaughlin & Lambert, 2017; McLaughlin et al., 2015; de Carvalho Tofoli et al., 2011; Sanchez & Pollak, 2009; Streeck-Fischer & van der Kolk, 2000).

Despite the negative impact ACEs have on development, these experiences do not harm all children, and many do not go on to engage in sexual and nonsexual criminal behavior. Although it is human nature to want a clear explanation for behavior that is not understood, the research conducted thus far suggests that this is not yet possible with juveniles who engage in SPB. In the end, this population appears relatively similar to non-sexually problematic juvenile offenders in both developmental experiences and risk and protective factors. Nevertheless, the next step in developing our understanding of this phenomenon is to examine the pathways youth can take to engaging in SPB. As will be elaborated upon, some pathways are more concerning than others. Analyzing these pathways can help determine how much resources should be devoted to the supervision and treatment of these individuals.

7.4 Pathway to Sexually Problematic Behavior

Although there are various paths to juvenile SPB, the work of Lussier et al. (2012) and Lussier (2017) suggest that there are two distinct developmental trajectories for sexually abusive youth: adolescent limited and high rate/slow desister. The adolescent-limited trajectory represents the vast majority of youth who engage in this type of behavior. These youth are unlikely to have sexual behavior problems and demonstrate normal sexual development. For most children and adolescents in this group, SPB is related to developmental and contextual issues that do not remain present for long and do not reflect sexually deviant interests or antisociality. Youth who follow this developmental trajectory are unlikely to reoffend sexually. While they overlap to some degree, the pathways to SPB for the adolescent-limited trajectory can be divided as follows: experimental, cognitive deficits, social deficits, mental health, and substance intoxication. It is important to note that separating youth into distinct pathways is artificial. Sexually abusive youth likely demonstrate aspects of several pathways at the same time. However, doing so allows evaluators and treatment providers to identify and target the main reasons for offending sexually.

The experimental pathway characterizes youth whose SPB reflects relatively normative experimentation that occurs in adolescents. These youth are likely curious about sex, have limited access to or opportunity for consensual or age-appropriate sexual partners, and are naive to the illegality of their actions (Hunter, 2006). The cognitive deficits pathway highlights youth with intellectual impairments who have not developed age-appropriate levels of judgment, insight, social comprehension, or the ability to tell right from wrong and generalize learning (Blasingame et al., 2015). Youth on this pathway may sexually offend because of difficulties understanding how, when or with whom to engage in sexual behavior and failure to understand the implication of age disparities between themselves and others or what consent entails. The social deficits pathway characterizes youth whose predominant issue is developing healthy sexual relationships with same-aged peers. These youth may be sheltered, limiting their opportunities to develop social skills. Their SPB may result from not being able to access consensual or age-appropriate sexual relationships due to poor social skills. With psychoeducation regarding healthy and unhealthy sexual behavior, increasing access to opportunities for and competence with healthy peer socialization, and the deterrent effect of intervention, youth who follow these pathways to SPB are unlikely to reoffend sexually.

The mental health pathway identifies youth who engage in SPB due to mental health problems. Aside from conduct disorder (to be discussed shortly) and paraphilic disorders (unlikely in adolescence), no diagnosis is more likely than any other to contribute to sexual offending. Yet, it is possible for most mental health issues to contribute to SPB, given the right circumstance. For example, youth who are clinically depressed and lack healthy sexual outlets may engage in SPB. Depressed youth may be less concerned about what happens to them, and sexual contact temporarily lifts their mood. Children and adolescents with high functioning autism may engage in SPB due to the social immaturity that accompanies this diagnosis and difficulties understanding social cues. In addition, if they develop intense, restricted interests in sex, the need to repetitively engage in this behavior could contribute to sexual offending (Allely & Creaby-Attwood, 2016; Brown et al., 2016).

The substance abuse pathway encompasses youth who engage in SPB while intoxicated. The disinhibitory effects of substance intoxication increase the likelihood that an adolescent will act in a sexually impulsive manner without considering the consequences of his actions. The severity of the substance abuse issue will determine the intensity of the intervention. For youth who do not regularly use drugs or alcohol, brief substance abuse intervention and testing for these substances may be warranted, depending on clinical assessment findings. More intensive intervention such as detoxification and inpatient substance abuse treatment may be necessary for youth with a moderate-to-severe substance use disorder.

The high-rate/slow-desister group of sexually abusive youth represent a minority of youth who engage in this behavior. It is hypothesized that their onset of sexual offending occurs in childhood. This group is likely to have been exposed to multiples ACEs and show atypical sexual behaviors and antisociality during childhood, contributing to sexual offending beyond childhood. Without intervention, these youth will continue to engage in illegal sexual and nonsexual behavior through and beyond adolescence. While these juveniles will eventually desist, the process will take much longer, and the high-rate/slow desister group is more likely to continue offending into adulthood (Lussier et al., 2012; Lussier, 2017; Seto & Lalumière, 2010). The pathways to SPB for this developmental trajectory are conduct disorder (CD) and sexual deviance. The youth of most concern are those who demonstrate both.

CD is a well-known but stigmatizing diagnosis a practitioner can ascribe to their child clients. Yet, most experts in the field agree that early identification, diagnosis, and treatment offer the greatest opportunity for successful outcomes in CD (Frick & Marsee, 2006). CD is a cyclical and persistent pattern of behavior where others' rights, societal rules, or age-appropriate expectations are disregarded and violated (American Psychiatric Association, 2013). This concerning behavior is often perpetrated against people, animals, or property and may include stealing, intentional injury, and forced sexual activity. The disorder's four hallmarks include aggression to people or animals, destruction of property, deceitfulness or theft, and serious violations of rules (e.g., truancy or running away).

CD may originate from disposition and or environment (Frick, 1998). Dispositional factors refer to the temperament, neuropsychological pathways, and biological characteristics of the individual. The four dispositional issues that have been empirically linked with the development of CD are genetic components (Dick et al., 2011; Moffitt, 2005), difficulty learning from punishment, and focusing on reward-based outcomes (Lykken, 1995; Daugherty & Quay, 1991, O'Brien et al., 1994), low intelligence, attention deficits, and poor academic achievement (Hinshaw, 1992; Moffitt, 1993, 2006; Frick et al., 1991), and hostile attribution bias towards behavior of their own and others (Dodge & Frame, 1982; Crick & Dodge, 1996). These individuals tend to see others' actions as malevolent and frequently act in kind to these perceived threats.

Environmental factors consider issues with parenting, the qualities of the individual's neighborhood, and peer interactions. Four important environmental considerations for CD include family dysfunction in the form of parental psychopathology, poor parental marital relationships, and the type of socialization and child-rearing practices (Kofler-Westergren et al., 2010; Lytton, 1990; Patterson et al., 1992), peer rejection and association with deviant peers (Coie et al., 1990; Keenan et al., 1995), living in highly disadvantaged areas and high crime neighborhoods that contribute to the environmental issues (Frick, 1998), and exposure to violence within the culture (Kersten et al., 2017).

However, there is no singular developmental cause of CD. When considering the numerous developing systems (social, interpersonal, and neurological) working in concert during this time in the life of juveniles, a multifaceted pathway is expected, which has been supported in the research literature (Frick, 2006, 2012; Pardini & Frick, 2013). There are several explanations for CD that include social learning and developmental propensity (Lahey et al., 2003). Social learning theorists suggest that CD is developed through recurring social relationships that promote delinquent behavior during the youth's formative years (Snyder et al., 2003). However, research suggests that conduct problems materialize based on the propensity and development of these behaviors that may influence the age of onset, course, and severity of the disorder (Lahey & Waldman, 2003). Individuals with lower executive functioning or prefrontal deficits may act out more impulsively and react with more characteristics of aggression than fleeing (Nigg & Huang-Pollock, 2003).

The developmental model developed by Moffitt and colleagues (Moffitt, 1993, 2006; Moffitt et al., 1996) identified the childhood-onset pathway (before age 10) and the adolescent-onset pathway (after age 10). The child-onset pathway characterizes vulnerable and difficult children raised in an environment of parental dysfunction. This may lead to a cyclical and transactional process of poor parent-child interactions. This turmoil often leads to the development of delinquent behavior and eschews opportunities for prosocial development. Conversely, the adolescent-onset pathway involves a heightened rebellion phase for the youth that stems from an emerging gap between the youth's physical maturation and cognitive immaturity combined with being viewed by society as an adult.

There tends to be more focus on the childhood-onset subtype, as this group's delinquent behavior typically continues into adulthood. The childhood-onset subtype tends to be a more homogenous group with the hallmark trait of callousness or an unemotional demeanor that often leads to more persistent delinquent behavior. In contrast, the adolescent pathway tends to be a more heterogeneous group that usually involves impulsivity, poor parental socialization, low intelligence, and social cognition deficits. This diverse mix of factors underlies the varied pathways to this subtype of CD.

Despite the heterogeneity amongst juvenile sexual offenders, a distinct group and pathway for SPB is related to delinquent or antisocial behavior (Rich, 2009, 2011). While not all youth who engage in SPB have CD, this pathway involves many of the youth that engage in this behavior. This group's SPB usually accounts for only a small percentage of their antisocial behavior. This is because it is often part of a broader behavior problem that involves difficulty managing impulses in multiple settings. As such, CD youth's SPB is not expressly or only a sexual problem (Yeoman et al., 2021). Research has found that juvenile sex offending is generally associated with rule-breaking and impulsivity (Seto & Lalumière, 2010) and that CD youth who engaged in sexually abusive behavior pose a much higher risk to engage in future nonsexual offenses than sex offenses (Reitzel & Carbonell, 2006). This group of youth requires a moderate degree of intervention, but primarily for nonsexual conduct problems. They are likely manageable in the community if the conduct disorder is not severe and intractable, and the family collaborates with the provider in order to be in alignment with treatment goals. Their treatment should focus on general impulse control and intrusive behavior issues (Yeoman et al., 2021).

The pure sexual deviance pathway characterizes youth who demonstrate a pattern of sexual arousal to and behavior with much younger children or those who repeatedly engage in and report arousal to nonconsensual sexual behavior. These youth have likely experienced many ACEs and exist in family or social environments where SPB was reinforced early. While there is limited literature on the prevalence of juveniles with deviant sexual interests, it likely represents a small group of juvenile sexual offenders. The existing literature on the phenomenon has been mixed with support for varying perspectives. Some research supports the notion that deviant sexual interests are associated with some juvenile sexual behavior (Seto et al., 2000; Zolondek et al., 2001; Clift et al., 2009; Seto & Lalumière, 2010). However, others did not find an association between juvenile sexual arousal and sexual recidivism (Gretton et al., 2001). They suggest that the research literature overestimates how deviant sexual arousal influences sexual offending in youth (Finkelhor et al., 2009). Juveniles who engage in SPB may not have fully developed or understood sexual interests (Clift et al., 2009).

In light of the research conducted thus far, the field has generally recognized that evidence of deviant sexual interests in juvenile sex offenders is an important risk factor to consider when present, but that most juvenile sexual offenses are *not* the result of deviant sexual interests. They are likely to be distressed by or ashamed of their sexual interest and behavior and, with intervention, demonstrate the motivation to manage these arousals. This group of youth requires a moderate degree of intervention if good motivation by the youth and family support are present. Risk management needs to be put in place, such as Internet monitoring and no unsupervised contact with children. Generally, the treatment of this group of youth should focus on sexual self-control issues (Yeoman et al., 2021).

A minority of youth can be characterized by sexual deviance and CD pathways to sexual offending. This small subgroup of youth likely demonstrates atypical sexual behaviors and antisociality during childhood. With exposure to risk factors (i.e., ACEs) and limited protective factors (e.g., prosocial attachment figure), they are most likely to show evidence of diversification of sexual and nonsexual offending in adolescence and young adulthood. Without intervention, they will show increasing specialization in sexual offending over time (e.g., targeting a specific victim type) and ongoing criminal behavior. Although research in this area is relatively limited, there are four studies of high-risk youth to our knowledge. Although it is unknown if all of the youth studied demonstrated CD and sexual deviance, based on the highly structured environments in which these studies were conducted, both are likely. These studies found recidivism rates of between 11.76% and 42%. These recidivism rates are significantly higher than those commonly found for the average youth who commits a sexually abusive act. This small subgroup of youth will likely need a secured, structured treatment setting, such as a residential treatment center. Treatment should focus on first reducing general conduct problems so that cooperation can be obtained for sexual-specific aspects of treatment (Yeoman et al., 2021).

While prospective longitudinal cohort studies are needed to validate Lussier et al.'s (2018) work, these developmental trajectories are supported by the empirical evidence produced thus far. While juveniles commit anywhere between roughly 15% and 30% of sex offenses (Phenix & Hoberman, 2016), and most sexual abuse and assault of children and adolescents are at the hands of other children and adolescents (76.7% for males and 70.1% for females; Gewirtz-Meydan & Finkelhor, 2020), only 5% of sexual offenses are committed by repeat offenders (Sandler et al., 2008) and only 3% of youth sexually reoffend (Caldwell, 2016). In addition, using both retrospective and prospective longitudinal data from a group of approximately 500 adjudicated sexually abusive youth, Lussier et al. (2012) examined sexual offending and nonsexual offending trajectories from age 12 to about age 32. Those authors identified that a two sexual offending trajectory model best fit the longitudinal data. A group similar to Lussier's (2017) adolescent-limited pattern characterized 89.6% of the youth, and a group that resembles the high-rate/slow-desister pattern represented 10.4%. While both groups had a similar proportion of sexual recidivists during adolescence, with few exceptions, only the high-rate/slow-desister group included adult sexual recidivists. These results support the conclusion that most youth's SPB is adolescent-limited, and the majority do not sexually reoffend.

7.5 Factors Protective Against Sexually Problematic Behavior

Resiliency theory helps us understand why many mistreated youths do not engage in SPB or repeat this behavior after relatively minor intervention (Garmezy, 1991; Masten et al., 2007; Rutter, 1987; Werner & Smith, 1982). From this perspective, there are variables in the lives of youth that disrupt maladaptive developmental trajectories. These promotive or protective factors can mitigate the deleterious effects of risk factors in their lives (Zimmerman, 2013). It seems that specific features of the stress experience, such as developmental timing, severity, controllability, predictability of the stressor, and the degree of caregiver involvement play a significant role in differentiating the outcomes of the stress experience (Cohodes et al., 2020; Smith & Pollack, 2020). By examining these features and their interactions, an understanding of how adolescents with very similar experiences diverge in their neurodevelopment, behavior, and outcomes can begin to be gained. An appreciation of the influence that certain features of an incident can play in not only buffering the impact of adversity but, in some cases, actually promoting resiliency can also begin.

Nowhere is this more prominent than in the role that parental involvement and positive attachment experiences play in promoting neurodevelopment and fostering resilience. The presence or absence of emotionally available, stable, and consistent caretaking influences the child's sense of safety, control, and predictability (Malter Cohen et al., 2013; Edmiston et al., 2011). Given the importance of strong attachments for healthy development, it is no surprise that de Vries Robbe et al. (2015) found multiple empirically supported protective factors that result from these experiences. In particular, there is scientific support for the protective effect of youth having a positive relationship with a parent or guardian, positive support by prosocial peers, positive support by other prosocial relationships (siblings, extended family, or other role models), a living environment that provides positive structure, support, and supervision, social competence, coping, self-control, and perseverance. While empirical research on the predictive validity of these protective factors is only starting to emerge (Tharp et al., 2013), they were incorporated into the Structured Assessment of Protective Factors in Violence Risk - Youth Version (SAPROF-YV). The SAPROF-YV is a structured professional judgment tool designed to structure clinical thinking around the empirically supported factors that appear to protect against nonsexual and sexual violence risk.

It seems clear that, based on both developmental theory and scientific research, early and ongoing positive attachment experiences are crucial. These experiences may prevent youth exposed to ACE's from engaging in SPB and reduce the likelihood that those who have will reoffend. As more research examines the neurobiological responses to developmental experiences, early attachment interactions would appear to be a central component influencing neurodevelopment, emotional and behavioral regulation, learning and problem solving, reward-seeking, social interaction, and one's capacity for trust and intimacy (Hanson et al., 2017; Pollak, 2015; Porges, 2011). Recognizing the neurodevelopmental impact of childhood stressors and the mediating role that attachment relationships in exacerbating the impact of those experiences or buffering the child from the effects can provide the context for understanding how positive developmental trajectories can be bolstered or derailed.

7.6 Application of Developmental Considerations for Sex Offending

Incorporating a current scientific understanding of juvenile SPB into policy and legal decisions is critical. Without doing so, myth and ignorance contribute to misguided and even harmful decisions for youth who have engaged in SPB. Although it varies from jurisdiction to jurisdiction, these types of decisions continue to be made based on misunderstanding and unsubstantiated claims about risk and intervention (Lussier, 2017). As Chaffin (2008) points out, these scientifically uninformed beliefs about youth who engage in SPBs contribute to policies that are unlikely to increase community safety or serve juvenile justice. In general, these youth are seen as a homogenous high-risk group that is unlikely to change without a great deal of specialized intervention. In some countries, these erroneous beliefs have contributed to broad community registration and notification requirements and a default stance from the legal system that sexually problematic youth require intensive long-term intervention.

Instead, policymakers are encouraged to consider the scientific findings outlined in this chapter. While a small group of high-risk sexually problematic youth requires a high intensity of supervision and intervention, the vast majority do not. It is clear that antisocial, pro-offending environments with inadequate, abusive or neglectful caregivers contribute to poor outcomes for youth. While implemented with good intentions, most correctional interventions and institutional settings mimic these experiences. At best, these environments suppress problematic behavior. In reality, they are likely to exacerbate the underlying psychological issues that contributed to SPB in the first place. Rather than repeating these experiences, it would be more beneficial to the health of these youth and the community's safety to bolster protective factors against future SPB. Providing these youth with prosocial environments and supportive, healthy attachment figures can achieve this aim. While this may not be possible for some youth within their families or communities, treatment environments that view sexually problematic youth from a developmental perspective rather than as dangerous individuals that need to be contained can be created.

References

Aebi, M., Landolt, M. A., Mueller-Pfeiffer, C., Schnyder, U., Maier, T., & Mohler-Kuo, M. (2015). Testing the "sexually abused-abuser hypothesis" in adolescents: A population-based study. *Archives of Sexual Behavior, 44*(8), 2189–2199. https://doi.org/10.1007/s10508-014-0440-x

Allely, C., & Creaby-Attwood, A. (2016). Sexual offending and autism spectrum disorders. *Journal of Intellectual Disabilities and Offending Behaviour, 7*, 35–51. https://doi.org/10.1108/JIDOB-09-2015-0029

American Psychiatric Association. (2013). *Diagnostic and statistical manual of mental disorders* (5th ed.). American Psychiatric Press.

Bagley, C., & Shewchuk-Dann, D. (1991). Characteristics of 60 children and adolescents who have a history of sexual assault against others: Evidence from a controlled study. *Journal of Child & Youth Care*, 43–52.

Baglivio, M. T., Wolff, K. T., & Piquero, A. R. (2015). The relationship between adverse childhood experiences and recidivism in a sample of juvenile offenders in community-based treatment. *International Journal of Offender Therapy and Comparative Criminology, 61*(11), 1210–1242. https://doi.org/10.1177/0306624x15613992

Bandura, A. (1977). *Social learning theory*. Prentice Hall.

Barra, S., Bessler, C., Landolt, M. A., & Aebi, M. (2018). Patterns of adverse childhood experiences in juveniles who sexually offended. *Sexual Abuse, 30*(7), 803–827. https://doi.org/10.1177/1079063217697135

Blasingame, G. D., Creeden, K., & Rich, P. (2015). *Assessment and treatment of adolescents with intellectual disabilities who exhibit sexual problems or offending behaviors*. Association for the Treatment of Sexual Abusers.

Borowsky, L. M., Hogan, M., & Ireland, M. (1997). Adolescent sexual aggression: Risk and protective factors. *Pediatrics, 100*, 1–8.

Bowlby, J. (1969/1982). *Attachment and loss: Vol. 1. Attachment* (2nd ed.). Basic Books.

Bowlby, J. (1973). *Attachment and loss: Vol. 2. Separation: Anxiety and anger*. Basic Books.

Brown, J., Ma, G., Anderson, L., Cooney-Koss, B., Hastings, H., Pickett, Neal, D., Martindale, J., Dodson, K., Dodson, L., & Barfknecht, L. (2016). Autism Spectrum Disorder and Sexually Inappropriate Behaviors: An introduction for caregivers and professionals. *The Journal of Special Populations, 1*.

Burton, D. L. (2008). An exploratory evaluation of the contribution of personality and childhood sexual victimization to the development of sexually problematic behavior. *Sexual Abuse, 20*(1), 102–115. https://doi.org/10.1177/1079063208315352

Burton, D. L., Duty, K. J., & Leibowitz, G. S. (2011). Differences between sexually victimized and nonsexually victimized male adolescent sexual abusers: Developmental antecedents and behavioral comparisons. *Journal of Child Sexual Abuse, 20*(1), 77–93. https://doi.org/10.1080/10538712.2011.541010

Burton, D. L., Miller, D. L., & Tai Shill, C. (2002). A social learning theory comparison of the sexual victimization of adolescent sexual offenders and nonsexual offending male delinquents. *Child Abuse & Neglect: The International Journal, 26*, 893–907. https://doi.org/10.1016/S0145-2134(02)00360-5

Bushman, B. J., Baumeister, R. F., & Phillips, C. M. (2001). Do people aggress to improve their mood? Catharsis beliefs, affect regulation opportunity, and aggressive responding. *Journal of personality and social psychology, 81*(1), 17.

Caldwell, M. F. (2016). Quantifying the decline in juvenile sexual recidivism rates. *Psychology, Public Policy, and Law, 22*(4), 414–426. https://doi.org/10.1037/law0000094

Carpentier, J., & Proulx, J. (2011). Correlates of recidivism among adolescents who have sexually offended. *Sexual Abuse, 23*(4), 434–455. https://doi.org/10.1177/1079063211409950

Center for Disease Control and Prevention. (2020, April 3). Adverse Childhood Experiences (ACEs). http://cdc.gov/violenceprevention/childabuseandneglect/acestudy/index.html

Chaffin, M., Berliner, L., Block, R., Johnson, T., Friedrich, W., Louis, D., Lyon, T., Page, J., Prescott, D., Silovsky, J., & Madden, C. (2008). Report of the ATSA Task Force on Children with Sexual Behavior Problems. *Child Maltreatment, 13*, 199–218. https://doi.org/10.1177/1077559507306718

Chaffin, M., Letourneau, E., & Silovsky, J. F. (2002). Adults, adolescents, and children who sexually abuse children: A developmental perspective. In J. E. B. Myers, L. Berliner, J. Briere, C. T. Hendrix, C. Jenny, & T. A. Reid (Eds.), *The APSAC handbook on child maltreatment* (2nd ed., pp. 205–232). Sage.

Chen, Y., & Baram, T. Z. (2016). Toward understanding how early-life stress reprograms cognitive and emotional brain networks. *Neuropsychopharmacology: Official Publication of the American College of Neuropsychopharmacology, 41*(1), 197–206. https://doi.org/10.1038/npp.2015.181

Clift, R. J. W., Rajlic, G., & Gretton, H. M. (2009). Discriminative and predictive validity of the penile plethysmograph in adolescent sexual offenders. *Sexual Abuse: A Journal of Research and Treatment, 21*, 335–362.

Cohodes, E., Kitt, E. R., Baskin-Sommers, A., & Gee, D. (2020). Influences of early-life stress on frontolimbic circuitry: Harnessing a dimensional approach to elucidate the effects of heterogeneity in stress exposure. *Developmental Psychology, 00*, 1–20.

Coie, J. D., Dodge, K. A., & Kupersmidt, J. B. (1990). Peer group behavior and social status. In S. R. Asher & J. D. Coie (Eds.), *Peer rejection in childhood* (pp. 17–59). Cambridge University Press.

Coon, D., & Mitterer, J. O. (2008). *Introduction to psychology: Gateways to mind and behavior* (p. 220). Cengage Learning. ISBN 9780495599111.

Costello, E. J., Erklani, A., Fairbank, J., & Angold, A. (2003). The prevalence of potentially traumatic events in childhood and adolescence. *Journal of Traumatic Stress, 15*, 99–112.

Creeden, K. (2018). Adjusting the lens: A developmental perspective for treating youth with sexual behavior problems. In A. Beech, A. Carter, R. Mann, & P. Rotshtein (Eds.), *The Wiley handbook of forensic neuroscience*. Wiley.

Creeden, K. (2020a, June 2). *Understanding child with problematic sexual behavior.* [PowerPoint slides]. Massachusetts Children's Alliance.

Creeden, K. (2020b). Trauma and young people who display sexually harmful behavior. In H. Elliott (Ed.), *Sexual crime and trauma*. Palgrave.

Crick, N. R., & Dodge, K. A. (1996). Social information processing mechanisms in reactive and proactive aggression. *Child Development, 67*, 993–1002.

Daugherty, T. K., & Quay, H. C. (1991). Response perseveration and delayed responding in childhood behavior disorders. *Journal of Child Psychology and Psychiatry, 32*, 453–461.

de Bellis, M. D., Woolley, D. P., & Hooper, S. R. (2013). Neuropsychological findings in pediatric maltreatment: Relationship of PTSD, dissociative symptoms, and abuse/neglect indices to neurocognitive outcomes. *Child Maltreatment, 18*(3), 171–183. https://doi.org/10.1177/1077559513497420

de Carvalho Tofoli, S. M., Von Werne Baes, C., Martins, C. M. S., & Juruena, M. (2011). Early life stress, HPA axis, and depression. *Psychology & Neuroscience, 4*(2), 229–234. https://doi.org/10.3922/j.psns.2011.2.008

de Vries Robbe, M., Geer, M., Stapel, M., Hilterman, E., & De Vogel, V. (2015). The Structured assessment of protective factors for violence risk-youth version (SAPROF-YV).

Dick, D. M., Aliev, F., Krueger, R. F., Edwards, A., Agrawal, A., Lynskey, M., Lin, P., Schuckit, M., Hesselbrock, V., Nurnberger, J., Jr., Almasy, L., Porjesz, B., Edenberg, H. J., Bucholz, K., Kramer, J., Kuperman, S., & Bierut, L. (2011). Genome-wide association study of conduct disorder symptomatology. *Molecular Psychiatry, 16*(8), 800–808. https://doi.org/10.1038/mp.2010.73

Dierkhising, C. B., Ko, S. J., Woods-Jaeger, B., Briggs, E. C., Lee, R., & Pynoos, R. S. (2013). Trauma histories among justice-involved youth: Findings from the National Child Traumatic Stress Network. *European Journal of Psychotraumatology, 4*. https://doi.org/10.3402/ejpt.v4i0.20274

Dodge, K. A., & Frame, C. L. (1982). Social cognitive biases and deficits in aggressive boys. *Child Development, 53*, 620–635.

Edmiston, E. E., Wang, F., Mazure, C. M., Guiney, J., Sinha, R., Mayes, L. C., & Blumberg, H. P. (2011). Corticostriatal-limbic gray matter morphology in adolescents with self-reported exposure to childhood maltreatment. *Archives of Pediatrics & Adolescent Medicine, 165*(12), 1069–1077. https://doi.org/10.1001/archpediatrics.2011.565

Elkovitch, N., Latzman, R. D., Hansen, D. J., & Flood, M. F. (2009). Understanding child sexual behavior problems: A developmental psychopathology framework. *Clinical Psychology Review, 29*, 586–598.

Evans-Chase, M. (2014). Addressing trauma and psychosocial development in juvenile justice-involved youth: A synthesis of the developmental neuroscience, juvenile justice, and trauma literature. *Laws, 3*, 744–758.

Farrington, D. P. (1995). The development of offending and antisocial behavior in childhood: Key findings from the Cambridge study in delinquent development. *Journal of Child Psychology and Psychiatry, 36*, 929–964.

Finkelhor, D., Ormrod, R., & Chaffin, M. (2009, December). Juveniles who commit sex offenses against minors. *OJJDP Juvenile Justice Bulletin*. U.S. Department of Justice, Office of Justice Programs.

Ford, J. D., Chapman, J., Connor, D. F., & Cruise, K. R. (2012). Complex trauma and aggression in secure juvenile justice settings. *Criminal Justice and Behavior, 39*(6), 694–724. https://doi.org/10.1177/0093854812436957

Fox, B. H. (2017). What makes a difference?: Evaluating the key distinctions and predictors of sexual and nonsexual offending among male and female juvenile offenders. *Journal of Criminal Psychology, 7*(2), 134–150. https://doi.org/10.1108/JCP-12-2016-0047

Frick, P. (2012). Developmental pathways to conduct disorder: Implications for future directions in research, assessment, and treatment. *Journal of Clinical Child & Adolescent Psychology, 41*(3), 378–389.

Frick, P. J. (1998). *Conduct disorders and several antisocial behavior*. Plenum Press.

Frick, P. J. (2006). Developmental pathways to conduct disorder. *Child and Adolescent Psychiatric Clinics of North America, 15*(2), 311–vii. https://doi.org/10.1016/j.chc.2005.11.003

Frick, P. J., Kamphaus, R. W., Lahey, B. B., Loeber, R., Christ, M., Hart, E. L., & Tannenbaum, L. E. (1991). Academic underachievement and the disruptive behavior disorders. *Journal of Consulting and Clinical Psychology, 59*(2), 289–294. https://doi.org/10.1037/0022-006X.59.2.289

Frick, P. J., & Marsee, M. A. (2006). Psychopathy and developmental pathways to antisocial behavior in youth. In C. J. Patrick (Ed.), *Handbook of psychopathy*. Guilford Press.

Garland, R. J., & Dougher, M. J. (1990). The abused/abuser hypothesis of child sexual abuse: A critical review of theory and research. In J. R. Feierman (Ed.), *Pedophilia: Biosocial dimensions* (pp. 489–509). Springer-Verlag.

Garmezy, N. (1991). Resilience and vulnerability to adverse developmental outcomes associated with poverty. *American Behavioral Scientist., 34*, 416–430.

Gewirtz-Meydan, A., & Finkelhor, D. (2020). Sexual abuse and assault in a large national sample of children and adolescents. *Child Maltreatment, 25*(2), 203–214. https://doi.org/10.1177/1077559519873975

Grady, M. D., Levenson, J. S., & Bolder, T. (2016). Linking adverse childhood effects and attachment: A theory of etiology for sexual offending. *Trauma, Violence, & Abuse, 18*, 433–444. https://doi.org/10.1177/1524838015627147

Gretton, H. M., McBride, M., Hare, R. D., O'Shaughnessy, R., & Kumka, G. (2001). Psychopathology and recidivism in adolescent sex offenders. *Criminal Justice and Behavior, 28*, 427–449.

Hanson, J. L., van den Bos, W., Roeber, B. J., Rudolph, K. D., Davidson, R. J., & Pollak, S. D. (2017). Early adversity and learning: Implications for typical and atypical behavioral development. *Journal of Child Psychology and Psychiatry, 58*, 770–778. https://doi.org/10.1111/jcpp.12694

Harms, M. B., Shannon Bowen, K. E., Hanson, J. L., & Pollak, S. D. (2018). Instrumental learning and cognitive flexibility processes are impaired in children exposed to early life stress. *Developmental Science, 21*(4), e12596. https://doi.org/10.1111/desc.12596

Hart, H., & Rubia, K. (2012). Neuroimaging of child abuse: A critical review. *Frontiers in Human Neuroscience, 6*, 52. https://doi.org/10.3389/fnhum.2012.00052

Hinshaw, S. P. (1992). Externalizing behavior problems and academic underachievement in childhood and adolescence: Causal relationships and underlying mechanisms. *Psychological Bulletin, 111*, 127–155.

Hoberman, H. M., & Phenix, A. (2016). Sexual offending: Predisposing antecedents, assessments and management. Springer.

Hunter, J. A. (2006). Understanding diversity in juvenile sexual offenders: Implications for assessment, treatment, and legal management. In R. E. Longo & D. S. Prescott (Eds.), *Current perspectives: Working with sexually aggressive youth and youth with sexual behavior problems* (pp. 63–77). NEARI Press.

Keenan, K., Loeber, R., Zhang, Q., VanKammen, W. B., & Southamer-Loeber, M. (1995). The influence of deviant peers on the development of boys' disruptive and delinquent behavior: A temporal analysis. *Development and Psychology, 7*, 715–726.

Kersten, L., Vriends, N., Steppan, M., Raschle, N. M., Praetzlich, M., Oldenhof, H., Vermeiren, R., Jansen, L., Ackermann, K., Bernhard, A., Martinelli, A., Gonzalez-Madruga, K., Puzzo, I., Wells, A., Rogers, J. C., Clanton, R., Baker, R. H., Grisley, L., Baumann, S., Gundlach, M., et al. (2017). Community violence exposure and conduct problems in children and adolescents with conduct disorder and healthy controls. *Frontiers in Behavioral Neuroscience, 11*, 219. https://doi.org/10.3389/fnbeh.2017.00219

Knight, R. A., & Sims-Knight, J. E. (2004). Testing an etiological model for male juvenile sexual offending against females. *Journal of Child Sexual Abuse, 13*, 33–55.

Kofler-Westergren, B., Klopf, J., & Mitterauer, B. (2010). Juvenile delinquency: Father absence, conduct disorder, and substance abuse as risk factor triad. *International Journal of Forensic Mental Health, 9*, 33–43.

Koss, K. J., & Gunnar, M. R. (2018). Annual Research Review: Early adversity, the hypothalamic-pituitary-adrenocortical axis, and child psychopathology. *Journal of Child Psychology and Psychiatry, and Allied Disciplines, 59*(4), 327–346. https://doi.org/10.1111/jcpp.12784

Lahey, B. B., Moffitt, T. E., & Caspi, A. (Eds.). (2003). *Causes of conduct disorder and juvenile deliquency*. The Guilford Press.

Lahey, B. B., & Waldman, I. D. (2003). A developmental propensity model of the origins of conduct problems during childhood and adolescence. In B. B. Lahey, T. E. Moffitt, & A. Caspi (Eds.), *Causes of conduct disorder and juvenile delinquency*. The Guilford Press.

Levenson, J. S., Baglivio, M., Wolff, K. T., Epps, N., Royall, W., Gomez, K. C., & Kaplan, D. (2017). You learn what you live: Prevalence of childhood adversity in the lives of juveniles arrested for sexual offenses. *Advances in Social Work, 18*(1), 313–334. https://doi.org/10.18060/21204

Levenson, J. S., Willis, G. M., & Prescott, D. (2016). Adverse childhood experiences in the lives of male sex offenders and implications for trauma-informed care. *Sexual Abuse: A Journal of Research & Treatment, 28*(4), 340–359. https://doi.org/10.1177/1079063214535819

Loeber, R. (1990). Development and risk factors of juvenile antisocial behavior and delinquency. *Clinical Psychology Review, 10*, 1–41.

Lussier, P. (2017). Juvenile sex offending through a developmental life course criminology perspective. *Sexual Abuse: A Journal of Research and Treatment, 29*(1), 51–80. https://doi.org/10.1177/1079063215580966

Lussier, P., Mccuish, E., Mathesius, J., Corrado, R., & Nadeau, D. (2018). Developmental trajectories of child sexual behaviors on the path of sexual behavioral problems. *Sexual Abuse: A Journal of Research and Treatment, 30*(6), 622–658. https://doi.org/10.1177/1079063217691963

Lussier, P., van den Berg, C., Bijleveld, C., & Hendriks, J. (2012). A developmental taxonomy of juvenile sex offenders for theory, research, and prevention. *Criminal Justice and Behavior, 39*, 1559–1581. https://doi.org/10.1177/0093854812455739

Lykken, D. T. (1995). *The antisocial personalities*. Erlbaum.

Lytton, H. (1990). Child and parent effects in boys' conduct disorder: A reinterpretation. *Developmental Psychology, 26*, 683–697.

Malter Cohen, M., Jing, D., Yang, R. R., Tottenham, N., Lee, F. S., & Casey, B. J. (2013). Early-life stress has persistent effects on amygdala function and development in mice and humans. *Proceedings of the National Academy of Sciences of the United States of America, 110*(45), 18274–18278. https://doi.org/10.1073/pnas.1310163110

Marshall, W. L., & Barbaree, H. E. (1990). An integrated theory of the etiology of sexual offending. In W. L. Marshall, D. R. Laws, & H. E. Barbaree (Eds.), *Handbook of sexual assault: Issues, theories, and treatment of the offender* (pp. 257–275). Plenum Press.

Masten, A., & Coatsworth, J. D. (1998). The development of competence in favorable and unfavorable environments: Lessons from research on successful and unsuccessful children. *American Psychologist, 53*, 205–220.

Masten, A. S., Cutuli, J. J., Herbers, J. E., & Reed, J. M.-G. (2007). Resilience in development. In S. J. Lopez & C. R. Snyder (Eds.), *The Oxford handbook of positive psychology* (pp. 117–131). Oxford University Press.

McCuish, E. C., Lussier, P., & Corrado, R. R. (2015). Examining antisocial behavioral antecedents of juvenile sexual offenders and juvenile non-sexual offenders. *Sexual Abuse, 27*(4), 414–438. https://doi.org/10.1177/1079063213517268

McEwen, B. S. (2017). Neurobiological and systemic effects of chronic stress. *Chronic Stress*. https://doi.org/10.1177/2470547017692328

McGuire, R. J., Carlisle, J. M., & Young, B. G. (1965). Sexual deviations as conditioned behavior: A hypothesis. *Behaviour Research and Therapy, 2*, 185–190.

McLaughlin, K. A., & Lambert, H. K. (2017). Child trauma exposure and psychopathology: Mechanisms of risk and resilience. *Current Opinion in Psychology, 14*, 29–34. https://doi.org/10.1016/j.copsyc.2016.10.004

McLaughlin, K. A., Peverill, M., Gold, A. L., Alves, S., & Sheridan, M. A. (2015). Child maltreatment and neural systems underlying emotion regulation. *Journal of the American Academy of Child and Adolescent Psychiatry, 54*(9), 753–762. https://doi.org/10.1016/j.jaac.2015.06.010

Milloy, C. (1994). *A comparative study of juvenile sex offenders and non-sex offenders*. Washington State Institute for Public Policy.

Miner, M. H., Robinson, B. E., Knight, R. A., Berg, D., Romine, R. S., & Netland, J. (2010). Understanding sexual perpetration against children: Effects of attachment style, interpersonal involvement, and hypersexuality. *Sexual Abuse: A Journal of Research and Treatment, 22*(1), 58–77. https://doi.org/10.1177/1079063209353183

Moffitt, T. E. (1993). Adolescence-limited and life-course-persistent antisocial behavior: A developmental taxonomy. *Psychological Review, 4*, 674–701.

Moffitt, T. E. (2005). Genetic and environmental influences on antisocial behaviors: Evidence from behavioral-genetic research. *Advances in Genetics, 55*, 41–104.

Moffitt, T. E. (2006). Life-course-persistent versus adolescence-limited antisocial behavior. In D. Cicchetti & J. Cohen (Eds.), *Developmental psychopathology: Risk, disorder, and adaptation*. John Wiley & Sons, Inc.

Moffitt, T. E., Caspi, A., Dickson, N., Silva, P., & Stanton, W. (1996). Childhood-onset versus adolescent-onset antisocial conduct problems in males: Natural history from ages 3 to 18 years. *Development and Psychopathology, 8*, 399–424.

Moody, J. E. E., Brissie, J., & Kim, J. (1994). Personality and background characteristics of adolescent sexual offenders. *Journal of Addictions & Offender Counseling, 14*(2), 38. https://doi.org/10.1002/j.2161-1874.1994.tb00090.x

Nigg, J. T., & Huang-Pollock, C. L. (2003). An early-onset model of the role of executive functions and intelligence in conduct disorder/delinquency. In B. B. Lahey, T. E. Moffitt, & A. Caspi (Eds.), *Causes of conduct disorder and juvenile delinquency*. The Guilford Press.

Novick, A. M., Levandowski, M. L., Laumann, L. E., Philip, N. S., Price, L. H., & Tyrka, A. R. (2018). The effects of early life stress on reward processing. *Journal of Psychiatric Research, 101*, 80–103. https://doi.org/10.1016/j.jpsychires.2018.02.002

O'Brien, B. S., Frick, P. J., & Lyman, R. D. (1994). Reward dominance among children with disruptive behavior disorders. *Journal of Psychopathology and Behavioral Assessment, 16*, 131–145.

Pardini, D., & Frick, P. J. (2013). Multiple developmental pathways to conduct disorder: Current conceptualizations and clinical implications. *Journal of the Canadian Academy of Child and Adolescent Psychiatry*.

Patterson, G. R., Reid, J. B., & Dishion, T. J. (1992). *Antisocial boys*. Castalia.

Pechtel, P., & Pizzagalli, D. A. (2011). Effects of early life stress on cognitive and affective function: An integrated review of human literature. *Psychopharmacology, 214*(1), 55–70. https://doi.org/10.1007/s00213-010-2009-2

Perlman, S. B., Kalish, C. W., & Pollak, S. D. (2008). The role of maltreatment experience in children's understanding of the antecedents of emotion. *Cognition and Emotion, 22*(4), 651–670. https://doi.org/10.1080/02699930701461154

Perry, B. D., Griffin, G., Davis, G., Perry, J. A., & Perry, R. D. (2018). The impact of neglect, trauma, and maltreatment. In A. Beech, A. Carter, R. Mann, & P. Rotshtein (Eds.), *The Wiley handbook of forensic neuroscience*. Wiley.

Pollak, S. D. (2015). Developmental psychopathology: Recent advances and future challenges. *World Psychiatry, 14*, 262–269. https://doi.org/10.1002/wps.20237

Porges, S. W. (2011). *The Norton series on interpersonal neurobiology. The polyvagal theory: Neurophysiological foundations of emotions, attachment, communication, and self-regulation*. W W Norton & Co.

Reitzel, L. R., & Carbonell, J. L. (2006). The effectiveness of sexual offender treatment for juveniles as measured by recidivism: A meta-analysis. *Sexual Abuse: A Journal of Research and Treatment, 18*(4), 401–421. https://doi.org/10.1177/107906320601800407

Rich, P. (2009). *Juvenile sex offenders: A comprehensive guide to risk evaluation*. John Wiley & Sons.

Rich, P. (2011). *Understanding, assessing, and rehabilitating juvenile sexual offenders*. John Wiley & Sons.

Righthand, S., Welch, C., Carpenter, E. M., Young, G. S., & Scoular, R. J. (2001). *Sex offending by Maine youth: Their offenses and characteristics*. Department of Corrections and Department of Human Services.

Romens, S. E., & Pollak, S. D. (2012). Emotion regulation predicts attention bias in maltreated children at-risk for depression. *Journal of Child Psychology and Psychiatry, and Allied Disciplines, 53*(2), 120–127. https://doi.org/10.1111/j.1469-7610.2011.02474.x

Rutter, M. (1987). Psychosocial resilience and protective mechanisms. *American Journal of Orthopsychiatry, 57*, 316–331. [PubMed: 3303954].

Ryan, G., Miyoshi, T. J., Metzner, J. L., Krugman, R. D., & Fryer, G. E. (1996). Trends in a national sample of sexually abusive youths. *Journal of the American Academy of Child & Adolescent Psychiatry, 35*(1), 17–25. https://doi.org/10.1097/00004583-199601000-00008

Sanchez, M. M., & Pollak, S. (2009). Socioemotional development following early abuse and neglect: Challenges and insights from translational research. In M. De Haan & M. R. Gunnar (Eds.), *Handbook of developmental social neuroscience*. Guilford Press.

Sandler, J. C., Freeman, N. J., & Socia, K. M. (2008). Does a watched pot boil? A time-series analysis of New York State's sex offender registration and notification law. *Psychology, Public Policy, and Law, 14*, 284–302.

Seto, M. C. (2008). Pedophilia and sexual offending against children: Theory, assessment, and intervention. *American Psychological Association*. https://doi.org/10.1037/11639-000

Seto, M. C., & Lalumière, M. L. (2010). What is so special about male adolescent sexual offending? A review and test of explanations through meta-analysis. *Psychological Bulletin, 136*(4), 526–575. https://doi.org/10.1037/a0019700

Seto, M. C., Lalumiere, M. L., & Blanchard, R. (2000). The discriminative validity of phallometric tests for pedophilic interests among adolescent sex offenders against children. *Psychological Assessment, 12*, 319–327.

Shackman, J. E., & Pollak, S. D. (2014). Impact of physical maltreatment on the regulation of negative affect and aggression. *Development and Psychopathology, 26*(4 Pt 1), 1021–1033. https://doi.org/10.1017/S0954579414000546

Silovsky, J. F., & Niec, L. (2002). Characteristics of young children with sexual behavior problems: A pilot study. *Child Maltreatment, 7*(3), 187–197. https://doi.org/10.1177/1077559502007003002

Smallbone, S. (2006a). Social and psychological factors in the development of delinquency and sexual deviance. In H. E. Barbaree & W. L. Marshall (Eds.), *The juvenile sex offender* (pp. 105–127). Guilford Press.

Smallbone, S. W. (2006b). An attachment-theoretical revision of Marshall and Barbaree's Integrated theory of the etiology of sexual offending. In W. L. Marshall, Y. M. Fernandez, L. E. Marshall, & G. A. Serran (Eds.), *Wiley series in forensic clinical psychology. Sexual offender treatment: Controversial issues* (pp. 93–107). John Wiley & Sons Ltd.

Smith, K., & Pollack, S. (2020). Rethinking concepts and categories for understanding the neurodevelopmental effects of childhood adversity. *Perspectives on Psychological Science*, 1–27. https://doi.org/10.1177/1745691620920725

Smith, W. R., & Monastersky, C. (1986). Assessing juvenile sexual offenders' risk for reoffending. *Criminal Justice and Behavior, 13*(2), 115–140. https://doi.org/10.1177/0093854886013002001

Snyder, J., Reid, J., & Patterson, G. (2003). A social learning model of child and adolescent antisocial behavior. In B. B. Lahey, T. E. Moffitt, & A. Caspi (Eds.), *Causes of conduct disorder and juvenile delinquency*. The Guilford Press.

Spaccarelli, S., Bowden, B., Coatsworth, J. D., & Kim, S. (1997). Psychosocial correlates of male sexual aggression in a chronic delinquent sample. *Criminal Justice and Behavior, 24*(1), 71–95. https://doi.org/10.1177/0093854897024001005

Streeck-Fischer, A., & van der Kolk, B. A. (2000). Down will come baby, cradle and all: Diagnostic and therapeutic implications of chronic trauma on child development. *Australian & New Zealand Journal of Psychiatry, 34*(6), 903–918. https://doi.org/10.1080/000486700265

Teicher, M. H., Samson, J. A., Anderson, C. M., & Ohashi, K. (2016). The effects of childhood maltreatment on brain structure, function and connectivity. *Nature Reviews. Neuroscience, 17*(10), 652–666. https://doi.org/10.1038/nrn.2016.111

Tharp, A. T., DeGue, S., Valle, L. A., Brookmeyer, K. A., Massetti, G. M., & Matjasko, J. L. (2013). A systematic qualitative review of risk and protective factors for sexual violence perpetration. *Trauma, Violence & Abuse, 14*(2), 133–167. https://doi.org/10.1177/1524838012470031

Thorndike, E. L. (1901). Animal intelligence: An experimental study of the associative processes in animals. *Psychological Review Monograph Supplement, 2*, 1–109.

Tottenham, N., & Sheridan, M. A. (2010). A review of adversity, the amygdala and the hippocampus: A consideration of developmental timing. *Frontiers in Human Neuroscience, 3*, 68. https://doi.org/10.3389/neuro.09.068.2009

Truscott, D. (1993). Adolescent offenders: Comparison for sexual, violent, and property offences. *Psychological Reports, 73*(2), 657–658. https://doi.org/10.2466/pr0.1993.73.2.657

Wanklyn, S. G., Ward, A. K., Cormier, N. S., Day, D. M., & Newman, J. E. (2012). Can we distinguish juvenile violent sex offenders, violent non-sex offenders, and versatile violent sex offenders based on childhood risk factors? *Journal of Interpersonal Violence, 27*(11), 2128–2143. https://doi.org/10.1177/0886260511432153

Ward, T., & Beech, A. R. (2016). The integrated theory of sexual offending–revised. In D. P. Boer (Ed.), *The Wiley handbook on the theories, assessment and treatment of sexual offending*. https://doi.org/10.1002/9781118574003.wattso006

Welch, C., Carpenter, E., & Young, S. (2001). *Sex Offending by Maine Youth Their Offenses and Characteristics*.

Werner, E. E., & Smith, S. (1982). *Vulnerable but not invincible: A study of resilient children*. McGraw-Hill.

Worling, J. R. (1995). Sexual abuse histories of adolescent male sex offenders: Differences on the basis of the age and gender of their victims. *Journal of Abnormal Psychology, 104*(4), 610–613. https://doi.org/10.1037/0021-843X.104.4.610

Yeoman, Z., Hiscox, H., & Witt, P. (2021). The relationship between juvenile sex offending and conduct disorder. *Sex Offender Law Report*.

Yoder, J., Dillard, R., & Leibowitz, G. S. (2017). Family experiences and sexual victimization histories: A comparative analysis between youth sexual and nonsexual offenders. *International Journal of Offender Therapy and Comparative Criminology, 62*(10), 2917–2936. https://doi.org/10.1177/0306624x17738063

Zakireh, B., Ronis, S., & Knight, R. (2008). Individual beliefs, attitudes, and victimization histories of male juvenile sexual offenders. *Sexual Abuse: A Journal of Research and Treatment, 20*, 323–351. https://doi.org/10.1177/1079063208322424

Zimmerman, M. A. (2013). Resiliency theory: A strengths-based approach to research and practice for adolescent health. *Health Education & Behavior: The Official Publication of the Society for Public Health Education, 40*(4), 381–383. https://doi.org/10.1177/1090198113493782

Zolondek, S. C., Abel, G. G., Northey, J. R., & Jordan, A. D. (2001). The self-reported behaviors of juvenile sexual offenders. *Journal of Interpersonal Violence, 16*, 73–78.

Chapter 8
Neuropsychological Considerations of Sexual Offending

Gilian Tenbergen

8.1 Introduction

This chapter provides a deep dive and review of the literature surrounding the neuropsychology of pedophilia and sexual offending against children. To help readers appreciate the relevance of neuropsychological assessment to the prevention of first- and recidivistic sexual offending behavior, articles will be discussed in light of their contribution to the Motivation-Facilitation Model of Sexual Offending as proposed by Seto (2017). Additionally, the Compositional Explanatory Theory of Pedophilia (Gannon, 2021) is used as an organizing framework to distinguish the studies used to explain sexual offending behavior from those explaining the development and phenomenology of pedophilia. Overall, this chapter is meant to provide clinicians, researchers, students, and those who work in the field of sexual abuse prevention with a solid theoretical foundation of how neuropsychology intersects with pedophilia and sexual offending behavior.

8.2 Pedophilia and Sexual Offending Against Children

Pedophilia is a paraphilia characterized by the ongoing sexual preference toward prepubertal children (Seto, 2008, 2018). Although the term *pedophilia* is often used synonymously with child sexual abuse (CSA), *pedophilia* itself refers only to the sexual preference (Tenbergen et al., 2015). According to the ICD-10 and the DSM-5,

---

G. Tenbergen, PhD (✉)
Department of Psychological Sciences, State University of New York at Oswego, Oswego, NY, USA
e-mail: gilian.tenbergen@oswego.edu

R. J. Tully et al. (eds.), *Best Practices in Sexual Offender Assessment and Management*, Dangerous Behavior in Clinical and Forensic Psychology,
https://doi.org/10.1007/978-3-031-83135-5_8

this paraphilia can be differentiated into two categories: Pedophilia and Pedophilic Disorder (APA, 2013; World Health Organization, 1992).

Pedophilia describes an intense sexual preference toward prepubescent children—in the absence of either acting upon that preference in any way, or experiencing distress or impairment related to the preference. Pedophilic Disorder, according to the DSM-5, requires that the individual reports that A) the urges and fantasies are distressing or life-impairing, B) that they have acted upon these urges by sexually abusing a child or by consuming child sexual abuse material (CSAM), or C) they have experienced both symptoms (distress and behavior). These symptoms must be present for at least 6 months and be primarily directed toward prepubescent children. Thus, "pedophilia" describes the sexual preference toward prepubescent children, while Pedophilic Disorder is a mental health diagnosis. An individual with pedophilia can have a gender preference (e.g., towards boys, towards girls, or towards both genders), can be exclusively attracted to children, or can also be attracted to individuals in other age groups (e.g., exclusive or non-exclusive pedophilia, respectively), and can be attracted to children within or outside of the family unit (APA, 2013).

A related term, Minor Attracted Person (MAP) has recently emerged in the scientific literature (B4U-Act, 2011). This term has social value, as it is less heavily stigmatized than the term "pedophile," however it is neither a scientific nor a clinical term. Therefore, for ease of understanding, the term pedophilia will be used throughout this chapter to refer to a sexual preference specific to prepubescent children.

A relevant distinction to make regarding pedophilia is that it can and does exist exclusive of offending behavior; that is, non-offending individuals with pedophilia exist and are an important subgroup to consider when testing hypotheses about the origins of sexual offending behavior. A non-offending individual is just that—a person who experiences pedophilia but who has neither consumed CSAM nor has committed a contact sexual offense against a child. This group is understudied relative to the wealth of knowledge available on individuals who have offended sexually. How they remain offense-free and what their mental health needs are is of critical importance to improve CSA prevention initiatives.

The next section provides a general discussion of what neuropsychology is, followed by an elaboration of the history of neuropsychological assessment among individuals who have (or have not) offended sexually against children.

8.3 Neuropsychological Assessment

Human neuropsychology is the scientific study of brain and behavior (Rourke, 1991) and aims to understand and explain the structural and functional mechanisms in the brain responsible for our outward behavior, including:

- Sensation and perception
- Memory

- Consciousness and
- Intelligence (Mahon & Caramazza, 2009)

Human neuropsychological functioning spans the entire human existence, as it attempts to explain how our psychology is represented in the brain. One component of neuropsychology is executive function—the construct of human behavior that explains the 'how' of behavioral expression—and it is this set of functions that has garnered much attention in the field of sexual offending against children (Hucker et al., 1986).

Although no single formal operational definition of executive functioning yet exists, scholars have defined executive functions over the years as consisting of attentional control, planning, carrying out goal-directed behavior, and effective behavior (Jurado & Rosselli, 2007). The subcomponents of these terms consist of shifting, updating, and inhibition (Jurado & Rosselli, 2007; Suchy, 2009). Executive functions are by their very nature highly effortful and costly in terms of energy use to the individual and as such are only used in situations that are truly novel and complex, thus precluding the individual from relying on learned or acquired skills and behaviors (Suchy, 2009).

The components of executive function include:

- *Attentional control*, which refers to the ability to sustain attention for longer periods of time, to selectively attend to certain stimuli at the expense of others, and the ability to withhold responses when instructed,
- *Planning*, which encompasses the ability to identify and organize steps and elements needed to complete a goal,
- *Set shifting and cognitive flexibility*, which include the ability to switch rapidly between different response sets,
- *Verbal fluency*, which refers to verbal initiative and productivity, and of all the components of executive functioning; this is the most easily influenced through exposure to the postnatal environment (Jurado & Rosselli, 2007).

These functions have associated neural correlates and are strongly implicated in the search for neuropsychological impairment, especially among sexual offenders (Hucker et al., 1988).

However, concerns arise when one attempts to measure 'executive functioning,' especially within a group for whom impairments have been, at best, questionable (Suchy et al., 2014). This is first because executive functions come 'online' only when the situation at hand is exceptionally novel or complex and testing is usually completed in laboratory settings with strict participation rules and instructions. Tests used for research rarely, if ever, measure the true meaning and capacity of an individual's executive functions (Jurado & Rosselli, 2007). Secondly, the concept of executive function impairment is misleading, insofar as impairments are usually seen as the cumulative effect of slight weaknesses across a range of executive functioning components, and thus require a number of different tasks and tests to discern whether an impairment truly exists (Suchy et al., 2014). A third concern is that these tests are quite sensitive (i.e. they detect problems when they exist), but they are not specific (i.e. the result involves more than just damage to the frontal lobe) (Suchy et al., 2014). This relates to task impurity, as many of the tests that have been developed to measure the different executive functioning components are often weakly defined and may lead to one test measuring two or even three different components of executive functioning, rather than the one for which it was developed (Jurado & Rosselli, 2007). These issues have direct implications for clinical work, as discussed later within this chapter.

8.4 The Motivation-Facilitation Model of Sexual Offending

The Motivation-Facilitation Model of Sexual Offending, developed by Seto (2017), attempts to explain the origins of sexual offending behavior through motivating traits and facilitating states that exist within an individual or their environment. As originally conceptualized by Seto (2017), motivating traits include existent paraphilias, high sex drive, and intense mating effort, and facilitating traits include personality (such as antisocial traits) and states (such as intoxication, access to a potential victim, etc.).

This 2017 model is an improvement over previous theories attempting to explain sexual offending behavior insofar as it integrates historical data with newer methods to advance our knowledge of sexual offending behavior, while also generating a plethora of new testable hypotheses. While this model is useful to test and explain behavior, it falls short in its ability to explain the origins of sexual preference development; to this end, Compositional Theory of Pedophilia, as proposed by Gannon (2021) is also available. This theory posits that the development of pedophilia is a complex interplay of biological, environmental, neurodevelopmental, and psychological factors. So far, this is one of few theories to attempt to explain how pedophilia develops separately from offending behavior, and thus can explain the existence of non-offending individuals with pedophilia.

For our purposes, the neuropsychology of sexual offending is broadly categorized as a set of facilitating factors (both trait and state) that increase the likelihood that a sexual offense against a child will occur for an individual with pedophilia. Pedophilia is treated as a motivating factor, as put forth in Seto (2017). Specifically, executive functions, inhibition, attention, visuospatial functioning, verbal functioning, working memory, cognitive flexibility, and affect recognition are theorized to act as facilitating factors that can differentiate between individuals who have and who have not offended sexually, based on the existence of the motivating trait of pedophilia. To ease readers into this complex—and often equivocal—field of research, studies will be grouped according to behavior (offense vs no offense), followed by preference status (pedophilic vs non-pedophilic).

8.5 Neuropsychology of Pedophilia and Pedophilic Disorder

A considerable amount of research has investigated the relationship among potential neuropsychological deficits, pedophilia, and sexual offending against children. As the early research into the neuropsychology of sexual offending is examined, it can be seen that many studies used mixed groups of individuals with sexual offense histories, often conflating sexual preference with sexual behavior and obscuring any differences that may be preference specific. To begin, two excellent systematic reviews on the role of neuropsychology on sexual offending behavior were recently published that warrant their own, separate discussions.

The first systematic review, published by Turner and Rettenberger (2020) offers an excellent review of the published literature on neuropsychology and sexual offending against children. What makes their contribution stand out is the inclusion of more recently published empirical studies. Their primary result—similar to the thesis of this chapter—is that offense status (i.e. the existence of behavioral action toward a desired sexual target) is the significant driver of neuropsychological differences between those who have offended and healthy controls. This applies both for individuals with pedophilia and those without who have offended sexually against children. The neuropsychological components most often implicated in the research were inhibition and set-shifting, which suggests that those who offend sexually have a weakened ability to disengage from activated behavior and may struggle with activating relevant coping strategies when circumstances change. This focus on offense status should be kept in mind while reading the review below.

The other relevant systematic review, written by Dillien et al. (2020) offers a unique take on previous theorizing on the relationship between neuropsychological impairment and offending behavior. These authors have developed typologies to address the existent differences between categories of sexual offenders against children. What they suggest is that, similar to Turner and Rettenberger (2020), individuals who have offended sexually against children (whether pedophilic or not) share a weakness in inhibition in common [this result was also found in Massau et al. (2017)]. It is with other neuropsychological constructs that differences can be observed between pedophilic and non-pedophilic individuals who have sexually offended against children. Extant literature suggests that individuals with pedophilia who have offended show disturbances in attention, processing speed, and visuospatial functioning. Non-pedophilic sexual offenders against children showed difficulties in cognitive flexibility, visuospatial working memory, verbal memory, and affect recognition. The major takeaway from both reviews is that these results are at best preliminary, and much research is still needed to establish reliability and validity. Please see Table 8.1 for a review of how neuropsychological components differ according to preference and offense status. This table was created based on data pulled from the literature and from the author's own research findings.

Table 8.1 Proposed differences between individuals who have or have not engaged in CSA, stratified by preference status (pedophilic or non-pedophilic)

	Contact CSA		Non-Contact CSA		Non-Offenders
	Pedophilic	*Non-Pedophilic*	*Pedophilic*	*Non-Pedophilic*	
Inhibition	X	X	X(?)		X(?)
Attention	X	-	-		?
Processing speed	X	-	-		?
Visuospatial functioning	X	-	-		?
Verbal functioning	X	X	-		?
Verbal memory	-	X	-		?
Cognitive flexibility	-	X	-		?
Visuospatial working memory	-	X	-		?
Affect recognition	-	X	-		?

X, identified weakness in the literature; X(?), plausible difference not yet verified; ?, no data exists yet. Blank cells represent no difference

8.5.1 Mixed Sexual Offense Studies

Over the last 20 years, many studies have investigated the relationship between neuropsychological function and child sexual abuse behavior. However, these studies should be interpreted cautiously. Like many neuroscientific inquiries into pedophilia, many participant samples were mixed for sexual preference disorders (i.e., confounding pedophilia with pedophilic disorder), and included victims of varying age ranges. Additionally, these studies often did not assess directly for pedophilia (e.g., Hucker et al., 1986, 1988), but instead it was assumed through offense status. The first studies in this category assumed neuropsychological differences between their groups of sexual offenders and controls, which was not supported (Abracen et al., 1991; Gillespie & McKenzie, 2000; Tarter et al., 1983). These early studies did not control for sexual preference (e.g., pedophilia) and contained mixed groups of offenders, potentially obscuring any differences that did exist. Therefore, the results must be interpreted considering behavioral consequences related to offense status, not sexual preference.

Among the first studies to find executive function differences, Joyal et al. (2007) found, in his study of mixed sexual offenders, prolonged Stroop effects that were indicative of stronger interference effects (i.e. reduced capacity for response inhibition and sustained attention) and impaired verbal skills. Comparisons between sexual offenders against children and sexual offenders against adults yielded interesting results. Both groups performed similarly on measures of cognitive flexibility and set shifting, visual-spatial integration, and verbal skills. However, sexual offenders against children exhibited deficits in response inhibition that were not present in sexual offenders against adults. As behavioral inhibition can be correlated with impulsivity, subsequent studies directly assessed whether pedophilia and/or child sexual abuse (CSA) are associated with impulsivity.

Cohen et al. (2002) found that heterosexual participants with pedophilia were slightly more impulsive than a healthy control participant group. The authors interpreted this as evidence of a potential increase in behavioral impulsivity in participants with pedophilia who had offended sexually against a child; however, without a control group of non-offending men with pedophilia, it is difficult to conclude whether pedophilia itself, or the act of committing child sexual abuse, is associated with impulsivity.

8.5.2 *Pedophilia Studies*

This next section reviews studies that include sexual preference disorders (i.e., pedophilia) as a factor for group differences. Previously, studies assumed that behavior was synonymous with preference and assumed that an individual who had committed CSA also had pedophilia. The next studies assess pedophilia directly and attempt to differentiate those weaknesses associated with pedophilia from those associated with offending behavior.

8.5.2.1 Pedophilia with Offense

Executive functioning differences were observed among incarcerated individuals with pedophilia exclusively attracted to prepubescent children with a history of contact sexual offenses against at least two victims (Kruger & Schiffer, 2011). While the differences on these tasks suggest executive functioning weaknesses in the pedophilic group as compared to the control group, the absolute values were within the normal range for all tasks. These results suggest that individuals with pedophilia who sexually offend against children are not driven by executive functioning impairments specifically, but rather cumulative slight weaknesses in various domains.

8.5.2.2 Pedophilia vs. Non-Pedophilia with Offense

In what may have been the first study to directly investigate executive functioning differences between pedophilic and non-pedophilic sexual offenders against children as compared to healthy adult male control participants, Suchy et al. (2009) found that their pedophilic subsample tended to perform better than their non-pedophilic subsample; however both groups still performed worse than the healthy control group. The group with pedophilia displayed slower processing speed times than both the non-pedophilic and control groups, however this finding did not hold for accuracy. That is, individuals with pedophilia required more time to complete the activity but were still as accurate as controls (non-pedophilic individuals scored worse in accuracy than controls, regardless of speed of information processing). Therefore, the pedophilic and non-pedophilic groups did show weaknesses in executive functions, consistent with previous literature (e.g., Cohen et al., 2002; Joyal et al., 2007). Schiffer and Vonlaufen (2011) found that relative to non-sexual offenders and healthy controls, the non-pedophilic sexual offender group exhibited global executive function impairments that were not seen in a group of sexual offenders with pedophilia. Specific performance deficits in non-pedophilic sexual offenders were noted in set-shifting, verbal memory, and response inhibition.

Historically, it seems as though, starting with the Suchy et al. (2009) study and the results of the Kruger and Schiffer (2011) study, researchers began to focus more on the differences between pedophilic and non-pedophilic sexual offenders against children, as phenomenological and psychological studies have demonstrated distinct reasons for offending across these two groups (Seto, 2009, 2017, 2018). Eastvold et al. (2011), as a follow-up to Suchy et al. (2009), found that individuals with pedophilia who had offended sexually do not show generalized executive functioning impairments, they instead show a distinct pattern of weaknesses. These differences include worse performance on behavioral inhibition measures, but improved performance in abstract reasoning measures and planning measures as compared to non-sexual offender and non-pedophilic sexual offender controls. The authors interpreted these results as neuropsychological support for grooming behavior (e.g., planning access to a victim without being apprehended), which could indicate a planning-oriented response style (Eastvold et al., 2011). More recent research does not appear to support this response style hypothesis (Massau et al., 2017), but does support the identified differences in response inhibition, abstract reasoning, and planning measures.

Future studies are urgently needed to carefully control for psychiatric comorbidities, incarceration status, and offender status, as few studies to date have examined neuropsychological deficits in these subsamples (Cantor & McPhail, 2016; Turner & Rettenberger, 2020). In order to determine whether these effects are related to the pedophilic sexual preference or whether they are mediating factors in the pathway to offending behavior, future studies must include samples of non-offending individuals with pedophilia—a hitherto neglected sub-population within pedophilia at large (Cantor & McPhail, 2016; Turner & Rettenberger, 2020).

In addition to investigating the effect of offense status on neuropsychological performance in pedophilia broadly, studies have also examined the role of offense *type*. The following discussion will highlight our current understanding about how different types of sexual offenses against children are correlated with neuropsychological differences.

8.5.2.3 Contact vs. Non-Contact vs. Non-Offense Studies

Emerging studies are investigating potential differences based on whether an individual with pedophilia has committed an offense, as well as comparing offense type (i.e., contact vs non-contact offenses; also referred to as offline vs online offenses). In this latter domain, contact sexual offenses refer to the presence of a physical victim. Non-contact offending—in this capacity—refers primarily to internet offenses (e.g., viewing and distributing CSAM, online solicitation offenses to interact with children online, etc.), while non-offenders refers to a complete absence of offending behavior, which is a very new subsample for research and clinical purposes (Cantor & McPhail, 2016; Seto, 2017; Tenbergen et al., 2015).

First, individuals with non-contact offenses are typically younger than contact offenders, and also more highly educated and have higher intelligence (Blanchard et al., 2007; Neutze et al., 2011). Babchishin et al. (2011) upheld this age difference in a meta-analysis and a subsequent review of child sexual exploitation material (CSEM) users (Babchishin et al., 2018). Individuals with non-contact offenses tended to possess significantly more paraphilic sexual interests than those with contact offenses. General sexual interest could explain this, where the sexual material sought out matches the sexual preferences of the consumer.

Additionally, Babchishin et al. (2011) postulated that individuals with non-contact sexual offenses have greater rates of self-control and are less impulsive than comparable individuals with contact offenses. This explanation is still under investigation, with previous studies providing equivocal results [some suggesting lowered rates of impulsivity (Elliott et al., 2009) versus others finding no differences between offense type (Howitt & Sheldon, 2007)]. In addition, it appears that the transition from non-contact to contact offending is very low (~2.0% of non-contact to contact transition offending), which could suggest some inhibitory mechanisms are present and functional (Seto, 2018; Seto et al., 2011) although this rate may be an underestimation based on reliance on either self-report, or apprehension, for both the non-contact and contact offending.

In a push to separate the effects of offense behavior from sexual preference, Massau et al. (2017) compared executive function across groups of offenders with and without pedophilia and found that impulsivity was the major difference among the groups. More specifically, contact offense history was associated with greater deficits in response inhibition, with non-pedophilic contact offenders displaying the greatest impairments in this domain.

Furthermore, non-contact pedophilic offenses (this group was mixed also with non-offenders) showed weaknesses only in reflection impulsivity, suggesting that they jump to conclusions more quickly. They did not differ from controls regarding their response inhibition abilities. Specifically, response inhibition is indicative of contact offending, whereas reflection impulsivity is associated with non-contact or non-offending pedophilia. These results implicate different forms of impulsivity in committing contact versus non-contact offenses.

Rosburg et al. (2021), in their recent update to the empirical literature, supported previous results demonstrating that inhibitory control is the neuropsychological factor that differentiates individuals with pedophilia who have from those who have not offended sexually. Risk-taking differentiated contact CSA from non-contact CSA, with non-contact (individuals who had used CSAM but had no contact offense) scoring lower on risk-taking measures. This is in line with previous research that suggests that most neuropsychological weaknesses are found in individuals who had committed a contact sexual offense against a child, especially those who are not pedophilic.

So far, no studies have been conducted examining specifically the executive functions of dark field offending (those who have engaged in criminal sexual activity but who are unknown to the criminal justice system i.e. have not been convicted) and non-offending individuals with pedophilia, thus leaving a large gap in knowledge regarding how these individuals differ to their incarcerated counterparts. What is urgently needed in the field are studies recruiting community dwelling (e.g., non-incarcerated) darkfield individuals with offenses and non-offenders, to truly differentiate incarceration/general criminality effects from those effects produced by pedophilia as a sexual preference.

8.5.2.4 Darkfield and Non-Offense Studies

As mentioned above, there is a dearth of literature specifically assessing neuropsychological functioning in darkfield offenders and especially individuals with pedophilia who have not engaged in any child sexual abuse related behaviors. There may be key differences between the neuropsychological functioning of those who are apprehended for sexual offending and those who are not apprehended, yet those who are apprehended are those who tend to be studied for obvious reasons. This is a ripe field for investigation and would stand to shed light on crucial questions related to the development of pedophilia, such as whether it is neurodevelopmental in origin and related to other disorders such as Autism Spectrum Disorders (ASD) or schizophrenia, as suggested by Fazio (2018) and Joyal et al. (2019), and could contribute to our development of theories to explain pedophilia's origins, such as Gannon's recent paper on the Compositional Explanatory Theory of Pedophilia (CEToP) (Gannon, 2021). Scholarship in this field will offer much to our understanding of pedophilia and its behavioral attributes.

8.5.3 Summary

The above sections detailed the myriad executive function differences observed between sexual preference groups (pedophilic or not pedophilic), divided by offense status (type of offense vs non-offense). The major takeaways are that many of the observed differences are related to offense status, meaning that those who have committed a sexual offense against a child are more likely to show executive functioning differences in inhibition, attention, processing speed, and verbal fluency. The data is still teasing out the relationship with sexual preference, but initial data suggests that pedophilia—on its own—is not related to executive function deficits. Clinicians and scholars urgently need answers to these questions to treat their clients most effectively. Future research should focus on including groups of individuals with pedophilia who have not offended to define these answers.

8.6 Common Referral Questions

Clinical readers engaged in sex-offender specific treatment (sex offender treatment programs; SOTP) may benefit from knowing how this neuropsychological research literature aids them in their treatment provision. For example, a common question is how this aggregate scientific knowledge can be used to treat specific individuals; knowing general trends from the literature can be translated into clinical use with minor modifications. Clinical referral questions include how to assess an individual's neuropsychological and executive functioning, what tools are available for this assessment, how to integrate this information into a patient's treatment plan, and how to interpret changes in function and behavior. Of particular importance regarding change in behavior is the existence of demarcation points and the mapping of degrees of change; for example, at what point can a client be considered to have improved sufficiently in their neuropsychological functioning to deem treatment completed?

This chapter has hopefully provided readers with a solid understanding of the relationship between neuropsychological performance and sexual offending behavior. However, a major limitation of this literature is the lack of direct translation studies, i.e., studies that seek to both quantify and qualify these neuropsychological differences relative for use in treatment. While it is useful to know that these differences among offense and/or preference groups exist, what will benefit treatment providers is knowing exactly what parameters are weakened for their clients, and what tools are available to them for intervention purposes. For example, since weaknesses in behavioral inhibition appear common among individuals who have committed child sexual abuse, how would a clinician go about integrating this as a treatment target and how would they know when the client has improved? Currently, no such quantified parameters exist. This is a major open area for future clinically driven scholarship.

8.7 Theoretical Implications

As discussed in depth above, a critical gap that must be addressed is how these neuropsychological differences apply to *non-offending individuals*. So far, all research on the neuropsychology of sexual offending and/or pedophilia have only included samples with individuals who have some type of child sexual abuse offense in their histories (e.g., contact or non-contact or mixed). While this rich history of research has given us great insight into how neuropsychology might function across different types of offense categories, it has not yet answered the question relative to sexual preference paraphilias (i.e., pedophilia). What research does exist suggests a complex relationship between offense type and sexual preference disorder. A comprehensive theory of how pedophilia as a sexual orientation may be explained has only relatively recently been offered (Gannon, 2021), but it is still short of an explanation for the role of neuropsychological differences as they apply to non-offending individuals with pedophilia. Future research should bear this in mind as a possible method to explain the etiology of pedophilia as a sexual preference and should test for how strong a role neuropsychology has with the relationship to offending behavior among individuals with pedophilia.

8.8 Conclusions and Future Directions

As has been seen in this chapter, the most pronounced neuropsychological differences appear to apply primarily to individuals who have committed contact child sexual abuse offenses *without* pedophilia. The critical point here is that these are individuals who have a contact offense but who do *not have* pedophilia—which suggests a more relevant role for neuropsychological weaknesses or impairments in the behavioral regard (i.e., CSA). It remains to be seen whether these differences are observed when groups of non-offending individuals with pedophilia are studied. This is a critical gap that must be addressed to further our understanding of how pedophilia as a sexual preference disorder develops, and to provide guidance regarding how to differentiate between those likely to transition to contact offenses and those who will not. A major question exists regarding the relationship of how these existing neuropsychological differences among different offense trajectories relates to the existence of a sexual preference disorder, i.e., exactly what markers differentiate those who offend from those who never do? Is there a set of neuropsychological markers that can explain—and hopefully predict—those non-offending individuals with pedophilia who will transition? If this question were to be addressed in the literature in a systematic manner, its results could be translated immediately into clinical preventive and supportive work with the population of non-offending persons with pedophilia.

Further areas ripe for scientific inquiry are translation and treatment studies. As mentioned earlier within this chapter, while significant gains have been made in the understanding of how neuropsychological function differs between individuals who have versus those who have not offended and how pedophilia may play a role, there is still a lack of studies that translate this knowledge into clinical use. Providing clinically useful research is paramount in our quest to prevent both onset and recidivistic offending. Translating these empirical differences into quantifiable measures (such as z-scores) that clinicians can use to measure treatment gains, and which can be used by recidivism scholars to determine treatment effectiveness, would be a massive addition to prevention efforts. Another relevant area for research would be the development and integration of clinically useful tools for the measurement of change in neuropsychological function. While this area of scholarship may be somewhat further removed from this field than those identified above, interdisciplinary studies on making tools more "user-friendly" is a hot topic in human-computer interaction domains.

Questions remain surrounding the origins of a pedophilic sexual preference. Much has been learned in the last decade regarding what cognitive differences exist among types of sexual offending and among individuals with and without pedophilia. Response inhibition will continue to be a direct target for scholars wishing to understand the role of general criminality and neuropsychological differences in pedophilia, with more complex and ecologically valid designs including diverse samples of individuals with pedophilia. It will be exciting to see a new era develop in pedophilia research that seeks to understand pedophilia itself—as well as its relationship to behavior, as this increased understanding will further the aim of promoting desistance from sexual offending.

References

Abracen, J., O'Carroll, R., & Ladha, N. (1991). Neuropsychological dysfunction in sex offenders? *The Journal of Forensic Psychiatry, 2*(2), 167–177. https://doi.org/10.1080/09585189108407646

APA. (2013). *Diagnostic and statistical manual of mental disorders* (5th ed.). American Psychiatric Association.

B4U-Act. (2011). *Mental health care and professional literature*. B4U-Act.

Babchishin, K. M., Hanson, R. K., & Hermann, C. A. (2011). The characteristics of online sex offenders: A meta-analysis. *Sexual Abuse: A Journal of Research and Treatment, 23*(1), 92–123. https://doi.org/10.1177/1079063210370708

Babchishin, K. M., Merdian, H. L., Bartels, R. M., & Perkins, D. (2018). Child sexual exploitation materials offenders. *European Psychologist, 23*(2), 130–143. https://doi.org/10.1027/1016-9040/a000326

Blanchard, R., Kolla, N. J., Cantor, J. M., Klassen, P. E., Dickey, R., Kuban, M. E., & Blak, T. (2007). IQ, handedness, and pedophilia in adult male patients stratified by referral source. *Sex Abuse, 19*(3), 285–309. https://doi.org/10.1007/s11194-007-9049-0

Cantor, J. M., & McPhail, I. V. (2016). Non-offending pedophiles. *Current Sexual Health Reports, 8*(3), 121–128. https://doi.org/10.1007/s11930-016-0076-z

Cohen, L. J., Nikiforov, K., Gans, S. W., Poznansky, O., McGeoch, P. G., Weaver, C., King, E. G., Cullen, K., & Galynker, I. (2002). Heterosexual male perpetrators of childhood sexual abuse: A

preliminary neuropsychiatric model. *Psychiatric Quarterly, 73*(4), 313–336. https://doi.org/10.1023/a:1020416101092
Dillien, T., Goethals, K., Sabbe, B., & Brazil, I. A. (2020). The neuropsychology of child sexual offending: A systematic review. *Aggression and Violent Behavior, 54*, 101406. https://doi.org/10.1016/j.avb.2020.101406
Eastvold, A., Suchy, Y., & Strassberg, D. (2011). Executive function profiles of pedophilic and nonpedophilic child molesters. *Journal of the International Neuropsychological Society, 17*, 295–307. https://doi.org/10.1017/S1355617710001669
Elliott, I. A., Beech, A. R., Mandeville-Norden, R., & Hayes, E. (2009). Psychological profiles of internet sexual offenders: comparisons with contact sexual offenders. *Sex Abuse, 21*(1), 76–92. https://doi.org/10.1177/1079063208326929
Fazio, R. L. (2018). Toward a neurodevelopmental understanding of pedophilia. *Journal of Sexual Medicine, 15*(9), 1205–1207. https://doi.org/10.1016/j.jsxm.2018.04.631
Gannon, T. A. (2021). A compositional explanatory theory of pedophilia. *Aggression and Violent Behavior, 61*, 101662. https://doi.org/10.1016/j.avb.2021.101662
Gillespie, N. K., & McKenzie, K. (2000). An examination of the role of neuropsychological deficits in mentally disordered sex offenders. *Journal of Sexual Aggression, 5*(1), 21–29. https://doi.org/10.1080/13552600008413293
Howitt, D., & Sheldon, K. (2007). The role of cognitive distortions in paedophilic offending: Internet and contact offenders compared. *Psychology, Crime & Law, 13*(5), 469–486. https://doi.org/10.1080/10683160601060564
Hucker, S., Langevin, R., Dickey, R., Handy, L., Chambers, J., Wright, S., Bain, J., & Wortzman, G. (1988). Cerebral damage and dysfunction in sexually aggressive men. *Annals of Sex Research, 1*(1), 33–47. https://doi.org/10.1007/BF00852881
Hucker, S., Langevin, R., Wortzman, G., Bain, J., Handy, L., Chambers, J., & Wright, S. (1986). Neuropsychological impairment in pedophiles. *Canadian Journal of Behavioural Science/Revue canadienne des sciences du comportement, 18*(4), 440–448. https://doi.org/10.1037/h0079965
Joyal, C. C., Black, D. N., & Dassylva, B. (2007). The neuropsychology and neurology of sexual deviance: A review and pilot study. *Sex Abuse, 19*(2), 155–173. https://doi.org/10.1177/107906320701900206
Joyal, C. C., Kärgel, C., Kneer, J., Amelung, T., Mohnke, S., Tenbergen, G., Walter, H., & Kruger, T. H. C. (2019). The neurobiological origins of pedophilia: Not that simple. *Journal of Sexual Medicine, 16*(1), 153–154. https://doi.org/10.1016/j.jsxm.2018.10.015
Jurado, M. B., & Rosselli, M. (2007). The elusive nature of executive functions: A review of our current understanding. *Neuropsychology Review, 17*(3), 213–233. https://doi.org/10.1007/s11065-007-9040-z
Kruger, T. H., & Schiffer, B. (2011). Neurocognitive and personality factors in homo- and heterosexual pedophiles and controls. *Journal of Sexual Medicine, 8*(6), 1650–1659. https://doi.org/10.1111/j.1743-6109.2009.01564
Mahon, B. Z., & Caramazza, A. (2009). Concepts and categories: A cognitive neuropsychological perspective. *Annual Review of Psychology, 60*, 27–51. https://doi.org/10.1146/annurev.psych.60.110707.163532
Massau, C., Tenbergen, G., Kargel, C., Weiss, S., Gerwinn, H., Pohl, A., Amelung, T., Mohnke, S., Kneer, J., Wittfoth, M., Ristow, I., Schiltz, K., Beier, K. M., Ponseti, J., Walter, M., Kruger, T. H. C., Walter, H., & Schiffer, B. (2017). Executive functioning in pedophilia and child sexual offending. *Journal of the International Neuropsychological Society, 23*(6), 460–470. https://doi.org/10.1017/s1355617717000315
Neutze, J., Seto, M. C., Schaefer, G. A., Mundt, I. A., & Beier, K. M. (2011). Predictors of child pornography offenses and child sexual abuse in a community sample of pedophiles and hebephiles. *Sexual Abuse: A Journal of Research and Treatment, 23*(2), 212–242. https://doi.org/10.1177/1079063210382043

Rosburg, T., Pflueger, M. O., Mokros, A., Boillat, C., Deuring, G., Spielmann, T., & Graf, M. (2021). Indirect and neuropsychological indicators of pedophilia. *Sexual Abuse, 33*(5), 579–605. https://doi.org/10.1177/1079063220931822

Rourke, B. P. (1991). Human neuropsychology in the 1990s. *Archives of Clinical Neuropsychology, 6*(1–2), 1–14. https://doi.org/10.1093/arclin/6.1-2.1

Schiffer, B., & Vonlaufen, C. (2011). Executive dysfunctions in pedophilic and nonpedophilic child molesters. *The Journal of Sexual Medicine, 8*(7), 1975–1984. https://doi.org/10.1111/j.1743-6109.2010.02140.x

Seto, M. C. (2008). *Pedophilia and sexual offending against children: Theory, assessment, and intervention* (Vol. 1). American Psychological Association.

Seto, M. C. (2009). Pedophilia. *Annual Review of Clinical Psychology, 5*, 391–407. https://doi.org/10.1146/annurev.clinpsy.032408.153618

Seto, M. C. (2017). The motivation-facilitation model of sexual offending. *Sex Abuse, 31*(1), 3–24. https://doi.org/10.1177/1079063217720919

Seto, M. C. (2018). *Pedophilia and sexual offending against children: Theory, assessment, and intervention* (2nd ed.). American Psychological Association.

Seto, M. C., Hanson, R. K., & Babchishin, K. M. (2011). Contact sexual offending by men with online sexual offenses. *Sexual Abuse: A Journal of Research and Treatment, 23*(1), 124–145. https://doi.org/10.1177/1079063210369013

Suchy, Y. (2009). Executive functioning: Overview, assessment, and research issues for non-neuropsychologists. *Annals of Behavioral Medicine, 37*(2), 106–116. https://doi.org/10.1007/s12160-009-9097-4

Suchy, Y., Eastvold, A. D., Strassberg, D. S., & Franchow, E. I. (2014). Understanding processing speed weaknesses among pedophilic child molesters: Response style vs. neuropathology. *Journal of Abnormal Psychology, 123*(1), 273–285. https://doi.org/10.1037/a0035812

Suchy, Y., Whittaker, J. W., Strassberg, D. S., & Eastvold, A. (2009). Neurocognitive differences between pedophilic and nonpedophilic child molesters. *Journal of the International Neuropsychological Society, 15*(02), 248–257. https://doi.org/10.1017/S1355617709090353

Tarter, R. E., Hegedus, A. M., Alterman, A. I., & Katz-Garris, L. (1983). Cognitive capacities of juvenile violent, nonviolent, and sexual offenders. *Journal of Nervous and Mental Disease, 171*(9), 564–567. https://doi.org/10.1097/00005053-198309000-00007

Tenbergen, G., Wittfoth, M., Frieling, H., Ponseti, J., Walter, M., Walter, H., Beier, K., Schiffer, B., & Kruger, T. H. C. (2015). The neurobiology and psychology of pedophilia: Recent advances and challenges [Review]. *Frontiers in Human Neuroscience, 9*(344). https://doi.org/10.3389/fnhum.2015.00344

Turner, D., & Rettenberger, M. (2020). Neuropsychological functioning in child sexual abusers: A systematic review. *Aggression and Violent Behavior, 54*, 101405. https://doi.org/10.1016/j.avb.2020.101405

World Health Organization. (1992). *The ICD-10 classification of mental and behavioural disorders: Clinical descriptions and diagnostic guidelines*. World Health Organization.

Chapter 9
Best Practices in Sexual Recidivism Risk Assessment

Mark E. Olver

9.1 Introduction

The assessment of risk for future sexual offending involves appraising a potentially broad swath of harmful and sexually criminal behaviors that include contact (e.g., sexual assault) or non-contact (e.g., indecent exposure) offenses with face-to-face victims, to online activity with virtual victims (e.g., child sexually explicit materials [CSEM], child luring), to non-human victims (e.g., bestiality). As a specific, albeit, diverse class of harmful behaviors, the base rates of sexual recidivism are comparatively lower than other broader categories of antisocial behavior (e.g., general violence, general criminal recidivism). Perhaps the largest and most representative database examining rates of sexual recidivism across 7225 individuals and 20 samples identified rates of 9.1% after 5 years, 13.3% at 10 years, 16.2% at 15 years, and 18.2% at 20 years (Hanson et al., 2018). Given the manifold societal and human costs and harms from sexual victimization, responsible and effective assessment and prevention is paramount.

The present chapter features an evidence-informed approach to sexual recidivism risk assessment, primarily for individuals who have some history of sexual offending with face-to-face victims. Although this population may have online offenses (e.g., possession of CSEM) as well, individuals who commit CSEM-based offenses exclusively tend to be lower risk with lower rates of recidivism, and caution is advised when using mainstream risk assessment measures with this population (e.g., Eke et al., 2019). That said, assessment considerations for men with CSEM offenses will also be discussed. This chapter begins with a definition and

M. E. Olver (✉)
Department of Psychology and Health Studies, University of Saskatchewan, Saskatoon, SK, Canada
e-mail: mark.olver@usask.ca

R. J. Tully et al. (eds.), *Best Practices in Sexual Offender Assessment and Management*, Dangerous Behavior in Clinical and Forensic Psychology,
https://doi.org/10.1007/978-3-031-83135-5_9

overview of sexual recidivism assessment and its intended purpose—sexual recidivism prevention—by way of linking assessment and intervention. The chapter then proceeds to discuss a number of best practice considerations that include use of multiple information sources, evaluating the accuracy and credibility of assessment information, assessing multiple domains of functioning, use of static and dynamic sexual recidivism risk assessment measures, consideration of nonsexual recidivism risk measures, applications of risk assessment information, applications to ethnocultural minorities, and consideration of additional risk mitigating agents. A representative, though not exhaustive, sampling, of static and dynamic sexual recidivism risk measures are covered, including a brief description of the measure along with its associated functions and features (e.g., norms, administrator materials) to guide the use of such measures in sexual recidivism risk assessment.

9.2 Sexual Recidivism Risk Assessment: Definition and Overview

A sexual recidivism risk assessment might be conceptualized as a dynamic process of gathering and integrating information from multiple sources, across multiple domains of functioning, using multiple measures to appraise the likelihood, imminence, and potential severity of a sexual offense, in order to prevent future sexual violence. Risk instruments are key to this process; however, a risk instrument is not equivalent to a risk assessment (Mills, 2017). The former is one, albeit, critical part of the latter, as it helps to structure the assessment information gathered in domains empirically, clinically, or theoretically relevant to sexual recidivism. Further, the purpose of sexual recidivism risk assessment is the prevention, as opposed to the prediction, of sexual violence. For instance, when an individual is appraised to be high risk for sexual violence, rather than waiting for a sexually violent prophecy to be carried out, efforts are made to contain and manage the risk to prevent a sexual offense.

Key to the risk management and recidivism prevention functions of sexual recidivism risk assessment is its integration with correctional treatment and risk management, per the principles of risk, need, and responsivity (RNR; Andrews & Bonta, 1994–2010; Bonta & Andrews, 2017a). Per the risk principle, the intensity of intervention efforts is matched to the risk level of the individual; obviously, risk assessments in this sense can prioritize service delivery as well as accurately distinguish higher risk, from lower risk individuals. Per the need principle, dynamic risk factors linked to sexual violence should be prioritized for treatment and management; risk assessments serve a vital role in identifying such targets. Finally, per the responsivity principle, risk reduction and management interventions should be tailored to the unique characteristics of clientele (e.g., motivation, learning style, culture) to maximize therapeutic buy-in and potential gains; risk assessment can serve a critical role identifying responsivity considerations in this regard. The next section discusses some of the best practice considerations sexual recidivism risk assessment through the lens of the RNR model with the ultimate goal of sexual violence prevention.

9.3 Best Practice Considerations

Sexual recidivism risk assessments entail a systematic and comprehensive process of gathering, appraising, and integrating information. This section speaks to a number of best practice considerations including use of multiple information sources, evaluating the accuracy and credibility of assessment information, assessing multiple domains of functioning, use of static and dynamic sexual recidivism risk assessment measures, consideration of nonsexual recidivism risk measures, applications of risk assessment information, applications to ethnocultural minorities, and consideration of additional risk mitigating agents.

9.3.1 Multiple Sources of Information

The start to any risk assessment is typically an institutional file review followed by an interview with the client that includes but is not limited to a sexual history taking, indicators of sexual deviance or hypersexuality, intimate relationships, peers and community supports, emotional regulation abilities, offense-related attitudes and cognitions, substance use history, mental health functioning, and treatment program participation. The interviews could be a standard clinical forensic risk assessment interview focusing on the aforementioned areas, but may also involve the use of a semi-structured interview schedule, such as that included in the Violence Risk Scale-Sexual Offense version (VRS-SO; Wong et al., 2003–2017), or other risk assessment measures with an interview schedule. Also, review of collateral source documents contained within the file such as criminal record(s), police reports, victim impact statements, past psychological or psychiatric assessment reports, treatment progress reports, institutional behavior reports, etc. is necessary. Other collateral sources to interview include, but are not limited to treatment providers, parole/probation officers, frontline correctional staff, and (if feasible) family members. If the client refuses to be interviewed, the quality and credibility of collateral information sources to complete a file-based risk assessment becomes particularly salient.

9.3.2 Ensuring Accuracy and Evaluating Information Credibility

It is critical to evaluate the credibility, relevance, and recency of information obtained from these sources and to corroborate these sources. Preferably there would be multiple lines of support for any conclusions generated from a risk assessment. The information should be as accurate and up to date as possible. Recent and relevant information, as available, should be emphasized over outdated or irrelevant information. For instance, whether or not an individual has complete veridical recall of every detail of a sex crime, consistent with police reports and victim impact statements, from 15 years ago more than likely matters less than an individual's awareness and understanding of their dynamic risk factors and development of new skills, supports, and strategies to live prosocially in the community without sexual violence. Care must also be taken not to perpetuate errors contained within reports; too often has this author come across (and have had clients complain to him), about mistaken or inaccurate details or misdiagnoses that get duplicated across reports and evaluations. It behooves us ethically to evaluate the credibility of information sources and to corroborate such information.

9.3.3 Assessing Multiple Domains of Functioning

The clinical interview and review of collateral information sources should occur with an eye toward identifying critical information domains relevant to sexual violence risk. Mann et al. (2010) use the term psychologically meaningful risk factors to refer to variables that are: (1) plausible, possible causes of sexual violence, and (2) that reliably predict sexual offense recidivism. Unique to sexual offending populations is the domain of sexual deviance, a robust predictor of sexual recidivism that connotes a pattern of atypical or illegal sexual interests or preferences (e.g., paraphilias), sexual preoccupation, and problems with sexual self-regulation (e.g., compulsive or hypersexuality; Hanson & Morton-Bourgon, 2009). Other general risk-need domains common to most correctional populations also predict sexual recidivism (Olver et al., 2014) and have relevance, such as Andrews and Bonta's (1994–2010; Bonta & Andrews, 2017b) *Central Eight* covariates of criminal conduct which include general criminal history and the dynamic need areas of antisocial peers, antisocial attitudes, antisocial personality pattern, family/marital, employment/education, substance abuse, and leisure/recreation. Finally, within the *Central Eight*, there are sexual offense specific counterparts that have unique relevance for sexual recidivism, such as attitudes and cognitions that are supportive of sexual violence (e.g., child sexual abuse distortions, rape myths; Helmus et al., 2013).

But in addition to risk relevant information, indicators of mental health and academic/neurocognitive functioning can be beneficial for risk assessment and management. The author frequently includes a section entitled "Responsivity

Considerations", or similar language, in his risk assessment reports, that is, an assessment of such personal characteristics that can impact response to services and risk. Multidimensional measures of personality and psychopathology such as the MMPI-2 or PAI can alert attention to certain mental health considerations (e.g., mood disorder, active symptoms of psychosis) and perhaps corroborate diagnostic information from interview. For instance, active symptoms of psychosis might have risk relevance, but if nothing else, they have responsivity relevance, such as difficulties in communication and attention (e.g., due to disorganized speech and thinking) or problems in interpersonal interactions with staff and patients (e.g., due to paranoid delusions and disorganized behavior); both of which can be therapeutically managed. Moreover, measures of cognitive and academic functioning might identify literacy or other neurocognitive deficits (as well as areas of relative strength, such as nonverbal problem-solving ability), which can inform the adaptation of services suited to the client's strengths and needs.

9.3.4 *Use of Static and Dynamic Sexual Recidivism Risk Measures*

Particularly critical to sexual recidivism risk assessment is the use of one or more structured static (i.e., offense histories and demographic variables that predict recidivism but are not treatment amenable) and/or dynamic (i.e., potentially changeable factors such as criminal attitudes and substance use) sexual recidivism risk assessment measures. This section begins with an overview of sexual recidivism risk tool classification and critical concepts in sexual violence risk assessment. A representative selection of the more commonly used sexual recidivism risk tools with an accumulated body of psychometric research are then reviewed, including: static actuarial measures, namely, Static-99R and Static-2002R and a CSEM specific measure, the Child Pornography Offender Risk Tool (C-PORT); dynamic actuarial measures, such as Violence Risk Scale-Sexual Offense version (VRS-SO) and STABLE 2007; and structured professional judgment (SPJ) measures, specifically the Sexual Violence Risk-20 (SVR-20) and Risk for Sexual Violence Protocol (RSVP).

9.3.4.1 *Sexual Recidivism Risk Tool Classification and Critical Concepts*

Unstructured professional judgment has been long repudiated for being subjective, unreliable, having poor accuracy, tendency to overclassify risk, leading to false positives (Grove et al., 2000; Hanson & Bussière, 1998; Meehl, 1954; Mossman, 1994). Hanson and Morton-Bourgon (2009) identify three types of structured sexual violence risk assessment measures: empirical actuarial, SPJ, and mechanical tools. These are essentially systematized collections of operationalized static and dynamic risk items, assembled into risk scales. Empirical actuarial measures are comprised of items that are scored numerically and summed to generate risk scores, which are then linked to recidivism estimates over a defined follow-up (e.g., 5 years, 10 years). The items may be statistically derived in an atheoretical manner, or be informed by theory and research, and such measures can be static (e.g., Static-99R; Helmus et al., 2012) or dynamic (e.g., Violence Risk Scale-Sexual Offense version; VRS-SO, Wong et al., 2003-2017; STABLE-2007; Hanson et al., 2007). SPJ tools, by contrast, are nonnumeric measures, where items are rated for their risk relevance, however, the items are not summed to generate risk scores (e.g., Sexual Violence Risk-20; SVR-20; Boer et al., 1997). Instead, the profile or configuration of item ratings, in tandem with other information sources, is used to generate a summary risk rating of low, medium, or high risk for future sexual violence. Finally, mechanical approaches do not refer to class of tool per se, but rather, involve taking a numeric approach to SPJ measures; specifically, summing the items of an SPJ tool to generate risk scores, however the scores are not linked to recidivism estimates.

It is important to use sexual recidivism specific measures when assessing sexual recidivism risk. The reasons for this are: (a) that they have sexual recidivism specific item content, (b) they predict sexual recidivism better than non-sexual recidivism risk tools, and (c) they are normed and validated on sexual offending populations (at least the actuarial tools, as SPJ tools do not have norms). Although the goal of sexual recidivism risk assessment is sexual violence prevention, a primary means of evaluating the efficacy or utility of risk measures is their capacity to predict the targeted criterion, namely, sexual recidivism. Two prediction concepts are key in this regard—discrimination and calibration—the applications of which will be applied to the measures discussed below. Discrimination, or relative risk, refers to what extent recidivists can be differentiated from non-recidivists (or higher risk from lower risk cases) on the basis of their risk scores. Common discrimination metrics include the area under the curve (AUC; and related metrics, such as Cohen's d, and point biserial correlation), percentile ranks, or hazard ratios from Cox regression. Effect size language can be used to evaluate the discrimination properties of these tools for certain metrics: small (AUC = 0.56, $d = 0.20$, $r_{pb} = 0.10$), medium (AUC = 0.64, $d = 0.50$, $r_{pb} = 0.24$), and large (AUC = 0.71, $d = 0.80$, $r_{pb} = 0.37$; Rice & Harris, 2005).

The results of the most comprehensive meta-analysis on the topic (Hanson & Morton-Bourgon, 2009) featured 118 studies that examined the predictive properties of risk tools in sexual offending samples. Broadly moderate effects were observed in the prediction of sexual recidivism for sexual offense specific risk tools, although larger effects were observed for empirical actuarial ($d = 0.67$, $k = 0.81$, $N = 24{,}089$) and mechanical ($d = 0.66$, $k = 29$, $N = 5838$) tools, than for SPJ measures ($d = 0.46$, $k = 6$, $N = 1131$). General violence and general risk-need tools had slightly smaller, significant effects in the prediction of sexual recidivism, such as the Level of Service Inventory (LSI) Measures ($d = 0.45$, $k = 4$, $N = 904$; see also Olver et al., 2014) and the Historical Clinical Risk-20 (summing the items, $d = 0.33$, $k = 04$, $N = 398$). By contrast, the LSI measures had stronger moderate effects in the prediction of violent ($d = 0.72$, $k = 3$, $N = 390$) and general recidivism ($d = 0.69$, $k = 3$, $N = 390$).

Calibration, or absolute risk, refers to the rates of recidivism associated with risk scores. Common calibration metrics include the E/O (expected/observed) index or logistic regression generated recidivism estimates on the basis of risk scores. The E/O index is a metric that represents the extent to which the rates of recidivism associated with risk scores expected from a reference group (e.g., normative sample) correspond to the rates of recidivism observed in a comparison group (Hanson, 2017). E/O index values of 1.0 indicate perfect calibration, while values significantly below 1.0 represent under-classification of recidivists, and above 1.0 represent over-classification of recidivists. Logistic regression is used to examine the association of one or more predictor variables (e.g., risk scores) to binary recidivism over a defined follow-up (e.g., 5 years). Using information from the logistic regression coefficients (B1) and base rate information (B0), a logistic function can be used to estimate rates of recidivism associated with specific combinations of risk scores. This has the advantage of decreasing error and bias, for instance, that might occur when using actual rates of recidivism for individual scores or groups of scores, owing to the instability of actual recidivism rates, particularly at extreme scores with small *n*.

A common language for risk assessment has been developed to integrate information concerning absolute and relative risk into non-arbitrary risk categories. The categories were originally formulated based on the frequency of cases, density of criminogenic need, anticipated rates of general recidivism over a 2-year follow-up, and recommended dosage or intensity level of intervention. The categories also apply to other more specific forms of recidivism, such as violent and sexual recidivism, however, adaptations to the model had to be made to sexual recidivism risk instruments, as will be outlined below, given the much lower base rates of sexual recidivism compared to general recidivism. The labels for the risk categories are framed employing functional less stigmatizing language, in contrast to the easily misinterpreted low, medium, and high categories.

Five levels have been identified (Hanson et al., 2016): Level I (very low risk) comprises about 5% of cases at the bottom of the distribution by risk, have few criminogenic needs, an anticipated 2% recidivism rate, and the need for few or no resources to manage risk. Level II (below average risk) comprises about 20% of cases, with a small number of isolated areas of risk and need, an anticipated 5–20% rate of general recidivism, and recommended targeted services at specific areas of concern. Level III (average risk) comprises the middle approximately 50% of the distribution, with several areas of risk and need requiring intervention, and an expected 20–49% recidivism rate. Level IV (above average risk) comprises the next upper 20% of individuals in terms of risk and need, with a large number of chronic areas requiring high intensity intervention, and an anticipated 50–84% rate of recidivism. Level V (well above average risk), comprises about the top 5% of the riskiest cases, who have chronic and severe areas of risk and need across most if not all areas, and an anticipated two-year rate of general recidivism of 85% or higher. Such cases require comprehensive high intensity services delivered over several hundred hours and multiple years. As noted above, given the comparatively low base rates of sexual recidivism, Hanson et al. (2017) proposed a Level IVa (denoting above average risk) and IVb (denoting well above average risk), as upper and lower tiers of Level IV for the purposes of risk communication about sexual violence risk.

9.3.4.2 *Static-99R and 2002R*

The Static-99R (Helmus et al., 2012, see also Hanson & Thornton, 1999, 2000) is an empirical actuarial sexual recidivism risk tool, comprising 10 items that cover content areas that include sexual and nonsexual criminal history and perpetrator and victim demographics. It is the most frequently used sexual recidivism risk assessment tool in the field (Kelley et al., 2020). Possible scores range from −3 to 12 and can be organized into the five risk levels of Level I (−3, −2), Level II (−1, 0), Level III (1–3), Level IVa (4, 5), and Level IVb (6–12; Hanson et al., 2017). Meta-analytic research supports the predictive properties of the Static-99R for sexual recidivism (AUC = 0.72, $k = 24$, 8390). A parallel tool is the Static-2002R, an extension of the Static-99R (Hanson & Thornton, 2003), revised by Helmus et al. (2012) in tandem with the Static-99R. The tool is less extensively used or researched, but a strong body of support attests to its predictive properties for sexual recidivism (AUC = 0.71). The score bands for the five levels for Static-2002R are Level I (−2, −1), Level II (0, 1), Level III (2–4), Level IVa (5, 6), Level IVb (6–14).

Norms for both relative and absolute risk exist for the Static-99R/2002R, available in a free online workbook that is routinely updated by the instrument developers (Helmus et al., 2021). These include percentile ranks and risk ratios (for relative risk), and logistic regression generated recidivism estimates for 5 and 10-year sexual recidivism associated with exact Static-99R/2002R scores (for absolute risk). Recidivism estimates are further organized into norms based on routine correctional samples and high risk-need samples, based on the density of unmeasured dynamic risk factors (e.g., based on referrals to high intensity treatment program), which impact recidivism estimates (i.e., the same Static-99R/2002R score will generate lower sexual recidivism estimates for routine samples than for high risk need samples). As such, is critical that users employ the appropriate reference group when using the recidivism norms.

Finally, the Static-99R has a time-free calculator (Thornton et al., 2021) that enables the generation of 20-year sexual recidivism estimates, based on meta-analytic estimates from Hanson et al. (2018) of 20-year rates of recidivism (available at www.saarna.org). The research examining the rate of decay or criminal desistence of sexual violence over time permits an examination of how much risk reduction is associated with each year time free in the community. The calculator further allows the estimation of 20-year rates of sexual recidivism, and natural decay over time, employing recidivism estimates from other tools (such as the VRS-SO, discussed below). Thus, the calculator is a useful application for the projection of long-term sexual recidivism estimates, as well as concordant reductions in risk with each passing year time free in the community, without sexually reoffending.

9.3.4.3 *Child Pornography Offender Risk Tool (C-PORT)*

The C-PORT (Seto & Eke, 2015) is a 7-item static actuarial risk tool designed to assess risk for sexual recidivism among men with CSEM offenses, including those with no contact offenses. The item content is a combination of age, criminal history, and evidence for preferential sexual interest in children and boys in particular. Research demonstrates that men with CSEM offenses tend to be lower risk and have lower rates of sexual recidivism, than men who have CSEM and contact offenses, underscoring the importance of tools developed for this population, such as the C-PORT (Eke et al., 2019). For instance, Eke et al. (2019) found men with CSEM and noncontact offenses only had a 5-year rate of sexual recidivism of 7.8–9.8% while men with CSEM and contact offenses had 5-year rates of sexual recidivism of 22.9–31.6%. Further, men with both CSEM and contact offenses scored nearly 2 SD higher on the C-PORT than men with CSEM and noncontact offenses only.

The validation research with this tool across three samples, two Canadian (Eke et al., 2019; Seto & Eke, 2015) and one Scottish (Savoie et al., 2021), have demonstrated C-PORT scores to have moderate to high predictive accuracy for sexual recidivism among men with CSEM and noncontact offenses (AUCs = 0.66–0.72). While the C-PORT is developed specifically for men with CSEM offenses, as a short actuarial tool, arguably it could be supplemented with a dynamic tool to provide a more comprehensive appraisal of risk; however, given that such measures have been developed largely on contact offending populations which have higher recidivism rates, indices of relative risk (e.g., percentile ranks) may be prioritized in lieu of indicators of absolute risk (i.e., sexual recidivism rates) to avoid inflating risk.

9.3.4.4 *Violence Risk Scale-Sexual Offense version (VRS-SO)*

The VRS-SO is a dynamic empirical actuarial tool designed to assess sexual recidivism risk, identify targets for treatment or risk management, and to evaluate changes in sexual recidivism risk from treatment or other change agents. It consists of 7 static and 17 dynamic factors, each of which is scored on a four-point (0, 1, 2, 3) ordinal scale. The items can be summed to generate scores for VRS-SO static (0–21), dynamic (0–51), and total (i.e., static + dynamic, 0–72). The five level system has also been developed for the VRS-SO (Olver, Mundt et al., 2018), including specifically the dynamic (Level I, 0–10.5; Level II 11–16.5; Level III, 17–27.5; Level IVa, 28–34.5; Level IVb, 35–51) and total (Level I, 0–14.5; Level II, 15–23.5; Level III, 24–39.5; Level IVa, 40–49.5; Level IVb, 50–72) scores. Factor analytic research demonstrates that the VRS-SO dynamic items can be arranged into three factors termed Sexual Deviance (i.e., a factor assessing patterns of atypical or deviant sexual interests and sexual self-regulation), Criminality (i.e., a general risk-need factor), and Treatment Responsivity (i.e., essentially an offense and treatment attitudes factor); there are additional items pertaining to relational and emotional functioning that do not consistently load on the factors (see Olver et al., 2021). The relevance of this is that the pattern of item scores on the factors informs case conceptualization, treatment planning, and risk management (Olver et al., 2007).

Change is assessed via a modified application of Prochaska et al.'s (1992) transtheoretical model of change, five stages of which have been operationalized for each dynamic item to capture the development of prosocial skills and strategies to reduce risk: precontemplation (lack of insight, denial of problem), contemplation (awareness of problem area), preparation (inconsistent and/or recent use of skills and strategies to manage problem area), action (sustained use of skills and strategies), and maintenance (generalization and transfer of learning across key high risk situations). Items with 2 or 3-point ratings are considered criminogenic; they are given a baseline stage of change rating, which is then re-rated upon each reassessment. Movement from one stage to the next is credited with a 0.5 deduction off the item score, 2 stages 1.0, and so on; the lone exception is movement from precontemplation to contemplation, where no risk reduction credit is provided, given that there is no behavioral change between the stages. The change ratings are the summed across each item to generate a change score.

Across eight predictive validity studies from five countries for the VRS-SO, Olver and Wong (2021) reported median AUCs of 0.69 for static scores, 0.67 for dynamic scores, and 0.72 for total scores. Although these studies all featured correctional samples of men convicted largely for contact sexual offenses, an unpublished doctoral thesis (Wielinga, 2022), found VRS-SO dynamic scores to have strong predictive validity for 5-year sexual recidivism (AUC = 0.72) in a community sample of men convicted for sexual offenses, many of whom had CSEM and noncontact offenses only. In turn, VRS-SO dynamic factor scores have demonstrated incremental predictive validity in the prediction of sexual, violent, and general recidivism controlling for static, baseline risk (e.g., Olver et al., 2007; Olver & Eher, 2020; Sowden & Olver, 2017). Finally, VRS-SO dynamic change scores have been found to be associated with decreased sexual and violent recidivism when controlling for baseline risk, supporting the risk relevance of change and dynamism of the VRS-SO dynamic factors (Olver, Mundt et al., 2018). These psychometric properties set the foundation for the VRS-SO norms.

The VRS-SO normative sample is based on four combined treated institutional samples of men with conviction histories of sexual offenses; three from Canada (Olver et al., 2007; Olver et al., 2014, 2020; Sowden & Olver, 2017) and one from New Zealand (Beggs & Grace, 2010, 2011). A total of 913 cases with a minimum 10 years follow-up were included to generate VRS-SO CL risk bands and a set of logistic regression algorithms to generate 5 and 10-year sexual recidivism estimates associated with VRS-SO scores (Olver, Mundt et al., 2018). A VRS-SO calculator has been developed (Mundt, 2015, available from www.psynergy.ca) to compute sexual recidivism estimates for specific combinations of risk and change scores with 95% CI. Given that the amount an individual can change is constrained by baseline score (i.e., higher risk individuals who have more room to move will generate larger change scores), yet individuals with higher scores are at greater risk to reoffend than individuals with lower scores, irrespective of the amount of change they make, this underscores the necessity of controlling for pretreatment (or Time1/baseline score), such as through regression modelling. As such, the calculator is set up in such a manner where baseline VRS-SO risk and change scores are entered as separate quantities; over repeated assessments, change is tracked cumulatively to update the recidivism calculator's projections. The Static-99R has been co-normed with the VRS-SO, which enables substitution of this measure in place of the VRS-SO's static items. The VRS-SO calculator also has a logistic regression equation which allows for the entry of specific scores for the Static-99R, pretreatment (time 1) dynamic, and change score to generate 5 and 10-year sexual recidivism estimates (Olver, Mundt et al., 2018). As with the Statc-99R/2002R an evaluators' workbook has been developed (Olver et al., 2020) with percentile ranks for static, dynamic, total, factor, and change scores, information on interpreting the tool and calculator estimates, and instructions for assigning a sexual recidivism risk level. The five level system is applied based on an integration of VRS-SO scores from the most recent assessment and the rate of sexual recidivism generated from the VRS-SO calculator associated with specific combinations of risk and change scores (Olver et al., 2020), and in this manner, it integrates information regarding both absolute and relative risk. VRS-SO dynamic risk levels can also be integrated with Static-99R risk levels (employing a 5 × 5 matrix) to generate an overall static-dynamic risk rating (see Olver et al., 2020, 2021 for details).

9.3.4.5 *STABLE 2007*

The STABLE 2007 is an empirical actuarial sexual recidivism risk measure, consisting of 13 dynamic items rated on a three-point (0, 1, 2) scale. Possible scores range from 0 to 24 for men without any child victims (only 12 out of 13 items are scored) or 0 to 26 for men with one or more child victims (with an additional item, *Emotional Congruence with Children*, that is scored only with this group). STABLE 2007 scores can change (Sowden & Olver, 2017), from treatment or other credible change sources, through rerating the items at subsequent assessment intervals. A recent meta-analysis of the STABLE 2007 (Brankley et al., 2021) from $k = 12$ samples and 6955 cases, examining hazard ratios (e^B) from Cox regression survival analysis found that STABLE 2007 scores had significant predictive validity for sexual ($e^B = 1.12$), violent, and general recidivism ($e^B = 1.10$). STABLE 2007 scores also incrementally predicted these three recidivism outcomes across the samples, controlling for Static-99R scores (Brankley et al., 2021).

A workbook has also been developed for the STABLE 2007 (Brankley et al., 2017). The STABLE 2007 normative sample is based on two large samples, one of probationers on community supervision for sexual offending (the Dynamic Supervision Project, DSP) and a second sample of men with community and custodial sentences from British Columbia Provincial Corrections for a combined sample of 3407 men; however, only data from the DSP on 611 men with five-year recidivism outcome information are used for sexual, violent, and general recidivism norms. STABLE 2007 scores can be arranged into three categories based on density of criminogenic need of low (0–3), moderate (4–11), and high (12–26); percentile ranks are also available for individual scores (Brankley et al., 2017). Although the STABLE 2007 is an empirical actuarial tool, it does not have recidivism rates linked to specific scores, and the tool is not intended to be used on its own without a static tool, specifically, the Static-99R, Static-2002R, or the Risk Matrix 2000. As such, pairings of exact STABLE 2007 scores can be integrated with exact Static-99R, 2002R, or Risk Matrix 2000 scores to generate global recidivism risk level from Level I through IVb per the common risk language scheme (Brankley et al., 2017). Each Static-STABLE risk level pairing, in turn, has associated 1, 3, and 5-year rates of sexual, violent, or general recidivism for each risk level (Brankley et al., 2017).

9.3.4.6 *Sexual Violence Risk-20 (SVR-20) and Risk for Sexual Violence Protocol (RSVP)*

The SVR-20 V1 (Boer et al., 1997) and V2 (Boer et al., 2017) both refer to a 20-item SPJ measure designed to assess risk for sexual violence. Items are rated on a three-point ordinal scale (0 no, 1 partially/possibly present, 2 present) and can be clustered into three domains corresponding to psychosocial adjustment (e.g., sexual deviance, psychopathy, substance abuse, employment history), sexual offenses (e.g., high density sex offenses, physical harm to victims, escalation), and future plans (e.g., lacks future goals). The two versions of the SVR-20 are very similar, both containing 20 items arranged into three sections with slight item modifications to V2 based on developments in the literature (Hart & Boer, 2021). As an SPJ tool, item ratings are not summed to yield risk scores, but rather, the pattern of items are scrutinized to generate a summary risk rating of low, medium, or high. A counterpart to the original SVR-20 is the Risk for Sexual Violence Protocol (RSVP, Hart et al., 2003), a 22-item SPJ-based sexual violence risk measure with similarities in item content. Items are scored on both sets of measures in terms of past relevance (prior to 12 months ago) or recent relevance (within the previous 12 months). The SVR-20 and RSVP each provide variations on guidelines for using and integrating the information obtained from the ratings and collateral sources (Hart & Boer 2021). The SVR-20 and RSVP can be used in conjunction with other static and/or dynamic risk tools, the results of which would need to be integrated in an SPJ type manner.

Psychometric research supports the predictive validity of the SVR-20 for sexual recidivism; most of this research, however, has examined it as a mechanical tool (i.e., summing item ratings). The Hanson and Morton-Bourgon (2009) meta-analysis reported medium effects in the prediction of sexual recidivism when the SVR-20 is examined in a mechanical manner ($d = 0.68$, $k = 10$, $n = 1699$) and a large effect in the small number of studies that have examined it in an SPJ manner ($d = 1.11$, $k = 3$, $n = 245$). Additional validation research for the RSVP and SVR-20, as summarized in Hart and Boer (2021), also provides support for their predictive properties for sexual violence.

9.3.5 Use of Other Forensic and Nonsexual Recidivism Risk Measures

Further it may be helpful to consider general violence and/or general recidivism measures to compliment specialized measures of sexual recidivism risk, such as an LSI variant (Andrews & Bonta, 1995), or general violence risk tools such as the HCR-20 (Douglas et al., 2013), Violence Risk Appraisal Guide-Revised (VRAG-R; Rice et al., 2013), Violence Risk Scale (VRS; Wong & Gordon, 1999-2003), or the Brief Assessment of Recidivism Risk-2002R (BARR-2002R; Babchishin et al., 2013), developed specifically to assess risk for nonsexual recidivism in sexual offending populations (Babchishin et al., 2016). Findings from meta-analyses (e.g., Hanson & Morton-Bourgon, 2009; Olver et al., 2014) demonstrate that these measures predict nonsexual outcomes as well or better than sexual recidivism risk tools, as well as sexual recidivism, although typically to a lesser degree. Not uncommonly an individual may pose a different level of risk for a different type of outcome (e.g., above average risk for future violence, but below average risk for sexual recidivism) that merits attention and management which may be identified through the consideration of an additional nonsexual recidivism risk measure.

Other measures such as the Hare Psychopathy Checklist-Revised (PCL-R; Hare, 1991, 2003) are not risk instruments, however, assess a clinical construct with a high level of criminal justice system relevance, and as such, the PCL-R is frequently used along with purpose-built risk measures in a risk assessment. When its use is informed by RNR principles, the PCL-R can be a useful adjunct to other sexual violence risk tools. The role and relevance of the psychopathy construct and the PCL-R in sexual offending populations is reviewed in detail in Chap. 18, and so this is only briefly discussed here. First, meta-analytic research, including a meta-meta-analysis of 18 PCL-R meta-analyses by DeMatteo and Olver (2021) found PCL-R total scores to have moderate predictive validity in the prediction of general (mean unweighted $d = 0.56$, k meta = 7) and violent (mean unweighted $d = 0.57$, k meta = 9) recidivism, as well as institutional violence (mean unweighted $d = 0.51$, k meta = 5) in correctional and forensic mental health samples; a level of predictive validity comparable to formalized risk measures. The predictive validity of PCL-R score for sexual recidivism was a small significant effect ($d = 0.39$, k meta = 3). Much of the predictive power of the PCL-R, however—which is most relevant to the RNR principles of risk and need—comes from the chronic antisocial lifestyle features of psychopathy as measured by Factor 2 and its Lifestyle and Antisocial facets (DeMatteo & Olver, 2021).

Although the interpersonal (e.g., superficial charm, grandiose, deceitful, manipulative) and emotional (e.g., callous lack of empathy, lack of remorse, shallow affect) features of psychopathy (collectively referred to as Factor 1 and, respectively, its Interpersonal and Affective facets), do predict various recidivism outcomes, the effect sizes tend to be small in magnitude. Per the RNR model, however, Factor 1 represents a set of responsivity issues (Wong et al., 2012) such as antagonistic behaviors toward staff and clients, staff splitting, boundary violations, intimidating and verbally abusive behavior, disruptive group behavior, evasiveness and manipulation, and so forth. As such, high Factor 1 scores can signal issues with treatment and risk management relevance such as the potential for decreased therapeutic gains (Sewall & Olver, 2019), increased risk for attrition (Olver & Wong, 2011), and weaker working alliances with service providers (DeSorcy et al., 2020). All of these issues have implications for risk and can be identified as potential responsivity considerations to be included in a comprehensive risk assessment.

9.3.6 *Applications of Sexual Recidivism Risk Assessment Information*

This section reviews the application of sexual recidivism risk assessment information in terms of some basic but important functions that include communicating the sexual recidivism risk level, identifying targets for sexual offense intervention and risk management, and reassessment and the evaluation of risk relevant change.

9.3.6.1 *Communicating the Sexual Recidivism Risk Level*

The risk level can be reported using either the verbal label or the five-level system, if it has been developed for the instrument at hand. As dynamic risk measures have demonstrated incremental predictive validity for future sexual violence above and beyond static measures (Brankley et al., 2021; Olver et al., 2021; van den Berg et al., 2018), arguably the inclusion of multiple measures (e.g., one static, one dynamic) not only strengthens prediction, but it generates a more comprehensive appraisal of risk since a larger number of risk-relevant domains receive coverage. It can also be helpful to report the percentile rank of an individual's score as a measure of relative risk, especially if done pretreatment-posttreatment, or other repeated assessment interval (e.g., annual review) to illustrate changes (or lack thereof) in risk.

The risk level informs the intensity of treatment services, risk management interventions, release decisions, and community supervision and restrictions, per the risk principle. Tools such as the Static-99R and VRS-SO have logistic regression generated estimates for 5 and 10-year sexual recidivism which can inform release and supervision considerations. When utilizing such information, it is recommended to frame the estimates relative to the normative group. For instance, Mr. X's score is associated with an estimated 24.2% rate of sexual recidivism over 5 years, and 32.6% over 10 years. (Some tools, such as the VRS-SO, also have the option to provide 95%CI for the recidivism estimates as a margin of error). It may be helpful to add that the rate of non-recidivism would be estimated at approximately 76% at 5 years, and 67% at 10 years. If there has been a change in risk level using the five level system, this should be documented (e.g., Level IVb Well Above Average Risk had been decreased to IVa Above Average Risk). Reassessments of risk should take into consideration changes in risk; for individuals in the community, this should take into consideration time free in the community, such as with the time free calculator.

9.3.6.2 *Identifying Targets for Sexual Offense Intervention and Risk Management*

It is essential not to focus solely on the score or summary risk rating, but also the individual risk factors deemed criminogenic, per the need principle. The pattern of items with high ratings, in turn, can serve as a criminogenic profile to drive services. For instance, one individual may have a pattern of sexual interest toward children, hypersexual arousal, and a lack of intimate relationships, however, they otherwise do not have issues with substance misuse, they can maintain a job and residence, have intact planning and problem solving, and are not aggressive or emotionally dysregulated. Another individual, by contrast, may have little or no evidence of paraphilia or deviant arousal, but have a series of shallow relationship contacts, protracted promiscuity, a history of nonsexual aggression and poor anger control, and a pervasive pattern of lifestyle impulsivity. Obviously, the treatment and risk management targets would be very different (e.g., arousal reconditioning, anti-androgen therapy, and relationship skills training vs. anger management, substance abuse, and cognitive problem-solving skills training, respectively).

9.3.6.3 *Reassessment and Evaluating Risk Relevant Change*

The previous example underscores the essentiality of linking assessment and intervention. When dynamic measures are administered, reassessments can be used to track and measure change. More recent assessments, in turn, have greater prognostic value, than older assessments (Babchishin & Hanson, 2020; Olver et al. 2021). Change information can be systematically incorporated into risk appraisals (e.g., via use of the VRS-SO calculator, or integration of common language risk levels across static and dynamic measures) to determine if risk has changed, to examine skills usage, and to identify any outstanding areas of risk and need to inform additional services. Change, however, needs to be risk-relevant to have prognostic value and to translate into meaningful reductions in the potential for future sexual violence.

The term offense analogue and offense replacement behaviors (OABs and ORBs) have been used to refer to manifestations of criminogenic needs in institutional or otherwise tightly controlled settings (OABs), as well as indicators of improvement and risk reduction that would suggest the presence of prosocial replacement behaviors (ORBs; Gordon & Wong, 2010; see Olver & Stockdale, 2020 as applied to the VRS-SO). For instance, a man with sexual interest in children in custody, but without ready access to the internet or potential child victims may still engage in deviant sexual fantasy and masturbation, he may develop child sexually explicit materials (e.g., deviant narratives, drawings), or engage in activities that can fuel deviant fantasy (e.g., watching television shows featuring children); all of which would serve as OABs for a deviant sexual interest in children. By contrast, prosocial replacement behaviors such as healthy fantasy and masturbation, avoiding triggering stimuli, use of healthy coping, and developing prosocial outlets as alternatives to CSEM could be examples of relevant ORBs.

As such, OABs and ORBs by definition have risk relevance; an increase in or the presence of substantial OABs would indicate the ongoing presence of concordant risks and needs, while a decrease in OABs and increase in ORBs would represent a decrease in risk and improvement in prosocial functioning. When conducting reassessment, it is then essential to evaluate the relative presence and absence of OABs and ORBs to appraise ongoing areas of risk and need, as well as to evaluate risk mitigation. As one such resource, an OAB/ORB guide (Olver et al., 2017) has been developed for the VRS-SO, although the guide can be used with other sexual recidivism risk measures to identify offense linked proxy behaviors or prosocial replacement behaviors.

9.3.7 Ethnoculturally Diverse Populations

Ethnocultural minority groups tend to be overrepresented in correctional systems internationally including Black and Hispanic persons in the US (Travis et al., 2014), and Indigenous persons in Canada, New Zealand, Australia, as well as the US (Anaya, 2015; Day et al., 2018; Nellis, 2016; Public Safety Canada, 2019). All of this occurs across a backdrop of systemic racism, social marginalization, and socioeconomic disadvantage by many ethnocultural minority groups, which is perpetuated by the criminal justice system (Travis et al., 2014). Accordingly, the use of risk assessment instruments in general, and sexual recidivism risk instruments, in particular, with ethnocultural minorities has been the focus of research, legal scrutiny, and debate (Gutierrez et al., 2016; Olver, 2016).

As such, risk measures should be used in a manner to aid, rather than hinder, service delivery and reintegration, with all persons, and the individual's cultural context should be taken into consideration when administering, scoring, and interpreting risk measures. Preferably measures with psychometric research with a given ethnocultural minority group should be employed. The Static-99R for instance has been validated with Canadian Indigenous (Lee et al., 2020), and US Black (Lee & Hanson, 2017; Varela et al., 2013) and Hispanic (Lee & Hanson, 2017; Leguizamo et al., 2015; Varela et al., 2013) sexual offending populations, and it has the greatest breadth of psychometric support with different ethnocultural groups. Further, the VRS-SO has been validated with Canadian Indigenous men with histories of sex crimes (Olver, Sowden et al., 2018), as has the STABLE 2007, along with other ethnocultural minority groups.

9.3.8 Consideration of Other Risk Mitigating Agents

Finally, it is important to consider other agents that could be risk mitigating and aid community reintegration, of which two will be discussed here; aging and protective factors. The age crime curve is well established such that risk and recidivism decline—including sexual recidivism—as a function of age, particularly as an individual reaches middle age (Nicholaichuk et al., 2014). For instance, relevant to sexual offending, age-related changes such as decreased sex drive, reduced victim access, and improved self-control may partly explain the lower rates of continued sexual offending (Hanson, 2002). Most risk assessment tools incorporate one or more age-related items to account for increasing risk as a function of young age, or decreasing risk, as a function of older age. To this end, age-related calibration research has been conducted on the Static-99R and VRS-SO. For instance, Hanson (2006) found that the Static-99, prior to development of new age weights with the 99R, had good discrimination properties for older men (age 60), however, the sexual recidivism rates were substantially lower than for men in younger age cohorts, even at the same score. Static-99R was then developed to account for decreasing risk associated with age through an age at release item that credits a decrease in points with certain age gradations (e.g., −3 for age 60+ at anticipated release). The VRS-SO static items also assign lower scores at the highest age bracket, and on the dynamic factors, risk-related changes need not only be the product of treatment, but may also reflect the forces of aging or other credible change agents.

Calibration research with the Static-99R/2002R demonstrates that such an adjustment for age improved calibration, such that the rates of sexual recidivism predicted by the Static-99R/2002R within a given age cohort, aligned well (via the E/O index) with those directly observed for that cohort (Helmus et al., 2012). Similar age-related calibration was done using the VRS-SO normative sample, comparing observed vs. predicted rates of 5 and 10-year sexual recidivism for the VRS-SO using either its own set of static factors or when these were substituted by the Static-99R (Olver et al., 2021); use of the latter slightly improved age-related calibration for men age 60 and up at time of release. Short of using measures with age-related calibration, the risk mitigating effects of increasing time free in the community over a long-term, 20-year forecast can be utilized through the time-free calculator using sexual recidivism estimates from any measure.

Protective factors refer to salutary characteristics that can mitigate risk and the potential for negative outcomes (e.g., a new sexual offense), while promoting health and wellness and increasing the potential for positive outcomes (e.g., sustaining employment, remaining offense free in the community, maintaining a residence or relationship). Relevant examples of protective factors may include internal characteristics, such as intact cognitive ability and literacy skills, secure attachments, good self-regulation, or having an arsenal of positive coping strategies, or external factors such as prosocial supports and peers, access to therapeutic services, or the availability of structures and supports (e.g., stable housing; de Vogel et al., 2009, 2011). While these may be assessed informally, measures such as the Structured Assessment of

Protective Factors (SAPROF; de Vogel et al., 2009)—a 17-item SPJ-based protective factors measure—permits the structured assessment of these competencies. A sexual offense specific variant has also been developed for sexual offending populations, the SAPROF-Sexual Offence version (SAPROF-SO; Willis et al., 2018). The results can then be integrated with one or more structured risk assessment tools. The existing research has demonstrated measures such as the SAPROF to predict decreased recidivism incrementally when controlling for baseline risk, and in some instances, for positive changes (signaling an improvement in protective factors) to be associated with deceased violent recidivism in violent (Coupland & Olver, 2020; de Vries Robbé et al., 2015) and sexual offending (Olver & Riemer, 2021) populations.

While different methods have been proposed for integrating protective factors with risk measures, such as integrating SPJ risk and protective judgments (de Vries Robbé et al., 2015), at the very least, a measure like the SAPROF can be administered and protective factors can be discussed explicitly within the context of a risk assessment and integrated into the broader case conceptualization to inform decision making and risk management. The consideration of protective factors and use of such language (e.g., in terms of health and wellness), can offset undue pessimism from an exclusively risk focused assessment and even provide some room for cautious optimism for the promotion of criminal desistance and client wellbeing.

9.4 General Conclusions

The present chapter provided an overview of some best practice considerations in sexual recidivism risk assessment. With an eye toward the prevention of future sexual violence, sexual recidivism risk assessments should be comprehensive, evidence informed evaluations, obtaining information from multiple credible sources, covering multiple domains of functioning, and using psychometrically substantiated measures. A number of sexual recidivism risk measures have been developed, static and dynamic, actuarial and SPJ, with good support for their predictive properties. The utility of a measure, however, can only be found in its application to guide service delivery through appraising baseline risk, identifying targets for intervention and risk management, and dynamically appraising changes in risk through reassessment to aid release and reintegration decisions. The various measures available vary in the concordant products and user materials available to facilitate their application, such as relative risk norms (e.g., percentiles), non-arbitrary risk categories, or recidivism calculators to compute long and short term recidivism estimates from risk assessment information.

Given the overrepresentation of ethnocultural minorities in the criminal justice system, and among persons who commit sexual offenses, the sociohistorical context, which often includes systemic racism and socio-economic marginalization, needs to be considered in sexual recidivism evaluations. Preferably, extant measures would have some psychometric data supporting their validity and reliability with different ethnocultural groups, and absent this, used with caution, sensitivity, and professional discretion to aid risk management, release, and reintegration, rather than perpetuating historical trauma. Further, the consideration of other risk mitigating agents, such as aging and protective factors, can be systematically incorporated into sexual recidivism assessments to facilitate a fuller and more balanced conceptualization of the client and their functioning. All of which is intended to decrease sexual victimization and to promote safer communities and client wellbeing.

References

Anaya, S. J. (2015). Report of the special rapporteur on the rights of indigenous peoples in the situation of Maori peoples in New Zealand. *Arizona Journal of International and Comparative Law, 32*, 1–26.

Andrews, D. A., & Bonta, J. (1994–2010). *The psychology of criminal conduct* (1st to 5th ed.). Anderson.

Andrews, D. A., & Bonta, J. (1995). *LSI-R: The level of service inventory-revised*. Multi-Health Systems.

Babchishin, K. M., & Hanson, R. K. (2020). Monitoring changes in risk of reoffending: A prospective study of 632 men on community supervision. *Journal of Consulting and Clinical Psychology, 88*, 886–898. https://doi.org/10.1037/ccp0000601

Babchishin, K.M., Hanson, K. R. & Blais, J. (2013). Guide for the Brief Assessment for Recidivism Risk – 2002R (BARR-2002R). Author.

Babchishin, K. M., Hanson, R. K., & Blais, J. (2016). Less is more: Using Static-2002R subscales to predict violent and general recidivism among sexual offenders. *Sexual Abuse, 28*(3), 187–217. https://doi.org/10.1177/1079063215569544

Beggs, S. M., & Grace, R. C. (2010). Assessment of dynamic risk factors: An independent validation study of the Violence Risk Scale: Sexual Offender Version. *Sexual Abuse: A Journal of Research and Treatment, 22*, 234–251. https://doi.org/10.1177/1079063210369014

Beggs, S. M., & Grace, R. C. (2011). Treatment gains for sexual offenders against children predicts reduced recidivism: A comparative validity study. *Journal of Consulting and Clinical Psychology, 79*, 182–192. https://doi.org/10.1037/a0022900

Boer, D. P., Hart, S. D., Kropp, P. R., & Webster, C. D. (1997). *Manual for the sexual violence risk-20: Professional guidelines for assessing risk of sexual violence*. Mental Health, Law, and Policy Institute, Simon Fraser University.

Boer, D. P., Hart, S. D., Kropp, P. R., & Webster, C. D. (2017). *Manual for version 2 of the sexual violence risk-20: Professional guidelines for assessing risk of sexual violence*. Protect International Risk and Safety Services Inc..

Bonta, J., & Andrews, D. A. (2017a). *The psychology of criminal conduct* (6th ed.). Routledge.

Bonta, J., & Andrews, D. A. (2017b). *The psychology of criminal conduct* (6th ed.). Anderson.

Brankley, A. E., Babchishin, K. M., & Hanson, R. K. (2021). STABLE-2007 demonstrates predictive and incremental validity in assessing risk-relevant propensities for sexual offending: A meta-analysis. *Sexual Abuse, 34*(1), 34–62. Advanced online publication. https://doi.org/10.1177/1079063219871572

Brankley, A. E., Helmus, L. M., & Hanson, R. K. (2017). *STABLE-2007 Evaluator Workbook – Revised 2017*. Ottawa, ON.

Coupland, R. B. A., & Olver, M. E. (2020). Assessing protective factors in treated violent offenders: Associations with recidivism reduction and positive community outcomes. *Psychological Assessment, 32*, 493–508. https://doi.org/10.1037/pas0000807

Day, A., Tamatea, A. J., Casey, S., & Geia, L. (2018). Assessing violence risk with Aboriginal and Torres Straight Islander offenders: considerations for forensic practice. *Psychiatry, Psychology, and Law, 25*, 452–464. https://doi.org/10.1080/13218719.2018.1467804

de Vogel, V., de Ruiter, C., Bouman, Y. H. A., & de Vries Robbe´, M. (2009). *SAPROF: Guidelines for the assessment of protective factors for violence risk*. Forum Educatief.
de Vogel, V., de Vries Robbe, M., de Ruiter, C., & Bouman, Y. H. A. (2011). Assessing protective factors in a forensic psychiatric practice: Introducing the SAPROF. *International Journal of Forensic Mental Health, 10*, 171–177. https://doi.org/10.1080/14999013.2011.600230
de Vries Robbé, M., de Vogel, V., Douglas, K. S., & Nijman, H. L. I. (2015). Changes in dynamic risk and protective factors for violence during inpatient forensic psychiatric treatment: Predicting reductions in postdischarge community recidivism. *Law and Human Behavior, 39*, 53–61. https://doi.org/10.1037/jhb0000089
DeMatteo, D., & Olver, M. E. (2021). Use of the psychopathy checklist-revised in legal contexts: Validity, reliability, admissibility, and evidentiary issues. *Journal of Personality Assessment., 104*(2), 234–251. https://doi.org/10.1080/00223891.2021.1955693
DeSorcy, D. R., Olver, M. E., & Wormith, J. S. (2020). Working alliance and psychopathy: Linkages to treatment outcome in a sample of treated sexual offenders. *Journal of Interpersonal Violence, 35*(7-8), 1739–1760. https://doi.org/10.1177/0886260517698822
Douglas, K. S., Hart, S. D., Webster, C. D., & Belfrage, H. (2013). *HCR-20V3: Assessing risk for violence–user guide*. Mental Health, Law, and Policy Institute, Simon Fraser University.
Eke, A. W., Helmus, L. M., & Seto, M. C. (2019). A validation study of the child pornography Offender Risk Tool (CPORT). *Sexual Abuse, 31*(4), 456–476. https://doi.org/10.1177/1079063218762434
Gordon, A., & Wong, S. C. P. (2010). Offense analogue behaviors and indicators of criminogenic need and treatment progress in custodial settings. In M. Daffern, L. Jones, & J. Shine (Eds.), *Offense paralleling behavior: An individualised approach to offender assessment and treatment* (pp. 171–184). Wiley.
Grove, W. M., Zald, D. H., Lebow, B. S., Snitz, B. E., & Nelson, C. (2000). Clinical versus mechanical prediction: A meta-analysis. *Psychological Assessment, 12*, 19–30. https://doi.org/10.1037/1040-3590.12.1.19
Gutierrez, L. L., Helmus, M., & Hanson, R. K. (2016). What we know and don't know about risk assessment with offenders of Indigenous heritage. *Journal of Threat Assessment and Management, 3*, 97–106. https://doi.org/10.1037/tam0000064
Hanson, R. K. (2002). Recidivism and age: Data from 4,673 sexual offenders. *Journal of Interpersonal Violence, 17*, 1046–1062. https://doi.org/10.1177/088626002236659
Hanson, R. K. (2006). Does Static-99 predict recidivism among older sexual offenders? *Sexual Abuse: A Journal of Research and Treatment, 18*, 343–355. https://doi.org/10.1177/107906320601800403
Hanson, R. K. (2017). Assessing the calibration of actuarial risk scales: A primer on the E/O index. *Criminal Justice and Behavior, 44*, 26–39. https://doi.org/10.1177/0093854816683956
Hanson, R. K., Babchishin, K. M., Helmus, L. M., Thornton, D., & Phenix, A. (2017). Communicating the results of criterion referenced prediction measures: Risk categories for the Static-99R and Static-2002R sexual offender risk assessment tools. *Psychological Assessment, 29*, 582–597. https://doi.org/10.1037/pas0000371
Hanson, R. K., Bourgon, G., McGrath, R. J., Kroner, D., D'Amora, D. A., Thomas, S. S., & Tavarez, L. P. (2016). *A five-level risk and needs system: Maximizing assessment results in corrections through the development of a common language*. Justice Center Council of State Governments.
Hanson, R. K., & Bussière, M. T. (1998). Predicting relapse: A meta-analysis of sexual offender recidivism studies. *Journal of Consulting and Clinical Psychology, 66*, 348–362.
Hanson, R. K., Harris, A. J. R., Letourneau, E., Helmus, L. M., & Thornton, D. (2018). Reductions in risk based on time offense free in the community: Once a sex offender, not always a sex offender. *Psychology, Public Policy, and Law, 24*, 48–63. https://doi.org/10.1037/law0000135
Hanson, R. K., Harris, A. J. R., Scott, T., & Helmus, L. (2007). *Assessing the risk of sex offenders on community supervision*. (User Report No. 2007-05). Public Safety and Emergency Preparedness Canada.

Hanson, R. K., & Morton-Bourgon, K. E. (2009). The accuracy of recidivism risk assessments for sexual offenders: A meta-analysis of 118 prediction studies. *Psychological Assessment, 21*(1), 1–21. https://doi.org/10.1037/a0014421

Hanson, R. K., & Thornton, D. (1999). *Static 99: Improving actuarial risk assessments for sex offenders*. (User Report 99-02). Department of the Solicitor General of Canada.

Hanson, R. K., & Thornton, D. (2000). Improving risk assessments for individuals convicted of sexual offences: A comparison of three actuarial scales. *Law and Human Behavior, 24*, 119–136. https://doi.org/10.1023/A:1005482921333

Hanson, R. K., & Thornton, D. (2003). *Notes on the development of Static-2002*. (User Report 2003-01). Department of the Solicitor General of Canada.

Hare, R. D. (1991). *Manual for the revised psychopathy checklist*. Multi-Health Systems.

Hare, R. D. (2003). *The hare psychopathy checklist-revised* (2nd ed.). Multi-Health Systems.

Hart, S. D., & Boer, D. P. (2021). Structured professional judgment guidelines for sexual violence risk assessment: The sexual violence risk-20 (SVR-20) Versions 1 and 2 and risk for sexual violence protocol (RSVP). In K. S. Douglas & R. Otto (Eds.), *Handbook of violence risk assessment* (2nd ed., pp. 322–358). Routledge.

Hart, S. D., Kropp, P. R., Laws, D. R., & Klaver, J. (2003). *The risk for sexual violence protocol (RSVP): Structured professional guidelines for assessing risk for sexual violence*. Mental Health, Law, and Policy Institute, Simon Fraser University.

Helmus, L., Hanson, R. K., Babchishin, K. M., & Mann, R. E. (2013). Attitudes supportive of sexual offending predict recidivism: A meta-analysis. *Trauma, Violence, & Abuse, 14*(1), 34–53. https://doi.org/10.1177/1524838012462244

Helmus, L., Thornton, D., Hanson, R. K., & Babchishin, K. M. (2012). Improving the predictive accuracy of Static-99 and Static-2002 with older sex offenders: Revised age weights. *Sexual Abuse: A Journal of Research and Treatment, 24*(1), 64–101. https://doi.org/10.1177/1079063211409951

Helmus, L. M., Lee, S. C., & Zabarauckas, C. L. (2021). *Do Static-99R and STABLE-2007 work with Indigenous people charged or convicted of sexual offences? A prospective field validity study.* Unpublished manuscript.

Kelley, S. M., Ambroziak, G., Thornton, D., & Barahal, R. M. (2020). How do professionals assess sexual recidivism risk? An updated survey of practices. *Sexual Abuse, 32*, 3–29. https://doi.org/10.1177/1079063218800474

Lee, S., & Hanson, R. K. (2017). Similar predictive accuracy of the Static-99R risk tool for White, Black, and Hispanic sex offenders in California. *Criminal Justice and Behavior, 44*(9), 1125–1140. https://doi.org/10.1177/0093854817711477

Lee, S. C., Hanson, R. K., & Blais, J. (2020). Predictive accuracy of the Static-99R and Static-2002R risk tools for identifying Indigenous and White individuals at high risk for sexual recidivism in Canada. *Canadian Psychology/Psychologie canadienne, 61*(1), 42–57. https://doi.org/10.1037/cap0000182

Leguizamo, A., Lee, S. C., Jeglic, E. L., & Clakins, C. (2015). Utility of the Static-99 and Static-99R with Latino sex offenders. *Sexual Abuse: A Journal of Research and Treatment*. Advance online publication. https://doi.org/10.1177/1079063215618377

Mann, R. E., Hanson, R. K., & Thornton, D. (2010). Assessing risk for sexual recidivism: Some proposals on the nature of psychologically meaningful risk factors. *Sexual Abuse: A Journal of Research and Treatment, 22*, 191–217. https://doi.org/10.1177/1079063210366039

Meehl, P. E. (1954). *Clinical vs. statistical prediction: A theoretical analysis and a review of the evidence*. University of Minnesota Press.

Mills, J. F. (2017). Violence risk assessment: A brief review, current issues, and future directions. *Canadian Psychology/Psychologie canadienne, 58*, 40–49. https://doi.org/10.1037/cap0000100

Mossman, D. (1994). Assessing predictions of violence: Being accurate about accuracy. *Journal of Consulting and Clinical Psychology, 62*, 783–792. https://doi.org/10.1037/0022-006X.62.4.783

Mundt, J. C. (2015). *VRS-SO calculator*. Retrieved at: www.psynergy.ca

Nellis, A. (2016). *The color of justice: Racial and ethnic disparity in state prisons*. The Sentencing Project.

Nicholaichuk, T. P., Olver, M. E., Gu, D., & Wong, S. C. P. (2014). Age, actuarial risk, and long-term recidivism in a national sample of sex offenders. *Sexual Abuse: A Journal of Research and Treatment, 26*, 406–428. https://doi.org/10.1177/1079063213492340

Olver, M., Kelley, S., Johnson, L., & Wong, S. (2020). *Violence risk scale-sexual offense version (VRS-SO): Users' workbook.* [Unpublished manual] Retrieved at: www.psynergy.ca

Olver, M. E. (2016). Some considerations on the use of actuarial and related forensic measures with diverse correctional populations. *Journal of Threat Assessment and Management, 3*, 107–121.

Olver, M. E., Beggs Christofferson, S. M., Nicholaichuk, T. P., & Wong, S. C. P. (2020). Predictive properties of the violence risk scale-sexual offense version as a function of age. *Assessment*, 1–23. Ahead of print publication. https://doi.org/10.1177/1073191120914405

Olver, M. E., & Eher, R. (2020). Predictive properties and factor structure of the VRS-SO: Results from an Austrian sample. *European Journal of Psychological Assessment, 36*, 748–757. https://doi.org/10.1027/1015-5759/a000551

Olver, M. E., Gordon, A., & Wong, S. C. P. (2017). *Offense analogue and offence replacement behavior (OAB/ORB) rating guide for Violence Risk Scale: Sexual Offense version.* Unpublished rating manual retrieved at: www.psynergy.ca

Olver, M. E., Kelley, S. M., Kingston, D. A., Beggs Christofferson, S. M., Thornton, D., & Wong, S. C. P. (2021). Incremental contributions of static and dynamic sexual violence risk assessment: Integrating Static-99R and VRS-SO common language risk levels. *Criminal Justice and Behavior, 48*(8), 1091–1110. https://doi.org/10.1177/0093854820974400

Olver, M. E., Mundt, J. C., Thornton, D., Beggs Christofferson, S. M., Kingston, D. A., Sowden, J. N., Nicholaichuk, T. P., Gordon, A., & Wong, S. C. P. (2018). Using the violence risk scale-sexual offense version in sexual violence risk assessments: Updated risk categories and recidivism estimates from a multisite sample of treated sexual offenders. *Psychological Assessment, 30*, 941–955. https://doi.org/10.1037/pas0000538

Olver, M. E., Nicholaichuk, T. P., Kingston, D. A., & Wong, S. C. P. (2014). A multisite examination of sexual violence risk and therapeutic change. *Journal of Consulting and Clinical Psychology, 82*, 312–324. https://doi.org/10.1037/a0035340

Olver, M. E., Nicholaichuk, T. P., Kingston, D. K., & Wong, S. C. P. (2020). A prospective multisite examination of dynamic sexual violence risk: An extension and update to Olver, Nicholaichuk, Kingston, and Wong (2014). *Journal of Consulting and Clinical Psychology, 88*, 362–371. https://doi.org/10.1037/ccp0000478

Olver, M. E., & Riemer, E. K. (2021). High psychopathy men with histories of sexual offending have protective factors too: But are they risk relevant and can they change in treatment? *Journal of Consulting and Clinical Psychology, 89*(5), 406–420. https://doi.org/10.1037/ccp0000638

Olver, M. E., Sowden, J. N., Kingston, D. A., Nicholaichuk, T. P., Gordon, A., Beggs Christofferson, S. M., & Wong, S. C. P. (2018). Predictive accuracy of VRS-SO risk and change scores in treated Canadian Aboriginal and non-Aboriginal sexual offenders. *Sexual Abuse: A Journal of Research and Treatment, 30*, 254–275. https://doi.org/10.1177/1079063216649594

Olver, M. E., & Stockdale, K. C. (2020). Assessing and managing offense analogue and offense replacement behaviors in correctional settings. *Advancing Corrections, 10(3)*, 42–55.

Olver, M. E., Stockdale, K. C., & Wormith, J. S. (2014). Thirty years of research on the level of service scales: A meta-analytic examination of predictive accuracy and sources of variability. *Psychological Assessment, 26*, 156–176. https://doi.org/10.1037/a0035080

Olver, M. E., Thornton, D., & Beggs Christofferson, S. M. (2021). Understanding the latent structure of dynamic risk: Seeking empirical constraints on theory development using the VRS-SO and the theory of dynamic risk. *Sexual Abuse.* Ahead of print publication https://doi.org/10.1177/10790632211002858

Olver, M. E., & Wong, S. C. P. (2011). Predictors of sex offender treatment dropout: Psychopathy, sex offender risk and responsivity implications. *Psychology, Crime & Law, 17*(5), 457–471. https://doi.org/10.1080/10683160903318876

Olver, M. E., & Wong, S. C. P. (2021). Two treatment and change oriented risk assessment tools: The violence risk scale and the violence risk scale-sexual offense version. In K. S. Douglas & R. Otto (Eds.), *Handbook of violence risk assessment* (2nd ed., pp. 206–223). Routledge.

Olver, M. E., Wong, S. C. P., Nicholaichuk, T., & Gordon, A. (2007). The validity and reliability of the violence risk scale-sexual offender version: Assessing sex offender risk and evaluating therapeutic change. *Psychological Assessment, 19*, 318–329. https://doi.org/10.1037/1040-3590.19.3.318

Prochaska, J. O., DiClemente, C. C., & Norcross, J. C. (1992). In search of how people change: Applications to the addictive behaviors. *American Psychologist, 47*, 1102–1114. https://doi.org/10.1037/0003-066X.47.9.1102

Public Safety Canada. (2019). *Corrections and conditional release statistical overview: 2018 annual report*. Public Safety Canada.

Rice, M. E., & Harris, G. T. (2005). Comparing effect sizes in follow-up studies: ROC area, Cohen's d, and r. *Law and Human Behavior, 29*, 615–620. https://doi.org/10.1007/s10979-005-6832-7

Rice, M. E., Harris, G. T., & Lang, C. (2013). Validation of and revision to the VRAG and SORAG: The Violence Risk Appraisal Guide—Revised (VRAG-R). *Psychological Assessment, 25*(3), 951–965

Savoie, V., Quayle, E., Flynn, E., & O'Rouke, S. (2021). Predicting risk of reoffending in persons with child sexual exploitation material offense histories: The use of Child Pornography Offender Risk Tool in a Scottish population. *Sexual Abuse*. Ahead of print publication https://doi.org/10.1177/10790632211047190

Seto, M. C., & Eke, A. W. (2015). Predicting recidivism among adult male child pornography offenders: Development of the child pornography offender risk tool (CPORT). *Law and Human Behavior, 39*(4), 416–429. https://doi.org/10.1037/lhb0000128

Sewall, L. A., & Olver, M. E. (2019). Psychopathy and treatment outcome: Results from a sexual violence reduction program. *Personality Disorders: Theory, Research, and Treatment, 10*(1), 59–69. https://doi.org/10.1037/per0000297

Sowden, J. N., & Olver, M. E. (2017). Use of the Violence Risk Scale Sexual Offender Version and the Stable 2007 to assess sexual offender treatment change. *Psychological Assessment, 29*, 293–303. https://doi.org/10.1037/pas0000345

Thornton, D., Hanson, R. K., Kelley, S. M., & Mundt, J. C. (2021). Estimating lifetime and residual risk for individuals who remain sexual offense free in the community: Practical applications. *Sexual Abuse, 33*(1), 3–33. https://doi.org/10.1177/1079063219871573

Travis, J., Western, B., & Redburn, F. S. (2014). *The growth of incarceration in the United States: Exploring causes and consequences. Committee on Law and Justice, Division of Behavioral and Social Sciences and Education*. National Academies Press.

van den Berg, J. W., Smid, W., Schepers, K., Wever, E., van Beek, D., Janssen, E., & Gijs, L. (2018). The predictive properties of dynamic sex offender risk assessment instruments: A meta-analysis. *Psychological Assessment, 30*, 179–191. https://doi.org/10.1037/pas0000454

Varela, J. G., Boccaccini, M. T., Murrie, D. C., Caperton, J. D., & Gonzalez, E., Jr. (2013). Do the Static-99 and Static-99R perform similarly for White, Black, and Latino sexual offenders? *International Journal of Forensic Mental Health, 12*, 231–243. https://doi.org/10.1080/14999013.2013.846950

Wielinga, F. (2022). *Use of dynamic risk instruments to assess sexual violence risk in a community-supervised sample of men with sexual violence convictions*.] Unpublished doctoral thesis data. University of Saskatchewan.

Willis, G., Thornton, D., Kelley, S., & de Vries Robbé, M. (2018). *Structured Assessment of Protective Factor for violence risk – Sexual Offence version*. Pilot manual.

Wong, S., & Gordon, A. (1999–2003). *The violence risk scale (VRS)*. Regional Psychiatric Centre and University of Saskatchewan.

Wong, S., Olver, M. E., Nicholaichuk, T. P., & Gordon, A. (2003–2017). *The violence risk scale: Sexual offense version (VRS-SO)*. Regional Psychiatric Centre and University of Saskatchewan.

Wong, S. C. P., Gordon, A., Gu, D., Lewis, K., & Olver, M. E. (2012). The effectiveness of violence reduction treatment for psychopathic offenders: Empirical evidence and a treatment model. *International Journal of Forensic Mental Health, 11*(4), 336–349. https://doi.org/10.1080/14999013.2012.476760

Chapter 10
Best Practices in the Assessment of Abuse-Related Sexual Interests

Zachary Yeoman, Greg Bohall, and David S. Prescott

> Some of the paraphilias are playful and harmless. Some are an unwelcome nuisance to a partner who does not share their fantasy content. Some are dangerous and destructive, even to a consenting partner. Some of those that are legally classified as sex offenses are violently dangerous, and some, like exhibitionism are harmless offenses against modesty. (Money, 1986, p. 168).

10.1 Introduction

In the Holy Bible, the Old Testament included a variety of sexual acts that were prohibited, including masturbation, cross-dressing, same-sex intimate sexual acts, and sex with animals (Gordon, 2008). Early writings in the medical field identified the dangers of masturbation, prostitution, and venereal diseases existing well before 1850 (Stolberg, 2000). During the Middle Ages and the Renaissance Period, the term *perversion* was used to identify an act that violates the laws of God (divine norm; De Block & Adriaens, 2013). In the nineteenth century, the *perversion* concept shifted to the link between sexual desire and sexual instinct (the instinct for propagating the species); it was seen as a functional disease of this instinct (De Block & Adriaens, 2013).

Psychopathia Sexualis, a work published in German by Richard von Krafft-Ebing (1965) in 1886, is often identified as the bible of nineteenth century sexology (Downing, 2010); it was not until the 12th edition that it was published in English. In his landmark work, Krafft-Ebing disagreed with most as he favored the view that *perversions* were caused by "hereditary taintedness" which led to disproportionate

Z. Yeoman (✉)
Somerset Psychological Group, P.A., Martinsville, NJ, USA
e-mail: zyeoman@somersetpsych.com

G. Bohall
Innovative Psychological Solutions, Orange County, CA, USA

D. S. Prescott
Consultant and Director of the Continuing Education Center, Safer Society Foundation, Brandon, VT, USA

R. J. Tully et al. (eds.), *Best Practices in Sexual Offender Assessment and Management*, Dangerous Behavior in Clinical and Forensic Psychology,
https://doi.org/10.1007/978-3-031-83135-5_10

levels between an individual's sexual instinct, their ability to inhibit, and potential subsequent aggravation by excessive masturbation (Oosterhuis, 2000). In *Psychopathia Sexualis,* Krafft-Ebing identified *perversions* as different ways of being a person as opposed to a defect within the person. He also distinguished between *perversions* and *perversities* whereas the former is seen as a disease and the latter a vice.

Given the focus from biologists, historians, physicians, and anthropologists, in the early 1900s, sexology became an intellectual discipline in Europe and the United States (Waters, 2006). Magnus Hirschfeld, the founder of the Institute for Sexual Science in Berlin, believed that deviations from sexual norms may not be pathological or dangerous to society at large (Steakley, 1997). This evolution of sexology further expanded to emphasizing that non-procreative sex was enjoyed by many and is relatively harmless (De Block & Adriaens, 2013). This was mirrored in America by Alfred C. Kinsey, an American biologist and founder of the Institute for Sex Research at Indiana University (1947; now known as the Kinsey Institute at Indiana University), as he believed that many "deviant" sexual practices were actually more common in the American population than once believed. In *Sexual Behavior in the Human Male* (Kinsey et al., 1948) and *Sexual Behavior in the Human Female* (Kinsey et al., 1953), Kinsey and colleagues, among other things, attempted to showcase that human sexuality is similarly varied to animal mating practices. In *Studies in the Psychology of Sex,* Ellis (1936) (1) discussed various sexual pathologies (e.g., transvestism, coprophilia, fellatio, etc.), (2) argued that the individual's desire (e.g., pleasure, pain, control, etc.) was related to normal sexual desires and (3) added that these sexual pathologies became harmful when another person was hurt.

In the mid-1900s, the popularity of psychoanalysis in the United States was evident in the first two editions of the *Diagnostic and Statistical Manual of Mental Disorders* (DSM) from the American Psychiatric Association (APA, 1952, 1968); these editions were inspired by mostly psychodynamic ideas and etiological theories as it related to sexual deviation. Specifically, the original DSM (APA, 1952) had minimal information regarding sexual deviations as they were identified as "sociopathic personality disturbances". The DSM-II (APA, 1968) exhibited increased specificity of sexual deviation by categorizing sexual interests when they were directed "(a) toward objects other than people of the opposite sex, (b) toward sexual acts not usually associated with coitus, or (c) toward coitus performed in bizarre circumstances" (APA, 1968, p. 44). The DSM-III (APA, 1980) maintained most of DSM-II's (APA, 1968) sexual deviations appearing now as *paraphilias* but also included gender identity disorders as well as psychosexual dysfunctions. Although the DSM-III (APA, 1980) was developed utilizing extensive field testing, its revision, the DSM-III-R (APA, 1987), provided much needed alterations that include (1) the removal of exclusivity or repetition of paraphilic behavior in order to diagnose (replaced with severity codes), (2) the inclusion of recurrent intense sexual urges and fantasies for at least six months, and (3) the inclusion of the individual either acting on these urges/fantasies or is markedly distressed by them. In a slight, but significant change, the DSM-IV (APA, 1994) removed the DSM-III-R's (APA,

1987) inclusion of acting on their sexual urges and input that their fantasies, urges, and/or behaviors result in clinically significant distress or impairment in important life areas. However, the DSM-IV-TR (APA, 2000) focused on the paraphilias with a nonconsenting victim (e.g., pedophilia, frotteurism, etc.) and reverted back to DSM-III-R's (APA, 1987) criteria where the individual is required to either act on their sexual urge/fantasy OR experience distress based on their urge/fantasy. Presently, paraphilic disorders included in the DSM-5-TR (APA, 2022) have a qualitative nature of the paraphilia (Criterion A; e.g., touching/rubbing against a nonconsenting individual in frotteuristic disorder) and a negative consequence due to the paraphilic behavior (Criterion B; e.g., distress or impairment in social, occupational, or other area of functioning due to frotteuristic behavior). Therefore, a situation may occur where an individual meets Criterion A (qualitative experience) of a paraphilic disorder but not for Criterion B (no distress); in this instance, the individual is said to have a paraphilia but not a paraphilic disorder.

Indeed, sexual behavior has undergone numerous conceptualizations and interpretations. Over time, it has been repeatedly shown that professionals continue to struggle distinguishing between what is considered to be a sexually deviant act(s)[1] and what is a mental disorder; this has significant implications on the assessment of abuse-related sexual interests. In this chapter, referral questions for assessing individuals with perceived paraphilic disorders as well as self-report, psychophysiological, and proxy measure approaches to clinical assessment will be reviewed.

10.2 Common Referral Questions

Referrals for the assessment of sexual deviance are rarely made outside of court involvement. While it could be relevant in clinical practice–for example, a non-offending client reports arousal to fantasies of illegal sexual acts–it could expose areas of concern that many mental health professionals are not qualified to address. This type of evaluation may also reveal information that the clinician is required to disclose. For instance, a self-report questionnaire may ask questions about past sexual abuse of minors. If endorsed, the clinician may be mandated to report this information, depending on the jurisdiction. In addition, the experienced clinician knows that this type of evaluation is psychologically intrusive and can even be physically invasive, as is the case with the penile plethysmograph (PPG; to be discussed later). Most practitioners will not want to subject their clients to this type of evaluation unless absolutely necessary, usually when someone is charged for engaging in illegal sexual behavior.

[1] The term "sexual deviance" is pejorative and can be harmful to the treatment process. However, its use is commonplace in our field and easily understood. As such, it will be used periodically in this chapter to efficiently and accurately communicate about this topic. But it will also be used interchangeably with "offense-related," "abuse related" and "illegal" sexual interests.

When a sexual offense is committed or alleged, a forensic evaluator may be requested at multiple points in the legal process. In the pre-adjudication phase, the forensic evaluator may be retained by the defense even before formal charges are lodged. The evaluator in such cases is asked to conduct a risk assessment and develop a treatment and management plan. Although rare at this stage, if the allegations are particularly alarming or the individual reports substantial distress about their sexual interests, the evaluator could be asked to assess sexual deviance directly. Although the assessment of sexual deviance at this stage in the legal process is unlikely to yield a meaningful result, stakeholders may believe an accurate evaluation of this issue is paramount because of its perceived impact on risk to the community. These evaluations can be extremely difficult due to the ethical considerations involved. For example, assessments that give the appearance of swaying a trier of fact in the direction of guilt or innocence are proscribed by professional organizations such as the Association for the Treatment and Prevention of Sexual Abuse (ATSA).

In the disposition phase of the legal process, many considerations are beyond the evaluator's purview. However, an evaluator can assist the court by providing a clinical opinion about the individual's supervision and management needs. Amongst other considerations such as level of risk, treatment motivation, and family support, an assessment of abuse-related sexual interests or preferences is particularly relevant for treatment planning. There are many pathways to sexual offending, abuse-related sexual arousal patterns being one of them. Understanding the presence and strength of the individual's offense-related sexual interests informs the development of an adequate management plan. Knowing if sexual interests in illegal behaviors are primary or secondary motivators help tailor the treatment to the specific individual's needs.

Pre-release evaluations may occur when the individual is being considered for release from incarceration or a secure level of care. In these evaluations, considerations are similar to other contexts in that the individual's level of risk to the community is a primary concern. Stakeholders can benefit from a thorough risk assessment. As part of that risk assessment, if there is reason to suspect that an offense-related sexual interest or preference contributed significantly to the offense, evaluation of the individual's current sexual arousal in the context of a comprehensive risk assessment may assist in determining the level of supervision they needed in the community.

All 50 states and the District of Columbia place individuals who have committed sex offenses under their version of Megan's Law, a community notification and registration law. Jurisdictions also vary as to how the individual is placed under the law. Some jurisdictions classify by nature and degree of the convicted offense; other jurisdictions use a risk assessment scale to determine the level of placement under the law. Sometimes, in those states where the law includes a risk assessment component, there is a dispute about the level of risk the individual presents to the community. Finally, some jurisdictions allow certain juveniles relief from registration if they meet certain criteria (Yeoman et al., 2020). As with pre-release evaluations, stakeholders may be concerned about continued arousal to illegal sexual acts.

Assessment of the individual's current sexual arousal in combination with a comprehensive risk assessment may increase the chances that an individual will be accurately classified or released from his registration requirement.

10.3 Approaches to Assessing Sexual Deviance

Several methods are available to aid in the assessment of an individual's current deviant sexual arousal, with no one measure sufficient to provide a stand-alone means of diagnosis. These include self-report questionnaires, polygraphy, viewing time measures (VT), and penile plethysmography (PPG). However, the availability of these instruments does not mean they will be helpful. Many of these measures were created and validated in laboratory settings or with client populations that, unlike most forensic examinees, do not have much to lose by participating in them. While they may demonstrate psychometric soundness during development, it is often the case that psychological instruments will not show the same utility when used in the field (Murrie et al., 2012). The average person undergoing forensic evaluation is more than likely aware of what is at stake if they report or demonstrate an offense-related sexual arousal (e.g., less favorable plea, sentenced more harshly, not granted parole, placed on tighter restrictions in the community, not released from sex offense registries). As a result, most will attempt to minimize or suppress evidence of concerning sexual interests consciously or unconsciously. As discussed in the following sections, while each method has built-in validity measures, they are far from foolproof. If someone is motivated to not show a deviant arousal on assessment measures, they usually will not.

10.3.1 Self-Report

Self-report instruments are those that individuals complete on their own. This occurs most often in the form of a standardized questionnaire. Often referred to as objective tests, these tests may be preferable to structured or unstructured interviewing because they reduce human bias. Some research also suggests people are more honest on tests than in interviews (Gribble et al., 1999). The field of psychology has a long history of using such instruments to evaluate psychopathology. In general, objective tests are developed with large populations of people–called samples–with and without the psychopathology in question. Patterns of responses or norms emerge for different populations. For instance, people with clinical depression answer the questions of these tests in systematically different ways than people who are not clinically depressed. Assuming that the samples were large enough and sufficiently diverse, the sample norms are believed to be representative of an entire population. So, when an individual takes an objective self-report test, if their results match the norms for clinically depressed samples, for example, it increases the likelihood that the individual is also clinically depressed. Each interpretive statement can be viewed in the following light: in one or more research studies, a clinically significant number of people with similar answers exhibited the stated characteristic(s) (Hoberman & Riedel, 2016).

However, using self-report instruments in forensic contexts poses additional threats to validity. As Greene (2007) indicates, research has demonstrated that examinees may respond differently depending on their perception of the allegiance of the evaluator. They are more likely to report fewer problems to an evaluator perceived as not allied with their interests. Consequently, in most evaluations of individuals who have committed or are alleged to have committed sexual offenses, reports to such evaluators should be considered as potentially distorted and a likely underestimation of an individual's possible characteristics. While the most robust and popular self-report psychological instruments (e.g., Personality Assessment Inventory) contain scales to detect response style distortion, they are far from perfect. A motivated, intelligent respondent can avoid detection on validity scales and still present a false impression of themselves. Even if the respondent receives elevated scores on validity scales suggesting attempts to portray themselves unrealistically, this cannot be interpreted as indicative of psychopathology. Most people in forensic contexts will naturally try to put their best foot forward, given what is at stake.

Developing self-report instruments for abuse-related sexual interests is also far more complicated and has received less attention. Fewer people have been detected for or reported these issues than general psychopathology. Even less are willing to participate in developing these instruments in situations where there is no clear incentive to present themselves in an overly positive light. In addition, although many inventories have been developed, few were created in the same manner and with the same psychometric rigor as objective tests that assess general psychopathology. The development of each more robust instrument will be discussed, as well as their strengths and weaknesses.

The Multiphasic Sex Inventory (MSI, Nichols & Molinder,1984) and MSI-II (Nichols & Molinder, 1996, 2002) were designed to measure the sexual characteristics of adult males who committed sexual offenses. The MSI-II is a 560-item self-report questionnaire of true or false questions that break down into six scales: validity, accountability, attitudes toward treatment, paraphilias, sexual dysfunction, and sexual knowledge and beliefs. The MSI-II was standardized using a nationally representative sample of 2000 individuals. Independent studies of the MSI-II have found it to be a valid measure (Tong, 2007, Stinson & Becker, 2008; Stinson et al., 2008).

The MSI-II has certain limitations. The questions are based on past behavior rather than current sexual interests, which may not be as correlated as once believed. In addition, self-reported information about sexual arousal may be unhelpful if the participant is not insightful, a common characteristic of those who commit sexual offenses. Furthermore, using the MSI-II is somewhat unwieldy as you must send the raw data to the authors and wait for the results to be returned (Hoberman & Riedel, 2016). The main problem, as Kalichman et al. (1992) noted, is that, despite validity scales, the MSI is highly face-valid or transparent, making the denial of abuse-related sexual interests likely in forensic contexts. Although it does a reasonable job of detecting minimization and denial, this information does little to help the evaluator. Minimization and denial are expected in forensic evaluation contexts and are not diagnostic; most people will do so with so much on the line.

The Multidimensional Inventory of Development, Sex, and Aggression (MIDSA, 2007) is a computerized self-report inventory normed on juveniles and adults who have and have not committed a sexual offense. It was standardized on more than 4000 men, women, and boys in correctional and community settings in several jurisdictions worldwide. The MIDSA includes several validity scales, including one triggered when the respondent responds too quickly. It is an extensive measure of general background information and sexual history and functioning, deviant sexual interests (with unique questions appropriate for and only administered to people with child victims), sexual preoccupation, criminal and other antisocial behaviors and values, relevant personality traits (e.g., impulsivity), substance abuse, use of sexually arousing material, history of aggression or violence, history of sexually abusive behavior, cognitive functioning and responsivity factors, and insight into offending dynamics. The MIDSA is not a risk assessment instrument but maps well onto dynamic risk assessment instruments, such as the STABLE-2007.

The MIDSA has several advantages over its competitors. Computer administration is superior to human interviewing in consistency and exhaustiveness. Respondents are only asked questions appropriate for them (i.e., only respondents who identify themselves as interested in children are administered the questions for people with child victims). An embedded reading test in the instructions (4th-grade reading level) automatically identifies people with reading problems. The MIDSA provides graphed standard scores comparing the individual to community controls and those who have committed sexual offenses. Finally, it includes more sophisticated validity scales than its predecessors. However, as with any self-report instrument, the questions are face valid; there is no subtle or ambiguous way to ask questions about these topics. If someone chooses not to disclose this information, it does not matter how sophisticated the self-report measure is; the evaluator will not know about it (Hoberman & Riedel, 2016).

10.3.2 Psychophysiological Procedures

Psychophysiological procedures attempt to assess sexual deviance more directly and objectively than self-report. These instruments appear more advantageous than self-report instruments because they are not confined to what someone is willing to disclose. If the respondent reacts to a question or demonstrates arousal to what they are shown that reaction will be quantified by their involuntary response during test administration. When these psychophysiological tools are used in tandem with other measures related to potential deviant sexual interests, the evaluator may obtain a more precise and comprehensive overview of the individual's sexual interests, arousals, and behavioral history (Maram & Koetting, 2004). While the appeal of these types of instruments is evident, as will be discussed, they may be deficient in significant ways.

10.3.2.1 Polygraph Examination

In the United States, pursuant to 18 U.S.C. §3563(b)(9), the court may provide that a defendant "undergo available medical, psychiatric, or psychological treatment" and that the court may provide that the defendant "satisfy such other conditions as the court may impose" (18 U.S.C. §3563(b)(22)). Conditions may be for the purposes of public protection, deterrence, and/or rehabilitation as pursuant to 18 U.S.C. §3553(a)(2)(B)-(D). The polygraph examination is oftentimes utilized in probation and supervised release settings as consistent with the aforementioned United States Codes in order to provide historical information on a defendant's past behavior(s) which can then be used for assessing risk, targeting intervention, and to increase disclosure of activities (Administrative Office of the United States Courts, 2024). The polygraph examination, when included in sexual offender management programs, can be used to investigate sexual history (involvement in unknown/unreported offenses), serve as a means for maintenance and monitoring (verify compliance), and/or for issue-specific purposes, such as to follow-up on previous unresolved/deceptive examinations (Administrative Office of the United States Courts, 2024).

There are two predominant types of polygraph examinations, the Comparative Question Test (CQT) and the Concealed Information Test (CIT); both use the same physical apparatus, however, they differ in their theoretical underpinning and their academic and commercial usage (Synnott et al., 2015). In the United States, the CQT polygraph examination is used as opposed to the CIT as CQT standards have been developed by the National Center for Credibility Assessment. The polygraph examination includes interview questions and subsequent measures of involuntary physiological reactions to stress as measured by patterns in cardiovascular activity (red line), respiratory activity (blue line), and electrodermal activity (green line).

When the polygraph examination is used to assess sexual deviance, it is an attempt to obtain the respondent's full disclosure of their sexual interests (Phenix & Hoberman, 2016). Outside of the civil commitment of sexual offenders, forensic psychologists rarely use polygraphy. First, it is not part of education in psychology, and second, psychologists without extensive knowledge of the polygraph literature generally believe that it lacks scientific validity (U.S. Congress Office of Technology Assessment, 1983). For psychologists with polygraph examination knowledge, they tend to also believe that it lacks scientific validity. For example, Iacono and Lykken (1997) completed a study where they conducted a survey of academic opinion regarding the polygraph examination. Survey respondents were from the Society for Psychological Research (SPR) and the American Psychological Association's General Psychology division (Division 1). Of respondents, for the CQT, 36% of members of the SPR and 30% of Division 1 considered the CQT to be based on sound psychological principles. Therefore, although this study is dated, most psychologists do not consider the CQT as scientifically valid. While multiple studies have found support for postconviction polygraphy (Elliott & Vollm, 2018; English et al., 2000; Rubin & Madson, 2006; Kokish et al., 2005; Raskin, 1988; Raskin et al., 1976), these studies are concerned with the disclosure of victims, not the assessment of current sexual deviance. Although one may be correlated with the other, many other factors contribute to their relationship.

If the polygraph is used to assist in the assessment sexual deviance, it typically occurs well after the individual has been convicted and is used for maintenance and monitoring. It is improbable that an attorney would let their client participate in a polygraph examination of this sort prior to legal dispositions. An adverse outcome is sure to be unfairly prejudicial to their client. For the polygraph to be accurate, it must ask questions about specific behaviors rather than simply if the individual is sexually aroused to children. For example, a good polygraph question would be, "in the past six months, have you masturbated to thoughts of children?" If the individual demonstrates a significant reaction to that question, it is assumed to be a reliable indicator of a current deviant sexual interest. However, as with the other measures discussed, having a significant reaction during the polygraph does not mean that the person has a sexual interest in children. It may mean that the individual was uncomfortable with one or more of their responses on the polygraph. One reason could be that they have engaged in the offense-related sexual behavior at issue. It could also mean that the question was worded poorly and triggered an unrelated response from the individual.

10.3.2.2 Viewing Time

Viewing time (VT) is a measure of sexual interest, not a direct measure of arousal (such as an increase in penis size in response to erotic and semi-erotic stimuli). It is believed that people look longer at images of people who are attractive to them. Researchers have investigated this phenomenon as early as 70 years ago (Brown, 1979; Glasgow et al., 2003; Harris et al., 1996; Quinsey et al., 1996; Rosenzweig, 1942; Zamansky, 1956). VT has been found to be a reliable and valid measure of sexual interest in men (Gray et al., 2015). Research indicates that the Affinity (Glasgow et al., 2003; Glasgow, 2007) and Abel Assessment for Sexual Interest (AASI; Abel et al., 1998) suite of tests were found to be similar to phallometry in its ability to discriminate between known groups of child abusers categorized by the sex and age of their victims (Abel, et al., 1998; Abel et al., 2001; Abel et al., 1994; Abel et al., 1999; Abel & Wiegel, 2009; Gray & Plaud, 2005; Johnson & Listiak, 1999; Letourneau, 2002; Maram, 2002; Seghorn & Weigel, 1999). Independent researchers also replicated these results in five centers, comparing VT with phallometry. Their results showed VT to be similar to phallometry in discriminating between known groups (Gray & Plaud, 2005; Johnson & Listiak, 1999; Letourneau, 2002; Maram, 2002; Seghorn & Weigel, 1999).

However, only one peer-reviewed study has reported that VT results predict sexual recidivism in the expected manner (Gray et al., 2015). If VT accurately measures deviant sexual arousal, and deviant sexual arousal is one of the strongest predictors of sexual recidivism (Hanson & Morton-Bourgon, 2005), one would expect more research findings supporting the connection between a positive VT result and sexual recidivism.

Although VT has demonstrated adequate validity in research contexts, its utility for most forensic psychologists conducting outpatient evaluations is questionable. Many forensic psychologists are hired to do evaluations when someone is charged with a sexual crime. At this phase of the legal process, the individual being evaluated is highly incentivized to suppress this type of arousal if present. Demonstrating a deviant sexual interest pretrial would be detrimental to a favorable outcome. While VT and similar instruments may be more useful postconviction, these individuals are still incentivized to suppress illegal sexual interests. For example, if someone in a parole-mandated sex offense-specific treatment (SOST) demonstrates ongoing illegal sexual interests on VT, it is likely to extend the amount of time they are required to participate in that program. As important, VT has not yet proven itself as an entirely useful approach "in the field" in treatment programs, although (as with every other approach) it certainly has its place.

10.3.2.3 Penile Plethysmography

The PPG measures sexual arousal by changes in penile engorgement or tumescence (e.g., relative blood flow into the penis) while the individual is viewing clothed or nude images of children, adolescents, and adults; listening to audio-recorded sexual stories involving children and sexual and nonsexual violence; or viewing and listening to these stimulus presentations. The PPG is a controversial assessment procedure, given its invasiveness. Although it has been criticized due to lack of standardization and ethical concerns (Phenix & Hoberman, 2016), several authorities advocate that the most well-established method for assessing sexual interest or arousal remains the PPG (O'Donohue & Letourneau, 1992; Rosen & Keith, 1978; Zuckerman, 1971). PPG results provide relatively accurate information for classifying child molesters and men who commit sexually coercive acts, such as rape, into more refined, delimited diagnostic groups and/or differentiate them from other sex offender and non-sex offender groups (Barbaree & Marshall, 1984; Fedora et al., 1992; Lalumière et al., 2003; Quinsey et al., 1975; Wormith, 1986). The PPG has been around for over 70 years, and there is a large body of research supporting its use as the best-validated tool for assessing pedophilia. A single standardized means of administering the test and published norms are lacking (Camilleri & Quinsey, 2008). However, the PPG is most valid when its use includes audio-plus-slide or slide-only presentation modalities and z-score indices to assess pedohebephilic interests. Effective PPG examinations rely on stimuli depicting nonviolent and noncoercive sexual interactions with a child, as well as stimuli depicting sexual violence toward a child (McPhail et al., 2019).

A problem with using the PPG is that individuals can be unlikely to participate in the PPG openly. It can be a highly invasive, even embarrassing process, and, for many, the result can profoundly impact their liberty. PPG developers understand this issue and have embedded various validity measures into the administration. These include monitoring for abnormalities in respiration and skin response as well as tasks to ensure that the individual is paying attention to what they are being shown and processing the information. That being said, if the individual shows signs that they were not paying attention or tried to suppress or obscure their physiological responses, all the evaluator can say is that the test results are invalid. While frustrating to stakeholders, the assumptions that can be made about the meaning of the invalid response are limited. Again, in most real-world contexts, it is entirely natural for the individual, consciously or not, to suppress indications of problematic sexual interests. An invalid result does not inherently mean they are hiding something. People with normative sexual interests may be so concerned about the possibility of accidentally producing a concerning result that it interferes with measuring their arousal. For others, it is expected that the person being evaluated would not be forthcoming with information so damning. This does not make them antisocial or indicate that they are inherently at increased risk; it means that they are human and want to avoid consequences like everyone else. In addition, while the PPG is more difficult to fake than self-report, it is also possible to do so (Looman et al., 1998).

As illustrated by the discussion so far, although measures developed to assess sexual deviance may demonstrate valid and reliable results, there has always been a large gap between demonstrating utility in research settings and applied settings (e.g., clinical work). Research settings are often artificial. Individuals may be incentivized to participate with extra privileges or money. Even if they are not offered compensation, in some cases, they are told that the evaluation results cannot be used against them in their case. In the latter scenario, individuals have nothing to lose and are more likely to respond honestly than in real-world situations when their liberty is at stake.

In most cases where forensic psychologists become involved, there is much at stake for the individual being assessed. It is improbable that the individual will enter such an assessment openly if they have something to hide. These individuals are put in a bind by being administered such tests: either they participate openly in the assessment and produce potentially damning results related to deviant sexual interests, or they suppress those interests, have their suppression efforts detected, and have their lack of cooperation used as evidence that they are non-compliant individuals, having something to hide, are high risk, etc. Given these unappealing outcomes, alternative and experimental measures of offense-related sexual arousal should be seriously considered.

10.3.3 Proxy Measures of Abuse-Related Sexual Interests

As discussed earlier, accurately and directly assessing sexual deviance is challenging when a positive result can lead to a loss of liberty. Individuals can circumvent embedded validity measures to produce false negatives if sufficiently motivated. It may be more helpful and economical to use scientifically validated proxies of sexual deviance. A proxy measure is scored based on the individual's documented history of behavior rather than a direct assessment of the individual. The items included in the proxy measure have been found to predict deviant sexual interests. Proxy measures can be developed by looking at the histories of those who have demonstrated positive results on direct measurements of sexual deviance in less high-stakes contexts.

The screening scale for pedophilic interests (SSPI and SSPI-2) was designed to measure pedophilic sexual interests among men (age 18+) who have committed at least one sexual offense against a child (someone younger than age 15, based on a self-report or criminal charge; Seto et al., 2016; Seto et al., 2017; Stephens, et al., 2019). SSPI-2 is almost identical to the SSPI, with the addition of an item related to the possession of child sexual exploitation material (CSEM). It was normed with a sample of 1900 Canadian men charged for sexual offenses against children (no overlap with the original sample used to construct the SSPI). The SSPI-2 consists of the following five items rated as "yes" or "no": Item 1: Any boy victim under the age of 15, Item 2: Multiple child victims under the age of 15, Item 3: Any child victim under the age of 12, Item 4: Any extrafamilial child victims under the age of 15, and Item 5: Any possession of child pornography. The individual can obtain a score from zero to five, with higher scores more suggestive of pedophilic interest. Individuals with a score of five were approximately four times more likely to show greater penile response to children than to adults than were individuals with an SSPI score of 0 (72% vs. 18%). The SSPI has been used in multiple research studies and typically shows expected correlations with other measures of sexual interest in children, including phallometrically assessed sexual arousal to child stimuli, relative viewing time measures, and self-report. Also, the SSPI-2 performed slightly better than the SSPI in predicting sexual re-arrest in a sample of 2416 individuals in New York (Seto, et al., 2016; Seto et al., 2017; Stephens, et al., 2019).

The correlates of admission of sexual interests in children (CASIC) is part of the Child Pornography Offender Risk Tool (CPORT-V2, 2018). It is scored when an individual caught with CSEM does not carry a diagnosis of a pedophilic disorder or does not admit this type of interest to the police. Most without a previous pedophilic disorder diagnosis are likely to deny this type of arousal, given the consequences of accepting it. As such, proxy variables that do not require self-report are more helpful at determining the presence of deviant sexual interests. The CPORT development team collected extensive information regarding the development sample's pornography and CSEM collections and collecting behaviors (Seto & Eke, 2015). They identified the following behavioral correlates (now the items of the CASIC) of admission of deviant sexual interests made by those studied. Item 1: Never married,

Item 2: Child pornography videos, Item 3: Child pornography stories, Item 4: evidence interest in child pornography spanned two or more years, Item 5: Volunteering in a role with high access to children, and Item 6: Engaging in online sexual communications with a minor or officer posing as a minor. If three or more of these are present, the individual receives one point on the CPORT item related to indications of pedophilic or hebephilic interests (Seto & Eke, 2017). Through data analysis, the research found that the CASIC was an adequate substitute for admission of sexual interest in children.

10.4 Conclusion

Effective management and intervention of deviant sexual behavior hinges on identifying and understanding underlying dysfunction, utilizing assessment techniques that provide insight into the etiology of deviant sexual behavior, and providing an accurate diagnosis so an appropriate intervention and management plan can be implemented in order to reduce sex-based criminality. This oftentimes includes the assessment of offender risk in the community. Although risk was not covered in this chapter, please review *Best Practices in Sexual Recidivism Risk Assessment* in this volume for further clarity. As reviewed previously, sexual behavior has undergone numerous conceptualizations and interpretations over time. Philosophically, as it relates to abuse-related sexual interests, defining a paraphilic disorder (disease) and healthy sexual behavior has been difficult to define. Although there are diagnostic criteria to aid in this, the criteria of a disorder has changed and those changes have also reverted back to previous definitions.

In this chapter, referral questions for assessing individuals with perceived paraphilic disorders as well as self-report, psychophysiological, and proxy measure approaches to clinical assessment were reviewed. Assessments of abuse-related sexual interests require considerable skill and knowledge of each individual's context and circumstances. Given the stakes involved, evaluators must remain aware of the implications of results and not produce even the appearance of unfounded conclusions. Further, as this review shows, no one approach or measure is adequate for diagnosing a sexual disorder, let alone determining an individual's risk for sexual re-offense.

References

Abel, G. G., Huffman, J., Warberg, B., & Holland, C. L. (1998). Visual reaction time and plethysmography as measures of sexual interest in child molesters. *Sexual Abuse: Journal of Research and Treatment, 10*(2), 81–95. https://doi.org/10.1023/A:1022063214826

Abel, G. G., Jordan, A., Hand, C. G., Holland, L. A., & Phipps, A. (2001). Classification models of child molesters utilizing the Abel Assessment for sexual interest™. *Child Abuse & Neglect, 25*, 703–718.

Abel, G. G., Lawry, S. S., Karlstrom, E., Osborn, C., & Gillespie, C. F. (1994). Screening tests for pedophilia. *Criminal Justice and Behavior, 21*, 115–131.

Abel, G. G., Phipps, A., Hand, C., & Jordan, A. (1999, September). *The reliability and validity of visual reaction time as a measure of sexual interest in children*. Paper presented at the 18th annual meeting of the Association for the Treatment of Sexual Abusers, Orlando, FL.

Abel, G. G., & Wiegel, M. (2009). Visual reaction time: Development, theory, empirical evidence and beyond. In F. Saleh, A. Grudzinskas, J. M. Bradford, & D. Brodsky (Eds.), *Sex offenders: Identification, risk assessment, treatment, and legal issues* (pp. 101–118). Oxford University Press.

Administrative Office of the United States Courts. (2024). *Overview of probation and supervised release conditions; Updated to include cybercrime guidance*. Author.

American Psychiatric Association. (1952). *Diagnostic and statistical manual: Mental disorders*. Author.

American Psychiatric Association. (1968). *Diagnostic and statistical manual of mental disorders* (2nd ed.). Author.

American Psychiatric Association. (1980). *Diagnostic and statistical manual of mental disorders* (3rd ed.). Author.

American Psychiatric Association. (1987). *Diagnostic and statistical manual of mental disorders* (3rd ed.). Author.

American Psychiatric Association. (1994). *Diagnostic and statistical manual of mental disorders* (4th ed.). Author.

American Psychiatric Association. (2000). *Diagnostic and statistical manual of mental disorders* (4th ed. Text Revision). Author.

American Psychiatric Association. (2022). *Diagnostic and statistical manual of mental disorders* (5th ed. Text Revision). Author.

Barbaree, H. E., & Marshall, W. L. (1984). Deviant sexual arousal, offense history, and demographic variables as predictors of reoffense among child molesters. *Behavioral Sciences and the Law, 6*, 267–280.

Brown, M. (1979). Viewing time of pornography. *Journal of Psychology, 102*, 83–95.

Camilleri, J. A., & Quinsey, V. L. (2008). Pedophilia: Assessment and treatment. In D. R. Laws & W. T. O'Donohue (Eds.), *Sexual deviance: Theory, assessment, and treatment* (pp. 183–212). The Guilford Press.

De Block, A., & Adriaens, P. R. (2013). Pathologizing sexual deviance: A history. *Journal of Sex Research, 50*(3-4), 276–298. https://doi.org/10.1080/00224499.2012.738259

Downing, L. (2010). John Money's "Normophilia": Diagnosing sexual normality in late-twentieth-century Anglo-American sexology. *Psychology & Sexuality, 1*(3), 275–287. https://doi.org/10.1080/19419899.2010.494904

Elliott, E., & Vollm, B. (2018). The utility of post-conviction polygraph testing among sexual offenders. *Sexual Abuse, 30*(4), 367–392. https://doi.org/10.1177/1079063216667922

Ellis, H. H. (1936). *Studies in the psychology of sex*. Random House.

English, K., Jones, L., Pasini-Hill, D., Patrick, D., & Cooley-Towell, S. (2000). *The value of polygraph testing in sex offender management*. National Institute of Justice, Colorado Department of Public Safety Division of Criminal Justice, Office of Research & Statistic.

Fedora, O., Reddon, J. R., Morrison, J. W., Fedora, S. K., Pascoe, H., & Yeudall, L. T. (1992). Sadism and other paraphilias in normal control and aggressive and nonaggressive sex offenders. *Archives of Sexual Behaviors, 21*, 1–31.

Glasgow, D. (2007). *The affinity measure of sexual interest-version 2.5*. Retrieved 15 May from http://www.pacific-psych.com/products/affinity.html

Glasgow, D. V., Osborne, A., & Croxen, J. (2003). An assessment tool for investigating paedophile sexual interest using viewing time: An application of single case methodology. *British Journal of Learning Disabilities, 31*, 96–102.

Gordon, H. (2008). The treatment of paraphilias: An historical perspective. *Criminal Behavior and Mental Health, 18*(2), 79–87. https://doi.org/10.1002/cbm.687

Gray, S. R., Abel, G. G., Jordan, A., Garby, T., Wiegel, M., & Harlow, N. (2015). Visual reaction time™ as a predictor of sexual offense recidivism. *Sexual Abuse: A Journal of Research and Treatment, 27*(2), 173–188. https://doi.org/10.1177/1079063213502680
Gray, S. R., & Plaud, J. J. (2005). A comparison of Abel Assessment for sexual interest™ and penile plethysmography in an outpatient sample of sex offenders. *Journal of Sexual Offender Civil Commitment, 1*, 1–10.
Greene, R. L. (2007). Forensic applications of the Minnesota multiphasic personality inventory-2. In A. M. Goldstein (Ed.), *Forensic psychology: Emerging topics and expanding roles* (pp. 73–96). John Wiley & Sons Inc.
Gribble, J. N., Miller, H. G., Rogers, S. M., & Turner, C. F. (1999). Interview mode and measurement of sexual behaviors: Methodological issues. *Journal of Sex Research, 36*.
Hanson, R. K., & Morton-Bourgon, K. E. (2005). The characteristics of persistent sexual offenders: A meta-analysis of recidivism studies. *Journal of Consulting and Clinical Psychology, 73*, 1154–1163.
Harris, G. T., Rice, M. E., Quinsey, V. L., & Chaplin, T. C. (1996). Viewing time as a measure of sexual interest among child molesters and heterosexual men. *Behaviour Research and Therapy, 34*, 389–394.
Hoberman, H. M., & Riedel, R. G. (2016). Structured psychological assessment in evaluations of sexual offenders: Nature and applications. In A. Phenix & H. Hoberman (Eds.), *Sexual offending*. Springer. https://doi.org/10.1007/978-1-4939-2416-5_1
Iacono, W. G., & Lykken, D. T. (1997). The validity of the lie detector: Two surveys of scientific opinion. *Journal of Applied Psychology, 82*(3), 426–433. https://doi.org/10.1037/0021-9010.82.3.426
Johnson, S. A., & Listiak, A. (1999). The measurement of sexual preference: A preliminary comparison of phallometry and the Abel assessment. In B. K. Schwartz (Ed.), *The sex offender* (Vol. III, Chapter 26, pp. 2–18). Civic Research Institute.
Kalichman, S. C., Henderson, M. C., Shealy, L. S., & Dwyer, M. (1992). Psychometric properties of the multiphasic sex inventory in assessing sex offenders. *Criminal Justice and Behavior, 19*, 384–396.
Kinsey, A., Pomeroy, W., & Martin, C. (1948). *Sexual behavior in the human male*. Saunders.
Kinsey, A., Pomeroy, W., Martin, C., & Gebhard, P. (1953). *Sexual behavior in the human female*. Saunders.
Kokish, R., Levenson, J. S., & Blasingame, G. D. (2005). Post-conviction sex offender polygraph examination: Client-reported perceptions of utility and accuracy. *Sexual Abuse: A Journal of Research and Treatment, 17*(2), 211–221.
Krafft-Ebing, R. (1965). *Psychopathia sexualis with special reference to the antipathic sexual instinct: A medico-forensic study*. Paperback Library. (Original work published in 1886)
Lalumière, M. L., Quinsey, V. L., Harris, G. T., Rice, M. E., & Trautrimas, C. (2003). Are rapists differentially aroused by coercive sex in phallometric assessments? In R. A. Prentky, E. S. Janus, & M. C. Seto (Eds.), *Sexually coercive behavior, understanding and management* (Vol. 989, pp. 211–224). Annals of the New York Academy of Sciences.
Letourneau, E. J. (2002). A comparison of objective measures of sexual arousal and interest: Visual reaction time and penile plethysmography. *Sexual Abuse: A Journal of Research and Treatment, 10*, 81–95.
Looman, J., Abracen, J., Maillet, G., & DiFazio, R. (1998). Phallometric nonresponding in sexual offenders. *Sexual Abuse, 10*, 325–336.
Maram, W. (2002, May). *Penile plethysmograph & Abel Assessment effectiveness: Research outcome*. Paper presented at the 5th Annual Conference of the California Coalition on Sexual Offending, San Diego, CA.
Maram, W. B., & Koetting, M. G. (2004). *Phallometry and visual reaction time: Criterion-related validity using phallometric change scores and visual reaction time*. Unpublished raw data.

McPhail, I. V., Hermann, C. A., Fernane, S., Fernandez, Y. M., Nunes, K. L., & Cantor, J. M. (2019). Validity in phallometric testing for sexual interests in children: A meta-analytic review. *Assessment, 26*(3), 535–551. https://doi.org/10.1177/1073191117706139

MIDSA Clinical Manual. (2007). Bend, OR: Augur Enterprises, Inc. www.midsa.us

Money, J. (1986). *Lovemaps: Clinical concepts of sexual/erotic health and pathology, paraphilia, and gender transposition in childhood, adolescence, and maturity*. Irvington Publishers.

Murrie, D. C., Boccaccini, M. T., Caperton, J., & Rufino, K. (2012). Field validity of the psychopathy checklist–revised in sex offender risk assessment. *Psychological Assessment, 24*(2), 524–529. https://doi.org/10.1037/a0026015

Nichols, H., & Molinder, I. (1984). *Manual for the multiphasic sex inventory*. Crime and Victim Psychology Specialists.

Nichols, H., & Molinder, I. (2002). *Multiphasic sex inventory II Handbook*. Nichols & Molinder Assessments.

Nichols, H. R., & Molinder, I. (1996). Multiphasic Sex Inventory II handbook. Tacoma, WA: Nichols and Molinder Assessments.

O'Donohue, W. T., & Letourneau, E. (1992). The psychometric properties of the penile tumescence assessment of child molesters. *Journal of Psychopathology and Behavioral Assessment, 14*(2), 123–174. https://doi.org/10.1007/BF00965172

Oosterhuis, H. (2000). *Stepchildren of nature: Krafft-Ebing, psychiatry, and the making of sexual identity*. University of Chicago Press.

Phenix, A. & Hoberman, H. (2016). Sexual Offending: Predisposing Antecedents, Assessments and Management. https://doi.org/10.1007/978-1-4939-2416-5

Quinsey, V. L., Ketsetzis, M., Earls, C., & Karamanoukian, A. (1996). Viewing time as a measure of sexual Interest. *Ethology and Sociobiology, 17*, 341–354.

Quinsey, V. L., Steinman, C. M., Bergersen, S. G., & Holmes, T. F. (1975). Penile circumference, skin conductance, and ranking responses of child molesters and "normals" to sexual and non-sexual visual. *Behavior Therapy, 6*(2), 213–219.

Raskin, D., Barland, G. H., & Podlesny, J. A. (1976). *Validity and reliability of detection of deception: Final report*. (Government Study Contract # 75-NI-00-0001). National Institute of Law Enforcement and Criminal Justice, Law Enforcement Assistance Administration, U.S. Department of Justice.

Raskin, D. C. (1988). Does science support polygraph testing? In A. Gale (Ed.), *The polygraph test: Lies, truth and science* (pp. 96–110). Sage.

Rosen, R. C., & Keith, F. J. (1978). The measure of human penile tumescence. *Psychophysiology, 15*, 366–376.

Rosenzweig, S. (1942). The photoscope as an objective device for evaluating sexual interest. *Psychosomatic Medicine, 4*, 150–157.

Seghorn, T. K., & Weigel, M. (1999, September). *Comparative use of Abel Assessments and penile plethysmograph laboratory assessments in an outpatient forensic practice*. Paper presented at the 18th Annual Research and Treatment Conference of the Association for the Treatment of Sexual Abusers, Lake Buena Vista, FL.

Seto, M. C., & Eke, A. W. (2015). Predicting recidivism among adult male child pornography offenders: Development of the Child Pornography Offender Risk Tool (CPORT). *Law and Human Behavior, 39*(4), 416–429. https://doi.org/10.1037/lhb0000128

Seto, M. C., & Eke, A. W. (2017). Correlates of admitted sexual interest in children among individuals convicted of child pornography offenses. *Law and Human Behavior, 41*(3), 305–313. https://doi.org/10.1037/lhb0000240

Seto, M. C., Sandler, J. C., & Freeman, N. J. (2016). The revised screening scale for pedophilic interests (SSPI-2): Concurrent and predictive validity. *Submitted to Sexual Abuse: A Journal of Research and Treatment, 29*, 636–657.

Seto, M. C., Stephens, S., & Lalumiere, M. (2017). Screening Scale for Pedophilic Interests. *Version, 2*, (SSPI-2).

Steakley, J. (1997). *Per scientiam ad justitiam:* Magnus Hirschfeld and the sexual politics of innate homosexuality. In V. A. Rosario (Ed.), *Science and homosexualities* (pp. 133–154). Routledge.

Stephens, S., Seto, M. C., Cantor, J. M., & Lalumière, M. L. (2019). The revised screening scale for pedophilic interests (SSPI-2) may be a measure of pedohebephilia. *Journal of Sexual Medicine, 16*(10), 1655–1663. https://doi-org.resources.njstatelib.org/10.1016/j.jsxm.2019.07.015

Stinson, J. D., & Becker, J. V. (2008). Assessing sexual deviance: A comparison of physiological, historical, and self-report measures. *Journal of Psychiatric Practice, 14*, 379–388.

Stinson, J. D., Sales, B. D., & Becker, J. V. (2008). *Sex offending: Causal theories to inform research, prevention, and treatment.* American Psychological Association. https://doi.org/10.1037/11708-000

Stolberg, M. (2000). Self-pollution, moral reform, and the venereal trade: Notes on the sources and historical context of Onania (1716). *Journal of the History of Sexuality, 9*(1).

Synnott, J., Dietzel, D., & Ioannou, M. (2015). A review of the polygraph: History, methodology, and current status. *Crime Psychology Review, 1*(1), 59–83. https://doi.org/10.1080/23744006.2015.1060080

Tong, D. (2007). The penile plethysmograph, Able assessment for sexual interest, and MSI-II: Are they speaking the same language? *The American Journal of Family Therapy, 35*, 187–202.

U. S. Congress Office of Technology Assessment. (1983). *Scientific validity of polygraph testing: A research review and evaluation: A technical memorandum.* November 1983 (OTA-TM-H-15). Author.

Waters, C. (2006). Sexology. In H. G. Cocks & M. Houlbrook (Eds.), *The modern history of sexuality* (pp. 41–63). Palgrave Macmillan.

Wormith, J. S. (1986). Assessing deviant sexual arousal: Physiological and cognitive aspects. *Advances in Behavior Research and Therapy, 6*, 101–137.

Yeoman, Z., Hiscox, H., & Witt, P. (2020). *The relationship between juvenile sex offending and conduct disorder. Sex Offender Law Report.*

Zamansky, H. S. (1956). A technique for measuring homosexual tendencies. *Journal of Personality, 24*, 436–448.

Zuckerman, M. (1971). Physiological measures of sexual arousal in the human. Psychological *Bulletin, 75*, 297–329.

Chapter 11
Clinical Versus Criminal Voyeurism, Exhibitionism, and Frotteurism: Theory, Assessment, Diagnosis, and Intervention

Leah E. Kaylor and Elizabeth L. Jeglic

11.1 Chapter Introduction

Voyeurism, exhibitionism, and frotteurism are recognized by the American Psychiatric Association (APA) as sexual paraphilias that involve sexual arousal derived from non-consenting individuals (APA, 2013). This chapter will focus on the Diagnostic and Statistical Manual of Mental Disorders, fifth edition [DSM-5] definitions of Voyeuristic, Exhibitionistic, and Frotteuristic Disorders. The diagnostic criteria were revised from DSM-IV-TR (2000) to DSM-5 (2013) to differentiate between paraphilic behaviors and paraphilic disorders (Balon, 2016). In the DSM-IV-TR, the paraphilias were referred to as Voyeurism, Exhibitionism, and Frotteurism (APA, 2000). To meet criteria for a paraphilic disorder in the DSM-5 either; (1) the individual must act on their urges and fantasies; or (2) an individual's urges and fantasies must cause clinically significant distress or impairment in social, occupational, or other important areas of functioning (APA, 2013). In contrast, paraphilic behaviors constitute the sexually deviant act, but if they do not cause significant distress or impairment or do not occur frequently enough, they do not warrant a diagnosis. Thus, in this chapter, any research conducted prior to the DSM-5 referring to a paraphilic diagnosis, will utilize the capitalized terms Voyeurism, Exhibitionism, or Frotteurism. When describing sexually deviant acts or behaviors that do not meet criteria for a diagnosis, they will be referred to as voyeuristic, exhibitionistic, and/or frotteuristic act(s) or behavior(s).

This chapter will be divided into two parts. In the first part, what is known about Voyeuristic, Exhibitionistic, and Frotteuristic Disorder in terms of diagnostic

L. E. Kaylor (✉)
PLLC, Uniontown, PA, USA

E. L. Jeglic
Department of Psychology, John Jay College of Criminal Justice, New York, NY, USA

R. J. Tully et al. (eds.), *Best Practices in Sexual Offender Assessment and Management*, Dangerous Behavior in Clinical and Forensic Psychology,
https://doi.org/10.1007/978-3-031-83135-5_11

criteria, prevalence, frequency, age of onset, and scope of the problem is presented separately by disorder. However, given the overlap between the disorders and the dearth of research about these paraphilias in general, the second part of the chapter will broadly discuss comorbidity, differential diagnosis, etiological theories, clinical assessment, and interventions for all three paraphilias in tandem and will conclude with recommendations for future research.

11.2 Part I

11.2.1 Voyeuristic Disorder

11.2.1.1 Diagnostic Criteria

All of the sexual paraphilias in this chapter were first recognized in the scientific literature in the 1800s; however, their existence has been observed throughout history. The term "voyeur" comes from the French word *voir* which translates into "to see" and was first referenced in the literature in the late 1800s (Janssen, 2018). Voyeurism was first included in the second edition of the DSM in 1968; but it did not have a definition until the third edition of the DSM in 1980 (Långström, 2010). The DSM-5 defines Voyeuristic Disorder as "recurrent and intense sexual arousal from observing an unsuspecting individual who is naked, in the process of disrobing, or engaging in sexual activity, as manifested by fantasies, urges, behaviors" for a period of at least six months (APA, 2013, p. 686). To be diagnosed with Voyeuristic Disorder, an individual has either: (1) "acted on these urges or fantasies with a nonconsenting person; or (2) the sexual urges or fantasies cause clinically significant distress or impairment" (APA, 2013, p. 686). The eleventh revision of the International Classification of Diseases (ICD-11) definition for Voyeuristic Disorder differs very little from the DSM-5 describing Voyeuristic Disorder as being "characterized by sustained, focused and intense pattern of sexual arousal—as manifested by persistent sexual thoughts, fantasies, urges, or behaviours—that involves observing an unsuspecting individual who is naked, in the process of disrobing, or engaging in sexual activities" (World Health Organization [WHO], 2020).

11.2.1.2 Prevalence

The prevalence of Voyeuristic Disorder is unknown as many perpetrators avoid detection; however, according to the DSM-5, the maximum possible lifetime prevalence rate of Voyeuristic Disorder derived from non-clinical samples is estimated to be 12% for males and 4% for females (APA, 2013). Similarly, in a study utilizing a non-clinical sample of Swedish adults (n = 2433), researchers found that 11.5% of men and 3.1% of women reported engaging in at least one incident of voyeurism where they became sexually aroused by spying on people partaking in sexual intercourse (Långström & Seto, 2006). There is debate as to whether watching pornography should be considered a voyeuristic act. The DSM-III explicitly stated that "watching pornography, filmed or live causes excitement, however, the people who are being observed are willingly in view, even though in fantasy the observer may imagine (but knows better) that the people are unsuspecting" (APA, 1980, p. 273; Balon, 2016). Despite the much wider availability of pornography, the DSM-5 does not make reference to whether viewing pornography falls into the category of voyeuristic behavior.

Much of the existing research on the prevalence of Voyeuristic Disorder has examined individuals who have come to the attention of legal authorities or therapeutic entities (Kaylor & Jeglic, 2019a). Compared to other sexual paraphilias, voyeuristic acts are easily relatable and do not provoke the same negative public reactions, which may account for the low reporting rates (Långström, 2010).

11.2.1.3 Frequency

Historically, voyeurism was considered a nuisance behavior and as such has received sparse empirical attention (Davis & Davis, 1976; Firestone et al., 2006; Kaylor & Jeglic, 2019a; Långström, 2010; Morin & Levenson, 2008; Murphy & Page, 2008). Research on voyeuristic acts and specifically the frequency of such acts is difficult to measure as it is often a covert behavior (Clark et al., 2016). Consequently, victims may not know they are being watched and therefore cannot report the crime. Despite these obstacles in measurement, the APA (2013) noted that voyeuristic acts are the most commonly occurring law-breaking sexual behavior. For example, Abel and Rouleau (1990) used self-report data to reveal that voyeurs reported an average of 849 voyeuristic acts. Research that relies on perpetrator self-report must be interpreted with caution as these numbers may be unreliable. Self-reports may over-or under-estimate true rates of behavior depending upon the individual's motivations. While the prevalence of Voyeuristic Disorder remains unknown, reports of voyeuristic behaviors are not uncommon.

11.2.1.4 Age of Onset

The DSM-5 added an age requirement, criterion C, in which the individual engaging in the voyeuristic act must be at least 18 years of age to meet criteria for Voyeuristic Disorder (APA, 2013; Balon, 2016). Adolescence is a time of sexual exploration (Kaylor et al., 2016; Sadhu, 2012); thus, the age requirement was implemented to avoid pathologizing normal sexual developmental curiosity (APA, 2013). To better understand the age of onset of voyeurism, a retrospective study asked individuals who engaged in voyeurism when they began to feel the urge to engage in voyeuristic acts. Overall, half (50%) of voyeurs had the urge to engage in voyeuristic acts before age 15 (Kaplan & Krueger, 1997; Mathis, 1972). Given the normative developmental interest in observing sexual behaviors during adolescence, longitudinal research is needed to tease apart normative adolescent curiosity from pathological behavior. This may help identify those who need therapeutic support or may pose future risks, from those who may not.

11.2.1.5 Scope of Problem

The stereotypical portrayal of a person engaging in voyeuristic behavior involves a man hiding in the bushes peering into the window of a stranger's home, otherwise known as a "Peeping Tom" (Hopkins et al., 2016). The sexual arousal stems from spying on individuals who do not know they are being watched. Common methods for spying on others include the use of binoculars, mirrors, and video recorders when looking through windows or peepholes (Balon, 2016). Since voyeuristic acts are often covert, the perpetrator can easily avoid detection (Kaylor & Jeglic, 2019a).

Voyeuristic behavior can be thought of as an umbrella term that encapsulates various subtypes of this behavior, such as scopophilia—the preference for viewing others undressing; scoptophilia—the preference for watching individuals engaging in sexual intercourse; troilism—the preference for viewing one's significant other partaking in sexual intercourse with another person; and coprophilia—the preference for watching others urinate or defecate (Hopkins, et al., 2016; Kaplan & Krueger, 1997; Kaylor & Jeglic, 2019a; Smith, 1976).

With the development of technology, such as personal webcams and video recording devices, the opportunity for engaging in voyeuristic acts has expanded dramatically (Bell et al., 2006). The Internet allows anyone to engage in voyeuristic behavior with websites that broadcast consensual live activities and sexual behaviors (e.g. Chatroulette, Snapchat; Hopkins et al., 2016). However, the arousal of voyeurism stems from watching unsuspecting individuals, thus the Internet has also allowed for the creation of video voyeurism websites (e.g. voyeurlounge.com; Kaylor & Jeglic, 2019a; Metzl, 2004). Some video voyeurism websites feature hidden camera footage displaying unsuspecting individuals in private areas, such as inside a person's home, public bathrooms, locker rooms, and hotel rooms (Stalking Resource Center, 2003). Cameras used to surreptitiously film unsuspecting individuals are becoming smaller and easier to hide allowing voyeurs endless opportunities (Kaylor & Jeglic, 2019a).

Technology has also allowed for hacking into and gaining control over personal webcams to watch selected individuals without detection or consent (Sophos Press Release, 2008; Zinni, 2012). Voyeurs may do so by tricking their desired target into downloading spyware which is disguised as trustworthy software. Once hacked, individuals are unaware they are being watched through their webcam (Zinni, 2012). Webcam hacking has grown to become a widespread problem. According to the Federal Bureau of Investigation (FBI) there are over half a million victims worldwide (Perez et al., 2014).

11.3 Exhibitionistic Disorder

11.3.1 Diagnostic Criteria

Exhibitionism comes from the Latin word *exhibere* which translates into "to show or to present" (Hanafy et al., 2016, p. e61). The term exhibitionist was coined in 300 B.C. by Theophrastus; however, it was not until 1824 that exhibitionistic acts became illegal in England under the *Vagrancy Act* (Hanafy et al., 2016). Exhibitionism was not specifically defined as a disorder until 1877 by French physician, Ernest-Charles Lasègue, as a person revealing parts of his body, but going no further (Lasègue, 1877; Murphy & Page, 2008). In 1965, German psychiatrist, Richard von Krafft-Ebing, further built upon the exhibitionism literature by including it as a sexually deviant act in his book *Psychopathia Sexualis* (Karfft-Ebing, 1906; Långström, 2010).

Exhibitionism was first included in the DSM in the third edition in 1980 (APA, 1980; Grant, 2005). Since its debut in the DSM-III, the definition of exhibitionism has remained relatively unchanged (Långström, 2010). In the DSM-5 Exhibitionistic Disorder is defined as "recurrent and intense sexual arousal from the exposure of one's genitals to an unsuspecting person, as manifested by fantasies, urges, or behaviors" (APA, 2013, p. 689). Over a period of at least six months, individuals with this disorder must have "acted on these sexual urges with a nonconsenting person, or the sexual urges or fantasies have caused clinically significant distress or impairment in social, occupational, or other important areas of functioning" (APA, 2013, p. 689). Similarly, the ICD-11 defines exhibitionism as "a sustained, focused and intense pattern of sexual arousal – as manifested by persistent sexual thoughts, fantasies, urges, or behaviours – that involves exposing one's genitals to an unsuspecting individual in public places, usually without inviting or intending closer contact" (WHO, 2020).

11.3.2 Prevalence

The prevalence of Exhibitionistic Disorder is unknown; however, it is estimated that the highest possible prevalence for exhibitionistic acts in males is between 2–4% (APA, 2013). Researchers examined the prevalence of exhibitionistic acts in a non-clinical sample ($n = 2433$) and found a lifetime prevalence of 3.1% of exhibitionistic behavior (2.1% for females and 4.1% for males; Långström & Seto, 2006). There is a dearth of literature on exhibitionistic acts committed by females; however, the prevalence is assumed to be a much lower compared to that of males (Kaylor & Jeglic, 2019b; Murphy & Page, 2008). Most individuals apprehended by authorities for exhibitionistic acts are male (Blair & Lanyon, 1981; Gebhard et al., 1965; McGrath, 1991; Swindell et al., 2011).

Despite the exact prevalence rates being unknown, exhibitionistic behavior is not uncommon (Firestone et al., 2006; Rabinowitz-Greenberg et al., 2002). There is research to suggest that exhibitionistic acts are the most commonly reported of all sexual offenses; accounting for one-third (Rooth, 1973) to two-thirds of all reported sex crimes (Abel et al., 1988; Firestone et al., 2006; Gebhard et al., 1965; McNally & Fremouw, 2014). Moreover, Riordan (1999) found 45% of victims of exhibitionistic acts did not report the crime to authorities, as such exhibitionistic acts may be even further underestimated in official statistics.

11.3.3 Frequency

It is hypothesized that many exhibitionists have exposed themselves on numerous occasions without arrest (Grant, 2005; Swindell et al., 2011). Researchers believe that acts of exhibitionism may occur up to 150 times more often that what is reflected in official police statistics and does not accurately capture the frequency and number of victims (Abel et al., 1988; Abel & Rouleau, 1990; Bader et al., 2008 Clark et al., 2016; Firestone et al., 2006; Kafka & Hennen, 1999; Långström & Seto, 2006; Rabinowitz-Greenberg et al., 2002). Perpetrator self-report has the potential to underestimate the frequency of exhibitionistic acts as clinical or criminal justice settings may motivate perpetrators to under-report deviant sexual behavior (Abel et al., 1987; Bader et al., 2008; Bhugra et al., 2010; Clark et al., 2016). Due to low reporting rates, and a high number of victims per perpetrator, researchers have taken to using victim self-reports as a more accurate way of calculating exhibitionistic acts. Victim self-reports differ greatly from that of official police statistic in that studies estimate the lifetime victimization for exhibitionistic acts range from 33–53% (Clark et al., 2016; Cox, 1988; Rhoads & Borjes, 1981; Riordan, 1999).

11.3.4 Age of Onset

Unlike voyeurism, a minimum age is not required to be diagnosed with Exhibitionistic Disorder (APA, 2013). Males who engage in exhibitionistic behavior often report becoming aware of the urge to expose their genitals to unsuspecting individuals during adolescence (Murphy & Page, 2008). Yet like the research on voyeurism, it may be difficult to differentiate between age-appropriate sexual curiosity, impulsive behavior during adolescence, and exhibitionistic behaviors (APA, 2013).

11.3.5 Scope of the Problem

Exposing one's genitals in public is legally a sexual offense in many countries. The perpetrator typically does not make physical contact with the victim when engaging in exhibitionistic acts, thus this act would be considered a noncontact or hands-off sexual offense (MacPherson, 2003; McNally & Fremouw, 2014). While it was originally considered a nuisance offense, there is evidence that victims can experience long lasting negative consequences resulting from the exhibitionistic act (Clark et al., 2016). It has been hypothesized that exhibitionistic acts serve to surprise, shock, or impress the target (Brown, 2019). Perpetrators typically target young females, with a preference for strangers (Clark et al., 2016; Cox, 1988; Freund et al., 1988; Riordan, 1999). It has been hypothesized that girls and young women are often targets for this deviant behavior as they may be scared and less likely to scream or report the crime (Clark et al., 2016). The location of exhibitionistic acts may vary based upon geographic location. In major cities, exhibitionistic acts often take place at public transportation stops (i.e., subway stations; Clark et al., 2016). In suburban and rural areas, exhibitionists may expose themselves in parking lots, public streets, parks, wooded areas, or while inside a vehicle (Bader et al., 2008; Gittleson et al., 1978).

Some individuals prefer exposing themselves to prepubescent children, while others prefer adults, or both children and adults (APA, 2013). While all exhibitionistic acts are problematic and illegal, researchers have found that individuals who masturbate during exposure, touch and/or communicate with their victim, or expose themselves to children were more likely to escalate to other sexually assaultive acts (Bader et al., 2008; McNally & Fremouw, 2014; Mohr et al., 1962; Petri, 1969; Sugarman et al., 1994).

Traditionally, exhibitionistic acts were thought to occur in public places; however, with developments in technology individuals can expose themselves to a much wider audience through the use of the Internet, webcams, and smartphones (Hanafy et al., 2016; Kaylor et al., 2016). It is believed that the anonymity of the Internet allows the individual to engage in exhibitionistic acts with little risk for detection (Kaylor et al., 2016).

11.4 Frotteuristic Disorder

11.4.1 Diagnostic Criteria

The earliest clinical discussions of frotteurism were written by European psychiatrists Magnan (1890) and von Krafft-Ebing (1906) to describe the act of rubbing against an unsuspecting person for sexual gratification (McAnulty, 2017; Ranger & Fedoroff, 2015). French psychiatrist, Valentin Magnan, coined the term "frotteur" from the French word *frotter* meaning "to touch or rub" (Ranger & Fedoroff, 2015).

Magnan (1890) described acts of frotteurism as a man rubbing his penis on the body of a stranger, typically in a public venue. Often, the frotteur is a male and the victim is a female (Patra et al., 2013).

Frotteurism appeared in DSM-III (1980) as an atypical paraphilia (McAnulty, 2017). Although there were some minor alterations to the diagnostic criteria, such as eliminating age ranges from the third to the current edition of the DSM, the definition of Frotteuristic Disorder remains largely unchanged (Ranger & Fedoroff, 2015). Currently, the DSM-5 defines frotteurism as a "recurrent and intense sexual arousal from touching or rubbing against a nonconsenting person, as manifested by fantasies, urges, or behaviors" (APA, 2013, p. 691). A diagnosis of Frotteuristic Disorder can be made if both of the following criteria are met: (1) fantasies, urges, or behaviors must be present for at least six months and (2) the "person has acted on these sexual urges with a nonconsenting person, or the sexual urges or fantasies cause clinically significant distress or impairment in social, occupational, or other important areas of functioning" (APA, 2013, pp. 691–692). Similarly, the ICD-11 defines Frotteuristic Disorder as "a sustained, focused and intense pattern of sexual arousal—as manifested by persistent sexual thoughts, fantasies, urges, or behaviours—that involves touching or rubbing against a non-consenting person in a crowded public place" (WHO, 2020). The ICD-11 specifically excludes consensual touching or rubbing.

The terms frotteurism and toucherism have been used interchangeably by some researchers (e.g., Freund, 1990; Freund et al., 1997) and distinguished as different behaviors by others (e.g., Adams & McAnulty, 1993). As such, frotteurism is the rubbing of one's genitals against an unsuspecting individual, whereas toucherism is the use of hands to fondle a female stranger's crotch or breasts, typically from behind (Horley, 2001; Lussier & Piché, 2008; McAnulty et al., 2001, McAnulty, 2017). Some researchers suggest toucherism is a subtype of frotteurism (Horley, 2001). It should be noted that both touching with the hands and rubbing with the penis would be considered frotteuristic acts in the DSM-5 and ICD-11.

11.4.2 Prevalence

According to the DSM-5 (APA, 2013), as much as 30% of the male population may have engaged frotteuristic acts; however, it is estimated that approximately 10–14% of adult men seen in outpatient settings for paraphilic disorders and hypersexuality have a presentation that will meet diagnostic criteria for Frotteuristic Disorder. Similar rates (35%) of self-reported frotteuristic acts (i.e., attempted touching or rubbing against a woman in a sexual manner in crowds) were found in a sample of undergraduate college students (Lussier & Piché, 2008; Templeman & Stinnett, 1991). Other studies revealed a much wider range for frotteuristic behavior. Johnson et al. (2014) reviewed four community studies on frotteurism and found the prevalence rates ranging from 7.9–35%. Prevalence studies that involve self-report have the potential to underestimate the frequency as many individuals may be motivated to under-report their engagement in sexually deviant behavior (Abel et al., 1987, Bader et al., 2008; Bhugra et al., 2010).

Despite the APA (2013) considering frotteuristic acts to be one of the more common paraphilias; there is sparse empirical research on the topic. Much of the scientific literature on this paraphilia is derived from single case studies (e.g., Allen, 1969; Bezeau et al., 2004; Fedoroff, 2003; Horley, 2001; Magnan, 1890; Myers, 1991; Perilstein et al., 1991). The existing research on the prevalence of Frotteuristic Disorder is sparse, methodologically inconsistent and limited by small sample sizes that are not nationally representative (Johnson et al., 2014). Additionally, many studies use different definitions of frotteurism or frotteuristic acts, thus limiting the generalizability of existing research (Lussier & Piché, 2008).

11.4.3 Frequency

To combat the underestimations that can result from self-report studies, many researchers rely on data from official police reports or information garnered from perpetrators mandated to receive treatment in order to estimate the frequency of the behaviors. This data has revealed that not only do perpetrators often have a high rate of engaging in frotteuristic acts, but that each perpetrator has offended against many victims (Abel & Rouleau, 1990; APA, 2000; Kafka & Hennen, 1999; Langstrom & Seto, 2006). There are methodological issues when determining the frequency of frotteurism as some studies report means, whereas others use medians in their results, and they are subject to recall bias. Given that the behavior is not normally distributed, this can result in skewed results (Lussier & Piché, 2008). For example, Abel et al. (1987) examined a sample of frotteurs ($n = 62$) and found a mean of 849 frotteuristic acts, but a median of 29. Consequently, similar to the other paraphilias, it is difficult to accurately assess the frequency of frotteuristic behavior.

11.4.4 Age of Onset

Like other facets of this paraphilia, there is debate about the age of onset. Abel et al. (1993) used retrospective data from 1025 patients with paraphilias in U.S. outpatient clinics and found that the average age of onset for acts of frotteurism was 20 years old ($n = 87$). Another study found that frotteurism/toucherism started at much younger age (11.7 years) (Zolondek et al., 2001). Other researchers report the age of onset ranges between 15 and 25 years old, (Anil, 2009; Ahuja, 2001; Bhatia et al., 2010; Vernon & Geverth, 2010) and postulate that acts of frotteurism decline after age 25 (Anil, 2009; Hyde & DeLamater, 2003). The general consensus for age of onset for frotteuristic acts is adolescence or emerging adulthood (APA, 2013; Guterman et al., 2011; Hyde & DeLamater, 2003).

11.4.5 Scope of the Problem

Although frotteurism is a poorly understood disorder, frotteuristic acts are a common occurrence within the general population that often go unnoticed or are overlooked as accidental bumps in crowded areas (Guterman et al., 2011; Patra et al., 2013). One explanation for the paucity of research in this area is the longstanding view that like exhibitionistic behavior, frotteuristic acts are nuisance behaviors and the limited available enforcement resources are instead directed towards sex crimes involving violence (Krueger & Kaplan, 2008).

Krueger and Kaplan (1997) put forth three general characteristics of individuals who engage in frotteuristic acts. First, individuals who engage in frotteuristic acts have many victims due to the anonymous and crowded context through which they commit unwanted sexual touching (Krueger & Kaplan, 2008; Ranger & Fedoroff, 2015). Second, individuals who engage in frotteuristic acts are rarely arrested, which may be due to a variety of factors (e.g., victims being unaware that they were victimized, victims unsure their complaint will be taken seriously by police). Lastly, even if convicted of frotteuristic behavior, individuals are unlikely to serve long sentences (Horley, 2001).

Typically, individuals who wish to engage in frotteuristic acts go to crowded venues (e.g., elevators, shopping malls, public transportation, busy sidewalks, events/festivals, nightclubs, etc.) to seek out unsuspecting targets (Adams & McAnulty, 1993; Fedoroff, 2003; Guterman et al., 2011; Patra et al., 2013; Ranger & Fedoroff, 2015). The situational context allows the frotteur to come into close physical contact with the target and act upon their sexual urges anonymously under the guise of moving through a crowded area (Lussier & Piché, 2008; Patra et al., 2013 Ranger & Fedoroff, 2015). Further, frotteurs choose these locales because they can easily escape into the crowd and minimize their chances of detection (Clark et al., 2016). To gain a better understanding of unwanted sexual touch that frequently happens to women, inventors created a 'smart dress' embedded with sensors to detect touch. Three women wore the smart dress to a nightclub in Brazil and data from the smart dress was transferred onto a computer to show the areas of the dress where unwanted touching occurred (Dickson, 2018). The smart dress revealed that men touched the women on their arms, back, and bottom. The women spent approximately four hours at the club and were collectively groped a total of 157 times (Dickson, 2018).

Unfortunately, frotteuristic acts have become so commonplace, that people who live in urban areas and regularly rely on public transportation may experience unwanted sexual contact as a daily occurrence which has the potential to desensitize victims and may result in less reporting to authorities (Clark et al., 2016). As such, frotteuristic acts are seldom reported to law enforcement (Guterman, et al., 2011). If reported to the authorities, frotteuristic acts are notoriously difficult to prosecute, since the crowded circumstances make finding witnesses difficult (Guterman et al., 2011; Krueger & Kaplan, 2008). Another obstacle for prosecution is proving the physical contact was intentional rather than accidental. Clark et al. (2016) found that more than three out of every four frotteuristic acts took place on a subway train or platform. In alignment with this research, the New York subway system (MTA) has reported that the most prevalent sex crime is forcible touching (McAnulty, 2017; Ryley & Donohue, 2014). The widespread phenomena of unwanted sexual contact on public transportation has led to the coining of terms such as "transit grinder" or "subway groper" (Bayone, 2010). The increase in frotteuristic acts in major cities such as Tokyo, Mexico City, and Rio de Janeiro has resulted in the creation of women-only passenger cars (Beech & Harkins, 2012; Guterman et al., 2011).

11.5 Part II

The second part of this chapter will cover Voyeuristic, Exhibitionistic, and Frotteuristic Disorders together due to the overlap between the disorders and the dearth of research differentiating these paraphilias. This section will broadly discuss comorbidity, differential diagnosis, etiological theories, clinical assessment, and interventions for all three paraphilias in tandem and will conclude with recommendations for future research.

11.5.1 Comorbidity

Known comorbidities for Voyeuristic, Exhibitionistic, and Frotteuristic Disorders are primarily based upon research derived from individuals convicted of sexually deviant behavior associated with their respective paraphilia. Therefore, these comorbid conditions may not be applicable to all individuals who are diagnosed with a paraphilic disorder (APA, 2013). Disorders and symptoms that often co-occur with Voyeuristic, Exhibitionistic, and Frotteuristic Disorder include depressive disorders, bipolar disorder, anxiety, substance use disorders, and antisocial personality disorder (APA, 2013). Attention-deficit/hyperactivity disorder has been found to be comorbid with Voyeuristic and Exhibitionistic Disorders, whereas conduct disorder has been found to be comorbid with Voyeuristic and Frotteuristic Disorders (APA, 2013).

Voyeuristic, Exhibitionistic, and Frotteuristic Disorders are highly comorbid with one another as well as with other sexual paraphilias (Abel & Rouleau, 1990; APA, 2013; Långström & Zucker, 2005; Price et al., 2002; Rye & Meaney, 2007). For example, a study of 241 individuals with exhibitionism found that 32% also engaged in voyeurism and 30% engaged in frotteurism (Bader et al., 2008; Freund, 1990). Hypersexuality is also cited as a comorbidity for Voyeuristic, Exhibitionistic, and Frotteuristic Disorders (APA, 2013; Kafka, 2010). Given the high rates of paraphilic comorbidity and comorbidity with hypersexuality, researchers favor the Courtship Disorder Hypothesis (see etiological theories below) to explain the high rates of overlap amongst paraphilias (McAnulty, 2017).

11.5.2 Differential Diagnosis

When making a diagnosis, other disorders that have similar or overlapping characteristics must be ruled out. Voyeuristic, Exhibitionistic, and Frotteuristic Disorders have symptoms or diagnostic criteria that overlap with certain other disorders that must be ruled out before a definitive diagnosis can be reached. For example, conduct disorder in adolescents and antisocial personality disorder in adults are both characterized by various law and norm-breaking behaviors; however, the specific interest in voyeuristic, exhibitionistic, or frotteuristic acts would be absent (APA, 2013). Similarly, individuals who are intoxicated or under the influence of substances may engage in a single voyeuristic, exhibitionistic, or frotteuristic act; however, when they are not under the influence of substances, it is unlikely they would be interested in engaging in paraphilic behavior (APA, 2013; (McAnulty, 2017; Patra et al., 2013).

Autism Spectrum Disorder (ASD) is a neurodevelopmental disorder in which adolescents have normal sexual desires and may engage in exhibitionistic acts. Such behaviors are likely to occur when the individual fails to distinguish appropriate from inappropriate behavior, specifically with regard to disrobing in public (Beddows & Brooks, 2016). It is normal for adolescents with ASD to have sexual curiosity; however, the inappropriate sexual behaviors may occur due to a variety of factors (e.g., sensory issues, social problems, puberty, severity of symptoms, differentiation of relationships, etc.; Beddows & Brooks, 2016). If the individual meets criteria for ASD and displays exhibitionistic acts, the individual would not meet criteria for Exhibitionistic Disorder as the inappropriate sexual behavior is a consequence of ASD and may be corrected through education and social skill development (Beddows & Brooks, 2016).

When assessing for Frotteuristic Disorder specifically, mental health professionals should rule out Bipolar I Disorder. During a manic episode, the individual has lower inhibition and less impulse control, which may leave the person at a greater likelihood of engaging in frotteuristic acts; however, such sexually deviant behavior should not be seen when the individual has returned to baseline or a depressive state (McAnulty, 2017). Similarly, those with traumatic brain injury (TBI) or neurological impairment may also engage in frotteuristic behaviors; however, researchers have pointed to neurological impairments being responsible for more widespread patterns of disinhibition rather than for frotteuristic behavior alone (Cannas et al., 2006; McAnulty, 2017; Simpson et al., 1999; Solla et al., 2015). Simpson et al. (1999) completed a retrospective file review of adults with TBI ($n = 445$) and found that 29 males engaged in at least one sexually aberrant behavior (i.e., exhibitionism, frotteurism/toucherism, or sexual assault) with the most common behavior being frottuerism/toucherism, accounting for over 64% of all inappropriate sexual behaviors (Lussier & Piché 2008; Simpson et al., 1999).

11.6 Etiological Theories

A comprehensive etiological theory for Voyeuristic, Exhibitionistic, or Frotteuristic Disorders does not exist, rather various theories have been offered as potential etiological pathways. Despite the dearth of literature on developmental pathways, this section will review popular theories including: courtship disorder hypothesis, psychoanalytic theory, evolutionary theory, social incompetence theory, behavioral and social learning theories, sex drive hypothesis, and physiological approaches as applicable to each paraphilia.

11.6.1 Courtship Disorder Hypothesis

Famous for his book, *Psychopathia Sexualis*, which translates into "Psychopathy of Sex", Austro-German psychiatrist, Richard von Krafft-Ebing, often used the terms perversion and deviancy in his case studies (Krafft-Ebing, 1906). To move toward less pejorative terminology, he later began using the term paraphilia. The Greek translation for the prefix *para* meaning beside or around, implying "missing the mark" and *philia* meaning love (Malin & Saleh, 2007). This translation of missing the mark for love as a cause for paraphilic behaviors is aptly captured by the Courtship Disorder Hypothesis.

According to the Courtship Disorder Hypothesis, the highly comorbid nature of sexual paraphilias can be explained because these acts are part of a larger sequence of deviant sexual behaviors mimicking normal courtship behaviors (Freund, 1990; Hopkins et al., 2016). A typical relationship begins with visually selecting a partner, followed by nonphysical interactions, leading to physical touching, culminating with sexual intercourse (Freund & Watson, 1990). Voyeuristic behaviors are the deviation from the normal courtship behavior of visually selecting a partner. Exhibitionistic acts are the deviation from the nonphysical stage. Frotteurism or toucherism are deviant modifications of the touching stage with rape representing the last nonconsensual stage of the Courtship Disorder Hypothesis (Clark et al., 2016; Freund, 1990; Freund & Watson, 1990; Hopkins et al., 2016; Kaylor & Jeglic, 2019a). Each of the paraphilic acts deviates from the normal relationship template in that it is pathological rather than conducive to the development of a consensual sexual relationship (Freund & Watson, 1990; Hopkins, et al., 2016). The highly comorbid nature of these paraphilias may be better conceptualized under the Courtship Disorder Hypothesis in that voyeurism, exhibitionism, frotteurism/toucherism, and rape are all progressive expressions of the same disorder (Freund & Watson, 1990; Kaylor & Jeglic, 2019a). Freund and Watson (1990) studied heterosexual males (N = 1572) including sex offenders (n = 1198) and individuals with no charges but who had requested counseling for an "anomalous erotic preference" (n = 374) seen at a psychiatric teaching hospital. The researchers found that the preferential rape pattern co-occurred with voyeurism, exhibitionism, and frotteurism/toucherism to a higher degree than other paraphilic behaviors. However, these results should be interpreted with caution as the authors note the large number of statistical comparisons was at significance level ($p < 0.01$) which may have led to spurious results and was not as rigorous as $p < 0.001$ (Freund & Watson, 1990).

11.6.2 Psychoanalytic Theory

According to Sigmund Freud's psychoanalytic theory of sexual development, all children go through a series of normal libidinal developmental stages (oral, anal, phallic, latency, and genital stages; Lantz & Ray, 2020). In the case of Voyeuristic Disorder, it is thought that the child experiences an internal conflict that they wish to resolve (Freund & Blanchard, 1986). Freud believed it was inevitable that a child would likely see their parents engaging in intercourse or their mother disrobing, which would create a threat of castration for the child (Metzl, 2004). As an attempt to resolve their castration anxiety, the individual watches others to distract from this fear. Psychoanalytic theory also posits the voyeur has a lack of control over their sexual behaviors which leads to a willingness to engage in risky sexual behavior despite the potential of being punished, as well as an inability to appreciate the gravity of getting caught (Meyer, 1995; Rye & Meaney, 2007).

Similarly, psychoanalytic theory posits that Exhibitionistic Disorder also stems from castration anxiety. By exposing one's genitals to others and receiving a response from the victim, the exhibitionist confirms that his penis exists and he has not been castrated (Blair & Lanyon, 1981; Enelow, 1969; Fenichel, 1964; Freud 1905, 1914; Holtzman & Kulish, 2012; Rosen, 1964). In the case of female exhibitionists, the exposure of breasts is viewed as a defense against the narcissistic wound from castration, effectively distracting the female exhibitionist from her lack of penis (Blair & Lanyon, 1981; Freud 1905, 1914; Holtzman & Kulish, 2012). Frotteuristic Disorder is not addressed in psychoanalytic theory.

11.6.3 Evolutionary Theory

From a Darwinian perspective, all sexual behavior is for reproductive purposes in that sexual interests underlying sexual behavior have been shaped over time by their reproductive success (Quinsey, 2012). However, it is unclear how those who surprise their victims with exhibitionistic acts and who covertly watch others through voyeuristic acts contribute to furthering their reproductive success. There is a dearth of literature on how evolutionary theory applies to Exhibitionistic Disorder. Some researchers have equated acts of exhibitionism to that of animal courtship; however, Mester (1984) argues that viewing exhibitionistic acts as a way for males to advertise their sexuality is a misinterpretation of the theory.

According to evolutionary theory, voyeuristic behavior stems from inane curiosity, which is a critical piece of the normative sexual experience. Researchers believe voyeuristic behavior is an extension of the evolutionary process of visually selecting a mate for reproductive purposes (Hopkins, et al. 2016; Kaplan & Krueger, 1997). Voyeuristic Disorder occurs in a higher proportion of males and as such evolution may be contributing towards men's proclivity to engage in this behavior as a means of eventual mating and reproduction (Buss 1998; Rye & Meaney, 2007). There is a lack of literature detailing how evolutionary theory may explain Frotteuristic Disorder.

11.6.4 Social Incompetence Hypothesis

The social incompetence hypothesis presumes individuals have social deficits that prevent them from forming consensual sexual relationships (McAnulty, 2017). Debate exists among researchers as to why an individual may be unable to form consensual relationships, but theories include developmental disabilities (Fedoroff, 2003), social anxiety (Brockman & Bluglass, 1996), poor social skills, self-esteem disturbances (Lee et al., 2001) and heterosocial inadequacy (Krafft-Ebing, 1906). There is a lack of research regarding how the social incompetence hypothesis may apply to acts of exhibitionism; however, some researchers believe that indecent exposure may be a reaction to rejection (Dietz et al., 1986) or a form of desire for interpersonal interaction (Lang et al., 1987).

Individuals who are socially incompetent tend to be shy and have difficulties interacting with others, especially members of the opposite sex. Moreover, social relationships may be avoided as they believe them to be confusing and unpredictable (Morrell et al., 2001). Despite the lack of literature on social incompetence theory of Voyeuristic Disorder, it could be speculated that viewing members of the opposite sex disrobing or engaging in sexual activity feels safer compared to socially interacting and developing a consensual sexual relationship with the victim.

This hypothesis has not been studied with a sample of individuals with Frotteuristic Disorder; however, it has been tested with other sexual paraphilias, such as pedophilia. Evidence from those studies showed that some people who engage in paraphilic acts have social skills deficits, insecure attachments, and loneliness (Marshall, 1989; Seto, 2004). O'Donohue and colleagues (1997) propose that acts of frotteurism allow for immediate sexual gratification with little cost, effort, or investment. Engaging in frotteuristic acts also allows the individual to protect themselves from being rejected by a potential partner. Another protective measure may be that those who engage in frotteurism select victims who are least likely to report the crime to avoid being apprehended (e.g., children, adolescents; Lussier & Piché, 2008).

11.6.5 Behavioral and Social Learning Theory

Learning theories focus on how people respond to events or stimuli. Behavioral learning theory encompasses operant conditioning which describes why humans repeat behaviors that benefit them (Staddon & Cerutti, 2003). Social learning theory builds upon this foundation by adding that behaviors are learned through observation (McLeod, 2016). Social learning theory posits that voyeuristic behaviors are learned through operant and classical conditioning as well as modeling. Operant conditioning occurs when viewing a person disrobing or engaging in sexual behavior is rewarded with sexual arousal (Rye & Meaney, 2007). One might be inhibited to engage in voyeuristic acts due to social controls which can serve as punishment or negative reinforcement. Bandura (1969) hypothesized that individuals will engage in voyeuristic acts when: (1) there is an opportunity; (2) previous voyeuristic acts have been rewarded; and (3) the benefits of engaging in voyeuristic behaviors outweigh the cost of potential punishment (Rye & Meaney, 2007).

Supporters of the behavioral theory of conditioning believe that individuals who engage in exhibitionistic acts first begin to engage in this behavior due to random chance when at an early age the person exposed their genitals to another person and found this experience to be pleasurable and sexually arousing (Bandura, 1982; Kinsey et al., 1953, 1955). Since this act was sexually stimulating, the behavior was reinforced. Three key events are thought to initiate the conditioning process: sharing a bathtub with other children when they are young, children looking at one another's genitals during early sex play, and appearing nude before family members (Swindell et al., 2011). Moreover, Bandura (1986) pointed to the experience of a post-pubertal male becoming sexually aroused by seeing his mother naked as a form of the mother engaging in an exhibitionistic act. This experience incorrectly has the post-pubertal male concluding that if he exposes himself to others, they too will become sexually stimulated (Swindell et al., 2011).

Similar to the social incompetence hypothesis, experts believe the Frotteuristic Disorder may develop initially from a random or accidental touch of another person's genitals. This accidental touch is sexually arousing for the individual which serves to reinforce and perpetuate continued touching of others without consent (Patra et al., 2013).

11.6.6 Sex Drive Hypothesis

The sex drive hypothesis suggests that some individuals have unusually high sex drives, also known as hypersexuality. Individuals with hypersexuality may have an increased libido, compulsively watch pornography, or masturbate excessively (Béreau, 2018). Researchers posit that individuals with hypersexuality may use sex to compensate for unfulfilled needs (Bancroft & Vukadinovic, 2004; Cortoni & Marshall, 2001). As such, individuals with hypersexuality may find impersonal sexual encounters especially desirable. Pulling from the literature on social incompetence theory, individuals who lack the social skills necessary to form a relationship may be especially prone to act on hypersexual impulses (McAnulty, 2017). Kafka (2010) considers hypersexuality to be a defining facet in many paraphilias. Långström and Hanson (2006) found an association between hypersexuality and engaging in paraphilic behaviors (i.e., exhibitionism and voyeurism) in a nonclinical Swedish sample. Over 2,000 Swedish adult men and women completed interviews and questionnaires on various sexual behaviors. The results revealed a strong association between rates of impersonal sex and the paraphilic interests of exhibitionism, voyeurism, and masochism/sadism (Långström and Hanson, 2006). Since those with hypersexuality may watch pornography excessively, engaging in voyeuristic acts may provide an even more thrilling experience as the target of their viewing is unsuspecting. With regard to Exhibitionistic Disorder, one could argue hypersexuality coupled with lack of awareness for socially appropriate boundaries may lead a person to act on exhibitionistic urges. A similar argument could be made for Frotteuristic Disorder, despite the lack of research on its relationship to hypersexuality (McAnulty, 2017).

11.6.7 Biological Theory

Physiological theories suggest chemical changes or structural damage in the brain can reduce one's control over their sexual behaviors (Duff, 2018). With regard to voyeuristic acts, a person is more likely to act on natural curiosity as the neurological changes in the brain make it more difficult to repress inappropriate sexual urges (Duff, 2018). Neuroscientists posit that exhibitionistic acts can be a result of excessive neuronal discharges in the subcortical areas of the brain, specifically within the limbic system (Blair & Lanyon, 1981; Monroe, 1976). Excessive neuronal discharges can be responsible for an individual impulsively acting upon deviant sexual urges (Monroe, 1976). There is some evidence that individuals who engage in Frotteuristic Disorder have low levels of serotonin, which is linked to high sexual arousal, impulsivity, and thrill seeking (Joyal & Ankfold, 2017). Testosterone, which is associated with aggressiveness and sex drive, interacts with the available serotonin. When low serotonin is paired with high levels of testosterone it may explain why men have a greater likelihood of developing a paraphilia compared to women (Joyal & Ankfold, 2017).

11.7 Clinical Assessment

There is no standard assessment battery for diagnosing Voyeuristic, Exhibitionistic, or Frotteuristic Disorder (Krueger & Kaplan, 2008). When assessing for paraphilic acts and disorders, a comprehensive clinical interview is currently considered the gold standard (See Table 11.1). Historically, evaluators have used assessment batteries created for contact sex offenders and applied them to paraphilic disorders. Experts have recommended that a comprehensive clinical interview for assessing and diagnosing paraphilic disorders should be comprised of psychological, behavioral, legal, medical, and sexual/paraphilic components (Adams & Sturgis, 1977; Adams et al., 1980; Barlow, 1977; Blair & Lanyon, 1981). Interviews with the individual as well as self-report measures rely heavily on honest self-disclosure (Krueger & Kaplan, 2008) and individuals who have been charged with a sexual offense may be motivated to minimize or deny certain aspects of their behavior (Schneider & Wright, 2004; Seto, 2004). To combat this problem, assessors should review any available records (i.e., arrest reports, victim statements, witness statements, legal history, etc.) prior to conducting the interview (Krueger & Kaplan, 2008; Risen, 1995). Another method of assessing truthfulness is the use of a polygraph (Konopasek, 2015). Although polygraphs are used in many sex offender treatment programs (McGrath et al., 2010), there is limited research examining the utility and validity of the polygraph during an assessment for Voyeuristic, Exhibitionistic, or Frotteuristic Disorders (McAnulty, 2017; Rosky, 2013).

Best practice dictates that certain strategies are utilized by clinicians when conducting psychosexual evaluations with individuals with possible paraphilic diagnoses. Since an interviewee may feel embarrassed about the sexual nature of the interview questions, it is recommended that the clinical interview begin with gathering general information from the client to establish rapport (Krueger & Kaplan,

Table 11.1 Comprehensive clinical interview topics and preparation

• Record review (i.e., arrest reports, victim statements, witness statements, legal history, etc.)
• Establish rapport
• Demographic and developmental history
• Typical and atypical sexual behaviors
• Range of other paraphilic behaviors
• Sexual preferences, attitudes, fantasies, and dysfunction
• Ability to self-regulate sexual behaviors
• Location of paraphilic acts, why location was chosen, level of activity/foot traffic, and types of people who frequent that location
• Behavioral plan when acting on paraphilic urge
• Level of intrusiveness for paraphilic act
• Number of paraphilic acts and frequency of acts (e.g., day, week, month)
• Number of victims and frequency of reoffending against the same victim
• Frequency of masturbation fantasies
• Precursors that led to sexually deviant behavior
• Rape fantasies or escalation behaviors to more aggressive sexual acts
• Previous treatment or pharmacological approaches, adherence, and degree to which it reduced paraphilic behaviors or fantasies
• Examination of lesser-telling charges (e.g., misdemeanor harassment)
• Comprehensive psychological history (e.g., substance use, prior mental health conditions)
• Neurological conditions, head injuries, and medications

2008). The assessor is encouraged to create a non-judgmental environment to gather as much information as possible, especially when inquiring about typical and atypical sexual behavior. Thus, it is recommended that caution should be used with specific language (e.g., sexually deviant) and that the assessor should choose their words carefully to maximize participation and engagement with the interviewee (McAnulty et al., 2001). Further, the assessor should begin by asking questions about normal sexual behavior, then gradually move onto questions about deviant sexual behavior (Lussier & Piché, 2008). As exemplified in the Courtship Disorder Hypothesis, various paraphilic behaviors may potentially overlap, thus it is advised that the assessor inquire about a range of paraphilic behaviors (McAnulty et al., 2001). Topics to be included in the interview should include (but are not limited to) sexual preference, attitudes, fantasies, sexual dysfunction, masturbation patterns, frequency of behaviors, and ability to self-regulate sexual behaviors.

Specific details about the nature of the paraphilic behaviors should be obtained to understand the quality and quantity of the behaviors. Quality refers to location of paraphilic acts, behavioral plan, fantasies, and level of intrusiveness (e.g., masturbation during exhibitionistic act, use of hands or penis during frotteuristic act; Lussier & Piché, 2008). The assessor is encouraged to gain an understanding of why the interviewee chose a specific location to engage in a paraphilic act. This discussion may include the use of a map and specific questions about the level of activity or foot traffic in that area (e.g., a very crowded area lends itself to undetected frotteuristic acts, areas with little foot traffic lends itself to exhibitionistic acts) and types of people who frequent the area. Quantity refers to the number of paraphilic acts, frequency of such acts over a period of time (e.g., day, week, month), number of victims, frequency of reoffending against same victim, and frequency of masturbation fantasies (Lussier & Piché, 2008).

A comprehensive clinical interview will also include questions about precursors that lead to the sexually deviant behaviors as well as escalation to more aggressive sexual acts (Lussier & Piché, 2008). It is crucial that the evaluator inquire about acts or fantasies involving rape behaviors (i.e., attempts, date rape, etc.) as this may be an indicator of possible escalation. If the interviewee has engaged in individual or group treatment, the assessor should inquire about adherence to treatment and medications. If medications were used, information should be gathered on the degree to which pharmacological methods were able to control paraphilic behavior and fantasies (Lussier & Piché, 2008).

Interviewees may deny engaging in paraphilic behaviors, however an effective indicator of a history of paraphilic acts is a record of two or more allegations of such behaviors. It should be noted that the absence of a criminal record does not exculpate the interviewee as some behaviors are more covert (e.g., voyeuristic acts) and may not have been detected by the victim or behaviors may have been plea bargained to a less-telling charge (e.g., misdemeanor harassment; McAnulty, 2017; McAnulty et al., 2001). If the offender has multiple arrests and convictions for a paraphilic act spanning more than six months, this information supports the diagnosis of a paraphilic disorder (Krueger & Kaplan, 2008).

There is a high likelihood that there will be comorbid psychiatric conditions among individuals who commit sexually deviant acts, thus the assessor must also obtain a comprehensive psychological history (Kafka & Hennen, 2002; Krueger & Kaplan, 2008; Raymond et al., 1999, 2003). As outlined in the differential diagnosis section, it is important to tease apart other possible mental health conditions that may influence future offending (e.g., substance use, conduct disorder, psychopathy, etc.; Kafka & Hennen, 2002). Similarly, some neuropsychiatric conditions have been associated with paraphilic acts such as Autism Spectrum Disorder, Parkinson's Disease, temporal lobe epilepsy, brain tumors, and disturbances in the limbic system (Beddows & Brooks, 2016; Langevin, 1992; Solla et al., 2015). Thus, the evaluator should inquire about head injuries, medications, and neurological symptoms as these may be connected to paraphilic behavior (Krueger & Kaplan, 2008).

Although there are no validated assessment tools for diagnosing Voyeuristic, Exhibitionistic, or Frotteuristic Disorders the following measures have been used with mixed results: Abel Assessment for Sexual Interests (Abel, 1995), Bancroft Sexual Interest and Activity Scale (Bancroft et al., 1974), Clark Sex History Questionnaire for Males (Langevin et al., 1985; Paitich et al., 1977), Clinical Global Impressions Scale (Guy, 1976), Coleman Compulsive Sexual Behavior Inventory (Coleman et al., 2001), Millon Clinical Multiaxial Inventory – III (Millon, 1992), Minnesota Multiphasic Personality Inventory – 2 (Butcher et al., 2001), Multiphasic Sex Inventory – II (Nicholas & Molinder, 1984), Psychopathy Checklist – Revised (Hare, 2003), and Yale—Brown Obsessive Compulsive Scale Modified for Compulsive Sexual Behavior (Wainberg et al., 2006). Evaluators often use assessment tools designed for contact sex offender to assess paraphilic offenders.

Another measurement tool frequently utilized with sexual offenders is the penile plethysmograph (PPG). A PPG measures penile physiology of sexual arousal during audio and visual stimuli (Wilson & Miner, 2016). There is no standardized set of audio descriptions or visual images that accompany the PPG (McAnulty, 2017). As such the psychometric properties of this tool cannot be determined (Murphy et al., 2015) and researchers have cautioned against its use for diagnostic and assessment purposes (Prentky et al., 2010), especially for diagnostic use with paraphilias (Kalmus & Beech, 2005; Marshall, 2014). Some researchers have developed customized stimuli to measure arousal to various paraphilias; however, these have not been normed or validated (Krueger & Kaplan, 2008).

11.8 Clinical Interventions

To date, there are no manualized treatments designed to treat individuals diagnosed with Voyeuristic, Exhibitionistic, or Frotteuristic Disorders. The most common interventions for paraphilias are cognitive and behavioral therapies and pharmacological treatment (McAnulty, 2017). Existing literature on the effectiveness of treating paraphilias has yielded mixed results (Krueger & Kaplan, 2008). The research examining the effectiveness of treatment for sexual paraphilias has historically been limited by small sample sizes, lack of standardized operational definitions, lack of control groups, and short or no follow-up periods (McManus et al., 2013).

Many individuals who engage in paraphilic behaviors often do not voluntarily seek professional help (APA, 2000; Malin & Saleh, 2007). Individuals who do engage in treatment are typically mandated to do so through a court order (Guterman et al., 2011). Some obstacles mental health professionals may face when treating individuals who engage in paraphilic behavior are resistance, denial, rationalization, and minimization (Hyde & DeLamater, 2003; Seligman & Hardenburg, 2000).

11.8.1 Therapeutic Techniques

One of the most commonly used treatments for those who are diagnosed with paraphilic disorders is cognitive behavioral therapy (CBT). CBT focuses on how thoughts can create and maintain dysfunctional behaviors and feelings (Guterman et al., 2011). CBT relies on the client to be reflective and become self-aware of the underlying motivations to engage in the sexually deviant behavior. This may be particularly difficult for many individuals who engage in paraphilic acts because they report that they feel as though they are forced to act on impulses outside of their control (Chopin-Marcé, 2001). While there is no CBT protocol for the treatment of paraphilic acts, there have been some adaptations of CBT designed for individuals who sexually abuse children that are utilized with individuals who engage in frotteuristic acts (Abel et al., 1984). For example, a mental health professional can challenge deviant frotteuristic thoughts and facilitate increased empathy for the victim (Krueger & Kaplan, 2008). The success of CBT largely depends upon the client's motivation and engagement in treatment (Chopin-Marcé, 2001).

While individual therapy can be tailored to meet the unique needs of the client, many sex offender programs rely on CBT-based group treatment format. A group format can reach a wider group of clients and allow for interaction and support among and between group members, while at the same time challenging dysfunctional thinking and confronting denial. Group sessions can take the form of psychoeducation, skill building, or processing. Group treatments that focus on social skills and self-esteem have been used for individuals who engage in paraphilic behaviors (Krueger & Kaplan, 2008). Social incompetence hypothesis posits that individuals engage in paraphilic acts because there is a deficit in the ability to form a consensual sexual relationship (McAnulty, 2017). For example, individuals who engage in exhibitionistic acts typically have poor interpersonal boundaries as reflected by their exposure behaviors as well as deficits in reading social cues (Morin & Levenson, 2008). As such, social skills training in either the individual or group modality can target inappropriate behaviors and educate clients on healthy boundaries and interpersonal communication. However, it is possible that due to the shame or stigma associated with sexually deviant behavior, these individuals may not be open to addressing this behavior in a group setting.

11.8.2 Behavioral Techniques

Mental health professionals may use behavioral techniques that use learning principles to replace deviant sexual interests with appropriate thoughts (Beech & Harkin, 2012). A treatment used specifically with individuals who engage in exhibitionistic acts is aversion therapy. Ammonia aversion acts as a positive punishment in which the inhalation of ammonia fumes create a pain-mediated response (Barker, 2001). This treatment entails the client carrying a small bottle of smelling salts and when the urge to expose oneself arises the individual is to inhale the ammonia mixture. While inhaling the client is to replace the offense-related thoughts with prosocial thoughts (Marshall, 2006). This treatment relies heavily on the client to diligently use the ammonia mixture, if the client is inconsistent, the exhibitionistic urges may return. It is important to note, aversion therapy is primarily based on case studies and there is no evidence demonstrating its overall efficacy at curbing exhibitionistic behavior (Marshall, 2006).

11.8.3 Pharmacological Treatments

Despite the lack of evidence-based therapeutic interventions to treat those with paraphilic disorders, there is some evidence to support the use of pharmacological methods. Researchers have recommended antidepressant medication, specifically selective serotonin reuptake inhibitors (SSRIs), for individuals who engage in paraphilic acts that have a compulsive quality (Kafka, 2003a, b; McAnulty, 2017). SSRIs are particularly useful for clients who also have depression or obsessive-compulsive disorder (Krueger & Kaplan, 2008). There is evidence that individuals who engage in frotteuristic acts respond well specifically to the SSRI, fluoxetine (Guterman et al., 2011; Perilstein et al., 1991).

There is very little published literature on the pharmacological treatment of voyeuristic behavior and as such there is little evidence supporting any particular treatment approach (Hanson & Harris, 1997). Abouesh and Clayton (1999) published a case study using paroxetine with an individual who had Voyeuristic Disorder with compulsive tendencies. The client reported an improvement in their ability to control their sexual impulses, followed by a reduction in the intensity and frequency of urges to engage in voyeurism.

Other pharmacological approaches have been tested with some success. Terao and Nakamura (2000) found low dose of trazadone, a serotonergic antidepressant, to reduce the impulse to expose one's genitals in a client with Exhibitionistic Disorder. Although trazadone was found to effective, trazadone has the potential to decrease sex drive, reduce libido, and cause erectile dysfunction, possibly resulting in client attrition (Terao & Nakamura, 2000).

11.8.3.1 Androgen-Reducing Agents

The use of androgen-reducing agents, such as gonadotropin-releasing hormone agonists, reduce sexual interest and performance and have shown some success in treating individuals with paraphilias, specifically those who engage in frotteuristic acts (Beech & Harkins, 2012; Krueger & Kaplan, 2008; Rosler & Witztum, 1998; Saleh et al., 2004). A significant side effect of androgen reduction therapy is the potential for osteopenia (thinning of the bones) and osteoporosis, and thus such treatments should be utilized with care (Gallagher & Rapuri, 2003; Krueger & Kaplan, 2008; O'Connell & Seaton, 2005).

Since many individuals who engage in paraphilic acts do not voluntarily seek treatment, the sparse outcome data relies on studies that are severely limited in various ways. While CBT based therapies have shown some promise, the success of treatment depends heavily on the client's engagement and motivation. Numerous pharmacological treatments have been used to treat paraphilias; however, many clients stop taking medication due to side effects that cause sexual dysfunction or physical problems. There is a great need for more controlled studies to evaluate therapeutic and pharmacological treatments for sexual paraphilias.

11.9 Conclusions and Future Directions

References to voyeuristic, exhibitionistic, and frotteuristic behaviors have existed for centuries; however, very little is still known about the prevalence, frequency, age of onset, scope, and etiology, assessment, and treatment of these disorders compared to other sexual paraphilias and rape. The lack of research knowledge about these paraphilias may be in part explained by the historical view that these acts were "nuisance behaviors" and as such were rarely reported to the authorities.

Without validated clinician administered or self-report measures for voyeuristic, exhibitionistic, and frotteuristic behaviors and their corresponding disorders the ability to gather adequate information about these disorders, their development, and their impact upon the perpetrator and their victims is limited. Consequently, knowledge about the relationship between paraphilic behaviors and possible escalation to more aggressive sexual acts is also limited. Without such validated measures our ability to accurately and consistently assess for their presence is constrained, which in turn has impacts the scope of established treatments.

What is clear is that in order to move forward and better understand these paraphilic disorders it is necessary first to establish a validated self-report measure. This would enable researchers to conduct large scale population-based studies to examine both the prevalence of voyeuristic, exhibitionistic, and frotteuristic behavior as well as their corresponding disorders in the general population. With this knowledge, those who endorse these behaviors and disorders could then be interviewed to better understand the etiological pathways to the development of each of the paraphilic disorders.

Once more information on the etiology of the disorder is obtained, then clinicians would be better able to understand the factors that led to the behaviors and develop interventions that could effectively address these paraphilic behaviors and disorders and conduct research to establish evidence-based treatments. Not only can the field of psychology benefit from a greater understanding of these paraphilic disorders, but additional research can aide in our ability to treat, manage, and potentially prevent recidivism and escalation to more egregious sexual offending.

References

Abel, G. G. (1995). The Abel assessment for sexual interest. *Adult sex offenders*, 1–23.

Abel, G. G., Becker, J. V., Cunningham-Rathner, J., Mittelman, M., & Rouleau, J. (1988). Multiple paraphilic diagnoses among sex offenders. *Bulletin of the American Academy of Psychiatry and the Law, 16*(2), 153–168.

Abel, G. G., Becker, J. V., Mittelman, M., Cunningham-Rathner, J., Rouleau, J. L.,& Murphy,W. D. (1987). Self-reported sex crimes of nonincarcerated paraphiliacs. Journal of Interpersonal Violence, 2, 3–25.

Abel, G. G., Becker, J. V., & Cunningham-Rathner, J. (1984). Complications, consent, and cognitions in sex between children and adults. *International journal of law and psychiatry.*

Abel, G. G., & Rouleau, J. L. (1990). The nature and extent of sexual assault. In W. L. Marshall, D. R. Laws, & H. E. Barbaree (Eds.), *Handbook of sexual assault: Issues, theories, and treatment of the offender* (pp. 9–21). Plenum.

Abel, G. G., Osborn, C. A., & Twigg, D. A. (1993). Sexual assault through the life span: Adult offenders with juvenile histories. In H. E. Barbaree,W. L. Marshall,&S.M. Hudson (Eds.), The juvenile sex offender (pp. 104–117). : Guilford Press.

Abouesh, A., & Clayton, A. (1999). Compulsive voyeurism and exhibitionism: A clinical response to paroxetine. *Archives of Sexual Behavior, 28*(1), 23–30.

Adams, H. E., & Sturgis, E. T. (1977). Status of behavioral reorientation techniques in the modification of homosexuality: A review. *Psychological Bulletin, 84*, 1171–1188.

Adams, H. E., Webster, J. S., & Carson, T. P. (1980). Appropriate behavioral assessment and modification of sexual deviation: A comment on "biosyntonic" therapy. *Journal of Consulting and Clinical Psychology, 48*, 106–108.

Adams, H. E., & McAnulty, R. D. (1993). Sexual disorders: The paraphilias. In Comprehensive handbook of psychopathology (pp. 563–579). Springer US.

Ahuja, N. (2001). *A short textbook of psychiatry* (4th ed., pp. 114–120). Jaypee Brothers.

Allen, C. (1969). *Atextbook of psychosexual disorders* (2nd ed.). Oxford University Press.

American Psychiatric Association. (1980). *Diagnostic and statistical manual of mental disorders* (3rd ed.). Author.

American Psychiatric Association. (2000). *Diagnostic and statistical manual of mental disorders* (4th ed., text rev. ed.). Author.

American Psychiatric Association. (2013). *Diagnostic and statistical manual of mental disorders* (5th ed.). Author.

Anil, A. (2009). *Forensic & medicolegal aspects of sexual crimes and unusual sexual practices* (pp. 183–184). CRC Press, Taylor & Francis Group, LLC.

Bader, S. M., Schoeneman-Morris, K. A., Scalora, M. J., & Casady, T. K. (2008). Exhibitionism: Findings from a Midwestern police contact sample. *International Journal of Offender Therapy and Comparative Criminology, 52*(3), 270–279.

Balon, R. (2016). Lack of clarity in the DSM-5 criteria of Voyeuristic Disorder. *Journal of Sex & Marital Therapy, 42*(5), 391.

Bancroft, J., & Vukadinovic, Z. (2004). Sexual addiction, sexual compulsivity, sexual impulsivity, or what? Toward a theoretical model. *Journal of Sex Research, 41*, 225–234.

Bancroft, J., Tennent, G., Loucas, K., & Cass, J. (1974). The control of deviant sexual behaviour by drugs: I. Behavioural changes following oestrogens and anti-androgens. *The British Journal of Psychiatry, 125*(586), 310–315.

Bandura, A. (1969). Principles of behavior modification.

Bandura, A. (1982). The psychology of chance encounters and life paths. *American Psychologist, 37*, 747–755.

Bandura, A. (1986). *Social foundations of thought and action, a social cognitive theory.* Prentice Hall.

Barlow, D. H. (1977). Assessment of sexual behavior. In R. A. Ciminero, K. S. Calhoun, & H. E. Adams (Eds.), *Handbook of behavioral assessment*. Wiley.

Barker, L. M. (2001). *Learning and behavior: Biological, psychological, and sociocultural perspectives* (3rd ed.). Prentice Hall.

Bayone, J. (2010, October 10). Crowded NYC subway not an excuse for groping. *Sandeep*. Retrieved from https://sandeep.journalism.cuny.edu/2010/10/15/crowded-nyc-subway-not-an-excuse/.

Beddows, N., & Brooks, R. (2016). Inappropriate sexual behaviour in adolescents with autism spectrum disorder: what education is recommended and why. *Early Intervention in Psychiatry, 10*(4), 282–289.

Beech, A. R., & Harkins, L. (2012). DSM-IV paraphilia: Descriptions, demographics and treatment interventions. *Aggression and Violent Behavior, 17*(6), 527–539.

Bell, V., Hemmens, C., & Steiner, B. (2006). Up skirts and down blouses: A statutory analysis of legislative responses to video voyeurism. *Criminal Justice Studies: A Critical Journal Of Crime, Law & Society, 19*(3), 301–314.

Béreau, M. (2018). Hypersexuality in neurological disorders: from disinhibition to impulsivity. In *Neurologic-psychiatric syndromes in focus-part I* (Vol. 41, pp. 71–76). Karger Publishers.

Bezeau, S. C., Bogod, N. M., & Mateer, C. A. (2004). Sexually intrusive behaviour following brain injury: Approaches to assessment and rehabilitation. *Brain Injury, 18*, 299–313.

Bhugra, D., Popelyuk, D., & McMullen, I. (2010). Paraphilias across cultures: Contexts and controversies. *Journal of Sex Research, 47*, 242–256.

Blair, C., & Lanyon, R. I. (1981). Exhibitionism: Etiology and treatment. *Psychological Bulletin, 89*, 439–463. https://doi.org/10.1037/0033-2909.89.3.439

Brockman, B., & Bluglass, R. (1996). A general psychiatric approach to sexual deviation. *Sexual Deviation, 3*, 1–42.

Brown, G. (2019). *Exhibitionism - Mental Health Disorders*. Retrieved July 27, 2020, from https://www.merckmanuals.com/home/mental-health-disorders/sexuality-and-sexual-disorders/exhibitionism

Buss, D. M. (1998). Sexual strategies theory: Historical origins and current status. *Journal of Sex Research, 35*, 19–31.

Butcher, J. N. (2001). *Minnesota Multiphasic Personality Inventory-2: Manual for administration, scoring, and interpretation*. University of Minnesota Press.

Cannas, A., Solla, P., Floris, G., Tacconi, P., Loi, D., Marcia, E., & Marrosu, M. G. (2006). Hypersexual behaviour, frotteurism and delusional jealousy in a young parkinsonian patient during dopaminergic therapy with pergolide: A rare case of iatrogenic paraphilia. *Progress in Neuro-Psychopharmacology and Biological Psychiatry, 30*(8), 1539–1541.

Chopin-Marcé, M. (2001). Exhibitionism and psychotherapy: A case study. *International Journal of Offender Therapy and Comparative Criminology, 45*(5), 626–633.

Clark, S. K., Jeglic, E. L., Calkins, C., & Tatar, J. R. (2016). More than a nuisance: The prevalence and consequences of frotteurism and exhibitionism. *Sexual Abuse, 28*(1), 3–19.

Coleman, M. M., Ohlerking, F., & Nancy Raymond, E. (2001). Compulsive Sexual Behavior Inventory: A preliminary study of reliability and validity. *Journal of sex & marital therapy, 27*(4), 325–332.

Cortoni, F., & Marshall, W. L. (2001). Sex as a coping strategy and its relationship to juvenile sexual history and intimacy in sexual offenders. *Sexual Abuse: A Journal of Research and Treatment, 13*, 27–43.

Cox, D. J. (1988). Incidence and nature of male genital exposure behavior as reported by college women. *Journal of Sex Research, 24*(1), 227–234.

Davis, S. K., & Davis, P. W. (1976). Meanings and process in erotic offensiveness: An expose of exposees. *Journal of Contemporary Ethnography, 5*, 377–396. https://doi.org/10.1177/089124167600500307

Dickson, E. J., (2018). A "Smart Dress" Proves What Women Already Know: Sexual Harassment Is A Problem, Vox., 29 November http://www.vox.com/the-goods/2018/11/29/18118402/ogilvy-schweppes-smart-dress-harassment

Dietz, P. E., Cox, D. J., Wegener, S., Curran, W. J., McGarry, A. L., & Shah, S. A. (1986). Male genital exhibitionism. *Forensic Psychiatry and Psychology*, 363–385.

Duff, S. (2018). *Voyeurism*. In *Voyeurism* (pp. 13–29). Palgrave Pivot.

Enelow, M. L. (1969). Public nuisance offenses: Exhibitionism, voyeurism and transvestism. In S. G. Kling (Ed.), *Sexual behavior and the law*. Pocket Books.

Fedoroff, J. P. (2003). Paraphilic worlds. In *Handbook of clinical sexuality for mental health professionals* (pp. 333–356). John Wiley & Sons, Inc.

Fenichel, O. (1964). On acting. *Psychoanalytic Quarterly, 15*, 144–160.

Firestone, P., Kingston, D. A., Wexler, A., & Bradford, J. M. (2006). Long-term follow up of exhibitionists: Psychological, phallometric, and offense characteristics. *Journal of the American Academy of Psychiatry and the Law, 34*, 349–359.

Freud, S. (1905). Three essays on sexuality. *SE, 7*, 130–243.

Freud, S. (1914). On narcissism: An introduction. *SE, 14*, 73–102.

Freund, K. (1990). Courtship disorders. In W. L. Marshall, D. R. Laws, & H. E. Barbaree (Eds.), *Handbook of sexual assault: Issues, theories, and treatment of the offender* (pp. 195–207). Plenum.

Freund, K., & Blanchard, R. (1986). The concept of courtship disorder. *Journal of Sex & Marital Therapy, 12*, 79–92.

Freund, K., & Watson, R. (1990). Mapping the boundaries of courtship disorder. *Journal of Sex Research, 27*, 589–606.

Freund, K., Watson, R., & Rienzo, D. (1988). The value of self-reports in the study of voyeurism and exhibitionism. *Sexual Abuse: A Journal of Research and Treatment, 1*(2), 244–262. https://doi.org/10.1177/107906328800100205

Freund, K., Seto, M. C., & Kuban, M. (1997). Frotteurism and the theory of courtship disorder. In D. R. Laws & W. T. O'Donohue (Eds.), *Sexual Devian ce: Theory, Assessment And Treatment* (pp. 111–130).

Gallagher, J. C., Rapuri, P. B., Haynatzki, G., & Detter, J. R. (2003). Effect of discontinuation of estrogen, calcitriol, and the combination of both on bone density and bone markers. *Alternative Medicine Review, 8*(1), 92–93.

Gebhard, P. H., Gagnon, J. H., Pomeroy, W. B., & Christenson, C. V. (1965). *Sex offenders: An analysis of types*. Heinemann.

Gittleson, N. L., Eacott, S. E., & Mehta, B. M. (1978). Victims of indecent exposure. *British Journal of Psychiatry, 132*, 61–66.

Grant, J. E. (2005). Clinical characteristics and psychiatric comorbidity in males with exhibitionism. *The Journal of Clinical Psychiatry, 66*(11), 1367–1371.

Geverth, V. J. (2010). *sex-related homicide & death investigation – Practical & clinical prospectives* (2nd ed., pp. 14–15). CRC Press, Taylor & Francis Group, LLC.

Guterman, J. T., Martin, C. V., & Rudes, J. (2011). A solution-focused approach to frotteurism. *Journal of Systemic Therapies, 30*(1), 59–72. https://doi.org/10.1521/jsyt.2011.30.1.59

Guy, W. (1976). Clinical global impressions scale. *Psychiatry*.

Hanafy, I., Clervoy, L., & Brenot, P. (2016). Exhibitionists, so much inhibition. *Sexologies: European Journal of Sexology And Sexual Health/Revue Européenne De Sexologie Et De Santé Sexuelle, 25*(4), e61–e63.
Hanson, R. K., & Harris, A. J. R. (1997). Voyeurism: Assessment and treatment. In *Sexual deviance: Theory, assessment, and treatment* (pp. 311–331). The Guilford Press.
Hare, R. D. (2003). Psychopathy checklist—revised. *Psychological assessment.*
Holtzman, D., & Kulish, N. (2012). Female exhibitionism: Identification, competition and camaraderie. *The International Journal of Psychoanalysis, 93*(2), 271–292.
Hopkins, T. A., Green, B. A., Carnes, P. J., & Campling, S. (2016). Varieties of intrusion: Exhibitionism and voyeurism. *Sexual Addiction & Compulsivity, 23*(1), 4–33.
Horley, J. (2001). Frotteurism: A term in search of an underlying disorder? *Journal of Sexual Aggression, 7*(1), 51–55.
Hyde, J. S., & De Lamater, J. D. (2003). *Understanding human sexuality* (8th ed.). McGraw-Hill.
Janssen, D. F. (2018). "Voyeuristic Disorder": Etymological and historical note. *Archives of sexual behavior*, 1–5.
Johnson, R. S., Ostermeyer, B., Sikes, K. A., Nelsen, A. J., & Coverdale, J. H. (2014). Prevalence and treatment of frotteurism in the community: A systematic review. *Journal of the American Academy of Psychiatry and the Law Online, 42*(4), 478–483.
Joyal, C., & Ankfold, J. (2017). Official Definitions of Paraphilias.
Kafka, M. P. (2003a). Sex offending and sexual appetite: The clinical and theoretical relevance of hypersexual desire. *International Journal of Offender Therapy and Comparative Criminology, 47*(4), 439–451.
Kafka, M. P. (2003b). The monoamine hypothesis for the pathophysiology of paraphilic disorders: An update. *Annals of the New York Academy of Sciences, 989*(1), 86–94.
Kafka, M. P., & Hennen, J. (1999). The paraphilia-related disorders: An empirical investigation of nonparaphilic hypersexuality disorders in 206 outpatient males. *Journal of Sex and Marital Therapy, 25*, 305–319.
Kafka, M. P., & Hennen, J. (2002). A DSM-IV Axis I comorbidity study of males (n = 120) with paraphilias and paraphilia-related disorders. *Sexual Abuse: A Journal of Research and Treatment, 14*, 349–366.
Kafka, M. P. (2010). Hypersexual disorder: A proposed diagnosis for DSM-V. *Archives of sexual behavior, 39*, 377–400.
Kalmus, E., & Beech, A. R. (2005). Forensic assessment of sexual interest: A review. *Aggression and Violent Behavior, 10*(2), 193–217.
Kaplan, M. S., & Krueger, R. B. (1997). Voyeurism: Psychopathology and theory. In D. R. Laws & W. O'Donohue (Eds.), *Sexual deviance: Theory, assessment, and treatment* (pp. 297–310). Guilford Press.
Kaylor, L., & Jeglic, E. (2019a). Non-contact paraphilic disorders and offending. In L. A. Craig & R. M. Bartels (Eds.), *Sexual deviance: Understanding and managing deviant sexual interest and paraphilic disorders*. Wiley-Blackwell.
Kaylor, L., & Jeglic, E. (2019b). Exhibitionists. In O'Donohue (Ed.), *Handbook of sexual assault and sexual assault prevention*. Springer.
Kaylor, L., Jeglic, E., & Collins, C. (2016). Examining the impact of technology on exhibitionistic behavior. *Deviant Behavior, 37*(10), 1152–1162. https://doi.org/10.1080/01639625.2016.1169828
Kinsey, A. C., Pomeroy, W. B., Martin, C. E., & Gebhard, P. H. (1953). *Sexual behavior in the human female*. W. B. Saunders.
Kinsey, A. C., Reichert, P., Cauldwell, D. O., & Mozes, E. B. (1955). The causes of homosexuality: A symposium. *Sexology, 21*, 558–562.
Konopasek, J. E. (2015). Expeditious disclosure of sexual history via polygraph testing: Treatment outcome and sex offense recidivism. *Journal of Offender Rehabilitation, 54*(3), 194–211.
Krafft-Ebing, R. (1906). *Psychopathia sexualis, translated by FJ Rebman*. Medical Art Agency.
Krueger, R. R., & Kaplan, M. (2008). Assessment and treatment. *Sexual Deviance, 150.*

Lang, R. A., Langevin, R., Checkley, K. L., & Pugh, G. (1987). Genital exhibitionism: Courtship disorder or narcissism? *Canadian Journal of Behavioural Science/Revue canadienne des sciences du comportement, 19*(2), 216.
Langevin, R., & Lang, R. A. (1987). The courtship disorders. In G. D. Wilson (Ed.), *Variant sexuality: Research and theory* (pp. 202–228). Johns Hopkins University Press.
Langevin, R. (1992). Biological factors contributing to paraphilic behavior. *Psychiatric Annals, 22*(6), 307–314.
Langevin, R., Handy, L., Paitich, D., Russon, A., & Langevin, R. (1985). Appendix A: A new version of the Clarke Sex History Questionnaire for males. In *Erotic preference, gender identity, and aggression in men: New research studies* (pp. 287–305). L. Erlbaum Associates.
Långström, N. (2010). The DSM diagnostic criteria for exhibitionism, voyeurism, and frotteurism. *Archives of Sexual Behavior, 39*(2), 317–324.
Långström, N., & Hanson, R. K. (2006). High rates of sexual behavior in the general population: Correlates and risk factors. *Archives of Sexual Behavior, 35*, 37–52.
Långström, N., & Seto, M. (2006). Exhibitionism and voyeuristic behavior in a Swedish national population survey. *Archives of Sexual Behavior, 35*, 427–435. https://doi.org/10.1007/s10508-006-9042-6
Långström, N., & Zucker, K. J. (2005). Transvestic fetishism in the general population: Prevalence and correlates. *Journal of Sex and Marital Therapy, 31*, 87–95.
Lantz, S. E., & Ray, S. (2020). Freud developmental theory. In *StatPearls [Internet]*. StatPearls Publishing.
Lasègue, C. (1877). *Les exhibitionnistes*. L'union Médicale. 709–714 [série 3–23].
Lee, J. K., Pattison, P., Jackson, H. J., & Ward, T. (2001). The general, common, and specific features of psychopathology for different types of paraphilias. *Criminal Justice and Behavior, 28*(2), 227–256.
Lussier, P., & Piché, L. (2008). Frotteurism: Psychopathology and theory. In D. R. Laws & W. T. O'Donohue (Eds.), Sexual deviance: Theory, assessment, and treatment (2nd ed., p. 131). Guilford Press.
MacPherson, G. J. (2003). Predicting escalation in sexually violent recidivism: Use of the SVR-20 and PCL:SV to predict outcome with noncontact recidivists and contact recidivists. *Journal of Forensic Psychiatry & Psychology, 14*(3), 615–627.
Magnan, V. (1890). Des exhibitionnistes. *Les Archives de l' Anthropologie Criminelle et de Sciences Pénales, 5*, 456–471.
Malin, H. M., & Saleh, F. M. (2007). Paraphilias: clinical and forensic considerations. *Psychiatric times, 24*(5), 32–32.
Marshall, W. L. (1989). Intimacy, loneliness and sexual offenders. *Behaviour Research and Therapy, 27*(5), 491–504.
Marshall, W. L. (2006). Ammonia aversion with an exhibitionist: A case study. *Clinical Case Studies, 5*(1), 15–24.
Marshall, W. L. (2014). Phallometric assessments of sexual interests: An update. *Current Psychiatry Reports, 16*(1), 428.
Mathis, J. L. (1972). Voyeurism. In *Clear thinking about sexual deviations* (pp. 41–52). Nelson-Hall Company.
McAnulty, R. (2017). Frotteurism. *Unusual and rare psychological disorders: A handbook for clinical practice and research*, (pp. 136–148). Oxford University Press.
McAnulty, R. D., Adams, H. E., & Dillion, J. (2001). Sexual deviation: Paraphilias. In P. B. Sutker & H. E. Adams (Eds.), *Comprehensive handbook of psychopathology* (3rd ed., pp. 749–773). Kuwer Academic/Plenum.
McGrath, R. J. (1991). Sex-offender risk assessment and disposition planning: A review of empirical and clinical findings. *International Journal of Offender Therapy and Comparative Criminology, 35*, 328–350.
McGrath, R. J., Cumming, G. F., Burchard, B. L., Zeoli, S., & Ellerby, L. (2010). Current practices and emerging trends in sexual abuser management. *The Safer Society, 24*.

McLeod, S. A. (2016, Febuary 05). *Bandura - social learning theory*. Simply Psychology. https://www.simplypsychology.org/bandura.html

McManus, M. A., Hargreaves, P., & Lee Rainbow, L. J. A. (2013). Paraphilias: Definition, diagnosis and treatment. *F1000prime Reports, 5*.

McNally, M. R., & Fremouw, W. J. (2014). Examining risk of escalation: A critical review of the exhibitionistic behavior literature. *Aggression and Violent Behavior, 19*(5), 474–485.

Mester, H. (1984). Phenomenology and history of the origin of exhibitionism. *Forensic and Neurological Psychiatry, 52*(7), 237–249.

Metzl, J. M. (2004). Voyeur nation? Changing definitions of voyeurism, 1950–2004. *Harvard Review of Psychiatry, 12*(2), 127–131.

Meyer, J. K. (1995). Paraphilias. In H. I. Kaplan & B. J. Sadock (Eds.), *Comprehensive textbook of psychiatry IV* (pp. 1334–1347). Williams & Wilkins.

Millon, T. (1992). Millon clinical multiaxial inventory: I & II. *Journal of Counseling & Development, 70*(3), 421–426.

Mohr, J. W., Turner, E. R., & Ball, R. B. (1962). Exhibitionism and pedophilia. *Corrective Psychiatry & Journal of Social Therapy, 8*(4), 172–186.

Monroe, R. R. (1976). Episodic sexual disorders. *Medical Aspects of Human Sexuality*, 55–64.

Morin, J., & Levenson, J. (2008). Exhibitionism: Assessment and treatment. In D. R. Laws & W. T. O'Donohue (Eds.), *Sexual deviance: Theory, assessment, and treatment* (2nd ed., pp. 76–107). Guilford Press.

Morrell, B., Mendel, M. P., & Fischer, L. (2001). Object relations disturbances in sexually abused males. *Journal of Interpersonal Violence, 16*(9), 851–864.

Murphy, L., Ranger, R., Fedoroff, J. P., Stewart, H., Dwyer, R. G., & Burke, W. (2015). Standardization of penile plethysmography testing in assessment of problematic sexual interests. *The Journal of Sexual Medicine, 12*(9), 1853–1861.

Murphy, W., & Page, I. (2008). Exhibitionism: psychopathology and theory. In D. R. In Laws & W. T. O'Donohue (Eds.), *Sexual Deviance: Theory, Assessment, and Treatment* (2nd ed., pp. 61–75). New York, NY.

Myers, W. A. (1991). A case history of a man who made obscene telephone calls and practiced frotteurism. In G. I. Fogel & W. A. Myers (Eds.), *Perversions and near perversions in clinical practice: Newpsychoanalytical practice* (pp. 109–123). Yale University Press.

Nichols, H. R., & Molinder, I. (1984). *Manual for the Multiphasic Sex Inventory*. Crime and Victim Psychology Specialists.

O'Connell, M. B., & Seaton, T. L. (2005). Pharmacotherapy: A Pathophysiologic Approach.

O'Donohue, W., Letourneau, E. J., & Dowling, H. (1997). Development and preliminary validation of a paraphilic sexual fantasy questionnaire. *Sexual Abuse: Journal of Research and Treatment, 9*(3), 167–178.

Patra, A. P., Bharadwaj, B., Shaha, K. K., Das, S., Rayamane, A. P., & Tripathi, C. S. (2013). Impulsive frotteurism: A case report. *Medicine, Science and the Law, 53*(4), 235–238. https://doi.org/10.1177/0025802412474813

Paitich, D., Langevin, R., Freeman, R., Mann, K., & Handy, L. R. R. D. R. (1977). The Clarke SHQ: A clinical sex history questionnaire for males. *Archives of Sexual Behavior, 6*, 421–436.

Perez, E., Prokupecz, S., & Cohen, T. (2014). More than 90 people nabbed in global hacker crackdown. *CNN Justice*. Retrieved from: http://www.cnn.com/2014/05/19/justice/us-global-hacker-crackdown/index.html?hpt=hp_t1

Perilstein, R. D., Lipper, S., & Friedman, L. J. (1991). Three cases of paraphilia responsive to fluoxetine treatment. *Journal of Clinical Psychiatry, 52*, 169–170.

Petri, H. (1969). Exhibitionism: Theoretical and social aspects and treatment with antiandrogens. *Nervenarzt, 40*(5), 220–228.

Prentky, R. A., Gabriel, A. M., & Coward, A. I. (2010). Sexual offenders. In *Handbook of clinical psychology competencies*.

Price, M., Kafka, M., Commons, M. L., Gutheil, T. G., & Simpson, W. (2002). Telephone scatological comorbidity with other paraphilias and paraphilia-related disorders. *International Journal of Law and Psychiatry, 25*, 37–49.

Quinsey, V. L. (2012). Pragmatic and Darwinian views of the paraphilias. *Archives of Sexual Behavior, 41*(1), 217–220.

Rabinowitz-Greenberg, S. R., Firestone, P., Bradford, J. M., & Greenberg, D. M. (2002). Prediction of recidivism in exhibitionists: Psychological, phallometric, and offense factors. *Sexual Abuse: Journal of Research and Treatment, 14*(4), 329–347.

Ranger, R. C., & Fedoroff, P. (2015). *Frotteurism*. Edited.

Raymond, N. C., Coleman, E., Ohlerking, F., Christenson, G. A., & Miner, M. M. (1999). Psychiatric comorbidity in pedophilic sex offenders. *American Journal of Psychiatry, 156*, 786–788.

Raymond, N. C., Coleman, E., & Miner, M. H. (2003). Psychiatric comorbidity and compulsive/impulsive traits in compulsive sexual behavior. *Comprehensive psychiatry, 44*(5), 370–380.

Rhoads, J., & Borjes, E. (1981). The incident of exhibitionism in Guatemala and the United States. *British Journal of Psychiatry, 139*(3), 242–244. https://doi.org/10.1192/bjp.139.3.242

Riordan, S. (1999). Indecent exposure: The impact upon the victim's fear of sexual crime. *Journal of Forensic Psychiatry, 10*, 309–316.

Risen, C. B. (1995). A guide to taking a sexual history. *Psychiatric Clinics of North America, 18*(1), 39–53.

Rooth, F. G. (1973). Exhibitionism, sexual violence, and paedophilia. *British Journal of Psychiatry, 122*(6), 705–710.

Rösler, A., & Witztum, E. (1998). Treatment of men with paraphilia with a long-acting analogue of gonadotropinreleasing hormone. *New England Journal of Medicine, 338*(7), 416–422.

Rosen, I. (1964). Exhibitionism, scopophilia and voyeurism. In I. Rosen (Ed.), *The pathology and treatment of sexual deviation*. Oxford University Press.

Rosky, J. W. (2013). The (f) utility of post-conviction polygraph testing. *Sexual Abuse, 25*(3), 259–281.

Rye, B. J., & Meaney, G. J. (2007). Voyeurism: It is good as long as we do not get caught. *International Journal of Sexual Health, 19*(1), 47–56.

Ryley, S., & Donohue, P. (2014, June 23). Grand Central more like sex crime central: Nearly half of all subway sex crimes reported along Lexington Avenue line in Manhattan. *New York Daily News*. Retrieved from https://www.nydailynews.com/new-york/nyc-crime/daily-news-analysis-reveals-perverted-subway-stations-article-1.1836952.

Sadhu, J. M. (2012). Sexting: The impact of a cultural phenomenon on psychiatric practice. *Academic Psychiatry, 36*(1), 76–81.

Saleh, F. M., Niel, T., & Fishman, M. J. (2004). Treatment of paraphilia in young adults with leuprolide acetate: A preliminary case report series. *Journal of Forensic Sciences, 49*(6), 1–6.

Schneider, S. L., & Wright, R. C. (2004). Understanding denial in sexual offenders: A review of cognitive and motivational processes to avoid responsibility. *Trauma, Violence, & Abuse, 5*(1), 3–20.

Seligman, L., & Hardenburg, S. A. (2000). Assessment and treatment of paraphilias. *Journal of Counseling & Development, 78*(1), 107–113.

Seto, M. C. (2004). Pedophilia and sexual offenses against children. *Annual Review of Sex Research, 15*(1), 321–361.

Simpson, G., Blaszczynski, A., & Hodgkinson, A. (1999). Sex offending as a psychosocial sequela of traumatic brain injury. *The Journal of Head Trauma Rehabilitation, 14*(6), 567–580.

Smith, R. S. (1976). Voyeurism: A review of literature. *Archives of Sexual Behavior, 5*, 585–608. https://doi.org/10.1007/BF01541221

Solla, P., Bortolato, M., Cannas, A., Mulas, C. S., & Marrosu, F. (2015). Paraphilias and paraphilic disorders in Parkinson's disease: A systematic review of the literature. *Movement Disorders, 30*(5), 604–613.

Sophos Press Release. (2008). *Four years jail for voyeur hacker who spied via webcam*. Retrieved from: http://www.sophos.com/en-us/press-office/press-releases/2008/08/webcam.aspx

Staddon, J. E., & Cerutti, D. T. (2003). Operant conditioning. *Annual Review of Psychology, 54*(1), 115–144.

Stalking Resource Center. (2003). In partnership with the National Center for Victims of Crime. *New Frontiers of Stalking-Video Voyeurism*. Retrieved from: http://www.victimsofcrime.org/docs/src/new-frontiers-of-stalking%2D%2D-video-voyeurism.pdf?sfvrsn=2

Sugarman, P., Dumughn, C., Saad, K., Hinder, S., & Bluglass, R. (1994). Dangerousness in exhibitionists. *Journal of Forensic Psychiatry, 5*, 287–296.

Swindell, S., Stroebel, S. S., O'Keefe, S. L., Beard, K. W., Robinett, S. R., & Kommor, M. J. (2011). Correlates of exhibition-like experiences in childhood and adolescence: A model for development of exhibitionism in heterosexual males. *Sexual Addiction & Compulsivity, 18*(3), 135–156.

Templeman, T. L., & Stinnett, R. D. (1991). Patterns of sexual arousal and history in a "normal" sample of young men. *Archives of Sexual Behavior, 20*, 137–150.

Terao, T., & Nakamura, J. (2000). Exhibitionism and low-dose trazodone treatment. *Human Psychopharmacology: Clinical and Experimental, 15*(5), 347–349.

Wainberg, M. L., Muench, F., Morgenstern, J., Hollander, E., Irwin, T. W., Parsons, J. T., & O'Leary, A. (2006). A double-blind study of citalopram versus placebo in the treatment of compulsive sexual behaviors in gay and bisexual men. *Journal of Clinical Psychiatry, 67*(12), 1968–1973.

Wilson, R. J., & Miner, M. H. (2016). Measurement of male sexual arousal and interest using penile plethysmography and viewing time. In *Treatment of sex offenders* (pp. 107–131). Springer.

World Health Organization. (2020). *International statistical classification of diseases and related health problems* (11th ed.) https://icd.who.int/

Zinni, M. (2012). *Hackers gain access to homes through webcams*. Retrieved from: http://fox8.com/2012/05/09/hackers-gain-access-to-homes-through-webcams/

Zolondek, S. C., Abel, G. G., Northey, W. F., Jr., & Jordan, A. D. (2001). The self-reported behaviors of juvenile sexual offenders. *Journal of Interpersonal Violence, 16*(1), 73–85.

Chapter 12
Clinical Versus Criminal Sexual Sadism: An Extended Review of Theory, Assessment, Diagnosis, and Intervention

Rajan Darjee and Michael R. Davis

12.1 Introduction

Sexual sadism (SS),[1] experiencing sexual pleasure through fantasies or acts of cruelty towards others, has a long, important, but elusive status in forensic clinical practice, our understanding of sexual violence, and wider societal responses to the cruel and horrific. Since its identification, naming, and reification as a clinical entity, over a century ago, the term "sadism" has been used narrowly and widely, precisely and imprecisely, sexually and non-sexually, normatively and pathologically, and forensically and non-forensically to cover a range of internal (thoughts, fantasies,

[1] The following terms and abbreviations are used in this chapter sexual sadism (SS), sexual sadism disorder (SSD), coercive sexual sadism (CSS), and coercive sexual sadism disorder (CSSD). The current authors generally prefer to use CSS or CSSD to emphasize reference to forensically relevant sexual sadism and the ICD-11 concept respectively. But SS and SSD are used, where the sources referenced and therefore the concepts being discussed, use these terms. The term BDSM (Bondage and Discipline/Domination and Submission/Sadism and Masochism) is used to refer to consensual sadomasochism.

R. Darjee (✉)
Forensic Behavioural Assessment and Consultation Services (FBACS), Melbourne, VIC, Australia

Centre for Forensic Behavioural Science, Swinburne University of Technology, Melbourne, VIC, Australia
e-mail: rdarjee@swin.edu.au

M. R. Davis
Centre for Forensic Behavioural Science, Swinburne University of Technology, Melbourne, VIC, Australia

Department of Psychiatry, Monash University, Clayton, VIC, Australia

Department of Psychiatry, The University of Melbourne, Parkville, VIC, Australia

R. J. Tully et al. (eds.), *Best Practices in Sexual Offender Assessment and Management*, Dangerous Behavior in Clinical and Forensic Psychology,
https://doi.org/10.1007/978-3-031-83135-5_12

and urges) and external (behaviours, acts, and offences) phenomena. Editions of the *Diagnostic and Statistical Manual* (DSM) of the American Psychiatric Association (APA) and *International Classification of Diseases* (ICD) of the World Health Organization (WHO) have incorporated it, but with changing labels and definitions, and questionable reliability. Confusion has been caused by conflating coercive sexual sadism (CSS), seen in forensic settings, with the consenting role play of BDSM (Bondage and Discipline/Domination and Submission/Sadism and Masochism), non-sexual cruelty, and sadistic personality traits. Using the terms sadism in clinical or forensic practice comes with connotations, assumptions, and predictions, about a person and their potential for harm. Therefore, precision, conceptual clarity, and understanding and knowledge of what research and practice indicate is important. Indeed, over the last couple of decades or so there have been important developments in our understanding of the nature and boundaries of SS, its identification and assessment, its origins and underlying psychopathology, aspects of prognostic utility and validity, but not so much its treatment and management (Mokros et al., 2019).

This chapter aims to provide a pragmatic and evidence-based account to aid practitioners with understanding SS but, more importantly, approaching cases in forensic and clinical contexts. The history, definitions, concept and structure of sexual sadism will be examined first. After this, boundaries and overlaps, including what it mimics, what mimics it and what complicates it will be considered, addressing differential diagnosis and comorbidity. Then the multi-faceted etiology of SS will be explored, before looking at its prevalence. Specific groups are considered next, including, perpetrators of sexual offences and homicides, young people and women, people who have not offended but present with concerning thoughts or behaviours, and separation from BDSM. Practical issues of clinical assessment, risk assessment, treatment, and management will then be addressed.

It may be helpful to set out what the current authors believe are important and evidence-based tenets, covered in more detail later, but which are important fundamentals to bear in mind when reading this chapter and considering SS:

1. An act may be cruel, controlling, or brutal without being indicative of *sadism*, if the primary purpose is not to bring pleasure to the person who acts that way. To be considered *sexual sadism* that pleasure must be associated with sexual arousal. And to be considered *coercive sexual sadism disorder* (CSSD; WHO, 2022) this must be associated with lack of consent, cause harm or distress, and be sustained, focused, and intense in pattern.
2. SS is not a natural taxon but part of a *dimension*, sitting at the top of an *agonistic continuum* of coercive and aggressive sexual interests and behavior. Therefore, categorical definition is arbitrary.
3. CSSD is fundamentally different from *BDSM*. For over a century, BDSM has been conflated with CSS, wrongly pathologizing and stigmatizing healthy mutual non-harmful kink, but also making interpreting the literature on SS problematic.
4. Categorical diagnosis with ICD-11 (WHO, 2022) or DSM-5-TR (APA, 2022) can be unreliable, and using *objective crime scene behavior scales,* such as the

Sexual Sadism Scale (*SESAS*), to anchor diagnostic assessment should now be considered best practice.

5. CSSD is associated with chronic, escalating, seriously harmful, and fatal sexual violence, and with serial sexual homicide (SH). Therefore, it is an important *risk factor* and has significant implications for legal adjudications, treatment, and management.

12.2 What Is Sexual Sadism?

So, what is sexual sadism? How has the concept developed, what are its elements and structure, what are the diagnostic criteria, and are the current diagnostic criteria valid and useful? This section will start with a historical overview, before addressing these issues in detail.

12.2.1 Historical Overview

In *Psychopathia Sexualis*, Krafft-Ebing (1886) coined the clinical term "sadism" after the Marquis de Sade (1969, 1971, 1990, 1996), whose late eighteenth century writings led to "*sadisme*" appearing in French dictionaries in the early nineteenth century, defined as a "terrible aberration of debauchery: a monstrous and antisocial system which revolts nature" (Boiste, 1835; Bourke, 2020). In Greek and Roman history and myth there were vivid descriptions of sadistic and serial sexual homicides (Felton, 2021). However, the first scholarly description of what is referred to as sadism today was likely in Seneca's treatise *De Clementia* [translated as 'On Mercy'] in 55 C.E., where the term '*insania*' was used to include those who took pleasure in inflicting pain on others: "This is why savagery should be detested above all: it first goes beyond customary limits, then beyond human limits, in searching out new forms of punishment, in calling on special talents to dream up the means of multiplying and prolonging pain, in taking pleasure in human misery. In the end, its diseased and loathsome thoughts are reduced to utter insanity [*insania*]: cruelty is converted into pleasure, committing murder becomes an actual delight." (Seneca, 2017). At the time *insania* was a level of 'insanity' less severe than *furens* [furiously mad] and was not considered exculpatory (McGlen et al., 2015).

The term 'perversion', with medieval roots, originally referred to any behavior considered unnatural, including sexual behavior, and prior to the nineteenth century, myth (e.g., lycanthropy and vampirism) or religion (sin, demons, and Satan) were invoked as explanations. Sadism was not amongst the six sexual "aberrations" identified in Kaan's *Psychopathia Sexualis* in 1844 (Kaan, 2016), which reinterpreted the Christian sexual sins (masturbation, bestiality, pederasty, homosexuality, violation of cadavers, and sex with statues) as mental diseases. Before the nineteenth century there were examples of sexually sadistic killings (e.g., Gilles de Rais in the fifteenth century; Wolf, 1980; Bataille, 1990) and in the early nineteenth century psychiatric concepts like homicidal monomania and moral insanity were sometimes applied in such cases (De Saussure, 1946). But SS was a non-existent concept, and sin, atavism and degeneracy were the explanations given for such primitive and beastly behavior. Ironically, punishments for such wrongdoers were public state sanctioned torture and killing, including acts which would be considered sadistic or sexually sadistic today (Briggs et al., 1996). Before Krafft-Ebing's *Psychopathia Sexualis* the strands of what would now be called BDSM and CSS were not entwined. Flagellation and other "sadomasochistic" behaviors, going back to ancient times, were seen as aphrodisiac, ecstasy inducing, part of religious discipline, or modes of punishment (Braun, 1967).

According to Krafft-Ebing (1886), sadism, "the association of active cruelty and violence with lust" was a "paraesthesia of the sexual feeling" or "perversion of the sexual instinct" (his terms for paraphilic disorders). He defined sadism as "the experience of sexual pleasurable sensations (including orgasm) produced by acts of cruelty, bodily punishment afflicted on one's own person or when witnessed in others, be they animals or human beings. It may also consist of an innate desire to humiliate, hurt, wound or even destroy others in order thereby to create sexual pleasure in oneself". It was innately sexual, tied to "lust", and so the antecedent "sexual" was unnecessary. He identified nine subtypes: "lust murder", "mutilation of corpses" (including necrophilia), "injury of women", "defilement of women", "other kinds of assault on females" ("symbolic sadism"), "ideal sadism", "sadism with other objects" (including "whipping of boys"), "sadistic acts with animals", and "sadism in woman". Several of these would not properly be considered sexually sadistic by modern forensic practitioners due to the lack of victim reaction (e.g., mutilation of corpses), but Krafft-Ebing (1886) nonetheless showed remarkable insight in identifying some of the more subtle forms of sadistic behavior (e.g., symbolic sadism and ideal sadism). Its origins were thought to be an exaggeration of the natural instinct of males to sexually subdue females, atavistic regression to a primitive animalistic state, and degeneration as expounded by Caesare Lombroso (Ellwood, 1912). Krafft-Ebing (1886) considered that "masochism and sadism represent perfect counterparts", but when co-occurring in an individual, one was always "markedly predominant", with the predominating one "original" and the other "acquired". He also differentiated lust murder from other sexual murders.

Alienists, sexologists, and psychoanalysts then grappled with the concept of sadism including its nature, etiology (particularly whether innate or acquired), medico-legal status, and relationship with and cooccurrence with masochism, and *algolagnia* and *algophilia* were terms used at the turn of the century emphasizing sexual pleasure from pain, actively in sadism or passively in masochism (von Schrenck-Notzing, 1892; Féré, 1904; Ellis, 1913; Crozier, 2002). Freud (1905), and the psychoanalysts that followed, saw sadism as innate in the infant, inherently sexual as bound to libidinal development, an integral part of normal development from childhood to adulthood, becoming manifest as a perversion where psychological development went awry, closely tied to masochism and usually coexisting with it, and described sadism as the most common sexual perversion. Psychoanalysts used the term more broadly than Krafft-Ebing (1886), including normal and pathological phenomena and behaviors blurring into lay concepts of sadism. Psychoanalytic concepts of sadomasochism are arguably at the root of the problematic status of SS at the end of the twentieth century, including conflation with BDSM, and lack of conceptual clarity. Stekel (1924), wrote two volumes on sadism and masochism, but the cases he described illustrate the broad psychoanalytic concept of sadomasochism, going far beyond what is recognized as CSSD today. Nonetheless, Stekel (1924) did make a major contribution to our understanding of SS by noting that the paraphilic focus was not on the infliction of pain. He stated that:

> An erroneous conception of the sadomasochistic complex makes pain the central factor for consideration and occupies itself with the phenomenon of gratification derived from pain. The expression *algolagnia* coined by Schrenck-Notzing, accords with this idea. We have ascertained, however, that the decisive thing in the phenomenon of sadomasochism is the affect... in the sadist, from his own sense of power in overcoming the resistance of another and from his feeling himself into the humiliation of his partner (p. 57).

Stekel's (1924) identification that the focus of SS is not on pain, but on feeling oneself into the humiliation, and by extension the suffering and degradation, of another was revolutionary. Surprisingly, this has been rarely cited in subsequent decades. However, similar descriptions of sexually sadistic behavior were described by Knoll and Hazelwood (2009), who described serial homicide offenders with SS who would "become the victim" during subsequent masturbation, acting out the prior offence from the perspective of their victims and even dressing in their clothes and binding themselves in similar ways. These are clear examples of the SS offender attempting to feel themselves into the suffering of their victim and experiencing the offending from their perspective. This underscores that the focus in SS is on victims' reactions to being humiliated, degraded, and made to suffer.

Other perspectives, some influenced by psychoanalysis, were formulations from forensic and sexological perspectives. Forensic clinicians described sexual sadism in association with sexual violence and homicide (Berg, 1945; de River, 1949; Karpman, 1954; East, 1955; Revitch, 1957; Drzazga, 1960; Traini, 1960; Slovenko, 1965; Podolsky, 1966; Brittain, 1970; Amir, 1971; Cohen et al., 1971; MacDonald, 1971; Rada, 1978; Groth, 1979; MacCulloch et al., 1983; Ressler et al., 1988), whilst sexologists described it alongside other sexual anomalies and behaviors (Hirschfeld, 1938; Kinsey et al., 1948; Masters & Lea, 1963; Messerman, 1969; Money, 1984). Meanwhile the original DSM (APA, 1952) included "sexual sadism (including rape, sexual assault, mutilation)" as part of "Sexual Deviation" under "Sociopathic Personality Disturbance", and DSM-II (APA, 1968) had SS as part of "Sexual Deviation", now separate from personality disorder. ICD-6 (WHO, 1948) and ICD-7 (WHO, 1955) included "sadism" as a sexual deviation, ICD-8

(WHO, 1965) included it within "Other Sexual Deviation" (Krueger, 2010; Krueger et al., 2017), and then similarly ICD-9 (WHO, 1977) included it as an inclusion term for "Other Sexual Deviation or Disorder" (Krueger et al., 2017). DSM-III (APA, 1980) included SS as a paraphilia, with the first definitional criteria (Krueger, 2010), then DSM-III-R (APA, 1987) had an operational definition setting the template for definitions to come (APA, 1994, 2000, 2013, 2022), whilst ICD-10 (1990) diagnostically amalgamated it with masochism as "sadomasochism". So, by the early 1990s there were psychoanalytic conceptualizations and descriptions, forensic and sexological descriptions, but very little empirical research (Grubin, 1994a, 1994b). In addition, consensual sadomasochism (only just named BDSM) and CSS were fully conflated and undifferentiated, contaminating and confusing conceptualization.

12.2.2 The Focus of Sexual Pleasure in Sexual Sadism

There has been disagreement about the focus of sexual pleasure in SS (Longpré et al., 2019). Candidates have included control, domination, fear, humiliation, suffering, pain, injury, and violence. Clearly these overlap and one may be inflicted to achieve another, but they primarily fall into four areas: control, humiliation, psychological suffering, and physical harm. Some have suggested the primacy of one of these, but if any aspect does have primacy, it is likely to be the infliction and savoring of fear and humiliation. Sexual fantasies, ritualism, and planning have also been considered hallmarks (Longpré et al., 2019), but they are more broadly related to SS being a paraphilia rather than specific to SS itself. Indeed, these are the behavioral core of most, if not all, paraphilic disorders. Suggested indicators of SS (Marshall & Hucker, 2006; Longpré et al., 2019) are listed in Table 12.1. There has been some variation in features considered core, necessary, sufficient, ancillary, or exclusionary by different authors (Longpré et al., 2019).

12.2.3 Categorical Diagnosis in DSM and ICD

Both DSM-5-TR (APA, 2022; Box 12.1) and ICD-11 (WHO, 2022; Box 12.2) attempt to focus on forensically and clinically relevant SS. Unfortunately, their attempts to be relevant to a wide range of situations that may involve SS behaviors leave them often too broad to provide appropriate guidance to practitioners. DSM-5-TR sexual sadism disorder (SSD) retains the arbitrary 6-month duration; focuses on suffering, not control or humiliation; and does not insist on non-consent

Table 12.1 Features that have been suggested as indicators of sexual sadism

Control	Humiliation	Psychological suffering	Physical harm	Other
Abduction **Bondage** Coercion **Confinement**[*] **Control**[*] **Domination**[*] Enslavement Force Non-consent **Power** Restraints Transportation of victim	**Degradation**[*] Disgusting treatment **Humiliation**[*] **Object insertion**[a]	Frightening Intimidation Terrifying Distressing **Prolonged in time** **Torture (psychological)**[*]	*Specific acts:* **Beating** **Whipping** Strangulation, asphyxiation or choking Using weapons Cannibalism Vampirism ***Degree of physical harm:*** **Expressive physical violence**[*] **Torture (physical)**[*] Infliction of pain Violence Killing ***Mutilation:*** **Non-sexual mutilation**[*] **Sexual mutilation**[*] Post-mortem mutilation	***Excessive cruelty:*** **Brutality** Gratuitousness **History of cruelty to humans or animals**[*] ***Other sexual behaviours:*** Consenting bondage or strangulation/choking **with sexual partners** Cross-dressing Post-mortem sex ***Evidence of fantasy:*** **Keeps trophies, records, or souvenirs**[*] **Planning**[*] **Ritualistic**[*] **Sadistic sexual arousal**[*] **Sadistic sexual fantasies**[*] Violent pornography use

These are clearly not mutually exclusive but capture the various features which have been suggested by psychiatrist and psychologists since Krafft-Ebing in 1886 (Marshall & Hucker, 2006; Longpré et al., 2019). The 'other sexual behaviors' have not been shown to be aspects of sexual sadism

[*] Features overtly appearing as, or within, items of part 1 and 2 of the Sexual Sadism Scale (SESAS; Mokros et al., 2012), although some non-asterisked ones clearly overlap with or contribute to the asterisked ones

where there is distress or poor functioning, so allows pathologization of BDSM practitioners distressed or impaired not by their consensual behavior, but by societal stigma (Wright, 2010). The "in a controlled environment" specifier seems unnecessary, and "in full remission" specifier may be misleading as there may be long periods without offending and offences may be hidden. Indeed, the suggestion that any paraphilic sexual interest that reached the magnitude of a paraphilic disorder would simply go into remission is controversial in the absence of compelling data. In practice, both of the current authors have had cases where paraphilic behaviors have returned in the form of offending after often lengthy periods of non-offending or any indication of concerns regarding deviant fantasies. As such, the current authors remain unconvinced that the "in full remission" specifier provides anything useful, other than stating that the individual has not been knowingly sexually sadistic for a seemingly arbitrary period of 5 years (and it is noted that the original proposal for DSM-5 was a period of just 6 months).

Box 12.1 DSM-5-TR criteria for sexual sadism disorder (F65.52) (APA, 2022)

A. Over a period of at least 6 months, recurrent and intense sexual arousal from the physical or psychological suffering of another person, as manifested by fantasies, urges or behaviors

B. The individual has acted on these sexual urges with a non-consenting person, or the sexual urges or fantasies cause clinically significant distress or impairment in social, occupational, or other important areas of functioning

Specify if:
In a controlled environment: This specifier is primarily applicable to individuals living in institutional or other settings where opportunities to engage in sadistic sexual behaviors are restricted
In full remission: The individual has not acted on the urges with a nonconsenting person, and there has been no distress or impairment in social, occupational, or other areas of functioning, for at least 5 years while in an uncontrolled environment

CSSD in ICD-11 (WHO, 2022) does better by requiring non-consensual coercion. Other differences include referencing "thoughts" as well as fantasies or urges, the term "sustained" for duration, including "focused", and clarifying boundaries. Although DSM-5 (APA, 2013) and DSM-5-TR (APA, 2022) attempted to de-pathologize diverse non-harmful sexuality by differentiating "paraphilias" from "paraphilic disorders", using SSD in relation to BDSM is problematic, and

DSM-5-TR references studies of BDSM when describing prevalence rates, which only contributes to the imprecision and turbidity of the construct of SSD.

Box 12.2 ICD-11 criteria for coercive sexual sadism disorder (6D33) (WHO, 2022)

Definition: *Coercive sexual sadism disorder* is characterised by a sustained, focused and intense pattern of sexual arousal—as manifested by persistent sexual thoughts, fantasies, urges or behaviours—that involves the infliction of physical or psychological suffering on a non-consenting person. In addition, in order for Coercive Sexual Sadism Disorder to be diagnosed, the individual must have acted on these thoughts, fantasies or urges or be markedly distressed by them. Coercive Sexual Sadism Disorder specifically excludes consensual sexual sadism and masochism

Coercive Sexual Sadism Disorder should not be diagnosed among **children** and should be diagnosed only with utmost caution among **adolescents**

The diagnosis of Coercive Sexual Sadism Disorder is generally not adequately supported when the evidence indicating a sustained, focused and intense pattern of sexual arousal consists solely of a **single or very limited number of instances** of coercive sadistic sexual behaviour, as there may be other explanations for specific occurrences

Boundaries with the following are specified: **(i)** Compulsive Sexual Behavior Disorder, (ii) Conduct-Dissocial Disorder, **(iii)** Disorders Due to Substance Use, **(iv)** other mental disorders, **(v)** sexual crimes that do not involve a Paraphilic Disorder

12.2.4 Problems with Reliability of Categorical Diagnosis

Research has previously questioned the reliability of diagnoses made using DSM-IV (APA, 1994) and ICD-10 (WHO, 1993) (Nitschke et al., 2013; Marshall et al., 2016). Potential reasons for this poor reliability include:

1. The rarity of SS, so professionals do not see many cases.
2. Over-reliance on self-report.
3. Lack of high stakes in clinical and research settings, compared to legal ones.
4. Vague criteria not adequately capturing or differentiating the condition.
5. Emphasis on arousal, fantasies, and urges rather than objective behavior.
6. Lack of consensus about core, defining, and necessary features.
7. Clinicians not applying the criteria properly, but using their own idiosyncratic ones in addition or instead.
8. Any disgusting or violent sexual offence being labelled sadistic.
9. Many sexual offences involve power, control, humiliation, and aggression.
10. Sadism being dimensional not a taxon, so the diagnostic threshold is arbitrary.
11. Conflating CSS with BDSM or non-sexual cruelty.
12. The statistical approach used to assess reliability (see Packard & Levenson, 2006).

DSM-5 (APA, 2013), DSM-5-TR (APA, 2022), and ICD-11 (WHO, 2022) are not immune from such issues, so clinicians must be aware that diagnoses may be of questionable reliability. In response, Marshall and Hucker (2006) suggested a dimensional approach using behavioral indicators may be a promising alternative.

12.2.5 The Status of Paraphilic Coercive Disorder and its Predecessors

A thorny issue has been the status, features, differentiation, validity, and utility of a paraphilic disorder diagnosis for arousal to non-sadistic coercion. Terms have included raptophilia (Balyk, 1997), rapism (Money & Lehne, 1983), paraphilic rape (Freund & Seto, 1998), biastophilia (Money, 1990), and paraphilic coercive disorder (PCD; Fuller et al., 1990). Unhelpfully, and further complicating the problems with defining SS, some definitions for these have included frightening, humiliating, surprising, assaulting, raping, struggling/resistance by victims or targeting strangers, in addition to coercion and lack of consent. There are men who commit sexual assault who experience relevant sexual arousal and fantasies, and this seems important in risk assessment and treatment (Thornton, 2010; Quinsey, 2010). But, differentiating them from SS phallometrically and clinically has been inconsistent and problematic (Knight et al., 2013), as has differentiating them from people who rape who do not have a strong or preferential sexual interest in coercion (Knight, 2010a). In addition, many men in general admit to coercive fantasies (Joyal et al., 2015). Concerns have been raised that PCD leads to the easy pathologization of most men who rape, particularly in the context of post-sentence commitment in the USA (Wollert, 2011). However, the rejection of PCD for inclusion in DSM-5, mirroring paraphilic rapism in DSM-III-R, has led to "paraphilic disorder not otherwise specified, nonconsent" being diagnosed, without specific criteria or a threshold, potentially leading to arbitrary ascertainment (Thornton, 2010; Frances & First, 2011).

The diagnostic manuals have been unable to agree upon criteria for non-sadistic paraphilic rape, and the proposed criteria often appear to be examples of "sadism-lite" or are difficult to differentiate from SS itself. However, it should be noted that there have been examples of non-sadistic, yet equally ritualistic and fantasy-driven, rape offenders described in the literature for more than half a century. Such offenders have been variously described as *Compensatory* (Cohen et al., 1969), *Power Reassurance* (Groth 1977; Hazelwood, 2017b), *Non-Sadistic Sexualization* (Knight, 1999, 2010b; Knight & Guay, 2006; Knight & Sims-Knight, 2016; Knight & Prentky, 1990; Prentky & Knight, 1991), and *Non-Sadistic Ritualistic* (Davis, 2012, 2018). Such individuals engage in considerable fantasy, comparable to that of SS, but their rape fantasies very often involve a relational component whereby the victim is going to enjoy their victimization and invite the offender to continue. Despite this theme of offence behavior being described for many decades, it is nonetheless a very different form of rape behavior than has been unsuccessfully proposed for the DSM editions.

12.2.6 Dimensionality and the Agonistic Continuum

Research, fueled by suggestions of dimensionality and PCD's uncertain status, has led to replicated findings, in different settings and samples, using different ways of measuring psychopathology and behavior, confirming that SS is dimensional, not a taxon, and is the extreme end of a continuum of coercive and aggressive sexual interests and behaviors, named the agonistic continuum, with PCD further down this (Knight et al., 2013; Longpré et al., 2018, 2020). This is presented in Fig. 12.1. It is unidimensional, cumulative, and hierarchically ordered (i.e., a Mokken or Guttman scale; Nitschke et al., 2009), so if there are features higher up, then those beneath are usually present. This underlying structure explains why SS and PCD have evaded discrimination and definition. Suggested categorical diagnoses capture different levels, but inevitably have features of ones below, and blur into each other.

Dimensionality has various implications. First, a categorical approach requires an arbitrary cut-off defined by interests, behaviors, or impact on functioning. Second, turning a dimension into a category loses information. Third, clinicians must use current diagnostic schemes knowing the underlying phenomenon is

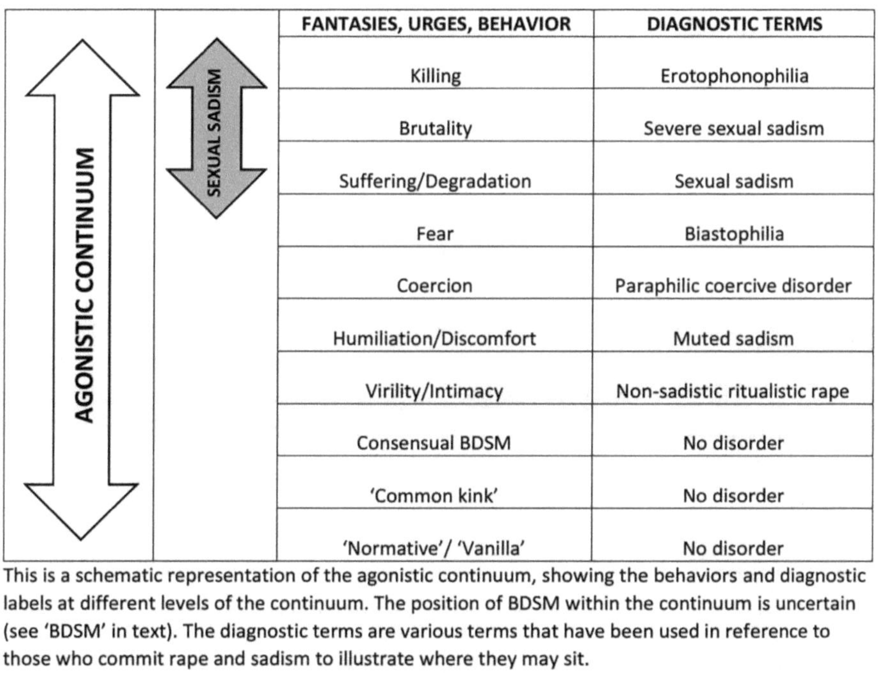

Fig. 12.1 The agonistic continuum. This is a schematic representation of the agonistic continuum, showing the behaviors and diagnostic labels at different levels of the continuum. The position of BDSM within the continuum is uncertain (see 'BDSM' in text). The diagnostic terms are various terms that have been used in reference to those who commit rape and sadism to illustrate where they may sit

dimensional. Fourth, validated scales based on relevant features and behaviors (e.g., the SESAS) should anchor assessments. Fifth, naturally dimensional phenomena have multiple interacting etiological factors. Sixth, the future approach to SS in DSM and ICD, like personality disorder (Hopwood et al., 2018), should be dimensional not categorical, but in a way practitioners can apply.

12.2.7 A Dimensional Approach to Diagnosis: 'coercive sexual agonistic disorder'

Table 12.2 gives a suggestion for a pragmatic dimensional approach to diagnosis, based on research on dimensionality, the personality disorders approach in ICD-11 (WHO, 2022) and the alternative DSM-5 model (APA, 2013), building on CSSD in ICD-11, but labelling the condition 'coercive sexual agonistic disorder' (CSAD). At low levels 'difficulty' is below the threshold for 'disorder', as is the case for personality difficulty versus disorder in ICD-11. Above difficulty are four disorder levels from mild to extreme. The lower two are equivalent to PCD and the higher two CSSD. There would be potential advantages in no longer using either term given the history of both, but it seems unlikely the field is ready to relinquish 'sadism'. Therefore, if retained, SS could be a specifier for 'extreme' or 'severe' cases. Before making the dimensional diagnosis, clinicians would consider all relevant information (see 'Assessment'—below); consider relevant aspects of control, humiliation,

Table 12.2 "Coercive Sexual Agonistic Disorder" (CSAD): a suggested approach to the future diagnosis of sexual sadism and paraphilic coercive disorder, taking a pragmatic dimensional approach

Level on the CSAD Continuum	DIAGNOSTIC CONDITION			INDICATIVE SYMPTOMS & BEHAVIORS SEXUALY AROUSING THOUGHTS, FANTASIES, URGES OR ACTS INVOLVING...				Indicative SESAS[1] Part I score
	Coercive agonistic	Coercive sexual sadism	Paraphilic coercive	Control	Humiliation	Psychological Suffering	Physical Harm	
0	**Absent (non-problematic)**	Absent	Absent	None	None	None	None	0-1
1	**Difficulty**	Absent	Mild (Sub-threshold)	Pressurise	Tease	Worry, upset	Discomfort	0-2
2	**Mild disorder**	Absent	Moderate	Coerce, force	Embarrass	Intimidate, bully	Hurt, pain	1-3
3	**Moderate disorder**	Mild (Sub-threshold)	Severe	Control, power	Demean	Scare, frighten	Injure or wound	2-4
4	**Severe[2] disorder**	Moderate	(Extreme)	Dominate, master	Degrade, debase	Terrify, horrify	Seriously harmful or life-changing	4-6
5	**Extreme[2] disorder**	Severe	(Extreme)	Subjugate, enslave, crush	Dehumanise	Terrorise, brutalise, destroy	Life-threatening or fatal injury	6-11

[1] SESAS = Sexual Sadism Scale (Mokros et al., 2012)

[2] If the term "sadism" is used, it is a qualifier for levels 4 and 5, which can be labelled 'severe CSAD – sexual sadism' and 'extreme CSAD – severe sexual sadism' respectively.

psychological suffering, and physical harm; and anchor diagnosis with a validated behavioral scale like the SESAS.

12.3 Boundaries, Overlaps and Apparent Similarities: Comorbidity, Undifferentiated Conditions, and Differential Diagnosis

Other conditions, phenomena and circumstances can complicate (occur at the same time as and perhaps exacerbate or mask), mimic (look similar too) and/or overlap with (have blurred boundaries with) SS. When these are mental disorders, the issues are comorbidity, differential diagnosis, and conceptual overlap respectively.

12.3.1 Personality and Personality Disorder

In the original DSM (APA, 1952), SS, as a sexual deviation, was classified under sociopathic personality disturbance (Krueger, 2010). Prior to that, terms like "sexual psychopathy" and "psychopathic personality with pathologic sexuality" were used, and since the late eighteenth century sexual perversion has been conflated with what would be called personality disorders today. Krafft-Ebing (1886) stated that whether a person acted on sadistic fantasies, and how, depended on being "weakened by original ethical defect, hereditary degeneracy, or moral insanity", i.e., personality disorder. Psychoanalytic formulations posit that paraphilic disorders arise from disrupted personality development (Yakely, 2021). Personality disorders and traits seem important in the etiology and development of CSS (i.e., predisposing), and in the expression of related behavior (i.e., facilitating or disinhibiting), which may be via response to particular contexts or triggers.

12.3.1.1 Sadistic Personality and Personality Disorder

Sadistic personality disorder (SPD) (Box 12.3) was considered for DSM-III-R, but only reached an appendix of proposed diagnoses needing further study (APA, 1987), and was not included in the subsequent DSM-IV (APA, 1994). This would appear to be largely due to concerns about the potential misuse of the diagnosis, rather than true clinical concerns, although there was also comparatively little in the way of research at the time (Fiester & Gay, 1991, 1995). This disorder was characterized by pervasive and persistent pattern of cruel, humiliating, and domineering behavior not associated with sexual pleasure or arousal. In essence, it was a non-sexual characterological form of sadism based on observations by clinicians working in forensic contexts. Research showed high co-occurrence with paranoid, antisocial, and narcissistic disorders (Fiester & Gay, 1991), suggesting lack of distinctiveness. Concerns included that it would stigmatize in criminal justice contexts and, conversely, absolve of responsibility in legal ones, which could be raised about most personality disorders. Despite this, Millon et al. (2015) retained it in the Millon Clinical Multi-Axial Inventory (MCMI), had pushed for inclusion in DSM, conceptualized it dimensionally (ranging from assertive, through abrasive, to sadistic), and had four subtypes: spineless (with avoidant features), tyrannical (with negativistic ones), enforcing (with compulsive ones), and explosive (with borderline ones).

Box 12.3 DSM-III-R criteria for sadistic personality disorder (APA, 1987)

A pervasive pattern of sadistic and cruel behavior that begins in early adulthood. It was defined by four of the following.

1. Has used physical cruelty or violence for the purpose of establishing dominance in a relationship (not merely to achieve some noninterpersonal goal, such as striking someone in order to rob him/her)
2. Humiliates or demeans people in the presence of others
3. Has treated or disciplined someone under his/her control unusually harshly
4. Is amused by, or takes pleasure in, the psychological or physical suffering of others (including animals)
5. Has lied for the purpose of harming or inflicting pain on others (not merely to achieve some other goal)
6. Gets other people to do what he/she wants by frightening them (through intimidation or even terror)
7. Restricts the autonomy of people with whom he or she has a close relationship, e.g., will not let spouse leave the house unaccompanied or permit teenage daughter to attend social functions
8. Is fascinated by violence, weapons, injury, or torture

This behavior must not be better explained by sexual sadism disorder and it must be directed towards more than one person

It is perhaps important to note that deriving pleasure from the suffering of others was just one of the eight criteria proposed in the DSM-III-R conceptualization of SPD. Some authors have, appropriately in our view, argued that this should be a compulsory or dominant criterion in order to differentiate SPD from antisocial personality disorder or contextually motivated sadistic acts (Berger et al., 1999; Kaminer & Stein, 2001; Myers et al., 2006). Indeed, identifying a non-sexual characterological satisfaction or pleasure from the suffering of others can be pragmatically useful, even when an individual meets formal criteria for SS and a personality disorder.

It is interesting to look back on SPD considering the dimensional nature of personality disorder (Hopwood et al., 2018), explaining the comorbidity, lack of distinctiveness, continuum with sub-clinical traits, and multiple subtypes. An unanswered clinical question is whether it is useful and of heuristic value in identifying a set of traits associated with pleasure in cruelty, beyond using other diagnoses? Recent findings of high rates of schizoid (detached), narcissistic (power/

humiliation) and obsessive-compulsive (controlling) traits in people who commit SH (Hill et al., 2006a; Chan et al., 2015; Darjee & Baron, 2018a) may reflect a sadistic trait conglomeration, similar to Brittain's (1970) sadistic murderer profile. As such, there may still be some heuristic and pragmatic value in considering sadistic personality features in addition to other personality disorder diagnoses. In our experience, such features are most certainly present in some offenders, but are almost always present in those that have other personality disorder diagnoses or prominent maladaptive personality features. Accordingly, they arguably have some explanatory value as additional personality and behavioral features.

While SPD was removed from the DSM nosology, research regarding such personality features has continued to occur. Indeed, Meloy (1997) noted that "the DSM-IV has tried to simplify things by eliminating sadistic personality disorder, but burning the map does not eliminate the territory" (p. 631). For example, Holt et al. (1999) found statistically significant relationships between differing measures of SPD and both factors of the Psychopathy Checklist-Revised (PCL-R; Hare, 1991; Hares, 2003). They also found a relationship between measures of SPD and SS, but this was of a lesser magnitude than the relationship between SPD and psychopathy.

Relationships between SPD, other personality disorders, and SS were also found by Berger et al. (1999). They found that over a quarter of men with serious sexual offences had SPD, it overlapped with borderline and antisocial disorders, criteria loaded on a factor with violent ones of antisocial personality, 42.1% of those with it had SS, and suggested SPD was not discrete but a subdimension of antisocial personality disorder. Amongst SH perpetrators, 17.5% had SPD, 36.7% SS, and the two were associated, with 36.1% of those with SS and 6.7% without having SPD (Hill et al., 2006b). Rates in non-forensic clinical samples have been 2.5–5% (Fiester & Gay, 1991).

Following the demise of SPD, at least in formal diagnostic manuals, there has been a resurgence of interest in sadistic personality in trait psychology. Characterological or everyday sadism has been added to the 'dark triad' of narcissism, Machiavellianism, and psychopathy, making a 'dark tetrad'. These have largely been researched in non-clinical non-forensic samples, are often labelled 'sub-clinical', and their associations investigated in normative not pathological personality contexts (e.g., see Thomas & Egan, 2022). This sadism is a tendency to derive pleasure (not sexual) from the distress or harm of others; there are several self-report measures of it (O'Meara et al., 2011; Buckels et al., 2013; Paulhus & Jones, 2015). It overlaps with, but is distinct from psychopathy, and correlates negatively with agreeableness, extraversion, conscientiousness, and openness to experience.

Sadistic personality traits may predispose one to the development of SS, or they may share similar etiological and developmental origins, such as traumatic experiences of humiliation and genetic predisposition to callousness, detachment, and control. Sadistic traits may disinhibit the expression of SS, particularly when need for power, order, and control is triggered by feeling humiliated or powerless.

12.3.1.2 Psychopathy

Psychopathy and SS are associated with each other but are distinct, usually present independently of each other, even in those who commit serious sexual violence (Meloy, 1997; Kirsch & Becker, 2007; Mokros et al., 2011; Darjee, 2019). Both entail empathy deficits (Kirsch & Becker, 2007), but whereas in SS a person puts themselves in the shoes of another, to perceive, feel and vicariously experience their suffering, delighting in this and becoming sexually aroused, in psychopathy the empathy deficit is underpinned by neurodevelopmental emotional under reactivity to fear and distress in others, leading to insensitivity to the effect of their behavior on others (Blair et al., 2005; Glenn & Raine, 2014). Put simply, sexual sadists take erotic pleasure from the suffering of others, while psychopaths just don't care about it, both predisposing to brutality. They share apparent callousness, but other features do not overlap (Mokros et al., 2011). Neither have deficits in theory of mind, although rarely comorbid autism complicates the picture.

Psychopathy and SS can co-occur (Robertson & Knight, 2014; Chan, 2020), such comorbidity is common in serial SH (Myers et al., 1993; Giannangelo, 1996; Cooke, 2001), and differentiates serial from single SH offenders (Hill et al., 2006a; Darjee, 2019; James & Proulx, 2014). The most prominent psychopathy facet in such cases is facet 2, the core empathy deficit, with other facets less consistently present (Hickey et al., 2018). There is overlap and co-occurrence between sadistic and psychopathic traits, which predispose to SS (Roberson et al., 2018), and facilitate acting on sadistic arousal and fantasy, due to tendencies such as grandiosity, conning and manipulation, lack of empathy, and/or impulsivity.

12.3.1.3 Other Personality Disorders

Most personality disorders have been found associated with SS in people who commit sexual violence: schizoid, schizotypal, borderline, antisocial, narcissistic, avoidant, and obsessive-compulsive (Berger et al., 1999; Proulx et al., 2007; Hill et al., 2006a; Darjee, 2019). These may predispose to developing sadistic fantasies in adolescence and adulthood due to emotional and social detachment, callousness, aggressiveness, introversion with retreat into fantasy, sensitivity to humiliation and need for power, lack of intimate connections, and/or being perfectionistic and controlling. Such traits overlap with sadistic and psychopathic ones, and may also trigger, facilitate, and disinhibit acting on fantasies in certain contexts.

In our experience, the most prevalent and notable personality traits that are found amongst those with CSSD *who commit sexual offences*, are notable levels of callous and unemotional personality features. Indeed, these are the features with considerable overlap amongst schizoid, psychopathic, narcissistic, and obsessive-compulsive personality disorders. Empathy is an important inhibitory mechanism when it comes to controlling urges or fantasies that may be harmful to others. As such, it is our view that a characterologically impoverished ability to empathize is an important component that permits those with sexually sadistic fantasies to engage in behavior consistent with their fantasies. This is demonstrated in Fig. 12.2, which is based on that described by Davis and Dietz (2024).

It is hypothesized that the level of callous/unemotional personality features interacts with the degree of coercion within sadistic fantasies to produce various forms of sexual and/or offending behavior. While these constructs should both be properly viewed as continua, the interaction can be viewed as having four broad quadrants. When both the degree of coercion in sadistic fantasy and the level of callous/unemotional personality features are low, this characterizes the modal BDSM practitioner (see below). When both are high, the behavior is that of the overt criminal with CSSD. When there is a low level of coercion in sadistic fantasies, but a high degree of callous/unemotional features, this characterizes the muted sadist (aroused by a victim's discomfort) or someone who engages in criminal acts of sexual bondage. Finally, when the degree of fantasized coercion is high, but there are minimal callous/unemotional traits, this characterizes an individual with ego-dystonic sadistic fantasies. There are case studies of the latter in the literature, who do not even date out of fear of harming someone (Revitch, 1980; Revitch & Schlesinger, 1989). Some case studies describe considerable planning to abduct and torture which ultimately ceases when the individual seeks treatment (Mullen et al., 2009). It is unclear just how many individuals there are in the wider society who do not offend but nonetheless have sadistic fantasies with high levels of coercion to the point of homicide. This will be considered in further detail below.

In people who commit sadistic sexual violence and homicide, comorbid personality disorder is ubiquitous (Berger et al., 1999). Amongst SH offenders, those with SS have higher rates than those without (Hill et al., 2006a), and serial sexual murderers predominantly have severe personality disorders and SS (Chan et al., 2015; Hill et al., 2006a). A comprehensive assessment of personality disorders is required in those who have committed, or are at risk of committing, sexually sadistic violence.

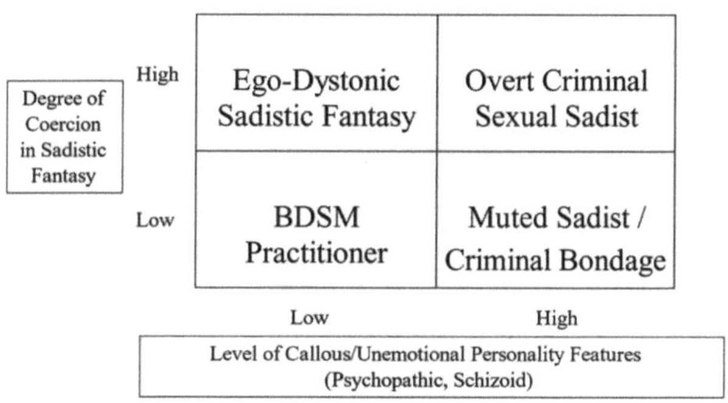

Fig. 12.2 Hypothesized Interaction between Personality, Sadistic Fantasy, and Behavior (Davis & Dietz, 2024)

12.3.2 Paraphilic Disorders

Amongst offenders with SS, comorbid paraphilic disorders are often described. Prentky et al. (1989) found rates in serial SH were: sadism 86%, voyeurism 75%, fetishism 71%, exhibitionism 25% and transvestic fetishism 25%; while in single victim cases: sadism 23%, voyeurism 43%, fetishism 33%, exhibitionism 7%, transvestic fetishism 0%. In an overlapping sample of sexually sadistic offenders Dietz et al. (1990) found an average of approximately three paraphilias per case. Hill et al. (2006b) found an average of 0.72 comorbid paraphilias in sadistic SH compared to 0.55 non-sadistic SH. Amongst the former the rate of masochism was 14.8%, transvestic fetishism 13.1% and voyeurism 11.5%, with lower rates perhaps due to most having just one victim. Gratzer and Bradford (1995) found higher rates of transvestism, voyeurism and exhibitionism amongst offenders with versus without SS. But most of these samples were extreme, exclusively or predominantly SH cases, so whether such associations hold for non-SH is unclear.

When considering co-occurrence, SS in an individual: (1) may be truly comorbid with other paraphilic disorders; (2) may have features which appear to be indicative of, or similar to, other paraphilic disorders but are primarily manifestations of SS; or (3) may be a misdiagnosis in the context of an alternative paraphilic disorder. When there is comorbidity, this may be due to common underlying factors, such as hypersexuality or personality problems. Necrophilia will be considered first, given its historic entanglement with sadism, before considering other disorders. PCD has already been considered above.

12.3.2.1 Necrophilia

Necrophilia can be diagnosed as "other specified paraphilic disorder, necrophilia" in DSM-5-TR (APA, 2022) and "other paraphilic disorder involving non-consenting individuals" in ICD-11 (WHO, 2022). 'True' or 'genuine' necrophilia involves sexual arousal by thoughts, fantasies, urges, or behaviors involving sexual interaction with a corpse, including viewing, touching, kissing, fondling or sexual penetration. This may involve fantasies only, behavior with already dead corpses ('regular' necrophilia or "necrostuprum"; Wulffen, 1910) or killing to have a corpse (necrophilic homicide; Rosman & Resnick, 1989). Genuine necrophilia has been differentiated from other situations where necrophilic behavior is not driven by recurrent, strong, or preferential sexual interest, the latter termed "pseudonecrophilia" (Meloy, 1996; Rosman & Resnick, 1989), although confusingly that term has also been used for sex with a person pretending to be dead and for fantasy only (Aggrawal, 2010). In addition to overtly sexual behavior with the dead, other behaviors have also been considered necrophilic, including sexual killing, mutilation, and consuming parts of the dead. So as well as the three types of genuine necrophilia, the terms necrophilia and necrophilic have referenced: getting sexual partners to act and appear like corpses (perhaps related to sex with sleeping or unconscious partners [somnophilia];

Knafo, 2015; Pettigrew, 2017; Deehan & Bartels, 2021); killing people for sexual pleasure (lust murder [Krafft-Ebing, 1886], erotophonophilia [Money, 1990], or sadistic pseudonecrophilia [Rosman & Resnick, 1989]); killing people and sexually interacting with them but without a persistent or intense pattern of necrophilic arousal (inhibited necrophilia after killing a partner [Jones, 1931]; or opportunistic or transitory pseudonecrophilia [Rosman & Resnick, 1989]); drinking blood (vampirism), eating human flesh (anthropophagy or cannibalism) or decaying flesh from the dead (necrophagy; Wulffen, 1910); mutilating, dismembering, disemboweling or eviscerating corpses (necrosadism or necromutilomania; Mellor, 2016); sexual attraction to corpses or killing of animals (necrozoophilia or necrobestiality). Aggrawal (2010) developed an elaborate theoretical classification of necrophilia, covering most of these, with 10 classes: "role players", "romantic necrophilia", "necrophilic fantisizers", "tactile necrophiles", "necromutilomaniacs", "opportunistic necrophiles", "regular necrophiles", "homicidal necrophiles", and "exclusive necrophiles". This covers behavior rather than necrophilia per se, and its empirical validity, or clinical or forensic utility is unknown. The use of the term necrophilia is further complicated by Fromm's (1973) non-sexual concept of "necrophilic personality", an orientation towards death, destruction, disease, and decay rather than a love of life.

The relationship between necrophilia and SS is complicated by the various concepts of each. In 1844 Kaan identified "violation of cadavers" as a common sexual "aberration", in his *Psychopathia Sexualis* (Kaan, 2016). Krafft-Ebing (1886) included necrophilia (including homicidal and non-homicidal necrophilia and mutilation of corpses) as a sub-category of sadism. Since then, the association between SS and necrophilia has been fraught with definitional problems and vagaries. On the one hand, sexual interaction with an unresisting and totally submissive body could be seen as an ultimate act of subjugation rooted in sadism (Bloch, 1935; Drzazga, 1960); on the other, a dead person cannot suffer (Moll, 1921; Ellis, 1936). And, how then should behavior towards a corpse, which if not dead would be sexually sadistic (such as mutilation; Mellor, 2016), be classified or conceptualized?

In our view SS involves inflicting and vicariously experiencing suffering, humiliation, degradation, and pain in a living person, while necrophilia involves sexual attraction to corpses which is not merely opportunistic, transitory, or due to a person dying during sexual intercourse. So, although many sexual murders involve perimortem sexual behavior (Higgs et al., 2017, 2017), this can be the culmination of sadistic arousal, spilling over after death (termed lust murder or erotophonophilia), rather than necrophilia per se; and homicides with extensive necrophilic behavior do not usually involve sadistic behavior pre-mortem. The 'spillover' mechanism maybe (1) getting carried away and consumed by arousal and behavior despite the victim's death; (2) merely a continuation of pre-mortem behavior, (3) a specific dénouement with final acts of domination, contempt, and humiliation; or (4) due to frustration or anger as death is anticlimactic.

Most individuals who have post-mortem sex with victims do not have necrophilia, their behavior being transitory, opportunistic or an extension of pre-mortem sadism (Rosman & Resnick, 1989). Stein et al. (2010) found no true necrophilia amongst 16 cases of SH with post-mortem sex. Chopin and Beauregard (2021) found four types of necrophilic behavior in SH: opportunistic, experimental, preferential, and sadistic, with the preferential (i.e., necrophilic) group smallest, only 15.6% of cases. Stefanska et al. (2022) described 25 SH cases with sexual activity only occurring post-mortem, of whom nine were sexually sadistic. These cases involved an extension of ante-mortem sadistic behavior post-mortem or 'sadistic' behaviors only inflicted after death; whilst non-sadistic cases included opportunistic and genuine necrophilia.

Apparent sadistic behavior towards corpses, whether also pre-mortem or not, and whether or not after homicide, has been subsumed under necrophilia (Mellor, 2016; Pettigrew, 2022). Corpse mutilation has long been considered a type or aspect of necrophilia (Krafft-Ebing, 1886; Wulffen, 1910), assuming sexual motivation, and termed necrosadism (Wulffen, 2010), necromanic (Rajs et al., 1998) or necromutilomania (Aggrawal, 2011). The term *splanchnophilia* has been used where there is sexual arousal to interacting with entrails (Dietz, 1992/2022). Most mutilation of victims is 'defensive', i.e., dismemberment to dispose of them, or obscure identifying features (Püschel & Koops, 1987; Rajs et al., 1998; Guggenheimer et al., 2021). Amongst the others are: 'aggressive', occurring due to disturbed emotions or mental state; and 'offensive', associated with sexual deviance. The latter manifesting as post-mortem removal of body parts, evisceration, disembowelment, or dismemberment. The term necrosadism for this behavior is problematic, as it has been defined variously, so some prefer the more descriptive necromutilophilia or necromutilomania. The term necrosadism may be better used where apparently sadistic behaviors are inflicted specifically post-mortem and not merely extending from pre- or peri-mortem sadism. One problem with otherwise extremely useful behavioral rating scales, like the SESAS, is there is no differentiation between pre- and post-mortem behavior. Although, Chopin and Beauregard (2021) found dismemberment in SH was primarily associated with indicators of sexual deviance, including SS and necrophilia, rather than avoiding detection, there has been little attention to whether indicators of sadism or deviance were present pre-, peri- or post-mortem.

12.3.2.2 Other Paraphilic Disorders

Vampirism, *necrophagy*, and *cannibalism* are sometimes considered rare forms of paraphilic disorders involving the consumption of blood, tissues, or organs, with necrophagy specifically decayed dead flesh, although Wulffen (1910) originally used the term for either cannibalism or mutilation. These behaviors are rare accompaniments to sexual violence, even SHs. When they occur, they are often unrelated to sexual arousal or fantasy. Although they are often considered manifestations of severe SS, when they occur in SHs they are more often associated with necrophilia (Carroll & Coston, 2021), due to a wish to assimilate, possess or prolong connection with victims; or with psychotic illness, to nourish and replenish in the context of delusions about the body deteriorating (Giordano et al., 2012). Biting, perhaps drawing blood, biting through flesh, or biting parts off a victim, is seen in SS to inflict pain and suffering, but not specifically to consume blood or flesh (Willmott et al., 2018). There are individuals primarily sexually aroused by eating the flesh of others, who seek this with the victim's consent where the victim may also be aroused by being eaten (Stampf, 2008), or by killing a victim to eat them (Kushner, 1997), but are not sadistic or necrophilic. Interestingly, people who kill and eat victims with pre- or post-mortem sexual activity more likely eat sexual organs (Carroll & Coston, 2021).

Erotophonophilia, coined by Money (1990) for lust murder, hence the alternative 'lust murderism' (Money, 1984), involves sexual arousal and gratification specifically through the act of killing (e.g., Peter Kurten in early twentieth century Germany; Wagner, 1935; Godwin, 1938; Berg, 1945; Skrapec 2001). However, lust murder is often used loosely to cover sadistic, necrophilic and necrosadistic homicide (Krafft-Ebing, 1886; Purcell & Arrigo, 2006), regardless of the primary sexual focus being killing the victim. As such, some, but arguably not all, erotophonophilic homicides may be committed by those with sexual sadism. Erotophonophilia is the very extreme end of the sadistic dimension, and, therefore, the agonistic continuum. Only a minority of SHs are erotophonophilic.

Piquerism (sexual arousal to the incising and piercing of flesh) occurs on its own without features of SS, but is often considered a form of SS, or one of a repertoire of behaviors used to cause pain, fear, suffering, or injury in SS. *Mutilomania* can be considered an extreme type of piquerism (see above; Pettigrew, 2022, 2023). Penetrating skin (piquerism) or other tissues (mutilomania) with a bladed implement can sexually arouse without direct sexual activity and may be conceptualized as substituting for or symbolizing penile penetration. So called "ripper" murders may involve piquerism and mutilomania, and differentiating such wounds from those due to angry overkill can be a challenge (Pettigrew, 2023), although the latter lack savoring and ritual. It should be noted that piquerism is a term that has arguably had more vague and contradictory definitions than sadism itself. Indeed, Davis (2016) argued that the term should be reserved for non-sadistic cases in which the incising of flesh was the paraphilic focus and proposed three sub-types of piquerism: *Piquer and Run* offenders, who stab the buttocks or breasts and quickly run away; *Post-Mortem Piquers*, who make many predominantly shallow knife wounds to genitalia or seemingly erotic body parts either post-mortem or perhaps peri-mortem; and *Ante-Mortem Face-to-Face Piquers*, who are clearly aroused by the incising of flesh rather than the victim's reaction (as would be the case in SS). The latter are the most difficult to differentiate from SS at the behavioral analysis stage, but some clear case studies have been described, including an individual who paid a 17 year-old approximately $6000 to be his "erotic pin-cushion" for an 18 month period (see Griffiths, 2015).

Partialism is a common sexual interest, with the focus on non-sexual parts of the body, such as hair (trichophilia) or feet (aretifism). This may be seen as a form of fetishism. In fact, partialism was added as a specifier to the diagnostic criteria of Fetishistic Disorder in DSM-5 (APA, 2013) under the term "body part(s)" (see Kafka, 2010a, 2010b). It is sometimes comorbid with SS, in its most rare extreme form may involve removing body parts, and may need to be differentiated from *acrotomophilia* (attraction to amputees or amputation; Money & Simcoe, 1984).

Cordophilia and *ligottism* are terms for a paraphilic interest in being physically bound or restrained, or binding or restraining others (Dietz et al., 1983). A related term is *bondage fetishism*. This is often associated with SS, and only warrants specification when it is prominent in the ritual of an individual (i.e., in fantasy or in offences), and are not merely functional (i.e., facilitating offence commission). Strangulation with bare hands or with a ligature is common in sadistic rape and SH, as it is intimate, controllable, and allows the perpetrator to see their victim's fear and distress; but may or may not be bound in with the deviant fantasy script. In our view, a diagnosis of cordophilia (ligottism) should only be made when the binding of the individual is clearly ritualistic and not simply functional or pragmatic. Behavioral indicators of cordophilia can include unnecessary bindings, such as the calves, forearms, or post-mortem binding, symmetry, neatness, or binding in a variety of positions (Hazelwood, 2006, as cited in Davis, 2022a).

Asphyxiophilia, also known as Kotzwarraism (Dietz et al., 1983) and previously hypoxyphilia,[2] usually described in the context of autoerotic asphyxia, can also reference arousal to asphyxiating others (although it is currently subsumed in the DSM-5-TR system as a specifier within the diagnosis of sexual masochism disorder). Asphyxiation is common in sadistic sexual violence, but as with other behaviors, it may or may not be central to fantasies and arousal. Autoerotic asphyxiation is associated with other paraphilic disorders, including transvestic fetishism, masochism, and bondage fetishism (Sauvageau & Racette, 2006). It has also been described with SS. In a series of sadistic serial SHs (Myers et al., 2008) where perpetrators practiced autoerotic asphyxia, striking parallels were seen between offences and autoerotic behavior. The latter allowed the experience of what it was like to be their victim, feeling terror, subjugation, pain and almost death from the victim's perspective, feeding their sadistic fantasies. Although like masochism they were aroused by being made to suffer, this was at their own hand, and only while experiencing what they inflicted on their victims. Moreover, this relates strongly to those with SS "becoming the victim" and feeling their way into their victim's experience (Stekel, 1924; Knoll & Hazelwood, 2009).

One aspect of SS is humiliation, including degrading and disgusting behavior. This may include getting victims to defecate, urinate or vomit; to have these cast on them; or being forced to consume them. *Coprophilia*, *urophilia* and *vomerophilia* are paraphilias focused on these respectively, are usually harmless solitary or mutual sexual interests, and rarely come to forensic or clinical attention. Where these occur in SS, they are usually a means to degrade, not a specific paraphilic focus, although occasionally they are prominent in fantasy and ritual (Bartholomew et al., 1975).

Sexual arousal to, and activity with, animals, *zoophilia* or *bestiality*, is often considered an extreme sexual deviance and placed alongside SS and necrophilia as concerningly taboo and dangerous. For example, where extreme pornography is legislated against, the specific behaviors included are these three paraphilias

[2] This was previously known as *Hypoxyphilia*, as it was thought that sexual arousal was associated with oxygen deprivation. However, Hucker (2011) noted that those that engage in this form of behavior are aroused by the restriction of breathing rather than hypoxia.

(McGlynn & Rackley, 2009). Despite grotesque connotations, most bestiality is not sexually penetrative or overtly physically harmful (Holoyda et al., 2018; Sandler, 2019; Bourke, 2020), and rates of sexual fantasies or behaviors in the population are relatively high at up to 10% (Holoyda et al., 2018; Bourke, 2020). Cases of sexually sadistic behavior towards larger mammals (e.g., cats, dogs, horses, cattle) arouse concern, may substitute for behavior towards humans, but can also be a developmental precursor, sometimes in childhood or adolescence, to targeting people (Dadds et al., 2002). Most are not specifically attracted to animals, so do not have zoophilia. However, rarely individuals' sadistic sexual fantasies and behavior are focused only on animals, and the term *zoosadism* has been used (Aggrawal, 2011). Indeed, this was one of the types of sadism originally identified by Krafft-Ebing (1886). Amongst people from the online community of zoophiles, 15% endorsed sadism as a paraphilic interest or behavior, and 'zoosadism' was identified as one of four subscales of the Sexual Interest in Animals-Self-Report (SIA-SR) scale, albeit demonstrating the least interest, the other three being 'zoophilia', 'opportunism' and 'furry sex' (Zidenberg & Olver, 2022). Individuals with SS may involve animals in behavior towards human victims. For example, forcing sexual interactions with animals, hurting or killing animals in front of victims, or using animal products, parts or corpses in disgusting, demeaning or frightening ways. Like feces and urine, this is usually a means to an end, rarely central to fantasy script.

Children and the elderly are more often victims of sexually sadistic crimes and SHs than young and middle-aged adults (Chopin et al., 2022). This may be due to vulnerability (being easier targets) and frailty (so more likely to suffer injuries and death). Amongst those who sexually abuse children a common distinction is between those with a sexual preference for children and without (Cohen et al., 1969; Knight, 1989; Lanning, 1992; see Chap. 13 of this volume for a detailed review). The former have *pedophilic disorder*, and amongst this group the smallest subgroup is sexually sadistic individuals (Knight, 1989; Lanning, 1992, 2010). They are focused on prepubescent or peri-pubescent children and commit most serial SHs of young children (Page et al., 2022). Children are integral to their deviant sexual scripts. Sexually sadistic offenders not attracted to children target adult and older teenaged victims, but rarely target younger children. When they do, the primary target is often the parent or guardian. Terrifying the parent or child, by harming the other, may be the purpose of harming or killing the person who is not the primary focus.

Sexual masochism has been entangled with SS since both were first named by Krafft-Ebing (1886). By the early twentieth century sadism and masochism were considered two sides of the same coin, both present to some degree in individuals with either, but conflation between BDSM and CSS, prevalent until very recently, has obscured understanding the relationship between them. The term sadomasochism has propagated the view they are related, either within an individual or between two individuals, and was a category in ICD-10 (WHO, 1992). Although in BDSM some people go between dominant and submissive roles, particularly females, and in any scene there will be a dominant and submissive, this does not apply to CSS. Few sadistic sexual aggressors have comorbid sexual masochism disorder even though they may engage in apparently masochistic behaviors. Clearly victims do not experience masochistic pleasure, and where offenders display apparent masochism, this is probably primarily to experience the suffering of victims, not to derive pleasure from their own suffering, as described for autoerotic asphyxia above. As such, masochistic behavior likely stimulates and fuels sadistic, not masochistic, fantasies.

Transvestic fetishism, fetishism, voyeurism, and exhibitionism are associated with SS in sexual aggressors (Prentky et al., 1989; Dietz et al., 1990; Gratzer & Bradford 1995; Hill et al., 2006b). The question is whether these are separate manifestations of underlying psychosexual disturbance in an individual who is polymorphously perverse (Abel et al., 1988), an early manifestation of an escalating paraphilic pattern, or intrinsically bound to a person's SS. So, some individuals cross-dress or involve fetish objects in sadistic fantasies and offences, but do not indulge in fetishism separately. Cross-dressing may occur with apparently masochistic behavior or autoerotic asphyxia in those who target girls or women, to identify with and experience victims' suffering. Very few individuals with voyeurism or exhibitionism commit contact sexual offences, let alone sadistic ones. An unanswered question is whether those with SS who exhibit these behaviors experience concomitant sadistic arousal and fantasies whilst exposing or watching others, so there is a different motivation and fantasy.

Schlesinger and Revitch (1999) described two types of *sexual burglaries*: fetish (handling and taking overtly sexual objects like underwear) and voyeuristic (looking around, inspecting drawers, often fantasizing about seeing woman naked). Both types may be associated with SS and escalate to serious sexual violence. In a third type sexual violence and burglary occur together in the victim's home (Davies & Dale, 1996; Vaughn et al., 2008; Pedneault et al., 2012). A quarter to a half of sexual offenders have past burglaries. While most of these are non-sexual, Harris et al. (2013) found a third of 762 burglaries (committed by 281 of 828 male serious sexual offenders) were, with 40 covert (including fetish and voyeuristic), 119 overt (involving sexual assault) and 65 combined. Interestingly, two thirds of the non-sexual burglaries did not involve stealing. Harris et al. (2013) highlighted several similarities between burglary and sexual violence feelings of power, intrusion, control or thrill, and planning and mental rehearsal, like ritualistic sexual offenders including those with SS. SS seems to have a particular relationship with stealing and then cutting up, destroying or soiling underwear.

12.3.3 Other Sexual Disorders

12.3.3.1 Compulsive Sexual Behavior Disorder

Compulsive sexual behavior disorder (CSBD) was introduced in ICD-11 (Briken, 2020), subsuming previous concepts, like sexual preoccupation, hypersexuality, sexual addiction and paraphilia-related disorders (Kafka, 2001, 2010a, 2010b). It is a persistent pattern of failure to control intense, repetitive sexual impulses or urges resulting in repetitive sexual behavior; repetitive sexual activity becomes a central focus, to the neglect and detriment of the person's health, personal care or other interests, activities, and responsibilities; leading to distress or impairment in personal, social, or occupational functioning. It is often comorbid with paraphilic disorders (Kafka & Hennen, 2002), may developmentally predispose to paraphilic disorders in adolescence, and shares with paraphilic disorders an uncoupling of sex and intimacy.

In the forensic experience of the current authors, it has been seen that compulsive masturbation and fantasizing is common amongst those with SS who have committed serial sexual offences. In addition, the literature indicates that there are high rates of CSBD in SH offenders. For example, Briken et al. (2010) found over half of SH offenders had paraphilia-related disorders and there was a significant association between these and SS. Prentky et al. (1989) found high rates of compulsive masturbation in a small sample of serial (70%) and single sexual murderers (50%), and Robertson et al. (2018) found hypersexuality was important in their etiological model of SS. When comorbid SS and CSBD are present, and the risk of sexual violence is high, pharmacological treatment is usually indicated.

12.3.3.2 Sexual Dysfunctions

Sexual dysfunction is no more or less likely in sexually sadistic versus non-sexually sadistic homicide offenders (Hill et al., 2006b), although one in five cases had sexual dysfunction, usually erectile dysfunction, at the higher end of the 5–20% in men who commit sexual offences (Briken & Turner, 2022; Eher et al., 2019; Phillips et al., 2015). There is no research on the association between SS and sexual dysfunction in other groups. Sexual dysfunction may trigger anger and violence during the commission of rape (Jones et al., 2010), but in SS may lead to increased coercion and infliction of suffering as less severe behaviors are not arousing enough, or to compensate for feeling humiliated and impotent. In addition, sexual dysfunction may lead to the use of more deviant fantasies to facilitate arousal (Briken & Turner, 2022), in SS heightening use of sadistic fantasies and behaviors.

12.3.4 Other Mental Disorders

We will consider various psychiatric disorders which may be associated with SS, facilitate the expression of SS, or present with thoughts or behaviors that look like SS, to help practitioners consider comorbidity, differential diagnosis, and formulation.

12.3.4.1 Psychotic Disorders

Psychosis has been described as rarely comorbid with SS (Meloy, 1997, 2000; Ressler et al., 1988). None of the sexually sadistic offenders described by Dietz et al. (1990) had psychosis, Ressler et al. (1988) found organized SH offenders were not mentally ill, Darjee (2019) found major mental disorder negatively associated with SS in SH, and psychosis occurs less in SH offenders than non-SH offenders (Lam et al., 2020; de Oliveira et al., 2023; Joynt & Darjee, 2023).

However, amongst 80 sexually violent men with *schizophrenia*, Smith (2000) found 9% were overtly sadistic whilst 7.5% were mutedly sadistic, but very few sadistic offences involved psychotic drive. Smith (1999) also found aggressive sexual fantasy, mostly sadistic, was associated with first committing sexual violence before illness onset, and more disturbed and adverse childhood experiences, particularly isolation and deviant sexual behavior.

Personality disorders associated with SS described above (schizoid, schizotypal, antisocial, and avoidant), predispose one to schizophrenia, contributing to an indirect connection. But psychosis does not precipitate, drive, or motivate sadistic sexual violence. When they commit homicides, psychotic individuals sometimes commit mutilation (Häkkänen & Laajasalo, 2006), but, unlike SS, this is without other sadistic features (e.g., control, humiliation, torture, ritual), rarely targeting sexual organs. SS, not schizophrenia, is associated with bizarre and more injurious behavior in sexual assaults.

12.3.4.2 Anxiety and Stress-Related Disorders

Individuals with *obsessive-compulsive disorder (OCD)* often have recurrent, intrusive, distressing, sexually violent obsessions (Grant et al., 2006), which are phenomenologically distinct from sadistic sexual fantasies. They are not pleasurable or sexually arousing, and although concern is often voiced about acting, there is no desire or motivation to, instead using avoidance behaviors (e.g., not going out, associating with women, or using knives) or compulsive rituals (e.g., counting or checking) to counteract obsessions. Some individuals with SS find their fantasies concerning or distressing (i.e., ego dystonic), but this is easy to differentiate from OCD as the former involves sexual arousal, sometimes with masturbation and overt sexual behavior. 'Obsession' is sometimes used to describe preoccupying and driving sexually sadistic fantasies, and 'compulsion' for the urge to act out such fantasies. Revitch and Schlesinger (1989) described sexual murderers with sadistic fantasies as "compulsive". But that usage is phenomenologically incorrect (Casey & Kelly, 2019) and can cause confusion. It is also important to differentiate obsessive-compulsive personality traits (such as being controlling, stubborn, abrasive and mean), seen in some sadistic sexual aggressors, from OCD, an anxiety disorder not associated with sexual violence nor with SS or SH, despite suggestions otherwise (Meloy, 2000).

People with CSSD often have adverse childhood experiences, including chronic and severe trauma, which seem to play an important etiological role in the genesis of sadistic fantasy and behavior (see 'Etiology'– below). However, post-traumatic stress disorder (PTSD) is not commonly encountered in these individuals. But abuse and trauma are important in the etiology of the personality disorders often seen. *Dissociative identity disorder (DID)* has been controversially diagnosed in several cases of serial sadistic SH in the context of unsuccessful insanity defenses (Ewing, 2008; Lewis, 2009). Many sexually sadistic offenders compartmentalize their behavior and can present a prosocial façade and lifestyle; identity disturbance and fragmentation is common in severe personality disorders, including those associated with SS; and the self-states in which they enact violence can be at variance with those they otherwise inhabit and manifest. However, these façades and shifts are often consciously enacted and not due to multiple split-off personalities. Questions are often asked as to what their true selves are, assuming their prosocial façade is a scam covering their true sadistic nature. However, the 'mask of sanity' is often more complex and nuanced. Humans adapt our personalities to situations, shifting states in different emotional and interpersonal contexts, both consciously and unconsciously, and are secretive at times. In the rare instances where such self-states seem disconnected and dissociated from each other, a more appropriate diagnosis is partial DID from ICD-11 (Tyrer, 2019), and legally the person is still considered to have consciously chosen to be sexually violent (Farrell, 2011; Scott et al., 2023).

12.3.4.3 Autism Spectrum Disorder

Emotional and social detachment, isolation and introversion, social avoidance and withdrawal, interpersonal distance and disconnection, low self-esteem and ostracization, and stubbornness and needing control are traits associated with CSS. But these overlap with or may be seen in autism spectrum disorder (ASD), raising a question whether this could factor in the development, maintenance and manifestation of SS. There has been no research on this, but it has been unconvincingly suggested that the serial murderer Jeffrey Dahmer had ASD (Silva et al., 2002), although no court expert diagnosed this (James, 2022) and the son of one expert described its application posthumously as "facile", "syllogistic", an "ill-advised attempt to make a diagnosis fit" and contributing "to the legend of solitary murderers as possibly suffering from an autism spectrum condition" (Palermo & Bogaerts, 2015). In addition, although he was diagnosed with SS by some psychiatric experts (Jentzen et al., 1994), others diagnosed necrophilia and paraphilic disorders focused on mutilating and eviscerating the dead (James, 2022). Another notorious SH perpetrator in the UK, diagnosed with ASD, along with schizophrenia, was Robert Napper (Alison & Eyre, 2009). But despite the grotesque nature of his crimes, it is unclear whether he was sexually sadistic, or, like Dahmer, behaviors occurred primarily post-mortem. A recent Australian case of SH by someone with both ASD and SS was Jaymes Todd who killed comedian Eurydice Dixon, with these diagnoses being important at sentencing (DPP v Todd, 2019; Todd v The Queen, 2020).

SS involves taking victims' perspectives, experiencing their pain, fear and suffering, so lack of theory of mind in ASD should mitigate against an association. In addition, callousness and lack of empathy, as opposed to poor perspective taking, are not features of ASD, and when present raise the possibility of comorbid psychopathy, described by Rogers et al. (2006) as a "double hit".

People with ASD may become fascinated by, and fixated on, images or videos depicting grotesque sexual violence, but this is not usually accompanied by sexual arousal or fantasy, or the motivation, willingness, ability or means to act, albeit this is troubling and disturbing to families or other supports who they sometimes openly show material to. Many of the few people in the UK arrested for viewing extreme pornography (depicting sadism, necrophilia, or bestiality) have autism.

In general, studies of ASD have shown high rates of problems with intimacy, paraphilic fantasies and behaviors, hypersexuality, and high rates of sadistic sexual fantasies and behavior (Fernandes et al., 2016; Turner et al., 2017, 2017; Schöttle et al., 2022). For example, 42.9% of males with high functioning ASD reported sadistic sexual fantasies and 28.6% sadistic sexual behavior (compared to 7.0% and 10.5% of healthy controls respectively; Schöttle et al., 2022). Suggested contributory factors include disregard of social norms, restricted social skills, lack of intimacy, isolation, sensory hypo-sensitivity, fixation and repetition, and associated hypersexuality. Given the methodology, one cannot assume these were coercive fantasies or behaviors, and although individuals with ASD who commit sexual offences are well recognized (Mogavero, 2016; Sevlever et al., 2013), there is no robust evidence of an association between ASD and sexual or violent offending (King & Murphy, 2014), let alone sexually sadistic offending.

12.3.4.4 Substance-Related Disorders and Behaviors

The role of substance misuse in sadistic sexual violence is unclear. High rates of substance, particularly alcohol, misuse and intoxication at offences characterize those who commit sexual violence (Kingree & Thompson, 2015) and SH (James & Proulx, 2014), and SH offenders are more likely to use alcohol than people who commit rape (Nicole & Proulx, 2007; Darjee & Baron, 2018a). However, those driven by SS seem less likely to be intoxicated than those who are opportunistic, impulsive or angry (Proulx et al., 2007; Darjee, 2019). Although alcohol intoxication may cause disinhibition and dysregulation, precipitating more violent and potentially fatal sexual violence, this does not seem to be primarily via disinhibiting SS. But it should be borne in mind that, although less so than others, those with SS have high rates of substance misuse and intoxication may play a role in offences (Proulx et al., 2007).

Although substances like gamma-hydroxy butyrate (GHB) and methamphetamine ("ice" or "meth"), can cause acute hypersexuality and associated disinhibition, leading to sexual violence, such offences are usually impulsive and disorganized and not sadistic. However, sexually sadistic offenders may use lower doses of GHB to heighten their sexual pleasure and arousal. Although not related to CSS, BDSM mixed with chem-sex (voluntary intake of certain psychoactive and non-psychoactive drugs with the intention of facilitating/enhancing the sexual encounter; McCall et al.,

2015), including the use of GHB and methamphetamine to heighten sexual arousal and drive, may lead to a fatal outcome. This is accidental and unintentional, but when a death is investigated, may lead to questions whether it was a sexually sadistic homicide. Examination of the antecedents of the individuals, history of involvement in BDSM amongst participants, and the crime scene, usually make it clear that CSS was not involved. Some sexually sadistic offenders, like other predatory individuals who commit sexual violence, use alcohol or other substances to make their victims easier to coerce, abduct, and control (LeBeau & Mozayani, 2001), or target individuals vulnerable through intoxication. But they do not like victims to be sedated unconscious as then they cannot experience or show fear and suffering.

12.3.4.5 Neurocognitive and Related Conditions

Most sexually sadistic offenders do not have overt neurocognitive disorders, although smaller medial temporal lobes and associated dilated anterior horns of the lateral ventricles, especially in the right brain, have been found in men who are sexually sadistic (see 'Etiology' - below). Briken et al. (2005) found 30% of sexual murderers had evidence of "brain abnormalities", broadly defined to include neurological disorders (epilepsy, traumatic brain injury, encephalitis/meningitis causing brain damage, genetic disorder), pathological neuroimaging and/or EEG results, and including cases that were mentioned as clearly pathologic but without a distinct diagnosis, who were included as "brain damage not specified". Those with brain abnormalities were significantly more likely to manifest DSM-IV SS, transvestic fetishism and paraphilia NOS, but the nature of the relationship (cause, effect, or epiphenomenon) between these abnormalities, paraphilic disorders and sexual violence was unclear. Interestingly the brain abnormalities group were also more isolated, less likely to abuse alcohol or substances, more likely to victimize strangers, commit serial offences and to display behaviors indicative of sadism (e.g., object insertion).

12.3.5 Non-sexually Sadistic Violence and Offending

It is important to distinguish sexually sadistic violence from other violence and other sexual violence. Where violence is shocking, excessive, grotesque, or cruel, sadism is easily invoked. However, most such violence is not sexually sadistic. Clearly sexual arousal and/or behavior are necessary, but may be covert, undetected, or undisclosed. In homicide cases, where there is no overt sexual activity or admitted sexual fantasies or arousal, the criteria of Ressler et al. (1988) can help in identifying whether there is a sexual element, although covert sexual dynamics (Greenall, 2012) can still be missed, and a lack of clothing obviously occurs in some non-SHs. Applying behavioral scales, such as the SESAS (Mokros et al., 2012) or in homicide cases the SADSEX-SH-R (Myers et al., 2019), can help identify SS. Sexually sadistic violence is usually prolonged and far beyond that necessary to rape or sexually assault. It is not usually over quickly or explosive, as the person is controlled, takes control, and savors the suffering. With rape offences, the groups which most often present difficulties in differentiating from SS are those with non-sadistic coercive rape fantasies (see 'PCD' - above) and those who have a vindictive motivation (see 'Rape' - below).

Practitioners also need to be aware that some apparently non-sexual offences may be manifestations of SS. Examples include assault, abduction, robbery, burglary, stalking, and murder. The sexual aspect may be missed, not warrant legal recognition, or a concomitant sexual offence dropped or pled away. This can be problematic both clinically and in legal contexts when assessing for the presence of SS. Again, applying structured behavioral rating scales can help identify SS and formulate hypotheses. People who have committed such offences or lawyers may object to a diagnosis of SS with no legally recognized sexual element, but given the implications of SS, practitioners would be remiss to ignore this when assessing and formulating.

12.3.6 Group Sexual Violence

When pairs or larger groups commit sexual violence or SH their behavior often manifests elements that appear to be like SS, such as prolonged offences, holding victims captive, tormenting and humiliating victims, escalation of violence, and more serious injuries (Horvath & Woodhams, 2013). Both rapes and SHs committed by multiple perpetrators are more apparently sadistic than those committed by single perpetrators (Clarkson et al., 2020; Horvath & Woodhams, 2013). Although it has been stated sexually sadistic offenders act alone (Brittain, 1970; MacCulloch et al., 1983), and the escalating violence and control may be a manifestation of the group dynamic, it may also be due to group leadership by someone with SS (Clarkson et al., 2020). It can also be a combination with a sexually sadistic individual initiating and driving, with escalation through the group dynamic. Clarkson et al. (2020) found most multiple perpetrator SHs looked behaviorally sadistic applying the SESAS, but not all pairs or groups included people with CSSD. When there was such an individual, they led the group and there was never more than one. When women are involved in sexually sadistic offending this is invariably committed with a man and he has SS (see 'Women - below). Cases where two sexual sadists have paired up and committed serial SHs are exceedingly rare (Jenkins, 1990). So, when assessing an individual involved in a multiple-perpetrator case where offence(s) appear sadistic, practitioners should consider whether this is primarily due to group dynamics or leadership by someone with CSSD. The latter may have a history of sadistic fantasy or solitary sadistic violence against animals or people.

12.4 Etiology

12.4.1 Biological Factors

There are many studies of neurobiological characteristics in people who commit sexual offences, but most focus on those with child victims or pedophilic sexual interests (Ramião et al., 2023). Studies rarely specifically examined SS. Below studies relevant to SS are considered, including the few addressing it directly, and those examining highly violent sexual offending including SH.

12.4.1.1 Genetic Factors

Genes play a role in sexual development (Blecher & Erickson, 2007), so likely play some role in paraphilic disorders, including SS, although studies have only addressed pedophilia and sexual offending (Långström et al., 2015; Kruger & Kneer, 2021). As with all complex and dimensional psychopathology, there are likely multiple genes involved, not specific to any paraphilic disorder, and other related aspects determined by hereditary factors, such as childhood temperament and adult personality, may mediate. Sex chromosome aneuploidies, XYY (Jacobs syndrome) and XXY (Klinefelter syndrome), may be important in a few cases.

Briken et al. (2006) reported three XYY cases amongst 166 SH perpetrators, of whom 13 had chromosome analysis. So, a rate of at least 2%, much higher than in offending samples (<1%) and the population (0.01%). All three had SS and psychopathy and two committed multiple SHs. Since the first report of a higher-than-expected rate of XYY in violent and sexual offenders (Jacobs et al., 1965), cases have been reported of sadistic sexual murderers with XYY syndrome: Manuel Delgado Villegas in Spain, Daniel Hugon in France, Sean Farley in the USA, Lawrence Edward Hannell and Robert Peter Tait in Australia (Saxe, 1969; Russell & Bender, 1970; Kraus, 1995). There have been reports of associations between XYY syndrome and sexual offending and homicide (Gosavi et al., 2009; Stockholm et al., 2012). But the vast majority of XYY males do not commit such offences (Re & Birkhoff, 2015). The most consistent finding in XYY males is large stature. Other associates, such as cognitive deficits and impulsive and aggressive behavior, are found inconsistently in a minority, although recently Joseph et al. (2018) found high rates of neurodevelopmental difficulties.

Cases have been reported of individuals with Klinefelter syndrome (47 XXY) with SS and homicidal offending (Davidson, 1994; Lauerma, 2001), including several serial sexual murderers: Francis Heaulme in France (Abgrall, 2010); Bobby Joe Long in the USA (Flowers, 2000); Mark Errin Rust in Australia (Fewster, 2014). Stochholm et al. (2012) found higher rates of offending, including homicide, sexual and violent offending, than in the general population in men with Klinefelter Syndrome and XYY syndrome. The association disappeared adjusting for sociodemographic factors for most offences, but not for sexual offending (or burglary or arson).

Klinefelter syndrome is associated with low testosterone and hypogonadism which is treated with testosterone replacement (although the cases reported were not on testosterone replacement when they offended), whilst XYY syndrome is associated with high testosterone, although there is no evidence of a mediating effect in sexual offending (Schiavi et al., 1984). Whether early and developmental perturbations in androgen function plays any role is unclear. However, associated neurocognitive deficits, physical issues (such as height, build and genital abnormalities), and effects on personality, when associated with other factors, such as abuse experiences, may predispose a few individuals to SS and related offending (Berlin, 1983; Kraus, 1995).

12.4.1.2 Structural and Functional Brain Abnormalities

CT scanning has shown an association between SS and right temporal lobe abnormalities (dilated inferior horn of lateral ventricle and reduced medial temporal volume): two in five versus one in 10 in controls (Hucker et al., 1988; Gratzer & Bradford, 1995). Using MRI, Aigner et al. (2008) found 59.4% of highly violent sexual offenders compared to 22.2% of low violence ones demonstrated brain abnormalities, with temporal abnormalities in three cases who were highly violent with SS. Temporal lobe abnormalities have been reported in association with other paraphilic disorders (Kruger & Kneer, 2021) and temporal-limbic pathways play an important role in aggression and sexual arousal (Siegel & Victoroff, 2009).

Garnett et al. (1988) compared a sexual sadist and two non-offending controls using positron emission tomography (PET) while presenting erotic and neutral auditory stimuli. They found right lateralized activity during both stimuli in non-sadists, whereas the sadist showed more bilateral activity. Harenski et al. (2012) compared eight sadists (identified using the SESAS) to seven nonsadists, all of whom had committed violent sexual offences, using functional magnetic resonance imaging to ascertain brain hemodynamic response to viewing depictions of a person in pain or not, whilst acquiring pain severity ratings. Sadism was associated with greater amygdala activation with pain pictures, high ratings of pain pictures, and positive correlation between pain severity ratings and anterior insula activity. So there was neurobehavioral evidence of unusually heightened sensitivity to the pain of others in SS, but the results may not indicate inherent brain abnormalities but rather context-dependent engagement of certain brain regions, and an atypical brain mechanism could result in sadism or vice versa.

12.4.1.3 Endocrine Factors

Although assumptions are made about the association between androgens, including testosterone, and sexual offending and paraphilic disorders, studies show inconsistent findings and a meta-analysis concluded there was no relationship between testosterone levels and sexual offending (Wong & Gravel, 2018). Testosterone is important in male sexual development and behavior, but its relationship with sexual aggression and deviance is likely complex and cannot be boiled down to simple differences in circulating testosterone levels. Testosterone is also important in non-sexual aggression, particularly that related to dominance, although perhaps less so in humans than in animals (Archer, 2006). However, it may be that dominance and winning lead to raised testosterone, rather than vice versa. Abnormal testosterone levels and activity may play a role at developmentally sensitive stages, such as in utero and adolescence, interacting with other developmental and contextual factors, predisposing to sexual aggression. There are context related brief elevations in testosterone in situations related to mating effort, with situational, motivational, and physiological variables moderating the interplay between social stimuli, testosterone reactivity, and behavior (Zilioli & Bird, 2017).

Three recent studies are relevant to SS. Kingston et al. (2012) studied 771 sexual offenders, finding free testosterone was somewhat related to level of violence (although not specifically sadism) and self-reported sex drive, while levels of luteinizing hormone (LH) and follicle stimulating hormone (FSH) related to hostility, and level of LH was related to offence violence and intrusiveness. Levels of FSH and LH also moderately predicted sexual and violent recidivism. But levels of all hormones were within normal limits, effect sizes were modest, and hormones do not explain sexual offending but interact with other factors. Weierstall et al. (2014), in students, found males responding with raised saliva testosterone when adopting a perpetrator perspective while listening to a violent story chose to view negative pictures (showing mutilation and dead bodies) for longer. They concluded testosterone moderates attraction to cruel and violent cues, although sexual cruelty was not specifically studied. Cazala et al. (2022) measured endocrine response while viewing a video of an individual in extreme distress in 23 male sexual offenders, finding that SESAS scores positively related to testosterone, but not oxytocin or adrenocorticotropic hormone, responses, concluding this was physiological evidence of atypical processing of distress cues in sadism, consistent with the role of testosterone in sexual arousal and aggressive behaviors.

So, the role of testosterone in SS (and sexual aggression and sexual deviance) is complex, cannot be simplified to differences in baseline testosterone levels, is context and developmental stage dependent, and interacts with other relevant biopsychosocial factors. Testosterone also plays a role in aggressive behavior, personality and sexual appetite, also in ways dependent on developmental stage and context, and interactions with other factors. Other hormones that regulate testosterone also seem important in this complex process.

12.4.1.4 Genital Abnormalities

Rettenberger et al. (2013) found 17.8% of perpetrators of SH had genital abnormalities, including phimosis, cryptorchidism, groin hernias, hypospadias, and retractile testis. Rates of all, except phimosis, were substantially higher than in the general population. Although they were associated with sexual dysfunction and sexual masochism, they were not specifically associated with SS, although more of those with abnormalities masturbated to sadistic and homicidal fantasies.

12.4.2 Early Abuse and Trauma

Studies have described high rates of abuse experiences in the childhoods of those who develop SS and those who commit homicidal sexual violence (Chopin et al., 2023), and early experiences of abuse, trauma and disrupted attachments have been linked to the development of sadistic sexual fantasy in theoretical models of SH (Burgess et al., 1986; Arrigo & Purcell, 2001; Hickey, 2015). However few studies compared individuals with SS to others with regards to such experiences.

More generally, those who experienced childhood sexual abuse are more likely to have various negative outcomes, including offending and sexual offending (Papalia et al., 2018), although this is likely not specific to sexual abuse, but related to the wider abusive context, including multiple other types of adverse experiences. Indeed, research has shown that having experienced multiple types of adverse experiences in childhood is associated with committing more serious and violent sexual offences. In a sample of men who had committed rape and SH, Delisi and Beauregard (2018) found experiencing more types of adverse childhood experiences correlated with SH versus rape, and this appeared to be mediated through effects on adolescent psychological difficulties and personality dysfunction (Chopin et al., 2023). Abusive experiences may lead directly to abnormal sexual functioning (including sexual preoccupation, hypersexuality and paraphilic disorders including SS), indirectly to problematic sexual behavior (via problems with intimacy, emotional functioning and distorted thinking about self and others), or other factors leading to acting out aggressive sexual behavior (such as personality dysfunction, substance misuse, anger, or violent attitudes). How abuse predisposes to SS and sexual violence has been considered in several theoretical models (see below).

Two types of abuse have been suggested to have particular relevance to SS: humiliation and maternal abuse. Some studies described high rates of humiliating experiences in the development of those who commit sexually sadistic crimes (Proulx et al., 2007), and clinically they often describe such experiences from parents, other care givers or family members, peers and/or those they are sexually attracted to in early adolescence. It is plausible that these lead to sadistic fantasies through identifying with their humiliator and/or through compensatory fantasies, although there must be other vulnerability factors as humiliated children rarely become sexually sadistic adults. Mothers of sexually sadistic individuals have been described as intrusive, overbearing, frightening, physically and sexually abusive, neglectful, chaotic and inconsistent, and absent. However, there is no consistent evidence sexual sadists have such relationships with mothers more often than with fathers or other adults, or than others who commit sexual violence. It seems likely their experience of their mother (whether objectively true or not) and internalized representation of her, is important in their internal representation (including in fantasy) of, and relationships with, women. This is emphasized in psychodynamic explanations (Yakely, 2021).

12.4.3 Psychodynamic Explanations

Psychodynamic concepts of sadism can be problematic due to the often broad conceptualization, incorporation of sadomasochism (and therefore BDSM), and the somewhat speculative and elusive nature of psychodynamic concepts, leading some to describe them as more literature than science (Grubin, 1994). Although "psychodynamic theories have not been subjected to or supported by empirical research, and have done little to advance our understanding of the etiology of sexual sadism" (Yates et al., 2008), clinically psychodynamic theory and practice can help understand SS in individuals, thinking about SS while understanding the complexities of human sexual development, and in dealing with the disturbing and complex transference and counter-transference issues that arise with SS (see 'Treatment' - below).

Freud (1905) initially proposed that we all start life perverse and subsequent defenses against infantile sexual impulses lead to personality development. The normal child was "polymorphously perverse" and then their sexual drives abate at the Oedipal phase due to unconscious factors like shame, disgust, guilt, and more mature ego defenses like repression and sublimation. So adult perversity occurs when infantile impulses escaped integration, repression, and sublimation due to biological and developmental vulnerabilities. He later conceived of perversion as a defence against castration anxiety leading to fetishism, whilst others extended the concept to earlier stages with primitive anxieties regarding the maternal relationship. Stoller (1976) considered perversion "the erotic form of hatred", with hostility the unconscious primary motivation, hidden behind the overt sexualization, representing a fantasy of revengeful triumph over childhood trauma, particularly relating to the mother. This trauma could be subtle, representing the risk of early attachment to her, who is over-involved, not allowing normal separation and development.

Yakely (2021) highlighted the roles of "the core complex", "corruption of the superego" and "confusion of boundaries" in paraphilic disorders. The core complex (Glasser, 1996), particularly relevant to SS, is a universal developmental stage relating to anxieties about abandonment and engulfment while separating and individuating from the mother. The complex is a primitive struggle between wishing to be close to her, while not being overwhelmed and obliterated. So, the individual either withdraws, feeling isolated and abandoned, or reacts aggressively in fantasy or reality for self-preservation. Aggression cannot be acted out towards her, so withdrawal into a self-absorbed state, becomes suffused with feelings of rejection again. Everyone experiences this, and it affects later intimate relationships, but it persists unmodified and intensely where there has been a pathological relationship with the mother. The resolution is to escape the vicious cycle, by sexualizing the hostility towards the mother, thus converting the initially defensive aggression into sadism. The object, initially the mother, is made to suffer and this gives pleasure, whilst the relationship with the object is preserved, does not need to be destroyed, but can be dominated and controlled. Acting on these fantasies in adulthood maintains an exciting interaction whilst warding off genuine intimate connection.

Turning specifically to SS, different psychoanalytic conceptualizations include fixation at the oral-biting stage of infancy (with the primitive urge to use mouth, lips and teeth as instruments of aggression, mastery and sexual gratification), fixation at the anal stage of psychosexual development (involving destruction of the object and its possession and control), development of mental impulses based on the fusion of aggression and sexuality, children viewing parental intercourse as involving subjugation or abuse, or arising not from the pleasure instinct (as per early conceptualizations) but the death instinct (Freud, 1905; Yates et al., 2008). Sadger (1926) proposed it developed during parental teaching regarding masturbation and toilet training when sexual pleasure was both denied and supported. Some theories have posited that SHs are symbolic or "displaced" matricides, where there is a lack of differentiation from the mother due to exploitative, controlling, aggressive or sexual maternal behavior, which in combination with the absence of a paternal figure, leads to feelings of hostility, rage, inadequacy, mistrust and fear of engulfment by females, ultimately expressed in the real world in SH (Revitch & Schlesinger, 1989; Meloy, 2000). This mirrors attempts to resolve the core complex.

12.4.4 The Role of Temperament and Personality

The role of personality disorder in predisposing to and facilitating the expression of SS was covered above. Childhood characteristics such as isolation, emotional detachment, feelings of inadequacy, cruelty to others, callousness, aggressiveness and/or disinhibition may be early manifestations of the personality traits described in association with SS. Such traits may be manifestations of or the result of neurobiological vulnerabilities and adverse childhood experiences and have been posited to play a role in the development of sadistic sexual fantasies and arousal (through isolation and compensatory fantasy which is sexualized in adolescence), problems in intimate and other relationships, and predisposition to act out violent sexual fantasies and urges.

12.4.5 Adolescence and the Emergence of Sadistic Sexual Fantasy and Arousal

Adolescence is a crucial phase in the development of sexual functioning and is considered crucial in the development of paraphilic disorders including SS. During adolescence sexual scripts, interests, and attitudes form; intimate and non-intimate relationships develop; sexual arousal, fantasy and behavior become manifest; and the differentiation of sexual and aggressive impulses needs to be achieved (Marshall & Barbaree, 1990). Developmental vulnerabilities due to problems in early and middle childhood lead to, and interact with, challenges and difficulties in these areas in adolescence. Although only a rare minority of individuals are primed to be aroused by sexually sadistic stimuli and behaviors in the context of such perturbations, most individuals with CSSD describe it emerging in adolescence. Although they may also experience arousal to non-sadistic fantasies and stimuli, sadistic ones tend to become salient and preferred, perhaps due to inherent predisposition, repeated pairing through fantasy and masturbation, compensatory feelings of mastery and power, and impaired development of mutual empathic intimate interactions and relationships. Adolescents who commit SH are equally, if not more likely, to manifest SS as adults, highlighting SS can be highly problematic relatively early (Myers & Blashfield, 1997).

12.4.6 Conditioning: Sexual Fantasy, Masturbation, and Behavioral Tryouts

From a behavioral perspective SS is seen as arising from the pairing of sexual arousal and orgasm with aggressive stimuli (classical conditioning) early in the development of an individual, which is then reinforced via sexual fantasy and masturbation (operant conditioning) (McGuire et al., 1965). MacCulloch et al. (1983) described these alleviating feelings of inadequacy, unassertiveness, and lack of control, arising from sexual failures and personality problems. With ongoing reinforcement through fantasy and masturbation sadistic fantasies escalated over time culminating in behavioral try outs, enacting aspects of fantasies, when disinhibitory factors allowed this. These lead to acting out progressively more fantasy congruent behaviors, but these cannot precisely match or fulfil the fantasies, so the fantasy must be restaged with further behaviors and victims. The fantasy is also shaped over time through reinforcement. Prentky et al. (1989) highlighted the importance of three social learning variables in this process: parental modelling of deviant behavior, repeated associations between the modeled behavior and a strong positive affective response in the child, and reinforcement of the child's deviant response.

To account for the initial development of sadistic sexual fantasies, rather than their maintenance and escalation, MacCulloch et al. (2000) posited that early childhood abuse along with classical and operant conditioning processes led to the development of sadistic sexual fantasy. Sadistic fantasy develops initially from "sensory preconditioning" a process where unrelated representations of stimuli that are concurrently active in cognition become associated with each other. Childhood abuse leads to fear, anxiety, and stress, along with atypical responses like sexual arousal. So, aggression/fear and sexual fantasy co-occur and with repeated abuse there are multiple such pairings, which become associated, leading via sensory preconditioning to a representation of sexual arousal which includes aggression/fear. Later aggression/fear invokes sexual arousal, and vice versa, leading to further reinforcement via classical and operant conditioning.

In terms of the transition from fantasy to acting in reality, it has been proposed that a decrease in the intensity and gratification of masturbation to fantasies results in a desire to act (Meloy et al., 1994), although sexually sadistic offenders often describe an escalation in deviant sexual fantasizing and masturbation in the lead up to offending (MacCulloch et al., 1983). Indeed, initial sexual fantasies may involve comparatively minor themes of humiliation that become progressively more extreme and involved over time. Fantasies have relational, paraphilic, situational, self-perceptual, and demographic components (Hazelwood & Warren, 2017) which shape aspects of offences including choice of victim.

12.4.7 Proximal Factors in Enacting Behavior

Some research has investigated the proximal or precipitating factors which are present in the lead up to committing sexual sadistic offences. Emotional states and situational cues and their interpretation have been suggested to result in behavioral acting out of sadistic sexual fantasies when an opportunity arises. However, a hallmark of sexually sadistic rapes and homicides is organized planning which individuals find sexually arousing while fantasizing about acting. Proulx et al. (2007) found that compared to non-sadistic offenders, sadistic ones were more likely to experience conflicts with women, anger, and deviant sexual fantasies in the 48 h before offences. They also did not uncommonly experience rejection, low self-esteem, and alcohol and drug misuse at this time, but no more frequently than non-sadists. Further, summarizing findings from several previous studies, Beauregard et al. (2007) described that in the pre-crime phase sexually sadistic SH offenders manifested high levels of unexpressed anger, elaborate sadistic fantasies, fantasy world being more important than reality, situational stress, blow to self-esteem, hunting their victims, selecting a specific victim after surveillance, premeditation of the offence, and consumption of alcohol; and in their small sample they found sadistic offenders more often manifested positive affect, separation from a partner, consuming pornography, indulging in deviant sexual fantasies and planning offences in the hours preceding their offences when compared with angry offenders.

12.4.8 Integrated Multifactorial Models

Several theoretical models have been proposed that integrate various of the factors described above in explaining the development of SS and its manifestation in sexually sadistic offending. Brittain's (1970) description of the "sadistic murderer" has been credited with providing a starting point for considering etiology and has been called a "syndrome" (MacCulloch et al., 2000). On the one hand, it is often cited as a "classic" or "seminal" paper on the topic, and some aspects have been borne out by subsequent empirical research. On the other, it is a descriptive pen picture, without details of cases or data, without reference to 90 years of literature that came before, and its validity has been questioned (Grubin, 1994b). The sexual sadist is described as secretive and concealing what he can from others, making him elusive and difficult to diagnose. He is obsessional, insecure, narcissistic, hypochondriacal, a loner, with a rich sexually sadistic fantasy life, but non-violent in everyday life. He dwells on atrocities, is fascinated by weapons and Nazi paraphernalia, uses pornography, is excited by cruelty, and draws his fantasies. He is single, often hates his mother, and shows sexual deviance early. He makes complex preparation to secure a victim and plan his methods of control, terror, killing and mutilation. Escaping detection leads to further offences, faithful to his established methods. In prisons or secure hospitals, he is a "model prisoner", leading the unwary to consider him no longer dangerous. Childhoods are characterized by overprotective controlling mothers and violent and authoritarian fathers, leading to insecurity and withdrawal. Sadistic sexual fantasy was central to Brittain's description, was linked to planning, and set the template for the behaviors manifested. But he did not really attempt to explain the emergence of the "syndrome" or the underlying mechanisms. Subsequently, MacCulloch et al. (1983, 2000) proposed models where sensory preconditioning in the context of experiencing childhood abuse, along with classical and operant conditioning, led to the establishment, maintenance, and escalation in sadistic sexual fantasy, leading to behavioral trial runs, and sexual violence and homicide (see above).

The "motivational model" of SH (Burgess et al., 1986; Ressler et al., 1988) has five components accounting for the development of sadistic sexual fantasy and homicidal behavior. It is based on the FBI's research on primarily serial SH. Firstly, there is an ineffective early environment in which healthy attachment and bonding is not facilitated, and problematic behavior is given facilitation. Parents or other care givers ignore, rationalize, or normalize behaviors in boys; support the boy's developing distortions and projections; do not provide nurture or protection; and are non-intervening and non-protective. Secondly, in this context, formative events occur in childhood and adolescence. These include trauma in the form of physical or sexual abuse; developmental failure with negative social attachment and diminished emotional response; and interpersonal failure with inconsistent care and contact with care givers, and deviant parental models. These two components lead to the third one, patterned responses in terms of how the individual functions and operates, which has two interacting subcategories: critical personality traits (social isolation, preference for autoeroticism, fetishes, rebelliousness, aggression, lying, entitlement) and cognitive mapping and processing (involving certain structures [daydreams, fantasies, imagery, nightmares], internal dialogue [strong limiting presuppositions, dealing in absolutes, generalizations], themes [dominance, revenge, violence, rape/molestation, power/control, death, torture, mutilation, inflicting pain], and kinesthetic arousal levels [requiring high levels of stimulation and high levels of aggressive experience]. The fourth component or phase is actions towards others, including in childhood (cruelty to animals, cruelty to children, aggressive repetitive play patterns, disregard of others, fire setting, stealing, destroying property) and adolescence/adulthood (assault, burglary, arson, abduction, rape, non-SH, SH). This leads to the fifth phase, a feedback filter linking back to the third component (patterned responses) where the individual justifies their acts, sorts out errors, discovers increased arousal states, discovers areas of dominance and power, and knows how to continue acts without detection or punishment.

In a similar vein to the FBI's motivational model are Hickey's (2015) "trauma control model" of serial murder, and Purcell's and Arrigo's (2006) "integrated theoretical model of paraphilias and lust murder". The trauma control model sets out predisposing factors, in the context of which traumatic events lead to dissociation and to low self-esteem and retreat into fantasy. This in turn leads to increasingly violent fantasies, in the context of facilitators, culminating in homicidal behavior. Homicidal behavior leads to trauma reinforcement, as does earlier dissociation, and this trauma reinforcement, along with other facilitators, reinforces low self-esteem, retreat into fantasy, increasingly violent fantasies, and further homicidal behavior. The integrated model posits that formative development leads to low self-esteem and early fantasy development, leading to paraphilic development. The paraphilic process involves interaction of paraphilic fantasy/stimuli, facilitators, and orgasmic conditioning, maintaining the paraphilic development, via an internal/external stimulus effect. A stressor or trigger acts on the paraphilic process, leading to its overt behavioral manifestation, increasingly violent fantasy, and further reinforcement through orgasmic conditioning. Although these models are interesting and tie in with some research findings, they are speculative and remain largely empirically untested.

Two recent empirically derived etiological models are worthy of note. Robertson et al. (2018) proposed an etiological model incorporating childhood psychological, physical, and sexual abuse; juvenile antisocial behaviors; and adolescent hypersexual behaviors and fantasies. They conducted structural equation modelling analysis using data derived from a comprehensive questionnaire (the Multidimensional Inventory of Development, Sex, and Aggression; MIDSA) administered to 219 adult male sexual offenders. Psychological abuse, physical abuse and sexual abuse showed substantial collinearity. Psychological and sexual abuse significantly contributed to juvenile externalizing, and physical abuse trended on significance. Psychological and sexual abuse approached significance in predicting hypersexuality. Juvenile externalizing and hypersexuality both significantly predicted SS which was made up of both fantasy and behavior. Overall, this developmental model explained 42% of the variance in SS, indicating that although it accounted for a sizeable proportion of the variance, additional variables contributing to the development of SS were not included. These likely cover various interacting biological, psychological and environmental factors involved in the development and maintenance of SS as described in this section. Longpré et al. (2018) studied 518 adult male sexual offenders assessed with the Massachusetts Treatment Center Sadism Scale (MTCSS; Longpré et al., 2019) and using structural equation modelling analyses found the best empirical solution explaining the development of SS was represented by 11 latent variables and 56 manifest variables. These variables covered three phases of development (childhood, adolescence, and adulthood). Having an antisocial father, unstable mother, suffering neglect and abuse, and experiencing family instability, were highly collinear, and were associated with early conduct problems. Which predisposed to problems at school and/or serious conduct problems in adolescence. Problems at school foreshadowed substance abuse in adulthood, whilst severe conduct problems foreshadowed adult narcissism. Adult narcissism and substance misuse represented two pathways to SS, labelled 'disinhibition path' and 'narcissistic-meaness path'. A third one involved a seclusive lifestyle in adulthood, labelled a 'schizoid path', not preceded by adolescent conduct problems, as these individuals are withdrawn and isolated. This empirically derived model highlights the role of early adverse experiences, problematic adolescent development, and heterogeneous adult pathways based on different personality profiles which predispose to the manifestation of sexually sadistic behavior.

12.5 Prevalence and Association with Offending

Given the problems with definition and reliability it is difficult to know the rates of SS in general and criminal justice populations. In addition, surveys and estimates of SS in the community have often included BDSM and related interests and behaviors, which as outlined below should not be conflated with forensic SS or CSSD. Kinsey et al. (1948) found 10–20% of men and 3–12% of women admitted sexual arousal to "sadomasochistic" narratives. Crépault and Couture (1980) found 14.9% of men had erotic fantasies of humiliating and 11.7% of beating up a woman during heterosexual activity, although only 2.1% and 1.1% respectively had such fantasies "often". Williams et al. (2009) found that in male college students, 62% had fantasies of "sadism" and 68% of sexual assault, using an adaptation of the Multidimensional Assessment of Sex and Aggression (MASA; Knight et al., 1994). Ahlers et al. (2011) found 21.8% of males had "sadistic" fantasies. Although more men than women have been found to have sexual fantasies involving force or dominance, reported by a quarter to a half in surveys (Leitenberg & Henning, 1995), this is not analogous to sadistic sexual fantasies, SS, or CSSD. Joyal et al. (2015) conducted an internet survey of 1516 adults (799 women and 717 men). In terms of fantasies that might possibly be considered related to SS, 59.6% of men and 46.7% of women had fantasized about dominating someone, 48.4% and 41.7% respectively about tying someone up, and 43.5% and 23.8% about spanking or whipping someone. So these are common fantasies and are not necessarily indicative of BDSM let alone CSSD. Baur et al. (2016) found 2.7% of a sample of the general population had a lifetime prevalence of at least one "sadistic behavior" although this would not equate with a diagnosis. Overall, it seems likely that well under 1% of males, and even less females, in the general population meet criteria for SSD or CSSD, although fantasies of coercion, force and domination are very common, especially in men.

Amongst men who commit sexual assaults and rape it has been estimated that about 2–5% have SSD (Quinsey et al., 1981; Yates et al., 2008). Proulx and Sauvetre (2007) found 7.9% of non-homicidal sexual aggressors against adult women met DSM-IV criteria for SS; Darjee and Baron (2018a) found that 1.9% of non-homicidal sexual offenders met DSM-IV criteria for SS and that group had an average SESAS part 1 score of 1 with no cases scoring 4 or above; Gonçalves et al. (2020) found that male sexual offenders had an average SESAS part 1 score of 2 with 14% scoring 4 or more, while 3.4% had a DSM-IV-TR or ICD-10 diagnosis of sadism. Using structured clinical interviews with 1346 incarcerated male sexual offenders, Eher et al. (2019) found 4.4% met DSM-IV-TR criteria for SS, 7.3% of offenders against adults and 1.5% of offenders against children.

Significantly higher rates of SS have been reported in SH offenders, with rates using DSM criteria of 16.7% (Proulx & Sauvetre, 2007), 23% (Prentky et al., 1989), 36.7% (Hill et al., 2006a), 37% (Stefanska et al., 2019), and 39.2% (Darjee & Baron, 2018a); and rates using the SESAS or SADSEX-SH-R of 28% (Reale et al., 2017), 26.9% (Stefanska et al., 2019), 29.4% (Darjee & Baron, 2018a), 31% (Eichinger & Darjee, 2021), and 45.5% (Chopin et al., 2022). Amongst serial SH offenders, rates have been even higher, with rates using DSM criteria of 66.7% (Hill et al., 2006a), 86% (Prentky et al., 1989) and 100% (Schlesinger et al., 2010). In their systematic review, James and Proulx (2014) found the average rate of SS (using various definitions) was 54.2% in single and 68.2% in serial SH offenders.

12.6 Special Groups

12.6.1 BDSM

The term BDSM originated in the early 1990s, referring to Bondage and Discipline (B&D), Dominance and Submission, (D/s) and/or Sadism and Masochism (SM or S&M). It covers a range of activities, specific subcultures where individuals participate in these and forms of interpersonal relationships involving domination and submission (Langdridge & Barker, 2007). The term is used commonly amongst participants, although the term sadomasochism has tended to be used more in the literature until recently. BDSM represents a wide range of behaviors and may be experienced very differently and hold different meanings among its practitioners, making it difficult to define in a unitary way, with the term embracing diverse practices. Additional aspects sometimes used to define BDSM are that it is undertaken in a safe, legal, and consensual manner, and as well as erotic arousal participants often seek to experience personal growth. As they participate with consenting adults and as mutual sexual activity, those involved have long campaigned for their sexual interests and behavior to be seen not as indicative of psychopathology, but rather part of human sexual diversity and intimacy. Although erotic arousal is often central, many participants use it for creative expression, some prefer the natural high provided by pain, others are drawn to the challenge or intense closeness with a sexual partner. Some prefer dominance or submission and stick to these roles, whereas others switch. Research in Finland on men found 7% were exclusively dominant, 18% predominantly dominant, 24% flexible, 36% predominantly submissive and 15% submissive (Paarnio et al., 2023). Many men and women have sexual fantasies involving coercion, domination or submission (Leitenberg & Henning, 1995). A survey of a representative sample of over a thousand people in Belgium (Holvoet et al., 2017) found just under half had ever performed at least one BDSM activity, just under a quarter had BDSM sexual fantasies, and one in eight performed a BDSM activity regularly. A quarter described themselves as interested in BDSM and 1 in 13 identified themselves as BDSM practitioners. BDSM interests were significantly higher in men than women. There are few high-quality studies, but figures from other countries over a number of decades indicate similarly high rates of BDSM interests and practice (De Neef et al., 2019; Paarnio et al., 2023). Phenomenologically the practice of BDSM may look superficially like behaviors seen in sadistic sexual and violent crimes, with examples of practices including blood play, bondage/restraint, body suspension, breath play, whipping, chaining, clamps, derogatory talk, electrical play, slapping/humiliation, fireplay, fisting, gagging, handcuffing, knife play and skin branding. But the context and focus of BDSM is very different from CSSD.

Risk taking is an intrinsic part of BDSM. Many of the activities could cause psychological or physical harm, serious injury and even death (Schori et al., 2022). Having control over these risks or giving someone else control over them is part of what excites and fulfils BDSM practitioners. Some have made an analogy between BDSM and participating in dangerous sports in terms of accepting and mitigating risk, and the responsibilities of those involved. In the face of discrimination, pathologization and criminalization, in the 1980s the phrase 'Safe, Sane and Consensual' (SSC) arose to get across the safe and ethical practice integral to BDSM, and to demarcate BDSM from criminal sexual abuse (Nielsen, 2010). SSC has been seen as a useful slogan to help those who do not practice BDSM understand it and not see it as abusive, pathological, dangerous, or subversive. As a general mantra many participants see it as an appropriate and useful framework to guide BDSM practice. However, SSC is sometimes viewed as referring strictly and absolutely to only allowing certain practices and not others deemed unsafe and setting a high threshold for the mental wellbeing and self-control required to participate. This strict and high threshold mantra is rejected by many BDSM practitioners. Another mantra adopted by some is Risk Aware Consensual Kink (RACK), sometimes described as the 'risk aware' approach (Williams et al., 2014). Consent is still crucial, but rather than emphasizing that practice must be safe, the RACK approach states practitioners should be aware of the risks, take personal responsibility for managing risks, but ultimately BDSM cannot be risk free. Some see RACK and SSC approaches as distinct and opposed approaches, with RACK practitioners getting involved in what some would see as less safe practices. Others see RACK as a more appropriate framework for practitioners of BDSM, whilst SSC is more useful for those outside BDSM to understand and accept the behavior. Others see RACK and SSC as complementary and largely overlapping. Particularly risky activities within BDSM are sometimes called 'edge play'. Those that see SSC and RACK as distinct, see this falling within the philosophy of RACK but not SSC. An example of edge play is breath play where the airway is restricted by various potential means (ligatures, smothering, gags, choking, strangulation).

Informed consent is integral to BDSM, no matter what the philosophy or preferences of the participants (Nielsen, 2010). Some see the approach to consent in BDSM as a model for consent in other types of sexual behavior. Some BDSM practitioners use safe words or signs to monitor how a submissive is and whether they wish to continue. Alternatively, a red, amber, and green approach may be taken. Those that see SSC and RACK as different describe safe words and signs as integral to SSC but not RACK. However, pros and cons to the use of safe words have also been highlighted, including situations where relying on safe words or signs can make BDSM more rather than less dangerous. For example, it has been suggested that remembering a safe word when at one's limit or distressed or on the verge of passing out may not be feasible, so it is better to just use everyday words. Safe words or signs cannot be used in certain activities (e.g., where a submissive is gagged) or they may be used too late, at a point where injury or harm has already occurred. So, although some BDSM practitioners use safe words and signs, many do not use them, and they are by no means ubiquitous. Some see it as more important to emphasize a trusting relationship between participants who know each other well. Others also emphasize the responsibility of both dominant and submissive to monitor and manage risk.

From the above description, it is obvious and stark that BDSM is very different from, and should not be conflated with, forensic SS or CSSD. Unfortunately, from when Krafft-Ebing (1886) defined and conceptualized SS the two were seen as related, similar, and often identical. Freud's (1905) and other psychoanalytic theories of sexuality and sadomasochism further contributed to this pathologization which continued until very recently. As outlined above, it is only recently that ICD-11 and DSM-5 have really attempted to exclude BDSM practitioners from receiving a paraphilic disorder diagnosis. Nonetheless, it must be stressed that the erotic focus on the consensual binding, paddling, whipping, or subjugation of a partner who is enjoying the activity, perhaps to the point of orgasm; has no relationship to a paraphilic focus on the humiliation, degradation, torture, and suffering of a non-consenting person who is pleading for the abuse to stop. The two activities are diametrically and fundamentally different.

Research into psychological and sexual characteristics of BDSM practitioners (De Neef et al., 2019), has found they no more likely have mental disorders, personality difficulties or sexual problems than the general population. Indeed, some research shows BDSM practitioners are happier and better adjusted than non-BDSM practitioners. With regards to personality, Wismeijer and Van Assen (2013) found, compared to the general population, BDSM practitioners were less neurotic, more extroverted, more open to new experiences, more conscientious, and less agreeable, and in terms of attachment styles less sensitive to rejection, more confident in relationships, with lower need for approval, and less anxious attachment. Although some research has shown somewhat higher rates of childhood abuse, it is not clear whether there is a relationship. Many BDSM-oriented people became aware of their BDSM related interests as teenagers and young adults, BDSM practitioners are usually highly educated, and while 90% of the general population identifies as heterosexual only two-thirds of the BDSM one do. BDSM practitioners often emphasize emotional and psychological aspects, many find BDSM and non-BDSM sexual activities equally satisfying, they often find BDSM deepens interpersonal connection, BDSM is more often associated with longer-term relationships, and some practitioners describe an addiction to the rush or "high" they experience (De Neef et al., 2019). It has been suggested that power dynamics, rather than pain, bondage, or humiliation, are central to BDSM. These findings in BDSM practitioners contrast with those in sexually sadistic offenders, which has found high rates of personality dysfunction, problems relating to others, psychopathology and sexual difficulties (see above).

So, what accounts for the differences between prosocial BDSM practitioners and sexually abusive individuals with CSSD, or do the two just have nothing in common? The findings above suggest several possibilities. Firstly, the two groups may have similar sexual fantasies but the way they act them out is different due to differences in personality, attachment, and social adjustment. An individual with sexual fantasies involving subjugation and pain, who cannot connect in a psychologically safe way with others or lacks empathy being more likely to indulge his fantasies through force without consent. Secondly, there may be a difference between the nature or severity of the sexual fantasies in BDSM versus CSSD. For example, BDSM practitioners do not fantasize about killing or disemboweling, they are not aroused by extreme fear or distress, but in CSSD non-consent is inherently linked to arousal and fantasy. Thirdly, the difference may be in degree of sexual fixation and preoccupation, with BDSM practitioners able to shift role, focus on the relational context, and have healthy sexual lives both within and out with BDSM. Fourthly, BDSM practitioners can see what they do as fantasy role play and a mutual game, whilst those with CSSD fantasize to cope with and hide from reality and turn their fantasies into harm to others who do not want to be involved or play the role.

Although BDSM and CSSD should not be conflated, there are some specific forensic implications of BDSM. Firstly, although extremely rare, having a BDSM interaction may be used as a pretext by predatory individuals who want to lure, abuse, and/or kill a vulnerable submissive (Dustin, 2023). Indeed, there are very likely a number of individuals with genuine SSD who spend time in the BDSM scene as a way of coping with their SS fantasies (Dietz, 2014); or even as veritable wolves in sheep's clothing. One of us has consulted in the past with BDSM practitioners who became appropriately concerned by play-partners who deviated from the consensually agreed script for a scene and, in one case, introduced a knife that they flashed in front of a bound partner's face. Secondly, individuals who are not involved in BDSM practices or relationships may attempt to use a "BDSM defense", most commonly after they have strangled a victim, claiming that a rape, assault, or homicide was a "sex game gone wrong", seen most often in the context of intimate partner homicide (Stefanska et al., 2021). An examination of the relationship between victim and perpetrator, their histories of involvement in BDSM, and analysis of the crime scene make it obvious BDSM was not involved. Thirdly, as BDSM is a risky activity, unfortunately there are rare situations where individuals are harmed or die (Schori et al., 2022). Such situations may lead to convictions for negligent manslaughter or be viewed legally as accidental. There have also been rare cases where, during a scene, a dominant goes beyond what a submissive has agreed to and/or a submissive has reacted violently to this, leading to fatality. Courts in the UK, North America and Australia have taken the view that one cannot consent to being seriously assaulted (except in medical and sporting contexts). So following the so-called Spanner case (R v Brown 1993; White, 2006), which has been viewed as stigmatizing, pathologizing and homophobic, BDSM practitioners can find themselves facing convictions for serious assault and manslaughter. Interestingly, in continental Europe a more open view is taken by the courts.

12.6.2 Rape

As mentioned above, few men who rape, approximately 2–5%, have CSSD. Most men who describe 'rape fantasies' leading to offending are not sadistic, rather their fantasies are primarily coercive and lower down the agonistic continuum (see PCD above), compensatory and about taking control while the victim submits willingly to the sexual encounter, primarily non-coercive and non-controlling in men with little sexual experience, or entirely situational when feeling inadequacy, betrayal, humiliation, or anger. Almost all typologies of rape behavior in the past seven decades have identified a sadistic type of offence and offender. These have variously been labeled sadistic (Guttmacher, 1951; Gebhard et al., 1965), sex-aggression-defusion (Cohen et al., 1969), anger excitement/anger excitation (Groth 1977), and overt sadistic (Knight & Prentky, 1990). However, the other "core" types that have been present in most typologies since that of Cohen et al. (1969) are the non-sadistic sexualization (compensatory or power-reassurance), opportunistic (power-assertive), and pervasively angry (anger-retaliatory; Hazelwood, 2017b; James & Proulx, 2020). More recent additions have included a vindictive type and a muted sadist. Figure 12.3 provides a schematic representation of these types, and intermediate types, which form a circumplex model based on two reasonably orthogonal primary dimensions (Davis, 2012, 2013, 2022b; Watson et al., 2024) similar to, but different from, the Massachusetts Treatment Centre Rape Typology Version 4 (MTC:R4; Knight & Sims-Knight, 2016). The types can be defined through their

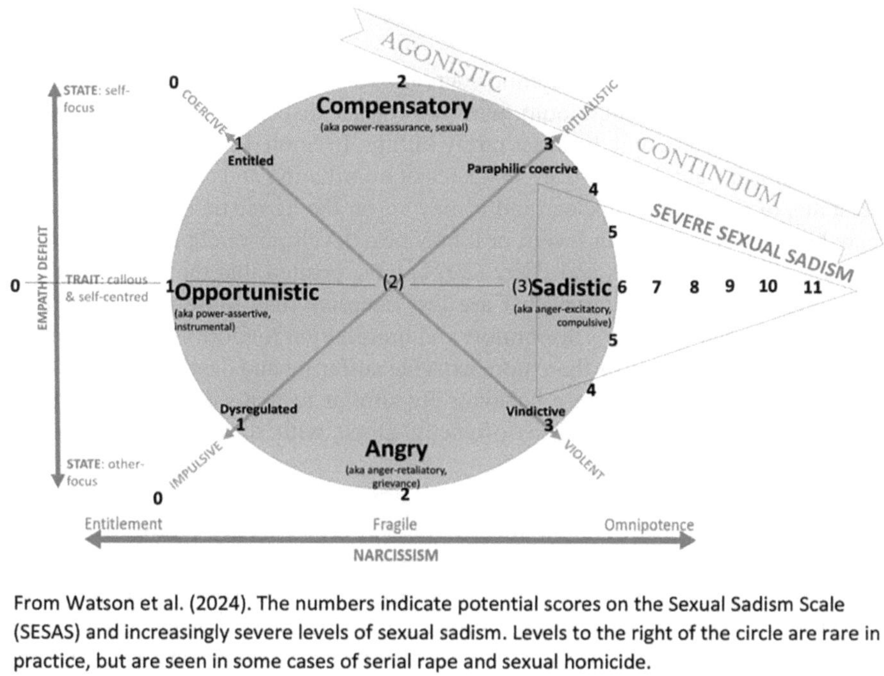

Fig. 12.3 An integrative meta-model of rape typologies and dimensions (based on Davis, 2012, 2013, 2022b). From Watson et al. (2024). The numbers indicate potential scores on the Sexual Sadism Scale (SESAS) and increasingly severe levels of sexual sadism. Levels to the right of the circle are rare in practice, but are seen in some cases of serial rape and sexual homicide

positions on two dimensions or axes: an impulsive-ritualistic axis (the degree to which offending is driven by and planned in fantasy), and a coercion-violence or instrumental-expressive/beyond instrumental axis (the degree to which force is primarily just enough to secure compliance versus far beyond that, excessive and expressive). The sexually sadistic type is thus highly ritualistic, and force/violence is excessive and expressive. Dimensions of empathy deficits and narcissism are also incorporated into the model, with sadistic cases empathically callous, and narcissistically omnipotent, and at the high end of the agonistic continuum.

Differentiating sadistic from proximal types can be challenging. Vindictive cases can use prolonged violence to exact revenge for perceived betrayal, often target current or former partners, but are not inherently sexually aroused by ritualistic fantasies; and angry rapists can be very violent and even kill, but their violence is reactive, explosive, and short lived. Davis (2022b) has posited that vindictive rape itself exists on a small continuum from the predominantly angry to the partially sadistic. The latter differs from overt SS because hybrid violent/sexual fantasies of punishing and raping females are at a macro level, as opposed to the more scripted and highly ritualistic fantasies, and resulting behaviors, of the SS offender. In essence, they punish females with both fist and phallus. Nonetheless, both variants of vindictive rape share the common feature that their offences are motivated by misogyny and a desire to punish females.

Differentiating SS from 'paraphilic coercion', as addressed above, is a matter of degree on the agonistic continuum, with the former displaying more degradation, brutality and violence, and the latter rarely killing. In 'muted sadism' overtly sadistic behavior is absent, but there are fantasies of humiliating and causing discomfort. The status of this type is unclear and it may sit on the agonistic continuum somewhere between SS and lower levels, or it may be a developmental precursor of overt SS. As noted above, Davis and Dietz (2024) have posited that the muted sadist is likely to have sadistic fantasies that are less coercive than those of the overt SS offender, such that a victim's discomfort and humiliation to more symbolic sadistic behaviors is arousing, rather than more extreme suffering and degradation. As such, these offences can appear more behaviorally similar to non-sadistic sexualization (compensatory/power reassurance) offences, albeit with some mild or symbolic sadistic elements.

It is usually easy to differentiate overtly sadistic rape from non-sadistic sexualization (compensatory/power reassurance) and opportunistic (power assertive) rape. Opportunistic rapists may be violent and sometimes (but rarely) commit homicide, to silence a victim or in response to victim resistance, but not due to inherent sexual arousal by violence. Compensatory rapists' ritualistic fantasies and crime scene behaviors are very different from sadists, as their primary fantasized focus is having control in a sexual encounter where the victim submits, adores them, and falls in love with them. They share with sadists ritual, planning, and associated sexual arousal. Using structured behavioral scales, like the SESAS, helps screen cases, assisting to identify those with SS. Although proximal types may score on some SESAS items, they rarely reach the threshold of 4 items. In our experience, it is only the partially sadistic variant of the vindictive type that scores highly on the SESAS without actually being primarily sexually sadistic. However, as noted above, analysis of offence behaviors in such cases invariably indicates that there was no elaborately detailed script and the seemingly sadistic behaviors simply reflected a misogynistic desire to punish females at a macro level.

12.6.3 Sexual Homicide

SS has been central in the conceptualization of SH over the last century and a half, to the extent the two have often been conflated (Ressler et al., 1988). Although, as outlined above, approximately one-third of SH offenders have CSSD, most do not. However, over three quarters of serial SH cases do. In keeping with our rape model in Fig. 12.3, the other two main subgroups of SH offenders are those driven by anger, grievance, or vindictiveness; and those who sexually assault opportunistically and kill accidentally, to silence a victim or reacting to victim resistance (Higgs et al., 2017, 2017, 2017). SHs with post-mortem sexual behavior involve either opportunistic sexual behavior while or after killing, or killing to then enact necrophilic sexual fantasies (see above). Factors associated with SS in SH include: higher rates of personality disorder including schizoid, avoidant, obsessive-compulsive and psychopathic traits, and lower rates of mental illness and intellectual disability; unprovoked, purposeful and planned offences; various sexual crime scene behaviors (including anal intercourse, fellatio, breast sucking, ejaculating on victims, inserting objects and stripping victims nude); biting, unusual, bizarre, controlling, and mutilating behaviors; using precautions to prevent detection; having a co-offender; deserted offence locations; less time to body recovery but also cases remaining unsolved; childhood enuresis/encopresis, isolation, and physical abuse; childhood and adolescent deviant sexual behavior and experiences of humiliation; sexual masochism; previous sexual and violent offences; stranger victims, attempted (versus completed) homicide, and multiple SHs (Hill et al., 2006b; Proulx et al., 2007; Reale et al., 2017; Darjee, 2019).

A question arises as to why some offenders with SS kill, especially as the dead cannot experience pain, suffering or humiliation, with death potentially anticlimactic. Indeed, two studies found SS more strongly related to very violent non-fatal sexual offences than SH (Healey et al., 2013; Darjee, 2019). Assault may lead to death for the same reasons as other SHs (i.e., accidentally, to silence victims, victim resistance, or anger); killing and perhaps post-mortem acts (such as mutilation) may be intrinsic to fantasy at the top of the agonistic/sadistic continuum (see erotophonophilia above); or associated traits, states or circumstances (e.g., callousness, intoxication or co-offenders) may lead to escalation to fatality. Chopin et al. (2022) found lethal outcome was associated with "crime escalation factors" (bringing a weapon), "victim vulnerability" (having a child or elderly victim) and "expressions of SS" (gratuitous violence/wounding, not degrading/humiliating victims, not being sexually aroused by the act, foreign object insertion, sexual and non-sexual mutilation), concluding that the deviant sexual process and escalation hypotheses were supported, but not the instrumental hypothesis (killing to avoid detection), and considered severe SS the most important predictor of death. Further, Chopin and Beauregard (2023), using latent class analysis, found four distinct patterns amongst sadistic SHs, with all four showing high levels of sexual domination and gratuitous/excessive violence. Almost half of cases were the "anal/oral sex" group who more often conned victims, consumed alcohol, and targeted males. Approximately one-fifth, the "inanimate object insertion" group, were socially well integrated, had fewer convictions, more likely assaulted acquaintances, used a blitz approach, and more often attacked the elderly in their homes. Another one-fifth, the "collector" group, took trophies, more likely used weapons, used coercive strategies, were socially competent, but had many convictions. One in eight, the "torture/mutilation" group, were more likely to be in a relationship, have alcohol problems, feel lonely, have previous convictions, have sexual dysfunction, con victims, have stranger victims, to have child victims, and to dismember and perform sexual acts post-mortem. In general, there were no differences between groups regarding situational factors, indicating the different manifestations reflected specific elements of fantasies and individual characteristics.

As with sexual assault and rape, using offence behavior scales, such as the SESAS and SADSEX-SH-R, can help identify SS, however some items, such as domination, expressive/gratuitous violence, and non-sexual mutilation, are not uncommon in non-sadistic SHs (Darjee, 2019), so some such cases can score three, four, or occasionally five on the SESAS. This highlights the importance of using such screens as a starting point before applying informed clinical judgement.

12.6.4 Sexual Violence Against Children

SS occurs in less than 1% of child victim sexual offending. Although typologies identify a sadistic type amongst offenders with pedophilic sexual preferences (Knight, 1989; Knight & King, 2012; Lanning, 1992), most child offenders, whether preferentially pedophilic or not, believe that they 'love' the children they abuse and are not overtly aggressive or cruel. Some non-sadistic individuals, who are introverted, inadequate, or morally indiscriminate with high levels of psychopathy, use non-sadistic violence and can kill children. Rates of SS in child SH are similar to adult SH, i.e., approximately one-third (Spehr et al., 2010; Ricono-Kaufhold et al., 2024), and indicators of SS are much more common in child SH than non-fatal child sexual abuse (Firestone et al., 1998; Chopin et al., 2021). Such offenders have sadistic pedophilic fantasies and are not sadists who target victims regardless of age (Reale et al., 2022). Chopin and Beauregard (2022) compared child SHs with and without SS, finding SS was associated with structured premeditation, stranger victims, offending and leaving bodies outdoors, more diverse sexual acts and unusual acts, specific methods of killing (strangulation, asphyxiation and drowning), and the partial use of forensic awareness strategies. These findings mirror those in adult SH. Reale et al. (2022) compared sadistic offenders with child versus adult victims, finding child ones primarily manifested features of pedophilia and sadism, while adult ones involved alcohol abuse, sexual dysfunction, and more structure to control victims and reduce risk of identification.

12.6.5 People Who Have Not Offended

Clinicians sometimes see individuals who appear to have CSSD who have not offended. Examples include individuals presenting with concerns about their sexual fantasies and urges, and those where others (e.g., parents, partners, professionals) are concerned after discovering what appear to be sadistic sexual interests (e.g., viewing sadistic pornography, drawing sexually sadistic pictures, identification with serial sexual killers, sadistic behavior towards others, cruelty to animals, stalking or breaking-in behaviors with a sexually sadistic element). They may not be under any officially sanctioned monitoring, supervision, or intervention. The two initial questions are does the person have CSSD and what risk do they pose?

Violent fantasies in general are not uncommon, and are usually used to regulate emotion and self-esteem, rather than being templates for action, but the latter may lead to future violence (Gilbert & Daffern, 2017). Apparent sadistic sexual fantasies or behavior must be differentiated from non-sexual violent fantasies, obsessions with sexually violent content, flashbacks to traumatic sexually violent experiences, delusions or hallucinations with sexually violent content, vengeful or rageful thoughts or urges, non-sexual cruelty, and, importantly, sexual fantasies with themes of domination or coercion which a person does not want to enact or only wants to enact with mutual consent (i.e., BDSM). If there have been acts they can be examined using a behavioral checklist, such as the SESAS. People who self-present are usually concerned and want help. Where concerns come from others, efforts have to be made to engage the person in assessment and see the benefit of any intervention offered.

Assessing risk can be difficult and structured professional judgment guidelines such as the Sexual Violence Risk-20 Version 2 (SVR-20 V2; Boer et al., 2017) or the Risk for Sexual Violence Protocol - Version 2 (RSVP-V2; Hart et al., 2022), can help structure consideration of relevant risk factors and formulate risk of sexual violence. Where there are concerns about sadistic or homicidal sexual violence, it can be helpful to compare the background, clinical presentation and behavior to factors identified in the research literature associated with such violence. In most cases the outcome will be that sexual violence is unlikely or implausible, however in a few there will be legitimate concern about a plausible risk of serious sexual violence, especially if overt planning for an abduction has commenced, including identifying a victim, choosing a venue, purchasing weapons, or obtaining restraints.

If there is a risk of sadistic sexual violence, the next question is whether the person wants intervention. Self-presenting individuals are often distressed, unhappy or at least ambivalent about acting on their fantasies. So, they can usually be engaged with treatment, support and monitoring to reduce risk. This is an established approach where there are concerns about sexual thoughts or urges towards children (Grant et al., 2019), but few clinical resources are available to help those with sexually violent thoughts towards adults, although some innovative services work with such individuals regardless of their legal status (McEwan & Darjee, 2021; Russell & Darjee, 2011). Unfortunately, many community forensic mental health services, who narrowly focus on case managing people with severe mental illnesses, will not work with such cases (see McEwan and Darjee (2021) for a case study).

Intervention is challenging when a person with CSSD poses a risk, but does not want treatment, support, or monitoring. This is rare, but may warrant engaging law enforcement, especially if there is an imminent risk of serious harm, particularly towards a specific person. In systems with good relationships between forensic mental health, law enforcement and other criminal justice agencies, actively working together to manage the risks posed by sexual and violent offenders in the community, such as Multi-Agency Public Protection Arrangements (MAPPA) in the UK (Kemshall & Hilder, 2020; Kemshall & Maguire, 2021), a knock-on benefit is that agencies are already familiar with each other, so when these "non-statutory" high risk cases arise, albeit rarely, inter-agency plans can be made. Even where individuals engage with services, this can help with risk management, and despite clinicians' concerns, do not necessarily erode, but usually enhance, clinical engagement and collaboration.

12.6.6 Adolescents

As outlined above, CSSD starts in adolescence, but most adolescents hide their fantasies and behaviors, or if they behave in a sexually abusive or violent way, underlying SS goes unrecognized. Therefore, most individuals with CSSD do not come to attention until adulthood, and rare sexually abusive adolescents, who are developing or manifesting SS, get the same responses and interventions as others.

A few studies have described juveniles who commit SH (Myers & Blashfield, 1997; Myers et al., 1998; Hunter et al., 2000; Myers, 2002; Cha et al., 2010; Chopin & Beauregard, 2020). Rates of SS are as high as, if not higher than, in adults who commit SH. Chan et al. (2010) found 59% of their sample of 22 juvenile sexual murderers had SS, and the three who subsequently committed further SHs on release all had SS. However, only one of eight cases described by Khachatryan et al. (2016) appeared to have SS. Myers (2002) suggested a typology of juvenile SH with four types, three with SS (explosive, predatory and displaced matricide) and one without (revenge). Chopin and Beauregard (2020) compared juvenile with adult perpetrated SH cases. Rates of SS, using the SADSEX-SH, were similar at about 30% in each. They derived four classes of juvenile SH using latent class analysis, with some similarities to Myer's (2002) ones: explosive-opportunistic, sadistic, overcontrolled-anger and predator. But only the one sadistic group evidenced SS.

12.6.7 Women

Research shows marked differences between men and women who commit sexual offences (Cortoni & Stefanov, 2020), factors relevant to males are either irrelevant to females or operate differently (Gannon & Cortoni, 2010), and risk assessment and treatment approaches for men cannot be applied to women (Cortoni & Gannon, 2016), whose rate of sexual recidivism is less than one percent (Cortoni et al., 2010). For a thorough review on female sexual offending, please see the chapter in this volume by 10 Bensel and Raptopolous (2024). Sexual arousal, fantasy and interest in females is also very different from males, and compared to males, females show "erotic plasticity" throughout the lifespan, so their sex drive is flexible and responsive, rather than relatively fixed and one-track in men (Baumeister, 2000). Women have, on average, a lower sex drive and are less likely to be sexually preoccupied or hypersexual (Baumeister et al., 2001). This has implications for the role of sexual arousal and fantasy in female perpetrated sexual abuse, and whether concepts of sexual deviance and paraphilic disorders developed in males apply to females.

Fundamentally deviant sexual arousal and behavior seems contextual and responsive, rather than driven by sexual preference or fantasy, and in females fantasy is less about visual imagery and more about narrative, emotions and senses (Ellis & Symons, 1990). Unlike men, sexual deviance and preoccupation are not significant factors in models of sexual offences committed by women (Gannon et al., 2008). Typologies of women do not feature sexual deviance, violence, or SS, with the largest group of women who sexually abuse those who act with others, usually males who take the lead or overtly coerce the female (McLeod & Dodd, 2022).

Women are less likely than men to have sexual fantasies or arousal related to coercion or force, although more often have submissive fantasies (Leitenberg & Henning, 1995). Where women commit sadistic sexual violence, this is usually co-offending with men, driven by the men's CSSD (Clarkson et al., 2020). Pflugradt and Allen (2012, 2013) studied five females who committed sexually sadistic offences, all of whom acted with men, out of 90 incarcerated female sexual offenders. Given what is known about female arousal, fantasy, and responsiveness, although they stated all five women met diagnostic DSM-IV-TR SS criteria, it is unlikely the women were inherently sexually sadistic, rather they were probably able to be aroused in the context of offences driven by the SS of men. The five women identified scored four to eight on the SESAS, but two "non-sadists" also scored four or more, and were considered additional cases of SS! Pflugradt and Allen (2012) found relational themes were important: co-offenders, known victims where they had caretaker roles, and arousal to psychological aspects, including control by creating emotional dependence. It is our view that these seemingly additional features of the five females identified with CSSD are likely to reflect underlying personality features interacting with the fact that they committed their offences as part of a dyad with a male, rather than aspects of any CSSD itself.

About 5–6% of SH perpetrators are female, with a high proportion acting with others, usually men (Chan & Frei, 2013; Chan et al., 2019; Skott et al., 2019; Clarkson et al., 2020; Eichinger & Darjee, 2021). The sparse data available does not point to SS being present when females commit SH (Chan & Frei, 2013; Skott et al., 2019). Where these women are involved in sexually sadistic homicides, the sadistic behavior is usually driven by male co-offenders, amplified by the pair or group dynamic, or driven by grievance or revenge (Clarkson et al., 2020). Females are then able to become sexually aroused in the context of such behavior, but do not have long-standing arousing sadistic sexual fantasies. In this context it is interesting to note females who commit serial homicide acting alone are rarely, if ever, sexually motivated (Hickey, 2015). Sex may be used to lure male victims and make them vulnerable, leading to homicide in a sexual context as part of the modus operandi, rather than sexual fantasy or arousal driving the ritual of the crime. Clarkson et al. (2020), in a study of multiple-perpetrator SH, with 23 groups (15 pairs and 7 of three or more), found all but one group had a male member, but 13 (21%) of 62 offenders were female. Four groups were led by women, all of whom were driven by grievance/revenge, behavioral indicators of sadism were often present, but none of the women had CSSD. Women who were "followers" were influenced or coerced by men who often had CSSD, with a crucial component of the modus operandi being using women to lure victims. This pattern matches that in partners of sexually sadistic men (Hazelwood et al., 1993; Warren & Hazelwood, 2002; Hazelwood, 2017a) and where couples commit serial SH (e.g., Fred and Rose West in the UK, David and Catherine Birnie in Australia, Gerald and Charlene Gallego in the USA, Ian Brady and Myra Hindley in the UK, and Paul Bernado and Karla Homolka in Canada; Williams, 1992; Woodrow, 2011; Davis, 2014; Cassidy, 2021). So, although females may be involved in sadistic offending, including SH, CSSD in women does not seem to play a role, and any sexually sadistic behavior and arousal are about the context of and response to the offence, rather than drivers.

12.7 Assessment

Although many of the principles and practical aspects of assessing people who may have sexual sadism are similar to those encountered with other complex people who pose a potential risk of violence or sexual violence, there are important specific considerations with sexual sadism, which are outlined here.

12.7.1 General Aspects

There are several contexts where practitioners assess individuals who may have CSSD. These include legal ones, such as to inform sentencing (with potential for longer or indeterminate sentences based on future risk), to determine if post-sentence measures should be made (e.g., civil commitment in the USA, and supervision or detention orders in Australia), or to determine whether individuals should be stepped down, conditionally or unconditionally released from prisons, forensic hospitals or supervision in the community. Within institutions assessments may inform security status and measures in prison or hospital, identification of treatment needs and targets, and whether leave (escorted or unescorted) should be granted. In the community assessments occur as part of ongoing monitoring and supervision, to determine treatment needs, and where individuals present with apparently sadistic sexual fantasies or behavior. In addition to these forensic and clinical contexts, one of us also works internationally with law enforcement to provide advice in the investigation of sexually violent and homicide cases and interviewing of suspects. Given that CSSD is related to repetition, escalation, and fatality in sexual violence, but is uncommon, care needs to be taken in identifying and diagnosing it, due to implications in terms of public safety, human rights, and treatment/management approach. Although forensic, clinical, and investigative contexts are distinct and different in important ways, there are commonalties relevant to assessment practice across all three. But there is a focus on forensic and clinical contexts here. The aims of assessment are to:

- identify whether SS is present and its nature and degree;
- identify and examine all other factors which are relevant to the development, maintenance and manifestation of SS;
- undertake a comprehensive clinical needs assessment, including a structured and evidence-based assessment of risk of sexual offending and violence, and to identify relevant responsivity issues;
- engage the individual in the process so they are as motivated, ready and responsive to any intervention as possible;
- formulate why the person has developed and acted on sexually sadistic fantasies and arousal how they have, when they have, in particular contexts;
- outline the risks the person poses to whom under what circumstances;
- make recommendations for intervention and management, including treatment, support, monitoring, supervision and victim safety planning;
- communicate the findings, formulation, and recommendations clearly and effectively to others, including courts, multi-disciplinary and multi-agency colleagues, and, importantly, to the individual being assessed.

This is no different from other assessments of those who have committed, or are at risk of committing, serious sexual or violent offences. Important comorbidities and differential diagnoses must be carefully assessed, including other paraphilic disorders, other sexual disorders (e.g., CSBD), personality disorders, and psychopathy.

It is important to prepare for interviews by reading collateral material, forming preliminary but tentative hypotheses that will need to be explored, considering challenges that might arise in the room, and strategies that may be required. Indeed, forensic assessment begins the instant that one begins reviewing collateral information, not at the start of the interview itself. Specific issues that may arise in interviews with sexually sadistic individuals are their need for dominance and control, secretiveness, bullying or intimidating the assessor, vicarious trauma in the assessor which the individual may enjoy, the assessor enjoying being embroiled in the sadistic world of the individual, and other extreme counter-transferential reactions. It is often important to: have more than one meeting; start with an open, flexible and less structured approach before using a more structured and closed one; give the person as much perceived control and power as possible; apply any tests necessary judiciously; if possible undertake assessment with another professional and at a minimum discuss the assessment and formulation with a colleague or supervisor; expect, accept and not be perturbed by one's reaction to the individual and case, both positive and negative. Comprehensive records and documents from multiple agencies and sources, and interviews with others (including family members and other professionals) are usually required where possible. Comprehensive descriptions of offences from records are usually sufficient, but it may sometimes be necessary to view photographs or videos, and if so, care must be taken to manage potential vicarious traumatization and identifying too much with the pleasure of sadism, so that the assessor can remain both objective and healthy.

Given the potential, although rare, genetic, neurological, and endocrine associations of CSSD, a comprehensive medical work up may be necessary, and will always be necessary if testosterone lowering medication is being considered.

12.7.2 Identifying and Assessing Sexual Sadism

Concerns have been raised about the reliability of SS, SSD or CSSD diagnoses using DSM or ICD (see above). Given serious consequences of under- or over-ascertainment, practitioners should be particularly careful, diligent, and thorough when considering if SS is present, mindful that it is the high end of the agonistic continuum, and reliability and validity are enhanced by using objective scales based on offence behaviors. These will be described below, with particular attention to the SESAS, given the evidence base for its use and our experience using it over the last decade.

A key issue in diagnosing CSSD, and other paraphilic disorders, is individuals may not disclose the nature and extent of their deviant sexual arousal and fantasies, due to shame, sexual internal world being private, being secretive, deceit, playing with the assessor, the potential implications of being open (i.e., damned if they do and damned if they do not disclose), and sometimes the lack of skill of assessors in approaching the topic sensitively, openly and confidently. Apart from a person's offences, evidence of sadistic sexual fantasy and behavior may be revealed in drawings, stories they write, books and magazines they read, models they obtain and make, diaries, auto-erotic behavior, pornography use, online searches and activity, engagement in conversations and forums online, and interviews with sexual partners. It is important that evidence of BDSM is not used to ascertain the presence of CSSD.

Most sexual violence is not reported, let alone prosecuted or convicted, although this is less so for SHs. Accordingly, when undertaking assessments, bear in mind that a person's official record may underestimate their history of sexual violence, ask individuals sensitively about previous relevant behaviors, and convictions such as assault, robbery and theft, may have been pled down or mask episodes of sexual offending. Obviously in legal contexts give advanced warning about the implications and admissibility of any self-disclosed non-adjudicated offences, and if there is dispute whether an act of sexual offending or violence occurred, the clinician is not arbiter of fact, so for legal purposes an assessment may need to be couched by giving an opinion if certain facts were true and another if they were not. Where there are convictions for assault, abduction, robbery, or attempted murder, there may be evidence from police reports or witness statements of sexually sadistic behavior. Clinicians should focus on the nature of behavior, rather than the conviction's label.

An important source of information is individual self-report gathered from clinical interviews, accounts to others, and perhaps self-report questionnaires, although self-report may not be reliable. The approach taken should facilitate open disclosure of relevant sexual history, fantasies, arousal and behavior, and descriptions of relevant offences. Clinicians should remember that SS goes well beyond control, coercion, abuse, aggression, and rape, and look for evidence of sexual arousal to subjugation, humiliation, causing fear, and inflicting physical pain. Reports of rape or violent fantasies need to be clarified and are not usually due to SS. Individuals with CSSD often describe feeling particularly aroused by the distress and fear they see in or hear from their victims, in fantasy and reality.

Self-report questionnaires can help gather information about sexual fantasies and behavior, but none focus exclusively or in detail on SS (Kalmus & Beech, 2005). Examples include: the Wilson Sex Fantasy Questionnaire (WSFQ; Wilson, 1978, 1988), the Sexual Interest Card Sort (Abel & Becker, 1979; Holland et al., 2000), the Sexual Deviance Card Sort (Laws, 1986), and the Paraphilic Sexual Fantasy Questionnaire (PSFQ; O'Donohue et al., 1997). There are also broader assessments including questions on deviant sexual interests and behavior, like the Clarke Sexual History Questionnaire (SHQ; Paitich et al., 1977); the Multiphasic Sex Inventory (MSI) I & II (Nichols & Molinder, 1984, 1996); the Multidimensional Assessment of Sex and Aggression (MASA; Knight et al., 1994; Knight & Cerce, 1999); the Explicit Sexual Interest Questionnaire (ESIQ; Banse et al., 2010; Schmidt & Perkins, 2021); and the Multidimensional Inventory of Development, Sex, and Aggression (MIDSA, 2011). All are transparent, rely on the individual's honesty, and lack validity scales (except the MIDSA), but can be used alongside relevant validity measures, such as the Paulhus Deception Scales (PDS; Paulhus, 1998), Minnesota Multiphasic Personality Inventory (MMPI; Ben-Porath & Tellegen, 2020; Ben-Porath et al., 2022) or Personality Assessment Inventory (PAI; Morey, 1991; Edens et al., 2001). Nonetheless, the current authors do not use sexual self-report scales in our forensic or clinical practice, preferring to slowly obtain crucially important sexual history information by means of a clinical interview that capitalizes on any rapport that has been built during personal history taking. However, as long as the assessment is thorough, and addresses all of the important areas of sexual development and interests in appropriate detail, it is our view that either approach is defensible.

12.7.3 Objective Assessment of Sexual Sadism

Due to the problems with self-report, so-called 'objective' measures have been developed to provide an assessment of sexually sadistic arousal or interests not reliant on self-report. The four main ones are: penile plethysmography (PPG); viewing time, visual reaction time and visual gaze/eye tracking measures; cognitive tasks (e.g., attentional capture, sexual content induced delay, implicit associations); and scales based on rating behaviors displayed at crime scenes. There may also be promise in using virtual reality and functional imaging (Renaud et al., 2002; Thornton et al., 2018; Trottier et al., 2019). The two of relevance are PPG and objective behavioral scales, as the others have been researched and developed primarily for pedophilia.

PPG or phallometry, where circumferential or volumetric erectile changes in response to sexual stimuli is measured, is validated as an objective measure of pedophilia, and is used to assess sexual interest in rape, violence and/or sadism in some centers (Murphy et al., 2015). But PPG's ablity to identify and measure SS has been inconsistent, with some studies showing discriminant validity (Fedora et al., 1992; Barbaree et al., 1994; Proulx et al., 2003, 2006), some no difference (Langevin et al., 1985; Seto & Kuban, 1996; Longpré et al., 2018) and one finding those without SS showed more deviant arousal than those with (Marshall et al., 2002). There are general and specific (to SS) issues that give context to such findings and question the utility of using PPG. General issues include individuals suppressing their sexual responses, low response rates, lack of standardized stimulus sets, inability to differentiate offenders from nonoffenders, and lack of consistent reliability and validity (Marshall & Hucker, 2006). Specific issues include the ethics of and ability to use SS stimuli depicting extreme scenarios, fantasies in SS involving highly idiosyncratic and therefore difficult to replicate or generalize scenarios, the use of "rape" stimuli or "violent" stimuli (images, videos, or narratives) which do not arouse those with SS, and the dimensional nature of SS and the agonistic continuum (Knight et al., 2013).

On the back of research showing SS is dimensional and the top of the agonistic continuum and questioning reliability and validity of ICD or DSM diagnosis, several dimensional scales have been developed. These include the Sexual Sadism Scale (SESAS; Mokros et al., 2012), the Massachusetts Treatment Centre Sadism Scale (MTCSS; Longpré et al., 2019), and the Sexual Homicide Crime Scene Rating Scale for Sexual Sadism (SADSEX-SH-R; Myers et al., 2019). Recently Longpré and Knight (in press) also developed and validated The Agonistic Continuum Scale (TACS). Given the evidence-base and utility of the SESAS, it is recommend that practitioners use it in all cases where SS is suspected. Therefore, it is described in detail below.

12.7.4 The Sexual Sadism Scale (SESAS)

The SESAS is a structured dimensional behavioral scale for objectively anchoring and guiding the clinical assessment of sexual sadism. It now has a substantial and growing evidence base in terms of reliability, validity and utility, and given the problems with all of these when making a clinical diagnosis or using other measures, the current authors always use it and recommend to practitioners that they always use it when sexual sadism is a relevant consideration in a case. The aim here is to provide detailed guidance on its use, although it is recommended that practitioners familiarize themselves with the instrument and have relevant experience and knowledge before using it, as they should do with any structured clinical decision-making tool. Training is available in using it, and both of us have trained forensic mental health, criminal justice, and law enforcement professionals to apply it in the field, but training is not necessary to use it.

12.7.4.1 Development of the SESAS

Marshall and Hucker (2006) developed an initial dimensional scale, their Sexual Sadism Scale (SSS) of 17 items, after asking professionals to evaluate the relevance of 35 candidate items. All were objective features ascertainable from information about offences, and some were given weightings based on how important and consistently professionals considered them in indicating SS. Nitschke et al. (2009) examined the 17-item SSS in 50 sexual offenders with SS and 50 without SS, developing an 11-item cumulative scale of severe SS from 10 of the items plus the additional item 'object insertion into orifices'. This included all five most heavily weighted items from the SSS, neither of two items indicating consensual strangulation or bondage with partners which are BDSM related, nor strangulation, choking or asphyxiation which are very common in SS but are non-specific. They found the scale highly reliable, a strong Guttman scale, and a cut-off of 4 items or more distinguished perfectly between the two evenly sized groups in the development sample. The scale was initially called the Severe Sexual Sadism Scale (SSSS) and limited to the 11 crime scene indicators. But subsequently these 11 items became Part I, three additional items to help with clinical judgement were added as Part II, and a manual of structured coding guidelines was produced for what was now called the Severe Sexual Sadism (SeSaS) scale, and then more recently just the Sexual Sadism Scale (SeSaS or SESAS).

12.7.4.2 Description of the SESAS

The SESAS has two parts (Table 12.3). Part I items, 11 in number, are ascertained from crime scene actions and form a cumulative dimensional scale of severe SS. A score of 4 or more suggests probable SSD. However, the final judgment as to presence of SS is made, anchored by this score, but also considering three additional part II indicators, and other relevant case features. Each item is coded present or

Table 12.3 Items of the Sexual Sadism Scale (SESAS; Mokros et al., 2012)

Part	Item number	Item label/description
Part I–Analysis of crime scene actions	1	Sexual arousal during the crime scene actions
	2	Exertion of power, control, domination
	3	Torturing the victim
	4	Degrading, humiliating behaviour towards the victim
	5	Mutilation of sexual parts of the victim's body
	6	Mutilation of other parts of the victim's body
	7	Expressive physical violence
	8	Insertion of objects into victim's bodily orifices
	9	Ritualistic behaviour
	10	Confinement of the victim
	11	Taking trophies
Part II—Additional indicators	12	Planned conduct
	13	Indications of sadistic acts in the past beyond the listed offences
	14	Arousability to sadistic fantasies or acts (either self-confessed or apparent through witness statements)

absent following the coding instructions, with a high threshold for presence, so if there is partial evidence or uncertainty it is scored absent. Thus, the SESAS is a set of structured professional judgement guidelines for ascertaining SS.

12.7.4.3 Psychometric Properties of the SESAS

The SESAS demonstrates high levels of inter-rater reliability and internal consistency (Nitschke et al., 2009; Mokros et al., 2012). In terms of concurrent validity, SESAS scores correlate with clinical diagnosis (Longpré et al., 2018; Gonçalves et al., 2020; Darjee, 2019), but not PPG assessed sadism (Longpré et al., 2018). From an amalgamation of four studies a cut score of 4 on part I has a sensitivity of 95% (95% CI: [66%, 99%]) and specificity of 99% (95% CI: [64%, 100%]) for predicting DSM-IV-TR SS (Nitschke et al., 2013), and the ROC-AUC was .93 (95% CI: [.90, .96]) (Mokros et al., 2014). However predictive validity for further sexual or violent offending is weak or absent (see below).

12.7.4.4 Using the SESAS in Applied Forensic and Clinical Settings

To bring objectivity, consistency, and an evidence-based approach to diagnosing SSD or CSSD clinicians should apply the SESAS to anchor their diagnostic judgements. The current authors usually apply the SESAS to collateral information available before interviews to help generate hypotheses to be tested at interview and if further information becomes available. A score of 4 on SESAS part I is a reliable indicator of probable SS. In terms of part II, item 12, 'planned conduct', is confirmatory of SS in those with high part I scores, whereas items 13, 'indications of sadistic acts in the past', and 14, 'arousability to sadistic fantasies or acts', highly indicate SS in themselves. In practice sometimes, but rarely, a person scores 3 on part I, but the presence of item 13 or 14, or other information such as the person describing being aroused by fear and distress in the eyes of their victim, leads to a judgment that SS is present. Conversely in some cases scores of 4, 5 or rarely even higher can be due to anger/vindictiveness or multiple perpetrators rather than SS. In the former items linked to sexual deviance (such as part I items 5, 9 and 11 [genital mutilation, ritual, and trophies]; and part II items 13 and 14) are absent and offences are not usually prolonged (Czarnietzki, et al., 2024); and in the latter it is important to look at each person, their role, and the impact of the group dynamic (Clarkson et al., 2020). In sexual homicide cases it has been suggested that a cut of 5 is used as the threshold rather than 4 (Consigliere et al., 2024).

It is crucial that the SESAS is used in a structured professional judgment (SPJ) fashion, involving informed clinical judgment, rather than simply looking for a cut-score of four or five. Indeed, as noted above, vindictive rape offences of the partially sadistic variant can have elevated SESAS scores, and the current authors have identified scores as high as six, but a thorough behavioral analysis, and lengthy assessment interview, both revealed that there were no ritualistic plans and the offending reflected a misogynistic desire to punish females, rather than CSSD. Thus, the assessing clinician should always ground their diagnostic opinion in the SESAS results, but is not entirely bound by it in a mechanical actuarial fashion.

12.8 Risk Assessment

An important task when assessing anyone who has committed a sexual offence or sexual violence is assessing the risk of further sexual or violent offending, to determine management strategies and interventions required to prevent these. Below specific considerations relevant to assessing risk in individuals with SS are highlighted.

12.8.1 Sexual Sadism as a Risk Factor for Recidivism

Five studies have examined whether SS, ascertained by DSM diagnosis, PPG or SESAS, predicts sexual or violent recidivism prospectively or pseudo-prospectively in released offenders (Hill et al., 2008; Kingston et al., 2010; Eher et al., 2016; Darjee et al., 2016; Gonçalves et al., 2020). Most found no effect or a small effect disappearing after adjusting for other risk relevant variables. This appears to question concerns and fears raised about further serious offending and escalation. Potential explanations are: SS is not strongly related to repetition of sexual violence, findings are confounded by treatment and management, low rates of SS in samples, SS being associated with non-release, and problems with reliability and validity of identifying SS. Even if SS is not related to recidivism, it can still be related to severity of harm if individuals do recidivate. In addition, replicated research findings show SS is associated with previous repeat violent and sexual offending, portends escalation in sexual violence, is far more common in those who commit SH than those who commit rape or sexual assault, and is even more common in those who commit repeat SH. It would be a brave and foolish clinician who downplayed the risk of serious sexual violence posed by an individual with CSSD who has already committed sexual violence. Unfortunately, the methodology of classic recidivism and risk studies is very limited and problematic for gauging this association. Myers et al. (2010), in a small study of recidivism in juvenile SH perpetrators, cautioned that SS could lead to further SH on release, and clinical experience and official serious case reviews indicate that some offenders with SS pose a long-term risk of serious sexual harm. In sexual violence risk assessment SS should be considered a red flag factor, along with a very high level of psychopathy, and the rare combination of both is always highly concerning. Although other factors may diminish with age, and frequency of sexual arousal and fantasy reduces, the nature and direction of sexual interest does not change, certainly not without intervention, and even if the use of fantasies has reduced or abated, when faced with relevant triggers in the future, such as loneliness, resentment, anger, feeling powerless, humiliation, conflict with women, or perceived rejection, they can re-emerge and the ability to not focus on them may diminish, given their power to alleviate such states. The cycle of fantasy, behavioral try outs and acting may therefore start again, even after many years.

12.8.2 Application of Risk Assessment Instruments

Actuarial risk assessment instruments, such as Static-99 (Hanson & Thornton, 1999), Static-99R (Phenix et al., 2016) and Risk Matrix-2000 (Thornton, 2007), should be used with caution, if at all, when assessing risk in offenders with SS (Doren, 2002), as they are atypical and rare in development and validation samples, and actuarial tools may give an indication of likelihood of recidivism but not risk of serious harm. Instruments focused on dynamic factors, such as Stable and Acute-2007 (Hanson et al., 2007) and Violence Risk Scale-Sexual Offence Version (Olver et al., 2007) can help for identifying relevant dynamic factors, including deviant sexual interests, and planning intervention. Structured professional judgement instruments (Hart & Boer, 2020), such as the SVR-20 V2 (Boer et al., 2017) and the RSVP-V2 (Hart et al., 2022) provide a good structure for considering relevant risk factors, formulating risk in atypical and concerning cases, assessing risk of serious harm, and planning individualized intervention and risk management. The current authors have used the RSVP (Hart et al., 2003), and recently RSVP-V2, for such cases in forensic and clinical contexts. Instruments that address risk of non-sexual violence, such as the Historical-Clinical-Risk Management Version 3 (HCR-20 V3; Douglas et al., 2013), may also be useful alongside, although many items overlap with the RSVP and RSVP-V2.

12.8.3 Risk assessment Outcome and Conclusions

The aim is to produce a concise but comprehensive formulation, articulating the role of SS in offending and future risk. This should answer the following: Why has this person, offended in these ways, against these victims, at those times, and not at other times? How could they plausibly offend in the future, why would they do it, against whom, under what circumstances and how? Why have they developed SS, how salient is fantasy related to SS, what triggers fantasy, how and why do they enact fantasy? The assessor should consider the nature and severity of SS; how central and dominant SS is in the formulation; the interaction between SS and other factors (such as sexual preoccupation, hypersexuality, callousness, narcissism, isolation, detachment, hostility, misogyny, anger, impulsivity, poor coping, feeling powerless/humiliated, substance use, and opportunity to access victims); and relevant internal, motivational, and external strengths and protective factors. Responsivity factors should be identified, particularly personality disorder traits.

12.9 Treatment

Much has been written and researched on the treatment of those who commit or pose a risk of committing sexual offences. Although the effectiveness of treatment is debated, multiple meta-analyses show modern treatments modestly reduces recidivism (Hanson et al., 2009; Schmucker & Lösel, 2015; Gannon et al., 2019), especially if they follow risk needs responsivity (RNR) principles (Hanson et al., 2009), focus on strengths and positive prosocial goals (Marshall, 2019; Olver et al., 2020;), are psychologically run and informed (Gannon et al., 2019), and incorporate interventions specifically addressing sexual deviance (Gannon et al., 2019). So best practice and an evidence-based approach can be adopted. Unfortunately, there has been little research and there is little guidance on treating SS (Yates et al., 2008; Berner et al., 2018). How treatment should be approached, adapted, and individualized with SS will now be focused on.

12.9.1 General Aspects

Much pessimism has been expressed regarding whether offenders with SS can be successfully treated. Treatment is likely to be long-term and should be based on best practice principles for treating people who have committed sexual abuse. Attention must be paid to readiness, engagement, and motivation to facilitate entry into and maintenance in treatment. Crucial responsivity factors include comorbid personality disorders, sometimes psychopathic traits. Although sexually sadistic offending is relatively rare, as outlined in this chapter, it is the culmination of complex interacting processes, so such individuals are heterogeneous, and there is no prescribable 'treatment for SS'. Therefore, treatment should be tailored to the individual formulation which should be informed by relevant etiological factors and assessment (see above). With individuals posing a high risk of serious harm, such as people with SS and/or psychopathy, it is important that treatment is also focused on prosocial outcomes they want to achieve. Therefore, integrating a "Good Lives" component to the dominant RNR focus may be appropriate. Treatment will often need to be multifaceted and multi-layered, involving individual approaches, group work, and wider milieu aspects; must adapt and pivot to changing aspects of the individual's internal world and external circumstances, by deciding the right moment for the right intervention (Berner et al., 2018); and often requires integrated pharmacological and psychological treatment. Treating people with SS can be extremely challenging and complex, with the potential for profound impacts on clinicians and teams, which must be attended to.

12.9.2 Psychological Treatment

Individual psychotherapy was traditionally psychodynamic in nature with a move towards more structured approaches, such as cognitive-behavioral therapy, over the last 30 or so years. Tardif et al. (2007) and Yakely (2021) have given contemporary accounts of working psychodynamically with SH perpetrators and individuals with paraphilic disorders, which may counterbalance the scathing commentary given to psychoanalytic attempts at treatment earlier in the twentieth century (Grubin, 1994a; Kingston & Yates, 2008). Berner et al. (2018) described the integration of psychodynamic understanding, concepts and processes in the treatment of two individuals with SS. Concepts with their origins in psychoanalysis are crucial to understanding and working with such individuals, including: transference and countertransference; the representation of early relationships in the mind and their impact on subsequent emotional, relational and sexual functioning; the acting out of unconscious drives and wishes. Such concepts are important in more recently developed therapies with an evidence base in treating people with personality disorders, such as schema therapy (Bernstein et al., 2019), transference-focused psychotherapy (Clarkin et al., 2023), mentalization-based psychotherapy (Bateman, 2022), and cognitive-analytic therapy (Pollock et al., 2006). Given high rates of personality disorders in people with CSSD and the role of personality dysfunction in the development and acting out of SS, these may be useful and effective in such cases.

Specific behavioral approaches have been used to treat and attempt to change the focus of sexual interest in people with paraphilic disorders, including SS (Kingston & Yates, 2008). These include aversive procedures, covert sensitization, orgasmic reconditioning, and satiation (Laws & Marshall, 2003; Marshall & Laws, 2003). Although some support for using these approaches has been presented in case studies and case series (Hayes et al., 1978; Laws et al., 1978), and individuals with SS engage with such approaches and report diminished use of sadistic fantasy and arousal, the research evidence for their effectiveness is limited (Quinsey & Marshall, 1983; Kingston & Yates, 2008), individuals have to be very motivated and committed to use them, their impact may be time limited and may not generalize, and gauging whether a person has been effectively treated is very hard. This is of particular concern when apparently successful treatment in an institutional setting may not be sustained on release to the community, which may be due to fading, lack of ongoing application of the technique, poor generalizability to other contexts, and/or the salience of previously long-standing sexually sadistic fantasies which are resorted to or re-emerge when people encounter isolation, conflict, lack of control, anger or perceived problems with potential victims in the community. Sometimes it may be due to sham engagement with treatment. Although a recent meta-analysis showed treatment programs are more effective at reducing recidivism if they incorporate behavioral techniques to address deviant sexual interests (Gannon et al., 2019), it is unclear whether this is directly due to the application of these approaches, a reflection that such programs pay more attention to the risk and needs principles of RNR, or more directly involved psychologists with a high level of experience and skill.

Some have raised concerns, like those previously raised about psychopathy (Salekin, 2002), relating to the treatment of people with SS in group programs. Such concerns include that they can get aroused by retelling their and hearing others' stories of sexual abuse reinforcing their deviant fantasies, that work on empathy may be ineffective given how attuned they are to the suffering of others or may even enhance their sadism, that they lead to destructive sadistic dynamics being acted out in the group, that their offences and fantasies are too disturbing for other group members to tolerate and may harm them, and that at best such treatment is ineffective and at worst increases risk of recidivism. Although such concerns are understandable, there are group treatment programs for high-risk high-needs sexual offenders internationally that do include those with SS, and the current authors have come across cases in the UK and Australia where these concerns have not eventuated in community and prison settings. However, whether the treatment was effective is unknown, and individuals usually received additional individual treatment, pharmacological treatment and multi-agency risk management, and a range of interventions over time. To address three of the specific concerns, firstly getting aroused by stories of sexual abuse in treatment is unlikely to reinforce what is already a salient sexual interest, albeit it will not lead to it diminishing, and will not be particularly therapeutic. Secondly, detailed offence accounts are not necessary in treatment, where the goal is to identify and ascertain treatment needs, not to get a detailed account which matches that of the victim or police report. Thirdly, understanding the impact on the victim and developing empathy are no longer considered evidence-based targets in treatment, given that neither are related to reducing recidivism. If work is going to be done on empathy, it has been suggested that the person focuses on someone close to them towards whom sexually sadistic fantasy has not been focused and towards whom such offending would be anathema (Marshall & Hucker, 2006). It may be, that just as for psychopathy (Sewall & Olver, 2019), treatment can be effective if it considers relevant RNR factors, is adapted to our understanding of SS, and attends to comorbid personality disorders.

12.9.3 Pharmacological Treatment

Medications used to treat individuals who have committed sexual offences include selective serotonin reuptake inhibitors (SSRIs) such as fluoxetine and sertraline, anti-androgens such as cyproterone acetate (CPA) and medroxyprogesterone acetate (MPA), and Gonadotrophin Releasing Hormone (GnRH) agonists such as triptorelin and leuprorelin. In addition, a GnRH antagonist, degarelix, has shown recent promise (Landgren et al., 2020). For recent comprehensive overviews of the pharmacological treatment of paraphilic disorders and those who commit sexual offences see Darjee and Quinn (2020), Thibaut et al. (2020), Turner and Briken (2021), Marshall et al. (2021) and Bradford & Saleh (2021). Darjee and Baron (2018c) described medical treatment of SH offenders.

In individuals who have committed sexual assault, rape or murder, in whom sexually sadistic arousal has been central to driving their offences, SS has had salience since adolescence or early adulthood, and there is an ongoing risk of re-emergence of sexually sadistic fantasy or acting on such fantasies or arousal to inflict serious harm, testosterone lowering medication in the form of an anti-androgen or GnRH agonist should usually be considered. The aim is to stop sexual fantasy, arousal, and related behavior. Anti-androgens cause worse side-effects and are more likely to lead to physical health complications than GnRH agonists, and cyproterone acetate has the disadvantage of primarily being used as a twice daily tablet taken by mouth, with the risk of a person forgetting to take it and non-adherence. In practice GnRH agonists are the most effective treatment and cause less side-effects and risk of medical complications. Recent international guidelines recommend that both an anti-androgen and a GnRH agonist are prescribed together where total suppression of sex drive is the goal in individuals who pose a high risk of very seriously harmful sexual violence (Thibaut et al., 2020). However, this is not warranted as a GnRH agonist on its own leads to libidinal suppression, so the anti-androgen adds nothing except side-effects and the risk of serious medical complications. They can be given by three- or six-monthly intramuscular injection, are well tolerated, and most individuals treated are grateful to be relieved of their fantasies and to be managed in a less restrictive environment.

Best practice is to prescribe medication on a voluntary basis, with initial medical work up and ongoing medical monitoring, and for them to be used in conjunction with psychological treatment. In the UK, Canada, Australia, and Western Europe they are prescribed in this way, however in some US states, some Eastern European countries, and some Asian countries they can be mandated (Turner et al. 2017, 2017). Concerns are sometimes raised about not being able to force people to take treatment and the risk of a person stopping treatment. In terms of the former, in individuals who pose a risk of committing rape or homicide without treatment, when assessing their suitability for stepping-down or conditional release, it can be put to them that medication gives them an opportunity to reduce the risk they pose so as to reassure those managing them that risk is manageable in less secure settings. Whether they accept treatment is up to them, as with psychological treatment, but may have implications for the assessment of the risk they currently pose and progression. The process then becomes one of negotiation and engagement with control remaining with the individual, rather than the dynamics of force, coercion or violation. If an individual wants to stop taking treatment then there will always be time to plan ongoing monitoring and management with a long-acting GnRH agonist, there may be reemergence of risk of sexually sadistic offending, but risk mitigation strategies such as increased psychological support, monitoring and supervision can be put in place, and then if dynamic risk factors increase or there is the emergence of risk related behaviors, appropriate action can be taken as for other high risk individuals managed in the community. There is some evidence that after several years of treatment risk is reduced despite people not taking treatment for the whole period of follow-up (Gallo et al., 2019), and two individuals with SS treated with GnRH agonists by one of us have come off medication after being on treatment for 4–5 years without committing further offences or being returned to custody.

The evidence base for the treatment of SS with GnRH agonists or anti-androgens is supportive but not comprehensive or robust. This is similar to the research evidence for the treatment of paraphilic disorders more generally (Darjee & Quinn, 2020). However, an understanding of the role of testosterone in sexual fantasy and behavior, the results of the observational studies and very few randomized controlled studies, and international practice of using these treatments, indicates that they can be very effective for treating people with paraphilic disorders and/or compulsive sexual behavior disorder who pose a risk of further sexual offending. Individuals who have been treated with and remain on GnRH agonists have shown very low rates of reoffending (Briken et al., 2003; Lewis et al., 2017; Turner & Briken, 2018), sexual fantasy and arousal is clearly central to the offending of those with SS, a recent long-term observational cohort study showed no re-offending amongst a high risk group with paraphilic disorders treated with leuprorelin, Bradford (2007) has described successful treatment in the community of SH cases, mirroring the experience of one of us treating similar cases (six individuals who had committed homicide, attempted homicide and/or serial rape) in the UK and Australia.

12.9.4 Contextual Aspects: Integration, Countertransference, and Supervision

It is very important that treatment approaches are integrated with each other and with the overall management plan, requiring ongoing multi-disciplinary and multi-agency communication, collaboration, and planning. No aspect of treatment or management can be considered or delivered in isolation from other aspects. For example, there is no point of undertaking masturbatory reconditioning of sexually sadistic fantasies while a person is prescribed triptorelin, and if a person is experiencing their confinement or restrictions in the community as controlling and humiliating, then this needs to be addressed in treatment, and ways to address this in the wider management plan need to be considered. It is also important that all disciplines and agencies are working to a joint formulation.

Individuals with SS cause some of the most difficult and disturbing countertransference reactions in those who work with them. These reflect their SS, severe personality difficulties, and personal and systemic anxiety about such cases, their offences and potential for further harm. Feelings of domination, omnipotence, terror, brutality, humiliation, intrusion, violation, and excitement can come immediately or belatedly in a confusing array. A capacity for reflective practice, a certain level of robustness, and good formal supervision and informal support from colleagues is essential. This can prevent practitioners from being negatively affected by the work (e.g., burn out, mental health problems, relationship problems, needing time off, or leaving the job), coming to distorted formulations and opinions, and not being able to work effectively. Such dynamics can also be played out in and reverberate around teams, services and agencies, and need to be recognized, reflected on and not acted out on others, if treatment and management are to be effective.

12.10 Management

Much has been written about managing people who commit violent and sexual offences (Harrison, 2010), including legal measures and processes, government policies, the impact of societal and political views and expectations, media representations, institutional management, management in the community, multi-agency collaboration, and specific strategies such as monitoring, supervision, imposing restrictions, providing supports, treatment, and community and victim safety planning. Those who commit sexually sadistic rapes and homicides are amongst the most notorious and difficult cases to manage locally, nationally, and internationally, and play a disproportionate role in shaping policy, and therefore practice, generally. Here some issues of specific relevance to SS are highlighted.

12.10.1 Court Issues

Although sexually sadistic offenders very rarely have comorbid serious mental illness and their sexual and personality disorders do not meet relevant thresholds, historically some have been successful in pleading the insanity defense (Bartholomew et al., 1975), despite psychiatrists and lawyers excluding SS from it (Kiernan, 1892, 1903; Crozier, 2002), and several notorious individuals who committed serial SH have attempted but failed with the defense (Ewing, 2008).

Many jurisdictions have partial defenses, such as diminished responsibility, the threshold for which can sometimes be reached by individuals with paraphilic disorders and/or personality disorders. Indeed, the leading case that defined the scope of diminished responsibility in England and Wales, R v Byrne (1960), dealt with a case of sadistic SH, although currently paraphilic disorders without comorbid mental disorders are unlikely to lead to diminished responsibility. In Germany severe paraphilic disorders can qualify for a finding of diminished criminal responsibility as, alongside personality disorders, they are considered "a serious abnormality", but only qualify for the partial defense if they are also considered to have "significantly reduced" the person's ability to understand or control their behavior (Dobbrunz et al., 2020). Guidelines have been suggested for the assessment of this including the nature and severity of the paraphilic disorder, its impact on the individual and the context of their offending, and the presence of comorbid conditions (Boetticher et al., 2005; Briken & Müller, 2014; Briken et al., 2019). Those found to have diminished responsibility may get a reduced sentence or indefinite placement in a forensic psychiatric clinic. There are similar procedures and practices in other European countries, such as the Netherlands (Barendregt et al., 2008). So, despite paraphilic disorders being irrelevant to criminal responsibility and mitigation in North America, Australia, and the UK, they are relevant in several European jurisdictions.

In several jurisdictions, rather than mitigation, a sexual element leads to more severe punishment in murder cases, reflecting views that such crimes are particularly "heinous". For example, 29 states in the USA stipulate co-occurring sexual assault as an aggravating factor for a potential death penalty (Kirchmeier, 1997, 2006), and in some jurisdictions a sexual element may lead to a life sentence without parole (Pettigrew, 2015), or a life rather than determinate sentence (Schartmueller, 2019). Sexually sadistic homicide is particularly likely to invoke such measures.

The other issue that comes up in criminal courts is risk assessment in relation to the likelihood of further offending, the associated risk to the community, and whether a person is likely to respond to rehabilitation efforts. Some jurisdictions have longer than normal sentences, extended periods of supervision, or indeterminate sentences that can be imposed on sexual or violent offenders deemed to pose an ongoing risk of serious harm (Jackson, 1996; Darjee & Russell, 2011). Sexually sadistic offenders are particularly liable to come within the ambit of such legislation (Langevin & Curnoe, 2014).

In criminal cases, it is important that psychiatric and psychological experts take due care and exercise diligence in identifying and diagnosing SS, assessing risk of further sexual violence and considering what risk management measures are required, given the implications for the individual and for community safety.

12.10.2 Institutional Management

Issues in institutional management include: the appearance of being a model prisoner and whether institutional behavior is relevant to future risk; risks to staff within the institution; the delivery of treatments and interventions in hospitals and prisons to reduce the risk of sexual violence in the community; collaborative working with community agencies when transitioning to the community; and determining when a person is ready and safe to step down, usually in a graded manner, and then be released, usually conditionally. None of these issues are unique to individuals with SS, but they are particularly pertinent in such cases.

12.10.3 Post-Sentence Commitment or Detention

In the USA, 20 states, plus Washington D.C. and the federal system, allow for the post-imprisonment civil commitment of people who have committed sexual offences, if there is a likelihood of future sexual, and a mental abnormality, broadly defined so including paraphilic disorders and personality disorders, predisposing them to sexual violence (Testa & West, 2010). It has often been in the context of assessments for civil commitment that concerns have been raised about the reliability of paraphilic and SS diagnoses, and the use of paraphilia not otherwise specified (NOS), nonconsent diagnoses for individuals who commit rape but fall short of the criteria for SS (King et al., 2014). Rates of SSD range from about 5% to 10% and paraphilia/paraphilic disorder NOS nonconsent range from a quarter to a half (Becker et al., 2003; Levenson, 2004; Jackson & Richards, 2007; Elwood et al., 2010).

In Australia and New Zealand post-sentence detention and supervision are available where sexual or violent offenders are assessed as posing an unacceptable risk of serious sexual or violent offending, but unlike the USA where detention is via civil commitment to what are designated as mental health facilities, those subject to the legislation are either detained in prison or supervised through the correctional system (Bartels et al., 2019). Like in the USA, the rate of SS in one study was 8% (Doyle et al., 2011). Although there is no legal requirement to make a diagnosis, in practice identifying and diagnosing relevant conditions, including SS, other paraphilic disorders and personality disorders, is an important part of the risk assessment and formulation process, but unlike the USA diagnosing paraphilia NOS, nonconsent, is rare.

12.10.4 Release Decision Making

Making assessments of whether an individual with SS who has committed rape or homicide is ready to have periods in the community or to be conditionally released, perhaps after decades in prison or a secure hospital, can be very challenging. They are often well behaved and described as model prisoners and sometimes, when their conviction has been for murder or manslaughter, or another "non-sexual" offence, their SS may be missed, and their risk of sexual violence not addressed through interventions in custody. It is incredibly difficult to gauge from institutional behavior or self-report whether a person has ongoing sexually sadistic fantasies or arousal. So, as outlined above, in cases where there is ongoing sadistic sexual fantasy or arousal, uncertainty about this, or a risk of the re-emergence of such fantasy or arousal on release, given the risk of serious harm, treatment with GnRH agonists should be offered. In practice this is all individuals with SS who have committed or pose a risk of committing serious sexual violence.

Making release decisions is easier where a person has been given graded exposure to less secure and restrictive settings and has started to engage with community management services. Ideally individuals should transition from high security, through medium security, low security, and open settings, with careful monitoring and testing out, before decisions are made about release by relevant legal bodies (e.g., parole tribunals, courts, or mental health tribunals). Some problems encountered with such cases are anxiety and horror that someone who has committed sadistic rape or SH might be given freedom, versus an over-focus on good institutional behavior and engagement particularly where the person has been detained for several decades. Although most sexually sadistic offenders can be transitioned safely to being managed in the community, those with very high levels of psychopathy and/or who have committed serial SH, who are rare even amongst the rare group of individuals with SS who offend, may never be safe for release to the community and the focus then needs to be on quality of life during lifelong incarceration (Völlm & Braun, 2019).

12.10.5 Legal Measures in the Community

In addition to criminal justice measures, other legal frameworks may also be relevant in some individuals with SS who pose a risk to others, such as sex offender registration and notification (Vess et al., 2014), sexual risk orders and similar orders police can use to impose restrictions where there is a risk of serious sexual harm (Kingston & Thomas, 2018), child protection procedures, and family court orders in child custody cases. Only a small minority of individuals subject to sex offender registration have committed seriously harmful offences and SS is rare. In an area of South East Scotland with a population of about a million people, with about 800 registered sex offenders, less than half a dozen of these individuals had SS (Darjee et al., 2016). Unfortunately, registration and prevention orders do not necessarily provide the means to prevent serious reoffending in such individuals when they are not subject to parole or potential recall to custody (Edinburgh, the Lothians, and Scottish Borders MAPPA Strategic Oversight Group, 2019).

A particularly challenging scenario is where an individual who has committed or poses a risk of committing serious sexual violence who is driven by sexually sadistic fantasies is in the community and subject to no legal measures. This can occur when a person is released at the end of a prison sentence without qualifying for, having rejected or after denial of parole; where intelligence becomes available that an individual has sexually sadistic fantasies and is planning an attack; and where individuals self-present to or are referred to services by concerned family or professionals (Darjee & Baron, 2018b; 2018c McEwan & Darjee, 2021). As outlined above, in these situations it is incumbent on professionals, including clinicians, to make the best assessment they can, to offer interventions to help the individual reduce risk, and work with colleagues from other agencies, including law enforcement to do what can be done under the circumstances to prevent serious sexual violence.

12.10.6 Multi-Agency Management

An important feature of modern forensic mental health and criminal justice practice in the community is multi-agency working. In some jurisdictions, such as in the UK, this is supported by legislation which lays out requirements for relevant agencies to co-operate with each other in the multi-agency management of sexual and violent offenders. In the UK these are called Multi-Agency Public Protection Arrangements (MAPPA) Kemshall & Hilder, 2020; Kemshall & Maguire, 2021). Such arrangements aim to ensure that, where an individual poses an ongoing or imminent risk of serious harm to others, necessary information is shared, agencies co-operate with each other, and joint management plans are made. The focus of these arrangements and associated resources is on the most high-risk individuals in the community. As with sex offender registration, the vast majority of individuals managed at MAPPA levels 2 and 3 (who are individuals deemed to pose a high or very high risk of causing serious harm imminently) are not sexually sadistic, but all sexually sadistic cases managed under MAPPA are usually managed, or should be managed, at those MAPPA levels, at least initially, as was the case in South East Scotland for the six cases alluded to above. Such arrangements allow a sharing of responsibility and risk and allow each agency to attend to its core task in collaboration with other agencies. Where SS is an issue though, the dynamics mentioned above can reverberate through the system, may lead to dysfunction, and need to be attended to, just as with transference and countertransference (see above). Clinicians can play a role in keeping such systems psychologically aware and psychologically informed by understanding the difficult dynamics of sadism and their impact, thus keeping the multi-agency team as healthy and non-dysfunctional as possible, and able to work effectively to optimize the person's psychosexual functioning and to reduce risk of serious sexual violence (Darjee et al., 2024).

12.11 Conclusion

Forensically and clinically relevant SS, or CSSD, is rare, but has important implications for the risk of serious harm posed by an individual. Conflation with BDSM and lack of understanding of its dimensional nature, have contributed to conceptual confusion, lack of clarity about its nature and development, and significant problems with reliability of diagnosis. It is a complex condition with multi-faceted etiology and development, likely involving interaction of genetics, neurobiology, endocrine functioning, trauma, attachment, temperament, personality, vulnerable developmental periods, and sexual development, which predispose to and lead to the manifestation of sexually sadistic fantasy, arousal, and behavior. It is very rare in the general population, although coercive sexual interests are not. It is uncommon in people who commit sexual assault and rape but forms an important typological group. It is much more common in people who commit SH, and almost ubiquitous in very rare individuals who commit serial SH. Therefore, even though recidivism studies point to an equivocal role for SS as a risk factor, it is related to chronic, escalating, violent, homicidal, and serially homicidal offending. So, despite and due to its rarity, it should be considered a red flag factor in sexual violence risk assessment.

SS is dimensional in nature and is at the top end of an agonistic continuum of coercive and aggressive sexual fantasies and behavior. As with personality disorder, future diagnostic approaches will need to embrace this dimensionality, whilst also being pragmatic. A potential future approach based on the dimensional and pragmatic approach of ICD-11 for personality disorders, the current ICD-11 approach to CSSD, looking at the key facets of SS (control, humiliation, psychological suffering, and physical harm), and anchoring identification and assessment using an objective dimensional scale, such as the SESAS is suggested. It is suggested that 'coercive sexual agonistic disorder' (CSAD) should be the term used for this dimensional diagnosis, given the baggage that comes with terms like SS and paraphilic coercion, and that SS should be a qualifier, defined and identified as the severe and extreme end of the diagnostic continuum. Such an approach could address the clunkiness, arbitrariness, inconsistency, and conceptual violation associated with current categorical diagnostic approaches.

Best practice in assessment is to use all available information, including that from interviews, collateral materials and information from others, to ascertain if SS is present, its degree and its nature, after first anchoring the assessment using an objective measure. The only objective measure with satisfactory evidence for reliability, validity, and utility is the SESAS, and in our view no assessment for SS should be made without using it. Other similar scales may emerge and be developed and validated, but the other ones available currently remain in the realm of research rather than translation into practice. The only other objective measure that has been widely used is PPG, but findings have been inconsistent, and there is little to recommend its use in SS. It is important to also assess for other paraphilic disorders, CSBD, personality disorders and psychopathy, and to assess risk with a focus on relevant dynamic factors using a structured professional judgment approach, while being wary of the applicability of actuarial instruments in such atypical cases. Unlike etiology, concept and structure, and assessment, there has been very little research to directly inform treatment and management, which must be based on best practice in working with people who have committed sexual offences who pose a high risk, have complex and high needs, and complex responsivity issues. It should involve integrated psychological, pharmacological, and systematic approaches, with skillful consideration of the stage the person is at, the case formulation, and relevant areas for treatment, while being mindful of the important transference and countertransference issues that arise. Pharmacological treatment with a GnRH agonist will usually be indicated where there is a history of serious sexual violence or homicide driven by SS; as without sexual fantasy, urges, or arousal sadistic sexual violence is very unlikely to recur. Case studies and series, qualitative studies, and observational cohort studies describing treatment and outcomes are desperately needed, given that a randomized controlled study of the psychological or pharmacological treatment of CSSD will never receive ethical approval.

References

Abel, G. G., & Becker, J. V. (1979). The sexual interest card sort. Unpublished manuscript.

Abel, G. G., Becker, J. V., Cunningham-Rathner, J., Mittelman, M., & Rouleau, J. L. (1988). Multiple paraphilic diagnoses among sex offenders. *Journal of the American Academy of Psychiatry and the Law, 16*(2), 153–168.

Abgrall, J. F. (2010). *Inside the mind of a killer*. Profile Books.
Aggrawal, A. (2010). *Necrophilia: Forensic and medico-legal aspects*. CRC Press.
Aggrawal, A. (2011). A new classification of zoophilia. *Journal of Forensic and Legal Medicine, 18*(2), 73–78.
Ahlers, C. J., Schaefer, G. A., Mundt, I. A., Roll, S., Englert, H., Willich, S. N., & Beier, K. M. (2011). How unusual are the contents of paraphilias? Paraphilia-associated sexual arousal patterns in a community-based sample of men. *The Journal of Sexual Medicine, 8*(5), 1362–1370.
Alison, L., & Eyre, M. (2009). *Killer in the shadows: The monstrous crimes of Robert Napper*. Pennant Books Ltd.
American Psychiatric Association. (1952). Diagnostic and statistical manual: Mental disorders.
American Psychiatric Association. (1968). Diagnostic and statistical manual of mental disorders (2nd ed.).
American Psychiatric Association. (1980). Diagnostic and statistical manual of mental disorders (3rd ed.).
American Psychiatric Association. (1987). Diagnostic and statistical manual of mental disorders (3rd ed., rev.).
American Psychiatric Association. (1994). Diagnostic and statistical manual of mental disorders (4th ed.).
American Psychiatric Association. (2000). Diagnostic and Statistical Manual of Mental Disorders (4th ed., text rev.).
American Psychiatric Association. (2013). Diagnostic and statistical manual of mental disorders (5th ed.). https://doi.org/10.1176/appi.books.9780890425596
American Psychiatric Association. (2022). Diagnostic and statistical manual of mental disorders (5th ed., text rev.).
Amir, M. (1971). *Patterns in forcible rape*. The University of Chicago Press.
Archer, J. (2006). Testosterone and human aggression: An evaluation of the challenge hypothesis. *Neuroscience & Biobehavioral Reviews, 30*(3), 319–345.
Arrigo, B. A., & Purcell, C. E. (2001). Explaining paraphilias and lust murder: Toward an integrated model. *International Journal of Offender Therapy and Comparative Criminology, 45*(1), 6–31.
Balyk, E. D. (1997). Paraphilias as a sub type of obsessive- compulsive disorder: A hypothetical bio-social model. *Journal of Orthomolecular Medicine, 12*(1), 29–42.
Banse, R., Schmidt, A. E., & Ciarbour, J. (2010). Indirect measures of sexual interest in child sex offenders: A multimethod approach. *Criminal Justice and Behavior, 37*(3), 319–335.
Barbaree, H. E., Seto, M. C., Serin, R. C., Amos, N. L., & Preston, D. L. (1994). Comparisons between sexual and nonsexual rapist subtypes: Sexual arousal to rape, offense precursors, and offense characteristics. *Criminal Justice and Behavior, 21*(1), 95–114.
Barendregt, M., Muller, E., Nijman, H., & De Beurs, E. (2008). Factors associated with experts' opinions regarding criminal responsibility in The Netherlands. *Behavioral Sciences & the Law, 26*(5), 619–631.
Bartels, L., Walvisch, J., & Richards, K. (2019). More, longer, tougher ... Or is it finally time for a different approach to the post-sentence management of sex offenders in Australia? *Criminal Law Journal, 43*(1), 41–57.
Bartholomew, A. A., Milte, K. L., & Galbally, F. (1975). Sexual murder: Psychopathology and psychiatric jurisprudential considerations. *Australian & New Zealand Journal of Criminology, 8*(2), 143–152.
Bataille, G. (1990). *The trial of Gilles de Rais*. Amok Books.
Bateman, A. W. (2022). Mentalizing and group psychotherapy: A novel treatment for antisocial personality disorder. *American Journal of Psychotherapy, 75*(1), 32–37.
Baumeister, R. F. (2000). Gender differences in erotic plasticity: The female sex drive as socially flexible and responsive. *Psychological Bulletin, 126*(3), 347.

Baumeister, R. F., Catanese, K. R., & Vohs, K. D. (2001). Is there a gender difference in strength of sex drive? Theoretical views, conceptual distinctions, and a review of relevant evidence. *Personality and Social Psychology Review, 5*(3), 242–273.

Baur, E., Forsman, M., Santtila, P., Johansson, A., Sandnabba, K., & Långström, N. (2016). Paraphilic sexual interests and sexually coercive behavior: A population-based twin study. *Archives of Sexual Behavior, 45*, 1163–1172. https://doi.org/10.1007/s10508-015-0674-2

Beauregard, E., Proulx, J., & St-Yves, M. (2007). Angry or sadistic: Two types of sexual murderers. In J. Proulx, E. Beauregard, M. Cusson, & A. Nicole (Eds.), *Sexual murderers: A comparative analysis and new perspectives* (pp. 123–142). Wiley.

Becker, J. V., Stinson, J., Tromp, S., & Messer, G. (2003). Characteristics of individuals petitioned for civil commitment. *International Journal of Offender Therapy and Comparative Criminology, 47*(2), 185–195.

Ben-Porath, Y. S., Heilbrun, K., & Rizzo, M. (2022). Using the MMPI-3 in legal settings. *Journal of Personality Assessment, 104*(2), 162–178.

Ben-Porath, Y. S., & Tellegen, A. (2020). *Minnesota multiphasic personality Inventory-3 (MMPI-3): Manual for administration, scoring, and interpretation*. University of Minnesota Press.

Berg, K. (1945). *The sadist, authorized translation by Olga Illner and George Godwin*. William Heinemann.

Berger, P., Berner, W., Bolterauer, J., Gutierrez, K., & Berger, K. (1999). Sadistic personality disorder in sex offenders: Relationship to antisocial personality disorder and sexual sadism. *Journal of Personality Disorders, 13*(2), 175–186.

Berlin, F. (1983). Sex offenders: A biomedical perspective. In J. G. Greer & I. R. Stuart (Eds.), *The sexual aggressor: Current perspectives on treatment*. Van Nostrand Reinhold.

Berner, W., Hill, A., & Briken, P. (2018). Sexual sadism: Pharmacological and psychotherapeutic approaches. In J. Proulx, A. Carter, E. Beauregard, J. James, R. Darjee, & A. Mokros (Eds.), *Routledge international handbook of sexual homicide studies* (pp. 317–326). Routledge.

Bernstein, D. P., Clercx, M., & Keulen-De Vos, M. (2019). Schema therapy in forensic settings. In D. L. L. Polaschek, A. Day, & C. R. Hollin (Eds.), *The Wiley international handbook of correctional psychology* (pp. 654–668). Wiley.

Blair, J., Mitchell, D., & Blair, K. (2005). *The psychopath: Emotion and the brain*. Blackwell Publishing.

Bloch, I. (1935). *Anthropological studies on the strange sexual practices of all races and all ages*. The Minerva Group, Inc.

Boer, D. P., Hart, S. D., Kropp, P. R., & Webster, C. D. (2017). Manual for version 2 of the sexual violence Risk-20: Structured professional judgment guidelines for assessing and managing risk of sexual violence. Protect International.

Boetticher, A., Nedopil, N., Bosinski, H. A. G., & Saß, H. (2005). Mindestanforderungen für Schuldfähigkeitsgutachten. *Neue Z. Strafrecht, 25*, 57–62.

Boiste, P. C. V. (1835). *Dictionnaire universel de la langue française, avec le latin et l'étymologie [Universal Dictionary of the French language, with Latin and etymology]*. J. P. Meline.

Bourke, J. (2020). *Loving animals. On bestiality, zoophilia and post-human love*. Reaktion Books.

Bradford, J. (2007). The biomedical treatment of sexual sadism and associated conditions. In Correctional services Canada, Sexual homicide and paraphilias: The Correctional Service of Canada's Experts Forum 2007 (pp. 213–238). Correctional Services Canada. https://www.csc--scc.gc.ca/research/shp2007-paraphil09-eng.shtml.

Bradford, J. M., & Saleh, F. M. (2021). Pharmacological treatment of paraphilic sex offenders. In F. M. Saleh, J. M. Bradford, & D. J. Brodsky (Eds.), *Sex offenders: Identification, risk assessment, treatment, and legal issues* (pp. 292–319). Oxford University Press.

Braun, W. (1967). *The cruel and the meek. A remarkable examination of sadism, masochism and flagellation*. The Anchor Press Ltd.

Briggs, J., Harrison, C., McInnes, A., Vincent, D., Briggs, J., Harrison, C., et al. (1996). Punishment. In J. Briggs, C. Harrison, A. McInnes, & D. Vincent (Eds.), *Crime and punishment in England: An introductory history* (pp. 73–86). Springer.

Briken, P. (2020). An integrated model to assess and treat compulsive sexual behaviour disorder. *Nature Reviews Urology, 17*(7), 391–406.
Briken, P., Boetticher, A., Krueger, R. B., Kismödi, E., & Reed, G. M. (2019). Current legal situation for patients with paraphilic disorders and implications of the ICD-11 for paraphilic disorders for Germany. *The Journal of Sexual Medicine, 16*, 1615–1622. https://doi.org/10.1016/j.jsxm.2019.07.011
Briken, P., Habermann, N., Berner, W., & Hill, A. (2005). The influence of brain abnormalities on psychosocial development, criminal history and paraphilias in sexual murderers. *ASTM International.*
Briken, P., Habermann, N., Berner, W., & Hill, A. (2006). XYY chromosome abnormality in sexual homicide perpetrators. *American Journal of Medical Genetics Part B: Neuropsychiatric Genetics, 141*(2), 198–200.
Briken, P., Hill, A., & Berner, W. (2003). Pharmacotherapy of paraphilias with long-acting agonists of luteinizing hormone-releasing hormone: a systematic review. *Journal of Clinical Psychiatry, 64*(8), 890–897.
Briken, P., Hill, A., Habermann, N., Kafka, M. P., & Berner, W. (2010). Paraphilia-related disorders and personality disorders in sexual homicide perpetrators. *Sexual Offender Treatment, 5*(1), 1–7.
Briken, P., & Müller, J. L. (2014). Beurteilung der Schuldfähigkeit bei paraphiler Störung. *Nervenarzt, 85*, 304–311. https://doi.org/10.1007/s00115-013-3901-x
Briken, P., & Turner, D. (2022). Erectile functioning as a risk factor for committing a sexual offense? *The Journal of Sexual Medicine, 19*(7), 1064–1066.
Brittain, R. P. (1970). The sadistic murderer. *Medicine, Science and the Law, 10*(4), 198–207.
Buckels, E. E., Jones, D. N., & Paulhus, D. L. (2013). Behavioral confirmation of everyday sadism. *Psychological Science, 24*, 2201–2209. https://doi.org/10.1177/0956797613490749
Burgess, A. W., Hartman, C. R., Ressler, R. K., Douglas, J. E., & McCormack, A. (1986). Sexual homicide: A motivational model. *Journal of Interpersonal Violence, 1*(3), 251–272.
Carroll, B. E., & Coston, C. T. (2021). The criminal cannibal: Examining the similarities of cannibalistic offenders. *UNC Charlotte Undergraduate Research Journal, 1*(1).
Casey, P., & Kelly, B. (2019). *Fish's clinical psychopathology: Signs and symptoms in psychiatry.* Cambridge University Press.
Cassidy, J. (2021). Killer couples: Ten couples who killed together. Independently published.
Cazala, F., Zak, P. J., Beavin, L. E., Thornton, D. M., Kiehl, K. A., & Harenski, C. L. (2022). Hormonal response to perceived emotional distress in incarcerated men with sexual sadism. *Personality and Individual Differences, 184*, 111180.
Chan, H. C. (2020). Sexual sadism and psychopathy in sexual homicide. In A. R. Felthous & H. Saß (Eds.), *The Wiley international handbook on psychopathic disorders and the law.* https://doi.org/10.1002/9781119159322.ch30
Chan, H. C., Beauregard, E., & Myers, W. C. (2015). Single-victim and serial sexual homicide offenders: Differences in crime, paraphilias and personality traits. *Criminal Behaviour and Mental Health, 25*(1), 66–78.
Chan, H. C., & Frei, A. (2013). Female sexual homicide offenders: An examination of an under researched offender population. *Homicide Studies, 17*(1), 96–118.
Chan, H. C., Heide, K. M., & Beauregard, E. (2019). Male and female single-victim sexual homicide offenders: Distinguishing the types of weapons used in killing their victims. *Sexual Abuse, 31*(2), 127–150.
Chan, H. C., Myers, W. C., & Heide, K. M. (2010). An empirical analysis of 30 years of US juvenile and adult sexual homicide offender data: Race and age differences in the victim–offender relationship. *Journal of Forensic Sciences, 55*(5), 1282–1290.
Chopin, J., & Beauregard, E. (2020). Juvenile sexual murderers: Examination and classification of the crime-commission process. *Journal of Forensic Sciences, 65*(5), 1627–1637.

Chopin, J., & Beauregard, E. (2021). Patterns of necrophilic behaviors in sexual homicide: A criminological perspective. *International Journal of Offender Therapy and Comparative Criminology, 65*(15), 1676–1699.
Chopin, J., & Beauregard, E. (2022). Sexual sadism: Its role in the crime-commission process of sexual homicide of children. *Journal of Interpersonal Violence, 37*(1–2) NP350-NP374.
Chopin, J., & Beauregard, E. (2023). Manifestation of sadism in sexual homicide: A criminological contribution. *Psychology, Crime & Law, 29*(3), 320–338.
Chopin, J., Beauregard, E., & DeLisi, M. (2021). Homicidal child sexual abuse: Identifying the combinations of factors predicting a lethal outcome. *Child Abuse & Neglect, 111*, 104799.
Chopin, J., Beauregard, E., & Dietz, P. (2022). Death in sadistic sexual crimes: A neural network analysis of factors associated with a lethal outcome. *Criminal Justice and Behavior, 49*(8), 1115–1133.
Chopin, J., DeLisi, M., & Beauregard, E. (2023). Developmental sequela for sexual homicide: Testing an integrated multi-theoretical model. *Journal of Interpersonal Violence, 38*(7–8), 5721–5747.
Clarkin, J. F., Meehan, K. B., De Panfilis, C., & Doering, S. (2023). Empirical developments in transference-focused psychotherapy. *American Journal of Psychotherapy, 76*(1), 39–45.
Clarkson, R., Eichinger, M., & Darjee, R. (2020). Multiple perpetrator sexual homicide in Australia and New Zealand: An exploratory study of groups, victims, offenders and offences. *Journal of Criminal Justice, 71*, 101726. https://doi.org/10.1016/j.jcrimjus.2020.101726
Cohen, M. L., Garofalo, R., Boucher, R., & Seghorn, T. (1971). The psychology of rapists. *Seminars in Psychiatry, 3*(3), 307–327.
Cohen, M. L., Seghorn, T., & Calmas, W. (1969). Sociometric study of the sex offender. *Journal of Abnormal Psychology, 74*(2), 249–255. https://doi.org/10.1037/h0027185
Consigliere, L., Kneißler, L. Z. M., Nanev, A., Davis, M., & Darjee, R. (2024). Assessing sexual sadism in sexual homicide offenders using behavioural dimensional scales, typological approaches and categorical diagnoses. *Sexual Offending: Theory, Research and Prevention.*
Cooke, D. J. (2001). Psychopathy, sadism and serial killing. In A. Raine & J. Sanmartín (Eds.), *Violence and psychopathy* (pp. 123–137). Springer. https://doi.org/10.1007/978-1-4615-1367-4_7
Cortoni, F., & Gannon, T. A. (2016). Female sexual offenders: An overview. In A. Phenix & H. M. Hoberman (Eds.), *Sexual offending: Predisposing antecedents, assessments and management* (pp. 213–224). Springer.
Cortoni, F., Hanson, R. K., & Coache, M. È. (2010). The recidivism rates of female sexual offenders are low: A meta-analysis. *Sexual Abuse, 22*(4), 387–401.
Cortoni, F., & Stefanov, G. (2020). Female sexual offenders. In J. Proulx, F. Cortoni, L. A. Craig, & E. Letourneau (Eds.), *The Wiley handbook of what works with sexual offenders: Contemporary perspectives in theory, assessment, treatment, and prevention* (pp. 279–293). Wiley.
Crépault, C., & Couture, M. (1980). Men's erotic fantasies. *Archives of Sexual Behavior, 9*, 565–581.
Crozier, I. (2002). James Kiernan and the responsible pervert. *International Journal of Law and Psychiatry, 25*(4), 331–350.
Czarnietzki, M., Ricono-Kaufhold, S., Nanev, A., Davis, M., & Darjee, R. (2024). Murdering the person closest to you: Similarities and differences between intimate partner sexual homicide and non-intimate partner sexual homicide. *Behavioral Science and Law*. https://doi.org/10.1002/bsl.2680
Dadds, M. R., Turner, C. M., & McAloon, J. (2002). Developmental links between cruelty to animals and human violence. *Australian & New Zealand Journal of Criminology, 35*(3), 363–382.
Darjee, R. (2019). Sexual sadism and psychopathy in sexual homicide offenders: An exploration of their associates in a clinical sample. *International Journal of Offender Therapy and Comparative Criminology, 63*(9), 1738–1765.
Darjee, R., & Baron, E. (2018a). Recent research on sexual homicide offenders in Scotland: Characteristics, crime scene themes and comparison with non-homicidal sexual aggressors. In

J. Proulx, A. Carter, E. Beauregard, J. James, R. Darjee, & A. Mokros (Eds.), *Routledge international handbook of sexual homicide studies* (pp. 419–432). Routledge.

Darjee, R., & Baron, E. (2018b). Managing perpetrators of sexual homicide in the community. In J. Proulx, A. Carter, E. Beauregard, J. James, R. Darjee, & A. Mokros (Eds.), *Routledge international handbook of sexual homicide studies* (pp. 419–432). Routledge.

Darjee, R., & Baron, E. (2018c). Pharmacological treatment of sexual homicide offenders. In J. Proulx, A. Carter, E. Beauregard, J. James, R. Darjee, & A. Mokros (Eds.), *Routledge international handbook of sexual homicide studies* (pp. 419–432). Routledge.

Darjee, R., Judge, J., & Kirkland, J. (2024). The importance of relationships in multi-agency working. In J. Marshall & J. Kirkland (Eds.), *Innovative practice in forensic settings: A cognitive analytic approach to effective relational work*. Pavillion Publishing & Media.

Darjee, R., & Quinn, A. (2020). Pharmacological treatment of sexual offenders. In J. Proulx, F. Cortoni, L. A. Craig, & E. Letourneau (Eds.), *The Wiley handbook on what works with sexual offenders: Contemporary perspectives in theory, assessment, treatment and prevention* (pp. 217–245). Wiley.

Darjee, R., & Russell, K. (2011). The assessment and sentencing of high-risk offenders in Scotland: A forensic clinical perspective. In B. McSherry & P. Keyzer (Eds.), *Dangerous people: Policy, prediction, and practice* (pp. 217–232). Routledge.

Darjee, R., Russell, K., Forrest, L., Milton, E., Savoie, V., Baron, E., & Stobie, S. (2016). Risk for sexual violence protocol (RSVP): A real-world study of the reliability, validity and utility of a structured professional judgement instrument in the assessment and management of sexual offenders in south East Scotland. Risk Management Authority and NHS Scotland Forensic Network.

Davidson, M. (1994). Case report: Sadistically motivated offending in an individual with chromosome constitution 47 XXY. *Journal of Forensic Psychiatry, 5*(1), 177–183.

Davies, A., & Dale, A. (1996). Locating the stranger rapist. *Medicine, Science and the Law, 36*(2), 146–156.

Davis, M. R. (2012, November). What is the point of paraphilic coercive disorder? [Paper presentation] Australian and New Zealand Association of Psychiatry, Psychology, and Law (ANZAPPL) 32nd annual congress, Melbourne, Australia.

Davis, M. R. (2013, November). A conceptual model for differentiating rapists and their offences. [Paper presentation]Australasian Association of Threat Assessment Professionals (AATAP) 3rd annual conference, Melbourne, Australia.

Davis, C. A. (2014). *Couples who kill*. Allison & Busby.

Davis, M. R. (2016, June). Getting to the point of piquerism. One hour invited address presented at the conference of the International Criminal Investigative Analysis Fellowship (ICIAF), FBI Academy, Quantico, Virginia, USA.

Davis, M. R. (2018, November). A cumulative behavioural rating scale for identifying non-sadistic ritualistic rape. [Paper presentation] Australian and New Zealand Association of Psychiatry, Psychology, and Law (ANZAPPL) 38th annual congress, Hobart, Australia.

Davis, M. R. (2022a, July). Identifying sexual deviance from crime scene and offense behavior. Professional development session presented to the International Criminal Investigative Analysis Fellowship (ICIAF) and Behavioral Analysis Unit (FBI), Virginia, USA (via video-link).

Davis, M. R. (2022b, November). Misogyny, anger, or sadism? Reconceptualising the vindictive rapist and their offences. [Paper presentation] Australian and New Zealand Association of Psychiatry, Psychology, and Law (ANZAPPL) 51st Annual Congress, Adelaide, Australia.

Davis, M. R., & Dietz, P. E. (2024). *The relationship between coercive fantasy, personality, and behavior in those with sexually sadistic interests* [Manuscript in preparation]. Centre for Forensic Behavioural Science, Swinburne University of Technology.

De Neef, N., Coppens, V., Huys, W., & Morrens, M. (2019). Bondage-discipline, dominance-submission and sadomasochism (BDSM) from an integrative biopsychosocial perspective: A systematic review. *Sexual Medicine, 7*(2), 129–144.

de Oliveira, G. C., Valença, A. M., Jones, T., Eichinger, M., Weise Valdés, I., Davis, M., & Darjee, R. (2023). What differentiates sexual homicide from nonsexual homicide? A case controlled comparative study. *Journal of Interpersonal Violence*.

de River, J. P. (1949). *The sexual criminal: A psychoanalytical study*. Charles C Thomas Publisher.

Douglas, K. S., Hart, S. D., Webster, C. D., & Belfrage, H. (2013). *HCR-20 V3: Assessing risk for violence*. Mental Health, Law, and Policy Institute, Simon Fraser University.

De Saussure, R. (1946). The influence of the concept of monomania on French medico-legal psychiatry (from 1825 to 1840). *Journal of the History of Medicine and Allied Sciences, 1*(3), 365–397.

Deehan, E. T., & Bartels, R. M. (2021). Somnophilia: Examining its various forms and associated constructs. *Sexual Abuse, 33*(2), 200–222.

Delisi, M., & Beauregard, E. (2018). Adverse childhood experiences and criminal extremity: New evidence for sexual homicide. *Journal of Forensic Sciences, 63*(2), 484–489.

Dietz, P. E. (1992/2022). Report re: State of Wisconsin v. In J. L. Dahmer & I. T. James (Eds.), *Dahmer: The psych reports*. SP Publishing.

Dietz, P. E. (2014). *Sexual sadism: A coping strategy model*. Proceedings of the American Academy of forensic sciences 66th annual scientific meeting (pp. 509–510), Seattle, WA, USA.

Dietz, P. E., Burgess, A. W., & Hazelwood, R. E. R. (1983). Autoerotic asphyxia, the paraphilias, and mental disorder. In R. R. Hazelwood, P. E. Dietz, & A. W. Burgess (Eds.), *Autoerotic fatalities* (pp. 77–100). Lexington Books.

Dietz, P. E., Hazelwood, R. R., & Warren, J. (1990). The sexually sadistic criminal and his offenses. *Bulletin of the American Academy of Psychiatry and the Law, 18*(2), 163–178.

Dobbrunz, S., Daubmann, A., Müller, J. L., & Briken, P. (2020). Predictive validity of operationalized criteria for the assessment of criminal responsibility of sexual offenders with paraphilic disorders—a randomized control trial with mental health and legal professionals. *Frontiers in Psychology, 11*, 613081.

Doren, D. M. (Ed.). (2002). *Evaluating sex offenders: A manual for civil commitments and beyond*. Sage Publications.

Doyle, D. J., Ogloff, J., & Thomas, S. (2011). Designated as dangerous: Characteristics of sex offenders subject to post-sentence orders in Australia. *Australian Psychologist, 46*(1), 41–48.

DPP v Todd [2019] VSC 585 (2 September 2019)

Drzazga, J. (1960). Necrophilia. In J. Drzazga & C. Charles (Eds.), *Sex crimes and their legal aspects*. Thomas.

Dustin, T. (2023). The wannabe serial killer: The true story of Colin Ireland. Amazon Digital Services LLC—KDP Print US.

East, N. (1955). *Sexual offenders*. Delisle.

Edens, J. F., Cruise, K. R., & Buffington-Vollum, J. K. (2001). Forensic and correctional applications of the personality assessment inventory. *Behavioral Sciences & the Law, 19*(4), 519–543.

Edinburgh, the Lothians, and Scottish Borders MAPPA Strategic Oversight Group. (2019). Independent significant case review commissioned by Edinburgh, the Lothians and Scottish Borders MAPPA Strategic Oversight Group relative to the management of person X. Edinburgh City Council. https://www.edinburgh.gov.uk/downloads/file/26560/significant-case-review-scr-executive-summary.

Eher, R., Rettenberger, M., & Turner, D. (2019). The prevalence of mental disorders in incarcerated contact sexual offenders. *Acta Psychiatrica Scandinavica, 139*(6), 572–581.

Eher, R., Schilling, F., Hansmann, B., Pumberger, T., Nitschke, J., Habermeyer, E., & Mokros, A. (2016). Sadism and violent reoffending in sexual offenders. *Sexual Abuse, 28*(1), 46–72.

Eichinger, M., & Darjee, R. (2021). Sexual homicide in Australia and New Zealand: A description of offenders, offences and victims. *Psychiatry, Psychology and Law, 28*(6), 885–908.

Ellis, H. (1913). Studies in the psychology of sex, volume 3. Analysis of the sexual impulse. Love and pain. The sexual impulse of women. Alpha Editions [Reprinted in 2018].

Ellis, H. (1936). *Studies in the psychology of sex* (Vol. 1). Random House.

Ellis, B. J., & Symons, D. (1990). Sex differences in sexual fantasy: An evolutionary psychological approach. *Journal of Sex Research, 27*(4), 527–555.

Ellwood, C. A. (1912). Lombroso's theory of crime. *Journal of the American Institute of Criminal Law and Criminology*, 716–723.

Elwood, R. W., Doren, D. M., & Thornton, D. (2010). Diagnostic and risk profiles of men detained under Wisconsin's sexually violent person law. *International Journal of Offender Therapy and Comparative Criminology, 54*(2), 187–196.

Ewing, C. P. (2008). *Insanity: Murder, madness, and the law*. Oxford University Press.

Farrell, H. M. (2011). Dissociative identity disorder: Medicolegal challenges. *Journal of the American Academy of Psychiatry and the Law, 39*(3), 402–406.

Fedora, O., Reddon, J. R., Morrison, J. W., Fedora, S. K., Pascoe, H., & Yeudall, L. T. (1992). Sadism and other paraphilias in normal controls and aggressive and nonaggressive sex offenders. *Archives of Sexual Behavior, 21*, 1–15.

Felton, D. (2021). *Monsters and monarchs. Serial killers in classical myth and history*. University of Texas Press.

Féré, C. (1904). *The evolution and dissolution of the sexual instinct*. Charles Carrington.

Fernandes, L. C., Gillberg, C. I., Cederlund, M., Hagberg, B., Gillberg, C., & Billstedt, E. (2016). Aspects of sexuality in adolescents and adults diagnosed with autism spectrum disorders in childhood. *Journal of Autism and Developmental Disorders, 46*, 3155–3165.

Fewster, S., (2014). Mark Errin Rust, who murdered Megumi Suzuki and Maya Jackic, will ask SA Supreme Court to grant him a non-parole period. Adelaide Advertiser. Retrieved 9 July 2017.

Fiester, S. J., & Gay, M. (1991). Sadistic personality disorder: A review of data and recommendations for DSM-IV. *Journal of Personality Disorders, 5*(4), 376–385.

Fiester, S. J., & Gay, M. (1995). Sadistic personality disorder. In W. J. Livesley (Ed.), *The DSM-IV personality disorders* (pp. 329–340). The Guilford Press.

Firestone, P., Bradford, J. M., Greenberg, D. M., Larose, M. R., & Curry, S. (1998). Homicidal and nonhomicidal child molesters: Psychological, phallometric, and criminal features. *Sexual Abuse: A Journal of Research and Treatment, 10*, 305–323.

Flowers, A. (2000). Bound to die: The shocking true story of Bobby Joe Long, America's most savage serial killer. Pinnacle Books.

Frances, A., & First, M. B. (2011). Paraphilia NOS, nonconsent: Not ready for the courtroom. *Journal of the American Academy of Psychiatry and the Law Online, 39*(4), 555–561.

Freud, S. (1905). Three essays on the theory of sexuality (1905). The standard edition of the complete psychological works of Sigmund Freud, volume VII (1901–1905): A case of Hysteria, three essays on sexuality and other works. (pp. 123–246).

Freund, K., & Seto, M. C. (1998). Preferential rape in the theory of courtship disorder. *Archives of Sexual Behavior, 27*, 433–443.

Fromm, E. (1973). The anatomy of human destructiveness. Picador.

Fuller, A. K., Fuller, A. E., & Blashfield, R. K. (1990). Paraphilic coercive disorder. *Journal of Sex Education and Therapy, 16*(3), 164–171.

Gallo, A., Abracen, J., Looman, J., Jeglic, E., & Dickey, R. (2019). The use of leuprolide acetate in the management of high-risk sex offenders. *Sexual Abuse, 31*(8), 930–951.

Gannon, T. A., Rose, M. R., & Ward, T. (2008). A descriptive model of the offense process for female sexual offenders. *Sexual Abuse, 20*(3), 352–374. https://doi.org/10.1177/1079063208322495

Gannon, T. A., & Cortoni, F. (Eds.). (2010). *Female sexual offenders: Theory, assessment and treatment*. Wiley.

Gannon, T. A., Olver, M. E., Mallion, J. S., & James, M. (2019). Does specialized psychological treatment for offending reduce recidivism? A meta-analysis examining staff and program variables as predictors of treatment effectiveness. *Clinical Psychology Review, 73*, 101752.

Garnett, E. S., Nahmias, C., Wortzman, G., Langevin, R., & Dickey, R. (1988). Positron emission tomography and sexual arousal in a sadist and two controls. *Sexual Abuse: A Journal of Research and Treatment, 1*(3), 387–339.

Gebhard, P. H., Gagnon, J. H., Pomeroy, W. B., & Christenson, C. V. (1965). *Sex offenders: An analysis of types*. Harper & Row, Publishers and Paul B. Hoeber, Inc., Medical Books.
Giannangelo, S. J. (1996). *The psychopathology of serial murder: A theory of violence*. Greenwood Publishing Group.
Gilbert, F., & Daffern, M. (2017). Aggressive scripts, violent fantasy and violent behavior: A conceptual clarification and review. *Aggression and Violent Behavior, 36*, 98–107.
Giordano, B., White, J., & Lester, D. (2012). A typology of criminal cannibalism. *American Journal of Forensic Psychology, 30*(3), 35–44.
Glasser, M. (1996). Aggression and sadism in the perversions. In I. Rosen (Ed.), *Sexual deviation* (3rd ed., pp. 279–299). Oxford University Press.
Glenn, A. L., & Raine, A. (2014). *Psychopathy: An introduction to biological findings and their implications* (Vol. 1). NYU Press.
Godwin, G. (1938). *Peter Kürten: A study in sadism*. Acorn Press.
Gonçalves, L. C., Rossegger, A., Gerth, J., Singh, J. P., & Endrass, J. (2020). Sexual sadism among sex offenders in Switzerland. *Sexual Abuse, 32*(1), 79–100.
Gosavi, S. R., Gajbe, U. L., Meshram, S. W., & Chimurkar, V. K. (2009). Cytogenetic study in criminals (murderers): Role of XYY chromosome in criminality. *Journal of Clinical and Diagnostic Research, 3*(6), 1911–1914.
Grant, B. J., Shields, R. T., Tabachnick, J., & Coleman, J. (2019). "I didn't know where to go": An examination of Stop It Now!'s sexual abuse prevention helpline. *Journal of Interpersonal Violence, 34*(20), 4225–4253.
Grant, J. E., Pinto, A., Gunnip, M., Mancebo, M. C., Eisen, J. L., & Rasmussen, S. A. (2006). Sexual obsessions and clinical correlates in adults with obsessive-compulsive disorder. *Comprehensive Psychiatry, 47*(5), 325–329. https://doi.org/10.1016/j.comppsych.2006.01.007
Gratzer, T., & Bradford, J. M. W. (1995). Offender and offense characteristics of sexual sadists: A comparative study. *Journal of Forensic Sciences, 40*(3), 450–455.
Griffiths, M. D. (2015, January). Life on a knife edge: A brief look at piquerism. *Psychology Today*. https://www.psychologytoday.com/us/blog/in-excess/201501/life-knife-edge
Greenall, P. V. (2012). Understanding sexual homicide. *Journal of Sexual Aggression, 18*(3), 338–354.
Groth, A. N. (1977). Rape: Power, anger, and sexuality. *American Journal of Psychiatry, 134*(11), 1239–1243.
Groth, A. N. (1979). *Men who rape: The psychology of the offender*. Plenum Press.
Grubin, D. (1994a). Sexual sadism. *Criminal Behaviour and Mental Health, 4*, 3–9.
Grubin, D. (1994b). Sexual murder. *The British Journal of Psychiatry, 165*(5), 624–629.
Guggenheimer, D., Caman, S., Sturup, J., Thiblin, I., & Zilg, B. (2021). Criminal mutilation in Sweden from 1991 to 2017. *Journal of Forensic Sciences, 66*(5), 1788–1796.
Guttmacher, M. S. (1951). *Sex offenses: The problem, causes, and prevention*. Norton.
Häkkänen, H., & Laajasalo, T. (2006). Homicide crime scene behaviors in a Finnish sample of mentally ill offenders. *Homicide Studies, 10*(1), 33–54.
Hanson, R. K., Harris, A. J. R., Scott, T.-L., & Helmus, L. (2007). *Assessing the risk of sexual offenders on community supervision: The dynamic supervision project (User Report No. 2007–05)*. Public Safety Canada. Retrieved from http://www.publicsafety.gc.ca/res/cor/rep/_fl/crp2007-05-en.pdf
Hanson, R. K., & Thornton, D. (1999). *Static 99: Improving actuarial risk assessments for sex offenders* (Vol. 2). Solicitor General Canada.
Hanson, R. K., Bourgon, G., Helmus, L., & Hodgson, S. (2009). The principles of effective correctional treatment also apply to sexual offenders: A meta-analysis. *Criminal Justice and Behavior, 36*(9), 865–891. https://doi.org/10.1177/0093854809338545
Harris, D. A., Pednault, A., & Knight, R. A. (2013). An exploration of burglary in the criminal histories of sex offenders referred for civil commitment. *Psychology, Crime and Law, 19*(9), 765–781. https://doi.org/10.1080/1068316X.2012.678850

Hazelwood, R. R., & Warren, J. I. (2017). The relevance of fantasy in serial sexual crimes investigation. In R. R. Hazelwood & A. W. Burgess (Eds.), *Practical aspects of rape investigation* (5th ed., pp. 67–77). CRC Press.

Hazelwood, R. R., Warren, J., & Dietz, P. E. (1993). Compliant victims of the sexual sadist. *Australian Family Physician, 22*(4), 474–479.

Hare, R. D. (1991). *The psychopathy checklist-revised (PCL-R)*. Multi-Health Systems.

Harenski, C. L., Thornton, D. M., Harenski, K. A., Decety, J., & Kiehl, K. A. (2012). Increased frontotemporal activation during pain observation in sexual sadism: Preliminary findings. *Archives of General Psychiatry, 69*(3), 283–292.

Hares, R. D. (2003). *The Hare psychopathy checklist-revised* (2nd ed.). Multi-Health Systems.

Harrison, K. (2010). *Managing high risk sex offenders in the community: Risk management, treatment and social responsibility*. Routledge.

Hart, S. D., & Boer, D. P. (2020). Structured professional judgment guidelines for sexual violence risk assessment: The sexual violence Risk-20 (SVR-20) versions 1 and 2 and risk for sexual violence protocol (RSVP). In K. S. Douglas & R. K. Otto (Eds.), *Handbook of violence risk assessment* (2nd ed., pp. 322–358). Routledge.

Hart, S., Kropp, P. R., Laws, D. R., Klaver, J., Logan, C., & Watt, K. A. (2003). *The risk for sexual violence protocol (RSVP): Structured professional guidelines for assessing risk of sexual violence*. The Institute Against Family Violence.

Hart, S. D., Kropp, P. R., Watt, K. A., Darjee, R., Davis, M. R., Klaver, J., Laws, D. R., & Logan, C. (2022). RSVP-V2: Version 2 of the risk for sexual violence protocol. *Protect International*.

Hayes, S. C., Brownell, K. D., & Barlow, D. H. (1978). The use of self-administered covert sensitization in the treatment of exhibitionism and sadism. *Behavior Therapy, 9*(2), 283–289.

Hazelwood, R. R. (2017a). Sexual sadists: Their wives and girlfriends. In R. R. Hazelwood & A. W. Burgess (Eds.), *Practical aspects of rape investigation: A multidisciplinary approach* (5th ed., pp. 385–392). CRC Press.

Hazelwood, R. R. (2017b). Analyzing the rape and profiling the offender. In R. R. Hazelwood & A. W. Burgess (Eds.), *Practical aspects of rape investigation: A multidisciplinary approach* (5th ed., pp. 97–121). CRC Press.

Healey, J., Lussier, P., & Beauregard, E. (2013). Sexual sadism in the context of rape and sexual homicide: An examination of crime scene indicators. *International Journal of Offender Therapy and Comparative Criminology, 57*(4), 402–424.

Hickey, E. W. (2015). Serial murderers and their victims. Cengage Learning.

Hickey, E. W., Walters, B. K., Drislane, L. E., Palumbo, I. M., & Patrick, C. J. (2018). Deviance at its darkest: Serial murder and psychopathy. In C. J. Patrick (Ed.), *Handbook of psychopathy* (pp. 570–584). The Guilford Press.

Higgs, T., Carter, A. J., Stefanska, E. B., & Glorney, E. (2017). Toward identification of the sexual killer: A comparison of sexual killers engaging in post-mortem sexual interference and non-homicide sexual aggressors. *Sexual Abuse, 29*(5), 479–499.

Higgs, T., Carter, A. J., Tully, R. J., & Browne, K. D. (2017). Sexual murder typologies: A systematic review. *Aggression and Violent Behavior, 35*, 1–12.

Higgs, T., Stefanska, E. B., Carter, A. J., & Browne, K. D. (2017). The developmental and criminal histories of subgroups of sexual murderers engaging, or not engaging, in post mortem sexual interference, compared to rapists. *Journal of Criminal Justice, 53*, 92–101.

Hill, A., Habermann, N., Berner, W., & Briken, P. (2006a). Psychiatric disorders in single and multiple sexual murderers. *Psychopathology, 40*(1), 22–28.

Hill, A., Habermann, N., Berner, W., & Briken, P. (2006b). Sexual sadism and sadistic personality disorder in sexual homicide. *Journal of Personality Disorders, 20*(6), 671–684.

Hill, A., Habermann, N., Klusmann, D., Berner, W., & Briken, P. (2008). Criminal recidivism in sexual homicide perpetrators. *International Journal of Offender Therapy and Comparative Criminology, 52*(1), 5–20.

Hirschfeld, M. (1938). *Sexual anomalies and perversions*. Encyclopaedic Press.

Holland, L. A., Zolondek, S. C., Abel, G. G., Jordan, A. D., & Becker, J. V. (2000). Psychometric analysis of the sexual interest cardsort questionnaire. *Sexual Abuse: A Journal of Research and Treatment, 12*, 107–122.
Holoyda, B., Sorrentino, R., Friedman, S. H., & Allgire, J. (2018). Bestiality: An introduction for legal and mental health professionals. *Behavioral Sciences & the Law, 36*, 687–697.
Holt, S. E., Meloy, J. R., & Strack, S. (1999). Sadism and psychopathy in violent and sexually violent offenders. *Journal of the American Academy of Psychiatry and the Law, 27*(1), 23–32.
Holvoet, L., Huys, W., Coppens, V., Seeuws, J., Goethals, K., & Morrens, M. (2017). Fifty shades of Belgian gray: The prevalence of BDSM-related fantasies and activities in the general population. *The Journal of Sexual Medicine, 14*(9), 1152–1159.
Hopwood, C. J., Kotov, R., Krueger, R. F., Watson, D., Widiger, T. A., Althoff, R. R., et al. (2018). The time has come for dimensional personality disorder diagnosis. *Personality and Mental Health, 12*(1), 82–86.
Horvath, M., & Woodhams, J. (Eds.). (2013). *Handbook on the study of multiple perpetrator rape: A multidisciplinary response to an international problem* (Vol. 4, p. Routledge).
Hucker, S. J. (2011). Hypoxyphilia. *Archives of Sexual Behavior, 40*, 1323–1326.
Hucker, S., Langevin, R., Dickey, R., Handy, L., Chambers, J., Wright, S., et al. (1988). Cerebral damage and dysfunction in sexually aggressive men. *Annals of Sex Research, 1*, 33–47.
Jackson, M. (1996). Sentencing of dangerous and habitual offenders in Canada. *The Federal Sentencing Reporter, 9*, 256.
Jackson, R. L., & Richards, H. J. (2007). Diagnostic and risk profiles among civilly committed sex offenders in Washington State. *International Journal of Offender Therapy and Comparative Criminology, 51*(3), 313–323.
Jacobs, P. A., Brunton, M., Melville, M. M., Brittain, R. P., & McClemont, W. F. (1965). Aggressive behaviour, mental sub-normality and the XYY male. *Nature, 208*(5017), 1351–1352.
James, T. (2022). *Dahmer: The psych reports. The complete psychiatric examination of the Milwaukee Cannibal*. SP Publishing.
James, J., & Proulx, J. (2014). A psychological and developmental profile of sexual murderers: A systematic review. *Aggression and Violent Behavior, 19*(5), 592–607.
James, J., & Proulx, J. (2020). Theories that explain sexual aggression against women. In J. Proulx, F. Cortoni, L. A. Craig, & E. Letourneau (Eds.), *The Wiley handbook on what works with sexual offenders: Contemporary perspectives in theory, assessment, treatment and prevention* (pp. 3–22). Wiley.
Jenkins, P. (1990). Sharing murder: Understanding group serial homicide. *Journal of Crime and Justice, 13*(2), 125–147.
Jentzen, J., Palermo, G., Johnson, L. T., Khang-Cheng, H., Stormo, K. A., & Teggatz, J. (1994). Destructive hostility: The Jeffrey Dahmer case: A psychiatric and forensic study of a serial killer. *The American Journal of Forensic Medicine and Pathology, 15*(4), 283–294.
Jones, J. S., Rossman, L., Wynn, B. N., & Ostovar, H. (2010). Assailants' sexual dysfunction during rape: Prevalence and relationship to genital trauma in female victims. *The Journal of Emergency Medicine, 38*(4), 529–535.
Jones, E. (1931). *On the nightmare*. Liveright.
Joseph, L., Farmer, C., Chlebowski, C., Henry, L., Fish, A., Mankiw, C., et al. (2018). Characterization of autism spectrum disorder and neurodevelopmental profiles in youth with XYY syndrome. *Journal of Neurodevelopmental Disorders, 10*(1), 1–11.
Joyal, C. C., Cossette, A., & Lapierre, V. (2015). What exactly is an unusual sexual fantasy? *The Journal of Sexual Medicine, 12*(2), 328–340.
Joynt, M., & Darjee, R. (2023). What is the association between sexual homicide and psychosis? *Journal of Forensic Psychiatry and Psychology*.
Kaan, H. (2016). *Heinrich Kaan's "Psychopathia Sexualis" (1844) A classic text in the history of sexuality*. Cornell University Press.

Kafka, M. P. (2001). The paraphilia-related disorders: A proposal for a unified classification of nonparaphilic hypersexuality disorders. *Sexual Addiction & Compulsivity: The Journal of Treatment and Prevention, 8*(3–4), 227–239.
Kafka, M. P. (2010a). Hypersexual disorder: A proposed diagnosis for DSM-V. *Archives of Sexual Behavior, 39*, 377–400.
Kafka, M. P. (2010b). The DSM diagnostic criteria for paraphilia not otherwise specified. *Archives of Sexual Behavior, 39*, 373–376.
Kafka, M. P., & Hennen, J. (2002). A DSM-IV Axis I comorbidity study of males (n= 120) with paraphilias and paraphilia-related disorders. *Sexual Abuse: A Journal of Research and Treatment, 14*, 349–366.
Kalmus, E., & Beech, A. R. (2005). Forensic assessment of sexual interest: A review. *Aggression and Violent Behavior, 10*(2), 193–217.
Kaminer, D., & Stein, D. J. (2001). Sadistic personality disorder in perpetrators of human rights abuses: A south African case study. *Journal of Personality Disorders, 15*, 475–486.
Karpman, B. (1954). *The sexual offender and his offenses*. Julian Press.
Kemshall, H., & Hilder, S. (2020). Effective systems and processes for managing violent offenders in the United Kingdom and the European Union. In J. S. Wormith, L. A. Criag, & T. E. Hogue (Eds.), *The Wiley handbook of what works in violence risk management: Theory, research and practice* (pp. 485–503).
Kemshall, H., & Maguire, M. (2021). Public protection, partnership and risk penality: The multi-agency risk management of sexual and violent offenders. In P. O'Malley (Ed.), *Governing Risks* (pp. 319–346). Routledge.
Khachatryan, N., Heide, K. M., Hummel, E. V., & Oliver Chan, H. C. (2016). Juvenile sexual homicide offenders: Thirty-year follow-up investigation. *International Journal of Offender Therapy and Comparative Criminology, 60*(3), 247–264. https://doi.org/10.1177/0306624X14552062
Kiernan, J. (1892). Responsibility in sexual perversion. *Chicago Medical Recorder, 3*, 185–210.
Kiernan, J. (1903). Responsibility in active algophily. *Medicine*, 269–273.
King, C., & Murphy, G. H. (2014). A systematic review of people with autism spectrum disorder and the criminal justice system. *Journal of Autism and Developmental Disorders, 44*, 2717–2733.
King, C. M., Wylie, L. E., Brank, E. M., & Heilbrun, K. (2014). Disputed paraphilia diagnoses and legal decision making: A case law survey of paraphilia NOS, nonconsent. *Psychology, Public Policy, and Law, 20*(3), 294–308.
Kingree, J. B., & Thompson, M. (2015). A comparison of risk factors for alcohol-involved and alcohol-uninvolved sexual aggression perpetration. *Journal of Interpersonal Violence, 30*(9), 1478–1492.
Kingston, D. A., Seto, M. C., Firestone, P., & Bradford, J. M. (2010). Comparing indicators of sexual sadism as predictors of recidivism among adult male sexual offenders. *Journal of Consulting and Clinical Psychology, 78*(4), 574.
Kingston, S., & Thomas, T. (2018). The sexual risk order and the sexual harm prevention order: The first two years. *Probation Journal, 65*(1), 77–88.
Kingston, D. A., & Yates, P. M. (2008). Sexual sadism: Assessment and treatment. In D. R. Laws & W. T. O'Donohue (Eds.), *Sexual deviance: Theory, assessment and treatment* (2nd ed., pp. 231–249). New York, Guildford Press.
Kinsey, A., Pomeroy, W. P., & Martine, C. E. (1948). *Sexual behavior in the human male*. Indiana University Press. Reprinted in 1998.
Kirchmeier, J. L. (1997). Aggravating and mitigating factors: The paradox of today's arbitrary and mandatory capital punishment scheme. *William & Mary Bill of Rights Journal, 6*, 345.
Kirchmeier, J. L. (2006). Casting a wider net: Another decade of legislative expansion of the death penalty in the United States. *Pepperdine Law Review, 34*, 1.
Kirsch, L. G., & Becker, J. V. (2007). Emotional deficits in psychopathy and sexual sadism: Implications for violent and sadistic behavior. *Clinical Psychology Review, 27*(8), 904–922.

Knafo, D. (2015). For the love of death: Somnophilic and necrophilic acts and fantasies. *Journal of the American Psychoanalytic Association, 63*(5), 857–886.
Knight, R. A. (1989). An assessment of the concurrent validity of a child molester typology. *Journal of Interpersonal Violence, 4*(2), 131–150.
Knight, R. A. (1999). Validation of a typology for rapists. *Journal of Interpersonal Violence, 14*(3), 303–330. https://doi.org/10.1177/088626099014003006
Knight, R. A. (2010a). Is a diagnostic category for paraphilic coercive disorder defensible? *Archives of Sexual Behavior, 39*, 419–426.
Knight, R. A. (2010b). Typologies for rapists—the generation of a new structural model. In A. M. Schlank (Ed.), *The sexual predator: Legal issues, assessment, treatment* (Vol. IV, pp. 17-1–17-28). Civic Research Institute.
Knight, R. A., & Cerce, D. D. (1999). Validation and revision of the multidimensional assessment of sex and aggression. *Psychologica Belgica, 39*(2/3), 135–161.
Knight, R. A., & Guay, J.-P. (2006). The role of psychopathy in sexual coercion against women. In C. J. Patrick (Ed.), *Handbook of psychopathy* (pp. 512–532). The Guilford Press.
Knight, R. A., & King, M. W. (2012). Typologies for child molesters—the generation of a new structural model. In B. K. Schwartz (Ed.), *The sex offender: Current trends in policy and treatment practice* (pp. 1–33). Civic Research Institute.
Knight, R. A., & Prentky, R. A. (1990). Classifying sexual offenders: The development and corroboration of taxonomic models. In W. L. Marshall, D. R. Laws, & H. E. Barbaree (Eds.), *Handbook of sexual assault: Issues, theories, and treatment of the offender* (pp. 23–52). Plenum Press.
Knight, R. A., Prentky, R. A., & Cerce, D. D. (1994). The development, reliability, and validity of an inventory for the multidimensional assessment of sex and aggression. *Criminal Justice and Behavior, 21*(1), 72–94.
Knight, R. A., & Sims-Knight, J. E. (2016). A theoretical integration of aetiological and typological models of rape. In D. Boer (Ed.), *The Wiley handbook on the theories, assessment and treatment of sexual offending* (pp. 73–102). Wiley.
Knight, R. A., Sims-Knight, J., & Guay, J. P. (2013). Is a separate diagnostic category defensible for paraphilic coercion? *Journal of Criminal Justice, 41*(2), 90–99.
Knoll, J. L., & Hazelwood, R. R. (2009). Becoming the victim: Beyond sadism in serial sexual murderers. *Aggression and Violent Behavior, 14*, 106–114.
Krafft-Ebing, R. (1886). *Psychopathia sexualis*. F.A.Davis.
Kraus, R. T. (1995). An enigmatic personality: Case report of a serial killer. *Journal of Orthomolecular Medicine, 10*(1), 11–24.
Krueger, R. B. (2010). The DSM diagnostic criteria for sexual sadism. *Archives of Sexual Behavior, 39*, 325–345.
Krueger, R. B., Reed, G. M., First, M. B., Marais, A., Kismodi, E., & Briken, P. (2017). Proposals for paraphilic disorders in the international classification of diseases and related health problems, eleventh revision (ICD-11). *Archives of Sexual Behavior, 46*, 1529–1545.
Kruger, T. H., & Kneer, J. (2021). Neurobiological basis of sexual deviance. In L. Craig & R. M. Bartels (Eds.), *Sexual deviance: Understanding and managing deviant sexual interests and paraphilic disorders* (pp. 67–88). Wiley.
Kushner, B. (1997). Cannibalizing Japanese media: The case of Issei Sagawa. *Journal of Popular Culture, 31*(3), 55–68.
Lam, A. A., Penney, S. R., & Simpson, A. I. (2020). A review of the prevalence of psychosis in sexual homicide. *The Journal of the American Academy of Psychiatry and the Law, 48*(1), 56–64.
Landgren, V., Malki, K., Bottai, M., Arver, S., & Rahm, C. (2020). Effect of gonadotropin-releasing hormone antagonist on risk of committing child sexual abuse in men with pedophilic disorder: A randomized clinical trial. *JAMA Psychiatry, 77*(9), 897–905. https://doi.org/10.1001/jamapsychiatry.2020.0440
Langdridge, D., & Barker, M. (Eds.). (2007). *Safe, sane and consensual: Contemporary perspectives on sadomasochism* (pp. 3–9). Palgrave Macmillan.

Langevin, R., Bain, J., Ben-Aron, M. H., Coulthard, R., Day, D., Handy, L., Heasman, G., Hucker, S. J., Purins, J. E., Roper, V., Russon, A. E., Webster, C. D., & Wortzman, G. (1985). Sexual aggression: Constructing a predictive equation. In R. Langevin (Ed.), *Erotic preference, gender identity and aggression in men: New research studies*. L. Erlbaum Associates.
Langevin, R., & Curnoe, S. (2014). Are dangerous offenders different from other offenders? A clinical profile. *International Journal of Offender Therapy and Comparative Criminology, 58*(7), 780–801. https://doi.org/10.1177/0306624X13481206
Långström, N., Babchishin, K. M., Fazel, S., Lichtenstein, P., & Frisell, T. (2015). Sexual offending runs in families: A 37-year nationwide study. *International Journal of Epidemiology, 44*(2), 713–720.
Lanning, K. V. (1992). *Child molesters: A behavioral analysis for law enforcement officers investigating cases of child sexual exploitation*. National Center for Missing and Exploited Children.
Lanning, K. V. (2010). *Child molesters: A behavioral analysis for law enforcement officers investigating cases of child sexual exploitation* (5th ed.). National Center for Missing and Exploited Children.
Lauerma, H. (2001). Klinefelter's syndrome and sexual homicide. *Journal of Forensic Psychiatry, 12*(1), 151–157.
Laws, D. R. (1986). Sexual deviance card sort. Unpublished manuscript, Tampa: Florida Mental Health Institute.
Laws, D. R., & Marshall, W. L. (2003). A brief history of behavioral and cognitive behavioral approaches to sexual offenders: Part 1. Early developments. *Sexual abuse: a journal of research and treatment, 15*, 75–92.
Laws, D. R., Meyer, J., & Holmen, M. L. (1978). Reduction of sadistic sexual arousal by olfactory aversion: A case study. *Behaviour Research and Therapy, 16*(4), 281–285.
LeBeau, M. A., & Mozayani, A. (Eds.). (2001). *Drug-facilitated sexual assault: A forensic handbook*. Academic Press.
Leitenberg, H., & Henning, K. (1995). Sexual fantasy. *Psychological Bulletin, 117*(3), 469–496.
Levenson, J. S. (2004). Sexual predator civil commitment: A comparison of selected and released offenders. *International Journal of Offender Therapy and Comparative Criminology, 48*(6), 638–648.
Lewis, D. O. (2009). *Guilty by reason of insanity: A psychiatrist explores the minds of killers*. Ivy Books.
Lewis, A., Grubin, D., Ross, C. C., & Das, M. (2017). Gonadotrophin-releasing hormone agonist treatment for sexual offenders: A systematic review. *Journal of Psychopharmacology, 31*(10), 1281–1293.
Longpré, N., Guay, J.-P., & Knight, R. A. (2018). The developmental antecedents of sexually sadistic behaviours. In J. Proulx, A. Carter, E. Beauregard, J. James, R. Darjee, & A. Mokros (Eds.), *Routledge international handbook of sexual homicide studies* (pp. 283–302). Routledge.
Longpré, N., Guay, J. P., & Knight, R. A. (2019). MTC sadism scale: Toward a dimensional assessment of severe sexual sadism with behavioral markers. *Assessment, 26*(1), 70–84.
Longpré, N., Guay, J. P., Knight, R. A., & Benbouriche, M. (2018). Sadistic offender or sexual sadism? Taxometric evidence for a dimensional structure of sexual sadism. *Archives of Sexual Behavior, 47*, 403–416.
Longpré, N. & Knight, R. A. (in press). Development and validation of a new agonistic continuum scale. [Personal communication 26th June 2023].
Longpré, N., Proulx, J., & Brouillette-Alarie, S. (2018). Convergent validity of three measures of sexual sadism: Value of a dimensional measure. *Sexual Abuse, 30*(2), 192–208.
Longpré, N., Sims-Knight, J. E., Neumann, C., Guay, J. P., & Knight, R. A. (2020). Is paraphilic coercion a different construct from sadism or the lower end of an agonistic continuum? *Journal of Criminal Justice, 71*, 101743.
MacCulloch, M., Gray, N., & Watt, A. (2000). Brittain's sadistic murderer syndrome reconsidered: An associative account of the aetiology of sadistic sexual fantasy. *The Journal of Forensic Psychiatry, 11*(2), 401–418.

MacCulloch, M. J., Snowden, P. R., Wood, P. J. W., & Mills, H. E. (1983). Sadistic fantasy, sadistic behaviour and offending. *The British Journal of Psychiatry, 143*(1), 20–29.
MacDonald, J. M. (1971). *Rape. Offenders and their victims*. Charles C. Thomas, Publisher.
Marshall, L. E. (2019). Effective sex offender treatment in correctional settings: A strengths-based approach. In D. L. L. Polaschek, A. Day, & C. R. Hollin (Eds.), *The Wiley international handbook of correctional psychology* (pp. 515–528). Wiley.
Marshall, W. L., & Barbaree, H. E. (1990). Integrated theory of the etiology of sexual offending. In W. L. Marshall, D. R. Laws, & H. E. Barbaree (Eds.), *Handbook of sexual assault: Issues, theories, and treatment of the offender* (pp. 257–275). Springer. https://doi.org/10.1007/978-1-4899-0915-2
Marshall, W. L., & Hucker, S. J. (2006). Issues in the diagnosis of sexual sadism. *Sexual Offender Treatment, 1*(2), 1–4.
Marshall, W. L., Hucker, S. J., Nitschke, J., & Mokros, A. (2016). Assessment of sexual sadism. In D. P. Boer (Ed.), *The Wiley handbook on the theories, assessment and treatment of sexual offending*. https://doi.org/10.1002/9781118574003.wattso039
Marshall, W. L., Kennedy, P., & Yates, P. (2002). Issues concerning the reliability and validity of the diagnosis of sexual sadism applied in prison settings. *Sexual Abuse: A Journal of Research and Treatment, 14*, 301–311.
Marshall, W. L., & Laws, D. R. (2003). A brief history of behavioral and cognitive behavioral approaches to sexual offender treatment: Part 2. The modern era. *Sexual Abuse, 15*(2), 93–120.
Marshall, E., Winder, B., Norman, C., & Blagden, N. (2021). Medication to manage problematic sexual arousal. In G. Akerman, D. Perkins, & R. M. Bartels (Eds.), *Assessing and managing problematic sexual interests: A practitioner's guide* (pp. 193–213). Routledge.
Marquis de Sade. (1969). Juliette. Grove Press. [Translated by Austryn Wainhouse. Original written in 1797].
Marquis de Sade. (1971). Philosophy in the bedroom. Grove Press. [Translated Richard Seaver and A. Wainhouse. Original written in 1795].
Marquis de Sade. (1990). The one hundred and twenty days of Sodom. Arrow Books Ltd. [Translated by A. Wainhouse & R. Seaver. Original written in 1785].
Marquis de Sade. (1996) Justine or the misfortunes of virtue. Woodsworth Classics [Translated by A. Wainhouse. Original written in 1791].
Masters, R. E. L., & Lea, E. (1963). *Sex crimes in history. Evolving concepts of sadism, lust-murder, and necrophilia—from ancient to modern times*. The Julian Press, Inc.
McCall, H., Adams, N., Mason, D., & Willis, J. (2015). What is chemsex and why does it matter? *BMJ, 3*(351). https://doi.org/10.1136/bmj.h5790
McEwan, T., & Darjee, R. (2021). The problem behaviour program. In J. Reid Meloy & J. Hoffman (Eds.), *International handbook of threat assessment* (2nd ed., pp. 536–553). Oxford University Press.
McGlen, M., Brown, J., Hughes, N., & Crichton, J. H. M. (2015). *The classical origins of the insanity defence*. John H. M. Crichton.
McGlynn, C., & Rackley, E. (2009). Criminalising extreme pornography: A lost opportunity. *Criminal Law Review, 4*, 245–260.
McGuire, R. J., Carlisle, J. M., & Young, B. G. (1965). Sexual deviations as conditioned behaviour: A hypothesis. *Behaviour Research and Therapy, 3*, 185–190.
McLeod, D. A., & Dodd, M. (2022). Modernized female sex offender typologies: Intrapsychic, behavioral, and trauma related domains. *Cogent Social Sciences, 8*(1), 2085360.
Mellor, L. (2016). Mincing words: Refining the language of mutilation. In L. Mellor, A. Aggrawal, & E. Hickey (Eds.), *Understanding necrophilia: A global multidisciplinary approach*. Cognella.
Meloy, J. R. (1996). Pseudonecrophilia following spousal homicide. *Journal of Forensic Sciences, 41*(4), 706–708.
Meloy, J. R. (1997). The psychology of wickedness: Psychopathy and sadism. *Psychiatric Annals, 27*(9), 630–633.

Meloy, J. R. (2000). The nature and dynamics of sexual homicide: An integrative review. *Aggression and Violent Behavior, 5*(1), 1–22.
Meloy, J. R., Gacono, C. B., & Kenney, L. (1994). A Rorschach investigation of sexual homicide. *Journal of Personality Assessment, 62*(1), 58–67.
Messerman, J. H. (Ed.). (1969). *Dynamics of deviant sexuality. Scientific proceedings of the American Academy of Psychoanalysis*. Grune & Stratton.
MIDSA Clinical Manual. (2011). Bend, OR: Augur Enterprises, Available at www.midsa.us.
Millon, T., Grossman, S., & Millon, C. (2015). *Millon clinical multi-axial inventory-IV MCMI-IV*. Pearson.
Mogavero, M. C. (2016). Autism, sexual offending, and the criminal justice system. *Journal of Intellectual Disabilities and Offending Behaviour, 7*(3), 116–126.
Mokros, A., Osterheider, M., Hucker, S. J., & Nitschke, J. (2011). Psychopathy and sexual sadism. *Law and Human Behavior, 35*(3), 188–199.
Mokros, A., Schilling, F., Eher, R., & Nitschke, J. (2012). The severe sexual sadism scale: Cross-validation and scale properties. *Psychological Assessment, 24*(3), 764.
Mokros, A., Schilling, F., Weiss, K., Nitschke, J., & Eher, R. (2014). Sadism in sexual offenders: Evidence for dimensionality. *Psychological Assessment, 26*(1), 138.
Mokros, A., Wessels, J., Hofmann, M., & Nitschke, J. (2019). Coercive sexual sadism: A systematic qualitative review. *Current Psychiatry Reports, 21*, 1–8.
Moll, A. (1921). Handbuch De Sexualwissenschaften. Vogel.
Money, J. (1984). Paraphilias: Phenomenology and classification. *American Journal of Psychotherapy, 38*(2), 164–179.
Money, J. (1990). Forensic sexology: Paraphilic serial rape (biastophilia) and lust murder (erotophonophilia). *American Journal of Psychotherapy, 44*(1), 26–36.
Money, J., & Lehne, G. K. (1983). Biomedical and criminal-justice concepts of paraphilia: Developing convergence. *Medicine and Law, 2*, 257–261.
Money, J., & Simcoe, K. W. (1984). Acrotomophilia, sex and disability: New concepts and case report. *Sexuality and Disability, 7*(1–2), 43–50.
Morey, L. C. (1991). *Personality assessment inventory: Professional manual*. Psychological Assessment Resources.
Mullen, P. E., Pathé, M., & Purcell, R. (2009). *Stalkers and their victims* (2nd ed.). Cambridge University Press.
Murphy, L., Ranger, R., Stewart, H., Dwyer, G., & Fedoroff, J. P. (2015). Assessment of problematic sexual interests with the penile plethysmograph: An overview of assessment laboratories. *Current Psychiatry Reports, 17*, 1–5.
Myers, W. C. (2002). *Juvenile sexual homicide*. Academic Press.
Myers, W. C., Beauregard, E., & Menard, W. (2019). An updated sexual homicide crime scene rating scale for sexual sadism (SADSEX-SH). *International Journal of Offender Therapy and Comparative Criminology, 63*(9), 1766–1775.
Myers, W. C., & Blashfield, R. (1997). Psychopathology and personality in juvenile sexual homicide offenders. *Journal of the American Academy of Psychiatry and the Law, 25*(4), 497–508.
Myers, W. C., Bukhanovskiy, A., Justen, E., Morton, R. J., Tilley, J., Adams, K., et al. (2008). The relationship between serial sexual murder and autoerotic asphyxiation. *Forensic Science International, 176*(2–3), 187–195.
Myers, W. C., Burgess, A. W., & Nelson, J. A. (1998). Criminal and behavioral aspects of juvenile sexual homicide. *Journal of Forensic Sciences, 43*(2), 340–347.
Myers, W. C., Burket, R. C., & Husted, D. S. (2006). Sadistic personality disorder and comorbid mental illness in adolescent psychiatric inpatients. *Journal of the American Academy of Psychiatry and the Law, 34*, 61–71.
Myers, W. C., Chan, H. C., Vo, E. J., & Lazarou, E. (2010). Sexual sadism, psychopathy, and recidivism in juvenile sexual murderers. *Journal of Investigative Psychology and Offender Profiling, 7*(1), 49–58.

Myers, W. C., Reccoppa, L., Burton, K., & McElroy, R. (1993). Malignant sex and aggression: An overview of serial sexual homicide. *Journal of the American Academy of Psychiatry and the Law Online, 21*(4), 435–451.
Nichols, H. R., & Molinder, I. (1984). Multiphasic sex inventory manual. (Available from Nichols & Molinder, 437 Bowes Drive, Tacoma, WA 98466).
Nichols, H. R., & Molinder, I. (1996). *Multiphasic sex inventory II*. Nichols and Molinder Assessments.
Nicole, A., & Proulx, J. (2007). The factors distinguishing sexual murderers from sexual aggressors: A multivariate analysis. In J. Proulx, E. Beauregard, M. Cusson, & A. Nicole (Eds.), *Sexual murderers: A comparative analysis and new perspectives* (pp. 87–97). John Wiley and Sons.
Nielsen, M. E. J. (2010). Safe, sane, and consensual—consent and the ethics of BDSM. *International Journal of Applied Philosophy, 24*(2), 265–288.
Nitschke, J., Mokros, A., Osterheider, M., & Marshall, W. L. (2013). Sexual sadism: Current diagnostic vagueness and the benefit of behavioral definitions. *International Journal of Offender Therapy and Comparative Criminology, 57*(12), 1441–1453.
Nitschke, J., Osterheider, M., & Mokros, A. (2009). A cumulative scale of severe sexual sadism. *Sexual Abuse, 21*(3), 262–278.
O'Donohue, W., Letourneau, E. J., & Dowling, H. (1997). Development and preliminary validation of a paraphilic sexual fantasy questionnaire. *Sexual Abuse: A Journal of Research and Treatment, 9*, 167–178.
Olver, M. E., Marshall, L. E., Marshall, W. L., & Nicholaichuk, T. P. (2020). A long-term outcome assessment of the effects on subsequent reoffense rates of a prison-based CBT/RNR sex offender treatment program with strength-based elements. *Sexual Abuse, 32*(2), 127–153.
Olver, M. E., Wong, S. C. P., Nicholaichuk, T., & Gordon, A. (2007). The validity and reliability of the violence risk scale—sexual offender version: Assessing sex offender risk and evaluating therapeutic change. *Psychological Assessment, 19*, 318–329. https://doi.org/10.1037/1040-3590.19.3.318
O'Meara, A., Davies, J., & Hammond, S. (2011). The psychometric properties and utility of the short sadistic impulse scale (SSIS). *Psychological Assessment, 23*(2), 523.
Paarnio, M., Sandman, N., Källström, M., Johansson, A., & Jern, P. (2023). The prevalence of BDSM in Finland and the association between BDSM interest and personality traits. *The Journal of Sex Research, 60*(4), 443–451.
Packard, R. L., & Levenson, J. S. (2006). Revisiting the reliability of diagnostic decisions in sex offender civil commitment. *Sexual Offender Treatment, 1*(3), 1–15.
Page, J., Tzani-Pepelasi, K., & Gavin, H. (2022). Characteristics of sexual homicide offenders focusing on child victims: A review of the literature. *Trauma, Violence, & Abuse*, 15248380221119511.
Paitich, D., Langevin, R., Freeman, R., Mann, K., & Handy, L. (1977). The Clarke SHQ: A clinical sex history questionnaire for males. *Archives of Sexual Behavior, 6*, 421–436.
Palermo, M. T., & Bogaerts, S. (2015). The dangers of posthumous diagnoses and the unintended consequences of facile associations: Jeffrey Dahmer and autism spectrum disorders. *International Journal of Offender Therapy and Comparative Criminology, 59*(14), 1564–1579.
Papalia, N., Luebbers, S., & Ogloff, J. R. (2018). Child sexual abuse and the propensity to engage in criminal behaviour: A critical review and examination of moderating factors. *Aggression and Violent Behavior, 43*, 71–89.
Paulhus, D. L. (1998). *Paulhus deception scales (PDS): The balanced inventory of desirable responding–7*. Multi-Health Systems.
Paulhus, D. L., & Jones, D. N. (2015). Measures of dark personalities. In G. J. Boyle, D. H. Saklofske, & G. Matthews (Eds.), *Measures of personality and social psychological constructs* (pp. 562–594). Academic Press.
Pedneault, A., Harris, D. A., & Knight, R. A. (2012). Toward a typology of sexual burglary: Latent class findings. *Journal of Criminal Justice, 40*(4), 278–284.

Pettigrew, M. (2015). Whole of life tariffs in the shadow of Europe: Penological foundations and political popularity. *The Howard Journal of Criminal Justice, 54*(3), 292–306.
Pettigrew, M. (2017). Comorbid, sequential, or different desires? Exploring the relationship between somnophilia and necrophilia. *Journal of Sexual Aggression, 23*(3), 351–359.
Pettigrew, M. (2022). Piquerism in homicide: A knife wound analysis of a sexually motivated serial killer. *Journal of Forensic Sciences, 67*(1), 408–415.
Pettigrew, M. (2023). Piquerism in overkill homicides: Identifying the sexual component in a series of 'ripper' killings. *Journal of Police and Criminal Psychology, 38*(2), 342–352.
Pflugradt, D., & Allen, B. (2012). A grounded theory analysis of sexual sadism in females. *Journal of Sexual Aggression, 18*(3), 325–337.
Pflugradt, D. M., & Allen, B. P. (2013). Identifying sadists among female sexual offenders using the cumulative scale of severe sexual sadism. *Sexual Offender Treatment, 8*(1), 1–12.
Phenix, A., Fernandez, Y., Harris, A. J. R., Helmus, M., Hanson, R. K., & Thornton, D. (2016). Static-99R coding rules revised—2016. http://www.static99.org/pdfdocs/Coding_manual_2016_v2.pdf.
Phillips, E. A., Rajender, A., Douglas, T., Brandon, A. F., & Munarriz, R. (2015). Sex offenders seeking treatment for sexual dysfunction—ethics, medicine, and the law. *The Journal of Sexual Medicine, 12*(7), 1591–1600.
Podolsky, E. (1966). Sexual violence. *Medical Digest, 34*, 60–63.
Pollock, P. H., Stowell-Smith, M., & Gopfert, M. (Eds.). (2006). *Cognitive analytic therapy for offenders: A new approach to forensic psychotherapy*. Routledge.
Potter De River, P. (1949). *The sexual criminal*. Charles C Thomas.
Prentky, R. A., Burgess, A. W., Rokous, F., Lee, A., Hartman, C., Ressler, R., & Douglas, J. (1989). The presumptive role of fantasy in serial sexual homicide. *American Journal of Psychiatry, 146*(7), 887–891.
Prentky, R. A., & Knight, R. A. (1991). Identifying critical dimensions for discriminating among rapists. *Journal of Consulting and Clinical Psychology, 59*(5), 643–661. https://doi.org/10.1037/0022-006X.59.5.643
Proulx, J., Blais, E., & Beauregard, E. (2003). Le sadisme sexuel. Manuscript in preparation.
Proulx, J., Blais, E., & Beauregard, E. (2006). Sadistic sexual aggressors. In W. L. Marshall, Y. Fernandez, L. Marshall, & G. Serran (Eds.), *Sexual offender treatment: Controversial issues* (pp. 61–77). Wiley.
Proulx, J., Blais, E., & Beauregard, E. (2007). Sadistic sexual offenders. In J. Proulx, E. Beauregard, M. Cusson, & A. Nicole (Eds.), *Sexual murderers: A comparative analysis and new perspectives* (pp. 107–122). Wiley.
Proulx, J., & Sauvetre, N. (2007). Sexual murderers and sexual aggressors: Psychopathological considerations. In J. Proulx, E. Beauregard, M. Cusson, & A. Nicole (Eds.), *Sexual murderers: A comparative analysis and new perspectives* (pp. 51–69). Wiley.
Purcell, C., & Arrigo, B. A. (2006). *The psychology of lust murder: Paraphilia, sexual killing, and serial homicide*. Elsevier.
Püschel, K., & Koops, E. (1987). Dismemberment and mutilation. *Archiv Für Kriminologie, 180*(3–4), 88–100.
Quinsey, V. L. (2010). Coercive paraphilic disorder. *Archives of Sexual Behavior, 39*, 405–410.
Quinsey, V. L., Chaplin, T. C., & Varney, G. E. O. R. G. E. (1981). A comparison of rapists' and non-sex offenders' sexual preferences for mutually consenting sex, rape, and physical abuse of women. *Behavioral Assessment, 3*(1), 27–135.
Quinsey, V. L., & Marshall, W. L. (1983). Procedures for reducing inappropriate sexual arousal: An evaluation review. In J. G. Greer & I. R. Stuart (Eds.), *The sexual aggressor: Current perspectives on treatment* (pp. 267–289). Van Nostrand Reinhold.
R v Brown. (1993). AC 1.
R v Byrne. (1960). 2 QB 396.
Rada, R. T. (Ed.). (1978). *Clinical aspects of the rapist* (pp. 21–58). Grune & Stratton.

Rajs, J., Lundström, M., Lindquist, O., Broberg, M., & Lidberg, L. (1998). Criminal mutilation of the human body in Sweden—a thirty-year medico-legal and forensic psychiatric study. *Journal of Forensic Sciences, 43*(3), 563–580.

Ramião, E., Figueiredo, P., Azeredo, A., Moreira, D., Barroso, R., & Barbosa, F. (2023). Neurobiological characteristics of individuals who have committed sexual offenses: A systematic review. *Aggression and Violent Behavior, 101858.*

Re, L., & Birkhoff, J. M. (2015). The 47, XYY syndrome, 50 years of certainties and doubts: A systematic review. *Aggression and Violent Behavior, 22*, 9–17.

Reale, K., Beauregard, E., & Martineau, M. (2017). Sadism in sexual homicide offenders: Identifying distinct groups. *Journal of Criminal Psychology, 7*(2), 120–133.

Reale, K. S., Chopin, J., Gauthier, A., & Beauregard, E. (2022). Sadistic sexual crimes against children: Comparing the manifestation of sexual sadism and crime-commission process. *International Journal of Offender Therapy and Comparative Criminology*, 0306624X221132225.

Renaud, P., Rouleau, J.-L., Granger, L., Barsetti, I., & Bouchard, S. (2002). Measuring sexual preferences in virtual reality: A pilot study. *CyberPsychology and Behavior, 5*, 1–9.

Ressler, R. K., Burgess, A. W., & Douglas, J. E. (1988). *Sexual homicide: Patterns and motives*. Simon and Schuster.

Revitch, E. (1957). Sex murder and sex aggression. *The Journal of the Medical Society of New Jersey, 54*(11), 519–523.

Revitch, E. (1980). Gynocide and unprovoked attacks on women. *Corrective and Social Psychiatry, 26*, 60–11.

Revitch, E., & Schlesinger, L. B. (1989). *Sex murder and sex aggression: Phenomenology, psychopathology, psychodynamics and prognosis*. Charles C Thomas.

Ricono-Kaufhold, S., Czarnietzki, M., Nanev, A., Brookes, N., Davis, M., & Darjee, R. (2024). Comparing child and adult sexual homicides in Australia and New Zealand: A retrospective study. *Behavioral Science and Law*. https://doi.org/10.1002/bsl.2665

Roberston, C. A., Graham, F. J., Krstic, S., & Knight, R. A. (2018). In J. Proulx, A. Carter, E. Beauregard, J. James, R. Darjee, & A. Mokros (Eds.), *Routledge international handbook of sexual homicide studies* (pp. 268–282). Routledge.

Robertson, C. A., & Knight, R. A. (2014). Relating sexual sadism and psychopathy to one another, non-sexual violence, and sexual crime behaviors. *Aggressive Behavior, 40*(1), 12–23.

Rogers, J., Viding, E., Blair, R. J., Frith, U. T. A., & Happe, F. (2006). Autism spectrum disorder and psychopathy: Shared cognitive underpinnings or double hit? *Psychological Medicine, 36*(12), 1789–1798.

Rosman, J. P., & Resnick, P. J. (1989). Sexual attraction to corpses: A psychiatric review of necrophilia. *Journal of the American Academy of Psychiatry and the Law Online, 17*(2), 153–163.

Russell, D. H., & Bender, F. H. (1970). Legal implications of the XYY syndrome. *Seminars in Psychiatry, 2*(1), 40–52.

Russell, K., & Darjee, R. (2011). Managing the risk posed by personality-disordered sex offenders in the community: A model for providing structured clinical guidance to support criminal justice services. In C. Logan & L. Johnstone (Eds.), *Managing clinical risk: A guide to effective practice* (pp. 88–114). Routledge.

Sadger, J. (1926). A contribution to the understanding of sadomasochism. *International Journal of Psycho-Analysis, 7*, 484–491.

Salekin, R. T. (2002). Psychopathy and therapeutic pessimism: Clinical lore or clinical reality? *Clinical Psychology Review, 22*(1), 79–112.

Sandler, D. J. (2019). Contemporary understanding of zoophilia—a multinational survey study. *Journal of Forensic and Legal Medicine, 62*, 44–51.

Sauvageau, A., & Racette, S. (2006). Autoerotic deaths in the literature from 1954 to 2004: A review. *Journal of Forensic Sciences, 51*(1), 140–146.

Saxe, D. B. (1969). Psychiatry, sociopathy and the XYY chromosome syndrome. *Tulsa Law Journal, 6*, 243–256.

Schartmueller, D. (2019). How long is life? Comparing the processes of release for life-imprisoned offenders in Denmark, Finland, and Sweden. *European Journal on Criminal Policy and Research, 25*(4), 391–408.

Schiavi, R. C., Theilgaard, A., Owen, D. R., & White, D. (1984). Sex chromosome anomalies, hormones, and aggressivity. *Archives of General Psychiatry, 41*(1), 93–99.

Schlesinger, L. B., Kassen, M., Mesa, V. B., & Pinizzotto, A. J. (2010). Ritual and signature in serial sexual homicide. *Journal of the American Academy of Psychiatry and the Law Online, 38*(2), 239–246.

Schlesinger, L. B., & Revitch, E. (1999). Sexual burglaries and sexual homicide: Clinical, forensic, and investigative considerations. *Journal of the American Academy of Psychiatry and the Law Online, 27*(2), 227–238.

Schmidt, A. F., & Perkins, D. (2021). Using the explicit and implicit sexual interest profile in applied forensic or clinical contexts. In G. Akerman, D. Perkins, & R. M. Bartels (Eds.), *Assessing and managing problematic sexual interests: A practitioner's guide* (pp. 57–81). Routledge.

Schmucker, M., & Lösel, F. (2015). The effects of sexual offender treatment on recidivism: An international meta-analysis of sound quality evaluations. *Journal of Experimental Criminology, 11*, 597–630.

Schori, A., Jackowski, C., & Schön, C. A. (2022). How safe is BDSM? A literature review on fatal outcome in BDSM play. *International Journal of Legal Medicine, 136*(1), 287–295.

Schöttle, D., Briken, P., Tüscher, O., & Turner, D. (2022). Sexuality in autism: Hypersexual and paraphilic behavior in women and men with high-functioning autism spectrum disorder. *Dialogues in Clinical Neuroscience*. https://doi.org/10.31887/DCNS.2017.19.4/dschoettle

Scott, C. L., Salem, A. M., Tindell, W. W., Neely, H. K., & Blum, A. W. (2023). The forensic assessment of dissociation: Distinguishing real from the unreal. *Behavioral Sciences & the Law*.

Seneca, L. A. (2017) On mercy. (Translated by D. Stewart). Independently published. (Original work published 55 C.E.).

Seto, M. C., & Kuban, M. (1996). Criterion-related validity of a phallometric test for paraphilic rape and sadism. *Behaviour Research and Therapy, 34*(2), 175–183.

Sevlever, M., Roth, M. E., & Gillis, J. M. (2013). Sexual abuse and offending in autism spectrum disorders. *Sexuality and Disability, 31*, 189–200.

Sewall, L. A., & Olver, M. E. (2019). Psychopathy and treatment outcome: Results from a sexual violence reduction program. *Personality Disorders: Theory, Research, and Treatment, 10*(1), 59.

Siegel, A., & Victoroff, J. (2009). Understanding human aggression: New insights from neuroscience. *International Journal of Law and Psychiatry, 32*(4), 209–215.

Silva, J. A., Ferrari, M. M., & Leong, G. B. (2002). The case of Jeffrey Dahmer: Sexual serial homicide from a neuropsychiatric developmental perspective. *Journal of Forensic Sciences, 47*(6), 1347–1359.

Skott, S., Beauregard, E., & Darjee, R. (2019). Female sexual homicide offenders: A descriptive and comparative study. *Journal of Forensic Sciences, 64*(1), 154–162.

Skrapec, C. A. (2001). Defining serial murder: A call for a return to the original *lustmörd*. *Journal of Police and Criminal Psychology, 16*(2), 10–24.

Slovenko, R. (1965). *Sexual behavior and the law*. Charles C. Thomas, Publisher.

Smith, A. D. (1999). Aggressive sexual fantasy in men with schizophrenia who commit contact sex offences against women. *The Journal of Forensic Psychiatry, 10*(3), 538–552.

Smith, A. D. (2000). Motivation and psychosis in schizophrenic men who sexually assault women. *The Journal of Forensic Psychiatry, 11*(1), 62–73.

Spehr, A., Hill, A., Habermann, N., Briken, P., & Berner, W. (2010). Sexual murderers with adult or child victims: Are they different? *Sexual Abuse, 22*(3), 290–314.

Stampf, G. (2008). *Interview with a cannibal: The secret life of the monster of Rotenburg*. Phoenix Books, Inc.

Stefanska, E., Bloomfield, S., & Carter, A. (2021). Our love was a two-person game. At least until one of us died, and the other became a murderer: Sexual homicide perpetrated by intimate partners. *Journal of Criminal Psychology, 11*(4), 301–314.
Stefanska, E., Carter, A., Pettigrew, M., & Higgs, T. (2022). Necrophilic crime scene behaviors in the context of sexual homicide: A multiple case study. *Journal of Forenic Psychology, 7*, 248–253. https://doi.org/10.35248/2475-319X.22.7.248
Stefanska, E. B., Nitschke, J., Carter, A. J., & Mokros, A. (2019). Sadism among sexual homicide offenders: Validation of the sexual sadism scale. *Psychological Assessment, 31*(1), 132.
Stein, M. L., Schlesinger, L. B., & Pinizzotto, A. J. (2010). Necrophilia and sexual homicide. *Journal of Forensic Sciences, 55*(2), 443–446.
Stekel, W. (1924). Sadism and masochism: The psychology of hatred and cruelty. In *Authorized English version* (Vol. 1 & 2). Liveright.
Stochholm, K., Bojesen, A., Jensen, A. S., Juul, S., & Gravholt, C. H. (2012). Criminality in men with Klinefelter's syndrome and XYY syndrome: A cohort study. *BMJ Open, 2*(1), e000650. https://doi.org/10.1136/bmjopen-2011-000650
Stoller, R. J. (1976). *Perversion: The erotic form of hatred*. The Harvester Press.
Tardif, M., Dassylva, B., & Nicole, A. (2007). Psychotherapeutic and psychodynamic issues with sexual murderers. In J. Proulx, E. Beauregard, M. Cusson, & A. Nicole (Eds.), *Sexual murderers: A comparative analysis and new perspectives* (pp. 213–228). Wiley.
ten Bensel, T., & Raptopolous, K. (2024). Special considerations: Female sexual offenders. In R. J. Tully, G. Bohall, & D. S. Prescott (Eds.), *Best practices in sexual offender assessment and management*. Springer.
Testa, M., & West, S. G. (2010). Civil commitment in the United States. *Psychiatry (Edgmont), 7*(10), 30.
Thibaut, F., Cosyns, P., Fedoroff, J. P., Briken, P., Goethals, K., Bradford, J. M., Task Force, W. F. S. B. P., & on Paraphilias. (2020). The world federation of societies of biological psychiatry (WFSBP) 2020 guidelines for the pharmacological treatment of paraphilic disorders. *The World Journal of Biological Psychiatry, 21*(6), 412–490.
Thomas, L., & Egan, V. (2022). A systematic review and meta-analysis examining the relationship between everyday sadism and aggression: Can subclinical sadistic traits predict aggressive behaviour within the general population? *Aggression and Violent Behavior, 65*, 1–32. https://doi.org/10.1016/j.avb.2022.101750
Thornton, D. (2007). Scoring guide for the risk matrix 2000. 9/SVC. https://www.birmingham.ac.uk/documents/college-les/psych/rm2000scoringinstructions.pdf.
Thornton, D. (2010). Evidence regarding the need for a diagnostic category for a coercive paraphilia. *Archives of Sexual Behavior, 39*(2), 411–418.
Thornton, D., Ambroziak, G., Kahn, R. E., & Mundt, J. (2018). Advances in the assessment of sexual deviance. *Current Psychiatry Reports, 20*, 1–8.
Todd v The Queen. (2020). VSCA 46.
Traini, R. (1960). *Murder for sex and cases of manslaughter under the new Act*. William Kimber & Co. Ltd.
Trottier, D., Goyette, M., Benbouriche, M., Renaud, P., Rouleau, J. L., & Bouchard, S. (2019). *Using virtual reality with child sexual offenders: Assessing deviant sexual interests. Virtual reality for psychological and neurocognitive interventions* (pp. 209–225).
Turner, D., & Briken, P. (2018). Treatment of paraphilic disorders in sexual offenders or men with a risk of sexual offending with luteinizing hormone-releasing hormone agonists: An updated systematic review. *The Journal of Sexual Medicine, 15*(1), 77–93.
Turner, D., & Briken, P. (2021). Pharmacological treatments for individuals with paraphilic disorders or at risk of sexual offending. In L. Craig & R. M. Bartels (Eds.), *Sexual deviance: Understanding and managing deviant sexual interests and paraphilic disorders* (pp. 282–294). Wiley.
Turner, D., Briken, P., & Schöttle, D. (2017). Autism-spectrum disorders in adolescence and adulthood: Focus on sexuality. *Current Opinion in Psychiatry, 30*(6), 409–416.

Turner, D., Petermann, J., Harrison, K., Krueger, R., & Briken, P. (2017). Pharmacological treatment of patients with paraphilic disorders and risk of sexual offending: An international perspective. *The World Journal of Biological Psychiatry*.
Tyrer, P. (2019). Dissociative identity disorder needs re-examination: Commentary on… dissociative identity disorder. *BJPsych Advances, 25*(5), 294–295.
Vaughn, M. G., DeLisi, M., Beaver, K. M., & Howard, M. O. (2008). Toward a quantitative typology of burglars: A latent profile analysis of career offenders. *Journal of Forensic Sciences, 53*(6), 1387–1392.
Vess, J., Day, A., Powell, M., & Graffam, J. (2014). International sex offender registration laws: Research and evaluation issues based on a review of current scientific literature. *Police Practice and Research, 15*(4), 322–335.
Völlm, B., & Braun, P. (Eds.). (2019). *Long-term forensic psychiatric care: Clinical, ethical and legal challenges*. Springer.
von Schrenck-Notzing, A. (1892). Suggestion therapy, translated by. C. G. Chaddock in 1895.
Wagner, M. S. (1935). *The monster of Dusseldorf. The life and trial of Peter Kurten*. Faber.
Warren, J. I., & Hazelwood, R. R. (2002). Relational patterns associated with sexual sadism: A study of 20 wives and girlfriends. *Journal of Family Violence, 17*, 75–89.
Watson, R., Darjee, R. D., & Davis, M. R. (2024). An integrative meta-model of rape typologies and dimensions: Practical and clinical applications [Manuscript in preparation]. Centre for Forensic Behavioural Science, Swinburne University of Technology.
Weierstall, R., Moran, J., Giebel, G., & Elbert, T. (2014). Testosterone reactivity and identification with a perpetrator or a victim in a story are associated with attraction to violence-related cues. *International Journal of Law and Psychiatry, 37*(3), 304–312.
White, C. (2006). The Spanner trials and the changing law on sadomasochism in the UK. In P. J. Klainplatz & C. Moser (Eds.), *Sadomasochism: Powerful pleasures* (pp. 167–187). Routledge.
Williams, E. (1992). *Beyond belief. The moors murderers: The story of Ian Brady & Myra Hindlay*. Pan Books.
Williams, K. M., Cooper, B. S., Howell, T. M., Yuille, J. C., & Paulhus, D. L. (2009). Inferring sexually deviant behavior from corresponding fantasies: The role of personality and pornography consumption. *Criminal Justice and Behavior, 36*(2), 198–222.
Williams, D. J., Thomas, J. N., Prior, E. E., & Christensen, M. C. (2014). From "SSC" and "RACK" to the "4Cs": Introducing a new framework for negotiating BDSM participation. *Electronic Journal of Human Sexuality, 17*(5), 1–10.
Willmott, D., Boduszek, D., & Robinson, R. (2018). A psychodynamic-behaviourist investigation of Russian sexual serial killer Andrei Chikatilo. *The Journal of Forensic Psychiatry & Psychology, 29*(3), 498–507.
Wilson, G. (1978). *The secrets of sexual fantasy*. J. M. Dent & Sons.
Wilson, G. D. (1988). Measurement of sex fantasy. *Sexual and Marital Therapy, 3*(1), 45–55.
Wismeijer, A. A. J., & Van Assen, M. A. L. M. (2013). Psychological characteristics of BDSM practitioners. *The Journal of Sexual Medicine, 10*(8), 1943–1952.
Wolf, L. (1980). *Bluebeard: The life and crimes of Gilles de Rais*. CN.
Wollert, R. (2011). Paraphilic coercive disorder does not belong in DSM-5 for statistical, historical, conceptual, and practical reasons. *Archives of Sexual Behavior, 40*(6), 1097–1098.
Wong, J. S., & Gravel, J. (2018). Do sex offenders have higher levels of testosterone? Results from a meta-analysis. *Sexual Abuse, 30*(2), 147–168.
Woodrow, J. C. (2011). *Rose West: The making of a monster*. Hodder & Stoughton.
World Health Organization. (1948). International classification of diseases (6th revision).
World Health Organization. (1955). ICD-7 international statistical classification of mental and behavioural disorders (7th revision).
World Health Organization. (1965). ICD-8 international statistical classification of mental and behavioural disorders (8th revision).

World Health Organization. (1977). International classification of diseases.1975 Revision (Vol. 1). (9th revision).
World Health Organization. (1992). The ICD-10 classification of mental and behavioural disorders. Clinical descriptions and diagnostic guidelines (10th revision).
World Health Organization. (1993). The ICD-10 classification of mental and behavioural disorders: Diagnostic criteria for research.
World Health Organization. (2022). ICD-11: International classification of diseases (11th revision). https://icd.who.int/.
Wright, S. (2010). Depathologizing consensual sexual sadism, sexual masochism, transvestic fetishism, and fetishism. *Archives of Sexual Behavior, 39*(6), 1229–1230.
Wulffen, E. (1910). Enzyklopädie der modernen Kriminalistik. Erich Langenscheidt.
Yakely, J. (2021). A psychoanalytic approach to paraphilic disorders, perversions and other problematic behaviours. In G. Akerman, D. Perkins, & R. M. Bartels (Eds.), *Assessing and managing problematic sexual interests: A practitioner's guide* (pp. 171–192). Routledge.
Yates, P. M., Hucker, S. J., & Kingston, D. A. (2008). Sexual sadism: Psychopathology and theory. In D. R. Laws & W. T. O'Donohue (Eds.), *Sexual deviance: Theory, assessment and treatment* (pp. 213–230). Guildford Press.
Zidenberg, A. M., & Olver, M. E. (2022). Measurement and correlates of zoophilic interest in an online community sample. *Archives of Sexual Behavior*. Advance online publication. https://doi.org/10.1007/s10508-022-02429-x
Zilioli, S., & Bird, B. M. (2017). Functional significance of men's testosterone reactivity to social stimuli. *Frontiers in Neuroendocrinology, 47*, 1–18.

Chapter 13
Clinical Versus Criminal Pedophilia: An Extended Review of Theory, Assessment, Diagnosis, and Intervention

Michael R. Davis and Rajan Darjee

13.1 Introduction

Pedophilia, having a sexual attraction to pre-pubescent children, is a misused term and those to whom it is attached are demonized. The term is often used lazily, angrily and disparagingly, by the media and the public, as synonymous with child sexual molestation. Thus, pedophilia and child sexual abuse (CSA) are wrongly conflated with each other, so all "child molesters" are seen as "pedophiles", and all "pedophiles" are considered "child molesters". There are few people in society who generate such fear, hatred and disgust, and this political, media and societal climate, though understandable, is unhelpful, and can infect professionals and services, creating an environment in which evidence-based, effective, rational, just and safe practice can be difficult. Unfortunately fears of "stranger danger" and the "moral panic" about CSA and pedophilia have played a greater role than the research

M. R. Davis (✉)
Centre for Forensic Behavioural Science, Swinburne University of Technology, Melbourne, VIC, Australia

Department of Psychiatry, Monash University, Clayton, VIC, Australia

Department of Psychiatry, University of Melbourne, Parkville, VIC, Australia
e-mail: mdavis.psych@gmail.com

R. Darjee
Centre for Forensic Behavioural Science, Swinburne University of Technology, Melbourne, VIC, Australia

Forensic Mental Health Service, Tasmanian Health Service, Hobart, TAS, Australia

Forensic Behavioural Assessment and Consultation Services (FBACS), Melbourne, VIC, Australia

R. J. Tully et al. (eds.), *Best Practices in Sexual Offender Assessment and Management*, Dangerous Behavior in Clinical and Forensic Psychology,
https://doi.org/10.1007/978-3-031-83135-5_13

evidence, and the reality of CSA and pedophilia, in directing and shaping policy and therefore practice.

CSA can have serious immediate and long-term effects on victims and prevention is rightly a very high priority. But it is important to bear in mind that only about half of those who commit CSA have a pedophilic sexual interest and many, perhaps most, people with a pedophilic sexual interest never sexually abuse children. However, pedophilia is clearly an important risk factor for CSA and for repeated child sexual offending. So, it is an important condition in clinical and forensic practice. Those who are sexually attracted to children, especially those who do not offend, often internalize societal prejudices, assumptions and stigma, leading to self-loathing and not seeking help or support. There have been significant developments and advances in our understanding of pedophilia, including its etiology, relationship with CSA, epidemiology, assessment, treatment and the prevention of CSA in the last quarter of a century, reflected in the contents of this chapter. This research and practice evidence base can help inform clinicians when they work with people with pedophilia, whether they have committed sexual abuse or not, to improve their mental health and social functioning, and to prevent CSA. This chapter aims to help practitioners in clinical and forensic contexts achieve these by adopting best and evidence-based practice.

Diagnostic criteria will be considered in detail later, but for now some terms which will be used throughout this chapter will be clarified. The term pedophilia will be used for a sexual attraction to prepubescent children and, following the *Diagnostic and Statistical Manual of Mental Disorders* (Fifth Edition [DSM-5]; American Psychiatric Association [APA], 2013), the *Diagnostic and Statistical Manual of Mental Disorders* (Fifth Edition Text Revision [DSM-5-TR]; APA, 2022) and the *International Classification of Diseases for Mortality and Morbidity Statistics* (11th Revision [ICD-11]; World Health Organization [WHO], 2022), the term *pedophilic disorder* will be used for individuals where pedophilia causes them distress, impairs social functioning or leads to harming others, including through committing sexual abuse. CSA will be used broadly to cover contact or non-contact, offline or online CSA. Contact CSA will be used where this abuse involves attempting to or actually physically touching a child. Child sexual abuse material (CSAM) will be used to refer to sexual images, videos or stories of children, usually now sourced or transmitted over the internet and stored electronically. CSAM offending is a non-contact form of CSA, along with other forms of sexual abuse, such as exposing oneself to a child or engaging with a child sexually, whether online or offline, through conversation or online chat. The use of technology to commit or facilitate CSA has become an increasing problem this century and its relationship with pedophilia will be referenced in this chapter. The boundaries and impacts of pedophilia will be considered, including the age of children a person is attracted to (including whether hebephilia—sexual attraction to children on the cusp of or in the early stages of puberty—is a useful concept), the exclusivity of the sexual interest in children (including whether pedophilia could or should be considered a sexual orientation for age rather than gender and/or a sexual interest like other paraphilias), relative sexual interest in children versus adults (taking in concepts such as interest, preference, attraction and exclusivity), acting on pedophilic arousal or urges (including factors related to committing sexual abuse and consideration of people who do not offend), and what can and should be done to prevent acting on pedophilic sexual interests (including assessment, treatment, management and prevention approaches). As it has become clear that many people with pedophilia do not come to the attention of law enforcement or criminal justice agencies, there has been increasing interest in this group, and the terms Minor Attracted Person (MAP) and Non-Offending MAP (NOMAP) have been used both by the individuals and by others. Technically the term MAP includes people attracted to anyone under the age of consent in their jurisdiction, but the vast majority of MAPS have pedophilia, a few are hebephilic, and a tiny minority could be considered ephebophilic (sexually attracted to post-pubertal teenagers), although such an attraction is indistinguishable from being teleiophilic (sexually attracted to adults) as both groups are physically sexually mature.

Some key points to bear in mind while reading this chapter are:

1. Pedophilia is a sexual attraction to prepubescent children and is not the same as CSA.
2. Hebephilia is a sexual attraction to children in the early stages of puberty, not teenagers per se, and although hebephilic disorder was rejected for inclusion in DSM-5-TR, clinically there are clearly individuals with a strong or primary sexual interest in children of this level of development. The term pedohebephilic has been used to cover people with pedophilia and/or hebephilia.
3. Pedophilic disorder is the diagnostic term used in DSM-5-TR and ICD-11 when pedophilia causes distress, problems with social functioning or harm to others, including via offending. So diagnosis is dependent on the psychosocial impact of the 'condition'.
4. Pedophilia is a predisposing factor which can motivate a minority of pedophilic individuals to commit contact and non-contact, online and offline CSA.
5. Pedophilic disorder is an important risk factor for further CSA in people who have already committed CSA. Therefore, pedophilic disorder has important implications for legal adjudications, treatment, management and prevention.
6. However, research has shown that although CSAM offenders have higher rates of pedophilic interests than contact CSA offenders, they have lower rates of sexual recidivism.
7. Most MAPs have pedophilia or pedophilic disorder but are not known to commit CSA.

Pedophilia will not be conflated with child sexual offending in this chapter and it will focus on pedophilia in clinical and forensic contexts. Sometimes reference will be made to research or practice relating to CSA, either as it is relevant to pedophilia or the literature makes it difficult to untangle them. But it will be endeavoured to be explicitly clear whether we are considering pedophilia or pedophilic disorder or CSA or offending or non-offending people with pedophilic sexual interests. An attempt to be morally neutral will also be made, reflecting the focus on prevention of CSA in practice and improving the lives of people who, through no fault of their own, find that they are sexually attracted to children. After all no one chooses who they are sexually attracted to, although every person is responsible for managing the expression of their sexual fantasies, urges, and sexual behavior.

13.2 What Is Pedophilia? History, Definition, and Concept

In this section a historical overview of the construct of pedophilia will be provided, the diagnostic criteria in both the DSM and ICD classification systems will be examined, and the status of the related construct of hebephilia will be reviewed. Differences, changes, and controversies in diagnostic criteria across the various nosologies will be discussed, along with recommendations for the future of diagnostic classification.

13.2.1 Historical Overview

Pedophilia, or "paedophilia" in Commonwealth countries, is a form of paraphilic or atypical sexual interest involving a sexual preference for prepubescent children. This can be manifested in the form of thoughts, fantasies, urges, or behavior. The name pedophilia is derived from the Greek terms for young children (pedeiktos) and love (philia). As is the case with many forms of paraphilic sexual interest, the term was first described in Richard von Krafft-Ebing's classic work *Psycopathia Sexualis* (1886) as *erotic paedophilia* (love of children). However, the use of the word "philia" has been questioned when describing paraphilias (other love or demented love) in general. Indeed, it has been suggested that the correct term should be *paralagnia*, meaning demented lust, as it is the sexual interest rather than love itself that is atypical (Aggrawal, 2009; Moser, 2001). This is perhaps an important distinction to keep in mind when considering pedophilia. While many of those with pedophilic sexual interests will have a seemingly genuine love for children, others will simply lust over children with no interest in intimacy or connection, although there is some evidence that those with pedophilia have a romantic attraction with the objects of their desire (i.e., children), more so than those with other paraphilic interests (Martijn et al., 2020). As such, the behavioral manifestations of pedophilia can vary considerably.

In recent years pedophilia has been viewed as one of the *chronophilias* (Money, 1986; Seto, 2017), whereby individuals have a sexual orientation towards a particular age, in conjunction with an orientation for gender. The chronophilias include nepiophilia (infants/toddlers), pedophilia (prepubescent children), hebephilia (pubescent children), ephebophilia (post-pubescent, sexually maturing adolescents), teleiophilia (young sexually mature adults), mesophilia (middle-aged adults), and gerontophilia (elderly adults). Clearly, only some of the chronophilias would be considered sexually deviant, and there has been some rigorous debate in the scholarly literature as to whether hebephilia, in particular, should be considered deviant in the same way as nepiophilia and pedophilia.

13.2.2 Conflation with Child Sexual Abuse

It is important to distinguish pedophilia from the concept of CSA as these terms are used interchangeably in wider society and the media. Unfortunately, CSA is far from a new phenomenon. Indeed, it is described as far back as the Old Testament, where it was also forbidden (see Book of Leviticus; 18). Killias (1991) reported that the laws of ancient Rome set the minimum age for getting married at 14 for boys and 12 for girls. Disturbingly by modern standards, during the Middle Ages, any child victim of sexual crimes, such as sodomy, was treated not as a victim, but as a participant that warranted equal punishment as that of their adult abuser. Killias (1991) further noted that it was not until the nineteenth century that youth was thought to be a distinct period of life and ages of consent increased.

In modern times, it is not unusual to see media reports of an adult victimizing a 15-, 16-, or 17-year-old being described as a "pedophile." However, no matter how destructive and, depending on the jurisdiction, illegal such behavior may be, this is clearly not a crime that reflects a preferential sexual interest in prepubescent children. In addition, not all of those who sexually abuse prepubescent children will have a preferential or persistent sexual interest in prepubescents. The literature suggests that approximately 50% of sexual offenders with child victims are likely to have pedophilic sexual interests, although this does vary between studies and how pedophilia is identified (see Seto, 2008, 2018). It is an unfortunate reality that males in particular will engage in sexual behavior with children for a range of different reasons and motivations, only one of which is a sexual preference for children. This has formed the basis of a number of typological systems that will be discussed later in this chapter.

While approximately half of sexual offenders with child victims will have pedophilic sexual interests, it must also be noted that there are an unknown number of people with pedophilic interests who do not engage in sexual behavior with children. The widespread proliferation of on-line child sexual abuse material in recent decades, and the surprisingly large number of people who have been found to have downloaded such material but never engaged in contact offending, indicates that there are many such individuals in the wider society. There are also likely to be pedophilic individuals who do not view child abuse material, but nonetheless engage in pedophilic fantasies whilst masturbating. It has been hypothesized that non-offending persons with pedophilia will likely differ in important ways from those who commit sexual offences (Seto, 2018), and there is some developing evidence for this opinion. For example, Szczypiński et al. (2022) found that those with pedophilic disorder and a history of CSA exhibited behavioral and neural abnormalities in regard to cognitive control during emotional interference. This was not found amongst those with pedophilic disorder who had not committed CSA. Moreover, the latter group did not differ from a sample of healthy controls. The involvement of the right dorsolateral prefrontal cortex was implicated in these results. Accordingly, those with pedophilic disorder are decidedly heterogenous. Not all with a pedophilic interest will sexually victimize children, and only half of those who sexually victimize children will have pedophilic interests. But there is an overlap between these two populations, which is where pedophilic individuals are most likely to be involved with forensic mental health professionals.

13.2.3 Diagnosis in DSM and ICD

The current diagnostic criteria for Pedophilic Disorder are highly congruent between the current DSM-5-TR (2022) and ICD-11 (2022) nosologies. DSM-5-TR (2022) has essentially kept the same diagnostic criteria since the DSM-IV-TR (2000) system, although there is now a crisp distinction made between *pedophilia* and *pedophilic disorder*. Pedophilia is defined by criterion A, whereby over a period of at least 6 months, there have been recurrent and intense sexually arousing fantasies, urges, or behaviors involving sexual activity with a prepubescent child or children. A general age of 13 or younger is provided for the child or children, but it is noted in text that this is approximate only and may vary from person to person. It is acknowledged that the onset of puberty has been declining over time and differs across cultures. While not mentioned in the diagnostic criteria itself, pedophilia and pedophilic disorder follow the overall DSM-5-TR (2022) approach to paraphilic disorders by noting that the sexual interests are "greater than or equal to nonparaphilic sexual interests" (p. 779).

Interestingly, the first printing of the previous DSM-5 (2013) explicitly stated that those that meet Criterion A have a "pedophilic sexual orientation" (p. 698). This was changed to "pedophilic sexual interest" following some public, rather than clinical, criticism (see Berlin, 2014 for discussion); with the doubtful claim that this was simply a text error that needed to be corrected. Nonetheless, it is our view that "orientation" is the correct conceptualization for *some* individuals with pedophilia, but not for others. This will be discussed in detail below.

Pedophilic Disorder is only diagnosed if Criterion B is met; where the individual has either acted on the urges with a child, or the urges or fantasies cause marked distress or interpersonal difficulty. The diagnosis is only made if the person is at least 16 years-of-age and at least 5 years older than the child or children to whom they are attracted. In addition, the diagnosis is not made if someone in late adolescence is involved in an ongoing sexual relationship with a 12- or 13-year-old child. Specifiers of "exclusive type" and "nonexclusive type" are included, with the former indicating that the individual is only attracted to children. Those making the diagnosis also specify if the individual is sexually attracted to males, females, or both genders, and a further specifier of "limited to incest" is made if appropriate.

It is perhaps important to note that diagnostic criteria for pedophilia and pedophilic disorder have seen some changes between various editions of the DSM system. For example, criterion A for what was then called Pedophilia in DSM-IV (1994) included fantasies, urges or behaviors, whilst Criterion B focused on the clinically significant distress or impairment that was caused by them. In what would appear to be a truly unintended consequence, these criteria meant that a diagnosis of pedophilia would not be made if someone acted on the urges with multiple children, but was not distressed by them (O'Donohue et al., 2000). This was also the case for other paraphilias that may involve non-consenting behaviors (i.e., Sexual Sadism, Frotteurism, Exhibitionism, and Voyeurism). As such, these paraphilias, including Pedophilia, were among the very few disorders to see changes to their diagnostic criteria in DSM-IV-TR (2000), such that Criterion B included acting on the urges or marked distress. This underscores the difficulties that can arise when creating diagnostic criteria for paraphilic disorders, including pedophilic disorder, where some individuals will be diagnosed on the basis of urges and fantasies alone, whilst others will engage in sexual offending behavior that raises the possibility of a diagnosis.

As is almost always the case, the ICD-11 (2022) criteria for Pedophilic Disorder are not nearly as detailed. However, they are congruent with the DSM-5-TR (2022) criteria and described "a sustained, focused, and intense pattern of sexual arousal—as manifested by persistent sexual thoughts, fantasies, urges, or behaviors—involving pre-pubertal children" (p. 564). No particular age range for the prepubescent children is included. As is the case with the DSM-5-TR (2022) criteria, a diagnosis is only made if the individual has acted on the urges or is markedly distressed by them.

It is important to note that ICD-11 (2022) criteria have changed in one important way from that outlined in the previous ICD-10 (1992) system. The ICD-10 (1992) criteria for what was then called *Paedophilia* described "a sexual preference for children, usually of prepubertal or early pubertal age" (171). It was noted that isolated incidents do not meet the criteria. However, surprisingly, men who have a sexual preference for adults but habitually turn to children as substitutes were included. The major difference to the DSM-III-R (1987) criteria at the time, and the current DSM-5-TR (2022) and ICD-11 (2022) criteria, was the inclusion of children of early pubertal age. This essentially expanded the construct of pedophilia to include individuals with a hebephilic sexual interest or preference. However, the subsequent *ICD-10 Diagnostic Criteria for Research* (1993), published the following year, only mentioned prepubescent children, so it is unclear if plans to remove the hebephilic aspect of the criteria were made this early, especially as ICD-11 (2022) was not published until 30 years after ICD-10 (1992).

13.2.4 The Status of Hebephilia

While the terms pedophilia and ephebophilia (sexual attraction to adolescents) have been in use for a long time, hebephilia was reportedly first termed as such by Glueck (1956) to refer to those with victims aged 12–15 years. The status of whether hebephilia should be considered a form of paraphilic disorder in diagnostic manuals has been vigorously debated over the past decade. As noted above, hebephilic sexual interest was subsumed in the ICD-10 (1992) diagnostic criteria for paedophilia, but has since been removed. It has never been included in the DSM system. However, there was a serious proposal to expand the pedophilia diagnosis to one known as *Pedohebephilic Disorder* for DSM-5 (2013).[1] The original proposed diagnostic criteria by Blanchard (2010a; see also Blanchard et al., 2009) involved an individual who is equally or more sexually attracted to children under the age of 15 years than to physically mature adults. Self-report, laboratory testing, or behavior could be used to determine criterion A. Criterion B was met if an individual was distressed or impaired by the attractions or had sought stimulation from children under 15 on three or more separate occasions. The specifiers were *Pedophilic Type* (attracted to children younger than 11), *Hebephilic Type* (attracted to children 11–14), and *Pedohebephilic Type* (attracted to both). Blanchard (2010b) acknowledged that the three-victim criterion emphasized specificity rather than sensitivity, such that it would tend to under-diagnose rather than over-diagnose pedohebephilia.

A subsequent revision of the proposed criteria in April 2012 (www.dsm5.org) saw the name changed to *Pedophilic Disorder* and the removal of the number of victims criterion as well as the age ranges. Instead, the pedophilic type was renamed the *Classic Type*, with an attraction to prepubescent children in Tanner stage one. The *Hebephilic Type* was described as an attraction to children in Tanner stages two-to-three. The *Pedohebephilic Type* remained for those sexually attracted to both age ranges. In and of itself, this was a very useful change from a pragmatic perspective as it moved away from ages and focused on developmental stages that more explicitly referenced prepubescence and early pubescence.

Despite the fact that this proposal would have simply made the DSM criteria consistent with those of the ICD at the time, Blanchard's proposal was met with considerable criticism in the literature that was sometimes extraordinarily caustic (e.g., Janssen, 2009). Indeed, Good and Burstein (2012) described it as the "construction of a fictitious diagnosis" (p. 492). It should be noted that many of the criticisms were wider than the proposed criteria themselves, and were more focused on topics such as whether hebephilia would meet the overall DSM criteria for a mental disorder (DeClue, 2009; Kramer, 2011; Moser, 2009; Tromovitch, 2009), or how the inclusion of hebephilia could be misused in civil commitment proceedings in the United States (Franklin, 2009; Zander, 2009).[2] Nonetheless, there was some pragmatic consideration of the proposal. For example, Prentky and Barbaree (2011) constructively suggested that there were three scenarios to consider. The first is an individual with sexual interests in prepubescent and early pubescent children, who

[1] The term *pedophebephilia* was first described under the name *paedo-hebephilia* by Freund et al. (1972) to describe individuals with an approximately equal sexual preference for prepubertal and pubertal children, compared to adolescents and physically mature adults.

[2] This was an arguably legitimate concern for many during the development of the DSM-5, particularly in regard to hebephilia, and perhaps more so, Paraphilic Coercive Disorder. Indeed, the *DSM-5 Work Group on Sexual and Gender Identity Disorders* included a lawyer involved in prosecuting sexually violent predator cases (see Stern, 2010).

would likely be deemed paraphilic. The second is an individual with a sexual interest in adults and young teenagers, who they believed would likely not be deemed paraphilic. The third was an individual with an exclusive sexual interest for young teenagers. They proposed that "when there is a specified minimum age differential or when the presumptive paraphilic is of a specified minimum age, exclusive interest may well reflect the kind of psychosexual and psychosocial deficits that constitute impairment" (p. 509). This scenario would appear to be of particular interest for forensic assessors when appraising the risk of reoffending.

Ultimately, the APA rejected the proposal for Pedohebephilic Disorder and chose to remain with the DSM-IV-TR (2000) criteria for Pedophilia, albeit with a new name of Pedophilic Disorder (Blanchard, 2013; Singy, 2015). However, it has been noted that the APA notably did not explicitly exclude hebephilia from continuing to be diagnosed under the residual category *Other Specified Paraphilic Disorder* (Stephens et al., 2018). Moreover, as has been noted in regard to other disorders that were removed or never formally part of the DSM, "burning the map does not eliminate the territory" (Meloy, 1997, p. 631). In fact, the past decade has seen ongoing research into hebephilia that has underscored its importance in applied forensic and clinical practice. For example, Stephens, Seto, et al. (2017) examined the convergent and divergent validity of a range of indicators of hebephilia and pedophilia (PPG indices, self-report, victim age) in a sample of 2238 men who had sexually offended. The various indicators of hebephilia showed considerable convergence, but there was poor divergence between the two sexual interests. While both the PPG Hebephilia and Pedophilia Indices differentiated those with a sexual interest in children from those without, both the indices accurately classified the other child sexual interest as well. Interestingly, those classified as pedohebephilic (both pedophilic and hebephilic) had the highest levels of sexual arousal toward prepubescent children and the lowest level of sexual interest in adults, suggesting that pedohebephilic individuals may have a more exclusive sexual interest in children.

A further study by Stephens et al. (2018), completed using the same sample, examined the age diversity amongst hebephilic and pedophilic individuals who had sexually offended. Whether identified by self-report or PPG indices, both hebephilia and pedophilia were moderately associated with a greater number of victims under the age of 11 years (hebephilia $r = .20$ and .24; pedophilia $r = .25$ and .44) and had a small but statistically significant association with more victims aged 11–14 (hebephilia $r = .07$ and .19; pedophilia $r = .09$ and .07). Both also had negative or no association with victims aged 17 or above. The main difference between the two groups was that hebephilia was more consistently, albeit still small in magnitude, related to a greater number of victims aged 15 or 16 years. These results were consistent with a sexual response gradient model, whereby individuals show some, but increasingly less, sexual interest as age deviates from their preference (Blanchard et al., 2012; Lykins et al., 2010). The authors concluded that:

> hebephilia and pedophilia are more similar than they are different. This raises the question of whether hebephilia should be viewed as distinct from pedophilia, or as an extension of pedophilic interest, as it is likely that a substantial proportion of individuals with sexual interest in children have interests in both prepubescent and pubescent children (p. 334).

A subsequent study by Stephens et al. (2019) investigated the PPG results of 1900 men with at least one child victim. Using a conservative *z*-score of > 0.25 for the hebephilia and pedophilia indices, denoting appreciably greater sexual arousal to either group, 25% met the pedophilia cut-off, 40% met the hebephilia cut-off, and 24% met both. Taken together, just one percent had only pedophilic interests, 16% had only hebephilic interests, and 24% were pedohebephilic. Using a less stringent but arguably more useful in applied settings *z*-score of >0.00 (indicating more arousal to children than adults), 36% met the pedophilia cut-score, 52% met the hebephilia cut-score, and 35% met both. Taken together, still just one percent were only pedophilic, 17% were only hebephilic, and 35% were pedohebephilic. Such results were again consistent with the sexual response gradient model, but also suggested that exclusive pedophilia, in and of itself, is comparatively rare.

It can be seen that, since the publication of DSM-5 (2013), the scholarly understanding of hebephilia has increased considerably. Indeed, there is substantial overlap between pedophilia and hebephilia, such that these sexual interests are arguably more alike than different. This contrasts with some of the earlier criticisms of the construct that suggested that hebephilic sexual interest was essentially normative (e.g., Good & Burstein, 2012; Rind & Yuill, 2012; Zander, 2009). These recent realizations have been reflected in the literature, whereby increasingly more papers are being published that consider pedohebephilia and newly developed risk assessment and diagnostic tools have included consideration of pedophilic or hebephilic sexual interests (e.g., Eke & Seto, 2016; Eke et al., 2018; Seto & Eke, 2017). This pragmatic approach to considering both pedophilia and hebephilia when assessing sexual interest in children is relevant for many clinical and forensic tasks, despite previous academic criticisms of the latter. Moreover, as Seto (2018) appropriately posited:

> There is a reasonable argument for considering pedophilia and hebephilia together as *pedohebephilia*. Puberty is a liminal event and thus hard to capture in clinical or scientific measurement. For many practical purposes, it might not matter much whether an individual's attraction is to prepubertal or pubertal children. It certainly would be hard to get it right without precisely knowing the Tanner (1990) stage of children… In other words, the distinction between pedophilia and hebephilia is real but might not be necessary for many practical purposes (p. 14).

13.2.5 Future of Diagnostic Classification

It is our opinion that the current diagnostic criteria for Pedophilic Disorder are overly sensitive and not particularly specific. Indeed, too many non-pedophilic individuals who commit situational sexual offences against children are likely to meet the rather woolly diagnostic criteria as they necessarily include fantasies, urges, or behaviors. In addition, the use of a general child age of 13 years or below is very likely to be, perhaps ironically, identifying a proportion of those with hebephilic interests (because many 11, 12, and 13 year-old children will have commenced puberty when victimized). Recent research has utilised an interest in children aged less than 11 years to approximate Tanner stage one (pedophilia) and 11–14 years to approximate Tanner stages two or three (hebephilia) when actual sexual development data regarding victims had been unavailable (Stephens, Seto, et al., 2017). If this imperfect proxy has any degree of accuracy, it would strongly suggest that the DSM-5-TR criteria will identify many hebephilic individuals as pedophilic.

Some of the remedies to this situation were already proposed in the final draft for DSM-5 that was rejected by the APA. One of these is to simply accept the clear overlaps between pedophilia and hebephilia and thereby also accept a dually considered diagnostic category of pedohebephilia (with or without pedophilic and hebephilic subtypes). In addition, a move away from arbitrary age differences to a focus exclusively on Tanner stages of development for identifying puberty and early pubescence would arguably increase specificity of both pedophilic and hebephilic interests. However, this is admittedly very difficult to determine in clinical practice as the Tanner stages of children in self-reported sexual behavior, documented offence behavior, and child abuse material offending is very often unavailable. Even then, recent literature has made it clear that hebephilic and pedophilic individuals have similar age correlates, and both self-reported and phallometrically identified hebephilia is slightly more associated with victims under the age of 11 years than those aged 11–14 years. So even knowing the Tanner stage of child sexual offence victims may still not wholly differentiate between the two interests. Nevertheless, if one wishes to identify the presence of a truly pedophilic preference, without consideration of hebephilic interests, identifying a clear preference for prepubescents in Tanner stage one would appear to be vital and improved methods for approximating Tanner stages would be invaluable.

Future diagnostic classifications should ideally focus on identifying those with a sexual preference for children, or at the very least an equal or greater sexual interest in children as to other age groups. One way of conceptualizing this, in regard to those that have sexually offended against children, is in the form of a continuum ranging from the situational and impulsive to the preferential and compulsive (Lanning, 2001, 2010). The use of behavioral rating scales is also a useful way of identifying preferential sexual interests and a fixation on children. At present there are several particularly useful behavioral rating scales that practitioners can readily utilize to identify preferential pedohebephilic and/or pedophilic sexual interests. These will be described in detail below.

13.3 Boundaries, Overlaps and Apparent Similarities: Comorbidity, Undifferentiated Conditions, and Differential Diagnosis

This section contains an examination of the overlap and comorbidity of pedophilic disorder with personality disorders, other paraphilic and sexual disorders, psychotic disorders, depression and suicide, anxiety and stress-related disorders, neurodevelopmental disorders, and neurocognitive disorders.

13.3.1 Personality and Personality Disorder

High rates of personality disorders have been reported in those who commit child sexual offences. Eher et al. (2019) found 43.1% of 671 contact child sexual offenders had personality disorders, significantly less than the 64.0% in adult sexual offenders. Rates of specific personality pathology in child offenders were: 7.6% cluster A, 34.3% cluster B (0.6% histrionic, 12.2% narcissistic, 17.9% borderline, 20.4% antisocial), 9.2% cluster C, and 17.6% personality disorder not otherwise specified. Rates of cluster B disorders were higher in adult offenders (although narcissistic was similar in both groups), cluster C disorders were higher in child offenders, and cluster A disorders were similar across both groups. This fits with adult offenders being more antisocial and disinhibited, while child offenders tend to be more introverted, anxious, and inhibited. The same group examined a smaller sample of 66 incarcerated online child sexual offenders finding 71.2% had personality disorders, with similar rates and profiles when comparing those with CSAM only offending to those with CSAM plus contact offending (Seiser et al., 2023), but the sample size was small, incarcerated CSAM offenders are probably not representative of CSAM offenders, and there is good evidence that those who commit both CSAM and contact offences are more antisocial than those who only commit CSAM offences (Babchishin et al., 2015). Although such studies point to a relationship between pedophilia and personality disorder, as less than half of contact offenders (Seto, 2018) and about two thirds of CSAM offenders have pedophilic disorder (Seto et al., 2006), extrapolating to pedophilia is not straightforward, as such personality traits may be related to acting on pedophilic sexual interest (in the real world or online) rather than having a pedophilic sexual interest.

Studies specifically examining pedophilia are largely confined to selected samples of men who have committed contact offences. Cohen et al. (2002) compared 20 pedophilic offenders to 24 healthy male controls, using the Millon Clinical Multiaxial Inventory-II (MCMI-II; Millon, 1987) finding higher rates of all clusters and disorders in the pedophilic group. Cohen et al. (2008) had similar findings when comparing pedophilic, substance dependent and health males using the Structured Clinical Interview for DSM-IV Axis-II Personality Disorders (SCID-II; First et al., 1995), although substance dependent individuals had higher rates of antisocial and borderline traits. They found significantly higher levels of psychopathy in those with pedophilia than health controls, but the substance dependent individuals scored higher, particularly on the behavioral factor. In a further study, Cohen et al. (2018) compared non-offending individuals with pedophilia, to offending individuals with pedophilia and health controls using the MCMI-II. Offenders scored highest on paranoid, antisocial and aggressive-sadistic traits; non-offending pedophilic individuals scored highest on avoidant, dependent and schizoid traits; and the two pedophilic groups were similar but higher than the controls on self-defeating, anxious, dysthymic and schizotypal traits. Controls scored lowest on all traits, except antisocial and sadistic-aggressive where they were similar or slightly higher than the non-offending pedophilic group. In a recent review Haugsand (2023) identified 13 studies of personality disorders in people with pedophilia, six of which were authored by Cohen's group, concluding that pervasive personality pathology across all clusters was present in people with pedophilia, particularly cluster C, followed by B, and then A. The rate of any personality disorder ranged from about 40 to 60%, but only three studies compared offending and non-offending people with pedophilia, finding similar rates but different profiles. There were more cluster C (particularly avoidant and obsessive-compulsive) traits in non-offenders, and more cluster B traits in offenders. Studies find lower rates of antisocial personality disorder in child sexual offenders with pedophilia compared to those without (Gerwinn et al., 2018). But in a non-offending sample, Abé et al. (2021) found a significantly higher rate of antisocial personality disorder in people with pedophilia (16%) compared to healthy controls (0%). Looking at the big five personality factors, Jahnke et al. (2019) found higher levels of emotional instability, introversion and conscientiousness in an online survey comparing men in the community with and without pedohebephilia. However, in offending samples, not necessarily all with pedophilia, lower conscientiousness and higher impulsivity have been found, along with higher neuroticism and lower extraversion (Dennison et al., 2001; Tenbergen et al., 2015).

Overall, the findings from these studies point to high rates of personality disorders in people with pedophilic sexual interests compared to the general population across all clusters, with non-offending associated with avoidant, obsessive-compulsive, and schizoid traits, and offending against children associated with antisocial traits. Antisocial traits are more common in child sex offenders who are not pedophilic, and avoidant, dysthymic, and schizotypal traits in those who are. Dysfunctional personality traits may share a common etiology with pedophilic sexual interests, e.g., resulting from experiences of abuse in childhood, genetic vulnerability or neurodevelopmental perturbations; they may predispose to developing a sexual interest in children, perhaps through diminishing capacity for adult intimacy; or they may disinhibit acting on pedophilic sexual arousal and urges, through impulsivity, antisociality, detachment or callousness. It may also be the case that having a pedophilic sexual preference predisposes to developing personality dysfunction due to impact on the development of identity, intimacy, interpersonal functioning, and self-perception and emotions related to shame and alienation as an adolescent. Personality dysfunction may underpin stable dynamic factors or criminogenic needs related to child sexual offending, e.g., problems with emotional and self-regulation, in relationships, and with attitudes and underlying schema focused on self, others and the world. Personality disorder is also an important responsivity factor relevant to motivation and readiness for, engagement with, and effectiveness of treatment. Assessing personality and personality disorder is therefore important in people with pedophilic disorder in offending and non-offending contexts.

13.3.2 Paraphilic Disorders

In this section the overlapping boundaries between pedophilia, hebephilia, and ephebophilia will be further examined; as well as comorbidity between pedophilic disorder and other paraphilic disorders.

13.3.2.1 Hebephilia and Ephebophilia

As noted above, consideration of hebephilia was proposed for inclusion in DSM-5 as part of Pedohebephilic Disorder, but was ultimately not accepted in the final manual. In addition, while sexual attraction to early pubescents was included in the ICD-10 criteria for paedophilia, the ICD-11 criteria for Pedophilic Disorder apply exclusively to prepubescent children. Nonetheless, recent research outlined above has illuminated the considerable overlaps between pedophilic and hebephilic sexual interests, such that some have advocated for a pragmatic consideration of pedohebephilia.

While the evidence is progressively growing that hebephilic sexual interests can be considered a form of sexual deviance, ephebophilia (sexual interest in older adolescents) is clearly not deviant. The literature has drawn a crisp and understandable distinction between Tanner stages two and three (hebephilia) and Tanner stages four and five (ephebophilia and teleiophilia; e.g., see Stephens et al., 2018). In fact, some of the arguments put forward against hebephilia being included in the DSM are arguably more relevant to ephebophilia. Indeed, a sexual interest in older adolescents may be socially sanctioned and appropriately illegal at the lower ages of adolescence, but a sexual interest in those in Tanner stage four is not sexually atypical. Adolescents in Tanner stage four more closely resemble adults in stage five than they do young pubescents in stages two or three.

13.3.2.2 Other Paraphilic Disorders

It is perhaps interesting to note that there is not a great deal of scholarly research addressing the comorbidity of pedophilic disorder and other paraphilic disorders. Paraphilic disorders very often co-occur and it is well known that certain conditions are frequently comorbid (e.g., Voyeurism, Exhibitionism, and Frotteurism; Sexual Sadism and Sexual Masochism; Fetishism and Transvestic Fetishism). However, there are no particularly common comorbidities with pedophilic disorder. We note that a classic paper by Abel et al. (1988) found that many pedophiles had engaged in several other sexually deviant behaviors, although this was less pronounced for female target incest offenders. Exhibitionism and Voyeurism were the most common comorbid behaviors, although it is unclear if these were simply behaviors that had been engaged in or were at the magnitude of a paraphilic disorder by modern criteria. Nonetheless, Seto (2018) noted that pedophilic individuals are more likely to engage in other paraphilic behavior than other men in the wider population. It was also noted that exhibitionistic and voyeuristic behaviors have been engaged in by those with pedophilic disorder. In addition, there are a thankfully small number of individuals that sexually victimize children who engage in sexually sadistic behaviors against them. It is unclear if they all meet formal criteria for both Pedophilic and Sexual Sadism Disorder, but this is a particularly problematic combination as the use of force and physically damaging coercion and violence is more likely.

The DSM-5-TR indicates that Pedophilic Disorder can be comorbid with a range of conditions, including other paraphilic disorders. None are specifically named, although an example is provided of an Exhibitionist exposing themselves to prepubescent children and thus meeting criteria for both Pedophilic Disorder and Exhibitionistic Disorder.

We note that Price et al. (2002) examined the comorbidity of *Telephone Scatologia* with other paraphilic and paraphilia-related disorders. While there was often notable comorbidity with conditions such as Exhibitionism and Voyeurism, and 95% engaged in compulsive masturbation, none of the 20 people in the telephone scatologia group had comorbid pedophilia (either incestuous or non-incestuous).

We have found in our own forensic clinical practice that some with pedophilic disorder have no other paraphilic conditions, whilst others have some additional paraphilic interests. Sometimes these arise after a period where the additional behavior had a functional role. For example, someone with pedophilic interests who peeps through a window at a child they are attracted to while they are disrobing or bathing. This initially has a functional quality, but becomes more arousing over time, to the point that thoughts of the voyeuristic activity itself are arousing. One may hypothesize that the more exclusive the pedophilic interest, particularly amongst those in whom pedophilic disorder is a more "hard-wired" sexual orientation (see below), comorbid paraphilic disorders may be less likely than they are amongst others with pedophilic disorder. However, this is admittedly speculative.

13.3.3 Other Sexual Disorders

13.3.3.1 Compulsive Sexual Behavior Disorder

Compulsive Sexual Behavior Disorder was introduced into the diagnostic lexicon in ICD-11 (2022). It is characterized by a persistent pattern of failure to control intense, repetitive sexual impulses or urges resulting in repetitive sexual behavior. An analogous condition known as *Hypersexual Disorder* was proposed for the DSM-5 (2013) nosology, but ultimately did not make the final version of the manual (Kafka, 2010). This was conceptualized as a "non-paraphilic sexual desire disorder with an impulsivity component" (Kafka, 2013, p. 377). In the more recently published ICD-11 (2022) conceptualization, *Compulsive Sexual Behavior Disorder* is classified as one of the impulse control disorders. Regardless of any slight theoretical differences between the proposed DSM-5 (2013) criteria and that published in the ICD-11 (2022), both would appear to be identifying the same condition.

Being a relatively new condition, at least formally, there is little published evidence regarding the overlap between compulsive sexual behavior disorder and pedophilia. Nonetheless, Kafka and Hennen (2003) investigated hypersexual desire in those with paraphilic disorders and paraphilia-related disorders. The sample of 120 included 20 with a diagnosis of pedophilia. Those with paraphilic disorders, mostly offenders, were found to have high levels of hypersexuality, sexual preoccupation, and compulsive masturbation. This is perhaps not too surprising. Indeed, as will be described below, sexual preoccupation is a particularly potent risk factor amongst sexual offenders, so some overlap is to be expected, although not all sexual offenders with pedophilic disorder will be hypersexual. The current authors have found in forensic practice that those who spend a lot of time viewing on-line child abuse material often become consumed by it and engage in compulsive masturbation. This is not inconsistent with those that report problematic use of legal pornographic material (e.g., see Sniewski et al., 2018).

13.3.4 Other Mental Disorders

In this section the comorbidity of pedophilia with psychotic disorders, depression and suicide, and anxiety and stress-related disorders will be examined. The importance of differentiating pedophilia from Obsessive-Compulsive Disorder with pedophilic content will also be emphasised.

13.3.4.1 Psychotic Disorders

Psychotic disorders are more common in men who commit sexual offences than men who do not (Alden et al., 2007; Fazel et al., 2007; Wallace et al., 1998), with rates in studies ranging from about 5 to 10% (Lewis & Dwyer, 2018), but many studies are potentially unrepresentative. Eher et al. (2019) found the rate of psychosis in contact child sexual offenders was 0.7%, lower than the 1.9% in adult victim offenders, and Seiser et al. (2023) found a rate of 3.0% in CSAM offenders. Rates of psychosis depend on factors like the setting of the study (correctional versus forensic mental health) and whether offenders with psychosis get diverted from the criminal justice to mental health system.

Overall psychosis seems no more or less common in child versus adult victim offenders and appears slightly more prevalent in child sex offenders than in the general population. But there are no studies specifically examining the relationship between pedophilia, in either offenders or non-offenders, and psychosis. Some studies point to lower rates of paraphilic disorders in sexual offenders with psychosis than in those without (Sorrentino et al., 2013), which fits with our clinical experience over the last two decades of finding comorbidity between pedophilia and psychosis rare, and when individuals with psychosis commit child sexual offences, they are almost always non-preferential. This is consistent with meta-analytic findings of higher rates of severe mental illness in contact versus CSAM offenders (Babchishin et al., 2015), as the latter have significantly higher rates of pedophilia than the former. This is despite some personality traits and disorders associated with pedophilia (see above) also being associated with schizophrenia (e.g., schizoid, schizotypal, and avoidant), and despite neurodevelopmental perturbations purportedly associated with pedophilia being similar to those associated with neurodevelopmental disorders like schizophrenia (see below). Rates of psychotic syndrome were not significantly higher in non-offending individuals with pedophilia compared with health controls (2% versus 0%; Abé et al., 2021).

Occasionally individuals with psychosis present with delusions that others believe them to be a pedophile or that they are a pedophile, and/or experience auditory hallucinations saying such things. This is usually easily differentiated from pedophilia. Although very rare in practice, RD treated a man with premorbid exclusive pedophilic interest and an intellectual disability, who developed schizophrenia, and then was taunted by hallucinatory voices about his pedophilia, who was distressed by both his sexual interest and the voices, but who never offended. A similar case was reported by Sorrentino et al. (2013).

13.3.4.2 Depression and Suicide

Relatively high rates of depression have been found in child sexual offenders compared to adult sexual offenders (Eher et al., 2019), in pedophilic child sexual offenders (Raymond et al., 1999), in CSAM offenders (Babchishin et al., 2015), and in non-offending individuals with pedophilia (Abé et al., 2021; Sorrentino &

Abramowitz, 2021; Stewart, 2022). Raymond et al. (1999) found over half of pedophilic sexual offenders had lifetime DSM-IV major depression. Factors related to the high prevalence of depression probably include: personality traits associated with pedophilia; experiences of childhood abuse and adversity; difficulties with relationships and intimacy in adolescence and adulthood potentially leading to rejection, alienation and loneliness; the impacts of being investigated, charged, and convicted; rejection and stigmatization due to their behavior and offending; and internalization of that stigma and associated shame.

Suicidal ideation and suicide attempts are common in non-offending people with pedophilia (Sorrentino & Abramowitz, 2021), CSAM offenders (Steel et al., 2022) and child sex offenders (Hoffer et al., 2010). The risk of suicide in child sexual offenders (contact and CSAM) may be a hundred times higher than in the general population (Key et al., 2021), with risk factors including shame, unique demographic characteristics (male gender, age between mid-thirties and early fifties, Caucasian, educated to a college degree level, employed in a professional role, married with children), absence of prior criminal contact, and the impact of a criminal investigation (Key et al., 2021). There appears to be a higher risk in CSAM offenders than in contact offenders, and a higher risk in people who only commit sexual offences against children versus those with more diverse offending. The highest risk period appears to be the 48 h to a month after becoming aware of investigations, along with when arrested, charged, tried, convicted, or sentenced, when the threat of public exposure or the reality of the legal process crystallizes.

13.3.4.3 Anxiety and Stress-Related Disorders

Anxiety disorders follow a similar pattern to depression, with higher rates in child sexual offenders than adult ones (Eher et al., 2019), in pedophilic child sexual offenders (Raymond et al., 1999), in CSAM offenders (Babchishin et al., 2015), and in non-offending individuals with pedophilia (Abé et al., 2021; Sorrentino & Abramowitz, 2021; Stewart, 2022). This is unsurprising given the strong association between depression and anxiety disorders (Saha et al., 2021), and the factors accounting for the association between pedophilia and anxiety disorders are likely similar to the ones outlined above for depression. There are few studies of specific anxiety disorders, but in a small sample of pedophilic sexual offenders (Raymond et al., 1999), lifetime rates were: 64% any DSM-IV anxiety disorder, 6.7% panic disorder, 37.8% social phobia, 26.7% simple phobia, 11.1% obsessive-compulsive disorder (OCD), 6.7% generalized anxiety disorder, and 33.3% post-traumatic stress disorder (PTSD). The average age of onset for all was in middle childhood (at 8–12 years old), except panic disorder in early adulthood, likely reflecting anxious, shy, and inhibited temperaments in childhood, and early experiences of trauma. Compared to the expected rates in the general population the two that particularly stand out are social phobia (now called social anxiety disorder) and PTSD. Abé et al. (2021), comparing 55 non-offending men with pedophilic sexual interests with 57 healthy controls, found rates were: 7% panic disorder, 29% social anxiety disorder, 15% generalized anxiety disorder, 18% OCD, and 2% PTSD; with significantly and much higher rates of OCD and social anxiety disorder.

Most studies have found that *social anxiety* is more common in child sexual offenders than in men generally or other types of offenders (Nunes et al., 2012; Porter et al., 2015), although results across studies are inconsistent, and most have not examined pedophilia specifically. The high rate of *PTSD* may partly reflect high rates of adverse childhood experiences (Levenson et al., 2016), although whether pedophilic individuals have higher rates than child sexual offenders or other sexual offenders is unknown. However, Marx et al. (2020) found higher rates of emotional and sexual abuse in the childhoods of people with pedophilia compared to psychotherapy outpatients and people from the general population. As detailed below (see Sect. 13.4) adverse childhood experiences, including sexual abuse, have been proposed as a major etiological factor in pedophilia and child sexual offending.

Obsessive-compulsive disorder may present with 'pedophilic content', i.e., intrusive thoughts, images or ruminations regarding child sexual abuse or being pedophilic (Bonagura et al., 2022; Bruce et al., 2018). However, in such cases there is no sexual fantasy or arousal to children, no masturbation to such fantasies or arousal, and no sexual behavior with children. In fact, in such cases people invariably go out of their way to avoid being in proximity with children reinforcing the condition. It is easily differentiated from ego-dystonic pedophilia, where there is actually sexual arousal to and fantasies about children, usually associated with masturbation and sometimes sexually abusive behavior, which the individual finds distressing. This is a common scenario in non-offending minor attracted people (NOMAPS), but not unusual in CSAM and contact offenders too. It is important to differentiate OCD from pedophilia (ego-dystonic or -syntonic) as OCD with 'pedophilic content' is not associated with offending, and taking a 'forensic' approach to such cases (referrals to forensic clinicians, instigating child protection or legal procedures) causes iatrogenic harm, because OCD becomes more entrenched by the confirmation of the fear that one is a danger to children, treatment involves exposure (Reid et al., 2016), and it wastes child protection, law enforcement and forensic resources (Bonagura et al., 2022). A basic phenomenological understanding of the person's experience, making the easy differentiation between obsession and sexual fantasy/arousal, should make identifying the correct diagnosis straightforward in all but very few cases. It is important that such individuals do not get unwittingly hooked into services and supports aimed at preventing child sexual abuse by people with concerning sexual thoughts, urges or behaviors towards children.

13.3.4.4 Developmental Disorders

In this section the prevalence of, and relationship between, pedophilia and developmental disorders, including Intellectual Disability, Autism Spectrum Disorder, and Attention-Deficit/Hyperactivity Disorder will be examined.

13.3.4.4.1 Intellectual Disability (ID)

Although it tends to be accepted that there is a relationship between ID and both child sexual offending and pedophilia, research findings have been inconsistent, probably due to the nature of samples studied and the methods used to ascertain ID and pedophilia. Some studies have focused on IQ scores, some on ID or equivalent diagnoses (generally with IQ under 70), some have included borderline ID, and others have included learning disorders or specific intellectual deficits.

In terms of IQ, Cantor et al. (2005), in a meta-analysis of 236 samples including 25,146 sexual offenders and controls, found that sexual offenders had lower IQs than controls, those with child victims had significantly lower IQs than those with adult victims, concluding that pedophilia was related to low IQ. They suggested previous discrepant findings were due to different prevalences of pedophilia in samples, and that the association was due to both low IQ and pedophilia being related to neurodevelopmental perturbations. Joyal et al. (2014), in a meta-analysis of 23 studies with 1756 participants examining neuropsychological measures other than IQ, found a high degree of heterogeneity suggesting that grouping together child and adult victim offenders and different specific neuropsychological measures should be avoided. All cognitive measures combined showed lower functioning in sexual offenders compared to the general population, but there were different patterns between adult and child victim offenders. Child offenders scored lower on tests of deduction and cognitive flexibility, better on tests of verbal fluency and control of internal interference, and similarly to adult offenders on motor speed. They were not able to specifically examine pedophilia though and highlighted that several studies found pedophilic sexual offenders to be less cognitively impaired than non-pedophilic ones, with some pedophilic offenders found to have higher IQs. In a study of 1462 sexual offenders in prison, Hocken (2020) unexpectedly found that sexual interest in children, beliefs supporting child sexual abuse and feeling more comfortable with children (dynamic risk factors indicative of pedophilia) were associated with higher IQ, whilst other dynamic factors (e.g., problems with self-regulation, with relationships, and with attitudes towards women) were associated with lower IQ. In addition, Hocken (2020) found that child sexual offenders were more likely to have superior IQs whilst adult offenders were more likely to have low IQs, although interestingly ID rates were similar in both groups at about 5%.

However, ID is specifically defined by having an IQ below 70 associated with problems with social and functional adaptation, so may show different associations from findings for overall IQ or specific cognitive measures. Mirroring Cantor et al. (2005)'s findings for IQ, several studies of sexual offenders have found that those with an ID are more likely to have apparent indicators of a pedophilic sexual interest, such as very young victims and male victims (Blanchard et al., 1999; Cassiani-Miranda et al., 2019; Reyes et al., 2011; Rice et al., 2008). However, Langevin and Curnoe (2008) found no difference in rates of ID or in IQ levels between child and adult victim offenders, that CSAM offenders had the highest IQs and lowest rate of ID of all sexual offenders, and overall although borderline ID (IQ 70–79) was over-represented amongst sexual offenders, ID was not. Learning disorders, defined as per the Wechsler Adult Intelligence Scale-Revised when "achievement on standard tests in reading, mathematics, or written expression is substantially below that expected for age, schooling, and level of intelligence" (Wechsler, 1981, as cited in Langevin & Curnoe, 2008, p. 402), were present in about 30% of all offenders, were much less frequent in CSAM offenders, were equally common in adult and child victim offenders overall, but were associated with having mixed genders of victims (whether children or adults). Hocken (2020) and Bradbury and Lievesley (2020) also failed to find an association between ID and indicators of pedophilia, and Vicenzutto et al. (2022) found no association between sexual deviance and ID, speculating that pedophilia seemed more common in the sexual offenders without ID. Carlstedt et al. (2009) found no association between having a learning disability and age of victim amongst sexual offenders who had victimized children.

An important issue when considering sexual offending in people with ID, particularly where victims are children or other people with ID, is the role of factors such as lack of sexual knowledge, poor social and interpersonal skills, limited opportunities to establish appropriate sexual relationships and express sexuality, and sexual naivety. The 'counterfeit deviance' hypothesis (Hingsburger et al., 1991) posits that such factors, rather than sexual deviance or antisociality, lead to inappropriate sexual behavior and sexual offending in people with intellectual disabilities, and has been very influential in the development of treatment services for sexual offenders with ID (Luiselli, 2000). Although studies comparing sexual offenders with ID with other people with ID and non-ID sexual offenders have cast doubt on the validity of this hypothesis (Galea et al., 2004; Lambrick and Glaser 2004; Michie et al., 2006; Talbot & Langdon, 2006), it seems likely that there are two groups of ID sexual offenders: those where such factors are relevant and those whose sexual offending is driven by similar factors to those that drive non-ID offenders (Coleman & Haaven, 2001; Craig & Moss, 2006; Day, 1997; Lunsky et al., 2007). Other important considerations in sexual offending in people with ID are a tendency for more indiscriminate offending with regards to age and gender of victims (Blanchard et al., 1999; Gilby et al., 1989; Griffiths et al., 1985), their own experiences of sexual abuse and learning inappropriate sexual behaviors particularly in institutional settings, and the potential role of comorbid medical conditions (Griffiths et al., 2010). So, when assessing apparently 'pedophilic behavior' it is important to bear such factors in mind when determining whether pedophilic disorder is present or not. In addition, it is likely that sexual offending by people with ID is more likely to come to the attention of authorities, but on the other hand such individuals are perhaps more likely to be diverted from the criminal justice system, affecting the representativeness of correctional samples (Griffiths et al., 2010).

Overall, then, the association between IQ level or ID and pedophilia is unclear, with contradictory evidence in the research literature. Specific problems have been a focus on sexual offenders, use of proxy measures of pedophilia, and the use of criminal justice samples. However, clinically it is important to differentiate between individuals with comorbid pedophilia and individuals with apparently pedophilic behavior unrelated to pedophilia. Although this is also important for individuals without ID, specific factors of relevance to ID must be considered in such cases.

Neuropsychological factors of potential relevance to the etiology of pedophilia will be described below (see Sect. 13.4).

13.3.4.4.2 Autism Spectrum Disorder (ASD)

Overall people with ASD appear no more likely to commit sexual offences than neurotypical people (King & Murphy, 2014), and there is no research indicating they have higher rates of sexual offending against children. However, people with ASD are perhaps more likely to commit, or be arrested for, CSAM offences (Dubin & Horowitz, 2017). Problems with communication and social interactions, restricted and repetitive sexual interests, lack of impulse control, naivety, difficulties understanding the actions of others, lack of intimate relationships, sensory issues, and sexual frustration may be relevant factors in people with ASD who commit sexual offences (Higgs & Carter, 2015; Margari et al., 2024; Mogavero, 2016). In a study comparing 96 people with and 96 without ASD, pedophilic sexual fantasies were more common in males (reported by over a quarter), but not females, with ASD, but pedophilic behavior did not occur (Schöttle et al., 2017). "Sexual interests towards children" was present in 5% of a sample of 76 males previously diagnosed with Asperger syndrome (Fernandes et al., 2016). However, reporting fantasies does not necessarily indicate that pedophilic disorder is present. Carlstedt et al. (2009) found that a third of child sex offenders had "autistic features" and no relationship with age of victim. Abé et al. (2021) compared 55 self-referred help-seeking men with pedophilia who had not offended with 57 age matched healthy controls using the Ritvo Autism and Asperger Diagnostic Scale (RAADS-14) screening tool (Eriksson et al., 2013), finding higher mean scores in the pedophilic group across all three subscales, and 60% (versus 9% of controls) screened in using a cut of 13 (13 or less rules out the diagnosis), whilst 32% (versus 4%) had a total score more than 23 (with a positive prediction rate for ASD of a third). These results imply that NOMAPS likely have higher rates of ASD than other people, but people who commit child sexual offences do not.

13.3.4.4.3 Attention Deficit Hyperactivity Disorder (ADHD)

Little is known about the relationship between ADHD and pedophilia. Turner et al. (2022) examined paraphilic fantasies and behaviors in 160 adults with ADHD and 75 without. Although the rate of pedophilic fantasies was somewhat higher in men, but not women, with ADHD, this was not significantly so. Abé et al. (2021) found that non-offending pedophilic men had higher rates of screening in for ADHD (38%) than healthy controls (16%). As ADHD is related to impulsivity, dysregulation, and antisocial personality traits, it may be relevant to offending by acting on pedophilic arousal and more generally. ADHD has been found to be associated with risky sexual behavior (Turner et al., 2022) and hypersexuality (Hertz et al., 2022).

However, there is no evidence that ADHD is related to offending in pedophilic or non-pedophilic child sexual offenders.

13.3.4.5 Neurocognitive Disorders

There has been an increasing number of studies of brain structure and function in child sexual offenders and people with pedophilia (see Sect. 13.4 below), with increasing interest in the brain circuits and structures that may underpin these. There have been descriptions of cases of 'acquired pedophilia' (Camperio Ciani et al., 2019; Scarpazza et al., 2021) in individuals who have displayed 'pedophilic behavior' after developing neurological conditions such as brain tumors, dementias, cerebrovascular disease, multiple sclerosis, or head injury (Scarpazza et al., 2021). In such cases there may seem to be the development of de-novo paraphilic sexual interests and behavior following the brain insult. However, the organic insult may lead to disinhibition, hypersexuality, lack of concern for others, and/or problems with communication/understanding, which either lead to child sexual abuse behavior in themselves or perhaps disinhibit an underlying pedophilic sexual interest that the person was not troubled by and did not act on previously. Scarpazza et al. (2021) found differences between people with 'acquired' versus 'developmental' (i.e., child sexual offenders without such neurological conditions) pedophilic behavior: older age, absence of previous psychiatric disorders, lack of previous sexual offences, lack of premeditation and masking, spontaneous confessions, and sense of guilt. Joyal (2023) described 64 cases found through a systematic review, finding an average age of 53 years, most cases committed other sexual and nonsexual impulsive acts, only a fifth showed evidence of premorbid pedophilia, and brain pathology mostly involved fronto-temporal regions associated with both sexual and impulsive behaviors. There was no evidence of new-onset pedophilic sexual fantasies or arousal. He concluded that such cases were either due to general disinhibition or disinhibition of pre-existing pedophilia, and/or hypersexuality, but not true modification of sexual interest, and that cases of acquired pedophilia were not adequate for inferring a neurological basis of pedophilia.

13.3.5 Non-preferential Child Sexual Offending

As noted above, approximately half of those who sexually victimize children will have a pedophilic sexual interest. Parsing the heterogeneity of those who commit sexual offences against children has seen considerable research attention over the past half century. Several useful typological systems have been developed that can assist clinicians and researchers to differentiate pedophilic sexual offenders from those who sexually victimize children for other motives. These will be described in detail below.

13.4 Etiology

Before looking at specific etiological factors and theoretical models, it is useful to consider some conceptual issues, before jumping into evidence regarding associations and potential causality. Firstly, as outlined above, child sexual abuse is not the same as pedophilia (Seto, 2018). Only about a half of people who commit contact child sexual offences could be considered to have pedophilia or pedophilic disorder (Seto, 2018), and about two thirds of those who commit CSAM offences (Babchishin et al., 2015; Seto et al., 2006). Therefore, although pedophilia is an important factor in understanding child sexual abuse, there are clearly factors unrelated to pedophilia which lead to such abuse. So, the questions 'what causes pedophilia?' and 'what causes child sexual abuse' have different, though somewhat related, answers.

Secondly, amongst individuals with pedophilia and pedophilic disorder are people (probably the majority) who do not commit child sexual abuse (who might be termed non-offending minor attracted persons or NOMAPS), people who commit CSAM offences but do not commit direct sexual abuse of children, and people (probably a small minority) who commit direct or contact sexual offences (Dombert et al., 2016). Factors related to being attracted to children are therefore different from those related to acting on that attraction in a criminal manner.

Thirdly, the current DSM-5-TR (2022) and ICD-11 (2022) definitions of pedophilic disorder focus on sexual arousal to pre-pubertal children. DSM-5-TR (2022) states that children should generally be aged 13 years or younger, but that such age guidelines are only approximate, given the range of ages that individuals go through puberty. Some white boys are still at Tanner stage 1 (i.e., prepubescent) at 16 years old and some white girls at 14 years old, while some white boys achieve Tanner stage 5 (adult genital development) at 12 and some white girls at 11 (Miller et al., 2020). Black children develop on average earlier than white children, with Hispanic, Pacific Islander and South Asian children in between, and East Asian children latest. So, it can be difficult to ascertain the physical maturity of children a person is attracted towards, particularly when primarily going on the age of a person's victims. If one was just to go by the suggested upper age of 13 years old, this would encompass people attracted to pre-pubertal, peri-pubertal, and sometimes post-pubertal children. So, this age range captures people who may be regarded as having pedophilic or hebephilic sexual interests, along with some individuals sexually attracted to physically developed children (who might be regarded as ephebophilic, although they cannot be readily differentiated from teleiophilic individuals). Sexual attraction to pre-, peri- and post-pubertal children seem very different both conceptually and etiologically.

Fourthly, pedophilia and pedophilic disorder are classified as types of paraphilia and paraphilic disorder in DSM and ICD, so they are types of 'sexual deviance' with 'atypical' sexual interests. But pedophilia has also been conceptualized as a sexual orientation (Fedoroff, 2020), specifically a sexual orientation to immaturity (Seto, 2012). Although these can be considered overlapping approaches, from an etiological and theoretical perspective this leads to questions as to whether models, precursors, associates, or causes are similar to, or the same as, those related to other paraphilic disorders on the one hand, or those related to sexual orientation for gender (e.g., heterosexuality, homosexuality, bisexuality) on the other. One potential outcome of viewing pedophilia as an orientation is to consider it immutable (Cantor & Fedoroff, 2018). However, our view is that both models apply to different people, with exclusive pedophilia being an orientation and non-exclusive pedophilia a sexual interest sharing characteristics with other paraphilic disorders.

Fifthly, there is the issue of dimensionality. The traditional approach to most psychiatric diagnoses, including paraphilic disorders, has been a categorical one. However, some diagnoses are clearly underpinned by dimensions, for example personality disorders (Hopwood et al., 2018) and sexual sadism disorder (see Chap. 12). Unlike sadism, research examining whether pedophilia is dimensional or categorical does not all point in the same direction. Some concluded pedophilia is taxonic (Blanchard et al., 2012; Brankley et al., 2022; McPhail et al., 2018; Schmidt et al., 2013) while others concluded it was dimensional (Mackaronis et al., 2011; Stephens et al., 2017). This might be accounted for by methodological issues, such as whether samples only included people with child sexual offences, measures of sexual interest in children, and which features of attraction to children were examined (e.g., just sexual interest/arousal or also emotional congruence with children). It may also be that both models are relevant to pedophilia. Exclusive or very strongly preferential sexual attraction to children may be a taxon, whilst non-exclusive (preferential and non-preferential) sexual attraction to children may be dimensional. This hybrid model chimes with our clinical and forensic practice experience, where individuals with an exclusive or very strongly preferential attraction to children seem relatively uncommon and different from those with a sexual attraction to children which is non-exclusive, even though it may be preferential and/or quite strong. It also fits with Gannon's (2021) recent etiological model of pedophilia outlined below. The non-exclusive dimension would, like the agonistic continuum (see Chap. 12) include people who are strongly (but not exclusively) pedophilic through to those who have minimal sexual attraction to children, and so may be relevant to both preferential child sexual offending and non-preferential child sexual offending (see Sect. 13.6.1 below). However, it may be that there are two pedophilic taxa: those with an exclusive pedophilic sexual interest and those with a non-exclusive interest (McPhail et al., 2018). Unlike sadism, the dimensional or taxonic nature of pedophilia has not yet been empirically resolved to the point where there are now clear ramifications for assessment, measurement, and diagnosis.

Sixth, an overlapping issue is the differentiation of individuals with no sexual attraction or arousability to children at all, those with some arousability to children but which is not strong or preferential, those with strong arousability to children but a preference for adults, those with a sexual preference for children but who can be aroused by adults, and those with an exclusive sexual attraction to children who are not sexually aroused by adults at all. In clinical practice you come across people with all these patterns, and it seems important to ascertain where a particular individual sits along this spectrum, regardless of whether pedophilia is dimensional or taxonic. A relevant question is whether sexual attraction to children and to adults are two different, and potentially independent variables or mutually dependent or just one variable (i.e., relative sexual attraction to children versus adults). A recent systematic review, with four meta-analyses, found that people with pedophilia who had committed offences against children (or assumed to have pedophilia from sample descriptions) were much less sexually attracted to adults, did not have a clear sexual preference for children over adults, but did have more absolute sexual interest in children (Schippers et al., 2023). The conclusion was that lack of sexual interest in adults may be a relevant factor in pedophilia. There may also be an interaction between a person's ability to be sexually attracted to or aroused by children (versus adults) and context and time, leading to a fluctuating level of sexual interest in or preference for children.

The primary focus of the following sections is on factors and models relevant to pedophilia and pedophilic disorder and not child sexual abuse in people without pedophilia. Readers should assume this chapter is referring to pedophilia unless explicitly stated otherwise. For recent comprehensive reviews see Seto (2018) and Gannon (2021). More expansive typological models and frameworks that differentiate between various motivations for child sexual victimization, including pedophilic and non-pedophilic, will be described in a different section later in this chapter.

13.4.1 Biological Factors

Most studies of neurobiological characteristics in people who commit sexual offences focus on those with child victims and/or pedophilic sexual interests (Kruger & Kneer, 2021; Ramião et al., 2023). The findings point to some broad conclusions. Neurobiological factors seem etiologically important in pedophilia, perhaps particularly in individuals who have an exclusive or very strong sexual preference for children and who act on that interest. Areas of the brain implicated overlap with those known to be important in sexual interest generally and those implicated in the small number of studies of non-pedophilic paraphilias. There is a suggestion that having an exclusive or very strong sexual preference for children is a neurodevelopmental condition sharing etiological characteristics with other neurodevelopmental perturbations. Factors related to contact sexual offending in men with pedophilia are like those linked to acting antisocially in other populations (e.g. sexual offending against adults and non-sexual offending) and discriminate between non-offending and offending people with a pedophilic sexual interest. The neurobiological substrates of pedophilia and acting on pedophilia may fall into three broad areas: those related to sexual arousal and interest (Kaplan & Krueger, 2010), those related to inhibiting or disinhibiting the acting out of behavioral urges (Graber et al., 1982), and perhaps those related to attachment and intimacy (Beech & Mitchell, 2005). Here the aim is to give an overview relevant to practice. For more detailed reviews of neurobiological factors in pedophilia and child sexual offending see Tenbergen et al. (2015), Jordan et al. (2020), Kruger and Kneer (2021), Saleh et al. (2021), Boschetti et al. (2023), and Ramião et al. (2023).

13.4.1.1 Genetic Factors

There is some evidence of a genetic contribution to sexual offending, child sexual offending and a sexual interest in children. This should be unsurprising given that brain development, structure and function, which underpins all aspects of psychological and behavioral functioning including sexual behavior and offending behavior, is dependent on genes. Långström et al. (2015), in a nationwide data linkage study with multigenerational family registers, examining sexual offending in male relatives, found that genetic factors explained 40% of the liability to sexual offending (non-shared environment explained 58% and shared environment 2%), with a greater genetic contribution for child sexual offending (46%) compared to rape of an adult (19%). Alanko et al. (2013), in a study of male twins and their male siblings in a population-based Finnish cohort, found that the variance in self-reported sexual interest in children attributable to heritability was 14.6%, also with nonshared environment accounting for most of the variance and but not shared environment. Alanko et al. (2016) further found several single-nucleotide polymorphisms (SNPs) linked to androgen, estrogen, prolactin, corticotropin, serotonin, and oxytocin were associated with self-reported sexual interest in children, but only before controlling for multiple testing. But Jakubczyk et al. (2017) failed to find an association between a history of a sexual offense and the distribution of genotypes or alleles in several analyzed polymorphisms, linked to neurotransmitters (dopamine, serotonin, monoamine oxidase A, and brain-derived neurotrophic factor). So, there is no definitive evidence regarding specific candidate genes yet and it is highly likely that multiple different genes are involved. It has also been suggested that epigenetics, how cells control gene activity without changing the DNA sequence of genes, is likely to play a role, explaining how an environmental factor (such as adverse childhood experiences) can affect gene expression (Jordan et al., 2020). Kruger et al. (2019) found evidence that epigenetic regulation of the androgen system, as indicated by methylation of the androgen gene, was altered in child sexual offenders, but not related to pedophilia per se.

13.4.1.2 Structural and Functional Brain Abnormalities

Some early studies found volume reductions in brain regions relevant to sexual behavior (amygdala, hypothalamus, limbic gyri, orbitofrontal cortex, ventral striatum, and insula) in pedophilic compared to non-pedophilic men, but did not distinguish between pedophilia and child sexual abuse, and all subjects had committed offences (Schiffer et al., 2007; Schiltz et al., 2007). More recent research has found that the brains of men sexually attracted to children are very similar in structure to those of men attracted to adults (Jordan et al., 2017; Mohnke et al., 2014; Tenbergen et al., 2015), and that brain abnormalities are related to child sexual abuse not pedophilia (Lett et al., 2018; Schiffer et al., 2017), likely reflecting deficient inhibitory control rather than sexual interest in children. So early magnetic resonance imaging studies (Cantor & Blanchard, 2012; Cantor et al., 2008) indicated decreased white matter generally, but perhaps specifically in the superior fronto-occipital fasciculus and the right arcuate fasciculus, confirmed with more sensitive diffusion tensor imaging (Cantor et al., 2015). But early findings of reductions in grey matter (summarized by Mohnke et al., 2014) have not been confirmed.

In a similar vein, functional imaging studies reveal diminished fronto-limbic functional connectivity at resting state is associated with child sexual offending rather than pedophilia (Kärgel et al., 2015; Kneer et al., 2019), linked to impaired inhibitory control, as also seen in other offenders (Rosell & Siever, 2015). Another area of functional imaging research has examined the hemodynamic brain responses to sexual stimuli in pedophilia, showing differences in activation of sexually relevant brain regions in pedophilic offenders (Sartorius et al., 2008; Schiffer et al., 2008; Walter et al., 2007), and that people with pedophilia show similar brain activation as healthy subjects while watching their preferred sexual stimulus (i.e., children rather than adults; Fonteille et al., 2019; Polisois-Keating & Joyal, 2013). Functional imaging with subliminally presented stimuli, that are not consciously perceived, has shown a high level of discrimination between pedophilic and non-pedophilic men, with both sexual (Ponseti et al., 2012) and face (Ponseti et al., 2016) images.

Cantor et al. (2016) demonstrated increased functional connectivity in the default mode network (areas of the brain that are activated when people are not engaged in any specific cognitive task, but rather are letting their minds wander at rest), with regional increases and decreases in the frontoparietal network in pedophilic sex offenders compared to non-sexual offenders and non-offenders. Most of these regions are known to respond to sexually relevant stimuli. Cantor et al. (2016) proposed a pattern of abnormal connectivity, rather than lack of connectivity, as a neuroanatomic substrate of pedophilia. In keeping with this, Cantor et al. (2015), using diffusion tensor imaging, found highly focused differences related to participants' genital responses to sexual depictions of children, but not to measures of psychopathy or to childhood histories of physical abuse, sexual abuse, or neglect, which they suggested confirmed pedophilia is characterized by neuroanatomical differences in white matter microstructure, over and above any neural characteristics attributable to psychopathy and childhood adversity.

Another area of functional imaging research relates to response inhibition (Habermeyer et al., 2013), with Kärgel et al. (2017) finding increased inhibition related activity in left posterior cingulate and left superior frontal cortex, areas associated with effective cognitive functioning in non-offending pedophiles compared to those who had offended. This fits with findings from neuropsychological studies (see below) demonstrating executive dysfunction associated with offending but not with pedophilia itself.

Studies using electroencephalography (EEG) have shown findings in keeping with failure of rapid attentional capture by adult erotic stimuli in pedophilic men (Knott et al., 2016), but that response inhibition, processing of stop-signals, and error detection were not necessarily impaired in child sex offenders although they may allocate less cognitive resources to the evaluation of committed errors, which might reflect a reduced sense of responsibility (Rosburg et al., 2018).

13.4.1.3 Endocrine Factors and Neurotransmitters

Wong and Gravel (2018) conducted a meta-analysis of seven studies and did not find a significant association between testosterone levels and sexual offending. Kruger et al. (2019) assessed markers of prenatal brain androgenization, genetic parameters of androgen receptor function, epigenetic regulation, and peripheral hormones in four groups: pedophilic sex offenders, non-pedophilic child sex offenders, pedophilic non-offenders, and non-offending controls. Independent of their sexual preference, child sexual offenders showed signs of elevated prenatal androgen exposure compared with non-offending pedophiles and controls. The methylation status of the androgen receptor gene was also higher in child sexual offenders, indicating lower functionality of the testosterone system, accompanied by lower peripheral testosterone levels. Markers of prenatal androgenization and the methylation status of the androgen receptor gene were correlated with the total number of sexual offenses committed. There were lower, but normal, testosterone levels in child sexual offenders than non-offenders independent of pedophilic preference. So, there were alterations of the androgen system on a prenatal, epigenetic, and endocrine level, related to child sexual offending, not pedophilia per se, supporting theories of testosterone-linked abnormalities in early brain development in delinquent behavior, and suggesting possible interactions of testosterone receptor gene methylation and plasma testosterone with environmental factors.

Interestingly four case studies of men with pedophilia treated with testosterone lowering medication have shown decreased activation in brain regions linked with sexual functions, with both overt (Habermeyer et al., 2012; Moulier et al., 2012; Schiffer et al., 2009) and subliminal (Jordan et al., 2014) stimuli. These findings accord with findings that older men treated with androgen deprivation for prostate cancer show less attention to sexually provocative stimuli assessed through eye-tracking (Palmer-Hague et al., 2017).

In terms of neurotransmitters, a monoamine (dopamine and serotonin) hypothesis of paraphilias has been proposed (Kafka, 2003), but although alterations of central monoamine neurotransmission can impact human sexual functioning, there is no specific evidence of alterations or abnormalities in people with paraphilias or pedophilia. Ristow et al. (2018), using magnetic resonance spectroscopy, found reduced gamma-aminobutyric acid (GABA)/creatinine (Cr) concentrations in the dorsal anterior cingulate cortex in pedophilic sex offenders compared to non-offending controls, associated with self-reported lower self-control. As GABA is an inhibitory neurotransmitter, this may be related to disinhibition and reduced behavioral control in pedophilic sex offenders, but as with other findings is unlikely to be linked to pedophilia per se.

13.4.1.4 Neuropsychology

As described above (see Sect. 13.3.4.4) the findings for the relationship between IQ and pedophilia are inconsistent, with most studies being of child sexual offenders or pedophilic offenders. Kruger et al. (2019) found pedophilic sex offenders had higher IQs than non-pedophilic child sex offenders, and that pedophilic non-offenders had higher IQs than non-pedophilic non-offenders, albeit that differences were not significant, and all groups had mean IQs in the average intelligence range.

Leverett and Tenbergen (2023) summarized findings from neuropsychological studies of pedophilia, highlighting that differences in neuropsychological function reported are driven primarily by offense status (e.g., whether someone has committed child sex abuse), not by sexual preference, and observed differences occurred mostly for impulsivity, specifically response inhibition. So, people who sexually offend against children demonstrate impaired response inhibition (Joyal et al., 2007; Turner et al., 2018) regardless of whether they are pedophilic or not. Studies comparing pedophilic offenders to healthy controls have demonstrated no significant differences for set shifting, attention, impulsivity or verbal fluency (Cohen et al., 2002), more errors in cognitive flexibility and abstract reasoning (Kruger & Schifer, 2011), weaknesses in executive functioning (response inhibition, cognitive flexibility, and working memory tasks; Suchy et al., 2009). Studies comparing pedophilic and nonpedophilic child sexual offenders found the former were weaker in processing speed perhaps suggesting a more deliberate response style, reflecting greater self-monitoring required to conceal sexual attraction to children in everyday life (Suchy et al., 2009), weaker inhibition driven by slower response times but better inhibition accuracy, abstract reasoning, and planning abilities (Eastvold et al., 2011), better set-shifting, verbal memory, and response inhibition (Schiffer & Vonlaufen, 2011), and better set shifting, similarly poor response inhibition and weaker reflection impulsivity (Massau et al., 2017), but without a control group of nonoffending pedophilia, it is difficult to conclude whether these are associations with pedophilia itself, with committing child sexual abuse, or with any of the confounds of general criminality or incarceration (Turner & Rettenberger, 2020). Studies comparing contact and noncontact child sexual offenders (online offenders who have mostly committed CSAM offences and generally have higher rates of pedophilia) have found the latter are more intelligent (Babchishin et al., 2015) and perhaps have better response inhibition (Babchishin et al., 2022). No studies have examined the neuropsychological functioning of pedophilic nonoffenders or undetected pedophilic offenders (Leverett & Tenbergen, 2023). Leverett and Tenbergen (2023) described several threats to the validity of findings in the literature. Internal threats were how pedophilia was ascertained, how executive function was defined and measured, and use of convenience samples; with external threats being the use of appropriate control groups and highly selected samples volunteering for research.

Another area of neuropsychological research of relevance to pedophilia, but more relating to assessment and ascertainment than its etiology, relates to tests based on salient sexual stimuli interfering with attentional tasks (Zappalà & Santtila, 2021) or sexual preferences leading to implicit associations revealed by the speed of pairing responses (Gray et al., 2005). The latter has led to the development of Implicit Association Test (IAT) measures of sexual preference for children (Babchishin et al., 2013), which are starting to be used in clinical practice alongside other measures (Schmidt & Perkins, 2021; see Sect. 13.7 below).

13.4.1.5 Other Evidence of Neurological Perturbations

A number of research findings point to potential early neurological perturbations in pedophilic sexual offenders, although it remains unclear if they apply to pedophilia itself. Some of these perturbations may be due to genetic and/or early embryonic environmental factors which impact neurodevelopment and have been described in various neurodevelopmental conditions. Higher rates of *non-right-handedness* have been described in child sex offenders and pedophilic offenders (Blanchard et al., 2007; Bogaert, 2001). Fazio et al. (2014) found associations between non-right-handedness and pedophilia, and between ambiguous handedness and hebephilia, in a large sample of phallometrically assessed sexual offenders. Higher rates of *minor physical abnormalities (MPAs)* have been found in pedophilic offenders relative to rates in people with schizophrenia and healthy controls (Dyshniku et al., 2015). MPA indices were positively associated with indicators of pedophilia, including phallometric responses to sexual stimuli, number of child but not adult victims, and possession of child sexual exploitation material. Pedophilic offenders have been found to have *shorter stature* and leg length compared to teleiophilic ones (Fazio et al., 2017). Using Swedish population-based registers, Babchishin et al. (2017) found that two *perinatal factors*, being small for gestational age and a small head circumference, were associated with risk of sexual, and non-sexual violent offenses. In addition, *congenital malformations* were associated with sexual offending against children, but not against adults, although this association also reached significance for non-sexual violent offenses. Babchishin et al. (2019) also compared child sexual exploitation material offenders (CSEM), individuals who had additionally committed contact child sexual offenses (mixed offenders) and matched controls. Congenital malformations were the only pregnancy-related independent risk marker for mixed offenders, but not for CSEM-exclusive offenders. Blanchard et al. (2002) found that pedophilic offenders were more likely to have suffered significant *head injuries* leading to unconsciousness in early childhood.

13.4.1.6 Implications of Neurobiological Findings

Based on some of these research findings several *neurobiological theories* of pedophilic offending have been suggested (Jordan et al., 2020; Joyal, 2023). The frontal-dysexecutive theory suggests damage or dysfunction of the frontal lobe causing behavioral disinhibition, leading to pedophilic behavior (Graber et al., 1982). The temporal-limbic theory suggests that lesions of temporal and limbic brain regions, which play a major role in sexual functions, are associated with atypical sexual interests or hypersexual behavior (Kaplan & Krueger, 2010). The dual-dysfunctional theory merges these two, with hypersexual behavior caused by temporal deficits and behavioral disinhibition caused by frontal deficits leading to pedophilic behavior. But these theories explain hypersexuality and disinhibition, not pedophilic interests per se (Caffo et al., 2021; Jordan et al., 2020; Joyal, 2023; Kruger & Kneer, 2021).

It has been suggested that findings regarding intelligence, neuropsychological dysfunction, white matter abnormalities, early brain injuries, epigenetics, stature, handedness, MPAs and congenital abnormalities point to a *neurodevelopmental* explanation of pedophilia (Fazio, 2018). This posits that pedophilic sexual preference begins prenatally, with early neurodevelopmental abnormalities resulting from various prenatal events, which are further shaped by experiences in childhood development. Similar neurodevelopmental models have been supported for conditions like schizophrenia, autism, and attention deficit hyperactivity disorder (ADHD). However, given that most findings supporting such a hypothesis are from studies of child sexual offenders, and findings that non-offending pedophilia is not associated with similar factors, it may be premature to adopt this as a model of, or pathway to, pedophilia per se (Joyal et al., 2019). Indeed, a recent study found no evidence for relevant neurodevelopmental perturbations in a community sample of pedohebephilic men compared to teleiophilic men, although those who reported convictions were shorter and less intelligent (Jahnke et al., 2023).

Jordan et al. (2020) asked if the neurobiological research on pedophilia and child sexual abuse indicated that there were valid *biomarkers*, that could support diagnostic and risk assessment, and treatment evaluation (Prata et al., 2014). The ones suggested as promising for diagnosing pedophilia were those related to longer viewing or preferential processing of sexually preferred stimuli, such as functional MRI or cognitive tasks, so not etiologically relevant neurobiological factors. Factors indicative of impaired inhibitory control were suggested as risk markers, but are not specific to pedophilia or child sexual abuse. The conclusion was that "currently none of the above discussed parameters and approaches is ready to serve as a clinically applicable diagnostic, response, or predictive biomarker for pedophilia and child sexual offending".

13.4.2 Early Abuse and Sexual Behavior

There has been considerable interest in the relationship between perpetrating child sexual abuse or pedophilia on the one hand and being a victim of child abuse on the other, particularly sexual abuse (Seto, 2018), the so-called "abused abuser theory of pedophilia" (Freund & Kuban, 1994). Childhood sexual abuse is linked to many adverse later outcomes, including psychiatric disorders and offending, but it is often difficult to tease out the specific contribution of sexual abuse versus other childhood adverse experiences often associated with it (Papalia et al., 2018). The research evidence regarding childhood sexual abuse portending later sexual offending against children is mixed, with a significant association in cross sectional studies (even when controlling for relevant confounders), but a weak or nonspecific association in longitudinal studies, particularly those that did control for confounders (Papalia et al., 2018; Seto, 2018). It has been suggested that the abused-abuser link might be moderated by pedophilia. Studies have found experiencing childhood sexual abuse associated with adult sexual offending against children rather than adults, with physical abuse linked to the latter (Jespersen et al., 2009), and adolescents sexual offending against boy victims (Worling, 1995), multiple child victims (Renshaw, 1994), and younger victims (Kaufman et al., 1996). In a study of paraphilic sexual offenders, Lee et al. (2002) found childhood sexual abuse was specifically associated with pedophilia, and adult sexual offenders who had bed been sexually abused as children were more likely to report sexual attraction to children (Fedoroff & Pinkus, 1996). Using phallometry, sexually abused adolescent sexual offenders have shown greater arousal to children than to adults (Hunter & Becker, 1994), and in adults being the victim of extrafamilial childhood sexual abuse was related to sexual arousal to children (Lussier et al., 2005). In community samples childhood sexual abuse has been found to be associated with pedophilia and hebephilia (Bagley et al., 1994; Freel, 2003; Santtila et al., 2015; Turner & Briken, 2015; Wurtele et al., 2014), but not in all studies (Savoie et al., 2021). Jahnke et al. (2023), in another community sample, highlighted that men with perceived non-coercive childhood sexual experiences with adults (PNCSE-A) or peers (PNCSE-P) did not necessarily consider themselves to have been victims of abuse, and while pedohebephilic men reported more child sexual abuse, PNCSE-A showed an inconsistent relationship with pedohebephilia and with offending. Pedohebephilic men reported more PNCSE-P than teleiophilic men, and offending pedohebephilic men reported more sexual and non-sexual child abuse than those who were non-offenders. Studies of CSAM offenders show somewhat discrepant findings, in that CSAM offenders have higher rates of pedophilia but lower rates of childhood sexual abuse than contact offenders (Babchishin et al., 2015), although mixed CSAM and contact offenders were found to have higher rates of sexual abuse than CSAM only and contact only offenders (Alanko et al., 2017). In addition, a systematic review comparing intrafamilial and extrafamilial child sexual offenders found the former had higher rates of experiencing sexual abuse in childhood while the latter had higher rates of pedophilia (Seto et al., 2015).

Clearly only a minority of individuals who experience sexual abuse in childhood go onto develop a pedophilic sexual interest or to commit child sexual abuse, so there has been interest in what factors make the association stronger in terms of personal vulnerabilities, the nature of the abuse experienced, and factors in adolescence and adulthood. As pointed out by Seto (2018), the most obvious vulnerability is male gender, as more girls are sexually abused than boys, yet pedophilia is much more prevalent in males. Salter et al. (2003) found that additional childhood adversities were more common in sexually abused boys who went on to commit sexual offences, but such adversities are linked to offending generally, and are unlikely to be related to pedophilia itself. Two studies have suggested different critical age windows in terms of when the abuse occurred. Grabell and Knight (2009) found that adolescent sexual offenders who had been sexually abused between 3 and 7 years old were more hypersexual, but Ogloff et al. (2012) found that boys who were sexually abused aged 12 years old or above were more likely to commit sexual offences but not specifically child sexual offences. In terms of the nature of the child sexual abuse experienced, factors found to be associated with later perpetration of sexual offending (not necessarily against children let alone associated with pedophilia) include being abused by both men and women, having a female abuser, perpetrators using violence, chronic sexual abuse, penetrative abuse, the child being required to be actively involved, and becoming sexually aroused while being abused (Burton et al., 2002; Grabell & Knight, 2009; Hall et al., 1998; Salter et al., 2003). But being sexually abused by a male has been found to be associated with markers of pedophilia in sexual offenders (Nunes et al., 2013).

The potential mechanisms of the association between being a victim of childhood sexual abuse and developing pedophilia include social learning through imitation, conditioning through pairing of sexual arousal and the sexual abuse experienced, effects on attitudes and beliefs about adult-child sex, the development of precocious and hyper-sexuality, genetic factors when the abuser has been intra-familial, other associated sexual experiences such as sexual behavior with peers or siblings in the context of poor familial or guardianship regulation of sexual behaviour, or perhaps the psychodynamic concept of identification with the abuser.

There is some evidence that pedophilia is associated with early sexual experiences with peers (Jahnke et al., 2023), higher frequency of sexual engagement with peers during childhood (Santtila et al., 2010), and earlier age of first ejaculation and masturbation (Breiling et al., 2020; Gerwinn et al., 2018), suggesting that early sexual activities with peers and/or precocious sexualization could be etiological precursors of pedophilia. It has been suggested that this is a more plausible conditioning scenario for sexual arousal to children than sexual activity with an adult (Jahnke et al., 2023; Santtila et al., 2010; Seto, 2018). But it could be that common factors lead to both, or that the underlying propensity to pedophilia leads to precocious sexual behavior.

13.4.3 Psychodynamic Explanations

Psychodynamic concepts of pedophilia predominated for most of the twentieth century, and their vestiges are seen in concepts such as "regressed" and "fixated" pedophilia, which have been important starting points in the development of typologies of child sexual abusers (Cohen et al., 1969). Psychoanalysts described the importance of identification of narcissistic object choices as defenses against destructive wishes directed toward the object in "sexual perversions" (Arlow, 1967) and readily applied such concepts to pedophilia (Phelan, 2018). So concepts included choosing an immature sexual object due to an unresolved oedipal complex (Freud, 1905), early loss of the breast with avoidance of castration anxiety by choosing a love object like one's self (Cassity, 1927), "narcissistic object choice" (Fenichel, 1945), fear of pubic hair in women (Karpman, 1950), defence against introjective and projective anxieties of early childhood, to eliminate anxiety, guilt, and pain (Socarides, 1959), attaching the self to "mirroring and idealizable objects" to prevent fragile and destructive archaic self-objects (parental images) from fragmenting the self and object structure (Juda 1986), either oedipal or pre-oedipal forms (Socarides 1988), and differentiation between the "pseudo-neurotic" (regressed) and "invariant" (fixated) "paedophile", as forms of "primary paedophilia" (seen as a "perversion") versus "secondary paedophilia" (where "ego disintegration" occurs due to other psychopathology or stresses; Glasser, 1987). Such psychodynamic formulations of pedophilia are dated and largely unvalidated, although broader, and perhaps less hokey and contrived constructs, such as internalization of early relationships, fearing, and turning away from adult intimacy, having a non-threatening and perfect love object, the secret and shameful sexual world of an individual, and the importance of transference and countertransference in treatment, are potentially useful.

13.4.4 The Role of Temperament and Personality

Findings of research on personality and its relationship with pedophilia, pedophilic offending, and child sexual abuse were described in detail above, along with potential mechanisms for associations (see Sect. 13.3.1). To reiterate, personality disorders and maladaptive personality features are common amongst those with pedophilic sexual interests. Antisocial traits are more common in child sex offenders who are not pedophilic; while avoidant, dysthymic, and schizotypal traits are common in those who are. From a broader "big five" perspective, higher levels of emotional instability, introversion and conscientiousness have been found in online surveys of men in the community with pedohebephilia (Jahnke et al., 2019). However, samples of those who engage in CSA (not necessarily all with pedophilia) have found lower conscientiousness and higher impulsivity, along with higher neuroticism and lower extraversion (Dennison et al., 2001; Tenbergen et al., 2015). As noted above, dysfunctional personality features may share a common etiology with pedophilic sexual interests. They may predispose one to developing a sexual interest in children, or they may disinhibit acting on pedophilic sexual arousal and urges. Conversely, it may also be the case that having a pedophilic sexual preference predisposes one to developing maladaptive personality features by affecting the development of identity, intimacy, interpersonal functioning, and self-perception.

13.4.5 Social Learning and Conditioning

The role of learning in the development of pedophilia has been tied to the impact of being sexually abused, witnessing sexual abuse and/or early sexualization (Seto, 2018). Classical conditioning, in the context of preparedness, with the pairing of sexual arousal with children due to sexual abuse or early sexual experiences with peers, has been suggested then to be operantly and intermittently reinforced through masturbation and orgasm (Laws & Marshall, 1990). This formulation of the development and maintenance of pedophilic sexual interest is central to behavior modification techniques which may show some success in treatment (McPhail & Olver, 2020).

In terms of social learning, there are three potential mechanisms (Bandura, 1977; McGuire, 1964). Direct modelling where the person has direct experience of the behavior through sexual abuse or early sexual play with other children; vicarious learning through observing or hearing about sexual behavior with children in one's environment or through pornography; and symbolic learning through imagining sexual scenarios with children.

The abused-abuser hypothesis has some empirical support (see above) and points to the potential role of both social learning and conditioning but given that most victims of sexual abuse do not develop pedophilia or commit sexual abuse, other factors must mediate or influence the social learning and conditioning process.

13.4.6 Adolescence and the Emergence of Pedophilic Sexual Interests

Adolescence is a crucial step in physical, psychological, and social sexual development, and most individuals with pedophilia describe sexual interest in children commencing in early adolescence. In vulnerable and predisposed individuals, which could be due to neurobiological factors and/or childhood sexual abuse/experiences, it has been suggested that problems negotiating sexual, relational, behavioral and intimacy development in adolescence may lead to paraphilias, including pedophilia, and sexual offending, including child sexual abuse (Marshall & Barbaree, 1990). Preparedness, sexual experiences in early adolescence, reinforcement through masturbation and emerging sexual behavior, difficulties with separation-individuation, and the impact of developing peer relationships may all be important factors.

13.4.7 Proximal Factors in Enacting Behavior

Factors relevant to whether someone with a pedophilic sexual interest actually manifests pedophilic behavior can be more distal and longstanding trait factors (such as personality factors and frontal dysfunction as outlined above) or state factors (such as disinhibition by alcohol and access to unsupervised children; Seto, 2019). Such factors are not etiological in terms of pedophilia, are shared with non-pedophilic sexual abuse, but are of relevance to the etiology of child sexual abuse and are important considerations in treatment and risk management. Potentially important, and overlapping, proximal factors include sexual preoccupation, heightened sexual arousal, negative emotions (anxiety, depression, anger), using sex to cope with negative emotions or situations, other dysfunctional coping such as drinking/taking drugs, relationship problems and breakdown, loneliness, withdrawal and isolation, increased use of pedophilic fantasy, having and/or seeking proximity to children (Babchishin et al., 2023; Nitsche et al., 2022). Different factors may be relevant to those who act situationally, impulsively, opportunistically, or planfully, who may be regarded as having different pathways, distally and proximally, to perpetrating child sexual abuse (Ward et al., 1995, 1998; Ward & Hudson, 2000; Ward & Siegert, 2002).

13.4.8 Integrated Models

There are several etiological models of child sexual offending, in most of which sexual interest plays an important role (Gannon, 2021; Seto, 2018), and typologies of child sex offenders all give prominence to differentiating individuals with pedophilia, sometimes described as fixated or preferential, from individuals without such a sexual preference (Knight et al., 1989; Knight & King, 2012, Lanning, 2010; Lim et al., 2021). But etiological models of child sexual abuse do not consider why and how pedophilic sexual interest develops, and there are few that specifically consider pedophilia (Gannon, 2021; Seto, 2018; Smid & Wever, 2017). In Seto's (2019) Motivation Facilitation Model (MFM) of child sexual abuse, pedophilia is considered a causal paraphilic motivator, which leads to sexual abuse in the context of state or trait facilitating factors, depending on situational context. Smid and Wever (2017, 2019) developed an incentive motivational model, in which pedophilia arises from a positive appreciation of a prepubescent child, triggering sexual arousal. This is partly evolutionarily determined but also shaped via learning and operant conditioning. Sexual arousal is seen as an emotional response, amplified by other emotions via 'excitation transfer' (Zillmann, 2008). So, pedophilia develops through experiencing endearment towards children which transfers prompting a sexual arousal response, particularly in overinhibited individuals. The emotionally stimulating experience of the child is transferred to and revisited for sexual arousal, leading to pedophilia through operant conditioning.

Quinsey and Lalumière's (1995) evolutionary account posits that men have a series of evolutionarily determined independent sexual preference brain "modules" to detect gender, youthful vigor, and physical build indicating sexual maturity (e.g. waist to hip ratio) to confer reproductive advantage. In pedophilia the physical build/sexual maturity module fails leading to a disconnection between youth and sexual maturity, so prepubescent children become attractive because the man sexually prefers the youthful characteristics (e.g., smooth flawless skin) without a module signaling sexual maturity.

Seto (2018) suggested there were two main approaches to explaining pedophilia, the first neurodevelopmental (encompassing many of the neurobiological factors described above), and the second behavioral (related to problems with sexual and social development, with learning a central mechanism). He emphasized that none of these were deterministic, that a number of risk factors influenced the probability of developing and acting on pedophilia, and that neurodevelopmental predisposition likely interacted with activating unusual early experiences. He suggested that both vulnerability and activation were necessary to develop pedophilia, explaining why most predisposed individuals, and most individuals with experience of sexual abuse or precocious sexualization do not develop pedophilia.

Gannon (2021) proposed a *Compositional Explanatory Theory of Pedophilia (CEToP)* using the Phenomena Detection Method of Theory Construction (Ward & Clack, 2019). Her 'explanatory target' was pedophilia conceptualized as a sexual interest in or sexual preference for prepubescent children, with the latter referring to a more powerful and extreme form of the former. The 'composition' of pedophilia describes the constellation of factors that constitute this sexual interest or preference from biological, environmental, neurological, and psychological domains. The CEToP suggests two 'pedophilia pathways', an environmental one and a biological one, which are not mutually exclusive, although one or other tends to predominate in an individual. Each pathway has stages of early development (early in childhood) and sexual orientation development (later in childhood and in adolescence). Foetal and childhood neurodevelopment may lead to an individual being biologically predisposed or not (in the environmental pathway) in terms of their early development. At the next stage in the environmental pathway, despite lacking biological predisposition, sexual and social experiences via learning impact emerging sexual orientation, and the person develops a sexual interest in children. At this stage of the biological pathway biological and neurological, including environmental-epigenetic processes, impact emerging sexual orientation leading to a sexual preference for children. Individuals on the environmental pathway develop non-exclusive or somewhat preferential sexual interest in children, while those on the biological pathway develop a strong preference for or exclusive sexual interest in children. It is suggested that late onset 'acquired pedophilia' is a late onset biological pathway to pedophilia. Gannon (2021) emphasized that throughout both pathways there are continued interactions between environment and biology. Although this model provides a very useful attempt to draw together etiological factors in a specific model of pedophilia, accounting for different factors (and their interactions) and degrees of pedophilic preference, it may be premature to infer a neurodevelopmental pathway to pedophilia as opposed to pedophilic behavior (Joyal et al., 2019), and, although clearly not Gannon's intention, may foster a belief in psychological and biological types of pedophilia, not necessarily supported by the literature, and a lack of integration between biological, psychological and social factors in individual cases.

In summary, the literature and available evidence strongly suggests that there are two primary pathways towards developing pedophilic sexual interests. One of these results in a sexual orientation to prepubescents that can be described as a genuinely exclusive form of pedophilia. The other pathway results in varying degrees of pedohebephilic interest that can be viewed as genuinely paraphilic and is developed in a similar way to other paraphilic disorders. Figure 13.1 presents a schematic metamodel that describes these pathways and a continuum from exclusive teleiophilia to

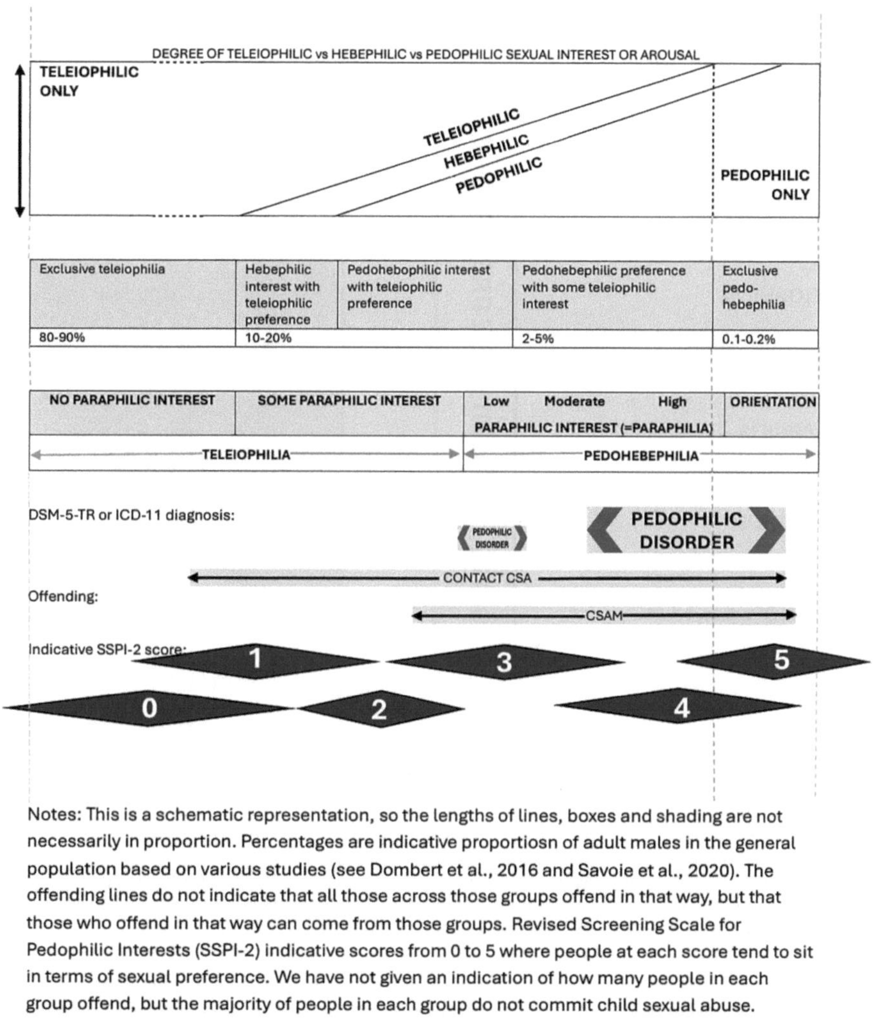

Fig. 13.1 Schematic meta-model of pedohebephilia, as both a sexual orientation in some people and a paraphilia in others. Notes: This is a schematic representation, so the lengths of lines, boxes and shading are not necessarily in proportion. Percentages are indicative proportion of adult males in the general population based on various studies (see Dombert et al., 2016; Savoie et al., 2020). The offending lines do not indicate that all those across those groups offend in that way, but that those who offend in that way can come from those groups. Revised Screening Scale for Pedophilic Interests (SSPI-2) indicative scores from 0 to 5 where people at each score tend to sit in terms of sexual preference. We have not given an indication of how many people in each group offend, but the majority of people in each group do not commit child sexual abuse

exclusive pedohebephilia. This figure also demonstrates where these various sexual interests are most likely to overlap with forms of offending behavior and indicate where scores on the Revised Screening Scale for Pedophilic Interests (SSPI-2; see below) are likely to be found. Figure 13.2 provides a further schematic

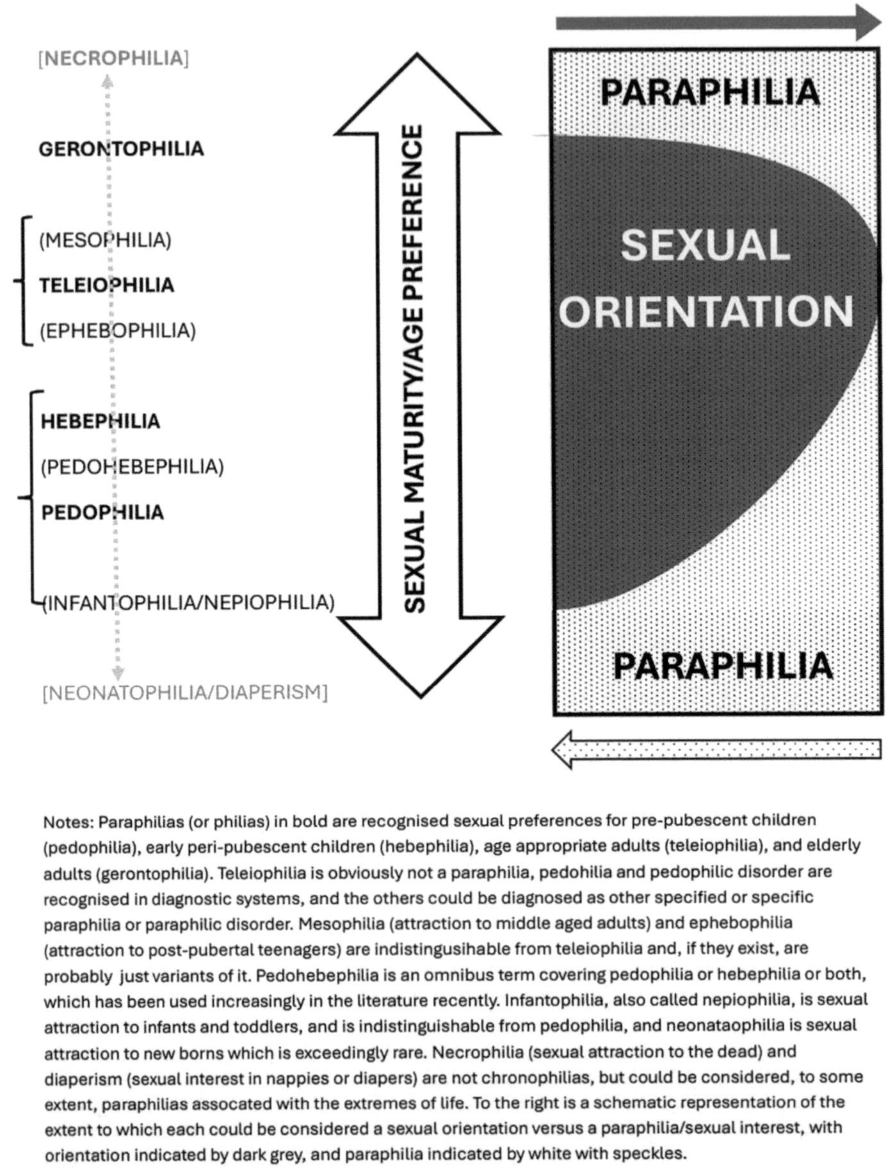

Fig. 13.2 Chronophilias: sexual maturity/age preference as sexual orientation or paraphilia. Notes: Paraphilias (or philias) in bold are recognised sexual preferences for pre-pubescent children (pedophilia), early peri-pubescent children (hebephilia), age appropriate adults (teleiophilia), and elderly adults (gerontophilia). Teleiophilia is obviously not a paraphilia, pedohilia and pedophilic disorder are recognised in diagnostic systems, and the others could be diagnosed as other specified or specific paraphilia or paraphilic disorder. Mesophilia (attraction to middle aged adults) and ephebophilia (attraction to post-pubertal teenagers) are indistingusihable from teleiophilia and, if they exist, are probably just variants of it. Pedohebephilia is an omnibus term covering pedophilia

representation of the extent to which the various chronophilias can be viewed as a sexual orientation or as a paraphilia.

13.5 Prevalence and Association with Offending

It is challenging to ascertain the prevalence of pedophilia and pedophilic disorder in the general population. Although there have been many studies examining rates of child related sexual thoughts and/or behaviors in community samples, different methods and criteria have been used. In a systematic review, including 30 studies from 1980 to 2020, Savoie et al. (2021) found a high risk of bias and poor external validity. Bearing this in mind, mean rates of sexual interest in pre-pubescent children (under 14 years old) were 2.1–7.0% and in pubescent children (14–16 years old) were 2.6%; for sexual fantasies 11.5% for prepubescent and 33.2% for pubescent; for masturbation to fantasies 2.9% for prepubescent and 2.6% for pubescent; for hypothetical sexual contact (if guaranteed not to be discovered) 3.4% with a prepubescent or pubescent child; and, for actual contact 7.3% with a prepubescent or pubescent child, but 2.0% excluding a highly biased outlying study. Putting all of the various elements together, they reported rates of 12.8 and 24% for sexual interest in prepubescent and pubescent children respectively, with correlates of these including male gender, adverse childhood experiences, distress and mental health problems. But given the methodological problems, the bottom line was that the rate of sexual interest in children was anywhere between 2 and 24%. These definitions do not map neatly on to pedophilia or pedophilic disorder. Seto (2018) estimated that the rate of pedophilia in men was probably about 1% and no higher than 3%, so the rate of pedophilic disorder, being lower as there must also be distress, impaired functioning or harm caused by the sexual interest in children, would likely be somewhere between 0.5 and 2.0%. It is even more difficult to estimate the rate of hebephilia in the community, but it is likely the same as or slightly higher than pedophilia, but will also overlap with pedophilia, so the rate of pedohebephilia is less than the sum of the two and perhaps 2–5%. As with most atypical sexual interests, rates are higher in men than women (Joyal et al., 2015; Joyal & Carpentier, 2017). For example, Joyal et al. (2015) found 1.8% of men and 0.8% of women stated that they had sexual fantasies about children under the age of 12 during their lives. Rates of pedophilic and hebephilic sexual interest and behavior are unsurprisingly high amongst MAPS and self-presenting people who are concerned about their sexual thoughts

Fig. 13.2 (continued) or hebephilia or both, which has been used increasingly in the literature recently. Infantophilia, also called nepiophilia, is sexual attraction to infants and toddlers, and is indistinguishable from pedophilia, and neonataophilia is sexual attraction to new borns which is exceedingly rare. Necrophilia (sexual attraction to the dead) and diaperism (sexual interest in nappies or diapers) are not chronophilias, but could be considered, to some extent, paraphilias assocated with the extremes of life. To the right is a schematic representation of the extent to which each could be considered a sexual orientation versus a paraphilia/sexual interest, with orientation indicated by dark grey, and paraphilia indicated by white with speckles

and/or behavior towards children, about two thirds to three quarters of whom are pedophilic and a third to a quarter hebephilic (Beier et al., 2015; Lievesley & Harper, 2021).

Between a third and three quarters of those who commit sexual offences against children are likely to be pedophilic (Seto, 2018), with most studies finding the rate to be around a half. In a recent study of a large sample of incarcerated sexual offenders in Austria, diagnosed according to DSM-5 (2013) using semi-structured interviews, of the 671 offenders against children, 67.1% had pedophilic disorder, of whom 20.9% preferred boys, 64.7% preferred girls, 14.4% had no gender preference, and 14.0% were exclusively attracted to children. Two percent of the 675 offenders against adults had pedophilic disorder, probably similar to the rate in males generally. Significantly higher rates of pedophilia have been reported in those who commit CSAM offences, ranging from two thirds to three quarters of individuals (Babchishin et al., 2015; Henshaw et al., 2018; Seiser et al., 2023; Seto et al., 2006). There have been few studies of online solicitation offenders, but Seto et al. (2012) found only 1.4% self-reported pedophilia (compared to 44.7% of CSAM and 13.2% of contact CSA offenders), while 30.0% self-reported hebephilia (compared to 52.6% of CSAM and 7.9% of contact CSA offenders), with a rate of pedohebephilia of 30.0% (compared to 65.8% of CSAM and 21.1% of contact CSA offenders). At the other extreme, rates of pedophilia in those who commit child sexual homicide are similar to those in contact CSA offenders, and unsurprisingly higher than in those with adult victims, with rates ranging from a third to a half of cases, and comorbid pedophilia and sexual sadism in a quarter to a half of cases (Beauregard et al., 2008; Chopin & Beauregard, 2019; Darjee & Baron, 2018; Page et al., 2023; Proulx et al., 2018; Ricono-Kaufhold et al., 2024; Spehr et al., 2010). Most serial sexual murderers of younger children are highly sexually sadistic and pedophilic, and have high levels of factor 1 (exploitative, manipulative, callous, lacking empathy) or just facet 2 (callousness and detachment) of psychopathy, a combination which thankfully occurs very rarely (Borowski, 2014; Wyre & Tate, 1995).

13.6 Special Groups

In this section, we describe various pedophilic and non-pedophilic motivations for CSA and provide an overview of typological systems that can assist in the assessment and formulation of those that commit such offences. These will be examined in detail. Those who engage in CSAM, Minor Attracted Persons (MAPs), and Non-Offending Minor Attracted Persons (NOMAPs) will also be examined, and the presence of pedophilic sexual interests amongst young people and females will be reviewed.

13.6.1 Child Sexual Abuse

As noted above, up to half of those that sexually victimize children are motivated by pedophilic sexual interests. Indeed, it is an unfortunate reality that adult males will engage in sexual behavior with prepubescent or pubescent children for a variety of reasons, only one of which is an atypical sexual interest in children. From a pragmatic clinical forensic perspective, identifying the motive for CSA, and identifying the presence of pedophilic or hebephilic sexual interests, is important for formulation, treatment planning, management, and risk assessment. To this end, a variety of typological systems have been developed over the past five decades to assist practitioners and researchers in identifying the motives behind child sexual victimization.

It must be stressed that those who sexually victimize children that are motivated by pedophilia or hebephilia are no worse or better than those who sexually victimize children for other motivations. Regardless of the behaviors exhibited by the child, or the motivation of the offender, every time an adult engages in sexual activity with a child, the adult is an offender and the child is a victim (Lanning, 2010). Without being cognizant of this, clinicians and investigators can significantly add to the subsequent shame, guilt, and embarrassment that victims of these offences can experience later in their lives.

13.6.1.1 Early Typological Systems

It is perhaps important to note that early typological systems made a clear distinction between *Fixated* and *Regressed* offenders. As the name suggests, fixated offenders have a long-standing sexual preference for children. Early descriptions of the term suggested that the offender had become stuck at an early stage of development, which was why very early typologies often focused on the immaturity of the offender. In contrast, regressed offenders regress to earlier stages of development and turn to children at times of stress. The vast majority of published typologies of child sexual offenders make this distinction, even if they use different terms and sometimes add additional types. For example, Groth (1981) described a typology with five groups in two major categories: *Child Molesters (fixated or regressed)* and *Child Rapists (anger, power, or sadistic)* with the latter groups essentially mirroring the three-fold typology of rape described in Groth and Birnbaum (1979). This distinction between paraphilic and non-paraphilic offenders has also been described for sexual offence behaviors in general, albeit using different terminology. For example, Dietz (1983) distinguished between *Preferential* sexual offenders who have paraphilic sexual interests, and *Situational* sexual offenders who offend in the context of intoxication, stress, or non-paraphilic mental disorders. Similarly, Hazelwood and Warren (2000) made a distinction between *Ritualistic* and *Impulsive* sexually violent offenders.

One of the earliest clinical attempts at categorizing those that sexually victimize children was described by Fitch (1962). This scheme involved five types, the first two of which appear analogous to the fixated/regressed distinction. It is these two types that comprised three-quarters of the sample of 147 males. The first type was the *Inadequate* who were described as being stuck at a childish level of psychosexual development and their offences were thought to be the acting out of infantile fantasies. The second type was the *Frustrated* whose offences were a reaction against frustration, whereby they would revert to primitive behaviors when insecure or rejected. It was noted that this type can be found in cases of incest. The third type was termed the *Sociopathic.* As the name suggests, these were individuals who had difficulties with social conformity and committed impulsive offences against complete strangers. They were not thought to be "sexual perverts" (p. 30). The fourth type was the *Pathological* who committed offences "as a result of psychosis, mental defect, organic impairment or premature senile deterioration" (pp. 30–31). A fifth *Miscellaneous* type was also described for isolated and impulsive acts that do not fit the other categories. Fitch (1962) noted that these categories were not mutually exclusive. Nonetheless, the majority of offenders in the sample could be classed as either the immature or frustrated types. Interestingly, 71% of the immature group targeted male victims, whilst 75% of the frustrated type targeted female victims. The immature group were also younger and had more previous sexual offences than the frustrated offenders. These findings are all congruent with what one would now expect to find amongst a group of pedophilic or hebephilic offenders in comparison to non-pedophilic offenders.

Interestingly, a paper from the same year by Kopp (1962) described two types of what they termed "pedophiliacs." These appeared analogous to those proposed by Fitch (1962), including a timid and immature type of offender and a more self-important type.

Gebhard and Gagnon (1964) presented a four-fold typology of offenders that targeted very young children aged 5 years or younger. The first type was termed *Pedophiles* who, perhaps strangely, may or may not prefer children (46%). The second was the *Mental Defectives* who did not have strong sexual drives but were the least capable of having adequate relationships with adults (25%). The third type was the *Sociosexually Undeveloped* who "turn to children as a last resort" (p. 579; no percentage was reported but would appear to be 19%). The final group were those that offend due to *Severe Alcohol Involvement*, although they had histories of other forms of criminality. This typology once again appears to include a largely preferential pedophilic type and three different situational types who were not offending due to a preference for children. Gebhard et al. (1965) followed this up with a highly descriptive typology 1 year later that simply identified groups based on heterosexual or homosexual victims, aggressive or non-aggressive offence behaviors, and the age of the victims (0–11 and 12–15). However, there were a range of sub-types within the various types.

Prentky and Burgess (2000) provided a detailed overview of child molester typologies and concluded that most included variants of three types. The *Fixated* type with an exclusive sexual preference for children; a *Regressed* type who regresses in response to severe stress; and an *Exploitative* or *Sociopathic* type who exploits children because it is easy to do so.

There are currently a range of typological systems that practitioners and researchers can utilize to assist in understanding offence behavior and differentiating between pedophilic and non-pedophilic individuals who sexually victimize children. This section will focus on three typologies in particular that have seen research attention or applied forensic use in recent years: The Massachusetts Treatment Center Child Molester Typology (MTC:CM3/4; Knight et al., 1989; Knight & King, 2012), Lanning's (1986, 2001, 2010) motivational continuum typology, and Canter et al.'s (1998) behavioral typology. These have all built upon the precursor systems described above and suggested useful indications of varying motives. It will be seen that there are often considerable overlaps between the various types in these systems, suggesting substantial convergent validity despite the quite different ways that each was developed.

13.6.1.2 The Massachusetts Treatment Center Child Molester Typology (MTC:CM3 and MTC:CM4)

The Massachusetts Treatment Centre (MTC) has been a leading institution for the development of typologies for sexual offenders. Indeed, their rapist typology is currently in its fourth iteration and is the most validated, and arguably most used, typology of rapist offenders and behaviors currently available (MTC:R3/MTC:R4; see Knight, 2010; Knight and Sims-Knight, 2017; see also Knight, 1999; Knight & Guay, 2006; Knight & Prentky, 1990; Prentky & Knight, 1991). The child molester typology has followed the same dual strategy used for the rapist typology. This involves both deductive/rational and inductive/empirical approaches to develop, implement, validate, integrate, and revise the typology (Knight, 1988; Knight & Prentky, 1990). It is important to note that the MTC:CM typologies were developed on samples of child sex offenders that did not include those that had committed exclusively incest offences. While it could be argued that the overall motivations and behavioral patterns in the MTC:CM are likely to apply to incest offenders, at least at a macro level, Prentky and Burgess (2000) suggested that criteria for the various dimensions of fixation, social competence, and contact with children would have to be changed to some degree when applying the model to such offenders. To this end, they provided some guidance on how that might be achieved.

The initial paper that described the first version of the MTC:CM typology (MTC:CM1; Cohen et al., 1969) appears to be the first publication to use the term "fixated" when referring to those that sexually victimize children. While it referred to all offenders in their sample as "pedophiles," the three groups identified were the *Pedophile-Fixated, Pedophile-Regressed,* and *Pedophile-Aggressive*. An additional group of *Pedophile-Aggressive or Sadistic* was later added (Cohen et al., 1979). This reportedly had some reliability difficulties, such that it was revised. The second version, the MTC:R2 (Knight, 1988), involved several steps to classification. The first was differentiating between instrumental and expressive aggression. For those using instrumental aggression in their offences, there were two primary types, the *Object-Related* and *Exploitative.* These were differentiated based on the nature of their relationship with the victim, the nature of the sexual behavior, and importantly, whether the offending involved planning and seduction or impulsivity and deception. Those using expressive aggression were divided into *Non-Sadistic* and *Sadistic* types based on whether there was eroticized aggression. All four types were further subdivided into *Fixated* and *Regressed* types based on both the degree of focus on children and the offender's level of social competence. However, this was still found to have reliability difficulties and a further revision was necessary (Knight & King, 2012).

The MTC:CM3 (Knight et al., 1989) resulted in a much more reliable typology, but required two axes, such that the authors themselves considered it "clinically unwieldy" (Knight & King, 2012, p. 8). The first axis required a decision as to whether there was high or low fixation, with clear manualized criteria as to how to identify the degree of fixation. While dichotomized, the authors noted that fixation existed on a continuum. Those high in fixation had clear evidence that children were a central focus of thoughts and fantasies and the decision reflected the strength of pedophilic interest. Each group also had a low and high social competence subgroup, with clear criteria, such that fixation and social competence were now considered to be separate constructs. This resulted in four types in axis one based on the degree of fixation (high/low) and the degree of social competence (high/low).

Axis II of the MTC:CM3 involved decisions as to whether there was high or low contact with children in both sexual and non-sexual contexts. Those with high contact were divided into two types: *Interpersonal* and *Narcissistic*. The *Interpersonal* type engaged in non-genital non-orgasmic sexual behaviors with children, knew their victims prior to the offence, often had multiple contacts with the victim, and engaged in a large degree of planning. The *Narcissistic* type engaged in phallic sexual behaviors, often targeted stranger victims in single encounters, tended to have many victims, and engaged in little planning.

For those with a low amount of contact with children, a further distinction was necessary to differentiate between low and high physical injury. Both groups were further sub-divided into low and high levels of sadism. The low injury/low sadism group constituted the *Exploitative* type. These showed no evidence of aggression being eroticized, phallic sexual behaviors, stranger victims, and little planning. The low injury/high sadism group constituted the *Muted Sadistic* type. These offenders engaged in relatively little serious physical injury, but the aggression was eroticized and suggested sadistic fantasies (i.e., the presence of bondage, spanking, urination, feces, or ritualistic acts).

The high injury/low sadism group constituted the *Aggressive* type, characterized by a high degree of physical injury, phallic sexual acts, no evidence of sadism or eroticized aggression, usually stranger victims, and very little evidence of planning. The high injury/high sadism group constituted the *Overt Sadistic* type, characterized by a high degree of physical injury, high arousal or pleasure from putting the victim in fear or subjecting them to pain; infliction of force, violence or threats of violence increasing arousal, typically stranger victims, and a high degree of planning.

The most recent revision to the MTC:CM system (the MTC:CM4) is described in detail in Knight and King (2012). While the various types currently remain, the way that they related to each other changed. Perhaps the most important research finding that contributed to the revision was the identification of the high fixation/low social competence type in Axis I as a cluster of offenders with increased neurodevelopmental difficulties, increased sexual preference for children (both using phallometric assessment and self-report), and higher levels of sexualization. The totality of these results indicated that the high fixation/low social competence type constituted a taxon that was meaningfully differentiated from the high fixation/high social competence type and the two low fixation types. In essence, this type in particular would constitute those with a pedophilic sexual orientation that have previously been found to be a taxon. It could be hypothesized that the remaining three types in Axis I cover those with little sexual preference for children, and others that have a preference for children, but not the conglomeration of neurodevelopmental indicators found amongst the taxon of more "hard-wired" pedophilic sexual orientation.

Axis II has become considerably less unwieldy in the MTC:CM4. The high/low contact and low/high injury distinctions have been subsumed by an externalization/emotional dysregulation dimension that is best explained by reference to the lifestyle impulsivity/antisocial factor of the Psychopathy Checklist-Revised (PCL-R Factor Two). This results in a continuum of aggression that has three clusters. The *Interpersonal* and *Narcissistic* (high contact) types involve low aggression, the *Exploitative* and *Muted Sadism* (low contact) types involve moderate aggression, and the *Aggressive* and *Overt Sadistic* (low contact) types involve high aggression.

The MTC:CM4 brings the two axes together in a cautious but interacting fashion. It is noted that externalization/PCL-R factor two and the amount of contact with children are unrelated to both fixation and the neurodevelopmental perturbations of the taxon. Low contact with children and low social competence are related to higher externalization. Knight and King (2012) presented a three-dimensional model that includes high-to-low dimensions of fixation, social competence, and externalization. The first two are orthogonal to each other, as are fixation and externalization. However, externalization is correlated with social competence. The authors believe that this new conceptualization is more compatible with known etiological models, whilst allowing for both taxonic and dimensional distributions of the three contributing scales.

While the MTC:CM4 appears to be an important improvement over the previous MTC:CM3 structure, there has unfortunately been no published research in the past decade that has further explored the new structure or identified a neurodevelopmental scale or optimal cut-offs for the taxon. Nonetheless, the identification that the high fixation/low social competence type constitutes a taxon has resulted in some researchers using this type as a diagnostic criterion for sexual interest in children (Lehmann et al., 2014, 2022). Interestingly, Lehmann (2022) suggested that this type may contain a more severe group of offenders with pedophilic disorder, because using this group as a diagnostic criterion for pedophilic disorder required slightly higher cut-scores on a pedophilic screening scale than did clinical diagnosis or penile plethysmography (PPG). It is thus important to acknowledge that the taxon identified in the MTC:CM4 does not identify all pedophilic offenders, although it may identify those with a more severe "hard-wired" pedophilic orientation.

From a practitioner perspective, the lack of recent research on the MTC:CM4 does not obviate its use in forensic clinical practice. Indeed, the various types from the MTC:CM3 still remain valid and the new guidance regarding externalization (PCL-R Factor Two) and the important identification of the high fixation/low social competence type as a likely taxon provides useful information that can assist in identifying the most appropriate type, developing a feasible formulation, and deciding upon the correct diagnosis.

13.6.1.3 Lanning's Motivational Continuum Typology (1986, 2001, 2010)

Lanning's (1986, 2001, 2010; see also Davis, 2013; Oliva, 2013) motivational typology is a rationally-derived system based on his considerable experience as an expert in the sexual victimization of children at what was previously known as the FBI's Behavioral Science Unit. This typology initially divided those who sexually abuse children into four *Situational* types and three *Preferential* types. This macro distinction was consistent with the previous fixation/regression distinction. However, Lanning's typology evolved over time and in 2001 it was reconceptualized to envisage those who sexually victimize children, as well as sexual offenders in general, on a motivational continuum from the situational to the preferential. This acknowledges the fact that behavioral patterns amongst such offenders are not mutually exclusive and there can be multiple motivations for committing such crimes. It is thus a particularly useful typology in applied settings, as individuals can be considered at any point along the continuum. While initially developed for use by law enforcement professionals, it is also of considerable use by forensic mental health professionals. In our experience, the use of this continuum approach greatly assists with formulation and is easily communicated to other practitioners and legal professionals alike.

13.6.1.3.1 Situational Offences

Those offences towards the situational end of the continuum are thought to reflect basic physiological sexual needs such as lust, or non-sexual needs such as power or anger. Such offenders usually do not have a genuine sexual interest in children, but may molest or otherwise sexually victimize them for a number of often complex reasons. Their offending is often impulsive and opportunistic. Three major patterns of offence behavior have been identified at the situational end of the continuum: *Regressed*, *Morally Indiscriminate*, and *Inadequate*.

The *Regressed* pattern of behavior involves individuals who do not have a sexual preference for children, but who turn to them as a sexual substitute. This often occurs during times of stress and such offenders tend to have poor coping skills and low self-esteem. Children are chosen due to their availability. Accordingly, incest offenders can often, though certainly not always, be characterized in this fashion. This type utilized the same name as the classic regressed offender in early typologies, but did not posit the same narrow theoretical explanation for the regression.

The *Morally Indiscriminate* pattern of behavior involves the sexual abuse of children as simply another form of antisocial behavior in the offender's life. A diagnosis of antisocial personality disorder, and elevated levels of psychopathic personality features, are often found in such offenders. Victims are chosen due to vulnerability and opportunity. Force, lures, or manipulation may be used and the victims may be abducted. Pubescent children are thought to be particular targets of such offenders.

Those who engage in the *Inadequate* behavior pattern include an array of withdrawn and "unusual" individuals such as eccentric personalities, psychotic individuals, or those with an intellectual disability or senility. It is of course important to note that most people with these difficulties will not sexually abuse children. The inadequate offender does not have a sexual preference for children, but targets them because he finds them to be non-threatening. As such, they may also target the elderly as well. Lanning (2010) reported that sexually-motivated child murders reviewed and profiled by the FBI usually involved either the morally indiscriminate or inadequate patterns of behavior.

13.6.1.3.2 Preferential Offences

Those offences at the preferential end of the motivational continuum reflect deviant sexual needs, most obviously a sexual preference for children, although one type (the "diverse") is motivated by other forms of atypical sexual interest. Four major patterns of offence behavior have been identified at the preferential end: *Seduction*, *Introverted*, *Sadistic*, and *Diverse*.

As the name suggests, the *Seduction* pattern of behavior characterizes individuals who essentially engage with children by seducing and grooming them with affection, attention, and presents. These offenders are able to identify with their victims. They know how to talk and listen to children and often target those who are neglected. Indeed, they are very adept at identifying children who are in need of attention and affection. Over time they gradually lower the child victim's sexual inhibitions until they are willing to engage in sexual behavior because of the benefits that they are receiving. Such offenders may simultaneously abuse multiple victims. If threats or physical violence are used they are likely to be instrumental in nature and are made to avoid identification or disclosure. Such offenders can abuse the same child for lengthy periods of time and may even find it difficult to get the child to leave when they age and become too old for the offender.

The *Introverted* behavioral pattern characterizes offenders who have a sexual preference for children but essentially lack the interpersonal skills required to successfully groom and seduce them. Such offenders are similar to the inadequate situational offender, but they do have deviant sexual preferences. As such, their selection of child victims is more circumscribed and predictable across multiple offences. The lack of interpersonal skills means that these offenders engage in minimal verbal communication with their victims, who are often strangers. Such offenders are more likely to attend playgrounds or other areas where children gather.

The *Sadistic* behavioral pattern involves offences in which the child's response to the infliction of suffering, humiliation, or pain is sexually arousing. Essentially, these offenders would meet formal diagnostic criteria for both Pedophilic Disorder and Sexual Sadism Disorder. Thankfully such offenders are rare. Perhaps unsurprisingly, they are more likely than other preferential offenders to abduct and murder their victims.

The *Diverse* behavioral pattern was previously termed 'sexually indiscriminate' and was initially thought to be a situational type as such offenders do not have a preferential sexual interest in children. Nonetheless, under the reconceptualized motivational continuum such offences are now situated toward the preferential end because their diverse sexual behaviors reflect sexual deviance and they may meet criteria for several paraphilic disorders. Indeed, the facetious term 'try-sexual' is also used to describe such offenders because they are indiscriminate in their sexual interests and willing to try a wide variety of sexual behaviors. There is some similarity to the morally indiscriminate situational offending pattern, however the diverse offender has deviant and indiscriminate sexual interests, but is often more discriminating in their non-sexual behaviors.

Given the range of behavioral patterns at either end of the continuum, it is perhaps clear that further dimensions beyond the situational-preferential dimension are needed for a truly comprehensive and academically rigorous typological system (and one may hypothesize that developments in the MTC:CM4 typology, as noted above, may be relevant in this regard). Nonetheless, from a pragmatic practitioner perspective, Lanning's typology provides a rich behavioral framework to consider the various motivations of those who sexually victimize children, and to assist in identifying those that are pedophilic or hebephilic. The various types on either side of the continuum reflect the marked heterogeneity of those who sexually victimize children. Furthermore, the notion of a motivational continuum is particularly useful in clinical practice as the need to awkwardly force offenders into discrete categories is removed. Indeed, some offenders can be properly envisaged as being toward the middle of this continuum, with a preferential sexual interest in children as well as an awareness of situational opportunities to offend.

13.6.1.4 Behavioral Typology

The behavioral typology of Canter et al. (1998) was developed using a form of non-metric multidimensional scaling (smallest space analysis) on 19 offence behaviors from 97 recorded child sexual offences in the United Kingdom. In hypothesizing the behavioral consistencies that may be found, they explicitly noted both Lanning's early typology and the MTC:CM3. Canter et al. (1998) found three themes of offence behavior with a common core behavior of the child being alone at the time of the offence which was found in more than 70% of cases. The first theme was *Intimacy* which was characterized by the behaviors promise of gifts/treats, reassurance, affection, desensitization, oral sex by offender on victim, and kissing. This behavioral them shows a clear overlap with Lanning's Seduction type of preferential offender. The second theme was *Aggression* (also known as *Hostile*; Alison et al., 2005), which was characterized by violence beyond level necessary, initial force used by offender, offender not deterred by victim reaction, threats of violence to victim, sexual or abusive language used, and anal penetration. The third behavioral theme was *Criminal-Opportunism* (also known as *Controlled*; Alison et al., 2005), which was characterized by stranger victim targeted, offence committed outdoors, one-off offence, and offender intoxicated at time of offence.

Canter et al. (1998) noted that there was a degree of behavioral similarity between the Aggressive and Criminal-Opportunism themes. Indeed, the behaviors "initial force" and "intoxication" appeared to be variables that were so close to the regional boundary that they were considered to be boundary variables shared by both themes. In addition, the variables "offender ejaculation during offence" and "vaginal penetration" were situated on the boundary of the Intimate and Aggressive themes, shared by both, but showing otherwise very different behavioral repertoires.

In testing this empirically-derived framework, each offence in the sample was assigned to a behavioral theme if they had more behaviors from that theme than both others combined. Using this approach, 45% were classified as Intimate, 14% as Aggressive, and 18% as Criminal-Opportunist. A total of 23% were not definitively assigned, although 17 of the 22 unclassifiable cases were deemed to be Aggressive/Criminal-Opportunism "hybrids."

The behavioral model provides a further useful framework for differentiating individuals who sexually victimize children. The strong emphasis on offence behaviors makes the behavioral model useful in applied practice, either when used on its own or in conjunction with the other typology frameworks. It provides useful information as to the rarity of particular offence behaviors as well as an indication of which behaviors are most likely to co-occur in individual cases.[3]

While the behavioral model does not explicitly make the distinction between preferential and situational offenders as do other typologies, this can nonetheless be inferred to some degree from the behaviors comprising the three themes. Indeed, the authors noted that this model demonstrates "that paedophilia exists both as a pathology and a form of criminality" (p. 552). Moreover, and as noted above, the Intimate theme is analogous to Lanning's Seduction pattern and similar to the MTC:CM's Interpersonal or Narcissistic types. The Criminal-Opportunism theme is similar to Lanning's Morally Indiscriminate pattern and the MTC:CM's Exploitative type. Finally, the Aggressive theme is potentially similar to Lanning's Sadistic pattern and/or the MTC:CM's Aggressive or Overt Sadistic types. As such, there is clear

[3] It should be noted that other behavioral models have been developed. For example, Lehmann et al. (2014) examined 424 cases of child sexual abuse in Germany and revealed four behavioral themes of *Fixation, Regression (Sexualization), Criminality,* and *(Sexualized) Aggression*. These also appear to have some clear overlaps with other typologies.

evidence of convergent validity between the three extant typological systems described here, despite the fact that they were developed in quite different ways, including a dual rational/inductive approach (MTC:CM3/4), a rational approach (motivational continuum), and a more empirical approach (behavioral model). As each model seems to provide slightly different insights into the behaviors and motivations of those that sexually victimize children, one could certainly use two or even all three to assist decision-making in the individual case.

13.6.2 Online Child Sexual Abuse

Since the late 1990s, with the emergence of public access to the internet, and faster, more powerful, and more sophisticated technology, there has been an exponential rise in the use of the internet and related technology to commit child sexual abuse (Henshaw et al., 2020). The most prolific activity is accessing, viewing, downloading, and sharing images and videos depicting child sexual abuse, or child sexual abuse material (CSAM) offences. However other behaviors include producing such material either through direct interaction with children or virtual interactions with children, communicating and interacting sexually with children perhaps with the intention of committing offline sexual abuse, live streaming the sexual abuse of children sometimes with the opportunity for remote viewers to direct the sexual abuse, and the use of the internet and technology in trafficking children for sexual abuse and sexual slavery. As technology accelerates and develops, so the landscape of online child sexual abuse changes, with recent developments and concerns centering around the role of artificial intelligence and virtual reality. There has been a proliferation of research on CSAM over the last two decades with a reasonable evidence base to inform aspects of practice. This is much less so for other types of online offending.

There are higher rates of pedophilia in CSAM offenders than in offenders who commit contact offences (Babchishin et al., 2015; Henshaw et al., 2018) with rates in contact offenders of up to a half and rates in CSAM offenders of over two thirds and often over three quarters (Henshaw et al., 2017; Seto et al., 2006). Offenders who commit both types of offences have similarly high rates of pedophilia as CSAM only offenders (Henshaw et al., 2018). Broadly, contact offenders are more likely to be antisocial, commit other offences, have attitudes that condone child sexual abuse, have poorer behavioral inhibition, and lack empathy; while those who commit CSAM offences are more likely to have problems with sexual regulation, emotional regulation, intimacy, self-esteem, and assertiveness. But those who do both have high rates of both those sets of characteristics, particularly pedophilia and antisociality (Babchishin et al., 2015; Henshaw et al., 2018). It has been suggested that viewing CSAM is a good marker for pedophilia (Seto et al., 2006) but is not in itself a risk factor for contact child sexual abuse. The latter is emphasized by the fact that despite having significantly higher rates of pedophilia, CSAM offenders are much less likely to reoffend than contact offenders, and CSAM offenders with no prior history of contact offending very rarely go on to commit contact offences (Eke et al., 2018; Elliot et al., 2019; Faust, et al., 2015; Seto & Eke, 2015; Seto et al., 2011; Savoie et al., 2022).

There is no convincing evidence that the proliferation of access to CSAM has led to an increased level of pedophilia or child sexual abuse. In fact, rates of contact child sexual abuse have reduced significantly over the last 30 years (Finkelhor, 2020). However, every CSAM image and video involves child sexual abuse, in jurisdictions where stories, cartoon images and artificially generated images are not illegal, so clearly prevention efforts, via reducing the behavior and law enforcement activity, is extremely important. In our view images, videos, stories and other material which do not involve real children at all in their production are probably not problematic, which may seem a very controversial statement. They may provide a non-abusive sexual outlet for people with a strong or exclusive sexual interest in children, and there is no evidence that exposure to such material desensitizes, leads to pedophilic sexual interest, or is a gateway to the sexual abuse of children. However, it is not yet known what the impact of such material on developing sexual behavior in children and adolescents is, where concerns are legitimate, but research evidence is scant.

There is some evidence that people who sexually solicit children online are more likely to be hebephilic or teliophilic than pedophilic (Seto et al., 2012), as most victims are teenagers, reflecting that older children are more active on social media, the internet and gaming platforms (Schulz et al., 2016, 2017), although the age of technological access and engagement is lowering. Seto et al. (2012) found that only 1% of solicitation offenders were pedophilic, whilst 30% were hebephilic, both lower than rates in CSAM offenders. Solicitation offenders have been found to have similar demographic and offence histories to CSAM offenders, although a high proportion, over a quarter, are female (Schulz et al., 2017). So unlike CSAM, pedophilia appears not to have a strong relationship with online solicitation of children, although there has been little research.

It is worth considering people who use child related materials for sexual stimulation, where the production of such material does not involve the sexual abuse of children in reality. Examples include cartoons, text-based stories, realistic images or videos generated by artificial intelligence, and anatomically correct child sex dolls. CSAM depicting real children involves children being exploited and abused, and accessing such material leads to further such exploitation and abuse by perpetuating the demand and market for such material. That is the primary and very legitimate justification for the prosecution and prevention of CSAM offending. Other purported justifications are that using such material leads to or reinforces pedophilic sexual arousal and interests, desensitizes the user and leads to more deviant arousal and behavior, and is a gateway to committing direct child sexual abuse. However recent research findings that a tiny minority of, if any, men who commit CSAM only offences go on to later commit contact child sexual abuse (Eke et al., 2019; Savoie et al., 2022), and that people who commit CSAM and contact offences usually commit contact offences first (Babchishin et al., 2022), bring such assumptions into question. In fact, most men with pedophilic sexual interests do not wish to cause harm to children, so do not commit contact sexual offences, and using child related sexual materials that do not involve sexual exploitation or abuse for their production may well be a non-abusive and non-harmful outlet for individuals who have a strong sexual attraction to children and minimal if any sexual attraction to adults. Our experience of working with such individuals, and the research evidence regarding CSAM, would, in our view, tend to support such conclusions. However, in many jurisdictions such material is viewed the same as CSAM depicting real children. There is a legitimate question as to whether this should be the case, and going further, whether using such material could prevent the use of material depicting real children and prevent contact sexual offending. A recent mixed methods study of teleiophilic and pedohephilic men who use anatomically correct sex dolls supports the latter hypothesis, challenging the view that such doll use is dangerously affecting human sexuality, rather suggesting they are used as a sexual outlet for potentially dangerous and illegal sexual fantasies (Desbuleux & Fuss, 2023). Relatedly it is important to note that as CSAM offending has escalated and diversified over the last 30 years (Westlake, 2020), there has been a reduction in contact sexual abuse (Finkelhor, 2020), and although one cannot conclude that the former has caused the latter, certainly the former cannot have fueled contact child sexual abuse, otherwise both would be escalating in parallel. In fact, the former probably reflects the unmasking of minor attracted persons in society who were relatively hidden before the internet became widely accessible, and the latter the general decline in crime and violence in westernized societies (Tonry, 2014).

13.6.3 Minor Attracted Persons (MAPs)

Rates of sexual interest in children in the general male population have been found to be between 2 and 24%, depending on definition, method of ascertainment and sample (Savoie et al., 2021). These rates do not necessarily indicate rates of pedophilia, as rates of sexual preference for children or exclusive sexual interest in children are lower (APA, 2022). The rate of pedophilic disorder in the general population has been estimated to be around 1% (Cantor & McPhail, 2016; Seto, 2018). In an online survey of a large sample of German males, Dombert et al. (2016) found that 5.5% had some sexual attraction to pre-pubescent children, but only 0.1% were exclusively sexually attracted to pre-pubescent children. In terms of behavior involving pre-pubertal children, 3.2% of men reported they had behaved in such a way, mostly through accessing CSAM (2.5%), although 1.5% reported sexual contact with children. Recently the concept of Minor Attracted Person (MAP) has been used increasingly (Sorrentino & Abramowitz, 2021). It was developed by and for people with a persistent sexual interest in children, most of whom do not commit offences, with the associated term NOMAPS for 'non-offending' MAPs. As the term MAP references adults attracted to children under the age of consent, not all MAPS are attracted to prepubertal children, so not all are pedophilic, although the vast majority are pedophilic or hebephilic. Virtuous Pedophiles (www.virped.org)

and B4U-ACT (www.b4uact.org) are internet-based organizations dedicated to supporting NOMAPs.

13.6.3.1 Characteristics of MAPS and NOMAPS

Grady and Levenson (2021) found the most common adverse childhood experiences (ACEs) in MAPs were verbal/emotional abuse and bullying by peers/siblings, rates of all ACEs except sexual abuse were much higher than seen in the general population, but compared to child sexual offenders MAPs had higher rates of emotional abuse/neglect and lower rates of sexual abuse and family dysfunction. Cohen et al. (2018) found that MAPs, regardless of whether they were NOMAPS, were more socially inhibited, had more cognitive distortions and experienced more sexual abuse than general population controls. But offending was associated with older age, longer duration of pedophilic attraction, more antisocial traits, greater attraction to boys, greater difficulty controlling their attraction, more positive attitudes toward adult-child sexual activity, prior mental health treatment, nonsexual offenses, and childhood sexual and nonsexual abuse. NOMPAS were more impulsive than controls. Culling (2018) also found that MAPs and convicted offenders presented with similarly high levels of cognitive distortions and this differed from non-MAP controls.

Suicidal ideation and acts are common in MAPS, seen in a third to a half of individuals, and particularly prevalent in 14–16-year-olds (B4U-ACT, 2011; Cohen et al., 2020; Levenson & Grady, 2019). Cohen et al. (2020) found suicidal ideation was not associated with history of sexually engaging with a child or contact with the criminal justice system. But it was correlated with young age, less education, prior mental health treatment, weaker attraction to adult women, history of sexual abuse in the participants' own childhood, and the psychosocial impact of perceived stigma against pedophilia. Stevens and Wood (2019) found high rates of addiction, anxiety, depression, self-harm, self-hatred, and suicidal thoughts and behaviors among MAPs, and Levenson and Grady (2019) found high rates of strong feelings of isolation and loneliness, extreme difficulty with concentration, significant anger and frustration, and struggling with feelings of detachment, which MAPS attributed to their minor attraction. Collins (2023) found MAPs tend to prefer avoidance techniques in potentially risky situation, utilizing complete avoidance or a buddy system. They experienced significantly more hopelessness and loneliness than non-MAPs, and less respect for authority.

Spriggs et al. (2018) found significant variability in perceptions of harm and of mitigating or aggravating factors in MAPS, concluding that understanding their subjective perspectives, range of attitudes, and issues they identify as pertinent is important for clinical efficacy in treating pedophilia. The heterogeneity of MAPS was explored by Stewart (2022), who developed a 'Vulnerability Typology'. Low vulnerability MAPs were largely healthy and unimpaired, moderate vulnerability MAPs displayed modest characteristic deficits, and MAPs in the high vulnerability group showed significant impairment for most measured vulnerability constructs across biopsychosocial and sexual factors. High vulnerability MAPs perceived themselves to pose the highest risk for acting, whereas lowest self-reported risk was found in low vulnerability MAPs. Use of maladaptive or adaptive coping strategies did not moderate the relationship between MAP clusters and self-perceived risk.

13.6.3.2 Stigma

Unsurprisingly MAPs are highly stigmatized, regardless of whether they have had sexual contact with a child. A public survey (Jahnke et al., 2015) found 39% believed that NOMAPs should be incarcerated, and 14% believed that they would be "better off dead." Pervasive societal misconceptions include that MAP sexual orientation is a choice, MAPs cannot resist their sexual urges, all MAPs have or inevitably will offend, MAPs will not respond to therapy, and MAPs are fundamentally predatory and immoral. An online psychoeducational text with the myths vs facts about MAPs increased rather than decreased stigma towards MAPS amongst members of the public in the USA (Jara & Jeglic, 2021). In a similar study in Australia McKillop and Price (2023) concluded educating the public may improve attitudes toward MAPs, but more knowledge is required on how to best disseminate messages to maximize impact. Lawrence and Willis (2022) were more optimistic in their study using a humanizing narrative (lived experience of an individual with sexual interest in children) and informative (fact-based information about pedophilia) anti-stigma interventions. Stigmatising and negative attitudes have also been found amongst professionals including clinical psychologists (Millar, 2022), primary medical, and mental health professionals (Lievesley et al., 2022), perhaps indicating a need for further training, focusing on increasing comfort around working with MAPs (Lievesley et al., 2022).

An important issue is the internalization of social stigma among MAPs with associated shame, guilt, hopelessness, and suicidal ideation (Grady et al., 2019; Lievesley et al., 2020), which may be associated with suppression of unwanted thoughts and a propensity to actively avoid children (Lievesley et al., 2020). In terms of labels, "minor-attracted person" and "pedophile/hebephile" were preferred by MAPs, in the context of themes of "contested self-labels," "person-first language and pathologizing sexuality/ identity," "stigma and shame," and "reclaiming the pedophile label," with difficulties associated with finding a non-stigmatizing label (Jahnke et al., 2022). Walker (2021) described the complex relationships between strategies for maintaining resilience to offending and strategies for maintaining emotional resilience in the face of ever-present societal stigma in MAPs. Such strategies introduced additional risks to physical or emotional health, especially when they involved seeking the help and support of others. Seeking support from friends and family involved the risk of suspicion and rejection, while seeking support from mental health practitioners exposed participants to additional risk to their wellbeing. Elchuk et al. (2022) found that loneliness and whether a person received a supportive response to a disclosure were important determinants of mental health in MAPS.

13.6.3.3 Barriers to Help Seeking

However, many MAPS express that they want help, to reduce the likelihood of offending and/or to improve their mental health, with barriers to help seeking including shame and stigma, accessibility and appropriateness of services, and the attitudes, knowledge and ability of professionals (Uzieblo & De Boeck, 2022). Moss (2019) found maladaptive coping decreased treatment motivation and this association was further intensified by higher levels of internalized stigma. Clinicians with forensic specialization expressed a higher willingness to provide treatment for MAPs compared with general clinicians and those with a sexology specialization, but there were no significant differences across clinician groups on explicit stigma, except for feelings of anger towards MAPs (Moss, 2019). More than half of social work students believed clients who identify as pedophiles must be automatically reported to the police, with implications for providers' understandings of the term "pedophile," and their knowledge of guidelines for when to break confidentiality (Walker et al., 2022). This was not significantly affected by taking ethics courses, nor courses that covered mandatory reporting guidelines. But contrarily, most did not think they had to report a client who had attractions to children, but had never committed an offense, most indicated a willingness to work with MAPs, and they indicated they wanted more information about MAPs and when to break client confidentiality in their study programs. Stigmatizing views amongst psychologists were associated with reduced support for the treatment of, willingness to work with, and more dehumanisation of MAPs (Millar, 2022). So professional practices around working with and service provision for MAPs are variable, with clinicians possessing low levels of knowledge about this population and unclear about treatment goals (Lievesley et al., 2022).

13.6.3.4 Support, Treatment, and Prevention

It is often assumed that the primary goal in intervention with MAPs is to prevent sexual offending by addressing criminogenic needs, as applied to those who have committed child sexual abuse. Stewart (2022) suggested criminogenic needs and destabilizing factors in domains of antisocial cognitions, deviant sexual interests, and psychosocial functioning may be relevant targets for prevention and wellness approaches among MAPs. An important issue in work with MAPs, and in prevention efforts, along with having professionals and services accessible and willing to do such work, is what the approach should be and what the focus of intervention should be.

In a study of treatment target prioritization amongst MAPs and professionals, Lievesley et al. (2023) (202found self-compassion drove many treatment targets prioritized by MAPs. They were typically focused on addressing mental health needs and treatment targets related to how to best live in a society that is heavily stigmatizing. The prioritization of such targets was predicted by lower levels of wellbeing and self-compassion, as well as more problem-focused coping. So those with lower levels of wellbeing and self-acceptance felt they needed the most support in relation to mental health concerns and ability to live with a stigmatized sexual attraction pattern. There was rejection of treatment targets related to controlling or changing of sexual attractions, probably due to the perceived immutability of sexual preference and being a group with good self-control. Sexual frustration was seen as a treatment target in those with better wellbeing perhaps indicating a secondary need after achieving self-compassion and self-acceptance. However, professionals highly prioritized all potential treatment targets, including criminogenic ones, probably reflecting confusion, lack of knowledge and lack of focus (Lievesley et al., 2022).

Lievesley and Harper (2022) suggested a desistance framework could help inform prevention, both in terms of improving mental health and prevention of sexual offending, with a wellbeing focus at the heart of preventative treatment for MAPs. This included decisive momentum and motivation when a person decides to seek help; rehabilitative approaches perhaps more focused on mental health, self-acceptance, and shame than on criminogenic needs; re-entry to and normalcy in society, including professionals not conflating minor attraction with child sexual abuse, and not fearing being reported for their attraction as opposed to actual abusive behavior. In a similar vein, Levenson and Grady (2019), based on their findings regarding ACEs, recommended a trauma informed approach for helping MAPs with their mental health and/or to reduce their risk of acting. Treatment and preventive interventions in practice will be considered further below

13.6.4 Young People

Most people who develop pedophilia and/or hebephilia describe sexual arousal to children emerging with developing sexual awareness in early adolescence, some describe an awareness of an attraction to prepubescent children before adolescence, but almost all have such fantasies and sexual attraction by early adulthood (Abel et al., 1985). However, adolescence is a period of dynamic transition with regards to sexuality, but also relationships, emotions, behavior and identity more generally. Sexual arousal, fantasy and masturbation emerge during this changeable and fluid period of discovery, shaped by the person's earlier development, family and peer environment, and sexual experiences, including abusive and precocious ones. In addition, adolescents tend to have higher levels of sexual arousal and sexual responsivity, and there is evidence that, as young as the age of seven, children can become aware of being attracted to others or behaviors, although this is not usually accompanied by sexual arousal. So, there can be sexual behaviors, including abusive and offending ones, some of which can appear paraphilic in nature, but which are not necessarily indicative of a longer standing or emerging paraphilic sexual interest, including apparently pedophilic or hebephilic ones. A degree of pedophilic or hebephilic sexual interest could be considered normal in 10–15-year-old boys and sexual play and exploration with peers is a normal part of human sexual development.

Therefore, it is obviously difficult for children, and their caretakers as well as clinicians, to disentangle emerging problematic sexual attraction to children (prepubescent or pubescent) from normal sexual development, concerning sexual behavior may be environment and developmental stage specific, but also the context, external and internal response to, and interventions made can shape emerging pedophilic sexual interests both positively and negatively.

DSM-5-TR (2022) specifies that a person must be at least 16 years old and 5 years older than the children they are sexually attracted to and excludes an individual in late adolescence in an ongoing sexual relationship with a 12- or 13-year-old. ICD-11 (2022) specifies that a diagnosis of pedophilic disorder "does not apply to sexual behaviors among pre- or post-pubertal children with peers who are close in age" (p. 566). The online "additional clinical features" section of ICD-11[4] further states that it "should not be diagnosed among children and should be diagnosed only with utmost caution among adolescents. Sexual experimentation is typical during adolescence and sexual acts may occur impulsively or opportunistically rather than representing a recurrent pattern of sexual arousal" (https://icd.who.int/browse/2024-01/mms/en#517058174). So, an understandably cautious approach is encouraged before labelling a child with pedophilia or pedophilic disorder. Most young people who commit sexual abuse against other children do not have pedophilia, and as with sexual offending and other offending more generally, where such offences occur most young people are not life-course persistent but are adolescent limited. Systemic issues, particularly within families and care environments need to be considered, so do developmental ones, and adolescent sexual interests and behavior have been described as a "moving target" (Miner et al., 2006). So, when assessing adults who have committed sexual abuse as children, sexual behaviors towards peers or siblings close to them in age should not be used as evidence of pedophilia or hebephilia, and other behaviors in childhood and adolescence with younger children, especially if not repeated, are rarely indicative of pedophilia.

Rates of sexual recidivism are lower in adolescents than in adults who commit sexual abuse (Caldwell, 2010; Reitzel & Carbonell, 2006). However, atypical (particularly pedophilic) sexual interest is associated with further sexual offending (Worling & Curwen, 2000), as it is in adults, and is associated with continuing to commit child sexual abuse into adulthood, although most juvenile sexual offenders do not become adult sexual offenders, and most adult sexual offenders were not juvenile sexual offenders (Beaudry-Cyr et al., 2017; Jennings et al., 2015; Lussier & Blokland, 2014; Lussier et al., 2016; Reingle, 2012). Accordingly, despite difficulties, and necessary caveats, ascertaining the presence of pedophilic sexual interest in young people, and the cautious approach directed by diagnostic manuals, is an important part of assessment, alongside identifying other relevant risk and protective factors in the young person and their networks. Given the natural history of pedophilia, in theory successful identification and intervention in adolescence could

[4] The on-line version of the ICD-11 includes considerably more detail beyond the criteria described in the published version. Indeed, the published edition refers to the on-line version as "the definitive version" (p. 1).

have an impact on pedophilia and perpetration of sexual abuse in adulthood. But the challenge is how to identify and then help young people without causing iatrogenic harm (to a person's mental health or sexual development), stigmatizing, and over-diagnosing. It should be noted that adolescent MAPS have been found to have particularly high levels of distress but also of wanting help, with the potential for intervention to improve mental health and prevent sexual abuse (see Sects. 13.6.3 and 13.11 below).

Adolescents who commit child versus peer sexual abuse have a less delinquent predisposition, less substance-abuse proneness and less antisocial functioning (Glowacz & Born, 2013), similar to differences between adults who offend against adults versus children. They are a heterogeneous group with factors such as antisociality, family dysfunction, histories of adverse experiences, substance misuse, cognitive and developmental difficulties, emotional problems and insecure attachment. Within this heterogeneity, Pullman and Seto (2012) identified a subgroup with unique risk and aetiological factors including childhood sexual abuse and atypical sexual interests. Seto and Lalumière (2010) concluded that although adolescent sexual offenders shared many of the same delinquency risk factors with other adolescent non-sex offenders, to explain why sexual abuse was committed required specific sexual factors: sexual abuse history, exposure to sex or pornography, and/or atypical sexual interests.

In terms of assessment approaches, PPG is not often used, even in the USA (McGrath et al., 2010), with concerns raised about the ethics of using such a sexually intrusive approach and exposing minors to sexually explicit material, which may be illegal in some jurisdictions. In addition, young people may respond to stimuli due to the general hypersexuality and heightened sexual responsiveness of adolescence, and may be more sexually responsive to stimuli which mirror their own sexual abuse experiences (Mackaronis et al, 2016). However, the lack of other methods to identify risky pedophilic interests, the apparent although questioned validity of PPG in assessing pedophilic interests in adolescents (Rice et al., 2012), and PPG assessed sexual arousal to children being associated with recidivism in adolescents (Clift et al., 2009), as it is in adults, have been argued to counterbalance such concerns (Bradford & Federoff, 2006). In a study of almost one hundred juvenile sex offenders, Hunter and Becker (1994) found similar associations between high levels of deviant arousal and having male child victims as would be seen in adults. But importantly, they stated their findings reflected greater fluidity in the offense patterns of juvenile offenders, and generally less correspondence between measured arousal and offense histories than would be expected in adults, suggesting caution in the interpretation of phallometric data with adolescents. Mackaronis et al. (2016) stated, that unlike for the assessment of pedophilia in adults, "The few research teams conducting empirical studies of PPG use with adolescents who have sexually offended, however, have not yet found clear evidence of the external validity of these PPG results." Overall, there are enough concerns and limits to the use of PPG in identifying and measuring pedophilic arousal and interest in adolescents that its appropriateness, utility, and validity are highly questionable. Less intrusive viewing time and visual reaction time measures are used more often in programs for adolescents in the USA, in about one in three programs (McGrath et al., 2010). Mackaronis et al. (2016) found that the Screening Scale for Pedophilic Interests (SSPI; Seto & Lalumière, 2001; see below) did not correlate with PPG or a viewing time measure, so had limited utility in adolescence, but PPG and viewing time category-level data were significantly positively correlated with each other, but only when comparing raw as opposed to ipsatized data. So other "objective" measures, which have shown validity and are used in adults, may not be applicable to adolescence.

In terms of interventions, there is some evidence for the effectiveness of cognitive behavioral therapy and multisystemic therapy in reducing risk of sexual recidivism in adolescents who commit sexual abuse (Thibaut et al., 2016), including those with child victims. So, such treatments, along with motivational interviewing and psychoeducation, are recommended for all adolescents with paraphilic disorders who sexually offend according to the World Federation of Societies of Biological Psychiatry (WFSBP; Thibaut et al., 2016) guidelines for the treatment of adolescent sexual offenders with paraphilic disorders. Thibaut et al. (2016) also recommended adjunctive treatment with SSRI medication (see below Sect. 13.9) in adolescents (aged 12 years old or more) with paraphilic disorders (including pedophilic disorder) who had committed low to moderate degrees of physical violence (e.g., indecent exposure, touching the body or genital parts of another person). Where there is a high risk of sexual violence (which would include repeated penetrative abuse of children and/or sexual abuse involving high degrees of violence), for those who had reached Tanner stage V (i.e., physical sexual maturity) treatment with an anti-libidinal medication (see Sect. 13.9 below) for 6 months at a time was recommended, whilst if Tanner stage V was reached and the person was over 16 years old anti-libidinals could be given without a time limit. For high-risk cases aged over 16 years old who were at Tanner stage IV or below, advice from a pediatric endocrinologist was recommended, before potential treatment with an anti-libidinal, after assessing completion of bone growth and epiphyseal closure. However, Thibaut et al. (2016) acknowledged "the low level of evidence available in the literature on which we have based our guidelines" and there are legitimate concerns about the use of medications to reduce sexual interest or drive in adolescents.

In terms of other international guidelines, the International Association for the Treatment of Sexual Offenders (IATSO), in its standards of care for juvenile sexual offenders, set out the following principles, which apply to adolescents with apparent pedophilic sexual interests or behavior as well as others who commit sexual abuse (Miner et al., 2006):

1. *Juveniles are best understood within the context of their families and social environments.*
2. *Assessment and treatment of juveniles should be based on a developmental perspective, should be sensitive to developmental change, and should be an ongoing process.*
3. *Assessment and treatment should include a focus on the youth's strengths.*

4. *The development of sexual interest and orientation is dynamic. The sexual interests of youth can change over the course of adolescence and this is the period when sexual orientation emerges.*
5. *Youth who have committed sexual offenses are a diverse population. They should not be treated with a "one size fits all" approach.*
6. *Treatment should be broad–based and comprehensive.*
7. *Labels can be more iatrogenic in children and adolescents than in adults. The juvenile and his/her family/primary care–giving system should be treated with respect and dignity.*
8. *Sexual offender registries and community notification, should not be applied to juveniles.*
9. *Effective interventions result from research guided by specialized clinical experience, and not from popular beliefs, or unusual cases in the media.*

The Association for the Treatment of Sexual Abusers (ATSA) has published comprehensive practice guidelines for assessment, treatment, and intervention with adolescents who have engaged in sexually abusive behavior (ATSA, 2017). In terms of assessment, it is noted that polygraph and PPG are not used regularly outside the USA, and "Without a clearly identified benefit and with a potential for harm, ATSA recommends against using polygraph or plethysmography with adolescents under age 18." Comprehensive, multi-source, holistic, developmentally appropriate and informed, and systemically informed assessment is recommended, incorporating appropriately validated and applied structured risk assessment measures (see Jung & Thomas, 2022). A risk-needs-responsivity (RNR) informed approach to intervention is recommended, nested within building on identified individual and ecological protective factors and strengths. Effective evidence-based treatment principles are set out:

- *Focusing on dynamic risk factors supported by current research*
- *Promoting safety while facilitating prosocial and developmentally appropriate skill development*
- *Using evidence-based interventions that match presenting risk and needs*
- *Including caregivers and other positive supports*
- *Addressing risk and protective factors across the adolescent's natural ecologies (e.g., family, peers, school)*
- *Occurring in the natural environment when possible to allow the adolescent and his/her caregivers to practice skills and use social supports in real-life situations*
- *Tailoring approaches to match individual characteristics and circumstances of the adolescent (e.g., developmental status, learning styles, gender, culture) and*
- *Addressing sexually abusive behavior problems as well as other conduct problems*

These principles apply to the treatment of adolescents who appear to have pedophilic sexual interests and behavior, as they do to other sexually abusive adolescents. For a recent overview of approaches to assessment and intervention with young people who engage in harmful sexual behavior see McPherson et al. (2024).

13.6.5 Women

The research literature regarding female sexual offenders is minuscule in comparison to what is known about males. While our understanding of female sexual offenders has increased dramatically in recent decades (Cortoni, 2014), it remains an unfortunate reality that very little is known about pedophilia in females. Even the most useful typologies for female sexual offenders do not really assign any importance to pedophilia or paraphilic disorders, other than when the female is being reportedly coerced by a male co-offender, although there are indications of some females with chronic histories of sexual abuse that subsequently offend within the family (Almond et al., 2017; Mathews et al., 1989; Matthews et al., 1991). What is known is that the recidivism rates for female sexual offenders are vanishingly low in comparison to males. A meta-analysis by Cortoni et al. (2010) found a 6 year recidivism rate of just 1.34%. Perhaps unsurprisingly, none of the extant risk assessment tools developed for use with male sexual offenders have demonstrated any predictive validity with female sexual offenders.

The DSM-5-TR (2022) notes that the prevalence of pedophilic disorder in females "is even more uncertain, but it is likely a small fraction of the prevalence in men" (p. 794). Indeed, the literature pertaining to female pedophilia primarily consists of case studies (e.g., Fedoroff et al., 1999). These indicate that preferential pedophilia does exist in females, but it is a seemingly rare phenomenon (Warren & McLeod, 2017). For example, Chow and Choy (2002) described a female who abused two 4 year-old girls whilst babysitting at the ages of 18 and 23 years. She performed oral sex on both and masturbated to orgasm whilst thinking of the second offence. She described being sexually aroused whilst bathing the girls and had fantasies of 3–4 year-old girls since she herself was a child, along with fantasies of adult females and males. She had fantasies or arousal to children 12 times each month but denied any sexual interest in her own two sons.

While understanding of female pedophilic sexual offenders is minimal, even less is known about those that have not come to the attention of the criminal justice system. There is clearly a dark figure of sexual crime involving female offenders. For example, Fromuth and Conn (1997) surveyed 546 female university students and found that four percent acknowledged at least one sexual experience with a child at least 5 years younger. Most physical contact involved touching and kissing. The mean age of the females was 12 years and of the victims was six. 70 percent of the victims were male and 69% were related to the females. Those who admitted to such contact were more likely to report an attraction to, or fantasies involving, children (18% *c.f.* 5%).

Wiegel et al. (2003) found that, in a sample of 242 females that admitted to committing a sexual offence, 70% had done so to a child (the rest involved obscene telephone calls, bestiality, exhibitionism, or voyeurism). More than half had one victim, but 10% admitted to five or more child victims. 17 percent who admitted to victimizing a child did so to their own and 35% victimized a niece or nephew. Only four percent victimized a stranger.

Peter (2009) looked at 345 cases of child abuse in Canada and indicated that 10.7% were committed by females. Females were responsible for the abuse of 9.3% of female victims and 14.1% of male victims. However, it is unclear how many of these females would meet formal criteria for pedophilic disorder or hebephilia. Moreover, there has been an unfortunate tendency to attempt to apply models and methods from research on male sexual offenders to females with often poor results. For example, the PPG has been found to be a useful approach when identifying the presence of pedophilic disorder, and other paraphilic interest, in males. However, Cooper et al. (1990) found that vaginal photoplethysmography did not discriminate between child and adult stimuli in a female sexual offender with multiple child victims.

13.7 Assessment

In this section there will be a focus on the assessment of pedophilic disorder and hebephilia. General aspects of the assessment process, including the importance of taking a thorough sexual history and knowing the details of any offending behavior will be discussed. An overview of objective methods for assessing pedophilic disorder will be provided and several behavioral rating scales that are particularly useful in applied forensic practice will be reviewed.

13.7.1 General Aspects

Diagnosing any paraphilic disorder, including pedophilic disorder, requires a thorough assessment. The most straightforward way of identifying atypical sexual interests is via self-report, be that in the form of an interview or a questionnaire. However, such topics are understandably highly sensitive and many interviewees are unlikely to readily admit to paraphilic fantasies or behaviors, particularly those involving children, at least without a great deal of minimization. This is why any forensic or clinical assessment interview must proceed cautiously. An assessment of atypical sexual interests must necessarily be part of a comprehensive overall assessment of the individual. In forensic practice, a great deal of time can be spent taking a personal history in order to both understand them and any personality features or signs of mental illness that may be present. When taken appropriately, the personal history taking builds rapport so that the interviewee is more comfortable when inevitable questions regarding their sexual life are asked later in the interviewee. Administering psychometric tests regarding personality functioning, clinical symptoms, or embedded deception scales, can also occur prior to taking a sexual history.

The importance of taking a thorough sexual history cannot be stressed enough. One does not simply focus on pedophilic fantasies or behaviors. It is important to carefully understand when the individual started masturbating, learned about sex, were first exposed to pornography, and first engaged in sexual behavior with others. Understanding the nature of sexual contacts, in both ongoing relationships and fleeting encounters, is important, along with any utilization of the services of sex workers and infidelity within intimate relationships. Identifying the extent and degree of various sexual behaviors is important along with asking about the major forms of atypical sexual activity. This needs to be conducted sensitively. In fact, one way of making the interviewee feel comfortable is to say "I am going to ask you some questions that I ask everyone during these assessments. I am going to describe some sexual behaviors and I want to know which of these you may have engaged in in the past."

We note that there are a number of clinical assessment measures, questionnaires, and sexual history inventories that some practitioners may wish to utilize in their assessments. These can be very helpful in ensuring that a thorough sexual history is taken and nothing is neglected. Some even include validity scales that can be particularly useful when assessing those in the criminal justice system. However, some practitioners prefer to slowly obtain the important information through a clinical interview that capitalizes on the rapport that has been built during personal history taking. In our view, as long as the assessment is thorough and addresses all of the important areas in appropriate detail, either approach is defensible.

If the individual being assessed has committed sexual offences, it is important, wherever possible, to know these offences in as much detail as the assessor can before the assessment. Indeed, forensic assessment begins when one starts to review collateral information, not when the interview commences. Formal summaries can be contrasted with the interviewee's version of events and questions can be asked about any discrepancies. The current authors have also found that knowing the offending behavior, and having some hypotheses regarding the presence, or lack thereof, of deviant sexual interests and motivation, can be a useful way of challenging any denial of atypical sexual interests, including pedohebephilic interests.

13.7.2 *Identifying and Assessing Pedophilic Disorder*

In addition to taking a thorough sexual history, there are a number of additional assessment approaches that can assist in identifying pedophilic disorder. In this section, objective assessment methods such as the PPG, indirect cognitive measures, the polygraph, viewing time measures, and behavioral rating scales will be reviewed.

13.7.3 *Objective Assessment of Pedophilic Disorder*

Due to the potential problems of relying on self-report to identify whether someone has atypical sexual interests, especially pedophilic sexual interests, several "objective" approaches have been developed which do not rely on what a person is willing to tell you. Most involve some form of equipment or technology, and all have been primarily researched and introduced for the assessment of pedophilic sexual interest and arousal. However, their use internationally is patchy and in many clinical and forensic settings access to such methods is very limited. For example, where the current authors have practiced, in Scotland and Australia, none of these approaches is used in practice although one or two are used in research. But given the reliability, validity and ease of application of behavioral scales based on a person's child sexual offending history, particularly the Screening Scale for Pedophilic Interests (SSPI) described in detail below, it is questionable whether the more sophisticated, time consuming, expensive and somewhat unwieldy approaches are necessary, and they certainly are not essential. These will be described briefly before focusing in more detail on the far more portable and user-friendly behavioral scales. For recent detailed reviews of most of these approaches see Carvalho et al. (2020) and Akerman et al. (2020), on which the following summary is based.

Penile plethysmography (PPG), also called phallometry or penile tumescence testing (PTT), measures male sexual arousal, via changes in penile volume or circumference, in response to being presented with sexual or neutral stimuli, in the form of images, videos or narratives. Relative sexual responses to different stimuli can be used to determine sexual interest in, for example, children versus adults. Stimuli may depict adult-child or adult-adult interactions, different degrees of coercion, clothed or nude individuals, and males and females of different ages. Some jurisdictions allow, but others prohibit, the use of nude images of children for PPG assessments. Due to this, and other factors, there are differences between the stimulus sets used in different laboratories. Deception countermeasures are often used to identify attempts to manipulate the results, such as suppressing arousal or trying to "fake good" by attempts to elicit an erection to a stimulus that is not actually sexually interesting. The setting in which the testing is completed, stimulus modality, level of sexual explicitness, and laboratory cutoff scores are important factors in determining presence and extent of response. Raw scores (of change in volume or circumference) or statistically normalized z-scores are used to quantify changes in penile blood flow. The degree of arousal compared to the flaccid state is measured, and indices of arousal can be used, comparing arousal to, for example, children versus adults, by either dividing or subtracting. Some clinicians consider PPG the "gold standard" and regard it as making a vital contribution to the assessment of pedophilia. However, others question the necessity of using such an intrusive and technical method, and whether it delivers information that can be more easily ascertained in other ways. PPG assessment can contribute to clinical assessment, risk assessment and measuring change with treatment, and pedophilic sexual interest as measured by PPG has been shown to be one of the strongest predictors of sexual reoffending in those who commit child sexual offences (Hanson & Morton-Bourgon, 2005; McPhail et al., 2019). A meta-analysis of 37 comparison samples and 16 predictive validity samples found several phallometric testing procedures were valid indicators of pedohebephilic interest, and features of testing associated with greater validity included slide or audio-plus-slide stimuli and z-score-based indices (McPhail et al., 2019). However, PPG should never be used in isolation and should form a part of a holistic multisource psychosexual assessment. It is also important to note that it cannot be used to determine guilt or innocence in relation to committing child sexual abuse. There are issues with standardization, with variations in assessment stimuli, testing protocols, analysis, and interpretation between laboratories, although some have standardized their stimulus sets and protocols, some standard stimulus sets are used internationally, and there have been recent moves towards the standardization between different countries globally. An equivalent for females, vaginal photoplethysmography (VPP), has been used as a general measure of female sexual arousal, but not yet in the context of assessing pedophilic sexual interest, although such use is being investigated. However, as noted above, Cooper et al. (1990) found that this did not discriminate between child and adult stimuli in a female sexual offender with multiple child victims, such that it may not have the same utility as the PPG does for males.

Indirect cognitive measures are of two types, Firstly, ones like the Implicit Association Task (IAT; Gray et al., 2005), which are based on the implicit unconscious cognitive link between labels (such as "sex" and "child"). Secondly, are tasks based on the disruption to attention (e.g., the rapid serial visual presentation task and the choice reaction time) due to pre-attentive processing and salience of sexual attributes. These tests bypass conscious appraisal and attendance to salient stimuli, so sidestep social desirability and conscious faking. The IAT involves classifying a series of attribute words as "sex" or "not sex" and as "adult" or "child" as quickly as possible using a computer, with the variable measured being reaction time, and faster reaction time indicating an implicit association, e.g., between "sex" and "child". The similar Picture Association Task (PAT) can be administered with the IAT. Evidence is promising in terms of identifying people with a pedophilic sexual interest, with some impressive effects sizes demonstrated, although not better than PPG (Snowden et al., 2011). The IAT is one of three components of the Explicit and Implicit Sexual Interest Profile (EISIP; see below). Although there have been some promising results with the attention disruption tasks, they have performed less well than the IAT, and are still very much in the realm of research rather than practice.

Eye-tracking measures use oculometric indicators, such as time to first fixation on a stimulus and pupil dilation, to indicate stimulus preference, and, as they rely on automatic processing, bypass manipulation and faking. A few studies have shown men with pedophilia demonstrated shorter fixation latencies and longer fixation times for child stimuli, indicating automatic and voluntary attention to children. But when combined with a cognitive challenge the task unexpectedly performed poorly. Although showing some initial promise these techniques have not been adopted in practice.

Viewing time measures assume that people look longer at preferred sexual stimuli, although the viewing time has actually been found to be the latency time for deciding whether a stimulus is sexually attractive, so a measure of attentional disruption. Two examples are the Abel Assessment for Sexual Interest Test (Abel Screening Incorporated, 2001) and the Affinity (Pacific Psychological Assessment Corporation, Inc, 2007). These computerized tests ask the person to rate the attractiveness of pictures of people of various ages and genders, while surreptitiously recording the time taken viewing each image. In a meta-analysis, Schmidt et al. (2017) reported that viewing time discriminated between child and nonchild sexual offenders with a moderate effect size and showed significant convergent validity with other measures of pedophilia. Validity was increased by using pedophilic difference scores rather than absolute scores. A variation of viewing time, visual reaction time, predicted sexual recidivism in 621 men evaluated while on probation or parole followed up for 7 or 15 years (Gray et al., 2015). Limitations include inconsistency in scoring systems, being easily manipulated when subjects are aware of the variable of interest, and inferiority to PPG. But viewing time measures are used in practice and such a measure is part of the EISIP (see below).

Virtual reality and *augmented reality* based assessment approaches (Laws, 2020), where an individual interacts with avatars in a virtual environment, or with computer generated stimuli in the real world, have been suggested as having potential. There have been a handful of interesting studies, some linking virtual reality stimuli with PPG, and studies have shown that people seek virtual proximity to others they find sexually attractive (Welsch et al., 2020). But these methods have not come to fruition yet in practice.

It has been suggested that *functional MRI* could be used to examine blood flow in brain regions associated with sexual arousal while presenting men with potential sexual stimuli to assess sexual interest and preference, and there have been case studies showing decreases in such blood flow after anti-libidinal treatment (see above in Sect. 13.4 for further details). But although functional MRI shows some promise for assessing the presence of pedophilia and response to treatment, further research and development will be required, and it is yet to be seen whether functional imaging will be introduced and used in clinical practice (Jordan et al., 2015).

Although *polygraph* interviews have been shown to increase disclosures of potentially risk relevant information (e.g., sexual fantasies about children) during post-conviction supervision in the community, and can be mandated in some jurisdictions (e.g., England and Wales, and most US States) for sexual offenders on probation and parole, there is no evidence that polygraph testing reduces recidivism, it may place an inappropriate focus on overcoming denial which is not an evidence based risk factor or treatment target, it may undermine the development of good supervisory and therapeutic relationships, and raises questions about how to appropriately respond to disclosures in individual cases when they occur (Elvin et al., 2021). Despite its enthusiastic adoption in the USA and in England and Wales, it is either used rarely or not at all in most other jurisdictions.

The *Explicit and Implicit Sexual Interests Profile (EISIP)* is a computerized assessment combining three approaches: three different IATs (men-women, girls-women, boys-men), a viewing time measure (based on 80 non-explicit semi-nude computer-manipulated pictures of males and females across the five Tanner stages), and the Explicit Sexual Interest Questionnaire (ESQ; Banse et al., 2010), with 40 items tapping into presence of sexual behaviors and sexual fantasies as an adult relating to young girls, young boys, women, and men (Schmidt & Banse, 2022; Schmidt & Perkins, 2021). The EISIP does not provide norms to compare assessment results against. So, profile interpretations are based on ipsative comparisons (within the person's own various responses on the three measures) of high and low points in the sexual interest profile. These can be used as a reference frame or baseline of the subjectively least and most sexually interesting categories within and across the EISIP measures. The EISIP profile is used alongside other information to help with diagnosis and case formulation in collaboration with the subject. The EISIP is used in clinical practice across several jurisdictions, although only by a relatively small number of practitioners.

13.7.4 Behavioral Rating Scales

In this section the use of behavioral rating scales for identifying pedophilic sexual interests from analysis of offence behaviors will be described. The MTC:CM3 processes for identifying fixation and social competence will be discussed and the use of the SSPI, the Revised Screening Scale for Pedophilic Interests (SSPI-2), the Screening Scale of Pedophilic Crime Scene Behavior (SSPC), and the Correlates of Admitted Sexual Interest in Children (CASIC) will be examined.

13.7.4.1 Behavioral Rating Scales for Identifying Pedophilic and Hebephilic Interests

Recent years have seen the development of several behavioral rating scales that can assist in the identification of pedophilic and hebephilic sexual interests amongst those that have committed sexual offences against children. Arguably the first is the Level of Fixation on Children decision embedded in the MTC:CM3 typology (Knight et al., 1989). While not a scale per se, the manual for the typology provides quite clear definitions for identifying "Low Fixation" and "High Fixation," and also provides guidance for some situations that may initially seem equivocal. The inter-rater reliability for the Fixation decision was found to be good (Kappa = .67).

In addition to the Fixation decision, the MTC:CM3 also provides useful guidance for identifying the Degree of Social Competence. Given that the combination of high fixation and low social competence has been identified as indications of a taxon of strong pedophilic interest, these guidelines may also be useful when identifying pedophilic interests. The inter-rater reliability for the Degree of Social Competence Decision was found to be excellent (Kappa = .84).

Since the development of the MTC:CM3, several more overtly behavioral rating scales have been developed for identifying the presence or degree of pedophilic, and in some cases hebephilic, sexual interests. In this section there will be a focus on four scales: the SSPI, SSPI-2, SSPC, and CASIC.

13.7.4.2 The Screening Scale for Pedophilic Interests (SSPI)

The SSPI (Seto & Lalumière, 2001) was initially developed as a triage for identifying male child sexual offenders who may require a penile plethysmograph assessment. The original version of the instrument included four easily scored offence behavioral variables: any male victim < 14; more than one victim < 14; any victim < 12; and any extrafamilial victims < 14. Each item was scored dichotomously (zero = not present, one = present), except for the male victim item, where the presence was worth two points due to the fact that this item had twice the weight of the other items in stepwise regression analysis. Accordingly, scores ranged from zero to five.

Interpreting the results of the SSPI is reasonably straightforward and logical. Each score can be viewed alongside the proportion of child sex offenders who had an equal or greater arousal to children on the penile plethysmograph. These were zero = 18%, one = 23%, two = 32%, three = 41%, four = 47%, and five = 72%. As such, those with scores of four or five suggest the presence of a preferential sexual interest in children. It was noted that those with a score of zero or one had very similar PPG results to non-offenders and rapists of adults. In contrast, those with scores of four or five showed a distinctly different profile, with lower responses to adult female stimuli and higher responses to stimuli that depicted prepubescent males.

The SSPI performed very well in its initial study, showing a good relationship with the results of the PPG Pedophilic Index (AUC = .70). Indeed, the SSPI was recognized by the authors of the Sex Offender Risk Appraisal Guide (SORAG) as an acceptable substitute for phallometric test results (Harris et al., 2015; Quinsey et al., 2006). In addition, a study by Helmus et al. (2015) recommended that a trichotomized SSPI score (0 = 0, 1–3 = 1, 4 or 5 = 2) could be used as a substitute to the STABLE-2007 Deviant Sexual Interests item.

13.7.4.3 The Revised Screening Scale for Pedophilic Interests (SSPI-2)

The SSPI was revised in 2015 (Seto et al., 2017) following research that had indicated that CSAM offending was a valid and possibly independent indicator of pedophilia (e.g., Seto et al., 2006). It is important to note that the criteria for several of the original items changed slightly, with an upper age range of below 15 rather than below 14 years. This was reportedly due to changes in the age of consent in Canada at the time that changed the nature of the samples at the clinic where the data was collected.

Analyses indicated that the male victim item should be changed to a simple dichotomous scoring like each of the other items. With the inclusion of any CSAM offending, the five items in the SSPI-2 are: any boy victim < 15; more than one child victim < 15; any child victim < 12; any extrafamilial child victim < 15; and child pornography offending (admission or charge). Total scores still range from zero to five.

Interpreting the results of the SSPI-2 is as straightforward and logical as the original SSPI. Each score can be viewed alongside the proportion of child sex offenders who had an equal or greater arousal to children on the penile plethysmograph. In the validation sample these were zero or one = 20%, two = 28%, three = 30%, four = 53%, and five = 60%. As such, those with scores of four or five still suggest the presence of a preferential sexual interest in children, and there is a clearer demarcation between the scores of four or five and a score of three.

The SSPI-2 had a statistically significant difference with the original SSPI in regard to their relationships with the PPG Pedophilic Index (AUC = .63 *c.f.* .59) and self-admitted pedophilic interest (AUC = .78 *c.f.* .73).

It is important to note that recent research by Stephens et al. (2019) indicated that the SSPI-2 is better viewed as a measure of pedohebephilia rather than just pedophilia. This is perhaps not too surprising given that the criteria for the revised version primarily involve consideration of victims under the age of 15 years. Exclusive pedophilia was vanishingly rare in the sample (just one percent) in comparison to 35% pedohebephilia and 17% hebephilia only. The SSPI-2 had a good relationship with pedohebephilia (AUC = .66) but not for exclusive hebephilia (AUC = .51).

13.7.4.4 The Screening Scale of Pedophilic Crime Scene Behavior (SSPC)

The SSPC (Dahle et al., 2014; Lehmann et al., 2018, 2022) was developed in Germany from an initial 22 crime scene variables that were identified as evidence of pedophilia. Using a stepwise regression process, seven of these items remained. The first four items are related to the offence history: number of victims (3+ victims younger than 14), number of offences (11+ separate offences against victim or victims younger than 14), victim aged 9 or younger, and child pornography (production or possession). The final three items relate to crime scene features in the index offence only: confidence approach (any indication of trust building), anal penetration, and offender using no threats. Each is scored dichotomously so that scores range from zero to seven.

Total scores of five or higher have been found to relate to a clinical diagnosis of pedophilia. Indeed, in German and Canadian samples 100% of those with scores of five or higher had diagnoses of pedophilia. It was only in a US sample that used a criterion of the MTC:CM4 high fixation/low social competence type where a score of six was necessary to capture all. However, a score of five still identified 62.5% that met the MTC:CM4 criterion. In addition, the SSPC and the SSPI added incremental validity to each other, indicating that there was at least some unique variance being accounted for by the two instruments, despite some overlap in variables. The authors suggested that the SSPC may be a more precise measure of pedophilia than the SSPI-2 which appears to be more of a measure of pedohebephilia.

13.7.4.5 Correlates of Admitted Sexual Interest in Children (CASIC)

The CASIC was developed as part of the Child Pornography Offender Risk Tool (CPORT; Eke et al., 2018; Eke & Seto, 2016; see below) as a proxy measure for admission of sexual interest in children amongst those that commit CSAM offences. It consists of six dichotomous items: never married, had child pornography videos, had child pornography text stories, child pornography activity spanning 2 or more years, volunteering in a role with high access to children, and engaging in online sexual communications with a minor or undercover officer posing as a minor. A conservative cut-score of three or more can be used as evidence that the CPORT item "indication of pedophilic or hebephilic sexual interests" is present. Seto and Eke (2017) found that the CPORT was slightly more accurate at predicting recidivism when the CASIC was used exclusively for this item (AUC = .775 *c.f.* .740 for any CSAM recidivism; AUC = .754 *c.f.* .724 for any sexual recidivism).

13.7.4.6 Using Behavioral Rating Scales in Applied Forensic and Clinical Settings

Behavioral rating scales have considerable utility in applied and clinical settings when the individual being assessed or treated has a history of sexual offending behavior against children under the age of 15 years. While these tools have cut-scores that suggest the possible presence of a preferential sexual interest in prepubescent or early pubescent children, the current authors would caution against anyone using these tools in a rigid actuarial fashion. Indeed, while they can provide often very useful information, they must be utilised in a Structured Professional Judgment (SPJ) fashion, where they are integrated with information gathered during a thorough forensic interview and considered in regard to typological considerations.

We have found that a combination of the SSPI-2 and the SSPC can provide particularly valuable information when there is some question as to whether an individual's atypical sexual interests are best conceptualized as pedophilic or hebephilic. Elevated scores on the SSPI-2 and low scores on the SSPC are often a useful indicator that hebephilic interests are more likely than pedophilic interests as the SSPI-2 is a measure of pedohebephilia and the SSPC focuses on pedophilia exclusively. In addition, lower scores on the SSPI-2 amongst an individual who has sexually victimized 14 year-olds can sometimes be an indicator that they have an ephebophilic sexual interest and have turned to available young pubescents in accordance with the sexual response gradient model. Furthermore, the current authors have found that in cases involving a *Diverse* pattern of offence behavior, where the primary paraphilic interests are not pedophilic but they have chosen to sexually offend against children, SSPI-2 scores of three are frequently found, which appears to correspond nicely with the notion of the diverse pattern of behavior (Lanning, 2010). In cases involving CSAM, the CASIC can provide valuable information regarding pedohebephilic sexual interests beyond its intended use embedded in the CPORT instrument (see below).

The development of these various behavioral rating scales has certainly been a very welcome addition to the armamentarium of forensic mental health professionals. When used correctly, they enable diagnostic opinions to have a more robust empirical foundation than was previously possible. However, they must be used in conjunction with all available information and not used in a mechanical actuarial fashion. A diagnosis of Pedophilic Disorder or Hebephilia can have serious consequences not only for the individual being assessed, but also for society as a whole. It is thus imperative that such diagnoses are only made on the basis of all available information.

13.8 Risk Assessment

An important task when assessing anyone who has committed a sexual offence or sexual violence is assessing the risk of further sexual or violent offending, to determine management strategies and interventions required to prevent these. Below specific considerations relevant to assessing risk in individuals with pedophilic or hebephilic sexual interests are highlighted.

13.8.1 Pedophilia as a Risk Factor for Recidivism

Paraphilic disorders and atypical sexual interests are the most potent risk factors for sexual recidivism amongst those that have committed sexual offences involving a live victim. This is a consistent finding across the literature. A meta-analysis by Hanson and Bussière (1998) found that any deviant sexual preference had a moderate relationship with sexual recidivism (r = .22). However, phallometric results showing a sexual interest in children was the single strongest predictor (r = .32). Phallometric results showing a sexual interest in boys were also statistically significant (r = .14), as was having a male child victim (r = .11).

A subsequent meta-analysis by Hanson and Morton-Bourgon (2004, 2005) once again found that a broadly defined category of sexual deviance was the most potent risk factor, with any deviant sexual interest (d = 0.31), sexual interests in children (d = 0.33), and sexual preoccupations (d = 0.39) being particularly noteworthy.

A further updated meta-analysis by Mann et al. (2010) further confirmed the importance of sexual deviance in general, and pedophilic sexual interests in particular, as risk factors for sexual recidivism. Indeed, sexual preoccupation (d = 0.39), any deviant sexual interest (d = 0.31), plethysmograph showing sexual preference for children (d = 0.32), multiple paraphilias (d = 0.21), and emotional congruence with children (d = 0.42) were all important risk factors for recidivism.

While paraphilic sexual interests in general, and pedophilic sexual interest in particular, are amongst the strongest risk factors in regard to their relationship with sexual recidivism, it should be stressed that they do not have demonstrably large predictive validity on their own. Indeed, effect sizes of $d = 0.21–0.42$ are, at best, small-to-medium in magnitude. As such, risk assessments should not be made solely on the basis of diagnosable sexual deviance. It is a reality that most sexual offenders do not re-offend, and pedophilic disorder or any other paraphilic disorder is just one of many risk factors that should ideally be considered when conducting a comprehensive risk assessment. For this reason, the use of formal risk assessment instruments, be they actuarial or structured professional judgment tools, must be used even if the individual has a clearly diagnosable paraphilic disorder. Risk assessments need to consider both static (historical and unchanging) and dynamic (changeable) risk factors in order to be comprehensive and track changes in risk over time. Moreover, in cases where the individual has exclusively committed online child sexual abuse material offences without involving actual children, they may be very likely to have a diagnosable pedophilic disorder, but still unlikely to re-offend on the basis of this sexual interest alone. As such, these offenders should also be assessed using an appropriate risk assessment tool.

13.8.2 Application of Risk Assessment Instruments

In this section an overview of the application of risk assessment instruments in those with pedophilic disorder who have sexually offended is detailed. The importance of utilising formal risk assessment instruments will be emphasized, including actuarial or structured professional judgment tools, and the risk assessment process for both CSA and CSAM offending is examined.

13.8.2.1 Risk Assessment in Contact Sexual Offenders

Risk assessment has become a very important aspect of the wider forensic assessment of those that have sexually offended. While it remains an empirical fact that unstructured clinical opinions regarding risk have little relationship with recidivism, actuarial and structured risk assessment schemes have demonstrated predictive validity that is considerably better.

Forensic assessors currently have at their disposal a range of different risk assessment tools from which to choose. These loosely fall into two categories. *Actuarial* tools involve a combination of risk factor scores that result in a total score that mechanically places individuals into a risk category. If the tool is a purely actuarial instrument they will also provide a probability estimate for reoffending, based on those with similar scores that reoffended, as well as percentiles and relative risk ratios. However, there are some mechanical tools that are developed in a rational, rather than strictly empirical, fashion. These will mechanically place an individual into a risk category, but recidivism estimates are not provided beyond the omnibus risk category in which they have been placed. In contrast, *Structured Professional Judgment (SPJ)* tools are rationally developed professional guidelines that serve as an aide-memoire that guides the assessor through coding of risk factors, determining their relevance to the individual, developing a formulation of sexual violence risk, identifying scenarios in which reoffending is most likely to occur, preparing management plans, and providing an informed clinical judgment of risk that is informed by the number of risk factors, but without any mechanical cut-scores. Indeed, the final risk level is determined by the clinician after working their way through the guidelines (Davis & Ogloff, 2008; Ogloff & Davis, 2020).

There has been considerable and often caustic debate in the literature regarding the relative merits of actuarial and SPJ approaches to risk assessment. Despite these spirited debates, it is generally the case that when it comes to the task of prediction, actuarial and SPJ tools perform the task with approximately equal accuracy. In some studies, the SPJ approach has been found to outperform the actuarial tool. For example, in a meta-analysis by Hanson and Morton-Bourgon (2007, 2009) the most accurate approach was structured judgments made on the basis of the Sexual Violence Risk-20 (SVR-20, Boer et al., 1997; $d = 1.11$). This was considerably better than the leading actuarial tools such as the Static-99 (Hanson & Thornton, 1999; $d = 0.67$) and the Risk Matrix 2000/S (Thornton, 2010; $d = 0.67$). However, in other studies there is no statistically significant difference found between actuarial and SPJ tools. SPJ instruments have traditionally been thought to have an advantage in that they consider both static and dynamic risk factors and can thus consider changes in risk factors over time. However, there are actuarial tools that include dynamic risk factors, some of which can be combined with actuarial tools in a further mechanical process to create a combined risk category. Regardless of the approach one chooses to use, a comprehensive risk assessment needs to consider a range of static and dynamic risk factors from several areas of the individual's life.

In the current authors' own forensic clinical practice, what is known as a *convergent* approach (Boer, 2006; Boer & Hart, 2009) has often been adopted, whereby an actuarial tool is utilized as a baseline measure of risk, as well as a comprehensive and detailed SPJ instrument that serves to ultimately individualize the assessment beyond the group-based conclusions of the baseline actuarial results. Such an approach can provide a rich and detailed explanation of the individual's offending, as well as a risk assessment that is both relative to other sexual offenders and action-oriented in terms of management and risk prevention strategies.

13.8.2.2 Risk Assessment in Online Child Sexual Abuse Material Offenders

As described above, although the rate of contact child sexual abuse is reducing the rate of online child sexual offending, especially that involving use of CSAM, is rising, and clinicians are often asked to assess risk in such cases, including risk of further CSAM offending and risk of contact offending. Although CSAM offenders have higher rates of pedophilia than contact CSA offenders, their rates of recidivism are much lower. Helmus (2023) collated recidivism data from 23 samples from North America, Europe, and Australasia. For all CSAM offenders, statistically estimated 5-year rates were 5.5% for sexual recidivism, 2.8% for contact sexual recidivism, and 2.7% CSAM recidivism; for CSAM only 3.9%, 1.4%, and 4.8% respectively; and for CSAM plus contact 10.0%, 3.4%, and 1.1% respectively. So, for CSAM offenders with contact offences rates of sexual recidivism and contact offending are similar to contact non-CSAM offenders and risk assessment instruments can be used as with other people who commit contact offences. However, CSAM only offenders have very low rates of contact recidivism, and if they do recidivate it is very likely to be further CSAM offending.

Another factor to bear in mind is the trajectory of offending in CSAM offenders who commit other sexual offences. Babchishin et al. (2022) examined 85 male CSAM offenders who had also committed another child sex offence. Almost half were "stable" committing a CSAM offence followed by another CSAM offence; two-fifths showed "de-escalation" committing an earlier contact offence and then a later CSAM offence; and only one in ten showed "escalation" from earlier CSAM to contact offending. All three groups were already serial offenders, so they had relatively high rates of further sexual offending (i.e., committing a third offence), about a third across the groups. But although the recidivism of the escalators was as likely to be contact as CSAM, the stable and de-escalation groups were twice and three times as likely to commit CSAM than contact offences. Accordingly, in addition to reoffending rates being low, even where a person also has a contact offence it is usually committed before the CSAM offence, in adolescence or early adulthood, and part of a de-escalation trajectory.

As contact sexual offending is so uncommon after a person has been charged with CSAM offending, the default for first time CSAM only offenders must be that they pose a low risk of recidivism, even though two thirds to three quarters are pedophilic. Unlike contact offenders, in CSAM offenders, pedophilia is a risk factor for further CSAM offending but not a risk factor for contact offending. In fact, the rate of future contact offending is so low that it is very difficult to get a large enough sample of CSAM offenders followed up for long enough to determine what the risk factors for future contact offending might be. They cannot be assumed to be the same ones that differentiate dual offenders (CSAM plus contact) from CSAM offenders, given that very few dual offenders are CSAM offenders who later commit contact offences. The factors associated with CSAM versus dual offending are higher occupational and educational functioning, being white and less ethnically diverse, less chronic and diverse offending histories, lower rates of substance use problems and severe mental disorder, lower rates of sexual and physical abuse, less likely to hold attitudes that support offending, more problems with sexual regulation and sexual deviance, and more self-esteem and assertiveness problems (Babchishin et al., 2015; Henshaw et al., 2018). These are very similar to the factors which differentiate non-offending MAPs from those who self-report having offended (Cohen et al., 2018), and reflect an association between antisociality, and dual offending, but not sexual deviance or sexual regulation problems.

So, can risk assessment instruments developed for sexual offenders generally be applied to those who commit CSAM offences? Although Helmus et al. (2024) concluded there was some evidence for the predictive validity of Risk Matrix 2000 (Thornton et al., 2003, 2023), with an adapted scoring method for three items (Thornton, 2017; Thornton et al., 2023), and perhaps some partial evidence for Static-99R (Hanson & Thornton, 2000; Helmus et al., 2012), those actuarial instruments would only be applied by the current authors where a person also has a contact offence to forecast risk of any sexual offence and would add a caveat with dual offenders that if the pattern is historical contact offending with current CSAM offending then the person is likely to be on a de-escalating trajectory. But for CSAM only offenders the actuarial instrument with the best predictive validity from multiple studies is the Child Pornography Offender Risk Assessment Tool (CPORT; Eke et al., 2018; Helmus, Eke, Farmus, et al., 2024; Seto & Eke, 2015).

The CPORT has seven items: (1) age 35 or younger, (2) prior criminal history, (3) failure on conditional release, (4) contact sexual offending, (5) pedophilic or hebephilic interests, (6) more boy than girl content in illegal material, (7) more boy than girl content in non-illegal material. As with other instruments for sexual offenders, broadly the items fall into two groups, ones related to antisociality and others relating to sexual deviance. When relevant diagnostic information is absent, item 5 can be scored using the specifically developed CASIC which, as noted above, is a behavioral scale like the SSPI-2, but specific to CSAM offenders, who cannot be rated using the SSPI-2 if they only have CSAM offences. The six items of the CASIC are described above. A CASIC score of 3 or more is indicative of pedophilic or hebephilic interests for scoring item 5 of the CPORT. The CPORT can be scored if only one item is missing and in most of our cases this is item 7 as getting information on non-illegal material can be challenging outside of a law enforcement context. Items 6 and 7 may also change between jurisdictions, given different definitions of CSAM. They have also been found to be unrelated to recidivism, unlike the other five items, in several validation studies.

The CPORT has been validated across nine studies from Canada, the USA, Iceland, Scotland, New Zealand, Spain and Germany. In a meta-analysis of all but two of these studies (Helmus, Eke, Farmus, et al., 2024) there was good predictive validity for sexual recidivism (AUC = .73) and for CSAM recidivism (AUC = .74), superior to RM2000/S (AUCs of .66 and .67 respectively), and much better than unstructured clinical judgment (estimated AUC .56). Predictive validity is slightly worse in CSAM only offenders (AUCs of .68 and .69 respectively) and better in dual offenders (AUCs of .72 and .77 respectively). Interestingly RM2000/S had similar predictive validity for dual offenders, as might be expected, but was inferior and no better than unstructured clinical judgement for CSAM only offenders.

The two studies since the meta-analysis of Helmus, Eke, Farmus, et al. (2024) have been somewhat unusual. Cohen (2023) used natural language processing and machine learning techniques to extract data from extensive file information in a large sample (N = 5768) from the USA and found a moderate but significant effect (AUC = .62) despite using what would be considered a modified or approximated version of the CPORT. In a German self-presenting non-convicted cohort of 132 men, where the CPORT ratings and recidivism were based on self-report rather than charges or convictions (von Franqué et al., 2023), and the base rate of reoffending was much higher than would be expected (contact 3.8% and CSAM 39.4% over 28 months average follow-up time), there was moderate predictive validity for contact (AUC = .69) and CSAM (AUC = .63) recidivism. In their review of risk assessment instruments for CSAM offenders, Helmus, Eke, and Seto (2024), concluded that there was sufficient evidence of good predictive validity and strong inter-rater reliability to make the CPORT the best current actuarial instrument for use with CSAM offenders across WEIRD (Western, educated, industrialized, rich and democratic) countries, including the USA, despite the reservations expressed by Scurich and Krauss (2023).

In terms of structured instruments capturing dynamic risk factors, there is one field study showing good predictive validity for Stable 2007 (Fernandez et al., 2014; Hanson et al., 2007) and Acute 2007 (Hanson et al., 2007) for predicting any sexual and CSAM recidivism in CSAM offenders (Babchishin et al., 2023). There is no research examining the predictive validity of other instruments which assess dynamic factors, such as the Violence Risk Scale: Sexual Offense version (VRS-SO; Olver et al., 2007), Sexual Violence Risk-20 Version 2 (SVR-20 V2; Boer et al., 2017), or Risk for Sexual Violence Protocol-Version 2 (RSVP-V2; Hart et al., 2022). However, the dynamic factors captured by Stable-2007 and Acute-2007 (covering social networks, sexual deviance, sexual regulation, general self-regulation, relationships, supervision, victim access and substance misuse) are all covered, but in slightly different ways, by the dynamic factors of the VRS-SO, SVR-20 V2 and RSVP-V2. So, it is likely that these other instruments cover the relevant dynamic factors, although that is empirically untested in CSAM offenders. Stable-2007 adds incremental predictive validity to Risk Matrix 2000/S (Thornton, 2010; Thornton et al., 2003) and Static-99R (Hanson & Thornton, 1999, 2000), with sexual offenders generally and the actuarial and dynamic risk ratings can be mechanically combined to give an overall risk level and recommendations for treatment targets and dosage. This may be the same with the CPORT, although is also untested. Stable-2007 can be used to identify relevant dynamic factors which can be targeted in treatment, and which may change with treatment, changes in circumstances and/or time. Acute-2007 can be used to pick up on proximal factors that are reassessed and monitored at each appointment by supervising staff, which may indicate an imminent risk and therefore a need for action.

There are two other instruments specifically designed for CSAM offenders. The Kent Internet Risk Assessment Tool—Version 2 (KIRAT) is an investigative case prioritization tool for law enforcement, which aims to identify CSAM offenders who are more likely to have a concurrent or previous contact offence, so immediate actions can be taken to protect those children, but does not predict future offending in CSAM offenders and so is not a risk assessment instrument which can be used to forecast future offending or to plan treatment or management in criminal justice or forensic mental health contexts (Long et al., 2016). The Estimated Risk for Internet Child Sexual Offending (ERICSO; Garrington et al., 2022) is a recent purported structured professional judgement instrument, described by the authors as "an empirically guided tool for estimating risk" in CSAM offenders, which has 46 factors, across four domains, hypothesized to be relevant based on literature review, surveying professionals and offender case studies. It lacks validation and is not appropriate to use in applied practice yet.

In clinical and forensic practice when assessing a CSAM only offender, the current authors would use the CPORT and the perpetrator factors of the RSVP-V2 to assess dynamic factors and before setting out the results of using these instruments would always state that the baseline reoffending rate in CSAM only offenders is low for CSAM and very low for contact offending. When applying the CPORT, although the current manual does not give risk levels, and suggests the instrument can be used to rank order cases in terms of risk, given the accumulating research and the rates of reoffending in people with different scores, the current authors would regard scores of 0–1 as low risk, 2–3 as moderate risk, and 4 and above as high risk. These levels indicate the likelihood of further sexual recidivism compared to the average CSAM offender, not compared to the average sex offender. Then relevant dynamic risk factors are identified using the RSVP-V2 and RSVP-V2 structured judgments are used relative to other sex offenders. So, the majority of CSAM only offenders are low likelihood, low severity, low imminence, and low case priority using the RSVP-V2, a few are rated moderate likelihood and very few are rated high likelihood. The relevant dynamic factors inform the case formulation, treatment targets and risk management planning. One of us sometimes uses Stable 2007 and Acute 2007 instead of, or alongside, the RSVP-V2, given the recent study. The important aspect of either approach is that risk assessment is grounded in a reasonably well validated actuarial tool comprised of static risk factors, which are supplemented by consideration of dynamic risk factors, and the results are considered in terms of CSAM and sexual offending in general.

For dual offenders the current authors use CPORT and either Risk Matrix 2000/S or Static-99R, along with RSVP-V2, as would be the case for other sexual offenders. But for dual offenders with early historic contact offending who have de-escalated to CSAM offending, relevant base rate information is set out and that that pattern is unlikely to lead to further contact offending. For the small number of dual offenders who commit CSAM and contact offences at the same time, or are the rare escalators who start with CSAM and then commit contact abuse, authors would be concerned and proceed as would be the case for contact offenders. In 40 years of practice between the current authors, assessing CSAM cases where there are concerns about risk, we have assessed nobody who has fitted the escalation pattern, but many on the de-escalation or repeat CSAM pathway have been seen. Due to the nature of the cases referred to the current authors, rarely has the typical first time prosocial CSAM only offender who make up 80–90% of cases been seen. The effect of further CSAM offending has never been discounted when it is a risk and does happen, as every image (of a real child) is a child being abused. But managing risk of further CSAM offending is different from managing risk of contact offending.

In terms of other types of online child sexual abuse, unlike CSAM offenders, most solicitation offenders are not pedophilic, a significant minority are hebephilic, but most are teleiophilic, and most victims are pubescent and postpubescent teenagers (Seto et al., 2012). There is little empirical research to guide practitioners in terms of recidivism rates, risk factors and application of structured instruments. Most solicitation offenders do not want to or plan to meet children offline, although some do. Exchanging images is often part of the solicitation process, so most are charged with CSAM offending concurrently. There are some indicators that solicitation offenders are more like CSAM offenders in terms of their lack of general antisociality. But overall, identifying and addressing pedophilia or pedophilic disorder is not the issue, as opposed to hebephilia. The field desperately needs empirical findings to inform risk assessment in solicitation offenders. In such cases, the current authors recommend using one or more risk assessment instruments that appear most relevant to the individual case, and including appropriate caveats both to their use and the resulting risk opinions derived from them.

13.8.3 Risk Assessment Outcome and Conclusions

Regardless of the actual risk assessment tools that the individual clinician chooses to use, it is imperative that the final risk opinion includes information as to the likelihood of risk that is relative to other offenders. However, the risk assessment should also provide an understanding of previous offending, identify likely scenarios for future offending, and be action-oriented by outlining how the assessed level of risk should be appropriately managed. Risk assessment without risk management is of little utility. In the case of an individual with an entrenched pedophilic disorder, ongoing fantasy management or even anti-libidinal medications may be appropriate, but much of the risk management plans will involve areas other than the pedophilic disorder itself. When present, this can be a potent risk factor for recidivism, and while it should always be identified and monitored over time, risk management plans may focus more on providing a more stable lifestyle with meaningful employment or leisure activities, the development of pro-social supportive relationships, and developing coping strategies to more successfully deal with stress.

13.9 Treatment

Multiple meta-analyses show modern offence specific treatments modestly reduce recidivism in sexual offenders (Gannon et al., 2019; Hanson et al., 2009; Schmucker & Lösel, 2015), especially if they follow the risk-needs-responsivity (RNR) principles (Hanson et al., 2009), have some added focus on strengths and positive prosocial goals (Marshall et al., 2017; Olver et al., 2020), are psychologically run and informed (Gannon et al., 2019), and incorporate interventions specifically addressing sexual deviance (Gannon et al., 2019). Most studies have included individuals who have child victims, and most samples have more offenders with child rather than adult victims. So many people with pedophilia are included in the host of treatment studies which have been undertaken, although none focus specifically on pedophilic sexual offenders per se. So best practice and an evidence-based approach can be adopted with people with pedophilia who commit sexual abuse. Given the high rates of histories of adverse experiences and personality difficulties it is also important to be trauma (Levenson, 2014) and personality (Craissati et al., 2021) informed in terms of engagement, readiness, responsivity, and therapeutic approach. Specific aspects of treatment in individuals with pedophilic disorder are focused on here.

A crucial issue in the treatment of individuals with pedophilic disorder is how to approach their sexual interest in children, particularly as pedophilic sexual interest is central to understanding child sexual offending (Seto, 2018), is a risk factor for further such offending (Hanson & Bussière, 1998; Hanson & Morton-Bourgon, 2005), and is an important criminogenic need (Mann et al., 2010; McPhail & Olver, 2020). A good assessment and formulation should allow an understanding of the degree of pedophilic sexual interest and preference relative to that for adults, the behaviors the person poses a risk of, the interaction between pedophilia and other factors which may increase or decrease pedophilic sexual arousal and fantasy (such as mood state or sexual preoccupation), the role of other factors that may facilitate or protect against acting on sexual arousal (such as intoxication, access to children or self-control), and what the person wants to achieve in relation to their sexual interest in children. Options with regard to the latter include: (1) continuing to be sexually aroused by children but not acting illegally, (2) continuing to be sexually aroused by children but not acting on that arousal problematically (illegally or legally), (3) having less sexual arousal to and fantasies involving children, (4) having more sexual arousal to and fantasies involving adults, (5) being less distressed by and more accepting of one's sexual preference for children, and (6) having less or no sexual arousal or fantasies of any type (to children or other stimuli). These options are not necessarily mutually exclusive.

Options available in treatment will depend on the person's relative sexual attraction to children and adults, for example sexually aroused by children but with a preference for adults, having a sexual preference for children although a degree of arousal to adults, or exclusively sexually aroused by children. In terms of direct treatments behavior modification techniques can reduce sexual interest in children while increasing sexual interest in adults (Kelly, 1982; Laws & Marshall, 1991; Marshall et al., 2009), and anti-libidinal medication can reduce or prevent sexual arousal and fantasy generally. Both can make it easier for an individual to manage and control their sexual fantasies and arousal (McPhail & Olver, 2020). Improvements in emotional and self-regulation, cognitions supportive of child sexual abuse, intimacy and relationships, and sexual regulation, can diminish the experience of and/or acting on sexual interest in children. Self-compassion and self-acceptance focused approaches can decrease the distress and despondency that can be associated with having a pedophilic sexual interest (Walton & Hocken, 2020).

Most individuals with pedophilia have some sexual arousal to and interest in adults, albeit often much less than to children, so there is the potential for treatment to increase sexual arousal to and behavior with adults, while diminishing that focused on children. However, in some individuals, with exclusive or very strongly preferential sexual arousal to children, that is not possible.

The approach to treatment of sexual offenders with pedophilia should be as per best practice for sexual offenders generally. Some criminogenic needs or dynamic factors that arise very commonly where there is pedophilia are emotional congruence with children, problems with adult intimacy, attitudes condoning sexual behavior with children, sex as coping, and sexual preoccupation. Improved understanding and awareness, skills development, and making relevant changes are important for these and any other relevant dynamic factors. Sexual interest in children should be specifically addressed in a way that is integrated with other aspects of treatment, although individual sessions with a specific focus on the behavioral technique, alongside or after group sessions, are usually required for effective behavior modification treatment (McPhail & Olver, 2020).

Although most sexual offending behavior programs are delivered in mixed groups (i.e., with people with child and adult victims) there is no convincing evidence that group treatment is more effective than individual treatment, albeit that it is more efficient (Gannon et al., 2019; Schmucker & Lösel, 2015). Wider institutional and community issues in terms of abuse of, threats to, and alienation of those who commit child sexual offences can impact the willingness and ability of a person to engage in and benefit from treatment and may impact group dynamics (Blagden et al., 2017). But treating child and adult victim offenders together is usual practice and is feasible. There is no evidence at this time that offence-specific treatment is more or less effective for child versus adult victim offenders.

Amongst contact offenders it can be useful to keep in mind typologies when formulating and treating individuals (Knight et al., 1989;Knight & King,2012; Lanning, 2010). Most pedophilic contact offenders "love" children, emotionally and in their distorted belief systems, and do not believe that they are causing harm at the time. Some such individuals are narcissistic and self-focused, while others see the interaction as mutual. Some introverted or antisocial individuals are oblivious to the physical and/or psychological harm they cause while sexually exploiting children to meet their sexual needs. Rarely pedophilic individuals are also sexually sadistic, enjoying and being sexually aroused by the suffering they cause (see Chap. 12 on Sexual Sadism). These differences have implications for both relevant treatment targets and responsivity.

Most CSAM offenders, the majority of whom have a pedophilic sexual interest, are low risk and their treatment needs are different from contact sexual offenders (Henshaw, Arnold, et al., 2020). It could be argued that the vast majority do not need offence specific treatment as they are very unlikely to commit further offences. Such individuals are generally prosocial, have been able to work, have relationships, and function reasonably well. Being arrested, charged, and convicted has the necessary deterrent effect. We have found that the primary offence-specific treatment need is usually to overcome the distorted belief that they are not hurting anyone by downloading such material. Indeed, once such offenders have addressed and accepted the fact that real children were sexually victimized in order to make the CSAM they were downloading, there is very often little else that needs to be addressed in treatment that would be deemed "offence-specific." The main challenge with such individuals is to get them through the criminal justice process with their lives relatively intact and trying to maintain their mental health and wellbeing. They may need some support and help with dealing with difficult emotions, with intimacy and relationships, with assertiveness and self-esteem, with managing their sexual behavior, and with managing their online behavior. They often also need help to deal with shame, rejection, alienation, depression, and suicidal ideation, especially during the court process. A smaller group of CSAM offenders repeatedly commit such offences, but do not escalate to commit contact sexual offences. They sometimes have historic contact offences, often as teenagers. They often have an exclusive or very strongly preferential sexual interest in children, very significant problems relating to others and dealing with emotions, and spend much of their lives on their own online. These individuals may benefit from offence specific treatment geared towards their specific needs rather than programs which are primarily geared towards contact offenders (Henshaw, Arnold, et al., 2020). A tiny minority of CSAM offenders, who also commit contact offences usually at the same time as online offences, have treatment needs identical to other contact child sexual offenders and usually have criminogenic needs across many domains. The treatment and support needs of NOMAPS have been described above and will be discussed further when considering prevention below.

People who commit CSA, including those with pedophilia, often feel a high degree of shame which may be associated with denial or minimization. These can present barriers to treatment especially if treatment requires the person to share extensive details of their offending, clinicians are perceived as judgmental and condemnatory and lacking genuine interest in people as humans and hope for the future, and clinicians do not take time to sensitively understand and help people to deal with feelings of shame. Particularly when talking about sexual attraction to children, sexual behavior and child sexual abuse, clinical skill, sensitivity, and discretion are helpful to promote engagement, obtain valid assessment information, and promote positive changes in sexual self-regulation (Marshall et al., 2011).

One specific and direct psychological intervention for pedophilic (or other deviant or atypical) sexual interest is via behavior modification. This is a set of approaches which aim to provide men with skills to manage or inhibit their sexual arousal to children in daily life. Those based on operant conditioning principles, include aversion therapies in which a noxious stimulus is paired with arousal to children or reinforcement therapies in which adult stimuli are associated with a rewarding experience (e.g., masturbation and orgasm; Marshall et al., 2009). Specific approaches include covert sensitization, olfactory aversion, orgasmic reconditioning, masturbatory satiation, and verbal satiation (Miner & Munns, 2021). Reviews indicate these interventions decrease sexual interest in children and increase interest in adults (Kelly, 1982; Laws & Marshall, 1991; Marshall et al., 2009). But findings from some studies indicate there are limited effects when it comes to increasing arousal to adults (Crolley et al., 1998; Johnston et al., 1992; Jones, 2014). As well as reducing arousal to children and perhaps increasing arousal to adults in the short to medium term, behavioral interventions have been described as potentially giving men a "portable skill" of having the capacity to control or inhibit arousal in the longer-term (McPhail & Olver, 2020). However, there is no evidence regarding the long-term effects of such treatment or whether improvements persist. There have also been no recent advances or innovations with behavior modification with most studies being from the twentieth century.

The other treatment specifically targeting sexual arousal to children is pharmacological (Darjee & Quinn, 2020). Broadly there are two types of medications which have some evidence for effectiveness: selective serotonin reuptake inhibitors (SSRIs) which potentiate serotonergic transmission in the brain and anti-libidinal medications which reduce testosterone activity in the body including the brain. The latter include anti-androgens which primarily block testosterone activity (e.g., cyproterone acetate and medroxyprogesterone acetate), gonadotrophin releasing hormone (GnRH) agonists (e.g., triptorelin, leuprorelin and goserelin), and GnRH antagonists (e.g., degarelix). SSRIs can reduce libido, decrease the intrusiveness of sexual thoughts, improve mood and reduce anxiety and so reduce sexual arousal as a means of dealing with negative emotions. It has been suggested that they can reduce deviant sexual interests while not having the same effect on non-deviant interests (Fedoroff, 2008). However their effects can be unpredictable and inconsistent, and their mechanism of action in reducing sexual urges is unknown. Anti-libidinal medications reduce sexual arousal, sexual fantasies, sexual urges, masturbation and sexual activity, which are all dependent on testosterone. High doses of anti-androgens and standard doses of GnRH agonists and antagonists can reduce testosterone activity to castrate levels and stop sexual fantasies and urges altogether. Medications can cause adverse effects, which can be particularly significant with anti-libidinal medications, although GnRH agonists are better tolerated than anti-androgens, and good medical monitoring can mitigate adverse effects. Anti-libidinal medications reduce all sexual interests and arousal and do not have a differential effect on deviant versus nondeviant sexual interests. Anti-libidinal medications can be helpful where there is comorbid hypersexuality or compulsive sexual behavior disorder, sexual urges that are subjectively very difficult to control and/or a pattern of serious sexual offending driven by pedophilic urges. Most experts agree that medications should be used voluntarily alongside other treatment and management strategies including psychological interventions. As medications reduce or stop fantasy, masturbation, and sexual activity, they cannot be used at the same time as initiating or implementing behavioral strategies. Where both approaches are utilized, behavioral interventions should be taught and implemented first, with pharmacological treatment later and prior to release to the community. Although the research evidence base for the use of medication is supportive, it is not necessarily robust, with positive (Lösel & Schmucker, 2005; McPhail & Olver, 2020; Turner & Briken, 2018), lukewarm (Landgren et al., 2022; Lewis et al., 2017) and negative systematic reviews (Khan et al., 2015; Schmucker & Lösel, 2015). The newest medication, degarelix, was shown, in a randomized control trial of self-presenting men with pedophilia, to quickly and significantly reduce pedophilic sexual interest, sexual preoccupation and the risk score for committing child sexual abuse (Landgren et al., 2020), with almost 60% of people treated reporting no further sexual interest in children after 12 weeks (Landgren et al., 2022), and the researchers concluding "degarelix holds potential to be a tolerable treatment with significant short-term risk-reduction effects in help-seeking patients with pedophilic disorder, including high-risk patients" (Rahm et al., 2020).

Two recent reviews have specifically looked at treatments targeting pedophilic sexual interest. McPhail and Olver (2020) undertook a meta-analytic review of the effectiveness of behavioral and pharmacological interventions for managing pedohebephilic arousal as measured by phallometric testing, including 1071 participants from 41 studies (18 of which were single case design studies). They found that both treatments showed moderate to large effects for reducing pedohebephilic arousal, and that men with high pretreatment pedohebephilic arousal showed the greatest reductions. However comprehensive treatment programs, which included programs which aimed to address multiple psychosocial risk factors including arousal control to reduce sexual recidivism, had small effects, but it was unclear whether this was due to these programs providing services to men without pedohebephilic interests, or potentially due to the treatment approach itself or a diluted effect from combining specialized interventions. None of the interventions had the effect of increasing sexual arousal to adults though. The authors were of the view that "changes on phallometric testing is likely best understood as a change in a person's ability to monitor and manage their arousal as opposed to representing a shift in sexual interest or orientation per se." Landgren et al. (2022) undertook a review of pharmacological treatment for pedophilic disorder and compulsive sexual behavior disorder, finding twelve studies conducted between 1974 and 2021 including studies of non-criminal samples, and concluded the studies provided some evidence that testosterone-lowering drugs reduced sexual activity in patients with pedophilia and compulsive sexual behavior disorder. But the body of evidence was described as "meager" with a need for studies using larger samples, specific criteria for inclusion, longer follow-up periods, and standardized outcome measures adhering to international reporting guidelines.

The debate as to whether pedophilia is a sexual orientation versus a sexual interest, as epitomized in the exchange between Cantor (2018) and Fedoroff (2018), has potential implications regarding the treatment of people with pedophilia. A sexual *orientation* is usually considered immutable, i.e., one cannot change the gender and age of the people one is sexually attracted to. The treatment task is then to help the individual to control and not act on their sexual attraction to children. However, sexual *interest* in children could be considered changeable by increasing sexual interest and activity with adults, reducing the barriers to adult intimacy, and reducing sexual interest and activity with children. On the one hand it is known that most individuals with a sexual attraction to children also have some sexual attraction to adults, on the other hand people with an exclusive or strong sexual preference for children just are not able to be attracted to adults. Rather than being two mutually exclusive alternatives, this heterogeneity, reflecting the reality of people encountered in clinical and forensic practice, means that some people can increase their interest and orientation towards adults and reduce that to children, while some unfortunately cannot.

13.10 Management

Management of people with pedophilia who have committed sexual offences, like other sexual and non-sexual offenders, involves a combination of some or all of the following: monitoring, supervision, restrictions, support, treatment and victim safety planning. Best practice would suggest that these risk management strategies should be tailored towards the level and nature of the risk posed by an individual, should target specific relevant risk factors, and build up a person's strengths, supports and protective factors. Management approaches should be effective (i.e., based on good research evidence as appropriately applied to an individual), only as restrictive as necessary and proportionate to the risk posed, balance the protection of others with the human rights of the individual, defensible (evidence-based, proportionate and following best practice) but not defensive (anxiety-based, back-covering and over-emphasizing reputational risk), aim to improve the psychological, sexual and social functioning of an individual, and should not, even inadvertently, increase the risk to others (through sexual offending) or to the individual (e.g., through suicide). There are few groups in society subject to more risk management approaches and processes than people considered to pose a sexual risk to children, and the drivers of this, unfortunately, are not primarily best practice approaches to clinical and forensic work and the prevention of child sexual abuse, but societal perceptions and concerns about the pervasive dangers posed by 'pedophiles' who are perceived as dangerous predators. Clinical and forensic practitioners must have an awareness of this societal and policy context, while striving to adhere to best practice within, and sometimes despite of, the legislative and policy contexts in which they work. This sometimes involves challenging orthodox, accepted, or required approaches, both overly punitive and risk averse ones, but also lax and dangerous ones, within teams, services, agencies, and inter-agency contexts, and in different clinical and forensic settings.

Societal concerns, as reflected in public discourse and political considerations (which are often far from considered), about the safety of children and CSA, have played a major role in shaping approaches to managing the risk posed by sexual offenders since the early 1990s. Central to this has been the fear of stereotypical 'predatory pedophiles' who purportedly groom, abduct, destroy the childhoods of, cause irreparable damage to, and sometimes kill their victims. Fear of "stranger danger" (Kitzinger, 2002; Moran et al., 1997) and a "moral panic" (Cohen, 2011; Fox, 2013) centered on pedophilia and pedophiles, alongside concurrent developments in risk assessment, have contributed to the adoption of a 'community protection model' (Connelly & Williamson, 2000) to manage the risk pose by sexual offenders generally and particularly those who target children, with the latter incorrectly conflated with pedophilia. High profile, but rare and atypical cases where children were killed by people who had previously committed child sexual offences have led to the adoption of sexual offender registration and notification (McPherson, 2016) laws, longer and indefinite sentencing (Padfield, 2017), post-sentence commitment (Jonathan, 2021) or supervision/detention (Bartels et al., 2019). The names of the children are well known and associated with inquiries, legislation or calls for action: Adam Walsh, Jacob Wetterling, Megan Kanka and Jessica Lunsford in the USA; Sarah Payne, Hollie Wells and Jessica Chapman in England; Scott Simpson and Mark Cummings in Scotland; Daniel Morcombe and Masa Vukotic in Australia. Over the last three decades such measures have become increasingly restrictive, driven by such horrific but unrepresentative child sexual homicide cases rather than research evidence or practice experience. At the same time concerns about child sexual abuse have also led to measures to protect children from adults who might cause sexual harm in care, work, and institutional settings (Erooga, 2012; Erooga et al., 2012, 2020; Kaufman et al., 2019).

It has been argued that the "pedophile panic" has been disproportionate to the actual risk posed to children, fueled by media sensationalism, erroneous perceptions that rates of child sexual abuse have escalated, and that those who sexually abuse children are incorrigible, unreformable, and irredeemable (West, 2000). Disgust, fear, hatred and othering of "pedophiles" has led to retributive and exclusionary policies, difficult to argue against when everything possible must be done to protect our children. In fact there has been a reduction in rates of child sexual abuse in developed countries over the last 30 years (Finkelhor, 2020) and rates of sexual abuse have probably been reducing for over 50 years (Fanslow et al., 2021); most child sexual abuse is committed by people without a previous history of such behavior (Lussier & Cale, 2013); much, if not most, child sexual abuse is not committed by people with pedophilia (Seto, 2018); most people who commit child sexual abuse do not recidivate (Dowling et al., 2021; Seto, 2018) and recidivism rates have reduced markedly over the last 50 years (Lussier et al., 2023); most people with a pedophilic sexual interest do not sexually abuse children (Dombert et al., 2016); and most child sexual abuse is perpetrated within families by males (particularly stepfathers, fathers and siblings) most of whom are not pedophilic (Seto et al.). Escalating rates of online CSAM offending (Kloess et al., 2014), survey findings that 5–10% of men have some sexual interest in children (Dombert et al., 2016; Savoie et al., 2021), and findings that experiences of and perpetration of child sexual abuse are very common and still at an unacceptably high level (Stoltenborgh et al., 2015) perhaps add fuel to the "pedophile panic". However, a legitimate question is whether westernized societies are wasting time, energy, resources, and money on measures that may have little impact in reducing CSA, or whether some of the measures introduced have contributed to the reduction in sexual abuse (Fanslow et al., 2021; Finkelhor, 2020). West (2000) suggested that the "punitive socio-legal policy" … "driven by public demand" had perhaps had negative effects on children, on the rehabilitation of child sex offenders, and on those with pedophilic sexual interests, through vigilantism, exclusion, rejection, and stigmatization.

Recently there has been increasing emphasis on adopting public health approaches in the prevention of crime generally (Sutton et al., 2021), sexual offending (Laws, 2000), and child sexual abuse specifically (Russell et al., 2020; Seto et al., 2024). Rather than focusing on tertiary prevention (intervening after sexual abuse has occurred) through compulsory measures and risk management, the public health approach focuses primarily on secondary prevention (intervening before sexual abuse has occurred or escalated) and on tertiary prevention approaches which are focused on treatment, rehabilitation, and social inclusion. Secondary prevention will be described below (see Sect. 13.11). Kemshall (2017) suggested that the overwhelming trend towards community protection approaches had recently been somewhat "mitigated" by desistance approaches, strengths promotion, and public health prevention methods.

Although at a policy level the community protection and public health approaches may seem antagonistic, in reality, when involved in the practical management of individuals in the community, practitioners have to strike the balance between, and integrate, rehabilitative and inclusionary approaches, and compulsory and restrictive measures (Kemshall, 2021). Restrictive measures should be the minimum required to prevent child sexual abuse based on an individualized and evidence-based risk assessment. Unfortunately, there can be a tension between this and legally mandated blanket measures, for example the compulsory reporting of specified behaviors, mandatory sentencing for certain offences, automatic placement on sexual offender registries and public notification, compulsory treatment programs, and non-discretionary community monitoring and restrictions. The problem with this is that precious risk management resources are then spread thinly across many individuals, rather than focusing on those who actually pose an ongoing risk to children. Especially as evidence-based risk assessment is pretty successful at identifying low risk offenders (Fazel et al., 2012), there is evidence that automatic public notification schemes increase the incidence of sexual offences in the area (Prescott & Rockoff, 2011; Zgoba & Mitchell, 2023), and blanket restrictions can mean that people who have committed sexual offences cannot live safe or stable lifestyles potentially increasing the likelihood of recidivism (Levenson, 2008).

In prison and other custodial settings people who commit child sexual offences are branded "pedophiles" and despised, as they are in society, not only by other prisoners, but also by staff. Sexual offenders are often kept in separate protection units, but even in these units those who offend against children are seen as the 'lowest of the low'. This creates barriers to treatment and rehabilitation, with treatment efforts easily undone, or not even possible, when people face hostility, abuse, and alienation (Blagden & Perrin, 2016). Prisons with an environment conducive to rehabilitation have staff with positive attitudes to offenders and who believe offenders can change, and an environment experienced as safe and positive by prisoners who have committed sexual offences (Blagden et al., 2016). This can be achieved by having prisons or units within prisons that specialize in the treatment and rehabilitation of sexual offenders, although some concerns in such settings are a sexually deviant "undercurrent" which normalizes sexual deviance and offending, staff concerns about relationships with sexual offenders, and offenders' concerns about the authenticity of staff (Blagden & Wilson, 2020). There are often fears that if child sexual offenders are allowed to spend time together that they will indirectly (through reinforcing attitudes, fantasies, or behaviors) or directly (through facilitating access to victims and forming pedophile networks and rings) increase the risk that they will reoffend. However, although there are cases where offenders act in pairs or groups (Harkins & Dixon, 2010), most child sexual offending is a solitary activity and co-offending in child sexual offenders is less common than in people who offend in every other way (Bright et al., 2022; Van Mastrigt & Carrington, 2019), and there is no convincing research evidence that associating with other individuals with similar offending or sexual interests facilitates further sexual offending. Indeed, Hanson and Harris (1998, 2000) found that, whether contact was ongoing or fleeting, association with other sexual offenders had no relationship with re-offending. This was found for both offenders that victimized children and those that victimized adult females. In fact, ongoing contact amongst girl victim CSA offenders was slightly negatively related to recidivism (i.e., less offending when there was contact), but was so close to zero it was not statistically significant. Accordingly, concerns regarding sexual offenders having contact with each other would seem to be based on "folk wisdom" rather than evidence-based practice. What is considerably more important from a risk assessment perspective is the overall number of significant social influences (i.e., net positive is protective and net negative is related to recidivism). Despite this, it is often an automatic condition that child sexual offenders are not allowed to associate with each other, even though whilst in prison they can only safely associate with each other, and then when released struggle to form other friendships and associations.

Many of the people who come within the ambit of special measures for high-risk sexual offenders, such as post-sentence civil commitment and indeterminate sentencing, have committed child sexual offences and have been assessed as posing an ongoing risk. Committing sexual offences against children rather than adults and having a diagnosis of pedophilic disorder have been found to be associated with selection for post-sentence civil commitment in the USA (Levenson, 2004). Offenders with child victims make up the majority of those who are civilly committed, and pedophilia is diagnosed in a third (Janus & Walbek, 2000; Levenson, 2004) to a half (Elwood et al., 2010; Jackson & Richards, 2007), and as many as two thirds (Becker et al., 2003) or three quarters (McLawsen et al., 2012) of cases. So, a diagnosis of pedophilia and treatment and management of sexual offenders with pedophilia is central to civil commitment regimes and facilities in the USA. Similarly, most offenders subject to post-sentence orders in Victoria, Australia, had previous and index sexual offences against children, whilst over half were diagnosed with pedophilia and almost one in ten hebephilia (Doyle et al., 2011). Obviously, it is important when assessing people for post-sentence measures that best practice is followed with regards to ascertaining and diagnosing pedophilia and assessing risk of further child sexual abuse. This is also important at sentencing in jurisdictions where long or indeterminate sentences or detention can be imposed on child sexual offenders who are deemed to pose a high risk of further sexual offending (Gailey et al., 2017; Valiquet, 2006).

Unfortunately, there can be conflation, confusion and translation between punitive/retributive and risk management/rehabilitative aims and measures in policy and practice. When treatment is touted by politicians in the name of retribution, this should be seen as very concerning. For example, chemical and surgical castration laws in the USA. As outlined above, pharmacological treatment can be effective in reducing pedophilic sexual interest and arousal and so contribute to rehabilitation and risk reduction in some people, alongside other interventions and rehabilitative strategies. But most experts agree that medication should be given on a voluntary and individualized basis and that clinically irreversible surgical castration has no advantage over pharmacological treatment with a GnRH agonist, forgetting about the punitive and mutilating connotations of the former. Laws are politically justified based on retribution, deterrence and risk management. Recent examples are Alabama's mandatory chemical castration law and Louisiana's mandatory surgical castration law. The latter requires a medical assessment at sentencing where a person has committed a serious sexual offence against a child under 13 years old, and then if an offender is mandated to be surgically castrated and refuses to have the procedure before they are released, they can be given a further 3–5 years in prison. There will clearly be complex ethical, clinical, and forensic issues to be negotiated and reconciled by psychiatrists and other health professionals who involve themselves in such assessments and some view these developments as a return to medieval punitive castration.

The risk management of people with a sexual attraction to children who pose a risk of harming children is relevant in several non-criminal contexts. These include family court proceedings in relation to child custody, child protection procedures where a child is potentially at sexual risk, preventing the risk of sexually harm potentially proposed in employment settings through background checks and measures taken by professional regulatory bodies where there may be a sexual risk to a child from a professional (e.g., teacher, doctor, psychologist, nurse, social worker). Although many who pose a sexual risk to children in such contexts, particularly family contexts, do not have pedophilia, about half of those who sexually abuse children do (Seto, 2018), most child sexual abuse is not reported or prosecuted (Cashmore et al., 2020), and a significant minority of minor attracted people in the community do report having had sexual contact with children (Dombert et al., 2016). Assessing for the presence of pedophilia, assessing risk of sexual harm, and determining if risk mitigation and protective measures are sufficient are essential in these situations. Where the issue is someone self-reporting or being discovered to have sexual thoughts about children, but without a history of committing child sexual abuse, it is important to ascertain the nature of the thoughts. As outlined above, in obsessive-compulsive disorder themes of child sexual interest or abuse are common but such individuals do not pose a sexual risk to children. However, the current authors have come across cases in all these settings where pedophilia-themed obsessive-compulsive disorder has led to sanctions and measures against individuals as they have been wrongly regarded as having pedophilia and posing a risk to children. In addition, a majority of minor attracted people do not commit sexual abuse and most CSAM offenders do not commit further child sexual abuse, so a balance has to be struck with such individuals and assumptions of risk are often unfounded. Assessing for the presence of pedophilia can be particularly challenging where there have been allegations but no official charges or convictions for child sexual abuse. Instruments like the SSPI-2 can be applied to the allegation information, with appropriate caveats, to give an initial indicator of the extent of sexual attraction to children. Risk assessment is often challenging in these contexts. When there are no charges or convictions or most allegations have not been officially recognized, actuarial instruments are of no use. The current authors use structured professional judgment (SPJ) instruments (Hart & Boer, 2020), such as the SVR-20 V2 (Boer et al., 2017) and RSVP-V2 (Hart et al., 2022), for these cases, scoring and applying these instruments twice or sometimes iteratively, starting with verified child sexual abuse then adding in alleged incidents, and then seeing what the outcomes of the assessment in terms of formulation, risk scenarios and risk level are with and without considering certain allegations. Then the decision maker, for example a court or tribunal, can decide what they are going to consider as valid facts, and then use the risk assessment accordingly to make their decisions.

Multi-agency management, interaction and communication are an integral part of the management of people who are considered to pose a risk of sexual harm in the community, whether they are in the criminal justice system, the forensic mental health system or child protection system. This can bring both benefits and challenges (Darjee et al., 2024), but where there is a high risk of harm should be considered an integral part of supporting and treating people and managing risk in the community. For example, in the UK statutory Multi-Agency Public Protection Arrangements (MAPPA) mandate that agencies like the police, community criminal justice, prisons, child protection, child protection, housing, social services and mental health services work together, sharing relevant information and making joint plans to manage the risk posed by the highest risk offenders in the community (Darjee et al., 2024; Kemshall & Maguire, 2021). Resources are targeted towards the small minority of people who pose an ongoing risk of serious harm and there is not a blanket approach to all sexual offenders. So, risk assessment plays a crucial role and less than five percent of registered sexual offenders receive high levels of multi-agency management. For people who do pose an ongoing risk of sexual harm to children such measures allow agencies to work together, not work in silos, share information, but crucially to develop trusting relationships with each other and to help each other. Some mental health professionals see such arrangements as a threat to the sanctity of their therapeutic relationships and patient confidentiality. However, in reality, if clinicians keep patients informed, share just what is required to manage risk, and approach this as agencies being on the same page and working together to help the individual and protect others (particularly children), then such threats do not actualize and despite the inherent tensions, multi-agency working can be supportive with a sense of shared risk across professionals, services and agencies.

The issue of what and when to disclose information or report to child protective services or the police can be anxiety provoking and challenging for clinicians. Laws, service policies, professional guidelines and ethical codes set out the frameworks to be followed, and clinicians need to be aware of those that apply to them in their jurisdiction. In some situations, reporting is mandatory without clinical discretion or judgment playing a role. For example, in Victoria, Australia, the law mandates that any adult who becomes aware of a sexual offence against a child must report this to the police or face a potential criminal charge. This includes CSAM offences. Most jurisdictions have a higher threshold for reporting, and some, for example Germany, do not mandate such reporting at all. This has implications when working with people sexually attracted to children who may disclose unreported offences, making it important to make patients aware of the obligations and responsibilities of the clinician. In some situations, disclosure or reporting is based on the risk the person poses, making evidence-based risk assessment important. However, it is important that people with concerns about their thoughts or behaviors, such as people with pedophilia-themed OCD and NOMAPS, are not automatically reported when no offences have been committed and there is no risk to children. Sometimes it is easier for professionals or services to take an unthinking all or nothing approach, either always reporting everyone where there is anything to do with sex with children, or always hiding behind confidentiality and never reporting anyone. In addition, most practitioners, including those working in mental health services, do not necessarily know the base rates, relevant risk factors. or how to assess risk. Forensic clinicians can play an important role in consulting, supporting, and educating their colleagues in these areas.

Based on the research evidence at the time, Seto (2018), believing a conservative approach was warranted, and made the following recommendations for the treatment and management of people with pedophilia who commit child sexual offences:

1. Risk assessment using a well-supported measure, for the purpose of triaging individuals in terms of placement, security, and intensity of any treatment and supervision.
2. Education of the client, his spouse or partner, family members, and close friends regarding risky situations and potential precursors for sexual offenses against children (e.g., the offender being alone with a child or consuming alcohol).
3. Behavioral treatments targeting pedophilic sexual arousal, when applicable, with "booster" sessions as needed on an ongoing basis.
4. Monitoring of access to child pornography, unsupervised contacts with children, and alcohol or drug use.
5. Anti-androgen treatments targeting sexual drive for higher-risk individuals who are not suitable for incapacitation. Though the evidence for such treatments is not strong, compliance with the regimen is a positive treatment-related indicator and could be used to adjust the intensity of other interventions.
6. Cognitive-behavioral and behavioral treatments targeting dynamic risk factors for general criminal behavior such as antisocial attitudes and beliefs, association with antisocial peers, and substance abuse.
7. Incapacitation of high-risk pedophilic sex offenders, especially those who have committed many sexual offenses against children or who have committed violent sexual offenses.

Although this is a useful summary of what one of the world's leading experts considered to be best practice, based on the scientific evidence, the current authors would clarify or adjust them as follows: offence specific psychological treatment to address sexual offending for people who pose a moderate or high risk of sexual recidivism rather than just focusing on antisociality; pharmacological treatment should be given voluntarily and considered as a treatment for people with relevant sexual regulation problems (including compulsive sexual behavior disorder and pedophilic disorder with difficulty inhibiting behavior) not a compliance measure; and there are different levels of incapacitation from imprisonment, and detention in other facilities, through to legally mandated restrictions and monitoring in the community.

13.11 Prevention

Prevention of CSA has been considered a societal priority over the last three decades. Until recently the primary approach to this was managing the risk posed by known child sexual offenders. These included providing treatment, monitoring and supervision to those who have committed child sexual offences, incapacitating and placing restrictions on those who have committed child sexual offences, checks placed on those who might work with or otherwise have access to children, and ensuring reporting of child sexual abuse along with appropriate child protection measures. Another approach has been to educate children about situations where they may be at risk and make environments safer for children. These are focused on how children can protect or advocate for themselves as potential victims, and what their caregivers, adult bystanders, and institutions can do to stop sexual abuse from occurring. None of these approaches are specific to pedophilia although about half of those targeted by such measures will have pedophilia. However, these approaches could be considered reactive tertiary prevention ones which primarily aim to prevent further sexual abuse by people who have already committed child sexual offences, decided to commit such offences, or placed themselves in situations where there is a heightened risk of such offending.

More recently there has been a focus on secondary prevention, through psychological, social, or educational interventions for those concerned about their sexual thoughts or behavior towards children. These are sometimes described as primary prevention measures for CSA, but in the context of considering pedophilia, they are more appropriately considered secondary prevention. Although these do not specifically target minor attracted people or people with pedophilia, most of those involved have a sexual interest in children and so have pedophilia or pedophilic disorder. Approaches include helplines, self-help websites, peer support groups, therapist-guided interventions using pre-created modules usually online, in-person treatment, institutional interventions (e.g., classroom sessions), and technology facilitated interventions, such as campaigns run by major technology and social media companies (Seto et al., 2024). They are all secondary prevention approaches, although they do not exclude those who may have committed child sexual abuse whether detected or not, particularly as most child sexual abuse is not officially reported or sanctioned.

Stop It Now! developed initially in the USA in the 1990s but there are now allied and affiliated Stop It Now! organizations in England and Wales, Scotland, Ireland, the Netherlands, Belgium, and Australia (Eisenberg et al., 2014; Grant et al., 2019; Hudson, 2018; Van Horn et al., 2015). These provide free confidential helplines and online self-help resources for people concerned about their sexual attractions, thoughts, or behaviors regarding children. They also provide resources for people concerned about the behavior of others. Some also provide remote or in person individual and group support and treatment. The longest running, most developed and best known in-person prevention program is the Prevention Program Dunkelfeld in Germany, which has been running since it started as a pilot project in Berlin 20 years ago, but now operates across Germany with some international extensions (Beier, 2018). Dunkelfeld translates to "darkfield" in English, with this referring to the dark figure of unreported child sexual abuse crimes. It provides confidential and free treatment, and its slogan is "You are not guilty because of your sexual desire, but you are responsible for your sexual behavior. There is help! Don't become an offender!" It has grown into a network of interventions in Germany (Kein Täter Werden—"Don't Offend"), interventions for adolescents, and online developments like Troubled Desire, an anonymous online intervention. Treatment has three main components. Patients are encouraged to accept that they have sexual interests in children, to integrate it into their self-concept, and to involve relatives or partners in the therapeutic process. Cognitive behavior therapy is used to improve coping skills, stress management, and sexual attitudes. In addition pharmacological treatments, such as SSRIs and anti-libidinal medications, may be offered.

In a description of 358 Dunkelfeld Project participants, 60% had pedophilia, 28% hebephilia, and 12% were teleiophilic. Although they had self-referred, 71% had committed contact sexual abuse or accessed CSAM. An initial evaluation by Beier et al. (2009) examined the outcomes of 53 patients treated for 12 months compared with 22 individuals who had been on the waiting list for 12 months using pre- and post-intervention ratings on 14 self-report measures representing dynamic factors related to sexual abuse. The control group showed no reductions, while the treatment group showed improvements in emotional deficits, offence supportive cognitions and sexual self-regulation. But almost all of those treated had committed CSAM or contact sexual abuse, and 20% of contact sexual abuse perpetrators and 90% of CSAM perpetrators continued with their behaviors. None of these offences were detected by legal authorities. The conclusion was that the intervention could reduce dynamic risk factors and related behaviors. However, Mokros and Banse (2019) reassessed the data focusing on the time by group interaction to ascertain the treatment effect, finding that at best there were weak non-significant treatment effects, and concluded the data did not show that treatment led to a reduction in proneness to commit child sexual abuse.

Project Bridge, which developed from Prevent It developed in Sweden, provides anonymous online therapist-created interventions in multiple languages (English, Spanish, German, Swedish, Finnish, Czech or Slovak). It is targeted at people over 18 years old concerned about their sexual urges involving minors who want help, and have used CSAM, whether they have been sanctioned or not. Individuals who sign up agree for their data to be used for research. The two interventions are *Mi Bridge* involving five text-chat motivational interviewing sessions exploring and eliciting the participants' reasons for change to facilitate help-seeking; and *ReDirection*, a 5-week self-help cognitive behavioral therapy program to help individuals decrease or stop using CSAM with text based chat support available if needed. It is available globally and is a collaboration between universities and a nongovernmental organization across the European Union. Prevent It was targeted more widely, including people who had not committed CSAM or contact sexual abuse, recruiting people through Darknet forums. A single blind randomized controlled trial with 160 participants from across the world, who had used CSAM in the previous week, showed a significant reduction in time viewing CSAM in the treatment group although the effect size was small (Lätth et al., 2022).

Some forensic mental health services and clinicians provide assessment and intervention for self-presenting individuals concerned about their sexual thoughts and behavior (McEwan & Darjee, 2021), although many such individuals are turned away by or do not receive the help they need or want when they present to primary care, mental health, or forensic services. This occurs as most health service clinicians lack the knowledge and skills necessary, they do not know who to refer people to, there are no services to refer people to, they stigmatize those with pedophilia and are overwhelmed by risk concerns, and/or do not believe that such individuals deserve or respond to mental health care. This even occurs when minor attracted people are seeking standard mental health or other health interventions rather than specialist input. Ideally the need for services should be based on clinical needs and risk, rather than whether a person has offended already. Barriers to MAPs seeking and receiving treatment and support have been described above (see Sect. 13.6.3 above).

Seto et al. (2024) conducted a systematic review of studies of the outcomes of child sexual abuse perpetration prevention interventions, identifying only seven studies, five focused on adults and two on children. Most studies had significant methodological limitations precluding drawing conclusions. There were no studies of helpline, self-help or peer support interventions, one of a therapist guided intervention, four of in-person treatment in adults (three of which were from the Prevention Project Dunkelfeld), one of in-person treatment with children, and one of institutional intervention for children. As expected, despite the "tremendous growth in the development and launch of CSA perpetration prevention" recently, there has been a lag in evaluating whether prevention efforts actually have the desired outcome in terms of preventing child sexual abuse. So, despite the enthusiasm for and rapid growth of such prevention programs evidence for effectiveness in preventing child sexual abuse is lacking although it is early days and methodologically stronger studies, some which are underway, are required. Most of the interventions include people who have not offended, people who have committed CSAM offences and people who have committed contact CSA, albeit usually without necessarily being apprehended so are a mixture of secondary and tertiary prevention.

Some of the clinical challenges in this work are assumptions that self-presenting people would have gone on to commit child sexual offences, when most, like CSAM offenders, probably would not. Initially the focus of preventive interventions was primarily on treatments like offence specific programs used for those who have committed sexual offences, focusing on engagement, motivation and criminogenic needs. More recently, in keeping with research on MAPS (see above), there has been increasing emphasis in some interventions on self-compassion, acceptance, reducing self-stigma, improving psychosocial functioning and preventing suicide. Mandatory reporting policies and legislation can present a barrier to such interventions. In Germany there are no such requirements so confidentiality can be maintained. However, many interventions elsewhere are delivered anonymously to avoid mandatory reporting, making it easier for people to contact programs and be open, but perhaps impairing the quality of relationships with professionals. Barriers to recruitment and retention include societal stigma and opprobrium, negative experiences when seeking help previously, and internalized stigma and lack of hope. So preventive programs must find ways to overcome these.

Some criticisms of currently available preventive interventions are that they target people with pedophilia (or hebephilia) rather than people who pose a risk of committing child sexual abuse, given that many if not most people who commit child sexual abuse do not have a primary sexual interest in children. Seto et al. (2024) suggested that there needed to be more of a focus on preventive interventions for parents and caregivers, perhaps particularly stepfathers, who tend not to have pedohebephilia. Despite the clinical challenges and lack of evidence of effectiveness it is important that services are available for people concerned about their sexual thoughts about or behaviors with children, as much to alleviate their distress and improve their psychosexual functioning rather than necessarily because they are likely to commit sexual abuse. Often the task for clinicians is to reassure people that they are unlikely to commit child sexual abuse especially as they have sought help. But relatedly, it is important that people with obsessive-compulsive disorder, focused on pedophilia or child sexual abuse, do not get entangled in these prevention interventions, if they call helplines or put themselves forward for interventions to address their perceived risk to children (see above).

In terms of primary prevention, specific measures to prevent people developing pedophilia may be no more feasible than trying to prevent people developing teleiophilia, particularly if one views pedophilia as an immutable sexual orientation. Some of the etiological research findings may point to the potential for interventions in early and prenatal life to prevent pedophilia or pedophilia leading to committing sexual abuse, although the current evidence base does not support any specific pedophilia targeted preventive measures. Potential measures could include improved perinatal care and the prevention of neurological perturbations, prevention of child sexual abuse and early sexualization, prevention of and interventions for more general adverse childhood experiences, and interventions with children showing early signs of problematic sexual behavior. But all those things are necessary to prevent poor psychosocial outcomes in children anyway. Preventive educational interventions in schools have shown some success in reducing peer-on-peer sexual harassment and abuse, and it has been suggested that incorporating a focus on preventing child sexual abuse perpetration at an age-appropriate level, in the context of sexual and relationship education, could be effective (Seto et al., 2024). Although this may not prevent pedophilia per se, it may prevent children growing up to become perpetrators of sexual abuse in the context of promoting healthy sexual attitudes, behaviors and functioning.

A further potential prevention target is the stigmatization of MAPs. Stigmatizing minor attracted people probably does nothing to prevent child sexual abuse and may even increase its likelihood. However, it is perhaps unrealistic to think that politicians, the media, and the public will accept that, while also crying out for more punitive and restrictive approaches for those who sexually abuse children. Making "myth busting" information available has not been shown to be effective or helpful (Jara & Jeglic, 2021) although there may be some promise in stigma reducing approaches (Lawrence & Willis, 2022; McKillop & Price, 2023). All professionals who work in relevant fields should make efforts to not conflate pedophilia or minor attraction with child sexual abuse. After all heterosexuality is not conflated with rape, even though most of those who commit rape are heterosexual teleiophilic men and over half of adults have coercive sexual fantasies!

13.12 Conclusion

Pedophilia and *Pedophilic Disorder* are terms that reflect a particular or preferential sexual interest in prepubescent children. In current diagnostic terminology, pedophilia refers to the nature of the fantasies, urges, or behaviors. However, this does not constitute a disorder unless the individual acts on the urges with a child or the fantasies cause marked distress or interpersonal difficulty. While they are often conflated, pedophilia and pedophilic disorder are not the same as child sexual abuse. Indeed, approximately half of the males who sexually victimize children have pedophilic sexual interests. The other half are motivated by a range of sexual and nonsexual motives. Conversely, there is likely a considerable number of individuals with pedophilic sexual interests who never engage in any sexual behaviors involving children.

Hebephilia refers to a sexual attraction to young pubescent children. Hebephilic interests were previously included in the diagnostic criteria for Paedophilia in ICD-10 and were proposed for inclusion in DSM-5. While this proposal was rejected for various reasons, and is no longer formally part of the DSM or ICD nosologies, the last decade has seen considerable research that has underscored the strong overlaps between pedophilic and hebephilic sexual interests, to the point that many researchers and practitioners refer to pedohebephilia.

It is estimated that between one and three percent of males will have pedophilic sexual interests, but the rate of Pedophilic Disorder, based on concomitant distress and impaired functioning caused by the sexual interest in children, is likely to be somewhere between 0.5 and 2.0%. It is difficult to estimate the rate of hebephilia in the community, but it is likely the same as, or slightly higher than, pedophilia, but will also overlap with pedophilia, so the rate of pedohebephilia is less than the sum of the two and perhaps between two and five percent.

This chapter has provided a detailed overview of the likely etiology of pedophilia and pedophilic disorder and concluded that there are likely two primary pathways in which such interests develop. One of these results in a sexual orientation to prepubescents that can be described as a genuinely exclusive form of pedophilia. The other pathway results in varying degrees of pedohebephilic interest that can be viewed as genuinely paraphilic and is developed in a similar way to other paraphilic disorders. Throughout the chapter several typological systems and behavioral rating scales have been described that can assist practitioners to differentiate sexual offenders with a preferential pedophilic interest from those with little such interest. These approaches can also provide some indication of the relative strength of pedophilic and pedohebephilic interests.

It is our opinion that the current diagnostic criteria for Pedophilic Disorder are overly sensitive and not particularly specific. Indeed, too many non-pedophilic individuals who commit situational sexual offences against children are likely to meet the rather woolly diagnostic criteria as they necessarily include fantasies, urges, or behaviors. In addition, the use of a general child age of 13 years or below is very likely to be, perhaps ironically, identifying a proportion of those with hebephilic interests. One potential remedy would be to simply accept the clear overlaps between pedophilia and hebephilia and thereby also accept a dually considered diagnostic category of pedohebephilia (with or without pedophilic and hebephilic subtypes). In addition, a move away from arbitrary age differences to a focus exclusively on Tanner stages of development for identifying puberty and early pubescence would arguably increase specificity of both pedophilic and hebephilic interests. Future diagnostic classifications should ideally focus on identifying those with a sexual preference for children, or at the very least those with an equal or greater sexual interest in children as to other age groups. Identifying those with a stronger or more preferential sexual interest in children than is currently possible will allow more focused insights and enhanced understanding of pedophilic and hebephilic sexual interests.

References

Abé, C., Adebahr, R., Liberg, B., Mannfolk, C., Lebedev, A., Eriksson, J., Långström, N., & Rahm, C. (2021). Brain structure and clinical profile point to neurodevelopmental factors involved in pedophilic disorder. *Acta Psychiatrica Scandinavica, 143*(4), 363–374. https://doi.org/10.1111/acps.13273

Abel, G. G., Becker, J. V., Cunningham-Rathner, J., Mittelman, M., & Rouleau, J.-L. (1988). Multiple paraphilic diagnoses among sex offenders. *Bulletin of the American Academy of Psychiatry and the Law, 16*(2), 153–168.

Aggrawal, A. (2009). *Forensic and medico-legal aspects of sexual crimes and unusual sexual practices*. CRC Press. https://doi.org/10.1201/9781420043099

Akerman, G., Perkins, D., & Bartels, R. M. (Eds.). (2020). *Assessing and managing problematic sexual interests*. Routledge. https://doi.org/10.4324/9780429287695

Alanko, K., Schmidt, A. F., Neutze, J., Bergen, E., Santtila, P., & Osterheider, M. (2017). Male sexual interest in and offending against children: The abused-abuser hypothesis. *Journal of Forensic Psychology Research and Practice, 17*(2), 128–144. https://doi.org/10.1080/24732850.2017.1286544

Alden, A., Brennan, P., Hodgins, S., & Mednick, S. (2007). Psychotic disorders and sex offending in a Danish birth cohort. *Archives of General Psychiatry, 64*(11), 1251–1258. https://doi.org/10.1001/archpsyc.64.11.1251

Alison, L., Goodwill, A., & Alison, E. (2005). Guidelines for profilers. In L. Alison (Ed.), *The forensic psychologist's casebook: Psychological profiling and criminal investigation* (pp. 235–277). Willan.

Almond, L., McManus, M. A., Giles, S., & Houston, E. (2017). Female sex offenders: An analysis of crime scene behaviors. *Journal of Interpersonal Violence, 32*(24), 3839–3860. https://doi.org/10.1177/0886260515603976

American Psychiatric Association. (1987). *Diagnostic and statistical manual of mental disorders* (3rd ed., rev.). Author.

American Psychiatric Association. (1994). *Diagnostic and statistical manual of mental disorders* (4th ed.). Author.

American Psychiatric Association. (2000). *Diagnostic and statistical manual of mental disorders* (4th ed., text rev.). Author.

American Psychiatric Association. (2013). *Diagnostic and statistical manual of mental disorders* (5th ed.). Author. https://doi.org/10.1176/appi.books.9780890425596

American Psychiatric Association. (2022). *Diagnostic and statistical manual of mental disorders* (5th ed., text rev.). Author.

Arlow, J. A. (1967). Perversion: Theoretical and therapeutic aspects. In H. M. Ruitenbeek (Ed.), *The psychotherapy of perversions* (pp. 56–63). Citadel Press.

B4U-ACT. (2011). *Awareness of sexuality in youth, suicidality, and seeking care*. Retrieved May 25, 2024, from http://www.b4uact.org/research/survey-results/spring-2011-survey

Babchishin, K. M., Dibayula, S., McCulloch, C., Hanson, R. K., & Helmus, L. M. (2023). ACUTE-2007 and STABLE-2007 predict recidivism for men adjudicated for child sexual exploitation material offending. *Law and Human Behavior, 47*(5), 606–618. https://doi.org/10.1037/lhb0000540

Babchishin, K. M., Hanson, R. K., & VanZuylen, H. (2015). Online child pornography offenders are different: A meta-analysis of the characteristics of online and offline sex offenders against children. *Archives of Sexual Behavior, 44*(1), 45–66. https://doi.org/10.1007/s10508-014-0270-x

Babchishin, K. M., Lee, S. C., Eke, A. W., & Seto, M. C. (2022). Temporal order of sexual offending is risk-relevant for individuals with child sexual exploitation materials offences. *Sexual Offending: Theory, Research, and Prevention, 17*, Article e7229. https://doi.org/10.5964/sotrap.7229

Babchishin, K. M., Nunes, K. L., & Hermann, C. A. (2013). The validity of Implicit Association Test (IAT) measures of sexual attraction to children: A meta-analysis. *Archives of Sexual Behavior, 42*(3), 487–499. https://doi.org/10.1007/s10508-012-0022-8

Babchishin, K. M., Seto, M. C., Fazel, S., & Långström, N. (2019). Are there early risk markers for pedophilia? A nationwide case-control study of child sexual exploitation material offenders. *Journal of Sex Research, 56*(2), 203–212. https://doi.org/10.1080/00224499.2018.1492694

Babchishin, K. M., Seto, M. C., Sariaslan, A., Lichtenstein, P., Fazel, S., & Långström, N. (2017). Parental and perinatal risk factors for sexual offending in men: A nationwide case-control study. *Psychological Medicine, 47*(2), 305–315. https://doi.org/10.1017/S003329171600249X

Bagley, C., Wood, M., & Young, L. (1994). Victim to abuser: Mental health and behavioral sequels of child sexual abuse in a community survey of young adult males. *Child Abuse and Neglect, 18*(8), 683–697. https://doi.org/10.1016/0145-2134(94)90018-3

Bandura, A. (1977). Self-efficacy: Toward a unifying theory of behavioral change. *Psychological Review, 84*(2), 191–215. https://doi.org/10.1037/0033-295x.84.2.191

Bartels, L., Walvisch, J., & Richards, K. (2019). More, longer, tougher . . . or is it finally time for a different approach to the post-sentence management of sex offenders in Australia? *43 Criminal Law Journal 41 SSRN Electronic Journal*. https://doi.org/10.2139/ssrn.3394599

Becker, J. V., Stinson, J., Tromp, S., & Messer, G. (2003). Characteristics of individuals petitioned for civil commitment. *International Journal of Offender Therapy and Comparative Criminology, 47*(2), 185–195. https://doi.org/10.1177/0306624X03251114

Beech, A. R., & Mitchell, I. J. (2005). A neurobiological perspective on attachment problems in sexual offenders and the role of selective serotonin re-uptake inhibitors in the treatment of such problems. *Clinical Psychology Review, 25*(2), 153–182. https://doi.org/10.1016/j.cpr.2004.10.002

Beier, K. M. (2018). Preventing child sexual abuse: The prevention project Dunkelfeld. *The Journal of Sexual Medicine, 15*(8), 1065–1066. https://doi.org/10.1016/j.jsxm.2018.03.008

Beier, K. M., Neutze, J., Mundt, I. A., Ahlers, C. J., Goecker, D., Konrad, A., & Schaefer, G. A. (2009). Encouraging self-identified pedophiles and hebephiles to seek professional help: First results of the Prevention Project Dunkelfeld (PPD). *Child Abuse and Neglect, 33*(8), 545–549. https://doi.org/10.1016/j.chiabu.2009.04.002

Berlin, F. S. (2014). Pedophilia and DSM-5: The importance of clearly defining the nature of a pedophilic disorder. *Journal of the American Academy of Psychiatry and the Law, 42*(4), 404–407.

Blagden, N., & Perrin, C. (2016). 'Relax lads, you're in safe hands here': Experiences of a sexual offender treatment prison. In C. Reeves (Ed.), *Experiencing imprisonment* (pp. 27–45). Routledge.

Blagden, N., Perrin, C., Smith, S., Gleeson, F., & Gillies, L. (2017). 'A different world' exploring and understanding the climate of a recently re-rolled sexual offender prison. *Journal of Sexual Aggression, 23*(2), 151–166. https://doi.org/10.1080/13552600.2016.1264633

Blagden, N., & Wilson, K. (2020). 'We're all the same here'—Investigating the rehabilitative climate of a rerolled sexual offender prison: A qualitative longitudinal study. *Sexual Abuse, 32*(6), 727–750. https://doi.org/10.1177/1079063219839496

Blagden, N., Winder, B., & Hames, C. (2016). 'They treat us like human beings'—Experiencing a therapeutic sex offenders prison: Impact on prisoners and staff and implications for treatment. *International Journal of Offender Therapy and Comparative Criminology, 60*(4), 371–396. https://doi.org/10.1177/0306624X14553227

Blanchard, R. (2010a). The DSM diagnostic criteria for pedophilia. *Archives of Sexual Behavior, 39*, 304–316. https://doi.org/10.1007/s10508-009-9536-0

Blanchard, R. (2010b). The specificity of victim count as a diagnostic indicator of pedohebephilia. *Archives of Sexual Behavior, 39*, 1245–1252. https://doi.org/10.1007/s10508-010-9659-3

Blanchard, R. (2013). A dissenting opinion on DSM-5 pedophilic disorder. *Archives of Sexual Behavior, 42*, 675–678. https://doi.org/10.1007/s10508-013-0117-x

Blanchard, R., Christensen, B. K., Strong, S. M., Cantor, J. M., Kuban, M. E., Klassen, P., Dickey, R., & Blak, T. (2002). Retrospective self-reports of childhood accidents causing unconsciousness in phallometrically diagnosed pedophiles. *Archives of Sexual Behavior, 31*(6), 511–526. https://doi.org/10.1023/A:1020659331965

Blanchard, R., Kolla, N. J., Cantor, J. M., Klassen, P. E., Dickey, R., Kuban, M. E., & Blak, T. (2007). IQ, handedness, and pedophilia in adult male patients stratified by referral source. *Sexual Abuse: A Journal of Research and Treatment, 19*(3), 285–309. https://doi.org/10.1177/107906320701900307

Blanchard, R., Kuban, M. E., Blak, T., Klassen, P. E., Dickey, R., & Cantor, J. M. (2012). Sexual attraction to others: A comparison of two models of alloerotic responding in men. *Archives of Sexual Behavior, 41*(1), 13–29. https://doi.org/10.1007/s10508-010-9675-3

Blanchard, R., Lykins, A. D., Wherrett, D., Kuban, M. E., Cantor, J. M., Blak, T., Dickey, R., & Klassen, P. E. (2009). Pedophilia, hebephilia, and the *DSM-V*. *Archives of Sexual Behavior, 38*, 335–350. https://doi.org/10.1007/s10508-008-9399-9

Blanchard, R., Watson, M. S., Choy, A., Dickey, R., Klassen, P., Kuban, M., & Ferren, D. J. (1999). Pedophiles: Mental retardation, maternal age, and sexual orientation. *Archives of Sexual Behavior, 28*(2), 111–127. https://doi.org/10.1023/a:1018754004962

Boer, D. P. (2006). Sexual offender risk assessment strategies: Is there a convergence of opinion yet? *Sexual Offender Treatment, 1*(2), 1–4.
Boer, D. P., & Hart, S. D. (2009). Sex offender risk assessment: Research, evaluation, 'best-practice' recommendations and future directions. In J. L. Ireland, C. A. Ireland, & P. Birch (Eds.), *Violent and sexual offenders: Assessment, treatment and management* (pp. 27–42). Willan.
Boer, D. P., Hart, S. D., Kropp, P. R., & Webster, C. D. (1997). *Manual for the sexual violence risk-20: Professional guidelines for assessing risk of sexual violence*. The British Columbia Institute Against Family Violence and The Mental Health, Law, and Policy Institute, Simon Fraser University.
Boer, D. P., Hart, S. D., Kropp, P. R., & Webster, C. D. (2017). *Manual for version 2 of the Sexual Violence Risk-20: Structured professional judgment guidelines for assessing and managing risk of sexual violence*. Protect International.
Bogaert, A. F. (2001). Handedness, criminality, and sexual offending. *Neuropsychologia, 39*(5), 465–469. https://doi.org/10.1016/S0028-3932(00)00134-2
Bonagura, A., Abrams, D., & Teller, J. (2022). Diagnostic differential between pedophilic-OCD and pedophilic disorder: An illustration with two vignettes. *Archives of Sexual Behavior, 51*(4), 2359–2368. https://doi.org/10.1007/s10508-021-02273-5
Boschetti, A., Camperio Ciani, A. C., & Scarpazza, C. (2023). Sexual offenses and the brain. *Handbook of Clinical Neurology, 197*, 161–179. https://doi.org/10.1016/B978-0-12-821375-9.00017-7
Bradbury, J., & Lievesley, R. (2020). *The risk factors and characteristics of men with intellectual disability convicted of sexual offences experiencing sexual preoccupation*. In K. Hocken, R. Lievesley, B. Winder, H. Swaby, N. Blagden, & P. Banyard (Eds.), *Sexual crime and intellectual functioning* (pp. 131–160). Palgrave MacMillan.
Brankley, A. E., Knight, R. A., & Hanson, R. K. (2022). Pedophilia is a taxon among 706 adult males assessed at a civil commitment center. *Journal of Psychopathology and Clinical Science, 131*(2), 209–220. https://doi.org/10.1037/abn0000735
Breiling, L., Rettenberger, M., & Turner, D. (2020). The relevance of sexual biographies in individuals convicted of child sexual abuse offenses for the development of pedosexual interests and sexual recidivism. *Sexual Offending: Theory, Research, and Prevention, 15*(1). https://doi.org/10.5964/sotrap.3711
Bright, D., Whelan, C., & Ouellet, M. (2022). Assessing variation in co-offending networks. *Global Crime, 23*(1), 101–121. https://doi.org/10.1080/17440572.2022.2047654
Bruce, S. L., Ching, T. H. W., & Williams, M. T. (2018). Pedophilia-themed obsessive–compulsive disorder: Assessment, differential diagnosis, and treatment with exposure and response prevention. *Archives of Sexual Behavior, 47*(2), 389–402. https://doi.org/10.1007/s10508-017-1031-4
Burton, D. L., Miller, D. L., & Shill, C. T. (2002). A social learning theory comparison of the sexual victimization of adolescent sexual offenders and nonsexual offending male delinquents. *Child Abuse and Neglect, 26*(9), 893–907. https://doi.org/10.1016/s0145-2134(02)00360-5
Caffo, E., Asta, L., & Scandroglio, F. (2021). Child abuse and exploitation: What we know about the problem and new perspectives. In E. Caffo (Ed.), *Online child sexual exploitation* (pp. 3–21). Springer. https://doi.org/10.1007/978-3-030-66654-5_2
Camperio Ciani, A. S. C., Scarpazza, C., Covelli, V., & Battaglia, U. (2019). Profiling acquired pedophilic behavior: Retrospective analysis of 66 Italian forensic cases of pedophilia. *International Journal of Law and Psychiatry, 67*, 101508. https://doi.org/10.1016/j.ijlp.2019.101508
Canter, D., Hughes, D., & Kirby, S. (1998). Paedophilia: Pathology, criminality, or both? The development of a multivariate model of offence behaviour in child sexual abuse. *Journal of Forensic Psychiatry, 9*(3), 532–555. https://doi.org/10.1080/09585189808405372
Cantor, J. M. (2018). Can pedophiles change? *Current Sexual Health Reports, 10*(4), 203–206. https://doi.org/10.1007/s11930-018-0165-2
Cantor, J. M., & Blanchard, R. (2012). White matter volumes in pedophiles, hebephiles, and teleiophiles. *Archives of Sexual Behavior, 41*(4), 749–752. https://doi.org/10.1007/s10508-012-9954-2

Cantor, J. M., Blanchard, R., Robichaud, L. K., & Christensen, B. K. (2005). Quantitative reanalysis of aggregate data on IQ in sexual offenders. *Psychological Bulletin, 131*(4), 555–568. https://doi.org/10.1037/0033-2909.131.4.555

Cantor, J. M., & Fedoroff, J. P. (2018). Can pedophiles change? Response to opening arguments and conclusions. *Current Sexual Health Reports, 10*(4), 213–220. https://doi.org/10.1007/s11930-018-0167-0

Cantor, J. M., Kabani, N., Christensen, B. K., Zipursky, R. B., Barbaree, H. E., Dickey, R., Klassen, P. E., Mikulis, D. J., Kuban, M. E., Blak, T., Richards, B. A., Hanratty, M. K., & Blanchard, R. (2008). Cerebral white matter deficiencies in pedophilic men. *Journal of Psychiatric Research, 42*(3), 167–183. https://doi.org/10.1016/j.jpsychires.2007.10.013

Cantor, J. M., Lafaille, S., Soh, D. W., Moayedi, M., Mikulis, D. J., & Girard, T. A. (2015). Diffusion tensor imaging of pedophilia. *Archives of Sexual Behavior, 44*(8), 2161–2172. https://doi.org/10.1007/s10508-015-0629-7

Cantor, J. M., & McPhail, I. V. (2016). Non-offending pedophiles. *Current Sexual Health Reports, 8*(3), 121–128. https://doi.org/10.1007/s11930-016-0076-z

Carlstedt, A., Nilsson, T., Hofvander, B., Brimse, A., Innala, S., & Anckarsäter, H. (2009). Does victim age differentiate between perpetrators of sexual child abuse? A study of mental health, psychosocial circumstances, and crimes. *Sexual Abuse, 21*(4), 442–454. https://doi.org/10.1177/1079063209346699

Carvalho, J., Bradford, J., Murphy, L., Briken, P., & Fedoroff, P. (2020). Measuring pedophilic sexual interest. *The Journal of Sexual Medicine, 17*(3), 378–392. https://doi.org/10.1016/j.jsxm.2019.12.008

Cashmore, J., Taylor, A., & Parkinson, P. (2020). Fourteen-year trends in the criminal justice response to child sexual abuse reports in New South Wales. *Child Maltreatment, 25*(1), 85–95. https://doi.org/10.1177/1077559519853042

Cassiani-Miranda, C. A., Quintero-Gómez, T. C., Burbano, A. L., & Eduard, A.-C. (2019). Pedophilia, substance-use disorder, and intellectual disability: A case report. *Addictive Disorders and Their Treatment, 18*(1), 58–62. https://doi.org/10.1097/ADT.0000000000000149

Cassity, J. H. (1927). Psychological considerations of pedophilia. *Psychoanalytic Review, 14*, 189–209.

Chow, E. W., & Choy, A. L. (2002). Clinical characteristics and treatment response to SSRI in a female pedophile. *Archives of Sexual Behavior, 31*(2), 211–215. https://doi.org/10.1023/a:1014795321404

Cohen, L. J., Grebchenko, Y. F., Steinfeld, M., Frenda, S. J., & Galynker, I. I. (2008). Comparison of personality traits in pedophiles, abstinent opiate addicts, and healthy controls: Considering pedophilia as an addictive behavior. *The Journal of Nervous and Mental Disease, 196*(11), 829–837. https://doi.org/10.1097/NMD.0b013e31818b4e3d

Cohen, L. J., McGeoch, P. G., Watras-Gans, S., Acker, S., Poznansky, O., Cullen, K., Itskovich, Y., & Galynker, I. (2002). Personality impairment in male pedophiles. *The Journal of Clinical Psychiatry, 63*(10), 912–919. https://doi.org/10.4088/jcp.v63n1009

Cohen, L., Ndukwe, N., Yaseen, Z., & Galynker, I. (2018). Comparison of self-identified minor-attracted persons who have and have not successfully refrained from sexual activity with children. *Journal of Sex and Marital Therapy, 44*(3), 217–230. https://doi.org/10.1080/0092623X.2017.1377129

Cohen, L. J., Wilman-Depena, S., Barzilay, S., Hawes, M., Yaseen, Z., & Galynker, I. (2020). Correlates of chronic suicidal ideation among community-based minor-attracted persons. *Sexual Abuse, 32*(3), 273–300. https://doi.org/10.1177/1079063219825868

Cohen, M. L., Boucher, R. J., Seghorn, T. K., & Mehegan, J. (1979). *The sexual offender against children.* Paper presented at the meeting of the Association for Professional Treatment of Offenders, Boston, MA, USA.

Cohen, M. L., Seghorn, T., & Calmas, W. (1969). Sociometric study of the sex offender. *Journal of Abnormal Psychology, 74*(2), 249–255. https://doi.org/10.1037/h0027185

Cohen, S. (2011). *Folk devils and moral panics*. Routledge. ISBN 978-0-203-82825-0. https://doi.org/10.4324/9780203828250

Cohen, T. H. (2023). Building a risk tool for persons placed on federal post-conviction supervision for child sexual exploitation material offenses: Documenting the federal system's past, current, and future efforts. *Federal Probation, 87*(1), 19–31. https://www.uscourts.gov/federal-probation-journal/2023/06/building-risk-tool-persons-placed-federal-post-conviction

Coleman, E. M., & Haaven, J. (2001). Assessment and treatment of learning disabled sexual abusers. In M. S. Carich & S. E. Mussack (Eds.), *Handbook for sexual abuser assessment and treatment* (pp. 194–209). Safer Society Foundation.

Collins, C. M. (2023). *Understanding minor attracted persons*. Unpublished doctoral dissertation. University of Ontario Institute of Technology. https://hdl.handle.net/10155/1700

Connelly, C., & Williamson, S. (2000). *Review of the research literature on serious violent and sexual offenders. Crime and criminal justice research findings no. 46.* Scottish Executive central Research Unit.

Cooper, A. J., Swaminath, S., Baxter, D., & Poulin, C. A. (1990). A female sex offender with multiple paraphilias: A psychologic, physiologic (laboratory sexual arousal) and endocrine case study. *The Canadian Journal of Psychiatry, 35*(4), 334–337. https://doi.org/10.1177/070674379003500411

Cortoni, F. (2014). What is so special about female sexual offenders? Introduction to the special issue on female sexual offenders. *Sexual Abuse: A Journal of Research and Treatment, 27*(3), 232–234.

Cortoni, F., Hanson, R. K., & Coache, M.-È. (2010). The recidivism rates of female sexual offenders are low: A meta-analysis. *Sexual Abuse: A Journal of Research and Treatment, 22*(4), 387–401. https://doi.org/10.1177/1079063210372142

Craig, L. A., & Moss, T. E. (2006, June). Categorising sexually inappropriate behaviour in men with learning disabilities. In *15th annual conference* (pp. 20–22). Division of Forensic Psychology.

Craissati, J., Ramsden, J., Ryan, S., Webster, N., & West, L. (2021). Intensive intervention and risk management services (IIRMS) three years on: What we need to do better in the offender personality disorder pathway. *The Journal of Forensic Practice, 23*(4), 385–396. https://doi.org/10.1108/JFP-08-2021-0042

Crolley, J., Roys, D., Thyer, B. A., & Bordnick, P. S. (1998). Evaluating outpatient behavior therapy of sex offenders: A pretest-posttest study. *Behavior Modification, 22*(4), 485–501. https://doi.org/10.1177/01454455980224003

Culling, H. (2018). *Informing the prevention of child sexual abuse: Comparing convicted offenders and minor-attracted persons*. Unpublished Master of Science thesis. University of Canterbury. https://doi.org/10.26021/8628

Dahle, K.-P., Lehmann, R. J. B., & Richter, A. (2014). Die Screening Scala Pädophilen Tatverhaltens. *Forensische Psychiatrie, Psychologie, Kriminolgie, 8*, 208–215. https://doi.org/10.1177/1079063214566715

Darjee, R., Judge, J., & Kirkland, J. (2024). Muti-agency public protection arrangements (MAPPA). In J. Marshall & J. Kirkland (Eds.), *Innovative practice in forensic settings. A cognitive analytic approach to effective relational work* (pp. 75–86). Pavilion.

Darjee, R., & Quinn, A. (2020). Pharmacological treatment of sexual offenders. In J. Proulx, F. Cortoni, L. A. Craig, & E. Letourneau (Eds.), *The Wiley handbook of what works with sexual offenders: Contemporary perspectives in theory, assessment, treatment and prevention* (pp. 217–245). Wiley.

Davis, M. R. (2013, October). Differentiating child sexual abusers. *InPsych: The Bulletin of the Australian Psychological Society, 35*(5), 14–15.

Davis, M. R., & Ogloff, J. R. P. (2008). Key considerations and problems in assessing risk for violence. In D. V. Canter & R. Žukauskienė (Eds.), *Psychology and law: Bridging the gap* (pp. 191–210). Ashgate.

Day, K. (1997). Clinical features and offense behavior of mentally retarded sex offenders: A review of research. *The NADD Newsletter, 14*(6), 86–90.

DeClue, G. (2009). Should hebephilia be a mental disorder? A reply to Blanchard et al. (2008). *Archives of Sexual Behavior, 38*, 317–318. https://doi.org/10.1007/s10508-008-9422-1

Dennison, S. M., Stough, C., & Birgden, A. (2001). The big 5 dimensional personality approach to understanding sex offenders. *Psychology, Crime and Law, 7*(3), 243–261. https://doi.org/10.1080/10683160108401796

Desbuleux, J. C., & Fuss, J. (2023). The self-reported sexual real-world consequences of sex doll use. *The Journal of Sex Research, 61*(8), 1261–1275. https://doi.org/10.1080/00224499.2023.2199727

Dietz, P. E. (1983). Sex offenses: Behavioral aspects. In S. H. Kadish (Ed.), *Encyclopedia of crime and justice* (pp. 1485–1493). Free Press.

Dombert, B., Schmidt, A. F., Banse, R., Briken, P., Hoyer, J., Neutze, J., & Osterheider, M. (2016). How common is men's self-reported sexual interest in prepubescent children? *Journal of Sex Research, 53*(2), 214–223. https://doi.org/10.1080/00224499.2015.1020108

Dowling, C., Morgan, A., & Pooley, K. (2021). Reoffending among child sexual offenders. *Trends and Issues in Crime and Criminal Justice, 628*, 1–16.

Dubin, L. A., & Horowitz, E. (2017). *Caught in the web of the criminal justice system: Autism, developmental disabilities, and sex offenses*. Jessica Kingsley.

Dyshniku, F., Murray, M. E., Fazio, R. L., Lykins, A. D., & Cantor, J. M. (2015). Minor physical anomalies as a window into the prenatal origins of pedophilia. *Archives of Sexual Behavior, 44*(8), 2151–2159. https://doi.org/10.1007/s10508-015-0564-7

Eastvold, A., Suchy, Y., & Strassberg, D. (2011). Executive function profiles of pedophilic and nonpedophilic child molesters. *Journal of the International Neuropsychological Society, 17*(2), 295–307. https://doi.org/10.1017/S1355617710001669

Eher, R., Rettenberger, M., & Turner, D. (2019). The prevalence of mental disorders in incarcerated contact sexual offenders. *Acta Psychiatrica Scandinavica, 139*(6), 572–581. https://doi.org/10.1111/acps.13024

Eisenberg, M., Mulder, J., van Horn, J., & Stam, J. (2014). Stop it now! Helpline Netherlands: A study of its use and effects—English summary. De Waag. https://www.stopitnow.org.uk/wp--content/uploads/2020/01/stop_it_now_nl_findings.pdf.

Eke, A. W., Helmus, L. M., & Seto, M. C. (2018). *Scoring guide for the Child Pornography Offender Risk Tool (CPORT): Version 2.*

Eke, A. W., Helmus, L. M., & Seto, M. C. (2019). A validation study of the child pornography offender risk tool (CPORT). *Sexual Abuse, 31*(4), 456–476. https://doi.org/10.1177/1079063218762434

Eke, A. W., & Seto, M. C. (2016). *Scoring guide for the Child Pornography Offender Risk Tool (CPORT).*

Elchuk, D. L., McPhail, I. V., & Olver, M. E. (2022). Stigma-related stress, complex correlates of disclosure, mental health, and loneliness in minor-attracted people. *Stigma and Health, 7*(1), 100–112. https://doi.org/10.1037/sah0000317

Elwood, R. W., Doren, D. M., & Thornton, D. (2010). Diagnostic and risk profiles of men detained under Wisconsin's sexually violent person law. *International Journal of Offender Therapy and Comparative Criminology, 54*(2), 187–196. https://doi.org/10.1177/0306624X08327305

Eriksson, J. M., Andersen, L. M., & Bejerot, S. (2013). RAADS-14 Screen: Validity of a screening tool for autism spectrum disorder in an adult psychiatric population. *Molecular Autism, 4*(1), 49. https://doi.org/10.1186/2040-2392-4-49

Erooga, M. (Ed.). (2012). *Creating safer organisations: Practical steps to prevent the abuse of children by those working with them*. Wiley.

Erooga, M., Allnock, D., & Telford, P. (2012). Sexual abuse of children by people in organisations: What offenders can teach us about protection. In M. Erooga (Ed.), *Creating safer organisations: Practical steps to prevent the abuse of children by those working with them* (pp. 63–84). Wiley.

Erooga, M., Kaufman, K., & Zatkin, J. G. (2020). Powerful perpetrators, hidden in plain sight: An international analysis of organisational child sexual abuse cases. *Journal of Sexual Aggression, 26*(1), 62–90. https://doi.org/10.1080/13552600.2019.1645897

Fanslow, J., Hashemi, L., Gulliver, P., & McIntosh, T. (2021). A century of sexual abuse victimisation: A birth cohort analysis. *Social Science and Medicine, 270*, 113574. https://doi.org/10.1016/j.socscimed.2020.113574
Fazel, S., Singh, J. P., Doll, H., & Grann, M. (2012). Use of risk assessment instruments to predict violence and antisocial behaviour in 73 samples involving 24 827 people: Systematic review and meta-analysis. *BMJ, 345*, e4692. https://doi.org/10.1136/bmj.e4692
Fazel, S., Sjöstedt, G., Långström, N., & Grann, M. (2007). Severe mental illness and risk of sexual offending in men: A case-control study based on Swedish national registers. *The Journal of Clinical Psychiatry, 68*(4), 588–596. https://doi.org/10.4088/jcp.v68n0415
Fazio, R. L. (2018). Toward a neurodevelopmental understanding of pedophilia. *The Journal of Sexual Medicine, 15*(9), 1205–1207. https://doi.org/10.1016/j.jsxm.2018.04.631
Fazio, R. L., Dyshniku, F., Lykins, A. D., & Cantor, J. M. (2017). Leg length versus torso length in pedophilia: Further evidence of atypical physical development early in life. *Sexual Abuse: A Journal of Research and Treatment, 29*(5), 500–514. https://doi.org/10.1177/1079063215609936
Fazio, R. L., Lykins, A. D., & Cantor, J. M. (2014). Elevated rates of atypical handedness in paedophilia: Theory and implications. *Laterality, 19*(6), 690–704. https://doi.org/10.1080/1357650X.2014.898648
Fedoroff, J. P. (2008). Treatment of paraphilic sexual disorders. In D. L. Rowland & L. Incrocci (Eds.), *Handbook of sexual and gender identity disorders* (pp. 563–586). Wiley.
Fedoroff, J. P. (2018). Can people with pedophilia change?: Yes they can! *Current Sexual Health Reports, 10*(4), 207–212. https://doi.org/10.1007/s11930-018-0166-1
Fedoroff, J. P. (2020). The pedophilia and orientation debate and its implications for forensic psychiatry. *Journal of the American Academy of Psychiatry and the Law, 48*, 146–150. https://doi.org/10.29158/JAAPL.200011-20
Fedoroff, J. P., Fishell, A., & Fedoroff, B. (1999). A case series of women evaluated for paraphilic sexual disorders. *The Canadian Journal of Human Sexuality, 8*(2), 127–140.
Fedoroff, J. P., & Pinkus, S. S. (1996). The genesis of pedophilia. *Journal of Offender Rehabilitation, 23*(3–4), 85–101. https://doi.org/10.1300/J076v23n03_06
Fenichel, O. (1945). *The psychoanalytic theory of neurosis*. Basic Books.
Fernandes, L. C., Gillberg, C. I., Cederlund, M., Hagberg, B., Gillberg, C., & Billstedt, E. (2016). Aspects of sexuality in adolescents and adults diagnosed with autism spectrum disorders in childhood. *Journal of Autism and Developmental Disorders, 46*(9), 3155–3165. https://doi.org/10.1007/s10803-016-2855-9
Fernandez, Y., Harris, A. J. R., Hanson, R. K., & Sparks, J. (2014). *STABLE-2007 coding manual—Revised 2014*. Unpublished report. Public Safety Canada.
Finkelhor, D. (2020). Trends in adverse childhood experiences (ACEs) in the United States. *Child Abuse and Neglect, 108*, 104641. https://doi.org/10.1016/j.chiabu.2020.104641
First, M. B., Gibbon, M., Spitzer, R. L., Williams, J. B. W., & Benjamin, L. S. (1995). *User's guide for the Structured Clinical Interview for DSM-IV axis II personality disorders*. American Psychiatric Publishing.
Fitch, J. H. (1962). Men convicted of sexual offences against children. *British Journal of Criminology, 3*(1), 18–37.
Fonteille, V., Redouté, J., Lamothe, P., Straub, D., Lavenne, F., Le Bars, D., Raverot, V., Moulier, V., Marchand, J.-J., Vittoz, A., Leriche, C., Pugeat, M., & Stoléru, S. (2019). Brain processing of pictures of children in men with pedophilic disorder: A positron emission tomography study. *NeuroImage. Clinical, 21*, 101647. https://doi.org/10.1016/j.nicl.2018.101647
Fox, K. J. (2013). Incurable sex offenders, lousy judges & the media: Moral panic sustenance in the age of new media. *American Journal of Criminal Justice, 38*(1), 160–181. https://doi.org/10.1007/s12103-012-9154-6
Franklin, K. (2009). The public policy implications of "hebephilia": A response to Blanchard et al. (2008). *Archives of Sexual Behavior, 38*, 319–320. https://doi.org/10.1007/s10508-008-9425-y

Freel, M. (2003). Child sexual abuse and the male monopoly: An empirical exploration of gender and a sexual interest in children. *British Journal of Social Work, 33*(4), 481–498. https://doi.org/10.1093/bjsw/33.4.481

Freud, S. (1905). *Three essays on the theory of sexuality* (Standard edition, 7). Hogarth Press.

Freund, K., & Kuban, M. (1994). The basis of the abused abuser theory of pedophilia: A further elaboration on an earlier study. *Archives of Sexual Behavior, 23*(5), 553–563. https://doi.org/10.1007/BF01541497

Freund, K., Seeley, H. R., Marshall, W. E., & Glinfort, E. K. (1972). Sexual offenders needing special assessment and/or therapy. *Canadian Journal of Criminology and Corrections, 14*(4), 345–365.

Fromuth, M. E., & Conn, V. E. (1997). Hidden perpetrators: Sexual molestation in a nonclinical sample of college women. *Journal of Interpersonal Violence, 12*(3), 456–465. https://doi.org/10.1177/088626097012003009

Gailey, Y., Martin, L., & Webb, R. (2017). 'An exceptional sentence': Exploring the implementation of the order for lifelong restriction. Contemporary sex offender risk management. *Perceptions, I*, 115–143.

Galea, J., Butler, J., Iacono, T., & Leighton, D. (2004). The assessment of sexual knowledge in people with intellectual disability. *Journal of Intellectual & Developmental Disability, 29*(4), 350–365. https://doi.org/10.1080/13668250400014517

Gannon, T. A. (2021). A compositional explanatory theory of pedophilia. *Aggression and Violent Behavior, 61*. ISSN 1359-1789. https://doi.org/10.1016/j.avb.2021.101662

Gannon, T. A., Olver, M. E., Mallion, J. S., & James, M. (2019). Does specialized psychological treatment for offending reduce recidivism? A meta-analysis examining staff and program variables as predictors of treatment effectiveness. *Clinical Psychology Review, 73*, 101752. https://doi.org/10.1016/j.cpr.2019.101752

Garrington, C., Kelty, S. F., Rickwood, D., & Boer, D. (2022). The development of the ERICSO—A proposed instrument for internet child abuse material offender assessment. *Journal of Forensic Practice, 24*(4), 453–470. https://doi.org/10.1108/JFP-07-2022-0033

Gebhard, P. H., & Gagnon, J. H. (1964). Male sex offenders against very young children. *American Journal of Psychiatry, 121*, 576–579. https://doi.org/10.1176/ajp.121.6.576

Gebhard, P. H., Gagnon, J. H., Pomeroy, W. B., & Christenson, C. V. (1965). *Sex offenders: An analysis of types*. Harper & Row and Paul B. Hoeber, Inc., Medical Books.

Gerwinn, H., Weiß, S., Tenbergen, G., Amelung, T., Födisch, C., Pohl, A., Massau, C., Kneer, J., Mohnke, S., Kärgel, C., Wittfoth, M., Jung, S., Drumkova, K., Schiltz, K., Walter, M., Beier, K. M., Walter, H., Ponseti, J., Schiffer, B., & Kruger, T. H. C. (2018). Clinical characteristics associated with paedophilia and child sex offending—Differentiating sexual preference from offence status. *European Psychiatry, 51*, 74–85. https://doi.org/10.1016/j.eurpsy.2018.02.002

Gilby, R., Wolf, L., & Goldberg, B. (1989). Mentally retarded adolescent sex offenders. A survey and pilot study. *Canadian Journal of Psychiatry. Revue Canadienne de Psychiatrie, 34*(6), 542–548. https://doi.org/10.1177/070674378903400611

Glasser, M. (1987). Psychodynamic aspects of paedophilia. *Psychoanalytic Psychotherapy, 3*(2), 121–135. https://doi.org/10.1080/02668738700700111

Glueck, B. (1956). *Final report: Research project for the study of persons convicted of crimes involving sexual aberrations. June 1952–June 1955*. State Department of Hygiene.

Good, P., & Burstein, J. (2012). Hebephilia and the construction of a fictitious diagnosis. *The Journal of Nervous and Mental Disease, 200*(6), 492–494. https://doi.org/10.1097/NMD.0b013e318257c4f1

Grabell, A. S., & Knight, R. A. (2009). Examining childhood abuse patterns and sensitive periods in juvenile sexual offenders. *Sexual Abuse, 21*(2), 208–222. https://doi.org/10.1177/1079063209333133

Graber, B., Hartmann, K., Coffman, J. A., Huey, C. J., & Golden, C. J. (1982). Brain damage among mentally disordered sex offenders. *Journal of Forensic Sciences, 27*(1), 125–134. https://doi.org/10.1520/JFS11457J

Grady, M. D., & Levenson, J. S. (2021). Prevalence rates of adverse childhood experiences in a sample of minor-attracted persons: A comparison study. *Traumatology, 27*(2), 227–235. https://doi.org/10.1037/trm0000273

Grant, B.-J., Shields, R. T., Tabachnick, J., & Coleman, J. (2019). 'I didn't know where to go': An examination of Stop It Now! *Journal of Interpersonal Violence, 34*(20), 4225–4253. https://doi.org/10.1177/0886260519869237

Gray, N. S., Brown, A. S., MacCulloch, M. J., Smith, J., & Snowden, R. J. (2005). An implicit test of the associations between children and sex in pedophiles. *Journal of Abnormal Psychology, 114*(2), 304–308. https://doi.org/10.1037/0021-843X.114.2.304

Gray, S. R., Abel, G. G., Jordan, A., Garby, T., Wiegel, M., & Harlow, N. (2015). Visual reaction timetm as a predictor of sexual offense recidivism. *Sexual Abuse, 27*(2), 173–188. https://doi.org/10.1177/1079063213502680

Griffiths, D. M., Fedoroff, P., & Richards, D. (2010). Sexual and gender identity disorders in people with intellectual disabilities. In L. A. Craig, W. R. Lindsay, & K. D. Browne (Eds.), *Assessment and treatment of sexual offenders with intellectual disabilities: A handbook* (pp. 111–135). Wiley-Blackwell. https://doi.org/10.1002/9780470665510.ch7

Griffiths, D., Hindsburger, D., & Christian, R. (1985). Treating developmentally handicapped sexual offenders: The York Behaviour Management Services treatment program. *Psychiatric Aspects of Mental Retardation Reviews, 4*(12), *49–52.*

Groth, A. N. (1981). *Sexual offenders against children.*. Forensic Mental Health Associates.

Groth, A. N., & Birnbaum, H. J. (1979). *Men who rape: The psychology of the offender.* Plenum Press.

Habermeyer, B., Esposito, F., Händel, N., Lemoine, P., Kuhl, H. C., Klarhöfer, M., Mager, R., Mokros, A., Dittmann, V., Seifritz, E., & Graf, M. (2013). Response inhibition in pedophilia: An fMRI Pilot Study. *Neuropsychobiology, 68*(4), 228–237. https://doi.org/10.1159/000355295

Habermeyer, B., Händel, N., Lemoine, P., Klarhöfer, M., Seifritz, E., Dittmann, V., & Graf, M. (2012). LH-RH agonists modulate amygdala response to visual sexual stimulation: A single case fMRI study in pedophilia. *Neurocase, 18*(6), 489–495. https://doi.org/10.1080/13554794.2011.627346

Hall, D. K., Mathews, F., & Pearce, J. (1998). Factors associated with sexual behavior problems in young sexually abused children. *Child Abuse and Neglect, 22*(10), 1045–1063. https://doi.org/10.1016/s0145-2134(98)00078-7

Hanson, R. K., Bourgon, G., Helmus, L., & Hodgson, S. (2009). The principles of effective correctional treatment also apply to sexual offenders: A meta-analysis. *Criminal Justice and Behavior, 36*(9), 865–891. https://doi.org/10.1177/0093854809338545

Hanson, R. K., & Bussière, M. T. (1998). Predicting relapse: A meta-analysis of sexual offender recidivism studies. *Journal of Consulting and Clinical Psychology, 66*(2), 348–362. https://doi.org/10.1037/0022-006x.66.2.348

Hanson, R. K., Harris, A. J. R., Scott, T.-L., & Helmus, L. (2007). *Assessing the risk of sexual offenders on community supervision: The Dynamic Supervision Project* (Corrections Research User Rep. No. 2007-05). Public Safety Canada.

Hanson, R. K., & Morton-Bourgon, K. E. (2004). *Predictors of sexual recidivism: An updated meta-analysis* (Corrections Research User Rep. No. 2004-02). Public Safety and Emergency Preparedness Canada.

Hanson, R. K., & Morton-Bourgon, K. E. (2005). The characteristics of persistent sexual offenders: A meta-analysis of recidivism studies. *Journal of Consulting and Clinical Psychology, 73*(6), 1154–1163. https://doi.org/10.1037/0022-006X.73.6.1154

Hanson, R. K., & Morton-Bourgon, K. E. (2007). *The accuracy of recidivism risk assessments for sexual offenders: A meta-analysis* (Corrections User Report No 2007-01). Public Safety and Emergency Preparedness Canada.

Hanson, R. K., & Morton-Bourgon, K. E. (2009). The accuracy of recidivism risk assessments for sexual offenders: A meta-analysis of 118 prediction studies. *Psychological Assessment, 21*(1), 1–21. https://doi.org/10.1037/a0014421

Hanson, R. K., & Thornton, D. (1999). *Static-99: Improving actuarial risk assessments for sex offenders* (Corrections User Report No 1999-02). Department of the Solicitor General of Canada.

Hanson, R. K., & Thornton, D. (2000). Improving risk assessments for sex offenders: A comparison of three actuarial scales. *Law and Human Behavior, 24*(1), 119–136. https://doi.org/10.1023/A:1005482921333

Harkins, L., & Dixon, L. (2010). Sexual offending in groups: An evaluation. *Aggression and Violent Behavior, 15*(2), 87–99. https://doi.org/10.1016/j.avb.2009.08.006

Harris, G. T., Rice, M. E., Quinsey, V. L., & Cormier, C. A. (2015). *Violent offenders: Appraising and managing risk* (3rd ed.). American Psychological Association. https://doi.org/10.1037/14572-000

Hart, S. D., & Boer, D. P. (2020). Structured professional judgment guidelines for sexual violence risk assessment: The Sexual Violence Risk-20 (SVR-20) versions. In K. S. Douglas & R. K. Otto (Eds.), *Handbook of violence risk assessment* (2nd ed., pp. 322–358). Routledge.

Hart, S. D., Kropp, P. R., Watt, K. A., Darjee, R., Davis, M. R., Klaver, J., Laws, D. R., & Logan, C. (2022). *RSVP-V2: Version 2 of the Risk for Sexual Violence Protocol*. Protect International.

Haugsand, I. B. (2023). *What is the prevalence of personality disorders and their associated traits in persons with pedophilia? A scoping review*. Masters thesis. Universitetet I Oslo. https://www.duo.uio.no/bitstream/handle/10852/109339/IBH-master-2023.pdf?sequence=11&isAllowed=y

Hazelwood, R. R., & Warren, J. I. (2000). The sexually violent offender: Impulsive or ritualistic? *Aggression and Violent Behavior, 5*(3), 267–279. https://doi.org/10.1016/S1359-1789(99)00002-6

Helmus, L., Ciardha, C. Ó., & Seto, M. C. (2015). The Screening Scale for Pedophilic Interests (SSPI): Construct, predictive, and incremental validity. *Law and Human Behavior, 39*(1), 35–43. https://doi.org/10.1037/lhb0000099

Helmus, L. M., Eke, A. W., Farmus, L., & Seto, M. C. (2024). The CPORT and Risk Matrix 2000 for Men Convicted of Child Sexual Exploitation Material (CSEM) offenses: A predictive accuracy comparison and meta-analysis. *Criminal Justice and Behavior, 51*(1), 3–23. https://doi.org/10.1177/00938548231208194

Helmus, L. M., Eke, A. W., & Seto, M. (2024). *What risk assessment tools can be used with Men Convicted of Child Sexual Exploitation Material (CSEM) Offenses? Recommendations from a review of current research*. CrimRxiv. https://doi.org/10.31234/osf.io/pngr9

Helmus, L., Hanson, R. K., Thornton, D., Babchishin, K. M., & Harris, A. J. R. (2012). Absolute recidivism rates predicted by Static-99R and Static-2002R sex offender risk assessment tools vary across samples: A meta-analysis. *Criminal Justice and Behavior, 39*(9), 1148–1171. https://doi.org/10.1177/0093854812443648

Henshaw, M., Arnold, C., Darjee, R., Ogloff, J. R., & Clough, J. A. (2020). Enhancing evidence-based treatment of child sexual abuse material offenders: The development of the CEM-COPE program. *Trends and Issues in Crime and Criminal Justice, 607*, 1–14. https://www.aic.gov.au/publications/tandi/tandi607

Henshaw, M., Darjee, R., & Clough, J. A. (2020). Online child sexual offending. In I. Bryce & W. Petherick (Eds.), *Child sexual abuse: Forensic issues in evidence, impact, and management* (1st ed., pp. 85–108). Academic Press.

Henshaw, M., Ogloff, J. R. P., & Clough, J. A. (2017). Looking beyond the screen: A critical review of the literature on the online child pornography offender. *Sexual Abuse: A Journal of Research and Treatment, 29*(5), 416–445. https://doi.org/10.1177/1079063215603690

Henshaw, M., Ogloff, J. R. P., & Clough, J. A. (2018). Demographic, mental health, and offending characteristics of online child exploitation material offenders: A comparison with contact-only and dual sexual offenders. *Behavioral Sciences and the Law, 36*(2), 198–215. https://doi.org/10.1002/bsl.2337

Hertz, P. G., Turner, D., Barra, S., Biedermann, L., Retz-Junginger, P., Schöttle, D., & Retz, W. (2022). Sexuality in adults with ADHD: Results of an online survey. *Frontiers in Psychiatry, 13*, 868278. https://doi.org/10.3389/fpsyt.2022.868278

Higgs, T., & Carter, A. J. (2015). Autism spectrum disorder and sexual offending: Responsivity in forensic interventions. *Aggression and Violent Behavior, 22*, 112–119. https://doi.org/10.1016/j.avb.2015.04.003

Hingsburger, D., Griffiths, D., & Quinsey, V. (1991). Detecting counterfeit deviance: Differentiating sexual deviance from sexual inappropriateness. *The Habilitative Mental Healthcare Newsletter, 10*(9), 51–54.

Hocken, K. (2020). Intellectual functioning and criminogenic factors for sexual offending. In K. Hocken, R. Lievesley, B. Winder, H. Swaby, N. Blagden, & P. Banyard (Eds.), *Sexual crime and intellectual functioning* (pp. 205–228). Palgrave MacMillan.

Hoffer, T. A., Shelton, J. L. E., Behnke, S., & Erdberg, P. (2010). Exploring the impact of child sex offender suicide. *Journal of Family Violence, 25*(8), 777–786. https://doi.org/10.1007/s10896-010-9335-3

Hopwood, C. J., Kotov, R., Krueger, R. F., Watson, D., Widiger, T. A., Althoff, R. R., Ansell, E. B., Bach, B., Michael Bagby, R., Blais, M. A., Bornovalova, M. A., Chmielewski, M., Cicero, D. C., Conway, C., De Clercq, B., De Fruyt, F., Docherty, A. R., Eaton, N. R., Edens, J. F., … Zimmermann, J. (2018). The time has come for dimensional personality disorder diagnosis. *Personality and Mental Health, 12*(1), 82–86. https://doi.org/10.1002/pmh.1408

Hudson, K. (2018). Preventing child sexual abuse through education: The work of Stop it Now! Wales. *Journal of Sexual Aggression, 24*(1), 99–113. https://doi.org/10.1080/13552600.2017.1383088

Hunter, J. A., Jr., & Becker, J. V. (1994). The role of deviant sexual arousal in juvenile sexual offending: Etiology, evaluation, and treatment. *Criminal Justice and Behavior, 21*(1), 132–149. https://doi.org/10.1177/0093854894021001009

Jackson, R. L., & Richards, H. J. (2007). Diagnostic and risk profiles among civilly committed sex offenders in Washington State. *International Journal of Offender Therapy and Comparative Criminology, 51*(3), 313–323. https://doi.org/10.1177/0306624X06292874

Jahnke, S., Blagden, N., & Hill, L. (2022). Pedophile, child lover, or minor-attracted person? Attitudes toward labels among people who are sexually attracted to children. *Archives of Sexual Behavior, 51*(8), 4125–4139. https://doi.org/10.1007/s10508-022-02331-6

Jahnke, S., Imhoff, R., & Hoyer, J. (2015). Stigmatization of people with pedophilia: Two comparative surveys. *Archives of Sexual Behavior, 44*(1), 21–34. https://doi.org/10.1007/s10508-014-0312-4

Jahnke, S., Schmidt, A. F., & Hoyer, J. (2023). Pedohebephilia and perceived non-coercive childhood sexual experiences: Two non-matched case-control studies. *Sexual Abuse, 35*(3), 340–374. https://doi.org/10.1177/10790632221098341

Jahnke, S., Schmitt, S., Geradt, M., & Hoyer, J. (2019). Big five personality factors among men with a sexual interest in children. *International Journal of Sexual Health, 31*(2), 164–169. https://doi.org/10.1080/19317611.2019.1609641

Jakubczyk, A., Krasowska, A., Bugaj, M., Kopera, M., Klimkiewicz, A., Łoczewska, A., Michalska, A., Majewska, A., Szejko, N., Podgórska, A., Sołowiej, M., Markuszewski, L., Jakima, S., Płoski, R., Brower, K., & Wojnar, M. (2017). Paraphilic sexual offenders do not differ from control subjects with respect to dopamine- and serotonin-related genetic polymorphisms. *The Journal of Sexual Medicine, 14*(1), 125–133. https://doi.org/10.1016/j.jsxm.2016.11.309

Janssen, D. F. (2009). Hebephilia plethysmographica: A partial rejoinder to Blanchard et al. (2008). *Archives of Sexual Behavior, 38*, 321–322. https://doi.org/10.1007/s10508-009-9479-5

Janus, E. S., & Walbek, N. H. (2000). Sex offender commitments in Minnesota: A descriptive study of second generation commitments. *Behavioral Sciences and the Law, 18*(2–3), 343–374. https://doi.org/10.1002/1099-0798(200003/06)18:2/3<343::aid-bsl395>3.0.co;2-g

Jara, G. A., & Jeglic, E. (2021). Changing public attitudes toward minor attracted persons: An evaluation of an anti-stigma intervention. *Journal of Sexual Aggression, 27*(3), 299–312. https://doi.org/10.1080/13552600.2020.1863486
Jespersen, A. F., Lalumière, M. L., & Seto, M. C. (2009). Sexual abuse history among adult sex offenders and non-sex offenders: A meta-analysis. *Child Abuse and Neglect, 33*(3), 179–192. https://doi.org/10.1016/j.chiabu.2008.07.004
Johnston, P., Hudson, S. M., & Marshall, W. L. (1992). The effects of masturbatory reconditioning with nonfamilial child molesters. *Behaviour Research and Therapy, 30*(5), 559–561. https://doi.org/10.1016/0005-7967(92)90043-G
Jonathan, S. (2021). Managing the monstrous: Sex offenders and the new penology. In P. O'Malley (Ed.), *Governing risks* (pp. 279–294). Routledge.
Jones, D. T. (2014). *An evaluation of the use of phallometric assessment for men incarcerated for sexually offending against children in New Zealand: Past results and future directions.* Unpublished doctoral dissertation. University of Waikato.
Jordan, K., Fromberger, P., Laubinger, H., Dechent, P., & Müller, J. L. (2014). Changed processing of visual sexual stimuli under GnRH-therapy—A single case study in pedophilia using eye tracking and fMRI. *BMC Psychiatry, 14*(1), 142. https://doi.org/10.1186/1471-244X-14-142
Jordan, K., Fromberger, P., & Müller, J. L. (2015). Could we measure sexual interest using functional imaging? *Sexual Offender Treatment, 10*(1) http://www.sexual-offender-treatment.org/index.php?id=141
Jordan, K., Fromberger, P., & Müller, J. L. (2017). Structural and functional magnetic resonance imaging in assessing sexual preference. In D. P. Boer (Ed.), *The Wiley handbook on the theories, assessment, and treatment of sexual offending* (pp. 925–964). Wiley-Blackwell. https://doi.org/10.1002/9781118574003.wattso043
Jordan, K., Wild, T. S. N., Fromberger, P., Müller, I., & Müller, J. L. (2020). Are there any biomarkers for pedophilia and sexual child abuse? A review. *Frontiers in psychiatry, 10*, 940. https://doi.org/10.3389/fpsyt.2019.00940
Joyal, C. C. (2023). The neuroanatomical bases of pedophilia and the importance of distinguishing genuine vs. acquired types: A systematic review. *Sexual Offending: Theory, Research, and Prevention, 18*, 1–21. https://doi.org/10.5964/sotrap.6989
Joyal, C. C., Beaulieu-Plante, J., & de Chantérac, A. (2014). The neuropsychology of sex offenders: A meta-analysis. *Sexual Abuse, 26*(2), 149–177. https://doi.org/10.1177/1079063213482842
Joyal, C. C., Black, D. N., & Dassylva, B. (2007). The neuropsychology and neurology of sexual deviance: A review and pilot study. *Sexual Abuse, 19*(2), 155–173. https://doi.org/10.1177/107906320701900206
Joyal, C. C., Kärgel, C., Kneer, J., Amelung, T., Mohnke, S., Tenbergen, G., Walter, H., & Kruger, T. H. C. (2019). The neurobiological origins of pedophilia: Not that simple. *The Journal of Sexual Medicine, 16*(1), 153–154. https://doi.org/10.1016/j.jsxm.2018.10.015
Juda, D. P. (1986). The usefulness of self psychology in understanding and treating a case of homosexual pedophilia. *Dynamic Psychotherapy, 4*, 99–123.
Kafka, M. P. (2003). The monoamine hypothesis for the pathophysiology of paraphilic disorders: An update. *Annals of the New York Academy of Sciences, 989*, 86–94.; discussion 144. https://doi.org/10.1111/j.1749-6632.2003.tb07295.x
Kafka, M. P. (2010). Hypersexual disorder: A proposed diagnosis for DSM-V. *Archives of Sexual Behavior, 39*, 377–400. https://doi.org/10.1007/s10508-009-9574-7
Kafka, M. P., & Hennen, J. (2003). Hypersexual desire in males: Are males with paraphilias different from males with paraphilia-related disorders? *Sexual Abuse: A Journal of Research and Treatment, 15*(4), 307–321. https://doi.org/10.1177/107906320301500407
Kaplan, M. S., & Krueger, R. B. (2010). Diagnosis, assessment, and treatment of hypersexuality. *Journal of Sex Research, 47*(2), 181–198. https://doi.org/10.1080/00224491003592863
Kärgel, C., Massau, C., Weiß, S., Walter, M., Borchardt, V., Krueger, T. H. C., Tenbergen, G., Kneer, J., Wittfoth, M., Pohl, A., Gerwinn, H., Ponseti, J., Amelung, T., Beier, K. M., Mohnke, S., Walter, H., & Schiffer, B. (2017). Evidence for superior neurobiological and behavioral

inhibitory control abilities in non-offending as compared to offending pedophiles. *Human Brain Mapping, 38*(2), 1092–1104. https://doi.org/10.1002/hbm.23443

Kärgel, C., Massau, C., Weiß, S., Walter, M., Kruger, T. H. C., & Schiffer, B. (2015). Diminished functional connectivity on the road to child sexual abuse in pedophilia. *The Journal of Sexual Medicine, 12*(3), 783–795. https://doi.org/10.1111/jsm.12819

Karpman, B. (1950). A case of paedophilia (legally rape) cured by psychoanalysis. *Psychoanalytic Review, 37*(3), 235–276.

Kaufman, K. L., Erooga, M., Mathews, B., & McConnell, E. (2019). Recommendations for preventing child sexual abuse in youth-serving organizations: Implications from an Australian Royal Commission review of the literature. *Journal of Interpersonal Violence, 34*(20), 4199–4224. https://doi.org/10.1177/0886260519869239

Kaufman, K. L., Hilliker, D. R., Lathrop, P., Daleiden, E. L., & Rudy, L. (1996). Sexual offenders' modus operandi: A comparison of structured interview and questionnaire approaches. *Journal of Interpersonal Violence, 11*(1), 19–34. https://doi.org/10.1177/088626096011001002

Kelly, R. J. (1982). Behavioral reorientation of pedophiliacs: Can it be done? *Clinical Psychology Review, 2*(3), 387–408. https://doi.org/10.1016/0272-7358(82)90020-4

Kemshall, H. (2017). The historical evolution of sex offender risk management. In K. McCartan & H. Kemshall (Eds.), *Contemporary sex offender risk management, Volume I. Perceptions*. Palgrave Macmillan. https://doi.org/10.1007/978-3-319-63567-5_1

Kemshall, H. (2021). Risk and desistance: A blended approach to risk management. *Academic Insights, 7*. HM Inspectorate of Probation. https://www.justiceinspectorates.gov.uk/hmiprobation/wp-content/uploads/sites/5/2021/06/Academic-Insights-Kemshall.pdf

Kemshall, H., & Maguire, M. (2021). Public protection, partnership and risk penality: The multi-agency risk management of sexual and violent offenders. In P. O'Malley (Ed.), *Governing risks* (pp. 319–346). Routledge.

Key, R., Underwood, A., Farnham, F., Marzano, L., & Hawton, K. (2021). Suicidal behavior in individuals accused or convicted of child sex abuse or indecent image offenses: Systematic review of prevalence and risk factors. *Suicide and Life-Threatening Behavior, 51*(4), 715–728. https://doi.org/10.1111/sltb.12749

Khan, O., Ferriter, M., Huband, N., Powney, M. J., Dennis, J. A., & Duggan, C. (2015). Pharmacological interventions for those who have sexually offended or are at risk of offending. *The Cochrane Database of Systematic Reviews, 2015*(2), CD007989. https://doi.org/10.1002/14651858.CD007989.pub2

Killias, M. (1991). The historic origins of penal statutes concerning sexual activities involving children and adolescents. *Journal of Homosexuality, 20*(1–2), 41–46. https://doi.org/10.1300/J082v20n01_5

King, C., & Murphy, G. H. (2014). A systematic review of people with autism spectrum disorder and the criminal justice system. *Journal of Autism and Developmental Disorders, 44*(11), 2717–2733. https://doi.org/10.1007/s10803-014-2046-5

Kitzinger, J. (2002). The ultimate neighbour from hell? Stranger danger and the media framing of paedophiles. In Y. Jewkes & G. Letherby (Eds.), *Criminology: A reader* (pp. 145–146). SAGE. ISBN 0-7619-4710-8.

Kloess, J. A., Beech, A. R., & Harkins, L. (2014). Online child sexual exploitation: Prevalence, process, and offender characteristics. *Trauma, Violence and Abuse, 15*(2), 126–139. https://doi.org/10.1177/1524838013511543

Kneer, J., Borchardt, V., Kärgel, C., Sinke, C., Massau, C., Tenbergen, G., Ponseti, J., Walter, H., Beier, K. M., Schiffer, B., Schiltz, K., Walter, M., & Kruger, T. H. C. (2019). Diminished fronto-limbic functional connectivity in child sexual offenders. *Journal of Psychiatric Research, 108*, 48–56. https://doi.org/10.1016/j.jpsychires.2018.01.012

Knight, R. A. (1988). A taxonomic analysis of child molesters. *Annals of the New York Academy of Sciences, 528*, 2–20. https://doi.org/10.1111/j.1749-6632.1988.tb42057.x

Knight, R. A. (1999). Validation of a typology for rapists. *Journal of Interpersonal Violence, 14*(3), 303–330. https://doi.org/10.1177/088626099014003006

Knight, R. A. (2010). Typologies for rapists—The generation of a new structural model. In A. M. Schlank (Ed.), *The sexual predator: Legal issues, assessment, treatment* (Vol. IV, pp. 17-1–17-28). Civic Research Institute.

Knight, R. A., Carter, D. L., & Prentky, R. A. (1989). A system for the classification of child molesters: Reliability and application. *Journal of Interpersonal Violence, 4*(1), 3–23. https://doi.org/10.1177/088626089004001001

Knight, R. A., & Guay, J.-P. (2006). The role of psychopathy in sexual coercion against women. In C. J. Patrick (Ed.), *Handbook of psychopathy* (pp. 512–532). Guilford Press.

Knight, R. A., & King, M. W. (2012). Typologies for child molesters—The generation of a new structural model. In B. K. Schwartz (Ed.), *The sex offender: Current trends in policy and treatment practice* (pp. 1–33). Civic Research Institute.

Knight, R. A., & Prentky, R. A. (1990). Classifying sexual offenders: The development and corroboration of taxonomic models. In W. L. Marshall, D. R. Laws, & H. E. Barbaree (Eds.), *Handbook of sexual assault: Issues, theories, and treatment of the offender* (pp. 23–52). Plenum Press.

Knight, R. A., & Sims-Knight, J. E. (2017). A theoretical integration of aetiological and typological models of rape. In D. P. Boer, A. R. Beech, T. Ward, L. A. Craig, M. Rettenberger, L. E. Marshall, & W. L. Marshall (Eds.), *The Wiley handbook on the theories, assessment, and treatment of sexual offending* (pp. 73–102). Wiley Blackwell.

Knott, V., Impey, D., Fisher, D., Delpero, E., & Fedoroff, P. (2016). Pedophilic brain potential responses to adult erotic stimuli. *Brain Research, 1632*, 127–140. https://doi.org/10.1016/j.brainres.2015.12.004

Kopp, S. B. (1962). The character structure of sex offenders. *American Journal of Psychotherapy, 16*(1), 64–70.

Krafft-Ebing, R. V. (1886). *Psycopathia sexualis with especial reference to the antipathic sexual instinct: A medico-forensic study* (1965 unexpurgated translation). Stein and Day.

Kramer, R. (2011). APA guidelines ignored in development of diagnostic criteria for pedohebephilia. *Archives of Sexual Behavior, 40*, 233–235. https://doi.org/10.1007/s10508-010-9683-3

Kruger, T. H. C., & Kneer, J. (2021). Neurobiological basis of sexual deviance. In L. A. Craig & R. M. Bartels (Eds.), *Sexual deviance: Understanding and managing deviant sexual interests and paraphilic disorders* (pp. 67–88). Wiley.

Kruger, T. H. C., Sinke, C., Kneer, J., Tenbergen, G., Khan, A. Q., Burkert, A., Müller-Engling, L., Engler, H., Gerwinn, H., von Wurmb-Schwark, N., Pohl, A., Weiß, S., Amelung, T., Mohnke, S., Massau, C., Kärgel, C., Walter, M., Schiltz, K., Beier, K. M., … Frieling, H. (2019). Child sexual offenders show prenatal and epigenetic alterations of the androgen system. *Translational Psychiatry, 9*(1), 28. https://doi.org/10.1038/s41398-018-0326-0

Lambrick, F., & Glaser, W. (2004). Sex offenders with an intellectual disability. *Sexual Abuse: A Journal of Research and Treatment, 16*(4), 381–392. https://doi.org/10.1177/107906320401600409

Landgren, V., Malki, K., Bottai, M., Arver, S., & Rahm, C. (2020). Effect of gonadotropin-releasing hormone antagonist on risk of committing child sexual abuse in men with pedophilic disorder: A randomized clinical trial. *JAMA Psychiatry, 77*(9), 897–905. https://doi.org/10.1001/jamapsychiatry.2020.0440

Landgren, V., Savard, J., Dhejne, C., Jokinen, J., Arver, S., Seto, M. C., & Rahm, C. (2022). Pharmacological treatment for pedophilic disorder and compulsive sexual behavior disorder: A review. *Drugs, 82*(6), 663–681. https://doi.org/10.1007/s40265-022-01696-1

Langevin, R., & Curnoe, S. (2008). Are the mentally retarded and learning disordered overrepresented among sex offenders and paraphilics? *International Journal of Offender Therapy and Comparative Criminology, 52*(4), 401–415. https://doi.org/10.1177/0306624X07305826

Långström, N., Babchishin, K. M., Fazel, S., Lichtenstein, P., & Frisell, T. (2015). Sexual offending runs in families: A 37-year nationwide study. *International Journal of Epidemiology, 44*(2), 713–720. https://doi.org/10.1093/ije/dyv029

Lanning, K. V. (1986). *Child molesters: A behavioral analysis for professionals investigating the sexual exploitation of children*. National Center for Missing and Exploited Children.
Lanning, K. V. (2001). *Child molesters: A behavioral analysis for professionals investigating the sexual exploitation of children* (4th ed.). National Center for Missing and Exploited Children.
Lanning, K. V. (2010). *Child molesters: A behavioral analysis for professionals investigating the sexual exploitation of children* (5th ed.). National Center for Missing and Exploited Children.
Lätth, J., Landgren, V., McMahan, A., Sparre, C., Eriksson, J., Malki, K., Söderquist, E., Öberg, K. G., Rozental, A., Andersson, G., Kaldo, V., Långström, N., & Rahm, C. (2022). Effects of internet-delivered cognitive behavioral therapy on use of child sexual abuse material: A randomized placebo-controlled trial on the darknet. *Internet Interventions, 30*, 100590. https://doi.org/10.1016/j.invent.2022.100590
Lawrence, A. L., & Willis, G. M. (2022). Understanding and influencing public attitudes surrounding people with a sexual interest in children. *Stigma and Health, 7*(3), 260–269. https://doi.org/10.1037/sah0000391
Laws, D. R. (2000). Sexual offending as a public health problem: A North American perspective. *Journal of Sexual Aggression, 5*(1), 30–44. https://doi.org/10.1080/13552600008413294
Laws, D. R. (2020). Virtual and augmented reality: Being there. In D. R. Laws (Ed.), *A history of the assessment of sex offenders: 1830–2020* (pp. 173–191). Emerald.
Laws, D. R., & Marshall, W. L. (1990). A conditioning theory of the etiology and maintenance of deviant sexual preference and behavior. In W. L. Marshall, D. R. Laws, & H. E. Barbaree (Eds.), *Handbook of sexual assault. Applied clinical psychology*. Springer. https://doi.org/10.1007/978-1-4899-0915-2_13
Laws, D. R., & Marshall, W. L. (1991). Masturbatory reconditioning with sexual deviates: An evaluative review. *Advances in Behaviour Research and Therapy, 13*(1), 13–25. https://doi.org/10.1016/0146-6402(91)90012-Y
Lee, J. K. P., Jackson, H. J., Pattison, P., & Ward, T. (2002). Developmental risk factors for sexual offending. *Child Abuse and Neglect, 26*(1), 73–92. https://doi.org/10.1016/s0145-2134(01)00304-0
Lehmann, R. J. B., Brouillette-Alarie, S., Pednault, A., & Knight, R. (2022). Validating the screening scale of pedophilic crime scene behavior. *Archives of Sexual Behavior, 51*, 4085–4096. https://doi.org/10.1007/s10508-022-02354-z
Lehmann, R. J. B., Dahle, K.-P., & Schmidt, A. F. (2018). Primer on the contribution of crime scene behavior to the forensic assessment of sexual offenders. *European Psychologist, 23*(2), 154–166. https://doi.org/10.1027/1016-9040/a0003424
Lehmann, R. J. B., Goodwill, A. M., Hanson, R. K., & Dahle, K.-P. (2014). Crime scene behaviors indicate risk-relevant propensities of child molesters. *Criminal Justice and Behavior, 41*(8), 1008–1028. https://doi.org/10.1177/0093854814521807
Lett, T. A., Mohnke, S., Amelung, T., Brandl, E. J., Schiltz, K., Pohl, A., Gerwinn, H., Kärgel, C., Massau, C., Tenbergen, G., Wittfoth, M., Kneer, J., Beier, K. M., Walter, M., Ponseti, J., Krüger, T. H. C., Schiffer, B., & Walter, H. (2018). Multimodal neuroimaging measures and intelligence influence pedophile child sexual offense behavior. *European Neuropsychopharmacology, 28*(7), 818–827. https://doi.org/10.1016/j.euroneuro.2018.05.002
Levenson, J. S. (2008). Collateral consequences of sex offender residence restrictions. *Criminal Justice Studies, 21*(2), 153–166. https://doi.org/10.1080/14786010802159822
Levenson, J. S. (2014). Incorporating trauma-informed care into evidence-based sex offender treatment. *Journal of Sexual Aggression, 20*(1), 9–22. https://doi.org/10.1080/13552600.2013.861523
Levenson, J. S., & Grady, M. D. (2019). Preventing sexual abuse: Perspectives of minor-attracted persons about seeking help. *Sexual Abuse, 31*(8), 991–1013. https://doi.org/10.1177/1079063218797713
Levenson, J. S., Willis, G. M., & Prescott, D. S. (2016). Adverse childhood experiences in the lives of male sex offenders: Implications for trauma-informed care. *Sexual Abuse, 28*(4), 340–359. https://doi.org/10.1177/1079063214535819

Leverett, S. D., & Tenbergen, G. (2023). Recent advances in the neuropsychology of pedophilia. *Sexual Offending: Theory, Research, and Prevention, 18*, 1–15. https://doi.org/10.5964/sotrap.10515

Lewis, A., Grubin, D., Ross, C. C., & Das, M. (2017). Gonadotrophin-releasing hormone agonist treatment for sexual offenders: A systematic review. *Journal of Psychopharmacology, 31*(10), 1281–1293. https://doi.org/10.1177/0269881117714048

Lewis, E. T., III, & Dwyer, R. G. (2018). Psychosis and sexual offending: A review of current literature. *International Journal of Offender Therapy and Comparative Criminology, 62*(11), 3372–3384. https://doi.org/10.1177/0306624X17740016

Lievesley, R., & Harper, C. (2021). Understanding minor attraction. In L. A. Craig & R. M. Bartels (Eds.), *Sexual deviance: Understanding and managing deviant sexual interests and paraphilic disorders* (pp. 132–144). Wiley-Blackwell. https://doi.org/10.1002/9781119771401.ch8

Lievesley, R., & Harper, C. A. (2022). Applying desistance principles to improve wellbeing and prevent child sexual abuse among minor-attracted persons. *Journal of Sexual Aggression, 28*(1), 1–14. https://doi.org/10.1080/13552600.2021.1883754

Lievesley, R., Harper, C. A., & Elliott, H. (2020). The internalization of social stigma among minor-attracted persons: Implications for treatment. *Archives of Sexual Behavior, 49*(4), 1291–1304. https://doi.org/10.1007/s10508-019-01569-x

Lievesley, R., Harper, C. A., Swaby, H., & Woodward, E. (2023). Identifying and working with appropriate treatment targets with people who are sexually attracted to children. *Journal of Sex and Marital Therapy, 49*(5), 497–516. https://doi.org/10.1080/0092623X.2022.2149437

Lievesley, R., Swaby, H., Harper, C. A., & Woodward, E. (2022). Primary health professionals' beliefs, experiences, and willingness to treat minor-attracted persons. *Archives of Sexual Behavior, 51*(2), 923–943. https://doi.org/10.1007/s10508-021-02271-7

Lim, Y. Y., Wahab, S., Kumar, J., Ibrahim, F., & Kamaluddin, M. R. (2021). Typologies and psychological profiles of child sexual abusers: An extensive review. *Children, 8*(5), 333. https://doi.org/10.3390/children8050333

Long, M., Alison, L., Tejeiro, R., Hendricks, E., & Giles, S. (2016). KIRAT: Law enforcement's prioritization tool for investigating indecent image offenders. *Psychology, Public Policy, and Law, 22*(1), *12–21*. https://doi.org/10.1037/law0000069

Lösel, F., & Schmucker, M. (2005). The effectiveness of treatment for sexual offenders: A comprehensive meta-analysis. *Journal of Experimental Criminology, 1*(1), 117–146. https://doi.org/10.1007/s11292-004-6466-7

Luiselli, J. K. (2000). Presentation of paraphilias and paraphilia related disorders in young adults with mental retardation: Two case profiles. *Mental Health Aspects of Developmental Disabilities, 3*, 42–46.

Lunsky, Y., Frijters, J., Griffiths, D. M., Watson, S. L., & Williston, S. (2007). Sexual knowledge and attitudes of men with intellectual disability who sexually offend. *Journal of Intellectual and Developmental Disability, 32*(2), 74–81. https://doi.org/10.1080/13668250701408004

Lussier, P., Beauregard, E., Proulx, J., & Nicole, A. (2005). Developmental factors related to deviant sexual preferences in child molesters. *Journal of Interpersonal Violence, 20*(9), 999–1017. https://doi.org/10.1177/0886260505278024

Lussier, P., & Cale, J. (2013). Beyond sexual recidivism: A review of the sexual criminal career parameters of adult sex offenders. *Aggression and Violent Behavior, 18*(5), 445–457. https://doi.org/10.1016/j.avb.2013.06.005

Lussier, P., McCuish, E., Proulx, J., Chouinard Thivierge, S., & Frechette, J. (2023). The sexual recidivism drop in Canada: A meta-analysis of sex offender recidivism rates over an 80-year period. *Criminology and Public Policy, 22*(1), 125–160. https://doi.org/10.1111/1745-9133.12611

Mackaronis, J. E., Strassberg, D. S., & Marcus, D. K. (2011, November). The latent structure of Multiphasic Sex Inventory-assessed pedophilic interest. *Psychological Assessment, 23*(4), 1017–1022. https://doi.org/10.1037/a0024625

Mann, R. E., Hanson, R. K., & Thornton, D. (2010). Assessing risk for sexual recidivism: Some proposals on the nature of psychologically meaningful risk factors. *Sexual Abuse, 22*(2), 191–217. https://doi.org/10.1177/1079063210366039

Margari, A., De Agazio, G., Marzulli, L., Piarulli, F. M., Mandarelli, G., Catanesi, R., Carabellese, F. F., & Cortese, S. (2024). Autism spectrum disorder (ASD) and sexual offending: A systematic review. *Neuroscience and Biobehavioral Reviews, 162*, 105687. https://doi.org/10.1016/j.neubiorev.2024.105687

Marshall, W. L., & Barbaree, H. E. (1990). An integrated theory of the etiology of sexual offending. In W. L. Marshall, D. R. Laws, & H. E. Barbaree (Eds.), *Handbook of sexual assault: Issues, theories, and treatment of the offender* (pp. 257–275). Plenum Press.

Marshall, W. L., Marshall, L. E., & Olver, M. E. (2017). An evaluation of strength-based approaches to the treatment of sex offenders: A review. *Journal of Criminal Psychology, 7*(3), 221–228. https://doi.org/10.1108/JCP-04-2017-0021

Marshall, W. L., Marshall, L. E., Serran, G. A., & O'Brien, M. D. (2011). *Rehabilitating sex offenders: A strength-based approach*. American Psychological Association.

Marshall, W. L., O'Brien, M. D., & Marshall, L. E. (2009). Modifying sexual preferences. In A. R. Beech, L. A. Craig, & K. D. Browne (Eds.), *Assessment and treatment of sexual offenders: A handbook* (pp. 311–327). Wiley.

Martijn, F. M., Babchishin, K. M., Pullman, L. E., & Seto, M. C. (2020). Sexual attraction and falling in love in persons with pedohebephilia. *Archives of Sexual Behavior, 49*, 1305–1318. https://doi.org/10.1007/s10508-019-01579-9

Marx, C. M., Tibubos, A. N., Brähler, E., & Beutel, M. E. (2020). Experienced childhood maltreatment in a sample of pedophiles: Comparisons with patients of a psychosomatic outpatient clinic and the general population. *The Journal of Sexual Medicine, 17*(5), 985–993. https://doi.org/10.1016/j.jsxm.2020.01.019

Massau, C., Tenbergen, G., Kärgel, C., Weiß, S., Gerwinn, H., Pohl, A., Amelung, T., Mohnke, S., Kneer, J., Wittfoth, M., Ristow, I., Schiltz, K., Beier, K. M., Ponseti, J., Walter, M., Krüger, T. H. C., Walter, H., & Schiffer, B. (2017). Executive functioning in pedophilia and child sexual offending. *Journal of the International Neuropsychological Society, 23*(6), 460–470. https://doi.org/10.1017/S1355617717000315

Mathews, R., Mathews, J., & Speltz, K. (1989). *Female sexual offenders: An exploratory study*. Safer Society Press.

Matthews, J. K., Mathews, R., & Spelz, K. (1991). Female sexual offenders: A typology. In M. Q. Patton (Ed.), *Family sexual abuse: Frontline research and evaluation* (pp. 199–219). Sage.

McEwan, T., & Darjee, R. (2021). The problem behaviour program. In J. R. Meloy & J. Hoffman (Eds.), *International handbook of threat assessment* (2nd ed., pp. 536–553). Oxford University Press.

McGuire, W. J. (1964). Inducing resistance to persuasion: Some contemporary approaches. In L. Berkowitz (Ed.), *Advances in experimental social psychology* (Vol. 1, pp. 191–229). Academic Press.

McKillop, N., & Price, S. (2023). The potential for anti-stigma interventions to change public attitudes toward minor-attracted persons: A replication and extension of Jara and Jeglic's study. *Journal of Child Sexual Abuse, 32*(6), 694–714. https://doi.org/10.1080/10538712.2023.2204864

McLawsen, J. E., Scalora, M. J., & Darrow, C. (2012). Civilly committed sex offenders: A description and interstate comparison of populations. *Psychology, Public Policy, and Law, 18*(3), 453–476. https://doi.org/10.1037/a0026116

McPhail, I. V., Hermann, C. A., Fernane, S., Fernandez, Y. M., Nunes, K. L., & Cantor, J. M. (2019). Validity in phallometric testing for sexual interests in children: A meta-analytic review. *Assessment, 26*, 535–551. https://doi.org/10.1177/1073191117706139

McPhail, I. V., & Olver, M. E. (2020). Interventions for Pedohebephilic arousal in men convicted for sexual offenses against children: A meta-analytic review. *Criminal Justice and Behavior, 47*(10), 1319–1339. https://doi.org/10.1177/0093854820916774

McPhail, I. V., Olver, M. E., Brouillette-Alarie, S., & Looman, J. (2018). Taxometric analysis of the latent structure of pedophilic interest. *Archives of Sexual Behavior, 47*(8), 2223–2240. https://doi.org/10.1007/s10508-018-1225-4

McPherson, L. (2016). The Sex Offender Registration and Notification Act (SORNA) at 10 years: History, implementation, and the future. *Drake Law Review, 64*, 741.

Meloy, J. R. (1997). The psychology of wickedness: Psychopathy and sadism. *Psychiatric Annals, 27*(9), 630–633.

Michie, A. M., Lindsay, W. R., Martin, V., & Grieve, A. (2006). A test of counterfeit deviance: A comparison of sexual knowledge in groups of sex offenders with intellectual disability and controls. *Sexual Abuse, 18*(3), 271–278. https://doi.org/10.1177/107906320601800305

Millar, C. (2022). *The stigmatisation of minor attracted persons*. Unpublished Doctor of Clinical Psychology thesis. University of Liverpool. https://doi.org/10.17638/03164547

Miller, B. S., Sarafoglou, K., & Addo, O. Y. (2020). Development of Tanner stage–age adjusted CDC height curves for research and clinical applications. *Journal of the Endocrine Society, 4*(9), bvaa098. https://doi.org/10.1210/jendso/bvaa098

Millon, T. (1987). *Millon clinical multiaxial inventory-II: Manual for the MCM-II* (2nd ed.). National Computer Systems.

Miner, M., Borduin, C., Prescott, D., Bovensmann, H., Schepker, R., Du Bois, R., Schladale, J., Eher, R., Schmeck, K., Langfedt, T., Smit, A., & Pfäfflin, F. (2006). Standards of care for juvenile sexual offenders of the International Association for the Treatment of Sexual Offenders. *Sexual Offender Treatment, 1*(3).

Miner, M. H., & Munns, R. (2021). Psychological treatments for paraphilias and compulsive sexual behavior. In L. A. Craig & R. M. Bartels (Eds.), *Sexual deviance: Understanding and managing deviant sexual interests and paraphilic disorders* (pp. 253–267). Wiley.

Mogavero, M. C. (2016). Autism, sexual offending, and the criminal justice system. *Journal of Intellectual Disabilities and Offending Behaviour, 7*(3), 116–126. https://doi.org/10.1108/JIDOB-02-2016-0004

Mohnke, S., Müller, S., Amelung, T., Krüger, T. H. C., Ponseti, J., Schiffer, B., Walter, M., Beier, K. M., & Walter, H. (2014). Brain alterations in paedophilia: A critical review. *Progress in Neurobiology, 122*, 1–23. https://doi.org/10.1016/j.pneurobio.2014.07.005

Mokros, A., & Banse, R. (2019). The "Dunkelfeld" project for self-identified pedophiles: A reappraisal of its effectiveness. *The Journal of Sexual Medicine, 16*(5), 609–613. https://doi.org/10.1016/j.jsxm.2019.02.009

Money, J. (1986). *Lovemaps: Clinical concepts of sexual/erotic health and pathology, paraphilia, and gender transposition in childhood, adolescence, and maturity*. Irvington.

Moser, C. (2001). Paraphilia: A critique of a confused concept. In P. J. Kleinplatz (Ed.), *New directions in sex therapy: Innovations and alternatives* (pp. 91–108). Taylor and Francis.

Moser, C. (2009). When is an unusual sexual interest a mental disorder? *Archives of Sexual Behavior, 38*, 323–325. https://doi.org/10.1007/s10508-008-9436-8

Moss, S. L. (2019). *Understanding the treatment barriers for minor-attracted persons living in the community*. Unpublished Master of Science thesis. St. Mary's University.

Moulier, V., Fonteille, V., Pélégrini-Issac, M., Cordier, B., Baron-Laforêt, S., Boriasse, E., Durand, E., & Stoléru, S. (2012). A pilot study of the effects of gonadotropin-releasing hormone agonist therapy on brain activation pattern in a man with pedophilia. *International Journal of Offender Therapy and Comparative Criminology, 56*(1), 50–60. https://doi.org/10.1177/0306624X10392191

Nitsche, K., Etzler, S., Balas, J., Eher, R., & Rettenberger, M. (2022). A field study of acute dynamic risk assessment in individuals convicted of sexual offenses. *Psychological Assessment, 34*(6), 583–594. https://doi.org/10.1037/pas0001123

Nunes, K. L., Hermann, C. A., Renee Malcom, J., & Lavoie, K. (2013). Childhood sexual victimization, pedophilic interest, and sexual recidivism. *Child Abuse and Neglect, 37*(9), 703–711. https://doi.org/10.1016/j.chiabu.2013.01.008

Nunes, K. L., McPhail, I. V., & Babchishin, K. M. (2012). Social anxiety and sexual offending against children: A cumulative meta-analysis. *Journal of Sexual Aggression, 18*(3), 284–293. https://doi.org/10.1080/13552600.2010.549243

O'Donohue, W., Regev, L. G., & Hagstrom, A. (2000). Problems with the *DSM-IV* diagnosis of pedophilia. *Sexual Abuse: A Journal of Research and Treatment, 12*(2), 95–105. https://doi.org/10.1177/107906320001200202
Ogloff, J. R., Cutajar, M. C., Mann, E. C., & Mullen, P. E. (2012). Child sexual abuse and subsequent offending and victimisation: A 45 year follow-up study. *Trends and Issues in Crime and Criminal Justice, 440*, 1–6.
Ogloff, J. R. P., & Davis, M. R. (2020). From predicting dangerousness to assessing and managing risk for violence: A journey through four generations. In J. S. Wormith, L. A. Craig, & T. Hogue (Eds.), *The Wiley handbook of what works in violence risk management: Theory, research and practice* (pp. 81–98). Wiley-Blackwell.
Oliva, J. R. (2013). *Sexually motivated crimes: Understanding the profile of the sex offender and applying theory to practice*. CRC Press.
Olver, M. E., Marshall, L. E., Marshall, W. L., & Nicholaichuk, T. P. (2020). A long-term outcome assessment of the effects on subsequent reoffense rates of a prison-based CBT/RNR sex offender treatment program with strength-based elements. *Sexual Abuse, 32*(2), 127–153. https://doi.org/10.1177/1079063218807486
Olver, M. E., Wong, S. C. P., Nicholaichuk, T., & Gordon, A. (2007). The validity and reliability of the Violence Risk Scale-Sexual Offender version: Assessing sex offender risk and evaluating therapeutic change. *Psychological Assessment, 19*(3), 318–329. https://doi.org/10.1037/1040-3590.19.3.318
Padfield, N. (2017). Preventive sentencing. In K. McCartan & H. Kemshall (Eds.), *Contemporary sex offender risk management, Volume I. Perceptions*. Palgrave Macmillan. https://doi.org/10.1007/978-3-319-63567-5_4
Palmer-Hague, J. L., Tsang, V., Skead, C., Wassersug, R. J., Nasiopoulos, E., & Kingstone, A. (2017). Androgen deprivation alters attention to sexually provocative visual stimuli in elderly men. *Sexual Medicine, 5*(4), e245–e254. https://doi.org/10.1016/j.esxm.2017.10.001
Papalia, N., Luebbers, S., & Ogloff, J. R. P. (2018). Child sexual abuse and the propensity to engage in criminal behaviour: A critical review and examination of moderating factors. *Aggression and Violent Behavior, 43*, 71–89. https://doi.org/10.1016/j.avb.2018.10.007
Peter, T. (2009). Exploring taboos: Comparing male- and female-perpetrated child sexual abuse. *Journal of Interpersonal Violence, 24*(7), 1111–1128. https://doi.org/10.1177/0886260508322194
Phelan, J. (2018). *Psychodynamic theory and therapy of male pedophilia: The role of object relations, structural conflicts, and narcissism*. Authorea Preprints.
Polisois-Keating, A., & Joyal, C. C. (2013). Functional neuroimaging of sexual arousal: A preliminary meta-analysis comparing pedophilic to non-pedophilic men. *Archives of Sexual Behavior, 42*(7), 1111–1113. https://doi.org/10.1007/s10508-013-0198-6
Ponseti, J., Granert, O., Jansen, O., Wolff, S., Beier, K., Neutze, J., Deuschl, G., Mehdorn, H., Siebner, H., & Bosinski, H. (2012). Assessment of pedophilia using hemodynamic brain response to sexual stimuli. *Archives of General Psychiatry, 69*(2), 187–194. https://doi.org/10.1001/archgenpsychiatry.2011.130
Ponseti, J., Granert, O., van Eimeren, T., Jansen, O., Wolff, S., Beier, K., Deuschl, G., Huchzermeier, C., Stirn, A., Bosinski, H., & Roman Siebner, H. (2016). Assessing paedophilia based on the haemodynamic brain response to face images. *The World Journal of Biological Psychiatry, 17*(1), 39–46. https://doi.org/10.3109/15622975.2015.1083612
Porter, S., Newman, E., Tansey, L., & Quayle, E. (2015). Sex offending and social anxiety: A systematic review. *Aggression and Violent Behavior, 24*, 42–60. https://doi.org/10.1016/j.avb.2015.04.005
Prata, D., Mechelli, A., & Kapur, S. (2014). Clinically meaningful biomarkers for psychosis: A systematic and quantitative review. *Neuroscience and Biobehavioral Reviews, 45*, 134–141. https://doi.org/10.1016/j.neubiorev.2014.05.010

Prentky, R., & Barbaree, H. (2011). Commentary: Hebephilia—A would-be paraphilia caught in the twilight zone between prepubescence and adulthood. *Journal of the American Academy of Psychiatry and the Law, 39*(4), 506–510.

Prentky, R. A., & Burgess, A. W. (2000). *Forensic management of sexual offenders*. Kluwer Academic/Plenum. https://doi.org/10.1007/978-1-4615-4159-2

Prentky, R. A., & Knight, R. A. (1991). Identifying critical dimensions for discriminating among rapists. *Journal of Consulting and Clinical Psychology, 59*(5), 643–661. https://doi.org/10.1037/0022-006X.59.5.643

Prescott, J. J., & Rockoff, J. E. (2011). Do sex offender registration and notification laws affect criminal behavior? *The Journal of Law and Economics, 54*(1), 161–206. https://doi.org/10.1086/658485

Price, M., Kafka, M., Commons, M. L., Gutheil, T. G., & Simpsons, W. (2002). Telephone scatalogia: Comorbidity with other paraphilias and paraphilia-related disorders. *International Journal of Law and Psychiatry, 25*, 37–49. https://doi.org/10.1016/s0160-2527(01)00095-4

Quinsey, V. L., Harris, G. T., Rice, M. E., & Cormier, C. A. (2006). *Violent offenders: Appraising and managing risk* (2nd ed.). American Psychological Association. https://doi.org/10.1037/11367-000

Quinsey, V. L., & Lalumière, M. L. (1995). Evolutionary perspectives on sexual offending. *Sexual Abuse, 7*(4), 301–315. https://doi.org/10.1007/BF02256834

Rahm, C., Landgren, V., & Arver, S. (2020). Does degarelix hold potential for the treatment of pedophilic disorder?—Reply. *JAMA Psychiatry, 77*(10), 1085–1085. https://doi.org/10.1001/jamapsychiatry.2020.2597

Raymond, N. C., Coleman, E., Ohlerking, F., Christenson, G. A., & Miner, M. (1999). Psychiatric comorbidity in pedophilic sex offenders. *The American Journal of Psychiatry, 156*(5), 786–788. https://doi.org/10.1176/ajp.156.5.786

Reid, A. M., Flores, C., Olsen, B., Barthle, M. A., Rahmani, M., Rakhshani, A. C., Nguyen, M., Geffken, G. R., & McNamara, J. P. (2016). Treatment of sexual obsessive–compulsive symptoms during exposure and response prevention. In E. A. Storch & A. B. Lewin (Eds.), *Clinical handbook of obsessive–compulsive and related disorders: A case-based approach to treating pediatric and adult populations* (pp. 23–38). Springer.

Renshaw, K. L. (1994). Child molesters: Do those molested as children report larger numbers of victims than those who deny childhood sexual abuse? *Journal of Addictions and Offender Counseling, 15*(1), 24–32. https://doi.org/10.1002/j.2161-1874.1994.tb00095.x

Reyes, J. R., Vollmer, T. R., & Hall, A. (2011). Replications and extensions in arousal assessments for sex offenders with developmental disabilities. *Journal of Applied Behavior Analysis, 44*(2), 369–373. https://doi.org/10.1901/jaba.2011.44-369

Rice, M. E., Harris, G. T., Lang, C., & Chaplin, T. C. (2008). Sexual preferences and recidivism of sex offenders with mental retardation. *Sexual Abuse, 20*(4), 409–425. https://doi.org/10.1177/1079063208324662

Rind, B., & Yuill, R. (2012). Hebephilia as mental disorder? A historical, cross-cultural, sociological, cross-species, non-clinical empirical, and evolutionary review. *Archives of Sexual Behavior, 41*, 797–829. https://doi.org/10.1007/s1-5-8-012-9982-y

Ristow, I., Li, M., Colic, L., Marr, V., Födisch, C., von Düring, F., Schiltz, K., Drumkova, K., Witzel, J., Walter, H., Beier, K., Kruger, T. H. C., Ponseti, J., Schiffer, B., & Walter, M. (2018). Pedophilic sex offenders are characterised by reduced GABA concentration in dorsal anterior cingulate cortex. *NeuroImage. Clinical, 18*, 335–341. https://doi.org/10.1016/j.nicl.2018.01.018

Rosburg, T., Deuring, G., Boillat, C., Lemoine, P., Falkenstein, M., Graf, M., & Mager, R. (2018). Inhibition and attentional control in pedophilic child sexual offenders—An event-related potential study. *Clinical Neurophysiology, 129*(9), 1990–1998. https://doi.org/10.1016/j.clinph.2018.06.029

Rosell, D. R., & Siever, L. J. (2015). The neurobiology of aggression and violence. *CNS Spectrums, 20*(3), 254–279. https://doi.org/10.1017/S109285291500019X

Russell, D., Higgins, D., & Posso, A. (2020). Preventing child sexual abuse: A systematic review of interventions and their efficacy in developing countries. *Child Abuse and Neglect, 102*, 104395. https://doi.org/10.1016/j.chiabu.2020.104395

Saha, S., Lim, C. C. W., Cannon, D. L., Burton, L., Bremner, M., Cosgrove, P., Huo, Y., McGrath, J., & J. (2021). Co-morbidity between mood and anxiety disorders: A systematic review and meta-analysis. *Depression and Anxiety, 38*(3), 286–306. https://doi.org/10.1002/da.23113

Salter, D., McMillan, D., Richards, M., Talbot, T., Hodges, J., Bentovim, A., Hastings, R., Stevenson, J., & Skuse, D. (2003). Development of sexually abusive behaviour in sexually victimised males: A longitudinal study. *The Lancet, 361*(9356), 471–476. https://doi.org/10.1016/S0140-6736(03)12466-X

Santtila, P., Antfolk, J., Räfså, A., Hartwig, M., Sariola, H., Sandnabba, N. K., & Mokros, A. (2015). Men's sexual interest in children: One-year incidence and correlates in a population-based sample of Finnish male twins. *Journal of Child Sexual Abuse, 24*(2), 115–134. https://doi.org/10.1080/10538712.2015.997410

Santtila, P., Mokros, A., Hartwig, M., Varjonen, M., Jern, P., Witting, K., von der Pahlen, B., & Sandnabba, N. K. (2010). Childhood sexual interactions with other children are associated with lower preferred age of sexual partners including sexual interest in children in adulthood. *Psychiatry Research, 175*(1–2), 154–159. https://doi.org/10.1016/j.psychres.2008.10.021

Sartorius, A., Ruf, M., Kief, C., Demirakca, T., Bailer, J., Ende, G., Henn, F. A., Meyer-Lindenberg, A., & Dressing, H. (2008). Abnormal amygdala activation profile in pedophilia. *European Archives of Psychiatry and Clinical Neuroscience, 258*(5), 271–277. https://doi.org/10.1007/s00406-008-0782-2

Savoie, V., Quayle, E., & Flynn, E. (2021). Prevalence and correlates of individuals with sexual interest in children: A systematic review. *Child Abuse and Neglect, 115*, 105005. https://doi.org/10.1016/j.chiabu.2021.105005

Savoie, V., Quayle, E., Flynn, E., & O'Rourke, S. (2022). Predicting risk of reoffending in persons with child sexual exploitation material offense histories: The use of child pornography offender risk tool in a Scottish population. *Sexual Abuse, 34*(5), 568–596. https://doi.org/10.1177/10790632211047190

Scarpazza, C., Finos, L., Genon, S., Masiero, L., Bortolato, E., Cavaliere, C., Pezzaioli, J., Monaro, M., Navarin, N., Battaglia, U., Pietrini, P., Ferracuti, S., Sartori, G., & Camperio Ciani, A. S. (2021). Idiopathic and acquired pedophilia as two distinct disorders: An insight from neuroimaging. *Brain Imaging and Behavior, 15*(5), 2681–2692. https://doi.org/10.1007/s11682-020-00442-z

Schiffer, B., Amelung, T., Pohl, A., Kaergel, C., Tenbergen, G., Gerwinn, H., Mohnke, S., Massau, C., Matthias, W., Weiß, S., Marr, V., Beier, K. M., Walter, M., Ponseti, J., Krüger, T. H. C., Schiltz, K., & Walter, H. (2017). Gray matter anomalies in pedophiles with and without a history of child sexual offending. *Translational Psychiatry, 7*(5), e1129. https://doi.org/10.1038/tp.2017.96

Schiffer, B., Gizewski, E., & Kruger, T. (2009). Reduced neuronal responsiveness to visual sexual stimuli in a pedophile treated with a long-acting LH-RH agonist. *The Journal of Sexual Medicine, 6*(3), 892–894. https://doi.org/10.1111/j.1743-6109.2008.01094.x

Schiffer, B., Paul, T., Gizewski, E., Forsting, M., Leygraf, N., Schedlowski, M., & Kruger, T. H. C. (2008). Functional brain correlates of heterosexual paedophilia. *NeuroImage, 41*(1), 80–91. https://doi.org/10.1016/j.neuroimage.2008.02.008

Schiffer, B., Peschel, T., Paul, T., Gizewski, E., Forsting, M., Leygraf, N., Schedlowski, M., & Krueger, T. H. C. (2007). Structural brain abnormalities in the frontostriatal system and cerebellum in pedophilia. *Journal of Psychiatric Research, 41*(9), 753–762. https://doi.org/10.1016/j.jpsychires.2006.06.003

Schiffer, B., & Vonlaufen, C. (2011). Executive dysfunctions in pedophilic and nonpedophilic child molesters. *The Journal of Sexual Medicine, 8*(7), 1975–1984. https://doi.org/10.1111/j.1743-6109.2010.02140.x

Schiltz, K., Witzel, J., Northoff, G., Zierhut, K., Gubka, U., Fellmann, H., Kaufmann, J., Tempelmann, C., Wiebking, C., & Bogerts, B. (2007). Brain pathology in pedophilic offenders: Evidence of volume reduction in the right amygdala and related diencephalic structures. *Archives of General Psychiatry, 64*(6), 737–746. https://doi.org/10.1001/archpsyc.64.6.737

Schmidt, A. F., & Banse, R. (2022). Using indirect measures of sexual interest in forensic contexts: Past, present, and Future. In K. Uzieblo, W. J. Smid, & K. McCartan (Eds.), *Challenges in the management of people convicted of a sexual offence* (Palgrave studies in risk, crime and society). Palgrave Macmillan. https://doi.org/10.1007/978-3-030-80212-7_5

Schmidt, A. F., Mokros, A., & Banse, R. (2013). Is pedophilic sexual preference continuous? A taxometric analysis based on direct and indirect measures. *Psychological Assessment, 25*(4), 1146–1153. https://doi.org/10.1037/a0033326

Schmidt, A. F., & Perkins, D. (2021). Using the Explicit and Implicit Sexual Interest Profile in applied forensic or clinical contexts. In G. Akerman, D. Perkins, & R. M. Bartels (Eds.), *Assessing and managing problematic sexual interests: A practitioner's guide* (pp. 57–81). Routledge/Taylor & Francis.

Schmucker, M., & Lösel, F. (2015). The effects of sexual offender treatment on recidivism: An international meta-analysis of sound quality evaluations. *Journal of Experimental Criminology, 11*(4), 597–630. https://doi.org/10.1007/s11292-015-9241-z

Schöttle, D., Briken, P., Tüscher, O., & Turner, D. (2017). Sexuality in autism: Hypersexual and paraphilic behavior in women and men with high-functioning autism spectrum disorder. *Dialogues in Clinical Neuroscience, 19*(4), 381–393. https://doi.org/10.31887/DCNS.2017.19.4/dschoettle

Schulz, A., Bergen, E., Schuhmann, P., & Hoyer, J. (2017). Social anxiety and loneliness in adults who solicit minors online. *Sexual Abuse: A Journal of Research and Treatment, 29*(6), 519–540. https://doi.org/10.1177/1079063215612440

Schulz, A., Bergen, E., Schuhmann, P., Hoyer, J., & Santtila, P. (2016). Online sexual solicitation of minors: How often and between whom does it occur? *Journal of Research in Crime and Delinquency, 53*(2), 165–188. https://doi.org/10.1177/0022427815599426

Scurich, N., & Krauss, D. A. (2023). Risk assessment of child-pornography-exclusive offenders. *Law and Human Behavior, 47*(4), 499–509. https://doi.org/10.1037/lhb0000537

Seiser, A., Eher, R., Turner, D., & Rettenberger, M. (2023). The prevalence of mental disorders among incarcerated adult men convicted of child sexual exploitation material offences. *CNS Spectrums, 28*(6), 719–725. https://doi.org/10.1017/S1092852923002262

Seto, M. C. (2008). *Pedophilia and sexual offending against children: Theory, assessment, and intervention*. American Psychological Association.

Seto, M. C. (2017). The puzzle of male chronophilias. *Archives of Sexual Behavior, 46*(3), 3–22. https://doi.org/10.1007/s10508-016-0799-y

Seto, M. C. (2018). *Pedophilia and sexual offending against children: Theory, assessment, and intervention* (2nd ed.). American Psychological Association.

Seto, M. C. (2019). The motivation-facilitation model of sexual offending. *Sexual Abuse, 31*(1), 3–24. https://doi.org/10.1177/1079063217720919

Seto, M. C., Babchishin, K. M., Pullman, L. E., & McPhail, I. V. (2015). The puzzle of intrafamilial child sexual abuse: A meta-analysis comparing intrafamilial and extrafamilial offenders with child victims. *Clinical Psychology Review, 39*, 42–57. https://doi.org/10.1016/j.cpr.2015.04.001

Seto, M. C., Cantor, J. M., & Blanchard, R. (2006). Child pornography offenses are a valid diagnostic indicator of pedophilia. *Journal of Abnormal Psychology, 115*(3), 610–615. https://doi.org/10.1037/0021-843X.115.3.610

Seto, M. C., & Eke, A. W. (2015). Predicting recidivism among adult male child pornography offenders: Development of the Child Pornography Offender Risk Tool (CPORT). *Law and Human Behavior, 39*(4), 416–429. https://doi.org/10.1037/lhb0000128

Seto, M. C., & Eke, A. W. (2017). Correlates of admitted sexual interest in children among individuals convicted of child pornography offenses. *Law and Human Behavior, 41*(3), 305–313. https://doi.org/10.1037/lhb0000240
Seto, M. C., & Lalumière, M. L. (2001). A brief screening scale to identify pedophilic interests among child molesters. *Sexual Abuse: A Journal of Research and Treatment, 13*(1), 15–25. https://doi.org/10.1177/107906320101300103
Seto, M. C., Roche, K., Rodrigues, N. C., Curry, S., & Letourneau, E. (2024). Evaluating child sexual abuse perpetration prevention efforts: A systematic review. *Journal of Child Sexual Abuse, 33*(7), 847–868. https://doi.org/10.1080/10538712.2024.2356194
Seto, M. C., Stephens, S., Lalumièrem, M. L., & Cantor, J. M. (2017). The Revised Screening Scale for Pedophilic Interests (SSPI-2); Development and criterion-related validation. *Sexual Abuse: A Journal of Research and Treatment, 29*(7), 619–635. https://doi.org/10.1177/1079063215612444
Seto, M. C., Wood, J. M., Babchishin, K. M., & Flynn, S. (2012). Online solicitation offenders are different from child pornography offenders and lower risk contact sexual offenders. *Law and Human Behavior, 36*(4), 320–330. https://doi.org/10.1037/h0093925
Singy, P. (2015). Hebephilia: A postmortem discussion. *Archives of Sexual Behavior, 44*, 1109–1116. https://doi.org/10.1007/s10508-015-0542-0
Smid, W. J., & Wever, E. C. (2017). Incentive theory of sexual motivation: A framework for the description of sexual offending behaviour and the role of sexual deviance. In D. P. Boer, A. R. Beech, T. Ward, L. A. Craig, M. Rettenberger, L. E. Marshall, & W. L. Marshall (Eds.), *The Wiley handbook on the theories, assessment, and treatment of sexual offending* (pp. 141–164). Wiley-Blackwell.
Sniewski, L., Farvid, P., & Carter, P. (2018). The assessment and treatment of adult heterosexual men with self-perceived problematic pornography use: A review. *Addictive Behaviors, 77*, 217–224. https://doi.org/10.1016/j.addbeh.2017.10.010
Snowden, R. J., Craig, R. L., & Gray, N. S. (2011). Indirect behavioral measures of cognition among sexual offenders. *The Journal of Sex Research, 48*(2–3), 192–217. https://doi.org/10.1080/00224499.2011.557750
Socarides, C. W. (1959). Meaning and content of a pedophiliac perversion. *Journal of the American Psychoanalytic Association, 7*(1), 84–94. https://doi.org/10.1177/000306515900700103
Socarides, C. W. (1988). *Preoedipal origin and psychoanalytic therapy of sexual perversions*. International Universities Press.
Sorrentino, R., & Abramowitz, J. (2021). Minor-attracted persons: A neglected population. *Current Psychiatry, 20*(7), 21–27. https://doi.org/10.12788/cp.0149
Sorrentino, R., Bauer, L., & Reilly, D. (2013). Psychotic and sexually deviant. *Current Psychiatry, 12*(5), 37.
Spriggs, S. A., Cohen, L. J., Valencia, A., Yaseen, Z. S., & Galynker, I. I. (2018). Qualitative analysis of attitudes toward adult-child sexual activity among minor-attracted persons. *Journal of Sex and Marital Therapy, 44*(8), 787–799. https://doi.org/10.1080/0092623X.2018.1474406
Steel, C. M. S., Newman, E., O'Rourke, S., & Quayle, E. (2022). Suicidal ideation in offenders convicted of child sexual exploitation material offences. *Behavioral Sciences and the Law, 40*(3), 365–378. https://doi.org/10.1002/bsl.2560
Stephens, S., Leroux, E., Skilling, T., Cantor, J. M., & Seto, M. C. (2017). Taxometric analyses of pedophilia utilizing self-report, behavioral, and sexual arousal indicators. *Journal of Abnormal Psychology, 126*(8), 1114–1119. https://doi.org/10.1037/abn0000291
Stephens, S., Seto, M. C., Cantor, J. M., & Lalumière, M. L. (2019). The Revised Screening Scale for Pedophilic Interests (SSPI-2) may be a measure of pedohebephilia. *The Journal of Sexual Medicine, 16*(10), 1655–1663. https://doi.org/10.1016/j.jsxm.2019.07.015
Stephens, S., Seto, M. C., Goodwill, A. M., & Cantor, J. M. (2017). Evidence of construct validity in the assessment of hebephilia. *Archives of Sexual Behavior, 46*, 301–309. https://doi.org/10.1007/s10508-016-0907-z

Stephens, S., Seto, M. C., Goodwill, A. M., & Cantor, J. M. (2018). Age diversity among victims of hebephilic sexual offenders. *Sexual Abuse, 30*(3), 322–339. https://doi.org/10.1177/1079063216665837

Stern, P. (2010). Paraphilic coercive disorder in the DSM: The right diagnosis for the right reasons. *Archives of Sexual Behavior, 39*, 1443–1447. https://doi.org/10.1007/s10508-010.9645-9

Stevens, E., & Wood, J. (2019). 'I despise myself for thinking about them.' A thematic analysis of the mental health implications and employed coping mechanisms of self-reported non-offending minor attracted persons. *Journal of Child Sexual Abuse, 28*(8), 968–989. https://doi.org/10.1080/10538712.2019.1657539

Stewart, H. (2022). *Characteristics of minor attracted persons in the community: Developing a biopsychosocial-sexual typology of men with sexual interests in children.* Unpublished PhD thesis. University of New Brunswick. https://unbscholar.lib.unb.ca/handle/1882/37442

Stoltenborgh, M., Bakermans-Kranenburg, M. J., Alink, L. R. A., & van Ijzendoorn, M. H. (2015). The prevalence of child maltreatment across the globe: Review of a series of meta-analyses. *Child Abuse Review, 24*(1), 37–50. https://doi.org/10.1002/car.2353

Suchy, Y., Whittaker, J. W., Strassberg, D. S., & Eastvold, A. (2009). Neurocognitive differences between pedophilic and nonpedophilic child molesters. *Journal of the International Neuropsychological Society, 15*(2), 248–257. https://doi.org/10.1017/S1355617709090353

Sutton, A., Cherney, A., White, R., & Clancey, G. (2021). *Crime prevention: Principles, perspectives and practices.* Cambridge University Press.

Szczypiński, J., Wypych, M., Krasoska, A., Wiśniewski, P., Kopera, M., Suszek, H., Marchewka, A., Jakubczyk, A., & Wojnar, M. (2022). Abnormal behavioral and neural responses in the right dorsolateral prefrontal cortex during emotional interference for cognitive control in pedophilic sex offenders. *Journal of Psychiatric Research, 151*, 131–135. https://doi.org/10.2016/j.jpsychires.2022.04.012

Talbot, T. J., & Langdon, P. E. (2006). A revised sexual knowledge assessment tool for people with intellectual disabilities: Is sexual knowledge related to sexual offending behaviour? *Journal of Intellectual Disability Research, 50*(7), 523–531. https://doi.org/10.1111/j.1365-2788.2006.00801.x

Tenbergen, G., Wittfoth, M., Frieling, H., Ponseti, J., Walter, M., Walter, H., Beier, K. M., Schiffer, B., & Kruger, T. H. C. (2015). The neurobiology and psychology of pedophilia: Recent advances and challenges. *Frontiers in Human Neuroscience, 9*, 344. https://doi.org/10.3389/fnhum.2015.00344

Thornton, D. (2010). *Scoring guide for Risk Matrix 2000.10/SVC.* Unpublished document.

Thornton, D. (2017). *Scoring guide for Risk Matrix 2000 S & V Scales: International Version.*

Thornton, D., Fernandez, Y. M., & Helmus, L. M. (2023). *Scoring guide for Risk Matrix 2000 S & V Scales: International Version.* www.saarna.org

Thornton, D., Mann, R., Webster, S., Blud, L., Travers, R., Friendship, C., & Erikson, M. (2003). Distinguishing and combining risks for sexual and violent recidivism. In R. A. Prentky, E. S. Janus, & M. C. Seto (Eds.), *Sexually coercive behavior: Understanding and management* (pp. 225–235). New York Academy of Sciences.

Tonry, M. (2014). Why crime rates are falling throughout the western world. *Crime and Justice, 43*(1), 1–63. https://doi.org/10.1086/678181

Tromovitch, P. (2009). Manufacturing mental disorder by pathologizing erotic age orientation: A comment on Blanchard et al. (2008). *Archives of Sexual Behavior, 38*, 328. https://doi.org/10.1007/s10508-008-9426-x

Turner, D., & Briken, P. (2015). Child sexual abusers working with children-characteristics and risk factors. *Sexual Offender Treatment, 10*(1), 1–12. http://www.sexual-offender-treatment.org/138.html

Turner, D., & Briken, P. (2018). Treatment of paraphilic disorders in sexual offenders or men with a risk of sexual offending with luteinizing hormone-releasing hormone agonists: An updated systematic review. *The Journal of Sexual Medicine, 15*(1), 77–93. https://doi.org/10.1016/j.jsxm.2017.11.013

Turner, D., Hertz, P. G., Biedermann, L., Barra, S., & Retz, W. (2022). Paraphilias in ADHD and their association with hypersexuality. Research Square. Preprint. https://doi.org/10.21203/rs.3.rs-2111503/v1.

Turner, D., Laier, C., Brand, M., Bockshammer, T., Welsch, R., & Rettenberger, M. (2018). Response inhibition and impulsive decision-making in sexual offenders against children. *Journal of Abnormal Psychology, 127*(5), 471–481. https://doi.org/10.1037/abn0000359

Turner, D., & Rettenberger, M. (2020). Neuropsychological functioning in child sexual abusers: A systematic review. *Aggression and Violent Behavior, 54*, Article 101405. https://doi.org/10.1016/j.avb.2020.101405

Uzieblo, K., & De Boeck, M. (2022). They need somebody, and not just anybody: help-seeking behaviour in minor-attracted persons. In K. Uzieblo, W. J. Smid, & K. McCartan (Eds.), *Challenges in the management of people convicted of a sexual offence* (pp. 191–206). Palgrave Macmillan. https://doi.org/10.1007/978-3-030-80212-7_12

Valiquet, D. (2006). *The dangerous offender and long-term offender regime*. Parliamentary Information and Research Service. Government of Canada. https://publications.gc.ca/collections/collection_2009/bdp-lop/prb/prb0613-1e.pdf

Van Horn, J. V., Eisenberg, M., Nicholls, C. M., Mulder, J., Webster, S., Paskell, C., Brown, A., Stam, J., Kerr, J., & Jago, N. (2015). Stop it now! A pilot study into the limits and benefits of a free helpline preventing child sexual abuse. *Journal of Child Sexual Abuse, 24*(8), 853–872. https://doi.org/10.1080/10538712.2015.1088914

Van Mastrigt, S. B., & Carrington, P. J. (2019). Co-offending. In D. P. Farrington, L. Kazemian, & A. R. Piquero (Eds.), *The Oxford handbook of developmental and life-course criminology* (pp. 125–146). Oxford Academic. https://doi.org/10.1093/oxfordhb/9780190201371.013.8

Vicenzutto, A., Joyal, C. C., Telle, É., & Pham, T. H. (2022). Risk factors for sexual offenses committed by men with or without a low IQ: An exploratory study. *Frontiers in Psychiatry, 13*, 820249. https://doi.org/10.3389/fpsyt.2022.820249

von Franqué, F., Bergner-Koether, R., Schmidt, S., Pellowski, J. S., Peterson, J. H., Hakak, G., & Briken, P. (2023). Individuals under voluntary treatment with sexual interest in minors: What risk do they pose? *Frontiers in Psychiatry, 14*, Article 1277225. https://doi.org/10.3389/fpsyt.2023.1277225

Walker, A. (2021). *A long, dark shadow: Minor-attracted people and their pursuit of dignity*. University of California Press. ISBN-10:0520306341.

Walker, A., Butters, R. P., & Nichols, E. (2022). 'I would report it even if they have not committed anything': Social service students' attitudes toward minor-attracted people. *Sexual Abuse, 34*(1), 52–77. https://doi.org/10.1177/1079063221993480

Wallace, C., Mullen, P. E., Burgess, P., Palmer, S., Ruschena, D., & Browne, C. (1998). Serious criminal offending and mental disorder. Case linkage study. *The British Journal of Psychiatry, 172*, 477–484. https://doi.org/10.1192/bjp.172.6.477

Walter, M., Witzel, J., Wiebking, C., Gubka, U., Rotte, M., Schiltz, K., Bermpohl, F., Tempelmann, C., Bogerts, B., Heinze, H. J., & Northoff, G. (2007). Pedophilia is linked to reduced activation in hypothalamus and lateral prefrontal cortex during visual erotic stimulation. *Biological Psychiatry, 62*(6), 698–701. https://doi.org/10.1016/j.biopsych.2006.10.018

Walton, J. S., & Hocken, K. (2020). Compassion and acceptance as interventions for paraphilic disorders and sexual offending behaviour. In G. Akerman, D. Perkins, & R. Bartels (Eds.), *Assessing and managing problematic sexual interests* (pp. 149–170). Routledge.

Ward, T., & Clack, S. (2019). From symptoms of psychopathology to the explanation of clinical phenomena. *New Ideas in Psychology, 54*, 40–49. https://doi.org/10.1016/j.newideapsych.2019.01.004

Ward, T., & Hudson, S. M. (2000). A self-regulation model of relapse prevention. In D. R. Laws, S. M. Hudson, & T. Ward (Eds.), *Remaking relapse prevention with sex offenders: a sourcebook* (pp. 79–101). Sage. https://doi.org/10.4135/9781452224954.n5

Ward, T., Hudson, S. M., & Keenan, T. (1998). A self-regulation model of the sexual offense process. *Sexual Abuse, 10*(2), 141–157. https://doi.org/10.1177/107906329801000206

Ward, T., Louden, K., Hudson, S. M., & Marshall, W. L. (1995). A descriptive model of the offense chain for child molesters. *Journal of Interpersonal Violence, 10*(4), 452–472. https://doi.org/10.1177/088626095010004005
Ward, T., & Siegert, R. J. (2002). Toward a comprehensive theory of child sexual abuse: A theory knitting perspective. *Psychology, Crime and Law, 8*(4), 319–351. https://doi.org/10.1080/10683160208401823
Warren, J. I., & McLeod, D. A. (2017). Female sex offenders. In R. R. Hazelwood & A. W. Burgess (Eds.), *Practical aspects of rape investigation: A multidisciplinary approach* (5th ed., pp. 337–353). CRC Press.
Welsch, R., von Castell, C., Rettenberger, M., Turner, D., Hecht, H., & Fromberger, P. (2020). Sexual attraction modulates interpersonal distance and approach-avoidance movements towards virtual agents in males. *PLoS One, 15*(4), e0231539. https://doi.org/10.1371/journal.pone.0231539
Westlake, B. G. (2020). The past, present, and future of online child sexual exploitation: Summarizing the evolution of production, distribution, and detection. In T. Holt & A. Bossler (Eds.), *The Palgrave handbook of international cybercrime and cyberdeviance* (pp. 1225–1253). Palgrave Macmillan. https://doi.org/10.1007/978-3-319-78440-3_52
Wiegel, M., Abel, G. G., & Jordan, A. (2003, October). *The self-reported behaviors of female child abusers*. Paper presented at the 22nd annual conference of the Association for the Treatment of Sexual Abusers (ATSA), St. Louis, USA.
Wong, J. S., & Gravel, J. (2018). Do sex offenders have higher levels of testosterone? Results from a meta-analysis. *Sexual Abuse: A Journal of Research and Treatment, 30*(2), 147–168. https://doi.org/10.1177/1079063216637857
World Health Organization. (1992). *International classification of diseases and related health problems* (10th revision; ICD-10). Author.
World Health Organization. (1993). *The ICD-10 classification of mental and behavioural disorders: Diagnostic criteria for research*. Author.
World Health Organization. (2022). *International classification of diseases for mortality and morbidity statistics* (11th revision; ICD-11). Author. https://icd.who.int/
Worling, J. R. (1995). Sexual abuse histories of adolescent male sex offenders: Differences on the basis of the age and gender of their victims. *Journal of Abnormal Psychology, 104*(4), 610–613. https://doi.org/10.1037/0021-843x.104.4.610
Wurtele, S. K., Simons, D. A., & Moreno, T. (2014). Sexual interest in children among an online sample of men and women: Prevalence and correlates. *Sexual Abuse, 26*(6), 546–568. https://doi.org/10.1177/1079063213503688
Zander, T. K. (2009). Adult sexual attraction to early-stage adolescents: Phallometry doesn't equal pathology. *Archives of Sexual Behavior, 38*, 329–330. https://doi.org/10.1007/s10508-008-9428-8
Zappalà, A., & Santtila, P. (2021). Using the rapid serial visual presentation to detect sexual interest. In G. Akerman, D. Perkins, & R. Bartels (Eds.), *Assessing and managing problematic sexual interests*. Routledge.
Zgoba, K. M., & Mitchell, M. M. (2023). The effectiveness of sex offender registration and notification: A meta-analysis of 25 years of findings. *Journal of Experimental Criminology, 19*, 71–96.
Zillmann, D. (2008). Excitation transfer theory. In W. Donsbach (Ed.), *The international encyclopedia of communication*. Wiley. https://doi.org/10.1002/9781405186407.wbiece049

Chapter 14
Sexual Homicide

Tamsin Higgs, Jonathan James, Jean Proulx, Adam J. Carter, and Rajan Darjee

14.1 Introduction

Sexual homicide stands out as a particular subcategory of sexual offending—even insofar as having a dedicated chapter in this and other volumes—commanding special attention in the minds of theorists, clinicians, criminal investigators, and the general public. Its incidence is relatively low, estimated at 0.09 per 100,000 people in the US annually and roughly comparable rates in other countries including Canada, England, and Wales (Proulx et al., 2007c; Stefanska et al., 2016). However, the tremendous personal harm caused to victims and their families as well as the wider societal damage resulting from any one case of sexual homicide is such that it necessarily demands devoted scholarly attention. But is sexual homicide so different from other types of sexual offending? Should our approach be any different from the assessment and management practices recommended for perpetrators of non-homicide sexual offenses? Beech et al. (2005) addressed these questions concluding that there was not sufficient evidence to consider that perpetrators of sexual

T. Higgs (✉)
Department of Psychology, University of Montreal, Montreal, QC, Canada
e-mail: tamsin.higgs@umontreal.ca

J. James
Department of Psychology, University of Quebec in Trois Rivières, Trois Rivières, QC, Canada

J. Proulx
School of Criminology, University of Montreal, Montreal, QC, Canada

A. J. Carter
His Majesty's Prison and Probation Service, London, UK

R. Darjee
Victorian Institute of Forensic Mental Health (Forensicare), Victoria, Australia

R. J. Tully et al. (eds.), *Best Practices in Sexual Offender Assessment and Management*, Dangerous Behavior in Clinical and Forensic Psychology,
https://doi.org/10.1007/978-3-031-83135-5_14

homicide may not benefit from sexual offending behavior interventions similarly to men having committed acts of non-fatal sexual aggression, and the evidence base is looked at again in this chapter. However, with the benefit of more than 15 years of additional research and reflection, deliberation is merited as to whether a different question should be asked. A focus has been on whether there is something that sets perpetrators of sexual homicide apart as a unique type of sexual offender (i.e., presenting specific criminogenic factors for sexual violence). The answer, albeit in a somewhat oversimplified sense, seems to be not necessarily so. And yet, not only have these men (the context of most sexual homicides being a male perpetrator and an adult female victim) sexually offended, but they have killed. Therefore, while there is sexual offending behavior alongside risk factors associated with it that need to be understood, the lethal aspect of the offense also needs to be evaluated. The approach taken by researchers has been to examine why some sexual aggressors kill but others do not. The question now considered is: Why do some individuals kill in a sexual context rather than in a non-sexual context?

To elaborate on how this question might be addressed, a brief overview of the sexual homicide research is needed. One thing that is known is that sexual homicide is a heterogeneous phenomenon, as is unpacked in the sections that follow looking at the role of anger, sadistic fantasy, and psychopathology in this type of offending. What this heterogeneity means is that in most cases the victim's death is circumstantial; whether or not sexual aggression was premeditated to some degree, killing was not. It is quite logical, then, to conceptualize sexual homicide on a continuum of sexual offending whereby perpetrators are generally not distinguishable from perpetrators of non-homicide sexual aggression: The question as to the uniqueness of sexual homicide as a type of sexual offense being answered here. That being so, killing plays a functional role in a certain subtype of sexual homicide and rather than being attributable to situational factors it represents the fusion of sexual and homicidal drives. Thus, there does seem to be a distinct group who might be thought of as extreme in the sense that their offending inevitably results in fatality, assuming no external impeding factor.

It is here that the current authors propose that a conceptual shift might be useful: What are the factors that precipitate these *sexualized killings* (this being a particular subtype of sexual homicide, discussed below), and do those same factors drive other types of extreme violence that do not involve a sexual element? In other words, are there psychosocial factors associated with extreme (fatal) violence that manifest in both sexual and non-sexual contexts? As well as examining whether perpetrators of sexual homicide are similar or different from perpetrators of non-homicide sexual aggression, the similarities and differences between perpetrators of sexual homicide, and perpetrators of other extreme acts of violence such as intimate partner (non-sexual) homicide, or homicide resulting from political or religious extremism might be explored. In this chapter, the work that has brought us to this line of thinking and suggest that this might be one future direction for further enquiry is looked at in more detail. Current evidence-based practice in the assessment and management of perpetrators of sexual homicide offenses is also discussed.

14.2 Classifications of Sexual Homicide

We have said that sexual homicide is a heterogeneous phenomenon, and that is because it is really an umbrella term for a number of quite different types of offenses given that sexual homicide is not a specific offense category in any legal jurisdiction, to our knowledge (Carter & Hollin, 2015). Rather, a sexual offense may be recorded as a secondary charge or aggravating factor relating to the homicide (e.g. murder or manslaughter) charge. Alternatively, there might be no sexual offense recorded at all, for example, if there was insufficient evidence meeting the legal threshold for a conviction for it. Therefore, broadly speaking, any homicide involving an apparent sexual element may be categorized as sexual homicide for criminal investigation, clinical, or research purposes, regardless of how integral the sexual element may or may not have been.

The operational definition most often used is that offered by Ressler et al. (1988), according to which a homicide may be considered sexual in nature when evidence or observations include "victim attire or lack of attire; exposure of the sexual parts of the victim's body; sexual positioning of the victim's body; insertion of foreign objects into the victim's body cavities; evidence of sexual intercourse (oral, anal, vaginal); and evidence of substitute sexual activity, interest, or sadistic fantasy" (from the preface, pp. xiii). These criteria discriminate to an acceptable degree between sexual and non-sexual homicide (Carter et al., 2016), but certain elements lack clarity and reliance on these criteria is open to both false negatives and false positives. That is, a homicide is falsely determined to be non-sexual when evidence is not clear from the crime scene and the perpetrator is not forthcoming with this information; identifying substitute sexual activity, interest, or sadistic fantasy is not necessarily a straightforward task and there is risk of subjective bias and error. Conversely, a decision to falsely determine that a homicide involved a sexual element is possible because of one or more misleading indications. For example, the victim was found fully or partially naked, although she was in this state because there had been consensual sex some time shortly before the incident that triggered her homicide. It could be argued that sexual homicide is indeed being talked about here; after all, fatal violence occurred following sexual activity, before the victim had managed to dress herself. On the other hand, it may be erroneous to attribute any relevance to the sexual aspect. Thus, a situational context analysis may be necessary to avoid misinterpretation of crime scene indicators (Clarke & Carter, 2000). Forensic case formulation involving such an analysis would be expected in any individual assessment and management plan but during criminal investigation and judicial proceedings, especially with a non-cooperative accused person, contextual information will not necessarily be available. Likewise, reliable classification can be problematic in a research context depending on the data source.

Aiming to arrive at a definition with perfect sensitivity and specificity is unrealistic since sexual behaviors are overt but sexual motivation is unobservable and does not reliably manifest in objectively measurable ways. However, the current authors propose a revised definition that retains components from Ressler et al. (1988) but also draws on subsequent work that clarifies that sexual activity may not necessarily be evident from only the victim's body (Meloy et al., 1994; Schlesinger, 2007) and might not even be present at the crime scene itself (Clarke & Carter, 2000). Thus, sexual homicide refers to all homicide (regardless of category according to different criminal codes) where a sexual element was identified due to evidence of sexual activity including touching the victim's genitals, penetration of the victim (vaginally, anally, and/or orally), insertion of foreign objects, mutilation of genitals, or other sexually exploitative activities or sexual contact; which may occur at any or all stages before, during, or after the killing; and in some cases evidence of sexual activity might be found near to the victim's body or may not be overtly available but sexual motivations may be disclosed by the perpetrator or identified from evidence collected during criminal investigation. This definition captures three subtypes of sexual homicide, namely:

1. Rape killing, which refers to sexual aggression and subsequent homicide for instrumental reasons such as to silence the victim, thus preventing her from being able to identify her attacker, or in response to situational factors such as where the victim dies of injuries sustained during a sexual offense or as she tries to escape it—in these cases there is only an indirect association between the sexual element of the offense and killing;
2. grievance killing, which is driven by angry schemas and an excessively aggressive response style—in these cases the sexual attack may use particularly violent force, but fatal violence is not necessarily a source of sexual excitement;
3. sexualized killing, referred to in this way to make explicit the direct relationship between killing and sexual arousal—in these cases the victim's suffering, the act of killing itself, and/or post mortem sexual interference are facets of the perpetrator's sexual deviancy (Higgs et al., 2017a).

14.3 The Role of Anger and Violence

As in other forms of sexual aggression, gratification of sexual urges less often represents a motivational explanation for sexual homicide, as opposed to other drives such as a perceived need to (re)instate sensations of power and control (e.g. Groth & Birnbaum, 1979). Indeed, the literature has evolved, using varying terminology, with a tendency to dichotomize sexual homicide suggesting a sadistic type and an angry type (e.g., Beauregard & Proulx, 2002). However, the role of anger requires scrutiny (Myers et al., 2006; Stefanska et al., 2018). That is, it is an insufficient explanation for sexual violence; high levels of trait anger have been found among perpetrators of sexual homicide, but the same has been observed in other forensic populations, such as offenders assessed to have a high number of psychopathic traits (e.g., Decuyper et al., 2009). In fact, anger is a characteristic of the perpetrator that fails to explain lethal sexual violence (Carter & Hollin, 2015), particularly considering that anger typically has a physiological inhibitory effect on sexual excitation (Myers et al., 2006).

Where a subtype of sexual homicide (grievance killing, as defined earlier in this chapter) is consistently empirically and clinically described to be characterized by anger, this relates to self-reported *pre-crime* general anger, or thoughts or fantasies revolving around resentment and/or anger specifically towards women, as well as being inferred from the type and extent of violence (overkill; anal rape) used in the offense (Higgs et al., 2017a). On the other hand, anger *during* the offense has been reported among perpetrators of both grievance killings and sexualized killings (Beauregard & Proulx, 2002; Stefanska et al., 2018). Consistent with the argument according to which anger and sexual arousal are incompatible physiological states (Myers et al., 2006), grievance killings tend to occur when anger is triggered because a victim rejects the perpetrator's sexual advances or resists rape; following an argument arising during or after consensual sex; or in the course of a sexual assault in response to something that the victim said or did (Stefanska et al., 2018). Anger in such scenarios therefore often has a role as an antecedent to sexual violence, in that angry rumination (and with it, perhaps power orientation, mollification, and other criminal thinking styles; Walters, 2012) favors the use of sex to cause harm, whereas anger *during* the offense has a role in the recourse to fatal violence. The role of anger in sexualized killings is seemingly more complicated. It might be that anger during a sexualized killing reflects frustration with a crime that is failing to correspond to or satisfy an entrenched sexual fantasy, or that alternatively, acting on such fantasies triggers angry emotions that precipitated the development of deviant fantasies in the first place (as discussed in the following section). Further research is necessary to test such hypotheses, but in these cases, when anger is experienced, it seems to either exacerbate sexual violence, or simply fails to diminish it. Despite the apparent contradiction at the physiological level, on the contrary it may be that here sexual arousal is a conditioned response to anger (Yates et al., 1984).

Further, the role of anger in sexual homicide can be understood by determining whether aggression was used reactively rather than proactively (Dodge, 1991; Dodge & Coie, 1987). Proactive aggression is that which has otherwise been called predatory, premeditated, or even cold-blooded; descriptions that may be applied to sexualized killing. By contrast, consistent with the concept of grievance killing, reactive aggression is an immediate behavioral response to frustration or perceived or actual threat, which is usually accompanied by high, uncontrolled autonomic arousal (i.e., physical symptoms of anger such as increased heart rate; Houston et al., 2003). Developmental criminological research has indicated a tendency towards reactive aggression among physically maltreated children (Connor et al., 2004; Dodge et al., 1997), who also experience rejection or victimization by peers (Dodge et al., 1997; Lamarche et al., 2007; Price & Dodge, 1989; Salmivalli & Nieminen, 2002; Schwartz et al., 1998), and characteristically interpret others' attitudes as hostile (Crick & Dodge, 1996; Dodge & Coie, 1987), while being susceptible to negative affect (Shackman & Pollak, 2014; Teisl & Cicchetti, 2008), and having difficulty controlling anger (McAuliffe et al., 2006; Moore et al., 2019). Concordantly, in a study of perpetrators of reactive and proactive aggression in the context of sexual homicide, childhood maltreatment beginning early in life (1–12 years) and continuing through adolescence, combined with exposure to inadequate parental behavior (intimate partner violence; problematic alcohol use; criminal behavior; allowing the child to witness parents' sexual contact or mother's sexual contact with clients as a sex worker), was associated with the use of reactive aggression during a sexual homicide offense, whereas maltreatment more typically occurred during adolescence among perpetrators of sexual homicide using proactive aggression (James et al., 2020). It appears, then, that environmental influences at different neurodevelopmental and psychosocial developmental stages differentially favor cognitive behavioral patterns that predispose a tendency towards either reactive or proactive aggression.

14.4 The Role of Sadistic Fantasy

Having stressed that sexual homicide does not equate to murderous sexual predation, sexual homicide being a heterogeneous phenomenon has also been commented on and a subtype, namely, sexualized killing, has been described wherein homicide occurs as a function of sexual deviancy. In some samples, this sexual deviancy strongly signifies a precipitating role of sadistic fantasy in the lead up to a premeditated sexually sadistic homicide (Beauregard et al., 2007). Indeed, in James et al.'s (2020) sample of perpetrators of sexual homicide having used proactive aggression, higher scores compared to perpetrators of sexual homicide having used reactive aggression were found on the Severe Sexual Sadism Scale (SeSaS; Mokros et al., 2012; Nitschke et al., 2009). High SeSaS scores predicted proactive as opposed to reactive aggression among perpetrators of sexual homicide even when controlling for psychopathy; Factor 1 Psychopathy Checklist-Revised (PCL-R; Hare, 2003) scores indicating manipulative, narcissistic, callous unemotionality traits also being associated with the use of proactive aggression in both perpetrators of sexual homicide (James et al., 2020) and other violent offenders (Declercq et al., 2012).

In other studies, sexualized killing is committed either by perpetrators acting out their sexual sadism or it may be a manifestation of sexual deviancy that is not necessarily sadistic (e.g. Stefanska et al., 2015). Some discordance in the empirical literature may be attributed to difficulties in defining sexual sadism and measurement variation (for a discussion, see Higgs et al., 2020). However, whether sexual fantasies reflect full sexual sadism disorder or otherwise bind sexual and homicidal thoughts without expanding to sadistic acts, research suggests that the use of deviant sexual fantasies operates as an antecedent to sexualized killing as a pathological coping strategy in the face of diverse problems of social disconnection (Higgs et al., 2015; Proulx et al., 2007b). Having likely suffered multiple forms of adverse childhood experiences, these are individuals who have been maltreated (importantly, in terms of biopsychosocial development, this may be during adolescence more so than in early childhood; James et al., 2020), have had difficulties forming relationships from an early age and have remained socially isolated as adults, and in this context develop sexual fantasies and cognitive schema characterized by low empathic concern for others and sexual entitlement (Higgs et al., 2015, 2017b). Indicative of a process that might involve desensitization, conditioned sexual excitement, and eventual dissatisfaction with an imagined scenario driving the perpetrator towards acting on homicidal ideation, perpetrators of sexualized killing tend to have planned their offense. As such, deviant sexual fantasy has a role in increasing susceptibility to commit sexualized killing, which either means subjecting the victim to sadistic acts as the perpetrator seeks to enact his fantasy, or that the victim is killed to enable, for example, post-mortem sexual acts. What this means for assessment and intervention planning is explored later in this chapter but, in brief, the starting point for forensic case conceptualization with a perpetrator of a sexualized killing will be to look to understand: a) whether/to what extent deviant sexual arousal (be it sadistic or a non-sadistic binding of sexual and homicidal drives) supersedes interest in consensual sexual intimacy, and; b) the function of deviant sexual fantasies and/or behaviors including sexualized murder beyond sexual gratification.

14.5 Key Distinctions Between Sexual Homicide of Women and Other Sex Offenses

In the 1980s and in the 1990s, researchers focused their attention on perpetrators of serial sexual homicide and of sadistic sexual homicide (Proulx et al., 2007b). In addition, they did not differentiate between perpetrators having adult female, adult male, or child victims. During the 2000s the main trend of empirical investigations focused on perpetrators of non-serial sexual homicide, recognizing that non-serial cases are more common that serial cases, and research began to take into account the type of victim (women, men, children). In addition, samples were usually larger and more representative of the population than the samples studied in the 1980s and 1990s.

Consequently, it is known that the victims of sexual homicide are most frequently adult women. Stefanska et al. (2016) carried out a systematic review of studies that compared perpetrators of non-serial sexual homicide of women to perpetrators of non-fatal sexual offenses against women. Among the 10 studies retained in their review, most came from three countries, namely Canada (Healey et al., 2013; Proulx et al., 2007a; Langevin, 2003), the United Kingdom (Higgs et al., 2017b; Milsom et al., 2003; Oliver et al., 2007; Vettor et al., 2014), and Germany (Koch et al., 2011). The results of this systematic review indicated that among *developmental characteristics*, the presence of deviant sexual fantasies (e.g., sexually sadistic fantasies), as well as social isolation in childhood and adolescence, are the factors that best distinguish perpetrators of sexual homicide from perpetrators of non-homicide sexual aggression. However, contradictory results were found in relation to sexual and physical victimization, as well as to low self-esteem. Therefore, although these factors seem to be frequently reported predisposing factors in sexual criminals, it may not be concluded that they are specific to the psychosexual development of perpetrators of sexual homicide. Regarding *criminal careers*, both perpetrators of sexual homicide and of non-homicide sexual offenses have extensive criminal records, and these two types of offender do not differ in terms of previous charges for sexual and violent crimes (Stefanska et al., 2016). In terms of *psychopathological profiles*, there were no significant differences between the two groups in the prevalence of any personality disorders. Except for sexual sadism, which is more frequent in sexual homicide than in non-homicide sexual aggression, the prevalence of paraphilias is low in both types of sexual offenders. Regarding *modus operandi*, several studies have reported the precrime phase to be characterized by anger in sexual homicide, and by premeditation in non-homicide sexual offenses. During the crime phase, the use of restraints and mutilation of the victim is more frequent in sexual homicide, whereas vaginal penetration and humiliation of the victim are more frequent in non-homicide sexual offenses.

There are only a few comparative studies of perpetrators of sexual homicide of children (Proulx et al., 2018). Firestone et al. (1998) indicate that these offenders have a much more pathological profile than perpetrators of non-homicide child sexual offenses. Perpetrators of child sexual homicide presented a higher proportion of antisocial personality disorder and sexual sadism than perpetrators of non-homicide child sexual offenses. However, pedophilia was present in similar proportions, approximately 50%, in both groups. In addition, perpetrators of child sexual homicide were found to have a higher mean PCL–R score (28.7) than perpetrators of non-homicide child sexual offenses (16.6). Finally, perpetrators of child sexual homicide were more likely than perpetrators of non-homicide child sexual offenses to have committed previous violent and sexual offenses.

Perpetrators of child sexual homicide have been compared to perpetrators of sexual homicide of women in four studies; two from Canada (Beauregard et al., 2008; Langevin, 2006), one from Germany (Spehr et al., 2010), and one from France (Proulx et al., 2018). In the Canadian and German samples there were only minor discrepancies in the results, which suggested that when victims are children, the perpetrator is typically a man who has been neglected, sexually abused, and had adjustment problems at school (e.g., disruption of class, victim of bullying). As an adult, he is socially isolated and feels rejected by others. Also, he indulges in pedophilic, sadistic, and homicidal sexual fantasies, and masturbates compulsively. He rarely has sexual contact with other adults. His criminal record mainly includes sexual offenses, both contact and non-contact. In the hours preceding the sexual homicide, he is overwhelmed by deviant sexual fantasies, views pornography, and carefully plans his offense. His modus operandi is characterized by strangulation as cause of death, and dismemberment and hiding of the victim's body. When victims are women, the perpetrator is a man who has been rejected and physically abused as a child, who suffered from enuresis, and was a daydreamer. As an adult, he is socially isolated and abuses both drugs and alcohol. He has psychopathic personality traits. Also, he has financial and relationship problems. His criminal record includes both sexual and violent charges. In the hours preceding the sexual homicide he is under the influence of psychoactive substances. Although his murder is rarely planned, he keeps items belonging to the victim. Finally, regardless of whether victims were women or children, these studies found low prevalence of humiliation, torture, and mutilation of the victims. How well does the portrait from the French sample concord with these descriptions? Homicidal fantasies and sexual sadism were much more frequent in perpetrators of sexual homicide of women than those with child victims. Psychopathy was quite prevalent in both groups. Therefore, looking at the profiles drawn from these four studies, a particularity that can be noted in relation to perpetrators of child sexual homicide is that sexual deviancy is typically pedophilic in nature, whereas sexual sadism is more frequently associated with sexual homicides of women.

14.6 Psychopathology

We turn our attention now to the psychopathological factors that characterize the samples of perpetrators of sexual homicide that have been studied. First, mediatization of sexual homicide favors conjecture that these are the acts of people who must be mentally unwell. Alternatively, if not mentally disordered, are not perpetrators of sexual homicide surely psychopaths? To answer these questions, empirical work examining serious mental disorders and personality disorders in sexual homicide perpetrators is reviewed.

14.6.1 Serious Mental Disorders

Contrary to a common-sense perspective, most researchers and clinicians consider very few of the perpetrators of sexual homicide whom they have evaluated or studied to be psychotic (Brittain, 1970; Darjee & Baron, 2018c; Hill et al., 2018; Meloy, 2000; Proulx et al., 2020). However, it must be noted that sexual homicide research is usually based on samples from correctional facilities, where all detainees have been judged criminally responsible for their acts.

Revitch (1965) claimed that 20% of sexual homicide perpetrators may be diagnosed with schizophrenia, while Rada (1978) believed the majority to exhibit psychotic symptoms. In fact, as Liebert (1985) pointed out, strict application of modern nosology would result in most perpetrators of sexual homicide being diagnosed with some sort of personality disorder rather than with a psychiatric disorder. As an example, in a study by Proulx and Sauvetre (2007), based on a sample of 40 Canadian non-serial sexual homicide perpetrators with adult female victims, the prevalence of psychosis was extremely low (3%), and completely absent for mood disorder. In Germany, Hill et al. (2018) also found a very low prevalence of psychotic disorders (3%) and mood disorders (9.6%) in their sample ($N = 166$). Finally, in Scotland, Darjee and Baron (2018c) reported 12% prevalence of schizophrenia and 6% for mood disorder ($N = 51$). Again, though, most if not all of the data in these studies came from participants in prisons or penitentiaries.

Sexual sadism appears to be the only serious mental disorder observed in a significant proportion of perpetrators of sexual homicide (Dietz, 1986; Geberth, 1996; Myers, 2002; Stone, 1998). In Proulx and Sauvêtre's (2007) study, the prevalence of sexual sadism was 16.7%, whereas in Darjee and Baron (2018c), it is 39.2% and in Hill et al. (2018) it is 36.7%. A possible explanation for the variation in the prevalence of sexual sadism is related to the composition of the samples. In Proulx and Sauvêtre's (2007) study, all cases were non-serial whereas in Darjee and Baron's (2018c) study and that of Hill et al. (2018), serial cases represent 25% and 21.7% respectively. Since sadistic sexual fantasies, common among sexual sadists, is a strong motivational factor for seriality, the higher proportion of serial cases in the German and Scottish studies may explain the higher percentage of sexual sadism in their samples.

14.6.2 Personality Disorder

The state of scientific knowledge concerning personality disorders among perpetrators of sexual homicide is not clear. Psychopathy (antisocial and narcissistic personality disorders) is most frequently reported (Darjee & Baron, 2018c; Dietz, 1986; Hill et al., 2018; Porter et al., 2003). According to Porter and Rose (2018), psychopaths are sensation seekers, and so sexual homicide may be a way to satisfy this need. In addition, during a sexual homicide there is an absence of victim empathy, and subsequently perpetrators are unlikely to feel either remorse or guilt. Finally, they have inflated self-confidence, thinking themselves to be so intelligent that they will not be caught by the police. But is this psychopathic psychological functioning found in all perpetrators of sexual homicide?

Brittain (1970) concluded, based on his clinical experience, that sadistic perpetrators of sexual homicide are anxiety-ridden, shy, and reserved in their interpersonal relations. They also tend to shun human company in favor of an imaginary world in which they are omnipotent. Applying the diagnostic criteria of the *Diagnostic and Statistical Manual of Mental Disorders* (5th ed.; *DSM-5;* American Psychiatric Association, 2013), one would probably classify these men as avoidant and schizoid. They behave psychopathically only toward their victims, therefore appearing to be distinct from psychopaths who are dominant, manipulative, and hostile in every sphere of their lives. There is empirical research that can add to Brittain's (1970) clinical observations and theoretical considerations. The adolescent perpetrator of sexual homicide in Myers and Blashfield's (1997) study exhibited schizoid (38%) and schizotypal (38%) personality disorders. In Proulx and Sauvêtre's (2007) adult sample, Millon Clinical Multiaxial Inventory (MCMI; Millon, 1983) results revealed that the most common personality disorders were schizoid (20%), avoidant (28%), and dependent (32%). Finally, in Darjee and Baron's (2018c) study, although narcissistic (60.7%) and antisocial (66.7%) were the personality disorders with the highest prevalence, schizoid personality disorder was present in 43.8% of their sample. These results suggest that the emotional detachment of many sexual murderers could be conceptualized as a form of schizoid, rather than psychopathic disorder.

According to Myers (2002), the impulsiveness, anger, emotional instability, and chaotic interpersonal relationships of serial sexual homicide offenders are evidence of borderline personality disorder. Other authors (Gacono & Meloy, 1994; Liebert, 1985; Schlesinger, 2000) also believe that at least some perpetrators of sexual homicide exhibit a borderline personality organization. Finally, in Proulx and Sauvêtre's (2007) study, 28.6% of the sample were diagnosed as having a borderline personality disorder (DSM-IV criteria; American Psychiatric Association, 1994).

Although these personality disorder findings may be interpreted as inconclusive, they may also be considered a genuine portrait of the situation, that is, heterogeneity in the personality profiles of these offenders. In fact, all of this research relies on samples of perpetrators of sexual homicide according to broad inclusion criteria, thereby combining sexualized killing, grievance killing, and rape killing. These different types of sexual homicide may be related to different profiles of personality disorders. Proulx & Beauregard (2014) carried out a study based on a sample of sexual aggressors of women (not distinguishing between those who had committed rape or sexual homicide). Sexual aggressors following a *sadistic pathway* were characterized by an anxious personality profile (i.e., avoidant, dependent, and schizoid personality traits) and deviant sexual preferences. Aggressors with such a personality profile have low self-esteem and believe that the people they meet, especially women, reject and humiliate them. Such cognitions trigger negative emotions (e.g., anger, humiliation, anxiety, suffering) that dominate their inner world. In reaction, they isolate themselves and withdraw into a world of sadistic fantasies. These fantasies constituted a motivation to offend, but also shaped the modus operandi, which is characterized by torture and humiliation of the victim. Sexual aggressors following an *angry pathway*, present a borderline personality disorder. Angry sexual aggressors had a general lifestyle that is as unstable as their self-image. Their lives are chaotic, and characterized by substance abuse, temper tantrums, and rebelliousness. Angry sexual aggressors did not plan their offense and no deviant sexual fantasies shaped their modus operandi. Typically, while she was not physically restrained or kidnapped, the victim was physically injured. Finally, sexual aggressors following an *opportunistic pathway* are characterized by a psychopathic personality disorder profile (antisocial, narcissistic). They are convinced that they are superior to other people whom they expect to fulfil their needs and admire them. Any obstacle to the immediate satisfaction of their needs is unfair and unacceptable. They therefore feel entitled to use any means necessary to achieve their goals. The modus operandi of the opportunistic aggressors is not shaped by anger or deviant sexual fantasies. In fact, any planning they do engage in is toward having sex with a willing partner. They use threats and a minimal amount of force to obtain victim compliance, and lethal violence to eliminate a witness. These three pathways illustrate how personality disorder heterogeneity is related to different modus operandi in perpetrators of both non-homicide sexual offenses and sexual homicide.

14.7 Serial Sexual Homicide

Most people can readily bring to mind the name of at least one individual who has committed multiple sexual homicides, whether it is Ted Bundy in the United States, Robert Pickton in Canada, Angus Sinclair in the United Kingdom, or Ivan Milat in Australia. These individuals have in common that they have committed at least two sexual homicides in separate events, which according to the U.S. Federal Bureau of Investigation (FBI; Morton, 2008) allows us to identify them as serial sexual homicide offenders (SSHOs).

Although in the collective imagination SSHOs constitute the prototypical perpetrator of sexual homicide, in reality it has been estimated that they represent only 2% of this population (Proulx et al., 2007c). Nevertheless, despite their relative rarity, these individuals have received sustained attention from several research teams: The first being affiliated with the FBI in the 1980s and 1990s (Burgess et al., 1986; Dietz et al., 1990; Ressler et al., 1983, 1986a, 1986b, 1988; Warren et al., 1996); another, more recently, being a team of French-Canadian researchers working in collaboration with the French Gendarmerie Nationale Behavioral Science Unit (James, 2020; James & Beauregard, 2018; James et al., 2018a, 2018b, 2019a, 2019b; Langevin et al., 2018). One of the reasons why SSHOs have received so much attention is that, beyond the extreme violence exhibited during their crimes, this minority of individuals are responsible for a significant proportion of sexual homicides. For example, in a random sample of perpetrators of sexual homicide in France ($N = 120$), it was found that although SSHOs made up less than one-third (27.5%) of the sample, they were responsible for more than half of the homicides committed (56.7%). Most committed two sexual homicides, but some were convicted of committing up to nine sexual homicides. In more extreme cases documented elsewhere, some individuals may be responsible for the deaths of dozens of people, as illustrated by the tragic example of Samuel Little, an individual who admitted to committing more than 90 sexual homicides in the USA between 1970 and 2005. This leads to the following conclusion: The prevention of sexual homicides depends in part on our ability to interrupt the criminal trajectory of offenders with the potential to become SSHOs. Consequently, the rapid identification by public safety services of perpetrators of sexual homicide after their first is a crucial prevention issue. However, in order to identify them effectively, it is essential to have a clear profile of the individuals sought. The above-mentioned collaboration between public security services and researchers has made it possible to draw up a detailed profile of SSHOs. This profile provides an overall understanding of their life trajectory and an understanding of who they are in everyday life. In the following paragraphs, their developmental characteristics, their general and sexual lifestyles in adulthood, their psychopathological profile, their offending process, and the difficulties they pose for criminal investigators are detailed.

During their youth, SSHOs tend to have been exposed to a wide range of problematic behaviors at a young age. They grew up in chaotic family environments characterized by parental neglect (e.g., nutritional deficiencies, poor supervision), psychological abuse (e.g., threats, insults, humiliation) and exposure to inappropriate role models (e.g., psychiatric problems, sexual activity). This set of adverse childhood conditions may partly explain the emergence of internalized (e.g., feelings of loneliness, daydreaming, low self-esteem, phobias) and externalized disorders, the latter of which may take the form of aggressive, violent, or criminal behaviors (e.g., tantrums, rebellions, vandalism, theft, fights, arson, self-harming) or non-violent problem behaviors (e.g., chronic lying, drug use, compulsive masturbation). In the community (e.g., school, neighborhood), these children are usually stigmatized and rejected because of their parents' bad reputation (e.g., excessive alcohol consumption, criminality), their own physical appearance (e.g., poor dress, poor personal hygiene), and their antisocial behaviors. Thus, the belief that they were not accepted by anyone may have increased their sense of inadequacy (e.g., social isolation) and encouraged the use of deviant sexuality (fantasies and behaviors) to manage their negative emotions (e.g., anxiety, anger, loneliness).

In adulthood, SSHOs are extremely violent in their daily lives, creating fear and pain in their relationships (they abuse their partners, including strangulation; they use sadistic sexual behaviors in intimate relationships) and commit a variety of violent criminal acts. However, they are also good manipulators with excellent criminal skills. Thus, although their deviant and criminal behaviors are known to their intimate partners, they go unnoticed by other community members and the police.

In terms of psychological functioning, SSHOs are particularly problematic; they are sadistic psychopaths whose psychopathological profile is characterized by emotional detachment (Facet 2; Psychopathy Checklist: Screening Version; PCL: SV, Hart et al., 1995) and psychosexual problems (hypersexuality, deviant sexual fantasies). Their interpersonal style is superficial (Facet 1; PCL: SV), their cognitions may favor the commission of a series of sexual offenses (they consider their sexual needs to be uncontrollable and women to be sexual objects), and their acting out appears to be primarily motivated by the need to act out a homicidal, sadistic, or rape fantasy. Thus, it is reasonable to assume that the simultaneous presence of these psychological components may increase the likelihood of the individual committing a series of sexual homicides.

In the year prior to the commission of the sexual homicide, SSHOs face a range of difficulties (e.g., family, work, legal) that affect their personal adaptation (e.g., anxiety), which they attempt to cope with through excessive alcohol or drug use. These consumption problems disinhibit their deviant sexual behaviors, favor the appearance of sexual dysfunctions (e.g., erectile and ejaculation dysfunctions) and thus deteriorate an already problematic psychosexual life (e.g., sexual disinhibition, sexual coercion). The accumulation of unsatisfactory life experiences leads SSHOs to invest heavily (e.g., sometimes for several hours a day) in a fantasy world in which they set up sexual aggression scenarios that will serve as a sexual script to which they will refer when acting out. Consequently, it is not surprising that their behaviors have an organized appearance and that their crimes are rigorously premeditated.

In the hours leading up to the sexual homicide, SSHOs feel anger and are proactive, assembling a kit to commit their crime (e.g., knife, gloves, rope), and looking for a potential target with specific characteristics (e.g., age, physical appearance) to attack in a preselected location (e.g., common areas of a building, parks, side roads). They contact their victims by manipulating them (e.g., asking for help, offering to help), confining them and tying them up in order to neutralize them and satisfy their deviant sexual needs. Such preparation and execution of the crime allows the individual to exert control over the criminal event, to possibly set up a ritual allowing him to carry out his fantasies (e.g., variety of sexual acts, torture, non-lethal strangulation, mutilation), to limit the probability that a third party will intervene or that a struggle will be engaged between the aggressor and the victim and, consequently, that witnesses or forensic traces will not lead to his identification by the police.

After the death of the victim, SSHOs are cautious and concerned about protecting their identity; they clean up, destroy, or conceal items that could lead to their detection by the police. As a result, they actively contribute to putting themselves in a position to commit a second sexual homicide if they so choose. Sexual homicides committed by SSHOs are thus difficult to solve. Given that their offenses are consistent with the content of their fantasies, it is not surprising that most of them have experienced sexual pleasure. Thus, if they are not detected by the police following the first sexual homicide (avoidance of punishment), the SSHOs' sense of impunity, coupled with the pleasure they experienced in the crime, could be likely to reinforce their behaviors and lead them to commit a series of sexual homicides.

Finally, the decisions that SSHOs make before, during, and after the sexual homicide do not appear to be the only factors that increase or decrease the likelihood that they will be quickly identified by the police and whether or not they will commit a series of sexual homicides. Indeed, it has been shown that the decisions that criminal investigators make may also increase or decrease the likelihood of rapid identification and consequently increase or decrease the likelihood of a second sexual homicide (James & Beauregard, 2018). This finding is disappointing, but realistic; to err is human, and criminal investigators are no exception to the rule. Indeed, it has been observed that non-optimal decisions made by criminal investigators can indirectly contribute to increasing the probability that a perpetrator of sexual homicide will commit a series of similar offenses. Thus, by analyzing a variety of types of decisions made by criminal investigators, it was found that sometimes, for example, neighborhood enquiries were not carried out, specimens taken from the crime scene were not analyzed, the location of missing victims was not analyzed, and the cause of death of the victim specified in the forensic report was inaccurate (e.g., suicide, overdose).

This detailed profile of SSHOs, together with an awareness of the difficulties that criminal investigators may face, can be advantageous in the prevention of sexual homicide as it allows us to better understand who these individuals are in everyday life and to act more effectively in preventative efforts in terms of interrupting the criminal trajectory towards serial sexual homicide.

14.8 Rehabilitating Perpetrators of Sexual Homicide: Assessment, Treatment and Management from Custodial Settings to the Community

Before consideration can be given to the reduction of risk of recidivism for those serving a sentence for a sexual homicide, correctional service/forensic mental health practitioners will first need to identify that a homicide was indeed sexual in nature. They then need to understand the connection between killing and the sexual element. This is firstly to help inform risk assessment (i.e. evaluation using appropriate measure(s) of sexual and/or general violence risk, noting that perpetrators of sexual homicides are likely to have been included in at least some instrument validation studies but no instrument has been specifically validated for this group). Secondly, such an understanding is necessary for risk reduction work (i.e., intervention adhering to risk, need, and responsivity principles; Bonta & Andrews, 2017). Given the absence of any legal definition of sexual homicide, courts are unable to convict individuals recording the crime in this way. Despite this, the term sexual homicide is applied by staff to cases where the offense seems to have had a sexual component. While identifying this sexual component can pose challenges when there has not necessarily been a sexual conviction (Carter & Hollin, 2015; Carter & Perkins, 2018; Grubin, 1994), research over the last few decades has led to more guidance and shared good practice to help with the undertaking of this task. There are three steps that can be followed in the assessment of a case of sexual homicide:

1. Identify if the case is clearly or potentially a sexual homicide;
2. Determine how integral the sexual element was to the homicide;
3. Apply typological theory to help with risk assessment, management and amelioration.

Starting with the first step, in the broadest terms, sexual homicide can be considered to have occurred when killing has taken place in connection with consensual or non-consensual sex. The definition of sexual homicide presented earlier in this chapter may be useful for this initial determination. If the definition is met, the next stage is to understand the connection between the sexual element and killing. The nature of this connection between the sexual behavior (intended or actual) and the killing is important; it has been shown to be relevant for informing assessment, rehabilitation and risk management. Carter and Hollin (2015) introduced the terms *direct* and *indirect* to help in determining the different ways that a homicide can be classified as sexual. The direct and indirect distinction has been developed as a classification of sexual homicide (Stefanska et al., 2017, 2020). In *direct* cases, the killing itself is central to the individual's pursuit of sexual gratification, whether or not this is achieved. On this basis, killing that is carried out for the perpetrator to carry out sexual acts with the body would also be considered as a *direct* case of sexual homicide. When killing has occurred which is not directly connected to the perpetrator's quest for sexual gratification, this would be classified as an *indirect* case. For example, if the victim is killed to eliminate the only witness to a sexual assault. There can be mixed *direct* and *indirect* cases, thus, the *direct/indirect* classification serves as a starting point to establish how integral the sexual behavior was at any stage of the homicide, accommodating the possibility that criminal events unfold in ways that the perpetrator may not necessarily have anticipated. Subsequently, typological theory can be used to generate hypotheses to help to determine the motivation for the offense and develop a case formulation, which enables the identification of targets for risk reduction work. For example, deviant sexual interests constitute a criminogenic factor for perpetrators of sexualized killings, whereas the management of negative emotions and addressing cognitive schema that favor sexual violence are likely primary treatment needs for perpetrators of grievance killings, and programs targeting sexual offending risk as well as general violence are recommended for perpetrators of rape killings.

The extent to which the assessor can develop an accurate and helpful formulation is dependent upon the information available. Much of this information needs to be gathered from interviews and here, steps can be taken to ensure this is a collaborative and beneficial process. Carter and Perkins (2018) advise that anyone carrying out such an assessment should first familiarize themselves with typological research and theories of sexual homicide. This is one of several steps they suggest for facilitating a collaborative approach to the process that also includes recommendations to work on building trust, beginning with understanding concerns the person may have about disclosing having committed a crime that will be classified as a sexual homicide, implications of this in terms of labelling as a sexual offender, and what ensues from this. Next, a detailed history needs to be established, which "should include background details along with psychological factors, such as the use of fantasy, loneliness, experience of negative mood states, attitudes towards women, and the ability to solve problems" (Carter & Hollin, 2015, p. 291). The assessment should inform a detailed treatment plan shaped by what is uncovered in the interview process. As treatment starts, more information and areas to work on may become apparent and can also inform the order that issues are tackled. Perkins and Carter (2018) illustrate how developmental experiences and ways of coping and behaving can be linked to more immediate antecedents to the killing. They can also create barriers to therapeutic change. For example, Perkins and Carter (2018) highlight how experiences of trauma and difficulties with trust may need to be addressed for individuals to develop therapeutic relationships. Addressing these factors may also help with unhelpful patterns of coping such as alcohol dependency and fantasy, and serve to attenuate risk. While psychologically driven treatment approaches including cognitive-behavioral programs addressing risk of sexual offending may form part of the treatment plan, certain individuals may require a medical treatment plan.

Pharmacological treatment has a role in addressing psychopathology in some perpetrators of sexual homicide, as one part of a holistic biopsychosocial approach to treatment and management. Where conditions such as psychosis or major mood disorders are present, treatment with antipsychotic, antidepressant, or mood stabilizing medication should be part of the treatment plan. Where symptoms such as emotional dysregulation/instability of affect, behavioral impulsivity/disinhibition, suspiciousness/paranoid thinking or reality distortion are prominent and problematic in people with personality disorder then, although the evidence base is equivocal, medication may be a useful adjunct to primarily psychosocial approaches (Darjee & Davidson, 2010; Paris, 2011). Where a paraphilic disorder and/or compulsive sexual behavior disorder (Briken, 2020) are identified, then alongside psychological treatment, as outlined above, consideration should be given to pharmacological treatment to reduce sexual drive (Darjee & Baron, 2018b; Darjee & Quinn, 2020).

Broadly there are two groups of medications used to treat paraphilic and compulsive sexual behavior disorders: (1) testosterone lowering anti-libidinal medications and (2) serotonin potentiating selective serotonin reuptake inhibitors (SSRIs). Anti-libidinal medications reduce testosterone levels and activity, thus reducing sexual drive and sexual fantasy, which are both dependent on testosterone circulating in the brain in men (Jordan et al., 2011). SSRIs reduce the intrusiveness of sexual thoughts and fantasies, and reduce libido, although their mechanism of action in relation to these is uncertain (Greenberg & Bradford, 1997). Anti-libidinals can be further subdivided into anti-androgens (cyproterone acetate and medroxyprogesterone acetate) and gonadotrophin releasing hormone (GnRH) agonists (triptorelin, leuprorelin and goserelin). Anti-libidinals as a group have very similar side-effects to each other, which are primarily due to the impact of low testosterone levels on the male body, but GnRH agonists tend to cause less troubling side-effects. Another potential advantage of GnRH agonists is that they can be given by long-acting injection once every three months. GnRH agonists usually cause complete cessation of sexual fantasizing with an associated lack of sexual urges, masturbation, and sexual behavior (Lewis et al., 2017; Turner & Briken, 2018). The research evidence base for anti-libidinal medication in the treatment of sexual offenders and paraphilic disorders is supportive but not robust (Darjee & Quinn, 2020). There is a dearth of randomized controlled trials, but our understanding of the underlying biological mechanism, clinical experience internationally and the results of cohort studies indicate they should be used where indicated, and international best practice guidelines recommend their prescription alongside psychological interventions (Thibaut et al., 2020). They are indicated where there is deviant sexual arousal (such as coercive sexual sadism disorder or pedophilic disorder) which a person has acted on or finds difficult to control (especially when acting has caused serious harm to others or has been repeated), and/or the person is sexually preoccupied or hypersexual, therefore meeting criteria for compulsive sexual behavior disorder according to the World Health Organization's (2019) *International Statistical Classification of Diseases and Related Health Problems* (11th ed.; *ICD-11*). Paraphilic disorders are often comorbid with each other and with compulsive sexual behavior disorder (Kafka & Hennen, 2003), including in perpetrators of sexual homicide (Briken et al., 2006).

With perpetrators of sexual homicide, given the potentially devastating consequences of sexual recidivism, if there is evidence of coercive sexual sadism disorder, pedophilic disorder, another relevant paraphilic disorder (such as erotophonophilia, extreme picquerism, necrophilia, or necrosadism) and/or compulsive sexual behavior disorder, then treatment with a GnRH agonist would usually be necessary. According to the World Federation of Societies of Biological

Psychiatry guidelines (Thibaut et al., 2020), where there is a risk of "catastrophic sexual violence" (such as sexual homicide) the aim should be complete suppression of testosterone activity with a GnRH agonist and an anti-androgen, although there is little scientific, empirical, or clinical justification for this 'double hit' treatment. A GnRH agonist on its own suffices to achieve testosterone suppression (Darjee & Baron, 2018b). It could be argued that when paraphilic sexual fantasies coupled with sexual compulsivity were central to offending, these should be extinguished or very significantly diminished and unlikely to return before such individuals may be released. This requires treatment with GnRH agonists. In some jurisdictions, treatment can be mandated, but in most it is given on a voluntary basis (Turner et al., 2017). Various ethical issues and duties need to be considered and balanced when treating men who have committed sexual homicide, who are subject to legally sanctioned coercion and control in institutions and the community, whether or not treatment is legally mandated (Darjee & Quinn, 2020). When released to the community, psychiatrists prescribing and monitoring medical treatment need to work closely with the other disciplines and agencies involved in community risk management (Darjee & Baron, 2018a, 2018b). In a German sample of perpetrators of sexual homicide 70% of cases had either a paraphilic disorder or compulsive sexual behavior disorder and 35% had both (Briken et al., 2006). The latter group would clearly be candidates for medical treatment and perhaps many of the 70% would be too, but not all, due to medical contraindications, refusal to take treatment, or due to their sexual disorders being less significant or responding to other interventions.

A further area where consideration of community treatment and management is relevant is the prevention of sexual homicide, not in people who have already committed this crime, but in people yet to kill (Darjee & Baron, 2018b; Beauregard & Reale, 2019). Although research over the last two decades has identified developmental, psychopathological, behavioral and situational precursors of sexual homicide, the rare people in society who will become perpetrators will never be identified with accuracy. However, considering what is known about people who commit sexual homicide, it is possible to suggest interventions that are likely to be preventative. Childhood abuse, trauma, adversity, and attachment disorders are preludes to the interpersonal, emotional, behavioral, and sexual difficulties that emerge in childhood and adolescence, which in turn herald the severe sexual and personality pathology, which put some individuals on pathways towards extreme sexual violence. The earlier that interventions can prevent or address trauma and identify and intervene with children with these vulnerabilities and behavioral disturbances, the fewer individuals will move along these pathways. Although few sexual offenders escalate to commit homicide (Francis & Soothill, 2000), between a quarter and a half of perpetrators of sexual homicide have a history of sexual offending (Beauregard & Martineau, 2016). Therefore, effective interventions to reduce recidivism in sexual offenders will prevent some sexual homicides. So will effective interventions for violent offenders, as many perpetrators of sexual homicide have previously committed non-sexual violent offenses (Beauregard & Martineau, 2016).

Scenarios where there may be specific concern about the potential for an individual to commit sexual homicide include:

1. Sexual offenders with sexually sadistic or homicidal fantasies or behaviors, who show high levels of anger/grievance particularly focused on women, or who are highly psychopathic (especially those who are very callous);
2. Perpetrators of intimate partner violence or stalking who are sexually sadistic or display high levels of sexual vindictiveness/possessiveness;
3. Young males who present with concerning sexual thoughts (such as sadistic, necrophilic, or homicidal sexual fantasies), who use extreme sexually violent pornography (with sadistic, necrophilic, or homicidal content), who appear to be preoccupied with sexual homicide or planning to sexually kill (perhaps demonstrated in their writings, drawings, or online activities), or are displaying concerning associated behaviors (e.g. 'try outs' such as sadistic abuse of animals, putting together a rape and murder kit, following or spying on potential victims, sexual burglary, or stealing and damaging underwear).

It should be noted that participation in consenting BDSM is not associated with the perpetration of violent sexual offenses (Higgs et al., 2021). Assessing and treating those who have not committed an offense yet, most of whom will not kill, can be challenging. Most mental health services do not cater for these anxiety provoking cases, but some innovative community forensic mental health services do (McEwan & Darjee, 2021; Russell & Darjee, 2012), using similar models for preventive clinical intervention as those for people with concerning sexual thoughts or behaviors towards children (Beier, 2019). The first step is to assess whether the person poses a plausible risk of sexual violence by undertaking a comprehensive psychosexual assessment, understanding the nature of the underlying psychopathology, and cautiously and thoughtfully applying relevant tools and empirical research findings. If the person has a paraphilic disorder (particularly sexual sadism), concerning personality traits, a significant number of risk factors for sexual violence and/or displays characteristics that are associated with sexual homicide offenders, then concerns may be justified and efforts should be made to engage the person in intervention, including psychological therapy and pharmacological treatment where relevant. Most individuals are eager and grateful to receive such help. Whether they would or would not have actually killed is irrelevant, as providing treatment to reduce their distress and risk and improve their lives is helpful to them, probably prevents sexual violence, and may save some lives. McEwan and Darjee (2021) give a detailed description of the assessment and treatment of such a case. Individuals with concerning indicators who do not come forward themselves but are identified by relatives, educational establishments, employment settings, mental health clinicians, or other individuals or organizations may be harder to engage in interventions. However, there should still be access to consultation and assessment from experts in threat and risk assessment in people with the potential for sexual violence, and where concerns cannot be alleviated from the information, available plans need to be put in place to manage the risk. In cases assessed as posing an immediate threat of serious sexual violence, this may involve contacting law enforcement and/or warning others. Fortunately, this scenario is rarely faced in practice.

14.9 Conclusion

Best practice in assessment and management when working with perpetrators of sexual homicide begins with recognition of the heterogeneity in this type of offense and the implications of this when reviewing the empirical evidence base and then when developing a case conceptualization and treatment plan. Some key points that summarize this chapter are that:

1. Serial sexual homicide has been the focus of considerable research but perpetrators of non-serial sexual homicide are more numerous than serial offenders;
2. There are nevertheless some similarities than can be observed in the offense and perpetrator characteristics between serial sexual homicide and non-serial sexual homicide when taking into account subtypes of the latter. Specifically, in sexualized killing, deviant sexual interest and the use of fatal violence are functionally related. This along with the psychosocial factors underlying it may favor repetition of the behavior if the perpetrator is not apprehended or if he is released without recidivism risk factors being properly addressed;
3. The psychopathological profiles of perpetrators of sexual homicide that have been discussed in the chapter may correspond more or less closely to different criminal careers and trajectories towards either sexualized killing, grievance killing, or rape killing. However, the majority of the empirical examinations of perpetrators of sexual homicide describe the population as a whole rather than by subtype meaning that there are a number of hypotheses that still need to be tested to understand sometimes contradictory research results.

In this chapter, some recommendations concerning treatment strategies and clinical objectives have also been made. Focusing on what can be achieved through psychological and pharmacological intervention is important because as Mossman (2008) explains, what makes a person more violent needs to be alleviated, in the knowledge that whether or not a rare event like sexual homicide will occur may not be predicted with accuracy. Recidivism studies are almost non-existent (with the most notable exception being a 20 year follow up of 139 offenders in Germany; Hill et al., 2008). In any case, having the specific goal of predicting a new sexual homicide, even a test that in most circumstances would be considered very accurate, that is, one that has high sensitivity and specificity, would greatly overestimate the likelihood of sexual homicide assuming that the base rate is as low as it would seem from the extremely limited information available: Three out of the 139 perpetrators of sexual homicide in Hill et al.'s (2008) study were reconvicted for homicide or attempted homicide, and none of an albeit very small sample ($N = 8$) in the United States were arrested for homicidal acts (Khachatryan et al., 2016). This means that it is necessary to treat the problems that have been discussed in this chapter as precursors to sexual homicide among perpetrators of sexual homicide as part of a recidivism risk reduction strategy, but also among certain violent and sexual offenders who have not necessarily committed a sexual homicide as a preventative strategy. In other words, this involves implementing "broad measures that reduce known risks for rare but harmful events" (Mossman, 2008, p. 39), while also being mindful when making recommendations that will be used for release planning that the majority of decisions will keep individuals who would not become serial sexual homicide perpetrators detained.

Finally, earlier in this chapter it was proposed that widening the frame of reference might be fruitful in continuing to work towards a better understanding of sexual homicide not only as a form of sexual crime, but also in terms of lethality, whether that manifests through sexual homicide or other forms of fatal violence. Through the chapter, certain environmental and psychological predisposing factors for sexual homicide have been outlined and now is is noted that several of the same themes have similarly been observed in samples of religious and political extremist offenders. These are also men (mostly) having had difficulty finding their place in society, being socially alienated, and frustrated with their failures in the workplace and in their social and intimate relationships (Bakker, 2006; Pressman, 2009). Alternatively, they may have been at least superficially well socially integrated, but their preoccupation with religious or political ideology and vengefulness towards perceived or actual opposers gives meaning to their lives (Dawson et al., 2016). This could be compared to entitlement and grievance thinking towards women among perpetrators of sexual homicide. Dawson et al. (2016) theorize that in religious extremism, terrorist ideology "offers a simple but definitive explanation for their angst, offers a grand solution, targets a culprit and prescribes a course of action" (p. 9). Thus, terrorist ideology does not function entirely differently to sexual deviance: Aggression is aimed at a different target and is expressed in a different form of violence, but a cognitive-behavioral functional analysis with a perpetrator of extremist violence and a perpetrator of sexual homicide may reach quite similar conclusions. From this, a hypothesis to be explored is that similar circumstances underlie extreme violence, with micro sociological as well as macro socio-political factors favoring trajectories towards either sexual or non-sexual violence. In fact, as predicted by chaos theory as applied to criminal behavior (e.g., Walters, 1999), trajectories towards sexual homicide or non-fatal sexual aggression, or towards sexual violence or non-sexual violence, are certainly sensitive to personal and social circumstances as well as situational factors during the criminal event, given the holistic and interactive nature of human conduct.

References

American Psychiatric Association. (1994). *Diagnostic and statistical manual of mental disorders* (4th ed.). American Psychiatric Association.

American Psychiatric Association. (2013). *Diagnostic and statistical manual of mental disorders* (5th ed.). American Psychiatric Association. https://doi.org/10.1176/appi.books.9780890425596

Bakker, E. (2006). *Jihadi terrorists in Europe, their characteristics and the circumstances in which they joined the jihad: An exploratory study*. Netherlands Institute of International Relations.

Beauregard, E., & Martineau, M. (2016). *The sexual murderer: Offender behavior and implications for practice*. Taylor & Francis.

Beauregard, E., & Proulx, J. (2002). Profiles in the offending process of nonserial sexual murderers. *International Journal of Offender Therapy and Comparative Criminology, 46*(4), 386–399. https://doi.org/10.1177/0306624X02464002

Beauregard, E., & Reale, K. S. (2019). Can we prevent sexual homicide? An examination of correlates of a lethal outcome in sexual assaults. In W. T. O'Donohue & P. A. Schewe (Eds.), *Handbook of sexual assault and sexual assault prevention* (pp. 645–660). Springer.

Beauregard, E., Proulx, J., & St-Yves, M. (2007). Angry or sadistic: Two types of sexual murderers. In J. Proulx, E. Beauregard, M. Cusson, & A. Nicole (Eds.), *Sexual murderers: A comparative analysis and new perspectives* (pp. 123–142). John Wiley & Sons.

Beauregard, E., Stone, M. R., Proulx, J., & Michaud, P. (2008). Sexual murderers of children: Developmental, precrime, crime, and postcrime factors. *International Journal of Offender Therapy and Comparative Criminology, 52*(3), 253–269. https://doi.org/10.1177/0306624X07303907

Beech, A. R., Oliver, C. O., Fisher, D., & Beckett, R. (2005). *STEP 4: The sex offender treatment programme in prison: Addressing the offending behavior of rapists and sexual murderers*. University of Birmingham.

Beier, K. M. (2019). Preventing child sexual abuse and the use of child abuse images: The prevention project Dunkelfeld as an international perspective. *The International Journal of Forensic Psychotherapy, 1*(1), 61–66. https://doi.org/10.33212/ijfp.v1n1.2019.61

Bonta, J., & Andrews, D. A. (2017). *The psychology of criminal conduct* (6th ed.). Routledge.

Briken, P. (2020). An integrated model to assess and treat compulsive sexual behavior disorder. *Nature Reviews Urology, 17*(7), 391–406. https://doi.org/10.1038/s41585-020-0343-7

Briken, P., Habermann, N., Kafka, M. P., Berner, W., & Hill, A. (2006). The paraphilia-related disorders: An investigation of the relevance of the concept in sexual murderers. *Journal of Forensic Sciences, 51*(3), 683–688. https://doi.org/10.1111/j.1556-4029.2006.00105.x

Brittain, R. P. (1970). The sadistic murderer. *Medicine, Science & the Law, 10*(4), 198–207.

Burgess, A., Hartman, C., Ressler, R., Douglas, J., & McCormack, A. (1986). Sexual homicide: A motivational model. *Journal of Interpersonal Violence, 1*(3), 251–272. https://doi.org/10.1177/088626086001003001

Carter, A. J., & Hollin, C. R. (2015). Assessment and treatment when sex is attached to a killing: A case study. In D. T. Wilcox, T. G. Garrett, & L. Harkins (Eds.), *Sex offender treatment: A case study approach to issues and interventions* (pp. 286–304). Wiley-Blackwell.

Carter, A. J., & Perkins, D. (2018). The assessment of perpetrators of sexual homicide for the purposes of risk reduction in secure psychiatric hospital and prison settings. In J. Proulx, E. Beauregard, A. J. Carter, A. Mokros, R. Darjee, & J. James (Eds.), *Routledge international handbook of sexual homicide studies* (pp. 356–369). Routledge.

Carter, A. J., Hollin, C., Stefanska, E. B., Higgs, T., & Bloomfield, S. (2016). The use of crime scene and demographic information in the identification of non-serial sexual homicide. *International Journal of Offender Therapy and Comparative Criminology, 61*(4), 1554–1569. https://doi.org/10.1177/0306624X16630313

Clarke, J., & Carter, A. J. (2000). Relapse prevention with sexual murderers. In D. R. Laws, S. Hudson, & T. Ward (Eds.), *Remaking relapse prevention with sex offenders: A sourcebook* (pp. 389–401). Sage.

Connor, D. F., Steingard, R. J., Cunningham, J. A., Melloni, R. H., Jr., & Anderson, J. J. (2004). Proactive and reactive aggression in referred children and adolescents. *American Journal of Orthopsychiatry, 74*(2), 129–136. https://doi.org/10.1037/0002-9432.74.2.129

Crick, N. R., & Dodge, K. A. (1996). Social information-processing mechanisms in reactive and proactive aggression. *Child Development, 67*(3), 993–1002. https://doi.org/10.1111/j.1467-8624.1996.tb01778.x

Darjee, R., & Baron, E. (2018a). Managing perpetrators of sexual homicide in the community. In J. Proulx, E. Beauregard, A. J. Carter, A. Mokros, R. Darjee, & J. James (Eds.), *Routledge international handbook of sexual homicide studies* (pp. 382–401). Routledge.

Darjee, R., & Baron, E. (2018b). Pharmacological treatment of sexual homicide offenders. In J. Proulx, E. Beauregard, A. J. Carter, A. Mokros, R. Darjee, & J. James (Eds.), *Routledge international handbook of sexual homicide studies* (pp. 419–432). Routledge.

Darjee, R., & Baron, E. (2018c). Recent research on sexual homicide in Scotland: Characteristics, crime scene themes, and comparison with non-homicidal sexual aggressors. In J. Proulx, E. Beauregard, A. J. Carter, A. Mokros, R. Darjee, & J. James (Eds.), *Routledge international handbook of sexual homicide studies* (pp. 196–218). Routledge.

Darjee, R., & Davidson, K. (2010). Personality disorders. In S. Lawrie, E. Johnston, M. Sharpe, & A. McIntosh (Eds.), *Companion to psychiatric studies* (8th ed., pp. 507–540). Churchill Livingstone.

Darjee, R., & Quinn, A. (2020). Pharmacological treatment of sexual offenders. In J. Proulx, F. Cortoni, L. A. Craig, & E. Letourneau (Eds.), *The Wiley handbook of what works with sexual offenders: Contemporary perspectives in theory, assessment, treatment and prevention* (pp. 217–246). Wiley.

Dawson, L. L., Amarasingam, A., & Bain, A. (2016). *Talking to foreign fighters: Socio-economic push versus existential pull factors*. Canadian Network for Research on Terrorism, Security and Society. https://www.tsas.ca/research/tsas-working-papers

Declercq, F., Willemsen, J., Audenaert, K., & Verhaeghe, P. (2012). Psychopathy and predatory violence in homicide, violent, and sexual offenses: Factor and facet relations. *Legal and Criminological Psychology, 17*(1), 59–74. https://doi.org/10.1348/135532510X527722

Decuyper, M., De Pauw, S., De Fruyt, F., De Bolle, M., & De Clerq, B. J. (2009). A meta-analysis of psychopathy-, antisocial PD- and FFM associations. *European Journal of Personality, 23*(7), 531–565. https://doi.org/10.1002/per.729

Dietz, P. E. (1986). Mass, serial and sensational homicides. *Bulletin of the New York Academy of Medicine, 62*(5), 477–491.

Dietz, P. E., Hazelwood, R. R., & Warren, J. (1990). The sexually sadistic criminal and his offenses. *Bulletin of the American Academy of Psychiatry and the Law, 18*(2), 163–178.

Dodge, K. A., & Coie, J. D. (1987). Social information processing factors in reactive and proactive aggression in children's peer groups. *Journal of Personality and Social Psychology, 53*(6), 1146–1158. https://doi.org/10.1037/0022-3514.53.6.1146

Dodge, K. A. (1991). The structure and function of reactive and proactive aggression. In D. Pepler & K. Rubin (Eds.), *The development and treatment of childhood aggression* (pp. 201–218). Lawrence Erlbaum Associates.

Dodge, K. A., Lochman, J. E., Harnish, J. D., Bates, J. E., & Pettit, G. S. (1997). Reactive and proactive aggression in school children and psychiatrically impaired chronically assaultive youth. Journal of Abnormal Psychology, 106, 37–51.

Firestone, P., Bradford, J. M., Greenberg, D. M., Larose, M. R., & Curry, S. (1998). Homicidal and nonhomicidal child molesters: Psychological, phallometric, and criminal features. *Sexual Abuse, 10*(4), 305–323. https://doi.org/10.1023/A:1022146105664

Francis, B., & Soothill, K. (2000). Does sex offending lead to homicide? *The Journal of Forensic Psychiatry, 11*(1), 49–61. https://doi.org/10.1080/095851800362355

Gacono, C. B., & Meloy, J. R. (1994). *The Rorschach assessment of aggressive and psychopathic personalities*. Lawrence Erlbaum.

Geberth, V. (1996). *Practical homicide investigation: Tactics, procedures, and forensic techniques* (3rd ed.). CRC Press.

Greenberg, D. M., & Bradford, J. M. (1997). Treatment of the paraphilic disorders: A review of the role of the selective serotonin reuptake inhibitors. *Sexual Abuse, 9*(4), 349–360. https://doi.org/10.1177/107906329700900407

Groth, A. N., & Birnbaum, H. J. (1979). *Men who rape: The psychology of the offender*. Plenum.

Grubin, D. (1994). Sexual murder. *British Journal of Psychiatry, 165*(5), 624–629. https://doi.org/10.1192/bjp.165.5.624
Hare, R. D. (2003). *The psychopathy checklist-revised manual* (2nd ed.). Mental Health Systems.
Hart, S. D., Cox, D. N., & Hare, R. D. (1995). Manual for the psychopathy checklist: Screening version (PCL: SV). Multi-Health Systems.
Healey, J., Lussier, P., & Beauregard, E. (2013). Sexual sadism in the context of rape and sexual homicide: An examination of crime scene indicators. *International Journal of Offender Therapy and Comparative Criminology, 57*(4), 402–424. https://doi.org/10.1177/0306624X12437536
Higgs, T., Carter, A., Stefanska, E., & Glorney, E. (2015). Toward identification of the sexual killer: A comparison of sexual killers engaging in post-mortem sexual interference and non-homicide sexual aggressors. *Sexual Abuse, 29*(5), 479–499. https://doi.org/10.1177/1079063215609935
Higgs, T., Carter, A. J., Tully, R. J., & Browne, K. D. (2017a). Sexual murder typologies: A systematic review. *Aggression and Violent Behavior, 35*, 1–12. https://doi.org/10.1016/j.avb.2017.05.004
Higgs, T., Stefanska, E., Carter, A. J., & Browne, K. D. (2017b). The developmental and criminal histories of subgroups of sexual murderers engaging, or not engaging, in post mortem sexual interference, compared to rapists. *Journal of Criminal Justice, 53*, 92–101. https://doi.org/10.1016/j.jcrimjus.2017.10.001
Higgs, T., Lord, A., Stefanska, E., & Perkins, D. (2020). Assessing sadism in sexual offenders. In J. Proulx, F. Cortoni, L. Craig, & E. Letourneau (Eds.), *The Wiley handbook on what works with sexual offenders: Contemporary perspectives in theory, assessment, treatment and prevention* (pp. 139–152). John Wiley & Sons.
Higgs, T., Proulx, J., Gauthier, A., Garant, E., & James, J. (2021). Sexual sadism and offending. In L. A. Craig & R. Bartels (Eds.), *Sexual deviance: Understanding, assessing and managing deviant sexual interests and paraphilic disorders* (pp. 189–206). John Wiley & Sons.
Hill, A., Habermann, N., Klusmann, D., Berner, W., & Briken, P. (2008). Criminal recidivism in sexual homicide perpetrators. *International Journal of Offender Therapy and Comparative Criminology, 52*(1), 5–20. https://doi.org/10.1177/0306624X07307450
Hill, A., Berner, W., & Briken, P. (2018). Perpetrators of sexual homicide in Germany: Medical, psychiatric, and psychological characteristics. In J. Proulx, E. Beauregard, A. J. Carter, A. Mokros, R. Darjee, & J. James (Eds.), *Routledge international handbook of sexual homicide studies* (pp. 219–236). Routledge.
Houston, R. J., Stanford, M. S., Villemarette Pittman, N. R., Conklin, S. M., & Helfritz, L. E. (2003). Neurobiological correlates and clinical implications of aggressive subtypes. *Journal of Forensic Neuropsychology, 3*(4), 67–87. https://doi.org/10.1300/J151v03n04_05
James, J. (2020). *Les caractéristiques individuelles, de l'événement criminel et de l'enquête criminelle en matière d'homicides sexuels sériels et non-sériels*. [Unpublished doctoral thesis]. Université de Montréal.
James, J., & Beauregard, E. (2018). Murderer vs investigator: Factors influencing the resolution of sexual homicide cases. *Police Practice and Research, 21*(2), 172–186. https://doi.org/10.1080/15614263.2018.1526683
James, J., Lussier, P., & Proulx, J. (2018a). Serial and non-serial sexual murderers: An exploratory study of developmental antecedents. In J. Proulx, E. Beauregard, A. J. Carter, A. Mokros, R. Darjee, & J. James (Eds.), *Routledge international handbook of sexual homicide studies* (pp. 70–91). Routledge.
James, J., Proulx, J., & Lussier, P. (2018b). A cross-national study of sexual murderers in France and Canada. In J. Proulx, E. Beauregard, A. J. Carter, A. Mokros, R. Darjee, & J. James (Eds.), *Routledge international handbook of sexual homicide studies* (pp. 171–195). Routledge.
James, J., Beauregard, E., & Proulx, J. (2019a). Sexual murderers in everyday life. *Journal of Criminal Justice, 60*, 64–73. https://doi.org/10.1016/j.jcrimjus.2018.12.001
James, J., Proulx, J., Vuidard, E., Renard, A., Le Maout, S., & Brunel-Dupin, M. L. (2019b). Sexual homicide in France. *International Journal of Offender Therapy and Comparative Criminology, 63*(9), 1575–1596. https://doi.org/10.1177/0306624X19834418

James, J., Higgs, T., & Langevin, S. (2020). Reactive and proactive aggression in sexual homicide offenders. *Journal of Criminal Justice, 71*, 101728. https://doi.org/10.1016/j.jcrimjus.2020.101728

Jordan, K., Fromberger, P., Stolpmann, G., & Müller, J. L. (2011). The role of testosterone in sexuality and paraphilia—A neurobiological approach. Part I: Testosterone and sexuality. *Journal of Sexual Medicine, 8*(11), 2993–3007. https://doi.org/10.1111/j.1743-6109.2011.02394.x

Kafka, M. P., & Hennen, J. (2003). Hypersexual desire in males: Are males with paraphilias different from males with paraphilia-related disorders? *Sexual Abuse, 15*(4), 307–321. https://doi.org/10.1023/A:1025000227956

Khachatryan, N., Heide, K. M., Hummel, E. V., & Chan, H. C. (2016). Juvenile sexual homicide offenders: Thirty-year follow-up investigation. *International Journal of Offender Therapy and Comparative Criminology, 60*(3), 247–264. https://doi.org/10.1177/0306624X14552062

Koch, J., Berner, W., Hill, A., & Briken, P. (2011). Sociodemographic and diagnostic characteristics of homicidal and nonhomicidal sexual offenders. *Journal of Forensic Sciences, 56*(6), 1626–1631. https://doi.org/10.1111/j.1556-4029.2011.01933.x

Lamarche, V., Brendgen, M., Boivin, M., Vitaro, F., Dionne, G., & Pérusse, D. (2007). Do friends' characteristics moderate the prospective links between peer victimization and reactive and proactive aggression? *Journal of Abnormal Child Psychology, 35*(4), 665–680. https://doi.org/10.1007/s10802-007-9122-7

Langevin, R. (2003). A study of the psychosexual characteristics of sex killers: Can we identify them before it is too late? *International Journal of Offender Therapy and Comparative Criminology, 47*(4), 366–382. https://doi.org/10.1177/0306624X03253848

Langevin, R. (2006). An actuarial study of recidivism risk among sex killers of adults and children: Could we have identified them before it was too late? *Journal of Forensic Psychology Practice, 6*(1), 29–49. https://doi.org/10.1300/J158v06n01_02

Langevin, S., James, J., Proulx, J., Vuidard, E., & Proulx, J. (2018). Sexual murderers' sexual lifestyle: An internal constraint to modus operandi? In J. Proulx, E. Beauregard, A. J. Carter, A. Mokros, R. Darjee, & J. James (Eds.), *Routledge international handbook of sexual homicide studies* (pp. 46–49). Routledge.

Lewis, A., Grubin, D., Ross, C. C., & Das, M. (2017). Gonadotrophin-releasing hormone agonist treatment for sexual offenders: A systematic review. *Journal of Psychopharmacology, 31*(10), 1281–1293. https://doi.org/10.1177/0269881117714048

Liebert, J. A. (1985). Contributions of psychiatric consultation in the investigation of serial murder. *International Journal of Offender Therapy and Comparative Criminology, 29*(3), 187–200. https://doi.org/10.1177/0306624X8502900303

McAuliffe, M. D., Hubbard, J. A., Rubin, R. M., Morrow, M. T., & Dearing, K. F. (2006). Reactive and proactive aggression: Stability of constructs and relations to correlates. *The Journal of Genetic Psychology, 167*(4), 365–382. https://doi.org/10.3200/GNTP.167.4.365-382

McEwan, T. E., & Darjee, R. (2021). The problem behavior program: Threat assessment and management in a community forensic mental health context. In J. R. Meloy & J. Hoffman (Eds.), *International handbook of threat assessment* (pp. 536–553). Oxford University Press.

Meloy, J. R. (2000). The nature and dynamics of sexual homicide: An integrative review. *Aggression and Violent Behavior, 5*(1), 1–22. https://doi.org/10.1016/S1359-1789(99)00006-3

Meloy, J. R., Gacono, C. B., & Kenney, L. (1994). A Rorschach investigation of sexual homicide. *Journal of Personality Assessment, 62*(1), 58–67. https://doi.org/10.1207/s15327752jpa6201_6

Millon, T. (1983). Millon clinical multiaxial inventory manual. Interpretive Scoring Systems.

Milsom, J., Beech, A. R., & Webster, S. D. (2003). Emotional loneliness in sexual murderers: A qualitative analysis. *Sexual Abuse, 15*, 285–296. https://doi.org/10.1023/A:1025095927047

Mokros, A., Schilling, F., Eher, R., & Nitschke, J. (2012). The severe sexual sadism scale: Cross-validation and scale properties. *Psychological Assessment, 24*(3), 764–769. https://doi.org/10.1037/a0026419

Moore, C. C., Hubbard, J. A., Bookhout, M. K., & Mlawer, F. (2019). Relations between reactive and proactive aggression and daily emotions in adolescents. *Journal of Abnormal Child Psychology, 47*(9), 1495–1507. https://doi.org/10.1007/s10802-019-00533-6

Morton, R. J. (2008). *Serial murder: Multi-disciplinary perspectives for investigators*. National Center for the Analysis of Violent Crime.

Mossman, D. (2008). Connecting *which* dots? Problems in detecting uncommon events. In A. J. R. Harris & C. A. Pagé (Eds.), *Sexual homicide and Paraphilias: The correctional service of Canada's experts forum 2007* (pp. 37–76). Correctional Service of Canada.

Myers, W. C. (2002). *Juvenile sexual homicide*. Academic Press.

Myers, W. C., & Blashfield, R. (1997). Psychopathology and personality in juvenile sexual homicide offenders. *Journal of the American Academy of Psychiatry and the Law, 25*(4), 497–508.

Myers, W. C., Husted, D. S., Safarik, M. E., & O'Toole, M. E. (2006). The motivation behind serial sexual homicide: Is it sex, power, and control, or anger? *Journal of Forensic Sciences, 51*(4), 900–907. https://doi.org/10.1111/j.1556-4029.2006.00168.x

Nitschke, J., Osterheider, M., & Mokros, A. (2009). A cumulative scale of severe sexual sadism. *Sexual Abuse, 21*(3), 262–278. https://doi.org/10.1177/1079063209342074

Oliver, C. J., Beech, A. R., Fisher, D., & Beckett, R. (2007). A comparison of rapists and sexual murderers on demographic and selected psychometric measures. *International Journal of Offender Therapy and Comparative Criminology, 51*(3), 298–312. https://doi.org/10.1177/0306624X06289157

Paris, J. (2011). Pharmacological treatments for personality disorders. *International Review of Psychiatry, 23*(3), 303–309. https://doi.org/10.3109/09540261.2011.586993

Perkins, D., & Carter, A. J. (2018). The treatment of sexual homicide offenders in secure psychiatric hospitals and prison settings for the purposes of risk reduction. In J. Proulx, E. Beauregard, A. Carter, A. Mokros, R. Darjee, & J. James (Eds.), *Routledge international handbook of sexual homicide studies* (pp. 370–381). Routledge.

Porter, S., & Rose, K. (2018). The sexual psychopath. In J. Proulx, E. Beauregard, A. J. Carter, A. Mokros, R. Darjee, & J. James (Eds.), *Routledge international handbook of sexual homicide studies* (pp. 37–48). Routledge.

Porter, S., Woodworth, M., Earle, J., Drugge, J., & Boer, D. (2003). Characteristics of sexual homicides committed by psychopathic and nonpsychopathic offenders. *Law and Human Behavior, 27*, 459–470. https://doi.org/10.1023/A:1025461421791

Pressman, D. E. (2009). *Risk assessment decisions for violent political extremism*. Public Safety Canada.

Price, J. M., & Dodge, K. A. (1989). Reactive and proactive aggression in childhood: Relations to peer status and social context dimensions. *Journal of Abnormal Child Psychology, 17*(4), 455–471. https://doi.org/10.1007/BF00915038

Proulx, J., & Beauregard, E. (2014). Pathways in the offending process of extrafamilial sexual aggressors against women. In J. Proulx, E. Beauregard, P. Lussier, & B. Leclerc (Eds.), *Pathways to sexual aggression* (pp. 85–123). Routledge.

Proulx, J., & Sauvetre, N. (2007). Sexual murderers and sexual aggressors: Psychopathological considerations. In J. Proulx, E. Beauregard, M. Cusson, & A. Nicole (Eds.), *Sexual murderers: A comparative analysis and new perspectives* (pp. 51–70). John Wiley & Sons.

Proulx, J., Beauregard, E., Cusson, M., & Nicole, A. (2007a). *Sexual murderers: A comparative analysis and new perspectives*. John Wiley & Sons.

Proulx, J., Blais, E., & Beauregard, E. (2007b). Sadistic sexual offenders. In J. Proulx, E. Beauregard, M. Cusson, & A. Nicole (Eds.), *Sexual murderers: A comparative analysis and new perspectives* (pp. 107–122). John Wiley & Sons.

Proulx, J., Cusson, M., & Beauregard, E. (2007c). Sexual murder: Definitions, epidemiology and theories. In J. Proulx, E. Beauregard, M. Cusson, & A. Nicole (Eds.), *Sexual murderers: A comparative analysis and new perspectives* (pp. 9–28). Wiley.

Proulx, J., James, J., Siwic, M., & Beauregard, E. (2018). Sexual murderers of children: Psychopathological and modus operandi factors. In J. Proulx, E. Beauregard, A. J. Carter,

A. Mokros, R. Darjee, & J. James (Eds.), *Routledge international handbook of sexual homicide studies* (pp. 117–132). Routledge.
Proulx, J., James, J., & Higgs, T. (2020). Sexual murderers. In J. Proulx, F. Cortoni, L. Craig, & E. Letourneau (Eds.), *The Wiley handbook of what works with sexual offenders: Contemporary perspectives in theory, assessment, treatment, and prevention* (pp. 295–310). John Wiley & Sons.
Rada, R. T. (1978). *Clinical aspects of the rapist*. Grune & Stratton.
Ressler, R. K., Burgess, A. W., & Douglas, J. E. (1983). Rape and rape-murder: One offender and twelve victims. *The American Journal of Psychiatry, 140*(1), 36–40. https://doi.org/10.1176/ajp.140.1.36
Ressler, R. K., Burgess, A. W., Douglas, J. E., Hartman, C. R., & D'Agostino, R. B. (1986a). Sexual killers and their victims: Identifying patterns through crime scene analysis. *Journal of Interpersonal Violence, 1*(3), 288–308. https://doi.org/10.1177/088626086001003003
Ressler, R. K., Burgess, A. W., Hartman, C. R., Douglas, J. E., & McCormack, A. (1986b). Murderers who rape and mutilate. *Journal of Interpersonal Violence, 1*(3), 273–287. https://doi.org/10.1177/088626086001003002
Ressler, R. K., Burgess, A. W., & Douglas, J. E. (1988). *Sexual homicide: Patterns and motives*. The Free Press.
Revitch, E. (1965). Sex murder and the potential sex murderer. *Diseases of the Nervous System, 26*(10), 640–648.
Russell, K., & Darjee, R. (2012). Managing the risk posed by personality-disordered sex offenders in the community: A model for providing structured clinical guidance to support criminal justice services. In C. Logan & L. Johnstone (Eds.), *Managing clinical risk: A guide to effective practice* (pp. 88–114). Routledge.
Salmivalli, C., & Nieminen, E. (2002). Proactive and reactive aggression among school bullies, victims, and bully-victims. *Aggressive Behavior, 28*(1), 30–44. https://doi.org/10.1002/ab.90004
Schlesinger, L. B. (2000). *Serial offenders: Current thought, recent findings*. CRC Press.
Schlesinger, L. B. (2007). Sexual homicide: Differentiating catathymic and compulsive murders. *Aggression and Violent Behavior, 12*(2), 242–256. https://doi.org/10.1016/j.avb.2006.09.007
Schwartz, D., Dodge, K., Coie, J. D., Hubbard, J. A., Cillessen, A. H. N., Lemerise, E. A., & Bateman, H. (1998). Social-cognitive and behavioral correlates of aggression and victimization in boys' play groups. *Journal of Abnormal Child Psychology, 26*, 431–440. https://doi.org/10.1023/A:1022695601088
Shackman, J. E., & Pollak, S. D. (2014). Impact of physical maltreatment on the regulation of negative affect and aggression. *Development and Psychopathology, 26*(4), 1021–1033. https://doi.org/10.1017/S0954579414000546
Spehr, A., Hill, A., Habermann, N., Briken, P., & Berner, W. (2010). Sexual murderers with adult or child victims: Are they different? *Sexual Abuse, 22*(3), 290–314. https://doi.org/10.1177/1079063210374346
Stefanska, E. B., Carter, A. J., Higgs, T., Bishopp, D., & Beech, A. R. (2015). Offense pathways of non-serial sexual killers. *Journal of Criminal Justice, 43*(2), 99–107. https://doi.org/10.1016/j.jcrimjus.2015.01.001
Stefanska, E. B., Beech, A. R., & Carter, A. J. (2016). A systematic review of the literature comparing male non-serial sexual killers and sexual aggressors: Examining homogenous and heterogenous characteristics of these groups. *Journal of Sexual Aggression, 22*(3), 323–341. https://doi.org/10.1080/13552600.2015.1126657
Stefanska, E. B., Higgs, T., Carter, A. J., & Beech, A. R. (2017). When is a murder a sexual murder? Understanding the sexual element in the classification of sexual killings. *Journal of Criminal Justice, 50*, 53–61. https://doi.org/10.1016/j.jcrimjus.2017.03.004
Stefanska, E. B., Higgs, T., Carter, A. J., & Beech, A. R. (2018). "We boil at different degrees": Factors associated with severity of attack in sexual killing. *Journal of Interpersonal Violence, 36*(5–6), 2409–2429. https://doi.org/10.1177/0886260518758333

Stefanska, E. B., Longpré, L., Bloomfield, S., Perkins, D., & Carter, A. J. (2020). Untangling sexual homicide: A proposal for a new classification of sexually motivated killings. *Journal of Criminal Justice, 71*, 101729. https://doi.org/10.1016/j.jcrimjus.2020.101729

Stone, M. (1998). Sadistic personality in murderers. In T. Millon, E. Simonsen, M. Birket-Smith, & R. Davis (Eds.), *Psychopathy: Antisocial, criminal and violent behavior* (pp. 346–355). The Guildford Press.

Teisl, M., & Cicchetti, D. (2008). Physical abuse, cognitive and emotional processes, and aggressive/disruptive behavior problems. *Social Development, 17*(1), 1–23. https://doi.org/10.1111/j.1467-9507.2007.00412.x

Thibaut, F., Cosyns, P., Fedoroff, J. P., Briken, P., Goethals, K., & Bradford, J. M. W. (2020). The World Federation of Societies of Biological Psychiatry (WFSBP) 2020 guidelines for the pharmacological treatment of paraphilic disorders. *World Journal of Biological Psychiatry, 21*(6), 412–490. https://doi.org/10.1080/15622975.2020.1744723

Turner, D., & Briken, P. (2018). Treatment of paraphilic disorders in sexual offenders or men with a risk of sexual offending with luteinizing hormone-releasing hormone agonists: An updated systematic review. *Journal of Sexual Medicine, 15*(1), 77–93. https://doi.org/10.1016/j.jsxm.2017.11.013

Turner, D., Petermann, J., Harrison, K., Krueger, R., & Briken, P. (2017). Pharmacological treatment of patients with paraphilic disorders and risk of sexual offending: An international perspective. *The World Journal of Biological Psychiatry, 20*(8), 616–625. https://doi.org/10.1080/15622975.2017.1395069

Vettor, S., Beech, A. R., & Woodhams, J. (2014). Rapists and sexual murderers: Combined pathways to offending. In J. Proulx, E. Beauregard, P. Lussier, & B. Leclerc (Eds.), *Pathways to sexual aggression* (pp. 285–315). Routledge.

Walters, G. D. (1999). Crime and chaos: Applying nonlinear dynamic principles to problems in criminology. *International Journal of Offender Therapy and Comparative Criminology, 43*(2), 134–153. https://doi.org/10.1177/0306624X99432002

Walters, G. D. (2012). *Crime in a psychological context: From career criminals to criminal careers*. SAGE.

Warren, J. I., Hazelwood, R. R., & Dietz, P. E. (1996). The sexually sadistic serial killer. *Journal of Forensic Sciences, 41*(6), 970–974. https://doi.org/10.1520/JFS14033J

World Health Organization. (2019). *International statistical classification of diseases and related health problems* (11th ed.). https://icd.who.int/). WHO.

Yates, E., Barbaree, H. E., & Marshall, W. L. (1984). Anger and deviant sexual arousal. *Behavior Therapy, 15*(3), 287–294. https://doi.org/10.1016/S0005-7894(84)80031-3

Chapter 15
Human Sex Trafficking

Mary C. Burke, Shannon White, Tina Krolikowski, and Susan O'Rourke

15.1 Introduction

Human trafficking is a transnational organized criminal enterprise in which people are exploited for profit (Roza, 2013). At the international level, the General Assembly of the United Nations (UN) adopted the Protocol to Prevent, Suppress and Punish Trafficking in Persons, especially Women and Children and entered it into force in December 2003 (United Nations Office on Drugs and Crime [UNODC], 2018). This protocol, referred to as the Palermo Protocol, supplemented the Convention against Transnational Organized Crime and was the first legally binding instrument at the global level to address human trafficking (UNODC, 2018). The Palermo Protocol defines human trafficking as "the recruitment, transport, transfer, harbouring or receipt of a person by such means as threat or use of force or other forms of coercion, abduction, fraud or deception for the purpose of exploitation." Sex trafficking is one form of human trafficking and according to the UN Global Report on Trafficking in Persons (2020), the majority of identified victims (50%) in 2018 were trafficked for sexual exploitation, 38% for forced labor, 7% for forced

For this chapter, the terms "woman," "women," and "girls" will be used to refer to those in the victim-survivor role in relation to sex trafficking and prostitution. While boys and men are also in the victim-survivor role, they are less represented in this population of violent crime survivors. Furthermore, victim-survivor will be used to refer to those exploited in sex trafficking.

M. C. Burke (✉) · S. White · T. Krolikowski
Department of Psychology, Counseling & Criminology, Carlow University, Pittsburgh, PA, USA
e-mail: mcburke@carlow.edu

S. O'Rourke
Center for Global Engagement, Carlow University, Pittsburgh, PA, USA

R. J. Tully et al. (eds.), *Best Practices in Sexual Offender Assessment and Management*, Dangerous Behavior in Clinical and Forensic Psychology,
https://doi.org/10.1007/978-3-031-83135-5_15

criminal activity including begging, forced marriages and organ removal. While sex and labor trafficking are the most common forms of trafficking, and while there is overlap between the two, most would say sexually-based offenses of any type are the most egregious of crimes, causing enduring harm to survivors. This is the case with sex trafficking, which is the focus of this chapter.

15.2 Overview of Sex Trafficking

Sex trafficking is the sexual exploitation of an individual, through coercion, threats, force, or intimidation of the individual providing the sexual acts, for a third party's economic gain (United States, 2000). The "third-party beneficiary" is someone in addition to the purchaser of sex (e.g., the john) who is involved and benefitting financially (Levy, 2018). This individual is the trafficker and is often a pimp, romantic partner, friend, or at times a family member. An exception to this is when someone under the age of 18 is involved, then force, fraud, or coercion need not be present to constitute trafficking (United States, 2000). This means, for example, a 16-year-old who reports being involved in a commercial sex act of their own accord, is not involved in prostitution, rather they are a sex trafficking victim. Sex trafficking is not limited to prostitution; victims of sex trafficking are forced into a number of different forms of sexual exploitation including for example pornography, sex tourism and trafficking for marriage.

Every nation is affected by sex and labor trafficking, whether through in-country trafficking or internationally as a country of origin, transit, destination, or some combination of the three. In the United States, involuntary servitude and slavery were abolished in 1865 through actions taken by President Abraham Lincoln, yet today human trafficking, a form of slavery, occurs in every jurisdiction in the country. The Trafficking Victims Protection Act (TVPA) of 2000 was drafted to address this issue in its present form in the U.S. It criminalizes all acts related to sex and labor trafficking, strengthens penalties for offenders and provides assistance to victims. Traffickers use a range of tactics to control victim-survivors, including emotional manipulation, physical and sexual abuse, blackmail, and the confiscation of identification papers in situations involving international trafficking (Administration for Children and Families [ACF], 2017). Sex trafficking occurs in a wide range of contexts and does not require the movement of the victim from one place to another, which is a common misconception related to the crime. Exploitation through sex trafficking can take place in a victim's home country, during migration or in a foreign country. A victim-survivor can be trafficked in their own home or the home of a trusted friend or romantic partner. Examples of sex trafficking locations include rural neighborhoods and extend to any number of places including massage businesses, escort services, residential brothels, strip clubs, hotels/motels, highway rest areas, truck stops, and city streets. This crime can be committed just about anywhere, where there are people.

15.2.1 Commercial Sex Acts

There is often confusion regarding sex trafficking and prostitution. When money is exchanged for sexual acts, this is referred to as a "commercial sex act," which can be further understood as prostitution, pornography, and any sexual performance done in exchange for money or any item deemed valuable such as food, clothing, shelter, drugs, etc. Prostitution (commercial sex act) is the performance of sexual acts in exchange for money, but without the use of force, fraud, or coercion. Sex trafficking, though variously defined, does not include sex acts for which consent is freely given. Consent is the essential difference between sex trafficking and prostitution. This distinction between the two is critical and hinges on the agency of the individual involved. While there is great difficulty in securing reliable prevalence data for both the incidence of sex trafficking and prostitution, the FBI Uniform Crime Report (2020) can provide a snapshot of the latter. For example, FBI records show that in 2019 there were 26,713 arrests for prostitution. This number can be misleading for a variety of reasons, including that it is possible that some of the arrests include unidentified victims of sex trafficking and that prostitution is difficult for law enforcement to detect.

15.2.2 Commercial Exploitation of Children

The involvement of children in commercial sex acts is a form of sex trafficking. According to the International Labor Organization (ILO, 2017), each year traffickers take advantage of approximately one million children worldwide for the purpose of sex trafficking. Within the United States, a relatively conservative estimate of the number of children involved in sex trafficking is approximately 200,000 each year (Goldberg & Moore, 2028). This includes involvement in sexual intercourse, escort services, pornography, stripping, and other acts that are sexual in nature. The National Center for Missing and Exploited Children (2018) estimates that 1 in every 7 missing children is likely a victim of sex trafficking. Additional estimates include that in 2018, 51.6% of human trafficking cases were in fact cases involving the sex trafficking of children (Feehs & Currier, 2019).

15.3 Dynamics of Sex Trafficking

Sex trafficking occurs in rural, suburban, and urban communities alike; regardless of the location, traffickers are skilled at maintaining covert recruitment and day-to-day operations (Cole & Sprang, 2015). Recruitment can occur at parties, public places, or within the victim's home by family members or other trusted familiar people in their lives (Rosenblatt, 2014). Other locations for recruitment can include schools, convenience stores, or faux modeling agencies (Rosenblatt, 2014). Recruitment occurs within the home when victims are sold into the industry by their families, oftentimes at the suggestion of friends, neighbors, and other community members (Jones et al., 2011). With regard to recruitment, traffickers demonstrate the ability to quickly adapt their strategies and target populations and regions in order to focus on those most vulnerable at a given time (Wheaton et al., 2010). The promise of an increased profit margin plays a role in trafficker motivation to quickly changes areas in which they work (Jakobsson & Kotsadam, 2013). An example of this adaption includes traveling across states in the U.S. in order to be near large, well-attended sporting events such as the Super Bowl.

Current research suggests that online recruitment is a common way victims are lured into the sex trade (Baird et al., 2020). This includes use of various online platforms and social media that includes but is not limited to Craigslist, Kijiji, Instagram, and Facebook (Baird et al., 2020; Rosenblatt, 2014). The rise of online recruitment has led to increased policing and surveillance to find and arrest perpetrators (Hadjiyanni et al., 2014). The internet has allowed for sex trafficking to occur virtually anywhere at any time.

Sex traffickers attract individuals through false advertisements for lucrative career opportunities, transportation to other countries, marriage proposals and educational opportunities (The National Trafficking Hotline, 2020; Deshpande & Nour, 2013; Kara, 2017). A more violent method is that of kidnapping, which occurs with frequency in some regions of the world (Deshpande & Nour, 2013; Kara, 2017). Another tactic sex traffickers use to secure victims is through the girls and women they are already victimizing (Brayley et al. 2011). Current victims may see themselves as the girlfriend or romantic partner of the trafficker, which is a perspective that is intentionally cultivated by the trafficker. The sex trafficker will leverage this connection and direct these girls and women to befriend others, who he in turn, victimizes in the same manner.

Researchers have noted that sex traffickers typically use one or a combination of five strategies or techniques to recruit and control victims. These strategies/techniques include (1) the façade of romantic relationships, (2) threats of false or inflated debt (shower with "free" gifts and then require the "debt" to be paid off), (3) induce victim drug addiction, (4) use of physical violence or the threat of physical violence, and (5) the assumption of power and a position of authority.

Once victimized through sex trafficking, it is very difficult to escape. Debt bondage, noted above and commonly used as a control tactic, involves the repayment of money owed through labor or services (Deshpande & Nour, 2013). Oftentimes the debt is falsely created, and victims are not aware of the debt until it has accumulated, causing the victim to feel stuck in the trafficking situation (Jones et al., 2011). Traumatic bonding, also referred to as Stockholm Syndrome, is also common within the context of sex trafficking. This bonding occurs when the trafficker ingrains a sense of gratitude and fear simultaneously within the victim (Deshpande & Nour, 2013). Other tactics used to control survivor-victims is threats of deportation or of violence to the victim and the victim's family members (Dovydaitis, 2010). "Watchers" are often used to escort trafficked victims to and from locations under the guise of ensuring safety, which in reality ensures that the victim cannot escape. Substantial physical abuse and ailments are common, including sexually transmitted infections, unsafe abortions, broken bones, burns, bruising, and dental complications (Dovydaitis, 2010). These experiences tend to lead victims to believe there are only three ways to leave the sex trade: become unprofitable to the trafficker due to pregnancy or debilitating emotional trauma, to be aided in an escape by a client, or death (Hughes & Denisova, 2001).

15.3.1 The Sex Traffickers

Understanding who the traffickers are and how they operate is imperative to preventing sex trafficking. Sex traffickers can be individuals working alone (e.g., pimp), small groups of people, loose-knit decentralized criminal networks, gangs, and international organized criminal operations. It is not uncommon for sex traffickers and their victims to be of the same national, ethnic, or cultural background. This shared background can serve to facilitate trust in the victim, thus making manipulation easier for the trafficker. Sex traffickers can be U.S. citizens or foreign nationals, male or female; they can be romantic partners, family members, acquaintances or strangers.

In cross-border trafficking situations, the added layer of discerning the link between the citizenship of victims and traffickers is another crucial data point necessary for prevention and intervention (UNODC, 2014). While most convicted traffickers are citizens of the country where they are arrested and convicted, it is interesting to note that 35% of convicted traffickers are foreigners, although their country of origin is typically located near the country where they were initially convicted. UNODC (2014) further reported that the percentage of those convicted of trafficking in foreign countries represents a higher rate than those convicted of other non-trafficking related crimes.

Sex traffickers who transport victims to new countries must create falsified documents, establish routes, and pay bribes to officials in order to operate (Wheaton et al., 2010). These individuals can hold a variety of responsibilities, including organizers, middlemen, business operators, and corrupt government administrators (Wheaton, et al., 2010). Some may be responsible for identifying and recruiting potential victims, transporting them, or purchasing the victims (Wheaton et al., 2010). In domestic sex trafficking, connectors, recruiters, and groomers help find new victims and prepare them for sexual exploitation. Other trafficked victims become members of the trafficker's business to collect money and carry out orders (Williamson & Prior, 2009). In sex trafficking, the term trafficker is often synonymous with the term pimp (Butler & Wilson, 2013). After recruiting the victim-survivor, the trafficker or pimp actively creates a pathological support network which may be reminiscent of the abusive childhood of some victims (Butler & Wilson, 2013).

Gang involvement in sex trafficking has been on the radar of law enforcement for a number of years. Gangs consider sex trafficking a source of income that has low overhead in terms of costs and often goes undetected by the authorities and thus presents less risk than other criminal enterprises. For example, the National Gang Center (NGC) is a project funded by the Office of Juvenile Justice and Delinquency Prevention (OJJDP), the Office of Justice Programs (OJP) and the U.S. Department of Justice (DOJ). Part of the work of the NGC is to collate information related to gang activity in the United States. Examination of data collected from this group shows how prostitution and trafficking cases with gang involvement have become increasingly common over the past ten years (NGC, 2020).

15.3.2 The Consumers

In sex trafficking, consumers include those who purchase sexual acts directly (sometimes referred to as Johns) and those purchasing indirectly, such as those consuming pornography that may involve sex trafficking victims. The focus here is on those purchasing sex directly, the Johns. It has been estimated that between 1% and 15% of men report paying for sexual services within the past year (Carael et al., 2006). Men who are 20–24 and men who live in urban environments are more likely to solicit sexual services (Carael et al., 2006). Sexual favors in exchange for money can occur in too many settings to name, some examples include brothels, strip clubs, massage parlors, and transit spaces, restaurants and bars, hotels and motels, and private residences (Hadjiyanni et al., 2014). Motivation for seeking paid sexual experiences include a need for stress relief, the belief that paying for sex would be easier than seeking it from other means, and the desire for entertainment (Pitts et al., 2004). Other reasons include the use of controlled substances, the guarantee of a short-term interaction, and loneliness (Malarek, 2011; Pitts et al., 2004).

Along with sex traffickers, Johns play a role in sex trafficking and often act as a source of abuse to survivor-victims. Johns often attempt to murder, rape, kidnap or engage in unusual sex acts with the trafficked individual (Cecchet & Thoburn, 2014). Some Johns refer to themselves as "hobbyists" and have been found to converse in anonymous online chat rooms (Milrod & Monto, 2017; Milrod & Monto, 2012; Milrod & Weitzer, 2012). Some Johns share a desire for romance, or what may be referred to as "the girlfriend experience" (Malarek, 2011). Such an experience gives the sense of a genuine relationship, though in reality exists only because of payment. The internet has provided an easy way for Johns to find those involved in the commercial sex industry, some of whom are victims of traffickers (Tidball et al., 2016).

15.3.3 Sex Trafficking Case Example

The true case below illustrates some of the tactics used by sex traffickers in the various stages of the trafficking process:

Department of Justice U.S. Attorney's Office
Central District of Illinois
Friday, January 29, 2021
Central Illinois Sex Trafficker Sentenced to Life in Prison
PEORIA, Ill.—U.S. District Judge James E. Shadid today sentenced a Central Illinois man, Franshon Stapleton, 48, to multiple life prison terms for trafficking young women for sex. Stapleton, of Springfield, ran his prostitution enterprise from a motel in Champaign where he lived, and used women he recruited from Champaign, Sangamon, and Peoria counties.
Prosecutors described the degradation and manipulation Stapleton used in 2017 and 2018, to exploit desperate young women, who were fighting drug addiction and homelessness, to force them to perform sex acts for money. Stapleton arranged the encounters, set the price, and collected the money. Stapleton used violence and threats of violence to force them to engage in sex with men. Through constant manipulation, Stapleton exploited his victims' desperation as he ensured the women were 'indebted' to him for the motel rooms, drugs, and food he provided.
At sentencing, Judge Shadid stated that a sentence of anything less than life would ignore the nature of the offense, the impact to the victims, the defendant's lack of remorse, his prior criminal history, and the sentencing guidelines.
U.S. Attorney John Milhiser commended the strength of the victims who provided critical evidence against the defendant and recognized the sustained efforts by federal and local law enforcement to locate, investigate and prosecute dangerous predators and remove them from the community.
Stapleton was ordered to serve a life sentence for each of the four counts of sex trafficking. The sentences will be served concurrently with additional five-year prison terms for each of the 13 related charges charged. Stapleton pleaded guilty to all the charges against him on Sept. 28, 2020, as his trial was set to begin. He has been in the custody of the U.S. Marshals Service since his arrest on the charges in May 2018.
The charges were investigated by U.S. Immigration and Customs Enforcement Homeland Security Investigations; the Urbana Police Department; the Champaign County Sheriff's Office; the Illinois State Police Forensics Laboratory; and, the Champaign Police Department with cooperation from Champaign County State's Attorney Julia Reitz. Assistant U.S. Attorneys Elly M. Peirson and Ryan Finlen represented the government in the prosecution.

15.4 Prevalence of Sex Trafficking

There are many challenges in obtaining data related to the prevalence of sex trafficking; these challenges include but are not limited to a lack of a shared definition of sex trafficking among researchers and those from whom they collect data, difficulty identifying survivor-victims and simply not enough research on the issue. To that end, any data on the prevalence of sex trafficking and related research must be interpreted with caution.

Many survivors of human trafficking identified globally are trafficked for sexual exploitation (United Nations International Labour Organization [ILO], 2017). This is particularly true in the Americas, East Asia, Europe, and the Pacific. In many other regions, labor trafficking is most prevalent, and in Central and South Asia, sex and labor trafficking appear to be equally prevalent. When attempting to interpret prevalence data, it is critical to keep in mind the somewhat common mistake of conflating sex trafficking and prostitution. The misinterpretation of this difference can lead to data that is misleading at best and in some instances completely inaccurate.

Prevalence can best be understood using three different but related perspectives—*point prevalence* (proportion of reported cases in a population with a specific time interval), *period prevalence* (specific time period), and *lifetime prevalence* (occurring during a time interval in someone's life). Each of these are essential to consider in order to ascertain the scope and magnitude of sex trafficking (Rothman, 2012).

According to the ILO (2017) report, at any given point in 2016, globally, there were 24.9 million people in forced labor (to include sex trafficking) of some form. Of these, 16 million individuals were involved in labor exploitation through the private sector (e.g., construction, restaurants, agriculture, and domestic work); eight million individuals were exploited in sex trafficking with the remaining four million individuals in forced labor that is "state-sponsored," meaning, in countries where the authorities sanction slavery. Girls and women and are disproportionately impacted by forced labor and are through to account for 99% of victims in the commercial sex industry and 58% of the victims in other sectors. Of those exploited through sex trafficking, one million are children, approximately 3.8 million are adults, and 99% (as noted earlier) are female. Considering these numbers in other terms, in 2016 there were 5.4 victims of slavery for every one thousand people in the world; there were 5.9 adult victims of for every one thousand adults in the world and there were 4.4 child victims for every one thousand children in the world (ILO, 2017).

Demographically, 70% of those exploited in the sex trade industry are in Asia and the Pacific, 14% are located in Central Asia and Europe, while 4% remain in the Americas (ILO, 2017). Overall, those forced into sex trafficking generate an estimated $99 billion worldwide (ILO, 2017). Sex trafficking generates revenue of $32 billion annually and is the most rapidly growing form of commerce (Deshpande & Nour, 2013). It is important to note that sex trafficking is recognized as organized crime and is ranked number three behind narcotics and arms sales across the entire conglomerate of activities that compromise organized crime (Deshpande & Nour, 2013).

The Polaris Project, a federally funded non-profit organization, serves as a hub of resources for both victims and social agencies supporting victims. The Polaris Project also operates the national trafficking hotline, through which they collect data about the problem as it exists within the country. In 2018 in the United States, 3178 cases of sex trafficking out of 5147 cases of human trafficking were reported via The Polaris Project national human trafficking hotline (Kelly, 2019). Data from the Polaris Project, while helpful, represents only a portion of cases in the United States. Therefore, this information should be interpreted with caution. Kelly (2019) further reported that there is currently no official estimate of sex trafficking survivors in the United States. Despite only a portion of the cases represented and no existence of an official estimate of sex trafficking survivors in the U.S., human trafficking most likely exists as the most underreported crime known and is thought to be the most horrific form of human trafficking (Polaris Project, 2021). It is clear that the gaps in information regarding prevalence points to the need for further research.

15.4.1 Demographic Locations of Sex Trafficking

Research on sex trafficking reflects its occurrence in every country worldwide and further reveals that while illegal in most places and a violation of human rights everywhere, sex trafficking thrives in countless locations. According to the UNODC (2014), in consideration of cross-border sex trafficking, one of the most common destinations for victims is Europe, while Asia remains the location with the greatest scope of sex trafficking. The Americas continue to exist as common for both the origin and destination of victims of sex trafficking. The United States is one of the most common locations for sex trafficking. According to Deshpande & Nour (2013), the US Department of State has consistently reported that approximately 14,500 to 17,500 individuals are trafficked annually in the United States, which does not account for victim-survivors for whom the U.S. is their country of origin. Victim-survivors are typically trafficked to the U.S. from Mexico and East Asia, the Union of Soviet Socialist Republics, numerous regions within the continent of Africa, Eastern Europe, Mexico, and South America (Deshpande & Nour, 2013). It bears mentioning that the portability of the trafficking industry is facilitated in industrialized countries because the well-developed infrastructure makes it easier to entrap, transport and sell victims (Deshpande & Nour, 2013). It is also important to note that regions where political climates are unsteady and the economy is depressed, tend to be the locations from which many victim-survivors are trafficked (Deshpande & Nour, 2013).

15.5 Conceptual Frameworks

Sex and labor trafficking are most often viewed through a criminal justice lens, with the focus primarily on legislation and resource allocation for the prosecution of traffickers. This results in victims being seen within this model, rather than at the center of the issue, with their needs being given primacy. Ideally, using different frameworks or theories will center survivors and broaden understanding of human trafficking, whether for sex, labor, or organs. These frameworks can be informed by different disciplines and used together, may provide ways to expand thinking about the underlying causes of trafficking, the contexts in which it thrives, unique vulnerabilities to victimization and how to design effective methods to prevent trafficking. What follows are examples of some conceptual frameworks that have been applied to different aspects of sex trafficking.

15.5.1 Macro-Economics: Supply and Demand Theory

Economics is a common lens through which the commercial sex industry is considered. Sex trafficking, while a criminal activity, is also a business and, operates in ways that are similar to other, non-criminal, legitimate industries. This similar manner of functioning allows us to apply macro-economic theory, particularly, supply and demand theory, which further allows for consideration of the influences causing shifts in supply and demand.

Whether virtual or physical, an economic market is where sellers and buyers are connected in mutually beneficial relationships. The seller is on the "supply" side of the market equation and the buyer on the "demand" side. The two can be connected directly or through an intermediary, in this case, the sex trafficker. Through this lens, like any market, the commercial sex market is driven predominantly by demand (Hughes, 2004). Meaning, that when there are people interested in paying for sex and sex acts, there will be a supply of those meeting that demand, either of their own accord or through force, fraud, or coercion.

Sex trafficking represents a unique business prototype, as adults and minors can be sold and forced to generate profits over the course of numerous years. This distinction alone sets this type of illegal trade apart from illegal profits earned via drug and narcotics sales, in which products are sold and used only once (Deshpande & Nour, 2013). In fact, a primary reason for the global expansion of the sex trafficking industry is the high-profit margin for traffickers, which is reified because of how the same "commodity" can be used repeatedly. Each trafficked woman can bring between $75,000 and $250,000 annually in profit, depending on the country's market in which the crime is being committed. For example, it has been estimated that a single victim-survivor trafficked in the United States can generate profits of as much as $100,000 annually (Zakhari, 2005).

15.5.2 Ecological Theory

Ecological Theory attends to the various environments in which the individual functions and the impact of these environments on the individual (Bronfenbrenner & Morris, 1998). In this theory, the five environmental systems included are (1) the individual, (2) microsystem, (3) mesosystem, (4) exosystem, and the (5) macrosystem. The microsystem is the immediate setting in which the individual lives and includes family, peers, school, church, etc. The mesosystem is characterized by the interactions between and among the microsystems. For example, the parent of a student (parent is in the student's microsystem) may interact with their teacher (parent and teacher interaction). The exosystem is made up of the connections between the social systems that directly impact the individual and do not hold an active position. Examples of the exosystem are friends of family, neighbors, media, government, etc. The macrosystem is the larger culture and social ideologies in which the individual resides. This theory is relevant in so much as it can help us to understand victim-survivor vulnerabilities to sex trafficking, means of support after sex trafficking, and points of possible intervention to prevent sex trafficking. Similarly, it can help us consider the trafficker and their experiences in systems that may have played into the development of becoming a perpetrator. Clinicians working with survivor-victims should consider all of the systems affecting the individual with attention to both strengths and areas of deficit within each system. In treatment planning, this will allow for leveraging resources that are in place as well as highlighting where additional support is necessary. For those involved in prevention and efforts to identify perpetrators, a similar scan of the systems in a given area can be done to focus this work (Fig. 15.1).

15.5.3 Conflict Theory

Conflict theory addresses power structures and how differences in power affect social inequality (Rössel, 2013). Conflict theory rests on the assumption that people are largely driven by self-interest and thus feel competitive for what is seen as scarce resources (Rössel, 2013). According to conflict theory, those in more well-resourced, wealthier classes are able to maintain power over less well-resourced, lower-income and ethnic minority groups, in part by allowing these groups to believe that the betterment of the other will be harmful to them, resulting in these groups playing into each other's oppression (Parillo, 2012).

As it relates to sex trafficking, conflict theory provides a framework for understanding how an imbalance of power, social inequality, and oppression occur, thereby creating a class of individuals who, unable to meet basic needs, are vulnerable to sex trafficking. This theory is often used to explain racism, classism, and sexism, all of which pertain to sex trafficking and those who find themselves struggling to meet basic needs and therefore at risk for both sex and labor trafficking.

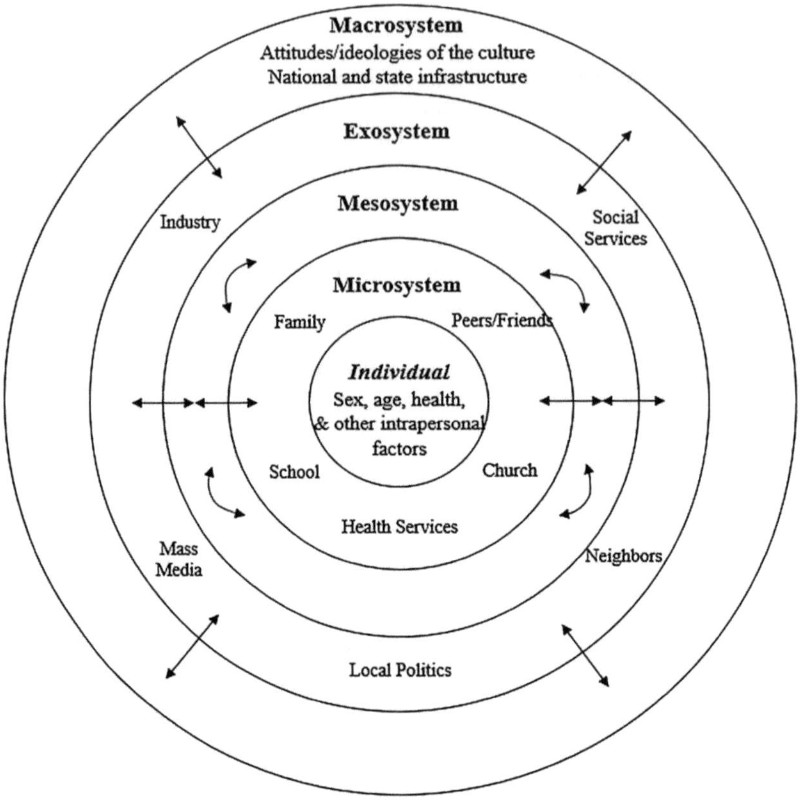

Fig. 15.1 Bronfenbrenner's Ecological Theory Model

Conflict theory can be used to explain vulnerability to sex trafficking on the community and state levels as well as internationally.

15.6 Vulnerability to Sex Trafficking

A number of factors create a risk to sex trafficking, all of which pertain in some form to an individual's ability to protect herself and to meet her basic needs. Research, time and time again, indicates that the majority of survivor-victims report being in a state of significant economic need (e.g., difficulty meeting basic survival needs) prior to being forced or otherwise recruited into sex trafficking (Dahal et al., 2015; Murphy, 2016; Silverman et al., 2007). This economic vulnerability is exploited by traffickers whose promises are designed to give the impression of providing solutions to the challenges facing survivor-victims. Additional risk factors include compromised support system, ability status, membership in a marginalized identity group, status as an immigrant or refugee, political instability, and natural disasters (ACF, 2018b; CDC, 2020; Polaris Project, 2021). The survivor-victim, in some situations, has a desire to be loved and has seen family members or neighbors engage in prostitution (Cecchet & Thoburn, 2014). This can lead to an initial openness to some types of employment opportunities used by traffickers as part of their deceit tactics for recruitment (Table 15.1).

While all victims of human trafficking have vulnerability that places them at risk, some populations are at increased danger for being trafficked. In the United States, these include those of American Indian/Alaska Native decent, lesbian-gay-bisexual-transgender-questioning (LGBTQ) youth, temporary guest workers, undocumented migrants, runaway/homeless youth and individuals with disabilities (USDS, 2022). Of these, LGBTQ+ youth, special needs individuals and native populations have received the least attention in the professional literature and therefore will be discussed briefly here.

15.6.1 LGBTQ+ Youth

The LGBTQ+ population is a steadily growing demographic of those marginalized within the United States. According to Jones (2022), among those who self-identify as non-heterosexual, there is an increase of 7.1%, double the percentage from 2012. Although the exact number of LGBTQ+ individuals in the United States is unknown, data from the Census Bureau's Household Pulse Survey (2022) indicates that approximately 20 million adults in this country may identify as lesbian, gay, bisexual, or transgender. Additionally, it is speculated that millions more may identify similarly with newer identity terms that are more broadly defined (e.g., pansexual, asexual, etc.). Persistent cultural biases against queer-identifying individuals foster

Table 15.1 Increased vulnerability: to sex trafficking is characterized by

• Poverty
• Instability in the living situation
• Status as a run away
• Involvement with the foster care or juvenile justice systems
• History of surviving domestic violence
• Sexual abuse history
• Family member or primary caregiver substance use difficulties
• Instability in immigration status
• Identification as LGBTQ+
• Identification as Native American
• History of criminal convictions
• Substance use issues
• Unaddressed mental health needs
• Cognitive and/or physical disability
• Isolation from family and friends

a climate that puts LGBTQ+ youth at risk for increased mental health challenges and for exploitation, including sex trafficking.

This group faces unique challenges due to their gender identity, sexual orientation, and age. Many experience aggression, hate, and rejection from family members, which can be exceptionally hurtful especially when coming from parents or others in an elder or parental role (Ream & Forge, 2014). Family members may evict the youth from the home or youth may runaway as a means of escaping mistreatment at home. Once on the street, LGBTQ+ youth are especially vulnerable to sex trafficking due to the combined impact of their minority status and their age. Due to their age, minors in particular are targeted by traffickers because they are often easier to manipulate and less able to protect themselves. In a study by Morton et al. (2018) it was found that LGBTQ+ youth had over two times the rate of early death among homeless youth and more than double the risk of homelessness compared to their non-LGBTQ+ peers. Additionally, LGBTQ+ youth who also identify as black or multiracial had some of the highest rates of homelessness. The researchers also found that among homeless youth, LGBTQ+ youth reported higher rates of trauma and adversity, with this being particularly true for youth identifying as transgender.

When away from home, LGBTQ+ youth are faced with finding ways to meet basic needs, such as securing food and shelter. Some may engage in commercial sex, sometimes referred to as survival sex, to secure funding and other resources to take care of themselves. Traffickers are known to target homeless youth and will find ways to take advantage of them for their own financial gain. For example, a trafficker may offer food or lodging to befriend and build trust with the individual. Having an adult offer support may be confusing for the youth, thereby making it more difficult to push back against instructions given by the trafficker. While there has been work done to prevent the sex trafficking of LGBTQ+ homeless youth and to aid them after victimization, more effort is needed in this area.

15.6.2 Individuals with Special Needs

Consistent with other types of violent crime, individuals with disabilities are three times more likely to be trafficked than their non-disabled peers, (Harrell, 2017). Multiple factors related to an individual's disability may contribute to this increased vulnerability. For example, limited access to transportation for individuals with physical disabilities increases the likelihood of isolation and in turn the desire for human connections, even when those appear suspicious of intent. Individuals with an intellectual development disorder may fail to understand authentic friendships or deceitful practices. Sensory impairments, such as blindness and deafness, limit a person's ability to recognize warnings of danger in their environments. Individuals with autism spectrum disorder, given their impairment in social-emotional reciprocity, nonverbal behaviors, and understanding relationships, are often quite literal and fail to understand when a person is lying. Furthermore, social skill impairment limits their ability to establish social networks which leaves them particularly vulnerable to seeking friendships and having a limited experience in the components of a healthy relationship.

Individuals with disabilities are more likely to be living in poverty because of limited employment opportunities (Morris, 2017). Women with disabilities are particularly more likely to live in poverty. This gender disparity, coupled with the disability disparity, results in a poverty rate of 31 percent for disabled women, compared to 26 percent for disabled men, (Morris, 2017). These statistics extend to persons of color where the poverty rate for the disabled is 40%, (Morris, 2017). The intersectionality of disability, social class, and poverty results in the increased likelihood of vulnerability being trafficked.

A recent study by the Department of Maternal and Child Health at the University of North Carolina at Chapel Hill (Franchino-Olsen et al., 2020a), found that minor girls in the U.S. with any disability had a higher prevalence of sex trafficking than their peers without disabilities. Furthermore, minor girls with severe disabilities and those with significant intellectual disabilities were trafficked considerably more than their disabled peers (Franchino-Olsen et al., 2020b). Reid (2018) discovered similar results analyzing records indicating that under-age girls with intellectual disabilities were easily manipulated by their traffickers often due to a lack of awareness around the risks associated with the relationship or an inability to recognize that they were victims. Individuals with disabilities—especially those with intellectual disabilities or behavioral disorders—may not recognize sexual abuse as being illegal or how to communicate the assault to a trusted care provider (Harrell, 2017).

Individuals with complex needs often rely on caregivers for their very survival. They may not feel comfortable reporting abuse if they believe that it will negatively impact their care which is necessary for their existence. Limited access to social networks and others who may learn of the abuse reduce their ability to file reports. Additionally, when reporting the victimization, they may not be viewed as credible. Non-verbal individuals are particularly limited as their communication attempts may be insufficient to be understood or considered reliable.

15.6.3 American Indian/Alaska Native Women

Around the world, Indigenous populations are at a higher risk of human trafficking than other diverse populations; this is true for both labor and sex trafficking (Administration for Children and Families, 2018a). In the United States, Indigenous groups include those of American Indian/Alaska Native, Native Hawaiian, Pacific Islander descent. Indigenous communities in the United States and elsewhere are impacted by historical trauma consequent of systematic oppression. One of the ways in which historical trauma impacts current generations is through the intergenerational transmission of the trauma and its effects (Coyle, 2014).

Indigenous people have experienced centuries of trauma and oppression including loss of their land, forced assimilation, and both physical and sexual violence. This systemic violence and trauma have impacted their ability to make progress by contributing to higher levels of family dysfunction, higher levels of poverty and higher levels of substance abuse and domestic violence. All of this combines to create vulnerabilities among Indigenous groups that has led to increased risk for exploitation, including risk for sex trafficking.

15.7 Trafficking as a Sexual Offense

In the United States, federal law in 10 U.S. Code § 920 defines sex crimes, including both sexual assault and rape. Additionally, this law includes important concepts that assist law enforcement and court officials in determining whether offenses not clearly noted in the law, count as sex crimes. The concepts are each relevant in qualifying the sex trafficker as a sexual offender and are as follows:

- Lack of consent: Consent must be given explicitly and free of pressure for each sexual event. Whether those involved had a prior relationship or the victim did not actively resist sexual activity is not relevant. It is important to note that legally, certain people are not qualified to consent, such as individuals who are asleep, unconscious, drug-impaired, or mentally incompetent. Under the law, any sexual acts committed upon these individuals are considered sexual assaults.
- Sexual contact: Sexual contact can be the behavior of sexually touching someone directly, and it can also be the behavior of causing someone else to make sexual contact (e.g., touch) with another person.
- Force: Force occurs when (1) there is use of a weapon, (2) physical strength leads to bodily harm, restraint, or overpowering another, or (3) the person is coerced by physical injury.

15.8 Sexual Offender Assessment

States vary with their guidelines for determining whether an offender meets the legal criteria as a sexual offender or a sexually violent predator (SVP). In most states, the law defines a SVP as someone convicted of a sexually violent offense and who is likely to engage in predatory sexually violent offenses again in the future. As described previously, this includes sex trafficking and related offenses. Some states implement a board comprised of psychologists in addition to other relevant professionals to make these determinations (Felthous & Ko, 2018). Board members are typically directed to consider the following in their assessment (Felthous & Ko, 2018):

1. Characteristics of the offender, including:
   (a) Age
   (b) Use of illegal drugs or psychological challenges
   (c) Patterns of behavioral characteristics related to the offender's conduct
2. Current Offense:
   (a) Whether the offense involved one or multiple victims
   (b) Whether the offender exceeded the means needed in order to accomplish the offense
   (c) Nature of sexual contact with the victim
   (d) Age of the victim
   (e) Relationship between the victim and the offender
   (f) Whether the offense included unusual cruelty by the offender
   (g) The mental capacity of the victim
3. Prior Offenses:
   (a) Offender's prior criminal record, sexual offenses, and sentences
   (b) Whether the individual uses available programs for sexual offenders

15.9 Conclusion

A combination of overarching sociocultural factors contribute to individual vulnerability to sex trafficking. On the individual level, poverty, social inequality, social exclusion, lack of family support and trauma are just a few of the experiences that render a person more likely to be exploited by sex traffickers. Using a human rights lens as well as perspectives afforded on the issue from various theories may help strengthen anti-sex trafficking efforts, nationally and abroad. Unfortunately, despite efforts spanning in part over the last twenty years and those that predate the 2000s, sex trafficking persists and remains misunderstood, under-researched and under-identified. Only through continued work of those in non-profits, the government, education and concerned citizens will greater strides be made to eliminate this crime.

References

Administration for Children and Families. (2017). *Fact Sheet: Human trafficking*. https://www.acf.hhs.gov/sites/default/files/documents/otip/fact_sheet_human_trafficking_fy18.pdf

Administration for Children and Families. (2018a). *Recognizing and responding to human trafficking among American Indian/Alaska Native and Pacific Islander communities [Memorandum]*. U.S. Department of Health and Human Services. https://www.acf.hhs.gov/sites/default/files/ana/ana_human_trafficking_im_2015_11_18.pdf

Administration for Children and Families. (2018b). *Trafficking prevention and response*. National Human Trafficking Training and Technical Assistance Center. https://nhttac.acf.hhs.gov/sites/default/files/2020-02/Trafficking%20Prevention%20and%20Disaster%20Response%20Literature%20Review.pdf

Baird, K., McDonald, K. P., & Connolly, J. (2020). Sex trafficking of women and girls in a southern Ontario region: Police file review exploring victim characteristics, trafficking experiences, and the intersection with child welfare. *Canadian Journal of Behavioural Science / Revue Canadienne Des Sciences Du Comportement, 52*(1), 8–17. https://doi.org/10.1037/cbs0000151

Brayley, H., Cockbain, E., & Laycock, G. (2011). The value of crime scripting: Deconstructing internal child se trafficking. *Policing, 5*, 132–143.

Bronfenbrenner, U., & Morris, P. (1998). The ecology of developmental processes. In W. Damon & R. Lerner (Eds.), *Handbook of child psychology* (Theories of development) (Vol. 4, pp. 999–1058). Wiley.

Butler, L., & Wilson, B. (2013). Running a gauntlet: A review of victimization and violence in the pre-entry, post-entry, and peri-/post-exit periods of commercial sexual exploitation. *Psychological Trauma: Theory, Research, Practice, and Policy, 5*(4), 1–11. https://doi.org/10.1037/a0032977

Carael, M., Slaymaker, E., Lyerla, R., & Sarkar, S. (2006). Clients of sex workers in different regions of the world: Hard to count. *Sexually Transmitted Infections, 82*(Suppl 3), iii26–iii33. https://doi.org/10.1136/sti.2006.021196

Cecchet, S. J., & Thoburn, J. (2014). The psychological experience of child and adolescent sex trafficking in the United States: Trauma and resilience in survivors. *Psychological Trauma: Theory, Research, Practice, and Policy, 6*(5), 482–493. https://doi.org/10.1037/a0035763

Centers for Disease Control and Prevention (CDC). (2020). *Human trafficking in the wake of a disaster*. https://www.cdc.gov/disasters/human_trafficking_info_for_shelters.html.

Cole, J., & Sprang, G. (2015). Sex trafficking of minors in metropolitan, micropolitan, and rural communities. *Child Abuse & Neglect, 40*, 113–123.

Coyle, S. (2014). Intergenerational trauma—Legacies of loss. *Social Work Today, 14*(3), 18. https://www.socialworktoday.com/archive/051214p18.shtml

Dahal, P., Joshi, S. K., & Swahnberg, K. (2015). 'We are looked down upon and rejected socially': A qualitative study on the experiences of trafficking survivors in Nepal. *Global Health Action, 8*, 29267–29267. https://doi.org/10.3402/gha.v8.29267

Deshpande, N., & Nour, N. (2013). Sex trafficking of women and girls. *Reviews in Obstetrics and Gynecology, 6*(1), 22–27. https://doi.org/10.3909/riog0214

Dovydaitis, T. (2010). Human trafficking: The role of the health care provider. *Journal of Midwifery & Women's Health, 55*(5), 462–467. https://doi.org/10.1016/j.jmwh.2009.12.017

Feehs & Currier. (2019). Federal Human Trafficking Report, Human Trafficking Institute 2020.

Felthous, A. R., & Ko, J. (2018). Sexually violent predator law in the United States. *East Asian Archives of Psychiatry, 28*(4), 159–173. https://doi.org/10.12809/eaap1835

Franchino-Olsen, H., Chesworth, B., Boyle, C., Rizo, C., Martin, S., Jordan, B., Macy, R., & Stevens, L. (2020a). The prevalence of sex trafficking of children and adolescents in the United States: a scoping review. *Trauma Violence & Abuse*. https://doi.org/10.1177/152483020933873

Franchino-Olsen, H., Silverstein, H. A., Kahn, N. F., & Martin, S. L. (2020b). Minor sex-trafficking of girls with disabilities. *International Journal of Human Rights in Healthcare, 13*(2), 97–108. Publisher: Emerald Publishing.

Goldberg, A., & Moore, J. (2028). Domestic minor sex trafficking. *Child and Adolescent Psychiatric Clinics 27*(1), 77–92.

Hadjiyanni, T., Povlitzki, M., & Preble, H. (2014). The placeness of sex trafficking-instilling consciousness through Minnesota's experience. *Journal of Interior Design, 39*(1), 1–16.

Harrell, E. (2017). *Crimes against persons with disabilities*. Bureau of Justice Statistics. https://www.bjs.gov/content/pub/pdf/capd0915st.pdf

Hughes, D. M. (2004). *Best practices to address the demand side of sex trafficking*. U.S. Department of State. https://www.popcenter.org/sites/default/files/problems/trafficked_women/PDFs/Hughes_2004a.pdf.
Hughes, D. M., & Denisova, T. A. (2001). The transnational political criminal nexus of trafficking in women from Ukraine. *Trends in Organized Crime, 6*(3/4), 43–67. https://doi.org/10.1007/s12117-001-1005-7
International Labour Office. (2017). *Global estimates of modern slavery: Forced labour and forced marriage*. International Labour Office (ILO).
Jakobsson, N., & Kotsadam, A. (2013). The law and economics of international sex slavery: Prostitution laws and trafficking for sexual exploitation. *European Journal of Law and Economics, 35*(1), 87–107. https://doi.org/10.1007/s10657-011-9232-0
Jones, J. (2022, February 19). LGBT. Identification in the U.S. Ticks Up to 7.1%. *Gallup*. https://news.gallup.com/poll/389792/lgbt-identification-ticks-up.aspx
Jones, L., Engstrom, D., Hilliard, P., & Sungakawan, D. (2011). Human trafficking between Thailand and Japan: Lessons in recruitment, transit and control. *International Journal of Social Welfare, 20*(2), 203–211. https://doi.org/10.1111/j.1468-2397.2009.00669.x
Kara, S. (2017). *Sex trafficking: Inside the business of modern slavery*. Columbia University Press.
Kelly, C. (2019, July 30). 13 sex trafficking statistics that explain the enormity of the global sex trade. *USA Today*. https://www.usatoday.com/story/news/investigations/2019/07/12-trafficking-statistics-enormity-global-sex-trade/1755192001/
Levy, A. R. (2018). *Federal Human Trafficking Civil Litigation: 15 years of the private right of action*. The Human Trafficking Legal Center. https://www.htlegalcenter.org/wp-content/uploads/Federal-Human-Trafficking-Civil-Litigation-1.pdf
Malarek, V. (2011). *The johns: Sex for sale and the men who buy it*. Arcade Pub.
Milrod, C., & Monto, M. (2012). The hobbyist and the girlfriend experience: Behaviors and preferences of male customers of internet sexual services providers. *Deviant Behavior, 33*, 792–810. https://doi.org/10.1080/01639625.2012.707502
Milrod, C., & Monto, M. (2017). Older male clients of female sex workers in the United States. *Archives of Sexual Behavior, 46*(6), 1867–1876. https://doi.org/10.1007/s10508-016-0733-3
Milrod, C., & Weitzer, R. (2012). The intimacy prism: Emotion management among the clients of escorts. *Men & Masculinities, 15*(5), 447–467.
Morris, M. (2017). Poverty and disability in America matter. *HuffPost*. Retrieved from: https://www.huffpost.com/entry/poverty-and-disability-in_b_9557142
Morton, M. H., Samuels, G. M., Dworsky, A., & Patel, S. (2018). *Missed opportunities: LGBTQ youth homelessness in America*. Chapin Hall at the University of Chicago.
Murphy, L. T. (2016). *Labor and sex trafficking among homeless youth: A ten-city study full report*. Retrieved from https://oag.ca.gov/sites/all/files/agweb/pdfs/ht/murphy-labor-sex-trafficking-homeless-youth.pdf.
National Gang Center. (2020). *Gangs and human trafficking*. Retrieved from https://nationalgangcenter.ojp.gov/insights/47/gangs-and-human-trafficking
National Human Trafficking Hotline. (2020). *The traffickers*. Retrieved from https://humantraffickinghotline.org/what-human-trafficking/human-trafficking/traffickers
Parillo, V. (2012). *Strangers to these shores* (10th ed.). Pearson Education, Inc..
Pitts, M. K., Smith, A. M. A., Grierson, J., O'Brien, M., & Misson, S. (2004). Who pays for sex and why? An analysis of social and motivational factors associated with male clients of sex workers. *Archives of Sexual Behavior, 33*(4), 353–358. https://doi.org/10.1023/B:ASEB.0000028888.48796.4f
Polaris Project. (2021). *Myths, facts, and statistics*. Retrieved from https://polarisproject.org/myths-facts-and-statistics/
Ream, G. L., & Forge, N. (2014). Homeless lesbian, gay, bisexual and transgender (LGBT) youth in New York City: Insights from the field. *Child Welfare, 93*(2), 7–22.

Reid, J. A. (2018). Sex trafficking of girls with intellectual disabilities: An exploratory mixed methods study sexual abuse. *Journal of Research and Treatment, 30*(2), 107–131. Publisher: Sage Publications.

Rosenblatt, K. (2014). Determining the vulnerability factors, lures, and recruitment methods used to entrap American children into sex trafficking. *Sociology and Criminology-Open Access, 2*, 1. https://doi.org/10.4172/2375-4435.1000108

Rössel, J. (2013). *Conflict theory*. Oxford Bibliographies in Sociology. https://doi.org/10.1093/OBO/9780199756384-0035

Rothman, K. J. (2012). *Epidemiology: An introduction* (2nd ed.). Oxford University Press.

Roza, P. (2013). Human trafficking: An issue of human and national security. *University of Miami National Security & Armed Conflict Law Review, 29*.

Silverman, J. G., Decker, M. R., Gupta, J., Maheshwari, A., Patel, V., Willis, B. M., & Raj, A. (2007). Experiences of sex trafficking victims in Mumbai, India. *International Journal of Gynecology & Obstetrics, 97*(3), 221–226. https://doi.org/10.1016/j.ijgo.2006.12.003

Tidball, S., Zheng, M., & Creswell, J. W. (2016). Buying sex on-line from girls: ngo representatives, law enforcement officials, and public officials speak out about human trafficking-a qualitative analysis. *Gender Issues, 33*(1), 53–68. https://doi.org/10.1007/s12147-015-9146-1

United Nations Office on Drugs and Crime. (2018). *United nations convention against transnational organized crime and the protocols thereto*. United Nations Office on Drugs and Crime. https://www.unodc.org/unodc/en/organized-crime/intro/UNTOC.html

United Nations Office on Drugs and Crime (UNODC). (2014). Global report on trafficking in persons. *United Nations Office on Drugs and Crime, Vienna*, 1–85. https://www.unodc.org/documents/data-and-analysis/glotip/GLOTIP_2014_full_report.pdf

United States. (2000). *Victims of trafficking and violence act of 2000*.

United States Census Bureau. (2022). Household Pulse Survey.

United States Department of State (USDS). (2022). *Trafficking in persons report*. https://www.state.gov/wp-content/uploads/2022/08/22-00757-TIP-REPORT_072822-inaccessible.pdf

Wheaton, E. M., Schauer, E. J., & Galli, T. V. (2010). Economics of human trafficking. *International Migration, 48*(4), 114–141. https://doi.org/10.1111/j.1468-2435.2009.00592.x

Zakhari, B. (2005). Legal cases prosecuted under the victims of trafficking and violence protection act of 2000. In S. Stoecker & L. Shelley (Eds.), *Human traffic and transnational crime: Eurasian and American perspectives*. Lanham.

Chapter 16
Neurodevelopmental Disorders and Sexual Offending

Melanie Clark Mogavero, Amanda Fenrich, Ragini Patel, and Samantha Etzi

16.1 Introduction

Sexual offending behavior is a serious social concern in which there has been increased attention towards specific treatment for those who commit such acts. Sexual offenses include a broad range of behaviors from non-contact offenses (e.g., exposing genitals in public, soliciting minors, indecent images of minors) to contact offenses (e.g., sexual assault, touching others sexually), against victims of various ages. The term, sexual offender (SO) is a broad-based term that refers to a heterogeneous group that engages in a broad spectrum of sexual offenses against adults and minors (Simons, 2015). Some who commit sexual offenses have various neurodevelopmental disorders (NDDs) in which standard evidence-based treatment practices may not be applicable or effective in reducing sexual offending behavior. Authors of this chapter specifically focus on sexual offending and treatment of adult male offenders with NDDs, specifically intellectual developmental disorder (ID) and autism spectrum disorder (ASD). Although females sexually offend, they account for less than 3.5% of sexual offenses (United States Department of Justice, 2018). A diagnosis of ASD or ID does not increase the risk of committing a sexual-related offense (Lindsay et al., 2014; O'Brien et al., 2010) and offending

M. C. Mogavero (✉)
Department of Crime and Justice Studies, Georgian Court University, Lakewood, NJ, USA
e-mail: mmogavero@georgian.edu

A. Fenrich
Graduate School of Arts and Sciences, Purdue University Global, West Lafayette, IN, USA

R. Patel
London, UK

S. Etzi
Graduate School of Social Work, University of Pittsburgh, Pittsburgh, PA, USA

R. J. Tully et al. (eds.), *Best Practices in Sexual Offender Assessment and Management*, Dangerous Behavior in Clinical and Forensic Psychology,
https://doi.org/10.1007/978-3-031-83135-5_16

behavior, in general, is rare among those with ID (Cantor et al., 2005) and ASD (Mouridsen, 2012; Scragg & Shah, 1994; Woodbury-Smith et al., 2006). As with any condition that questions *mens rea* or criminal intent, one must examine whether characteristics of said condition are directly or indirectly related to those who commit such offenses to mitigate Criminal Justice System (CJS) sanctions and how they should be handled in the CJS and mental health system.

This chapter provides a comprehensive overview of sexual offending behaviors exhibited among those with NDDs. The chapter begins with a summary of the definitions of ID and ASD to demonstrate how the terminology has changed over time and to clear any confusion with previous terminology. Authors provide prevalence rates of ID and ASD in the general population, CJS or mental health populations to highlight the scope of problematic sexual behavior among those with NDDs.

Authors reviewed the empirical research of sexual offending behaviors among those with ID and/or ASD and provide evidence-based best practices, which include risk assessments commonly used, theoretical frameworks, clinical intervention recommendations, and other considerations for sexual offending behaviors. Authors provide a range of case studies based on real-life examples to demonstrate the sexual offending behaviors those with ASD and/or ID engage in, the adaptations necessary for them to address their risk factors, and any other challenges they may present in the community, in correctional settings, or forensic mental health settings.

16.2 Defining Neurodevelopmental Disorders

NDDs were introduced as an umbrella category in the fifth edition of the Diagnostic and Statistical Manual of Mental Disorders (DSM-5) published by the American Psychiatric Association (APA) in 2013 and in the eleventh edition of the International Classification of Diseases and Related Health Problems (ICD) first published by the World Health Organization (WHO) in 2018. The DSM-5 Text Revision (DSM-5-TR) published in 2022 and the 2022 version of the ICD-11 are the current versions of the diagnostic manuals. NDDs are disabilities primarily associated with the functioning of the neurological system and the brain with an onset during a child's developmental period (APA, 2022; WHO, 2018/2022). NDD's encompass a wide range of disorders that effect one's development, communication, and present general deficits in functioning. Examples of NDDs include ASD, ID, attention-deficit/hyperactivity disorder (ADHD), specific learning disabilities, communication and speech disorders, conduct disorders, cerebral palsy, and vision and hearing disabilities (APA, 2022; WHO, 2018/2022). This chapter focuses on sexual offending behavior and treatments among two prevalent NDDs in the research, ID and ASD.

16.2.1 *Intellectual Disability: Evolution of Terminology*

Intelligence and cognitive ability (mostly children's) have been measured since the early twentieth century. In 1905, Binet and Simon created the first standardized test to measure one's intellect and used the intelligence quotient (IQ) to diagnose conditions related to intelligence officially. In 1948, the WHO added the condition "mental deficiency" to the sixth edition of the ICD (WHO, 1948). The APA published the first DSM, in 1952, which also recognized this condition as "mental deficiency" (APA, 1952). Clinicians in the United States (US) and North America use the DSM, and most countries outside North America use the ICD to diagnose various mental and cognitive disabilities.

A variety of terms describing cognitive deficits throughout history includes developmental disability, mental handicap, mental deficiency, mental retardation, cognitive disability, and intellectual disability. The specific terms used differ according to geographical region and time period. Due to the change in the political and social views over the last decade, mental retardation, the previous diagnostic term, was replaced with intellectual disability (ID). ID became the preferred term by various professionals, the lay public, and advocacy groups prior to the APA making the change official in the DSM-5 in 2013. On October 5, 2010, US President Barack Obama signed *S. 2781,* known as Rosa's Law, which amended several Federal Acts and required the terms "mental retardation" and "mentally retarded" to be removed from federal use.

There have also been significant progressions in the terminology, placement of the condition in the ICD and DSM, and the classification of defining characteristics of diagnosing one with ID, including terms to indicate the degree of severity based on IQ scores. The DSM-1 (1952) included levels ranging from mild (.Q 70–85) to severe (IQ under 50), with additional labels for those with scores under 50. In 1965, the WHO replaced the term "mental deficiency" with "mental retardation" in the ICD-8, and in 1968, the APA made this change in the DSM-II with the same IQ ranges. IQ scores for severity ranges (APA, 1968; WHO, 1967). "Mental retardation" was removed when the APA published the DSM-5 in 2013, and when the WHO published the first ICD-11 in 2018 (APA, 2013; WHO, 2018/2022). The current diagnosis in the DSM-5-TR is Intellectual Developmental Disorder (Intellectual Disability, ID) and Disorder of Intellectual Development (DID) in the ICD-11 (APA, 2022; WHO, 2018/2022). Both the DSM-5-TR and the ICD-11 still determine cognitive ability and diagnose using IQ scores; however, adaptive functioning is now used to determine the severity of ID (i.e., mild, moderate, severe, and profound).

16.2.1.1 Diagnostic Criteria for Intellectual Disability

Although both the ICD and DSM are authoritative guides for professionals, the DSM is specific to mental health conditions and, therefore, the authors list diagnostic criteria from DSM. According to the DSM-5-TR, clinicians diagnose a person with ID using both clinical assessment and standardized tests. To receive the diagnosis, one must demonstrate deficits in intellectual functioning (e.g., reasoning, problem-solving, planning, abstract thinking, judgment, academic learning, and learning from experience). Clinicians also confirm the diagnosis when an individual demonstrates deficits in adaptive functioning or the failure to meet developmental and sociocultural standards for personal independence and social responsibility (e.g., communication, social participation, independent living) across multiple environments (e.g., home, school, community). The onset of intellectual and adaptive deficits occurs during childhood or adolescence (APA, 2022).

16.2.2 Autism Spectrum Disorder: Evolution of Terminology

ASD was not formally recognized as a diagnosis until the APA published the DSM-5 in 2013. This diagnostic term evolved over decades before recognizing autism as a spectrum of symptoms or characteristics. In the DSM-II, this condition was referred to as schizophrenia reaction, childhood type (APA, 1952). The WHO added infantile autism to the ICD-8 in 1967 and was also listed as a subtype of schizophrenia (WHO, 1967). Infantile autism was recognized as a separate diagnosis in 1980 when the APA published the DSM-III, but under the umbrella term, pervasive development disorders (PDD). In 1987, the revised DSM-III-TR replaced infantile autism with autism disorder (AD). The DSM-III-TR included a broader and mild diagnosis of pervasive developmental disorder-not otherwise specified (PDD-NOS) for children who presented characteristics and showed significant impairments but did not meet the full diagnostic criteria of AD (APA, 1987).

In 1994, the APA added Asperger's syndrome (AS) to the DSM-IV (APA, 1994) as another PDD. The DSM-IV (1994) and the DSM-IV-TR (2000) were the first editions to categorize AD as a spectrum with varying functioning levels with or without ID. AS and AD share many diagnostic features but individuals with AS are of average to above-average intelligence. They do not have a significant delay in language, cognitive development, or self-help skills. Children with AS have adequate grammar and vocabulary but may exhibit an inappropriate use of speech and may respond inappropriately in conversations (APA, 2000). The APA recognized that AS, AS, and PDD-NOS were a spectrum the same condition. With the reclassification of the PDD, ASD, AD, AS, and PDD-NOS were removed from the DSM and ICD and both diagnostic manuals use the term ASD (APA, 2022; WHO, 2018/2022).

16.2.2.1 Diagnostic Criteria for Autism Spectrum Disorder

ASD is characterized by two groups of features: (1) persistent impairment in reciprocal social communication and social interaction and (2) restricted, repetitive patterns of behavior, both present in early childhood (APA, 2022). Both areas are described by one of three severity levels indicated by levels of required support. The social communication and social interaction deficits include (1) lack of social-emotional reciprocity (e.g., failure to initiate or respond to social interactions), (2) nonverbal communication (e.g., abnormalities in eye contact and nonverbal communication), and (3) developing, maintaining, and understanding relationships (e.g., difficulty adjusting behavior to various social contexts; APA, 2022). The restricted, repetitive patterns of behavior, interests, or activities include, (1) insistence on sameness, inflexible adherence to routines, or ritualized patterns of behavior, (2) highly restricted, fixated interests that are abnormal in intensity or focus (e.g., strong attachment to or preoccupation with unusual objects, and (3) hyper- or hypo-reactivity to sensory input or unusual interests in sensory aspects of the environment (e.g., excessive smelling or touching of objects; APA, 2022). Individuals are given a diagnosis of ASD with or without ID.

16.3 Prevalence Rates

The prevalence rates of children and adults with ASD and ID in the general population vary by country and region (McKenzie et al., 2016). Prevalence rates for NDDs are difficult to establish, due to the heterogeneity of study settings, methodologies, age groups included, definitions and diagnostic criteria used (i.e., ICD or DSM), changes to diagnostic criteria, accessibility to diagnostic services, and motivation to be assessed given potential social and economic implications. The following section provides an overview of research that estimated the prevalence rates of NDDs in the general and forensic populations.

16.3.1 Intellectual Disability

The APA (2022) estimates that approximately 1% of the overall general population have ID. Two meta-analyses of studies across North America, Europe, Australia, and Asia published between 1980 and 2009 (Maulik et al., 2011) and between 2010 and 2015 (McKenzie et al., 2016) supported this 1% estimate. Maulik et al. (2011) revealed a prevalence rate of 1.37% from their meta-analysis of 52 studies. McKenzie et al. (2016) provided a more conservative range of estimated prevalence of 0.05 to 1.55% from a systematic review of 20 studies (McKenzie et al., 2016). The APA also noted that ID is more commonly diagnosed in males, both mild forms (1.6 to 1 ratio) and severe forms (1.2 to 1 ratio; APA, 2022).

Similar prevalence rates of ID were found in CJSs worldwide. Fazel et al. (2008) conducted a systematic review of a total sample of 12,000 inmates across five regions (Australia, Dubai, New Zealand, United Kingdom, United States) and found between 0.5%–1.5% of prisoners had ID. The results were consistent with the proportions found in the general population for the same age-group and, therefore, one can reasonably conclude that offenders with ID are not overrepresented in the CJS. However, those with other NDD's or cognitive disabilities appear to be overrepresented in the CJS. According to the most recent report published by the United States Department of Justice, Bureau of Justice Statistics (BJS; 2018), approximately 19.5% of those in prison have a cognitive disability (which includes ID and other NDDs). In this report, BJS found that these rates are higher among those in jail, with more than 30% having a cognitive disability (Bronson & Berzofsky, 2015).

Several researchers have attempted to measure prevalence rates of ID among those who have committed sexual offenses to determine whether sexually inappropriate behavior is more common. An early review of the literature by Murphy et al. (1983) revealed a prevalence rate of 10–15% of the ID population had committed a sexual offense. Ward et al. (2001) surveyed 243 community service agencies that served a total of 17,767 people with ID or other developmental disabilities, of which, 914 (5%) engaged in sexually inappropriate or sexual offending behavior, and of those, only 194 (15%) had ever been incarcerated. O'Brien et al. (2010) reviewed the records of 477 individuals with learning disabilities referred to forensic treatment facilities throughout the UK of which, 314 (66%) had ID or borderline ID (n = 80, 17%). More recently, Ray et al. (2019) estimated the prevalence in forensic psychiatric populations to be 9.2%.

16.3.2 Autism Spectrum Disorder

Elsabbagh et al. (2012) conducted a systematic review of epidemiological surveys and estimated the global prevalence of ASD is 62/10,000 or about 0.62%. The Center for Disease Control and Prevention (CDC) indicates a prevalence between 1–2% of the population in North America, Europe, and Asia (CDC, n.d.). The APA (2022) estimates that approximately 1% of the general population is diagnosed with ASD; males are more likely than females (4:1 ratio) to be diagnosed with ASD.

The data collected by Bronson and Berzofsky (2015) on disabilities among incarcerated individuals are aggregated, so the number of those with ASD counted in the cognitive disability statistics is unknown. To date, there are no comprehensive U.S. studies to estimate the percentage of incarcerated individuals with an official ASD diagnosis. Fazel et al. (2008) assessed the prevalence of possible ASD in one maximum-security prison in the U.S. and estimated 4.4% have a possible diagnosis of ASD. A similar study in the U.K. found that the prevalence of those incarcerated with possible ASD was similar to the general population (Underwood et al., 2016).

Several researchers examined the prevalence of ASD in forensic mental health populations, and rates varied from 1.4% (Søndenaa et al., 2014), 2.3%–2.4% (Hare et al., 1999; Scragg & Shah, 1994), 10% (Lindsay et al., 2014), 13% (Anckarsäter et al., 2008), to as high as 12–15%, (Siponmaa et al., 2001). Based on this data, one can reasonably conclude that individuals with ASD are overrepresented in the CJS. There is some evidence that those with ASD may be overrepresented among those who commit sexual offenses. Sutton et al. (2012) conducted a pilot study of 37 adolescent males adjudicated for sexual offenses and revealed that 60% met the diagnostic criteria for ASD. Hart-Kerkhoffs et al. (2009) compared a sample of 175 juveniles who have committed sexual offenses to age-matched control samples of 91 individuals with ASD and 500 non-offending peers without ASD. After screening all three groups for ASD, Hart-Kerkhoffs et al. (2009) found juveniles who have committed sexual offenses had more ASD characteristics than the non-offending control group. The exact reasons why people with ASD are overrepresented in the CJS remains unknown, but such reasons may include the possibility of being more likely to be apprehended than those without ASD; more research is necessary.

16.4 Inappropriate Sexual Behavior and Sexual Offending

The social and communication deficits among those with NDDs may result in some unknowingly engaging in inappropriate or illegal sexual behavior, particularly when pursuing romantic interests. Such behaviors could result in formal accusations, which may involve the criminal justice system. Although no direct association exists between individuals with NDD and criminal sexual behavior, harassment, stalking, such behaviors may be the result of the social and communication deficits associated with NDDs (Mogavero, 2016).

16.4.1 Harassment and Stalking

According to the United States Department of Justice Office on Violence Against Women (USDOJ OVW), stalking refers to a "course of conduct directed at a specific person that would cause a reasonable person to fear for his or her safety or the safety of others or suffer substantial emotional distress" (n.d.). Mullen et al. (1999) examined the records of 145 patients in a psychiatric hospital with stalking in their criminal "incompetent stalker." "Incompetent stalkers" sought to establish relationships but displayed loneliness, a lack of social competence, and obsessional characteristics (Mullen et al., 1999). MacKenzie et al. (2010) examined a sample of 160 stalkers using Mullen et al.'s (1999) types and noted the incompetent type had the lowest IQ scores among the sample.

Research on dating and courtship behaviors among those with ASD have noted "stalking-type" behaviors. Stokes et al. (2007) revealed that those with ASD continued to pursue a person of interest when the person of interest did not respond or rejected them longer than their typically developed (TD) peers. Stokes and Kaur

(2005) and Stokes and Newton (2004) used parental reports to compare adolescents and adults with ASD and their TD peers to understand differences in romantic behaviors and revealed that those with ASD were more likely to engage in inappropriate courting behaviors, including touching the person of interest inappropriately, making inappropriate comments, or "stalking" behaviors (e.g., monitoring activities, following, making threats). Mogavero and Hsu (2020) compared individuals with and without ASD and found that those with ASD had more social impairments with romantic relationships, less knowledge about initiating romantic relationships, and engaged in more "stalking-type" behaviors while pursuing romantic interests.

Inappropriate courtship behaviors with others have been self-reported among those with ASD, which has led to contacts with police (Mogavero & Hsu, 2020; Stokes et al., 2007). In a literature review, Mogavero (2016) linked many deviant courtships and sexual behaviors to the social and communication deficits commonly associated with ASD and noted that many had no malicious intent. Naiveté about sexual behavior and pursuing sexual relationships may lead to inappropriate behaviors. For example, Mehzabin & Stokes (2011) reported among a sample with ASD that they learned about sex by "making mistakes." Awareness of an offender's diagnosis has implications on how they are handled in the CJS, as this may influence other's perceptions of the offender's ability to form intent. Mogavero and Hsu (2018) revealed that those who were aware of one's ASD diagnosis, they were less inclined to agree to harsher punishments for stalking behaviors, regardless of their level knowledge of ASD.

Cantor et al. (2004) examined the records of 473 male patients where 24% had engaged in inappropriate courtship behaviors, which included voyeuristic behaviors, exposing themselves, and making obscene phone calls. Of the inappropriate courtship behaviors, stalking is not particularly common among those with ID. O'Brien et al. (2010) reviewed the records of 477 individuals with learning disabilities referred to forensic treatment facilities throughout the UK of which, 314 (66%) had ID or borderline ID. Of the 477 cases, stalking was the least common crime against a person, with only nine individuals (2%) having this offense in their records.

16.4.1.1 Case 1: Stalking and Criminal Sexual Contact

Johnson[1] is a 65-year-old African American male with a diagnosis of ID. He stalked a woman (stranger) for several weeks. He followed her in a park, approached her, forced her against a tree, and touched her breasts. He pleaded guilty and was convicted of Indecent Liberties with Forcible Compulsion and was sentenced to a prison term of 3 years. Johnson has an extensive criminal history of stalking

[1] Note: case studies incorporate the descriptions of actual cases of men who have committed sexual offenses. All identifying information has been changed to protect the anonymity of these individuals. Some case details have been omitted and the specific countries or states of these cases were not specified for additional privacy.

behavior and admitted that following women was something that he found pleasurable. Due to his low intellect and cognitive disabilities, he stated that he did not know that following (i.e., stalking) at the time of his arrest or that touching women's breasts without their consent was illegal.

Johnson's treatment program included addressing appropriate physical and sexual boundaries and the concept of consent. He required adapted treatment assignments and activities to understand his risk and interventions due to his lower intellect. He practiced role-plays around stalking behaviors and learned how to develop healthy relationships. Even though he was eventually able to verbally explain how his behaviors increased his risk of sexually re-offending, he will require continued treatment in the community to reinforce the skills he learned in SO treatment continuously.

16.4.2 Child Molestation and Solicitation of Minors

Those who are socially and emotionally delayed may gravitate towards minors which places them at risk of committing statutory offenses or other sexual offenses. The link between sexual interest in minors and low IQ has been well-documented in the research (Cantor et al., 2005; O'Brien et al., 2010). O'Brien et al. (2010) clearly states that low cognitive functioning does not cause a sexual interest in children, but deviant sexual interest is correlated with low cognitive functioning. Those with ASD are often years behind their TD peers in their social and emotional development, and many adults with ASD are emotionally or developmentally "trapped" in adolescence (Attwood et al., 2014; Mahoney, 2009). The social and communication deficits inherent in ASD have led to more anxiety in meeting potential dating partners (Hancock et al., 2020); however, the internet has provided a means to avoid these anxieties (Roth & Gillis, 2015). The increase in the use of the internet to meet potential dating or sexual partners, combined with delayed maturity, could place those with ASD at risk for meeting minors online and face various legal consequences.

Ward et al. (2001) reported among their sample with ID that sexual offenses involving minors were reported by nearly half the respondents (42.6%), and such offenses included solicitation of minors, viewing child pornography, and child molestation. Rice et al. (2008) compared 69 SOs with ID and 69 offenders with average intelligence and revealed that those with ID had a greater sexual preference towards prepubescent children. Cantor et al. (2005) conducted a large meta-analysis comparing IQ scores and various types of SOs to non-offenders and found that child SOs, particularly with victims under the age of 12, had lower IQs than both adult SOs and non-offenders. Cantor et al. (2004) compared cognitive ability among pedophiles (sexual interest in prepubescent children), hebephiles (sexual interest in pubescent children; see Glueck, 1955), and teleiophiles (sexual interest in adults; see Blanchard et al., 2000) found that the pedophilia group scored the lowest and the association between poor brain functioning and a sexual interest in prepubescent children was associated with lower IQ (Cantor et al., 2004).

16.4.2.1 Case 2: Soliciting Minor

Jake is a Caucasian male in his mid-20 s who began emailing whom he thought was a 14-year-old girl after posting an ad online. Unbeknownst to Jake, he was emailing an undercover officer as part of a sting operation. Jake's email conversations with the "girl" were sexual in nature, and he later sent explicit images of himself. According to the email conversations, Jake was aware of the "girl's" age and was aware of potential consequences. He and the "girl" arranged to meet for sex, and he was arrested at the agreed location. Jake was charged with several offenses, including attempted involuntary indecent sexual intercourse, and attempted statutory sexual assault, among other charges. Jake reluctantly entered a plea deal with the prosecutor and pleaded guilty to two misdemeanors. Jake was also required to register as a SO.

Jake underwent a psychological evaluation due to the nature of the offense. On intelligence tests, he scored well above average but scored extremely low in various memory tests. He showed many of the ASD criteria (e.g., deficits in emotional reciprocity, initiating social interactions, developing/maintaining relationships, social awkwardness, repetitive patterns of behavior/interests), and was diagnosed with possible ASD.[2] He was also diagnosed with two learning disorders, Unspecified Neurodevelopmental Disorder, and Unspecified Obsessive-Compulsive Disorder. The clinician noted that he had various addictive and compulsive tendencies, particularly regarding internet use. After his arrest, he began participating in therapy where the clinician focused on motivation, relationships, responsibility, obsessive-compulsive disorder, and addictive behaviors. Jake's clinician noted he had dependent, "people-pleasing" personality traits and underlying addiction-like behavior patterns involving sex. His treatment goals focused on reducing his need to gain approval from others, increase his self-image, and increase his assertiveness. Jake also participated in group therapy sessions to practice assertiveness.

16.4.3 Indecent Images of Minors

Legal problems develop when those with ID or ASD, due to their cognitive deficits or a comorbidity, unknowingly or unintentionally view indecent images of minors. Alley et al. (2019) highlighted several legal cases of individuals with ASD charged with indecent images of children related offenses to demonstrate how ASD characteristics were presented during legal arguments and how they impacted legal liability. Some are naïve about the content on the internet as well as its availability. Some individuals with ASD reported they believed that internet search engines would not allow anything illegal (Payne et al., 2020) or that police would not let such material

[2] Autism is reliably diagnosed in childhood and is more difficult to diagnosis in adults. See https://www.nimh.nih.gov/health/topics/autism-spectrum-disorders-asd/index.shtml.

be available (personal communication, M. Mahoney, November 16, 2017). Others may be unaware that the children in the images are being harmed or are even victims (Attwood et al., 2014). Woodbury-Smith et al. (2005) revealed that some adults with ASD had an impaired ability to recognize emotional facial expressions and explained how this might explain the inability to perceive children in the indecent images as victims.

The legality of pornography depends on the age of the individual portrayed in the image. Due to the social and emotional developmental delays, adults with ASD may see prepubescent children or adolescents as peers (Attwood et al., 2014). Those with ASD and/or ID must be able to determine the age of the individual portrayed in the image despite the aforementioned delays to avoid committing a crime. This becomes difficult when pornographic images often portray adult women to look much younger and depicting prepubescent girls to look much older (Mahoney, 2009). Steel (2015) emphasized that the ASD diagnosis alone, especially when the diagnosis was post-indictment, should not be used to excuse criminal behavior. Alley et al. (2019) noted the importance of determining criminal liability and the appropriateness of sentences for individuals with ASD convicted of indecent images of children related offences.

For those with NDDs, including ID or ASD, viewing indecent images of minors may not be due to a sexual interest in minors. If those with ID and/or ASD exhibit compulsive behaviors, downloading indecent images may become a compulsion, not necessarily for sexual gratification or sexual interest in minors. Because individuals with ASD have a propensity for repetitive and ritualized activities, it is possible that pornography or other sexual behaviors could become one of their narrow interests or activities (Brown et al., 2018; Mesibov & Sreckovic, 2017).

16.4.3.1 Case 3: Indecent Images of Minors

Anthony is a Caucasian male in his early 50s who was diagnosed with ASD in middle adulthood. Several years before his arrest, he developed compulsive behavior of downloading pirated material on the internet. He began downloading and hoarding music files, progressed to TV shows, movies, images of bands, musicians, actresses, and actors. The downloading of images and movies led him to pornography, which eventually led to indecent images of children. He often found that he was downloading many files simultaneously, often unaware of the content.

Police arrived at Anthony's apartment, responding to an unrelated complaint. While speaking with Anthony, police noticed images on his computer that looked suspicious. After obtaining a search warrant, police seized his computer and found thousands of explicit images of underage girls. Anthony admitted that he had been downloading images for years, but often unaware of the specific content. He was charged with and pleaded guilty to possessing indecent images of children. After his arrest, he received a psychological evaluation where his clinician scored him in the low-risk category. The clinician also described his behavior of downloading indecent images as compulsive, not sexual. The clinician's assessment and evaluation persuaded the court to reduce his SO registration from a level-2 (moderate risk) to a level-1 (low-risk). The clinician also evaluated his sexual interests and concluded that Anthony's sexual interests were consistent with "normal adult heterosexual men." Anthony also denied engaging in any paraphilias, and his sexual fantasies did not include any of the paraphilias. Anthony was sentenced to 10 years of probation, in which the conditions included compliance with treatment and required him to register as a SO. For relapse prevention, his clinician addressed his cognitive distortions and self-defeating thoughts. Currently, Anthony presents no deviant sexual urges, and his treatment focuses on depression, anxiety, and feelings of hopelessness using rational-emotive behavior therapy.

16.4.4 Sexually Inappropriate Touching and Public Lewdness

Although sexual offending behavior among those with ID and ASD are rare, such behaviors have been reported by caregivers and have been found in official records of those in forensic settings. Among samples of males with ID who have committed sexual offenses, the most common offenses were indecent exposure, touching sexually over victim's clothing, and rape or attempted rape (Heaton & Murphy, 2013; Johnson, 2008). Of the 473 patients examined by Cantor et al. (2004), 28% engaged in contact sexual offending behaviors, including various forms of unwanted physical contact. According to the survey by Ward et al. (2001), the most common sexual behaviors in those with ID were inappropriate sexual behaviors in public (e.g., exposure, masturbation; 62.2%) and touching others inappropriately (e.g., touching genitals; 42.6%). Hypersexuality has been reported to play a role in the motivation for committing sexual offenses; however, little research exists on high sex drive and sexual offending (Seto, 2019).

Some individuals with ASD engage in inappropriate sexual behaviors, and some of the more common behaviors reported by parents and caregivers were sexually touching others (Mehzabin & Stokes, 2011; Stokes & Kaur, 2005), exposing their private parts in public, and/or masturbating in public (Hellemans et al., 2007; Nichols & Blakeley-Smith, 2010; Van Bourgondien et al., 1997). Hellemans et al. (2007) interviewed caregivers of 24 individuals with ASD and found that some caregivers were unable to distinguish between consensual and non-consensual touching; it was also noted that none of those who sexually touched others expressed care or concern that the other party consented to be touched. In a follow-up study, Hellemans et al. (2010) compared samples of those with ID and ASD and found that 37% of those with ID and 25% of those with ASD touched others sexually; of those, there were differences regarding emotional reciprocity or consent. Specifically, 80% of those with ASD lacked reciprocity, compared to only 42% of those with ID. This failure to distinguish undesired contact (i.e., consent) is a common feature associated with social skill deficits. In-depth interviews of nine individuals with ASD convicted of sexual offenses reported that social difficulties were factors in their offending (e.g., understanding boundaries, how to approach others appropriately; Payne et al., 2020).

16.4.4.1 Case 5: Burglary with Intent to Commit a Sexual Offense

Allen is a Caucasian male in his early 30 s and was diagnosed with ASD as a child. He was incarcerated for burglary with intent to commit a sexual offense. Allen entered a female neighbor's residence, dragged her into the bedroom, held her down on the bed, and struggled to remove her clothing. A neighbor heard screams, called the police, and police arrived before Allen completed the sexual assault.

Allen's experience with courtship has been limited to communicating via the internet, and he has also been accused of stalking women, which escalated to his index offense. Allen revealed that he had never been in a long-term relationship, and his experience with sexual gratification had been limited to viewing pornography and visiting adult entertainment clubs. Allen's lack of knowledge and his exposure to erotica hindered his awareness of socially appropriate behavior regarding courtship and the ability to initiate relationships. He was not engaged in group treatment and had little insight into his risk factors. He often responds with "I don't know" when asked questions about the motive of his index offense. Allen's clinician learned to accept the "I don't know" responses as Allen may not be able to recall information. His clinician was patient and provided him time to respond to questions at his own pace. Because he lacked participation in the group setting, his clinician added individual sessions where Allen was able to share his thoughts and emotions more comfortably.

16.5 Explanations for Deviant and Criminal Sexual Behavior

Inappropriate or illegal sexual behaviors may be explained by common characteristics of NDDs, such as diminished emotional or social reciprocity, repetitive patterns of behavior and interests, naïveté in courtship and romantic relationships, an inability to grasp social mores with regards to socially appropriate behavior, including diminished social skills to appropriately to handle rejection. Such explanations are not intended to excuse criminal sexual behavior, but to instead, provide a better understanding of intent to determine appropriate interventions.

16.5.1 Diminished Theory of Mind

Clinicians and professionals working in the CJS should consider other explanations when establishing *mens rea* of individuals with ID or ASD. One consideration is whether an individual has a diminished theory of mind (ToM). ToM is a communication deficit associated with developmental and neurological disorders (Leslie, 1992) and refers to the "ability to recognize and understand the thoughts, beliefs, desires, and intention of others" (Attwood, 2007, p. 112). Essentially, ToM deficits inhibit one's ability to recognize that others have thoughts and feelings of their own.

ToM has been described as a core deficit among those with ASD, but research has found that those with ID also have diminished ToM. Leslie (1992) compared ToM tasks among children with ASD, ID, and TD children; it was found that the TD children outperformed both groups, and the ID children outperformed the children with ASD. Yirmiya et al. (1998) conducted a meta-analysis testing ToM among those with ASD, ID, and TD individuals and revealed that the TD individuals outperformed both ASD and ID groups and mixed results when comparing those with ASD and ID. Additionally, authors found that in some ToM tasks, those with ID outperformed those with ASD, and in some tasks, there was no significant difference. Mintah and Parlow (2018) tested Leslie's (1992) ToM model and revealed that autistic traits predicted inappropriate courtship. A diminished ToM predicted whether one perceived another's body language as "flirtatious." An individual with a diminished ToM may engage in inappropriate behavior when they misrepresent or cannot understand others' views and intentions. For example, an individual with ID may perceive a smile as an invitation for sexual contact. Understanding consent may be difficult when a victim did not verbally say "no" but physically resisted during the sexual assault and explaining these concepts to reduce reoffending risk is essential.

16.5.1.1 Case 4: Indecent Exposure and Criminal Sexual Contact

George is a Hispanic adult male with ID and has an extensive criminal history of masturbating in public, dating back to when he was a juvenile. Some of his offending behavior includes becoming sexually aroused at a park after observing a woman in a bikini and masturbating. For his index offense, George was in a park and noticed a woman sitting on a bench. He approached the woman (after exposing his genitals), grabbed her breasts, forced her down on the bench, and kissed her. George pled guilty to criminal sexual contact and was incarcerated. George's intellect and cognitive difficulties made it difficult for him to determine the setting in which a legal behavior (e.g., masturbating) is deemed illegal. At the time of his arrest, George reported that he was unaware that masturbating in public or that touching others without their consent were illegal.

George's inappropriate behavior continued while he was incarcerated. Several female correctional officers lodged complaints regarding inappropriate behavior and statements towards them. George's diminished ToM led him to misinterpret smiles and friendly behavior from female officers as them being romantically interested in him. George's treatment assignment focused on improving problem-solving, appropriate sexual behaviors, including the concept of consent, and misinterpretation of various social cues. George has since learned that masturbating in public and touching others without consent is inappropriate and illegal. Using concrete concepts, repetition, and role-playing exercises, George began to understand that simply because someone is friendly to him does not necessarily mean they want to be touched sexually. Reinforcing socially appropriate sexual behaviors is essential to help reduce the risk that George will, for example, masturbate in public or touch others without consent.

16.5.2 Lack of Sexual Knowledge

Individuals with ASD and ID physically mature, enter puberty and possess similar sexual desires as their typically developed peers (Fawley & Wilson, 2016; Schaafsma et al., 2017; Stokes et al., 2007). Studies have demonstrated that those with ASD experience more difficulties expressing their sexuality appropriately than their TD peers (Dekker et al., 2017; Peterson et al., 2007; Sullivan & Caterino, 2008). These differences can be explained, in part, by the reality that many with ASD do not have the same sexual outlets throughout their development as their TD peers. Similarly, researchers have noted this pattern among those with ID (Hammond & Beail, 2020; Lindsay et al., 1998a, 1998b) and ASD (Konstantareas & Lunsky, 1997). Those with ID desire to have an intimate partner but often struggle due to a lack of knowledge and social skills (Schaafsma et al., 2017). Social and communication deficits tend to result in more social rejection and social isolation that prevent learning opportunities (Attwood et al., 2014; Brown-Lavoie et al. 2014; Mehzabin & Stokes, 2011).

Studies that examined means of learning about sex and romantic relationships showed that fewer individuals with ASD reported they learned from their peers, and those with ASD more often gained knowledge via their own observations in the media (Hancock et al., 2020; Mogavero & Hsu, 2020; Stokes & Kaur, 2005). Few reported having sexual education from parents (Hancock et al., 2020; Mogavero & Hsu, 2020; Stokes & Kaur, 2005), and it has been found that parents of children with ASD often lack the necessary skills and training to provide sufficient sexual education to them (Ballan, 2012; Nichols & Blakeley-Smith, 2010). Ballan (2012) reported that parents of children with ASD did not believe their children should have sexual education, as some believed it was not necessary (will not become sexually active) while others feared sex might become a specialized interest.

To obtain sexual knowledge, some often turn to non-social sources such as television and the internet (Brown-Lavoie et al., 2014), where they may be exposed to inaccurate or inappropriate sexual education. A concern with the increased use of the internet to explore one's sexuality is viewing pornography. Geradin and Thibaut (2004) cautioned that those juveniles exposed to pornography might develop a maladaptive concept of appropriate sexual behavior, which may lead to sexual offending behavior. Similar challenges can arise for those with intellectual or social difficulties. This should not be interpreted as a cause and effect; however, the correlation between pornography and sexual offending has been documented in the systematic review conducted by Mellor and Duff (2019) and should be discussed with clients during treatment.

Professionals working with individualswith ID should explain the harm of viewing or sharing these indecent images with others (Dewson et al., 2018). Clinicians can use this opportunity to address risk and assist the individual in developing interventions should they develop compulsive behavior to view pornography or use pornography inappropriately. Clinicians must explain the risks of sending sexually-explicit images of themselves to others as a form of courtship, as this could have legal consequences if the recipients of the images are minors or if the images are unwanted. Pornography may be used to cope with negative emotions or stress, or clients with ASD and/or ID may use pornography to meet their sexual needs in lieu of developing a healthy relationship.

16.5.3 Paraphilic Disorders

Clinicians typically diagnose individuals with paraphilic disorders in forensic settings, usually after an arrest for a sexually related offense (First, 2014). The DSM-5 contains eight specific paraphilic disorders, divided into three subcategories, courtship disorders, anomalous target disorders, and algolagnic disorders. The courtship disorders resemble distorted components of courtship behavior and include Voyeuristic Disorder (spying on others in private activities), Exhibitionistic Disorder (exposure of genitals to unsuspecting strangers), and Frotteuristic Disorder (touching and rubbing against non-consenting persons). Algolagnic disorders (sexual arousal dependent on pain/suffering) include Sadism (inflicting pain/suffering on others) and Masochism (other inflicting pain/suffering on oneself). Anomalous target disorders illustrate sexual preferences directed elsewhere such as a preference for objects or clothing (Transvestic and Fetishistic Disorder), or persons (Pedophilic Disorder: involving prepubescent children, generally age 13 and younger). Pedophilic and voyeuristic disorders account for the most sexual offenses (APA, 2022). The disorders listed in the DSM-5 do not exhaust the list of possible paraphilic disorders, as clinicians have identified and named dozens of other paraphilic disorders.

16.5.3.1 Counterfeit Deviance

First used by Hingsburger et al. (1991), counterfeit deviance differentiates clinical assessments of individuals with ID or other NDDs. Griffiths et al. (2013) explain that counterfeit deviance occurs when clients exhibit behaviors that appear to meet the DSM diagnostic criteria of a paraphilic disorder, "but served a function that was not related to paraphilia sexual urges or fantasies" (p. 471). Counterfeit deviance's primary concept is that people with ID and other NDDs may engage in inappropriate sexual behavior for reasons other than malice or deviance. The concept of counterfeit deviance does not deny that paraphilic diagnoses exist among persons with disabilities, and some may develop sexualized interests and behavior that meet the diagnostic criteria of a paraphilic disorder (Cantor et al., 2004).

Clinicians, attorneys, and judges should explore whether counterfeit deviance could explain deviant or criminal sexual behaviors. When establishing criminal intent, behaviors may not necessarily be acts of sexual deviance, but due to their characteristics related to their diagnosis, they could be counterfeit deviance. Individuals who exhibit counterfeit deviance may have sexual naiveté, poor social skills, and few chances to develop sexual relationships (Lindsay et al., 2020). Sexual preoccupation is commonly identified as a risk factor for SOs, including those with ID and ASD. Pornography can become one of the preoccupations, or repetitive and fixated interests for someone with ASD, which could present similar problems for those with ID due to their adaptive deficits. For those with cognitive and social impairments consistent with ID and/or ASD, viewing pornography, particularly by those with a sexual offending history, can be a dangerous combination. Clinicians must use caution when applying a paraphilia diagnosis to those with ASD and/or ID (Griffiths et al., 2013). Although the DSM-5 acknowledges that specific individuals may have a decrease in judgment, social skills, or impulse control that may lead to unusual sexual behavior, it does not include a "counterfeit deviance" explanation of said behavior.

16.5.4 Suggestibility and Confabulation

Individuals with ID and/or ASD are particularly vulnerable to suggestibility and confabulation, particularly during police questioning, leading to false or misleading statements (Cloud et al., 2002; Gudjonsson, 1984; North et al., 2008). Interrogative suggestibility, first defined by Gudjonsson and Clark (1986), is 'the extent to which, within a closed social interaction, people come to accept messages communicated during formal questioning, as the result of their subsequent behavioral response is affected' (p. 84). Research has shown that individuals with ID are at increased risk of providing false confessions (National Registry of Exonerations, 2019; Perske, 2011), particularly among those alleged to have committed sexual offenses (Mogavero, 2020).

This increased vulnerability is likely due to controversial police interrogation techniques that use an accusatory style along with coercion and deceit to extract information. In the US, this type of deception is permissible (see Frazier v. Cupp, 1969 and Colorado v. Connelly, 1986). Such techniques can confuse people with ID or ASD into providing misleading statements or false confessions, particularly those who tend to be "concrete-thinkers" (Debbaudt, 2004; Haney-Caron et al., 2018; Redlich et al., 2010).

Statements provided to police can develop into confabulations, a memory processing problem where people unintentionally replace memory gaps with imaginary experiences. Confabulations may include distortions (i.e., major changes) to details of an existing memory, fabrications, a novel memory, or new element to the narrative (Gudjonsson, 2018). Confabulation is often facilitated by imaginational exercises aided by the interrogator, where the suspect converts a statement or admission into a detailed confession with the help of second-hand sources (e.g., crime scene photos, overheard conversations) (Kassin, 2007; Kassin & Kiechel, 1996).

Clinicians are commonly asked to ascertain the reliability of statements made to the police during questioning and to assess whether suspects have any vulnerabilities that may result in inaccurate statements (North et al., 2008). Although clients are encouraged to discuss their criminal histories, clinicians should be mindful of suggestibility and confabulation. Those with ID and ASD also tend to be highly compliant, meaning they are more eager to please and acquiescent, and may simply agree to statements to avoid confrontation or disapproval from others (Kranendonk et al., 2019; North et al. 2008). ASD and ID are "hidden disabilities" meaning that some individuals with ID and/or ASD may present to non-clinicians, in a way that their disability is not identified, and interviewers may be unaware of any limitations concerning communication or comprehension. Although those with ID may have low intellect, they tend to be "streetwise" and can effectively hide their disability, often due to embarrassment or stigma (Kranendonk et al., 2019). Kranendonk et al. (2019) recommend having individuals paraphrase statements back to the interviewer in their own words. If a clinician already has prior knowledge about the offense and asks the client if they engaged in specific behaviors, the client may respond with, "I guess I did" or "if that's what it says." Responses such as this can indicate that clients are not prepared to discuss the details of their offense.

In some cases, clients respond in this manner because they have no memory of the offense and trust the statements of authority (e.g., law enforcement, clinicians), what Gudjonsson and MacKeith (1982) refer to as "memory distrust syndrome." Individuals may agree that something did or did not happen because they want the questioning to end, which may occur in both clinical settings (Brown et al., 2019) and CJS settings (Leo & Davis, 2010). Speaking about sexual offenses can be uncomfortable and may increase anxiety; therefore, by agreeing to the questions, the client or individual may believe they can end the interview sooner. In both clinical and CJS settings, interviewers should avoid leading questions, negatively framing questions, or make any suggestions that the client/suspect repressed memories of the offense, as they can increase suggestibility during the interview (Brown et al., 2019; Leo & Davis, 2010). Proper interviewing techniques should use simple open-ended questions, visual tools, and/or instructions, allow time for a response, and accept "I don't know" as a valid response (Brown et al., 2019; Kranendonk et al., 2019).

16.6 Sexual Offense Recidivism

Researchers have found that individuals with ID commit sexual offenses at a higher rate compared to individuals without (Blasingame, 2016). However, whether they recidivate at a higher rate remains unknown, as re-offending is measured differently in various studies. Lindsay et al. (2002) reviewed records of 62 individuals with ID who committed sexual offenses and revealed that after being discharged from treatment, 4% either sexually re-offended or there was suspicion of a sexual re-offending after 1 year, 13% after 3 years, and 21% after 4 years. McGrath et al. (2007) examined 103 adult males with ID who committed sexual offenses in Vermont and found after a follow-up period of almost 6 years, 10.7% were reconvicted of a sexual offense. These recidivism rates are higher than the general population of of those who committed sexual offenses according to a less conservative definition of recidivism (re-arrest). Alper and Durose (2019) of the BJS tracked incarcerated individuals convicted of sexual offenses in 30 states after their release from prison. They found that only 1.9% were re-arrested for another sexual offense after 1 year, 4.4% after 3 years, 5.1% after 4 years, 6.3% after 6 years, and 7.7% after 9 years.

16.6.1 Assessing Sexual Offense Recidivism Risk

Risk assessment tools predict recidivism risk and are administered at various stages of the CJS. These tools have a significant role in determining treatment needs, appropriate sentences, and appropriate distribution of resources, but have several limitations when administered to those with ID (Johnston, 2002). As the outcome of interest in sexual offending is recidivism, clinicians often consider the tool's predictive validity when deciding on which risk assessment to use. However, few have examined the predictive validity of these assessments when administered with ID and ASD clients. According to Gunasekara and Chaplin (2012), risk assessment tools have been validated for those with mental illnesses such as schizophrenia, but not those with various developmental disorders, including ID or ASD, and the tools were designed with items that assume a level of functioning consistent with those without ID.

16.6.1.1 Actuarial Risk Assessment Tools

The Static-99 and the updated Static-99R (Hanson & Thornton, 2000) were designed to predict sexual and violent recidivism in adult males. Two subsequent versions of the Static-99R have also been developed, the Static-2002 (Hanson & Thornton, 2003) and the Static-2002R (Phenix et al., 2015); however, these will not be addressed in this chapter, as few studies have explored the use of these updated versions with individuals with ID (Baldry et al., 2012) due to the lack of research with ID and ASD samples.

The Static-99/99R is the most frequently employed risk assessment in the U.S. (Archer et al., 2006) and is recommended for those with ID (Stephens et al., 2018). The original samples used to validate the Static-99 included some individuals with ID, but this sub-group was not separately analyzed (Harris et al., 2003). A meta-analysis of 536 findings (from 16 countries) found the Static-99 to be the "best supported" tool (Hanson & Morton-Bourgon, 2009, p. 10) and demonstrated significant predictive validity and large effect sizes in a cumulative meta-analysis on those with ID (Hanson et al., 2013).

The Stable-2007/2007-R is another tool to assess sexual recidivism risk (Fernandez et al., 2014; Hanson et al., 2015) and can identify risk factors in the ID population that the Static-99-R cannot (Delforterie et al., 2019). Delforterie et al. (2019) compared the Static-99-R and Stable-2007 among those with ID to those with above-average IQs and found few significant differences in both static risk factors and the total Static-99-R score. The Stable-2007, however, revealed that those with ID scored significantly higher on the items measuring impulsive acts, problem-solving skills, and concern for others (Delforterie et al., 2019). In contrast, those with above average IQs scored significantly higher on measures of deviant sexual interests. Delforterie et al. (2019) concluded the differences between the two groups might be due to adaptive skills deficits, and the elevated scores on "lack of concern for others" may be due to lower social-emotional functioning. Delforterie et al. (2019) and Fernandez et al. (2014) stated that clinicians should be mindful of how characteristics of NDDs skew risk assessment scores and must use caution when interpreting scores of those with cognitive deficits. Three previous reviews of primary studies explored the risk of sexual and violent recidivism by individuals with ID (Camilleri & Quinsey, 2011; Keeling et al., 2006; Lindsay & Taylor, 2005). Findings indicated that the Static-99 (Hanson & Thornton, 1999) and Violence Risk Appraisal Guide (VRAG, Quinsey et al., 2006) demonstrated good predictive validity for those with ID but recommended validating the tools to incorporate ID-specific characteristics. Mathur-Patel (2015) conducted a literature review of eight studies to determine which risk assessment factors had superior predictive validity for sexual recidivism among those with ID. She concluded that static risk factors with good effect sizes in individuals without ID are also valid predictors of recidivism in those with ID. Still, both static and dynamic risk factors should be assessed (Mathur-Patel, 2015).

Several structured professional judgment (SPJ) tools have been developed to assess the risk of sexual recidivism. Mathur-Patel's (2015) findings from her literature review indicated that instruments measuring dynamic risk factors developed specifically for those with ID demonstrated greater effect sizes than actuarial or SPJ tools. However, SPJ tools generally do not provide explicit instructions or guidelines for risk indicators when assessing those with ID and/or ASD (Boer et al., 2010). The SVR-20 (Boer et al., 2010) has guidelines developed for the administration for people with ID, but they have yet to be empirically supported and validated. Importantly, Boer et al. (2010) included guidelines for those displaying challenging behaviors that have not previously been involved in the CJS. The VRAG and SVR-20 have been revised since the reviews included in the literature review were conducted (SVR-20 Version 2, Boer et al., 2012; VRAG- Revised, Rice, et al., 2013), however, no further reviews regarding use with ID/ASD have been conducted to the authors' knowledge.

Clinicians assessing risk of those with ID should consider tools designed specifically for the identification and risk management of sexually inappropriate behavior, such as the Assessment of Risk and Manageability with Intellectually Disabled Individuals Who Offend Sexually (ARMIDILO-S; Boer et al., 2012) or the Dynamic Risk Assessment and Management System (DRAMS; Lindsay et al., 2004b). The ARMIDILO-S contains stable and acute dynamic risk factors divided into four sub-domains: stable client (e.g., supervision compliance), acute client (e.g., changes in compliance with supervision or treatment), stable environment (e.g., attitude towards the ID client), and acute environment (e.g., changes in social relationships).

For each item, the presence of both risk and protective factors are scored on a 3-point scale. The DRAMS consists of stable dynamic risk factors (e.g., self-regulation, therapeutic alliance) and acute dynamic risk factors (e.g., victim access, sexually inappropriate behaviors) rated on a problem continuum from, "no" to "extreme." At the very least, no matter what tool is applied, special consideration should be given to ID-specific factors or how ID may affect the rating of other items within a risk tool, so that risk assessment is fully responsive to the person's ID presentation.

16.6.1.2 Limitations of Risk Assessment Tools for Those with Neurodevelopmental Disorders

Heterogeneous diagnostic samples from prison settings have been used to validate risk assessments and develop norms (Singh, 2013); however, specific characteristics common among those with ID and/or ASD may impact the weightings assigned to such static factors (Gunasekara & Chaplin, 2012; Lindsay et al., 2006). For example, risk ratings using age may be positively skewed, as offenders with ID tend to be younger or report a younger age at first offense (Keeling et al., 2006; Lindsay et al., 2006). Those with ID and/or ASD tend to have less relationship experience, particularly if they have been institutionalized (Wilcox et al., 2009), and items relating to relationship status may positively skew risk (Craig, 2010). Those with ID who have been institutionalized in single-sex settings may also increase the likelihood of male victims, sometimes younger than themselves (Wilcox et al., 2009), which may positively skew ratings for victim type. Justice-involved individuals with ID may have a higher incidence of psycho-social adversities (e.g., history of childhood abuse or neglect and behavior problems at school; Craig, 2010; Lindsay et al., 2004a, 2004b) which may positively skew risk level. Clinicians may consider adding the Questionnaire on Attitudes Consistent with Sexual Offending (QACSO; Lindsay et al., 2020). The QACSO is a psychometric rather than risk measure, which consists of seven scales assessing permissive attitudes, cognitive distortions, covers themes of intent, responsibility, and victim awareness, and has been standardized on those with ID (Lindsay et al., 2007b), and can help inform risk assessment.

Characteristics of ASD, such as preoccupations, stereotyped behaviors, or sensitivities, may lead to aggressive or violent behavior and may positively skew risk (Gunasekara & Chaplin, 2012). Clinicians may also consider using a Framework for the Assessment of Risk and protection in offenders with ASD (FARAS; Al-Attar, 2019) as a supplementary aid when assessing this population. The FARAS provides clinicians guidance regarding seven facets of ASD that can be explored, understood, and considered to contextualize risk and how they may be understood as a risk or protective indicator. The seven facets include (1) circumscribed interests, (2) visual fantasy and impaired social imagination, (3) need for order, rules, routines, and predictability, (4) obsessionality, repetition and collecting, (5) social interactions and communication difficulties, (6) cognitive styles (difficulties and strengths), and

(7) sensory hyper and hypo-sensitivity. Such guidance can improve the efficacy of the risk assessment and have clinical utility for intervention planning.

16.6.1.3 Measures of Deviant Sexual Arousal

Measuring deviant sexual arousal and pedophilic sexual interests is an important process in overall risk assessment among those who committed sexual offenses, particularly those with ID (Rice et al., 2008). Because of communication and other cognitive difficulties, assessing deviant sexual interests among those with NDDs via self-report or other non-objective measures can be challenging. Therefore, clinicians should consider adding objective measures, such as the Abel Assessment of Sexual Interest Revised (AASI-3, Abel, 1995) or phallometric assessments. The AASI-3 is a computer-based test that includes both objective and self-report measures. The objective measure is the visual reaction time (VIT), which measures a sexual interest in children based on the length of time they look at an image. The VIT consists of a series of 160 slides of people in different situations. The longer a person looks at an image, the more interest they have in those stimuli.

Another objective measure is the phallometric assessment, which measures changes in the penis when exposed to visual stimuli. Early phallometric assessments measured penile engorgement (Laws & Marshall, 2003) while current phallometric assessments measure penile circumference (Reyes et al., 2017). Phallometric assessments are widely used in sexual offending assessments and treatment interventions due to their objectivity, accuracy, and reliability. For example, the phallometric assessment can identify a specific demographic one is aroused by (e.g., boys aged 6–7 years). Reyes et al. (2006) examined ten males with ID who have committed one or more sexual offenses and presented them with video clips (not intended to be sexual) of male and female children of various ages ranging from five to teenage years, or adults and sexual videos of adults. Their results demonstrated three patterns of arousal among the participants; differential deviant arousal (particular gender and age), undifferential deviant arousal (aroused by deviant and non-deviant images), and no deviant arousal (only aroused by adult stimulus). Four of the participants demonstrated differentiated deviant arousal, two participants demonstrated undifferentiated deviant arousal, and four participants had no arousal to deviant stimuli. However, all the participants demonstrated arousal towards sexually explicit stimuli of adults. Follow-up studies by Reyes et al. (2011a), Reyes et al. (2011b), and Reyes et al. (2017) yielded similar results. The authors concluded that phallometric assessments could be valid and reliable measures of deviant sexual arousal among those with ID (Reyes et al., 2006, 2011a, 2011b, 2017). An important finding regarding the validity of such assessments Reyes et al. (2011b) noted was that participants could artificially lower their arousal levels when they were allowed to masturbate before the assessment. Clinicians should have procedures to supervise clients before assessments.

16.7 Treatment Frameworks

Two leading frameworks in treating and assessing those who commit sexual offenses are the Risk Need Responsivity Model (RNR; Andrews et al., 1990) and the Good Lives Model (GLM; Ward & Stewart, 2003). The RNR model, outlines three principles for effective rehabilitation: the risk principle (program intensity as it relates to the individual's risk level), the needs principle (target criminogenic needs), and the responsivity principle (intervention corresponds with individual's learning abilities; Andrews & Bonta, 2010; Andrews et al., 2011). A criticism of the RNR model was the focus on criminogenic needs over basic human needs, such as employment and interpersonal relationships. Ward and Stewart (2003) identified the primary goals of the GLM to assist justice-involved individuals in living more fulfilling lives, thereby reducing the likelihood of recidivism.

16.7.1 Risk Need Responsivity Model

There are various treatment frameworks clinicians follow to guide the development of treatment plans for recidivism prevention based on risk level and the client's specific treatment needs. The RNR model has been utilized in the field for over three decades as an effective correctional assessment and treatment framework, proving to reduce recidivism (Andrews et al., 2011; Looman & Abracen, 2013). The RNR model is one framework to manage those in the forensic population. The framework's first application is the risk principle, which uses risk assessment tools to identify individual's appropriate intervention and treatment level (e.g., prioritize the highest risk to more intense services). The needs principle indicates that intervention should be targeted towards the individual's criminogenic needs using evidence-based interventions. Wilson and Yates (2009) stated that a decrease in recidivism is directly linked to targeting one's criminogenic needs. The appropriate level of treatment intensity not only prioritizes the allocation of resources (Harkins et al., 2012; Wilson & Yates, 2009) but an incorrect or unnecessary treatment intensity can not only waste valuable resources but in some cases, increase offending. Bonta and Andrews (2007) argue under-treating (providing less intense programming to those at high recidivismrisk) can lead to increased offending, while over-treating (over programming those at low recidivismrisk) can lead to destabilization and an increase in recidivism. The responsivity principle refers to the consideration of the individual's learning needs using evidence-based interventions. Specific characteristics of the individual, such as cognitive ability and maturity, must be a focal point in tailoring the treatment for the individual's responsivity, particularly for those with ID and ASD. The RNR framework is not without criticisms. Concerns with the RNR include a lack of emphasis on prosocial supports, successful community reintegration, an individual's engagement and motivation, and compartmentalizing individuals into specific risk categories (McWhinnie et al., 2013; Ward et al., 2007a; Wilson & Yates, 2009).

16.7.2 Good Lives Model

The Good Lives Model (GLM; Ward & Stewart, 2003) is another treatment framework commonly used for those who commit sexual offenses (Harkins et al. 2012; Lindsay et al., 2007a; Wilson & Yates, 2009) and is also recommended for those with ID (Aust, 2010). According to Ward and Stewart (2003), the GLM is an effective way to reduce recidivism as it provides those who have been released into the community with the tools needed to create more fulfilling lives, including housing, employment, and meaningful interpersonal relationships. Ward and Stewart (2003) described these as primary human goods and detailed nine goals developed from a biological, psychological, and anthropological perspective that humans strive for (life, knowledge, excellence in play and work, excellence in agency, inner peace, relatedness, spirituality, happiness, and creativity; Ward & Gannon, 2006). Secondary goods are the methods used to obtain the primary goods. The GLM theorizes sexual offending can occur when individuals attempt to acquire these goals or goods in an inappropriate or maladaptive manner or when frustrated when they are unable to obtain the goals (Harkins et al., 2012). One may choose to commit a criminal offense to achieve these desirable human goods and may lack opportunities and/or capabilities to do so in using socially acceptable methods.

The GLM approach in treatment focuses on instilling knowledge and developing prosocial skills to lead a fulfilling life (Harkins et al., 2012). In contrast, the RNR purports that the criminogenic needs may be viewed as symptoms or effects of inappropriate means to achieve the goods (Lindsay et al., 2007a; Wilson & Yates, 2009). The GLM does not seek to change the prosocial goals but helps the offender develop proper ways to attain the goal. By creating a positive approach, clinicians emphasize the client's strengths to increase self-worth and treatment engagement (Harkins et al., 2012) while reducing the likelihood of re-offending (Lindsay et al., 2007a).

Criticisms of the GLM approach include a lack of focus on risk factors and more emphasis on obtaining goods (Harkins et al., 2012; Ogloff & Davis, 2004). Harkins et al. (2012) surveyed facilitators of the GLM, and many (73%) did not believe the model was appropriate for all individuals who committed sexual offenses, specifically those deemed high-risk, or those with no prior treatment participation, as they lacked the skills and terminology to participate effectively. GLM requires a balance between focusing on promoting human goods and reducing risk, but individuals may focus on attaining needs through criminal behavior (Harkins et al., 2012).

16.7.3 Risk Need Responsivity Model *and* Good Lives Model

Although research has demonstrated that the RNR and the GLM model have been effective in reducing sexual recidivism (Ogloff & Davis, 2004; Ward et al., 2007b; Wilson & Yates, 2009). Researchers have suggested pairing the two frameworks to increase engagement and reduce recidivism, while focusing on the individual's autonomy and values (Andrews et al., 2011; Ward & Stewart, 2003; Ward et al., 2001; Wilson & Yates, 2009). The integration of the two models would reduce recidivism while increasing the individual's self-efficacy, successful community reintegration, and increase public safety (Wilson & Yates, 2009). The RNR model has greater focus on the criminogenic needs of the offending with less emphasis on the individual's engagement and well-being while adding the GLM will allow a greater focus on individual's human goods (Harkins et al. 2012). By integrating the two frameworks, treatment focuses on reducing the likelihood of recidivism by emphasizing risk factors, while encouraging client participation for a holistic approach (Lindsay et al., 2007a; Wilson & Yates, 2009). Applying the two models for those with ID or ASD is particularly useful, as these individual's have specific needs and responsivity, which require additional supports to acquire human goods. Human goods can be incredibly difficult for those convicted of sexual offenses due to the severe stigma of their SO status and harsh punishments. This may increase the risk of offending due to stressors involving the desire for peer acceptance (Baldry et al., 2011; Jones, 2007). For some with NDDs residing in the community, the demands of community-living may increase the risk of offending (Jones, 2007), which are further hindered by poor social skills and poor impulse control (Lambrick & Glasser, 2004). Formal and informal sanctions coupled with the SO specific legislation are often counterproductive to the person's treatment plan and recidivism prevention. Clinicians provide effective treatment frameworks and must advocate for appropriate sanctions and communicate the recidivism risks of failing to obtain human goods to prosecutors, judges, and probation or parole officers.

16.8 Treatment Modalities

To change one's behavior, behavioral and cognitive therapies have been the most common treatment modality since their inception decades ago. There are several treatment techniques clinicians use to help change one's behavior and better manage emotions and impulses. The strategies of these modalities have evolved and have been adapted to treat those who engage in various sexually deviant behaviors. Behavior modification (BM), applied behavior analysis (ABA), cognitive behavioral therapy (CBT; Beck, 1963, 1970), and dialectical behavioral therapy (DBT; Linehan, 1993) are the most common evidenced-based and effective treatment approaches for sexual offending behavior. These treatment modalities have also beneficial for individuals with NDDs and to further assist this population, some of these treatment modalities have been simplified and sometimes combined.

16.8.1 Behavioral Techniques

Behavioral techniques, including BM and ABA refer to evidence-based approaches to eliminate or reduce maladaptive behavior in children or adults. These terms became prominent in the 1950s and 1960s, and are based on classical conditioning theories (Pavlov, 1897/1902; Watson, 1913) and operant conditioning (Skinner, 1938). While some therapies such as cognitive therapies (described in more detail below) focus on changing thought processes that can affect behavior, BM/ABA focuses on changing specific behaviors through reinforcement and/or punishment. Such behavioral interventions have shown to be effective across settings and behaviors (Wilson et al., 2001), including inappropriate sexual behavior (Fyfee et al., 2004). Wolfe et al. (2009) acknowledge that ABA is an evidence-based practice that could be successfully applied to reduce socially appropriate sexual behaviors and increase socially acceptable, legal, and safe expressions of sexual behaviors. Although research on the use of ABA among those who committed sexual offenses is limited, results from a sample of juveniles adjudicated for sexual offenses suggests it may be promising (Brogan et al., 2018).

An effective but controversial behavioral technique used specifically for those who have engage in deviant sexual behavior includes aversion therapy or covert sensitization. Individuals are presented with deviant stimuli to evoke arousal, then followed immediately by an aversive stimulus. Using the phallometric assessment, Weinrott et al. (1997) revealed significant reductions in deviant sexual arousal among juveniles. Although Rea et al. (2003) found that covert sensitization (aversion) techniques successfully reduced deviant sexual arousal, authors questioned whether the results were able to be generalized from the laboratory to the natural environment. To the authors' knowledge, such aversion therapy techniques have yet to be tested on ID and ASD populations for effectiveness in reducing deviant sexual arousal. Also, aversion therapy is not a permanent change and often requires follow-up to maintain effects, thus, requires a cooperation and motivation by the individual.

In clinical settings, principles of behaviorism can be applied to the treatment programs for those who committed sexual offenses. Serran et al. (2003) noted that such individuals are typically reluctant to take responsibility for their actions as they minimize the harm, they have caused their victims. A typical treatment goal would be for the client to accept responsibility, which can be reinforced by rewarding clients for their honesty with positive statements (e.g., "I am impressed with the honesty of your account" (Serran et al., 2003, p. 373). By consistently rewarding honesty and outlining the benefits of honesty encourages clients to accept responsibility for their offending behavior. Clinicians should avoid confrontational approaches, as they could have a negative and opposite effect. For example, Lindsay (2009) highlights the importance of facilitators being aware of how the message is being conveyed to the client.

16.8.2 Cognitive Techniques

Cognitive therapy techniques refer to a class of intervention techniques and include Rational Emotive Behavior Therapy (Ellis, 1955), CBT (Beck, 1963, 1970), and DBT (Linehan, 1993). The core premise of these behavioral therapies pioneered by Beck (1963, 1970) and Ellis (1955, 1962) posits that maladaptive thoughts contribute to the underlying cause and continuance of emotional distress and behavioral problems. CBT is the primary treatment modality used to treat those with ID who have committed sexual offenses (Marotta, 2017). Adapted treatment approaches that use visuals, repetition, focus on social skills, and simple/concrete language is essential to help this population work on their risk factors and interventions. Lindsay et al. (2020) provided suggestions for clinicians providing treatment to those with ID who have sexually offended. DBT is a type of CBT that provides clients with new skills to manage painful emotions and decrease conflict in relationships. DBT specifically focuses on providing therapeutic skills in four key areas: mindfulness of the present, skills to improve one's tolerance to distress, emotion regulation and management, and effective communication techniques (Linehan, 1993). DBT has been adapted for individuals with developmental disabilities by using shorter sentences and visual aids, allowing clinicians to teach skills such as emotion regulation, distress tolerance, interpersonal skills, coping skills, and mindfulness more effectively (Dykstra & Charlton, 2008). Sakdalan and Collier (2012) combined elements of CBT and DBT to treat those with ID who have sexually offended. They demonstrated a reduction in cognitive distortions and attitudes supportive of sexual offending upon program completion.

Regardless of the treatment modality, when speaking with individuals with ID or ASD, it is important to use short sentences with a single concept and words with fewer than three syllables. Individuals with ID have difficulty learning information quickly and may have slower cognitive processing. Frequent repetition and visual aids are often necessary to learn concepts and information, particularly for those with ASD, who tend to process information visually. Having clients paraphrase or summarize what they have learned is standard practice to determine comprehension. Roleplaying exercises are useful for those to practice the skills acquired in treatment and become more comfortable speaking about high-risk behaviors. A clinician's skill and level of patience are important characteristics to consider with populations that require treatment materials to be delivered at a slower pace. Clinicians should develop flexible methods to deliver CBT and other treatment modalities to engage clients with limited attention spans.

According to Lindsay (2009), treatment length is an essential consideration for clients with ID, as he noted that with ID are typically in SO treatment for 18 months to 2 years. Lindsay and Smith (1998) compared two groups of participants, one in treatment for one year and the other for two years and noted those in treatment for one year had significantly poorer progress. Lindsay and Smith (1998) concluded that two years of treatment would likely result in a better outcome for those with ID, and Lindsay (2009) later concluded that any less than two years was "a waste of time" (p. 113).

16.9 Conclusions and Recommendations

There is little doubt that sexually offending behavior produces negative emotions such as anger among community members and creates fear, psychological, and physical harm to victims. In response, the community tends to demand punishment for such criminal behavior (Taylor et al., 2009). According to Mouridsen (2012), when examining sexual offenses, clinicians, attorneys, and judges must examine the motivation behind it and differentiate one's ID or characteristics as a causal factor in sexually inappropriate behavior, rather than presuming sexual perversion as a motivation. Clinicians are tasked with assessing risk, offering recommendations, providing appropriate interventions, while considering public safety and legislative requirements that may vary between jurisdictions. Due to the varied needs of those with NDDs who commit sexual offenses, multidisciplinary and multimodal approaches are necessary.

16.9.1 Recommendation 1: Individualized Treatment Across Settings

Specific treatment addressing sexual offending can occur in various settings; many individuals participate in treatment in correctional settings, while others are diverted from the CJS to forensic mental health systems or the community. Others may be subject to both settings, in which either during or after the completion of their sentence, they are involuntarily civilly committed to a psychiatric facility for treatment. Those with or without disabilities can be placed in a community-based services program based on their needs and characteristics or seriousness of the offense. The location or setting often determines the treatment format.

Some enter the CJS without a diagnosis. Therefore, prior to any discussions of plea agreements or the development of a treatment plan, clients must have evidence-based comprehensive assessments to determine their needs, whether they have deviant sexual interests and risk level. For example, Jake had no known diagnoses at the time of his arrest. It was not until Jake's parents read an article that they suspected that ASD may explain Jake's behavior. Jake had various learning, addiction, and neurodevelopmental disorders that explained his sexual offending behavior. Jake's defense attorney shared the full psychological reports with the prosecutor to assist with the plea agreement and his treatment plan.

Professionals working with individuals with NDDs should be cognizant that those with ID and ASD are a heterogeneous population with a range of needs and should have person-centered individualized treatment plans and be handled individually in the CJS. A specific treatment framework based on the individual's level of risk, needs, and responsivity issues, including their ability to comprehend and comply with treatment demands. As shown in the research and cases studies, individuals have various risk levels and various motives for their sexual offending behavior. For example, naiveté may be due to a lack of cognition or intellect, a lack of social skills, or an impulse control disorder.

Many treatment programs addressing sexually-deviant behavior use a group therapy format due to the cost-effectiveness and when individual sessions are unfeasible due to a lack of resources (Stinson & Becker, 2013). Group therapy can be particularly useful with adults and mature adolescents but should be applied judiciously with adolescents and/or those with NDDs (Dishion et al., 1999; Fago, 2003). Some clients may require individual sessions. For example, for those who are disruptive to the group setting (e.g., perseverates on their interest area or other behavioral issues, poor hygiene), or those who find the group environment stressful (e.g., creates anxiety, easily distracted), individual sessions may be more appropriate. For example, Allen found the group setting stressful, intimidating, and it was not a therapeutic environment. His clinician added individual sessions to build trust, develop a therapeutic relationship so that he could begin to share his thoughts. Over time, Allen was able to become more comfortable speaking about his sexual urges in both individual and group setting to learn new skills to develop relationships in a safe and legal manner.

16.9.2 Recommendation 2: Advocate for Individualized Treatment Plan

Individuals from various disciplines are involved in the treatment of justice-involved individuals with ID or ASD. Representatives from the CJS, such as prosecutors, defense attorneys, probation or parole officers, and judges, may not interact with this population frequently. This population requires certain considerations pertaining to sentencing and treatment options. Treatment options are limited, given their offense type, as well as the diagnosis of ASD or ID.

Professionals in the CJS may not have all the same goals as treatment providers. Clinicians work directly with this population and become familiar with each client's learning capabilities and limitations. Treatment providers must work in conjunction with the CJS to determine the best outcome for these individuals, for members of the community, and must balance the safety of the community and with the rehabilitation of their client. Oftentimes, sexual offending treatment is court-ordered and a clinician may recommend treatment options that the prosecutor or Judge does not agree with. For example, prosecutors may demand a client participate in group treatment as a condition to the plea agreement. However, sexually-offending specific treatment or group treatments may not appropriate. Over or under treatment may lead to an increase in re-offending behavior (Bonta & Andrews, 2007). Therefore, defense attorneys and assessing clinicians must advocate for their clients, particularly those who present with counterfeit deviance. Sexual offending-specific treatment is not necessary for all individuals who commit sexual offenses. For example, Anthony's psychological evaluation concluded that he has no deviant sexual interests. His offense of possessing child pornography was the result of his compulsion to downloading files from the internet. This compulsion manifested because of depression, feelings of hopelessness, and low self-worth. His clinician advocated that a sexual offending group treatment program was not appropriate, and this setting could lead to self-defeating thoughts and exacerbate his depression.

16.9.3 Recommendation 3: Assess Sexual Knowledge and Include Sexual Education

Some sexual offending behavior could be the result of naiveté about sex or naiveté as to how to initiate romantic relationships. Treatment programs for those with NDDs should include measures of sexual knowledge, and if necessary, a variety of sexual education options. The Socio-Sexual Knowledge and Attitudes Test-Revised (SSKAAT-R; Griffiths & Lunksy, 2003) has shown to be a valid tool among those with ID (Hammond & Beail, 2020; Thompson et al., 2016) and includes various measures of sexual knowledge, safe sex practices, and sexual boundaries (e.g., inappropriate touching). The General Sexual Knowledge Questionnaire (GSKQ; Talbot & Langdon, 2006) is another useful tool to measure sexual knowledge in individuals with and without ID, and Bender et al. (1983) developed a shorter version of this tool. For those with a lack of sexual knowledge, providing them with sex education can increase awareness of sexual safety, inform them of illegal sexual behavior, and help them develop healthy intimate relationships (Schwartz & Robertson, 2019; Turner & Crane, 2016).

Research has shown that sexual education has successfully improved sexual knowledge; however, those with ID may not retain this information long-term (Lindsay et al., 1992). Lindsay examined individuals with ID in treatment over 7 months and found no significant improvement in their sexual knowledge (Lindsay, 2009). Individuals with ID can improve their sexual knowledge, but treatment programs must include methods to reinforce the information (Lindsay et al., 1992). Such methods may consist of videos and role-playing exercises to reinforce the concepts of consent, victim resistance, and social/sexual cues (Schwartz & Robertson, 2019). For example, Johnson engaged in various illegal courtship behavior for years due to his naiveté about sex and initiating relationships. His treatment plan included sexual education including concepts of consent. Due to his low intellect, his education and treatment assignments were delivered at a slower place and included role-playing exercises. For Johnson to retain this information, he must continue his education and treatment long-term.

16.9.4 Recommendation 4: Specialized Skills, Training, and Leadership Support

When working with clients with ASD and/or ID, specific skills training is necessary, as the treatment must be delivered at a slower pace, with materials such as visual aids, and with the clinician having a more active facilitator role. Such training should include specific strategies as to how to develop timelines to deliver the treatment at a slower pace and how to prepare for individual and group sessions. Because these individuals require more planning and resources, supervisors should allow for smaller groups to provide clinicians more time to create and adapt evidence-based materials for clients.

To provide the support for both clinicians and their clients, it is imperative for those in leadership positions to also learn about justice-involved individuals with ID and/or ASD as this population poses unique challenges to the CJS and clinical settings. By acquiring this knowledge, supervisors can better support their supervisees and advocate for adequate funding to provide the necessary resources to meet these individuals' needs. The attitudes of leadership towards those with ID and/or ASD who commit sexual offenses can influence how staff's perceptions of working with these clients.

The clinician's role in the group is often engaging, with clinicians moving around the room to engage clients and increase their attention span. For clients with literacy problems, clinicians may use visual aids and drawings to convey treatment concepts. Clinicians may have to read documents or materials to clients, while pausing frequently to paraphrase what they just read. Because of this slower delivery pace, it is imperative that clinicians possess the ability to be patient, flexible, and be able to develop more creative ways to teach various skills. Some clinicians may find it difficult to think critically and create adapted treatment approaches and this rigidity can create frustration for both parties. Training must also include information to better understand how one's diagnosis affects treatment outcomes so that clinician can adapt and revise the timeline for treatment delivery.

Although tedious, repetition of terms and concepts is crucial as those with neurodevelopmental disorders may initially present as though they understand the material when, in reality, they do not. Many adults with ID have learned to model the behaviors of others to avoid any stigma or mistreatment. Therefore, they may present well and hide their disability because they do not want to appear unintelligent when they do not understand something (Kranendonk et al., 2019). This behavior often presents itself in treatment, where clients with ID pretend to understand what is asked of them when they actually do not. For example, they may be able to repeat information, but unable to do so in their own terms. As Kranendonk et al., (2019) recommended, individuals should paraphrase statements back to the clinician in their own words to ensure comprehension. Clinicians should avoid asking close-ended, "yes" or "no" questions, as this may lead to acquiescence. For example, Allen struggled to answer questions and gave "I don't know" responses. His clinician was cautious with follow-up questions to avoid suggestibility or acquiescence. Clinicians may also address this acquiescence by encouraging clients to advocate for themselves when they do not understand. Jake had a "people-pleasing" personality, and his approach to his clinician was no exception. Jake had to learn to practice advocating for himself, expressing his needs to become more assertive.

16.9.5 Recommendation 6: Consider Effects of Sexual Offender Legislation

Ward and Stewart (2003) noted that successful community re-integration for released offenders involves stable housing, employment, and meaningful interpersonal relationships. However, SOs are subject to legislation that often hinder obtaining these goods, as many with sexual offense convictions have experienced severe stigma due to the nature of their offense (Tewksbury, 2005). Zgoba (2011) explained how the additional stress of not being able to find stable housing can result in destabilization, which can hinder treatment efforts and increase recidivism. Given that social isolation and interpersonal difficulties appear to affect sexual recidivism (Ward & Brown, 2004; Ward & Gannon, 2006), clinicians must be mindful of how SO legislation may actually increase recidivism risk (Levenson & D'Amora, 2007).

Similarly, probation conditions that are too harsh may also hinder successful integration and treatment. For example, Anthony's probation conditions prohibited him from entering locations where children may be present (e.g., parks, churches). However, Anthony was an active member of his church and every week, he played the guitar and sang in the church choir. His clinician feared that removing this support system could lead to further destabilization and strongly advocated to remove this probation condition.

Those subject to public SO registration have experience feelings of shame, vulnerability, and stigma, which may lead to social isolation (Tewskbury & Lees, 2006). Individuals with ID and ASD often experience shame, stigma, and social rejection due to the characteristics of their condition, and the additional label of a SO exacerbates this stigma. The prosecutor in Anthony's case recommended he register as a moderate risk SO, and in his jurisdiction, the public were alerted to moderate and high-risk SOs. Because his clinician concluded that he was low-risk, his clinician advocated that his risk level be downgraded from a level-2 (moderate risk) to a level-1 (low-risk), which would not be made public.[3] Anthony's clinician argued that the possible stigma related to the public registry could increase his depression, anxiety, and feelings of self-worth. The prosecutor in Jake's case offered a plea deal in which he could receive probation and be required to register as low-

[3] All 50 states had implemented their own version of Sex Offender Registration and Notification, with a great deal of variability among them. Some registries make public all risk levels, whereas some only make public moderate-risk (level-2) and high-risk (level-3) levels.

risk, but his jurisdiction made public low, moderate, and high-risk levels on the registry. Having to register as a SO created a great deal of anxiety and began to negatively affect Jake's self-image. Jake's legal team and clinician worked together and recommended that he accept the probation deal and move to a jurisdiction where low-risk levels on the registry are not made public.

16.9.6 Recommendation 7: More Research Is Necessary

Empirical research on those with NDDs involved in the CJS for sexual offending is lacking, particularly areas surrounding specific offending behavior among those with ID, and assessment and treatment for those with ASD. More research on the prevalence of those with NDDs who have committed sexual offenses, forensic mental health population, and CJS is needed to better understand the scope of this problem. Further, more recidivism research is needed with consistent definitions, and should include self-reported offending, rearrests, and reconvictions to make valid and reliable comparison across settings and jurisdictions.

References

Abel Assessment of Sexual interest Revised (AASI-3). (1995).

Al-Attar, Z. (2019). Introducing the FARAS—A framework to aid risk assessment with offenders on the autistic Spectrum. 18th international conference on offenders with an intellectual and/or developmental disability, Birmingham, April 2011.

Alley, C. S., Kennedy, S., & Warren, I. (2019). A legal analysis of Australian criminal cases involving defendants with autism spectrum disorder charged with online sexual offending. *International Journal of Law and Psychiatry, 66*, 1–11. https://doi.org/10.1016/j.ijlp.2019.101456

Alper, M., & Durose, M. R. (2019). *Recidivism of sex offenders released from state prison: A 9-year follow-up (2005–14)*. Bureau of Justice Statistics.

American Psychiatric Association. (1952). *Diagnostic and statistical manual of mental disorders* (1st ed.).

American Psychiatric Association. (1968). *Diagnostic and statistical manual of mental disorders* (2nd ed).

American Psychiatric Association. (1980). *Diagnostic and statistical manual of mental disorders* (3rd ed.).

American Psychiatric Association. (1987). *Diagnostic and statistical manual of mental disorders* (3rd ed. Revised).

American Psychiatric Association. (1994). *Diagnostic and statistical manual of mental disorders* (4th ed.).

American Psychiatric Association. (2000). *Diagnostic and statistical manual of mental disorders* (4th ed. Text Revision).

American Psychiatric Association. (2013). *Diagnostic and statistical manual of mental disorders* (5th ed.). https://doi.org/10.1176/appibooks.9780890425596

American Psychiatric Association. (2022). *Diagnostic and statistical manual of mental disorders* (5th ed. Text Revision). https://doi.org/10.1176/appi.books.9780890425787

Anckarsäter, H., Nilsson, T., Saury, J. M., Råstam, M., & Gillberg, C. (2008). Autism spectrum disorders in institutionalized subjects. *Nordic Journal of Psychiatry, 62*(2), 60–167. https://doi.org/10.1080/08039480801957269

Andrews, D. A., & Bonta, J. (2010). Rehabilitating criminal justice policy and practice. *Psychology, Public Policy, and Law, 16*(1), 39–55. https://doi.org/10.1037/a0018362

Andrews, D. A., Bonta, J., & Hoge, R. D. (1990). Classification for effective rehabilitation: Rediscovering psychology. *Criminal Justice and Behavior, 17*(1), 19–52. https://doi.org/10.1177/0093854890017001004

Andrews, D. A., Bonta, J., & Wormith, J. S. (2011). The Risk-need-responsivity (RNR) model: Does adding the good lives model contribute to effective crime prevention? *Criminal Justice and Behavior, 38*(7), 735–755. https://doi.org/10.1177/0093854811406356

Archer, R. P., Buffington-Vollum, J. K., Stredny, R. V., & Handel, R. W. (2006). A survey of psychological test use patterns among forensic psychologists. *Journal of Personality Assessment, 87*(1), 84–94. https://doi.org/10.1207/s15327752jpa8701_07

Attwood, T. (2007). *The complete guide to Asperger's syndrome*. Jessica Kingsley Publishers.

Attwood, T., Henault, I., & Dubin, N. (2014). *The autism spectrum, sexuality, and the law*. Jessica Kingsley Publishers.

Aust, S. (2010). Is the good lives model of offender treatment relevant to sex offenders with a learning disability? *Journal of Learning Disabilities and Offending Behaviour, 1*(3), 33–39. https://doi.org/10.5042/jldob.2010.0627

Baldry, E., Dowse, L., & Clarence, M. (2011). People with mental and cognitive disabilities: Pathways into prison. In *Background paper for the National Legal Aid Conference Darwin 2011*. University of NSW, School of Social Sciences and International Studies.

Baldry, E., Dowse, L., & Clarence, M. (2012). *People with intellectual and other cognitive disability in the criminal justice system*. University of New South Wales.

Ballan, M. S. (2012). Parental perspectives of communication about sexuality in families of children with autism spectrum disorders. *Journal of Autism and Developmental Disorders, 42*, 676–684. https://doi.org/10.1007/s10803-011-1293-y

Beck, A. T. (1963). Thinking and depression: Idiosyncratic content and cognitive distortions. *Archives of General Psychiatry, 9*(4), 324–333. https://doi.org/10.1001/archpsyc.1963.01720160014002

Beck, A. T. (1970). Cognitive therapy: Nature and relation to behavior therapy. *Behavior Therapy, 1*(2), 184–200. https://doi.org/10.1016/S0005-7894(70)80030-2

Bender, M. P., Aitman, J. B., Biggs, S. J., & Haug, U. (1983). Initial findings concerning a sexual knowledge questionnaire. *Journal of the British Institute of Mental Handicap, 11*(4), 168–169.

Blanchard, R., Barbaree, H. E., Bogaert, A. F., Dickey, R., Klassen, P. E., Kuban, M. E., & Zucker, K. J. (2000). Fraternal birth order and sexual orientation in pedophiles. *Archives of Sexual Behavior, 29*(5), 463–478. https://doi.org/10.1023/a:1001943719964

Blasingame, G. D. (2016). Assessment, diagnosis, and risk management of sexual offenders with intellectual disabilities. In A. Phenix & H. M. Hoberman (Eds.), *Sexual offenders: Predisposing conditions, risk assessment and management* (pp. 227–246). Springer.

Boer, D. P., Frize, M., Pappas, R., Morrissey, C., & Lindsay, W. R. (2010). Suggested adaptations to the SVR-20 for offenders with intellectual disabilities. In L. A. Craig, W. R. Lindsay, & K. D. Browne (Eds.), *Assessment and treatment of sexual offenders with intellectual disabilities: A handbook* (1st ed., pp. 177–192). John Wiley & Sons, Ltd.

Boer, D. P., Haaven, J. L., Lambrick, F., Lindsay, W. R., McVilly, K. R. Sakdalan, J., & Frize, M. (2012). ARMIDILO-S Manual: Web Version 1.1 2013. Retrieved January 4, 2014, from http://www.armidilo.net/files/Web-Version-1-1-2013-Intro-Manual.pdf

Bonta, J., & Andrews, D. A. (2007). Risk-need-responsivity model for offender assessment and rehabilitation. Public Safety Canada. Retrieved from https://www.publicsafety.gc.ca/cnt/rsrcs/pblctns/rsk-nd-rspnsvty/rsk-nd-rspnsvty-eng.pdf

Brogan, K. M., Richling, S. M., Rapp, J. T., Thompson, K. R., & Burkhart, B. R. (2018). Collaborate efforts by the Auburn University applied behavioral analysis program in the treatment of adolescents adjudicated for illegal sexual behavior. *Behavior and Social Issues, 27*, 11–15. https://doi.org/10.5210/bsi.v.27i0.8267

Bronson, J., & Berzofsky, L. M. (2015). *Disabilities among prison and jail inmates, 2011–12*. Bureau of Justice Statistics.

Brown, J., Anderson, G., Cooney-Koss, L., Hastings, B., Pickett, H., Neal, D., Martindale, J., Dodson, K. D., & Barfknecht, L. (2018). Autism spectrum disorder and sexually inappropriate behaviors: An introduction for caregivers and professionals. *The Journal of Special Population, 1*(2), 1–8.

Brown,J.,Fenrich,A.,Haun,J.,&Carter,M.(2019).Clientsuggestibility:Abeginner'sguideformental health professionals. Counseling Today, Member Insights. Retrieved from https://ct.counseling.org/2019/08/client-suggestibility-a-beginners-guidefor-mentalhealth-professionals/

Brown-Lavoie, S. M., Viecili, M. A., & Weiss, J. A. (2014). Sexual knowledge and victimization in adults with autism Spectrum disorders. *Journal of Autism and Developmental Disorders, 44*(9), 2185–2196. https://doi.org/10.1007/s10803-014-2093-y

Camilleri, J. A., & Quinsey, V. L. (2011). Appraising the risk of sexual and violent recidivism among intellectually disabled offenders. *Psychology, Crime & Law, 17*(1), 59–74. https://doi.org/10.1080/10683160903392350

Cantor, J. M., Blanchard, R., Christensen, B. K., Dickey, R., Klassen, P. E., & Beckstead, A. L. (2004). Intelligence, memory, and handedness in pedophilia. *Neuropsychology, 18*(1), 3–14. https://doi.org/10.1037/0894-4105.18.1.3

Cantor, J. M., Blanchard, R., Robichaud, L. K., & Christensen, B. K. (2005). Quantitative reanalysis of aggregate data on IQ in sexual offenders. *Psychological Bulletin, 131*(4), 555–568. https://doi.org/10.1037/0033-2909.131.4.555

Cloud, M., Shepherd, G. B., Barkoff, A. N., & Shur, J. V. (2002). Words without meaning: The constitution, confessions, and mentally retarded suspects. *The University of Chicago Law Review, 69*(2), 495–624. https://doi.org/10.2307/1600500

Colorado v. Connelly, 479 U.S. 157. (1986).

Craig, L. A. (2010). Controversies in assessing risk and deviancy in sex offenders with intellectual disabilities. *Psychology, Crime & Law, 16*(1–2), 75–101. https://doi.org/10.1080/10683160802621982

Debbaudt, D. (2004). Beyond guilt or innocence, forum paper published by Autism New Zealand Inc. Retrieved from http://autismnz.org.nz/police/Pol_BeyGuilt.pdf

Dekker, L., van der Vegt, E., van der Ende, J., Tick, N., & Louwerse, A. (2017). Psychosexual functioning of cognitively-able adolescents with autism spectrum disorder compared to typically developing peers: The development and testing of the teen transition inventory – A self- and parent report questionnaire on psychosexual functioning. *Journal of Autism and Developmental Disorders, 47*(6), 1716–1738. https://doi.org/10.1007/s10803-017-3071-y

Delforterie, M., Willem van den Berg, J., Bolt, B., van den Hazel, T., Craig, L., & Didden, R. (2019). Comparing STATIC-99R and STABLE-2007 between persons with and without intellectual disabilities. *Journal of Intellectual Disabilities and Offending Behavior, 10*(3), 58–68. https://doi.org/10.1108/jidob-01-2019-0003

Dewson, H., Rix, K. J., Le Gallez, I., & Choong, K. A. (2018). Sexual rights, mental disorder and intellectual disability: Practical implications for policy makers and practitioners. *BJPsych Advances, 24*(6), 386–397. https://doi.org/10.1192/bja.2018.40

Dishion, T. J., McCord, J., & Poulin, F. (1999). When interventions harm: Peer groups and problem behavior. *American Psychologist, 54*(9), 755–764. https://doi.org/10.1037/0003-066X.54.9.755

Dykstra, E. J., & Charlton, M. (2008). Dialectical behavior therapy skills training: Adapted for special populations [Unpublished manuscript]. Aurora Mental Health Center. https://mha.ohio.gov/Portals/0/assets/HealthProfessionals/About%20MH%20and%2Adiction%20Treatment/TIC/ResourceLibrary/DBTSP%20Skills%20Training%20Manual%20v3%204.pdf

Ellis, A. (1955). New approaches to psychotherapy techniques. *Journal of Clinical Psychology, 11*(3), 207–260. https://doi.org/10.1002/1097-4679(195507)11:3<207::AID-JCLP2270110302>3.0.CO;2-1

Ellis, A. (1962). Reason and emotion in psychotherapy. Lyle Stuart.

Elsabbagh, M., Divan, G., Koh, Y. J., Kim, Y. S., Kauchali, S., Marcín, C., Montiel Nava, C., Patel, V., Paula, C. S., Wang, C., & Yasamy, M. T. (2012). Global prevalence of autism and other pervasive developmental disorders. *Autism Research, 5*(3), 160–179. https://doi.org/10.1002/aur.239

Fago, D. P. (2003). Evaluation and treatment of neurodevelopmental deficits in sexually aggressive children and adolescents. *Professional Psychology: Research and Practice, 34*(3), 248–257. https://doi.org/10.1037/0735-7028.34.3.248

Fawley, P., & Wilson, N. (2016). Young people with intellectual disability talking about sexuality education and information. *Sexuality & Disability, 34*, 469–484. https://doi.org/10.1007/s11195-016-9460-x

Fazel, S., Xenitidis, K., & Powell, J. (2008). The prevalence of intellectual disabilities among 12,000 prisoners: A systematic review. *International Journal of Law and Psychiatry, 31*(4), 369–373. https://doi.org/10.1016/j.ijlp.2008.06.001

Fernandez, Y., Harris, A. J. R., Hanson, R. K., & Sparks, J. (2014). *STABLE-2007 coding manual: Revised 2014*. Public Safety Canada.

First, M. B. (2014). DSM-5 and paraphilic disorders. *Journal of the American Academy of Psychiatry and the Law, 42*(2), 191–201.

Frazier v. Cupp, 394 U.S. 731. (1969).

Fyfee, C. E., Kahng, S. W., Fittro, E., & Russell, D. (2004). Functional analysis and treatment of inappropriate sexual behavior. *Journal of Applied Behavior Analysis, 37*(3), 401–404. https://doi.org/10.1901/jaba.2004.37-401

Geradin, P., & Thibaut, F. (2004). Epidemiology and treatment of adolescent sexual offending. *Pediatric Drugs, 6*(2), 79–91. https://doi.org/10.2165/00148581-200406020-00002

Glueck, B. C. (1955). *Final report: Research project for the study and treatment of persons convicted of crimes involving sexual aberrations, June 1952 to June 1955*. New York State Department of Mental Hygiene.

Griffiths, D., Hingsburger, D., Hoath, J., & Ioannou, S. (2013). Counterfeit deviance revisited. *Journal of Applied Research in Intellectual Disabilities, 26*(5), 471–480. https://doi.org/10.1111/jar.12034

Griffiths, D., & Lunksy, Y. (2003). *Sociosexual knowledge and attitudes assessment tool (SSKAAT-R)*. Stoelting.

Gudjonsson, G. H. (1984). A new scale of interrogative suggestibility. *Personality and Individual Differences, 5*(3), 53–58. https://doi.org/10.1016/0191-8869(84)90069-2

Gudjonsson, G. H. (2018). *The psychology of false confessions: Forty years of science and practice*. John Wiley & Sons.

Gudjonsson, G. H., & Clark, N. (1986). Suggestibility in police interrogation: A social psychological model. *Social Behaviour, 1*(2), 83–104.

Gudjonsson, G. H., & MacKeith, J. A. C. (1982). False confessions. Psychological effects of interrogation. A discussion paper. In A. Trankell (Ed.), *Reconstructing the past: The role of psychologists in criminal trials* (pp. 253–269).

Gunasekara, S., & Chaplin, E. (2012). Autism spectrum disorders and offending. *Advances in Mental Health and Intellectual Disabilities, 6*(2), 308–313. https://doi.org/10.1108/20441281211285955

Hammond, S., & Beail, N. (2020). The relationship between cognitive variables and offending behaviour in adults with intellectual disabilities: A systematic review. *Journal of Applied Research in Intellectual Disabilities, 33*(4), 779–792. https://doi.org/10.1111/jar.12738

Hancock, G., Stokes, M. A., & Mesibov, G. B. (2020). Differences in romantic relationship experiences for individuals with an autism spectrum disorder. *Sexuality and Disability, 38*(2), 231–245. https://doi.org/10.1007/s11195-019-09573-8

Haney-Caron, E., Goldstein, N. E. S., & Mesiarik, C. (2018). Self-perceived likelihood of false confession: A comparison of justice-involved juveniles and adults. *Criminal Justice and Behavior, 45*(12), 1955–1976. https://doi.org/10.1177/0093854818799806

Hanson, R. K., Helmus, L. M., & Harris, A. J. (2015). Assessing the risk and needs of supervised sexual offenders: A prospective studying using STABLE-2007, STATIC—99R, and STATIC-2002R. *Criminal Justice and Behavior, 42*(12), 1205–1224. https://doi.org/10.1177/0093854815602094

Hanson, R. K., & Morton-Bourgon, K. E. (2009). The accuracy of recidivism risk assessments for sexual offenders: A meta-analysis of 118 predictions studies. *Psychological Assessment, 21*(1), 1–21. https://doi.org/10.1037/a0014421

Hanson, R. K., Sheahan, C. L., & VanZuylen, H. (2013). Static-99 and RRASOR predict recidivism among developmentally delayed sexual offenders: A cumulative meta-analysis. *Sexual Offender Treatment, 8*(1), 1–14.

Hanson, R. K., & Thornton, D. (1999). *Static-99: Improving actuarial risk assessments for sex offenders. (User report 99-02)*. Department of the Solicitor General of Canada.

Hanson, R. K., & Thornton, D. (2000). Improving risk assessments for sex offenders: A comparison of three actuarial scales. *Law and Human Behavior, 24*(1), 119–136. https://doi.org/10.1023/A:1005482921333

Hanson, R. K., & Thornton, D. (2003). *Notes on the development of Static-2002. Corrections Research User Rep. No. 2003–01*. Department of the Solicitor General of Canada.

Hare, D. J., Gould, J., Millis, R., & Wing, L. (1999). *A preliminary study of individuals with autistic spectrum disorders in three special hospitals in England*. National Autistic Society.

Harkins, L., Flak, V. E., Beech, A. R., & Woodhams, S. (2012). Evaluation of a community-based sex offender treatment program using a good lives model approach. *Sexual Abuse: A Journal of Research and Treatment, 24*(6), 519–543. https://doi.org/10.1177/1079063211429469

Harris, A. J. R., Phenix, A., Hanson, R. K., & Thornton, D. (2003). Static-99 coding rules—Revised. Retrieved May 12, 2014, from www.static99.org

Hart-Kerkhoffs, L. A., Jansen, L. M., Doreleijers, T. A., Vermeiren, R., & Minderaa, R. B. (2009). Autism spectrum disorder symptoms in juvenile suspects of sex offenses. *Journal of Clinical Psychiatry, 70*(2), 266–272. https://doi.org/10.4088/jcp.08m04635

Heaton, K. M., & Murphy, G. H. (2013). Men with intellectual disabilities who have attended sex offender treatment groups: A follow-up. *Journal of Applied Research in Intellectual Disabilities, 26*(5), 489–500. https://doi.org/10.1111/jar.12038

Hellemans, H., Colson, K., Verbraeken, C., Vermeiren, R., & Deboutte, D. (2007). Sexual behavior in high-functioning male adolescents and young adults with autism spectrum disorder. *Journal of Autism and Developmental Disorders, 37*(2), 260–269. https://doi.org/10.1007/s10803-006-0159-1

Hellemans, H., Roeyers, H., Leplae, W., Dewaele, T., & Deboutte, D. (2010). Sexual behavior in male adolescents and young adults with autism spectrum disorder and borderline/mild mental retardation. *Sexual Disability, 28*(2), 93–104. https://doi.org/10.1007/s11195-009-9145-9

Hingsburger, D., Griffiths, D., & Quinsey, V. (1991). Detecting counterfeit deviance: Differentiating sexual deviance from sexual inappropriateness. *The Habilitative Mental Healthcare Newsletter, 10*, 51–54.

Johnson, P. R. (2008). Sexual offences of men with intellectual disabilities: A view from private practice. Journal on Developmental Disabilities, 14(2), 79–86.

Johnston, S. J. (2002). Risk assessment in offenders with intellectual disability: The evidence base. *Journal of Intellectual Disability Research, 46*(1), 47–56. https://doi.org/10.1046/j.1365-2788.2002.00003.x

Jones, J. (2007). Persons with intellectual disabilities in the criminal justice system: Review of issues. *International Journal of Offender Therapy and Comparative Criminology, 51*(6), 723–733. https://doi.org/10.1177/0306624X07299343

Kassin, S. M. (2007). Internalized false confessions. In M. P. Toglia, J. D. Read, D. F. Ross, & R. C. L. Lindsay (Eds.), *The handbook of eyewitness psychology* (*Memory for events*) (Vol. 1, pp. 175–192). Lawrence Erlbaum Associates Publisher.

Kassin, S. M., & Kiechel, K. L. (1996). The social psychology of false confessions: Compliance, internalization, and confabulation. *Psychological Science, 7*(3), 125–128. https://doi.org/10.1111/j.1467-9280.1996.tb00344.x

Keeling, J. A., Beech, A. R., & Rose, J. L. (2006). Assessment of intellectually disabled sexual offenders: The current position. *Aggression and Violent Behavior, 12*(2), 229–241. https://doi.org/10.1016/j.avb.2006.08.001

Konstantareas, M. M., & Lunsky, Y. J. (1997). Sociosexual knowledge, experience, attitudes, and interests of individuals with autistic disorder and developmental delay. *Journal of Autism and Developmental Disorders, 27*(4), 397–413. https://doi.org/10.1023/A:1025805405188

Kranendonk, R., Malsch, M., de Poot, C., Teeuwen, M., & Elffers, H. (2019, November 13–16). Suspects with intellectual disability in police interviews: Risks of interviewing techniques for the reliability of suspects statements [Paper Presentation]. American Society of Criminology 75th Annual Meeting, San Francisco, CA. United States.

Lambrick, F., & Glasser, W. (2004). Sex offenders with an intellectual disability. *Sexual Abuse: A Journal of Research and Treatment, 16*(4), 381–392. https://doi.org/10.1177/107906320401600409

Laws, D. R., & Marshall, W. L. (2003). A brief history of behavioral and cognitive behavioral approaches to sexual offenders: Part 1. *Early developments. Sexual Abuse: A Journal of Research and Treatment, 15*(2), 75–92. https://doi.org/10.1023/A:1022325231175

Leo, R. A., & Davis, D. (2010). From false confession to wrongful conviction: Seven psychological processes. *Journal of Psychiatry & Law, 38*(1–2), 9–56. https://doi.org/10.1177/009318531003800103

Leslie, A. M. (1992). Pretense, autism, and the theory-of-mind module. *Current Directions in Psychological Science, 1*(1), 18–21. https://doi.org/10.1111/1467-8721.ep10767818

Levenson, J. S., & D'Amora, D. (2007). Social policies designed to prevent sexual violence: The emperor's new clothes? *Criminal Justice Policy Review, 18*, 168–199. https://doi.org/10.1177/0887403406295309

Lindsay, W. R. (2009). *The treatment of sex offenders with developmental disabilities: A practice workbook*. Wiley-Blackwell.

Lindsay, W. R., Bellshaw, E., Culross, G., Staines, C., & Michie, A. (1992). Increases in knowledge following a course of sex education for people with intellectual disabilities. *Journal of Intellectual Disability Research, 36*(6), 531–539. https://doi.org/10.1111/j.1365-2788.1992.tb00571.x

Lindsay, W., Carson, D., O'Brian, G., Holland, A., Taylor, J. L., Wheeler, J. R., & Steptoe, L. (2014). A comparison of referrals with and without autism spectrum disorder to forensic intellectual disability services. *Psychiatry, Psychology & Law, 21*(6), 947–954. https://doi.org/10.1080/13218719.2014.918081

Lindsay, W. R., Craig, L., & Griffiths, D. M. (2020). *The Wiley handbook on what works for offenders with intellectual and developmental disabilities: An evidence-based approach to theory, assessment and treatment*. John Wiley & Sons.

Lindsay, W. R., Elliot, S. F., & Astell, A. (2004a). Predictors of sexual offence recidivism in offenders with learning disabilities. *Journal of Applied Research in Intellectual Disabilities, 17*(4), 299–305. https://doi.org/10.1111/j.1468-3148.2004.00217.x

Lindsay, W. R., Marshall, I., Neilson, C., Quinn, K., & Smith, A. H. (1998a). The treatment of men with a learning disability convicted of exhibitionism. *Research in Developmental Disabilities, 19*(4), 295–316. https://doi.org/10.1016/s0891-4222(98)00010-9

Lindsay, W. R., Murphy, L., Smith, G., Murphy, D., Edwards, Z., Chittock, C., Grieve, A., & Young, S. J. (2004b). The dynamic risk assessment and management system: An assessment of immediate risk of violence for individuals with offending and challenging behavior. *Journal of Applied Research in Intellectual Disabilities, 17*(4), 267–274. https://doi.org/10.1080/1068316X.2017.1324029

Lindsay, W. R., Olley, S., Jack, C., Morrison, F., & Smith, A. H. (1998b). The treatment of two stalkers with intellectual disabilities using a cognitive approach. *Journal of Applied Research in Intellectual Disabilities, 11*(4), 333–344. https://doi.org/10.1111/j.1468-3148.1998.tb00041.x

Lindsay, W. R., & Smith, A. H. W. (1998). Response to treatment for sex offenders with intellectual disability: A comparison of men with 1-and 2-year probation sentences. *Journal of Intellectual Disability Research, 42*(5), 346–353. https://doi.org/10.1046/j.1365-2788.1998.00147.x

Lindsay, W. R., Smith, A. H. W., Law, J., Quinn, K., Anderson, A., Smith, A., Overend, T., & Allan, R. (2002). A treatment service for sex offenders and abusers with intellectual disability: Characteristics of referrals and evaluation. *Journal of Applied Research in Intellectual Disabilities, 15*(2), 166–174. https://doi.org/10.1046/j.1468-3148.2002.00111.x

Lindsay, W. R., Steele, L., Smith, A. H. W., Quinn, K., & Allan, R. (2006). A community forensic intellectual disability service: Twelve-year follow-up of referrals, analysis of referral patterns and assessment of harm reduction. *Legal and Criminological Psychology, 11*(1), 113–130. https://doi.org/10.1348/135532505X55669

Lindsay, W. R., & Taylor, J. L. (2005). A selective review of research on offenders with developmental disabilities: Assessment and treatment. *Clinical Psychology and Psychotherapy, 12*(3), 201–214. https://doi.org/10.1002/cpp.450

Lindsay, W. R., Ward, T., Morgan, T., & Wilson, I. (2007a). Self-regulation of sex offending, future pathways and the good lives model: Applications and problems. *Journal of Sexual Aggression, 13*(1), 37–50. https://doi.org/10.1080/13552600701365613

Lindsay, W. R., Whitefield, E., & Carson, D. (2007b). An assessment for attitudes consistent with sexual offending for use with offenders with intellectual disabilities. *Legal and Criminological Psychology, 12*(1), 55–68. https://doi.org/10.1348/135532505x85882

Linehan, M. M. (1993). *Cognitive-behavioral treatment of borderline personality disorder*. The Guilford Press.

Looman, J., & Abracen, J. (2013). The risk need responsivity model of offender rehabilitation: Is there really a need for a paradigm shift (2013). *International Journal of Behavioral Consultation and Therapy, 8*(3–4), 30–36. https://doi.org/10.1037/h0100980

MacKenzie, R. D., James, D. V., McEwan, T. E., Mullen, P. E., & Ogloff, J. R. P. (2010). Stalkers and intelligence: Implications for treatment. *The Journal of Forensic Psychiatry & Psychology, 21*(6), 852–872. https://doi.org/10.1080/14789949.2010.503900

Mahoney, M. J. (2009). Asperger's Syndrome and the criminal law: The special case of child pornography, 1–81. Retrieved July 14, 2015, from http://www.harringtonmahoney.com/documents/Aspergers%20Syndrome%20and%20the%20Criminal%20Law%20v26.pdf

Marotta, P. L. (2017). A systematic review of behavioral health interventions for sex offenders with intellectual disabilities. *Sexual Abuse, 29*(2), 148–185. https://doi.org/10.1177/1079063215569546

Mathur-Patel, R. (2015). *Assessing risk in sexual offenders with intellectual disabilities. [Unpublished doctoral dissertation]*. University of Nottingham.

Maulik, P. K., Mascarenhas, M. N., Mathers, C. D., Dua, T., & Saxena, S. (2011). Prevalence of intellectual disability: A meta-analysis of population-based studies. *Research in Developmental Disabilities, 34*(2), 419–436. https://doi.org/10.1016/j.ridd.2010.12.018

McGrath, R. J., Livingston, J. A., & Falk, G. (2007). Community management of sex offenders with intellectual disabilities: Characteristics, services, and outcome of a statewide program. *Intellectual and Developmental Disabilities, 45*(6), 391–398. https://doi.org/10.1352/1934-9556(2007)45[391:CMOSOW]2.0.CO;2

McKenzie, K., Milton, M., Smith, G., & Ouellette-Kuntz, H. (2016). Systematic review of the prevalence and incidence of intellectual disabilities: Current trends and issues. *Current Developmental Disorders Reports, 3*, 104–115. https://doi.org/10.1007/s40474-016-0085-7

McWhinnie, A. J., Wilson, R. J., & Brown, R. E. (2013). Circles of support and accountability: Dimensions of practice, research, and interagency collaboration in prisoner reentry. *Journal of Community Corrections, 22*(2), 5–15.

Mehzabin, P., & Stokes, M. A. (2011). Self-assessed sexuality in young adults with high-functioning autism. *Research in Autism Spectrum Disorders, 5*(1), 614–662. https://doi.org/10.1016/j.rasd.2010.07.006

Mellor, E., & Duff, S. (2019). The use of pornography and the relationship between pornography exposure and sexual offending in males: A systematic review. *Aggressive and Violent Behavior, 46*, 116–126. https://doi.org/10.1016/j.avb.2019.02.003

Mesibov, G., & Sreckovic, M. (2017). Child and juvenile pornography and autism spectrum disorder. In A. Lawrence, J. D. Dubin, & E. Horowitz (Eds.), *Caught in the web of the criminal justice system: Autism, developmental disabilities, and sex offenses* (pp. 64–93). Jessica Kingsley Publishers.

Mintah, K., & Parlow, S. E. (2018). Are you flirting with me? Autistic traits, theory of mind, and inappropriate courtship. *Personality and Individual Differences, 128*, 100–106. https://doi.org/10.1016/j.paid.2018.02.028

Mogavero, M. C. (2016). Autism, sexual offending, and the criminal justice system. *Journal of Intellectual Disabilities and Offending Behavior, 7*(3), 116–126. https://doi.org/10.1108/JIDOB-02-2016-0004

Mogavero, M. C. (2020). An exploratory examination of intellectual disability and mental illness associated with alleged false confessions. *Behavioral Sciences & The Law, 38*(4), 299–316. https://doi.org/10.1002/bsl.2463

Mogavero, M. C., & Hsu, K. H. (2018). Autism spectrum disorder and harassment: An application of attribution theory. *International Journal of Criminology and Sociology, 7*, 260–274. https://doi.org/10.6000/1929-4409.2018.07.19

Mogavero, M. C., & Hsu, K. H. (2020). Dating and courtship behaviors among those with autism spectrum disorder. *Sexuality and Disability, 38*(2), 355–364. https://doi.org/10.1007/s11195-019-09565-8

Mouridsen, S. E. (2012). Current status of research on autism spectrum disorders and offending. *Research in Autism Spectrum Disorders, 6*(1), 79–86. https://doi.org/10.1016/j.rasd.2011.09.003

Mullen, P. E., Pathe, M., Purcell, R., & Stuart, G. W. (1999). Study of stalkers. *American Journal of Psychiatry, 156*(8), 1244–1249. https://ajp.psychiatryonline.org/doi/10.1176/ajp.156.8.1244

Murphy, W. D., Coleman, E. M., & Haynes, M. R. (1983). Treatment and evaluation issues with the mentally retarded sex offender. In J. G. Greer & I. R. Stuart (Eds.), *The sexual aggressor: Current perspectives on treatment* (pp. 22–41). Van Nostrand Reinhold.

National Registry of Exonerations. (2019). Age and mental status of exonerated defendant who confessed. Retrieved from https://www.law.umich.edu/special/exoneration/Documents/Age%20and%20Mental%20Status%20of%20Exonerated%20Defendants%20Who%20Falsely%20Confess%20Table.pdf

Nichols, S., & Blakeley-Smith, A. (2010). "I'm not sure we're ready for this …": Working with families toward facilitating healthy sexuality for individuals with autism spectrum disorders. *Social Work and Mental Health, 8*(1), 72–91. https://doi.org/10.1080/15332980902932383

North, A. S., Russell, A. J., & Gudjonsson, G. H. (2008). High functioning autism spectrum disorders: An investigation of psychological vulnerabilities during interrogative interview. *The Journal of Forensic Psychiatry & Psychology, 19*(3), 323–334. https://doi.org/10.1080/14789940701871621

O'Brien, G., Taylor, J. L., Lindsay, W. R., Holland, A. J., Carson, D., Steptoe, L., Price, K., Middleton, C., & Wheeler, J. (2010). A multi-Centre study of adults with learning disabilities referred to services for antisocial or offending behaviour: Demographic, individual, offending and service characteristics. *Journal of Learning Disabilities and Offending Behaviour, 1*(2), 5–15. https://doi.org/10.5042/jldob.2010.0415

Ogloff, J. R., & Davis, M. R. (2004). Advances in offender assessment and rehabilitation: Contributions of the risk-needs-responsivity approach. *Psychology Crime and Law, 10*(3), 229–242. https://doi.org/10.1080/10683160410001662735

Pavlov, I. P. (1897/1902). *The work of the digestive glands*. Griffin.

Payne, K. L., Maras, K., Russell, A. J., & Brosnan, M. J. (2020). Self-reported motivations for offending by autistic sexual offenders. *Autism, 24*(2), 307–320. https://doi.org/10.1177/1362361319858860

Perske, R. (2011). False confessions from 53 persons with intellectual disabilities: The list keeps growing. *Intellectual and Developmental Disabilities, 46*(6), 468–479. https://doi.org/10.1352/2008.46:468-479

Peterson, C., Slaughter, V., & Paynter, J. (2007). Social maturity and theory of mind in typically developing children and those on the autism spectrum. *Journal of Child Psychology and Psychiatry, 48*(12), 1243–1250. https://doi.org/10.1111/j.1469-7610.2007.01810.x

Phenix, A., Helmus, L., & Hanson, K. (2015). Static-99R and Static-2002R evaluator's workbook. In V. L. Quinsey, G. T. Harris, M. E. Rice, & C. A. Cormier (Eds.), *(2006). Violent offenders: Appraising and managing risk* (2nd ed.). American Psychological Association.

Quinsey, V. L., Harris, G. T., Rice, M. E., & Cormier, C. A. (2006). *Violent offenders: Appraising and managing risk* (2nd ed.). American Psychological Association.

Ray, I., Simpson, A. I. F., Jones, R. M., Shatokhina, K., Thakor, A., & Mulsant, B. H. (2019). Clinical, demographic, and criminal behavior characteristics of patients with intellectual disabilities in a Canadian forensic program. *Frontiers in Psychiatry, 10*, 3–9. https://doi.org/10.3389/fpsyt.2019.00760

Rea, J. A., Williams, D., Saunders, K. J., Dixon, M., Wright, K., & Spradlin, J. E. (2003). Covert sensitization: A generalization analysis in the laboratory and natural environment through the use of a portable-penile plethysmograph. *The Behavior Analyst Today, 4*(2), 192–201. https://doi.org/10.1037/h0100119

Redlich, A. D., Summers, A., & Hoover, S. (2010). Self-reported false confessions and guilty pleas among offenders with mental illness. *Law and Human Behavior, 34*(1), 79–90. https://doi.org/10.1007/s10979-009-9194-8

Reyes, J. R., Vollmer, T. R., & Hall, A. (2011a). Replications and extensions in arousal assessments for sex offenders with developmental disabilities. *Journal of Applied Behavior Analysis, 44*(2), 369–373. https://doi.org/10.1901/jaba.2011.44-369

Reyes, J. R., Vollmer, T. R., & Hall, A. (2011b). The influence of presession factors in the assessment of deviant arousal. *Journal of Applied Behavior Analysis, 44*(4), 707–717. https://doi.org/10.1901/jaba.2011.44-707

Reyes, J. R., Vollmer, T. R., & Hall, A. (2017). Comparison of arousal and preference assessment outcomes for sex offenders with intellectual disabilities. *Journal of Applied Behavior Analysis, 50*(1), 27–37. https://doi.org/10.1002/jaba.364

Reyes, J. R., Vollmer, T. R., Sloman, K. N., Hall, A., Reed, R., Jansen, G., Carr, J., & Stoutmour, M. (2006). Assessment of deviant arousal in adult male sex offenders with developmental disabilities. *Journal of Applied Behavior Analysis, 39*(2), 173–188. https://doi.org/10.1901/jaba.2006.46-05

Rice, M. E., Harris, G. T., & Lang, C. (2013). Validation of and revision of the VRAG and SORAG: The violence risk appraisal guide—Revised (VRAG-R). *Psychological Assessment, 25*(3), 951–965. https://doi.org/10.1037/a0032878

Rice, M. E., Harris, G. T., Lang, C., & Chaplin, T. C. (2008). Sexual preferences and recidivism of sex offenders with mental retardation. *Sexual Abuse: A Journal of Research and Treatment, 20*(4), 409–425. https://doi.org/10.1177/1079063208324662

Rosa's Law, Pub. Law. No. 111-256, Stat. 2781 (2010). https://www.govinfo.gov/app/details/PLAW-111publ256

Roth, M. E., & Gillis, J. M. (2015). "Convenience with the click of a mouse": A survey of adults with autism spectrum disorder on online dating. *Sexuality & Disability, 33*(1), 133–150. https://doi.org/10.1007/s11195-014-9392-2

Sakdalan, J. A., & Collier, V. (2012). Piloting an evidence-based group treatment programme for high risk sex offenders with intellectual disability in New Zealand setting. *New Zealand Journal of Psychology, 41*(2), 6–12. Retrieved from https://www.psychology.org.nz/journal-archive/Sakdalan1.pdf

Schaafsma, D., Kok, G., Stoffelen, J. M. T., & Curfs, L. M. G. (2017). People with intellectual disabilities talk about sexuality: Implications for the development of sex education. *Sexuality and Disability, 35*(1), 21–38. https://doi.org/10.1007/s11195-016-9466-4

Schwartz, R. J., & Robertson, R. E. (2019). A review of research on sexual education for adults with intellectual disabilities. *Career Development and Transition for Exceptional Individuals, 42*(3), 148–157. https://doi.org/10.1177/2165143418756609

Scragg, P., & Shah, A. (1994). Prevalence of Asperger's syndrome in a secure hospital. *British Journal of Psychiatry, 165*(5), 679–682. https://doi.org/10.1192/bjp.165.5.679

Serran, G., Fernandez, Y., Marshall, W. L., & Mann, R. E. (2003). Process issues in treatment: Application to sexual offender programs. *Professional Psychology: Research and Practice, 34*(4), 368–374. https://doi.org/10.1037/0735-7028.34.4.368

Seto, M. C. (2019). The motivation – Facilitation model of sexual offending. *Sexual Abuse, 31*(1), 3–24. https://doi.org/10.1177/1079063217720919

Simons, D. A. (2015). *Adult sex offender typologies*. U.S. Department of Justice. Office of Justice Programs.

Singh, J. P. (2013). Predictive validity performance indicators in violence risk assessment: A methodological primer. *Behavioral Sciences & the Law, 31*(1), 8–22. https://doi.org/10.1002/bsl.2052

Siponmaa, L., Kristiansson, M., Jonson, C., Nyden, A., & Gillberg, C. (2001). Juvenile and young adult mentally disordered offenders: The role of child neuropsychiatric disorders. *Journal of American Academy of Psychiatry Law, 29*(4), 420–426.

Skinner, B. F. (1938). *The behavior of organisms: An experimental analysis*. Appleton-Century.

Søndenaa, E., Rasmussen, K., Helverschou, S. B., Steindal, K., Nilson, B., & Nøttestad, J. A. (2014). Violence and sexual offending behavior in people with Autism Spectrum disorder who have undergone a psychiatric forensic examination. *Psychological Reports: Disability & Trauma, 115*(1), 32–43. https://doi.org/10.2466/16.15.PR0.115c16z5

Steel, C. (2015). The Asperger's defence in digital child pornography investigations. *Psychiatry, Psychology and Law, 23*(3), 473–482. https://doi.org/10.1080/13218719.2015.1080150

Stephens, S., Newman, J. E., Cantor, J. M., & Seto, M. C. (2018). The Static-99R predicts sexual and violent recidivism for individuals with low intellectual functioning. *Journal of Sexual Aggression, 24*(1), 1–11.

Stinson, J. D., & Becker, J. V. (2013). *Treating sex offenders: An evidence-based manual*. The Guilford Press.

Stokes, M. A., & Kaur, A. N. (2005). High-functioning autism and sexuality: A parental perspective. *Autism, 9*(3), 266–289. https://doi.org/10.1177/1362361305053258

Stokes, M. A., & Newton, N. (2004). Autistic spectrum disorders and stalking. *Autism, 8*(3), 337–338. https://doi.org/10.1007/s10803-006-0344-2

Stokes, M. A., Newton, N., & Kaur, A. N. (2007). Stalking, and social and romantic functioning among adolescents and adults with Autism Spectrum disorder. *Journal of Autism and Developmental Disorders, 37*(10), 1969–1986. https://doi.org/10.1007/s10803-006-0344-2

Sullivan, A., & Caterino, L. (2008). Addressing the sexuality and sex education of individuals with autism spectrum disorders. *Education and Treatment of Children, 31*(3), 381–394. http://www.jstor.org/stable/42899984

Sutton, L. R., Hughes, T. L., Huang, A., Lehman, C., Paserba, D., Talkington, V., Taormina, R., Walters, J. B., Fenclau, E., & Marshall, S. (2012). Identifying individuals with autism in a state facility for adolescents adjudicated as sexual offenders: A pilot study. *Focus on Autism and Other Developmental Disabilities, 28*(3), 175–183. https://doi.org/10.1177/1088357612462060

Talbot, T. J., & Langdon, P. E. (2006). A revised sexual knowledge assessment tool for people with intellectual disabilities: Is sexual knowledge related to sexual offending behaviour? *Journal of Intellectual Disability Research, 50*(7), 523–531. https://doi.org/10.1111/j.1365-2788.2006.00801.x

Taylor, K., Mesibov, G., & Debbaudt, D. (2009). Autism in the criminal justice system. *North Carolina Bar Journal, 14*(4), 32–36.

Tewksbury, R. (2005). Collateral consequences of sex offender registration. *Journal of Contemporary Criminal Justice, 21*(1), 67–81. https://doi.org/10.1177/1043986204271704

Tewskbury, R., & Lees, M. (2006). Perceptions of sex offender registration: Collateral consequences and community experiences. *Sociological Spectrum, 26*(3), 309–334. https://doi.org/10.1080/02732170500524246

The Center for Disease Control and Prevention. (n.d.). *Autism spectrum disorder.* The United States Department of Health and Human Services. Retrieved from https://www.cdc.gov/ncbddd/autism/index.html

Thompson, V. R., Stancliffe, R. J., Broom, A., & Wilson, N. J. (2016). Clinicians' use of sexual knowledge assessment tools for people with intellectual disability. *Journal of Intellectual & Developmental Disability, 41*(3), 243–254. https://doi.org/10.3109/13668250.2016.1164303

Turner, G. W., & Crane, B. (2016). Pleasure is paramount: Adults with intellectual disabilities discuss sensuality and intimacy. *Sexualities, 19*(5–6), 677–697. https://doi.org/10.1177/1363460715620573

Underwood, L., McCarthy, J., Chaplin, E., Forrester, A., Mills, R., & Murphy, D. (2016). Autism spectrum disorder traits among prisoners. *Advance in Autism, 2*(3), 106–117. https://doi.org/10.1108/AIA-11-2015-0023

United States Department of Justice. (2018). *Crime in the United States, 2018*. Federal Bureau of Investigation.

United States Department of Justice. Office of Violence Against Women (n.d.). *Stalking*. Retrieved from https://www.justice.gov/ovw/stalking

Van Bourgondien, M. E., Reichle, N. C., & Palmer, A. (1997). Sexual behavior in adults with autism. *Journal of Autism and Developmental Disorders, 27*(2), 113–125. https://doi.org/10.1023/A:1025883622452

Ward, T., & Brown, M. (2004). The Good Lives Model and conceptual issues in offender rehabilitation. Psychology, Crime & Law, 10(3), 243–257. https://doi.org/10.1080/10683160410001662744

Ward, T., & Gannon, T. A. (2006). Rehabilitation, etiology, and self-regulation: The comprehensive good lives model of treatment for sexual offenders. *Aggression and Violent Behavior, 11*(1), 77–94. https://doi.org/10.1016/j.avb.2005.06.001

Ward, T., Mann, R. E., & Gannon, T. A. (2007b). The good lives model of offender rehabilitation: Clinical implications. *Aggression and Violent Behavior, 12*(1), 87–107. https://doi.org/10.1016/j.avb.2006.03.004

Ward, T., Melser, J., & Yates, P. M. (2007a). Reconstructing the risk-need-responsivity model: A theoretical elaboration and evaluation. *Aggression and Violent Behavior, 12*(2), 208–228. https://doi.org/10.1016/j.avb.2006.07.001

Ward, T., & Stewart, C. A. (2003). The treatment of sex offenders: Risk management and good lives. *Professional Psychology: Research and Practice, 34*(4), 353–360. https://doi.org/10.1037/0735-7028.34.4.353

Ward, K. M., Trisher, L., & Pfeuffer, C. K. (2001). Community services, issues, and service gaps for individuals with developmental disabilities who exhibit inappropriate sexual behaviours. *Mental Retardation, 39*(1), 11–19. https://doi.org/10.1352/0047-6765(2001)039<0011:CSIASG>2.0.CO;2

Watson, J. B. (1913). Psychology as the behaviorist views it. *Psychological Review, 20*(2), 158–177. https://doi.org/10.1037/h0074428

Weinrott, M. R., Riggan, M., & Frothingham, S. (1997). Reducing deviant arousal in juvenile sex offenders using vicarious sensitization. *Journal of Interpersonal Violence, 12*(5), 704–728. https://doi.org/10.1177/088626097012005007

Wilcox, D. T., Beech, A., Markall, H. F., & Blacker, J. (2009). Actuarial risk assessment and recidivism in a sample of UK intellectually disabled sexual offenders. *Journal of Sexual Aggression, 15*(1), 97–106. https://doi.org/10.1080/13552600802578577

Wilson, D. B., Gottfredson, D. C., & Najaka, S. S. (2001). School-based prevention of problem behaviors: A meta-analysis. *Journal of Quantitative Criminology, 17*(3), 247–272. https://doi.org/10.1023/A:1011050217296

Wilson, R. J., & Yates, P. M. (2009). Effective interventions and the good lives model: Maximizing treatment gains for sexual offenders. *Aggression and Violent Behavior, 14*(3), 157–161. https://doi.org/10.1016/j.avb.2009.01.007

Wolfe, P. S., Condo, B., & Hardaway, E. (2009). Sociosexuality education for persons with autism Spectrum disorders using applied behavior analysis. *Teaching Exceptional Children, 42*(1), 50–61. https://doi.org/10.1177/004005990904200105

Woodbury-Smith, M. R., Clare, I. C. H., Holland, A. J., & Kearns, A. (2006). High functioning autistic Spectrum disorders, offending and other law-breaking: Findings from a community sample. *The Journal of Forensic Psychiatry & Psychology, 17*(1), 108–120. https://doi.org/10.1080/14789940600589464

Woodbury-Smith, M. R., Clare, I. C. H., Holland, A. J., Kearns, A., Staufenberg, E., & Watson, P. (2005). A case-control study of offenders with high functioning autistic Spectrum disorders. *The Journal of Forensic Psychiatry & Psychology, 16*(4), 747–763. https://doi.org/10.1080/14789940500302554

World Health Organization. (1948). *International classification of diseases and related health problems* (6th ed.).

World Health Organization. (1967). *International classification of diseases and related health problems* (8th ed.).

World Health Organization. (2018/2022). *International classification of diseases and related health problems* (11th ed.).

Yirmiya, N., Erel, O., Shaked, M., & Solomonics-Levi, D. (1998). Meta-analyses comparing theory of mind abilities of individuals with autism, individuals with mental retardation, and normally developing individuals. *Psychological Bulletin, 124*(3), 283–307. https://doi.org/10.1037/0033-2909.124.3.283

Zgoba, K. M. (2011). Residence restriction buffer zones and the banishment of sex offenders: Have we gone one step too far? *Criminology & Public Policy, 10*(2), 391–400. https://doi.org/10.1111/capp.2011.10.issue-2

Chapter 17
Personality Disorders, Psychopathy, and Sexual Offending

Mark E. Olver and Emily K. Riemer

17.1 Introduction

Mental health diagnoses tend to be overrepresented in correctional and forensic populations on a global scale, and among persons with histories of sexual offending (Moulden et al., 2014). The relationship between mental disorder and crime is reciprocal and complex; however, for reasons that will become apparent shortly, certain classes or categories of psychopathology, such as personality disorders (PDs) are much more likely to have high representation in sexual offending populations. In turn, knowledge of PD diagnosis, or particularly serious PD variants such as psychopathy, can inform assessment, case formulation, and intervention with persons who have sexually offended.

This chapter covers the role and relevance of PD in general, and psychopathy in particular, for sexual offending behavior. It begins with a review of the clinical and etiologic relevance of PD in sexual offending, including base rates of PD in forensic and correctional adult male sexual offending samples. The chapter proceeds with a review of the psychopathy construct, its role and relevance in the commission of sexual violence, and its representation in sexual offending populations as moderated by victim profile. The risk-relevance of PD and psychopathy in sexual violence risk assessment and management, including the intersection of these diagnoses with other clinically and forensically meaningful risk constructs (e.g., sexual deviance) will then be reviewed. Finally, sexual violence treatment and risk management considerations for psychopathy in sexual offending populations, including a model for treatment and a review of recent treatment outcome research, is discussed.

M. E. Olver (✉) · E. K. Riemer
Department of Psychology and Health Studies, University of Saskatchewan, Saskatoon, SK, Canada
e-mail: mark.olver@usask.ca

R. J. Tully et al. (eds.), *Best Practices in Sexual Offender Assessment and Management*, Dangerous Behavior in Clinical and Forensic Psychology,
https://doi.org/10.1007/978-3-031-83135-5_17

17.2 Personality Disorder in Sexual Offending Samples

PDs represent an enduring and inflexible pattern of behavior and inner experience (cognition and perception) that: (i) depart considerably from societal norms, (ii) persist across multiple social and interpersonal situations and contexts, (iii) generate clinically meaningful distress and/or impairment in relational, occupational, or other important areas of functioning, and (iv) demonstrate stability across the lifespan, being traceable back to adolescence or emerging adulthood (American Psychiatric Association [APA], 2013). The components of interpersonal impairment, rigidity, and stability over the lifespan typify PD. The Diagnostic and Statistical Manual of Mental Disorders fifth edition (DSM-5; APA, 2013) recognizes three clusters of PD, each of which represent different symptom profiles and constellations of maladaptive personality traits: Cluster A, Odd and Eccentric (paranoid, schizoid, and schizotypal PD), Cluster B, Dramatic, Emotional, and Erratic (antisocial, borderline, narcissistic, histrionic), and Cluster C, Anxious and Fearful (avoidant, dependent, obsessive compulsive).

PDs represent a fundamental disturbance in identity and interpersonal functioning; PDs are ultimately relational disorders, and without relationships, PDs arguably would not exist. After all, without some interpersonal context, to whom would someone avoid, be dependent upon, antisocial towards, manipulative of, grandiose around, paranoid of, or attention seeking from? Conceptualizations of personality in terms of the Big Five and the Circumplex model lean toward stable and characteristic aspects of self and other. Therefore, it can be reasonably concluded that certain PDs are overrepresented in people who engage in harmful or destructive behavior to others such as intimate partner violence, general interpersonal violence, and sexual violence. Sexual offenses are ultimately relational offenses, with the individual imposing themselves sexually upon another non-reciprocating individual, and the presence of a PD may catalyze such interactions. A person who is avoidant or dependent may lack the interpersonal maturity for adult relationships and seek out children for sexual and social outlets. Further, an individual who is narcissistic, emotionally dysregulated, or self-centered and rule defying may use sexual coercion to satisfy their own immediate sexual urges, exact revenge, or inflict harm.

17.2.1 Base Rates of Personality Disorders in Sexual Offending Samples

As with general and correctional forensic samples, PDs in general and cluster B PDs in particular are overrepresented in sexual offending populations, with the highest prevalence being ASPD by a considerable margin, followed by lower frequencies of diagnoses from the B and C clusters, as well as PD not otherwise specified (PD NOS). There is a great deal of jurisdictional and regional variation in base rates of PD in adult male sexual offending samples. At least four studies in German prison or forensic hospital settings of men convicted of sexual offenses have reported high lifetime prevalence rates of PD ranging from about 40–60% (Dudeck et al., 2007; Harsch et al., 2006; Leue et al., 2004; Schroeder et al., 2013). ASPD had the highest base rate of all PD diagnoses in three out of four studies (26–36%), followed by other cluster B including borderline (5–19%), narcissistic (7–37%), or avoidant from Cluster C (4–24%; Dudeck et al., 2007; Harsch et al., 2006; Leue et al., 2004; Schroeder et al., 2013). In a small forensic inpatient sample in The Netherlands (40% of whom were convicted for sexual offenses), two-thirds of the sample met criteria for any PD, diagnosed from the DSM-IIIR Personality Disorders Questionnaire, with the highest base rate PD diagnoses being ASPD (60%), Paranoid (52%), and Borderline (50%; Derks, 1996). Bogaerts et al. (2008), in a Belgian sample of 70 men convicted for child sexual offenses, found that those with paraphilia diagnoses had a greater presence of borderline, histrionic, obsessive compulsive, and depressive PD symptomatology than nonparaphilic child sexual abusers.

A large Canadian study of 747 men convicted for sexual offenses found the overall base rate of ASPD to be about 17%, however, the highest base rates were found in men who had committed sexual homicides (51%), violent sexual offenses (41%), and who were sadistic (39%), vs. the large majority of men who did not employ excessive force or aggression (11%; Langevin, 2003). A Canadian study that examined profiles of mental illness among incarcerated and hospitalized men with sex offenses (N = 134) found an overall base rate of 41% for any PD and the highest prevalence being ASPD (18%), with a slightly higher prevalence of in men with adult victims vs. those who had offended against children (21% vs. 15%, respectively; Moulden et al., 2014). Finally, a Canadian study of two treated sexual offending samples, one a high intensity program of federally sentenced men (n = 394, study 1), the other a sample of men convicted for sexual offenses assessed at a sexual behaviors clinic (n = 586, study 2), found elevated rates of PD in general (74% and 14%, respectively) and for the high intensity sample, ASPD (56%) in particular (Kingston et al., 2015).

Additionally, some studies have examined PD prevalence using the MCMI-III base rate cut scores with sexual offending samples. A UK study comparing samples of men convicted for rape (n = 112) vs. sexual murder (n = 58) found both groups had high base rates of antisocial, depressive, and avoidant PD traits (16–24%) as well as anxiety and alcohol problems (Oliver et al., 2007). Similarly, a US prison inmate sample (N = 695), found men convicted for sex offenses also to have high MCMI-III base rates (24–37%) of antisocial, depressive, avoidant, or dependent PD traits (Alhmeyer et al., 2003) with base rates of internalizing PD symptomatology was highest among men with child victims.

In conclusion, ASPD is the norm rather than the exception, ASPD is most common, and individuals who are higher risk, commit more violent offenses, and are in higher security settings tend to have higher base rates of the diagnosis. Other cluster B diagnoses (narcissistic, borderline) are also overrepresented compared to the general community population but tend to be lower in frequency. Some cluster C diagnoses (avoidant) may have etiologic relevance by virtue of relational impairment and rejection sensitivity, accounting for higher rates particularly among men who sexually abuse children.

17.3 Psychopathy in Sexual Offending Samples

17.3.1 Psychopathy: Conceptualization, Diagnosis, and Measurement

Psychopathy is a serious personality disorder overrepresented in correctional and forensic settings that is characterized by a constellation of problematic interpersonal, affective, and behavioral features. The most widely used operationalization of the psychopathy construct is Hare's Psychopathy Checklist-Revised (PCL-R; Hare, 1991, 2003), a 20-item symptom construct clinical rating scale developed to assess psychopathy. Items are rated from institutional file and/or clinical interview and scored on a three-point scale of 0 (trait absent), 1 (possibly, partially present), or 2 (yes, trait present). Total scores range from 0 to 40 and represent the extent to which the person assessed resembles a prototypical psychopathic individual. Although research has demonstrated psychopathy to be a dimensional construct (Edens et al., 2006), cut-off scores ranging from 25 (file based, research purposes) to 30 (with interview) have been used to characterize psychopathy. The mean score for North American male offenders is approximately 22 and SD of 8, and SEM of approximately 3–4 points.

Confirmatory factor analytic research of the PCL-R and its derivatives (PCL: Screening Version, Hart et al., 1995; PCL: Youth Version, Forth et al., 2003) provide evidence for a correlated four factor model corresponding to interpersonal (e.g., superficial charm, grandiosity, deceitful, manipulative), affective (e.g., lack of remorse, callous, shallow emotions, doesn't accept responsibility), lifestyle (e.g., need for stimulation, parasitic, lacks goals, impulsivity, irresponsibility), and antisocial (e.g., poor behavior controls, early behavior problems, juvenile delinquency, release failure, criminal versatility) dimensions (Neumann et al., 2014). Two items, sexual promiscuity and multiple short-term marital relationships—both of which have particular salience to sexual offending populations—do not typically load on any of the factors. Further, the four factors (often referred to as facets in the psychopathy literature) are subsumed by two broad factors, with Factor 1 (the personality and emotional style of psychopathy) subsuming the interpersonal and affective facets and Factor 2 (chronic antisocial lifestyle) subsuming the lifestyle and antisocial facets.

ASPD and psychopathy are not synonymous (Hart & Hare, 1996; Hare & Neumann, 2008). The DSM-5 criteria for ASPD, as with its predecessors, is behaviorally based and essentially captures the Factor 2 (lifestyle and antisocial) features of psychopathy with few features of Factor 1 (Hare & Neumann, 2008; Ogloff, 2006; Ogloff et al., 2016). Psychopathy can be distinguished by the prominence of the interpersonal and affective features; some have used the term sociopathy (and akin to ASPD) to refer to persons who have prominent Factor 2 features but relatively few Factor 1 traits (Hare & Neumann, 2008). As such, most individuals with psychopathy will also have ASPD along with traits or even diagnoses of narcissistic and histrionic PD; however, only a proportion of individuals with ASPD will be psychopathic (Hart & Hare, 1989; Ogloff et al., 2016).

PCL-R measured psychopathy is associated with most criminal behavioral criteria including violent recidivism (Campbell et al., 2009; Yang et al., 2010), general recidivism (Leistico et al., 2008), institutional behavior problems, including violence (Olver et al., 2020), and both instrumental and reactive violence (Blais et al., 2014). Hare (1999) has commented that psychopathy is conducive to forms of instrumental violence such as sexual offending in particular, and that base rates of PCL-R measured psychopathy should be elevated in sexual offending populations.

17.3.2 Psychopathy Base Rates and PCL-R Profiles in Sexual Offending Samples

Table 17.1 presents a summary of PCL-R psychopathy ratings in incarcerated samples of men convicted for sexual offenses. The table is organized by victim profile and PCL-R score components for the sample. Median values presented at the bottom of each victim profile group provide an aggregate of PCL-R factor, total scores, and base rate. Several themes are noteworthy. First, the most frequent cut-off employed was 25 given that these were file-based ratings and 8 out of the 11 studies featured Canadian samples. Second, the median base rate was approximately one quarter (24.5%) of sexual offending samples, with a total score of approximately 20 (out of 40) and Factor 1 and 2 scores similarly proportioned at around 8 (out of 16) and 10 (out of 20) points, respectively. Given the small number of studies that reported scores on the individual facets, these are not presented. Third, Table 17.1 also shows that the base rate and PCL-R profiles vary as a function of victim profile. Men who had adult sexual offense victims (i.e., most typically sexual assault of adult women) or who were polymorphous in their victim selection (i.e., having at least one adult and one child victim, aka the "mixed" profile) had: (i) substantially higher psychopathy base rates (upwards of 1/3 overall), and (ii) higher PCL-R total (by approximately 1SD) and factor scores (especially Factor 2, by about 1SD, about 1/3SD for Factor 1), compared to men with intrafamilial or extrafamilial child victims. The psychopathy base rates are about twice that for men sexually assaulting adults or both adults and children compared to the general prison population, and the median PCL-R score was consistent with the North American male offender average reported in Hare (2003). Men with the mixed profile had slightly higher median PCL-R total scores overall than men with only the adult victim profile which could be accounted for by higher Factor 1 scores (approximately 1/3 SD).

Table 17.1 PCL-R scores and psychopathy base rates as a function of sexual offense victim profile

Study	Country	PCL-R cut-off	Victim profile	n	BR	PCL-R score M (SD)		
						Total	Factor 1	Factor 2
Beggs and Grace (2008)	New Zealand	25	Overall	216	4.6	8.2 (7.3)	–	–
Brown et al. (2015)	USA	30	Overall	719	22.3	23.6 (7.1)	8.9 (3.3)	12.2 (4.3)
Brown and Forth (1997)	Canada	30	Overall	60	35.0	24.9 (6.7)	8.6 (4.0)	12.1 (2.9)
Hildebrand et al. (2004)	Netherlands	26	Overall	94	35.1	22.2 (7.3)	7.7 (3.5)	11.8 (4.7)
Langton et al. (2006)	Canada	25	Overall	418	15.8	15.6 (7.2)	–	–
Looman et al. (2005)	Canada	25	Overall	272	41.5	22.3 (7.7)	–	–
Olver and Riemer (2021)	Canada	25	Overall	426	17.8	18.2 (6.6)	6.8 (3.5)	9.3 (4.1)
Olver and Wong (2006)	Canada	25	Overall	156	28.8	20.2 (7.4)	6.0 (3.3)	10.0 (4.3)
Porter et al. (2000)	Canada	30	Overall	229	26.8	24.1 (6.7)	10.1 (3.5)	10.3 (4.3)
Rice and Harris (1997)	Canada	25	Overall	288	–	16.7 (7.8)	–	–
Serin et al. (1994)	Canada	29	Overall	65	9.9	15.3 (8.4)	5.5	8.3
			Median		24.5	20.2	7.7	10.3
Brown et al. (2015)	USA	30	Adult	468	25.5	24.3 (7.0)	9.2 (3.3)	12.6 (4.1)
Brown and Forth (1997)	Canada	30	Adult	60	35.0	24.9 (6.7)	8.6 (4.0)	12.1 (2.9)
Hildebrand et al. (2004)	Netherlands	26	Adult	94	35.1	22.2 (7.3)	7.7 (3.5)	11.8 (4.7)
Olver and Riemer (2021)	Canada	25	Adult	195	24.1	19.3 (6.7)	6.7 (3.7)	10.5 (3.9)
Olver and Wong (2006)	Canada	25	Adult	76	36.8	21.9 (7.3)	6.3 (3.5)	11.1 (4.1)
Porter et al. (2000)	Canada	30	Adult	103	35.9	25.9 (5.9)	10.1 (3.4)	12.0 (3.3)
Rice and Harris (1997)	Canada	25	Adult	88	–	18.8 (9.0)	–	–
Serin et al. (1994)	Canada	29	Adult	33	12.2	17.1 (8.6)	6.2	9.4
			Median		35.0	22.1	7.7	11.8
Brown et al. (2015)	USA	30	Mixed	40	32.5	26.7 (6.2)	10.4 (3.1)	13.6 (3.5)

(continued)

Table 17.1 (continued)

Study	Country	PCL-R cut-off	Victim profile	n	BR	PCL-R score M (SD) Total	Factor 1	Factor 2
Olver and Riemer (2021)	Canada	25	Mixed	54	17.6	20.0 (5.3)	7.1 (3.3)	10.7 (3.2)
Olver and Wong (2006)	Canada	25	Mixed	26	42.3	22.7 (7.3)	6.4 (3.9)	11.4 (3.5)
Porter et al. (2000)	Canada	30	Mixed	25	64.0	29.0 (6.5)	11.8 (4.2)	12.3 (3.0)
Rice and Harris (1997)	Canada	25	Mixed	58	–	21.5 (8.1)	–	–
			Median		37.4	22.7	8.8	11.9
Beggs and Grace (2008)	New Zealand	25	EF child	92	6.5	9.5 (8.1)	–	–
Olver and Riemer (2021)	Canada	25	EF child	86	15.1	17.7 (6.8)	7.3 (3.7)	8.4 (3.9)
Olver and Wong (2006)	Canada	25	EF child	25	4.0	15.9 (5.8)	5.5 (2.9)	7.8 (3.5)
Porter et al. (2000)	Canada	30	EF child	48	6.3	20.9 (6.1)	9.3 (3.6)	8.3 (4.0)
Beggs and Grace (2008)	New Zealand	25	IF child	124	3.2	7.2 (6.4)	–	–
Olver and Riemer (2021)	Canada	25	IF child	91	7.7	15.2 (6.2)	6.5 (3.1)	6.8 (3.9)
Olver and Wong (2006)	Canada	25	IF child	29	17.2	17.7 (6.8)	5.3 (2.8)	7.8 (4.8)
Porter et al. (2000)	Canada	30	IF child	37	10.8	21.2 (6.4)	10.2 (3.2)	7.6 (4.5)
Brown et al. (2015)	USA	30	EF/IF child	211	13.7	21.3 (7.5)	7.9 (3.4)	11.2 (4.8)
Rice and Harris (1997)	Canada	25	EF/IF child	142	–	13.4 (6.9)	–	–
Serin et al. (1994)	Canada	29	EF/IF child	32	7.5	13.2 (7.8)	4.7	7.0
			Median		7.6	15.9	6.9	7.8

Note: BR = base rate of psychopathy (%)

In short, men who target adult victims, or who are indiscriminate in the age profile of their victims are likely to have a history of nonsexual criminality, other dynamic risk factors relevant to sexual and nonsexual offending (e.g., substance abuse, antisocial peers, education/employment), consistent with other prison inmates without sexual crimes and also consistent with Factor 2 (Olver & Wong, 2006). It also makes sense that men with the mixed offense profile, with a history of sexually abusing both children and adults, may be higher on some of the interpersonal and affective features (e.g., callousness, lack of remorse) than other sexual offending groups. This group also showed the greatest variability in psychopathy base rates (ranging from about 1/5 to 2/3 of samples), part of which may be attributable to range restriction in some of the samples (e.g., Olver & Riemer, 2021). Such profiles would be consistent with concordant diagnoses of ASPD or other cluster B PDs such as narcissistic and histrionic diagnoses.

Further, Knight and Guay (2018) suggest that psychopathy's propensity for sexual violence—particularly toward women—represents intersecting dimensions of callous-manipulativeness and hypersexuality, which may underpin the psychopathy deviance nexus, its relation to sexual violence, and the higher representation of psychopathy among mixed and adult rape victim profiles. From an evolutionary standpoint, indicators of hypersexuality such as short-term relationships, high mating effort, and low parental investment, are characteristic of psychopathy, and particularly for sexual aggression toward adult women (in evolutionary terms, there would high potential for reproductive payoff). Moreover, features such as callous-manipulativeness would facilitate the commission of violent sexual acts, tolerance of (or indifference to) victim distress, and the use of whatever violent means necessary to obtain victim compliance and obtain sexual gratification (Knight & Guay, 2018).

Men who targeted solely child victims either in the context of extrafamilial child molestation or intrafamilial sexual abuse, tended to have considerably lower PCL-R scores overall. They had lower Factor 1 scores by about 1/3 to 2/3 SD, but the largest disparity from the other sexual offense profile groups was in terms of Factor 2, where the median score across samples was approximately 1 full SD lower than the adult or mixed victim profile groups. Men who target children are more likely to have social skills deficits and emotional congruence with children (McPhail et al., 2013); such social and emotional pathology would seem to be consistent with other PDs found to be elevated in sexual offending samples such as avoidant and dependent (in addition to ASPD). They have less nonsexual criminal history and tend to have less propensity for violence and aggression. Elements of their sexual offending would invariably involve a considerable degree of manipulativeness (e.g., victim grooming, secretiveness) as well as callousness and self-centeredness (particularly if abusing their own children or relatives). There are important psychological differences between intrafamilial and extrafamilial child sexual abusers (Seto et al., 2015), in terms of PCL-R score, this is more likely to appear in terms of higher Factor 2 scores for extrafamilial subtypes as seen in the table and reported elsewhere (Seto et al., 2015).

17.4 Psychopathy and Personality Disorder in Sexual Offense Risk Assessment

17.4.1 Risk Relevance and Predictive Validity of Personality Disorder

What is the role and relevance of psychopathy and PD in sexual offense risk assessment? The available literature shows that non-substance related mental disorders (NSMD), such as anxiety, depression, and psychosis without concordant concerns with substance misuse to be weak predictors of recidivism in general correctional populations (Bonta et al., 1998, 2014; Rezansoff et al. 2013), as well as among sexual offending samples in particular (Hanson & Bussière, 1998; Kingston et al., 2015; Mann et al., 2010). By contrast, diagnoses of PD in general, and ASPD in particular, have demonstrated robust associations with recidivism in sexual offending and general correctional samples. For instance, in their landmark meta-analysis of sexual offense recidivism predictor variables across 61 studies and more than 23,000 individuals with histories of sexual offending, Hanson and Bussière (1998) found any PD and ASPD to each be significantly predictive of sexual (r_w = .16 and .14, respectively), general (r_w = .21 and .16, respectively), and nonsexual violent (r_w = .19, ASPD only) recidivism.

Moreover, in a pair of studies examining diagnostic and risk predictors of recidivism in large Canadian samples of men incarcerated for sexual offenses (*N*s = 390 and 586), Kingston et al. (2015) found that any PD diagnosis was associated with a more than twofold increase in the odds of violent or general recidivism, although it was not significantly predictive of sexual recidivism. Further, in one sample with ASPD diagnostic information available (*N* = 390), the presence of this diagnosis was associated with a similar twofold increase in the odds of violent or general recidivism, but again not sexual recidivism. In Cox regression analyses, ASPD diagnoses also predicted violent and general recidivism after controlling for posttreatment dynamic risk scores on the Violence Risk Scale-Sexual Offense version (VRS-SO; Wong et al., 2003–2017). In all, the sexual offense risk literature has demonstrated PD and ASPD have risk relevance (as does SUD), but NSMDs do not.

17.4.2 Risk Relevance and Predictive Validity of PCL-R Measured Psychopathy

The psychopathy and sexual offending literature has yielded similar conclusions. Hare (1999) has written extensively on a psychopathic individual's penchant for instrumental violence, including sexual violence. In what he termed the "deadly combination", Hare (1999) advanced that the combination of high psychopathy and high sexual deviance (e.g., sadism, pedophilia, or other pedophilias) potentiates risk for future sexual violence. A combination of high psychopathy and sexual deviance has featured prominently in both real life and fictitious examples of serial sexual murderers, such as Ted Bundy, Kenneth Bianchi, Edmund Kemper, Jeffrey Dahmer, Richard Ramirez, John Wayne Gacy, as well as notorious Canadian examples such as Clifford Olson, Paul Bernardo, and Colonel Russell Williams.

At least four meta-analyses have examined the predictive validity of the PCL-R and its variants for recidivism in sexual offending samples. In these prediction studies, small effects are characterized by Area Under the Curve (AUC) = .56, point biserial correlation (r_{pb}) = .10, and standardized mean difference (d) = .20; medium effects AUC = .64, r_{pb} = .24, d = .50; and large effects AUC = .71, r_{pb} = .37, d = .80

(Rice & Harris, 2005). The most comprehensive meta-analysis, Hawes et al. (2013), also examined the PCL-R psychopathy and sexual deviance nexus and its association with recidivism. Across 20 studies and over 5300 sexual offenders, the PCL-R total score had a significant small to moderate effect for predicting sexual recidivism (d = .40) and a moderate effect for predicting violent recidivism (ds = 55). Across a smaller subset of studies, Factor 1 had subthreshold effects for both sexual and violent recidivism (ds = .17 and .08, respectively) while Factor 2 had broadly moderate effects for these outcomes (d = .44 and .63, respectively). Other meta-analyses have similarly found PCL total scores to have moderate predictive effects for general and violent recidivism (Hanson & Morton-Bourgon, 2004) and small effects (d < .20) for sexual recidivism (Hanson & Morton-Bourgon, 2005; Mokros et al., 2014; Walters, 2003). Hawes et al. (2013) identified 7 studies that had examined the interaction of psychopathy and sexual deviance in their relationship, and found a 2.80 to 3.21 increase in the odds of sexual recidivism when both psychopathy and sexual deviance were present vs. one or fewer domains.

To contextualize these findings, it is important to consider the primary domains underpinning sexual violence risk: (i) sexual deviance, a constellation of atypical or illegal sexual interests, compulsive sexuality, and problems with sexual self-regulation; and (ii) general criminality or antisociality, a general risk-need domain akin to the Central Eight (Andrews et al., 2006) that taps a broad propensity for rule violation (Hanson & Morton-Bourgon, 2005). Studies have found inconsistent associations between PCL-R total and factor scores with the sexual deviance construct, with several studies finding small or negligible associations (rs ≤ .10 s) (Looman et al., 2013; Olver & Wong, 2009; Seto et al., 2004) and others detecting a positive association (Hildebrand et al., 2004; Serin et al., 1994). However, PCL-R total and factor scores, particularly Factor 2, have consistently demonstrated positive moderate to large correlations (rs = .30–.50+) with measures of general risk and need in sexual offending (Barbaree et al., 2001; Olver & Wong, 2009), violent offending (Douglas et al., 2005; Wong & Gordon, 2006), and general correctional (Simourd & Hoge, 2000) samples. Some research as well has shown Factor 1 to have moderate to large correlations with measures of sexual offense attitudes and poor treatment responsivity (Olver & Wong, 2009). Factor 2 thus captures the general criminality or antisociality domain of sexual violence risk well (which has shared variance with Factor 1), while the instrument would not capture the sexual deviance domain, and other components of the tool likely covary with other less prominent domains of sexual violence risk (e.g., offense supportive attitudes, intimacy deficits).

As an indication of this, the PCL-R has been found to incrementally predict sexual recidivism beyond a measure of sexual deviance in some sexual offending samples (e.g., Hildebrand et al., 2004; Olver & Wong, 2006; Seto et al., 2004). Formal examinations of incremental predictive validity have found, however, that PCL-R total scores tend not to be incrementally predictive of sexual recidivism after introducing a more comprehensive control for sexual violence risk such as Static-99R (Looman et al., 2013) or the VRS-SO (Olver & Wong, 2009; Sewall &

Olver, 2019), while the purpose built sexual offense risk measures do uniquely predict this outcome, likely given that they capture both the sexual deviance and criminality domains of sexual violence risk. That said, for broader outcomes such as general violence and general criminal recidivism, the PCL-R and sexual violence risk tools have each been found to incrementally predict such outcomes. In a sexual offense treatment sample of 272 men, Looman et al. (2013) found the Static-99R and PCL-R each significantly predicted violent recidivism, while Sewall and Olver (2019), in a similarly treated sample of 296 men, found the PCL-R and VRS-SO total scores also each uniquely predicted general violence.

17.4.3 Use of the PCL-R in Sexual Violence Risk Assessment

So, what is the place for the PCL-R and its derivatives, and more broadly, ASPD and other cluster B diagnoses in sexual violence risk assessment? First, the PCL-R and these diagnoses have a place given that they have general risk and need ramifications; on their own they are predictive of sexual recidivism, and when paired with a sexual violence risk measure, these variables are still frequently predictive of violent and general recidivism. The PCL-R can complement a sexual violence risk measure (or measures) well in this regard; its combination with high sexual deviance has been demonstrated to elevate risk for sexual recidivism. Similarly, a low PCL-R score can be highly informative in terms of risk for nonsexual offending outcomes or potential for institutional behavioral or management concerns; importantly, the tool needs to be used in tandem with one or more measures of recidivism risk.

Second, PCL-R scores and PD diagnoses can inform correctional and release planning. High PCL-R scores will generally be indicative of high criminogenic need, which in turn, can be directly assessed via a dynamic risk assessment tool such as the VRS-SO, STABLE 2007 (Hanson et al., 2007), or the Sex Offender Treatment Information and Progress Scale (SOTIPS; McGrath et al., 2012). Third, and relatedly, the PCL-R and the use of one or more sexual violence risk tools can drive treatment planning, particularly the presence of high psychopathy and high deviance (or above average sexual violence risk in general), would suggest a high intensity sexual offense treatment program (per the risk principle), that is comprehensive in its treatment foci (per the need principle), and the potential for a number of potential challenging treatment-related behaviors that would need to be nimbly addressed to promote client retention and to maximize gain (per the responsivity principle). It is this final section of treatment issues with sexual offending high psychopathy and PD clientele to which this chapter now turns.

17.5 Psychopathy and Personality Disorder in Sexual Offense Treatment

17.5.1 Psychopathy, Therapeutic Pessimism, and Service Integrity

PD is of often viewed as synonymous with treatment resistance, and similarly, there is a long history of psychopathy and therapeutic pessimism in the literature and clinical practice (Olver, 2016). Indeed, research from meta-analyses demonstrates that PCL-R scores, ASPD diagnosis, and any PD diagnosis are each significantly associated with increased drop out from sexual offense treatment as well as other types of correctional programming (Olver et al., 2011). Research that has dug a little deeper into examining treatment dynamics of psychopathy in correctional programs has found that different aspects of the syndrome seem to interfere in treatment response in different ways. For instance, Factor 1 traits may give rise to treatment challenges as the interpersonal and affective features do not bode well for forming or maintaining quality relationships with co-patients or staff (e.g., therapeutic alliance; DeSorcy et al., 2020). Further, per Factor 1, high PCL-R scoring men can be abrasive and antagonistic in their interpersonal relations, they may be superficially charming and adept at manipulation, pushing boundaries, and creating friction or division between staff members. And behaviorally, high psychopathy men may lack motivation, display poor therapeutic work ethic, be verbally abusive or intimidating, or behave disruptively in group therapy settings (Olver, 2016; Olver et al., 2020; Olver & Riemer, 2021).

While the aforementioned treatment correlates may be established within research, this is not to say that high psychopathy individuals may not similarly benefit from evidence informed correctional services as demonstrated by other high risk, high need populations (Olver, 2016). For instance, the principles of risk (i.e., treatment intensity matched to a client's correctional risk level), need (i.e., dynamic risk factors, aka criminogenic needs, are prioritized for intervention), and responsivity (i.e., interventions are individualized to promote engagement and motivation) for correctional intervention has well established reductions in recidivism across client groups (Andrews & Bonta, 2010; Olver, 2016).

Even with well-established models of service delivery such as RNR in place for some time, high profile treatment outcome evaluations, sometimes featuring questionable treatment regimes, have held much traction in the past and the psychopathy treatment field has been slow to adjust. One vivid example is an archival review by Rice et al. (1992) examining a therapeutic community (TC) program delivered at a secure mental health facility in Ontario, Canada. High psychopathy men attending the program had significantly higher rates of violent recidivism post release (77%) compared to similarly psychopathic men who did not attend the program (55%). Conversely, low psychopathy men who attended the TC had lower rates of violent recidivism over the follow up (22%) than those who did not (39%). As Simourd and Hoge (2000) note, however, the psychopathy treatment field has been "short on quantity and long on lore" (p. 270), with most outcome studies failing to adhere to RNR, such as was the case for the TC examined by Rice et al. (1992). The program simply did not follow RNR principles; high and low risk men were intermixed, there were no structured psychological interventions, and the clients were left to confront each other without prosocial modeling or involvement from staff.

17.5.2 Psychopathy and RNR Based Services: The 2-C Model

Research emerging subsequent to the Rice et al. (1992) evaluation, including quantitative reviews, has painted a more optimistic picture showing that although high psychopathy men are harder to treat, the majority do improve in some form with treatment (Olver, 2016; Salekin, 2002; Wong, 2016). In short, programs that appear to hold the greatest promise are integrated RNR-based programs, with service intensity and dosage matched to risk level, criminogenic treatment foci, and a comprehensive and multimodal approach to service delivery using cognitive behavioral treatment (CBT) methods of change. In recent years, there appears to be a shift in the therapeutic zeitgeist toward "what works" for treating high psychopathy client populations, including men with histories of sexual offending. As part of this movement, a Two-Component (2-C) model has been formulated for the treatment of psychopathic clientele (Wong, 2016; Wong et al., 2012; Wong & Hare, 2005).

The 2-C model maps onto the two-factor model of the PCL-R and reflects characteristics of correctional CBT programs that are grounded in RNR principles. The overarching rationale of the model is that treatment should target something that is changeable as well as risk relevant to future violence or sexual violence; the model is arranged into an interpersonal component (Component 1 or C-1) and a criminogenic component (Component 2 or C-2). For instance, Factor 1 tends to be more stable over time (Harpur & Hare, 1994) and a weaker predictor of recidivism, and therefore less risk relevant, than other features of psychopathy (Yang et al., 2010). Factor 1, however, has therapeutic relevance; for instance, high scores on the PCL-R's affective facet (corresponding to prominent callous, unemotional features) have been associated with adverse therapeutic outcomes such as decreased treatment progress (Olver et al., 2013; Sewall and Olver, 2019), increased attrition (Daly, 2017), and weaker working alliances between client and therapist (DeSorcy et al., 2020; Olver et al., 2020).

Accordingly, the focus of C-1 is to manage the characteristics of Factor 1 (e.g., superficiality, grandiosity, deceitfulness, lack of empathy, etc.) per the responsivity principle, rather than trying to fundamentally alter the character structure of psychopathy (Olver & Riemer, 2021). Management of these behaviors can be done through consistent staff communication, mutual support, and boundary maintenance to offset attempts at staff-splitting or manipulation. Further, increasing treatment buy-in using techniques such as motivational interviewing and through the management of countertransference may decrease attrition and increase client retention (DeSorcy et al., 2020). Cultivating a positive working relationship while maintaining a realistic tether to workable goals aimed at reducing risk, combined with an emphasis on tasks conducive to completing treatment components, may have promise in driving change (Olver, 2016; Polaschek & Daly, 2013).

C-2 is based on the notion that the lifestyle and antisocial features of psychopathy measured by Factor 2 tend to change over time (Harpur & Hare, 1994) and are a better predictor of recidivism than Factor 1 (Yang et al., 2010), thus having risk relevance. As such, C-2 involves directly targeting criminogenic, and therefore risk relevant, dynamic needs associated with Factor 2 by developing prosocial living skills and behaviors within the course of treatment (Olver, 2016; Olver & Riemer, 2021). Changeability per C-2 also reflects the general crime curve and associated age-related declines in Factor 2 (impulsivity, lack of realistic goals, poor behavioral controls, etc.) over time, lending further support to the importance of prioritizing these domains for intervention within the context of sexual offense specific treatment (Olver 2016; Wong, 2016). Per C-2, sexual-offense specific targets such as arousal reconditioning are also integrated with general CBT skills (e.g., anti-criminal thinking, prosocial problem solving) to reduce both general and sexual recidivism risk.

The use of pharmacotherapy in tandem with psychological interventions, may also be employed to target other risk-relevant domains per C-2, such as reducing sexually deviant fantasies and behaviors. For instance, selective serotonin reuptake inhibitors (SSRIs) are commonly used for arousal management when there are comorbid disorders or features such as anxiety or depression (Khan et al., 2015; Schmucker & Losel, 2015). Steroidal antiandrogens and luteinizing hormone-releasing hormone agonists (LRHRA) are similarly used as they suppress serum testosterone concentrations and reduce the biological functions related to sexual fantasies and behaviors (Turner & Bricken, 2015). Research into the long-term effectiveness in pharmacotherapy is limited, however, and although there are promising preliminary findings, further research is required to better substantiate the use of pharmacological interventions, particularly among high risk, high need, high psychopathy sexual offending populations (Khan et al., 2015; Schmucker & Lösel, 2015; Turner & Bricken, 2015).

17.5.3 Psychopathy and Sexual Offense Treatment Outcome: Some Recent Findings and Conclusions

There is emerging evidence to date suggesting that correctional programs that adhere to RNR principles, consistent with the 2-C model, have shown pre-post changes in risk indicative of decreased recidivism, demonstrating that if high psychopathy clientele can be retained in treatment despite the interpersonal challenges they bring, there is potential for benefit (Olver & Wong, 2009; Sewall & Olver, 2019). Much of the recent psychopathy sexual offense treatment outcome literature has come from Canada's federal correctional department, the Correctional Service of Canada (CSC). The programs evaluated here broadly subscribe to the "what works" philosophy (i.e., RNR), and by extension the 2-C model. For instance, Olver and Wong (2009) found that most (73%) psychopathic men who were admitted to a high intensity sexual offense program at Saskatchewan's Regional Psychiatric Centre (RPC), completed it, and treatment change was significantly negatively correlated with violent recidivism ($r_{pb} = -.40$). Further, in an expansion of this study on a larger sample and increased follow-up, Sewall and Olver (2019) found that while high PCL-R-scoring clients were more likely than less psychopathic men to discontinue treatment, 70% did successfully complete the program. In both evaluations, pre-post changes in risk measured by the VRS-SO were significantly associated with decreased sexual and violent recidivism, controlling for baseline risk and PCL-R total score.

Moreover, Looman et al. (2005) examined the association of psychopathy and risk-related treatment change in another high intensity treatment service in Ontario's Regional Treatment Centre, finding that psychopathic men judged as having lowered their risk at the end of treatment had lower rates of violent recidivism (at 30%) compared to psychopathic men who did not lower their risk (50%). In a prison-based sexual offense treatment program at another Ontario facility, Langton et al. (2006) similarly found that psychopathic men who displayed poor treatment behavior had a significantly higher and faster rate of sexual recidivism than psychopathic men who displayed positive treatment behavior. There was about a twofold increase in the failure rates for sexual recidivism in the poor response/high psychopathy group compared to the other groups. Finally, Olver and Riemer (2021) found that high psychopathy men attending sexual offense programming at sites across CSC, made significant pre-post changes in protective factors with treatment. Improvements in protective factors were also associated with reductions in violent recidivism, controlling for psychopathy and baseline protection scores.

In all, while psychopathy represents a challenging subset of forensic clientele to work with, the emerging research suggests that integrating evidence-based practice (per RNR/2-C) into program delivery has the potential to improve client retention and promote change on risk-relevant dimensions, which in turn, may translate into successful community reintegration and reduced recidivism.

17.6 General Conclusions

PD, particularly ASPD, and psychopathy are overrepresented in sexual offending populations. Conceptually, this makes sense given the interpersonal and affective symptomatology that is endemic to PD and characteristic of crimes of a sexual nature. Psychopathy in particular, along the dimensions of callous-manipulativeness and hypersexuality, would increase the potential for sexual aggression against adults as well as crimes of sexual opportunism. PD and psychopathy have risk and need relevance for future sexual violence, given that they broadly predict a range of recidivism criteria and correlate meaningfully with measures of sexual violence risk and criminogenic need; these clinical entities, however, do need to be contextualized within a comprehensive sexual violence risk assessment that addresses both static and dynamic factors. On its own, psychopathy is not a strong predictor of sexual violence, and most men convicted for sex crimes who are high on psychopathy will not be charged or convicted for a new sexual offense. The combination of psychopathy and sexual deviance, however, has been demonstrated to potentiate sexual violence risk, which in turn, can be an important driver of risk management services and psycholegal decision making.

Perhaps above all, are the responsivity ramifications of PD and psychopathy for client retention and treatment gain. The interpersonal and affective symptoms of personality pathology tend not to foster optimism for treatment, particularly for psychopathy; but people cannot benefit from services if they are not retained in, and given sufficient opportunity to engage in, such services. Accordingly, an emerging body of evidence suggests that cautious optimism may be warranted for evidence informed approaches backed by the RNR principles in general, and direct therapeutic applications such as the 2-C model of psychopathy treatment. These lines of research and practice suggest that high psychopathy people can develop working alliances, be retained in treatment, and make risk-relevant changes—stability in personality traits, notwithstanding.

References

Alhmeyer, S., Kleinsasser, D., Stoner, J., & Retzlaff, P. (2003). Psychopathology of incarcerated sex offenders. *Journal of Personality Disorders, 17*, 306–318. https://doi.org/10.1521/pedi.17.4.306.23969

American Psychiatric Association. (2013). *Diagnostic and statistical manual for mental disorders* (5th ed.). Author.

Andrews, D. A., & Bonta, J. (2010). Rehabilitating criminal justice policy and practice. *Psychology, Public Policy, and Law, 16*, 39–55. https://doi.org/10.1037/a0018362

Andrews, D. A., Bonta, J., & Wormith, J. S. (2006). The recent past and near future of risk and/or needs assessment. *Crime and Delinquency, 52*, 7–27. https://doi.org/10.1177/0011128705281756

Barbaree, H. E., Seto, M. C., Langton, C. M., & Peacock, E. J. (2001). Evaluating the predictive accuracy of six risk assessment instruments for adult sex offenders. *Criminal Justice and Behavior 28*(4), 490–521. https://doi.org/10.1177/009385480102800406

Beggs, S. M., & Grace, R. C. (2008). Psychopathy, intelligence and recidivism in child molesters: Evidence of an interaction effect. *Criminal Justice and Behavior, 35*, 683–695. https://doi.org/10.1177/0093854808314786

Blais, J., Solodukhin, E., & Forth, A. E. (2014). A meta-analysis exploring the relationship between psychopathy and instrumental versus reactive violence. *Criminal Justice and Behavior, 41*, 797–821. https://doi.org/10.1177/0093854813519629

Bogaerts, S., Daalder, A., Vanheule, S., Desmat, M., & Leeuw, F. (2008). Personality disorders in a sample of paraphilic and nonparaphilic child molesters. *International Journal of Offender Therapy and Comparative Criminology, 52*, 21–30. https://doi.org/10.1177/0306624X07308261

Bonta, J., Blais, J., & Wilson, H. A. (2014). A theoretically informed meta-analysis of the risk for general and violent recidivism for mentally disordered offenders. *Aggression and Violent Behavior, 19*, 278–287. https://doi.org/10.1016/j.avb.2014.04.014

Bonta, J., Law, M., & Hanson, K. (1998). The predication of criminal and violent recidivism violent recidivism among mentally disordered offenders: A meta-analysis. *Psychological Bulletin, 123*, 123–142. https://doi.org/10.1037/0033-2909.123.2.123

Brown, A. R., Dargis, M. A., Mattern, A. C., Tsonis, M. A., & Newman, J. P. (2015). Elevated psychopathy scores among mixed sexual offenders: Replication and extension. *Criminal Justice and Behavior, 42*, 1032–1044. https://doi.org/10.1177/0093854815575389

Brown, S. L., & Forth, A. E. (1997). Psychopathy and sexual assault: Static risk factors, emotional precursors, and rapist subtypes. *Journal of Consulting and Clinical Psychology, 65*, 848–857. https://doi.org/10.1037/0022-006X.65.5.848

Campbell, M. A., French, S., & Gendreau, P. (2009). The prediction of violence in adult offenders: A meta-analytic comparison of instruments and methods of assessment. *Criminal Justice and Behavior, 36*, 567–590. https://doi.org/10.1177/0093854809333610

Daly, T. E. (2017). *Why are psychopaths difficult to treat? Testing the two-component model for the treatment of PCL psychopaths [Unpublished doctoral dissertation]*. Victoria University of Wellington.

Derks, F. C. H. (1996). A forensic day treatment program for personality-disordered criminal offenders. *International Journal of Offender Therapy and Comparative Criminology, 40*, 123–134. https://doi.org/10.1177/0306624X96402005

DeSorcy, D. R., Olver, M. E., & Wormith, J. S. (2020). Working alliance and psychopathy: Linkages to treatment outcome in a sample of treated sexual offenders. *Journal of Interpersonal Violence, 35*, 1739–1760. https://doi.org/10.1177/0886260517698822

Douglas, K. S., Yeomans, M., & Boer, D. P. (2005). Comparative validity analysis of multiple measures of violence risk in a sample of criminal offenders. *Criminal Justice and Behavior, 32*, 479–510. https://doi.org/10.1177/0093854805278411

Dudeck, M., Spitzer, C., Stopsack, M., Freyberger, H. J., & Barnow, S. (2007). Forensic inpatient male sexual offenders: The impact of personality disorder and childhood sexual abuse. *The Journal of Forensic Psychiatry and Psychology, 18*, 494–506. https://doi.org/10.1080/14789940701491495

Edens, J. F., Marcus, D. K., Lilienfeld, S. O., & Poythress, N. G. (2006). Psychopathic, not psychopath: Taxometric evidence for the dimensional structure of psychology. *Journal of Abnormal Psychology, 115*, 131–144. https://doi.org/10.1037/0021-843X.115.1.131

Forth, A. E., Kosson, D. S., & Hare, R. D. (2003). *Psychopathy checklist: Youth version (PCL: YV)*. Multi-Health Systems.

Hanson, R. K., & Bussière, M. T. (1998). Predicting relapse: A meta-analysis of sexual offender recidivism studies. *Journal of Consulting and Clinical Psychology, 66*, 348. https://doi.org/10.1037/0022-006X.66.2.348

Hanson, R. K., Harris, A. J. R., Scott, T., & Helmus, L. (2007). *Assessing the risk of sex offenders on community supervision. (User Report No. 2007-05)*. Public Safety and Emergency Preparedness Canada.

Hanson, R. K., & Morton-Bourgon, K. (2004). *Predictors of sexual recidivism: An updated meta-analysis. (User Report 2004-02)*. Public Safety and Emergency Preparedness Canada.

Hanson, R. K., & Morton-Bourgon, K. (2005). The characteristics of persistent sexual offenders: A meta-analysis of recidivism studies. *Journal of Consulting and Clinical Psychology, 73*, 1154–1163. https://doi.org/10.1037/0022-006X.73.6.1154

Hare, R. D. (1991). *Manual for the revised psychopathy checklist*. Multi-Health Systems.

Hare, R. D. (1999). Psychopathy as a risk factor for violence. *Psychiatric Quarterly, 70*, 181–197. https://doi.org/10.1023/A:1022094925150

Hare, R. D. (2003). *The Hare psychopathy checklist-revised* (2nd ed.). Multi-Health Systems.

Hare, R. D., & Neumann, C. S. (2008). Psychopathy as a clinical and empirical construct. *Annual Review of Clinical Psychology, 4*, 217–246. https://doi.org/10.1146/annurev.clinpsy.3.022806.091452

Harpur, T. J., & Hare, R. D. (1994). Assessment of psychopathy as a function of age. *Journal of Abnormal Psychology, 103*, 604–609. https://doi.org/10.1037/0021-843X.103.4.604

Harsch, S., Bergk, J. E., Steinert, T., Keller, F., & Jockusch, U. (2006). Prevalence of mental disorders among sexual offenders in forensic psychiatry and prison. *International Journal of Law and Psychiatry, 29*, 443–449. https://doi.org/10.1016/j.ijlp.2005.11.001

Hart, S. D., Cox, D. N., & Hare, R. D. (1995). *The Hare psychopathy checklist: Screening version (PCL: SV)*. Multi-Health Systems.

Hart, S. D., & Hare, R. D. (1989). Discriminant validity of the psychopathy checklist-revised in a forensic psychiatric population. *Psychological Assessment: A Journal of Consulting and Clinical Psychology, 1*, 211–218. https://doi.org/10.1037/1040-3590.1.3.211

Hart, S. D., & Hare, R. D. (1996). Psychopathy and antisocial personality disorder. *Current Opinion in Psychiatry, 9*, 129–132.

Hawes, S. W., Boccaccini, M. T., & Murrie, D. C. (2013). Psychopathy and the combination of psychopathy and sexual deviance as predictors of sexual recidivism: Meta-analytic findings using the psychopathy checklist—Revised. *Psychological Assessment, 25*, 233–243. https://doi.org/10.1037/a0030391

Hildebrand, M., de Ruiter, C., & de Vogel, V. (2004). Psychopathy and sexual deviance in treated rapists: Association with sexual and nonsexual recidivism. *Sexual Abuse: A Journal of Research and Treatment, 16*, 1–24. https://doi.org/10.1177/107906320401600101

Khan, O., Ferriter, M., Huband, N., Powney, M. J., Dennus, J. A., & Duggan, C. (2015). Pharmacological interventions for those who have sexually offended or are at risk of offending. *Cochrane Database of Systematic Reviews, 2015*(2), CD007989. https://doi.org/10.1002/14651858.CD007989.pub2

Kingston, D. A., Olver, M. E., Harris, M., Wong, S. C., & Bradford, J. M. (2015). The relationship between mental disorder and recidivism in sexual offenders. *International Journal of Forensic Mental Health, 14*, 10–22. https://doi.org/10.1080/14999013.2014.974088

Knight, R. A., & Guay, J. (2018). The role of psychopathy in sexual coercion against women: An update and expansion. In C. J. Patrick (Ed.), *Handbook of psychopathy* (2nd ed., pp. 662–681). Guilford.

Langevin, R. (2003). A study of the psychosexual characteristics of sex killers: Can we identify them before it is too late? *International Journal of Offender Therapy and Comparative Criminology, 47*, 366–382. https://doi.org/10.1177/0306624X03253848

Langton, C. M., Barbaree, H. E., Harkins, L., & Peacock, E. J. (2006). Sex offenders' response to treatment and its association with recidivism as a function of psychopathy. *Sexual Abuse: Journal of Research and Treatment, 18*, 99–120. https://doi.org/10.1177/107906320601800107

Leistico, A. M. R., Salekin, R. T., DeCoster, J., & Rogers, R. (2008). A large-scale meta-analysis relating the Hare measures of psychopathy to antisocial conduct. *Law and Human Behavior, 32*, 28–45. https://doi.org/10.1007/s10979-007-9096-6

Leue, A., Borchard, B., & Hoyer, J. (2004). Mental disorders in a forensic sample of sexual offenders. *European Psychiatry, 19*, 123–130. https://doi.org/10.1016/j.eurpsy.2003.08.001

Looman, J., Abracen, J., Serin, R., & Marquis, P. (2005). Psychopathy, treatment change, and recidivism in high-risk, high-need sexual offenders. *Journal of Interpersonal Violence, 20*, 549–568. https://doi.org/10.1177/0886260504271583

Looman, J., Morphett, N. A. C., & Abracen, J. (2013). Does consideration of psychopathy and sexual deviance add to the predictive validity of the Static-99R? *Journal of Offender Therapy and Comparative Criminology, 57*, 939–965.

Mann, R. E., Hanson, R. K., & Thornton, D. (2010). Assessing risk for sexual recidivism: Some proposals on the nature of psychologically meaningful risk factors. *Sexual Abuse: A Journal of Research and Treatment, 22*, 191–217. https://doi.org/10.1177/1079063210366039

McGrath, R. J., Lasher, M. P., & Cumming, G. F. (2012). Sex offender treatment intervention and Progress scale (SOTIPS): Psychometric properties and incremental predictive validity with Static-99R. *Sexual Abuse: A Journal of Research and Treatment, 24*, 431–458. https://doi.org/10.1177/1079063211432475

McPhail, I. V., Hermann, C. A., & Nunes, K. L. (2013). Emotional congruence with children and sexual offending against children: A meta-analytic review. *Journal of Consulting and Clinical Psychology, 81*, 737–749. https://doi.org/10.1037/a0033248

Mokros, A., Vohs, K., & Habermeyer, E. (2014). Psychopathy and violent reoffending in German-speaking countries: A meta-analysis. *European Journal of Psychological Assessment, 30*, 117–129. https://doi.org/10.1027/1015-5759/a000178

Moulden, H. M., Chaimowitz, G., Mamak, M., & Hawes, J. (2014). Understanding how sexual offenders compare across psychiatric and correctional settings: Examination of Canadian mentally ill sexual offenders. *Journal of Sexual Aggression, 20*, 172–181. https://doi.org/10.1080/13552600.2013.794903

Neumann, C. S., Hare, R. D., & Pardini, D. A. (2014). Antisociality and the construct of psychopathy: Data from across the globe. *Journal of Personality, 83*, 678–692. https://doi.org/10.1111/jopy.12127

Ogloff, J. R. P. (2006). Psychopathy/antisocial personality disorder conundrum. *Australian and New Zealand Journal of Psychiatry, 40*, 519–528. https://doi.org/10.1080/j.1440-1614.2006.01834.x

Ogloff, J. R. P., Campbell, R. E., & Shepherd, S. M. (2016). Disentangling psychopathy from antisocial personality disorder: An Australian analysis. *Journal of Forensic Psychology Practice, 16*, 198–215. https://doi.org/10.1080/15228932.2016.1177281

Oliver, C. J., Beech, A. R., Fisher, D., & Beckett, R. (2007). A comparison of rapists and sexual murderers on demographic and selected psychometric measures. *International Journal of Offender Therapy and Comparative Criminology, 51*, 298–312. https://doi.org/10.1177/0306624X06289157

Olver, M. E. (2016). Treatment of psychopathic offenders: Evidence, issues, and controversies. *Journal of Community Safety and Well-Being, 1*, 75–82. https://doi.org/10.35502/jcswb.25

Olver, M. E., & Riemer, E. K. (2021). High-psychopathy men with a history of sexual offending have protective factors too: But are these risk-relevant and can they change in treatment? *Journal of Consulting and Clinical Psychology, 89*, 406–420. https://doi.org/10.1037/ccp0000638

Olver, M. E., Stockdale, K. C., Neumann, C. S., Hare, R. D., Mokros, A., Baskin-Sommers, A., Brand, E., Folino, J., Gacono, C., Gray, N. S., Kiehl, K., Knight, R., Leon-Mayer, E., Logan, M., Meloy, J. R., Roy, S., Salekin, R. T., Snowden, R., Thomson, N., Tillem, S., Vitacco, M., & Yoon, D. (2020). Reliability and validity of the Psychopathy Checklist-Revised in the assessment of risk for institutional violence: A cautionary note on DeMatteo et al. *Psychology, Public Policy, and Law, 26*, 490–510. https://doi.org/10.1037/law0000256

Olver, M. E., Stockdale, K. C., & Wormith, S. J. (2011). A meta-analysis of predictors of offender treatment attrition and its relationship to recidivism. *Journal of Consulting and Clinical Psychology, 79*, 6–21. https://doi.org/10.1037/a0022200

Olver, M. E., & Wong, S. C. P. (2006). Psychopathy, sexual deviance, and recidivism among sex offenders. *Sexual Abuse: A Journal of Research and Treatment, 18*, 65–82. https://doi.org/10.1177/107906320601800105

Olver, M. E., & Wong, S. C. P. (2009). Therapeutic responses of psychopathic sexual offenders: Treatment attrition, therapeutic change, and longterm recidivism. *Journal of Consulting and Clinical Psychology, 77*, 328–336. https://doi.org/10.1037/a0015001

Olver, M. E., Lewis, K., & Wong, S. C. P. (2013). Risk reduction treatment of high-risk psychopathic offenders: The relationship of psychopathy and treatment change to violent recidivism. *Personality Disorders, Theory, Research, and Treatment, 4*, 160–167. https://doi.org/10.1037/a0029769

Polaschek, D. L. L., & Daly, T. E. (2013). Treatment and psychopathy in forensic settings. *Aggression and Violent Behavior, 18*, 592–603. https://doi.org/10.1016/j.avb.2013.06.003

Porter, S., Fairweather, D., Drugge, J., Hervé, H., Birt, A., & Boer, D. P. (2000). Profiles of psychopathy in incarcerated sexual offenders. *Criminal Justice and Behavior, 27*, 216–233. https://doi.org/10.1177/0093854800027002005

Rezansoff, S. N., Moniruzzaman, A., Gress, C., & Somers, J. M. (2013). Psychiatric diagnoses and multiyear criminal recidivism in a Canadian provincial offender population. *Psychology, Public Policy, and Law, 19*, 443–453. https://doi.org/10.1037/a0033907

Rice, M. E., & Harris, G. T. (1997). Cross-validation and extension of the violence risk appraisal guide for child molesters and rapists. *Law and Human Behavior, 21*, 231–241. https://doi.org/10.1023/A:1024882430242

Rice, M. E., & Harris, G. T. (2005). Comparing effect sizes in follow-up studies: ROC area, Cohen's d, and r. *Law and Human Behavior, 29*, 615–620. https://doi.org/10.1007/s10979-005-6832-7
Rice, M. E., Harris, G. T., & Cormier, C. A. (1992). An evaluation of a maximum security therapeutic community for psychopaths and other mentally disordered offenders. *Law and Human Behavior, 16*, 399–412. https://doi.org/10.1007/BF02352266
Salekin, R. T. (2002). Psychopathy and therapeutic pessimism: Clinical lore or clinical reality? *Clinical Psychology Review, 22*, 79–112. https://doi.org/10.1016/S0272-7358(01)00083-6
Schmucker, M., & Lösel, F. (2015). The effects of sex offender treatment on recidivism: An international meta-analysis of sound quality evaluations. *Journal of Experimental Criminology, 11*, 597–630. https://doi.org/10.1007/s11292-015-9241-z
Schroeder, M., Simeon Iffland, J., Hill, A., Berner, W., & Briken, P. (2013). Personality disorders in men with sexual and violent criminal offense histories. *Journal of Personality Disorders, 27*, 519–530. https://doi.org/10.1521/pedi_2012_26_050
Serin, R. C., Malcolm, P. B., Khanna, A., & Barbaree, H. E. (1994). Psychopathy and deviant sexual arousal in incarcerated sexual offenders. *Journal of Interpersonal Violence, 9*, 3–11. https://doi.org/10.1177/088626094009001001
Seto, M. C., Babchishin, K. M., Pullman, L. E., & McPhail, I. V. (2015). The puzzle of intrafamilial child sexual abuse: A meta-analysis comparing intrafamilial and extrafamilial offenders with child victims. *Clinical Psychology Review, 39*, 42–57. https://doi.org/10.1016/j.cpr.2015.04.001
Seto, M. C., Harris, G. T., Rice, M. E., & Barbaree, H. E. (2004). The screening scale for pedophilic interests predicts recidivism among adult sex offenders with child victims. *Archives of Sexual Behavior, 33*, 455–466. https://doi.org/10.1023/B:ASEB.0000037426.55935.9c
Sewall, L. A., & Olver, M. E. (2019). Psychopathy and treatment outcome: Results from a sexual violence reduction program. *Personality Disorders: Theory, Research, and Treatment, 10*, 59–69. https://doi.org/10.1037/per0000297
Simourd, D. J., & Hoge, R. D. (2000). Criminal psychopathy: A risk-and-need perspective. *Criminal Justice and Behavior, 27*, 256–272. https://doi.org/10.1177/0093854800027002007
Turner, D., & Bricken, P. (2015). Treatment of paraphilic disorders in sexual offenders or men with a risk of sexual offending with a luteinizing hormone-releasing hormone agonist: An updated systematic review. *Journal of Sexual Medicine, 15*, 77–93. https://doi.org/10.1016/j.jsxm.2017.11.013
Walters, G. D. (2003). Predicting institutional adjustment and recidivism with the psychopathy checklist factor scores: A meta-analysis. *Law and Human Behavior, 27*, 541–558. https://doi.org/10.1023/A:1025490207678
Wong, S. C. P. (2016). Treatment of violence prone individuals with psychopathic personality traits. In J. Livesley, G. Dimaggio, & J. Clarkin (Eds.), *Integrated treatment of personality disorder: A modular approach* (pp. 345–376). Guildford.
Wong, S. C. P., & Gordon, A. (2006). The validity and reliability of the violence risk scale: A treatment-friendly violence risk assessment tool. *Psychology, Public Policy, and Law, 12*, 279–309. https://doi.org/10.1037/1076-8971.12.3.279
Wong, S. C. P., Gordon, A., Deqiang, G., Lewis, K., & Olver, M. E. (2012). The effectiveness of violence reduction treatment for psychopathic offenders: Empirical evidence and a treatment model. *The International Journal of Forensic Mental Health, 11*, 336–349. https://doi.org/10.1080/14999013.2012.746760
Wong, S., & Hare, R. D. (2005). *Guidelines for a psychopathy treatment program*. Multi-Health Systems.
Wong, S., Olver, M., Nicholaichuk, T., & Gordon, A. (2003–2017). *Violence risk scale: Sexual offense version*. University of Saskatchewan and Regional Psychiatric Centre.
Yang, M., Wong, S. C. P., & Coid, J. (2010). The efficacy of violence prediction: A meta-analytic comparison of nine risk assessment tools. *Psychological Bulletin, 136*, 740–767. https://doi.org/10.1037/a0020473

Chapter 18
Special Considerations: Problem Sexual Behavior and Offending Patterns by Adolescents

Addison R. Kobie, Eunsuhk Choi, Lisa L. Sample, and Zachary K. Hamilton

18.1 Introduction

Juveniles who commit sexual offenses has been the subject of public concern and research for many years (Letourneau & Miner, 2005; Miner, 2002; Przybylski & Lobanov-Rostovsky, 2015). These youths, often called Juvenile Sex Offenders (JSOs), engender much public fear and, in turn, have been subjected to many of the policies created for their adult counterparts. For example, JSOs in some states are subjected to sex offender registry and notification laws as required under the Sex Offender Registration and Notification Act (SORNA; U.S. Department of Justice, 2008). However, research has found that these laws do little to assuage juveniles from first time or repeat sex offending (Letourneau et al., 2019, 2010) Further, for many years, JSO treatment was modeled after adult modalities, until juvenile behavior became differentiated from adult behavior along ecological (i.e., social) systems (Miner & Munns, 2005). Unlike adult behavior, juvenile behaviors are more influenced by systems such as the family, schools, religion, neighborhoods, and peers (Cauffman & Steinberg, 2000).

Risk assessment for JSOs emulates prediction for adult sexual reoffending, which relies on current and past sexual interests and behaviors (Hanson & Morton-Bourgon, 2009; Olver et al., 2021; Seto & Pullman, 2012). Based on this

A. R. Kobie (✉) · L. L. Sample · Z. K. Hamilton
Department of Criminology and Criminal Justice, University of Nebraska-Omaha, Omaha, NE, USA
e-mail: akobie@unomaha.edu; lsample@unomaha.edu; zhamilton@unomaha.edu

E. Choi
Police Policy Research Division, Police Science Institute, Thornhill, ON, Canada

Korean National Police University, Asan-si, Chungcheongnam-do, Republic of Korea
e-mail: eunsuhk.choi@wsu.edu

R. J. Tully et al. (eds.), *Best Practices in Sexual Offender Assessment and Management*, Dangerous Behavior in Clinical and Forensic Psychology,
https://doi.org/10.1007/978-3-031-83135-5_18

assumption, assessment tools are typically developed for, and applied to, those who have a history of sex offending. However, problem sexual behavior as a juvenile is often not a lifelong propensity (Caldwell, 2010, 2016; McCuish & Lussier, 2017; Zimring et al., 2009). Furthermore, JSOs exhibit different types of offending and non-offending patterns (Ybarra & Petras, 2021). For example, many youths desisting from sexual offending before adulthood (Caldwell, 2016; Kleeven et al., 2022; Reale et al., 2020; Vandiver, 2006) and/or observed to commit crimes other than sexual recidivism; however, they are nevertheless considered sex offenders (SO) above anything else (Carpentier & Proulx, 2011; Fanniff et al., 2017; Leibowitz et al., 2016). Additionally, it is often overlooked that youth committing other offense types can also reoffend sexually. These Juvenile Non-Sexual Offenders (JNSOs), unless classified based on a prior sex offense, are rarely assessed for sexual offending propensity, and not considered for interventions until they are adjudicated for a sex crime. These disparities between practical assumptions and youth reoffending patterns presents three critical issues: (1) risk item feature selection lacks empirical support, (2) tool development and application are almost exclusively focused with JSOs, and (3) prediction modeling is designed for a solitary outcome.

Further, much like issues found in risk assessments predicting sexual recidivism, treatment interventions historically resemble those for adults (Worling & Curwen, 2001; Przybylski, 2015). However, there has more recently been a push to establish treatments for JSO with regard to their specific needs (Aebi et al., 2022, Worling et al., 2010). Limited research suggests sex offender treatments are distinct from, but bear promise at reducing sex crimes by juveniles (Kettrey & Lipsey, 2018; Dopp et al., 2015; Przybylski, 2015). Further, studies often find that JSO treatments vary in provision of interventions (i.e., skill attainment, therapeutic interventions, duration of treatment). Moreover, while JSOs possess an increased likelihood to recidivate generally, most interventions target sexual recidivism specifically, questioning the effectiveness of specified treatments (Kettrey & Lipsey, 2018; Dopp et al., 2015; Caldwell, 2016). Overall, treatments attempting to prevent inappropriate sexual behavior is an underdeveloped area of research.

In this chapter the differences between inappropriate sexual behavior and sexual offending are reviewed. Additionally, the relevance of this conceptual distinction for juvenile justice agencies is provided. Furthermore, the scope of the problem is reviewed and the impact of labeling SOs is explored. Lastly, clinical assessment considerations and techniques as well as recommended interventions are provided.

18.2 The Distinction Between Problem Sexual Behavior and Sexual Offending

Prior to discussing risk assessment and treatment for JSOs, it is necessary to discuss the difference between problem sexual behavior and the narrower definition of sexual offending. It is important to note that developmentally there is a range of behavior which is expected with youths as they grow older and is considered relatively normed for their age range (i.e. touching genitals in public/home, trying to look at others who are nude, and encroaching boundaries by standing to close to others; Elkovitch et al., 2009). In contrast, problem sexual behavior is distinct from appropriate sexual behavior, and is behavior considered abnormal for youths within a spectrum in which the most serious acts are those that rise to the level of sexual offending (Bonner et al., 2001, Chaffin et al., 2008; Kellogg & Committee on Child Abuse and Neglect, 2009; Elkovitch et al., 2009). Although all problem sexual behaviors are considered abnormal for the development of the youth and should be contrasted with age-appropriate sexual behavior, the severity or level of seriousness of the acts should be considered when intervening (Chaffin et al., 2008). In other words, although all sexual offenses would fall under the umbrella of problem sexual behavior and lead to legal consequences for juveniles, not all of these behaviors reach this level. For example, non-coercive sexual acts with other youth is inappropriate for a child, however, it generally does not rise to the same legal consequences as sexually violent actions, such as rape or sexual assault (Bonner et al., 2001). Thus, although both actions would be classified as problematic and requiring intervention, one is clearly more severe than the other.

18.3 Impact of Labeling

In most aspects of the criminal justice system, juveniles who have committed offenses are perceived to be amendable to change, however, there is a notable exception for youths that commit sexual offenses (Chaffin, 2008; Caldwell, 2016; Caldwell & Caldwell, 2022). Juveniles with sexual criminal histories are often perceived as unamendable to rehabilitation efforts, at high risk of sexual recidivism, and are a homogenous group (Chaffin, 2008). These labels are not substantiated by empirical evidence provided by the field overall (Caldwell, 2010, 2016). Specifically, findings overall suggest that JSOs are less likely to recidivate than other youth (Caldwell, 2010; Kettrey & Lipsey, 2018). Further, studies have found that JSOs are not a homogenous group, suggesting that there are high, moderate, and lower risk individuals (Chaffin, 2008).

While treatment to help reduce sexual offending among juveniles holds promise; policies regarding JSOs often do not reflect a hopeful perception. As Chaffin (2008) discusses in his seminal commentary on JSO practices, often these juveniles face laws and policies that label them as SOs. One such policy places JSOs on SO registries, which are now widespread via SORNA (U.S. Department of Justice, 2008; Parker, 2014). This overarching policy allows youths above the age of 14 to be placed on the registry, in some cases, for life (Parker, 2014). This labeling can severely impact JSOs as they face legal and interpersonal consequences such as isolation from peers and increased stigmatization (Chaffin, 2008). In other words, the JSO label can prevent youth from engaging with common societal institutions (i.e., work, school, social groups) and reduce the ability to build pro-social bonds. Public perception of those labeled as a JSO can further show how this label is attached (Harris & Socia, 2016). For example, Harris and Socia (2016) found in a representative survey of 1000 U.S. adults that when a juvenile was labeled as a JSO there was increased general agreement among respondents with registering these youths as well as notifying the public with an internet notification. They further note that in both conditions, juveniles, when compared to adults, were still considered more likely to recidivate (Harris & Socia, 2016). This finding suggests that juveniles who obtain this label are seen by the public as more dangerous and overall, further isolates them.

Overall, when trying to understand how to reduce juvenile sex offending, awareness must be in place that these labels can fundamentally change how society perceives JSOs and, in turn, outline the importance of narrowly defining this label if it must be used (Parker, 2014). Instead, greater focus should be on rehabilitation and how to adequately program juveniles to reduce recidivism to reduce future behavior and stigma (Parker, 2014).

18.4 Contemporary Risk Assessment of Juvenile Sexual Offenders

Risk assessment tool development for JSOs burgeoned around the year 2000 (Rasmussen, 2013). The three most commonly cited risk assessment instruments used for JSOs (Krause et al., 2021; Ozkan et al., 2020; Prentky et al., 2016; Viljoen et al., 2012): the Juvenile Sex Offender Assessment Protocol-II (J-SOAP-II; Prentky & Righthand, 2003), the Estimate of Risk of Adolescent Sexual Offense Recidivism (ERASOR; Worling, 2004), and the Juvenile Sexual Offender Recidivism Risk Assessment Tool-II (JSORRAT-II; Epperson & Ralston, 2015). Additionally, there are two newer fully dynamic assessments: Protective + Risk Observations For Eliminating Sexual Offense Recidivism (PROFESOR; Worling, 2017) and the Youth Needs and Progress Scale (YNPS; Prentky et al., 2020). The following subsections include each tool's features, items, predictive validity, and development methods. The receiver operating characteristics area under curve (ROC AUC) is used as an index of predictive strength[1] as it is the psychometric industry standard, and commonly reports prediction abilities of risk assessment tools (American Educational Research Association [AERA]; American Psychological Association [APA]; National Council on Measurement in Education [NCME], 2014).

[1] The magnitude of AUC values ranges from 0.5 to 1 (Rice & Harris, 2005). Values below 0.55 are considered 'negligible,' values between 0.56 and 0.63 are considered 'small,' values between 0.64 and 0.71 are considered 'moderate,' and 'strong' values are indicated at 0.72 or above (Rice & Harris, 2005).

18.4.1 J-SOAP-II

The J-SOAP-II was developed by Prentky and Righthand (2003). It is one of the most widely used tools to assess youth sexual recidivism (McGrath et al., 2010; Miccio-Fonseca, 2013). It was designed to assess sexual and nonsexual re-offense risk in juveniles who have a history of sexually coercive behavior (Viljoen et al., 2012). It can be used in the context of community supervision or in treatment (Prentky & Righthand, 2003). The current version of the J-SOAP-II was developed for adjudicated and non-adjudicated males ages 12 to 18 (Miccio-Fonseca, 2013).

The J-SOAP-II is a 28-item instrument (16 static and 12 dynamic risk factors), comprising four scales: Sexual Drive/Preoccupation (Scale 1), Impulsive/Antisocial Behavior (Scale 2), Clinical Intervention (Scale 3), and Community Stability/Adjustment (Scale 4; see Table 18.1). Each scale is composed of five to eight items. Items are rated on a 3-point scale (ranging from 0 to 2). The items in Scale 1 and 2 are summed for a Static Scale Score and the items in Scale 3 and 4 are summed for a Dynamic Scale Score. As the J-SOAP-II does not provide cutoff scores, evaluators have discretion to determine level of risk in combination with other sources of assessment (Miccio-Fonseca, 2013).

Studies on the predictive ability of the J-SOAP-II have revealed mixed results. Schwartz-Mette et al. (2020) compared findings from 12 studies and presented the AUCs of the J-SOAP-II total score for sexual recidivism ranging from .51 to .80. However, the authors reported their own results of the J-SOAP-II's prediction ability, an AUC value of .76, by following the youth sample into their adult years. Additionally, a recent study found an AUC value of .74 with an Australian male sample (Molnar et al., 2020).

The J-SOAP-II is an empirically guided tool, not an actuarially developed one (Miccio-Fonseca, 2013). The developers used research conducted in the mid- to late 1990s and identified risk factors of boys aged 12 to 18 (Prentky et al., 2000). While clinical professionals created the structured checklist through a review of the literature (Miccio-Fonseca, 2013; Prentky et al., 2000), their judgment was involved in selecting, scoring, and weighting items (Epperson & Ralston, 2015).

18.4.2 ERASOR

The ERASOR is a 25-item instrument (Worling & Curwen, 2001) that comprises 9 static and 16 dynamic factors. The items on the ERASOR fall into five scales: (a) Sexual Interests, Attitudes, and Behaviors, (b) Historical Sexual Assaults, (c) Psychosocial Functioning, (d) Family/Environmental Functioning, and (e) Treatment (Worling et al., 2012; see Table 18.1). It was designed to provide a short-term estimate of risk for sexual recidivism in youth aged 12–18 in community supervision and/or treatment (Hemple et al., 2013; Worling, 2004). Since the ERASOR consists primarily of dynamic factors, the developers claimed that this

Table 18.1 Risk assessment instruments and items for Juvenile Sex Offenders

J-SOAP-II 16 static and 12 dynamic items	ERASOR 9 static and 16 dynamic items	JSORRAT-II 12 static items
1. Sexual drive/preoccupation Prior legally charged sex offenses Number of sexual abuse victims Male child victim Duration of sex offense history Degree of planning in sexual offense(s) Sexualized aggression Sexual drive and preoccupation Sexual victimization history 2. Impulsive, antisocial behavior Caregiver consistency Pervasive anger School behavior problems History of conduct disorder before age 10 Juvenile antisocial behavior (age 10–17) Ever charged or arrested before age 16 Multiple types of offenses History of physical assault and/or exposure to family violence 3. Intervention Accepting responsibility for offense(s) Internal motivation for change Understands risk factors Empathy Remorse and guilt Cognitive distortions Quality of peer relationships 4. Community stability/adjustment Stability of current living situation Stability in school Evidence of positive support systems Management of sexual urges and desire Management of anger	1. Sexual interests, attitudes, and behaviors Deviant sexual interest Obsessive sexual interests Attitudes supportive of sexual offending Unwillingness to alter deviant sexual interests 2. Historical sexual assaults Ever sexually assaulted 2 or more victims Ever sexually assaulted same victim 2 or more times Prior adult sanctions for sexual assault(s) Threats of, or use of, excessive violence/weapons Ever sexually assaulted a child Ever sexually assaulted a stranger Indiscriminate choice of victims Ever sexually assaulted a male victim Diverse sexual-assault behaviors 3. Psychosocial functioning Antisocial interpersonal orientation Lack of intimate peer relationships/social isolation Negative peer associations and influences Interpersonal aggression Recent escalation in anger or negative affect Poor self-regulation of affect and behavior 4. Family/environmental functioning High-stress family environment Problematic parent-offender relationships Parent(s) not supporting sexual-offense-specific assessment/treatment Environment supporting opportunities to reoffend sexually 5. Treatment No development or practice of realistic prevention plans/strategies Incomplete sexual-offense-specific treatment	1. Offending history and characteristics Number of adjudications for sex offenses Number of victims in charged sex offenses Duration of charged sexual offending history Any charged sexual offense committed under supervision Any felony-level, charged sexual offense committed in a public place Sexual offense preceded by deception or grooming Number of juvenile adjudications for non-sexual offenses 2. Abuse history Number of hands-on sexual abuse incidents experienced as the victim Number of incidents of physical abuse experienced as the victim 3. School history Any special education placements in K-12 Number of different educational periods with discipline problems 4. Treatment history Sexual offender treatment program status prior to index offense

tool was proper to check youth progress and recommended reassessing youth at 6-month intervals (Worling & Curwen, 2001).

The ERASOR developers (Worling & Curwen, 2001) described its development processed in a similar way of creating an adult tool (Sexual Violence Risk-20 [SVR-20], Boer et al., 1997). Additionally, the ERASOR was developed based on a structured professional judgment model (Viljoen et al., 2009). This means that assessors have discretion to determine the levels of risk (low, moderate, or high risk) with total scores as well as other sources of assessment (Krause et al., 2021; Viljoen et al., 2009). Thus, tool scoring may be inherently subjective in determining risk levels and the utility of assessment results (Krause et al., 2021).

The literature shows an inconsistent pattern of predictive validity for the ERASOR. Recent studies yielded some promising results. Worling et al. (2012) found that dynamic total score on the ERASOR significantly predicted sexual reoffending (AUC = .73). Barra et al. (2018) reported the highest predictive validity of the total ERASOR score for sexual recidivism (AUC = .78). However, in a meta-analysis with 10 studies by Viljoen et al. (2012), the average AUC for sexual recidivism was .66 (ranging from .61 to .72). Risk levels decided by assessors also presented moderate effect sizes on average (AUC = .66, ranging from .60 to .71; Viljoen et al., 2012).

18.4.3 JSORRAT-II

The JSORRAT-II is a 12-item instrument designed to assess short-term risk of sexual reoffending in adjudicated male JSOs 12 to 18 years old (Epperson & Ralston, 2015). Compared to the J-SOAP-II and ERASOR, the JSORRAT-II has several unique features: (a) it was the first tool for JSOs using an actuarial approach (Ralston et al., 2017), (b) comprises only 12 static risk factors (Epperson & Ralston, 2015), (c) was cross-validated (Rasmussen, 2018), and (d) provides cutoff scores for risk levels (Rasmussen, 2018).

In development, Epperson and Ralston (2015) focused on offense characteristics and individual background information since the literature on dynamic risk factors for youth sexual recidivism was still exploratory. The authors identified a total of 10 domains: history of sexual offending, sexual offense characteristics, sexual offender treatment, child abuse, special education, discipline problems at school, family instability, mental health diagnoses, mental health treatment, and history of nonsexual offending. Using statistical methods (i.e., chi-square, biserial correlation, and logistic regression), the authors selected 12 static items (see Table 18.1). The first six items measure behavior regarding sexual offending, while the other six reflect history of abuse, school, and treatment. This tool was initially validated with Utah samples (Epperson & Ralston, 2015) and cross-validated in Iowa (Ralston et al., 2017).

The JSORRAT-II demonstrates mixed levels of predictive strength, where moderate findings for the validation sample (AUC = .65) and slightly larger effects

(AUC = .70) in a cross-validation study (Ralston et al., 2016). Yet, recent study findings identified shrinkage (AUC = .57; Rasmussen, 2018), indicating a substantial reduction in predictive strength for a sample of JSOs with a higher base rate (17.4%) than that of the development sample (13.2%) and cross-validation sample (6.4%).

A logical assumption regarding the relationship between research findings and tool items is that the stronger predictors are found in the literature, the more items are commonly used and contribute to stable predictive ability. However, the tools and items discussed demonstrate that types of risk factors in use and predictive strengths vary substantially from instrument to instrument. For instance, although all three tools include items regarding sexual offending history, the quantitative and qualitative features of risk factors significantly differ. Questions regarding victims are 'number of sexual abuse victims' and 'male child victim' in the J-SOAP-II, 'ever sexually assaulted two or more victims', 'ever sexually assaulted same victim two or more times', 'ever sexually assaulted a child', 'ever sexually assaulted a stranger', 'indiscriminate choice of victims', and 'ever sexually assaulted a male victim' in the ERASOR, and 'number of victims in charged sex offenses' in the JSORRAT-II. Additionally, each tool also has its unique domain; the Community Stability/Adjustment of J-SOAP-II, Psychosocial Functioning of ERASOR, and Abuse History of JSORRAT-II. With this heterogeneity of risk factors across tools, a youth has the potential to be categorized as higher risk in one tool and lower in another.

18.4.4 Other Contemporary Assessments

The following subsections will briefly discuss these newer non-risk based assessments, the PROFESOR (Worling, 2017) and YNPS (Prentky et al., 2020). Given how recently both assessments were developed, there is overall no information about the performance of AUC and other indicators of predictive strength for either assessment. Nevertheless, these assessments do provide a new and interesting look at how other types of assessments are being developed and what they may contribute to the discussion of assessment and treatment.

18.4.4.1 PROFESOR

The PROFESOR is a structured checklist developed by Worling (2017). It was designed to identify dynamic risk and protective behaviors (e.g., 'bipolar factors') of individuals engaged in or accused of illegal or otherwise abusive sexual behaviors (Worling, 2020). The assessment was developed for ages 12–25 and is notably developed to provide information on the intensity of treatment needed and planning interventions and not be predictive of future offending (Worling, 2020).

Table 18.2 Assessment instruments items for PROFESOR and YNPS

PROFESOR 20 dynamic items	YNPS 22 dynamic items
1. Hope regarding healthy sexual future	1. Understanding appropriate sexual behavior
2. Sexual environment	2. Understanding the consequences of sexual abuse
3. Sexual beliefs and attitudes	3. Sexual thoughts—Frequency x
4. Sexual interests—Focus	4. Sexual interests—Age and consent
5. Sexual interests—Frequency	5. Sexual attitudes & beliefs x
6. Knowledge of Laws and Procedures for respectful sexual relationships	6. Sexual behavior management
7. Knowledge of consequences of sexual offending	7. Compassion for others x
8. Strategies to prevent sexual offending	8. Relationships with peers
9. Compassion for others	9. Emotion management x
10. General values and attitudes	10. Social skills
11. Self-regulation	11. Self-confidence x
12. Problem solving	12. Commitment to school / work
13. Responsivity to guidance and support	13. Use of unstructured time x
14. Self-esteem	14. Nonsexual behavior attitudes & beliefs
15. Intimacy and friendship	15. Nonsexual behavior management
16. Relationship with parent/caregiver	16. Client view of primary caregiver relationship
17. Parent/caregiver practices	17. Client view of supportive adult relationships
18. Engagement in school/work	18. Family functioning
19. Engagement in organized leisure activity	19. Living situation—Safety & stability
20. Living arrangement	20. Involvement in community resources
	21. Mental health management
	22. Participation in interventions

The PROFESOR contains 20 factors (20 dynamic factors) that cover both protective and risk characteristics. Factors are rated on a 3-point scale (ranging from 'protective,' 'neutral,' and 'risk') and involve 20 items (see Table 18.2, Worling, 2017). This information is gathered from the individual's functioning in the last 2 months. The individual is then categorized into Predominantly Protective, More Protective than Risk, Predominantly Balanced, More Risk than Protective, and Predominantly Risk. With each category, the tool provides a suggested interpretation of intervention ranging from Very Low intensity, if any, to Very High intensity.

Worling (2020) noted that the assessment has not yet been empirically tested. Further, the PROFESOR was not developed to be a 'risk-prediction' tool and, as such, is not intended to be a predictor of future behavior. Instead, the assessment is designed to measure treatment over time. Therefore, the assessment, although innovative with the use of all dynamic factors, needs empirical testing.

18.4.4.2 YNPS

The YNPS, developed by Prentky et al. (2020), was initially tested by Kang et al. (2019) under the name Treatment Needs and Progress Scale (TNPS). The tool was developed to assess dynamic risk and protective factors of individuals aged 12 to 25 who have engaged in abusive sexual behavior (Prentky et al., 2020). Notably, the assessment is not designed to predict recidivism but instead focuses on identifying factors that may be criminogenic needs for individuals and providing recommended interventions for sexual and general delinquent behavior.

The final assessment has 22 items covering both factors associated with general and sexual offending (Prentky et al., 2020) broken into four scales: General Behavior, Sexual Behavior, Sociological Supports & Stability, and Specific Responsivity Needs. These items are scored on a 4-point scale: No intervention needed (0), Possible/Limited Intervention need (1), Moderate Intervention needed (2), and Strong Intervention Needed (3). The assessments further focus on the individual functioning during the past 3 months. Overall, the assessment is designed to inform management strategies.

Much like the other tool in this section the YNPS has not received much, if any empirical testing. However, there have been two significant critiques of the pilot study (Lee Rasmussen & Fagundes, 2022; Miccio-Fonseca, 2021). Specifically, critiques indicate a lack of empirical support for individuals that are 18–25 age group, not addressing the needs of high-risk youth, and a lack of psychometric testing (Lee Rasmussen & Fagundes, 2022; Miccio-Fonseca, 2021).

18.5 Risk Feature Selection Lacking in Empirical Support

When risk assessment instruments are created, tool developers typically begin with a literature review on risk factors to identify potential variables for item or feature selection. Research on predictors plays a key role in tool development as the predictive power of each risk factor contributes to the tool's validity. Regarding youth sexual recidivism prediction, studies have focused on unique traits of JSOs (McCuish & Lussier, 2017). Predictors are sought within the specific population with the assumption that they will reoffend sexually.

Traditionally, the effort to discover risk factors for sexual recidivism in youth has examined between-group heterogeneity. The typological studies classified juvenile offenders by previous offense type and sought similarities and differences in risk items through comparisons between JSOs and JNSOs. Seto and Lalumière (2010) reviewed 59 studies that examined a wide range of risks and concluded that only a few indicators were associated with JSOs. In this study, authors found that while sexual abuse, deviant sexual interests, anxiety, and low self-esteem were common for JSOs, these youth tended to have less extensive criminal histories, fewer antisocial peers, and fewer substance use issues. Fanniff et al. (2017) also found few differences in risk items for sexual recidivism between JSOs and JNSOs including, less history of antisocial behavior, fewer antisocial peers, and fewer substance use problems in JSOs, while they showed many similarities in reoffending patterns. Those predictors identified are a few, and possibly, insufficient to fully inform risk assessment for sexual re-offense. Additionally, the majority of distinguishable risk factors indicated less criminogenic needs of JSOs (i.e., fewer antisocial peers or less substance abuse) than their counterparts. Overall, findings from between-group heterogeneity inform JSOs' strengths and weaknesses in rehabilitation, rather than providing JSOs' specific risk.

Another method used for selection, is the use of risk items derived from adult samples. For instance, like Andrews and Bonta's development of the Level of Service Inventory (LSI, Andrews, 1982) and subsequent revised version (LSI-R, Andrews & Bonta, 1995), the J-SOAP-II was developed by first selecting items identified from prior literature (Prentky & Righthand, 2003). However, due to a lack of youth specific research, items were selected based on adult findings (Miccio-Fonseca, 2013). Although the use of adult sources is logical where no evidence exists, subsequent research has identified that the J-SOAP-II and similarly created tools that rely on adult samples, do not show consistent prediction. Additionally, Miccio-Fonseca (2013) expressed caution regarding the J-SOAP-II's use for youth under 12, stating concerns of applying adult risk factors to preadolescent children.

As neither the traditional youth group comparisons nor the adult predictors sufficiently assess youth risk, there is an effort to alter the approach to identify risk factors. An emerging theory, developmental life course (DLC), attempts to provide a path to sexual offending, incorporating developmental criminology and the life course approach (Lussier, 2017; Lussier et al., 2018; McCuish & Lussier, 2017). While developmental criminologists focus on how past behavior informs future behavior (i.e., LeBlanc & Fréchette, 1989; Loeber & LeBlanc, 1990), life course researchers look at how life events and transitions affect individual criminal trajectories (Farrington, 2003; Sampson & Laub, 2005). Studies applying the DLC analyses have identified significant risk factors of sexual reoffending which corresponds with developmental profiles such as criminal history, frequency of violence, onset of sexual offending, and aspects of sexual behavior (see Cale et al., 2016; McCuish et al., 2016; Rosa et al., 2020; van Den Berg et al., 2017). However, these predictors are available for distinguishing trajectories within sexual offending, not transitions between different types of offenses. As the DLC approach is more likely to focus on juveniles labeled as JSOs and their continuity/discontinuity of sexual offending (McCuish & Lussier, 2017), rigorous examinations have yet to be conducted examining how the occurrence of other offense types may interrupt the perceived developmental stages of sexual offending.

The lack of findings regarding risk factors resulted in poor utility of significant predictors as well as the use of items without empirical support. Research suggests that items for adolescent tools should be selected from a pool focusing on adolescent population characteristics, such as delinquent patterns (Butler & Seto, 2002; Seto & Lalumière, 2010; van der Put et al., 2013), heterogeneity (Caldwell, 2002, 2007; Chaffin, 2008), and developmental trajectory (Caldwell, 2010; Hunter et al., 2003; Riser et al., 2013; Vandiver, 2006; van Den Berg et al., 2017). It can thus be argued that tool developers should seek new predictor sources to better develop theories of youth sexual reoffending, potentially reflecting youth transitions to desistance, or more serious offense types.

18.6 Tool Development and Application Preoccupied with JSOs

Emulating adult sexual offender risk assessment, practice for JSOs has been preoccupied with the assumption that a single sexual offense of a youth indicates a high risk of future sexual recidivism. The use of instruments, developed for, and applied to, this specific population is rationalized by answering the following questions: (a) does an assessment's development sample include all likely JSOs? and (b) without intervention, are subjects more likely to recidivate with a sexual offense than other types of offenses? However, recidivism patterns of juvenile offenders do not support current risk assessment practices for sexual recidivism, indicating a potential mismatch between rational prediction targets and actual assessment subjects in practice.

JSOs are not the only group that sexually reoffends. While a recent study quantifying the average rate of juvenile sexual reoffending revealed that less than 5% of JSOs recidivated sexually (Caldwell, 2016), however, JNSOs have an equivalent rate of sexual reoffending (Caldwell, 2007; Caldwell et al., 2008; Calleja, 2015; Chu & Thomas, 2010; Fanniff et al., 2017). Sexual re-offenses committed by JNSOs are the majority in noted empirical findings and JNSOs are often a larger population (Calleja, 2015; Chu & Thomas, 2010; Fanniff et al., 2017). Current assessment tools do not include all likely juvenile offenders because the population is limited to those with sexual histories, which, in turn, miss a large proportion of future sex offenses.

Furthermore, recidivism patterns revealed that re-offense types of JSOs are versatile. Caldwell (2016) reviewed 106 studies and calculated that the nonsexual recidivism rate for JSOs was eight times greater than the sexual recidivism rate on average. Although there are a few studies that attempt to predict JSOs general recidivism risk, there is no tool validated for these outcomes. Thus, current risk assessment tools and practices may not align with recidivism patterns of JSOs.

This common development practice not only has the potential to mislabel delinquent youth as sex offenders, but also excludes a group of juvenile offenders that may recidivate sexually. It has therefore been argued that risk assessment practice should be rearranged to focus on future offense types, not simply reflective of prior offense types alone (Miccio-Fonseca, 2013). It can thus be argued that the targets for sexual recidivism risk assessments should include all juvenile offenders, no matter their adjudications. Further, it is critical to assess versatile re-offense risk patterns of juvenile offenders, which include sexual recidivism.

18.6.1 Prediction Modeling Design for a Solitary Outcome

The biggest challenge in attuning the assessment practice to youth reoffending patterns derives from the contemporary tool development framework, or the single-model approach for solitary outcome prediction (i.e., rearrest or reconviction regardless of types of crime committed). The major prediction constraints in single-model risk assessment involves structural limitations that are unable to reflect offense versatility. Traditionally, single-model risk assessment instruments fall into one of two categories: broadband (assessment for general reoffending) or narrowband (prediction for a specific offense type; Brennan et al., 2009; Duwe, 2014). With narrowband instruments, sexual recidivism is predicted only for JSOs. Although it is possible to assess JSOs' risk of general reoffending with broadband tools, this practice largely ignores re-offense versatility as tools are not designed to identify heterogeneity among JSOs' reoffending patterns. Consequently, a single prediction model, which does not account for youth heterogeneity, has reduced predictive ability.

In the field of youth sexual recidivism prediction, narrowband tools are commonly used, designed to and applied to JSOs. As previously reviewed, the contemporary risk assessment instruments have not demonstrated consistent performance. Regarding the ERASOR, although it was considered as one of the most commonly used tools, the developer, James Worling, renounced its further use due to predictive performance loss (2017).

Furthermore, while there are some empirical findings of non-sexual reoffending rates of JSOs, suggesting a degree of opportunistic offending, few studies have attempted to estimate JSOs' risk of general recidivism with broadband tools. Viljoen et al. (2009) assessed 193 male youths who were enrolled in a residential SO program with the Youth Level of Service/Case Management Inventory (YLS/CMI). The authors found a moderate prediction strength (AUC = .66) of the YLS/CMI total score for their general recidivism. Additionally, Schmidt et al. (2016) also examined the YLS/CMI with a sample of Canadian JSOs. The YLS/CMI strongly predicted both violent (AUC = .78) and nonviolent recidivism (AUC = .71) of the JSOs (Schmidt et al., 2016). Although the study results are limited, they imply the potential utility of broadband tools for JSOs, predicting general reoffending where the estimate of failure is irrespective of the qualitative type of re-offense. While assessments reveal strengths and weaknesses of youth in rehabilitation, the results are translated without re-offense types, which is often the most crucial information in deciding intervention types.

One approach to this issue is to use multiple tools, one to predict general reoffending and another for more specific offense types when deemed relevant. However, this practice assumes relative agreement and consistent use of differently designed tools built from varying populations, where if risk levels from various tools are consistent, then the results give confidence in decision-making in aggregate (Mills & Kroner, 2006; Vrieze & Grove, 2010). However, this assumption can be erroneous, as demonstrated by empirical research showing divergent assessment results. Vrieze and Grove (2010) observed the risk discrepancy for an individual when comparing assessment results of eight different instruments (PCL-R, VRAG, SORAG, MnSOST-R, Static-99, RRASOR, SVR-20, and HCR-20). Delineating each instrument result, they attempted to combine risk factors and yield a comprehensive risk estimate. However, authors observed a wide variety of risk prediction for each subject, failing to identify a common level of risk across tools. The researchers concluded that the inconsistent risk estimates were likely irresolvable, as each instrument provides various decision-making points spawning variability in scoring as well as rater differences.

Barbaree et al. (2006) also observed divergent risk levels of subjects across five different actuarial risk instruments (RRASOR, Static-99, VRAG, SORAG, and MnSOST-R). Assessing 262 sex offenders, the researchers provided percentile rank of individual scores for each instrument and applied similar risk level cut point demarcations across the five instruments. The top 25% of the sample was defined as the high-risk group and bottom 25% of the sample was classified as low risk for each instrument. Authors found that over 95% of subjects demonstrated inconsistent risk levels across the five instruments. These noted discrepancies suggest that the use of multiple instruments has the potential to lead to mis-specified classification, as risk level is largely dependent on the instrument utilized.

In sum, neither broadband nor narrowband instruments alone provide universally consistent prediction of recidivism. While it is common for both broad and narrowband tools to predict general and specific outcomes (Hanson & Morton-Bourgon, 2009), the choice of tool and its development sample drives the consistency of future prediction in the new, or applied population. In addition, the common practice of using multiple tools to predict multiple outcomes also suffers from an absence of guidelines and may produce conflicting results. Further, prediction of recidivism, when limited to samples of offenders with similar prior offense patterns, misses the risk of future crime, which may be unrelated to the present crime and present a pattern of opportunistic offending. To create risk prediction models unfettered by sexual offense history, tool development practices should be explored and updated from the single to multiple bands, where a single set of risk items can be used to more consistently predict multiple recidivism types for a single population.

18.7 Clinical Assessment Considerations and Techniques

As indicated, any justice involved youth can reoffend sexually. When this assumption replaces the old rationale, that only JSOs are likely to commit sex offenses, an extensive youth population can more effectively be used to develop an assessment. The suggested practice shifts the focus from JSOs' sexual recidivism to the reoffending patterns of all youth. Extending the discussion of prior sections, two areas of needed innovation are outlined: (1) risk item selection from comprehensive juvenile characteristics and (2) an assessment focusing on re-offense types with multiband tools.

18.7.1 Risk Factor Selection from Comprehensive Juvenile Characteristics

The limited theoretical approaches to youth sexual recidivism suggests a new strategy for risk feature selection; an item pool that operates across, rather than confined within a narrow or broadband theoretical boundary. Using this approach, the potential item pool can be collected based on a variety of sources such as existing risk assessment tools for general delinquency, literature exploring youth sexual recidivism and heterogeneity, as well as research findings regarding developmental trajectories. This strategy enables empirical tests for youth characteristics that have not been fully investigated for sexual recidivism.

Choi (2020) examined a large number of assessment features (k = 126) for a Washington State youth sample, identifying items that were predictive of sexual recidivism. The analyses resulted in newly identified risk factors for sexual recidivism such as 'youth's belief in education', 'suicide ideation', and 'employment aspirations'. As the selection pool included items traditionally used for JSOs, some common narrowband risk factors were also identified as predictive (i.e., sexual desire, history of sexual abuse, and impulse). Incorporating all predictive items, Choi (2020) created a new prediction model for sexual recidivism. Applied to a group of JSOs and JNSOs, findings indicated moderate predictive strength (AUC = 0.67). More importantly, the results implied that risk factors can predict sexual offending for JNSOs. Further, new predictors of youth sexual recidivism included common broadband tool predictors, such as: use of free time, employment history, and alcohol/drug related indicators. Although replication is needed, findings suggested that restricting risk items to only those demonstrating a prior offense type history, unnecessarily confines predictions within an isolated theoretical boundary, which has the potential to misclassify youth, prevent needed intervention, and increase the potential for future harm.

We argue that the use of more extensive item pools will revitalize youth assessment development. Miccio-Fonseca and Rasmussen (2018) further emphasized needed investigation of protective factors, where broadband tools may provide said indicators not commonly assessed in sex-offender specific tools. With this said, there is no strongly established theoretical basis for youth sexual recidivism (Rasmussen, 2013). Exploring a large pool of items can provide an alternative route for a risk prediction model creation. This suggests a new development path to data driven research, with routinely collected assessment data, likely leading to a greater understanding of both unique and general prediction youth delinquency patterns. Creating new measures and tools is now more feasible due to the extensive data collected for youth and adults, with multiple tools, spanning decades of subjects. Therefore, it is crucial to create and use an item pool that opens possibilities of the data driven analyses for more advanced prediction models.

18.7.2 Risk Assessment Focusing on Re-offense Types with Multi-band Tools

In terms of risk assessment practice, narrow-band tools were developed for adults to reflect offense specialization, typically for either violence or sex offending (Hamilton et al., 2017b). As described, using history of sex offense as the criterion to apply tools has been problematic for juveniles. Specifically, a single offense does not denote a specialization, and, depending on their next offense, individuals may change their group membership. Thus, if a juvenile, labeled a JSO, non-sexually reoffends, risk assessment based on prior group membership fails. As such, tools developed and applied exclusively for JSOs, demonstrate limited utility (Hamilton et al., 2017b; Duwe, 2014). This is a common limitation, inherent for tools developed absent of risk items with a general application for JNSOs or recidivism prediction generally. Thus, it is argued that assessment standards for populations and practice should expand to predict both narrow and broadband reoffending patterns of youth with a mix of specific and general recidivism prediction features.

This strategy develops an instrument with multiple prediction models is termed 'multi-band', assessing a variety of outcomes separately but from the same item pool. First outlined by Duwe (2014), multi-band tools use a variety of statistical models computing a new outcome for each, selecting and weighting items in the pool to specifically predict each re-offense type (see also, Hamilton et al., 2016; 2019). These models, like all risk models place individuals on a continuum, rating their likelihood of either general or specific recidivism types. Their distinction from narrowband models is that multi-band prediction is made for each specific offense type, which is a portion of the larger, general offending, base rate. When developed with the full sample, the content of items selected are those for the specific outcome and capture the content overlap of general offending as well. Further validation can then be compared across sub-populations, examining the assessment's predictive strength for both theoretical (i.e., JSO) and atheoretical (i.e., JNSO) populations.

A risk assessment tool developed with such strategies serves practitioners with clear guidance on intervention, prioritizing programming for those with the greatest risks and for more serious outcomes (Hamilton et al., 2017b). For example, a JSO can be assessed for different recidivistic outcomes, including violent, sex, and drug-related reoffending, simultaneously. Results from these multiple models contribute to case management, as a multi-model risk tool may demonstrate a JSO at high risk for committing a future violent crime. Assessment results via multiple models serve as objectively sound criteria to select a proper program from among a wide range of interventions that are not limited to sexual recidivism prevention.

While applying multiple prediction models seems formidable in development stages, application will likely not result in increased labor, and may reduce it for agencies that deploy individual assessments for each outcome. Once a multi-band instrument is created, the use of multiple models provides results for each outcome. Further, agencies can select model's order of importance in risk classification, creating what is termed a 'hierarchical classification system' (Hamilton et al., 2017a; Hamilton et al., 2016). As a way of explaining the proposed system, Fig. 18.1 provides a visual. The hierarchy can reflect agencies' priorities in case management. The models presented in the figure (left side) are the crime types that an agency mainly focuses on. Using a multi-band method to develop hierarchical models, one is provided with a variety of risk levels for an individual (right side). Once this system is established, the assessment process is as follows: (a) assess all youth with an item pool which consists of predictors from each model in aggregate, (b) enter youth responses to all items into an assessment system, and (c) for a given outcome,

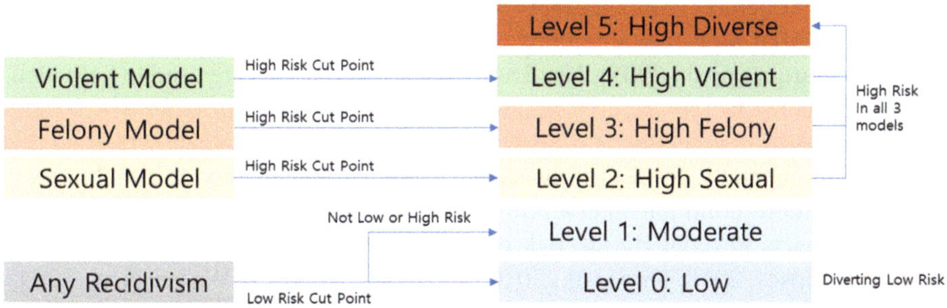

Fig. 18.1 An example of hierarchical classification system

select items and weight scores, following the new model schematics. An advantage of this approach, is that assessment instruments are built based on a robust item pool, align decision-making processes with genuine characteristics of youth delinquency, and help allot resources effectively by selecting appropriate targets for interventions.

18.8 Treatment Interventions for Preventing Sexual Recidivism

The first SO treatment program for youth was created in 1975, but it was not until the National Task Force on Juvenile Sex Offending (1988) that legislators began urging treatment programs for adjudicated youths (Worling & Curwen, 2001). This mandate occurred largely before empirical evidence was available and/or suggested treatment changed juvenile offenders' motives for offending or influenced their reoffending rates. Nonetheless, growth in both residential and outpatient juvenile SO treatment programs continued over the next 30 years. Although there are still sizeable proportions of juveniles who quit general offending and sexual reoffending without therapeutic treatment at all (Zimring et al., 2009), there are still some common elements that can be found in JSO treatment (Przybylski & Lobanov-Rostovsky, 2015).

One of the most popular therapies is psychotherapy, specifically cognitive behavior therapy (CBT), which addresses irrational thoughts and beliefs of individuals by practicing opportunities to model and engage in prosocial behavior and problem thinking skills in a group setting (Kolko et al., 2004; Przybylski, 2015). As a community-based intervention, multisystemic therapy (MST) is commonly employed to target juveniles' socialization processes and interpersonal transactions (Borduin et al., 2009). MST involves working with juveniles' families in their natural environment to provide parents with the skills needed to address problem behavior. Lastly, most programs include relapse prevention modalities that target risk and need factors of youths (Hanson & Morton-Bourgon, 2009). For example, a program may highly structure group therapy sessions that help individuals identify and address potential high-risk situations that may lead to sexual offending (see, for example, Marques et al., 2005). Need assessment instruments are used to help identify criminogenic factors underlying problematic sexual behavior, after which treatment is matched to juveniles' abilities and learning styles, thus acknowledging that not all youth mentally develop at the same rate or learn using the same techniques.

Overall, these common interventions with this population have demonstrated positive impacts in reducing the risk of re-offense with JSOs (Dopp et al., 2015; Kettrey & Lipsey, 2018; Kim et al., 2016; Sneddon et al., 2020; Walker et al., 2004). For example, Walker et al.'s (2004) meta-analysis of 10 studies found that CBT had the largest effect sizes of the interventions compared. It should be noted however, that they were limited in the amount of MST treatments at the time, and that they suggested comparing them against MST and other modalities. Moreover, Dopp et al.'s (2015) through a systematic review of ten studies examined CBT and MST and their effectiveness in reducing sexual recidivism. They found that MST for problem sexual behavior was relatively effective, suggesting that the therapy targeting critical socialization processes were likely one of the effective treatment components for targeting problem sexual behavior. In this review, limited support was found for CBT programs.

However, specified treatments that focus solely on juvenile sexual offending vary widely in effectiveness; specifically, how much more effective these narrow treatments are from more generalizable treatments (Sorrentio et al., 2018). For example, much of the literature notes that MST and CBT do reduce recidivism overall, however, these studies are substantially different in methodology and study populations which is a concern when attempting to establish best practices (Kettrey & Lipsey, 2018; Sneddon et al., 2020; Kim et al., 2016). Therefore, it is necessary to discuss some treatment intervention issues to better understand the context of the individual juveniles and their needs.

18.8.1 Treatment Intervention Issues for JSOs

There are numerous methodological problems when determining if and how SO treatment reduces sexual motives and reoffending. These problems have, in turn, limited the general knowledge of what is effective for this population and causes significant caution when interpreting findings regarding program efficacy for this population. In this section, some of the issues that limit the field in accurately assessing the state of the literature regarding these available treatment options are highlighted.

18.8.1.1 Methodological Issues with Current Studies

Although there has been significant research assessing interventions for this population, it is difficult to determine generalizability from program-to-program and specifically understand what mechanisms of a program improves outcomes. For example, Dopp et al. (2015) evaluated CBT and MST, specified to JSOs, finding that out of the ten studies that met inclusion criteria, there were still significant methodological issues with the studies that limited their generalizability. A key issue in evaluating the effectiveness of JSO programming is statistical power, namely having requisite sample size to determine statistically significant effects. Dopp et al. (2015) identified that the number of individuals in prior studies ranged from 16 to 285 participants. Further, comparison groups were often problematic, ranging from dropouts from the program to another type of therapy (i.e., individual therapy, outpatient therapy CBT when compared to MST therapy), and failing to examine sexual offenses as the individual transitions to an adult (Dopp et al., 2015). Sneddon et al.'s (2020) research further reiterates these findings as their review of the literature could only include four randomized control trials, none that included girls, and all having less than 40 participants. In this way, it is difficult to note what programmatic elements may have been effective as there is there is a lack of studies across multiple population types which therefore, limit generalizability.

Specialized treatments also vary widely in scope and dosage, making it difficult to know what aspects of the programs might be effective (i.e., skill attainment vs. therapeutic interventions) and the duration and number of sessions needed for an effective dose (Kettrey & Lipsey, 2018). For example, in Kim et al.'s (2016) meta-analysis, authors found that program types for juveniles and adults ranged from classical behavioral interventions to surgical and hormonal treatments. This range of interventions is also undermined by fidelity to a specific program modality. For example, Reitzel and Carbonell (2006) caution that in their meta-analysis of nine studies there was a lack of evidence that programs were manualized which is a common consideration of program fidelity. This was further expressed by Winokur et al.'s (2006) meta-analysis of 11 studies which found drastically different lengths in treatment dosages ranging from 3–24 months. Given the findings of this meta-analysis, authors identified that it can be difficult to find recommended lengths of treatment of any one type. Further, as Przybylski (2015) suggests, there has been a lack of replication in juvenile treatment studies, which can limit many of the findings. Overall, few studies have academic rigor regarding treatment for JSOs despite the wide adoption of specialized treatments for youths (See, Kettrey & Lipsey, 2018; Dopp et al., 2015).

18.8.1.2 JSOs as Generalists

Further, as Kettrey and Lipsey (2018) addressed, the current literature seems to suggest that juveniles with sexual histories are more similar to their more generalist counterparts than adult offenders. Specifically, there is a significant contention that many of the treatments given to JSOs are limited in effectiveness because they only focus on sexual history and the prevention of sexual recidivism and not recidivism overall (Kettrey & Lipsey, 2018). Specifically, in their meta-analysis comparing specialized and generalized treatment, Kettrey and Lipsey (2018) found that specialized interventions were no more effective than generalized treatments for JSOs. Although limited by the number of programs that were eligible for the analysis, their findings suggest that juveniles with sexual criminal histories are like those without general deviant histories. Therefore, specialized treatment may be too narrowly applied for the population. In other words, the sexual offense committed by the JSO could be an isolated incident and not indicative of future offending patterns that require specialized intense treatment (Przybylski, 2015). Therefore, with more specified risk assessments, as suggested in this chapter, researchers may potentially limit this critique by only placing those who are at high risk for sexual recidivism in treatment. For example, Aebi et al.'s (2022) randomized control trial found that treatments that focused on attaining specific skills that focused on the sexual offense were helpful in reducing sexual recidivism but not general recidivism. This finding suggests that these types of programs can be narrowly applied to those who are more likely to sexually recidivate.

18.8.2 Potential Avenues of Treatment Interventions for JSOs

Although prior findings of JSO treatments have significant caveats, there are some indications of potential positive effects of treatment for this population (Kettrey & Lipsey, 2018). Overall, individuals do seem be amendable to psychological treatment (Sneddon et al., 2020; Kettrey & Lipsey, 2018; Kim et al., 2016; Schmucker & Lösel, 2015; Dopp et al., 2015; Winokur et al., 2006; Reitzel & Carbonell, 2006; Lösel & Schmucker, 2005; Walker et al., 2004; Hanson et al., 2002; Aebi et al., 2022; Worling et al., 2010). Given this general finding, there are a few avenues in which these treatments could be more amendable. Specifically, understanding their criminogenic risks and further using MST related treatments.

18.8.2.1 Matching Individuals on Criminogenic Risk

Overall, there is significant consideration that juveniles are generalists and therefore more general treatment plans could be effective. For example, as shown by Kettrey and Lipsey (2018), generalized treatment plans may be effective for JSOs. Moreover, with more accurate assessments, it may be possible to better match individuals with programming based on their criminogenic needs and therefore follow a more general treatment model (Bonta & Andrews, 2016). For example, by using more accurate risk assessments, treatment providers could more narrowly apply specialized sexual recidivism treatment to individuals at high risk for sexual recidivism and a more generalized treatment plan for those who are not instead of providing the narrow program to all individuals (Bonta & Andrews, 2016). In this way, instead of matching juveniles by crime type and history they can instead match by criminal needs and risk type.

18.8.2.2 Use of Multisystemic Therapy

Although psychotherapeutic programs seem promising, and many programs are effective with the use of CBT, more recent meta-analysis have suggested that MST therapeutic models may provide a greater impact (Dopp et al., 2015; Borduin et al., 2009). For example, Henggeler et al. (2009) found that when compared to other psychological treatments (i.e., CBT, individual therapy), youths in MST exhibited a greater decrease in antisocial behavior and deviant sexual interest. The authors' suggested MST is effective in using caregivers to identify negative peers' groups and empower follow-through on planned discipline (Henggeler et al., 2009, see also; Borduin et al., 2009). In other words, this therapeutic intervention lends itself well to target not only reducing the irrational thoughts and behaviors of the youths but also target other areas of risk such as peers. Although research is limited, these findings suggest that general recidivism programming and intensive therapeutic interventions can help JSO populations, whose sexual offending behavior is amenable for treatment.

18.9 Conclusions

Much of the popular narrative around JSOs has suggested that they are at high risk for re-offense inherently and are categorically different from other juvenile delinquents (Chaffin, 2008). Because of this perception, research has treated JSOs fundamentally differently than their peers and employed assessment tools to evaluate risk and prioritize treatment. Most policies, in turn, have sought to label and ostracize this population from society to limit their potential risk to others, such as SO registries (Chaffin, 2008). Luckily, as shown in this chapter, this narrative seems demonstrably unsupported by research.

Indeed, it has been proposed that multi-band instruments could potentially allow for both narrow and broadband outcomes to be used across a wide a variety of youth populations. In this way, the assessment can predict sexual recidivism more accurately and adequately account for the level of risk among this population. Specifically, with multi-band modeling, it can be possible to avoid misperceptions surrounding youth sexual offending and accurately depict risk with criminogenic needs and prioritizing targeted interventions. This way, overdue updates to SO and general assessments may hold a key to improved programming and prevention efforts.

Moreover, there are indications of promising treatment effects for this population, and there is significant evidence to support the claim that they are amendable to change (Kettrey & Lipsey, 2018). Specifically, evidence shows that JSOs are similar to their other juvenile counterparts, where psychological interventions such as CBT and MST are effective in reducing recidivism overall, and that intensive treatment seems to be most effective (Dopp et al., 2015; Kettrey & Lipsey, 2018). However, there are still potential caveats with current findings, suggesting the need for additional research with greater methodological rigor (Kettrey & Lipsey, 2018). As JSO assessment and programming moves forward, it is hoped that this chapter provides readers a concise overview of the current state of research findings and suggested directions for future work.

References

Aebi, M., Krause, C., Barra, S., Vogt, G., Vertone, L., Manetsch, M., Imbach, D., Endrass, J., Rossegger, A., Schmeck, K., & Bessler, C. (2022). What kind of therapy works with juveniles who have sexually offended? A randomized-controlled trial of two versions of a specialized cognitive behavioral outpatient treatment program. *Sexual Abuse, 34*(8), 1–30. https://doi.org/10.1177/10790632211070804

American Educational Research Association, American Psychological Association, National Council on Measurement in Education. (2014). *Standards for educational and psychological testing*. American Educational Research Association.

Andrews, D. A. (1982). *The level of supervisory inventory LSI*. Ontario Planning and Support Services Division.

Andrews, D. A., & Bonta, J. L. (1995). *LSI-R: The level of service inventory manual*. Multi-Health Systems.

Barbaree, H. E., Langton, C., & Peacock, E. J. (2006). Different actuarial risk measures produce different risk rankings for sexual offenders. *Sexual Abuse: A Journal of Research and Treatment, 18*, 423–440.

Barra, S., Bessler, C., Landolt, M. A., & Aebi, M. (2018). Patterns of adverse childhood experiences in juveniles who sexually offended. *Sexual Abuse, 30*(7), 803–827.

Boer, D. P., Hart, S. D., Kropp, P. R., & Webster, C. D. (1997). *Manual for the sexual violence risk – 20: Professional guidelines for assessing risk of sexual violence*. The Mental Health, Law, & Policy Institute.

Bonner, B. L., Walker, C. E., & Berliner, L. (2001). Children with sexual behavior problems: Assessment and treatment. National Clearinghouse on Child Abuse and Neglect Information.

Bonta, J., & Andrews, D. A. (2016). *The psychology of criminal conduct*. Routledge.

Borduin, C. M., Schaeffer, C. M., & Heiblum, N. (2009). A randomized clinical trial of multisystemic therapy with juvenile sexual offenders: Effects on youth social ecology and criminal activity. *Journal of Consulting and Clinical Psychology, 77*(1), 26.

Brennan, T., Dieterich, W., & Ehret, B. (2009). Evaluating the predictive validity of the COMPAS risk and needs assessment system. *Criminal Justice and Behavior, 36*, 21–40.

Butler, S. M., & Seto, M. C. (2002). Distinguishing two types of adolescent sex offenders. *Journal of the American Academy of Child and Adolescent Psychiatry, 41*, 83–90.

Caldwell, M. (2002). What we do not know about juvenile sexual re-offense risk. *Child Maltreatment: Journal of the American Professional Society on the Abuse of Children, 7*, 291–302.

Caldwell, M. (2007). Sexual offense adjudication and recidivism among juvenile offenders. *Sexual Abuse: A Journal of Research and Treatment, 19*, 107–113.

Caldwell, M. (2010). Study characteristics and recidivism base rates in juvenile sex offender recidivism. *International Journal of Offender Therapy and Comparative Criminology, 54*(2), 197–212.

Caldwell, M. (2016). Quantifying the decline in juvenile sexual recidivism rates. *Psychology, Public Policy, and Law, 22*, 414–426.

Caldwell, M. F., & Caldwell, B. M. (2022). The age of redemption for adolescents who were adjudicated for sexual misconduct. *Psychology, Public Policy, and Law, 28*(2), 167–178. https://doi.org/10.1037/law0000343

Caldwell, M., Zempke, M., & Vitacco, M. (2008). An examination of the sex offender registration and notification act as applied to juveniles: Evaluating the ability to predict sexual recidivism. *Psychology, Public Policy, and Law, 14*(2), 89–114.

Cale, J., Smallbone, S., Rayment-McHugh, S., & Dowling, C. (2016). Offense trajectories, the unfolding of sexual and non-sexual criminal activity, and sex offense characteristics of adolescent sex offenders. *Sexual Abuse: A Journal of Research and Treatment, 28*, 791–812.

Calleja, N. G. (2015). Juvenile sex and non-sex offenders: A comparison of recidivism and risk. *Journal of Addictions & Offender Counseling, 36*(1), 2–12.

Carpentier, J., & Proulx, J. (2011). Correlates of recidivism among adolescents who have sexually offended. *Sexual Abuse, 23*, 434–455.

Cauffman, E., & Steinberg, L. (2000). (Im) maturity of judgment in adolescence: Why adolescents may be less culpable than adults. *Behavioral Sciences & the Law, 18*(6), 741–760.

Chaffin, M. (2008). Our minds are made up—Don't confuse us with the facts: Commentary on policies concerning children with sexual behavior problems and juvenile sex offenders. *Child Maltreatment, 13*, 110–121.

Chaffin, M., Berliner, L., Block, R., Johnson, T. C., Friedrich, W. N., Louis, D. G., & Madden, C. (2008). Report of the ATSA task force on children with sexual behavior problems. *Child Maltreatment, 13*(2), 199–218.

Choi, E. (2020). Enhancing the integrated treatment assessment for youth sexual recidivism prediction: Toward a Washington State-unified risk assessment system [Doctoral dissertation, Washington State University]. ProQuest Dissertation and Thesis Global.

Chu, M. C., & Thomas, S. D. M. (2010). Adolescent sexual offenders: The relationship between typology and recidivism. *Sexual Abuse: A Journal of Research and Treatment, 22*, 218–233.

Dopp, A. R., Borduin, C. M., & Brown, C. E. (2015). Evidence-based treatments for juvenile sexual offenders: Review and recommendations. *Journal of Aggression, Conflict, and Peace Research, 7*(4), 223–236.

Duwe, G. (2014). The development, validity, and reliability of the Minnesota screening tool assessing recidivism risk (MnSTARR). *Criminal Justice Policy Review, 25*(5), 579–613.

Elkovitch, N., Latzman, R. D., Hansen, D. J., & Flood, M. F. (2009). Understanding child sexual behavior problems: A developmental psychopathology framework. *Clinical Psychology Review, 29*(7), 586–598.

Epperson, D. L., & Ralston, C. A. (2015). Development and validation of the juvenile sexual offense recidivism risk assessment tool–II. *Sexual Abuse: A Journal of Research and Treatment, 27*(6), 529–558.

Fanniff, A. M., Schubert, C. A., Mulvey, E. P., Iselin, A. R., & Piquero, A. R. (2017). Risk and outcomes: Are adolescents charged with sex offenses different from other adolescent offenders? *Journal of Youth Adolescence, 46*, 1394–1423.

Farrington, D. P. (2003). Developmental and life-course criminology: Key theoretical and empirical issues-the 2002 Sutherland award address. *Criminology, 41*, 221–225.

Hamilton, Z., Campagna, M., Tollefsbol, E., van Wormer, J., & Barnoski, R. (2017a). A more consistent application of the RNR model: The strong-R needs assessment. *Criminal Justice and Behavior, 44*(2), 261–292.

Hamilton, Z., Tollefsbol, E., Campagna, M., & van Wormer, J. (2017b). Customizing criminal justice assessments. In F. S. Taxman (Ed.), *Handbook on risk and need assessment: Theory and practice* (pp. 333–377). Taylor & Francis Group.

Hamilton, Z., Kigerl, A., Campagna, M., Barnoski, R., Lee, S., van Wormer, J., & Block, L. (2016). Designed to fit: The development and validation of the STRONG-R recidivism risk assessment. *Criminal Justice and Behavior, 43*(2), 230–263.

Hamilton, Z., Kowalski, M. A., Kigerl, A., & Routh, D. (2019). Optimizing youth risk assessment performance: Development of the modified positive achievement change tool in Washington state. *Criminal Justice and Behavior, 46*(8), 1106–1127.

Hanson, R. K., Gordon, A., Harris, A. J. R., Marques, J. K., Murphy, W., Quinsey, V. L., & Seto, M. C. (2002). First report of the collaborative outcome data project on the effectiveness of psychological treatment for sex offenders. *Sexual Abuse: A Journal of Research and Treatment, 14*, 169–194.

Hanson, R. K., & Morton-Bourgon, K. E. (2009). The accuracy of recidivism risk assessments for sexual offenders: A meta-analysis of 118 prediction studies. *Psychological Assessment, 21*(1), 1–21. https://doi.org/10.1037/a0014421

Harris, A. J., & Socia, K. M. (2016). What's in a name? Evaluating the effects of the "sex offender" label on public opinions and beliefs. *Sexual Abuse, 28*(7), 660–678.

Hemple, I., Buck, N., Cima, M., & van Marle, H. (2013). Review of risk assessment instruments for juvenile sex offenders: What is next? *International Journal of Offender Therapy and Comparative Criminology, 57*(2), 208–228.

Henggeler, S. W., Letourneau, E. J., Chapman, J. E., Borduin, C. M., Schewe, P. A., & McCart, M. R. (2009). Mediators of change for multisystemic therapy with juvenile sexual offenders. *Journal of Consulting and Clinical Psychology, 77*(3), 451.

Hunter, J., Figueredo, A., Malamuth, N., & Becker, J. (2003). Juvenile sex offenders: Toward the development of a typology. *Sexual Abuse: A Journal of Research and Treatment, 15*, 27–48.

Kang, T., Beltrani, A., Manheim, M., Spriggs, S., Nishimura, B., Sinclair, S., Stachniuk, M., Pate, E., Righthand, S., Prentky, R., & Worling, J. (2019). Development of a risk/treatment needs and progress protocol for juveniles with sex offenses. *Translational Issues in Psychological Science, 5*(2), 154–169. https://doi.org/10.1037/tps0000191

Kellogg, N. D., & Committee on Child Abuse and Neglect. (2009). Clinical report—The evaluation of sexual behaviors in children. *Pediatrics, 124*(3), 992–998.

Kettrey, H. H., & Lipsey, M. W. (2018). The effects of specialized treatment on the recidivism of juvenile sex offenders: A systematic review and meta-analysis. *Journal of Experimental Criminology, 14*, 361–387.

Kim, B., Benekos, P. J., & Merlo, A. V. (2016). Sex offender recidivism revisited: Review of recent meta-analyses on the effects of sex offender treatment. *Trauma, Violence, & Abuse, 17*(1), 105–117.

Kleeven, A. T. H., de Vries Robbé, M., Mulder, E. A., & Popma, A. (2022). Risk assessment in juvenile and young adult offenders: Predictive validity of the SAVRY and SAPROF-YV. *Assessment. American Psychological Association, Society for Clinical Psychology, 29*(2), 181–197.

Kolko, D. J., Noel, C., Thomas, G., & Torres, E. (2004). Cognitive-behavioral treatment for adolescents who sexually offend and their families: Individual and family applications in a collaborative outpatient program. *Journal of Child Sexual Abuse: Research, Treatment, & Program Innovations for Victims, Survivors, & Offenders, 13*(3–4), 157–192.

Krause, C., Roth, A., Landolt, M. A., Bessler, C., & Aebi, M. (2021). Validity of risk assessment instruments among juveniles who sexually offended: Victim age matters. Sexual Abuse, 33(4), 379-405.

LeBlanc, M., & Fréchette, M. (1989). *Male criminal activity from childhood through youth: Multilevel and developmental perspectives*. Springer.

Lee Rasmussen, L. A., & Fagundes, M. (2022). A critique of the youth needs and progress scale and its applicability to individuals ages 18 to 25 with sexually abusive behavior. *Journal of Aggression, Maltreatment & Trauma, 31*(6), 734–752.

Leibowitz, G. S., Akakpo, T., & Burton, D. L. (2016). Comparison of non-sexual crimes committed by juvenile sexual offenders and delinquent youth. *Journal of Sexual Aggression, 22*(1), 66–81.

Letourneau, E. J., Bandyopadhyay, D., Armstrong, K. S., & Sinha, D. (2010). Do sex offender registration and notification requirements deter juvenile sex crimes? *Criminal Justice and Behavior, 37*(5), 553–569.

Letourneau, E. J., & Miner, M. H. (2005). Juvenile sex offenders: A case against the legal and clinical status quo. *Sexual Abuse: A Journal of Research and Treatment, 17*(3), 293–312.

Letourneau, E. J., Shields, R. T., Nair, R., Kahn, G., Sandler, J. C., & Vandiver, D. M. (2019). Juvenile registration and notification policies fail to prevent first-time sexual offenses: An extension of findings to two new states. *Criminal Justice Policy Review, 30*(7), 1109–1123.

Loeber, R., & LeBlanc, M. (1990). Toward a developmental criminology. *Crime and Justice, 12*, 375–473.
Lösel, F., & Schmucker, M. (2005). The effectiveness of treatment for sexual offenders: A comprehensive meta-analysis. *Journal of Experimental Criminology, 1*(1), 117–146.
Lussier, P. (2017). Juvenile sex offending through a developmental life course criminology perspective: An agenda for policy and research. *Sexual Abuse: A Journal of Research and Treatment, 29*(1), 51–80.
Lussier, P., McCuish, E., Mathesius, J., Corrado, R., & Nadeau, D. (2018). Developmental trajectories of child sexual behaviors on the path of sexual behavioral problems. *Sexual Abuse, 30*(6), 622–658.
Marques, J. K., Wiederanders, M., Day, D. M., Nelson, C., & Van Ommeren, A. (2005). Effects of a relapse prevention program on sexual recidivism: Final results from California's Sex Offender Treatment and Evaluation Project (SOTEP). *Sexual Abuse: A Journal of Research and Treatment, 17*(1), 79–107.
McCuish, E. C., & Lussier, P. (2017). Unfinished stories: From juvenile sex offenders to juvenile sex offending through a developmental life course perspective. *Aggression and Violent Behavior, 37*, 71–82.
McCuish, E., Lussier, P., & Corrado, R. (2016). Criminal careers of juvenile sex and non sex offenders: Evidence from a prospective longitudinal study. *Youth Violence and Juvenile Justice, 14*, 199–224.
McGrath, R. J., Cumming, G. F., Burchard, B. L., Zeoli, S., & Ellerby, L. (2010). *Current practices and emerging trends in sexual abuser management: The safer society 2009 north American survey*. Safer Society Foundation.
Miccio-Fonseca, L. C. (2013). MEGA♪: A new paradigm in risk assessment tools for sexually abusive youth. *Journal of Family Violence, 28*, 623–634.
Miccio-Fonseca, L. C. (2021). A critical assessment of the youth needs and Progress scale. *Journal of Child Sexual Abuse, 30*(7), 765–784. https://doi.org/10.1080/10538712.2021.1914260
Miccio-Fonseca, L. C., & Rasmussen, L. A. (2018). Scientific evolution of clinical and risk assessment of sexually abusive youth: A comprehensive review of empirical tools. *Journal of Child Sexual Abuse, 27*(8), 871–900. https://doi.org/10.1080/10538712.2018.1537337
Mills, J. F., & Kroner, D. G. (2006). The effect of base-rate information on the perception of risk for re-offense. *American Journal of Forensic Psychology, 24*(3), 45–56.
Miner, M. H. (2002). Factors associated with recidivism in juveniles: An analysis of serious juvenile sex offenders. *Journal of Research in Crime and Delinquency, 39*(4), 421–436.
Miner, M. H., & Munns, R. (2005). Isolation and normlessness: Attitudinal comparisons of adolescent sex offenders, juvenile offenders, and nondelinquents. *International Journal of Offender Therapy and Comparative Criminology, 49*(5), 491–450.
Molnar, T., Allard, T., McKillop, N., & Rynne, J. (2020). Reliability and predictive validity of the Juvenile Sex Offender assessment protocol-II in an Australian context. *International Journal of Offender Therapy and Comparative Criminology, 66*(10–11), 1051–1070. https://doi.org/10.1177/0306624X19900978
National Task Force on Juvenile Sexual Offending. (1988). Preliminary report. *Juvenile and Family Court Journal, 39*(2), 1–67.
Olver, M. E., Thornton, D., & Christofferson, S. M. B. (2021). Understanding the latent structure of dynamic risk: Seeking empirical constraints on theory development using the VSO-SO and the theory of dynamic risk. *Sexual Abuse, 34*(2), 227–254.
Ozkan, T., Clipper, S. J., Piquero, A. R., Baglivio, M., & Wolff, K. (2020). Predicting sexual recidivism. *Sexual Abuse, 32*(4), 375–399. https://doi.org/10.1177/1079063219852944
Parker, S. C. (2014). Branded for life: The unconstitutionality of mandatory and lifetime juvenile sex offender registration and notification. *Virginia Journal of Social Policy & the Law, 21*(1), 167–206.
Prentky, R. A., Harris, B., Frizzell, K., & Righthand, S. (2000). An actuarial procedure for assessing risk with juvenile sex offenders. *Sexual Abuse: Journal of Research and Treatment, 12*, 71–93. https://doi.org/10.1177/107906320001200201

Prentky, R. A., & Righthand, S. (2003). *Juvenile Sex Offender Assessment Protocol (J-SOAP-II): Manual*. Justice Research Institute.

Prentky, R. A., Righthand, S., & Lamade, R. (2016). Sexual offending: Assessment and intervention. In K. Heilbrun, D. E. DeMatteo, & N. E. Goldstein (Eds.), *APA handbook of psychology and juvenile justice* (pp. 641–672). American Psychological Association. https://doi.org/10.1037/14643-029

Prentky, R., Righthand, S., Worling, J., & Kang, T. (2020). Final report: Development and implementation of the Youth Needs and Progress Scale (YNPS). Office of Sex Offender Sentencing, Monitoring, Apprehending, Registering, and Tracking (SMART). Grant Number: 2016-AW-BX-K004. http://www.ncjrs.gov/App/publications/abstract.aspx?ID=279050

Przybylski, R. (2015). The effectiveness of treatment for juveniles who sexually offend. Office of Sex Offender Sentencing, Monitoring, Apprehending, Registering, and Tracking.

Przybylski, R., & Lobanov-Rostovsky, C. (2015). Unique considerations regarding juveniles who commit sexual offenses.

Ralston, C. A., Epperson, D. L., & Edwards, S. R. (2016). Cross-validation of the JSORRAT-II in Iowa. *Sexual Abuse: A Journal of Research and Treatment, 28*, 534–554.

Ralston, C. A., Sarkar, A., Philipp, G. T., & Epperson, D. L. (2017). The impact of using documented but uncharged offense data on JSORRAT-II predictive validity. *Sexual Abuse: Journal of Research and Treatment, 29*(2), 186–202.

Rasmussen, L. A. (2013). Young people who sexually abuse: A historical perspective and future directions. *Journal of Child Sexual Abuse, 22*, 119–141. https://doi.org/10.1080/10538712.2013.744646

Rasmussen, L. A. (2018). Comparing predictive validity of JSORRAT-II and MEGA♪ with sexually abusive youth in long-term residential custody. *International Journal of Offender Therapy and Comparative Criminology, 62*(10), 2937–2953.

Reale, K., McCuish, E., & Corrado, R. (2020). The impact of juvenile sex offending on the adult criminal career. *Sexual Abuse: A Journal of Research and Treatment, 32*(4), 400–422.

Reitzel, L. R., & Carbonell, J. L. (2006). The effectiveness of sexual offender treatment for juveniles as measured by recidivism: A meta-analysis. *Sexual Abuse, 18*(4), 401–421.

Rice, M. E., & Harris, G. T. (2005). Comparing effect sizes in follow-up studies: ROC Area, Cohen's d, and r. Law and human behavior, 29, 615

Riser, D. K., Pegram, S. E., & Farley, J. P. (2013). Adolescent and young adult male sex offenders: Understanding the role of recidivism. *Journal of Child Sexual Abuse, 22*, 9–31.

Rosa, M., Fox, B., & Jennings, W. G. (2020). Do developmental life course theory risk factors equally predict age of onset among juvenile sexual and nonsexual offenders? *Sexual Abuse, 32*(1), 55–78.

Sampson, R. J., & Laub, J. H. (2005). A life-course view of the development of crime. *Annals of the American Academy of Political and Social Science, 602*, 12–45.

Schmidt, F., Sinclair, S. M., & Thomasdóttir, S. (2016). Predictive validity of the youth level of service/case management inventory with youth who have committed sexual and nonsexual offenses: The utility of professional override. *Criminal Justice and Behavior, 43*(3), 413–430. https://doi.org/10.1177/0093854815603389

Schmucker, M., & Lösel, F. (2015). The effects of sexual offender treatment on recidivism: An international meta-analysis of sound quality evaluations. *Journal of Experimental Criminology, 11*, 597–630.

Schwartz-Mette, R. A., Righthand, S., Hecker, J., Dore, G., & Huff, R. (2020). Long-term predictive validity of the juvenile sex offender assessment protocol–II: Research and practice implications. *Sexual Abuse, 32*(5), 499–520.

Seto, M. C., & Lalumière, M. (2010). What is so special about male adolescent sexual offending? A review and test of explanations through meta-analysis. *Psychological Bulletin, 136*, 526–575.

Seto, M. C., & Pullman, L. (2012). Assessment and treatment of adolescent sexual offenders: Implications of recent research on generalist and versus specialist explanations. *Child Abuse & Neglect, 36*, 203–209. https://doi.org/10.1016/j.chiabu.2011.11.003

Sneddon, H., Gojkovic Grimshaw, D., Livingstone, N., & Macdonald, G. (2020). Cognitive-behavioural therapy (CBT) interventions for young people aged 10 to 18 with harmful sexual behaviour. The Cochrane database of systematic reviews, 6(6), CD009829. https://doi.org/10.1002/14651858.CD009829.pub2

Sorrentino, R., Brown, A., Berard, B., & Peretti, K. (2018). Sex offenders: General information and treatment. *Psychiatric Annals, 48*(2), 120–128. https://doi.org/10.3928/00485713-20171220-01

U.S. Department of Justice. (2008). The national guidelines for sex offender registration and notification: Final guidelines. Retrieved from http://www.ojp.usdoj.gov/smart/pdfs/final_sornaguidelines.pdf

van Den Berg, C., Bijleveld, C., & Hendriks, J. (2017). The juvenile sex offender: Criminal careers and life events. *Sexual Abuse, 29*, 81–101.

van der Put, C. E., van Vugt, E. S., Stams, G. J. J. M., Devokic, M., & van der Laan, P. H. (2013). Differences in the prevalence and impact of risk factors for general recidivism between different types of juveniles who have committed sexual offenses (JSOs) and juveniles who have committed nonsexual offenses (JNSOs). *Sexual Abuse: A Journal of Research and Treatment, 25*, 48–68.

Vandiver, D. M. (2006). A prospective analysis of juvenile male sex offenders: Characteristics and recidivism rates as adults. *Journal of Interpersonal Violence, 21*, 673–688.

Viljoen, J. L., Elkovitch, N., Scalora, M. J., & Ullman, D. (2009). Assessment of re-offense risk in adolescents who have committed sexual offenses: Predictive validity of the ERASOR, PCL: YV, YLS/CMI, and Static-99. *Criminal Justice and Behavior, 36*(10), 981–1000.

Viljoen, J. L., Mordell, S., & Beneteau, J. L. (2012). Prediction of adolescent sexual reoffending: A meta-analysis of the J-SOAP-II, ERASOR, JSORRAT-II, and Static-99. *Law and Human Behavior, 36*(5), 423–438.

Vrieze, S. I., & Grove, W. M. (2010). Multidimensional assessment of criminal recidivism: Problems, pitfalls, and proposed solutions. *Psychological Assessment, 22*(2), 382–395.

Walker, D. F., McGovern, S. K., Poey, E. L., & Otis, K. E. (2004). Treatment effectiveness for male adolescent sexual offenders: A meta-analysis and review. *Journal of child sexual abuse, 13*(3–4), 281–293.

Winokur, M., Rozen, D., Batchelder, K., & Valentine, D. (2006). Juvenile sexual offender treatment: a systematic review of evidence-based research.

Worling, J. R. (2004). The Estimate of Risk of Adolescent Sexual Offense Recidivism (ERASOR): Preliminary psychometric data. *Sexual Abuse: A Journal of Research and Treatment, 16*(3), 235–254.

Worling, J. R. (2017, June 14). PROFESOR: Protective + risk observations for eliminating sexual offense recidivism. Retrieved from https://www.profesor.ca/history–rationale.html

Worling, J. R. (2020). Protective + risk observations for eliminating sexual offense recidivism: User's Guide 1.0. Retrieved from https://www.profesor.ca/uploads/8/7/7/6/8776493/profesor_user_guide_1.0_2020.pdf

Worling, J. R., Bookalam, D., & Littlejohn, A. (2012). Prospective validity of the estimate of risk of adolescent sexual offense recidivism. *Sexual Abuse: A Journal of Research and Treatment, 24*(3), 203–223.

Worling, J. R., & Curwen, T. (2001). Adolescent sexual offender recidivism: Success of specialized treatment and implications for risk prediction. *Child Abuse & Neglect, 24*(7), 965–982.

Worling, J. R., Litteljohn, A., & Bookalam, D. (2010). 20-year prospective follow-up study of specialized treatment for adolescents who offended sexually. *Behavioral Sciences & the Law, 28*(1), 46–57.

Ybarra, M., & Petras, H. (2021). Groups of sexual violence perpetration in a national sample of youth 13–25 years of age. *Prevention Science, 22*(2), 205–215.

Zimring, F. E., Jennings, W. G., Piquero, A. R., & Hays, S. (2009). Investigating the continuity of sex offending: Evidence from the second Philadelphia birth cohort. *Justice Quarterly, 26*, 58–76.

Chapter 19
Special Considerations: Female Sexual Offenders

Tusty ten Bensel and Kilby Raptopoulos

19.1 Scope of the Problem

Since the 1990s, a number of sex offender (SO) laws have been passed to control and reduce sexual offending in the United States (Berman, 2005; Sample & Bray, 2003; see Wright, 2014). Laws such as offender registration, community notification, civil commitment, residency restrictions, and electronic monitoring were enacted to protect and inform the public, manage and supervise, and reduce recidivism rates among this population (Sample & Bray, 2003). The proliferation of SO laws has increased research on SOs; however, this body of research has been predominately gender-specific often minimizing the existence and seriousness of female sexual offending (Denov, 2001, 2003a; Fromuth & Holt, 2008; King & Roberts, 2017; Leone et al., 2018; Mellor & Deering, 2010; Rogers & Davies, 2007; Steely & ten Bensel, 2020; Zack et al., 2018). In reality, official statistics indicate that females represent about 2–12% of the SO population and some scholars have argued that the true estimate is likely to be much higher due to underreporting (Cortoni et al., 2017; Stemple et al., 2017).

The limited research on female sex crimes can be attributed to several factors such as cultural and societal perceptions that women are incapable of committing such crimes (Broussard et al., 1991; Denov, 2003a; Hetherton, 1999), lack of reporting by victims and often, female sex crimes are viewed in conjunction with male accomplices (Vandiver & Kercher, 2004). The lack of reporting by victims could be a result of multiple barriers which prevent them from reporting abuse (Denov, 2003b). Many sex offenses occur within the home making reporting female sex

T. ten Bensel (✉) · K. Raptopoulos
School of Criminal Justice and Criminology, University of Arkansas-Little Rock,
Little Rock, AR, USA
e-mail: ixzohra@ualr.edu

R. J. Tully et al. (eds.), *Best Practices in Sexual Offender Assessment and Management*, Dangerous Behavior in Clinical and Forensic Psychology,
https://doi.org/10.1007/978-3-031-83135-5_19

crimes even more difficult for victims (William & Bierie, 2015). Young boys are often reluctant to report sexual abuse by an older female as society has glamorized this type of abuse (Reid, 2012). Furthermore, society has historically been unwilling to view females as capable of sexual violence despite research documenting their dangerousness (Budd & Bierie, 2017; Denov, 2001, 2003a, 2004; Rudin et al., 1995; ten Bensel et al., 2019). Consequently, these perceptions continue to reinforce the sexual scripts in society, which undermine the accurate scope and threat of female SOs (Mellor & Deering, 2010; Denov, 2001, 2003a). More recently, however, research has found that societal perceptions of female SOs may be shifting. Zack et al. (2018) found that despite the public's willingness to minimize the threat of female perpetrated sexual abuse, their sample believed females should receive equal punishments compared to male SOs. It could be that the public is starting to hold more punitive attitudes toward female SOs.

Although research on female SOs has been scant, it has been growing over the past several decades; scholars have examined offender, victim, and offense characteristics (Darling et al., 2018; Comartin et al., 2018; Faller, 1987; Gannon et al., 2008; Marshall & Miller, 2019; Steely & ten Bensel, 2024; ten Bensel et al., 2019; Vandiver & Kercher, 2004; Vandiver & Walker, 2002; Wijkman et al., 2010), typologies (Faller, 1987; Gannon et al., 2008; Gannon et al., 2014; Mathews et al., 1989; Nathan & Ward, 2002; Steely & ten Bensel, 2024; Vandiver & Kercher, 2004), societal perceptions of female SOs (Denov, 2001; Mellor & Deering, 2010), comparative research between various types of female offenders (Rush-Burkey & ten Bensel, 2015; Gillespie et al., 2015; Muskens et al., 2011; ten Bensel et al., 2019; Vandiver, 2006), and offense severity and judicial sentencing disparities (Darling et al., 2018; Gibbs & ten Bensel, 2022; ten Bensel et al., 2019). There has also been some research on female perpetrated sexual abuse within the educational setting (Darling et al., 2018; Darling & Hackett, 2020; Ratliff & Watson, 2014; Steely & ten Bensel, 2020). In this chapter, the authors review this body of research, as well as provide assessment and intervention consideration for this population.

19.2 Female Sex Offender Characteristics

Studies have found that female SOs are typically in their late 20s-to-early-to-mid-30s (Darling et al., 2018; Comartin et al., 2018; Faller, 1987; Gannon et al., 2008; Marshall & Miller, 2019; ten Bensel et al., 2019; Vandiver & Kercher, 2004; Vandiver & Walker, 2002; Wijkman et al., 2010), white (Comartin et al., 2018; Faller, 1995; Gannon et al., 2008; ten Bensel et al., 2019; Vandiver & Kercher, 2004; Vandiver & Walker, 2002), and exhibit high rates of past abuse, trauma, and mental health issues (Christopher et al., 2007; Elliott et al., 2010; Faller, 1987; Green & Kaplan, 1994; Johansson-Love & Fremouw, 2009; Kaplan & Green, 1995; Levenson et al., 2015; Lewis & Stanley, 2000; Miccio-Fonseca, 2000; Strickland, 2008; ten Bensel et al., 2019; Wijkman et al., 2010). Thus far, there has been mixed results on the marital status (Faller, 1995; Kaplan & Green, 1995; Lewis & Stanley, 2000), level of school performance, and IQ among female SOs (Bumby & Bumby, 1997; Lewis & Stanley, 2000; McCarty, 1986; Travis et al., 1990; Wijkman et al., 2010). In addition, some studies have found female SOs are likely to be unemployed, experience unstable employment, or have minimum wage employment (Faller, 1987).

19.2.1 Prior Abuse and Trauma

Female SOs often have a history of previous abuse and trauma (Elliott et al., 2010; Gannon et al., 2008; Green & Kaplan, 1994; Johansson-Love & Fremouw, 2009; Lewis & Stanley, 2000; Nathan & Ward, 2002; ten Bensel et al., 2019; Strickland, 2008; Wijkman et al., 2010). They tend to have higher rates of past childhood sexual abuse than male SOs and female offenders convicted of non-sex offenses (Christopher et al., 2007; Green & Kaplan, 1994; Johansson-Love & Fremouw, 2009; Kaplan & Green, 1995; Levenson et al., 2015; Strickland, 2008). For example, Levenson et al. (2015) examined a sample of 47 female SOs who were in outpatient, secured SO treatment programs across the United States. They found that female SOs had greater odds of experiencing childhood sexual abuse, verbal abuse, and emotional neglect than the general female population. Christopher et al. (2007) also examined a sample of 142 females, which included 61 SOs and 81 non-SOs in a Midwest women's prison. They found the female SOs had higher rates of prior sexual abuse when compared to the non-SO sample. Additionally, those who were in the SO sample experienced childhood abuse that lasted longer in duration than those in the non-SO group.

Female SOs typically experience sexual abuse at a younger age and in conjunction with other forms of abuse such as physical abuse, verbal abuse, and neglect (Elliott et al., 2010). They have a high rate of intimate partner abuse (IPA) in their past and current relationships (Rush-Burkey & ten Bensel, 2015; Comartin et al., 2018; Gannon et al., 2008), which include physical and sexual abuse, verbal threats, as well as intimidation (Rush-Burkey & ten Bensel, 2015; Comartin et al., 2018; West et al., 2011). Comartin et al. (2018) analyzed data on 60 female SOs who were incarcerated in a Midwestern state. The majority of their sample (70%; n = 42) experienced some form of IPA, such as physical violence, intimidation, and sexual victimization. In their sample, IPA was higher among female SOs who were in a co-offending relationship (e.g., committing an offense with a partner, often romantic). These types of partner abuse could make female SOs vulnerable to participate in male-coerced sexual abuse by threat or violence (Rush-Burkey & ten Bensel, 2015). Childhood abuse and trauma, as well as IPA have been documented to increase the likelihood of mental health concerns and issues with substance abuse misuse, especially among female SOs (Bickart et al., 2019; Green & Kaplan, 1994; Lewis & Stanley, 2000; McLeod, 2015; Strickland, 2008; Wijkman et al., 2010).

19.2.2 Mental Health and Substance Abuse/Misuse

Over the past few decades, researchers have noted the relationship between prior victimization and a variety of mental health and substance abuse/misuse (Bickart et al., 2019; Green & Kaplan, 1994; Lewis & Stanley, 2000; McLeod, 2015; Strickland, 2008; Wijkman et al., 2010). Bickert et al. (2019) examined psychosocial and offense data for 98 women who were incarcerated for online sexual offenses. They found that approximately 60% of their sample experienced sexual abuse, while 46% indicated that they were victims of physical abuse. Moreover, about 62% of their sample reported a history of mental health treatment (47% outpatient and 15% inpatient).

Studies have also found that when compared to females who co-offend, solo female SOs were more likely to exhibit higher levels of mental and mood disorders, as well as substance abuse issues (Gillespie et al., 2015; Muskens et al., 2011). Gillespie et al. (2015), for example, examined a sample of female SOs (20 solo and 20 co-offenders) in the United Kingdom. They found that solo and co-offenders were similar in their developmental (relationship with parents, childhood context, and experiences with abuse) and psychological traits (self-control, offense cognitions, management); however, differed in their "distal personal factors" (p. 14). When compared to the co-offenders in the sample, solo offenders exhibited higher levels of depression, difficulties with substance abuse/misuse, and other types of mental health issues. Additionally, females also had more difficulties with anxiety, depression, low self-esteem, loneliness, and assertiveness when compared to male SOs (Miller et al., 2009; Vandiver & Walker, 2002).

Research has yielded mixed results regarding female SOs and substance abuse issues specifically (Fazel et al., 2010; Johansson-Love & Fremouw, 2009; McLeod, 2015; Strickland, 2008; ten Bensel et al., 2016). ten Bensel et al. (2016) examined 223 solo and co female SOs who were convicted of sex crimes between 1995 and 2013. They found 57% (n = 126) of their sample self-reported some type of drug and/or alcohol abuse and the majority of those who had issues with substance abuse/misuse were solo offenders (62%; n = 78) when compared to co-offenders. Other researchers have documented high rates of substance abuse among female SO samples (Fazel et al., 2010; Green & Kaplan, 1994; McLeod, 2015; Strickland, 2008). Yet, the research is not conclusive regarding rates of substance abuse among female SOs compared to other offending groups. For example, research has indicated female SOs have comparable rates of substance abuse compared to female non-SOs (Fazel et al., 2010; Green & Kaplan, 1994; Strickland, 2008) and male SOs (McLeod, 2015); however, Johansson-Love and Fremouw's (2009) research did not indicate differences in rates of substance abuse among female SOs when compared to female non-SOs, male SOs, and male non-SO samples.

19.3 Victim Characteristics of Female Sex Offenders

Female SOs have been found to victimize both males and females (Comartin et al., 2018; Faller, 1987; Gannon et al., 2008; Vandiver & Kercher, 2004; Vandiver, 2006) and results are mixed in this area (Bader et al., 2010; Vandiver, 2006; Wijkman et al., 2010; William & Bierie, 2015). Some studies have found that female SOs have a high percentage of female victims, but this could be a result of females abusing youth with male co-offenders (Faller, 1995; McLeod, 2015; Vandiver & Kercher, 2004). ten Bensel et al. (2016) found that solo female offenders were more likely to have male victims, while those who committed their offense with male offenders were more likely to target female victims.

Victims of female SOs are typically 18 years old or younger, with an average age of 12 years old (Faller, 1995; Kaplan & Green, 1995; Lewis & Stanley, 2000; Vandiver, 2006; Wijkman et al., 2010), although ages ranged from 9 to 17 years old (Ferguson & Meehan, 2005; McLeod, 2015; Vandiver & Kercher, 2004). Research has found that female offenders are likely to offend against family members or close acquaintances (Comartin et al., 2018; Faller, 1987; Gannon et al., 2008; Kaplan & Green, 1995; Lewis & Stanley, 2000; Vandiver & Kercher, 2004; Vandiver, 2006). In fact, most female SOs have some sort of known relationship with their victims (Comartin et al., 2018; Faller, 1987; Gannon et al., 2008; Lewis & Stanley, 2000; Vandiver, 2006) and are victimized within the SO's home (Nathan & Ward, 2002). For example, Lewis and Stanley's (2000) entire sample of female SOs had some known relationship with their victims, while over half of Denov's (2003b) sample of female SOs had abused their own children. Further, previous sexual abuse among female SOs has shown similar rates (Elliott et al., 2010; Kaplan & Green, 1995).

19.4 Offense Characteristics and Severity

Female SOs commit a wide range of sex crimes from no contact offenses (such as permitting abuse of a minor) to violent sexual abuse (Nathan & Ward, 2002; Sandler & Freeman, 2009; ten Bensel et al., 2019), which are often against their own children and/or close acquaintances (Denov, 2003b; Nathan & Ward, 2002). Additionally, some female SO's commit their sexual acts alone; however, many females offend in conjunction with a male partner. Some female SO's feel compelled to participate under duress by a male partner (Comartin et al., 2018; Nathan & Ward, 2002; ten Bensel et al., 2016). Research has found that solo offenders typically have one victim (Wijkman et al., 2010) and were likely to victimize a non-familial victim when compared to co-offenders (Muskens et al., 2011; ten Bensel et al., 2016; Vandiver, 2006). The range of sexual abuses can range from fondling to sexual penetration (Vandiver & Kercher, 2004).

19.4.1 Criminal Histories and Recidivism

As research on female SOs continues to grow, a better understanding of their criminal histories has been gained. In fact, studies have found that prior non-sexual crimes range from 16% (Elliott et al., 2010) to 63% (Bader et al., 2010), while a previous history of sex crimes range from 1% (Bickart et al., 2019) to 5% (Elliott et al., 2010; ten Bensel et al., 2019). Female SOs also have lower recidivism rates compared to male SOs and those who are likely to reoffend tend to be older and have prior non-sexual convictions (Sandler & Freeman, 2009). Sandler and Freeman (2009) conducted a meta-analysis examining recidivism rates of female SOs using a five-year follow up period and found only 1.8% of their sample had been rearrested for a new sexual offense. Similarly, Cortoni and Hanson (2005) found recidivism rates for female SOs around 1% for future sex crimes at a five-year follow-up period. These recidivism statistics could be a result of a lack of reporting due to barriers faced by victims or it could be as a result of females taking their criminal justice sanctions and treatment seriously (Denov, 2004).

19.4.2 Sentencing Outcomes

Despite their serious offenses, previous research on judicial sentencing decisions have largely been comparative in nature and focused on differential treatment between female and male SOs (Berliner et al., 1995; Embry & Lyons, 2012; Hassett-Walker et al., 2014; Shields & Cochran, 2020; Thompson et al., 2019). These studies have found that females were charged more leniently than male SOs who committed similar crimes (Hassett-Walker et al., 2014) and were more likely to receive lighter sentences or probation in lieu of incarceration when compared to male SOs (Embry & Lyons, 2012; Hassett-Walker et al., 2014; Shields & Cochran, 2020; Thompson et al., 2019). Shields and Cochran (2020) analyzed over 10,000 SOs through precision matching and found that female SOs were approximately 57% less likely to be incarcerated than their male counterparts. In addition, females who were incarcerated received 17% shorter sentences than male SOs. This could be an extension of public perception about female dangerousness reaching the confines of the courtroom. These findings could also be explained by the chivalry hypothesis (Anderson, 1976; Chesney-Lind, 1986; Embry & Lyons, 2012; Hassett-Walker et al., 2014), which postulated that females are viewed to be weaker than men and thus, not necessarily responsible for their behaviors and require the protection of men (Embry & Lyons, 2012; Curry et al., 2004; Chesney-Lind, 1986).

Only a handful of studies have solely focused on the variations of female SO sentencing decisions (Darling et al., 2018; Gibbs & ten Bensel, 2022). Darling et al. (2018) analyzed 71 female SOs in England, Scotland, and Wales. The results indicated that 73% of their sample were incarcerated, approximately 60% were taken into custody after conviction, and 27% of the sample had their sentence suspended.

Gibbs and ten Bensel (2022) examined records of 262 female SOs between 1996 and 2018 in a southern state. They found that females who were convicted of more serious sex crimes, had a higher number of charges, and a greater extent of prior arrests were more likely to receive a prison sentence. In addition, females who had younger victims and more likely to victimize their own children, were perceived to be the most dangerous type of offender and received the most serious punishment.

Based on offender, victim, and offense characteristics, SOs have been classified into typologies, or "subtypes," to help scholars study patterns, behaviors, and motivations for offending (Nathan & Ward, 2002). Female SOs are considered a heterogenous group of offenders who offend for a variety of reasons (Vandiver & Kercher, 2004). Some scholars have studied female SOs in terms of solo versus co-offending (Comartin et al., 2018; Gillespie et al., 2015; ten Bensel et al., 2016; William & Bierie, 2015), while others have developed more typological groups based on various offender, victim, and context characteristics (Faller, 1987; Mathews et al., 1989; Nathan & Ward, 2002; Vandiver & Kercher, 2004).

19.5 Typologies of Female Sexual Offenders

Similar to male SOs, several typologies have been developed to explain female sexual offending (Faller, 1987; Mathews et al., 1989; Nathan & Ward, 2002; Steely & ten Bensel, 2024; Vandiver & Kercher, 2004). For example, Faller (1987) proposed a five-category female typology, which included poly-incestuous abusers—females who offend with another (usually a male perpetrator) and have more than one victim. A single parent abuser assaults their own children, while a psychotic abuser suffers from "out-of-control libidinal impulses" and justifies sexually inappropriate behaviors through a delusional system (Faller, 1987, p. 167). Furthermore, adolescent offenders are youth who struggle with peer relationships and lack appropriate sexual outlets; therefore, they choose younger friends and seek opportunities, such as babysitting. Having access to these opportunities is a means for self-gratification while non-custodial offenders are mothers who do not have custody of their children and assault them during parental visitation.

The more widely known female SO typology was proposed by Mathews et al. (1989), which included the teacher/lover, male coerced, predisposed offenders, experimenter/exploiter, and psychologically disturbed. The following information on each of these subtypes is from their work. First, teacher/lover offenders claim to feel genuine affection for their victims and believe it is their obligation to teach their victims about sex. They deny causing their victims any harm and believe they are in a romantic relationship with their victim. The predisposed molester offenders, like the teacher/lover offenders, are solo offenders who sexually abused their victims alone. These offenders have extensive histories of past sexual abuse, typically by family members, and likewise, these offenders in turn abuse their own family members. Male-coerced offenders also have extensive histories of past sexual abuse as children typically by males and currently have difficult relationships with current male partners marked by interpersonal violence. These offenders feel powerless and fearful of their male partners as they usually are completely dependent on them for their financial needs; therefore, they placate their husbands through their abuse. In this subtype, male partners of the female SOs utilize domination and coercion to the point where the female SOs feel the need to make them happy to keep their relationships intact. The experimenter/exploiter offenders are more likely to be juveniles, between 12 and 16 years old, and abuse their victims while babysitting or taking care of younger children. These offenders are less likely to have extensive sexual abuse histories or prior sexual knowledge. They claim their abuse is a form of sexual exploration. The psychologically disturbed offenders are those more likely to have experienced past or current psychological diagnoses, (i.e., depression or suicide attempt), that could potentially progress into antisocial conduct into adulthood. This typology is corroborated with research indicating female SOs do have higher rates of psychological disturbances (Green & Kaplan, 1994; Lewis & Stanley, 2000); however, this is not yet conclusive (Nathan & Ward, 2002).

Nathan and Ward (2002) proposed a modification to Mathews et al.'s (1989) typology. In their work, they found that most of their female SO's committed offenses in conjunction with a male SO and did so of their own accord. These women did not feel compelled to commit their crimes out of coercion, but rather had their own motivations for their sexual offenses. This prompted these researchers to create an additional category titled male-accompanied: the rejected/revengeful offender to include females who abused their victims actively alongside their male partners. Comartin et al. (2018) also found support for this additional typology subcategory. Their female SO sample was also comprised of a considerable number of female SOs who actively participated in the abuse without coercion from a male partner (Comartin et al., 2018). These female SOs histories were characterized by poor parental relationships like incarceration, parental drug and alcohol abuse, and divorce (Comartin et al., 2018).

Most typologies are based on small sample sizes with a limited number of SOs in the study. Vandiver and Kercher (2004), however, created a typology for female SOs using a large data set comprised of 471 female SOs by examining offender and victim characteristics. While their data was limited due to the unavailability of information regarding offending with or without a male accomplice, they were able to statistically analyze a much larger data set compared to most other typologies. Their research led to the creation of six sub-types of female SOs: heterosexual nurturers, noncriminal homosexual offenders, female sexual predators, young adult child exploiters, homosexual criminals, and aggressive homosexual offenders.

The most frequent female offender was the heterosexual nurturer; this is similar to Mathew's et al. (1989) teacher/lover offender. These females typically victimized males around 12 years of age and were more likely to have some type of authority over their victim (i.e., teacher; Vandiver & Kercher, 2004). They also did not have lengthy criminal histories as they were the least likely group to have been arrested previously for a sexual offense and had low arrest rates for new sexual offenses. The second most frequent offender was the noncriminal homosexual offender. Similar to heterosexual nurturers, these offenders had victims who were about 12 years old and were more likely to abuse female victims. Also, these females did not have extensive criminal histories, had low arrest rates for new sexual offenses and low rates of total number of arrests. Researchers were unable to draw strong conclusions regarding these females' motivations for offending because the data lacked information concerning whether offenders were acting alone or co-offending with a male partner.

The third largest category of female offenders was the female sexual predator. These offenders had extensive criminal histories and were more likely to resemble other non-sexual female offenders leading the researchers to conclude their sexual offending was part of a broader pattern of criminal behavior. They were most likely to be arrested for future crimes and had high rates in the total number of offenses. Victims were, on average, 11 years old and male; however, these offenders victimized both males and females.

The young adult child exploiters comprised the fourth largest category and included females who were younger and more likely to abuse younger victims. These offenders also had a high number of victims that were related to them, leading researchers to conclude there was probably a considerable amount of incestuous abuse among these offenders. They hypothesized that perhaps mothers abused their own children, which would correlate with Mathews et al. (1989) predisposed molester offenders (Vandiver & Kercher, 2004). Here again, researchers remarked that more information regarding the presence of a male accomplice would have given them more insight into this category of offenders.

The homosexual criminals were older, had lengthier criminal histories, and were more likely to victimize female victims. Apart from having high rates of subsequent arrests, they were also most likely to encounter the police compared to the other five categories. The offenders did not have a high rate of violent sexual crimes leading the researchers to conclude these offenders might have offended for economic reasons. Many of them committed crimes that forced their victims into prostitution. The sixth and smallest category of offenders included the aggressive homosexual offenders who were older offenders and victimized older victims, as well. They primarily offended against adult females, with an average victim's age of 31 years old. Thus, it is important to make the distinction that not all female sex offending is perpetrated against children.

19.6 Offending in Educational Settings

Beyond the broader research on female SOs, scholars have also focused on the context in which sex crimes occur such as within school settings. Research has found the majority of child sexual abuse which have occurred within an educational setting was committed by male SOs assaulting female victims (Jaffe et al., 2013); however, emerging research has also indicated that a considerable number of these offenses are committed by female SOs, as well (Ratliff & Watson, 2014). For example, female educational abuse varies from 25% (Ratliff & Watson, 2014) to 43% (Shakeshaft, 2004).

Female offenders who sexually abuse in an educational setting are more likely to be in their mid-thirties, with a higher SES and more education compared to female SOs who offend outside of an educational setting (Darling et al., 2018; Steely & ten Bensel, 2020). They are also less likely to have been convicted of a previous offense (Christensen & Darling, 2020) and more likely to be a solo offender (Darling et al., 2018; Steely & ten Bensel, 2020). Victims of female sexual abuse within an institutional context are typically male, with an average age of 15 years old (Darling et al., 2018; Steely & ten Bensel, 2020).

Research has also indicated that females who sexual assault within an educational setting might use grooming tactics, such as gaining trust of parents/guardians or bribing victims which is similar to male child SOs (Steely & ten Bensel, 2020). For example, Steely and ten Bensel (2020) conducted a qualitative study examining female teachers who sexually assaulted their students. They analyzed personal history questionnaires and interviews for 35 women who had been convicted of sex crimes and were being assessed for the state's SO registry. The researchers focused specifically on the onset of abuse and found that many of the female offenders used grooming tactics to gain the trust of their victims prior to the abuse. For example, 19% of the sample reported befriending their victims by establishing a nonsexual relationship with the victim and/or victim's family before the abuse started. These abuses began in a nonsexual context (i.e., school club activities or through tutoring sessions) and progressed to a more intimate nonsexual friendship. Technology was a common medium for communication with the offenders texting the victim or using social media as an outlet for communication and eventually abuse. The majority of the sample admitted to manipulating their victims into opportunities for sexual encounters (Steely & ten Bensel, 2020).

These offenders were also characterized by mental health challenges (Christensen & Darling, 2020), low self-esteem (Darling et al., 2018; Steely & ten Bensel, 2020), and problems with relationships (Steely & ten Bensel, 2020). Several motivating factors for their offending were in part attempting to fill a lack of sexual gratification and intimacy in their current relationships (Christensen & Darling, 2020; Darling et al., 2018; Steely & ten Bensel, 2020). In Steely and ten Bensel's (2020) research, a motivating factor for many of their female offenders was a need for emotional support, which for some stemmed from troubled relationships (Steely & ten Bensel, 2020). Examples included offenders who felt a need for sexual intimacy following a divorce or when a relationship ended, low self-esteem and insecurity about their sexuality, and feelings of loneliness. Similarly, Christensen and Darling (2020) conducted a mixed methods study examining a sample of male and female teachers who had been referred for investigation for allegedly sexually abusing a student to the National College for Teaching and Leadership, a regulatory organization that oversees certifying and de-certifying teachers in England. They too found that some of their female offenders initiated nonsexual relationships with their victims prior to the abuse. Further, their female sample also experienced mental health challenges like depression and trouble coping with stress, which is a prevalent finding for this population.

19.7 Clinical Assessment Considerations and Techniques

Currently, there are no validated assessment instruments specifically designed for female SOs. Given the percentage of females who commit sex offenses and the low rates of sex crime recidivism rates, it may be difficult to develop an instrument for this population (Cortoni & Gannon, 2013, 2016). Clinicians and SO management agents often use tools that were developed for male SOs; however, this is problematic because male and female offenders vary in their offending rates, patterns, typologies, prior victimization, mental and cognitive health issues, as well as substance abuse/misuse history (Cortoni & Gannon, 2013, 2016). The use of instruments developed for male SOs on their female counterparts are likely to lead to inaccuracies in assessment and treatment of this population. Some scholars have argued that there is a need for an assessment tool that captures the unique offender, victim, and offense characteristics of female SOs (Nathan & Ward, 2002; Vandiver, 2006).

Gannon et al. (2008) proposed the Descriptive Model of Female Sexual Offending (DMFSO) that incorporated three distinct patterns for female sex offending. It included an explicit-approach (calculated, premeditated, minimal to no coercion needed), directed-avoidant (women were coerced into involvement; negative experience), and implicit-disorganized (little to no planning, impulsive, mixed experience). In conjunction with this model, Gannon et al. (2012) developed an Offense Pathway Checklist that focused on essential offense characteristics that may assist clinicians and criminal justice agents in assessment and intervention needs.

In addition, the Adverse Childhood Experiences (ACE) may be another instrument clinicians can utilize when working with female SOs. The 10-item ACE scale was designed to assess the presence of childhood abuse, (physical, sexual, and emotional), neglect, and household dysfunction such as domestic violence, parental substance and incarceration, and divorce (Levenson et al., 2015). Given that female SO's have been found to exhibit high rates of previous abuse, trauma, and neglect (Gannon et al., 2008; Wijkman et al., 2010), the use of this instrument is likely to provide clinicians insight when working and treating female SOs.

Lastly, researchers have found the Level of Service Inventory-Revised (LSI-R) instrument to be useful in predicting recidivism among this population. The LSI-R is a risk/needs assessment instrument that has been commonly used among the correctional population (Andrews & Bonta, 1995), although not necessarily among female SOs. More recently, Marshall et al. (2021) utilized this instrument with a sample of female SOs in Texas and found a significant relationship between the total instrument score and recidivism. Although this instrument was created to be gender neutral, more research is needed to understand the predictive utility of the LSI-R for female SOs.

19.8 Clinical Intervention

The importance of effective interventions and treatments for SOs cannot be overstated. Treatment strategies have salient practical implications for public safety with the goal to reduce recidivism among this population, as well as encourage desistance. In particular, treatment and intervention strategies for female SOs can be quite complex given the array of mental, cognitive, physical, and substance use issues that impact this population. Clinical and criminal justice agents must holistically understand the most effective way to prevent these types of crimes from occurring in the future and consider treatment options that focus on the myriad of issues exhibited by this population. Specific treatment options should consider addressing offense supportive cognitions, abuse/negative relationship dysfunctions, issues of self-worth, dependency, and negative coping strategies, mental health disorders, substance abuse/misuse, as well as deviant sexual interests (Cortoni & Gannon, 2013, 2016; Mathews et al., 1989; Vandiver & Kercher, 2004; Wijkman et al., 2010). Childhood abuse and current trauma from intimate partner violence have consistently been a pattern for female SOs, which have often led to mental health issues, as well as substance abuse/misuse (Bicket et al., 2019; Green & Kaplan, 1994; Lewis & Stanley, 2000; McLeod, 2015; Strickland, 2008; Wijkman et al., 2010). Strickland (2008) stated,

> Trauma disrupts the normal developmental pathways needed to build appropriate coping skills…social relationships, and feelings of self-worth. Childhood trauma has been linked to a number of adult dysfunctions, including the development of personality disorders, post-traumatic stress disorder, depression, aggression, and substance abuse. (p. 483)

Treatment strategies for this offender population should account for previous abuse and the way trauma gets re-invited and projected onto others (i.e., cycle of violence; ten Bensel et al., 2019). Intervention initiatives could also focus on targeting more offense supportive cognitions by restructuring thinking through Cognitive Behavioral Therapy (CBT). CBT is an evidence-based treatment strategy that has garnered some positive results in treating SOs with issues of anxiety disorders, depression, and anger and reducing recidivism. Through this process, offenders are asked to challenge their offense-supportive cognitive distortions and deviant thought processing that support sexual offending tendencies (Marshall, 1999). CBT techniques have been found to be effective in changing inappropriate cognitions, which has resulted in a reduction of recidivism among SO, in general (Hanson et al., 2005; Harrison et al., 2020; Losel & Schmucker, 2005).

The practice framework of the Good Lives Model (GLM) has been more recently reconstructed (Ward & Durrant, 2021) to provide practitioners detailed and clear strategies of implementing organized interventions (Prescott & Willis, 2022). The GLM was originally introduced as a rehabilitative theory (Ward, 2002) that proposed a "strength-based overarching framework for rehabilitation" (Prescott & Willis, 2022, p. 1). At the core of this theoretical framework, its ethical values included human dignity, rights and agency, primary human goods values, risk reduction, and wellbeing (Prescott & Willis, 2022). Although the GLM has been around for decades, the recently reconstructed practice framework of the GLM provides a framework for explicit strategies for intervention implementation that practitioners can use to assist various correctional populations, including female SOs. Building on the ethical values discussed above, the practice framework has "three interconnected levels" which include "core values and principles, knowledge related assumptions…. and intervention guidelines" (Prescott & Willis, 2022, p. 1). It focuses on the goals and aspirations of those who are in treatment when building future life plans. This model could be a pathway for treatment strategy for practitioners who work with female SOs.

19.9 Conclusions and Recommendations

There are numerous misconceptions about female SOs. In reality, the true estimates of female sex crimes are unknown, largely because of these misconceptions. Society, must move beyond these myths about female SOs to prevent future sex crimes from occurring and to help women who need treatment. Research has shown that women are capable of committing sex crimes and should be held accountable for their behaviors. Researchers need to continue conducting sound research on this population to understand the context and dynamics of these crimes, as well as how to provide gender-focused, holistic treatment. Female SOs exhibit an array of mental, emotional, and physical abuse issues. Their needs are complex and a "one shoe fits all" strategy is likely to be less effective than intervention that is gender-focused and specifically tailored to this population.

References

Anderson, E. A. (1976). The "chivalrous" treatment of the female offender in the arms of the criminal justice system: A review of the literature. *Social Problems, 23*(3), 350–357. https://doi.org/10.2307/799780

Andrews, D. A., & Bonta, J. (1995). *The level of service inventory–Revised*. Multihealth Systems.

Bader, S. M., Welsh, R., & Scalora, M. J. (2010). Recidivism among female child molesters. *Violence and Victims, 25*(3), 349–362. https://doi.org/10.1891/0886-6708.25.3.349

Berliner, L., Schram, D., Miller, L. L., & Milloy, C. D. (1995). A sentencing alternative for sex offenders: A study of decision making and recidivism. *Journal of Interpersonal Violence, 10*(4), 487–502. https://doi.org/10.1177/088626095010004007

Berman, D. A. (2005). Distinguishing offense conduct and offender characteristics in modern sentencing reforms. *Stanford Law Review, 58*(1), 277–291.

Bickart, W., McLearen, A. M., Grady, M. D., & Stoler, K. (2019). A descriptive study of psychosocial characteristics and offense patterns in females with online child pornography offenses. *Psychiatry, Psychology and Law, 26*(2), 295–311. https://doi.org/10.1080/13218719.2018.1506714

Broussard, S., Wagner, W. G., & Kazelskis, R. (1991). Undergraduate students' perceptions of child sexual abuse: The impact of victim sex, perpetrator sex, respondent sex, and victim response. *Journal of Family Violence, 6*(3), 267–278. https://doi.org/10.1007/BF00980533

Budd, K. M., & Bierie, D. M. (2017). Injury matters: On female-perpetrated sex crimes. *Journal of Interpersonal Violence, 35*(19–20), 3735–3766. https://doi.org/10.1177/0886260517711178
Bumby, K. M., & Bumby, N. H. (1997). Adolescent female sexual offenders. *The Sex Offender, 2*, 10–11.
Chesney-Lind, M. (1986). "Women and crime": The female offender. *Signs, 12*(1), 78–96. https://doi.org/10.1086/494298
Christensen, L. S., & Darling, A. J. (2020). Sexual abuse by educators: A comparison between male and female teachers who sexually abuse students. *Journal of Sexual Aggression, 26*(1), 25–35. https://doi.org/10.1080/13552600.2019.1616119
Christopher, K., Lutz-Zois, C. J., & Reinhardt, A. R. (2007). Female sexual-offenders: Personality pathology as a mediator of the relationship between childhood sexual abuse history and sexual abuse perpetration against others. *Child Abuse and Neglect, 31*, 871–883. https://doi.org/10.1016/j.chiabu.2007.02.006
Comartin, E. B., Burgess-Proctor, A., Kibiak, S., & Kernsmith, P. (2018). Factors related to co-offending and coerced offending among female sex offenders: The role of childhood and adult trauma histories. *Violence and Victims, 33*(1), 53–74. https://doi.org/10.1891/0886-6708.33.1.53
Cortoni, F., Babchishin, K. M., & Rat, C. (2017). The proportion of sexual offenders who are female is higher than thought: A meta-analysis. *Criminal Justice and Behavior, 44*(2), 145–162. https://doi.org/10.1177/0093854816658923
Cortoni, F., & Gannon, T. A. (2013). What works with female sexual offenders. In L. A. Craig, L. Dixon, & T. A. Gannon (Eds.), *What works in offender rehabilitation: An evidence based approach to assessment and treatment* (pp. 271–284). Wiley-Blackwell. ISBN 9781119974567.
Cortoni, F., & Gannon, T. A. (2016). Female sexual offenders: An overview. In *Sexual offending* (pp. 213–224). https://doi.org/10.1007/978-1-4939-2416-5_10
Cortoni, F., & Hanson, R. K. (2005). *A review of the recidivism rates of adult female sexual offenders*. Correctional Service of Canada: Public Safety and Emergency Preparedness Canada.
Curry, T. R., Lee, G., & Rodriguez, S. F. (2004). Does victim gender increase sentence severity? Further explorations of gender dynamics and sentencing outcomes. *Crime and Delinquency, 50*(3), 319–343. https://doi.org/10.1177/0011128703256265
Darling, A. J., & Hackett, S. (2020). Situational factors in female-perpetrated child sexual abuse in organisations: Implications for prevention. *Journal of Sexual Aggression, 26*(1), 5–22. https://doi.org/10.1080/13552600.2019.1695968
Darling, A. J., Hackett, S., & Jamie, K. (2018). Female sex offenders who abuse children whilst working in organizational contexts: Offending, conviction, and sentencing. *Journal of Sexual Aggression, 24*(2), 196–214. https://doi.org/10.1080/13552600.2018.1476601
Denov, M. A. (2001). A culture of denial: Exploring professional perspectives on female sex offending. *Canadian Journal of Criminology, 43*(3), 303–309. https://doi.org/10.3138/cjcrim.43.3.303
Denov, M. S. (2003a). The myth of innocence: Sexual scripts and the recognition of child sexual abuse by female perpetrators. *The Journal of Sex Research, 40*(3), 303–314. https://doi.org/10.1080/00224490309552195
Denov, M. S. (2003b). To a safer place? Victims of sexual abuse by females and their disclosures to professionals. *Child Abuse and Neglect, 27*, 47–61. https://doi.org/10.1016/S0145-2134(02)00509-4
Denov, M. S. (2004). The long-term effects of child sexual abuse by female perpetrators: A qualitative study of male and female. *Victims. Journal of Interpersonal Violence, 19*(10), 1137–1156. https://doi.org/10.1177/0886260504269093
Elliott, I. A., Eldridge, H. J., Ashfield, S., & Beech, A. R. (2010). Exploring risk: Potential static, dynamic, protective and treatment factors in the clinical histories of female sex offenders. *Journal of Family Violence, 25*, 595–602. https://doi.org/10.1007/s10896-010-9322-8
Embry, R., & Lyons, P. M. (2012). Sex-based sentencing: Sentencing discrepancies between male and female sex offenders. *Feminist Criminology, 7*(2), 146–162. https://doi.org/10.1177/1557085111430214

Faller, K. C. (1987). Women who sexually abuse children. *Violence and Victims, 2*(4), 263–276. https://doi.org/10.1891/0886-6708.2.4.263

Faller, K. C. (1995). A clinical sample of women who sexually abuse children. *Journal of Child Sexual Abuse, 4*(3), 13–28. https://doi.org/10.1300/J070v04n03_02

Fazel, S., Sjöstedt, G., Grann, M., & Långström, N. (2010). Sexual offending in women and psychiatric disorder: A national case–control study. *Archives of Sexual Behavior, 39*(1), 161–167. https://doi.org/10.1007/s10508-008-9375-4

Ferguson, C. J., & Meehan, D. C. (2005). An analysis of females convicted of sex crimes in the state of Florida. *Journal of Child Sexual Abuse, 14*(1), 75–89. https://doi.org/10.1300/J070v14n01_05

Fromuth, M. E., & Holt, A. R. (2008). Perception of teacher sexual misconduct by age of student. *Journal of Child Sexual Abuse, 17*(2), 163–179. https://doi.org/10.1080/10538710801916663

Gannon, T. A., Hoare, J. A., Rose, M. R., & Parrett, N. (2012). A re-examination of female child molesters' implicit theories: Evidence of female specificity? *Psychology, Crime & Law, 18*(1–2), 209–224. https://doi.org/10.1080/10683161003752303

Gannon, T. A., Rose, M. R., & Ward, T. (2008). A descriptive model of the offense process for female sexual offenders. *Sexual Abuse: A Journal of Research and Treatment, 20*(3), 352–374. https://doi.org/10.1177/1079063208322495

Gannon, T. A., Waugh, G., Taylor, K., Blanchette, K., O'Connor, A., Blake, E., & Ciardha, O. (2014). Women who sexually offend display three main offense styles: A reexamination of the descriptive model of female sexual offending. *Sexual Abuse: A Journal of Research and Treatment, 26*(3), 207–224. https://doi.org/10.1177/1079063213486835

Gibbs, B. R., & Ten Bensel, T. (2022). Sentencing females convicted of sex offenses: Examining measures of perceived dangerousness and the decision to incarcerate. *Criminal Justice and Behavior, 49*(1), 58–76. https://doi.org/10.1177/00938548211032708

Gillespie, S. M., Williams, R., Elliott, I. A., Eldridge, H. J., Ashfield, S., & Beech, A. R. (2015). Characteristics of females who sexually offend: A comparison of solo and co-offenders. *Sexual Abuse, 27*(3), 284–301. https://doi.org/10.1177/1079063214556358

Green, A. H., & Kaplan, M. S. (1994). Psychiatric impairment and childhood victimization experiences in female child molesters. *Journal of the American Academy of Child and Adolescent Psychiatry, 33*(7), 954–961. https://doi.org/10.1097/00004583-199409000-00004

Hanson, R., & Morton-Bourgon, K. E. (2005). The characteristics of persistent sexual offenders: A meta-analysis of recidivism studies. *Journal of Consulting and Clinical Psychology, 73*, 1154–1163. https://doi.org/10.1037/0022-006X.73.6.1154

Harrison, J. L., O'Toole, S. K., Ammen, S., Ahlmeyer, S., Harrell, S. N., & Hernandez, J. L. (2020). Sexual offender treatment effectiveness within cognitive-behavioral programs: A meta-analytic investigation of general, sexual, and violent recidivism. *Psychiatry, Psychology and Law, 27*(1), 1–25. https://doi.org/10.1080/13218719.2018.1485526

Hassett-Walker, C., Lateano, T., & Di Benedetto, M. (2014). Do female sex offenders receive preferential treatment in criminal charging and sentencing? *Justice System Journal, 35*(1), 62–86. https://doi.org/10.1080/0098261X.2013.868278

Hetherton, J. (1999). The idealization of women: Its role in the minimization of child sexual abuse by females. *Child Abuse & Neglect, 23*(2), 161–174. https://doi.org/10.1016/S0145-2134(98)00119-7

Jaffe, P., Straatman, A. L., Harris, B., Georges, A., Vink, K., & Reif, K. (2013). Emerging trends in teacher sexual misconduct in Ontario 2007–2012. *Education & Law Journal, 23*(1), 19–39.

Johansson-Love, J., & Fremouw, W. (2009). Female sex offenders: A controlled comparison of offender and victim/crime characteristics. *Journal of Family Violence, 24*, 367–376. https://doi.org/10.1007/s10896-009-9236-5

Kaplan, M. S., & Green, A. (1995). Incarcerated female sexual offenders: A comparison of sexual histories with eleven female nonsexual offenders. *Sexual Abuse: A Journal of Research and Treatment, 7*(4), 287–300. https://doi.org/10.1007/BF02256833

King, L. L., & Roberts, J. J. (2017). The complexity of public attitudes toward sex crimes. *Victims and Offenders, 12*, 71–89. https://doi.org/10.1080/15564886.2015.1005266

Leone, C., Hawkin, L. B., & Bright, M. (2018). Minimizing mistreatment by female adults: The influence of gender-based social categories and personality differences on attitudes about child sexual abuse. *The Journal of Psychology, 153*(4), 361–382. https://doi.org/10.1080/00223980.2018.1541439

Levenson, J. S., Willis, G. M., & Prescott, D. S. (2015). Adverse childhood experiences in the lives of female sex offenders. *Sexual Abuse: A Journal of Research and Treatment, 27*(3), 258–283. https://doi.org/10.1177/1079063214544332

Lewis, C. F., & Stanley, C. R. (2000). Women accused of sexual offenses. *Behavioral Sciences & the Law, 18*, 73–81. https://doi.org/10.1002/(SICI)1099-0798(200001/02)18

Lösel, F., & Schmucker, M. (2005). The effectiveness of treatment for sexual offenders: A comprehensive meta-analysis. *Journal of Experimental Criminology, 1*, 117–146. https://doi.org/10.1007/s11292-004-6466-7

Marshall, W. L. (1999). Current status of north American assessment and treatment programs for sexual offenders. *Journal of Interpersonal Violence, 14*, 221–239. https://doi.org/10.1177/088626099014003002

Marshall, E. A., & Miller, H. A. (2019). Examining gender-specific and gender-neutral risk factors in women who sexually offend. *Criminal Justice and Behavior, 46*(4), 511–527. https://doi.org/10.1177/0093854818796872

Marshall, E. A., Miller, H. A., & Grubb, L. (2021). Examining the utility of the LSI-R in a sample of women who have sexually offended. *Criminal Justice and Behavior, 49*(3), 311–329. https://doi.org/10.1177/00938548211054031

Mathews, R., Matthews, J., & Speltz, K. (1989). *Female sexual offenders: An exploratory study*. Safer Society Press.

McCarty, L. M. (1986). Mother-child incest: Characteristics of the offender. *Child Welfare, 65*, 447–458.

McLeod, D. A. (2015). Female offenders in child sexual abuse cases: A national picture. *Journal of Child Sexual Abuse, 24*(1), 97–114. https://doi.org/10.1080/10538712.2015.978925

Mellor, D., & Deering, R. (2010). Professional response and attitudes toward female-perpetrated child sexual abuse: A study of psychologists, psychiatrists, probationary psychologists and child protection workers. *Psychology, Crime & Law, 16*(5), 415–438. https://doi.org/10.1080/10683160902776850

Miccio-Fonseca, L. C. (2000). Adult and adolescent female sex offenders: Experiences compared to other female and male sex offenders. *Journal of Psychology and Human Sexuality, 11*(3), 75–88. https://doi.org/10.1300/J056v11n03_08

Miller, H. A., Turner, K., & Henderson, C. E. (2009). Psychopathology of sex offenders: A comparison of males and females using latent profile analysis. *Criminal Justice and Behavior, 36*(8), 778–792. https://doi.org/10.1177/0093854809336400

Muskens, M., Bogaerts, S., van Casteren, M., & Labrijn, S. (2011). Adult female sexual offending: A comparison between co-offenders and solo offenders in a Dutch sample. *Journal of Sexual Aggression, 17*(1), 46–60. https://doi.org/10.1080/13552600.2010.544414

Nathan, P., & Ward, T. (2002). Female sex offenders: Clinical and demographic features. *The Journal of Sexual Aggression, 8*(1), 5–21. https://doi.org/10.1080/13552600208413329

Prescott, D. S., & Willis, G. M. (2022). Using the good lives model (GLM) in clinical practice: Lessons learned from international implementation projects. *Aggression and Violent Behavior, 63*, 101717. https://doi.org/10.1016/j.avb.2021.101717

Ratliff, L., & Watson, J. (2014). A descriptive analysis of public school educators arrested for sex offenses. *Journal of Child Sexual Abuse, 23*(2), 217–228. https://doi.org/10.1080/10538712.2014.870275

Reid, S. S. (2012). Bad bad teacher!: How judicial lenience, cultural ignorance, and media hype have inevitably lead to lighter sentences, underreporting and glamorization of female sex offenders. *Whittier Journal of Child and Family Advocacy, 11*(2), 353–374.

Rogers, P., & Davies, M. (2007). Perceptions of victims and perpetrators in a depicted child sexual abuse case. *Journal of Interpersonal Violence, 22*(5), 566–584. https://doi.org/10.1177/0886260506298827

Rudin, M. M., Zalewski, C., & Bodmer-Turner, J. (1995). Characteristics of child sexual abuse victims according to perpetrator gender. *Child Abuse and Neglect, 19*(8), 963–973. https://doi.org/10.1016/0145-2134(95)00058-G

Rush-Burkey, C., & ten Bensel, T. (2015). An examination and comparison of rationalizations employed by solo and co-offending female sex offenders. *Violence and Gender, 2*(3), 168–178. https://doi.org/10.1089/vio.2015.0018

Sample, L. L., & Bray, T. M. (2003). Are sex offenders dangerous? *Criminology & Public Policy, 3*(1), 59–82. https://doi.org/10.1111/j.1745-9133.2003.tb00024.x

Sandler, J. C., & Freeman, N. J. (2009). Female sex offender recidivism: A large-scale empirical analysis. *Sexual Abuse: A Journal of Research and Treatment, 21*(4), 455–473. https://doi.org/10.1177/1079063209347898

Shakeshaft, C. (2004). Educator sexual misconduct: A synthesis of existing literature. Policy and Program Studies Service. US Department of Education. Retrieved from https://files.eric.ed.gov/fulltext/ED483143.pdf

Shields, R. T., & Cochran, J. C. (2020). The gender gap in sex offender punishment. *Journal of Quantitative Criminology, 36*(1), 95–118. https://doi.org/10.1007/s10940-019-09416-x

Steely, M., & Ten Bensel, T. (2020). Child sexual abuse within educational settings: A qualitative study on female teachers who sexually abuse their students. *Deviant Behavior, 41*(11), 1440–1453. https://doi.org/10.1080/01639625.2019.1624288

Steely Smith, M. K., & ten Bensel, T. (2024). Sexual grooming behavior and processes of women who commit sexual offenses against children. Journal of interpersonal violence, 08862605241239450.

Stemple, L., Flores, A., & Meyer, I. H. (2017). Sexual victimization perpetrated by women: Federal data reveal surprising prevalence. *Aggression and Violent Behavior, 34*, 302–311. https://doi.org/10.1016/j.avb.2016.09.007

Strickland, S. M. (2008). Female sex offenders: Exploring issues of personality, trauma, and cognitive distortions. *Journal of Interpersonal Violence, 23*(4), 474–489. https://doi.org/10.1177/0886260507312944

ten Bensel, T., Gibbs, B., & Burkey, C. (2016). Female sex offenders: Is there a difference between solo and co-female sex offenders? *Journal of Interpersonal Violence, 34*(19), 4061–4084. https://doi.org/10.1177/0886260516674202

ten Bensel, T., Gibbs, B., & Raptopoulos, K. (2019). The role of childhood victimization on the severity of adult offending among female sex offenders. *Victims and Offenders, 14*(6), 758–775. https://doi.org/10.1080/15564886.2019.1630044

Thompson, L., Rydberg, J., Cassidy, M., & Socia, K. M. (2019). Contextual influences on the sentencing of individuals convicted of sexual crimes. *Sexual Abuse, 32*, 1–28. https://doi.org/10.1177/1079063219852936

Travis, S., Cullen, K., & Potter, B. (1990). Female sex offenders: Severe victims and victimizers. *Journal of Forensic Sciences, 35*, 140–150. https://doi.org/10.1520/JFS12811J

Vandiver, D. M. (2006). Female sex offenders: A comparison of solo offenders and co-offenders. *Violence and Victims, 21*(3), 339–354. https://doi.org/10.1891/vivi.21.3.339

Vandiver, D. M., & Kercher, G. (2004). Offender and victim characteristics of registered female sexual offenders in Texas: A proposed typology of female sexual offenders. *Sexual Abuse: A Journal of Research and Treatment, 16*(2), 121–137. https://doi.org/10.1023/B:SEBU.0000023061.77061.17

Vandiver, D. M., & Walker, J. T. (2002). Female sex offenders: An overview and analysis of 40 cases. *Criminal Justice Review, 27*(2), 284–300. https://doi.org/10.1177/073401680202700205

Ward, T. (2002). Good lives and the rehabilitation of offenders: Promises and problems. *Aggression and Violent Behavior, 7*, 513–528. https://doi.org/10.1016/S1359-1789(01)00076-3

Ward, T., & Durrant, R. (2021). Practice frameworks in correctional psychology: Translating causal theories and normative assumptions into practice. *Aggression and Violent Behavior, 58*, 1–9. https://doi.org/10.1016/j.avb.2021.101612

West, S. G., Friedman, S. H., & Kim, K. D. (2011). Women accused of sex offenses: A gender-based comparison. *Behavioral Sciences & the Law, 29*(5), 728–740. https://doi.org/10.1002/bsl.1007

Wijkman, M., Bijleveld, C., & Hendriks, J. (2010). Women don't do such things? Characteristics of female sex offenders and offender types. *Sexual Abuse: A Journal of Research and Treatment, 22*(2), 135–156. https://doi.org/10.1177/1079063210363826

William, K. S., & Bierie, D. M. (2015). An incident-based comparison of female and male sexual offenders. *Sexual Abuse: A Journal of Research and Treatment, 27*(3), 235–257. https://doi.org/10.1177/1079063214544333

Wright, R. (Ed.). (2014). *Sex offender laws: Failed policies, new directions*. Springer Publishing Company.

Zack, E., Lang, J. T., & Dirks, D. (2018). "It must be great being a female pedophile!": The nature of public perceptions about female teacher sex offenders. *Crime Media Culture, 14*(1), 61–79. https://doi.org/10.1177/1741659016674044

Chapter 20
Special Populations: Aging and Sexual Offending

Rebecca Crookes, Carlo Tramontano, Sarah Brown, Kate Walker, and Hayley Wright

20.1 Introduction

Research typically shows that as age increases, the likelihood of engaging in offending behaviour decreases (e.g., Barbaree et al., 2009; Farrington, 1986). However, the last decade has seen a rapid increase in the number of older prisoners globally (Allen & Watson, 2017; Baidawi et al., 2011; Bedard et al., 2017; Bureau of Justice Statistics, 2016; PMJ5, French Prison Authority, cited in Combalbert et al., 2018; Penal Reform International, 2015; Walmsley, 2016; Williams et al., 2012). Plausible reasons for this trend include the global aging population, people now living longer, the likelihood of longer custodial sentences (Howse, 2003), and an increase in the number of older individuals being convicted and sentenced for historical sexual offenses (House of Commons Justice Committee, 2013).

Individuals convicted of sexual offenses are over-represented among older prisoners globally (Fazel et al., 2001b; Morton, 1992; Uzoaba, 1998). Yet, research on this group is limited, so tailored treatment and interventions are lacking. Theories, intervention programmes, and risk assessment methods are generally based on younger men; hence may be inappropriate, ineffective, or irrelevant for older men.

R. Crookes (✉) · C. Tramontano
Centre for Global Learning, Coventry University, Coventry, Warwickshire, UK
e-mail: r.crookes@soton.ac.uk

S. Brown
Sexual Violence Research and Prevention Unit, University of the Sunshine Coast, Sunshine Coast, QLD, Australia

K. Walker
Northamptonshire NHS Foundation Trust (UK), Kettering, Northamptonshire, UK

H. Wright
Centre for Intelligent Healthcare, Coventry University, Coventry, Warwickshire, UK

R. J. Tully et al. (eds.), *Best Practices in Sexual Offender Assessment and Management*, Dangerous Behavior in Clinical and Forensic Psychology,
https://doi.org/10.1007/978-3-031-83135-5_20

A literature review (Chua et al., 2018) highlighted that first time older individuals (aged 65+ years) convicted of sexual offenses tend to victimise vulnerable individuals and can be differentiated from individuals who have repeatedly offended throughout their lifetime but were convicted at a later stage of life, and individuals with neurocognitive disorders. This review offered an essential insight into the characteristics of first-time older individuals convicted of sexual offenses but does not consider sub-populations within the broad older adult sexual offending population. This chapter provides a comprehensive overview of: (1) the demographic, psychological, offense, risk, and treatment characteristics of older adults (aged 60+) convicted of sexual offenses; and, (2) the similarities and differences of these characteristics among adults convicted of sexual offenses across the lifespan.

20.2 Method and Procedure

The review included any study either focused on: (1) older individuals convicted of sexual offenses (OSOs); (2) on age differences across the adult sexual offending population; and (3) comparisons among age bands groups (representing the adult lifespan). Search results were limited to peer-reviewed articles, primary studies, meta-analyses, books/book chapters, and dissertations/thesis[1] written in English and published after 1990, presenting data on adult male aged 60+ years, convicted of sexual offences, and not having any learning disability.

20.2.1 Search Methods

Searches were completed in: Academic Search Complete; CINAHL; PsycINFO; ProQuest Nursing and Allied Health; and PubMed.

Variants of the following search terms were used: ((sex* offen*) AND ("age" OR "aging"OR "ageing"OR "elder*" OR "old*")). Broad search terms ensured inclusion of a wide range of studies.

20.2.2 Data Collection and Analysis

The first search was conducted on 11th December 2017. Figure 20.1 outlines the implemented search strategy.

The first author initially screened all the studies. To ensure the reliability of the selection of papers, the third author applied the inclusion/exclusion criteria to 10%

[1] Systematic literature reviews were excluded to avoid the duplication of studies.

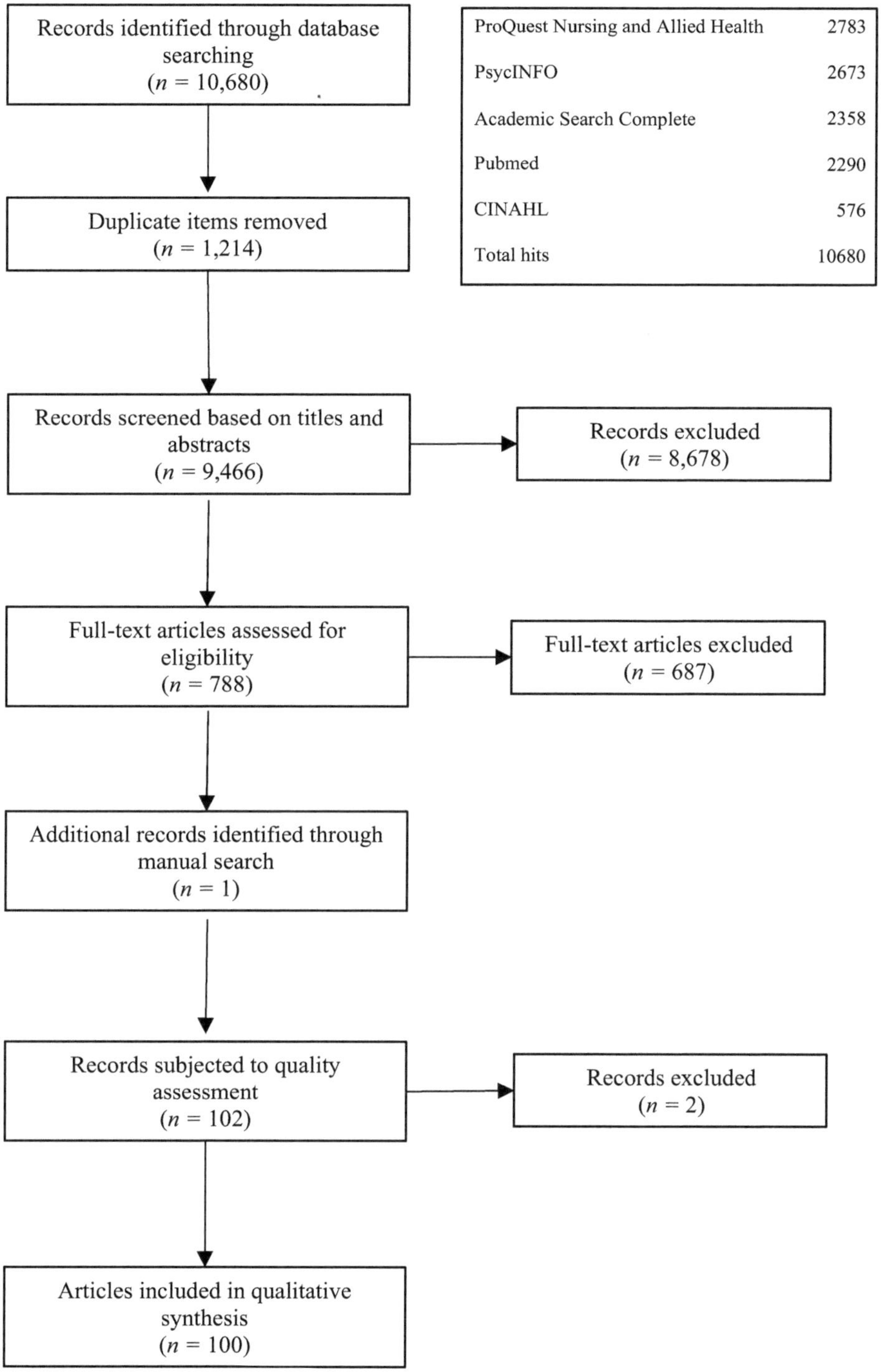

Fig. 20.1 Search strategy of the systematic review

of the 10,680 hits ($n = 1068$), with disagreement on only 3 decisions. Minor differences were addressed through discussion of the papers by both authors until an agreement was reached.

20.2.3 *Quality Assessment*

Studies were subjected to quality assessment using the Mixed Methods Appraisal Tool (MMAT; Hong et al., 2018). This tool aims to assess the risk of bias, and to appraise and describe the methodological quality of qualitative, quantitative, and mixed methods studies, but is not suitable for meta-analyses.

The process of using the MMAT results in a classification of the study from one to five stars. Two papers were excluded on the basis of this quality assessment. Forty-two studies were classed as five star, 22 as four star, 19 as three star, 7 as two star, and 3 as one star. Six meta-analyses and one book chapter could not be quality assessed using MMAT but are still included.

20.2.4 *Data Extraction and Synthesis*

The final studies were reviewed and categorised into research themes. A narrative synthesis uncovered four areas of research focus: age of onset; individual and offense characteristics; age and risk of reoffending; and treatment.

20.3 Findings

The final review included 100 studies. Samples included individuals convicted of offenses against children and adults, for contact (including rape and child molestation) and non-contact (e.g., involving child sexual abuse material) offenses. Studies were mostly conducted in Canada ($n = 38$), the United States ($n = 23$), and the United Kingdom ($n = 13$); and fewer from Australia (7) and Europe (Austria = 4; New Zealand = 5; Sweden = 3; Italy = 2; Spain = 2; Germany = 1; Brazil = 1; and France = 1).

Of the 100 studies, 87 implemented a quantitative methodology, including using phallometric assessments, psychometric assessments, questionnaires, and meta-analyses. Secondary data analyses of case file data (e.g., police/national crime databases, prison or facility records) were common, including offender demographic, risk assessment outcomes, and data on reoffending. Six studies used a qualitative approach, all with semi-structured interviews, and five employed a mixed-methods design, typically using interviews that were supplemented by questionnaires, secondary data, or psychometric measures/tools.

20.3.1 Area 1: Age of Onset

Eighteen studies (11 of which were deemed "higher quality") examined the age of onset of offending behaviors and the prevalence of OSOs. Collectively, the studies suggest that average age of onset of sexual offending ranged from mid-twenties to mid-thirties, demonstrating that the onset of sexual offending declines as individuals' age, thus supporting the age-crime effect (see Mathesius & Lussier, 2014). Smallbone et al. (2008) suggested that there are two distinct populations based on age of onset of sexual offending: (1) individuals who first sexually offended during adolescence but stopped offending as they emerged into adulthood, and (2) individuals who started offending during adulthood and who had a peak risk period of late thirties.

Conversely, earlier research showed that early onset of problematic sexual behaviors was one of the strongest predictors of deviant behavior later in life (Marshall et al., 1991). In a sample of 50 individuals convicted of sexual offenses, Doyle et al. (2011) found that 34% started sexually offending aged <18 years, 32% started between age 18–24 years, 6% between ages 24–30 years, 18% between ages 31–40 years, and 10% at age 40+ years. More recent research shows only 8% started to sexually offend over the age of 50 (McKillop et al., 2015). These stages of life relate to the emergence of sexual exploration and peer activities in adolescence, and changes in family, work and social circumstance in adulthood, which may explain why people may begin offending at different ages.

Those convicted of *child* sex offenses have an older age of onset compared to those convicted of *adult* sex offenses. Harris (2012) found that individuals whose first recorded offense was for a sexual offense against a child had the latest age of onset (25.48 years old). One study shows those convicted of both adult and child sexual offenses had their first conviction at a younger age (mean = 23 years), than those who exclusively offended against children (mean = 30 year; Woodworth et al., 2013). The age of the first adult sexual offense ranged from 18 to 55 years (mean age = 26) and the age of the first nonsexual offense ranged from 11 to 53 years (mean age = 18). Individuals convicted of extrafamilial offenses had a significantly earlier onset of sexual offending (mean age = 29) compared to those convicted of intrafamilial offenses (mean age = 34; Smallbone & Wortley, 2004). Moreover, individuals convicted of intrafamilial child sexual offenses tended to be older (mean age = 40 years) than individuals convicted of extrafamilial child sexual offenses (mean age = 34 years) and those convicted of both types of offenses (mean age = 35). Men who targeted stranger (i.e. extrafamilial) victims had an earlier actual onset than those offending within their biological family. Mathesius and Lussier (2014) concluded that differences in age of onset might reflect situational factors, such as intimate relationships and access to children/victims. However, disclosure should also be considered as a factor, as many cases of sexual assault and child sexual abuse largely go unreported.

Smallbone and Wortley (2004) reported that for approximately 80% of their sample, the first convicted offense was nonsexual. Seven studies (e.g., Doyle et al.,

2011; Harris, 2012 found that males who were convicted of prior nonsexual offenses had a much earlier age of onset than those who had a first conviction of a sexual offense. Harris (2012) reported that individuals who started their criminal career with property crime (such as burglary or theft) were convicted at a significantly younger age (mean age = 16 years) than at their first charge of violent (mean age = 19 years) and sexual (mean age = 24 years) offenses. Similar trends were found by Cann et al. (2007), where on average, men were older (mean age = 37 years) when they began sexually offending than when offending in general (mean age = 30 years). Moreover, Redondo et al. (2007) found that, of the sample of 123 individuals convicted of sexual offenses, those who recidivated (in this case, of general crimes) were significantly younger (average 25.2 years old) compared to non-recidivists (average 34.3 years old) when committing their first sexual (convicted) offense. Furthermore, individuals convicted of sexual offenses released at a younger age were more likely to commit general crimes, whereas those released at an older age were more likely to be 'sexual offense specialists' (Thornton, 2006).

However, the actual age of onset of offending behavior (i.e., offender's age at the time of their first sexual offense) may differ from the official onset age (i.e., age when convicted and incarcerated for a sexual offense). Mathesius and Lussier (2014) reported an average 7.5 year gap between the actual (32 years) and official (40 years) onset of sexual offending. The authors suggested that this gap is significant because "it allows offenders to remain at-risk of offending including sexual offenses; it increases the difficulty in obtaining forensic evidence for the initial conviction(s), and; it may contribute to offenders' lowering their perception about the risk of sex offending" (Mathesius & Lussier, 2014, p. 140). However, it is difficult to ascertain a 'true' age of onset, given the reliance on the accuracy of data, and the legitimacy of disclosure and honesty of the individuals convicted of sexual offending.

20.3.2 Area 2: Characteristics of Individuals Convicted of Sexual Offenses and of the Offense

Forty-three studies (22 of which were deemed 'higher quality') reported on the characteristics of individuals convicted of sexual offenses and on offense characteristics. Factors such as age, relationship and employment status, and mental health were discussed for the characteristics of individuals convicted of sexual offenses. Offence type, age of the victim and the relationship to the victim were also examined for the offense characteristics.

20.3.2.1 Characteristics of Individuals Convicted of Sexual Offences

Thirteen studies examined the characteristics of OSOs compared to characteristics of other age groups, whereas others did not use a comparison group. Collectively, the studies found that OSOs tended to be: white, unemployed, or retired at the time of offense, had a history of steady and continuous employment (more recently employed as a car or truck driver and have military experience); and tended to have a high educational level (e.g., Fazel et al., 2001b; Rayel, 2000; Tsagaris et al., 2017).

In contrast to studies characterizing OSOs as unemployed or retired, two studies investigated professionals (e.g., physicians, teachers) who were convicted of sexual offenses. Dehlendorf and Wolfe (1998) found that physicians who were disciplined for sex-related offenses were, on average, older than the national physician population. Among all physicians, 35% were aged between 45 and 64 years, whereas 58% of disciplined physicians were in this age group. However, in the 64+ age group, there was no significant difference in the proportion of physicians disciplined for sex-related offenses and the national physician population. Additionally, Sullivan and Beech (2004) found that physicians tended to be older and more intelligent when compared to the broad population of individuals convicted of SOs.

Younger individuals convicted of sexual offenses were less likely to be in long-term relationships or have children (Brouillette-Alarie & Proulx, 2013). This would limit their access to intrafamilial victims and provides one explanation for younger men being more likely to have extrafamilial and adult victims. Mathesius and Lussier (2014) suggested the typical adult male convicted for the first-time for a sexual offense tended to be aged late 30 s, have limited education, unemployed, more likely to have offended against females, have on average two victims, have offended approximately 10 times within their familial environment, and be married. Clark and Mezey (1997) found that 77% of their sample were unmarried, though all had been married at some point in their life. This was reflective of Rayel (2000), who found in their sample of individuals aged over 55 convicted of sexual offenses and were admitted to a maximum-security forensic hospital, 86% were unmarried at the time of admission to the hospital. These two studies also found a history of sexual or physical abuse in childhood or adulthood was low for the OSO population (8% in Clark & Mezey, 1997; 14% in Rayel, 2000).

Regarding mental health, there were low rates of depression but no evidence of other mental illnesses within the OSO population (Clark & Mezey, 1997). OSOs were more likely to have dementia and have a previous psychiatric history, compared to younger persons convicted of a sexual offense (Fazel et al., 2001a). Further, OSOs were less likely to abuse substances, both for drugs and alcohol, compared to individuals not convicted of sexual offenses (Fazel et al., 2001a).

Two studies (Harkins et al., 2013; Marshall, 2010) reported OSOs were more likely to score lower on the Psychopathy Checklist-Revised (PCL-R) than younger individuals convicted of sexual offenses. Additionally, Marshall (2010) reported that OSOs: scored lower on the PCL-R Factor 2 (demonstrating lower criminal lifestyle), scored lower on the measure for treatment needs, and had a greater number of victims. A significant statistical difference was found in phallometric assessments, evidencing that convicted OSOs, at the time of assessment, had more sexually deviant interests than younger persons convicted of sexual offenses. Professionals (e.g., offender managers) reported that OSOs had a variety of issues with mobility, physical health, mental health, and sexual health (the latter finding contradicting previous findings; Bows & Westmarland, 2016). For instance, these men tended to experience erectile dysfunction, which can often lead to feelings of frustration, leading these men to actively seek children to fantasize about in order to achieve an erection.

In interviews with OSOs, Mann (2012) found that this population tended to justify their sexual offending behaviors, or avoid taking responsibility, by blaming external factors such as marital issues or alcohol abuse. Moreover, they tended to deny having caused any injury to their victims, and blamed society for negatively labelling them a "sex offender". These attitudes, combined with a higher level of intelligence, led to the participants exhibiting arrogance and dismissive attitudes, as well as being self-assured and proud of their actions (Mann, 2012).

20.3.2.2 Offense Characteristics

The majority of OSOs were known to their victim, had a greater number of victims and sex crimes, and were more likely to offend against children than adults. OSOs were more likely to be convicted of incest offenses or child sexual offenses, with rapists being younger and underrepresented within this population of OSOs (Firestone et al., 2000; Harry et al., 1993; Langevin & Curnoe, 2008; Marshall et al., 1991). One reason for OSOs offending against children could be that their victims are weaker and easier to overpower and manipulate, and because the OSO themselves have less strength (Hanson, 2006). Indeed, Poortinga et al. (2007) reported that OSOs experienced difficulties in overpowering victims over the age of 12 years.

Two small-scale studies explored the sexual abuse of older victims (Browne et al., 2018; Jeary, 2005). Browne et al. (2018) found that those who were convicted of sexual offenses against older adults were significantly younger than those who sexually offended against children, indicating that the young age of the offender may be an aggravating risk factor for this type of offense.

20.3.3 Area 3: Age and Risk of Reoffending

All the studies examining aging and reoffending (n = 44, 30 of which rated were deemed 'higher quality') that were included in this review demonstrated that as age increases, the likelihood of reoffending decreases (e.g., Eher et al., 2016; Hanson, 2006; Hanson, 2006). This trend is evident cross-culturally and using different risk assessment instruments (e.g., Static-99, Risk Matrix 2000, RRASOR) and cohorts.

However, there is debate around the rate of decline in reoffending. For example, Hanson (2006) demonstrated a negative linear relationship between aging and reoffending for men convicted of rape and incest, with higher recidivism rates between the ages of 18 and 24 years. For men convicted of extra-familial child sexual offenses, the highest peak was between the ages of 25 and 35 years. Prentky and Lee (2007) found that rates of sexual reoffending for rapists remained stable (around 28%) until the end of their 30 s, continuing to steadily decline thereafter, with no reoffending recorded in the oldest group (aged over 60). For the child molesters, those aged between 18 and 29 years had the lowest overall sexual re-offense rate (21%). This rapidly increased to 42% for those released in their thirties, thereafter steadily declining, dropping to 36% for those released in their 40 s, 23% in their 50 s, and 17% in their 60 s; similar to the pattern observed by Hanson (2006). Likewise, Rettenberger et al. (2015) found that recidivism rates dropped in their oldest group. In terms of violent recidivism, there was a consistent decrease in the proportion of recidivists with age, with a stronger aging effect in the rapist subgroup than the child. Similarly for sexual recidivism, Thornton (2006) observed the highest rate between ages 18 and 25 years (80%), which rapidly decreased thereafter.

Many explanations for the declining pattern of recidivism have been suggested. According to studies using phallometric assessments, the strength of male sexual arousal peaks in post-pubescence and decreases with age (Blanchard & Barbaree, 2005), with the fastest rate of decline between adolescence and the age of 30 (Barbaree et al., 2003). Decline in sexual arousal could be one reason for sexual recidivism declining with age. Further, in a study examining desistance from sexual crime, participants reported they would not reoffend because they were too old, too tired, and no longer had "it in them" (Harris, 2016, p. 1724). Hanson (2006) attributed the decline to three factors: self-control increases with age, opportunity for sexually offending decreases with age for rapists (as people often associate with others their own age, and most rape victims are young women who are known to the perpetrator), and sexual deviancy. However, the opportunity to offend may increase for individuals convicted of child sex offenses, as more opportunities for offending can arise (e.g., having grandchildren).

20.3.3.1 Age as a Variable in Risk Assessment Tools

Studies have reported that the 'age-at-release' effect (as age increases, offending rates decrease) was evidenced in numerous actuarial assessments (e.g., Barbaree et al., 2003; Eher et al., 2016; Wakeling et al., 2011), and actuarial risk assessment instruments (e.g., Static-99, RRASOR, SORAG and the Risk Matrix 2000) in which this age variable pattern is accounted (Craig, 2011; Hanson, 2006). Thus, this apparent pattern supports the age-crime trend in actuarial assessments.

However, the applicability of risk assessment tools for different age groups is questionable (Fazel et al., 2006), as the weightings for 'age at release' items may be overestimated for OSOs (Helmus et al., 2012). Researchers have urged consideration of age in understanding base rates of offending, and have argued that predictive accuracy could be improved if the age effect was taken into account (Lussier & Healey, 2009). Therefore, rather than using 'age at release', risk assessment instruments could use historical or unchanging factors (for instance, age of onset of criminal activity). 'Age at release' does not provide incremental predictive validity over actuarial risk assessment scores, and therefore age of onset is a better risk marker (i.e., individuals who have earlier onset of offending display an increased risk of reoffending; Harris & Rice, 2007). However, 'age of onset' and 'age at release' were strongly related, as those who start offending earlier, were more likely to be released younger than those who start offending later.

20.3.3.2 OSOs and Risk

Two studies (rated four and five stars) specifically examined the role of risk within the OSO population. Marshall (2010) found that first-time OSOs were at greater risk for recidivism compared to older men convicted of non-recent sexual offenses (i.e., those who ceased their offending behavior without receiving any form of intervention). The men convicted of non-recent sexual offences showed ability to stop and manage their sexual behavior, suggesting they were at a lower risk of sexual recidivism. OSOs were more sexually deviant than younger individuals convicted of sexual offenses, but there were no differences in deviant sexual interest found between men convicted of their first offence, those who recidivated, and those who committed historical offenses. Therefore, treating deviant sexual arousal may not be useful for the OSO population; if deviant sexual interests are a factor for an individual to sexually offending, it can be assumed that OSOs who committed historical offenses would have reoffended since their last known offense, and first-time OSOs would have offended at a much earlier opportunity. Therefore, opportunity for offending may be a significant contributing factor for sexually offending later in life (Marshall, 2010), supporting Hanson (2006).

In terms of managing the risk posed by OSOs in the community, with care or support needs, offender managers reported one of the main challenges was the 'trustworthiness' of OSOs (Bows & Westmarland, 2016). OSOs were more likely to exploit the appearances that result from their medical needs and portray themselves as being unlikely to harm others. Questions regarding three risk-related issues were identified: (1) managing the risk for individuals diagnosed with dementia, as any conditions, restrictions, or treatments may be forgotten; (2) managing the individualized risks of OSOs who are housed in care homes; for instance, grandchildren may frequently visit their relatives housed in the same facility; and (3) how their care needs will be met in the community (Bows & Westmarland, 2016).

20.3.4 Area 4: Treatment

Only three Canadian studies examined the role of age in treatment and whether OSOs could benefit from treatment programs and interventions. Two studies found no evidence linking age, risk, and treatment completion to outcome (Langevin, 2006; Olver et al., 2012). In general, treated OSOs had a significantly lower risk compared to those who were untreated (i.e., those who were not officially documented as having completed a sex offender treatment program; Olver et al., 2012). In support of previous risk and recidivism research findings, younger men (< 50 years) reoffended at higher rates than OSOs (50+ years), regardless of whether they attended treatment or not. However, it appeared that the younger individuals gained more from treatment than the OSOs, though this could be due to OSOs being a lower risk group, and that individuals wanting and attending treatment tended to be younger.

The type of offense (i.e., recidivist, first-time, and non-recent) should match the appropriate treatment level to individual OSOs (Marshall, 2010). For instance, recidivist OSOs (demonstrate a lack of control over their sexual behavior) should participate in a higher intensity treatment than first-time or non-recent OSOs. First-time and recidivist OSOs were at greater risk of recidivism than non-recent OSOs, as they went against the trend of the age-effect, having committed their offenses more recently. Non-recent OSOs were able to desist from their sexual offending behaviors without intervention, further suggesting that (1) non-recent OSOs are at a lower risk of recidivism, or (2) they had, essentially, grown out of offending. However, as Marshall (2010) stated, OSOs could be recidivists who "represent the most deviant and persistent sexual offenders" (p. 63). An exploration into first-time (factors responsible for onset of offending), non-recent (factors associated with cessation of offending in absence of legal intervention) and recidivist (factors for maintenance of sexually offensive behavior after judicial sanction) OSOs is essential for predicting sexual offending and informing treatment programs.

20.4 Discussion and Conclusions

This chapter presents a comprehensive overview of characteristics in OSO. It explored the similarities and differences among adult individuals convicted of sexual offenses across the lifespan, including offender and offense characteristic, the role and impact of age on the risk of reoffending, and the impact of treatment on OSOs.

The peak adult age of onset of sexual offending behaviors ranged from mid-twenties to mid-thirties. However, there is a limited knowledge about the actual prevalence rate of older individuals convicted of sexual offenses, and in particular about the proportion who start to offend at a later stage of life (e.g., 8% of the sample in McKillop et al., 2015). For this sub-population it is also unclear what factors trigger the late onset and those that sustain the offending behavior.

OSOs tend to be: unmarried; unemployed or retired at the time of offense; more highly educated; scoring lower on the PCL-R; and more likely to sexually offend against children who were known to them (e.g., a family member or an acquaintance). It is paramount to explore the mental health needs as well as the role of psychosocial factors for this population. A better understanding of the impact of mental health conditions, dementia and cognitive deterioration could inform tailored interventions. Similarly, given the initial evidence suggesting that OSOs tend to be highly intelligent, have low psychopathy, low depression, with sexually deviant interests, there is call for a more in-depth investigation of dynamic and changeable individual dimensions.

Findings confirmed the well-established pattern of the risk of reoffending decreasing as age increases. However, first-time OSOs did not conform to this trend, so their actual level of risk and the risk assessment tools need to be reviewed accordingly. Depending on whether the OSO is non-recent, recidivist or first-time, or the age at release or first offense, different tools and different risk categories may be appropriate. Further exploration of recidivism rates for first time OSOs is needed, as well as an understanding as to whether this group are more sexually deviant compared to younger individuals convicted of sexual offenses.

Finally, the few studies that explored treatment and age identified that there was no link between age, risk, and treatment completion to outcome. However, treatment needs of the OSOs population are still not understood, and this lack of association might rather be due to the misalignment between treatments and needs, as opposed to OSOs being lower risk. Therefore, an examination of the effectiveness of risk assessment measures for first time OSOs is essential, in order to identify whether such assessments accurately predict recidivism within this subgroup, assess whether first time OSOs are riskier, and to readdress the level of intervention they should be provided.

The findings from this review largely support the principles of the Motivation-Facilitation Model of Sexual Offending (MFM; Seto, 2019). The MFM identifies three primary sexual motivations: (1) paraphilias (e.g., pedophilia); (2) high sex drive; and (3) intense mating effort. Facilitation factors overcome any trait (e.g., self-regulation problems and hostile masculinity) or state (negative affect and alcohol use) inhibitions that prevent individuals from acting upon the motivations. Situational factors play a key role in an individual's propensity to sexually offend; individuals who are strongly motivated to sexually offend are more likely to create opportunities to offend (Seto, 2019). Further research is encouraged to explore factors such as individual differences, self-control and cognitive distortions (Ciardha & Ward, 2013; Szumski et al., 2018). Moreover, longitudinal studies are needed to examine the factors that contribute to the onset of offending, perhaps using a multifactoral approach such as the Integrated Theory of Sexual Offending (ITSO; Ward & Beech, 2016).

20.4.1 Limitations

From the studies included in this review, it was difficult to ascertain whether factors were unique to the OSO population, as numerous studies did not use a comparison group. Further, the use of standard deviation when reporting the age of the samples (and not reporting the age range) impacted on the inclusion criteria. Studies that did not report age range were excluded, and it is possible that some may have been relevant. Finally, there was no standard definition within the literature for what age is considered 'older', with findings being reported on OSOs aged 50+ and 60+ years.

20.4.2 Implications for Future Research and Clinical Practice

There is a need to develop a theory to explain why OSOs start their offending behavior at a later stage of life (contrary to the age-crime effect), and to understand the physical and mental health needs of OSOs. This will inform the development of appropriate and effective risk assessments and interventions for OSOs.

Future research should also report the prevalence of OSOs, as well as the proportions of first-time, recidivist, and non-recent OSOs, as these are currently unclear. A comprehensive exploration of the demographics and characteristics of 'younger' and 'older' individuals convicted of sexual offenses would elucidate the similarities and differences between the two populations. Again, this could improve the effectiveness of risk assessment and interventions, and target prevention strategies. This would also add to the development of a theory of how and why non-recent OSOs stopped offending without intervention, or why non-recent OSOs stopped then re-started offending when older.

References[2]

*Ackerman, A. R., Harris, A. J., Levenson, J. S., & Zgoba, K. (2011). Who are the people in your neighborhood? A descriptive analysis of individuals on public sex offender registries. *International Journal of Law & Psychiatry, 34*(3), 149–159. https://doi.org/10.1016/j.ijlp.2011.04.001. [1].

Allen, G., & Watson, C. (2017). *UK prison population statistics*. House of Commons Library.

*Amirault, J., & Lussier, P. (2011). Population heterogeneity, state dependence and sexual offender recidivism: The aging process and the lost predictive impact of prior criminal charges over time. *Journal of Criminal Justice, 39*(4), 344–354. https://doi.org/10.1016/j.jcrimjus.2011.04.001. [2].

*Babchishin, K. M., Hanson, R. K., & Blais, J. (2016). Less is more: Using static-2002R subscales to predict violent and general recidivism among sexual offenders. *Sexual Abuse: Journal of Research and Treatment, 28*(3), 187–217. https://doi.org/10.1177/1079063215569544. [3].

[2] References marked with an asterisk (*) indicate the studies included in the final review.

Baidawi, S., Turner, S., Trotter, C., Browning, C., Collier, P., O'Connor, D., & Sheehan, R. (2011). Older prisoners—A challenge for Australian corrections. *Trends & Issues in Crime and Criminal Justice, 426*, 1–8. Retrieved from: https://aic.gov.au/publications/tandi/tandi426

*Baltieri, D. A., & de Andrade, A. G. (2008). Drug consumption among sexual offenders against females. International Journal of Offender Therapy & Comparative Criminology, 52(1), 62–80. https://doi.org/10.1177/0306624X07299345. [4].

*Barbaree, H. E., Blanchard, R., & Langton, C. M. (2003). The development of sexual aggression through the life span: The effect of age on sexual arousal and recidivism among sex offenders. *Annals of the New York Academy of Sciences, 989*, 59–71. https://doi.org/10.1111/j.1749-6632.2003.tb07293.x. discussion 144–153. [5].

*Barbaree, H. E., Langton, C. M., Blanchard, R., & Boer, D. P. (2008). Predicting recidivism in sex offenders using the SVR-20: The contribution of age-at-release. *The International Journal of Forensic Mental Health, 7*(1), 47–64. https://doi.org/10.1080/14999013.2008.9914403. [6].

*Barbaree, H. E., Langton, C. M., Blanchard, R., & Cantor, J. M. (2009). Aging versus stable enduring traits as explanatory constructs in sex offender recidivism: Partitioning actuarial prediction into conceptually meaningful components. *Criminal Justice and Behavior, 36*(5), 443–465. https://doi.org/10.1177/0093854809332283. [7].

*Beauregard, E., Deslauriers-Varin, N., & St-Yves, M. (2010). Interactions between factors related to the decision of sex offenders to confess during police interrogation: A classification-tree approach. *Sexual Abuse: A Journal of Research & Treatment, 22*(3), 343–367. https://doi.org/10.1177/1079063210370707. [8].

*Becerra-García, J. A., & Egan, V. (2014). A cross-sectional study of the relationships between age and personality in sex offenders against children. *Sexologies: European Journal of Sexology and Sexual Health / Revue Européenne De Sexologie Et De Santé Sexuelle, 23*(2), e31–e34. https://doi.org/10.1016/j.sexol.2013.10.005. [9].

Bedard, R., Metzger, L., & Williams, B. (2017). Ageing prisoners: An introduction to geriatric health-care challenges in correctional facilities. *International Review of the Red Cross, 98*(903), 917–939. https://doi.org/10.1017/S1816383117000364

*Blanchard, R., & Barbaree, H. E. (2005). The strength of sexual arousal as a function of the age of the sex offender: Comparisons among pedophiles, hebephiles, and teleiophiles. *Sexual Abuse: Journal of Research and Treatment, 17*(4), 441–456. https://doi.org/10.1177/107906320501700407. [10].

*Blatier, C., Sellon, C., Gimenez, C., & Paulicand, M. (2016). The assessment of incarcerated sexual delinquents' risk of recidivism. *European Review of Applied Psychology / Revue Européenne De Psychologie Appliquée, 66*(4), 189–198. https://doi.org/10.1016/j.erap.2012.03.001. [11].

*Bourke, P., Ward, T., & Rose, C. (2012). Expertise and sexual offending: A preliminary empirical model. *Journal of Interpersonal Violence, 27*(12), 2391–2414. https://doi.org/10.1177/0886260511433513. [12].

*Bows, H., & Westmarland, N. (2016). Older sex offenders- Managing risk in the community from a policing perspective. *Policing and Society 28*(1), 62–74. https://doi.org/10.1080/10439463.2016.1138476. [13].

*Broadhurst, R., & Loh, N. (2003). The probabilities of sex offender re-arrest. *Criminal Behaviour & Mental Health, 13*(2), 121. https://doi.org/10.1002/cbm.535. [14].

*Brouillette-Alarie, S., & Proulx, J. (2013). Predictive validity of the static-99R and its dimensions. *Journal of Sexual Aggression, 19*(3), 311–328. https://doi.org/10.1080/13552600.2012.747630. [15].

*Browne, K. D., Hines, M., & Tully, R. J. (2018). The differences between sex offenders who victimise older women and sex offenders who offend against children. *Aging & Mental Health, 22*(1), 11–18. https://doi.org/10.1080/13607863.2016.1202892. [16].

Bureau of Justice Statistics. (2016). *Aging of the State Prison Population, 1993–2013*. US Department of Justice. Retrieved from www.bjs.gov/content/pub/pdf/aspp9313_Sum.pdf

*Calkins Mercado, C., Alvarez, S., & Levenson, J. (2008). The impact of specialized sex offender legislation on community re-entry. *Sexual Abuse: A Journal of Research and Treatment, 20*(2), 188–205. https://doi.org/10.1177/1079063208317540. [17].

*Cann, J., Friendship, C., & Gozna, L. (2007). Assessing crossover in a sample of sexual offenders with multiple victims. *Legal and Criminological Psychology, 12*(1), 149–163. https://doi.org/10.1348/135532506X112439. [18].

Carabellese, F., Candelli, C., Vinci, F., Tamma, M., & Catanesi, R. (2012). Elderly sexual offenders: Two unusual cases elderly sexual offenders: Two unusual cases. *Journal of Forensic Sciences (Wiley-Blackwell), 57*(5), 1381–1383. https://doi.org/10.1111/j.1556-4029.2012.02129.x. [19].

*Castonguay, L. G., Proulx, J., Aubut, J., McKibben, A., & Campbell, M. (1993). Sexual preference assessment of sexual aggressors: Predictors of penile response magnitude. *Archives of Sexual Behavior, 22*(4), 325–334. https://doi.org/10.1007/BF01542121. [20].

Chua, J., Cheung, G., Hatters Friedman, S., & Taylor, S. (2018). What are the characteristics of first time older sexual offenders? *International Psychogeriatrics, 30*(5), 647–662. https://doi.org/10.1017/S1041610217002186

Ciardha, C., & Ward, T. (2013). Theories of cognitive distortions in sexual offending: What the current research tells us. *Trauma, Violence & Abuse, 14*(1), 5–21. https://doi.org/10.1177/1524838012467856

*Clark, C., & Mezey, G. (1997). Elderly sex offenders against children: A descriptive study of child sex abusers over the age of 65. *Journal of Forensic Psychiatry, 8*(2), 357–369. https://doi.org/10.1080/09585189708412017. [21].

*Cohen, L. J., Frenda, S., Mojtabai, R., Katsavdakis, K., & Galynker, I. (2007). Comparison of sexual offenders against children with sexual offenders against adolescents and adults: Data from the New York state sex offender registry. *Journal of Psychiatric Practice, 13*(6), 373–384. https://doi.org/10.1097/01.pra.0000300123.83945.76. [22].

Combalbert, N., Pennequin, V., Ferrand, C., Armand, M., Anselme, M., & Geffray, B. (2018). Cognitive impairment, self-perceived health and quality of life of older prisoners. *Criminal Behaviour and Mental Health, 28*, 36–49. https://doi.org/10.1002/cbm.2023

*Coxe, R., & Holmes, W. (2009). A comparative study of two groups of sex offenders identified as high and low risk on the static-99. *Journal of Child Sexual Abuse, 18*(2), 137–153. https://doi.org/10.1080/10538710902743925. [23].

*Craig, L. A. (2011). The effect of age on sexual and violent reconviction. International Journal of Offender Therapy and Comparative Criminology, 55(1), 75–97. https://doi.org/10.1177/0306624X09353290. [24].

*Curtice, M., Parker, J., Wismayer, F. S., & Tomison, A. (2003). The elderly offender: An 11-year survey of referrals to a regional forensic psychiatric service. *Journal of Forensic Psychiatry & Psychology, 14*(2), 253–265. https://doi.org/10.1080/1478994031000077989. [25].

Dehlendorf, C. E., Wolfe, S. M. (1998). Physicians disciplined for sex-related offenses: JAMA Journal of the American Medical Association, 279*(23), 1883–1888. https://doi.org/10.1001/jama.279.23.1883. [26].

*Dickey, R., Nussbaum, D., Chevolleau, K., & Davidson, H. (2002). Age as a differential characteristic of rapists, pedophiles, and sexual sadists. *Journal of Sex & Marital Therapy, 28*(3), 211–218. https://doi.org/10.1080/009262302760328253. [27].

*Doyle, D. J., Ogloff, J., & Thomas, S. (2011). Designated as dangerous: Characteristics of sex offenders subject to post-sentence orders in Australia. *Australian Psychologist, 46*(1), 41–48. https://doi.org/10.1111/j.1742-9544.2010.00006.x. [28].

*Eher, R., Schilling, F., Hansmann, B., Pumberger, T., Nitschke, J., Habermeyer, E., & Mokros, A. (2016). Sadism and violent reoffending in sexual offenders. *Sexual Abuse: Journal of Research and Treatment, 28*(1), 46–72. https://doi.org/10.1177/1079063214566715. [29].

*English, K., Jones, L., Patrick, D., & Pasini-Hill, D. (2003). Sexual offender containment: Use of the postconviction polygraph. *Annals of the New York Academy of Sciences, 989*, 411–427. https://doi.org/10.1111/j.1749-6632.2003.tb07322.x. [30], discussion 441–445.

Farrington, D. (1986). Age and crime. *Crime and Justice, 7*, 189–250.

Fazel, S., Hope, T., O'Donnell, I., & Jacoby, R. (2001b). Hidden psychiatric morbidity among elderly prisoners. *British Journal of Psychiatry, 179*, 535–539. https://doi.org/10.1192/bjp.179.6.535

*Fazel, S., Hope, T., O'Donnell, I., & Jacoby, R. (2002). Psychiatric, demographic and personality characteristics of elderly sex offenders. *Psychological Medicine*, *32*(2), 219–226. https://doi.org/10.1017/S0033291701005153. [32].

Fazel, S., Hope, T., O'Donnell, I., Piper, M., & Jacoby, R. (2001a). Health of elderly male prisoners: Worse than the general population, worse than younger prisoners. *Age and Ageing, 30*, 403–407. https://doi.org/10.1093/ageing/30.5.403

*Fazel, S., O'Donnell, I., Hope, T., Gulati, G., & Jacoby, R. (2007). Frontal lobes and older sex offenders: A preliminary investigation. *International Journal of Geriatric Psychiatry, 22*(1), 87–89. https://doi.org/10.1002/gps.1648. [31].

*Fazel, S., Sjöstedt, G., Långström, N., & Grann, M. (2006). Risk factors for criminal recidivism in older sexual offenders. *Sexual Abuse: Journal of Research and Treatment, 18*(2), 159–167. https://doi.org/10.1177/107906320601800204. [33].

*Felson, R., & Cundiff, P. (2014). Sexual assault as a crime against young people. *Archives of Sexual Behavior, 43*(2), 273–284. https://doi.org/10.1007/s10508-013-0127-8. [34].

*Firestone, P., Bradford, J. M., Greenberg, D. M., & Serran, G. A. (2000). The relationship of deviant sexual arousal and psychopathy in incest offenders, extrafamilial child molesters, and rapists. *Journal of the American Academy of Psychiatry and the Law, 28*(3), 303–308. [35].

*Freedman, D. B. (2012). Determining the long-term risks of recidivism and registration failures among sexual offenders'. *Federal Probation, 76*(1), 14–18. [36].

*Freeman, N. J. (2007). Predictors of rearrest for rapists and child molesters on probation. *Criminal Justice and Behavior, 34*(6), 752–768. https://doi.org/10.1177/0093854806298280. [37].

*Fruehwald, S., Eher, R., Frottier, P., Aigner, M., Gutierrez, K., & Dwyer, S. M. (1998). The relevance of self-concepts discriminating in long-term incarcerated sex offenders. *Journal of Behavior Therapy and Experimental Psychiatry, 29*(4), 267–278. https://doi.org/10.1016/S0005-7916(98)00026-3. [38].

*Garombo, M. F., Salvadori, S., Contarino, A., Castellino, N., Molinaro, S., Garofano, P., Molo, M.T., Veglia, F., & Rosso, C. (2016). Factorial analysis of risk matrix 2000 on an Italian sample of sexual offenders. *Journal of Sexual Aggression, 22*(2), 137–146. https://doi.org/10.1080/13552600.2015.1047908. [39].

*Hanson, R. K. (2002). Recidivism and age: Follow-up data from 4673 sexual offenders. *Journal of Interpersonal Violence, 17*(10), 1046. [41].

*Hanson, R. K. (2006). Does static-99 predict recidivism among older sexual offenders? *Sexual Abuse: Journal of Research and Treatment, 18*(4), 343–355. https://doi.org/10.1177/107906320601800403. [42].

*Hanson, R. K., & Bussière, M. T. (1998). Predicting relapse: A meta-analysis of sexual offender recidivism studies. *Journal of Consulting and Clinical Psychology, 66*(2), 348–362. https://doi.org/10.1037/0022-006X.66.2.348. [40].

*Hanson, R. K., Harris, A. J. R., Letourneau, E., Helmus, L. M., & Thornton, D. (2018). Reductions in risk based on time offense free in the community: Once a sexual offender, not always a sexual offender. *Psychology, Public Policy, and Law* 24, 48. https://doi.org/10.1037/law0000135. [43].

*Harkins, L., Beech, A. R., & Thornton, D. (2013). The influence of risk and psychopathy on the therapeutic climate in sex offender treatment. *Sexual Abuse: A Journal of Research & Treatment, 25*(2), 103–122. https://doi.org/10.1177/1079063212443384. [44].

*Harris, D. A. (2012). Age and type of onset of offending: Results from a sample of male sexual offenders referred for civil commitment. International Journal of Offender Therapy and Comparative Criminology, 57(10), 1226–1247. https://doi.org/10.1177/0306624X12448649. [45].

*Harris, D. A. (2016). A descriptive model of desistance from sexual offending. International Journal of Offender Therapy & Comparative Criminology, 60(15), 1717–1737. https://doi.org/10.1177/0306624X16668176. [46].

*Harris, G.T., & Rice, M.E. (2007). Characterizing the value of actuarial violence risk assessments. *Criminal Justice and Behavior, 34*(12), 1638–1658. https://doi.org/10.1177/0093854807307029. [47].

*Harry, B., Pierson, T. R., & Kuznetsov, A. (1993). Correlates of sex offender and offense traits by victim age. *Journal of Forensic Sciences, 38*(5), 1068–1074. https://doi.org/10.1520/JFS13509J. [48].

*Helmus, L., & Thornton, D. (2016). The MATS-1 risk assessment scale: Summary of methodological concerns and an empirical validation. *Sexual Abuse: Journal of Research and Treatment, 28*(3), 160–186. https://doi.org/10.1177/1079063214529801. [49].

*Helmus, L., Thornton, D., Hanson, R. K., & Babchishin, K. M. (2012). Improving the predictive accuracy of static-99 and static-2002 with older sex offenders: Revised age weights. *Sexual Abuse: Journal of Research and Treatment, 24*(1), 64–101. https://doi.org/10.1177/1079063211409951. [50].

Hong, Q. N., Pluye, P., Fabregues, S., Bartlett, G., Boardman, F., Cargo, M., & O'Cathain, A. (2018). *Mixed methods appraisal tool (MMAT), version 2018*. IC Canadian Intellectual Property Office, Industry Canada.

House of Commons Justice Committee. (2013). *Older prisoners: Fifth report of session 2013–14*. Online. Accessed November 07, 2013, from www.publications.parliament.uk/pa/cm201314/cmselect/cmjust/89/89.pdf

Howse, K. (2003). *Growing old in prison: A scoping study on older prisoners*. Centre for Policy on Ageing and Prison Reform Trust.

*Janka, C., Gallasch-Nemitz, F., Biedermann, J., & Dahle, K. (2012). The significance of offending behavior for predicting sexual recidivism among sex offenders of various age groups. *International Journal of Law & Psychiatry, 35*(3), 159–164. https://doi.org/10.1016/j.ijlp.2012.02.002. [51].

*Jeary, K. (2005). Sexual abuse and sexual offending against elderly people: A focus on perpetrators and victims. *Journal of Forensic Psychiatry & Psychology, 16*(2), 328–343. https://doi.org/10.1080/14789940500096115. [52].

*Langevin, R. (2006). Acceptance and completion of treatment among sex offenders. International Journal of Offender Therapy and Comparative Criminology, 50(4), 402–417. https://doi.org/10.1177/0306624X06286870. [56].

*Langevin, R., & Curnoe, S. (2008). Assessing neuropsychological impairment among sex offenders and paraphilics. *Journal of Forensic Psychology Practice, 8*(2), 150–173. https://doi.org/10.1080/15228930801963960. [53].

*Langevin, R., & Curnoe, S. (2011). Psychopathy, ADHD, and brain dysfunction as predictors of lifetime recidivism among sex offenders. International Journal of Offender Therapy & Comparative Criminology, 55(1), 5–26. https://doi.org/10.1177/0306624X09360968. [54].

*Langevin, R., & Curnoe, S. (2012). Lifetime criminal history of sex offenders seen for psychological assessment in five decades. International Journal of Offender Therapy & Comparative Criminology, 56(7), 997–1021. https://doi.org/10.1177/0306624X11420084. [55].

*Levenson, J. S., Sandler, J. C., & Freeman, N. J. (2012). Failure-to-register laws and public safety: An examination of risk factors and sex offense recidivism. *Law and Human Behavior, 36*(6), 555–565. https://doi.org/10.1037/b0000002. [57].

*Looman, J., & Abracen, J. (2010). Comparison of measures of risk for recidivism in sexual offenders. *Journal of Interpersonal Violence, 25*(5), 791–807. https://doi.org/10.1177/0886260509336961. [58].

*Lussier, P., Deslauriers-Varin, N., & Râtel, T. (2010). A descriptive profile of high-risk sex offenders under intensive supervision in the province of British Columbia, Canada. International Journal of Offender Therapy & Comparative Criminology, 54(1), 71–91. https://doi.org/10.1177/0306624X08323236. [62].

Lussier, P., Gress, C., Deslauriers-Varin, N., & Amirault, J. (2014). Community risk management of high-risk sex offenders in Canada: Findings from a quasi-experimental study: JQ: Justice Quarterly, 31*(2), 287–314. https://doi.org/10.1080/07418825.2011.649694. [63].

Lussier, P., & Healey, J. (2009). Rediscovering quetelet, again: The "Aging" offender and the prediction of reoffending in a sample of adult sex offenders: JQ: Justice Quarterly, 26*(4), 827–856. https://doi.org/10.1080/07418820802593360. [59].

*Lussier, P., & McCuish, E. (2016). Desistance from crime without reintegration. International Journal of Offender Therapy & Comparative Criminology, 60(15), 1791–1812. https://doi.org/10.1177/0306624X16668179. [60].

*Lussier, P., Proulx, J., & Leblanc, M. (2005). Criminal propensity, deviant sexual interests and criminal activity of sexual aggressors against women: A comparison of explanatory models. *Criminology, 43*(1), 249–281. https://doi.org/10.1111/j.0011-1348.2005.00008.x. [61].

*Malcolm, P. B., Andrews, D. A., & Quinsey, V. L. (1993). Discriminant and predictive validity of phallometrically measured sexual age and gender preference. *Journal of Interpersonal Violence, 8*(4), 486–501. https://doi.org/10.1177/088626093008004004. [64].

*Mancini, C., Reckdenwald, A., Beauregard, E., & Levenson, J. S. (2014). Sex industry exposure over the life course on the onset and frequency of sex offending. *Journal of Criminal Justice, 42*(6), 507–516. https://doi.org/10.1016/j.jcrimjus.2014.09.002. [65].

*Mann, N. (2012). Ageing child sex offenders in prison: Denial, manipulation and community. *Howard Journal of Criminal Justice, 51*(4), 345–358. https://doi.org/10.1111/j.1468-2311.2012.00705.x. [66].

*Marshall, L. E. (2010). *Aging and sexual offending: An examination of older sexual offenders.* (2011-99,200-238). Retrieved from http://search.ebscohost.com/login.aspx?direct=true&db=psyh&AN=2011-99200-238&site=ehost-live. [67]

*Marshall, W. L., Barbaree, H. E., & Eccles, A. (1991). Early onset and deviant sexuality in child molesters. *Journal of Interpersonal Violence, 6*(3), 323–335. https://doi.org/10.1177/088626091006003005. [68].

*Mathesius, J., & Lussier, P. (2014). The successful onset of sex offending: Determining the correlates of actual and official onset of sex offending. *Journal of Criminal Justice, 42*(2), 134–144. https://doi.org/10.1016/j.jcrimjus.2013.09.004. [69].

*Mattek, R., & Hanson, R. K. (2018). Committed as a violent sexual predator in his tenth decade: A case study. *Archives of Sexual Behavior, 47*(2), 543–550. https://doi.org/10.1007/s10508-017-1041-2. [70]

*McKillop, N., Brown, S., Smallbone, S., & Pritchard, K. (2015). Similarities and differences in adolescence-onset versus adulthood-onset sexual abuse incidents. *Child Abuse & Neglect, 46*, 37–46. https://doi.org/10.1016/j.chiabu.2015.02.014. [71].

Morton, J. (1992). *An administrative overview of the older inmate*. U.S. Department of Justice, National Institute of Corrections.

*Navarro, J. N., & Jasinski, J. L. (2015). Demographic and motivation differences among online sex offenders by type of offense: An exploration of routine activities theories. *Journal of Child Sexual Abuse, 24*(7), 753–771. https://doi.org/10.1080/10538712.2015.1077363. [72].

*Nicholaichuk, T. P., Olver, M. E., Gu, D., & Wong, S. C. P. (2014). Age, actuarial risk, and long-term recidivism in a national sample of sex offenders. *Sexual Abuse: Journal of Research and Treatment, 26*(5), 406–428. https://doi.org/10.1177/1079063213492340. [73].

*Nilsson, T., Carlstedt, A., Baudin, C., Jakobsson, C., Forsman, A., & Anckarsäter, H. (2014). Intra- and extra-familial child sexual abusers and recidivism in Sweden: A 10- to 15-year follow-up study. *Journal of Forensic Psychiatry & Psychology, 25*(3), 341–361. https://doi.org/10.1080/14789949.2014.911945. [74].

*Olver, M. E., Nicholaichuk, T. P., Gu, D., & Wong, S. C. P. (2012). Sex offender treatment outcome, actuarial risk, and the aging sex offender in Canadian corrections: A long-term follow-up. *Sexual Abuse: Journal of Research and Treatment, 25*(4), 396–422. https://doi.org/10.1177/1079063212464399. [75].

Penal Reform International. (2015). *Alternatives to the death penalty information pack*. Penal Reform International.
Poortinga, E., Lemmen, C., & Majeske, K. (2007). A comparison of criminal sexual conduct defendants based on victim age. *Journal of Forensic Sciences, 52*(6), 1372–1375. https://doi.org/10.1111/j.1556-4029.2007.00571.x. [76].
*Prentky, R. A., & Lee, A. F. S. (2007). Effect of age-at-release on long term sexual re-offense rates in civilly committed sexual offenders. *Sexual Abuse: Journal of Research and Treatment, 19*(1), 43–59. https://doi.org/10.1177/107906320701900105. [77].
*Proulx, J., Pellerin, B., Paradis, Y., McKibben, A., Aubut, J., & Ouimet, M. (1997). Static and dynamic predictors of recidivism in sexual aggressors. *Sexual Abuse: Journal of Research and Treatment, 9*(1), 7–27. https://doi.org/10.1007/BF02674889. [78].
*Rayel, M. G. (2000). Elderly sexual offenders admitted to a maximum-security forensic hospital. *Journal of Forensic Sciences, 45*(6), 1190–1192. [79].
*Redondo, S., Luque, E., Navarro, J. C., & Martínez, M. (2007). An empirical study of characteristics and reoffence-risk factors in a sample of imprisoned sex offenders. *Psychology in Spain, 11*(1), 95–105. [80].
*Rettenberger, M., Briken, P., Turner, D., & Eher, R. (2015). Sexual offender recidivism among a population-based prison sample. International Journal of Offender Therapy & Comparative Criminology, 59(4), 424–444. https://doi.org/10.1177/0306624X13516732. [82].
*Rettenberger, M., Haubner-Maclean, T., & Eher, R. (2013). The contribution of age to the static-99 risk assessment in a population-based prison sample of sexual offenders. *Criminal Justice and Behavior, 40*(12), 1413–1433. https://doi.org/10.1177/0093854813492518. [81].
*Rodriguez, M., Boyce, P., & Hodges, J. (2017). A neuropsychological study of older adult first-time sex offenders. *Neurocase (Psychology Press), 23*(2), 154–161. https://doi.org/10.1080/13554794.2017.1334802. [83].
*Romano, E., & De Luca, R. V. (1997). Exploring the relationship between childhood sexual abuse and adult sexual perpetration. *Journal of Family Violence, 12*(1), 85–98. https://doi.org/10.1023/A:1021950017920. [84].
*Ryan, J., Wilson, N., Kilgour, G., & Reynolds, N. (2014). Balancing efficiency and accuracy: Guidelines for the psychological assessment of extended supervision orders for child sex offenders in New Zealand. *Psychiatry, Psychology and Law, 21*(1), 139–157. https://doi.org/10.1080/13218719.2013.793154. [86].
Seto, M. C. (2019). The Motivation-Facilitation model of sexual offending. *Sexual Abuse, 31*(1), 3–24. https://doi.org/10.1177/1079063217720919
*Seto, M. C., & Eke, A. W. (2015). Predicting recidivism among adult male child pornography offenders: Development of the child pornography offender risk tool (CPORT). *Law and Human Behavior, 39*(4), 416–429. https://doi.org/10.1037/lhb0000128. [87].
Sjöstedt, G., & Långström, N. (2001). Actuarial assessment of sex offender recidivism risk: A cross-validation of the RRASOR and the static-99 in Sweden. *Law and Human Behavior, 25*(6), 629–645. https://doi.org/10.1023/A:1012758307983. [88].
*Skelton, A., & Vess, J. (2008). Risk of sexual recidivism as a function of age and actuarial risk. *Journal of Sexual Aggression, 14*(3), 199–209. https://doi.org/10.1080/13552600802267098. [89].
Smallbone, S. W., Marshall, W. L., & Wortley, R. (2008). Explaining child sexual abuse: A new integrated theory. In S. W. Smallbone, W. L. Marshall, & R. Wortley (Eds.), *Preventing child sexual abuse: Evidence, policy and practice* (pp. 21–45). Willan Press. [90].
*Smallbone, S. W., & Wortley, R. K. (2004). Onset, persistence, and versatility of offending among adult males convicted of sexual offenses against children. *Sexual Abuse: Journal of Research and Treatment, 16*(4), 285–298. https://doi.org/10.1177/107906320401600403. [91].
*Stephens, S., Cantor, J. M., Goodwill, A. M., & Seto, M. C. (2017). Multiple indicators of sexual interest in prepubescent or pubescent children as predictors of sexual recidivism. *Journal of Consulting & Clinical Psychology, 85*(6), 585–595. https://doi.org/10.1037/ccp0000194. [92].

*Sullivan, J., & Beech, A. (2004). A comparative study of demographic data relating to intra- and extra-familial child sexual abusers and professional perpetrators. *Journal of Sexual Aggression, 10*(1), 39–50. https://doi.org/10.1080/13552600410001667788. [93].

*Swinburne Romine, R. E., Miner, M. H., Poulin, D., Dwyer, S. M., & Berg, D. (2012). Predicting reoffense for community-based sexual offenders: An analysis of 30 years of data. Sexual Abuse: A Journal of Research & Treatment, 24(5), 501–514. https://doi.org/10.1177/1079063212446514. [85].

Szumski, F., Bartels, R., Beech, A. R., & Fisher, D. (2018). Distorted cognition related to male sexual offending: The multi-mechanism theory of cognitive distortions (MMT-CD). *Aggression and Violent Behavior, 39*, 139–151. https://doi.org/10.1016/j.avb.2018.02.001

*Thornton, D. (2006). Age and sexual recidivism: A variable connection. *Sexual Abuse: Journal of Research and Treatment, 18*(2), 123–135. https://doi.org/10.1177/107906320601800202. [94].

*Tsagaris, G. S., Bach, J. E., & Cimino, C. (2017). The characteristics of federal offenders sentenced for sexual exploitation of children within a large urban metropolitan region. *Journal of Sexual Aggression, 23*(2), 181–194. https://doi.org/10.1080/13552600.2017.1307463. [95].

Uzoaba, J. (1998). *Managing older offenders: Where do we stand?* Correctional Services of Canada.

*van Gijn-Grosvenor, E. L., & Lamb, M. E. (2016). Behavioural differences between online sexual groomers approaching boys and girls. *Journal of Child Sexual Abuse, 25*(5), 577–596. https://doi.org/10.1080/10538712.2016.1189473. [96].

*Wakeling, H. C., Freemantle, N., Beech, A. R., & Elliott, I. A. (2011). Identifying predictors of recidivism in a large sample of United Kingdom sexual offenders: A prognostic model. *Psychological Services, 8*(4), 307–318. https://doi.org/10.1037/a0025516. [97].

Walmsley, R. (2016). *World prison population list*. International Centre for Prison Studies.

Ward, T., & Beech, A. R. (2016). The integrated theory of sexual offending-revised. In D. P. Boer (Ed.), *Theories, assessment, and treatment of sexual offending* (pp. 123–137). John Wiley & Sons.

Williams, B. A., Goodwin, J. S., Baillargeon, J., Ahalt, C., & Walter, L. C. (2012). Addressing the aging crisis in U.S. criminal justice healthcare. *Journal of the American Geriatrics Society, 60*, 1150–1156. https://doi.org/10.1111/j.1532-5415.2012.03962.x

*Willis, G. M., & Ward, T. (2011). Striving for a good life: The good lives model applied to released child molesters. *Journal of Sexual Aggression, 17*(3), 290–303. https://doi.org/10.1080/13552600.2010.505349. [98].

*Woodworth, M., Freimuth, T., Hutton, E. L., Carpenter, T., Agar, A. D., & Logan, M. (2013). High-risk sexual offenders: An examination of sexual fantasy, sexual paraphilia, psychopathy, and offence characteristics. *International Journal of Law & Psychiatry, 36*(2), 144–156. https://doi.org/10.1016/j.ijlp.2013.01.007. [99].

*Wortley, R., & Smallbone, S. (2014). A criminal careers typology of child sexual abusers. *Sexual Abuse: Journal of Research and Treatment, 26*(6), 569–585. https://doi.org/10.1177/1079063213503689. [100].

Chapter 21
Special Considerations: Child Sexual Abuse by Catholic Clergy

Natalie A. Ross, Elizabeth M. Bryant, and Anthony D. Perillo

21.1 Introduction

In 2002, *The Boston Globe* released a series of news stories detailing sexual abuse of children perpetrated by clergy within the Catholic Church ("Church" is used in the remainder of this chapter to denote the Catholic Church) and ways the Church protected the clergy responsible for the abuse (see Boston Globe, 2002). The news led to both public outcry and loss of trust in the Church. Within 1 year, a survey of Church parishioners revealed that 70% believed sexual abuse was more prevalent in the Church than most people would estimate, 84% believed the church responded inappropriately to instances of abuse, and 81% believed the church actively tried to cover-up the abuse and deceive parishioners (Wells, 2003).

In response to criticisms within and outside the Church, the United States Conference of Catholic Bishops (USCCB) created a charter declaring the Church's intent to investigate the nature and scope of sexual abuse within the Church. The USCCB and John Jay College of Criminal Justice collaborated on this investigation through extensive analysis of documented allegations of sexual abuse across dioceses over the preceding five decades (John Jay College, 2004). The *Nature and Scope Study* (John Jay College, 2004) revealed that from 1950 to 2002, approximately 4% of clergy—or 4392 active clergy over that time—had documented and substantiated allegations of sexually abusing children. These documented allegations included 10,667 documented victims and over 3000 additional

N. A. Ross (✉) · E. M. Bryant
Psychology Department, Indiana University of Pennsylvania, Indiana, PA, USA
e-mail: nbkbc@iup.edu

A. D. Perillo
Department of Psychiatry and Behavioral Sciences, University of New Mexico Health Sciences Center, Albuquerque, NM, USA

R. J. Tully et al. (eds.), *Best Practices in Sexual Offender Assessment and Management*, Dangerous Behavior in Clinical and Forensic Psychology,
https://doi.org/10.1007/978-3-031-83135-5_21

victims not formally documented (i.e., additional victims noted in a documented victim's allegations).

Although the John Jay *Nature and Scope Study* focused on North American dioceses, sexual abuse of children by clergy was soon observed to be a worldwide issue. Reports of abuse by clergy were documented in countries across different regions and cultures. Data from a similar investigation in Germany revealed parallel rates of documented allegations in North America: 4.4% between the years of 1946 and 2014, with similar victim characteristics to those observed within the United States (Dressing et al., 2019). These findings highlighted sexual abuse by clergy as both widespread and pervasive over time.

This chapter provides an overview of our current understanding of sexual abuse by clergy and directions for addressing abuse within the Church. It should be noted that although *sexual misconduct* issues (sexual behavior by clergy that is not necessarily illegal but considered unethical or otherwise morally problematic, such as consensual sex with an adult parishioner) are noted within the Church and relevant to clinical practice with clergy, this chapter focuses specifically on sexual abuse of children by Catholic clergy. First, literature on identified trends of clergy sexual abuse (including trends about victims, abuse incidents, and clergy themselves) and how these trends might explain sexual abuse within the Church is reviewed. Additionally, findings on clinical assessment with sexually abusive clergy are provided, including the application of various psychological and sexual risk assessment instruments. Treatment with sexually abusive clergy is then addressed, including the (limited) data on treatment efforts and how current sexual offense treatment models might apply to sexually abusive clergy. The chapter concludes with a summary of the current research on sexual abuse in the Church and the prospects of using this information to address and reduce sexual abuse by Catholic clergy.

21.2 Trends in Clergy Sexual Abuse

This section overviews different trends identified (or not identified) in the abuse patterns of sexually abusive clergy. Patterns of clergy sexual abuse against children of different ages and genders, as well as implications of these patterns are covered first. Next, detailed trends that inform on the potential roles of power and status, grooming, and celibacy in clergy sexual abuse are provided. Lastly, the implications of these trends and how they may be understood within the context of the assessment and treatment of sexually abusive clergy are reviewed.

21.2.1 Victim Age

Available information suggests the majority of clergy sexual abuse victims tend to be either in the midst of puberty or post-pubescent adolescents. The *Nature and Scope Study* (John Jay College, 2004) found that half of the victims (50.9%) were between ages 11 and 14, with this rate relatively stable across the five decades analyzed. The next common age range consisted of adolescents between the ages of 15 and 17 (27.3%), followed by children between the ages of 8 and 10 (16%). Relatively few victims were age seven or younger (6%). Available data from the Anglican Church of Australia (from 1990 to 2008) reveal similar overall trends: most victims (51%) were younger than 14, but only 11% were younger than 10 years old (Parkinson et al., 2012).

Trends highlighting the age of child victims, however, do not directly inform on rates of pedophilia among clergy who sexually abused children. Age preferences are considered to fall on a continuum. Pedophilia refers to individuals who experience attraction/urges/fantasies toward prepubescent children and is distinct from ephebophilia, which includes attraction/urges/fantasies toward postpubescent adolescents still going through sexual maturation (Seto, 2017). Hebephilia, which bridges the gap between pedophilia and ephebophilia, refers to attraction/urges/fantasies toward pubescent children in the midst of puberty (Seto, 2017). Because sexual maturation is a slow, gradual process, the lines distinguishing pedophilia from hebephilia from ephebophilia can blur and be difficult to distinguish from one another.

Furthermore, committing acts of sexual abuse against an adolescent or child is not directly indicative of sexual preference. The prevalence of adolescent victims—being the majority of victims of clergy sexual abuse— conflicts with the technical perception of pedophilia being a prominent factor in sexual abuse by clergy. In fact, Tallon and Terry (2008) analyzed clergy abuse patterns and contended, based exclusively on patterns of victim age, only 2.2% of abusive clergy did so exclusively against prepubescent children, and only 10.8% did so exclusively against postpubescent adolescents.

Some evidence suggests exposure to children might be proactively sought by some who sexually abused children in the context of their profession. Calkins et al. (2015), for example, found that clergy who had sexually abused children were more likely to specifically seek opportunities to work with children, adolescents, and the families of children and adolescents. Motivations for seeking these opportunities were not explicitly explored.

Additional information suggests children sexually abused by clergy are more victims of opportunity than victims of preference. In general, the majority of people who have sexually abused children in the context of their employment (including clergy) do not report being exclusively attracted to children (e.g., a 24% rate reported by Sullivan & Beech, 2004). Within the Church, clergy who abused ten or more children showed no observable pattern of preference toward age or gender (Tallon & Terry, 2008), often having victims of different ages. The John Jay College (2004) *Nature and Scope Study* also highlights the variable ages of clergy victims that line up more with opportunity and unsupervised access than targeted attraction to children. Overall, the ages of children abused by clergy have appeared to be more motivated by opportunity and unsupervised access (e.g., children participating in the altar service) than by targeted attraction to a particular age group.

21.2.2 Victim Gender and Issues of Preference Vs. Opportunity

Contrary to trends among sexual abuse in the community, the John Jay College (2004) *Nature and Scope Study* noted victims of sexual abuse by clergy have been predominantly boys (81%). Follow-up data from Australia revealed similar patterns; 87% of victims of clergy sexual abuse were boys (Parkinson et al., 2012). Direct comparisons with community samples of people who sexually abuse have indeed found notably higher rates of male victims for clergy who commit acts of sexual abuse. Haywood et al. (1996a) found the rates of male victims to be 77% for clergy and 38–50% for non-clergy. Perillo et al. (2017) noted 79% of the clergy in their sample had at least one male victim, whereas only 17% of their community sample did.

These higher rates of sexual abuse of boys among clergy might have fueled another common misconception of the "predatory homosexual priest" based on assumptions that victim characteristics implied victims of preference (e.g., assuming without a sexual preference towards boys, there would be equal rates of victimization for both male and female children in the Church). Other broad studies with higher representation of clergy in the sample, however, have found different trends. Sullivan and Beech (2004) found that within a sample of professionals who sexually abused children in the context of their work, the rate of those who exclusively abused boys (73%) did not match the rate of endorsing sexual interest in boys (56%). If the abuse of males were due to preference alone, then the proportion of boys who were sexually abused would be expected to better align with the proportion of attraction toward male children. An alternative explanation would be if victims of different genders were chosen more as a product of opportunity because of increased unsupervised access rather than preference.

Indeed, when examining victim gender trends in clergy sexual abuse throughout the decades, notable patterns emerge. The *Causes and Contexts Study* (John Jay College, 2006) revealed two relative peaks in the victimization of girls: the 1950s to 1960s and the 1990s to early 2000s. When considering this pattern, it is important to note that during the 1950s and 1960s clergy spent increased time in the homes of their parishioners, which provided them with access to all children. The peak victimization during this time period was girls, which suggests that when provided with increased opportunity to abuse children of any gender, clergy abuse of girls, relative to boys, substantially increased.

By the 1970s it became less common for clergy to spend time in the homes of their parishioners, so clergy most commonly had unsupervised time with children through professional roles like the altar service. During this time, only boys were allowed to be altar servers. Clergy therefore had more unsupervised time with boys through the altar service, and this period coincides with another relative increase in male victimization. In 1994, girls were allowed to join the altar service. The second peak in female victimization– the 1990s to 2000s– coincides with girls receiving the opportunity to join the altar service and, in turn, unsupervised time with clergy (John Jay College, 2006).

Clergy frequently interacted with male children during church activities, especially prior to 1994, but during this timeframe clergy had far fewer naturally occurring times to interact with unsupervised female children. Clergy, therefore, would have more ample opportunities to abuse male children within the Church compared to the opportunity to abuse female children, which would need to be purposeful and involve interaction outside of church activities. In both of these situations, however, clergy would have increased unsupervised time with potential victims. Overall, a pattern emerges where the relative percentage of boys as victims of clergy sexual abuse goes down as clergy had more unsupervised access with children of any gender. Indeed, a deeper analysis of a 50-year period of clergy abuse data from the John Jay College *Nature and Scope Study* (2004) noted the evidence suggested victim gender was much better explained by environmental factors and opportunity, with no evidence of a distinct targeting of boys across clergy (Holt & Massey, 2013).

When examining abuse patterns as a whole, clergy sexual abuse appears to be more explained by situational factors and opportunity as opposed to specific victim preferences or targets. Examining data from the *Nature and Scope Study* (John Jay College, 2004), Terry (2008a) argues that based on the combination of location of abuse, the trend of clergy being older at the time of their first offense, low rates of chronic offending/paraphilic behaviors, and targeting of adolescent boys— the victims to whom clergy would have the most access— instances of clergy sexual abuse appear primarily situational. Even among clergy with more-chronic abuse patterns, situational trends are more apparent than targeting specific types of victims. Clergy who sexually abused multiple children were more likely to abuse children within a private setting (Colombino & Mercado, 2009), with the majority of offenses occurring at the clergy's residence, the child's residence, or within religious facilities (Firestone et al., 2009). In addition, police reports reveal that clergy who abused multiple children were more likely to offend against children living in residential homes or group homes (Firestone et al., 2009). Examining these trends, it appears clergy tend to seek victims from vulnerable situations lacking supervision and perpetrate this abuse in a private or isolated location. These trends were supported by Holt and Massey (2013), whose examination of situational factors in sexual abuse incidents by clergy suggested victim gender was better explained by opportunity than deliberate planning.

Although gender preference has not been identified as a driving factor in sexual abuse perpetration by clergy, some differences in abuse incidents for victims of different genders could be possible. Holt and Massey (2013) observed that clergy who sexually abused female children often did so outside the Church; they tended to socialize more with the victim's family and perpetrate abuse within the victim's home. Clergy who sexually abused male children, in contrast, often did so within the Church; they tended to meet and abuse their victims during church-related activities. These trends were not consistent overall with an analysis of abuse trends for clergy with many victims (Mercado et al., 2008). Clergy with a single victim were more likely to abuse girls but also more likely to commit abuse within the Church. Clergy with ten or more victims, however, were more likely to abuse boys but also more likely to commit abuse within the victim's homes.

Substance use might be one particular factor in clergy sexual abuse against children of different genders. When sexually abusing boys, clergy were 150% more likely to be under the influence of drugs or alcohol compared to abusing girls (Holt & Massey, 2013). Substance use was also a factor in the model used to predict clergy who exclusively sexually abused male children (Perillo et al., 2008). Substance use during the commission of sexual abuse can serve many different purposes, including grooming victims, lowering inhibitions of the victim, or lowering inhibitions of the perpetrator. It is thus unclear what these trends might suggest about how to address clergy sexual abuse. Overall, however, these and other trends across abuse incidents suggest that clergy might perpetrate abuse differently based on their victim's gender.

21.2.3 Clergy Power Dynamics and Status

The power that clergy have through their position within the church and their relation to parishioners has been argued to play a role in the proliferation of clergy sexual abuse. One proposed theory draws parallels between clergy sexual abuse and incest between fathers and daughters (Blanchard, 1991) in that both types of sexual abuse involve large age gaps and an inherent power differential between the child and a male paternal figure with authoritative qualities. Another theory applies an abuse of power model, in which clergy who work with children and commit sexual abuse were likely to feel emasculated and powerless prior to abuse (Colton & Vanstone, 1998). Sexual abuse of children in these contexts is argued to be motivated by an attempt to regain power by taking power from those more vulnerable than themselves. In both of these theories, the emphasis of abuse relied on the power differential between the clergy and the children they abused.

After the release of the John Jay College studies (2004, 2006), additional theories explaining clergy sexual abuse were brought into discussion. As opposed to examining sexual abuse primarily through a power lens, these new conceptualizations of clergy incorporated a violation of trust. One such conceptualization compared clergy who sexually abuse children to those who commit white-collar offenses, as both involve a violation of trust within the individual's work role (Piquero et al., 2008). Though power differentials are still considered, the main focus falls upon taking advantage of the trust of others to "successfully" sexually abuse children (i.e., commit abuse without detection or consequence). Clergy are viewed as role models and provided with unsupervised access to children in ways not common in most professions. Clergy who commit acts of sexual abuse can thus be perceived as breaking the trust placed upon them to both protect and care for others (including the very children they abuse).

21.2.4 Grooming by Clergy

Grooming refers to the processes someone engages in to prepare a potential victim, the environment, and/or potential overseeing adults prior to committing sexual abuse (Craven et al., 2006). Grooming methods can include befriending the child or their family, giving the child gifts, and emotional manipulation (e.g., suggesting to the child that the behavior they engaged in was a secret and that it is bad to share secrets). Research has found that men who have sexually abused children through their profession use a variety of grooming behaviors in a variety of settings (Colton & Vanstone, 1998). This extends to sexually abusive clergy, who research suggests often use grooming behaviors within their role as a role model or protector of children. Most commonly, clergy have reportedly groomed their victims with enticements such as offering them access to alcohol or other substances, giving them money or gifts, or inviting them to spend the night at the clergy's residence (Terry, 2008b). Although threats were also sometimes used as a method of grooming, these threats were more likely to have a spiritual or psychological element to them rather than being physical threats.

Previously discussed issues of power and status are relevant to grooming. Data from Canada revealed the vast majority of clergy who had sexually abused children in their sample (90.9%) appeared to have used their power and authority as a member of the clergy as a form of psychological manipulation (Firestone et al., 2009). Befriending children by providing extra attention, gifts, or money were also common grooming behaviors in this sample. Socializing outside their professional context with victims or their families has also been observed in many incidents of clergy sexual abuse (Tallon & Terry, 2008). This socialization does not appear to be an attempt to intimidate children from reporting abuse. On the contrary, Smith et al. (2008) found that clergy's use of socialization with victims' families did not impact rates of reporting abuse. Socialization was instead used as a means to abuse by simultaneously gaining the trust of the child's family members while also providing themselves with additional opportunities to access the child. Socialization as a grooming technique therefore increased the opportunities for clergy to commit sexual abuse.

Spraitz et al. (2018) analyzed documentation from clergy, victims, attorneys, clinicians, and Church personnel covering specific incidents of sexual abuse within the Church and concluded sexually abusive clergy demonstrated several grooming methods. Clergy often built relationships by spending time with victims' families, presenting themselves as a mentor or friend to victims, and giving them gifts. Clergy also built trust through these mentorship roles and relationships with families. Psychological control was built through increased attention (playing favorites) and taking advantage of the respect and reverence clergy had acquired through their position and increased relationship with the victim. Inviting victims for isolated overnight stays also exuded control by making any potential escape more difficult. Finally, inhibitions were often lowered through normalizing physical contact (that would later progress to sexual contact) and/or providing victims substances (e.g., alcohol). Follow-up analysis of 18 additional clergy sexual abuse incidents found at least one of these grooming behaviors in documented abuse cases for 17 of 18 clergy, with most clergy demonstrating use of multiple grooming behaviors (Spraitz & Bowen, 2019).

21.2.5 The Potential Role of Celibacy

Most clergy in the Church are required to maintain a celibate lifestyle (though, it is important to note, not all clergy; married deacons are an exception, for example). Mandated celibacy has often been discussed as a potential force behind clergy sexual abuse. A lack of research on how the mandated celibacy impacts the psychosexual and psychological health of clergy — who like other people are sexual beings — led to calls for more research within this area and for open dialogues within seminaries about sexual issues (Loftus, 2004). Anonymous surveying of clergy suggests a divide in opinions of how celibacy contributes positively or negatively to the well-being of clergy (Baumann et al., 2017). In general, however, evidence fails to suggest celibacy within the Church serves as an overarching explanation for clergy sexual abuse (Doyle, 2006).

In terms of sexuality, Haywood et al. (1996a) found that clergy who sexually abused children reported lower sex drives than others who sexually abused children and non-abusive clergy. Qualitative research, however, suggests clergy who commit sexual abuse report being raised in a childhood environment where sex was demonized and considered taboo, and these clergy report joining the clergy was in part motivated by attempts to suppress their sexuality (D'Alton et al., 2013). This self-selection of clergy seeking mandated celibacy as an incentive to repress sexuality has also been noted by treatment providers of clergy (see Adams, 2003). Indeed, psychosexual concerns and deficits, some evident before entering the clergy, have been identified as potential risk factors for clergy misconduct (Kappler et al., 2020) and sexual abuse specifically (Anderson, 2015). Nonetheless, analysis of clergy abuse across time notes fluctuations that follow situational and environmental changes, suggesting the stable standard of mandated celibacy itself should not be viewed as causing clergy sexual abuse (John Jay College, 2004).

An alternative theory is that celibacy's relevance to clergy sexual abuse is not in the actual practice of celibacy, but celibacy's contribution to the emotional health of clergy. Doyle (2006) describes notions that celibacy directly explains why clergy sexually abuse children to be "naive and even preposterous" (p. 195). Instead, Doyle contends that the culture in the Church highlights celibacy as difficult, virtuous, and requiring more internal strength and dedication than a non-celibate life. As a result, a celibate lifestyle may serve as a symbol that clergy are more virtuous and morally and emotionally superior to others. Celibacy within the Church, therefore, may be theorized to serve as one of several messages fueling narcissistic tendencies, which then increases risk for exploitation and entitlement (including sexual exploitation of children). Mercado et al. (2011) urge researchers to further explore cultural patterns that might explain patterns in clergy sexual abuse. In all, though, celibacy is unlikely to be identified as an overarching, direct contributor to clergy sexual abuse.

21.3 Clinical Assessment of Clergy

Little research has been disseminated around the clinical assessment of sexually abusive clergy. Among clergy who have undergone clinical evaluations following sexual abuse allegations, narcissistic personality traits have been identified as potentially elevated (Irons & Laaser, 1994). The status of clergy opens them to high admiration from others and deference to them as an authority figure. Clergy are held in quite high regard within the Church, which has been theorized to both attract those high in narcissism and feed into narcissistic tendencies. Relatively elevated levels of dependent personality traits have also been assessed among these clergy (Irons & Laaser, 1994; Plante et al., 1996). Clergy have a strict set of rules that dictate many details, big and small, of their adult life. This restricted autonomy has been suggested to attract people who are highly dependent and further fuel and increase dependency issues.

In contrast, very low rates of Antisocial Personality Disorder have been observed across a range of studies (Irons & Laaser, 1994; Langevin et al., 2000; Plante & Aldridge, 2005). One direct comparison of diagnoses among clergy and non-clergy who committed sexual offenses found the prevalence of Antisocial Personality Disorder among sexually abusive clergy to be remarkably lower compared to others who have committed sexual offenses (Langevin et al., 2000). The stringent process for entering the clergy, combined with the social and behavioral conflicts at the core of Antisocial Personality Disorder, makes it unlikely for an individual with Antisocial Personality Disorder to complete the process of entering the clergy. Low rates of Antisocial Personality Disorder, however, are notable in that they suggest clergy are unlikely to commit acts of sexual abuse primarily through antisocial motivations.

21.3.1 Paraphilic Assessment

Contrary to general stereotypes expressed by the public, evidence of pedophilia among sexually abusive clergy is overall weakly correlated. Although many clergy in the above studies were determined to have paraphilic disorders, other non-paraphilic sexual disorders, or other sex-related concerns, evidence of pedophilia specifically (which involves specific attraction to prepubescent children) was very uncommon (Irons & Laaser, 1994; Plante et al., 1996). Low prevalence of pedophilia suggests clergy who sexually abuse children are generally more motivated by factors other than a specific attraction toward prepubescent children. Given the low rates of pedophilia and Antisocial Personality Disorder among clergy who commit sexual abuse, there is little evidence to suggest attraction to children or general criminality explain sexual abuse by clergy. Instead, any internal factors are more likely to be explained by a complex set of intrapersonal and interpersonal factors. Such research, however, is generally lacking.

21.3.2 Psychological Assessment

Many clergy complete psychological assessments even outside the context of responding to sexual or other behavioral concerns (e.g., suitability for certain cleric placements). Special considerations, however, must be addressed when administering assessments to clergy who have committed sexual abuse against a child. Clinicians must consider the purpose of their assessment and the scope of any assessment instruments used. Many assessment instruments can be used with clergy, but assessing, for example, risk for sexually abusing children is a precise question that has not been validated to be addressed with most general clinical instruments. Terry and Freilich (2012) further stress that neither assessments nor diagnoses of disorders alone discriminate between clergy who do or do not sexually abuse children. In practice, assessment with sexually abusive clergy might thus include a comprehensive, multimethod approach (e.g., clinical interview, personality measures, projective measures; Songy, 2003) supplemented with sexual-specific measures (e.g., risk assessment).

Some research has been conducted examining the psychological testing results of clergy presenting with sexual or non-sexual issues. The MMPI-2 (Hathaway & McKinley, 1989) and its updated versions have been validated to assess personality and psychopathology, but it would be beyond the scope of the measure to use results to assess on sexual abuse risk. Clergy with allegations of sexual abuse or sexual misconduct were likely to respond defensively on the MMPI-2, as noted by elevations on the L, K, and R scales (Langevin et al., 2000; Plante & Aldridge, 2005). There are numerous explanations for why clergy who commit sexual abuse would present as defensive, including a minimization of their role in the abuse and defensiveness toward the treatment environment.

When comparing clergy and non-clergy who had sexually abused children, sexually abusive clergy had fewer clinical elevations on the MMPI-2 (1.8) than non-clergy (4.1); compared to others who had sexually abused, sexually abusive clergy were more likely to have elevations on the Masculinity-Femininity scale and less likely to have elevations on the Psychopathic Deviate or Schizophrenia scales (Haywood et al., 1996b). Other analyses noted clergy who sexually abused children presented as less neurotic on the MMPI-2 than their peers, with lower levels of anxiety and obsessiveness and higher levels of extraversion and passivity (Camargo,

1997; Loftus & Camargo, 1993). Loftus and Camargo (1993) also observed two common clusters of MMPI-2 elevations with clergy who sexually abused children, which they refer to as a Depressed Cluster (with a high elevation on the Masculinity-Femininity Scale and elevations on Depression, Psychopathic Deviate, Psychasthenia, and Schizophrenia scales) and an Extroverted Cluster (with a high elevation on the Masculinity-Femininity Scale, low Social Introversion, and subclinical elevations on both the K and Psychopathic Deviate scale). Elevations on the Masculinity-Femininity scale for clergy who sexually abuse children, however, should not be mistaken for informing on sexuality, no differences have been observed in the MMPI-2 profiles of clergy applicants who identified as heterosexual or homosexual (Plante, 2007).

Other analysis of the MMPI-2 and other personality measures with sexually abusive clergy (Falkenhain et al., 1999) noted a diverse set of profile results. Four general profiles were identified from these testing results, which the authors labeled as "Sexually and Emotionally Underdeveloped," "Significantly Psychiatrically Disturbed," "Undefended Characterological," and "Defended Characterological." Differences among these profiles, however, did not appear to proactively predict membership in certain groups. In a recent study of clergy personality profiles (Amrom et al., 2017), different MMPI-2 trends were observed between clergy who were receiving treatment and those with no treatment history. There were no distinct patterns, however, to discriminate among clergy receiving treatment for different issues. Specifically, no MMPI-2 trends were identified that differentiated clergy receiving treatment for sexual abuse, broader sexual misconduct, or general clinical issues.

Rossetti et al. (1996) used factor analyses to devise a 16-item scale on the MMPI-2 to differentiate clergy determined to have ephebophilia from both clergy receiving treatment for general psychological conditions and control groups. While this scale failed to discriminate between clergy classified with different paraphilias (e.g., pedophilia vs. ephebophilia), it discriminated between those with paraphilias, those with general mental disorders, and those without mental disorders. A large amount of false positives, however, limited the scale's validity in practice.

Similar to the MMPI-2, the MCMI-III (Millon, 1997) and other iterations of the MCMI have not been demonstrated to be sensitive enough to discriminate clergy who commit sexual abuse or clergy at elevated risk to do so. Differences have been observed on the MCMI-III between clergy receiving treatment and other clergy not in treatment, but the MCMI-III failed to discriminate between clergy receiving treatment for specific issues (general psychological conditions, sexual misconduct, or sexual abuse; Amrom et al., 2017). Similarly, neither MCMI scales nor individual items differentiated sexually abusive clergy from clergy receiving treatment for nonsexual reasons (Musser et al., 1995). When examining and comparing the MCMI profiles of members of the clergy who committed sexual abuse from intake to 6 years post-treatment, there were no major changes in the profiles observed years after receiving treatment (Fones et al., 1999).

In all, some descriptive trends have been identified in various analyses of personality testing with clergy and sexually abusive clergy specifically. These measures, however, should not be used as a discriminatory tool for clergy who commit sexual abuse and are not intended to detect abnormality associated with engaging in sexual abuse.

21.3.3 Sexual Risk Assessment

The Static-99R (Helmus et al., 2012) and its predecessor (Static-99; Hanson & Thornton, 1999) are the most commonly used measures for assessing sexual recidivism risk for people convicted of sex offenses. Static-99R norms, however, are based heavily on people sanctioned within the criminal justice system and may be less applicable to clergy who commit sexual abuse. In the little research applying sexual risk measures to clergy, the scoring and distribution of scores on risk measures like the Static-99R and Minnesota Sex Offender Screening Tool-Revised revealed different distributions of sum scores for sexually abusive clergy than others (Perillo et al., 2017).

There have been concerns specifically about the restricted range of risk scores among clergy, which can be apparent from looking at the specific items of the Static-99R. For example, it might be expected for essentially all clergy to have "unrelated victims" and extremely few to have ever been married or cohabitated with a lover for 2 years (though these scenarios are conceivable). Indeed, in a treatment sample of sexually abusive clergy, 72% received the same score on the Static-99 (3; Montana et al., 2012). Notably, of the clergy who fell into that same risk category for a score of 3 (at the time, "Medium-High") or a higher risk category, 84% did not reoffend.

Seeing little variability in risk scores for sexually abusive clergy would raise concerns about using risk scores to distinguish clergy at higher or lower risk of additional sexual abuse. Consistent with these concerns and different score distributions overall, the Static-99 poorly predicted recidivism in clergy, over-predicting 15-year and 10-year absolute risk of re-offense four and three times higher than actual rates of re-offense, respectively (Montana et al., 2012). The notable overestimation of recidivism suggests current risk measures might not be valid for use with clergy, yet the sexual recidivism rates among the clergy sample in Montana et al. (2012) suggest risk assessment is similarly important to assess for sexually abusive clergy as in the general community.

Due to discrepancies between the items on the Static-99 and the composition of individuals within the clergy, there is weak evidence currently for using the Static-99R with sexually abusive clergy. Perillo et al. (2017) suggest risk measures focusing on sexual behavior and thoughts associated with recidivism risk are more likely to show promise in assessing sexually abusive clergy than measures that incorporate many non-sexual items, such as general antisocial behaviors. If so, measures like the Static-99R and STABLE-2007, which primarily focus on sexual behavior, could provide a foundation for assessing clergy in the future if there were new normative samples available (such as a sample that is representative for clergy) or revised scoring procedures that would allow more accurate risk assessment.

21.4 Clinical Intervention

The Church has long faced criticism for its response to allegations of sexual abuse, including inconsistent intervention efforts for clergy who sexually abused children. At the time of the Boston Globe coverage in 2002, fewer than half (40%) of clergy found to have sexually abused a child received treatment (Terry, 2008b). Relative to others who have sexually abused, a comparison of sexually abusive clergy and a state-wide sample of men incarcerated for sexual offenses suggested slightly (but significantly) fewer clergy completed sexual offense treatment (Perillo et al., 2017). Among clergy that do receive treatment, many are temporarily referred to designated treatment facilities for clergy with a number of clinical service needs; however, treatment approaches have been highly variable. Records suggest clergy have received several different treatment modalities, including individual or group psychotherapy, relapse prevention programs, spiritual counseling, and specialized programs for sexual offending (Terry, 2008b). In all, there are numerous inconsistencies in the treatment sexually clergy receive, including if they receive treatment at all.

21.4.1 Potential Approaches to Treatment

Different frameworks for treatment with sexually abusive clergy might be adapted from existing sexual offense treatment models. The Risk-Need-Responsivity Model (RNR; Andrews et al., 1990) of treatment notes three core principles for successful offending rehabilitation that essentially inform on the intensity, content, and delivery of treatment. First, the intensity of an individual's treatment should be in line with the intensity of their risk for relapse (the *risk* principle). In practice, this principle suggests high-intensity treatments be reserved for those at high risk for engaging in future sexual abuse, and those at lower risk for engaging in future sexual abuse should receive less intensive levels of intervention. Treatment should also be tailored to issues with a functional connection to sexual offending (the *needs* principle), both the broader criminogenic needs for engaging in sexual offending and the specific individual's needs that contributed to their offenses. Lastly, actual delivery of treatment should account for contextual factors such as individuals' insight, mental and emotional capacity, additional service needs, and receptiveness to treatment (the *responsivity* principle). The RNR Model has been demonstrated to effectively reduce sexual recidivism across multiple studies (Hanson et al., 2009).

Adapting the risk principle of the RNR model to sexually abusive clergy is complicated by the limited evidence for the effectiveness of current sexual risk measures with clergy; it is unclear how well current risk assessment approaches can inform on the level of service needs for sexually abusive clergy. Regarding treatment needs, noted concerns about psychosexual awareness, emotional insight, feelings of shame from perfectionistic standards, and distress coping skills have been discussed as functionally relevant to sexual abuse and misconduct in the Church (Anderson, 2015; Loftus & Camargo, 1993; Kappler et al., 2020). These issues are thus potential areas of focus that would be particularly relevant for treatment with sexually abusive clergy. Some of these clergy criminogenic needs would seemingly also factor into delivering treatment. In particular, issues into psychosexual and emotional insight would impact distress coping, addressing shame and perfectionistic tendencies, and psychosexual education. Effective treatment would also require treatment provider competence and awareness of cultural issues affecting views of sex, negative emotions, and broader spirituality among clergy.

The Good Lives Model (GLM) of treatment (Ward et al., 2007) is a strength-based approach to offense rehabilitation focusing directly on an individual's goals and values that, when fulfilled, reduce risk for future offending. This approach theorizes that sexual offending occurs when an individual lacks prosocial means for meeting their life goals, has goals or values that come into conflict, or attempts to meet life goals through unhealthy manners. GLM treatment focuses on insight into an individual's personal goals and values for their life, motivation to achieve these goals in ways that do not compromise their other values, and development of skills and resources to fulfill goals and values in prosocial ways (Barnao et al., 2016). Some contend the GLM overlaps considerably with RNR, just framed differently (see Andrews et al., 2011), and other research questions specific elements of the "good life" framework (Harper et al., 2020). Nonetheless, evidence suggests the GLM is at least as effective as other methods of offense rehabilitation (Mallion et al., 2020) and is well-received by those being treated.

Adapting the GLM for treatment with sexually abusive clergy would be based on each individual clergy's prioritized goals and values, but some particular "goods" might be expected to be particularly relevant across clergy. Given suggestions of psychosexual and emotional insight limitations (e.g., Anderson, 2015), strengthening prosocial connections with others could be suggested to fulfill goods of friendship and community that would decrease risk for committing sexual abuse. Distress coping skills and increased insight into one's own emotions and prosocial ways of addressing negative mood could similarly fulfill the good of inner peace. Integrating prosocial fulfillment of these goods with highly valued goods of many clergy—which could include knowledge, excellence in work, and spirituality— could assist clergy in balancing their highly valued goods in ways that would promote healthy emotional bonds and in turn reduce risk for additional abuse. None of these treatment considerations would require deviation from GLM protocol or principles.

Whatever treatment approach is used with sexually abusive clergy, contextual considerations of what increases risk for sexual abuse in the Church would allow for better precision of treatment in line with the needs of clergy. As noted, some scholars have argued that a critical component of treatment for sexually abusive clergy is psychoeducation about sex and sexual boundaries (Anderson, 2015), given documented limits in sexual knowledge for abusive and non-abusive clergy (Loftus &

Camargo, 1993). Songy (2003) advocates for additional psychological and spiritual components of treatment, stressing the importance of the Church and clinicians collaborating when treating a clergy who committed sexual abuse to address both psychological and spiritual needs. Such treatment could promote recognizing oneself both as a spiritual individual who is a member of the Church and as a human who has agency and responsibility for their own behaviors. Along this line, treatment could promote clergy's awareness of themselves as individuals independently from their role within the Church and encourage self-accountability, which could then promote reconciliation of their actions and their impact. Restorative justice programs— which could include Circles of Support and Accountability, Healing Circles, the Just Care Program, or mediation between the clergy and the victim— have also been argued to promote healing for both those who experienced and perpetrated abuse within the Church (Anderson, 2015).

21.4.2 Treatment Outcomes

Little research on treatment outcomes with sexually abusive clergy is available beyond feedback results from small samples of those receiving treatment (e.g., Fones et al., 1999). The minimal research on specific treatment outcomes with clergy who have sexually abused children limits our understanding of how effective current treatments are. An encouraging sign is the relatively low recidivism rates for clergy who received treatment after sexually abusing a child in Montana et al. (2012); however, without a comparison to recidivism rates for clergy who never received treatment, how effective treatment specifically was in these low recidivism rates cannot be assessed. That being said, a number of studies have found sexual offense treatment to be effective at reducing future sexual abuse (e.g., Hanson et al., 2009; Mallion et al., 2020). Considering unique needs of sexually abusive clergy (e.g., affective development, psychosexual development) would be critical to effectively implementing current sexual offending treatment models with sexually abusive clergy. Fortunately, empirically supported treatments rooted in RNR or GLM principles allow— and in fact, require— consideration of many of the unique contexts and circumstances of the individual being treated, suggesting current models for effective sexual abuse treatment can be adapted when working with sexually abusive clergy.

21.4.3 Primary Prevention Efforts

Beyond intervention efforts to prevent additional offending from those clergy who have abused, broader social, structure efforts can promote strategies to reduce sexual abuse within the Church more broadly. Situational Crime Prevention framework (Wortley & Smallbone, 2006) suggests that people at risk for sexual perpetration assess the risks and benefits of engaging in sexual abuse. Setting up an environment that reduces opportunities to engage in sexual abuse— or at least reduces opportunities to engage in sexual abuse without being held accountable— is theorized to reduce sexual abuse in that environment. These efforts have been found to both reduce child sexual abuse (LeClerc et al., 2016) and reduce the potential severity when abuse does occur (e.g., shorter duration and less physical contact; LeClerc et al., 2015).

Situational Crime Prevention strategies have been discussed as a potential primary prevention technique specifically within the Church. Terry and Ackerman (2008) note four broad strategies within a situational framework to reduce child sexual abuse. One, reducing acceptance or permissibility of abuse could be facilitated through psychosexual education with clergy (e.g., survivor experiences, issues of consent, consequences of abusing a child). Two, blocking situational factors that increase risk for child sexual abuse could include restricting unsupervised time between clergy and children and increasing guardianship or security during clergy-child interactions (e.g., having parents present, leaving doors open and windows uncovered). Three, increasing the effort needed to put children at risk for abuse could include these security strategies and also giving increased effort to identifying clergy at higher risk for abuse. Clergy identified as at-risk should then be restricted from having unsupervised time with children. Four, increasing the risk of being held accountable for sexual abuse can be accomplished through psychoeducation for parents, clergy, and members of the congregation about sexual abuse, how to identify potential abuse, and how to report abuse. Situational Crime Prevention strategies would allow clergy and members of the congregation alike to become active in preventing instances in which abuse could occur. Some evidence suggests clergy indeed weigh situational risk in ways that reduce their vulnerability to engage in misconduct (Guerzoni, 2018), suggesting potential to reduce clergy sexual abuse through broader structural and environmental efforts that block opportunities to abuse children.

21.5 Conclusions

Clergy who commit sexual abuse are a heterogenous group, both unique from each other and, as a group, unique from others who have sexually abused children. Although some general victim trends have been observed, the evidence overall suggests that sexually abusive clergy choose victims more as a function of opportunity than of specific targeted interest. That is, although the most common victim of clergy sexual abuse has been a boy between the ages of 11 to 14, the age and gender of victims appear more driven by opportunities for unsupervised access and grooming than by specific sexual desire toward boys or children in that age range. In fact, contrary to common public dialogue, sexually abusive clergy being driven by paraphilic desires (e.g., pedophilia or hebephilia) appears to be the exception, not the rule; little evidence exists to suggest high rates of pedophilia or paraphilic disorders among sexually abusive clergy.

Although paraphilic disorders do not appear to be a strong contributor to the broader scope of clergy sexual abuse, some evidence suggests other sexual issues might be relevant. Issues related to psychosexual maturity, insight into sexuality, and distress coping have all been identified as deficits that exacerbated risk for many clergy who have sexually abused children. These issues do not suggest sexually abusive clergy have deviant sexual proclivities. Instead, these issues more likely suggest deficits in sexual and emotional development that are common targets of sexual abuse treatment.

As a group, the current literature suggests sexually abusive clergy tend to demonstrate less antisociality and perpetrate abuse at an older age relative to people convicted of sexual offenses in the community (Langevin et al., 2000; Piquero et al., 2008). Although likely in part an artifact of the criteria for entering the clergy, these and other clinically relevant differences complicate our generalization of patterns from the sexual offending literature to clergy who commit sexual abuse. This in turn complicates our application of existing clinical management practices to sexually abusive clergy.

21.5.1 Implications for Clinical Management

Notable differences between clergy and others who sexually abuse children affect how existing measures (developed with broader community samples) can be used to assess recidivism risk for clergy. At this point, no assessment instruments have strong evidence for validly assessing sexual risk for clergy specifically. Clergy with behavioral or emotional concerns do appear to respond differently on personality assessment measures like the MMPI-2, suggesting some potential to identify concerns at least on a broader scale. Current personality and psychopathology measures, however, are not valid assessments of sexual offending risk for clergy or non-clergy. These measures should not be used to screen clergy who may be at risk to sexually abuse children.

Part of what limits prospects of screening for clergy at risk for committing sexual abuse is the limited knowledge in place for identifying those at risk for first-time sexual perpetration in general. In contrast, there is a vast body of information on factors relevant to sexual reoffending among people convicted of sexual offenses. Existing sexual risk assessment measures would seem to have more potential, then, in assessing recidivism risk of sexually abusive clergy. That being said, because most sexual abuse in the Church has long been addressed within the Church rather than the criminal justice and mental health systems, clergy are not well-represented in the recidivism literature or the normative samples of sexual risk measures. This lack of representation in the literature (and the unique contextual factors with clergy sexual abuse) impacts current sexual risk measures' validity with sexually abusive clergy. Indeed, instruments like the Static-99 have thus far demonstrated less variance of scores with clergy, which could limit their ability to assess relative risk. At this point, it is unclear how to best assess sexual risk of clergy. Considerations that could be explored include examining clergy-level norms for current risk measures, developing alternative forms of current measures (e.g., adding/removing/modifying items, adjusting scoring methods), or developing a measure specifically for clergy based on the patterns and contextual factors observed across clergy sexual abuse.

Just as there is little research on risk assessment with clergy, a similar gap can be seen in research on clinical interventions for clergy who have sexually abused a child. The broader literature on sexual offense treatment, however, appears to be more readily applicable to clergy than the assessment literature. Leading treatment frameworks allow for (and expect) unique tailoring to the specific needs and contextual factors for the individual being treated. Documented factors that appear relevant to the broad scope of clergy sexual abuse— including psychosexual deficits, emotional deficits, poorly developed interpersonal relationships, and poorly developed coping skills— are all issues currently considered in empirically supported sexual offense treatments. The prospects of using a RNR or GLM framework with sexually abusive clergy appears promising. At the same time, treatment with clergy must include consideration of religious and other cultural contexts that can impact the delivery or focus of treatment (e.g., religious beliefs related to healthy sexual functioning).

As improving clinical management efforts with sexually abusive clergy is attempted, it is important to note that the majority of the information about clergy who commit sexual abuse stems from the Church itself. Much of the data on clergy sexual abuse, including those from the extensive John Jay College investigations (2004, 2006), are based on sexual abuse incidents from decades ago that were handled primarily within the Church. Very few clergy during that time were actually charged or received any services within the criminal justice or community mental health systems (Piquero et al., 2008). As a result, very little is known about clergy who were removed from the Church after instances of sexual abuse and treated within the community— whether in the criminal justice system, private practice, community clinics, or inpatient hospitals. It is thus unclear how patterns of abuse, treatment outcomes, and subsequent abuse by clergy would translate for clergy in the broader community who were not remaining in the exact same system (i.e., within the Church). The extensive coverage of decades of clergy sexual abuse remains informative and helpful in understanding the broader issue of clergy sexual abuse, but continued examinations must be made with information from management efforts with present-day clergy in present-day environments.

21.5.2 Broader Prevention Efforts

As it currently stands, our assessment instruments and literature on first-time offending offer little in terms of screening to identify at-risk clergy. Instead, broader environmental strategies consistent with situational crime prevention appear to have particular promise in reducing sexual abuse within the Church. The framework outlined by Terry and Ackerman (2008) offers specific implementation strategies for setting up an environment within the Church that would reduce risk for sexual abuse. Increased psychosexual education efforts within the Church; less access to unsupervised, "closed door" situations with children; and increased clinical services are all pieces of a broader culture to reduce clergy sexual abuse. At the same time, psychoeducation to both parishioners and clergy that highlights what abuse is, instances in which abuse are more likely to occur, how to recognize when a child might have been abused, and how to address suspected victimization could increase accountability as part of a situational framework. Consistent with this framework, children within the church could also benefit from age-appropriate discussions about when it might be appropriate or inappropriate to be alone with adults, appropriate and inappropriate behavior by others, and what they can do or say if they think an adult might be doing something inappropriate. Building an environment that reduces risk for sexual abuse and increased accountability when it does, combined with continued research with clergy in the present-day, appears to be our best avenue toward reducing sexual abuse by clergy.

References

Adams, K. M. (2003). Clergy sex abuse: A commentary on celibacy. *Sexual Addiction & Compulsivity, 10*, 91–92. https://doi.org/10.1080/10720160390230583

Amrom, A., Calkins, C., & Fargo, J. (2017). Between the pew and the pulpit: Can personality measures help identify sexually abusive clergy? *ATSA, 31*(6), 686–706.

Anderson, J. (2015). Comprehending and rehabilitating Roman Catholic clergy offenders of child sexual abuse. *Journal of Child Sexual Abuse: Research, Treatment, & Program Innovations for Victims, Survivors, & Offenders, 24*(7), 772–795.

Andrews, D. A., Bonta, J., & Hoge, R. D. (1990). Classification for effective rehabilitation: Rediscovering psychology. *Criminal Justice and Behavior, 17*, 19–52.

Andrews, D. A., Bonta, J., & Wormith, J. S. (2011). The risk-need-Responsivity (RNR) model: Does adding the good lives model contribute to effective crime prevention? *Criminal Justice and Behavior, 38*(7), 735–755. https://doi.org/10.1177/0093854811406356

Barnao, M., Ward, T., & Robertson, P. (2016). The good lives model: A new paradigm for forensic mental health. *Psychiatry, Psychology and Law, 23*(2), 288–301. https://doi.org/10.1080/13218719.2015.1054923

Baumann, K., Jacobs, C., Frick Sj, E., & Büssing, A. (2017). Commitment to celibacy in German Catholic priests: Its relation to religious practices, psychosomatic health and psychosocial resources. *Journal of Religious Health, 56*(2), 649–668. https://doi.org/10.1007/s10943-016-0313-9

Blanchard, G. T. (1991). Sexually abusive clergymen: A conceptual framework for intervention and recovery. *Pastoral Psychology, 39*(4), 237–246. https://doi.org/10.1007/BF01040925

Boston Globe. (2002). *Betrayal: The crisis in the Catholic Church*. Little, Brown and Company.

Calkins, C., Fargo, J., Jeglic, E., & Terry, K. (2015). Blessed be the children: A case–control study of sexual abusers in the Catholic church. *Behavioral Sciences & the Law, 33*(4), 580–594. https://doi-org.proxy-iup.klnpa.org/10.1002/bsl.2193

Camargo, R. J. (1997). Factor, cluster, and discriminant analyses of data on sexually active clergy: The molesters of youth identified. *American Journal of Forensic Psychology, 15*(2), 5–24.

Colombino, N., & Mercado, C. C. (2009). Sex offender perpetration patterns. *Sex Offender Law Report, 10*(4), 49–62.

Colton, M., & Vanstone, M. (1998). Sexual abuse by men who work with children: An exploratory study. *British Journal of Social Work, 28*(4), 511–523.

Craven, S., Brown, S., & Gilchrist, E. (2006). Sexual grooming of children: Review of literature and theoretical considerations. *Journal of Sexual Aggression, 12*(3), 287–299. https://doi.org/10.1080/13552600601069414

D'Alton, P., Guilfoyle, M., & Randall, P. (2013). Roman Catholic clergy who have sexually abused children: Their perceptions of their developmental experience. *Child Abuse & Neglect, 37*(9), 698–702. https://doi.org/10.1016/j.chiabu.2012.12.001

Doyle, T. P. (2006). Clericalism: Enabler of clergy sexual abuse. *Pastoral Psychology, 54*(3), 189–213. https://doi.org/10.1007/S11089-006-6323-X

Dressing, H., Dölling, D., Hermann, D., Kruse, A., Schmitt, E., Bannenberg, B., Whittaker, K., Hoell, A., Voss, E., & Salize, H. J. (2019). Child sexual abuse by Catholic priests, deacons, and male members of religious orders in the Authority of the German Bishops' conference 1946–2014. *Sexual Abuse, 33*(3), 274–294. https://doi.org/10.1177/1079063219893371

Falkenhain, M. A., Duckro, P. N., Hughes, H. M., Rossetti, S. J., & Gfeller, J. D. (1999). Cluster analysis of child sexual offenders: A validation with Roman Catholic priests and brothers. *Sexual Addiction & Compulsivity, 6*(4), 317–336.

Firestone, P., Moulden, H. M., & Wexler, A. F. (2009). Clerics who commit sexual offences: Offender, offense, and victim characteristics. *Journal of Child Sexual Abuse, 18*(4), 442–454.

Fones, C. S. L., Levine, S. B., Althof, S. E., & Risen, C. B. (1999). The sexual struggles of 23 clergymen: A follow-up study. *Journal of Sex and Marital Therapy, 25*(3), 183–195.

Guerzoni, M. A. (2018). A situational crime analysis of Anglican clergy's child protective practices. *Child Abuse & Neglect, 77*, 85–98. https://doi.org/10.1016/j.chiabu.2017.12.016

Hanson, R. K., Bourgon, G., Helmus, L., & Hodgson, S. (2009). The principles of effective correctional treatment also apply to sexual offenders: A meta-analysis. *Criminal Justice and Behavior, 36*, 865–891. https://doi.org/10.1177/0093854809338545

Hanson, R. K., & Thornton, D. (1999). *STATIC-99: Improving actuarial risk assessments for sex offenders (User Report No. 19999-02)*. Department of the Solicitor General of Canada.

Harper, C. A., Lievesley, R., Blagden, N., Akerman, G., Winder, B., & Baumgartner, E. (2020). Development and validation of the good lives questionnaire. *Psychology, Crime, and Law, 27*(7), 678–703. https://doi.org/10.1080/1068316X.2020.1849695

Hathaway, S. R., & McKinley, J. C. (1989). *The Minnesota multiphasic personality Index-2*. National Computer Systems.

Haywood, T. W., Kravitz, H. M., Grossman, L. S., Wasyliw, O. E., & Hardy, D. W. (1996a). Psychological aspects of sexual functioning among cleric and noncleric alleged sex offenders. *Child Abuse & Neglect, 20*(6), 527–536.

Haywood, T. W., Kravitz, H. M., Grossman, L. S., Wasyliw, O. E., & Hardy, D. W. (1996b). Cycle of abuse and psychopathology in cleric and noncleric molesters of children and adolescents. *Child Abuse & Neglect, 20*(12), 1233–1243.

Helmus, L., Thornton, D., Hanson, R. K., & Babchishin, K. M. (2012). Improving the predictive accuracy of Static-99 and Static-2002 with older sex offenders: Revised age weights. *Sexual Abuse: A Journal of Research and Treatment, 24*(1), 64–101. https://doi.org/10.1177/1079063211409951

Holt, K., & Massey, C. (2013). Sexual preference or opportunity: An examination of situational factors by gender of victims of clergy abuse. *Sexual Abuse, 25*(6), 606–621.

Irons, R., & Laaser, M. (1994). The abduction of fidelity: Sexual exploitation by clergy- experience with inpatient assessment. *Sexual Addiction & Compulsivity, 1*(2), 119–129.

John Jay College of Criminal Justice. (2004). *The nature and scope of sexual abuse of minors by Catholic priests and deacons in the United States, 1950–2000*. United States Conference of Catholic Bishops.

John Jay College of Criminal Justice. (2006). *The nature and scope of sexual abuse of minors by Catholic priests and deacons in the United States-supplementary data analysis*. United States Conference of Catholic Bishops.

Kappler, S., Talitman, E., Cavaliere, C., DeLonghi, G., Sy, M., Simpson, M., & Roncadin, S. (2020). Underdeveloped affective maturity and unintegrated psychosexual identity as contributors to clergy abuse and boundary violations: Clinical observations from residential treatment of Roman Catholic clergy at the Southdown institute. *Spirituality in Clinical Practice, 7*(4), 302–309. https://doi.org/10.1037/scp0000234

Langevin, R., Curnoe, S., & Bain, J. (2000). A study of clerics who commit sexual offenses: Are they different from other sex offenders? *Child Abuse & Neglect, 24*(4), 535–545.

LeClerc, B., Chiu, Y., & Cale, J. (2016). Sexual violence and abuse against children: A first review through the lens of environmental criminology. *International Journal of Offender Therapy and Comparative Criminology, 60*(7), 743–765. https://doi.org/10.1177/0306624X14564319

LeClerc, B., Smallbone, S., & Wortley, R. (2015). Prevention nearby: The influence of the presence of a potential guardian on the severity of child sexual abuse. *Sexual Abuse: A Journal of Research and Treatment, 27*(2), 189–204. https://doi.org/10.1177/1079063213504594

Loftus, J. A. (2004). What have we learned? Implications for future research and formation. In T. G. Plante (Ed.), *Sin against the innocents: Sexual abuse by priests and the role of the Catholic Church* (pp. 85–96). Praeger Publishers/Greenwood Publishing Group.

Loftus, J. A., & Camargo, R. J. (1993). Treating the clergy. *Sexual Abuse: A Journal of Research and Treatment, 6*(4), 287–303.

Mallion, J. S., Wood, J. L., & Mallion, A. (2020). Systematic review of "good lives" assumptions and interventions. *Aggression and Violent Behavior, 55*, 101510. https://doi.org/10.1016/j.avb.2020.101510

Mercado, C. C., Tallon, J. A., & Terry, K. J. (2008). Persistent sexual abusers in the Catholic Church: An examination of characteristics and offense patterns. *Criminal Justice and Behavior, 35*(5), 629–642. https://doi.org/10.1177/0093854808314389

Mercado, C. C., Terry, K., & Perillo, A. D. (2011). Sexual abuse in the Catholic church and other youth-serving organizations. In D. P. Boer, R. Eher, L. A. Craig, M. H. Miner, & F. Pfäfflin (Eds.), *International perspectives on the assessment and treatment of sexual offenders: Theory, practice, and research* (pp. 525–541). Wiley-Blackwell. https://doi-org.proxy-iup.klnpa.org/10.1002/9781119990420.ch28

Millon, T. (1997). *MCMI-III: Manual*. NCS Pearson, Inc.

Montana, S., Thompson, G., Ellsworth, P., Lagan, H., Helmus, L., & Rhoades, C. J. (2012). Predicting relapse for catholic clergy sex offenders: The use of the static-99. *Sexual Abuse: Journal of Research and Treatment, 24*(6), 575–590. https://doi.org/10.1177/1079063212445570

Musser, P., Cimbolic, P., & Rossetti, S. (1995). Ephebophilia and the MCMI-II. *Sexual Addiction & Compulsivity, 2*(3), 214–222.

Parkinson, P. N., Oates, R. K., & Jayakody, A. A. (2012). Child sexual abuse in the Anglican Church of Australia. *Journal of Sexual Abuse, 21*(5), 553–570. https://doi.org/10.1080/10538712.2012.689424

Perillo, A. D., Laake, A. L. W., & Calkins, C. (2017). Understanding sexually abusive clergy as a unique offender subgroup: Risk-based comparisons across the course of offending. *The International Journal of Forensic Mental Health, 16*(1), 58–68. https://doi-org.proxy-iup.klnpa.org/10.1080/14999013.2016.1236304

Perillo, A. D., Mercado, C. C., & Terry, K. J. (2008). Repeat offending, victim gender, and extent of victim relationship in Catholic Church sexual abusers: Implications for risk assessment. *Criminal Justice and Behavior, 35*(5), 600–614.

Piquero, A. R., Piquero, N. L., Terry, K. J., Youstin, T., & Nobles, M. (2008). Uncollaring the criminal: Understanding criminal careers in criminal clerics. *Criminal Justice and Behavior, 35*(5), 583–599.

Plante, T. G. (2007). Homosexual applicants to priesthood: How many and are they psychologically healthy? *Pastoral Psychology, 54*(4), 495–498.

Plante, T. G., & Aldridge, A. (2005). Psychological patterns among Roman Catholic clergy accused of sexual misconduct. *Pastoral Psychology, 54*(1), 73–80.

Plante, T. G., Manuel, G., & Bryant, C. (1996). Personality and cognitive functioning among hospitalized sexual offending Roman Catholic priests. *Pastoral Psychology, 45*(2), 129–139.

Rossetti, S., Anthony, P., Cimbolic, P., & Wright, T. L. (1996). Development and preliminary validation of the MMPI-2 scale for same-sex priest child molesters. *Sexual Addiction & Compulsivity, 3*(4), 341–356.

Seto, M. C. (2017). The puzzle of male chronophilias. *Archives of Sexual Behavior, 46*, 3–22. https://doi.org/10.1007/s10508-016-0799-y

Smith, M. L., Rengifo, A. F., & Vollman, B. K. (2008). Trajectories of abuse and disclosure: Child sexual abuse by Catholic Priests. *Criminal Justice and Behavior, 35*(5), 570–582.

Songy, D. (2003). Psychological and spiritual treatment of Roman Catholic clerical sex offenders. *Sexual Addiction & Compulsivity, 10*(2–3), 123–137. https://doi.org/10.1080/10720160390230655

Spraitz, J. D., & Bowen, K. N. (2019). Examination of a nascent taxonomy of priest sexual grooming. *Sexual Abuse, 31*(6), 707–728. https://doi.org/10.1177/1079063218809095

Spraitz, J. D., Bowen, K. N., & Strange, L. (2018). Proposing a behavioral taxonomy of priest sexual grooming. *International Journal for Crime, Justice and Social Democracy, 7*(1), 30–43. https://doi.org/10.5204/ijcjsd.v7i1.387

Sullivan, J., & Beech, A. (2004). A comparative study of demographic data relating to intra- and extra- familial child sexual abusers and professional perpetrators. *Journal of Sexual Aggression, 10*(1), 39–50.

Tallon, J. A., & Terry, K. J. (2008). Analyzing paraphilic activity, specialization, and generalization in priests who sexually abused minors. *Criminal Justice and Behavior, 35*(5), 615–628.

Terry, K. J. (2008a). Understanding the sexual abuse crisis in the Catholic Church: Challenged with prevention policies. *Victims & Offenders, 3*(1), 31–44. https://doi-org.proxy-iup.klnpa.org/10.1080/15564880701750482

Terry, K. J. (2008b). Stained glass: The nature and scope of sexual abuse crisis in the Catholic Church. *Criminal Justice and Behavior, 35*(5), 549–569.

Terry, K. J., & Ackerman, A. (2008). Child sexual abuse in the Catholic Church: How situational crime prevention strategies can help create safe environments. *Criminal Justice and Behavior, 35*(5), 643–657.

Terry, K. J., & Freilich, J. D. (2012). Understanding child sexual abuse by Catholic priests from a situational perspective. *Journal of Child Sexual Abuse: Research, Treatment, & Program Innovations for Victims, Survivors, & Offenders, 21*(4), 437–455. https://doi-org.proxy-iup.klnpa.org/10.1080/10538712.2012.693579

Ward, T., Mann, R. E., & Gannon, T. A. (2007). The good lives model of offender rehabilitation: Clinical implications. *Aggression and Violent Behavior, 12*(1), 87–107. https://doi.org/10.1016/j.avb.2006.03.004

Wells, K. (2003). A needs assessment regarding the nature and impact of clergy sexual abuse conducted by the interfaith sexual trauma institute. *Sexual Addiction & Compulsivity, 10*(2–3), 201–217. https://doi-org.proxy-iup.klnpa.org/10.1080/10720160390230691

Wortley, R. K., & Smallbone, S. (2006). Applying situational principles to sexual offenses against children. In R. K. Wortley & S. Smallbone (Eds.), *Situational prevention of child sexual abuse* (pp. 7–36). Criminal Justice Press.

Chapter 22
Special Considerations: Internet Sexual Offenders

Sarah Paquette

22.1 Introduction

The internet is not only part of our everyday activities and interactions but is also used in criminal acts involving vulnerable persons. It has added a new dimension to sexual crimes as the sexual abuse of children can now be captured with digital photography and disseminated worldwide, while access to potential victims often takes place in what appears to be complete anonymity. The sexual exploitation of children has become a major societal problem, revealed by thousands of official reports of such activities: the Canadian Centre for Child Protection (CCCP) receives an average of 4000 reports of online sexual exploitation of children monthly and the National Center for Missing and Exploited Children (NCMEC) in the United States receives up to 1 million (CCCP, 2017). This chapter provides an overview of the phenomenon of online sexual exploitation of minors with a focus on those who commit such crimes, their behaviors, and strategies for assessment, prevention, and treatment. It is important not only to distinguish online from offline sexual offenders but also to recognize intra-group differences among online offenders as some target young children while others prey on teenagers, a difference that has important implications for both assessment and intervention.

S. Paquette (✉)
Department of Psychology, University of Portsmouth, Portsmouth, Hampshire, UK

R. J. Tully et al. (eds.), *Best Practices in Sexual Offender Assessment and Management*, Dangerous Behavior in Clinical and Forensic Psychology,
https://doi.org/10.1007/978-3-031-83135-5_22

22.2 Offending Behaviors Against Minors over the Internet

This section covers the many facets of the sexual behaviors committed through the internet, with a focus on its legal parameters. It defines the behaviors related to the use of child pornography, the solicitation of children and adolescents on the internet and social networks, as well as other offenses that facilitate the sexual abuse of minors.

22.2.1 The Use of Child Sexual Exploitation Material (CSEM)

Among the most prevalent behaviors associated with online sexual behaviors that involve children are those related to child pornography, from its access to its possession, distribution, and production. Child pornography refers to any representation of a person under the age of (or depicted as being under the age of) 18 years engaging in sexually explicit activity or whose genitals are exposed for a sexual purpose (Cournoyer & Ouimet, 2017). Although the term "child pornography" is commonly used in legal matters in some countries, it has been criticized for giving the "impression that children being abused are complicit in the abuse" (CCCP, 2016, p. 4), diminishing the seriousness of the exploitative acts involved. The terms "indecent images of children" (IIOC) or "child sexual exploitation material" (CSEM) are more accurate and are now commonly used in the scientific literature. Two criteria are used to determine whether an image is illegal: the age of the victim and the sexual nature of the image. While it may be easy to distinguish younger children from adults through physical cues, such as short stature, preliminary stages of dental development, lack of pubic hair, or level of maturation of genitals (Cooper, 2011; Sun et al., 2002), distinguishing adolescents from adults can be much more complex. Given this, while the majority of illegal content available on the internet depicts adolescents rather than young children (Steel, 2009; Wolak et al., 2005), relatively few of these representations lead to court action (Ratnayake et al., 2014) or are even reported to the authorities. The majority of those officially classified as victims of sexual exploitation in the collections of men charged with possession of pornography are prepubescent children: approximately 50% are aged 7 years or younger and the percentage increases to 78% when victims aged 8 to 11 are included (CCCP, 2016).

To meet the sexual criteria for classification as CSEM, the image has to depict explicit sexual activities involving underage persons, have a sexual purpose, or focus on genitals. The most common cases of CSEM are representations of direct abuse of children, including contact (penetration or touching) between adults and children, or children and other children (Byrne Hessick, 2014). Some non-contact acts are also classified as CSEM, such as masturbation or close-ups of children's genitals. In other cases, it is more difficult to determine whether the main characteristic of an image is the depiction of a minor for a sexual purpose: for instance, in some contexts a picture might be classified as CSEM, while in another context it would not. Consider a series of representations of a child who, as the images progress, is gradually undressed and engaged in increasingly explicit sexual activities. While the last images in such a series would clearly constitute child pornography, the first images, seen in isolation, might not seem illegal. They would, however, meet this definition if considered in context as they were produced for a sexual purpose (Fortin & Corriveau, 2015). In an analysis of 43,760 instances of CSEM, the CCCP (2016) found that half involved sexual posing, while the other half involved explicit (47.8%) and extreme (2.2%) sexual assault of minors. In their analysis of 59 collections belonging to individuals convicted of possessing CSEM, which contained over 80,000 child sexual exploitation images, Fortin and Proulx (2018) found that 89.8% of the images depicted non-contact sexual activities with minors and 10.2% showed contact sexual abuse with children, adults, and animals or brutality.

CSEM can take many forms, as depictions of child sexual exploitation are not limited to photographs or videos but can also include any other form of visual, written, or audio depictions and can portray both real and fictional children. Photographs and videos have been declared illegal in most countries, but this is not always true for other forms.

Anecdotal cases of individuals convicted of writing or possessing sexual scenarios involving children, ordering child-sized sex dolls, or even collecting sexual cartoons of children have been reported worldwide. In Krone et al.'s (2017) study in Australia, 32% of their sample of men convicted of online sexual offences ($n = 152$) had text-written CSEM. In Spain, written and fictional CSEM is legal (see Soldino et al., 2020).

22.2.2 Child Sexual Luring and Solicitation

Another online offending behavior occurs when someone—of any age—engages in communication with a person who is, or is perceived to be, under the age of 18 years with the intention of facilitating further online (e.g., distribution of CSEM) or offline crime (e.g., abduction, contact sexual offending, exhibitionism, bestiality). Child luring (the formal legal term used in Canada for this offence) focuses solely on the communication that facilitates a potential crime. No actual crime has to occur or be attempted. For an online communication to qualify as child luring, a number of parameters must be met, the most important of which is the perceived age of the person involved in the conversation. For instance, while the purpose of luring is facilitation of a sexual offence, the communication itself does not have to be sexual in nature but only has to groom the child, preparing him/her to engage in a further behavior and fostering a suitable context for sexual exploitation. The actual age of the suspect is not a factor in this offence as anyone who communicates in such a way with a person whom he or she believes to be a minor is liable to criminal sanctions, including minors. Finally, unlike other jurisdictions, Canadian law does not require that the victim be identifiable or even proven to be a minor: believing or having been informed by the person involved that she/he is underage is sufficient to lay charges. Convictions for this type of behavior have sometimes been obtained for individuals who had solicited "virtual" victims whose real identities were never investigated or victims impersonated by undercover officers.

22.2.3 *Other Internet-Related Behaviors*

In 2012, in an attempt to expand legislation for the protection of children, the Canadian criminal code was adapted to include new laws condemning online sexual exploitative behaviors involving minors (Quebec Ministry of Public Security, 2013). Using telecommunication technologies to make an arrangement or agreement with someone else to commit other online or offline crimes against children is now also prohibited. A concrete example of this behavior is an adult chatting with another adult about his intention to "lend" him his child for the purpose of engaging in sexual activity. Finally, making sexually explicit material available to children with the intention of facilitating further online or offline crimes against children is also illegal in Canada. An example of such behavior would be displaying material from an adult pornographic website to a child as part of the grooming process in order to desensitize the child and "teach" him/her how to engage in sexual activities, an activity that has been identified in numerous studies of child grooming in both online and offline environments (e.g., Elliot, 2017; Klain et al., 2001; O'Connell, 2003). Internationally, similar laws are being made and criminal codes being adapted, to respond to the ever-evolving nature of online offending behavior and exploitation of minors.

22.3 Scope of the Problem

According to the CCCP (2016), 98% of the reports they receive involve CSEM-related behaviors. The number of online child sexual solicitation offences, while still a small percentage of reported crimes, has, however, increased dramatically—in the United States, during the 4-year period from 2004 to 2008, reports of such crimes increased by 230% (U.S. Department of Justice, 2010). The over-representation of CSEM crimes is reflected in the scientific literature, where the vast majority of studies examine this type of offence, almost to the exclusion of child luring and solicitation. There do not appear to have been any studies having examined behaviors related to the arrangement and agreement of sexual exploitation of children by adults. The lack of studies that deal with men who sexually solicit minors was noted by Paquette and Cortoni (2019), whose study highlights the difficulty of identifying individuals who have committed only luring offences: most of those included in their study had also committed CSEM-related or contact sexual offences. Men charged with child solicitation tend to be considered as either "online offenders" whose behaviors and victims are virtual or "contact offenders" for whom the online communication is only an initial step to offline crimes. Failing to make clear distinctions in the nature of the crimes committed by individuals who sexually exploit children has several implications in terms of assessment and intervention (see subsequent sections) and may obscure important aspects of such offences, particularly given the preliminary evidence for important distinctions between subgroups of offenders as well as the specific characteristics of their victims.

22.3.1 *Profiles of Online Sexual Offenders Against Minors*

Individuals who engage in sexually exploitative behaviors against children over the internet are in large majority male (approximately 99%; Seto, 2013), although there have been anecdotal reports of female involvement in solo or co-offending behaviors (e.g., Eke et al., 2011; Prat et al., 2014). While men who engage in online sexual solicitation of minors rarely limit their activities to this and also collect sexual images of minors or engage in contact sexual activities with them (Krone et al., 2017; Malesky, 2007; Paquette & Cortoni, 2019; Seto et al., 2011), many who use CSEM never engage in contact sexual offending against children (Seto & Eke, 2015; Seto et al., 2011). Examining crime rates among online sexual offenders ($n = 4464$) a majority of whom had been convicted of CSEM-related offences and a minority of child solicitation, Seto et al. (2011) found that one in eight (12%) had an official history of contact sexual offences against children and one in two (55%) in a subsample ($n = 523$) had self-revealed such behaviors. As for recidivism, only 2% of their follow-up subsample ($n = 2630$) had been convicted of a new contact sexual offence against children. Looking specifically at men with CSEM offences only at the time of the index crime, recidivism rates range from 0.7% to 4% over follow-up periods up to 13 years (the average follow-up period is usually 4 to 5 years; Elliot et al., 2019; Eke et al., 2011; Faust et al., 2015; Krone et al., 2017; Seto & Eke, 2015). Recidivism rates for CSEM-related offences tend to be higher, although remaining quite low (e.g., 6.8% during a 4.1-year period; Eke et al., 2011).

Given that there is little scientific literature on men who engage in online sexual solicitation of children, it is not surprising that data on their recidivism rates has been slow to appear. Preliminary investigations, however, suggest low rates of prior and reoffending convictions. In Briggs et al.'s (2011) study, 5.9% of men who solicited children had prior convictions, 3.9% specifically for sexual offences. In an exploration of the criminal careers of 1596 men charged with either or both CSEM-related and solicitation offences, Bergeron et al. (2020) found that among the 18% ($n = 292$) of men who had engaged in child luring offences, 18% had previously committed a contact sexual offence against children and 6% had at least one further charge for such offences. The authors identified crime-based patterns of internet sexual offending that can be usefully combined with knowledge from studies on psychologically meaningful risk factors in order to help develop profiles of those who commit internet sexual offences against minors. This may be beneficial in the consideration of the psychological treatment needs of such offenders, and also in considering their risk levels.

22.3.2 CSEM Users: The Importance of Atypical Sexuality

To understand more clearly why some individuals decide to engage in online, or even offline, sexually exploitative behaviors against children, it is essential to examine and isolate risk factors by comparing non-offenders with online and contact sexual offenders. Such a comparison is important because one of the major concerns for both researchers and practitioners is to determine what leads someone who engages in online sexual offending activities to also commit offline contact sexual crimes against children. One of the major findings from studies comparing CSEM users to other groups of sexual offenders against children is that CSEM users exhibit a deviant sexual profile but without being particularly antisocial. In a meta-analysis of 4604 offenders that compared CSEM users and contact sexual offenders against children, Babchishin et al. (2015) found that CSEM users were less likely to exhibit antisocial tendencies as evidenced by fewer indications of criminal history, problems with supervision, and substance abuse, as well as lower hostility levels and unemployment rates. They were also younger, more educated, and more likely to be Caucasian. However, while CSEM users tend to endorse fewer antisocial cognitions supportive of contact sexual behaviors against children (Babchishin et al., 2015), they exhibit more cognitions specifically supportive of online sexual exploitative activities with children (Paquette & Cortoni, 2019). CSEM users appeared to be more sexually preoccupied, exhibited more paraphilias, including pedophilia, and more often indulged in sexual fantasies or behaviors—deviant or not—as a way to cope with stress or negative states (Babchishin et al., 2015; Webb et al., 2007).

An atypical sexuality and a propensity toward antisociality are now empirically established as the most important indicators of risk of sexual offending (Hanson & Morton-Bourgon, 2005). From a theoretical perspective, atypical sexuality may be seen as the main motivation for sexual offending (Seto, 2008, 2019), although it is not the only explanatory factor, as shown by the fact that many individuals who are sexually attracted to children never engage in offending behaviors (Cantor & McPhail, 2015). Other personal characteristics, including being antisocial, act to facilitate motivations to engage in sexual offending behaviors (Seto, 2008, 2019). The virtual and "distal" nature of looking at CSEM over the internet have, incidentally, been reported by offenders as being less harmful than engaging in contact offences (Paquette & Cortoni, 2020a, 2020b). Thus, the decision to engage in online rather than contact sexual offending against children may be an alternative choice for the more prosocial individuals, at least for some who experience issues about their sexuality.

The difficulties with emotions and relationships that have been reported for those who commit sexual offenses against children—although the studies generally do not discriminate between CSEM users and contact offenders (Babchishin et al.,

2015)—may also explain their engagement in internet activities, as the medium provides a secure environment away from perceived dangers offline. Negative emotions and difficulties in relationships with adults are frequently found among men who engage in sexual offending against children (Henry et al., 2010; Middleton et al., 2006). For CSEM users, who tend to use sexuality as a way to cope with negative moods, using the internet to look at sexualized images of children is a way to escape an unpleasant offline reality (Bartels & Merdian, 2016), while restoring a sense of well-being. Taken together, such personal and interpersonal difficulties may partly explain why online CSEM users, in comparison with contact sexual offenders, tend to be more preoccupied with use of the internet (Babchishin et al., 2015).

22.3.3 *Mixed Offenders: A High-Risk Subgroup*

Another important finding from comparison studies is that mixed or dual offenders—men who engaged in both forms of sexual offending (use of CSEM and contact offences)—tend to be much more problematic in terms of atypical sexuality and antisocial tendencies than those who engage in only one form of sexual offending behavior (Babchishin et al., 2015), constituting a higher-risk group. This is supported empirically by studies that show that overall rates of crime and recidivism are higher for such individuals (Babchishin et al., 2015). Eke et al. (2011) found that mixed offenders (n = 206) reoffended significantly more often than CSEM-users (n = 228) in terms of contact sexual offences (8.7% vs 1.3%), violent offences (12.1% vs 2.6%), and failure to abide by the conditions of conditional release (35.4% vs 10.5%). No significant difference was observed in terms of CSEM-related reoffending. Over a fixed period of 5 years, Elliot et al. (2019) found that mixed offenders (n = 106) were more likely to reoffend than CSEM-users for both general crimes (20.8% vs 12.5%) and sexual offenses (14.2% vs 2.7%). No difference was noted in violent and non-violent/sexual reoffending.

22.3.4 *Online Sexual Solicitors: Opportunity More than Deviance?*

While victimization surveys provide a great deal of information about those who are victims of internet luring and solicitation to obtain sexual images or sexually arousing conversation (e.g., Gámez-Guadix et al., 2018; Kloess et al., 2019), there is only limited access to the perpetrators of such crimes and therefore know very little about them. Preliminary evidence, however, points towards a less deviant profile in comparison with other subgroups of offenders. For one thing, men who sexually solicit minors over the internet primarily target teenagers, not children (Wurtele, 2017). In the National Juvenile Online Victimization (N-JOV) study, 99% of victims of online solicitation were aged between 12 and 17, 76% between 13 and 15 years old (Wolak et al., 2004). While it might be argued that young children are simply not present on the internet and social medias, studies show that those involved in solicitation are more likely to exhibit hebephilia (sexual interest in adolescents) than pedophilia (Briggs et al., 2011; Seto et al., 2011). Looking at the few available "traditional" studies of men who engage in contact sexual offences against adolescents, measuring sexual deviance by hebephilia failed to discriminate those who offended from those who did not (e.g., Freund & Costell, 1970; Quinsey et al., 1975)—adolescents might thus be, for some, an "alternative" choice of target in the absence of the preferred choice (Guay et al., 2001; Stephens et al., 2017), a consenting adult. This hypothesis may also apply to some of those who engage in online sexual solicitation of minors, as many of these offenders also use the internet to solicit adults (49% in Briggs et al.'s study, 2011). In a survey on the use of social media by sexual offenders, Dowdell et al. (2011) found that more than half (57%; $n = 113$) of internet offenders solicited minors who were present in "appropriate-age" chat rooms; i.e., adult ones. Lack of opportunity to engage in sexual activities with adults might lead some to turn to adolescents, particularly as many internet sexual offenders see adolescents as less judgmental or rejecting than adults (Paquette & Cortoni, 2020a). The Motivation-Facilitation model of sexual offending stresses the importance of sexually driven motivation and antisocial tendency (or other problematic traits, e.g., substance abuse), but also asserts that situational factors, particularly an opportune environment, are important in the commission of sexual crimes, (Seto, 2008, 2019). This is further evidenced by meta-analytic findings that have shown that online offenders have more access to the internet than contact offenders, while offline offenders have more direct access to children (Babchishin et al., 2015).

Those interested in the solicitation of children online have been found to be more sexually preoccupied than contact sexual offenders against children, but less preoccupied than CSEM users (Seto et al., 2011). Many online offenders engage in sexually soliciting communications with more than one youth at a time (Krone et al., 2017), sometimes with hundreds and thousands—both minors and adults—in a short period of time (see, for example, C. v. Poitras, 2019 QCCQ 5672). Given the rapid and easy access provided by the internet, it is possible that sexually preoccupied individuals engage opportunistically in sexual communications with anyone, regardless of age. As well, those convicted of solicitation of minors were more likely to use CSEM than those convicted of contact offences (Seto et al., 2012). Given that a large proportion of those who engage in solicitation do so in order to obtain sexual images of their adolescent victims (60% in a national study conducted by the NCMEC, 2017), these images may be collected, again opportunistically, to fulfill a general sexual urge rather than to address a specific pedophilic or hebephilic interest. However, empirical investigation of these hypotheses is needed.

Individuals who have been convicted of soliciting minors exhibit prosocial profiles, as evidenced by low instances of criminal history, violent behavior, and unemployment as well as low rates of substance abuse (Briggs et al., 2011, Wolak et al.,

2005). Comparisons of CSEM users and contact sexual offenders against children found no differences in levels of antisocial indicators (Seto et al., 2012).

In terms of emotional and relational difficulties, men who sexually solicit minors over the internet were less likely to have ever lived with an intimate partner than offline contact sexual offenders but more likely than CSEM users (Seto et al., 2012). As CSEM users tend to fear the offline world and offline adult relationships (Bartels & Merdian, 2016; Paquette & Cortoni, 2020a), the internet may provide a positive virtual social environment for individuals who lack offline social interactions. Many offenders use online networks not only for technological tips on how to access their targets of choice (e.g., sexual images, youths within chatrooms) or avoid getting caught, but also to meet other individuals who share similar interests (see Fortin et al., 2018). These networks make it possible for individuals to create a favorable image of themselves, an image that may be different from the reality. In the N-JOV study, up a quarter of the sample (n = 129) were deceptive in their online communications: 25% claimed to be younger than they were, 26% lied about their physical appearance or aspects of their identity, and 21% lied about their sexual motives (Wolak et al., 2004). In Dowdell et al.'s (2011) survey, 70.6% of online sexual solicitation offenders were somewhat dishonest in the information they provided: 83% of this group lied systemically about their name or age, while 17% did so occasionally.

22.4 Clinical Intervention

The Risk-Need-Responsivity framework holds that treatment for individuals involved in sexual offending should be offered at an intensity related to an offender's level of risk of reoffending, target specific needs, and take into consideration factors that influence an individual's ability to benefit from treatment (Bonta & Andrews, 2017). Adopting these principles has been found to be effective in reducing recidivism (Hanson et al., 2009). Inversely, inappropriate treatment, during which, for instance, a low-risk offender is involved in a highly intense program or a therapist focuses on non-criminogenic aspects (e.g., lack of empathy) rather than criminogenic ones, may not only be counter-productive but may also increase the risk of reoffending (Bonta et al., 2000).

22.4.1 Assessing Offenders' Level of Risk

Actuarial assessment tools have been found to be more accurate in determining the risk of reoffending than unstructured clinical judgments (e.g., Grove et al., 2000; Hanson & Morton-Bourgon, 2009). However, this is the case when the assessing tools have good psychometric properties and are used with the populations for which they were originally developed. The STATIC-99, one of the most frequently used tools (Hanson & Thornton, 2000), measures the risk of reoffending based on static factors (e.g., age, prior convictions, victim gender) and was designed for use with sexual offenders with *known* victims. When used with CSEM users, it has been found to overestimate their level of risk (Osborn et al., 2010). The STATIC-99 might be of use with those convicted of online solicitation given that their victims are assumed to be *known*. However, additional studies are required to further test its validity with this specific subgroup as many solicitation offenders limit their behavior to online communications and, unlike most of those considered in developing the tool, do not engage in contact offences. The Risk Matrix 2000 (Thornton et al., 2003), originally developed for use with contact sexual offenders, has also been found to overestimate the risk posed by CSEM users, although an adapted version in which two items were removed (stranger victims and non-contact sexual offences) seems promising for classifying offenders according to their risk level (Osborn et al., 2010). Seto and Eke (2015) developed the Child Pornography Offender Risk Tool (CPORT) specifically for use with CSEM users. It considers the offender's age, prior and index convictions, evidence of pedophilia, and preference for male victims as evidenced by a higher proportion of images of boys in a collection. During its development and in subsequent validation studies conducted with Canadian samples (n = 346) over a 5-year fixed follow-up period, the CPORT was found to accurately predict sexual recidivism of CSEM users for contact (AUC = .72) or non-contact (AUC = .66) sexual offences (Eke et al., 2018). It did not, however, predict sexual reoffending for men with CSEM offences only (AUC = .63, Seto & Eke, 2015). In a validation study conducted in Spain, CPORT was found effective—although with a small effect size—in predicting new CSEM offences among men with no other offences (n = 255; AUC = .57; Soldino et al., 2020).

22.4.2 *Targeting Offenders' Needs by Identifying Dynamic Risk Factors*

Because those who offend sexually online have different profiles, an accurate assessment of their needs is crucial; such an assessment requires empirically linking risk factors to recidivism (Andrews & Bonta, 2010). Traditional tools that measure dynamic risk factors have not yet been validated for men who engage in online sexual offending against children. However, the STABLE-2007, the tool most widely used in Canada and the United States to assess sexual recidivism according to dynamic risk factors (e.g., Bourgon et al., 2018; Kelley et al., 2018), was used in a meta-analysis that examined its validity among sexual offenders and found that it successfully predicted sexual recidivism among a subsample of CSEM users (n = 72), suggesting it may be suitable for use with this population (Brankley et al., 2019).

Atypical sexuality, as previously discussed, is an important component to consider in evaluating those who use CSEM. Sexual interest in children among this population has been measured using several different methods (i.e., psychometric questionnaires, penile plethysmograph (PPG), interviews, polygraphs; Babchishin et al., 2011; Seto et al., 2006). PPG, which is recognized as an accurate way to assess pedophilia, has been found to provide good discriminant, convergent, and predictive validity (McPhail et al., 2020). In developing the CPORT, Seto and Eke (2015) found that self-admission and indications of sexual interest towards children (as reported by police officers) were predictive of sexual recidivism (AUC ranges of from = .60 to .81). To provide a substitute for self-admission of pedophilia, which offenders may be reluctant to disclose to authorities and therapists, the authors developed the Correlates for Admitted Sexual Interest in Children (CASIC), a behavior scale that has been found to be effective at measuring such interest (AUC = .71; Seto & Eke, 2017). Paquette and McPhail (2020) found that the Sexual Interest Card Sort (SIC; Abel & Becker, 1979) showed good psychometric properties for measuring typical and atypical sexual interests, including pedophilia, among online sexual offenders. The Revised Screening Scale for Pedophilic Interests (SSPI-2; Seto, Stephens et al., 2017) may also be used to assess pedophilic interests with dual sexual offenders given its positive associations with PPG outcomes of sexual arousal to children, as well as its predictive validity for sexual reoffending (Seto et al., 2004; Seto et al., 2017a, 2017b). However non-significant associations between the SSPI-2 and indicators of pedophilia were found in other studies (e.g., McPhail et al., 2020). As well, this scale has not been validated for men with CSEM-related offences only. Special attention should be paid to victim age when assessing sexual interest given the different risk-profiles of online sexual offenders. In a validation study of the SSPI-2, those who engaged in sexual activities with adolescents aged 15 and 16 years old (n = 149) were found to exhibit greater sexual arousal toward adults than toward children (Seto et al., 2017b). In this context, determining the presence of hebephilia or teleiophilia (sexual preference for adults) would be of particular importance in evaluating those involved in solicitation.

The other components that characterize atypical sexuality should also be considered. Some individuals are not driven by a specific sexual stimulus (e.g., children) but may exhibit more general sexual interest or a preoccupation with sexual fantasies or behaviors. There appear to be no validated tools designed specifically to assess the sexual preoccupations of online sexual offenders. Paquette and Cortoni (2020a, 2020b) used the Sexual Preoccupation subscale (SP; Snell & Papini, 1989) with a sample of online sexual offenders and found that it showed good internal consistency (α = .90) in measuring the tendency to be obsessed with sexual thoughts and behaviors. In a study of both undetected and detected CSEM users, the researchers used the Sexual Behavior Involving Minors Scale (SBIMS; α = .74; Neutze et al., 2011) which has one item that assesses frequency of CSEM use (Neutze et al., 2012). Other studies have used the sex-drive item of the STABLE-2007 (Seto et al., 2006, 2012) or self-admission (Lee et al., 2012) as a way to assess this construct. Furthermore, men who sexually offend against children, both online and offline, were found to exhibit poor coping strategies for stress or negative emotional states (Cortoni & Marshall, 2001; Webb et al., 2007).

Some of the same problems arise in attempting to assess the sexual coping strategies of online sexual offenders; again there appears to be no validated tool specifically developed to deal with this. A study by Paquette and Cortoni (2020b) used the Coping Using Sex Inventory (CUSI; Cortoni & Marshall, 2001) and found good internal consistency ($\alpha = .81$). Future examination of how this tool might be used with online sexual offenders should explore whether adding other relevant components, perhaps the use of the internet for sexual purposes, would allow a more complete assessment of how this population copes with stress or negative emotional states.

Dynamic risk factors other than atypical sexuality should also be taken into account, including the offence-supportive cognitions that have been empirically established to be associated with sexual recidivism among contact sexual offenders (Helmus et al., 2013) and sexual exploitative behaviors of children on the internet (Paquette & Cortoni, 2020b). Several specific tools have been developed and initially validated for use with internet offenders. The Child & Sexual Activities scale (C&SA; Howitt & Sheldon, 2007) deals with cognitive distortions commonly reported by CSEM users as well as contact and dual sexual offenders. The Internet Behaviors and Attitudes Questionnaire (IBAQ; O'Brien & Webster, 2007) covers both the internet-related behaviors and cognitions of CSEM users. The Cognitions of Internet Sexual Offending scale (C-ISO; Paquette & Cortoni, 2019) was developed to assess beliefs supportive of both CSEM-related behaviors and internet sexual solicitation of minors. Finally, the Cognitive and Emotional Congruence with Children scale (C-ECWC; Paquette & McPhail, 2020) was developed and initially validated to assess the cognitions of both online and contact sexual offenders in terms of their self-identification with children.

The internet's properties of anonymity, affordability, and accessibility—described as the 'Triple-A Engine' (Cooper, 1998)—have been hypothesized to facilitate online sexual offending against children (Cooper et al., 2000; Quayle & Taylor, 2003; Seto, 2013). This would be consistent with findings that online offenders are more preoccupied with, and have more access to, the internet than offline offenders (Babchishin et al., 2015) and that they exhibit specific, internet-related cognitions supportive of their offending behaviors, including the ideas that the virtual environment is not reality and that the internet's content and accessibility are outside their control (Paquette & Cortoni, 2020a). There is, however, no empirical evidence to indicate that the characteristics of the internet can be used to predict online sexual offending or are linked to sexual recidivism. Paquette and Cortoni (2020b) examined whether perceived online anonymity was associated with online sexual offending against children but found no significant association. However, they used the Perceived Anonymity scale (PA; Yun, 2006), which was originally developed to assess how the non-offending population sees the anonymity of online networks and it is possible that this scale is not appropriate to accurately assess whether online sexual offenders, as opposed to offline sexual offenders or non-offenders, feel anonymous when engaging in child exploitative behaviors. Participants in the study had all been convicted of online sexual offences against children so it is possible they no longer felt anonymous or, alternatively, perceived anonymity may not be linked with online sexual offending against children.

More research is needed to better understand the criminogenic role of the internet in online sexual offending. Until this information is available, practitioners should be cautious about placing undue emphasis on the effect of the internet when assessing and treating offenders, particularly given findings that treatments are more effective when focused on the reduction of empirically based risk factors (Andrews & Bonta, 2006; Hanson et al., 2009).

22.4.3 Responsiveness to Treatment

According to the Risk-Need-Responsivity framework, effective treatment should match styles and modes of intervention with learning style and ability to receive treatment (Bonta & Andrews, 2017). Many factors, both internal and external, can influence an individual's responsiveness to treatment (see Looman et al., 2005 for a review). Individual factors include (among others) age, ethnicity, motivation, mental health, personality, and recognition—or denial or minimization—of the problematic situations that led to the therapy. Among external factors are therapist characteristics, such as being empathetic and supportive; therapists who demonstrate these characteristics promote a therapeutic alliance that contributes to reducing recidivism (Bonta, 1995). The responsivity principle also recommends focusing on efficient therapies, such as structured and cognitive-behavioral intervention methods, which are recognized as having been effective with sexual offenders (Hanson et al., 2009; McGrath et al., 1998).

22.4.4 iHorizon Treatment Programme

The iHorizon (formerly named Internet Sex Offender Treatment Programme (iSOTP) which was developed in accordance with Risk-Need-Responsivity principles, has been accredited by the National Probation Service of England and Wales (Middleton et al., 2009). The iHorizon, like the majority of programs for online sexual offenders, is an adaptation of programs designed for contact sexual offenders by the addition of new components, in this case aimed at managing problematic use of the internet. As men with CSEM-related offences only are assumed to have a lower risk for recidivism, those in this subgroup are generally enrolled in less intensive therapy. Those at higher risk, as evidenced by, for instance, high levels of atypical sexuality and antisociality or having engaged in both online and offline sexual offending against children, are generally prescribed more intensive therapy. In their study of treatment effectiveness, Middleton et al. (2009) looked at whether there were significant changes in the criminogenic needs of 264 individuals convicted of online sexual offences following treatment. Their results are promising, as significant changes in dynamic risk factors (e.g., offence-supportive cognitions) were found. However, other factors, such as offenders' sexual fantasies and emotional congruence with children, remained unchanged. This last finding suggests there is a need for further investigations of relevant risk factors among online sexual offenders and development of assessment tools that can help create better and more efficient treatment programs.

22.5 Police Intervention

While the major concern for clinical practitioners is reducing recidivism, for those in law enforcement it is how to prioritize cases, as the number of accusations is much greater than the number of officers available to investigate them. Most of the work on determining risk factors for sexual offenders has involved psychological research conducted directly with offenders. Police officers, however, rarely have such access to their suspects and thus cannot rely on personal factors (e.g., paraphilias) in assessing risk but must rely instead on physical evidence. This is one reason that the CPORT, which was developed to be used by both clinicians and those in law enforcement, includes items whose presence can be coded based on more than one source; for instance, the item "indication of pedophilic interest" can be determined on the basis of an official diagnosis, self-admission, or indications from responses to the CASIC (Eke & Seto, 2016).

Unlike traditional tools for evaluating the risk of recidivism, the Kent Internet Risk Assessment Tool (KIRAT-2; McManus et al., 2015; Long et al., 2016) was designed specifically to help with prioritizing police workloads. KIRAT-2 is divided into two sections: the first assesses organisational risk, and the second the likelihood that an adult male suspected of a CSEM-related offence has committed an undetected previous or concurrent contact sexual offence against a child. The latter section includes items that deal with an offender's official and non-official criminal history, access to children, involvement in online and/or offline grooming behavior, and other relevant risk factors (Long et al., 2016). In a validation study conducted with a sample ($n = 374$) of both CSEM-only and dual offenders, KIRAT-2 was found to be effective in accurately classifying levels of risk (AUC = .91; Long et al., 2016). It is not, however, useful for assessing risk of reoffending or providing information that makes it possible to prioritize a CSEM case in relation to cases involving other types of crime.

22.6 Ongoing Prevention and Research Initiatives and Future Directions

The fight against the sexual exploitation of children over the internet has mobilized researchers, clinicians, police officers, justice agents, and those involved in protecting children across the globe with the common goal of reducing harm to children and adolescents. Several ongoing initiatives have been created over the years to increase information in the field and to develop new strategies for prevention and intervention. Some of these are described below.

Krone et al. (2020) have pointed to the need to work with situational factors in dealing with prevention. While the authors acknowledge that individual risk factors are important in sexual offending, they stress the importance of opportunity. While contact sexual offenders have greater direct access to children, online offenders have greater access to the internet (Babchishin et al., 2015). Using previous findings, Krone et al. (2020) suggest that a perceived absence of internet regulations (Rimer, 2017) as well as the common belief among offenders that what happens on the internet is not real (Paquette & Cortoni, 2020a; Rimer, 2019) may create an opportunity for abusive behaviors online. In this context, crime prevention should focus on reducing or monitoring opportunities on the internet as well as targeting dynamic factors that may facilitate offending behaviors (Krone et al., 2020). Such strategies include forcing those responsible for providing access to the internet to implement clear and rigorous rules against the diffusion of CSEM and for the denunciation of offenders (Taylor & Quayle, 2008). Others, based on the situational prevention model (Cornish & Clarke, 2003), suggest making it more difficult to commit such crimes (e.g., blocking inappropriate websites) and increasing the risk associated with offending behaviors (e.g., increasing oversight of the internet by law enforcement), as well as suppressing potential incentives (e.g., removing CSEM from the internet) and making it more difficult to offer offence-supportive excuses (e.g., providing clear messaging about the illegality of such behavior and creating stricter policies and codes of conduct) (Quayle & Koukopoulos, 2018; Smallbone & Cale, 2016; Taylor & Quayle, 2008; Wortley, 2012; Wortley & Smallbone, 2006; see Krone et al., 2020 for a review).

In 2016 the CCCP launched the Arachnid Project, whose goal is to remove sexual offensive content on the internet and, incidentally, decrease the rewards available to potential offenders. A virtual website crawler was designed to detect CSEM available online. The web hosting company is then asked to delete any images or videos detected. Electronic service providers are given access to Shield, a tool that notifies companies if images and videos that have been identified as contained CSEM are posted on their web service/domain. As of August 7, 2020, 6.1 million removal requests related to over 125 billion images had been sent to internet providers, leading to a significant number of removals. Approximately 85% of the notifications involved child victims who had not yet been identified by law enforcement (see CCCP website for further details about Arachnid; https://projetarachnid.ca/en/).

The Dunkelfeld project, a prevention initiative launched in Germany in 2005, provides confidential pharmacological and psychological help to individuals sexually attracted to children and adolescents who are attempting to avoid engaging in sexually exploitative behaviors with minors (Beier et al., 2015). Preliminary data on the effectiveness of this treatment was promising, as men attending treatment ($n = 53$) showed improvement in most areas of criminogenic risk (i.e., emotional deficits, offence-supportive cognitions, atypical sexuality; Beier et al., 2015). However, perhaps due to low statistical power, research failed to demonstrate that these changes were the result of therapy (Mokros & Banse, 2018), highlighting the need for further research on the effectiveness of this treatment. Mokros and Banse (2018), have suggested combining results from treatment sites across Germany to increase research sample size and help detect any changes resulting from this form of treatment.

Lastly, PRESEL (an acronym derived from the French title of a research project on the online sexual exploitation of children) is a collaborative research project between the Quebec provincial police and academics. It is aimed at improving understanding of adult males who engage in sexually offensive behaviors against children and adolescents through the internet. Closed cases in police files are thoroughly analyzed in three main areas: characteristics of offenders and victims (e.g., sociodemographic and psychological features, nature of use of the internet), characteristics of the online criminal investigation, and the nature and outcome of police interrogations of online offenders. Ultimately, PRESEL hopes to identify risk factors for both online and contact sexual offending against minors, outline efficient police intervention strategies, and design case prioritization tools that can be used with for those who access CSEM or are involved in child luring or sexual solicitation (see Paquette et al., 2023 for further details about the project).

In conclusion, there are several avenues of research that need further exploration. In particular, additional research is needed to learn more about men who solicit children over the internet. The finding that an important percentage of these men engage in either or both use of CSEM and contact sexual offending raises the question of whether their use of the internet is an alternative to other offences or a specific crime. Data on such men is limited and much more study is needed to better understand their psychological and offending profiles, their motivations, and the level of risk they present. Just as with those who use CSEM only, research should be aimed at developing risk and case prioritisation tools for those who solicit minors both on and offline. Furthermore, while much of the research available at the moment focuses on the distinctive characteristics of online sexual offenders as compared with contact sexual offenders, future research should also consider non-sexual offenders and individuals from the general population to determine if online offenders' distinctiveness is due to a propensity for sexual offending, for general offending, or neither. As well, much more effort is needed in the development and validation of assessment tools. Many of the traditional tools designed to assess psychologically meaningful risk factors (e.g., sexual coping, sexual preoccupation) may be suitable for online offenders but need to be validated for this population. Finally, a number of relevant hypotheses still need to be empirically tested, such as the role the internet plays in facilitating sexually exploitative behaviors against minors.

References

Abel, G. G., & Becker, J. V. (1979). *The sexual interest card sort*. Unpublished manuscript.

Andrews, D. A., & Bonta, J. (2006). *The psychology of criminal conduct* (4th ed.). LexisNexis.

Andrews, D. A., & Bonta, J. (2010). Rehabilitating criminal justice policy and practice. *Psychology, Public Policy, and Law, 16*, 39–55. https://doi.org/10.1037/a0018362

Babchishin, K. M., Hanson, R. K., & Hermann, C. A. (2011). The characteristics of online sex offenders: A meta-analysis. *Sexual Abuse: A Journal of Research and Treatment, 23*, 92–123. https://doi.org/10.1177/1079063210370708

Babchishin, K. M., Hanson, R. K., & VanZuylen, H. (2015). Online child pornography offenders are different: A meta-analysis of the characteristics of online and offline sex offenders against children. *Archives of Sexual Behaviour, 44*, 45–66. https://doi.org/10.1007/s10508-014-0270-x

Bartels, R. M., & Merdian, H. L. (2016). The implicit theories of child sexual exploitation material offenders: An initial conceptualization. *Aggression and Violent Behavior, 26*, 16–25. https://doi.org/10.1016/j.avb.2015.11.002

Beier, K. M., Grundmann, D., Kuhle, L. F., Scherner, G., Konrad, A., & Amelung, T. (2015). The German Dunkelfeld project: A pilot study to prevent child sexual abuse and the use of child abusive images. *The Journal of Sexual Medicine, 12*, 529–542. https://doi.org/10.1111/jsm.12785

Bergeron, A., Fortin, F., & Paquette, S. (2020). A crime-based classification of men charged with online child sexual exploitation material and solicitation. *Submitted for publication.*

Bonta, J. (1995). The responsivity principle and offender rehabilitation. Forum on Corrections Research, 7. https://www.researchgate.net/publication/285503766

Bonta, J., & Andrews, D. A. (2017). *The psychology of criminal conduct* (6th ed.). Routledge.

Bonta, J., Wallace-Capretta, S., & Rooney, R. (2000). A quasi-experimental evaluation of an intensive rehabilitation supervision program. *Criminal Justice and Behavior, 27*, 312–329. https://doi.org/10.1177/0093854800027003003

Bourgon, G., Mugford, R., Hanson, R. K., & Coligado, M. (2018). Offender risk assessment practices vary across Canada. *Canadian Journal of Criminology and Criminal Justice, 60*, 167–205. https://doi.org/10.3138/cjccj.2016-0024

Brankley, A. E., Babchishin, K. M., & Hanson, R. K. (2019). STABLE-2007 demonstrates predictive and incremental validity in assessing risk-relevant propensities for sexual offending: A meta-analysis. *Sexual Abuse, 33*(1), 1–29. Advance online publication. https://doi.org/10.1177/1079063219871572

Briggs, P., Simon, W. T., & Simonsen, S. (2011). An exploratory study of internet-initiated sexual offenses and the chat room sex offender: Has the internet enabled a new typology of sex offender? *Sexual Abuse, 23*, 72–91. https://doi.org/10.1177/1079063210384275

Byrne Hessick, C. (2014). The limits of child pornography. *Indiana Law Journal, 89*, 1437–1484.

C. v. Poitras. (2019). QCCQ 5672 (CanLII). http://canlii.ca/t/j2jbh

Canadian Center for Child Protection. (2016). *Child sexual abuse images on the internet*. Canadian Centre for Child Protection.

Canadian Center for Child Protection. (2017). *Survivors' survey*. Canadian Centre for Child Protection.

Cantor, J. M., & McPhail, I. V. (2015). Sensitivity and specificity of the phallometric test for hebephilia. *The Journal of Sexual Medicine, 12*, 1940–1950. https://doi.org/10.1111/jsm.12970

Cooper, A. (1998). Sexuality and the internet: Surfing into the new millennium. *Cyberpsychology & Behavior, 1*, 187–193. https://doi.org/10.1089/cpb.1998.1.187

Cooper, S. W. (2011). The medical analysis of child sexual abuse images. *Journal of Child Sexual Abuse, 20*, 631–642. https://doi.org/10.1080/10538712.2011.627829

Cooper, A., Delmonico, D. L., & Burg, R. (2000). Cybersex users, abusers, and compulsives: New findings and implications. *Journal of Sexual Addiction & Compulsivity, 7*, 5–27. https://doi.org/10.1080/10720160008400205

Cornish, D. B., & Clarke, R. V. (2003). Opportunities, precipitators and criminal decisions: A reply to Wortley's critique of situational crime prevention. *Crime Prevention Studies, 16*, 41–96.

Cortoni, F., & Marshall, W. L. (2001). Sex as a coping strategy and its relationship to juvenile sexual history and intimacy in sexual offenders. *Sexual Abuse: A Journal of Research and Treatment, 13*, 27–44. https://doi.org/10.1177/107906320101300104

Cournoyer, G., & Ouimet, G. (2017). *Code criminel annoté [Annotated Criminal Code] 2018*. Éditions Yvon Blais.

Dowdell, E. B., Burgess, A. W., & Flores, J. R. (2011). Online social networking patterns among adolescents, young adults, and sexual offenders. *The American Journal of Nursing, 111*, 28–36. https://doi.org/10.1097/01.NAJ.0000399310.83160.73

Eke, A. W., Helmus, L. M., & Seto, M. C. (2018). A validation study of the child pornography offender risk tool (CPORT). *Sexual Abuse, 31*(4), 456–476. Advance online publication.. https://doi.org/10.1177/1079063218762434

Eke, A. W., & Seto, M. C. (2016). Scoring guide for the child pornography offender risk tool (CPORT). https://www.researchgate.net/project/Child-Pornography-Offender-Risk-Tool-CPORT

Eke, A. W., Seto, M. C., & Williams, J. (2011). Examining the criminal history and future offending of child pornography offenders: An extended prospective follow-up study. *Law and Human Behavior, 35*, 466–478. https://doi.org/10.1007/s10979-010-9252-2

Elliot, I. A. (2017). A self-regulation model of sexual grooming. *Trauma, Violence, & Abuse, 18*, 83–97. https://doi.org/10.1177/1524838015591573

Elliot, I. A., Mandeville-Norden, R., Rakestrow-Dickens, J., & Beech, A. R. (2019). Reoffending rates in a U.K. community sample of individuals with convictions for indecent images of children. *Law and Human Behavior, 43*, 369–382. https://doi.org/10.1037/1hb0000328

Faust, E., Bickart, W., Renaud, C., & Camp, S. (2015). Child pornography possessors and child contact sex offenders: A multilevel comparison of demographic characteristics and rates of recidivism. *Sexual Abuse: A Journal of Research and Treatment, 27*, 460–478. https://doi.org/10.1177/1079063214521469

Fortin, F., & Corriveau, P. (2015). *Who is Bob_34?: Investigating child Cyberpornography*. UBC Press.

Fortin, F., Paquette, S., & Dupont, B. (2018). From online to offline sexual offending: Episodes and obstacles. *Aggression and Violent Behavior, 39*, 33–41. https://doi.org/10.1016/j.avb.2018.01.003

Fortin, F., & Proulx, J. (2018). Sexual interests of child sexual exploitation material (CSEM) consumers: Four patterns of severity over time. *International Journal of Offender Therapy and Comparative Criminology, 63*, 55–76. https://doi.org/10.1177/0306624X18794135

Freund, K., & Costell, R. (1970). The structure of erotic preference in the nondeviant male. *Behaviour Research and Therapy, 8*, 15–20. https://doi.org/10.1016/0005-7967(70)90029-X

Gámez-Guadix, M., Almendros, C., Calvete, E., & De Santisteban, P. (2018). Persuasion strategies and sexual solicitations and interactions in online sexual grooming of adolescents: Modeling direct and indirect pathways. *Journal of Adolescence, 63*, 11–18. https://doi.org/10.1016/j.adolescence.2017.12.002

Grove, W. M., Zald, D. H., Lebow, B. S., Snitz, B. E., & Nelson, C. (2000). Clinical versus mechanical prediction: A meta-analysis. *Psychological Assessment, 12*, 19–30. https://doi.org/10.1037/1040-3590.12.1.19

Guay, J., Proulx, J., Cusson, M., & Ouimet, M. (2001). Victim-choice polymorphia among serious sex offenders. *Archives of Sexual Behavior, 30*, 521–533. https://doi.org/10.1023/A:1010291201588

Hanson, R. K., Bourgon, B., Helmus, L., & Hodgson, S. (2009). The principles of effective correctional treatment also apply to sexual offenders: A meta-analysis. *Criminal Justice and Behavior, 36*, 865–891. https://doi.org/10.1177/0093854809338545

Hanson, R. K., & Morton-Bourgon, K. E. (2005). The characteristics of persistent sexual offenders: A meta-analysis of recidivism studies. *Journal of Consulting and Clinical Psychology, 73*, 1154–1163. https://doi.org/10.1037/0022-006X.73.6.1154

Hanson, R. K., & Morton-Bourgon, K. E. (2009). The accuracy of recidivism risk assessments for sexual offenders: A meta-analysis of 119 prediction studies. *Psychological Assessment, 21*, 1–21. https://doi.org/10.1037/a0014421

Hanson, R. K., & Thornton, D. (2000). Improving risk assessments for sex offenders: A comparison of three actuarial scales. *Law and Human Behavior, 24*, 119–136. https://doi.org/10.1023/A:10054882921333

Helmus, L. H., Hanson, R. K., Babchishin, K. M., & Mann, R. E. (2013). Attitudes supportive of sexual offending predict recidivism: A meta-analysis. *Trauma, Violence & Abuse, 14*, 34–53. https://doi.org/10.1177/1524838012462244

Henry, O., Mandeville-Norden, R., Hayes, E., & Egan, V. (2010). Do internet-based sex offenders reduce to normal, inadequate and deviant groups? *Journal of Sexual Aggression, 16*, 33–46. https://doi.org/10.1080/13552600903454132

Howitt, D., & Sheldon, K. (2007). The role of cognitive distortions in paedophilic offending: Internet and contact offenders compared. *Psychology, Crime and Law, 13*, 469–486. https://doi.org/10.1080/10683160601060564

Kelley, S. M., Ambroziak, G., Thornton, D., & Barahal, R. M. (2018). How do professionals assess sexual recidivism risk? An updated survey of practices. *Sexual Abuse, 32*(1), 3–29. Advance online publication. https://doi.org/10.1177/1079063218800474

Klain, E. J., Davies, H. J., & Hicks, M. A. (2001). *Child pornography: The criminal-justice-system response*. American Bar Association Center on Children and the Law for the National Center for Missing & Exploited Children.

Kloess, J. A., Hamilton-Giachritsis, C. E., & Beech, A. R. (2019). Offense processes of online sexual grooming and abuse of children via internet communication platforms. *Sexual Abuse, 31*, 73–96. https://doi.org/10.1177/1079063217720927

Krone, T., Smith, R. G., Cartwright, J., Hutchings, A., Tomison, A., & Napier, S. (2017, January). *Online child sexual exploitation offenders: A study of Australian law enforcement data* (Report to the Criminology Research Advisory Council). https://www.researchgate.net/publication/320415930_Online_child_sexual_exploitation_offenders_A_study_of_Australian_law_enforcement_data

Krone, T., Spiranovic, C., Prichard, J., Watters, P., Wortley, R., Gelb, K., & Hunn, C. (2020). Child sexual abuse material in child-centred institutions: Situational crime prevention approaches. *Journal of Sexual Aggression, 26*, 91–110. https://doi.org/10.1080/13552600.2019.1705925

Lee, A. F., Li, N. C., Lamade, R., Schuler, A., & Prentky, R. A. (2012). Predicting hands-on child sexual offences among possessors of internet child pornography. *Psychology, Public Policy, and Law, 18*, 644–672. https://doi.org/10.1037/a0027517

Long, M., Alison, L., Tejeiro, R., Hendricks, E., & Giles, S. (2016). KIRAT: Law enforcement's prioritization tool for investigating indecent image offenders. *Psychology, Public Policy, and Law, 22*, 12–21. https://doi.org/10.1037/law0000069

Looman, J., Dickie, I., & Abracen, J. (2005). Responsivity issues in the treatment of sexual offenders. *Trauma, Violence, & Abuse, 6*, 330–353. https://doi.org/10.1177/1524838005280857

Malesky, L. A. (2007). Predatory online behavior: Modus operandi of convicted sex offenders in identifying potential victims and contacting minors over the internet. *Journal of Child Sexual Abuse, 16*, 23–32. https://doi.org/10.1300/J070v16n02_02

McGrath, R. J., Hoke, S. E., & Vojtisek, J. E. (1998). Cognitive-behavioral treatment of sex offenders. *Criminal Justice and Behavior, 25*, 203–225. https://doi.org/10.1177/0093854898025002004

McManus, M. A., Long, M. L., Alison, L., & Almond, L. (2015). Factors associated with contact child sexual abuse in a sample of indecent image offenders. *Journal of Sexual Aggression, 21*, 368–384. https://doi.org/10.1080/13552600.2014.927009

McPhail, I. V., Olver, M. E., Nicholaichuk, T. P., & Haynes, A. (2020). Convergent and predictive associations of three measures of pedophilic interest. Sexual Abuse. https://www.researchgate.net/publication/341031043_Convergent_and_Predictive_Associations_of_Three_Measures_of_Pedophilic_Interest

Middleton, D., Elliott, I. A., Mandeville-Norden, R., & Beech, A. R. (2006). An investigation into the applicability of the Ward and Siegert pathways model of child sexual abuse on internet offenders. *Psychology, Crime, and Law, 12*, 589–603. https://doi.org/10.1080/10683160600558352

Middleton, D., Mandeville-Norden, R., & Hayes, E. (2009). Does treatment work with internet sex offenders? Emerging findings from the internet sex offender treatment Programme (i-SOTP). *Journal of Sexual Aggression, 15*, 5–19. https://doi.org/10.1080/13552600802673444

Mokros, A., & Banse, R. (2018). The "Dunkelfeld" project for self-identified pedophiles: A reappraisal of its effectiveness. *The Journal of Sexual Medicine, 16*, 609–613. https://doi.org/10.1016/j.jsxm.2019.02.009

National Center for Missing & Exploited Children. (2017). The online enticement of children: An in-depth analysis of CyberTipline reports. https://www.missingkids.org/gethelpnow/cybertipline

Neutze, J., Grundmann, D., Scherner, G., & Beier, K. M. (2012). Undetected and detected child sexual abuse and child pornography offenders. *International Journal of Law and Psychiatry, 35*, 168–175. https://doi.org/10.1016/j.ijlp.2012.02.004

Neutze, J., Seto, M. C., Schaefer, G. A., Mundt, I. A., & Beier, K. M. (2011). Predictors of child pornography offenses and child sexual abuse in a community sample of pedophiles and hebephiles. *Sexual Abuse: A Journal of Research and Treatment, 23*, 212–242. https://doi.org/10.1177/1079063210382043

O'Brien, M. D., & Webster, S. D. (2007). The construction and preliminary validation of the internet Behaviours and attitudes questionnaire (IBAQ). *Sexual Abuse: A Journal of Research and Treatment, 19*, 237–256. https://doi.org/10.1177/107906320701900305

O'Connell, R. (2003). *A typology of cyber sexploitation and online grooming practices*. Cyberspace Research Unit. University of Central Lancashire.

Osborn, J., Elliott, I. A., Middleton, D., & Beech, A. R. (2010). The use of actuarial risk assessment measures with UK internet child pornography offenders. *Journal of Aggression, Conflict, and Peace Research, 2*, 16–24. https://doi.org/10.5042/jacpr.2010.0333

Paquette, S., Chopin, J., & Fortin, F. (2023). *Crimes sexuels en ligne, délinquants et victimes: théorie, recherche et pratique*. Les Presses de l'Université Laval.

Paquette, S., & Cortoni, F. (2019). The development and validation of the cognitions of internet sexual offending (C-ISO) scale. *Sexual Abuse, 32*(8), 907–930. Advance online publication.. https://doi.org/10.1177/1079063219862281

Paquette, S., & Cortoni, F. (2020a). Offense-supportive cognitions expressed by men who use internet to sexually exploit children: A thematic analysis. *International Journal of Offender Therapy and Comparative Criminology, 66*(6–7), 647–669. https://doi.org/10.1177/0306624X20905757. Advance online publication.

Paquette, S., & Cortoni, F. (2020b). *Offense-supportive cognitions, atypical sexuality, problematic self-regulation, and the perceived anonymity among online and contact sexual offenders against children*. Under Review.

Paquette, S., & McPhail, I. V. (2020). Construction and preliminary validation of the cognitive and emotional congruence with children (C–ECWC) scale. *Psychological Assessment, 32*(8), 739. Advance online publication. https://doi.org/10.1037/pas0000832

Prat, S., Bertsch, I., Chudzik, L., & Réveillère, C. (2014). Women convicted of a sexual offence, including child pornography production: Two case reports. *Journal of Forensic and Legal Medicine, 23*, 22–24. https://doi.org/10.1016/j.jflm.2014.01.002

Quayle, E., & Koukopoulos, N. (2018). Deterrence of online child sexual abuse and exploitation. *Policing: A Journal of Policy and Practice, 13*, 345–362. https://doi.org/10.1093/police/pay028

Quayle, E., & Taylor, M. (2003). Model of problematic internet use in people with a sexual interest in children. *Cyberpsychology & Behavior, 6*, 93–106. https://doi.org/10.1089/109493103321168009

Quebec Ministry of Public Security. (2013). Rapport annuel de gestion 2012–2013. Retrieved from http://www.securitepublique.gouv.qc.ca/ministere/publications-statistiques/rapports-

annuels/2012-2013/resultats-2012-2013/suivis-du-plan-strategique-et-du-plan-de-gestion-des-depenses.html
Quinsey, V. L., Steinman, C. M., Bergersen, S. G., & Holmes, T. F. (1975). Penile circumference, skin conductance, and ranking responses of child molesters and "normal" to sexual and nonsexual visual stimuli. *Behavior Therapy, 6*, 213–219. https://doi.org/10.1016/S0005-7894(75)80143-2
Ratnayake, M., Obertová, Z., Dose, M., Gabriel, P., Bröker, H. M., Brauckmann, M., Barkus, A., Rizgeliene, R., Tutkuviene, J., Ritz-Timme, S., Marasciuolo, L., & Cattaneo, C. (2014). The juvenile face as a suitable age indicator in child pornography cases: A pilot study on the reliability of automated and visual estimation approaches. *International Journal of Legal Medicine, 128*, 803–808. https://doi.org/10.1007/s00414-013-0875-y
Rimer, J. R. (2017). Internet sexual offending from an anthropological perspective: Analysing offender perceptions of online spaces. *Journal of Sexual Aggression, 23*, 33–45. https://doi.org/10.1080/13552600.2016.1201158
Rimer, J. R. (2019). "In the street they're real, in a picture they're not": Constructions of children and childhood among users of online child sexual exploitation material. *Child Abuse & Neglect, 90*, 160–173. https://doi.org/10.1016/j.chiabu.2018.12.008
Seto, M. C. (2008). *Pedophilia and sexual offending against children: Theory, assessment, and intervention*. American Psychological Association.
Seto, M. C. (2013). *Internet sex offenders*. American Psychological Association. https://doi.org/10.1037/14191-000
Seto, M. C. (2019). The motivation-facilitation model of sexual offending. *Sexual Abuse, 31*, 3–24. https://doi.org/10.1177/1079063217720919
Seto, M. C., Cantor, J., & Blanchard, R. (2006). Child pornography offenses are a valid diagnostic indicator of pedophilia. *Journal of Abnormal Psychology, 115*, 610–615. https://doi.org/10.1037/0021-843X.115.3.610
Seto, M. C., & Eke, A. W. (2015). Predicting recidivism among adult male child pornography offenders: Development of the Child Pornography Offender Risk Tool (CPORT). *Law and Human Behavior, 39*, 416–429. https://doi.org/10.1037/lhb0000128
Seto, M. C., & Eke, A. W. (2017). Correlates of admitted sexual interest in children among individuals convicted of child pornography offenses. *Law and Human Behavior, 41*, 305–313. https://doi.org/10.1037/lhb0000240
Seto, M. C., Hanson, R. K., & Babchishin, K. M. (2011). Contact sexual offending by men with online sexual offenses. *Sexual Abuse: A Journal of Research and Treatment, 23*, 124–145. https://doi.org/10.1177/1079063210369013
Seto, M. C., Harris, G. T., Rice, M. E., & Barbaree, H. E. (2004). The screening scale for pedophilic interests predicts recidivism among adult sex offenders with child victims. *Archives of Sexual Behavior, 33*, 455–466. https://doi.org/10.1023/B:ASEB.0000037426.55935.9c
Seto, M. C., Sandler, J. C., & Freeman, N. J. (2017b). The revised screening scale for pedophilic Interests-2 (SSPI-2): Predictive and concurrent validity. *Sexual Abuse, 29*, 636–657. https://doi.org/10.1177/1079063215618375
Seto, M. C., Stephens, S., Lalumière, M. L., & Cantor, J. M. (2017a). The revised screening scale for pedophilic interests (SSPI-2): Development and criterion-related validation. *Sexual Abuse, 29*, 619–635. https://doi.org/10.1177/1079063215612444
Seto, M. C., Wood, J. M., Babchishin, K. M., & Flynn, S. (2012). Online solicitation offenders are different from child pornography offenders and lower risk contact sexual offenders. *American Psychological Association, 36*, 320–330. https://doi.org/10.1037/h0093925
Smallbone, S., & Cale, J. (2016). Situational theories. In D. Boer (Ed.), *The Wiley handbook on the theories, assessment and treatment of sexual offending* (pp. 289–312). John Wiley & Sons.
Snell, W. E., & Papini, D. R. (1989). The sexuality scale: An instrument to measure sexual-esteem, sexual-depression, and sexual-preoccupation. *The Journal of Sex Research, 26*, 256–263. https://doi.org/10.1080/00224498909551510

Soldino, V., Carbonell-Vayá, E. J., & Seigfried-Spellar, K. C. (2020). Spanish validation of the child pornography offender risk tool. *Sexual Abuse, 33*, 1–26. https://doi.org/10.1177/1079063220928958

Steel, C. M. S. (2009). Child pornography in peer-to-peer networks. *Child Abuse & Neglect, 33*, 560–568. https://doi.org/10.1016/j.chiabu.2008.12.011

Stephens, S., Reale, K. S., Goodwill, A. M., & Beauregard, E. (2017). Examining the role of opportunity in the offense behavior of victim age polymorphic sex offenders. *Journal of Criminal Justice, 52*, 41–48. https://doi.org/10.1016/j.jcrimjus.2017.07.010

Sun, S. S., Schubert, C. M., Chumlea, W. C., Roche, A. F., Kulin, H. E., Lee, P. A., Himes, J. H., & Ryan, A. S. (2002). National estimates of the timing of sexual maturation and racial differences between US children. *Pediatrics, 110*, 911–919. https://doi.org/10.1542/peds.110.5.911

Taylor, M., & Quayle, E. (2008). Criminogenic qualities of the internet in the collection and distribution of abuse images of children. *The Irish Journal of Psychology, 29*, 119–130. https://doi.org/10.1080/03033910.2008.10446278

Thornton, D., Mann, R., Webster, S., Blud, L., Travers, R., Friendship, C., & Erikson, M. (2003). Distinguishing and combining risks for sexual and violent recidivism. *Annals of the New York Academy of Sciences, 989*, 225–235. https://doi.org/10.1111/j.1749-6632.2003.tb07308.x

U.S. Department of Justice. (2010). *The National Strategy for child exploitation prevention and interdiction: A report to congress*. U.S. Department of Justice. www.hsdl.org/?view&did=20763

Webb, L., Crassini, J., & Kreen, S. (2007). Characteristics of internet child pornography offenders: A comparison with child molesters. *Sexual Abuse: A Journal of Research and Treatment, 19*, 449–465. https://doi.org/10.1177/107906320701900408

Wolak, J., Finkelhor, D., & Mitchell, K. J. (2004). Internet-initiated sex crimes against minors: Implications for prevention based on findings from a national study. *Journal of Adolescent Health, 35*, 424.e11–424.e20.

Wolak, J., Finkelhor, D., & Mitchell, K. J. (2005). *Child pornography possessors arrested in internet-related crimes: Findings from the National Juvenile Online Victimization Study (Report CV81)*. National Center for Missing and Exploited Children. www.unh.edu/ccrc/pdf/jvq/CV81.pdf

Wortley, R. (2012). Situational prevention of child abuse in the new technologies. In E. Quayle & K. M. Ribisl (Eds.), *Understanding and preventing online sexual exploitation of children* (pp. 188–203). Routledge.

Wortley, R., & Smallbone, S. (2006). Applying situational principles to sexual offenses against children. In R. Wortley & S. Smallbone (Eds.), *Situational prevention of child sexual abuse* (pp. 7–35). Criminal Justice Press.

Wurtele, S. K. (2017). Preventing cyber sexual solicitation of adolescents. In R. Alexander (Ed.), *Research and practices in child maltreatment prevention* (Vol. 1, pp. 361–393). STM Learning, Inc.

Yun, H. (2006). The creation and validation of a perceived anonymity scale based on the social information processing model and its nomological network test in an online social support community. (Doctoral thesis, Michigan State University, 2006).

Chapter 23
Victimology and Rehabilitation

Claire Barker and Daniel Taggart

23.1 Introduction

While there is often a separation between the study and treatment of victims, and research into perpetrators, this chapter argues that such a position hinders understanding in both fields. As Lauritsen and Laub (2007) suggest, "neither victimization, nor offending can be understood without full consideration of the other" (p. 56). As such, whilst the rest of this volume has looked at the offender and theories of offending, this chapter will focus upon our understanding of victims and their experiences, before addressing issues of treatment.

Whilst this volume looks at offenders and victims as separate groups, the authors of this chapter recognize that there is overlap between them and that some victims are also offenders, with some research identifying figures of between 20% and 35% of perpetrators of sexual offences also reporting their own childhood victimization (Glasser et al., 2001; Fedoroff & Pinkus, 1996). This will be discussed as a potential impact of experiencing sexual abuse alongside a discussion of treatment implications, while recognizing that the vast majority of victims of sexual violence do not go on to perpetrate crimes themselves.

C. Barker (✉)
Private Practice, Oxfordshire, UK
e-mail: claire.barker@tullyforensicpsychology.com

D. Taggart
Clinical Psychology Program, University of Essex, Wivenhoe, UK

R. J. Tully et al. (eds.), *Best Practices in Sexual Offender Assessment and Management*, Dangerous Behavior in Clinical and Forensic Psychology,
https://doi.org/10.1007/978-3-031-83135-5_23

23.2 Theories of Victimology

There are a number of different theories of victimology, which are discussed below. These include victim precipitation, lifestyle theory, routine activities theory and deviant place theory. Each of these will be presented in turn and critiqued from the authors' perspectives. Furthermore, the authors will discuss repeat victimization and how this may relate to the theories presented.

23.2.1 Victim Precipitation

The theory of victim precipitation is the controversial idea that victims may initiate the actions which lead to their harm (Petherick, 2017). This theory relies upon the ideas of victim facilitation (that victims may act in ways that make them more vulnerable) and victim provocation (that victims may act first, to initiate the offences against them). Whilst there may be an argument within the context of some types of offences, for example in the context of peer-on-peer assault, there may be circumstances where the victim of the violence, did indeed act first or provoke the other individual. However, in the context of this chapter, when sexual assault, including child sexual abuse (CSA) is considered, the idea of victim precipitation would appear to be victim blaming. It would be easy to question in which circumstances one would consider that a child, whom is unable to consent to sex, could initiate and provoke sexual assault. Timmer and Norman (1984) summarize the consequences of accepting this theory in the ideology of victim precipitation as "blaming the individual crime victim only serves to divert attention and resources away from the structural causes of crime and the structural changes required by a less criminogenic society, and renders the existing social, political and economic orders more legitimate" (p. 63). It is also dangerous to accept this argument from those who are responsible for the crime as it serves them as well as it prevents them from accepting responsibility for their actions. Ultimately, it may keep them from addressing those risk factors within themselves which caused the crime and may lead them to offend again in future.

There is a strong history of victim blaming in the field of CSA that needs to be challenged. The 'Memory Wars' of the 1990s saw academic psychologists question the veracity of testimony of CSA disclosed in therapeutic contexts, using experimental empirical findings from non-trauma related fields to justify assertions that these memories were 'false' and created in the context of unsafe therapeutic practices (Rouf & Taggart, 2021). It is important to draw attention to more contemporary evidence suggesting that the False Memory case is overstated and the experimental evidence is not valid in the area of traumatic memories (Brewin et al., 2020). What the ongoing controversy reveals is the highly contested nature of victim testimony regarding CSA in particular and sexual violence in general. It is clinically unhelpful and ethically problematic to compound the huge struggle victims already have in achieving any form of justice by casting doubt on the veracity of their disclosures in therapeutic contexts and suggesting they have somehow created the conditions for the crimes committed against them. While exploring how victims of sexual violence can keep themselves safe can be helpful in individual clinical work, it is not helpful for it to bleed into conceptualizations of victimology that are of relevance to perpetrators.

23.2.2 Lifestyle Theory

Lifestyle theory suggests that people may become the victims of crime because of their lifestyles and choices (Hindelang et al., 1978). Using data from the National Crime Survey (now the National Crime Victimization Survey), Hindelang et al. (1978) found that victimization is not evenly distributed across the population and that certain characteristics are more associated with experiencing victimization. For example, victimization was increased amongst those under 20 years of age, being three times the rate of those aged over 65. Similarly, gender was found to have an impact, with the rate of victimization of men being 50% greater than that for women. These authors relate these findings back to the lifestyle choices made by different populations i.e. with younger people choosing to spend more time outside of the home than older people and, therefore, having more time “at risk” in public.

In relation to sexual victimization, the lifestyle theory might suggest that victimization occurs when individuals make choices that place them at risk, for example, being out, alone, late at night or mixing with strangers (Hindelang et al., 1978) or belong to groups that are at increased risk such as being homeless. However, as with the victim precipitation theory, care needs to be applied in the exploration of experiences of victims not to blame their experience upon the choices that they made. For example, research may find that being out alone at night may be linked to an increased likelihood of being a victim of an offence, it is not the fault of the victim that they encountered this, that responsibility lies solely with the offender. This idea appears to be better understood within the routine activity theory, which will be discussed below.

23.2.3 Routine Activities Theory

Routine activities are defined as “any recurrent and prevalent activity which provide for basic population and individual needs, whatever their biological or cultural origin” (Cohen & Felson, 1979, p. 593), including going to work, school, college etc. This theory relies upon the idea that changes in routine and daily activities have an impact upon criminal activity and that the probability of victimization increases when there is a meeting in time and space of three elements: the motivated offender, the suitable target, and the absence of a capable guardian. Alone, this theory would suggest that activities that bring the victim into contact with the offender, increases risk of victimization. In relation to sexual assault, this may be best applied to examples such as children who are abused in schools or churches by teachers or religious leaders.

23.2.4 Deviant Place Theory

As with the routine activities theory, the deviant place theory also overlaps with the lifestyle theory. This theory posits that individuals are most at risk of victimization when exposed to dangerous areas (Stark, 1987). The focus of this theory is not on the behavior of the victim, but the place that offences occur, identifying that some areas are higher risk for victimization than others and that more frequent visiting to these areas increases the risk of victimization. An example of deviant place theory can be found by looking at crime statistics for different areas or states, to identify those where rates of sexual offences might be higher. The National Crime Victimization Survey shows that the highest number of sexual assaults across all U.S. states occur in Alaska (Williams, 2016) and, therefore, this could be identified as a risky state to visit or reside, according to deviant place theory. Seigel (2006) suggests that, as victimization is due to the neighborhood and not victim behavior, safety precautions are of little use in these areas.

23.2.5 A Mixed-Theory Approach

As opposed to subscribing to one theory to understand victimization, the authors of this chapter suggest that a better understanding can be gained by combining different elements from a combination of these theories. Cohen et al. (1981) combine both the routine activities theory and lifestyle theory to understand sexual victimization in “The Opportunity Model of Predatory Victimization”. In linking these two theories, these researchers suggest that victimization is linked to four concepts; exposure, proximity, guardianship, and target attractiveness. This would suggest that victimization most often occurs in situations where the victim engages in activity that exposes them (i.e. in a high risk area), is in close proximity to offenders where protection from others is absent, and where they may be seen as an easy or vulnerable target. An example of this is found within the research of Mustaine and Tewksbury (2002) who identified the risk posed to female college students, who are amongst the most common victims of sexual assault. These researchers found that risk of victimization was influence by the proximity of female college students, or the amount of exposure that they had, to rape-supportive male peer groups in the absence of any guardianship. They also found that membership of a greater number of clubs, going out at night for leisure, and using drugs in public were all factors which increased risk of sexual assault. This study demonstrates that victimization can be better understood by including an understanding of the environment and the offender themselves, as opposed to purely focusing on the behavior of the victim.

23.2.6 Repeat Victimization

Within the theories above, what is not included is an understanding of repeat victimization. Research has identified that victims of violent offences are, unfortunately, more likely to be repeatedly victimized (Farrell, 2005). Research by Weisel (2005) conducted over a 25-year period found that 25% of assaults had been experienced by only 11% of victims i.e. that this small number of individuals were assaulted on repeated occasions. In relation to sexual assaults in particular, Myhill and Allen (2002) found that 41% of women who reported sexual victimization experienced multiple incidents. Repeated victimization was most likely to be experienced by those who reported their assault as having involved a partner or previous partner. This research did not explore whether the perpetrator of the further assaults was the same partner. However, other researchers have identified factors which may increase the risk of an individual being vulnerable to repeated assaults, including those from different perpetrators. Of particular importance is an individual's psychological wellbeing following an initial experience of abuse, particularly with regards to the impact of ongoing trauma symptomatology on current psycho-social functioning (Graham-Kevan et al., 2015). Therefore, how well someone copes with an experience and the support they receive can impact the risk of them experiencing future traumatic events. These researchers also found that where the first incident of victimization occurs in childhood, risk of repeated victimization is higher, supporting the work of Widom et al. (2008) who identified that early life trauma from "interpersonal victimization" was associated with higher lifetime victimization. There are also important social variables such as gender, patriarchy, institutional corruption and poverty that are important mediating factors that leave some people more at risk of repeat victimization, by making escape or protection by others more challenging (Graham-Kevan et al., 2015).

Based upon the research outlined, it is suggested that those who have been victimized as children and present with trauma symptomatology as adults may be at increased risk of re-victimization (Graham-Kevan et al., 2015). If re-victimization is also considered alongside theories of victimology, it could also be suggested that environmental factors may influence the time the victim spends "at risk" or with whom they associate and, therefore, some groups of victims may experience repeated trauma due to these factors. Repeat victimization is important to note as, when the impact upon victims is considered in the remainder of this chapter, a single experience of sexual violence in their lifetime is not always being referred to.

23.3 The Impacts of Sexual Assault

The Independent Inquiry into Child Sexual Abuse (IICSA) was established as a Statutory Inquiry in 2015 to investigate institutional failings in relation to CSA in England and Wales. As part of the Inquiry, the Truth Project was established to hear directly from victims and survivors of abuse. At the time of writing, the Truth Project has heard over 6000 accounts from victims and survivors who have shared their experiences of abuse and its effects, making it both the largest public participation in a UK Inquiry and one of the largest data sets on CSA in the world. Within this chapter anonymous quotes from those accounts shared with the Truth Project (Independent Inquiry into Child Sexual Abuse, 2017) are used to demonstrate the lived experience of individuals affected by sexual offences and to illustrate the findings of empirical research.

Research has established a variety of impacts as a result of being the victim of sexual abuse, whether these are due to CSA or assault experienced in adulthood. Whilst this chapter will focus upon the effects upon victims, it is also important to note that Domhardt et al. (2015) have suggested that up to 50% of victims and survivors do not evidence any clinical symptomatology at all. As such, it is not suggested that all victims will experience the trauma symptoms identified below, but that the impact may be mitigated by a variety of different factors which may promote resilience, including education, attachment and social support (Domhardt et al., 2015). There are also strong structural factors that appear to mediate impacts, such as social and economic status (Metzler et al., 2017), gender (Karatzias et al., 2019) and cumulative effects of multiple forms of childhood adversity (Dube et al., 2003). Three, interlocking sets of impacts are described below; psychological, physical and social. These form a triad of impacts that need to be conceptualized as part of assessment and treatment (Taggart et al., 2021).

23.3.1 The Psychological Impact

> It's with you forever, and it has effects. I can't prove that it has effects in various ways, but I suspect a lot of the things that I feel and do go back to that. (A male survivor participating in the Truth Project)

In 2017, the Truth Project reported having heard from a sample of participants that 82% experienced mental health problems including PTSD, depression, psychosis and anorexia. This sample described associated symptoms as being anxiety, panic attacks, phobias, self-harm and suicidal ideation or attempts.

> I don't think there's anything that it doesn't impact and I don't think there's anything that it doesn't have some significance. (A male survivor participating in the Truth Project)

Kilpatrick et al. (1979) identified high levels of anxiety within female rape victims and survivors, including feelings of dread, nervousness, tenseness and unease as well as experiences of panic attacks and phobias. The level of anxiety has also been found to be higher within sexually abused samples when compared to those who have experienced non-sexual (emotional) abuse (Fitzpatrick et al., 2010) and, amongst survivors of CSA, Spröber et al. (2014) found anxiety to be reported in between 14.7 and 19.4% of cases, with this being the most commonly mentioned diagnosis amongst the sample.

Kilpatrick et al. (1979) also found that, alongside anxiety, their sample reported higher levels of depression when compared to a sample of women who had not experienced rape. This is supported by other studies where depression has also been commonly noted (Carr et al., 2010; Hillberg et al., 2011) and, in some studies, this has been identified as the most commonly diagnosed psychological symptoms amongst those who have been sexually abused (Spröber et al., 2014). Benedict et al. (1996) found depression was self-reported by 67.6% of a sample of children in foster care who had experienced child abuse, compared to 25.3% of those who had not. Other diagnoses identified to be more prominent amongst child abuse survivors include mood disorders (Wolfe et al., 2006) and personality disorders (Carr et al., 2010).

The link between PTSD and sexual assault has been widely established. Wolfe et al. (2006) found that 42% of their male sample of victims of institutional abuse suffered from PTSD at some point in their life and Knefel et al. (2015) found that 21.4% of their victim sample met the criteria for Complex PTSD. Research by Resick (2016) for The National Victim Center and the Crime Victim's Research and Treatment Center found that 31% of women who have been raped go on to develop PTSD. This researcher suggested that this findings amounts to some 3.8 million American women with rape-related PTSD and a further 1.3 million with rape induced PTSD, highlighting the immense impact of psychological trauma associated with experiencing sexual assault.

> Flashbacks are so real in your head, I could literally feel him on top of me and smell his breath, and wake up and be trying to push him off. And that was years after. (A female survivor participating in the Truth Project)

Suicidal ideation and attempts have also been identified as common responses to experiences of sexual abuse.

> I think by the age of eight I had tried to kill myself 12 times. The first time I tried to hang myself with do you remember the old AV SCART leads you put in the tellies? The second time I bashed my head in with a dumbbell. The third time bleach, fourth time cut the main artery. The fifth time was SCART lead again. Sixth was stab myself with some glass. Seventh I jumped out of a window. Eighth I had put … I smashed my head into a radiator about 55 times. Nine I tried to suffocate myself with a plastic bag. And then I tried to suffocate myself with a belt. (A male survivor participating in the Truth Project)

The Irish Commission to Inquire into Child Sexual Abuse found this prevalent amongst 51% of their sample. In their report, the Commission outlined the evidence of one witness who described 17 of his 39 classmates having committed suicide since leaving the school (Commission to Inquire into Child Abuse, 2009). In many cases, suicidality has been exacerbated by substance use and social isolation of survivors (O'Riordan & Arensman, 2007). In the case of substances, these have been identified to serve as coping strategies or a form of escapism from the trauma experienced (Danielson et al., 2010; Draucker & Mazurczyk, 2013). However, the use of substances can also be associated with increased mental health problems and physical health effects, increasing the difficulties which a victim and survivor may be trying to cope with in the longer-term.

23.3.2 The Impact on Physical Health

One of the most obvious physical health implications of sexual assault is the result of pregnancy. Pregnancy rates have been documented from research across varying cultures. In the US, Holmes et al. (1996) found that the rape-related pregnancy rate amongst a sample of 4008 women aged 12 to 45, who were followed for 3 years, was 5.0% per rape. This amounts to an estimated 32,101 pregnancies resulting from rape each year. In Mexico a figure of between 15 and 18% of rapes are reported to result in pregnancy, which is similar to the reported 17% of those adolescents raped becoming pregnant in Ethiopia (Mulugeta et al., 1998). In Lima, 90% of all new mothers aged 12–16 in a maternity hospital reported that the pregnancy was a result of rape (O'Toole, 1997).

> The abuse had got progressively worse and when I was 14, the group, eight of them … and they all had sex with me, and they made me deliberately pregnant with a baby. (A female survivor participating in the Truth Project)

In research looking at the impact of sexual abuse within intimate relationships, Wingood et al. (2000) found that women suffering from both sexual and physical abuse were more likely to have contracted multiple sexually transmitted diseases within their abusive relationship than those experiencing physical abuse alone. Long-term chronic pelvic pain has been found to be an ongoing symptom for more women who have experienced sexual abuse than those who had not (Collett et al., 1998; Walling et al., 1991). Further, Collet et al. (1998) found that those reporting pelvic pain were also found to suffer from more sexual problems, including dyspareunia, loss of interest in sex, post-coital pain, and vaginismus. Thurston et al. (2018) presented their study at The North American Menopause Society (NAMS) annual meeting in which they had found that women who had previously experienced sexual harassment presented with an increased risk of high blood pressure, high triglycerides, and clinically poorer sleep quality.

A link between CSA and eating disorders is also well established, including bulimia nervosa and anorexia nervosa (Dyer et al., 2013; Bankoff et al., 2013; Jaite et al., 2012). However, Jaite et al. (2012) suggest that binge eating is more common amongst survivors than disorders associated with restriction of food.

23.3.3 Interpersonal, Social and Economic Impacts

Victims of abuse have reported poorer academic achievement when compared to non-abused groups (Paolucci et al., 2001).

> I have trouble, I can't read and write, it took everything away from me. (A male survivor participating in the Truth Project)

Lower educational achievement amongst victims of abuse have been noted in longitudinal studies (Mersky & Topitzes, 2010, Boden et al., 2007). A key study by Bode and Goldman (2012) explored the impact of historic child abuse on education, interviewing ten male victims of sexual abuse in a residential care home. Nine of these men directly linked their experiences of abuse with their educational attainments, as a result of their inability to concentrate and fear of authority. Only two of these individuals had progressed past primary school level. Goldman and Bode (2012) reported similar findings amongst females, of which all ten females interviewed reported feeling that their abuse has significantly impacted upon their later opportunities in life.

> I lost out on going to college. I stopped going to college. I lost out on my education. I didn't return to education until I was 36. I never got a flat. I never got my independence. I didn't get any of that. He destroyed my whole fucking life at that point. (A female survivor participating in the Truth Project)

Many victims and survivors of sexual abuse have reported problems in maintaining healthy relationships in the future (Benedict et al., 1996; Commission to Inquire into Child Abuse, 2009).

> Yeah. I mean it's kind of devastating really and it's probably had an impact on, kind of, every aspect of my life, the most being not able to form stable and trusting relationships, you know. (A male survivor participating in the Truth Project)

Research by Carr et al. (2009) found that, from a sample of 247 adult survivors of CSA, 44% reported a fearful attachment style. This style was linked with low levels of marital satisfaction. This is supported by the research of Godbout et al. (2009) whose work supports the link between experiences of CSA, an insecure attachment style and later, marital distress. They further identified that the impact upon attachment in future relationships was greater for victims and survivors who had perceived their own parents to be unsupportive after the abuse, indicating that a poor familial response to experiences of abuse can increase psychological distress and an insecure attachment style.

23.3.4 Victims Who Offend

As mentioned within the introduction to this chapter, there is an overlap between victims of sexual abuse and offenders, in that some victims are also perpetrators of sexual abuse themselves. The authors of this chapter do not seek to provide an excuse for offenders nor suggest that all victims will commit sexual offences. However, there is some overlap and it is important that this is acknowledged. Although research findings vary in this area, what appears to be a relatively common finding is the link between childhood sexual abuse and the development of a sexual interest in children (Freund et al., 1990; Bagley et al., 1994). This does not suggest that all individuals who are victimized as children will go on to develop a sexual interest in children themselves, or offend against them, as an adult, a number of factors have been identified that increase the likelihood of victims becoming perpetrators. Plummer and Cossins (2016) identify these factors to include the individual having been abused when they are 12 years or older, being subject to frequent and serious sexual abuse and being abused by someone, such as a father figure, with whom they have a relationship of dependency. However, what is important to note is that, when looking at the research regarding risk factors associated with sexual offending, being the victim of a sexual offence is only one factor, of a number identified, that is linked and therefore should not ever be considered in isolation.

23.4 Treatment Implications

The field of study into treatment for victims of sexual violence is dominated by psychological, psychosocial, and psychotherapeutic treatments, and it is recognized that unlike other areas of mental health care that medication is an addendum rather than primary treatment of choice (Laddis, 2011). Treatment options vary and will be discussed in more detail below but the majority of treatment programs adhere to a three stage model of trauma work (Herman, 1998). The three stage model involves firstly the establishment of emotional and physical safety for both clinician and client in order to provide a secure base from which the trauma can be processed. The second stage, variously described as 'mourning', retelling and processing involves discussion of the traumatic events and can include remembering specific details of the trauma that have been presenting themselves in the form of symptoms such as flashbacks, intrusive thoughts, and nightmares. The final phase is the reconnection of the survivor back into their community and a reengagement with the social world.

While the three phases are not straightforwardly linear, the establishment of a safe and trusting relationship is seen as key before any trauma processing work can begin (Courtois & Ford, 2016). This may be even so the case in the context of interpersonal abuse as the abuse occurs in a relationship where trust has been betrayed and so any future, intimate relationships will also be at risk of boundary issues and feelings of intrusion leading to a lack of safety in the victim. Therefore working relationally is at the heart of any trauma treatment, as relational disruption is a central feature of the harm caused by the interpersonal abuse.

23.4.1 Interpersonal and Relational Considerations

As John Bowlby pointed out, psychological harm that occurs in the context of relationships requires relational healing; "...the human psyche, like human bones, is strongly inclined towards self-healing. The psychotherapist's job...is to provide the conditions in which self-healing can best take place." (2012, p. 172). This is perhaps even more the case in the context of CSA and sexual violence as there is such a fundamental betrayal of trust (Freyd, 1996) in other people that can result from the intrusion that suspicion and vigilance become adaptive strategies for survival (Fonagy & Allison, 2014). Therefore, irrespective of which treatment modality is used, the establishment and maintenance of trust is a central therapeutic task and is one measure of how successful the intervention has been (Menschner & Maul, 2016). Therapeutic trust is one of the key ingredients in a Trauma Informed Approach (Sweeney & Taggart, 2018), an organizational level intervention that provides a framework for working with traumatized patients.

23.4.2 Trauma Informed Approaches

Trauma Informed Approaches (TIAs) are system level interventions that are designed to provide safe and effective services to survivors of trauma in a way that minimizes risk of re-traumatization. Re-traumatization is a risk for people engaging in helping services where there are conditions of coercion and control that can mirror aspects of the original abuse, or support services that "cause or exacerbate feelings of threat, a lack of safety, violation, feelings of shame and powerlessness" (Edmund & Bland, 2011, p. 2). For example, in psychiatric services women survivors have been subjected to enforced medicalization and restraint, a loss of control and invasion of privacy which have features in common with the loss of control and intrusion of sexual violence (Harris & Fallot, 2001). Re-traumatization has been described as, "one's reaction to a traumatic exposure that is colored, amplified, intensified or shaped by one's reaction or adaptational style to previous traumatic experiences" (Danielli, 2010, p. 195).

In the context of sexual violence there may be an additional layer of epistemic vigilance (Fonagy & Allison, 2014) and mistrust towards professionals born from a suspicion that staff might present themselves as helpers but actually be hiding other intentions that only become apparent later once vigilance has been dropped. This again is a reenactment of the original abuse dynamics (Fonagy & Allison, 2014). This leads on to another central feature of TIAs, that rather than perceiving trauma symptomatology as evidence of maladaptive behavior or pathology, this can be seen as evidence of adaptive strategies for survival that were necessary in light of the abuse but which may be counterproductive in less threatening relationships. For example, in youth justice settings young people with abuse histories may have learnt that the rubric of survival has to take priority over the rubric of adapting to social norms, however this is unlikely to be an effective strategy in negotiating the rule bound institution they find themselves in (Ford, 2015). From this perspective, it is less the behavior than the context in which it is deployed that is crucial in appraising its utility, and the apparently bizarre or counterproductive actions of an abuse survivor may have been a sensible and necessary strategy for survival in a previous context. Therefore, in any TIA system, a trauma lens is needed to understand the abuse survivor's experience in this broader historical context.

For the reasons set out above, the avoidance of re-traumatization and the understanding of trauma history as a way to assess symptomatology and behavior, are two key components of a TIA. The other components set out in the literature are summarized in Table 23.1 and include interlinked concepts such as the development of trust and transparency, ceding control of the process to the survivor, an emphasis on empowerment, and the development of partnerships with other survivors. In addition to describing the particular attributes of each component, the reasons behind them have been included, as well as an illustration of how this might be experienced by a survivor.

The use of TIA principles at an organizational and individual practitioner level can be used to frame specialist treatment and also to act as a philosophy and practice of standard care in the absence of trauma specific intervention. Below specialist treatment options are discussed.

23.4.3 Specialist Trauma Treatments

The evidence base for psychological treatments for sexual abuse and violence tends to focus on diagnosis and not the underlying aetiological reason for the problem, in this case sexual assault(s). The population-based evidence suggests that for women victims of sexual violence, particularly poly-victimization, and for people who are sexually abused in childhood there are risks that they will develop complex post traumatic stress disorder (C-PTSD) as opposed to PTSD (Karatzias et al., 2019). C-PTSD has recently been added to the ICD-11 as a sibling diagnosis but one that has additional symptoms in three areas of functioning; interpersonal problems, self-organization and emotional regulation (Ford, 2015).

Therefore this section focuses primarily on evidence based treatments for C-PTSD. It is also acknowledged however that for a significant amount of women victims of sexual violence across the lifespan, another commonly used diagnosis is emotionally unstable personality disorder (EUPD). While there is a well-developed critique of the victim blaming and silencing potential of this diagnosis for victims of sexual violence, including from survivors themselves (Shaw & Proctor, 2005), a brief overview of the treatment options for this group is also included.

There is an argument made for flexible, multi-modular treatment based on a number of empirically supported interventions to address the range of problems people with C-PTSD present with (Karatzias & Cloitre, 2019). This approach is based on recognition that different problem constellations may require different

Table 23.1 An overview of the ten key principles of TIAs

Principle	Description	Why?	How this might feel[a]
Recognition of trauma	See through a 'trauma lens' by understanding potential links between current difficulties and past experiences. This includes routine, sensitive and appropriate enquiries about trauma, and being able to recognize the signs of trauma (e.g. dissociation). Having trauma recognized in appropriate ways can help survivors feel validated, safe and hopeful.	The majority of people in contact with health and social care services are likely to have experienced significant trauma which impacts current functioning.	"I am being seen and believed"
Preventing re-traumatization	Understand the way in which service policies (e.g. around risk management) and power differences between staff and adults can re-traumatize all involved, and take steps to reduce re-traumatization and vicarious trauma (see Sect. 23.4).	Re-traumatization (sometimes known as iatrogenic harm) through contact with services is common and often subtle. Staff too are vulnerable to re-traumatization and vicarious trauma.	"They are not like the people that hurt me"
Cultural, historical and gender contexts	Services should be culturally and gender sensitive and appropriate, recognizing the role of intersectionalities.	Different groups of people are likely to experience different forms of trauma e.g. on account of their gender, race, sexual orientation, disability and so on. Cultural resources and taboos may mean that people respond to trauma in different ways.	"They thought about me as a unique person. Me as a whole person"

(continued)

Table 23.1 (continued)

Principle	Description	Why?	How this might feel[a]
Trustworthiness and transparency	Decisions taken at individual and service levels should be open and transparent with the aim of building trust.	Trauma is often defined by secrecy and betrayal, disrupting survivors' ability to form trusting relationships.	"When they say they will do something they do it"
Collaboration and mutuality	Relationships should be collaborative and mutual, based on respect, trust, connection and hope. There should be a clear move away from 'helper-helpee' roles which reinforce helplessness/power dynamics.	The inherent power imbalance between staff and survivors can mimic that of abusive relationships. Having experienced powerlessness in the past can lead to ongoing feelings of disconnection, hopelessness, mistrust and fear in the present.	"We are working through this difficult stuff together"
Empowerment, choice, and control	Adopt strengths based approaches that acknowledge the coping and adaptive skills survivors have developed in order to get to this point. Ensure people are supported to take control of their lives, and make meaningful, genuine choices.	To experience trauma is to experience an absolute absence of control. Coping strategies are often critical adaptations that have enabled a person to make it through (e.g. self-harm, heavy drug or alcohol use) but can be viewed negatively by staff.	"I am taking control of my life now"
Safety	Everyone within a service—staff and adult—should feel and be physically, emotionally, psychologically, socially and culturally safe. To achieve this, the above principles should be enacted, such as cultural and gender competence, choice and control, transparency and so on.	Experiencing trauma fundamentally disrupts a person's ability to feel safe at any given moment, with 'flight, flight or freeze' mechanisms typically highly sensitized. People who identity as part of a minority group e.g. LGBTQ may feel particularly unsafe in mainstream services.	"I feel like I can finally begin to trust people again" "It might be worth seeing if they're trustworthy"

(continued)

Table 23.1 (continued)

Principle	Description	Why?	How this might feel[a]
Survivor partnerships	Organizations should work in partnership with survivors and users to design, deliver and evaluate services using coproduction approaches. Peer support should be a fundamental part of any service.	Peer support and the coproduction of services mean that mutuality, empowerment, collaboration and fairness/justice become part of the response to trauma. Partnership working allows for control to be returned to the survivor, after being taken away in the original abuse.	"Meeting other people like me makes me feel less alone" "I am making a contribution to service development so things can be different for future generations."
Pathways to specialist trauma treatment (trauma specific support)	Trauma-informed services do not treat the impacts of trauma. Survivors should be signposted, and supported to access, trauma-specific treatments (where desired). Services should cultivate good links with these trauma-specific organizations to facilitate referrals.	Survivors often find accessing trauma specific support very difficult.	"I go somewhere safe to talk through and understand what happened to me"

[a]Adapted from Taggart (2018)

treatment modalities and that all can sit within a relational, three stage trauma model described above. The trauma informed principles of survivor choice and control are also served by a flexible model, meaning that treatment can be collaboratively negotiated.

23.4.3.1 Psychoeducation

Phase 1 of trauma treatment, irrespective of modality, will include significant levels of education before other stages of the intervention can safely begin. If basic principles are looked at, that trauma is at its core a response to situations that are psychologically and emotionally overwhelming for the person, then it can be understood why helping them understand what happens in a traumatized state is the first step towards them regaining control.

There are a plethora of resources available for practitioners and patients alike, some have been developed specifically by survivors themselves. Here some core components of psychoeducation for complex trauma are listed and some examples of available resources are provided; these can be found in Table 23.2.

Some education about the neuropsychology of traumatic experience is crucial in beginning to help the person make sense of how their current difficulties link to their

Table 23.2 Online resources for Psychoeducation

Adverse Childhood Experiences Video- NHS Scotland	https://www.youtube.com/watch?v=VMpIi-4CZK0
Trauma and the brain video	https://www.youtube.com/watch?v=4-tcKYx24aA
Understanding child trauma- American set of resources containing infographics on trauma and its impacts	https://www.samhsa.gov/child-trauma/understanding-child-trauma
Understanding CSA- online resources for understanding CSA and its impacts	https://www.nctsn.org/what-is-child-trauma/trauma-types/sexual-abuse

abuse. Affect identification, regulation and modulation are central therapeutic tasks, and can be framed in terms of what is happening at a neurobiological level. Concepts such as 'survival brain' that get activated under stress to protect us and yet undermine our capacity to differentiate current threat from associations with past threat, can help people understand their anxiety in a non-stigmatizing light but also learn to begin to demilitarize their threat systems (Panksepp, 1998).

While this Phase 1 treatment involving psychoeducation has an important role in establishing a sense of safety, one study found that it had only a small effect on treatment outcomes (Mahoney et al., 2020).

Eye Movement Desensitization and Reprocessing (EMDR) is a psychotherapeutic method that accesses and reprocesses traumatic memories through bilateral stimulation (usually eye movements), thus alleviating experiences of distress (Shapiro, 1989). Maxfield (2007) identifies EMDR as successful in the treatment of PTSD across a number of randomized controlled studies. The findings of these studies indicate that EMDR is effective in addressing trauma-related distress for individuals who have experienced a variety of different and complex traumatic experiences. However, more specific research has also indicated that EMDR is effective in addressing sexual trauma amongst adult female survivors of CSA (Edmond et al., 1999; Edmond & Rubin, 2004) and adult female rape victims (Rothbaum et al., 2005).

In comparison to Trauma focused CBT, Jaberghaderi et al. (2004) found that in a group of sexually abused Iranian girls, both treatments resulted in a reduction of trauma symptoms. However, fewer sessions of EMDR were needed for this and the participants generally self-reported favoring the EMDR approach. Generally, progress within fewer EMDR sessions, when compared to CBT based therapies, has been identified by a number of studies regarding EMDR for PTSD (not sexual specific), with de Roos et al. (2011) identifying this amongst their sample of disaster exposed children and Nijdam et al. (2012) in an adult sample.

23.4.3.2 Exposure-Based Therapy

The majority of therapeutic treatments for C-PTSD involve some form of exposure therapy in the Phase 2 element. EMDR offers one set of techniques to enable the patient to process trauma-related experience in the context of a safe, boundaried treatment. Other forms of psychological therapy offer different techniques of achieving the same goal of enabling the person to tolerate and talk about elements of the abusive experiences in a carefully structured way. The goal is more than cathartic, it is the re-experiencing of the trauma-related emotions and physical sensations so these can be integrated and thus reduce the unwarranted intrusions that characterizes a traumatized state (Courtois & Ford, 2016). It is hypothesized that engagement with the trauma-related memories, sensations and emotions can help the patient learn that these experiences can be tolerated without them becoming overwhelmed again, and also that habituation to them reduces affective intensity (Carey, 2011).

Prolonged exposure and cognitive processing therapy are two forms of exposure treatment that rely upon a graded approach to retelling and tolerating increasingly intense trauma memories. There is some evidence to support both sets of techniques in the treatment of CPTSD, including for the treatment of sexual violence and childhood abuse. However a broad range of other therapeutic treatments also use the principles of exposure to achieve trauma memory and emotion processing, and there is no consensus yet about the superiority of one form of this over others (Courtois & Ford, 2016).

23.5 Conclusions and Recommendations

This chapter has examined the theories of victimology, impact of being victimized, and treatment implications. It is argued that there is no single theory of victimology explaining why some individuals experience sexual assault and others do not. There are a broad range of factors that may influence the likelihood of being victimized, including age, lifestyle factors, social and economic position, location, associations, and previous life experiences. What is vital when working with victims is that theories which place the responsibility for the experience upon the victim (i.e. blaming them for the incident) are neither reliable nor helpful. Whilst some behaviors or routines may bring a victim into contact with a perpetrator, the responsibility for the sexual assault lies solely with that perpetrator. The stigma of sexual assault reduces disclosures and is fueled in part by prejudicial attitudes from others towards victims. It is vital that practitioners in the field lead the way in victim centered approaches.

Research findings have very clearly identified the broad range of impacts of sexual assault, whether this is experienced as a child or an adult. The main psychological, physical, interpersonal, social, and economic consequences have been set out, but it is important to note that every victim and survivor copes differently and, as such, the impacts will vary between individuals. There are also individuals who are more resilient and able to move forward without adverse consequences. However, where negative consequences are endured, these can affect an individual across the lifespan and across multiple facets of their lives, which in turn may increase the risk of them encountering further traumatic events.

There are a variety of treatment options available for those seeking to address the psychological impact of their experiences. However, effective interventions should be trauma informed, whether these are to address the individual trauma-related symptoms or to look at the traumatic incident itself. The focus of treatment may vary according to the client's individual presentation but what is most important is that consideration is given to avoiding re-traumatization and, therefore, careful thought needs to be given to the selection of the approach used and the timing of the engagement.

A final point to end on is one emergent lesson from the IICSA Truth Project that has been cited here to provide survivor accounts. The Truth Project involved survivors of CSA coming forward to share their experiences of abuse, the impacts that it has had on them, and the recommendations they wanted to make to IICSA. The support model behind the Truth Project was trauma-informed and participants were offered support before and after the session itself. What is noteworthy is that survivors of CSA, properly supported, were able and willing to share their experiences once provided with a safe environment and a practitioner who was prepared to believe them and treat them with respect. This challenges long held beliefs among professionals that CSA survivors will become destabilized if they talk about their experiences and that asking will 'open a can of worms'. While asking about childhood trauma needs to be handled sensitively, the Truth Project demonstrates that given choice and control over the process, survivors can talk about their experiences as one part of their ongoing recovery. It would be helpful for this learning to be incorporated into practice by professionals working in the field of forensic psychology.

References

Bagley, C., Wood, M., & Young, L. (1994). Victim to abuser: Mental health and behavioral sequels of child sexual abuse in a community survey of young adult males. *Child Abuse & Neglect, 18*, 683–697.

Bankoff, S. M., Valentine, S. E., Jackson, M. A., Schacht, R. L., & Pantalone, D. W. (2013). Compensatory weight control behaviors of women in emerging adulthood: Associations between childhood abuse experiences and adult relationship avoidance. *Journal of American College Health, 61*(8), 468–475.

Benedict, M. I., Zuravin, S., Somerfield, M., & Brandt, D. (1996). The reported health and functioning of children maltreated while in family foster care. *Child Abuse & Neglect, 20*(7), 561–571.

Bode, A., & Goldman, J. D. G. (2012). The impact of child sexual abuse on the education of boys in residential care between 1950 and 1975. *Pastoral Care in Education: An International Journal of Personal, Social and Emotional Development, 20*(4), 331–344.

Boden, J. M., Horwood, J., & Fergusson, D. M. (2007). Exposure to childhood sexual and physical abuse and subsequent educational achievement outcomes. *Child Abuse & Neglect, 31*, 1101–1114.
Bowlby, J. (2012). *A secure base*. Routledge.
Brewin, C. R., Andrews, B., & Mickes, L. (2020). Regaining consensus on the reliability of memory. *Current Directions in Psychological Science, 29*(2), 121–125. https://doi.org/10.1177/0963721419898122
Carey, T. (2011). Exposure and reorganization: The what and how of effective psychotherapy. *Clinical Psychology Review, 31*(2), 236–248.
Carr, A., Dooley, B., Fitzpatrick, M., Flanagan, E., Flanagan-Howard, R., Tierney, K., White, M., Daly, M., & Egan, J. (2010). Adult adjustment of survivors of institutional child abuse in Ireland. *Child Abuse & Neglect, 34*(7), 477–489.
Carr, A., Flanagan, E., Dooley, B., Fitzpatrick, M., Flanagan-Howard, R., Shevlin, M., Tierney, K., White, M., Daly, M., & Egan, J. (2009). Profiles of Irish survivors of institutional abuse with different adult attachment styles. *Attachment & Human Development, 11*(2), 183–201.
Cohen, L. E., & Felson, M. (1979). Social change and crime rate trends: A routine activity approach. *American Sociological Review, 44*, 588–608.
Cohen, L. E., Kluegel, J. R., & Land, K. C. (1981). Social inequality and criminal victimization. *American Sociological Review, 46*, 505–524.
Collett, B. J., Cordle, C. J., Stewart, C. R., & Jagger, C. (1998). A comparative study of women with chronic pelvic pain, chronic nonpelvic pain and those with no history of pain attending general practitioners. *British Journal of Obstetrics and Gynaecology, 105*(1), 87–92.
Commission to Inquire into Child Abuse. (2009). *Commission to inquire into child abuse report*. The Stationery Office.
Courtois, C., & Ford, J. (2016). *Treatment of complex trauma: A sequential relationship based approach*. Guilford Press.
Danielli, Y. (2010). *International handbook of multigenerational legacies of trauma*. Springer.
Danielson, C. K., Macdonald, A., Amstadter, A. B., Hanson, R., de Arellano, M. A., Saunders, B. E., & Kilpatrick, D. G. (2010). Risky behaviors and depression in conjunction with – or in the absence of – lifetime history of PTSD among sexually abused adolescents. *Child Maltreatment, 15*(1), 101–107.
de Roos, C., Greenwald, R., den Hollander-Gijsman, M., Noorthoorn, E., van Buuren, S., & de Jongh, A. (2011). A randomised comparison of cognitive behavioural therapy (CBT) and eye movement desensitisation and reprocessing (EMDR) in disaster-exposed children. *European Journal of Psychotraumatology, 2*, 5694. https://doi.org/10.3402/ejpt.v2i0.5694
Domhardt, M., Münzer, A., Fegert, J. M., & Goldbeck, L. (2015). Resilience in survivors of child sexual abuse: A systematic review of the literature. *Trauma, Violence & Abuse, 16*, 476–493.
Draucker, C. B., & Mazurczyk, J. (2013). Relationships between childhood sexual abuse and substance use and sexual risk behaviors during adolescence: An integrative review. *Nursing Outlook, 61*(5), 291–310.
Dube, S. R., Felitti, V. J., Dong, M., Chapman, D. P., Giles, W. H., & Anda, R. F. (2003). Childhood abuse, neglect, and household dysfunction and the risk of illicit drug use: The adverse childhood experiences study. *Pediatrics, 111*(3), 564–572. https://doi.org/10.1542/peds.111.3.564. PMID: 12612237.
Dyer, A., Borgmann, E., Kleindienst, N., Feldmann, R. E., Vocks, S., & Bohus, M. (2013). Body image in patients with posttraumatic stress disorder after childhood sexual abuse and co-occurring eating disorder. *Psychopathology, 46*, 186–191.
Edmond, T. E., & Rubin, A. (2004). Assessing the long-term effects of EMDR: Results from an 18-month follow-up study with adult female survivors of CSA. *Journal of Child Sexual Abuse, 13*, 69–86.
Edmond, T. E., Rubin, A., & Wambach, K. G. (1999). The effectiveness of EMDR with adult female survivors of childhood sexual abuse. *Social Work Research, 23*, 103–116.

Edmund, D., & Bland, B. (2011). Real tools: Responding to multi abuse trauma, Alaska network on domestic violence and sexual assault. https://andvsa.org/wp-content/uploads/2013/02/11d-Mental-Health-Concerns.pdf

Farrell, G. (2005). Progress and prospects in the prevention of repeat victimisation. In N. Tilley (Ed.), *Handbook of crime prevention and community safety*. Willan.

Fedoroff, J. P., & Pinkus, S. (1996). The genesis of pedophilia: Testing the 'abuse to abuser' hypothesis. *Journal of Offender Rehabilitation, 23*, 85–101.

Fitzpatrick, M., Carr, A., Dooley, B., Flanagan-Howard, R., Tierney, K., White, M., Daly, M., Shavlin, M., & Egan, J. (2010). Profiles of adult survivors of severe sexual, physical and emotional institutional abuse in Ireland. *Child Abuse Review, 19*(6), 387–404.

Fonagy, P., & Allison, E. (2014). The role of mentalizing and epistemic trust in the therapeutic relationship. *Psychotherapy, 51*(3), 372–380.

Ford, J. (2015). Complex PTSD: Research directions for nosology/assessment, treatment and public health. *European Journal of Psychotraumatology, 6*(1), 27584. https://doi.org/10.3402/ejpt.v6.27584

Freund, K., Watson, R., & Dickey, R. (1990). Does sexual abuse in childhood cause pedophilia: An exploratory study. *Archives of Sexual Behavior, 19*, 557–568.

Freyd, J. J. (1996). *Betrayal trauma: The logic of forgetting childhood abuse*. Harvard University Press.

Glasser, M., Kolvin, I., Campbell, D., Glasser, A., Leithch, I., & Farrelly, S. (2001). Cycle of child sexual abuse: Links between being a victim and becoming a perpetrator. *British Journal of Psychiatry, 179*, 482–494.

Godbout, N., Sabourin, S., & Lussier, Y. (2009). Child sexual abuse and adult romantic adjustment: Comparison of single- and multiple-indicator measures. *Journal of Interpersonal Violence, 24*(4), 693–705.

Goldman, J. D. G., & Bode, A. (2012). Female survivors' perceptions of lifelong impact on their education of child abuse suffered in orphanages. *International Journal of Lifelong Education, 31*(2), 203–221.

Graham-Kevan, N., Brooks, M., Willan, V. J., Lowe, M., Robinson, P., Khan, R., Stokes, R., Irving, M., Karwacka, M., & Bryce, J. (2015). Repeat victimisation, retraumatisation and victim vulnerability. *The Open Criminology Journal, 8*, 36–48.

Harris, M., & Fallot, R. D. (2001). Envisioning a trauma-informed service system: A vital paradigm shift. *New Directions for Mental Health Services, 89*, 3–22. https://doi.org/10.1002/yd.23320018903. PMID: 11291260.

Herman, J. (1998). Recovery from psychological trauma. *Psychiatry and Clinical Neurosciences, 52*(1), S98–S103. https://doi.org/10.1046/j.1440-1819.1998.0520s5S145.x

Hillberg, T., Hamilton-Giachritsis, C., & Dixon, L. (2011). Review of meta-analyses on the association between child sexual abuse and adult mental health difficulties: A systematic approach. *Trauma, Violence, & Abuse, 12*(1), 38–49.

Hindelang, M. J., Gottfredson, M. R., & Garofalo, J. (1978). *Victims of personal crime: An empirical foundation for a theory of personal victimization*. Ballinger Pub. Co.

Holmes, M. M., Resnick, H. S., Kilpatrick, D. G., & Best, C. L. (1996). Rape-related pregnancy: Estimates and descriptive characteristics from a national sample of women. *American Journal of Obstetrics and Gynecology., 175*(2), 320–324.

Independent Inquiry into Child Sexual Abuse. (2017). *Victim and survivor voices from the truth project*. IICSA. https://www.iicsa.org.uk/document/victim-and-survivor-voices-truth-project

Jaberghaderi, N., Greenwald, R., Rubin, A., Zand, S. H., & Dolatabadi, S. (2004). A comparison of CBF-BT and EMDR for sexually-abused Iranian girls. *Clinical Psychology and Psychotherapy, 11*, 358–368.

Jaite, C., Schneider, N., Hilbert, A., Pfeiffer, E., Lehmkuhl, U., & Salbach-Andrae, H. (2012). Etiological role of childhood emotional trauma and neglect in adolescent anorexia nervosa: A cross-sectional questionnaire analysis. *Psychopathology, 45*, 61–66.

Karatzias, T., & Cloitre, M. (2019). Treating adults with complex posttraumatic stress disorder using a modular approach to treatment: Rationale, evidence, and directions for future research. *Journal of Traumatic Stress, 32*(6), 870–876. https://doi.org/10.1002/jts.22457

Karatzias, T., Hyland, P., Bradley, A., Cloitre, M., Roberts, N., Bisson, J., & Shevlin, M. (2019). Risk factors and comorbidity of ICD-11 PTSD and complex PTSD: Findings from a trauma-exposed population based sample of adults in the United Kingdom. *Depression and Anxiety, 36*(9), 887–894. https://doi.org/10.1002/da.22934. PMID: 31268218.

Kilpatrick, D. G., Veronen, L. J., & Resick, P. A. (1979). The aftermath of rape: Recent empirical findings. *American Journal of Orthopsychiatry., 49*(4), 658–669.

Knefel, M., Garvert, D. W., Cloitre, M., & Lueger-Schuster, B. (2015). (in press)). Update to an evaluation of ICD-11 PTSD and complex PTSD criteria in a sample of adult survivors of childhood institutional abuse by Knefel & Lueger Schuster (2013): A latent profile analysis. *European Journal of Psychotraumatology, 4*(1), 22608.

Laddis, A. (2011). Medication for complex posttraumatic disorders. *Journal of Aggression, Maltreatment & Trauma, 20*(6), 645–668. https://doi.org/10.1080/10926771.2011.596137

Lauritsen, J. L., & Laub, J. H. (2007). Understanding the link between victimization and offending: New reflections on an old idea. In M. Hough & M. Maxfield (Eds.), *Surveying crime in the 21st century* (pp. 55–75). Criminal Justice/Willow Tree Press.

Mahoney, A., Karatzias, T., Halliday, K., & Dougal, N. (2020). How important are phase 1 interventions for complex interpersonal trauma? A pilot randomized control trial of a group psychoeducational intervention. *Clinical Psychology & Psychotherapy, 27*(4), 597–610.

Maxfield, L. (2007). Current status and future directions for EMDR research. *Journal of EMDR Practice and Research, 1*(1), 6–14.

Menschner, C., & Maul, A. (2016). *Key ingredients for successful trauma informed care*. Centre for Healthcare Strategies.

Mersky, J. P., & Topitzes, J. (2010). Comparing early adult outcomes of maltreated and non-maltreated children: A prospective longitudinal investigation. *Children and Youth Services Review, 32*, 1086–1096.

Metzler, M., Merrick, M. T., Klevens, J., Ports, K. A., & Ford, D. C. (2017). Adverse childhood experiences and life opportunities: Shifting the narrative. *Children and Youth Services Review, 72*, 141–149. https://doi.org/10.1016/j.childyouth.2016.10.021

Mulugeta, E., Kassaye, M., & Berhane, Y. (1998). Prevalence and outcomes of sexual violence among high school students. *Ethiopian Medical Journal, 36*(3), 167–174.

Mustaine, E. E., & Tewksbury, R. (2002). Sexual assault of college women: A feminist interpretation of a routine activities analysis. *Criminal Justice Review, 27*(1), 89–123.

Myhill, A., & Allen, J. (2002). *Rape and sexual assault of women: The extent and nature of.* Home Office.

Nijdam, M. J., Gersons, B. P., Reitsma, J. B., de Jongh, A., & Olff, M. (2012). Brief eclectic psychotherapy v. eye movement desensitisation and reprocessing therapy for post-traumatic stress disorder: Randomised controlled trial. *British Journal of Psychiatry, 200*(3), 224–231.

O'Riordan, M., & Arensman, E. (2007). *Institutional child sexual abuse and suicidal behaviour: Outcomes of a literature review, consultation meetings and a qualitative study*. National Suicide Research Foundation. Retrieved from http://www.nosp.ie/institutional_07.pdf

O'Toole, L. (Ed.). (1997). *Gender violence: Interdisciplinary perspectives* (p. 235). New York University Press.

Panksepp, J. (1998). *Series in affective science. Affective neuroscience: The foundations of human and animal emotions*. Oxford University Press.

Paolucci, E. O., Genuis, M. L., & Violato, C. A. (2001). A meta-analysis of the published research on the effects of child sexual abuse. *The Journal of Psychology, 135*, 17–36. https://doi.org/10.1080/00223980109603677

Petherick, W. (2017). Victim precipitation: Why we need to expand upon the theory. *Forensic Research & criminology International Journal, 5*(2), 00148.

Plummer, M., & Cossins, A. (2016). The cycle of abuse: When victims become offenders. *Trauma, Violence and Abuse, 22*(2016), 1–19.

Resick, P. A. (2016). The psychological impact of rape. *Journal of Interpersonal Violence, 8*(2), 223–255.

Rothbaum, B. O., Astin, M. C., & Marsteller, F. (2005). Prolonged exposure versus eye movement desensitization and reprocessing (EMDR) for PTSD rape victims. *Journal of Trauma Stress, 18*(6), 607–616.

Rouf, K., & Taggart, D. (2021). Recovered memories: Shooting the messenger—20 years on. In V. Sinason (Ed.), *Memory and trauma: Who's dispute?* Routledge.

Seigel, L. J. (2006). *Criminology* (10th ed.). University of Massachusetts, Lowell. Thomson Wadsworth.

Shapiro, F. (1989). Efficacy of the eye movement desensitization procedure in the treatment of traumatic memories. *Journal of Trauma Stress, 2*, 199–223.

Shaw, C., & Proctor, G. I. (2005). Women at the margins: A critique of the diagnosis of borderline personality disorder. *Feminism & Psychology, 15*(4), 483–490. https://doi.org/10.1177/0959-353505057620

Spröber, N., Schneider, T., Rassenhofer, M., Seitz, A., Liebhardt, H., König, L., & Fegert, J. F. (2014). Child sexual abuse in religiously affiliated and secular institutions: A retrospective descriptive analysis of data provided by victims in a government-sponsored reappraisal program in Germany. *BMC Public Health, 14*, 282–294.

Stark, R. (1987). Deviant places: A theory of the ecology of crime. *Criminology, 25*, 893–909. Strain.

Sweeney, A., & Taggart, D. (2018). (Mis)understanding trauma-informed approaches in mental health. *Journal of Mental Health, 27*(5), 383–387. https://doi.org/10.1080/09638237.2018.1520973

Taggart, D. (2018). Trauma informed care for young people, research in practice, Darlington.

Taggart, D., Rouf, K., Duckworth, L., Hassan, I., & Sweeney, A. (2021). Trauma, mental health and the Covid 19 crisis: Are we all in it together? *Journal of Mental Health, 30*(4), 401–404. https://doi.org/10.1080/09638237.2021.1875415

Thurston, R. C., Chang, Y., Matthews, K. A., von Känel, R., & Koenen, K. (2018). Association of sexual harassment and sexual assault with midlife women's mental and physical health [published online October 3, 2018]. *JAMA Internal Medicine, 179*(1), 48–53.

Timmer, D., & Norman, W. H. (1984). The ideology of victim precipitation. *Criminal Justice Review, 9*, 63–68.

Walling, M. K., Reiter, R. C., O'Hara, M. W., Milbum, A. K., Lilly, G., & Vincent, S. D. (1991). Abuse history and chronic pain in women: Prevalence of sexual abuse and physical abuse. *Obstetrics & Gynaecology, 84*, 193–199.

Weisel, D. L. (2005). Analyzing repeat victimisation. In The Office of Community Oriented Policing Services (Ed.), *Problem-oriented guides for police: Problem-solving tool series (no. 4)*. U.S. Department of Justice.

Widom, C., Czaja, S., & Dutton, M. (2008). Childhood victimisation and lifetime revictimisation. *Child Abuse & Neglect, 32*, 785–796.

Williams, C. (2016). Rape in Alaska. *Undergraduate Research Journal, 20*, 11.

Wingood, D., DiClemente, R., & Raj, A. (2000). Adverse consequences of intimate partner abuse among women in non-urban domestic violence shelters. *American Journal of Preventive Medicine, 19*(4), 270–275.

Wolfe, D., Francis, K., & Straatman, A. (2006). Child abuse in religiously-affiliated institutions: long-term impact on men's mental health. *Child Abuse and Neglect, 30*, 205–212.

Chapter 24
The Public Health Approach to SV

Elijah P. Morrow and Kelly Bonnar

24.1 Introduction

Sexually abusive behavior places a heavy burden on society. While precise prevalence rates have been difficult to ascertain (United States Department of Justice, 2020), the World Health Organization ([WHO]; 2018) estimated that nearly 30% of all women had been subjected to sexual violence (SV). Within the United States, it is estimated that approximately 25% of girls and 5% of boys are subject to sexual violence (Finkelhor et al., 2014). Such experiences increase a victim's likelihood of physical health issues such as heart disease and obesity (Norman et al., 2012), as well as mental health disorders such as depression and posttraumatic stress disorder (Leeb et al., 2011). The prevalence and impact of SV is not isolated, but widespread.

There is a financial cost to SV, as well. Letourneau et al. (2018) calculated the economic burden of child SV in the United States in 2015, factoring in a 20.3% loss of adult earnings for victims, suicide death costs, increased adult medical costs for victims, and the increase in special education enrollment for victims in comparison with children that had no maltreatment record. Their report identified the total economic burden in 2015 alone amounted to $9.3 billion. The impact of SV has been identified as contributing to 0.7% of the United States' total burden of disease (U.S. Burden of Disease Collaborators, 2013). The financial burden is not isolated to the United States, with the estimated annual cost being $3.9 billion in Australia (Taylor et al., 2008) and 3.2 billion pounds in the United Kingdom (Saied-Tessier, 2014). Clearly, adopting sound public policy aimed at reducing the rate and impact of SV could not only result in a populace less burdened by physical disease and

E. P. Morrow (✉)
California Department of Corrections and Rehabilitation, Coalinga, CA, USA

K. Bonnar
Department of Public Health & Human Performance, SUNY Potsdam, Potsdam, NY, USA

R. J. Tully et al. (eds.), *Best Practices in Sexual Offender Assessment and Management*, Dangerous Behavior in Clinical and Forensic Psychology,
https://doi.org/10.1007/978-3-031-83135-5_24

more prone to developing mental disorders, but one where more are able to realize their economic potential, producing more healthy and prosperous communities.

24.2 Categories of Prevention

SV is committed by a heterogenous population with a range of motivating factors. Consequently, effective public policy requires the development and implementation of interventions at varied junctures in the offending process to ensure maximal efficiency. Adopted from the field of public health, there exists three different categories in which interventions may fall: primary, secondary, or tertiary. Each level of prevention is categorized based upon 'when' the strategy is implemented and to 'whom' it is targeted. Primary prevention aims to stop SV before it occurs and involves wide-scale initiates aimed at the public. Primarily implemented as awareness raising and education, primary prevention is targeted at populations not affected by SV or absent significant risk factors for it. Secondary prevention involves the application of strategies targeted at those who are at risk of engaging in SV. This early intervention is designed to minimize the impact of SV or its occurrence by reducing risk factors. Finally, tertiary prevention is a reactionary approach after SV has occurred and aims to prevent SV from reoccurring. The goals of tertiary prevention are often long-term, implemented after SV has occurred, and are directed at those who have been victimized or who have perpetrated (Laws, 2000; Wortley & Smallbone, 2006). This chapter will explore the public policy efforts that have been made to intervene at these different junctures and review the efficacy of the interventions.

The dividing line between primary, secondary, and tertiary is not always simple. Interventions which are broadly primary may instead serve a secondary purpose if those referred are all done so due to concerning behaviors that could place them at a higher risk of SV or signify that SV may be occurring in secret. Similarly, if an individual who has already engaged in SV, detected or otherwise, were enrolled in a primary prevention program this would still count as a tertiary intervention despite the primary aim of the program being preventative. Thus, some of the policies and programs discussed in this chapter may also be placed in alternative categories depending on who was referred and the reason for the referral. The programs discussed here, however, are categorized based upon their primary intent despite potential broader applications.

24.3 Primary Prevention

Primary prevention is the first juncture for intervention and refers to strategies or interventions that aim to stop SV before it occurs (Centers for Disease Control and Prevention [CDC], 2004). Methods of primary prevention have been successfully utilized with various public health concerns, including cancer prevention (McCracken et al., 2013), substance abuse (Kumpfer, 2014), and weight management (Carlson et al., 2012) and have been proven to be a cost-effective method of managing both mental and physical health concerns. To this end, the WHO (2014) released a report detailing potential primary prevention areas for SV. To assess the current state of primary prevention strategies implemented, 133 countries were surveyed which accounted for 88% of the world's population. However, despite the interest that primary prevention methods have occasionally attracted, they have not been implemented with the same fervor as are tertiary interventions. For example, while 99% of the surveyed countries had a law punishing those who had engaged in statutory rape, only 35% of countries had implemented a prevention program for SV for schools and college populations (WHO, 2014). Thus, these interventions may pose an underutilized but nonetheless valuable method by which to reduce SV.

Primary prevention methods, to be maximally effective, should target factors known to be contributory towards eventual SV. In identifying factors leading to SV, the social-ecological model (Krug et al., 2002) identifies four interconnected levels that require targeting for long-term prevention of SV: individuals, relationships, communities, and societies. These levels represent segments of the populace in which to intervene.

Individual-level interventions aim at treating personal factors within both potential perpetrators and victims, with the goal that these factors should never accumulate to the threshold in which an individual is at risk of engaging in SV. Topics covered in this level include alcohol and drug use, preference for impersonal sex, hostility towards women (WHO, 2014), or consent in sexual relationships (e.g., the U.S. Child Assault Prevention [CAP] programs; see http://njcap.org/category/programs/).

Interventions which target the relationship level recognize that friends of individuals at risk of victimization or perpetration can intervene to prevent SV. Relationship interventions aim to broaden responsibility of SV prevention beyond potential victims and perpetrators (Foubert et al., 2010). Such interventions cover family environment factors such as emotional support or physical violence at home, to associations with negative peer influences such as those promoting sexually aggressive behavior (WHO, 2014).

Community-level interventions aim at developing policies which reduce the likelihood of social risk factors and instead promote protective factors. Examples of this level of intervention include developing policies addressing such factors as poverty, general tolerance of SV within the community, or lack of employment opportunities (WHO, 2014).

The final category for intervention, societal factors, addresses norms supportive of SV and attempts to instill healthy and accurate cultural norms for sexual engagement. Examples of some such cultural norms supportive of SV, often referred to as "rape culture", include 'no does not mean no,' 'sexual encounters are permissible when the victim under the influence of alcohol gives verbal consent', 'sexual aggression is warranted if the victim is dressed provocatively,' and 'removing consent midway through a sexual encounter is not permissible.' These widely held rape myths, if acted upon, result in SV being perpetrated.

Each of the above categories will be discussed below and some examples of available programs will be given. These examples are, in no means meant to be exhaustive but can serve to demonstrate primary prevention interventions implemented by public policy.

24.3.1 Primary Prevention—Individual Factor Intervention

Primary intervention strategies for individual factors have focused on potential victims of SV, potential perpetrators, or both. For example, *The Body Safety Program* is a school-based program that focuses on potential victims, aiming to build skills within children to be able to recognize, prevent, and respond to sexual advances from adults (Eriksen, n.d.). This program has been adopted by several counties across America such as in Fairfax County, Virginia and Oakland County, Michigan as a program delivered free of charge to the community (e.g., Eriksen, n.d.).

Some programs have instead focused on teaching appropriate sexual behavior to both potential perpetrators and victims. Such programs include *Shifting Boundaries* (Taylor et al., 2008) and *Safe Dates* (Foshee et al., 1996) which were designed to be delivered to middle school children. *Shifting Boundaries* addresses policy-based Safety concerns within the school, such as identifying areas of concern for increased monitoring, and publishing posters to increase awareness of dating violence (Taylor et al., 2008). Meanwhile, *Safe Dates* is a 10-session curriculum addressing attitudes, social norms, and healthy relationship skills, concluding in a 45-minute student play about dating violence and a poster contest (Foshee et al., 2004).

Finally, some programs have focused largely on potential perpetrators. One such program, *Coaching Boys Into Men*, uses athletic coaches to teach gender equality, recognition of abusive behavior, and that strength as a male does not equate violence to student athletes (*Coaching Boys Into Men—Respect. Integrity. Nonviolence*, 2018).

24.3.2 Primary Prevention—Relationships Factor Intervention

The relationships factor for primary prevention of SV has by and large focused upon the bystander effect. The bystander effect describes the phenomenon in which individuals are less likely to give assistance when others are present (Williams & Law, 2007) and, by addressing it, the aim is to broaden the perspective of the problem of SV.

Two examples of this type of intervention are *Bringing in the Bystander* (Baynard et al., 2007) and *Green Dot* (Coker et al., 2011). These programs were developed to be implemented with college students and provide education and training in breaking the barrier which the bystander effect can erect between being aware of an issue and intervening. These programs aim to provide participants with the skills necessary to act when they see behaviors which put others at risk or speak out against rape myths and sexist language. Additionally, several of the individual factor primary prevention programs discussed contain interventions on the bystander effect as well. For example, *Coaching Boys Into Men* not only provides strategies and resources regarding healthy and respectful relationships, but trains participants to be able to intervene when witnessing abusive behavior (*Coaching Boys Into Men—Respect. Integrity. Nonviolence*, 2018). Thus, many of the individual factor interventions, if administered widely enough, can have an impact on the relationship factors as well as they bring awareness of healthy sexual norms both to those who might eventually have engaged in such behavior, and those who might eventually witness such behavior.

24.3.3 Primary Prevention—Communities Factor Intervention

Many of the factors targeted by community and societal interventions are not explicitly described to be attempting to reduce future SV. For example, interventions aimed at employment opportunities or poverty may not be undertaken with the stated goal of reducing SV. However, a report by WHO described that "[p]overty is linked to both the perpetration of SV and the risk of being a victim of it" (Jewkes et al., 2002, p. 161). The report goes on to describe that those trapped in poverty with little opportunity for social mobility may feel thwarted in their expectations of masculine success, reshaping community ideals to emphasize misogyny, substance abuse, and participation in crime. Thus, strategies that aim to increase economic mobility of families or social assistance programs may reduce SV. Programs such as *Early Head Start Programs* (2020) that provide intensive and comprehensive child development and family support services to low-income infants and toddlers and their families may provide crucial services towards this end. Similarly, job training programs such as the *Employment Development Department* (n.d.) in California can provide economic mobility if effectively delivered to those in need.

24.3.4 Primary Prevention—Societies Factor Intervention

Societal factors for primary prevention focus on norms and socially held beliefs regarding sexuality. Such norms are often expressed in adopted legislation or policies related to SV. A noted purpose of adopted law is to express messages about morality, solidarity, and other more absolute ideological values. These ideological values are meant to convey community sanctions against the perpetration of SV and maintain moral consensus (Hermstad, 2013).

Commitment to communicating this value is often reflected in an emphasis on police training or appropriate allocation of police resources to SV. Similarly, laws and policies that address gender equality communicate values antithetical to hostility towards women. Finally, social norms can create an impact on the occurrence of future SV. Culturally accepted belief systems regarding where responsibility lies for sexual assault, age of consent, or ideologies promoting male entitlement towards sexual contact can all increase the likelihood of SV. Indeed, societies in which the ideology of male superiority is strong, rape is more common (Murnen et al., 2002).

While societal norms may be more ambiguous and thus more difficult to intervene upon, some efforts should be discussed. Most notably, the *#MeToo* movement sought to change societal norms through open discussion of experiences and public naming of those alleged to have committed sexual harassment, with measurable change occurring within public consciousness (Rasmussen & Yaouzis, 2019). While such a movement is beyond public policy discussions, adopted norms are carried and communicated subtly through interactions and behaviors (Nolan, 2011), thus changes in social norms through such movements permeate future public policy decisions and execution.

24.3.5 Primary Prevention—Efficacy

While multiple primary prevention programs exist and have prima facie validity, little empirical evidence has been produced on their efficacy. Of the programs discussed, three have been submitted to rigorous evaluation design; *Safe Dates*, *Shifting Boundaries*, and *Coaching Boys Into Men*. The evidence produced indicates that primary prevention remains an effective avenue of intervening in SV. For example, results from a 4-year follow-up study utilizing randomized controlled trial for *Safe Dates* demonstrated that participants in the program were significantly less likely to be both victims and perpetrators of SV (Foshee et al., 2004). Specifically, participants reported that they experienced between 56% and 92% less dating violence victimization and perpetration compared to controls at follow-up. Similarly, *Shifting Boundaries* has been reported to have been effective in reducing perpetration and victimization of sexual harassment and peer SV, as well as SV victimization but not perpetration by a dating partner (Taylor et al., 2008).

Finally, for *Coaching Boys Into Men*, a 3-month follow-up study utilizing randomized assignment to a control group demonstrated that participants were more likely to intervene in SV (Miller et al., 2012), and that 1 year later those who participated were less likely to report abuse perpetration and negative bystander behaviors when witnessing abusive or disrespectful behavior among peers (Miller et al., 2013). Thus, while empirical evidence is lacking, available evidence does appear to support the utility of primary prevention for SV.

24.3.6 Public Policy Support for Primary Interventions

Primary prevention strategies are a somewhat hodgepodge collection of communal initiatives with some scattered governmental backing. Public policy could collaborate more consistently with non-profit and community groups through grants or supportive legislation. For example, *Stop It Now!* is a non-profit with international sites, including the United States and Scotland, and strives to seek out root causes of SV and identify ways to prevent abuse before a child is harmed (Brown et al., 2014; Eisenberg et al., 2014). In 2022, *Stop it Now!* received a research award from the CDC to evaluate the effectiveness of abuse prevention programs in youth sports leagues. *Stop it Now!* planned to implement Circles of Safety, a curriculum they had designed, to teach individuals to identify boundary violations and feel confident speaking up before a concerning behavior escalates to abuse. Thus, public policy funding of non-profit organizations could provide valuable community interventions as well as important data on their efficacy to ensure that governmental aid is well spent. However, funding has remained miniscule, with the federal budget recently adding just $1.5 million dedicated to child SV prevention for fiscal year 2021 (Letourneau et al., 2022).

Further, such programs could be implemented into school and community centers, ideally from a state or federal level to ensure comprehensive coverage. With an increased population on whom these interventions would be delivered, the resulting shift in rates of SV and modifications of social norms could produce a generation with significantly lowered mental, physical, and fiscal costs incurred due to SV.

24.4 Secondary Prevention

The second juncture for SV intervention is secondary prevention. Secondary prevention is aimed at those with particular risk factors which make them likely to offend (Laws, 2000). A corollary example from another public health concern would be a program to assist those with pre-diabetes to decrease their risk of developing diabetes, such as through lipid intake control or smoking cessation. It has been argued that a lack of attention and resources have been dedicated to secondary prevention initiatives for SV, focusing instead on primary and tertiary initiatives. This has left a dearth of research on the efficacy of this stage of intervention as well as a reduced number of enacted programs, although some promising interventions have been developed. Perhaps one of the most important secondary preventions for SV is self-referred individual psychotherapy. Such interventions have been demonstrated to be helpful in reducing the risk of sex offending (e.g., Lampalzer et al., 2021). Despite an exploration of self-referrals being largely beyond the scope of a public policy chapter, the importance of those who brave fears of stigmatization and self-refer should not be overlooked.

24.4.1 Secondary Prevention—Criminal Justice

Criminal justice has four main goals: retribution, rehabilitation, incapacitation, and deterrence. The fourth of these goals, deterrence, aims to prevent those considering criminal behavior from acting due to the knowledge that there will be stiff penalties. Thus, criminal sanctions for SV can serve a secondary prevention purpose. There appears to be some evidence to substantiate this claim, as criminal sanctions became increasingly "uniquely punitive" towards individuals convicted of a sex offense in conjunction with a rise in public concern over the frequency of sex offending (Cochran et al., 2020, p. 105). Increasing sentence length may thus partly reflect an attempt to reduce the frequency of SV by attempting to make the consequences far outweigh any momentary benefit perpetrating may yield.

Despite the seeming validity of such an approach, available research indicates that severity of punishment does not consistently deter offending (Nagin, 2013). Concernedly, some research indicates that sentence length is positively related to recidivism for all forms of sex offending, while time served is negatively related to recidivism (Budd & Desmond, 2013). Thus, this approach appears to result in increased occurrences of SV rather than a reduction.

In noting that increased sentence length may increase SV, it is important to recognize that long sentences are enacted for more purposes than just deterrence. Sentence length expresses moral condemnation of certain behaviors as well as solidarity with victims and recognition of their pain. These are important public policy aims. However, if the current strategy increases frequency of SV, it may have the unfortunate outcome of multiplying pain rather than causing it to abate. Careful balancing must be made between the societal purpose that long sentences have and their potential deleterious effects. It is important that public policy not overly invest in a strategy demonstrated to not deter but occasionally increase SV.

While sentence length may not deter criminal behavior, the certainty of punishment can (Nagin, 2013). Knowing that one will be punished for criminal behavior appears to operate as a better deterrence than the threat of long periods of incarceration. However, for sex offending, conviction rates remain low. For example, in 2021 the United Kingdom Government released a report suggesting that only 1.6% of rape accusations ever result in anybody being charged (*The end-to-end rape review report on findings and actions*). Thus, criminal justice may serve an important role in reducing future SV by increasing conviction rates for the abuse that has already occurred. To do this, barriers to victims coming forward could be addressed. For example, the 'rape shield law' is the common term for evidentiary statutes that prevents cross-examination of rape victims about past sexual behavior to impeach their credibility as a witness. Several jurisdictions across the globe have enacted similar statutes (e.g., Philippines, Canada, Australia, United States). These statutes can have the effect of causing victims to feel more comfort in reporting abuse and testifying during trials, thereby increasing conviction rates, and further decreasing future offenses through deterrence.

24.4.2 *Secondary Prevention—Public Policy Support for Community Groups*

Other public policy initiatives for secondary prevention remain scarce. However, supportive legislation has been demonstrated to be a viable strategy. For example, Prevention Project Dunkelfeld (PPD) is an effort founded in Berlin to provide clinical and support services to individuals who are sexually attracted to children. While this program relies predominately on self-referral, it appears to be supported by legislation. Specifically, Germany requires that therapists maintain strict confidentiality regarding any past child SV disclosed by patients, and specifically exempts mandatory reporting for planned future child SV offenses unless the plan includes murder (Beier et al., 2009). Unless there is imminent or current child endangerment, these mandatory reporting requirements permit patients to securely disclose past and future abuse. This ensures that adequate interventions can be worked on collaboratively with therapists to prevent offending without the fear of immediate criminal justice involvement. Participants in PPD can feel more assured in seeking help as any breaches of confidentiality by a therapist will almost certainly be penalized unless the breach clearly serves to avert imminent endangerment. Other jurisdictions have lower thresholds for mandatory reporting which can impact a patient's comfort in seeking professional assistance. For example, a 1989 Maryland statute required that all patient disclosures of child SV, including ones that occurred before treatment, be reported. A 1991 study found that the change in the law caused a drop in self-referrals to one clinic from a total of 73 over a ten-year period to zero (Berlin et al., 1991). It appears that low or unclear bars for when mandatory reporting is triggered can leave potential patients as well as therapists unsure whether past or future offenses spoken about need be reported. While enacted with the best of intentions, namely preventing victims and punishing offenders, these requirements may instead deter treatment and not offending. Increased clarity in statutory language and changes in mandatory reporting requirements can allow organizations similar to PPD to operate more confidently, and potential patients can be more certain about the risks of seeking professional assistance.

24.4.3 *Secondary Prevention—Efficacy*

Little is known of the efficacy of secondary prevention approaches for SV. Kewley et al. (2021) sought to remedy this by surveying available literature on secondary prevention and performing a thematic analysis on the empirical studies. The authors highlight challenges which exist in the study of such programs, including the "embryonic nature" of the programs as well as ethical difficulties in establishing an appropriate control group study (p. 26). Nevertheless, some studies have been carried out. For example, in 2016, a study was conducted evaluating treatment of adult men who self-reported sexual interest in minors with no prior offense history. It was noted that dynamic risk factors did appear to reduce through treatment (Beier et al., 2016). Additionally, a 10 year follow up program for children ages 5 through 12 displaying sexual behavior problems indicated that both cognitive behavioral therapy and play therapy reduced problem behaviors (Carpentier et al., 2006). Similarly, PPD has also seen some promising results, with a 2014 study identifying significant decreases in emotional deficits and offense-supportive cognitions in comparison with a control group (Beier et al., 2015). Research in this area may be hampered by the inherent difficulty of measuring reductions in offending that may have eventually happened but for treatment. However, the available research appears to indicate that problem behaviors have reduced with longitudinal studies and that risk factors associated with offending have been similarly mitigated.

Overall, secondary prevention remains one of the least investigated as well as ethically and legally fraught intervention areas for SV. Having an identified group of individuals who are contemplating SV rightly provokes anxiety. This has arguably resulted in higher criminal sentencing, less investment in secondary prevention programs, and mandatory reporting requirements which deter treatment and not sexual offending. While far from being in an ideal state, several advances have been made which reveal that this prevention area is receiving more attention. Enacted criminal procedure laws may make the process of prosecuting SV easier for victims, and some community organizations are collaborating with their legislature to create safe self-referral programs for those at risk of SV. Continued development in this area may see novel approaches to intervening with those vulnerable to offending.

24.5 Tertiary Prevention

Where primary prevention is implemented before the problem occurs and secondary prevention involves the application of strategies designed to intervene early, tertiary interventions are designed to treat the problem after it has occurred. These strategies are typically long-term and directed at those who have perpetrated or at providing services to those victimized.

24.5.1 Tertiary Prevention—Policy

Since 1947, policy in the United States regarding the management of those who commit sexually based crimes have proliferated (Wang, 2015). Policy in the case of sexual crimes is a tertiary initiative because it is implemented after the sex crime occurs and is designed as a long-term effort reduce offenders' risk for recidivism, and so, in theory, rehabilitate (CDC, 2004). Recidivism is defined in the criminal justice system as "acts that resulted in rearrest, reconviction or return to prison with or without a new sentence during a 3-year period following the person's release"

(National Institute of Justice, 2022). Many policies currently exist to address this goal.

Since the early 1990s, a bevy of federal, state, and local legislation related to individuals convicted of sex offenses has been enacted. For example, the Jacob Wetterling Crimes Against Children Act and Sexually Violent Offender Registration Act (Adam Walsh Act, Public Law No: 109–248) were created to help law enforcement officials track individuals convicted of sex offenses and thus, theoretically, reduce the likelihood that they would recidivate. Title 1 of AWA, called the Sex Offender Registration and Notification Act (SORNA) was designed to improve the quality of state registries partially by mandating that individuals convicted of sex offenses register and verify their current names and addresses with local police. The United Kingdom (UK) similarly enacted the Sex Offender Act in 1997 which provided the groundwork for the UK registration system before it was later supplemented in 2000 by the Criminal Justice and Court Services Act which provided further arrangements to provide for the effective management of the registry. These acts set the template for others to follow in Canada, France, Australia, the Republic of South Africa, the Republic of Ireland, and elsewhere (Thomas, 2011).

In May 1996, amendments to the Wetterling Act were made when Megan's Law (Pub L No. 104–145) were passed. Megan's Law required states to establish community notification systems that made the sex offender registry information available to the public. Megan's Law required states to publish photographs, names, and addresses of individuals registering as sex offenders (IRSOs) so they are available to the public in forms such as the Internet. Extending from this was The Pam Lychner Sexual Offender Tracking and Identification Act of 1996 that established the National Sex Offender Registry at the Federal Bureau of Investigation (FBI) and in 1998, the Department of Commerce, Justice, and State, the Judiciary, and Related Agencies Appropriations Act of 1998 required those convicted of a sex crime to register in a new state if they move.

In 2000, the Jacob Wetterling Crimes Against Children Act and the Cleary Act were modified to mandate those convicted of sex crimes to notify their campus of their conviction if they attend an institution of higher education. In 2003, the PROTECT (Prosecutorial Remedies and Other Tools to End the Exploitation of Children Today) Act was passed and requires states to maintain a public sex offender registry website. Contrary to the United States, the UK does not allow any public access to their registry but does provide a more limited system of discretionary disclosure to individual members of the public if it is believed that it will prevent a crime or safeguard children (Thomas, 2013).

On July 27, 2007, President Bush signed the Adam Walsh Protection Act (AWA), a federal law mandating State registration requirements. AWA, which has six Titles, streamlined the tracking of sex offenders and notification requirements at the federal level. Under AWA, all states must implement AWA, or lose 10% of the Byrne grants they receive to fight crime. AWA had provisions for issues including but not limited to minimum registration and community notification procedures, registration of employment and education addresses, inclusion of a tiered risk level classification system, how often sex offenders must register, and consequences for failure to register. In addition, Title III of the AWA mandates civil commitment for certain dangerous offenders and Title IV of the Act makes it illegal for an IRSO to sponsor a family member, such as a wife, husband, or child, for Permanent Residency in the United States.

Since the passage of AWA, the laws have been modified to include the KIDS Act (October 2008; Public Health Law 110–400) to address the issue of online safety and instituted a mandate requiring IRSO's to report their online and social media identifiers, the Military Sex Offender Reporting Act (Congressional Research Service, 2021) requiring the Department of Defense to report information about sex offenders in the military, and International Megan's Law (February 8, 2015; Public Law 114–119) to address and restrict international travel by registered sex offenders. Those required to register as sex offenders are often bound by other policies like residency restrictions, GPS tracking, and restrictions related to attendance at institutions of higher education (Zgoba & Mitchell, 2021).

Finally, civil commitment laws, sometimes called Sexually Violent Predator (SVP) or Sexually Dangerous Person laws, have existed in the United States since 1990 when Washington passed the Washington State's Community Protection Act. As of 2023, 21 jurisdictions within the United States (20 states and the federal government) had enacted sex offender civil commitment laws. Similar programs are also found in Australia, England, and Germany (Harrison, 2013). Within the United States, the enacted statutes hold that individuals serve their original prison sentence until they are evaluated prior to their release into the community. If found to have met certain criteria, such as having an elevated risk to re-offend sexually due to a mental abnormality or personality disorder, they are detained, typically in secure residential facilities, until they are deemed to have no longer met criteria for continued detainment. Given the lack of a definite time limit to a stay, civil detainees often stay in detainment for many years, with recent data from the California Department of State Hospitals (DSH) indicating that patients remained for a mean of just under 6 years, with approximately 25% being detained for 11 additional years after the conclusion of their sentence (Sreenivasan et al., 2022).

24.5.2 Tertiary Prevention—Policy Effectiveness

The philosophy of these tertiary policies is that society must be protected against a group of criminals who pose a high risk for re-offense. The idea is that SV is pervasive because those with a proclivity for sexually deviant behavior will always be oriented to engage in it. In review, one of the primary goals of tertiary policies is to rehabilitate and so reduce or eliminate the risk for recidivism and with that theoretically driven purpose, yet the laws have proliferated to include more restrictions on those convicted of sexually based offenses. Recently, interest has grown in exploring the value these policies have at meeting this goal. In public health, the efficacy of such polices would be measured by the population-wide reduction in the prevalence of SV. In the criminal justice domain, that efficacy is measured by a reduction in recidivism among those required to abide by the SORNA.

Empirical research examining these policies has shown AWA and other IRSO policies have had no impact on the national rates of SV (Bonnar, 2010). In fact, since 1996, reports of SV have continued to increase (FBI, 2022). It is important to keep in mind that sexual crimes are among the most underreported, and so there are more actual cases of SV than those reported to the police (Bonnar, 2010). Given that, in the following examples, the data is less important than the trends over time. According to the FBI (2022), in 1996 there were 89, 411 rapes reported in the United States, much less than the 139, 390 reported in 2018. The FBI reported that "this estimate was 2.7 percent higher than the 2017 estimate and 18.1 percent higher than the 2014 estimate" (n.p.). Furthermore, data from the 2016/2017 National Intimate Partner and SV Survey suggested that SV continues to be pervasive, with 26.8% of women and 3.8% of men reporting being sexually assaulted at some point in their lifetime (Leemis, et al., 2022). Thus, during the period over which these policies were enacted, sex offending continued to increase rather than result in reduced frequencies.

As discussed, one method for examining the efficacy of these tertiary policies is to explore their influence on recidivism. SV recidivism occurs then when someone previously convicted of a sex crime, commits another sexual crime. There exists ample research examining recidivism for individuals convicted of a sex offense, with results holding up rather unanimously that the recidivism risk among sexual offenders is quite low (Ohio Public Safety, 2006; Stalans et al., 2002; Valentine & Huebner, 2006, Valle, 2018; United States Department of Justice, 2003; Center for Sex Offender Management, 2007). Many of these efficacy studies conclude that, while IRSO's can be re-arrested for crimes related to registration, such as failure to register on time or notify the police about a new address (Pryzbylski, 2015), IRSOs are rarely returned to prison for another sexual crime (Arizona Department of Corrections, 2007; Harris & Hanson, 2007; State of New York Department of Corrections, 2015; United States Department of Corrections, 2003). According to Harris and Hanson (2007), sexual offenders have a 3.5% rate of recidivism which decreases to 0% after 20 years. As such, policy effectiveness for an already low recidivism risk is challenging. However, in a meta-analysis of 18 studies examining SORNA effectiveness, Zgoba and Mitchell (2021) concluded that 25 years of SORNA implementation has had no deterrent effect on sexual offending.

24.5.3 Tertiary Prevention—Recommendations

Given that the SORNA and related policies have little to no impact on the rates at which SV and recidivism are occurring, any minimal benefit must be compared with the costs associated with their implementation. A cost-to-benefit analysis can aid in determining whether these policies are sound investments. For the incarceration of people convicted of sex crimes against children in state and federal prisons and civil commitment, Letourneau et al. (2022) estimated that American taxpayers spend nearly $5.4 billion annually. This total does not include the amount spent by states and the federal government to monitor IRSOs within the community, with the

National Justice Policy Institute (2009) reporting that the costs for implementing SORNA in the first year alone would cost up to $900 million. When utilizing figures provided by Letourneau et al. (2022), which excludes community monitoring, the American taxpayer invests in tertiary interventions over primary interventions at an approximate ratio 3600 to one. It should be emphasized than this investment serves only to reduce future SV in a population known to recidivate at low levels and intervenes only after the damage of at least one offense has occurred. For policies showing little efficacy, it seems money could be more effectively applied to primary and secondary prevention initiatives.

24.6 Conclusion

As seen, priority in public policy is often given to tertiary interventions which detain and monitor perpetrators of SV. The focus on tertiary interventions to the exclusion of additive primary and secondary interventions has persisted and escalated despite available literature noting that these policies overall have not reduced the rate of offending and sometimes have the effect of increasing recidivation. Public policies informed by scientific evidence are more likely to be effective in achieving goals of community protection (Levenson & D'Amora, 2007), and evidence-based approaches to public policy should be a goal for all practitioners and lawmakers. Given that the bulk of available evidence has not supported current tertiary interventions in proportion to its financial investment, the question remains as to why this approach persists.

The answer to this question may lie in public perception of individuals convicted of sex offenses. Public perception influences policy development (Zgoba & Mitchell, 2021), and public perception of individuals convicted of sex offenses remains largely tainted by popular myths. For example, Levenson et al. (2007) found widespread myth acceptance within directly surveyed community members. These myths include beliefs that convicted sex offenders will reoffend, that offenders reoffend at higher rates than other criminals, and that half of treated sex offenders will recidivate (Levenson et al., 2007). Other surveys have similarly identified high frequencies of endorsed myths, such as that sexual assaults are largely committed by strangers (Forney et al., 2007). Thus, the public appears to be largely misinformed on the topic of SV and these misperceptions may be a driving force behind current policy.

Given public perception that individuals convicted of sex offenses are strangers who will reoffend, it is no wonder that interventions have focused largely on increasing punishment and monitoring of perpetrators. As these policies seek to address a largely inaccurately perceived problem, it is also little wonder that they have not demonstrated more efficacy. However, the myth of 'stranger danger' hides the disturbing reality that victims are at much greater risk of being sexually abused by those known and trusted rather than by strangers lurking by schoolyards or in alleyways. More accurate and effective intervention would thus require more than identification and segregation of those already convicted and would require a broadening of solutions.

In addition to broadening of enacted solutions, the scope of disbursement should increase to include more than those already convicted or even those likely to offend. While perpetrators bear the bulk of the responsibility for SV, communities and non-perpetrating individuals can also have a substantial impact upon the occurrence of SV. From intervening when interpersonal boundaries are being crossed to educating youth about healthy sexual behavior, highly effective interventions may be overlooked when focusing on perpetrators alone. Implementing primary interventions which educate on how SV occurs and how to intervene or prevent it may thus be an appropriate place to start. An educated public would not only be less inclined to be victims or perpetrators themselves, but can better drive public policy in the future, specifically policies which more accurately address causes of SV.

References

Arizona Department of Corrections. (2007, August 31). *Sex offender recidivism*. http://www.adc-prisoninfo.az.gov/Recidivism.htm

Banyard, V., Moynihan, M., & Plante, E. (2007). Sexual violence prevention through bystander education: An experimental evaluation. *Journal of Community Psychology*, 35(4), 463481. https://doi.org/10.1002/jcop.20159.

Beier, K. M., Ahlers, C. J., Goecker, D., Neutze, J., Mundt, I. A., Hupp, E., & Schaefer, G. A. (2009). Can pedophiles be reached for primary prevention of child SV? First results of the Berlin Prevention project Dunkelfeld (PPD). *Journal of Forensic Psychiatry & Psychology, 20*(6), 851–867. https://doi.org/10.1080/14789940903174188

Beier, K. M., Grundmann, D., Kuhle, L. F., Scherner, G., Konrad, A., & Amelung, T. (2015). The German dunkelfeld project: A pilot study to prevent child SV and the use of child abusive images. *International Society for Sexual Medicine, 12*(2), 529–542. https://doi.org/10.1111/jsm.12785

Beier, K. M., Oezdemir, U. C., Schlinzig, E., Groll, A., Hupp, E., & Hellenschmidt, T. (2016). "Just dreaming of them": The Berlin project for primary prevention of child SV by juveniles (PPJ). *Child Abuse & Neglect, 52*, 1–10. https://doi.org/10.1016/j.chiabu.2015.12.009

Berlin, F. S., Malin, H. M., & Dean, S. (1991). Effects of statutes requiring psychiatrists to report suspected SV of children. *American Journal of Psychiatry, 148*(4), 449–453. https://doi.org/10.1176/ajp.148.4.449

Bonnar, K. K. (2010). Sexual offender laws and prevention of SV or recidivism. *American Journal of Public Health, 100*(3), 12–419. https://doi.org/10.2105/AJPH.2008.153254

Brown, A., Jago, N., Kerr, J., Nicholls, C. M., Paskell, C., & Webster, S. (2014). Call to keep children safe from sexual abuse: A Study of the use and effects of the Stop It Now! UK and Ireland Helpline. Retrieved from https://www.stopitnow.org.uk/files/stop_it_now_evaluation_uk_findings.pdf.

Budd, K., & Desmond, S. A. (2013). Sex offenders and sex crime recidivism. *International Journal of Offender Therapy and Comparative Criminology, 58*(12), 1481–1499. https://doi.org/10.1177/0306624x13507421

Carlson, J. A., Sallis, J. F., Ramirez, E. R., Patrick, K., & Norman, G. J. (2012). Physical activity and dietary behavior change in internet based weight loss interventions: Comparing two multiple-behavior change indices. *Preventative Medicine, 54*, 50–54.

Carpentier, M. Y., Silovsky, J. F., & Chaffin, M. (2006). Randomized trial of treatment for children with sexual behavior problems: Ten-year follow-up. *Journal of Consulting and Clinical Psychology, 74*(3), 482. https://doi.org/10.1037/0022-006X.74.3.482

Center for Sex Offender Management. (2007, November 25). *Managing challenges of sex offender re-entry*. http://www.csom.org/pubs/reentry_brief.pdf

Centers for Disease Control and Prevention. (2004). *SV prevention: Beginning the dialogue*. Author.
Coaching Boys into Men – Respect. Integrity. Nonviolence. (2018). Retrieved September 09, 2020, from http://www.coachescorner.org/
Cochran, J. C., Toman, E. L., Shields, R. T., & Mears, D. P. (2020). A uniquely punitive turn? Sex offenders and the persistence of punitive sanctioning. *Journal of Research in Crime and Delinquency, 58*(1), 74–118. https://doi.org/10.1177/0022427820941172
Coker, A. L., Cook-Craig, P. G., Williams, C. M., Fisher, B. S., Clear, E. R., Garcia, L. S., & Hegge, L. M. (2011). Evaluation of green dot: An active bystander intervention to reduce SV on college campuses. *Violence Against Women, 17*(6), 777–796. https://doi.org/10.1177/1077801211410264
Congressional Research Service. (2021, August 2). *Federal requirements for state and Military Registered Sex Offender Management*. https://sgp.fas.org/crs/misc/R46863.pdf
Department of Justice. (2020). *National crime victimization survey*, 2015–2019.
Early Head Start Programs. (2020, March 30). Retrieved September 14, 2020, from https://eclkc.ohs.acf.hhs.gov/programs/article/early-head-start-programs
Eisenberg, M., Mulder, J., van Horn, J., & Stam, J. (2014). Stop it now! Helpline Netherlands: A study of its use and effects—English summary. Utrecht, NL: De Waag.
Employment Development Department State of California. (n.d.). Retrieved September 14, 2020, from https://edd.ca.gov/
Eriksen, E. (n.d.). Body Safety Program. Retrieved September 09, 2020, from https://www.fairfaxcounty.gov/familyservices/children-youth/volunteer-partner-services/body-SVfety
Federal Bureau of Investigations. (2022, November 8). Crime in the United States, 2018. https://ucr.fbi.gov/crime-in-the-u.s/2018/crime-in-the-u.s.-2018/tables/table-1
Finkelhor, D., Shattuck, A., Turner, H. A., & Hamby, S. L. (2014). The lifetime prevalence of child SV and sexual assault assessed in late adolescence. *Journal of Adolescent Health, 55*(3), 329–333. https://doi.org/10.1016/j.jadohealth.2013.12.026
Forney, T., Levenson, J., Brannon, Y., & Baker, J. N. (2007). Myths and facts about sexual offenders: Implications for treatment and public policy. *Sexual Offender Treatment, 2*(1), 1–17.
Foshee, V. A., Bauman, K. E., Ennett, S. T., Linder, G. F., Benefield, T., & Suchindran, C. (2004). Assessing the long-term effects of the safe dates program and a booster in preventing and reducing adolescent dating violence victimization and perpetration. *American Journal of Public Health, 94*(4), 619–624. https://doi.org/10.2105/ajph.94.4.619
Foubert, J. D., Tabachnick, J., & Schewe, P. A. (2010). Encouraging bystander intervention for SV prevention. In K. L. Kaufman (Ed.), *The prevention of SV: A practitioner's sourcebook* (pp. 121–134). NEARI Press.
Harris, A. J. R., & Hanson, R. K. (2007). Sex offender recidivism: A simple question. https://www.publicSVfety.gc.ca/cnt/rsrcs/pblctns/sx-ffndr-rcdvsm/index-en.aspx
Harrison, K. (2013). Sentencing sex offenders: An international comparison of sentencing policy and legislation. In K. Harrison & B. Rainey (Eds.), *The Wiley-Blackwell handbook of legal and ethical aspects of sex offender treatment and management* (pp. 150–167). essay, John Wiley & Sons, Ltd.
Hermstad, K. (2013). Sexual offenses, law and morals. In K. Harrison & B. Rainey (Eds.), *The Wiley-Blackwell handbook of legal and ethical aspects of sex offender treatment and management* (pp. 3–17). John Wiley & Sons.
Jewkes, R., Sen, P., & Garcia-Moreno, C. (2002). SV. In E. G. Krug, L. L. Dahlberg, J. A. Mercy, A. B. Zwi, & R. Lozando (Eds.), *World report on violence and health* (pp. 147–181). World Health Organization.
Justice Policy Institute. (2009). *What will it cost states to comply with the Sex Offender Registration and Notification Act?* https://www.njjn.org/uploads/digital-library/resource_840.pdf
Kewley, S., Mhlanga-Gunda, R., & Van Hout, M.-C. (2021). Preventing child SV before it occurs: Examining the scale and nature of secondary public health Prevention approaches. *Journal of Sexual Aggression, 29*, 1–33. https://doi.org/10.1080/13552600.2021.2000651
Kumpfer, K. L. (2014). Family-based interventions for the prevention of substance abuse and other impulse control disorders in girls. *ISRN Addiction, 2014*, 1–23.

Krug, E. G., Mercy, J. A., Dahlberg, L. L., & Zwi, A. B. (2002). World report on violence and health . *World Health Organization*. https://doi.org/10.1016/S0140-6736(02)11133-0.
Lampalzer, U., Tozdan, S., von Franqué, F., & Briken, P. (2021). Hypersexuality and impulsivity in self-referred men with sexual interest in minors: Are they related? Do they change during treatment? An exploratory pilot study. *Sexual Medicine, 9*(5), 100429. https://doi.org/10.1016/j.esxm.2021.100429
Laws, D. R. (2000). Sexual offending as a public health problem: A north American perspective. *Journal of Sexual Aggression, 5*, 30–44. https://doi.org/10.1080/13552600008413294
Leeb, R. T., Lewis, T., & Zolotor, A. J. (2011). A review of physical and mental health consequences of child abuse and neglect and implications for practice. *American Journal of Lifestyle Medicine, 5*(5), 454–468. https://doi.org/10.1177/1559827611410266
Leemis, R. W., Friar, N., Khatiwada, S., Chen, M. S., Kresnow, M., Smith, S. G., Caslin, S., & Basile, K. C. (2022, October). The National Intimate Partner and SV survey: 2016/2017 report on intimate partner violence. Atlanta, GA: National Center for Injury Prevention and Control, Centers for Disease Control and Prevention. https://www.cdc.gov/violenceprevention/pdf/nisvs/nisvsreportonipv_2022.pdf
Letourneau, E. J., Brown, D. S., Fang, X., Hassan, A., & Mercy, J. A. (2018). The economic burden of child SV in the United States. *Child Abuse & Neglect, 79*, 413–422. https://doi.org/10.1016/j.chiabu.2018.02.020
Letourneau, E. J., Roberts, T. W., Malone, L., & Sun, Y. (2022). No check we won't write: A report on the high cost of sex offender incarceration. *Sexual Abuse, 35*, 107906322210783. https://doi.org/10.1177/10790632221078305
Levenson, J. S., Brannon, Y., Fortney, T., & Baker, J. (2007). Public perceptions about sex offenders and community protection policies. *Analyses of Social Issues and Public Policy, 7*(1), 1–25.
Levenson, J. S., & D'Amora, D. A. (2007). Social policies designed to prevent SV: The Emperor's new clothes? *Criminal Justice Policy Review, 18*(2), 168–199.
McCracken, J. L., Friedman, D. B., Brandt, H. M., Adams, S. A., Xirasagar, S., Ureda, J. R., Mayo, R. M., Comer, K., Evans, M., Fedrick, D., Talley, J., & Hebert, J. R. (2013). Findings from the community health intervention program in South Carolina: Implications for reducing cancer-related health disparities. *Journal of Cancer Education, 28*, 412–419.
Miller, E., Tancredi, D. J., Mccauley, H. L., Decker, M. R., Virata, M. C., Anderson, H. A., O'Connor, B., & Silverman, J. G. (2013). One-year follow-up of a coach-delivered dating violence prevention program. *American Journal of Preventive Medicine, 45*(1), 108–112. https://doi.org/10.1016/j.amepre.2013.03.007
Miller, E., Tancredi, D. J., Mccauley, H. L., Decker, M. R., Virata, M. C., Anderson, H. A., Stetkevich, N., Brown, E. W., Moideen, F., & Silverman, J. G. (2012). "Coaching boys into men": A cluster-randomized controlled trial of a dating violence prevention program. *Journal of Adolescent Health, 51*(5), 431–438. https://doi.org/10.1016/j.jadohealth.2012.01.018
Murnen, S. K., Wright, C., & Kaluzny, G. (2002). If "boys will be boys," then girls will be victims? A meta-analytic review of the research that relates masculine ideology to sexual aggression. *Sex Roles, 46*, 395–375. https://doi.org/10.1023/A:1020488928736
Nagin, D. S. (2013). Deterrence in the twenty-first century. *Crime and Justice, 42*(1), 199–263. https://doi.org/10.4324/9780203045510
National Institute of Justice. (2022). Recidivism. https://nij.ojp.gov/topics/corrections/recidivism
Nolan, J. M. (2011). The cognitive ripple of social norms communications. *Group Processes & Intergroup Relations, 14*(5), 689–702. https://doi.org/10.1177/1368430210392398
Norman, R. E., Byambaa, M., De, R., Butchart, A., Scott, J., & Vos, T. (2012). The long-term health consequences of child physical abuse, emotional abuse, and neglect: A systematic review and meta-analysis. *PLoS Medicine, 9*(11), e1001349. https://doi.org/10.1371/journal.pmed.1001349
Ohio Public Safety. (2006). *Report to the Ohio criminal sentencing commission: Sex offenders*. https://www.ohiomemory.org/digital/collection/p267401ccp2/id/1494
Pryzbylski, R. (2015, July). Recidivism of adult sexual offenders. https://smart.ojp.gov/sites/g/files/xyckuh231/files/media/document/recidivismofadultsexualoffenders.pdf

Rasmussen, K. B., & Yaouzis, N. O. (2019). #MeToo, social norms, and sanctions. *The Journal of Political Philosophy, 28*(3), 273–295.
Saied-Tessier, A. (2014). Estimating the costs of child SV in the UK. NSPCC, 1–44. Retrieved from: https://www.nspcc.org.uk/globalassets/documents/research-reports/estimating-costs-child-sexual-abuse-uk.pdf.
Sreenivasan, S., Cahan, J., Azizian, A., & Weinberger, L. E. (2022). Applying collaborative justice to sexually violent predator civil commitment. *The Journal of the American Academy of Psychiatry and the Law, 50*(4), 496–508. https://doi.org/10.29158/JAAPL.200023-20
Stalans, L. J., Seng, M., & Yarnold, P. (2002, November). Long-term impact evaluation of specialized sex offender probation programs in Lake, Dupage, Winnebago counties. https://www.ojp.gov/ncjrs/virtual-library/abstracts/long-term-impact-evaluation-specialized-sex-offender-probation
State of New York Department of Corrections. (2015). 2014 Releases: Three year post-release follow-up. https://doccs.ny.gov/system/files/documents/2021/03/inmate-releases-three-year-out-post-release-follow-up-2014.pdf
Stop It Now! (2022, December 1). *Center for violence prevention research awarded CDC grant to evaluate the effectiveness of abuse prevention programs in a youth sports league*. Retrieved December 10, 2022, from https://drive.google.com/file/d/10LcchMp-EEtMQt9xfbQsxiQRwLhYSVcB/view
Taylor, P., Moore, P., Pezzullo, L., Tucci, J., Goddard, C. D., & Bortoli, L. (2008). *The cost of child abuse in Australia. Australian Childhood Foundation and Child Abuse Prevention Research Australia: Melbourne*. Retrieved from https://www.researchgate.net/publication/264546577_The_Cost_of_Child_Abuse_in_Australia
The End-to-End Rape Review Report on Findings and Actions. (2021, July). Accessed September 12, 2022, from https://assets.publishing.service.gov.uk/government/uploads/system/uploads/attachment_data/file/1001417/end-to-end-rape-review-report-with-correction-slip.pdf
Thomas, T. (2011). *The registration and monitoring of sex offenders: A comparative study*. Routledge.
Thomas, T. (2013). Sex offender registration in the United States and the United Kingdom. In K. Harrison & B. Rainey (Eds.), *The Wiley-Blackwell handbook of legal and ethical aspects of sex offender treatment and management* (pp. 356–371). essay, John Wiley & Sons, Lt.
U.S. Burden of Disease Collaborators. (2013). The state of U.S. health, 1990–2010: Burden of diseases, injuries, and risk factors. *JAMA, 310*, 591–606.
United States Department of Justice. (2003, November). Recidivism of sex offenders released from prison in 1994. https://www.ojp.gov/bjs/pub/pdf/rsorp94.pdf
Valentine, D., & Huebner, B. (2006, June 30). Sex offender recidivism in Missouri and community corrections options. https://www.moSVc.mo.gov/file/SOrecidivism.pdf
Valle, A. (2018). Expanded view of recidivism in Alaska. *Alaska Justice Forum, 34*(3) https://scholarworks.alaska.edu/bitstream/handle/11122/8091/ajf.343d.expanded-view-recidivism-alaska.pdf
Wang, J. (2015). Paying the piper: The cost of compliance with the federal sex offender registration and notification act. *NYLS Law Review, 50*(4), 681–705. https://digitalcommons.nyls.edu/cgi/viewcontent.cgi?article=1139&context=nyls_law_review
Williams, K. D., & Law, A. T. (2007). Bystander effect. In R. F. Baumeister & K. D. Vohs (Eds.), *Encyclopedia of social psychology* (pp. 132–134). SVGE Publishing.
World Health Organization. (2014). *Global status report on violence prevention 2014*. World Health Organization. https://www.who.int/publications/i/item/9789241564793
World Health Organization. (2018). (rep.). *Violence against women prevalence estimates, 2018*.
Wortley, R., & Smallbone, S. (2006). *Situational prevention of child SV*. Criminal Justice Press.
Zgoba, K. M., & Mitchell, M. M. (2021). The effectiveness of sex offender registration and notification: A meta-analysis of 25 years of findings. *Journal of Experimental Criminology, 19*(6), 1–26. https://doi.org/10.1007/s11292-021-09480-z

Index

R. J. Tully et al. (eds.), *Best Practices in Sexual Offender Assessment and Management*, Dangerous Behavior in Clinical and Forensic Psychology,
https://doi.org/10.1007/978-3-031-83135-5